THE EYE OF THOMAS JEFFERSON

THE EYE OF THOMAS JEFFERSON

William Howard Adams

Editor

Thomas Jefferson Memorial Foundation, Inc., Charlottesville, Virginia
and
University of Missouri Press, Columbia and London

5 4 3 2 1   96 95 94 93 92

This catalogue was produced by the Editor's Office, National
Gallery of Art, Washington, D.C.
Designed by Susan Lehmann, Washington, D.C.
Printed by Garamond Pridemark Press, Baltimore, Maryland
Set in Linotype Electra (designed by W. A. Dwiggins, 1935) by the
Monotype Composition Company, Inc., Baltimore, Maryland. Display
type designed by J. F. Rosart in 1743 for the Enschedé Foundry,
Haarlem.
Jacket for 1992 edition designed by Rhonda Miller.

∞™ This paper meets the requirements of the American National
Standard for Permanence of Paper for Printed Library Materials,
Z39.48, 1984.

Library of Congress Cataloging-in-Publication Data

Eye of Th. Jefferson.
    The eye of Thomas Jefferson : [exhibition] / William Howard Adams,
editor.
        p.   cm.
    Originally published: Washington : National Gallery of Art, 1976.
    ISBN 0-8262-0879-7
    1. Jefferson, Thomas, 1743–1826—Art collections—Exhibitions.
2. Neoclassicism (Art)—Europe—Exhibitions. 3. Neoclassicism
(Art)—United States—Exhibitions. I. Adams, William Howard.
II. National Gallery of art (U.S.)
E332.2.E88   1992   92-20309
973.4′6′092—dc20   CIP

Frontispiece: Catalogue number 526.

CONTENTS

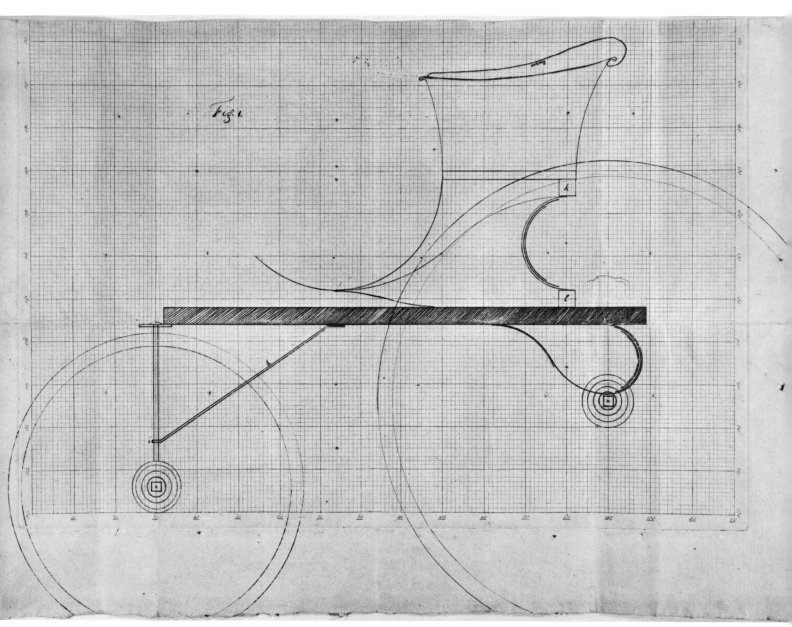

Fig. 1.

532

FOREWORD

A national gallery of art has, for us as a nation, a peculiar responsibility. It is more than a pleasure dome, though one hopes it will always be that too. It must somehow represent our best selves; it must embody our values, and help provide some inkling of who we are by bearing witness to who we have been. This anagogical role, more felt than definable concretely, jumps to the fore when the nation, and this institution, are faced with the phenomenon of a Bicentennial.

Who is there more logical to keep what Yeats called "the ceremony of innocence" alive than just such a national gallery, there on the national Mall, at the very foot of the Capitol itself? Yes, but what, exactly, should it be doing as July 4, 1776, floats two hundred years away?

The obvious first suggestion was, years ago when all this had to be decided, a super-survey of American art. Nothing wrong with that, certainly; it would take its place among other and wholly admirable exhibitions of a similar sort throughout the land. But the National Gallery of Art presents as a matter of course a survey of American painting of its own; it had had a loan show on that theme borrowed from Boston and New York not long before; there exists together among museums of Washington a truly extraordinary representation of this field; we would want to be as generous as possible in lending our own American objects at just that time to Bicentennial shows in this country and abroad, while other institutions would be scrambling for the material we would need; and furthermore, the event being commemorated happened not during the past two centuries but in that one year, two hundred years ago.

We are, by nature, an historical institution, and might not it be our particular responsibility to face that historical challenge head-on?

One solution might have been to have an exhibition of American art—perhaps all the American arts—in the year 1776. Interesting archaeologically, no doubt, but one has to be realistic: the major creative achievement of this polity in that year was not in its artistic output.

The idea thus emerged of exploring the possibility of an exhibition dedicated to all the visual manifestations of what might be called *The World in 1776*. There was Captain Cook, after all, discovering fascinating artifacts; there was the sophistication of the Chinese at the court of Emperor Ch'ien Lung; there was the tension between neoclassicism and romanticism in the creative centers of Europe.

It was in pursuing this that we instituted a series of discussions with leading scholars of the eighteenth century, probing this and alternative concepts that might help illustrate the broader cultural context out of which our revolutionary experiment emerged. Limiting a show to that one year, or even to a few on either side, turned out to be strangely unproductive. The very dynamics of the shift from the rococo to emerging neoclassical and romantic developments could not be documented by examples drawn from a time-frame that sat so near the still center of that stylistic cyclone. Seventeen-seventy-six turned out to be a good year for declarations but not a particularly outstanding one for art.

One day, when Frederick Cummings, Jr., a specialist in eighteenth-century French painting (and subsequently Director of the Detroit Art Institute) was here to worry this bone with us, the discussion kept coming back to Thomas Jefferson as one of the inescapable forces in not just American, but the world's intellectual and artistic life. And then everything came clear. Who was there more central to the fourth day of July 1776 than the author of the Declaration of Independence himself? And yet Jefferson's reach, through his reading, looking, travels, and own artistic output, could encompass the whole visual context we wanted to present, most particularly so by putting it into the perspective of antiquity so that our visitors, by arching back into their own heritage, might learn by the example of the value placed by our founding fathers on theirs.

Since then, this institution has been extremely fortunate in the help offered it in bringing this concept to fruition. An international scholarly Steering Committee was formed under the able chairmanship of Sir Francis Watson, meeting in Washington and London; other renowned scholars have contributed essays, catalogue entries and information; lenders from this country and abroad have been generous beyond our fondest hopes; the Exxon Corporation has helped underwrite the exhibition and funded a film so that the show can reach an audience not limited by time and space; and we are particularly fortunate to have had on our own staff, overseeing the whole undertaking for the Gallery, the talented W. Howard Adams, assisted by a very dedicated team.

Alfred North Whitehead, in his *Rhythm of Education*, stressed the value of "the habitual contemplation of greatness." An art gallery, at any time, is or should be in that business. For a national art gallery, in a Bicentennial summer, Thomas Jefferson will give us all the chance to contemplate a greatness in which one cannot help but find, in his own words, "the ring of eternity."

J. CARTER BROWN, *Director*

ix

ORGANIZATION

ORGANIZATION OF EXHIBITION

INTERNATIONAL STEERING COMMITTEE

Sir Francis Watson, Chairman
William Howard Adams, curator and editor
James A. Bear, Jr.
J. Carter Brown
Frederick J. Cummings
Italo Faldi
Basil Greenhill
Hugh Honour
Graham Hood
Frederick D. Nichols
Merrill D. Peterson
Sir Nikolaus Pevsner
Jules David Prown
Pierre Rosenberg
Robert Rosenblum
Jean Seznec
Adolf Max Vogt
Gabriel White

STAFF

Ross Watson
Janice C. Janis

Installation

John Bedenkapp
Elroy Quenroe

ORGANIZATION OF CATALOGUE

STAFF

Susan H. Baker
Linda Peterson
Ross Watson

CONTRIBUTORS

William Howard Adams   WHA
H. H. Arnason   HHA
Susan H. Baker   SHB
Silvio A. Bedini   SAB
William L. Beiswanger   WLB
Arnauld Bréjon de Lavergnée   ABdeL
Alfred Bush   AB
William P. Campbell   WPC
J. M. Edelstein   JME
John Fesperman   JF
Peter Fusco   PF
Elizabeth Garrett   EG
Charles Granquist   CG
Irma B. Jaffe   IBJ
Donald C. Hand   DH
Eileen Harris   EH
John Harris   JH
Seymour Howard   SH
Thomas J. McCormick   TJMCC
Eleanor McPeck   EM
Jean-Marie Pérouse de Montclos   PdeM
Frederick D. Nichols   FN
Linda Peterson   LP
Howard C. Rice   HCR
Pierre Rosenberg   PR
Andrew Robison   AR
Barbara Schnitzer   BS
Charles C. Sellers   CS
Anatole Senkevitch   AS
Thomas E. Thorne   TT
Gilbert Vincent   GV
Anna M. Voris   AMV
Sir Francis Watson   FW
Ross Watson   RW

ACKNOWLEDGMENTS

It is a tribute to the scale and range of Thomas Jefferson's intellectual and aesthetic topography that the writing and organization of material for this exhibition and catalogue has required the cooperation, imagination and assistance of so many scholars, museum colleagues, and collectors both in this country and abroad. Without the matchless contributions to Jefferson scholarship of Dumas Malone and Julian Boyd, especially, this presentation of Jefferson's world would have been impossible.

From the first meeting of the Steering Committee, the exhibition and catalogue have been a remarkable collaboration of international scholars. The patience and humor—not to mention his knowledge of the eighteenth century—of the committee's chairman, Sir Francis Watson, has given that collaboration an extra dimension. Jefferson's five years in France presented a unique opportunity to explore some neglected corners of art history during the 1780s, and this was made possible by the enthusiasm of Pierre Rosenberg. His contribution to the catalogue in his essay on the Salons and his enlisting the advice of Jean-Marie Pérouse de Montclos in the section on visionary architecture has immeasurably enriched the enterprise. In the United Kingdom we were most fortunate in having the experience of Gabriel White to assist us in the arrangement of loans. A complete list of the scholars (with their initials) who have written entries will be found on page x.

We are particularly grateful for the contributions of Alfred Bush, Harold E. Dickson, Judge Edward Dumbauld, Frederick D. Nichols, Paul Foote Norton, George G. Shackelford, Sir Francis Watson and Walter Muir Whitehill, who have written special essays, to be published separately, on aspects of Thomas Jefferson's life and achievements for this Bicentennial celebration.

My debt in regard to the many details in preparing the catalogue extends particularly to Linda Peterson and Susan Baker, who have assisted in research and editing; Ross Watson, who has assisted in the organization of the exhibition as well as of the catalogue; Anne Poulet, who not only did the translation of the French contributions to the catalogue but brought to the task her own considerable knowledge of the period; and Janice Janis, who gathered together the hundreds of photographs while tending to the daily demands of the exhibition's correspondence. Janet Goodman's quiet and efficient help has untangled all of the traffic and typing jams of my own work. John Bedenkapp and his assistant, Elroy Quenroe, have been responsible for the design of the exhibition installation, and valuable critics and allies in the production of the catalogue as well. The formidable task of producing the exhibition catalogue lay with the Editor's Office at the National Gallery where Frances P. Smyth, Polly Ravenscroft and Melanie Ness discharged their editorial tasks with energy and patience. In addition to those scholars who have contributed so richly to the catalogue and to the planning of the exhibition, I offer my deepest gratitude to the following persons for their help and advice:

Thomas Boylston Adams, Jean Adhémar, Luigi Amaduzzi, Richard T. Arndt, Andrew Ash, Jan Baculewski, Richard Bales, Helene Baltrusaitis, Julius P. Barclay, Françoise Baron, James A. Bear, Jr., Silvio A. Bedini, William Beiswanger, Luciano Berti, Victor Beyer, Daniel Boorstin, Patrick Bracco, Arnauld Bréjon de Lavergnée, Bennie Brown, Jr., Kathryn Buhler, R. Le Gette Burris, Jeanne Butler, Lyman H. Butterfield, Laura Byers, Janet Byrne, Elliott Carroll, Beverly Carter, Edward C. Carter, II, Clement E. Conger, John Sherman Cooper, Jean Coural, Walker Cowan, Julia F. Davis, Joan Dolmetsch, J. Gaube du Gers, The Most Reverend Giovanni Fallani, Joseph C. Farber, The Reverend Michael F. Farina, Leonard C. Faber, Alan M. Fern, John Fesperman, Robert Fisher, Malcolm Freiberg, M. Frerebeau, Ambassador Roberto Gaja, Wendell Garrett, Barbara Gould, Charles Granquist, Guy Greenwell, O. B. Hardison, Donald R. Haynes, Morrison H. Heckscher, Bruce Henry, Helen R. Hollis, Seymour Howard, Richard H. Howland, Carlisle H. Humelsine, Robert F. Illing, Monsignor Jean Jadot, John M. Jennings, Gregory Johnson, Patrick J. Kelleher, Ambassador Jacques Kosiusko-Morizet, Pierre Lemoine, William Matheson, Elizabeth B. McDougall, Eleanor McPeck, Mr. & Mrs. Paul Mellon, Ellen Miles, Robert C. Moeller, Phillippe de Montebello, Stephanie Munsing, Edward Munves, Jr., Keith Murphy, Ambassador Egidio Ortona, James Parker, Marian Peck, Charles Pickett, Buford L. Pickens, Jane Preger, Jean Preston, Eleanor S. Quandt, Ambassador Sir Peter Ramsbotham, Howard C. Rice, Jr., Stephen T. Riley, Elizabeth Roth, Carol Shackelford, Alan Shestack, Romaine Somerville, James A. Steed, Dawn Stilgoe, Gerald Straley, Teresa Sulerzyska, Joseph Ternbach, William R. Tyler, Mary Ann Thompson, Mario Valmarana, Gérald Van der Kemp, John A. Volpe, Christopher White, Walter Muir Whitehill, Dora Wiebenson, Jacques Wilhelm and Thomas S. Wragg.

WILLIAM HOWARD ADAMS

LENDERS

Academy of Natural Sciences, Philadelphia
Mr. Charles Francis Adams, Dover, Massachusetts
Albright-Knox Art Gallery, Buffalo
Allen Memorial Art Museum, Oberlin College
American Institute of Architects, Washington
American Philosophical Society, Philadelphia
Archives municipales, Bordeaux
Archives nationales, Paris
Baltimore Museum of Art, Maryland
The Governor & Company of the Bank of England, London
Biblioteka Universyteckiej, Warsaw
Bibliothèque nationale, Paris
Guardians of the Standard of Wrought Plate in Birmingham
    (The Birmingham Assay Office), England
Bodleian Library, Oxford
Mr. and Mrs. Philip W. Bonsal, Washington
Boston Athenaeum
British Embassy, Washington, the Honorable Sir Peter Ramsbotham,
    KCMG, British Ambassador
Trustees of the British Museum, London
British Museum of Natural History, London
Bruton Parish Church, Williamsburg, Virginia
Burnley Borough Council, Towneley Hall Art Gallery and Museum,
    England
Mrs. John M. Carter, Wayne, Pennsylvania
Walter Chatham, Washington
Trustees of the Chatsworth Settlement, Devonshire Collection,
    England
Cincinnati Art Museum, Ohio
City Art Gallery, Bristol, England
College of William and Mary in Virginia
Colonial Williamsburg Foundation, Virginia
Columbia Historical Society, Washington
Thomas Jefferson Coolidge, Jr., Boston
Cooper-Hewitt Museum of Design, Smithsonian Institution,
    New York
Thomas Coram Foundation for Children, London
Corcoran Gallery of Art, Washington
M Robert de Crèvecoeur, Listrac-Médoc
Department of State, Washington
Dumbarton Oaks Garden Library, Washington
Ecole des Beaux-Arts, Paris
Mr. and Mrs. John Page Elliott, Charlottesville, Virginia
Fine Arts Museums of San Francisco
Fine Arts Library of the Harvard College Library, Cambridge,
    Massachusetts
Fitzwilliam Museum, Cambridge, England
M J. Gaube du Gers, Paris

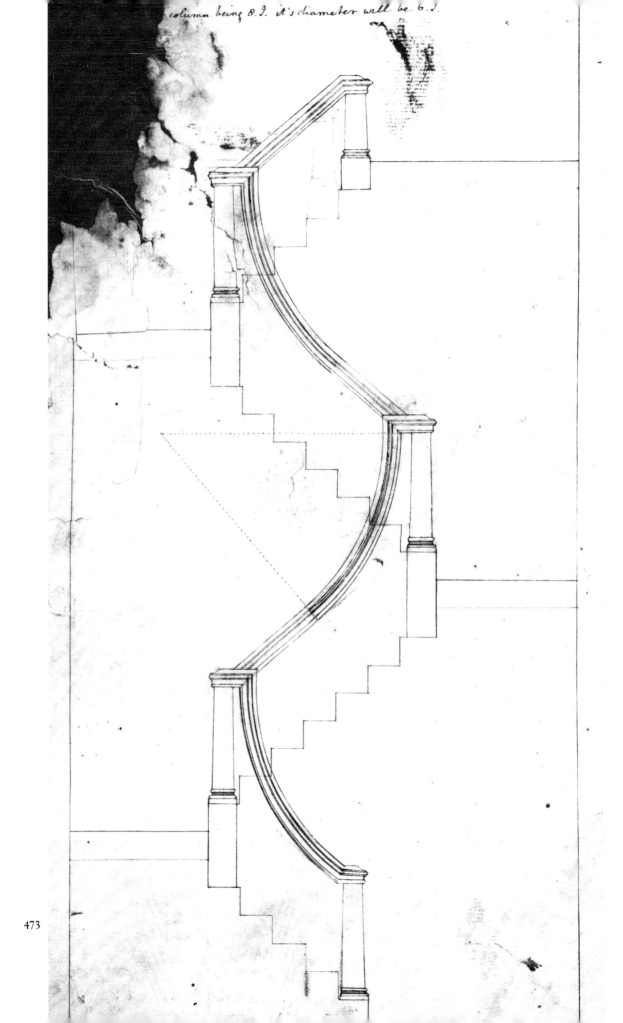

column being 8.9. it's diameter will be 6.9.

473

CHRONOLOGY

JEFFERSON IN AMERICAN HISTORY 1743–1826

Year		Concurrent Events in the Arts
1743	Thomas Jefferson born at Shadwell, Virginia, the son of Peter Jefferson and Jane Randolph	
1744		Bach, *Well Tempered Clavier*, Book II
1746	Peter Jefferson made the executor of the estate of William Randolph of Tuckahoe; established there with his family	
1747		Handel, *Judas Maccabeus*
1748	End of War of Austrian Succession (King George's War)	Gainsborough, *Cornard Wood*
1749		Johnson, *The Vanity of Human Wishes*
1750		Gray, *Elegy in a Country Churchyard*
1751	Peter Jefferson returns to Shadwell with his family	
1752	Jefferson at school of Rev. William Douglas of St. James Parish, Northam	
1753		Completion of Tiepolo's frescoes at the Residenz, Würzburg
1754	Peter Jefferson made county lieutenant of Albemarle County	
1756	Outbreak of Seven Years' War (French and Indian War)	
1757	Death of Peter Jefferson	Soufflot's Sainte-Geneviève (Panthéon) begun
1758	Jefferson begins attending school of Rev. James Maury, Albemarle County	
1759	Capture of Quebec	Voltaire, *Candide* Johnson, *Rasselas*
1760	Death of George II, accession of George III Jefferson enters College of William and Mary	Rousseau, *La Nouvelle Héloïse*
1762	Jefferson begins to study law with George Wythe	Rousseau, *Emile*
1763	By the Treaty of Paris, French relinquish Canada	
1764		Completion of Tiepolo's fresco in the throne room of the Royal Palace, Madrid
1765	Stamp Act Patrick Henry speech against the Stamp Act	
1766	Jefferson visits Annapolis, Philadelphia and New York Begins his *Garden Book*	
1767	Jefferson admitted to the Bar	
1768	Work begun at Monticello (building) Death of Governor Fauquier; arrival of Lord Botetourt as governor of Virginia	Royal Academy of Arts founded in London

Year		Concurrent Events in the Arts
	Jefferson elected burgess for Albemarle County to Virginia Assembly	
1769	Jefferson signs the Association, an agreement not to import or consume goods from England	
1770	Shadwell destroyed by fire Jefferson appointed lieutenant of Albemarle County by Lord Botetourt Jefferson moves to Monticello Death of Lord Botetourt Boston Massacre Lord North becomes British prime minister Repeal of colonial duties except that on tea	Gainsborough, The Blue Boy Burke, Thoughts on the Cause of the Present Discontents Goldsmith, The Deserted Village
1771	Jefferson reelected to Virginia Assembly	Completion of Ledoux's Pavillon de Madame du Barry at Louveciennes
1772	Jefferson marries Martha Skelton Birth of first child Martha Burning of British schooner Gaspée while chasing a smuggler at Providence, Rhode Island Samuel Adams forms Committees of Correspondence for action against the British	Choderlos de Laclos, Les Liaisons Dangereuses Haydn, "Farewell Symphony" Completion of Ledoux's Hôtel Guimard
1773	Jefferson involved in the creation of a Committee of Correspondence of the Virginia Assembly and meets with a group of younger radicals at the Raleigh Tavern, Williamsburg Death of Dabney Carr, Jefferson's close friend and brother-in-law British Parliament passes Tea Act Boston Tea Party	First cast-iron bridge in Coalbrookdale, Shropshire, England Goldsmith, She Stoops to Conquer
1774	Birth of Jefferson's second daughter Jane Randolph Jefferson writes "A Summary View of the Rights of British America" Through division of his wife's property, including Poplar Forest, Jefferson becomes a substantial landowner; acquires Natural Bridge Boston Port Bill closes Boston to trade First Continental Congress meets in Philadelphia, resolves to ban trade with Britain Death of Louis XV; accession of Louis XVI	Glück, Iphigenia in Aulis Goethe, The Sorrows of Werther Lord Chesterfield, Letters to His Son
1775	Jefferson elected to Continental Congress in Philadelphia Asked to draft a Declaration on the Necessity of Taking up Arms Draws up reply to Lord North's conciliatory motion Death of second daughter Jane Randolph Battles of Lexington and Concord Capture of Fort Ticonderoga Second Continental Congress in Philadelphia Washington appointed commander-in-chief of American forces Battle of Bunker Hill	Beaumarchais, The Barber of Seville produced in Paris Completion of Gabriel's Place Louis XV (Place de la Concorde)
1776	Jefferson drafts Declaration of Independence British evacuate Boston Thomas Paine publishes "Common Sense," urging independence of the 13 colonies Battle of Trenton Jefferson appointed a commissioner together with Franklin and Deane to negotiate a treaty with France, but declines	Adam Smith, An Inquiry into the Nature and Causes of the Wealth of Nations Gibbon, Decline and Fall of the Roman Empire

Year		Concurrent Events in the Arts
1777	Birth of Jefferson's only son who dies after a few weeks Battle of Princeton Marquis de Lafayette joins Washington's army Surrender of Burgoyne to Gates at Saratoga	Bélanger, Bagatelle
1778	Birth of Jefferson's third daughter Mary (Maria) Treaty of Alliance between United States and France War between Britain and France British peace offers rejected by Congress	Sheridan, The School for Scandal
1779	Jefferson elected governor of Virginia War between Britain and Spain	
1780	Birth of Jefferson's fourth daughter Lucy Elizabeth	David, Count Potocki
1781	Death of fourth daughter Lucy Elizabeth Tarleton raid on Monticello Jefferson appointed to commission for peace settlement with Great Britain, but declines Surrender of Cornwallis to Washington at Yorktown	Legrand and Molinos' dome to the Halle aux Bleds Rousseau, Confessions
1782	Birth of Jefferson's fifth daughter Lucy Elizabeth Death of Jefferson's wife Martha Jefferson appointed peace commissioner to Europe but unable to sail Lord North's government resigns British open peace negotiations with Vergennes and Franklin in Paris Florida conquered by Spain	Completion of Falconet's statue of Peter the Great in St. Petersburg
1783	Jefferson elected to Congress Treaty of Versailles brings Revolutionary War to a close and establishes recognition of the independence of United States by Great Britain William Pitt the Younger becomes British prime minister at age of 24	Montgolfier launches first manned balloon
1784	Jefferson appointed one of commissioners in Europe to draw up treaties of commerce Jefferson settles in Paris at Cul-de-sac Taitbout Death of Jefferson's fifth daughter Lucy Elizabeth	David, Oath of the Horatii Beaumarchais, The Marriage of Figaro Reynolds, Mrs. Siddons as the Tragic Muse Completion of Chalgrin's Sainte-Philippe du Roule Antoine Rousseau, Hôtel de Salm, Paris
1785	Jefferson appointed to succeed Franklin as minister to France and moves to Hôtel de Langeac, Paris Publication of Notes on the State of Virginia Diamond necklace scandal in France leads to greater unpopularity of Marie-Antoinette	
1786	Jefferson visits England, and goes on tour of gardens Bill for Religious Freedom passed by Virginia Assembly	Mozart, The Marriage of Figaro
1787	Jefferson tours south of France and northern Italy; sends a model based on the Maison Carrée at Nîmes for the new state capitol at Richmond Jefferson attends Assembly of French Notables which meets to resolve financial difficulties of the government without success United States Constitution drawn up	Mozart, Don Giovanni David, Death of Socrates in Salon
1788	Jefferson goes on a tour of the Rhineland and visits Holland with John Adams to negotiate a loan for the United States	Mozart, last three Symphonies, Nos. 39, 40, and 41 Goethe, Egmont

Year		Concurrent Events in the Arts
1789	Jefferson returns to the United States on leave, but, asked by Washington to be his secretary of state, never returns to Paris Meeting of the Estates General at Versailles Storming of the Bastille and outbreak of the French Revolution; French Declaration of the Rights of Man; abolition of feudal privilege George Washington inaugurated as first president of the United States	Mozart, *Cosi Fan Tutte* Blake, *Songs of Innocence* David, *The Lictors Returning the Sons of Junius Brutus*
1790	Jefferson appointed secretary of state and settles in Philadelphia at 274 High Market Street Marriage of Jefferson's eldest daughter Martha to Thomas Mann Randolph	Burke, *Reflections on the Revolution in France*
1791		Paine, *Rights of Man* Mozart, *Magic Flute* and Requiem (left incomplete at death) Boswell, *Life of Johnson*
1792	Enmity between Jefferson and Hamilton comes into the open and Jefferson attacked in the Federalist press Birth of Jefferson's first grandchild	Haydn begins writing and performing 6 "London" Symphonies Mary Wollstonecraft, *Vindication of the Rights of Women*
1793	Jefferson resigns as secretary of state Execution of Louis XVI and Marie-Antoinette	David, *Death of Marat* Canova, *Cupid and Psyche* Foundation stone of capitol laid, Washington
1794	Jefferson returns to Monticello and sets up nailery Is offered and refuses post as special envoy to Spain to negotiate treaty	Haydn, "Military" & "Clock" Symphonies Stuart and Revett, *The Antiquities of Athens*
1795	Jay's treaty with Great Britain which Jefferson condemns	Goethe, *Wilhelm Meister*
1796	Jefferson defeated in presidential election by John Adams, and elected vice-president	Haydn, "Mass in Time of War" David, portraits of *Monsieur and Madame Sériziat*
1797	Marriage of Jefferson's second surviving daughter to John Wayles Eppes Inauguration of Jefferson as vice-president Retirement of Washington as president; accession of Adams	
1798	Jefferson drafts Kentucky Resolutions in response to Alien and Sedition Acts	Wordsworth and Coleridge, *Lyrical Ballads*
1799	Death of Washington	Goya, *Los Caprichos* published
1800	Jefferson and Burr have a tied vote for the presidency	Beethoven, Symphony No. 1 David, *Portrait of Mme Récamier* Goya, *Family of Charles IV* David, *Napoleon Crossing the Great Saint-Bernard*
1801	The House of Representatives votes Jefferson president; beginning of his first term Jefferson elected member of the Académie des Sciences, Paris	Arrival in London of the Elgin marbles from the Parthenon Chateaubriand, *Atala* Peale's mastodon shown to American Philosophical Society
1802		Girodet, *Ossian Receiving Napoleon's Dead Generals*
1803	Jefferson concludes purchase of Louisiana from France Prepares instructions for Lewis and Clark Robert Fulton's first steamboat operated on the Seine	
1804	Jefferson reelected to the presidency Death of Maria Jefferson Eppes Alexander Hamilton killed in a duel by Aaron Burr Alexander von Humboldt visits Jefferson Lewis and Clark Expedition sets out from St. Louis	Beethoven, 3rd Symphony ("Eroica")

Year		Concurrent Events in the Arts
1805	Jefferson begins second term as president	Scott, *The Lay of the Last Minstrel*
1806	Lewis and Clark Expedition returns	
1807	Jefferson averts war with Britain over "Chesapeake" affair Embargo Act imposed on Britain and France Jefferson awarded a medal for his mouldboard plough by the French Society of Agriculture	Mme de Staël, *Corinne*
1808	Import of slaves from Africa forbidden	Canova, *Pauline Borghese as Venus* Ingres, *La Grande Baigneuse* Beethoven, 5th Symphony Goethe, *Faust*, part 1 Prud'hon, *Justice Pursuing Crime*
1809	Congress passes Non-Intercourse Treaty refusing to trade with Britain and France Jefferson retires to Monticello after second term as president and is succeeded by Madison	Beethoven, Piano Concerto No. 5 ("Emperor")
1810		Mme de Staël, *De l'Allemagne* Goya begins engraving *The Disasters of War* Scott, *The Lady of the Lake* Overbeck founds The Nazarenes
1811		Jane Austen, *Sense and Sensibility*
1812	Jefferson resumes correspondence and friendship with John Adams War declared with Great Britain	Byron, *Childe Harold's Pilgrimage* Grimm Brothers, *Fairy Tales*
1813		Schubert, Symphony No. 1 Jane Austen, *Pride and Prejudice* Byron, *The Giaour* and *The Bride of Abydos* Shelley, *Queen Mab*
1814	Burning of the public buildings in Washington by the British George Stephenson constructs an effective steam locomotive	Géricault, *The Wounded Cuirassier* Ingres, *La Grande Odalisque* Goya, *Dos Mayo* and *Tres Mayo* Byron, *The Corsair* Scott, *Waverley* Jane Austen, *Mansfield Park*
1815	Jefferson sells a large part of his library to the Library of Congress	Canova, *Three Graces* Goya, *Tauromaquia* (engravings) Nash begins Brighton Pavilion
1816		Rossini, *The Barber of Seville* Jane Austen, *Emma* Coleridge, *Kubla Khan* Scott, *The Antiquary* and *Old Mortality*
1817	Founding of University of Virginia	Constable, *Flatford Mill* Byron, *Manfred*
1818		Jane Austen, *Persuasion* and *Northanger Abbey* (posthumous) Keats, *Endymion* Scott, *Heart of Midlothian* and *Rob Roy* Byron, *Don Juan*
1819	Jefferson suffers financially in the Panic of 1819	Schubert, "Trout" quintet Géricault, *Raft of the "Méduse"* Gérard, *Corinne at Cape Misenium*

Year		Concurrent Events in the Arts
1820		Washington Irving, *Sketch Book of Geoffrey Crayon Gent*
		Keats, *The Eve of St. Agnes* and *Ode to a Nightingale*
		Lamb, *Essays of Elia*
		Shelley, *Prometheus Unbound* and *Ode to the West Wind*
		Scott, *Ivanhoe*
1821		Constable, *Hay Wain*
		Goethe, *Wilhelm Meister's Wanderjahre*
		Heine, *Poems*
		Shelley, *Adonaïs*
		Weber, *Der Freischütz*
1822		Delacroix, *Dante and Virgil in Hell*
		Schubert, Symphony No. 8 ("Unfinished")
1823		Beethoven, *Missa Solemnis* and Symphony No. 9
		Ingres, *La Source*
1824	Visit of Lafayette to the United States, including Monticello	Death of Byron at Missolonghi
		Delacroix, *Les Massacres de Scio*
1825	The University of Virginia opens its doors	Manzoni, *I Promessi Sposi*
		Pushkin, *Boris Gudunov*
1826	Death of Thomas Jefferson	Beethoven, Last Quartets
		Mendelssohn, incidental music for *Midsummer Night's Dream*

223
Thomas Jefferson,
Brown

64 *The Lord Mayor's Procession, Canaletto*

167 The Declaration of Independence, Trumbull

106 The Astronomer, Lépicié

129 *Indian Chief of the Little Osages,* Saint-Mémin

150 The Maison Carrée, Robert

197 *The Construction of the Hôtel de Salm*

331 *The Death of Socrates*, David

333 *Marius Imprisoned at Minturnae, Drouais*

510 *The Elevation of the Rotunda, Randolph*

528 *Coffee Urn, Leguay*

600 *Rubens Peale with a Geranium, Peale*

INTRODUCTION

1

WILLIAM HOWARD ADAMS

Of all the Founding Fathers, with their remarkable talents, learning and accomplishments, Jefferson stands alone in his life-long commitment to the arts, "panting" after them, as his kinsman Edmund Randolph wrote, and in the end, leaving us a legacy not only of concrete achievements in his architecture and designs but more importantly, the record of a uniquely creative man whose example is unmatched in the first two hundred years of the Republic. Lewis Mumford has called him "one of the true figures of the Renaissance," and the remarkable range of his abilities and training stands as the exemplar of the ideal humanist education. His capacity for learning was evident from an early age, and by his mid-thirties he had already assembled a library that had few equals in the colonies for its scope and organization.

Philosophy, history and languages were natural and inevitable fields of study for a young Virginia squire marked for leadership in a society that was as English in its culture as that of the English themselves, and that valued the standard cultivated attributes of an eighteenth-century gentleman in the Renaissance tradition. But the ideal classical education in America was grafted onto a native stock that had been bred and trained for survival on the frontier, where hunting, surveying, soldiering, breaking horses and building shelters were skills of practical necessity. Both these strains were a part of Jefferson's inherited tradition: the love of pure learning encouraged by his father, who insisted on a correct classical training, and the necessity, through his father's example, of the mastery of those exacting tasks demanded of the pioneer. The joy, intelligence and skill with which he combined these qualities in architecture, design and the organization of his surroundings, whether it was a drawing room, a garden, an anatomy theater, a university or a set of goblets, can be seen in the works themselves. The development of that eye and the mind and imagination behind it is the subject of this exhibition.

An aesthetic biography of a man such as Thomas Jefferson poses many problems, since his personality and interests reflected some of the strongest tendencies as well as paradoxes of the complex age in which he lived. We look back from the other end of the telescope, reducing and distorting through the prism of our own twentieth-century eyes the lost world that shaped his remarkable vision and the hopes for the political experiment in which he played such a creative role. Nor can we neatly separate the artist from the political activist, the architect of the capitol at Richmond from the author of the Declaration, the master de-signer of the "academical village," the University of Virginia, from the drafter of the Statute of Virginia for Religious Freedom. The spirit of the Revolution, which Jefferson articulated and em-bodied, was to create the framework of a new society reflecting in its constitution, statutes, buildings, furniture, songs and mottoes, the sober, republican, civic virtues drawn from the ancient examples of Greece and Rome. The Revolutionary general Charles Lee spoke for many when he said that he once regretted "not being thrown into the World in the glorious third or fourth century of the Romans but now it seemed that the ancient republican dreams at length bid fair to being realiz'd."

Jefferson's life stretches across one of the most revolutionary periods in the history of art as well as government. He was born before the artist David and survived the poet Byron, and it is not surprising to find his interests and tastes combining by turns the elements of the classicist and the romantic. The more we study the evidence, the supposed polarities of romanticism and classicism that once were thought to identify and explain the strange emotional energy of the art of the late eighteenth century are not so clearly discernible. The duality, "the merging paradoxes," that more accurately characterize the late Enlightenment, in the words of Henry Steele Commager, can be traced in Jefferson's own personality through his letters, his libraries, and his aesthetic predilections. But because of his looming historical presence as a principal figure in the American Revolution, as third president of the United States, and as the visionary negotiator of the Louisiana purchase and because of the ubiquitous portrait impressions which each generation of Americans absorbs on stamps and currency, it is all the more difficult to come close to the creative wellsprings of such a person and to assess his contributions to the American tradition in the field of the arts.

First of all and lest anyone be misled, Jefferson was educated and trained as a lawyer, not as an artist or architect. His artistic skills were learned in the Renaissance tradition of the amateur coupled with the practical necessities of conveying visual ideas, plans and designs to workmen who could carry them out. He seems to have taken a certain pleasure in the use of his hands, to translate or to record with pen, to try the etcher's tools or to simply manipulate a set of carpenter's tools which he kept in his study in the president's house. There is a letter written from Paris saying that he had been unable to finish some drawings for a carriage because the weather had not permitted him to work in the light of the open courtyard, but it is the only glimpse we have of his personal working habits, as far as drawing is concerned. Both his granddaughter, Cornelia Randolph, and the young architect, Robert Mills, who practiced their draftsmanship at Monticello under Jefferson's eye, ended by being more accomplished than their tutor. Except for his encouragement, however, there are no references to his own personal contribution to their instruction.

In his essay "Jefferson and the Arts," Fiske Kimball points out the paucity of artistic stimulation in Jefferson's Virginia and in his education. It may well have been the memory of these shortcomings that prompted him to include instruction in art in his proposed reforms for the curriculum at the College of William and Mary. The eighteenth century was, nevertheless, an age of speculation on the theory of art and its function in an ideal society, and from his readings in Hogarth, Burke and Lord Kames among others, Jefferson indulged his taste in the philosophical analysis of abstract systems fashionable at the time.

It would again be misleading to claim, however, that Jefferson subscribed to any particular aesthetic ideas, nor can we conveniently identify him with our latter-day academic labels as a romantic or neoclassicist. As Eleanor Berman put it,

Jefferson had no philosophy of art any more than he had a philosophy in our twentieth century concept of that discipline. His writings do not contain a body of knowledge about art organized into a clearly constructed, formal system. His aesthetic ideas express in effect a constellation of attitudes which are communicated via hundreds of observations occuring in all sorts of other connections throughout his voluminous writings. . . . Their formal inconsistencies cannot be counted as they change from one decade to the next in the context of the experiences of that long and active life.

We must substitute conjecture for fact in much of what we know about Jefferson's earliest interest in the arts and the haphazard aesthetic experiences open to a clever, rich young man growing up in Virginia in the 1750s and 1760s on the very edge of European civilization. His only significant travel beyond the narrow fringe of the settled Tidewater and the sparser reaches of the Piedmont, where he was born, was a trip to Philadelphia in 1766 to be inoculated against smallpox. While he was in Philadelphia, it was Jefferson's good fortune to meet Dr. John Morgan, who had studied in Edinburgh, London and Paris before taking the Grand Tour of Italy, bringing back a respectable collection of paintings, prints and books on architecture. All this represented a visual and intellectual feast for the young Virginian and was perhaps his first serious introduction into the arts as a concrete experience, undreamed of in the rural society that Jefferson had known.

Three years later, when Jefferson began his first plans for Monticello, he designed the central room as a gallery for paintings and sculpture. As the plans of the house evolved and changed over the years, it was in this west room and the later reception hall that he assembled what has been called the first art collection in America. Undoubtedly he had been inspired by Dr. Morgan during that first visit to Philadelphia as well as by his own wide reading in the art guides of the day. Because he grew up in a province with almost no paintings or sculpture, it is remarkable that Jefferson was able to develop an eye for the visual arts at all. In the surviving but incomplete inventory of his collection there are over sixty paintings listed, not to mention the sculpture of first rank, which included seven of Houdon's masterpieces. When he returned from France he brought some eighty crates of Louis XVI furniture to enrich the Monticello collection further, making it incomparable in America up to that time.

It requires the utmost imagination to reconstruct the scanty resources that Jefferson could have found or known in that provincial society to stimulate his eye or imagination in the years before he began his collecting and the building of his own private museum on the Virginia mountaintop. Here and there a few great houses of some architectural pretensions were oases of culture in an endless forest, the houses surrounded perhaps with formal gardens such as existed at Mt. Airy or Rosewell where Jefferson's friend, John Page, grew up. More often, civilization was represented by a cluster of less imposing frame or stone structures, organized into a self-contained, working village with its network of shops, barns, cribs, slave quarters, and occasionally, near the mansion, a neat family schoolhouse like the one that still survives at Tuckahoe, where Jefferson first encountered the world of books. Perhaps it was some memory of the spirit of this intimate, human, village setting of his earliest educational experience that informed his brilliant plans for the University of Virginia near the end of his life.

Books of philosophy, poetry, natural science and history with words and few pictures were the standard classroom fare. If we accept the proposed library that Jefferson drew up for his friend, Robert Skipwith, in 1771 as describing his own intellectual topography and interests in his late twenties, then we can get a reasonable picture of his development and tastes during his formative years. At an early age, he began "to collect a library, not merely amassing a number of books, but distinguishing them in subordination to early art and science," Edmund Randolph later wrote. In the chapter on painting in the list of books recommended to Skipwith are such standard eighteenth-century studies as Webb's *Essay on Painting*, an *Inquiry into the Beauties of Painting*, Jonathan Richardson's *Theory of Painting and Essay on a Connoisseur*, Leonardo da Vinci's *Treatise of Painting*, William Gilpin's *Essay on Prints* and Hogarth's *Analysis of Beauty*.

The importance of Jefferson's early reading and of the aesthetic inspirations he received from literary sources as he shaped his own taste in art, particularly sculpture, architecture, and landscape design, becomes all the more obvious when one attempts to identify the few works of art which Jefferson would have known as a young man beyond commonplace family portraits and engravings.

In 1781, he wrote in his *Notes on the State of Virginia* that, as far as architecture in the former colony was concerned, "the first principles of the art are unknown and there is scarcely a model among us sufficiently chaste to give an idea of them." But he could have directed the criticism to painting and sculpture as well. Even when the first copies of old masters to be shown in Virginia were exhibited in the Kings Arms Tavern at Williamsburg in June 1773, we can only say that Jefferson, who was in the neighborhood, might have seen young Mathew Pratt's copy of Benjamin West's copy of Correggio and Guido Reni. But his own letters and Journals of that date are absolutely silent.

Jefferson's enthusiasm for sculpture and for public commissions in particular, which he was later to champion with a critical eye that chose Houdon and Canova over more mediocre sculptors, may have been kindled by Lord Botetourt's statue ordered for Williamsburg by the colony in 1771, but he left no record of that possible spark of inspiration. In the same year he had completed the "hermit's" room, the first structure at Monticello, and it was probably during that spring that he drew up a list of famous sculpture he desired to decorate the grounds in casts or copies. As Professor Seymour Howard has suggested, perhaps the two niches in the west drawing room that Jefferson included in his original plans were actually designed to hold the *Venus de' Medici* and the *Apollo Belvedere*. Again the importance of books and engravings, the only source of study of antique sculpture, is evident, for not even plaster copies of such famous examples had yet appeared in the American colonies. Richardson and Addison provided critical descriptions of a number of the pieces; such as the *Venus de' Medici*, the *Apollo Belvedere*, the *Antinous* and the *Farnese Hercules*, but Jefferson's library catalogue also lists Spence's *Polymetis*, which first appeared in 1747 with its suggestive description of the antique. François Perrier's earlier folio *Signa et Statua Antiqua* with a hundred engravings of antique works was

also among the books of the young lawyer's library. At least one statue listed in his building notebook, *Hercules and Antaeus*, was taken from a book on anatomy by Chelseldon.

His earliest plans for the landscape and gardens at Monticello were sprinkled with grottoes, falls, springs and antique sculpture, in which the young Jefferson revealed his most susceptible romantic imagination. If a vision of the *Venus de' Medici* and the *Apollo Belvedere* planted on the edge of the wilderness, where buffalo might have been seen only a few years before, suggests the imagination of an American William Beckford, what are we to say when the same scheme for Monticello included Greek, Gothic and Chinese temples among the cascades and grottoes, with a memorial column taller than that of Trajan to stand as the central architectural element?

In 1770, the year before Jefferson had allowed his poetic musings to populate the top of Monticello mountain with gods and goddesses from the ancient world, Shadwell, the house where he was born, had burned. It is likely that he had already completed some of the basic plans for a new house before the fire and had determined that it should be placed on the nearby mountain to face the vast reaches of the wilderness that stretched westward to the Blue Ridge and beyond.

By the spring of 1771, Jefferson had completed a small pavilion where he lived alone in "one room, which like the cobler's serves me for parlor, for kitchen and hall. I may add, for bedchamber and study too . . . I have hope, however, of getting more elbow room this summer," he wrote in his first letter dated from Monticello. The original Monticello, as we know it from the earliest surviving drawings dated 1771, was a relatively small classical villa with a central gallery for works of art, and the dreams for the grounds show a sympathy with and understanding of the new English romantic landscape school which was without precedent in America as far as we know.

Probably the earliest books on architecture that Jefferson acquired were Gibbs' *Rules for Drawing in Architecture* and Leoni's *The Architecture of A. Palladio; in four books*, and it was to Palladio that he was to affirm his lifelong allegiance. It was a creative alliance of profound consequences. Through Palladio's plates, which conveyed an architecture of timeless proportion and mathematical harmony, Jefferson envisioned a style and form based on antiquity but with a purity which left behind history's corrupting influences of rotten governments, benighted rulers and unenlightened institutions. With the building and rebuilding of Monticello throughout his life, Jefferson indulged his pleasure of creation, tested and absorbed the inspirations from Palladio, Gibbs and the new examples of buildings he was to see in Paris, and carried on his practical studies of the theory and history of architecture as a designer and builder, acquiring a knowledge of the subject that went beyond the experience of any American of his generation.

The opportunities for architectural and landscape design presented by the new estate at Monticello not only appealed to Jefferson's earliest creative instincts but they represented areas where he could test some of the more experimental notions which were beginning to find new and astonishing expression in England

and on the Continent. The idea of the purification of nature, which was first advanced by the philosophers and poets in the late seventeenth century and the first quarter of the eighteenth century, was central to the new concept of the neoclassical landscape. The tradition of a literary inspiration for the ideal landscape was itself rooted in the study of the classical poets from Homer to Virgil, who were, of course, familiar to Jefferson from his earliest studies of Latin and Greek.

Milton's poetic vision of nature in the Garden of Eden has long been recognized as one of the seminal modern literary sources of the romantic school of landscape design. Jefferson may well have been reading Milton when he was drafting his first plans for the gardens at Monticello. In a letter ordering some pomegranates, written in the spring of 1771 to a friend in Williamsburg, he apparently evoked Milton's verse, for the recipient Mrs. Drummond replied that ". . . No pen but Yrs., cou'd, (surely so butiful discribe) espeshally, those few lines, in the Miltonic Stile. Thou wonderful Young Man, so piously entertaining, thro out that, exalted Letter. Indeed," she concluded with astonishing prescience, "I shal' think, Spirits of an higher order, inhabits Yr. Aerey Mountains. . . ."

Perhaps it was inevitable for a young boy with a keen mind, a romantic imagination and curiosity and a natural bent for detached observation, growing up on the very edge of civilization, to perfect a special visual faculty. From the Indian down through the whole mythology of the frontiersman, the celebration of an almost preternaturally acute use of the senses, especially sight and sound, has become a part of our national folklore. Jefferson's father, who had died relatively young, had such a reputation in Albemarle County from his days as an explorer and surveyor.

While it could scarcely be expected that any kind of rudimentary training in the fine arts, even classroom sketching, would have been offered in the schools that Jefferson attended, his mind was well stocked with poetry and literature. He undoubtedly developed at least a literary sense of proportion and rhythm from his professors of rhetoric, and it is not without significance that his favorite studies were mathematics and music. All this was useful when he applied his skills to the organization of his first architectural plans by formulas and mathematics, as Fiske Kimball has observed. Across the back of many of his drawings are "set down in his precise handwriting the result of those calculations." The general idea may have been inspired by Palladio, Gibbs or perhaps Robert Morris, but the details and direction for realization of the designs would have been distinctly Jefferson's own creation.

Some of the first books that Jefferson acquired as a young man were volumes of engraved plates of architecture or scenes from the antique. A few of these volumes may have come from the libraries of early Virginians like William Byrd of Westover. Others were ordered directly from England, for the sources of study, at best second hand, were not easily available in that outpost of European culture.

Robert Rosenblum makes the provocative observation that the most radical innovators in the neoclassical movement of the late eighteenth century, such as the Scottish painter, Gavin

Hamilton, and the Scandinavians, Johannes Wiedenwelt, Nicolai Abildgaard and Carl August Ehrensvard, came from the periphery of European art. It is not farfetched to see Jefferson's own precocious and romantic imagination, fed largely by literature and the engravings of the antique, filtered through the Augustan sensibilities of an earlier generation, developing also along the same perimeter in a similar intellectual environment but at another angle of the compass. Palladio, Herculaneum, Rome and the Maison Carrée were, at least in the imagination, as far from Edinburgh and Stockholm as they were from Philadelphia or Williamsburg.

When Jefferson wrote his critical indictment of Virginia architecture in his *Notes on the State of Virginia* in 1781, he was as thoroughgoing as in his bill of particulars against the king of England, five years before. "The private buildings are very rarely constructed of stone or brick, much the greatest portion being of scantling and boards, plastered with lime. . . . it is impossible to devise things more ugly, uncomfortable and happily more perishable," he observed, and even for those houses with any architectural pretense, there were but "two or three plans, on one of which, according to its size, most of the houses in the state are built."

When he wrote this, Virginia's architectural heritage, it should be noted, included some of the greatest eighteenth-century monuments of the North American colonies; not only the public buildings of Williamsburg—the capitol, the palace, the college—but, along the rivers, Rosewell, Mt. Airy, Stratford, Gunston Hall and Westover hardly constituted a catalogue of expendable cottages and "brick kilns," such as he dubbed the College of William and Mary, his alma mater.

Just as he had allied himself with the politics of revolution in establishing national independence, so it is clear that his eye early and easily responded to change when it came to the arts. When he wrote that his favorite amusement was "putting up and pulling down," he was referring specifically to architecture, but it was an attitude of innovation that characterized much of his life's accomplishments and interests.

From Williamsburg to Paris, no house that he ever occupied, including the new president's mansion in Washington, escaped his critical attention and alterations. And if there were immediate grounds or gardens to be reformed or improved as there were on the Champs Elysées in Paris and along Pennsylvania Avenue in Washington, then the environment itself had to accept his sensitive reorganization and attention. In the 1790s after he returned from Europe, the earlier more academic version of Monticello was pulled down to make way for a more complex solution reflecting the refinements of his eye during his travels. The gardens themselves were redesigned, and the romantic, natural schemes of the gardens he had seen in England bcame the model he hoped to adapt to his Virginia estate.

Because our own distant view of Jefferson and his presumed world is so dominated by classical features—Palladian villas, Roman temples, Vitruvian orders, antique manners and austere neoclassical profiles—it is difficult to recapture the profoundly romantic environment the American wilderness itself presented to the susceptible imagination of the young Jefferson, who devoured Sterne, Rousseau, Shenstone, McPherson's *Ossian* and other early romantic writers. Jefferson's Virginia, its "aery mountains," and "smooth blue horizon at an infinite distance," with rivers below pouring through valleys in a "riot and tumult roaring around" then passing into silence and calm, was the quintessential romantic landscape that European artists and poets dreamed about and invented on canvas and in poems. Jefferson had only to open his front door and step onto the portico. For him, John Locke's "tabula rasa" did not have to be created out of the overgrown accumulations of decayed societies, to begin a new epoch of government or of architecture. The primeval purity of the environment was simply waiting for the creative imagination of the New American whose "faith in the senses" and the rule of reason would produce a new era.

Jefferson's vivid perceptions of the contrast between the presumed corrupting influences of the Old World, which could only recapture its innocence and purity through drastic revolution, and "the tranquil, permanent felicity with which domestic society in America blesses most of its inhabitants," allowing its citizens "to follow those pursuits which health and reason approve," was reinforced wherever he turned when he arrived "on the vaunted scene of Europe" in 1784. He was like an eighteenth-century Henry James as he set down in letters the first impressions of how "this new scene has struck a savage of the mountains of America." But whatever the political and social oppression and squalor that frequently offended the congenial democrat, he could not find words "to tell . . . how much I enjoy their architecture, sculpture, painting and music." He shared with James that distinctive American gift that the latter described as "our moral consciousness, our unprecedented spiritual lightness and vigour" allowing us to "deal freely with forms of civilization not our own, and pick and choose and assimilate and in short claim our property." For the next five years and with a "lightness and vigour" that would have exhausted James, Thomas Jefferson went about claiming whatever aesthetic and cultural property that he deemed worthy to furnish the new American nation that was coming into view for all the world to marvel at.

With his obvious enthusiasm in exploring the remains of European civilization which most, like John Adams, assumed was in the last stages of its Roman decline as described by Gibbon, Jefferson maintained a detachment that underlined his self-consciousness as an American who was also intent on salvaging from Europe's bankrupt past its last great legacy, the Enlightenment. The "vaunted scene" and "the general fate of humanity" had not struck him "advantageously." He himself had escaped the corrupting dangers of a European education at an early age, unlike some of his Virginia contemporaries. "An American coming to Europe for education," he warned a young friend, "loses in his knowledge, in his morals, in his health, in his habits, and in his happiness." But for all of his preaching, and his often ambivalent observations on the European artistic scene, he was determined to identify and to select those things that would be useful and beneficial to the new republic—from new French architectural technology to the politically suggestive and even

revolutionary designs of the English romantic landscape. Jefferson responded with an engaging innocence and sometimes with critical acumen to the artistic experiments that were beginning to alter the aesthetic ideals and values of Europe. The "cold and icy star" of David immediately caught his eye. "I do not feel an interest in any pencil but that of David," he wrote enthusiastically. In sculpture, only Houdon "among the foremost or perhaps the foremost artist in the world," was equal to creating a monument to General Washington in his native state, the first public commission of sculpture in America. Later Canova, "considered by all of Europe as without a rival," would also receive Jefferson's recommendation for a similar commission in North Carolina. Sculpture, like architecture, had a symbolic, elevating role to play in a republic to remind a free people of its achievements and sacrifices, and it would be important for future generations to have the very best examples of creative genius.

In his *Notes on the State of Virginia*, an enquiry and agenda setting forth his philosophy and proposals to achieve an American Enlightenment in a land "kindly separated by Nature and a wide ocean from the exterminating havoc of one quarter to the globe," Jefferson significantly included some observations on architecture. "The genius of architecture seems to have shed its maledictions over this land. . . . Perhaps a spark may fall on some young subjects of natural taste, kindle up their genius, and produce a reformation in this elegant and useful art." Architecture was obviously important in a new country setting about to build new seats of government as symbols of virtue, to house legislatures and all the other administrative apparatus from jails to city halls. But the quick and inevitable growth of population required new and unprecedented skills if domestic housing was to rise above the "rude, misshapen piles" that constituted most of the architecture of his own Virginia. "As we double our numbers every 20 years we must double our houses. Besides we build of such perishable materials that one half of our houses must be replaced in every space of 20 years," he observed.

The classical vocabulary of the new French idealistic architecture, combined with a reductive simplicity that was beginning to manifest itself in Paris in the 1780s when Jefferson arrived, immediately attracted his eye. He would gaze for hours on Pierre Rousseau's new hotel for Prince Salm-Kyrburg opposite the Tuileries gardens, which had been completed in 1782. Nor was it his only affair with a building while he was in France. He sent a model of the little Maison Carrée at Nîmes—he later called "noble beyond expression"—to the state commissioners in Richmond, who were about to build the first structure designed specifically to house the basic functions of a modern republic. Jefferson's inspiration was to give the fledgling government a building of unprecedented symbolic monumentality in a temple form with the "ring of eternity" thus launching the classic revival in the United States.

Jefferson's architectural vocabulary of the classic form is as remote to us as the antique Roman models, so it is difficult to appreciate the impact of his innovations. Just as morality and civic humanism became the motivating force of the social and political philosophy of the Founding Fathers, the same neoclassical

Platonic concepts worked their visual reformation on the architecture of the new republic. Truth, honesty, abstract simplicity and antique virtues translated into red brick, stone and native clapboard produced models across the land equal to the new political ideals.

It was important to study the ancient sources themselves in their purest form, rather than relying on secondhand interpretations in books and engravings. His advice to young Americans always included admonitions to study ancient ruins and artifacts whenever possible during their travels in Europe. For as his advisor on the plans of the capitol at Richmond, the French architect Charles-Louis Clérisseau, had earlier remarked, "Let us learn from the ancients how to submit the rules of genius. Let us wipe out the mark of servitude and mimicry which disfigures our works." These were the lofty ideals to which Jefferson wholeheartedly subscribed and which were to inform his own experiments in design and construction.

Jefferson, the Puritan, agreed with the marquis de Chastellux that the European luxury, overrefinement and effeminacy expressed in much of contemporary art was a threat to the morals and the public happiness of the people and their representatives in the new American government. The dilemma was how to establish a foundation for the arts in America without accepting the time-honored conditions of wealth and rank in which they flourished. Jefferson, the statesman, revolutionary and philosopher believed with Chastellux that "whether we consider the fine arts . . . a delicious ambrosia that the Gods have thought proper to share with us, or . . . a dangerous poison, this liquor, whether beneficial or harmful, will always be modified by the vessel which receives it."

Painting, while not an essential element of an enlightened society, especially in its formative stages, could in Jefferson's words, "give a pleasing and innocent direction to accumulations of wealth which could otherwise be employed in the nourishing of coarse and vicious habits." In a more positive view, artists could also provide posterity with an accurate record of its great events and the men who participated in them. Jefferson's collaboration with young John Trumbull on his painting of *The Signing of the Declaration of Independence* reflects his appreciation of this useful function of the artist and the social role of art to portray the epic events of history. While he encouraged Trumbull in his work and even offered him the post of secretary to the minister in Paris so that he could continue his artistic studies, Jefferson was not at all sure that conditions were ripe for a successful professional career in America. There were too many other practical necessities to deal with in a new country. He warned his young countrymen, Rutledge and Shippen, that painting and sculpture were "too expensive for the state of wealth of our country. It would be useless, therefore, and preposterous for us to make ourselves connoisseurs in those arts." It was much like his earlier advice to family friends not to allow their sons to travel in Europe before they were thirty. It was simply too heady and dangerous an experience for youth. So it was perhaps in the same vein, that he thought some maturity would be necessary before the new nation could accommodate and absorb painters

and sculptors into the body politic on a useful and productive footing.

But for all of his reservations, Jefferson, like the young Henry James, went about "claiming his property" wherever his alert and finely tuned eye led him, from the moment he stepped onto the European scene. His famous love letter to Maria Cosway in the form of a dialogue between the "Head" and "Heart," is as revealing a guide to some of the new architectural experiments then taking place in Paris, as to the deeper revelations of Jefferson's own emotions. The new glass and frame dome of the Halle aux Bleds, as it was known in the eighteenth century, in which Jefferson and Mrs. Cosway first met, would later appear in Jefferson's suggestions to Latrobe for the design of the roof for the House of Representatives. The subtle arrangement of the apartments in de Monville's giant broken column in the strange, surreal gardens of the Désert de Retz, where the couple picnicked, was recalled by Jefferson when he drew up the plans for the rotunda at the University of Virginia, years later. Even the trellised "bowers of Marly," where he and Maria walked, may have been an unconscious influence, when he designed the arcaded passageways between the pavilions at the University of Virginia.

Even though he could not discern the limits of the intellectual and aesthetic revolution, the French philosopher d'Alembert had noted as early as 1759 that "a most remarkable change in our ideas is taking place, one of such rapidity that it seems to promise a greater change to come." When Jefferson arrived in Paris in the fall of 1784, those changes in architecture, painting and sculpture as well as philosophy could be seen advancing throughout the studios, workshops, galleries, and streets of Europe. The "tabula rasa" of his own provincial imagination responded easily to the new style that coalesced in the neoclassical masterpieces created during the decade of the 1780s. David's *Oath of the Horatii* with all of its vigorous purity was completed in 1784, and Jefferson and young Trumbull immediately went to admire it.

Claude-Nicolas Ledoux carried out his radically advanced designs for the king's tollhouses in the new wall constructed around Paris beginning in 1783. In their pure geometry, Ledoux plumbed the most primitive sources of antiquity for inspiration. Jefferson's brief reference to the wall condemned it on what appear to be political grounds while recognizing its beauty, for the clarity of Ledoux's work concealed under the decoration at Louveciennes and the Hôtel Guimard was in fact admired by the American minister, the latter inspiring his design for Pavilion IX at the University of Virginia.

The third artist to capture his attention and to break new ground in the decade of the 1780s was the Italian sculptor, Antonio Canova. He, like David, studied in Rome, and David was working on the *Oath* about the time that Canova began his model of the monument for Clement XIV to be placed in St. Peter's. Jefferson may have heard of the sculptor through David, who had known Canova in Rome. He was at least aware of Canova's reputation and accomplishments in 1816, when he insisted that the state of North Carolina give its commission for a monument to Washington to "old Canova," the best sculptor of the age.

Of all the discoveries the Enlightenment lays claim to or the rediscoveries that were its unique enterprise, it was the rediscovery of the ancient world through its literature, its philosophy and its art that Jefferson could most easily respond to when he arrived in Europe. There is no need to labor the point about his classical education, his erudition in Latin, his predilection for Greek and Roman authors, the translation of Greek poetry as he stood beside the fireplace at Monticello in his old age. As Professor Commager put it, "The Founding Fathers knew the ancient world better, perhaps, than they knew the European or even the British world, better, in all likelihood, than they knew the American outside their own section."

The historical and moral world of Greece and Rome was the basic foundation of all eighteenth-century education, and this extended to farmers and tradesmen as well as lawyers, clergymen and statesmen. When an English journal claimed the invention of making the circumference of a wheel from a single piece of wood, Jefferson wrote off immediately to St. John de Crèvecoeur that the practice has long been followed in New Jersey by farmers who in turn had discovered the technique in the classics. "Ours are the only farmers who can read Homer," he declared, then closes by quoting the appropriate lines in Greek from the *Iliad* on chariot making.

The classics had done more than furnish Jefferson's mind with basic appointments of philosophy and history, however. They had also educated his eye and imagination to appreciate the universal beauty and truth that Winckelmann had pursued and that architects from Palladio to Clérisseau had appropriated from the ruins of Rome, Palestrina, Nîmes and Spalatro. The works of Palladio, Lord Burlington and Piranesi had provided the most tempting early introduction to the subject in Virginia, so it is not surprising that Jefferson's travels in France and northern Italy were filled with the pleasure of ruins, as well as notes on building canals, growing rice and the price of good wine. "From Lyon to Nîmes I have been nourished with the remains of Roman Grandeur," he wrote to the comtesse de Tessé, and in the same letter he confessed that he had fallen in love with the Maison Carrée. "I am immersed in antiquities from morning to night," he continued, and if he was recalled from his reveries in the past to the eighteenth century it was only "by the recollection of your goodness and friendship." Statues, urns, fallen columns and bronze artifacts were carefully sought out and studied. Ancient coins which he collected in his travels were later given to the American Philosophical Society and the Roman askos he saw in the museum at Nîmes was to be translated into a splendid silver vessel for the dining table at Monticello.

Ten years before he had begun his affair with the temple at Nîmes, his imagination and pen were playing with perhaps the first neoclassical architectural project in America, at least on paper. It involved the palace at Williamsburg, which he had put down in his *Notes on the State of Virginia* as a building "not handsome without . . . but capable of being made an elegant seat." In a series of studies and measured plans of the palace, which were probably done before the American Revolution, the young architect-politician proposed to remodel the old house into a temple with immense porticos on both the front and back, whose eight columns would extend the full height of two stories. Had it been carried out, it would have become an architectural landmark of the first rank as the first temple-form house in the neoclassical movement, with inspiration drawn directly from antique sources, rather than adapting the more conventional Palladian and English baroque interpretation.

Coming to Europe as he did at the age of forty-one, having been until then removed from the aesthetic center of things, Jefferson was able to combine a kind of intellectual and visual purity with a practical experience in architecture and landscape design that was singular in its focus. With no accumulation of past styles and cultural relics to confuse his vision or shape his taste, beyond the modest buildings of Virginia and his own selective library of literature and engravings, he sailed with remarkable skill through the confusing and often contradictory currents of artistic expression in Europe during the five years of his visit. His own taste for the classics inevitably guided his eye to those examples, both new and old, that fit the mode. Through his awareness of the purely literary origins of the romantic landscape in his early reading and with his own youthful poetic narrative evoking an arcadian elysium in his landscape plans for Monticello, Jefferson was probably closer to the origins of the English romantic landscape movement than later interpretations, which emphasized the importance of the landscape painting of Claude and Salvator Rosa to the exclusion of literary sources and guidebook discriptions.

Jefferson's freedom from tradition, combined with his frontiersman's bold imagination, allowed him to roam, with an innocence that we can admire, through the studios and galleries, picking and choosing with confident abandon, not as an academic connoisseur but as an "enthusiast on the subject of the arts."

When Jefferson returned to the United States and became secretary of state, his enthusiasm and experience were valuable assets which the new government quickly recognized. For L'Enfant, he assembled the best city plans of Europe as a clue to the alternative directions L'Enfant might consider as he carved up the ten mile square that had been recently surveyed. The citizens of Georgetown might be able to lift their own aesthetic sights, Jefferson suggested, if the fledgling government would distribute free engravings of outstanding European buildings. When it came to the president's house, it was Jefferson who proposed an architectural competition and laid down its rules, submitting an anonymous plan of his own based on Palladio's Villa Rotonda but with a dome that reflected Legrand's radical glass and wood enclosure of the Halle aux Bleds.

As president, Jefferson saw the need to recruit professional architects to the service of the Federal government so he created the post of surveyor of the public buildings, and appointed the well-trained Benjamin Latrobe to the office.

From his earliest reforms of the College of William and Mary, Jefferson had thought deeply about the philosophy of education in the republic, the needs of the students and scholars, and the relationship between the educational program and the architecture that was to house it. The final project of his old age, the University of Virginia, was to be his last great achievement in celebration of "the important truths that knowledge is power, that knowledge is safety, and that knowledge is happiness. . . ."

"This institution of my native state," he wrote with pride, "the hobby of my old age, will be based on the illimitable freedom of the human mind to explore and to expose every subject susceptible of its contemplation." And he was determined that the institution of such lofty purpose should be properly housed. "A barn for a college and log huts for accommodations" would never do, no matter what the cost or obstacles.

While most American colleges and academies were either one or two large buildings, if not barns or huts, to house all of the functions of teaching, living and administration, Jefferson had something else in mind which was unique in academic architectural planning. "The plan of the building is not to erect one single magnificent building to contain everybody and everything, but to make of it an academical village in which every professor should have his separate house (or 'pavilion'), containing his lecture room with two or three or four rooms for his own accommodation according as he may have a family or no family, with kitchen, garden, etc.; distinct dormitories for the students, not more than two in a room; and separate boarding houses for dieting them by private housekeepers."

His calling the university a "village" shows how clearly he saw the necessity of organizing the individual buildings into a unified whole, which respected both the symbolic functions and the human scale. The arrangement of the pavilions for the professors, their classrooms and living quarters, connected by the arcades and gardens to the students' quarters, its library housed in the rotunda at the head, with a theater in the dome to trace the course of the stars, projects a vital order of extraordinary creative power and imagination. Again he turned to his chief architectural authority and lifelong companion in his library, Andrea Palladio. "Pavilion No. X [is to be modeled on the] East Doric of the Theatre of Marcellus. The columns to have no bases . . . I have never seen an attic pilaster with the measures of its parts minutely expressed except that of the Temple of Nerva Trojan (Palladio, Book III, Plate 18)." Even if the goals were of the highest, the success of the plan and of the individual buildings must be evident in the smallest detail.

Working from a carefully defined collegiate program that was far in advance of its time, Jefferson was able to orchestrate its wise, practical and aesthetic elements into a unified whole of extraordinary balance and beauty. Again and again, his own range of experience, knowledge and human delight is revealed in garden walls, concealed walks, symbolic friezes and modulated façades of the most satisfying scale and rhythm imaginable.

One could spend a good part of a lifetime sorting out and cataloguing all of the details of the university and following them to their source—from Louis XIV's garden at Marly to the Theater of Marcellus and the Pantheon in Rome. In the capitals, façades, railings and pediments, each carries a part of its creator's history and experience—his books, his plans, his love affairs of the heart as well as the head, his dreams, above all, for a new nation—into a biography of an eye that still sets, by its example, a course for the human spirit to follow.

1 Thomas Jefferson

JEAN ANTOINE HOUDON 1741–1828
Marble 1789
54.5 (21½) high
Inscribed under left shoulder:
houdon f. 1789.

Lent by The Museum of Fine Arts, Boston

Probably in the early summer of 1789 Jefferson sat for Houdon in Paris. The original clay maquette modeled from life was discarded in the process of making the mold from which plaster examples were cast and finished by Houdon. But a plaster bust was regarded by the sculptor as only a temporary and intermediate stage in the production of a final portrait in a more permanent substance, which was in this instance Saravezza marble. This final stage of the life portrait was completed sometime between the opening of the Salon and the end of the year.

This superb likeness of Jefferson by the greatest portraitist of his time has been displayed in many versions in public and private collections since its original exhibition. It shaped an enduring visual image, which adequately encompasses the full range of Jefferson's accomplishments.

The image was given extensive currency from its inception. Copies in *biscuit de Sèvres* were reproduced commercially by the Manufacture de Sèvres during Houdon's lifetime. The presidential portrait on the 1801 Indian peace medal by John Reich was, as Jefferson himself reported, "taken from Houdon's bust." A century after examples of this medal were distributed by Lewis and Clark to important Indian leaders met in the course of their expedition, the Reich medal was used as the basis of the obverse of the Jefferson dollar, which was minted in 1903 to commemorate the centennial of the Louisiana Purchase. Thirty-five years later another medalist, Felix Schlag, also chose the Houdon portrait for the representation of Jefferson on the nickel. Since its first issue in 1938, this version of Houdon's portrait has become one of the most widely circulated of all Jefferson likenesses. A.B.

2 Thomas Jefferson

THOMAS SULLY 1783–1872
Oil on canvas 1821
76.2 x 63.5 (30 x 25)

Lent by the West Point Museum Collections, United States Military Academy, West Point

In January 1821 Jefferson was informed of the desire of the "Superintendent, Officers, Professors, Instructors, and Cadets of the U. States Mil. Academy" to commission Thomas Sully to paint a portrait of him, to be added to those hanging in the "Academic Library" as "being alike one of the Founders, and Patrons of both . . . Our Republic . . . and the Mil. Academy." Jefferson responded cordially, and though he felt that the trouble of Sully's journey would be "illy bestowed on an ottamy of 78," he nevertheless agreed to the sitting, which took place at Monticello in March 1821. According to Dunlap, the thirty-seven-year-old Sully "was an inmate of Monticello twelve days, and left the place with the greatest reluctance."

The life portrait, a half-length now at the American Philosophical Society, was used by Sully as an intermediary step for the production of this great full-length portrait—one of only two portrayals executed during Jefferson's lifetime. The full-length conveys the imposing stature that was so memorable an aspect of his presence. James Fenimore Cooper, who was not an admirer of Jefferson, wrote of the effects of this portrait on him during his visit to West Point in April 1823: "There was a dignity, a repose, I will go further, and say a loveliness, about this painting, that I never have seen in any other portrait. . . . I saw . . . Jefferson, standing before me, not in red breeches and slovenly attire, but a gentleman, appearing in all republican simplicity, with a grace and ease on the canvas, that to me seem unrivalled."

As its frequent reproduction bears testimony, Sully's portrait offers us the finest image of Jefferson in his last years. The portrait, which survives in perfect condition, is an unusually reliable record of Jefferson's coloring, depicting accurately his fresh complexion and the traces of the sandy hue still in his hair and eyebrows. A.B.

THE
LAND
OF
PROMISE

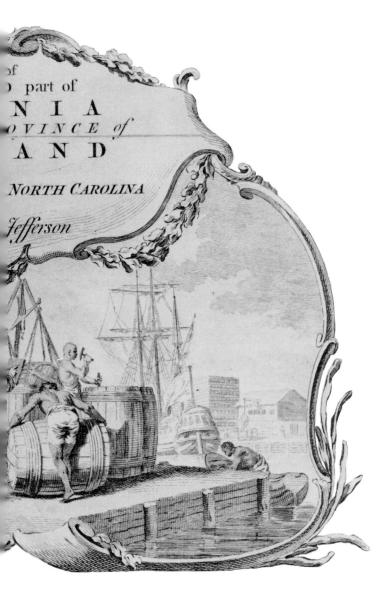

of
) part of
NIA
OVINCE of
AND

NORTH CAROLINA

Jefferson

VIRGINIA

Certainly it must be a happy climate, since it is very near the same latitude with the "Land of Promise."

ROBERT BEVERLY, *The History of the Present State of Virginia, 1705*

When Thomas Jefferson was born at Shadwell, his father's middle Piedmont tobacco plantation, in 1743, Great Britain's largest American colony, Virginia, had created a complex society with its own distinct characteristics on the periphery of European culture. The Virginia of Jefferson's youth was, in his own words, "a country isolated from the European world insulated from its sister colonies, with whom there was scarcely any intercourse, little visited by foreigners. . . ."

With a network of aristocratic families firmly established in the Tidewater along the coastal rivers and a new, plain, aggressive society growing along the western edges toward the mountains, the colony was a self-contained and yet divided "country." Jefferson's family ties ran both ways, for his mother was a Randolph with all of the Tidewater family connections the name implied, while his father, Peter Jefferson, with a less pretentious background, made a fortune in farming, land speculation, and surveying on the edge of the "wilderness."

Jefferson's earliest education began in the small frame school building at Tuckahoe Plantation above the fall line on the James River where his father had moved to raise both his own and the orphaned family of his best friend, William Randolph, who had died suddenly in 1745. The foundation of his studies was the conventional dose of Latin and Greek provided by Scottish tutors, but the rich, wild natural setting of Shadwell and Tuckahoe with their vast fields provided an even greater stimulant to the attentive eyes and eager imagination of the young Jefferson.

After his father died in 1757, leaving him at the age of fourteen with a considerable fortune, he continued his studies with the Reverend James Maury, "a correct classical scholar" and clergyman of some prominence. At the age of sixteen, he traveled to Williamsburg and enrolled at the College of William and Mary. "It was my great good fortune . . . ," Jefferson wrote later in his *Autobiography*, "that Dr. William Small of Scotland was then professor of Mathematics, a man profound in most of the useful branches of science, with a happy talent of communication correct and gentlemanly manners, & an enlarged & liberal mind. . . . He was the first who ever gave in that college regular lectures in Ethics, Rhetoric and Belles lettres."

Frances Fauquier, that amiable, cultivated lieutenant governor and sometime London gambler, had arrived in Williamsburg the same year as Small in 1758, and through Small, Jefferson was introduced to the governor's circle and joined his "familiar table" along with George Wythe, forming the celebrated *partie quarrée* and attic society recalled in Jefferson's memoirs.

The year that Jefferson entered the college, an English traveler noted that the town "does not contain more than one thousand souls, whites and negroes; and is far from being a place of any consequence. . . . there are ten or twelve gentlemen's families, constantly residing in it, besides merchants and tradesmen: and at the time of the assemblies, and general courts, it is crowded with the gentry of the country: on those occasions there are balls and other amusements; but as soon as business is finished, they return to their plantations and the town is in a manner deserted."

Whatever its shortcomings as an urban center, Williamsburg did provide Jefferson the student with libraries, bookshops, intellectual mentors of considerable achievement, and companions like John Page of Rosewell and Thomas Nelson who shared Jefferson's youthful enthusiasm for poetry, music and architecture, as well as the theater, dancing, card playing and fox hunting.

After five years of study of the law with Mr. Wythe, Jefferson returned to Shadwell and sometime before 1770 conceived the grand scheme to build himself a house on top of the mountain left to him by his father. The main dwelling was not completed when he brought his bride, Martha Wayles, there in January 1772. In its design, site and general landscape plan, nothing like Monticello had been seen before in America. The marquis de Chastellux, with his customary perception, wrote in his journal a dozen years later, after a visit to the new house, that Jefferson was "the first American who has consulted the Fine Arts to know how he should shelter himself from the weather."

The sources he consulted, the inspiration to his eye as well as of his mind during these years—Jefferson was not yet thirty when he first dreamed of the new dwelling—are important to us as a means of understanding Jefferson's aesthetic judgment, his lifelong affair with the role of the arts in a democracy, and as an artist his deep concern with the shaping of the image of the new Republic. The things he saw, the books he read, the places he lived or visited, the appearance of his immediate ancestors and contemporaries in their stiff, uncompromising poses, the nature of the Virginia countryside, the first tentative tracings and drawings of building designs, the poetic reveries set down as romantic landscape plans, all contribute to reconstructing something of the now fractured mosaic of Jefferson's eighteenth-century Virginia.

The Virginia planters, like the English lords or the Venetian aristocrats, demanded appropriate country seats as the center of their vast, productive estates along the Virginia rivers. Architecture and household furnishings were important in the grander establishments whose English factors kept up a steady shipment of chairs, chests, silver, porcelain and engravings. "The chief magnificence of the Virginians," Chastellux noted, "consists in furniture, linens and silver plate, in which they resemble our own [French] forefathers who had no private apartments in their castles, but only a well stored wine cellar and handsome sideboards." Paintings, except for portraits, were scarce. Neither Jefferson's father, mother nor wife were painted during their lifetime and his own first likeness was not done until he went to London in 1786.

In Jefferson's famous Notes on the State of Virginia, the arts in any form do not figure in the inventory of assets of the former colony. As for architecture, Jefferson observed, "The first principles of the art are unknown, and there exists scarcely a model among us sufficiently chaste to give an idea of them."

Jefferson's criticism of architecture extended to the public buildings of Williamsburg, especially the college which to his eye "would be taken for brick-kilns," if they did not have roofs. Aside from Monticello, some of his earliest architectural projects were for Williamsburg, including a bold proposal to reshape the governor's palace with a double portico and an octagonal chapel for the college, both without precedent in American colonial design.

If Virginia planters were short on paintings, and sculpture was nonexistent until Governor Botetourt's monument arrived in 1773, cheap engravings were popular and, more importantly, handsomely illustrated books, especially on classical subjects and architecture, were available in the better libraries of the gentry. The College of William and Mary had benefited from gifts of books from Governor Spotswood, Fauquier and others, including a copy still preserved of Descriptions des Châteaux et Parcs de Versailles, de Trianon, et de Marly, by Piganiol de la Force, describing royal parks that would later fascinate the American minister in Paris.

In Jefferson's list of 150 books for Robert Skipwith, compiled in 1771, works on the fine arts such as Burke's On the Sublime and the Beautiful, Hogarth's Analysis of Beauty and Lord Kames' Elements of Criticism are included.

When it came to the subject of architecture, Jefferson turned instinctively to the work of Palladio and his English followers as instruments to mold his own vision and aesthetic development. Gibbs, Morris, Kent and Halfpenny were bought and studied by a receptive student whose philosophy and outlook were attuned to the new classicism as the perfect symbol for a republic that was to humbly model itself on the political traditions of the ancients. Jefferson's aesthetic vision paralleled his political vision, seeing that man could plan and shape his physical environment along rational lines, just as he could construct new political machinery to confirm the rights of man in his "pursuit of happiness" and freedom.

At the close of the Revolution in 1782, having concluded his military duties at Yorktown, Chastellux wrote an essay in the form of a letter to the Reverend James Madison called "The Progress of the Arts and Sciences in America" as an enquiry on the future of the enlightenment in America. Jefferson received a copy and was so impressed that he urged his philosopher friend to include it as a postscript to the marquis' travels when it was published.

Jefferson understood the larger context of the purposes for the enquiry, for the rest of the world wondered in books, pamphlets, speeches and letters what the full implications and measure of the American experiment were to hold for mankind. What were to be the artistic standards in a democracy? What was the role of the artist? Who was to be his patron? For whom did he speak?

These questions were raised in Virginia two hundred years ago, and they deeply intrigued the young Jefferson, as they engage our own concern in 1976.

Jefferson's response to the measured enquiry and argument of an informed member of the French enlightenment on the future of the arts must be viewed against the eighteenth-century colonial background. If his early education in Virginia was conventional for the age, its thrust was cultural in detail as his library recommendations to his friend, Robert Skipwith, reveal.

In shaping his philosophy of art and determining its value, the strict classical ideals supplied by the examples of antiquity must be weighed with the frontiersman's faith in utility. Explaining his inclusion of contemporary novels along with Cicero and Homer, the young moralist wrote to Skipwith:

A little attention to the nature of the human mind evinces that the entertainments of fiction are useful as well as pleasant. That they are pleasant when well written, every person feels who reads. But wherein is its utility, asks the reverand sage, big with the notion that nothing can be useful but the learned lumber of Greek and Roman reading with which his head is stored? I answer everything is useful which contributes to fix in the principles and practices of virtue. . . . The field of imagination is thus laid open to our use and lessons may be formed to illustrate and carry home to the heart every moral rule of life.

In the arts as well as politics, Jefferson's life spanned a period of tumultuous change, from the rational order of the classic enlightenment as reflected in the Virginia society of his youth to the romantic revolution of his mature years. In his pursuit of the arts, he took his stand with the party of revolt. As Edmund Randolph wrote of his young kinsman, "he panted after the fine arts, and discovered a taste in them not easily satisfied with such scanty means as existed in a colony, for it was 'a part of Mr. Jefferson's pride to run before the times in which he lived.' " W.H.A.

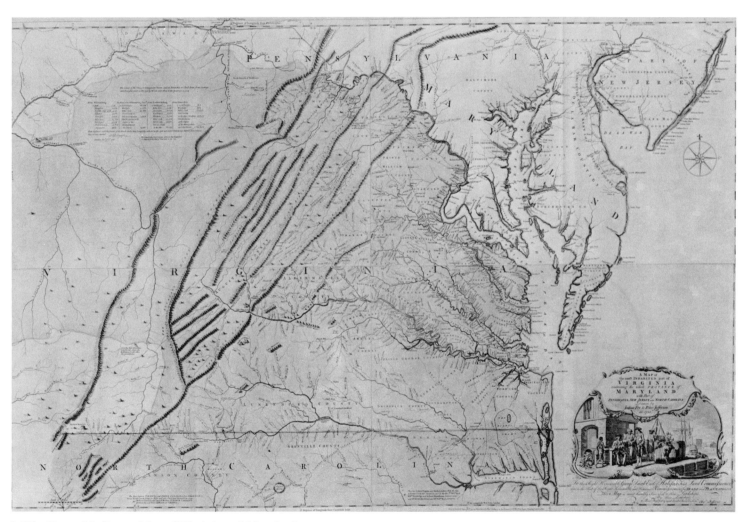

3 The Fry and Jefferson Map of Virginia and Maryland

JOSHUA FRY 1700?–1754, and
PETER JEFFERSON 1707/08–1757
Engraving 2nd ed. 1755
77.5 x 122 (30½ x 48)
Signed: Engraver—Robert Sayer at
No. 53 Fleet Street, London

Lent by Wilton Museum House,
Richmond. National Society of the
Colonial Dames of America in the
Commonwealth of Virginia. Gift of
Mrs. Cabell Mayo Tabb

The Fry and Jefferson map, recognized
in its time as the most accurate
rendering of the face of the new
country Virginia, represents an achievement of no small measure. That
Peter Jefferson was singularly equal to
the task of mapping the remote and
often inhospitable wilderness beyond
the Tidelands is suggested by the
account of his background and enterprising spirit contained in his son's
Autobiography: "The tradition in my
father's family was that their ancestor
came to this country from Wales, and
from near the mountain of Snowdon,
the highest in Gr. Br. . . . My father's
education had been quite neglected;
but being of a strong mind, sound

judgment and eager after information, he read much and improved himself insomuch that he was chosen with Joshua Fry professor of Mathem. in W. & M. college to continue the boundary line between Virginia & N. Caroline which had been begun by Colo Byrd, and was afterwards employed with the same Mr. Fry to make the 1st map of Virginia which had ever been made, that of Capt Smith being merely a conjectural sketch. . . . He was the 3d or 4th settler of the part of the country in which I live, which was about 1737."

The youngest of three sons of Captain Thomas Jefferson, Peter Jefferson first came to the upper reaches of the James River in about 1731 to take up his inheritance of lands at Fine Creek in Goochland County, about midway between Dungeness, the holdings of Isham Randolph, and Tuckahoe, the estate of Isham's nephew William Randolph, both across the James on the north bank. He had already begun to expand his lands and had held office both as justice of the peace and sheriff when he married Isham Randolph's eldest daughter, Jane Randolph, in 1739. They settled still further up the James at a choice site on the north fork of the Rivanna, obligingly ceded by Jefferson's friend William Randolph. There in about 1741 Peter began to build Shadwell, named for the London parish where Jane Randolph was born, and it was here that Thomas Jefferson, their third child and eldest son, was born on April 13, 1743. Shadwell lay in the new county of Albemarle, carved out of the larger Goochland County in 1744, and Peter Jefferson soon became an office holder of importance, serving as justice of the peace, judge of the court of chancery and lieutenant colonel.

Living nearby at Viewmont, about thirteen miles from Shadwell, on the Hardware River was Joshua Fry, presiding magistrate, county lieutenant and county surveyor of Albemarle. Born in Somerset and probably educated at Wadham College, Oxford, Fry had in 1737 resigned his appointment at William and Mary to seek his family's fortune in the back settlement. The two men became friends, and between 1746 and 1751 their names were linked in a series of important surveying exploits. They were both of the party which in 1746 set the western boundary of the great holdings of Lord Fairfax, known as the Northern Neck, running the Fairfax Line seventy-six rugged miles from the source of the Rappahannock to the headsprings of the Potomac. In 1749 they set off together to carry the line between Virginia and North Carolina ninety miles beyond the point reached by Byrd and his party

twenty-one years before. The extreme hardships of this journey—attacks by wild beasts, sleep snatched among the branches of trees—passed into the legends of the Jefferson family and doubtless would have been among the early memories of Thomas Jefferson, who was six years old at the time. In view of their intimate knowledge of the land, Fry and Jefferson were afterwards appointed by Acting Governor Lewis Burwell to satisfy a directive from the Lords of Trade calling for a map of the inhabited part of Virginia. Their map was completed and sent to London in 1751, and the first edition appeared sometime after March 1752, perhaps not until as late as 1754. A second edition of 1755, the version most widely used in Thomas Jefferson's time, contained additions by John Dalrymple, mainly indications of wagon roads.

Fry was called to the west in 1754 as commander-in-chief of the Virginia forces dispatched against the French, only to die in camp at Wills Creek on May 31. George Washington, his second in command, succeeded him. Peter Jefferson was named his executor, and part of Fry's legacy to him was the surveying instruments they had used together. He inherited as well the offices left vacant by his friend's death—county lieutenant, county surveyor and membership in the House of Burgesses. Peter Jefferson, too, died before his time in 1757, his strong constitution defeated by illness, leaving to his son—along with land and provisions for his education—a small library and his mathematical instruments, among them probably the surveying instruments that played such an essential part in the making of the map of 1751.

The Fry and Jefferson map lived on as the most authoritative map of Virginia. When Thomas Jefferson, then minister to France, decided to publish his *Notes on the State of Virginia*, first in a French and then in an English edition of 1787, he had the map reengraved, for the occasion, with some additions to extend its range, speaking of it with justifiable pride as more valuable than the book in which it was to appear. L.P.

4 William Randolph I

BRITISH SCHOOL
Oil on canvas c. 1695
91.4 x 72.3 (36 x 28½)

Lent by the Virginia Historical Society, Richmond

The immigrant William Randolph I of Turkey Island, Thomas Jefferson's great-grandfather, was born in Warwickshire, England, in about 1650, the son of a cavalier whose fortunes had faltered in the English Civil War. He came to Virginia in about 1670, joining his uncle, Henry Randolph, who was already an established and well-respected member of the Virginia gentry. William settled at Turkey Island in Henrico County on the north bank of the James River, a score of miles below Richmond, where over the years he built an imposing seat. He succeeded his uncle as the clerk of the Henrico County court sometime before 1675, for in that year he officially signed the inventory of John Perrin. This was but one of a long train of public offices and honors that came to him as a person of consequence and ability: magistrate, coroner,

lieutenant colonel of the militia, member of the House of Burgesses and speaker of that body, attorney general of the colony, clerk of the House of Burgesses, visitor of the College of William and Mary and member of the governor's council. In about 1678 he took a wife from nearby Bermuda Hundred, Mary Isham "of the antient and eminent family of Ishams of Northamptonshire."

William and Mary Randolph have been called the Adam and Eve of Virginia, and indeed their seven sons and two daughters were to establish the name and line of the Randolphs as preeminent in Virginia. Intermarrying with other patrician families—the Pages, the Nelsons, the Grymeses, the Lees and the Harrisons, among many others—they produced "a constellation of ability seldom rivaled in the history of the American colonies." William and Mary's third son, Isham Randolph, was to become the maternal grandfather of Thomas Jefferson, one of the brightest stars of this constellation.

The Randolphs and the Jeffersons

were bound by the ties of friendship as well as by intermarriage. William and Mary's second son, Thomas, was the father of William Randolph of Tuckahoe, neighbor and close friend of Thomas Jefferson's father Peter. When Peter Jefferson thought to build his first house, Shadwell, his friend William Randolph agreed to convey to him from his adjacent holdings a particularly choice site, the consideration to be "Henry Wetherburne's biggest bowl of Arrack punch" at the Raleigh Tavern in Williamsburg. The amiable proprietor of Tuckahoe died in 1745, entrusting his children and his estate to Peter Jefferson. Thus it was that the Jeffersons moved to Tuckahoe in 1745 for a stay of some six years, and that Thomas Jefferson spent his youngest years on Randolph lands and among his Randolph second cousins.

In his *Autobiography*, written late in life, Jefferson summed up his distinguished antecedents on the Randolph side in a single sentence: "They trace their pedigree far back in England & Scotland, to which let every one ascribe the faith & merit he chooses."

Portrayed on a "Kit-cat" size canvas made popular by Kneller, the sitter is painted as an imposing figure with a full-bottomed wig, Steinkirk cravat and coat with vented sleeve and elaborate ornamental frogging, all characteristic of the costume of the last decade of the seventeenth century. If this portrait is of William Randolph and if it was painted from life, it must be dated before his death in 1711. The portrait is obviously of British origin, and a suggested date would be c. 1695. T.T.

5 Mary Isham Randolph

Attributed to JOHN WOLLASTON
active 1735–1767
Oil on canvas
91.4 x 71 (36 x 28)
Lent by the Virginia Historical Society, Richmond

Mary Isham Randolph, great-grandmother of Jefferson, was the daughter of Henry and Catherine Isham of Bermuda Hundred, a plantation on the south side of the James River nearly opposite Turkey Island, the estate of her future husband. She came of an old Northamptonshire family which traced its name to the fourteenth-century manor of de Isham. The common ancestor of the Ishams was Robert Isham of Pytchley, who died in 1424, and the Lamport branch of the family were created baronets in 1627. The Ishams were thus a family of distinction and substance when Henry Isham came to Henrico County in about 1656. A merchant and militia officer, he signed his name "Gentleman," and his wife Catherine's will, made in 1686 and sealed with the Isham arms, bequeathed a quantity of silver to her heirs.

Mary Isham's marriage to William Randolph, although not recorded, must have taken place about 1678. The will of her brother Henry, dated November 13, 1678, and proved June 5, 1680, includes bequests to his sister "Mrs. Mary Randolph," indicating that the marriage had already taken place. William Randolph was in fact executor of the will and received a large part of the estate.

This unsigned painting, attributed to John Wollaston, poses a problem with regard to the identity of the sitter. If the portrait is indeed of Mary Isham Randolph, as family tradition holds, it must be a free copy of an earlier likeness; alternatively, the painting could be a portrait of some other member of the Randolph family from whom it descended for generations through various branches. The difficulties of assigning the painting become apparent when it is noted that Mary Isham Randolph died in 1735, whereas Wollaston came to the colonies in 1749 and to Virginia only after 1753.

Perhaps because of the many repainted areas of the canvas, the portrait has sometimes been attributed to

John Hesselius, who was active in Virginia at various times between 1750 and 1778. However, the head of the sitter, which in an eighteenth-century portrait usually displays the painter's most obvious characteristics, shows little of the direct observation of the face generally found in the work of Hesselius.

The "Kit-cat" size of the canvas matches that of the portraits identified by family tradition as being of Mary Randolph's husband and son. T.T.

6 Isham Randolph

BRITISH SCHOOL
Oil on canvas
86.3 x 66 (34 x 26)
Lent by the Virginia Historical Society, Richmond

Isham Randolph, Thomas Jefferson's maternal grandfather, was the third son of William and Mary Randolph, born in 1685, presumably at the ancestral seat of Turkey Island. Like five of his brothers he was educated at the College of William and Mary, for the Randolphs, aristocrats that they were, saw to it that their sons were properly prepared for their inheritance of lands and public duties. Of all the Randolph sons, Isham seems to have been a particular favorite of their distinguished neighbor, William Byrd II of Westover (see no. 7) who was eleven years his senior. Byrd's diary shows that Isham was often at Westover, accompanying Byrd on his rounds of the plantation, dining and talking, and for a time taking up Byrd's offer of lessons in French and making fair progress. When Isham decided on a career at sea, it was William Byrd who helped him realize his ambition by recommending him to the command of a ship. By September 1710 Isham called at Westover as Captain Randolph and took on board a cargo of tobacco.

Sometime prior to 1718 Isham Randolph was appointed the colonial agent for Virginia in England. He established a residence in London, probably in White Chapel Parish just outside Aldgate. Here he met Jane Rogers, daughter of Charles Rogers and Jane Lilburne, of the same family as the noted radical "Freeborn John" Lilburne, and married her in 1718. Their first daughter, Jane Randolph, later the wife of Peter Jefferson and the mother of Thomas Jefferson, was baptized at St. Paul's in Shadwell district on February 20, 1720.

By 1736 Isham decided to forsake the sea, and after a last voyage in the spring of that year, he returned to his large holdings in Goochland County. There, on the north side of the James River about thirty or forty

miles above the falls and a few miles below the point where the river forks into the Rivanna and the Fluvanna, he established his estate Dungeness, apparently naming it for the southern-most tip of Kent, where a lighthouse marked the entrance into the Straits of Dover. In November 1738, he was pressed into public service as a mem-ber of the House of Burgesses and in the same month became adjutant general of the colony, being "a Gentle-man well known & universally ac-ceptable in the Country."

It was in 1738, too, that he received at Dungeness the naturalist John Bartram, who had been recommended to Isham by his friend Peter Collin-son in London and with whom he later carried on a cordial correspond-ence. Collinson's instructions to Bartram offer a glimpse of the fastidi-ous society he might expect to find in Virginia: "One thing I must desire of thee, and do insist that thee must oblige me therein; that thou make up that drugget clothes to go to Virginia in, and no appear to disgrace thyself or me; for though I should not esteem thee the less to come to me in what

dress thou will, yet these Virginians are a very gentle, well dressed people, and look, perhaps, more at a man's outside than his inside. For these and other reasons pray go very clean, neat, and handsomely dressed to Virginia."

Isham Randolph died in 1742, providing in his will for the payment of £200 promised to Peter Jefferson on his marriage to Jane. He rests at Turkey Island, where his epitaph confirms Bartram's mention of his generosity and good nature:

The distinguishing qualities of the Gentleman he possessed in an eminent degree: To justice probity & honour so firmly attached That no view of secular interest or Worldly advantage, no discouraging frowns of fortune could alter his steady purpose of heart. By an easy compliance and obliging deportment he knew no enmey, but gained Many friends, thus in his life meriting an universal esteem. He died as uni-versally lamented Nov'r, 1742 age 57 Gentle Reader go & do likewise.

This portrait of a "Kit-cat" size was

probably intended as a companion to the portraits of William and Mary Randolph, Isham's mother and father, and shows a man of about forty years of age. Very competently but thinly painted, it could be the work of one of the many London artists using the Kneller formula for their portraits. T.T.

7 William Byrd II
Attributed to the Studio of
SIR GODFREY KNELLER 1646–1723
Oil on canvas
127 x 106.6 (50 x 42)

Lent by the Virginia Historical Society, Richmond

William Byrd II of Westover, son of the immigrant William Byrd, was born at his father's plantation near the falls of the James River on March 28, 1674. His father had already made the name of Byrd distinguished in colonial Virginia, and he had high ambitions for his eldest son. William Byrd the younger was accordingly sent to England for his education, where he read law at the Middle Temple. Under the patronage of Sir Robert Southwell, he mingled in aristocratic circles and received the unusual accolade of election to the Royal Society in recognition of his scientific interests at the young age of twenty-two. He frequented literary circles as well and knew Wycherley, Congreve, Swift and Pope. All these associations made William Byrd the most cultivated member of Virginia society, when he was recalled to America to take up his inheritance with the death of his father in 1704.

Marrying Lucy Parke, daughter of Colonel Daniel Parke, in 1706, he furnished an elegant model for his neighbors and fellow planters as master of Westover. He replaced his father's earlier house with a brick mansion of great distinction and set about ex-panding his remarkable library, which grew to four thousand volumes and was one of the largest in the colonies. Some of these volumes eventually reached Jefferson's first library by purchase. The sophistication of his gardens, reflecting his love of botanic studies, made them worthy of a visit by John Bartram in his southern tour of 1738. A portrait gallery contained not only the faces of his family but those of his many valued friends among the English gentry. One of the closest of these friends was Charles Boyle, Earl of Orrery, to whom this portrait was originally presented. For him Byrd described the bucolic yet demanding life of the Virginia planter in a letter of July 1726: "Like one of the patriarchs, I have my flocks and my herds, my bondmen and bond-

women, and every sort of trade amongst my own servants, so that I live in a kind of independence of everyone but Providence. However this sort of life is without expense, yet it is attended with a great deal of trouble. I must take care to keep all my people to their duty, to set all the springs in motion, and to make everyone draw his equal share to carry the machine forward. But then 'tis an amusement in this silent country. . . ."

Byrd's political career was not neglected, for he felt strongly the obligations of his position. In 1696 he was elected to the House of Burgesses, and shortly after he came into his inheritance he was appointed as receiver-general for the crown in Virginia. Three times he served as official agent of Virginia in London, and from 1709 until his death in 1744 he was a member of the governor's council. When the question of the boundary between Virginia and North Carolina became troublesome, he headed the survey of the line (a line later extended by the work of Thomas Jefferson's father Peter and Joshua Fry), an undertaking which he im-mortalized in his *History of the Dividing Line,* which circulated in manuscript during his lifetime. But he enjoyed perhaps most of all the dignity of his position as commander-in-chief of the colony's militia. "Everyone showed me an abundance of respect," he reported with evident satisfaction on reviewing his troops in 1711. William Randolph of Turkey Island—Byrd's neighbor and father of his young friend Isham Randolph, who was later to be the grandfather of Thomas Jefferson—was one of his lieutenants. Among his captains was Thomas Jefferson of Henrico County, Jefferson's other grandfather, and Byrd records in his diary that on one occasion he partook of a dinner of roast beef at Captain Jefferson's house.

The enormous number of portraits produced by Kneller's studio make an accurate attribution of any work to Kneller extremely difficult in the absence of documentation or signature. Ellis Waterhouse has said of Kneller's workshop that "his studio was a model factory. Kneller himself would draw the face from his sitter and transfer it to the canvas, while the rest, as often as not, was finished off by a multitude of assistants." The portrait of William Byrd exhibits some of the characteristics of Kneller and his studio, such as the striving for likeness, a kind of naturalism, and the elim-ination of lines in the face in the manner of the Italians. The finely drawn head dominates the portrait, a mark of Kneller's work noted by Horace Walpole in his *Anecdotes of Painting:* "In general, even where he took pains, all the parts are affectedly

kept down, to throw greater force in the head."

William Byrd's patron, Sir Robert Southwell, sat for Kneller in 1679, was host to the artist in 1685 at the Southwell country estate and was again painted by Kneller in 1690. Many of Byrd's intimate friends were painted by the artist, and certainly it is possible that the finest gentleman of the colonies was a sitter in Kneller's studio.

In a lively characterization of himself entitled "The Enamored Bird" Byrd describes himself for the most part with fidelity, and his verbal portrait is borne out by this painting: "His Person was agreable enough tho he had a certain cast of pride in his look, which clouded some of the grace of it." T.T.

8 Model of Rosewell
Conjectural drawing for model

Rosewell, the Page family seat on the York River in Gloucester County, was the largest and one of the finest of all Virginia houses. It was begun before 1726 by Mann Page I, whose second wife was the daughter of powerful Robert ("King") Carter of Corotoman. King Carter's will of 1726 provides £300 toward furnishing a brick house for his son-in-law, confirming that Rosewell was then under construction. It stood unfinished at Page's death in 1730, and both the financial burden and the glory of completing the magnificent seat passed to his son Mann Page II. In 1744 the Virginia Assembly passed an act to break the entail, allowing land to be sold to support the finishing of the house. Rosewell was therefore completed sometime after that date and descended in due course to Mann Page II's eldest son John Page, friend of Thomas Jefferson. John Page had married Francis Burwell of Isle of Wight County in about 1765, and by May 1769 he mentions to his London agent that he is laboring under "the necessary Expences of an encreasing Family joined to the Commencement of Housekeeping in a large House."

Jefferson was a frequent visitor at Rosewell, and it is in this setting, in one of the most impressive buildings in colonial America, that their "philosophical evenings" took place. On the roof of Rosewell they spent many evenings absorbed in Page's favorite pursuit of astronomy, and it was there also that Page, with his inexhaustible interest in all the activities of the heavens, conducted the first measurements of rainfall in America. Such were the pleasures of these visits that when Jefferson's own Shadwell burned he "cherished some treasonable thoughts of leaving these my native hills. Indeed I should be much happier were I nearer to Rosewell. . . . However the gods I fancy were apprehensive that if we were placed together we should pull down the moon or play some such devilish prank with their works."

The house passed out of the hands of the Page family in 1838, with the death of John Page's second wife, and was drastically "modernized" by a certain Thomas Booth, who removed both the paneling and the superb roof. Rosewell succumbed finally to fire in 1916, but portions of the walls and foundation have survived. Evidence shows that in addition to the main house there were two dependencies, on the east and on the west, and a stable. An insurance policy of 1802 described the east outbuilding as a structure measuring 24 by 60 feet,

one story high; the brick stable is listed as covered with wood and measuring 24 by 120 feet. The material of the roof is identified as lead, a rare luxury for the time.

Seven years later a more informative policy was issued. This correctly gives the dimensions of the main house as 60 by 60 and shows two L-shaped dependencies, reproduced in the model. The connecting passageways between the main house and the dependencies were apparently never built. Rosewell was still standing "like an old deserted English castle, in solitary grandeur" when Bishop Meade saw it sometime prior to 1906, and an engraving in his Old Churches, Ministers and Families of Virginia shows two cupolas on the roof. The design of the cupolas on the model is necessarily conjectural.

Together with Christ Church in Lancaster County, probably by the same craftsman, Rosewell contained the finest brickwork in all of North America. Flemish bond was used throughout, with random glazed headers, and all corners and jambs were of rubbed brick. In the splendid doorways were gauged brick, chosen for color and rubbed smooth on all faces. Rosewell's doorways are similar to those of Christ Church. Both are similar to plates 23 and 27 of William Salmon's Palladio Londinensis, but as this was published in London in 1734, it could not have been the exact precedent for Rosewell. Gauged brick was also used at Rosewell on the belt courses, sill aprons and segmented window arches.

The window treatment of Rosewell was unusual. The arrangement of two long façades with wider windows in the center is found only in the dependencies of Shirley. This motif is also to be seen in the reconstructed governor's palace in Williamsburg. The high arched windows gracing the end pavilions, resembling the windows of Christ Church, are, in Virginia, unique in their placement except for those in the Peyton Randolph house in Williamsburg.

Stone was used to emphasize the structural element, playing a decorative as well as a functional role. Probably imported from Portland, England, it was used for pilaster bases and capitals in the doorways as well as for windowsills, keystones, the rim of the parapet, chimney caps and the flight of steps at the entrance.

It has been proposed that the design of Rosewell, if not its execution, was the work of an English architect, but thus far he has not been identified, nor has a corresponding plate from an English plan book. More than any other Virginia mansion, Rosewell reflected the basic tenets of the English Palladians, and although

Jefferson carefully studied their published schemes, his earliest architectural drawings depart from the strict formula, if not the ideals, laid down by the architectural books. Aside from his great attachment to the place, there is nothing in the record to suggest that Rosewell offered much in the way of architectural inspiration to the young Jefferson.

Photographs taken before the fire indicate that the interiors were very fine. The great stairway on the far left as one entered had a magnificent terminal scroll, twisted balusters and step ends enriched with C scrolls and feathering. The newel posts were carved with vines and flowers, and the superb fascia on the second floor had scrolls, flowers and feathered leaves carved on the surface.

Little remains—beyond small fragments—of the interior, or indeed of the walls, but there is a description by one who knew them. John Page's youngest daughter, Anne Page Saunders, wrote that "The grand staircase was . . . an object of admiration to all who saw, or ascended it, and looked down upon the large hall, with its wainscoted walls of mahogany, and pillasters of Corinthian order, and the great hearth and marble mantelpiece. All the rooms were wainscoted with wood of different colors, and had marble mantels, the ceilings were also of great height." F.N.

9 John Page of Rosewell
JOHN WOLLASTON
active 1735–1767
Oil on canvas
121.9 x 96.5 (48 x 38)
Lent by the College of William and Mary, Williamsburg, Virginia

John Page, eldest son of Mann Page II and Alice Grymes, was born on April 17, 1743, at the magnificent family estate of Rosewell, which he was later to inherit. "Dear Page," as Jefferson addressed him in their exuberant letters, was one of the closest friends of his youth. Like Jefferson, John Page was a student of the illustrious Dr. William Small at the College of William and Mary, and the love of mathematics there imbibed led Page on to a lifelong attachment to astronomy. He was later a founder of the Society for the Promotion of Useful Knowledge, formed in Williamsburg in 1773 and modeled on the Royal Society in London. Jefferson was often at the Page family seat—"I reflect often with pleasure on the philosophical evenings . . . at Rosewell"—and Page was his chosen companion not only for philosophical and astronomical pursuits but in the difficulties of his unsuccessful courtship of Rebecca Burwell, Jefferson's "Belinda." It was Page whom Jefferson fancifully invited to share an antidotal voyage to "England Holland France Spain Italy (where I would buy me a good fiddle) and Egypt" in a vessel named the *Rebecca*, or again to inhabit a small castle in the air with room for Belinda should she reconsider: "I think to build. No castle though I assure you, only a small house which shall contain a room for myself and another for you, and no more, unless Belinda should think proper to favor us with her company. . . ."

In about 1765 Page married Frances Burwell, daughter of Robert Burwell of Isle of Wight County, a member of the governor's council. On her mother's side she was the grand-daughter of Thomas ("Scotch Tom") Nelson, first of that name in Virginia. No fewer than five of the Pages' nine surviving children married into the family of Thomas Nelson, and the Nelsons launched John Page's political career by bringing their young kinsman to the attention of Lord Botetourt and later Lord Dunmore, whose displeasure Page earned by his "Whiggish principles" while serving on Dunmore's council.

As the Revolution gathered force, Page played a prominent part in the events within Virginia. He was a member of the Virginia convention that simultaneously called for independence and set about drafting a state constitution—the first in the country —on May 15, 1776. The framing of a new government at Williamsburg was a project close to Jefferson's heart, and though he was then in Philadelphia at the Continental Congress, he drafted three versions and sent the final one on by George Wythe in mid-June 1776. In almost the same period of time, he was working on the Declaration of Independence, and it is believed that Page was one of a few friends favored with a copy of the first draft. "I am highly pleased with your Declaration. God preserve the united States. We know the Race is not to the swift nor the Battle to the strong. Do you not think an Angel rides in the Whirlwind and directs this storm?"

Meanwhile Virginia had elected its first governor, Patrick Henry, and Page himself was voted lieutenant governor. One of his first responsibilities was that of contriving a state seal, an enterprise about which he consulted Jefferson. The two friends opposed each other in the contest of 1779 for governorship, but "it was their competition, not ours," as Jefferson said, and when Jefferson won by a small margin their old affection was unimpaired. Page served as a representative of Virginia to the first four Congresses, from 1789 to 1797, and in 1802 became governor of Virginia, succeeding James Monroe.

This portrait is one of the finest productions of the English face-painter John Wollaston. Within a very personal style the artist has observed the accessories of gun, powder flask, hat and brace of quail with such accuracy that the mechanism of the fowling piece could be recreated by a good gunsmith. George Groce calls this interest in objects the "Americanization" of John Wollaston. The portrait probably dates from about 1756 or 1757, when the artist was painting practically the whole Page family. One can imagine that the sittings took place in the sumptuous setting of Rosewell.

Wollaston's distinctive drawing of the eye in oriental fashion, characteristic of most of his portraits, might be explained in part by a passage from Hogarth's *Analysis of Beauty* of 1753: "Some features are formed so as to make this or that expression of a passion more or less legible: for example, the little narrow Chinese eye suits a loving or laughing expression best." The painter found this "smiling eye" convention most suitable for the portrayal of the prosperous and contented aristocrats of the colonies. T.T.

10 Mann Page III and His Sister Elizabeth

JOHN WOLLASTON
active 1735–1767
Oil on canvas
124.4 x 101.6 (49 x 40)

Lent by the Virginia Historical Society, Richmond

Mann Page, the third of that name, was the eldest son of Mann Page II and his second wife, Anne Corbin Tayloe of Mount Airy, and thus half-brother to John Page. He was born at the family seat of Rosewell in about 1749 and was educated at the College of William and Mary.

Mann Page, Jr., as he was styled, had already taken his place in the House of Burgesses by the spring of 1774, when the news of the Boston Port Act swept south to Williamsburg. Jefferson and other members proposed a solemn day of fasting and prayer to mark the depth of Virginia's outrage at this treatment of her sister colony, and on May 24 the House of Burgesses passed the Fast Day Resolution. Lord Dunmore lost little time in dissolving that body, and the members adjourned as usual to the Apollo Room, where on May 27, 30 and 31

Mann Page set his signature beside Jefferson's in a series of documents expressing Virginia's full support for the inhabitants of Massachusetts in their "most piteous and melancholy Situation." These were the turbulent months which saw delegates elected for the first Congress, among them Jefferson, who wrote his *Summary View of the Rights of British America* for the occasion.

In 1777 Mann Page was a delegate to the Continental Congress with Jefferson, Thomas Nelson and George Wythe. He had married his cousin Mary Tayloe of Mount Airy in 1776 and had inherited the great Page house, Mannsfield, in Spotsylvania County near Fredericksburg. The architect Benjamin Henry Latrobe dined there soon after his arrival in Virginia in 1796 and left one of the few contemporary descriptions: "I dined with Mr. Minor at Mr. Man Page's at Mansfield where I met several gentlemen of the town and of the neighborhood. Mr. Page's house is of stone of a good but coarse grit in the style of the Country Gentlemen's house in England of 50 years ago."

Mann Page's sister Elizabeth, called

Betsey, was born at Rosewell in about 1762, the sixth of seven children of this marriage. At about age twenty she became the second wife of Benjamin Harrison of Brandon (1743–1807), Jefferson's good friend of college years, whose first wife was Anne Randolph of Wilton. It seems almost certain that Jefferson obliged his friend with advice in the building of Brandon, his handsome estate on the James River. A sketch believed to be of the central building survives among Jefferson's architectural drawings.

Although this double portrait is unsigned, there is no doubt that the painting belongs in Wollaston's oeuvre, for all the distinctive stylistic traits of the artist are present. The almond eye, the graceful fingertips, the slashing highlights on the drapery, the preference for warm colors, the casually painted lace—"all tell the hand of Wollaston was there," as Francis Hopkinson wrote in his poem of 1758 in praise of the painter.

About the same time that the artist painted the Page children, he completed another half-length of two children for the Custis family which can be dated with certainty before October 1757, when the artist signed a receipt of payment from Martha Custis. The same composition, a standing boy and a seated girl, was used in both paintings. In both, the extended left arm of the boy serves as a means of uniting the two figures. Cardinals fluttering on the boys' wrists —the exotic "Virginia red-bird" so prized by the fashionable in France and England at this period—are almost identical.

Mann Page's sister is seated, holding the ubiquitous Wollaston doll. This accessory first appears in the New York portrait of Isabella Morris of c. 1750. In 1753, when Wollaston was working at Annapolis, the doll appeared again as a prop in the painting of Rebecca Calvert; and finally, the doll was used in several Virginia portraits, including those of Elizabeth Randolph and Mary Lightfoot. T.T.

11 The Children of Philip Grymes of Brandon

Attributed to JOHN HESSELIUS
1728–1778
Oil on canvas c. 1750
165.1 x 137.1 (65 x 54)

Lent by the Virginia Historical Society, Richmond

Lucy Grymes, daughter of Colonel Philip and Mary Randolph Grymes of Brandon, the Grymes family seat on the Rappahannock River in Middlesex County, is portrayed here at about age seven in the company of her three brothers, Philip Ludwell, John Randolph and Charles. On July 29, 1762, she became the wife of Jefferson's friend Thomas Nelson and later traveled with him to Philadelphia, where Nelson signed the Declaration of Independence as a member of the Virginia delegation. They were to have eleven children, five of whom married sons and daughters of John Page of Rosewell. The marquis de Chastellux, an admirer of Thomas Nelson, spoke well of Lucy Nelson's cordial manner, when he paid the family a visit at their modest country retreat Offley in

April 1782, shortly after Nelson's term as governor. Thomas Nelson was absent on business, but so many members of the Nelson family gathered to do the marquis honor, he reported, "all called Nelsons, and distinguished only by their Christian names . . . that . . . during the two days which I spent in this truly patriarchal house, it was impossible for me to find out their degree of relationship." Lucy Nelson lived to the venerable age of eighty, surrounded by her many children and their descendants.

The paths of Lucy's brothers Philip and John, both educated at Eton, were later to part under the pressures of the Revolution. Philip Ludwell Grymes, the elder, went on to complete his schooling at Oxford and later inherited Brandon Plantation. He was a burgess for Middlesex County, when Lord Botetourt dissolved the House of Burgesses in 1769, and joined his brother-in-law Thomas Nelson and Thomas Jefferson in signing the historic Nonimportation Resolutions drafted by George Mason. John Randolph Grymes, here still in

skirts, eventually sided with the Loyalists, allying himself with Lord Dunmore's attempt to regain his position by force. Dunmore regarded Grymes as an ornament to his cause, writing to Lord George Germaine that he had the support of a member of the first family of Virginia, a gentleman of fortune, amiable character and strict honor. John Randolph Grymes served as a major in the Queen's Rangers until 1778, when he resigned and moved to England. There he married his cousin Susanna Randolph, daughter of John Randolph, once attorney general of Virginia and, like Grymes, a Loyalist refugee. In England, Grymes served as an officer in the corps of American Loyalists raised in anticipation of Napoleon's invasion of England. He later returned to Virginia and prospered as a planter in Orange County.

This very large, unsigned group portrait of four colonial children has been attributed variously to Charles Bridges and to John Hesselius, but the size and unsophisticated composition of the painting have no parallels in

12 Thomas Nelson

Attributed to MASON CHAMBERLIN
d. 1787
Oil on canvas
74.8 x 61.4 (29½ x 24⅜)

Lent by the Virginia Museum of Fine Arts, Richmond

Thomas Nelson was born into the influential Nelson family of Yorktown on December 26, 1738, the eldest son of William Nelson, president of the governor's council, and Elizabeth Burwell. His grandfather, Thomas ("Scotch Tom") Nelson, was a founder of Yorktown. At the age of fourteen he was sent abroad to be educated at the Hackney School in London and Christ's College, Cambridge. While on the voyage homeward in 1761 he was elected to the House of Burgesses as a representative of York County. When he and Thomas Jefferson became acquainted in Williamsburg, Nelson was the elder by five years, already with the polish of a British education and responsibilities in the legislature. By 1763, when Jefferson was hesitating between his Belinda and his dream of a trip to England, Nelson was a settled married man, having taken Lucy Grymes of Middlesex County as his wife on July 29, 1762. But the two were good friends, and when Jefferson lost his library and papers in the fire that destroyed Shadwell in 1770, Nelson wrote to assure him that "nothing can give me so much pleasure as to render you every service that is in my power."

Together Nelson and Jefferson signed the Nonimportation Resolutions of 1769 and nearly every other important document in Virginia's progress to revolution. At the Virginia constitutional convention of 1776, it was Nelson who introduced the resolution calling on Congress to declare the colonies free and independent, and when the resolution was passed on May 15, he carried the historic instructions to the other Virginia delegates in Philadelphia. His name appears with theirs on the Declaration of Independence. He was forced to resign his seat in Congress in May 1777 due to ill health. But Admiral Howe threatened the shores of Virginia, and by August Nelson was serving as commander-in-chief of the Virginia forces. When Congress urgently requested troops, he raised them at his own expense and marched with them to Philadelphia in 1778. He returned to Congress in 1780, but again ill health forced him to retire to Virginia, where he reorganized the militia and supported by his extensive credit the large sums needed to maintain two Virginia regiments and the French fleet and armaments.

The perceptive Chastellux, who met Thomas Nelson at the siege of Yorktown, pronounced him "a good and gallant man in every possible respect," and the closing actions of his public life confirm this. In 1781 he succeeded Jefferson as governor of Virginia, at Jefferson's recommendation, in a time of great military crisis. He brought forces to the aid of Washington at Yorktown and did not hesitate to lead the firing on the Nelson mansion, which was being used by Cornwallis as a headquarters. He was at Washington's side to receive the surrender of Cornwallis on October 19, 1781. His service to the Revolution complete and his fortune exhausted, he retired to Offley, a small wooden house in Hanover County which served as a refuge for his family during the Revolution.

Although the painting of Thomas Nelson is unsigned, the family tradition that it was painted in London by Mason Chamberlin has never been questioned. Chamberlin drew his patronage from the merchant class, and Thomas Nelson's father had many business connections in London. In the early part of his life Chamberlin was employed as a clerk in a merchants' counting house; later he studied painting with Francis Hayman. Edward Edwards wrote of him, "He painted portraits with tolerable success, some of which possess great force and resemblance."

This handsome portrait of Thomas Nelson was painted in the decade between 1752 and 1762 and is one of the early works assigned to Chamberlin. The artist has observed the sitter carefully and has rendered with careful control the details of the costume, allowing the head, with its rather florid coloring, to dominate the painting.

Peter Pindar (John Wolcot) in *Ode VI to the Royal Academicians* flatters Chamberlin, though with some reservations:

Thy Portraits, Chamberlin, maybe
A likeness, far as I can see
  But, faith, I cannot raise a single
    feature:
Yet, when it so shall please the Lord
  To make his people out of board,
Thy pictures will be tolerable nature.

                    T.T.

---

the known work of either painter. Charles Bridges can be eliminated from authorship, since he died in England in 1747. The painting cannot be of the sitters listed and still be painted before about 1750, for Lucy, the little girl in adult costume, was born in 1743. Her brother Philip was born in 1746, John the following year and baby Charles in 1748/1749. The attribution to John Hesselius seems the best that can be made in the known circumstances. He seems to have been in Williamsburg in 1750 and at Yorktown in the spring of 1751, since postal records reveal that his father Gustavus received letters from someone, possibly John, from these places during these years.

John Hesselius, the American son of the Swedish painter Gustavus Hesselius of Philadelphia, was born in 1728. With the minimal training given to him by his father, and at only twenty-two years of age, he ventured into Virginia seeking employment as a portrait painter. His presence in Virginia is confirmed by his signed works of 1751 for the Fitzhugh family.

The young artist must be forgiven the simple composition of the portrait and the general oddity of the background landscape and architectural details. The individual children were drawn and painted separately, with great attention given to the heads. The features of their faces are lined up on a central vertical axis, giving a slightly concave effect. This characteristic manner of drawing is found again and again in the paintings of John Hesselius and gives his work a certain naive charm. T.T.

13 Francis Fauquier

BENJAMIN WILSON 1721–1788
Oil on canvas c. 1757
91.5 x 71 (36 x 28)

*Collection of the Thomas Coram
Foundation for Children, London*
NOT IN EXHIBITION

Jefferson greatly admired Governor
Francis Fauquier (1704?–1768),
whom he regarded as "the ablest man
who had ever filled that office."
Fauquier arrived in Virginia in 1758.
Before that he had been a successful
merchant as a director of the South
Sea Company and had then spent
some time in the army. His interest in
science earned him a Fellowship of
the Royal Society, and he continued
to send reports back to London on
natural phenomena in the New World.
The governor became a popular
figure, not only socially, but politically,
for he was sympathetic to Virginian
views and acted as the colony's spokes-
man with the imperial government.
In the controversy over the Stamp Act
of 1765, Fauquier played a moderat-
ing role, explaining that the protests
to the king and to Parliament sent by
the Virginia Assembly were merely
the Virginians "praying to be per-

mitted to tax themselves." He managed to preserve his dignity and
popularity in the difficult time when
the obnoxious stamps actually arrived in Williamsburg, and by tact
prevented any of the scenes of violence
which took place in other American
colonies. Fauquier died in Williamsburg and was buried in Bruton
Church. His will showed both his
scientific and humanitarian mind, for
he permitted his body to be opened
if the cause of his death could not be
established, and he arranged for his
slaves to be kept together as families
and to choose their new masters.

Jefferson was at the College of
William and Mary from 1760 to 1762
and remained in Williamsburg for
another three years to study law with
George Wythe. Perhaps as an under-
graduate he was introduced to the
governor. Certainly, together with
Wythe and William Small, professor
of natural philosophy at William
and Mary, Jefferson became a frequent
visitor at the palace. For the young
and still impressionable Jefferson,
Fauquier represented a larger and more
cultivated world than he had hitherto
experienced. The conversation at

the governor's hospitable table ranged
over many subjects, including science,
religion and philosophy, where no
doubt Jefferson heard unfamiliar
points of view and so enlarged his
mind. He said many years later that
"at these dinners I have heard more
good sense, more rational and philosophical conversation than in all my
life besides." In the broader field of
good manners and gentlemanly com-
portment, Fauquier's example gave an
additional polish and tone to Williamsburg society where he lived in
considerable state, and Jefferson
acknowledged that it was "the finest
school of manners and morals that
ever existed in America."

Fauquier was a governor and bene-
factor of the Foundling Hospital,
London, and presented this portrait to
it in 1757 shortly before leaving
for Virginia. The painting was at one
time believed to be by Richard Wilson
the landscape painter. Portraits of
Fauquier and his wife are included in
Hogarth's *The Wollaston Family*
of 1730. R.W.

14 Lord Botetourt

WILLIAM HOARE c. 1707–1792
Oil on canvas
122.2 x 99 (49⅛ x 39)
*Lent by His Grace the Duke of
Beaufort*

The appointment of Norbonne
Berkeley, Lord Botetourt (1717–
1770), as governor-general of Virginia
in 1768 caused some adverse comment in England, because of his
questionable financial position, and in
the *Letters of Junius* he was described
as "a cringing, bowing, fawning,
sword-bearing courtier." Such strictures were exaggerated, for Botetourt
received his peerage and the political
office of Lord of the Bedchamber in
return for his active support of the
government. Lord Botetourt's decision
to go to Virginia, as the first resident
governor-general for nearly seventy-five
years, was extremely flattering to the
colony, and he was well received in
Williamsburg. This set the tone for his
administration, which was at a time
of strained relations between the
imperial government and the colonies,
in the aftermath of the Stamp Act
(1765) and the Townshend Acts
(1767), and Botetourt's tact and
charm helped to smooth over the
differences. Social life in Williamsburg
became more elaborate and sophisticated under his urbane leadership, and
something of the more polished atmosphere of the metropolis was
introduced to Virginia. The governor's
extensive entertaining was done not
only for the obvious pleasure he took
in convivial living but also with the
political aim of creating support
through personal contact with the
leading men of the colony. It also
served to enhance the dignity of his
position. Much of eighteenth-century
politics and business was conducted
at the dinner table and the long
potations afterwards, and sometimes
over fifty people sat down together
at the palace.

Jefferson was in Williamsburg at
the time of the governor's arrival and
shortly afterwards began his political
career as a burgess for Albemarle
County in the assembly of 1769.
Although so recently elected, Jefferson
prepared the resolution for the address of thanks to the governor at the
opening of the session. Botetourt's
graciousness did not prevent the
assembly asserting in respectful, but
determined, language the rights of
Virginia and their support for Massachusetts then embroiled with the
British administration. The governor
had no option but to dissolve the
assembly. Opposition was not, however, subdued, for the burgesses moved
to the Raleigh Tavern and there
formed an association for the non-

importation of British goods. Jefferson was one of the signers of the agreement.

The next session of the House of Burgesses also took place in 1769 and Jefferson was again returned. Relations between the British government and the colonies had temporarily improved, and Botetourt's conciliatory behavior created an atmosphere of harmony. Consequently, on his sudden death in 1770, Lord Botetourt was genuinely mourned, and his funeral was the most elaborate ceremony ever seen in colonial Virginia. A statue was erected to him, as "the best of Governors and the best of Men," and stood outside the Williamsburg capitol building.

Later Jefferson believed that "Lord Botetourt's great respectability, his character for integrity, and his general popularity, would have enabled him to embarrass the measures of the patriots exceedingly. His death was, therefore, a fortunate event for the cause of the Revolution." R.W.

15 The Botetourt gold medal
MC CARTNEY and BAYLEY
Gold
4.3 (1 11⁄16) diam.
Inscribed on obverse: REGNANTE GEORGIO TERTIO MUSIS AMICO, and beneath bust: QUAESITUM MERITIS. On reverse: GUL· ET MAR· TRADUNT BLARO CHART· COL·, and beneath group: ANNO REGNI/QUARTO

Lent by the Virginia Historical Society, Richmond

Governor Botetourt established two gold medal prizes for classical studies

and mathematics at the College of William and Mary. They were awarded for four years from 1772 to 1775. The present example was given to James White for mathematics in 1775. James Madison, afterwards president of the college and first Episcopal bishop of Virginia, who had been at school with Jefferson, won the classical gold medal in 1772. The medal has the effigy of George III with a dedication in Latin "Friend of the Muses," which is not excessive flattery, for the king was a patron of the arts. On the reverse is shown a representation of President James Blair, founder of the college, receiving the royal charter from William III and Mary. The dies still survive and are signed by the makers McCartney and Bayley.

The classics formed the basis of a gentleman's education at school or university in the eighteenth century. Mathematics was the other main subject taught, but it assumed less importance. Jefferson studied both at the College of William and Mary, having already been well grounded in Greek and Latin at the school run by the Reverend James Maury, "a correct classical scholar." Francis Walker Gilmer, a school fellow, recorded, "Even when at school he used to be seen with his Greek Grammar in his hand while his comrades were enjoying relaxation in the interval of school hours." Jefferson, looking back on his youth, wrote of his debt to the classics: "Among the values of classical learning, I estimate the luxury of reading the Greek and Roman authors in all the beauties of their originals, And why should not this innocent and elegant luxury take its preeminent stand ahead of all those addressed merely to the senses? I think myself more indebted to my father for this than for all the other luxuries his cares and affections have placed within my reach. . . . When the decays of age have enfeebled the useful energies of the mind, the classic pages fill up the vacuum of *ennui*, and become sweet composers to that rest of the grave into which we are all sooner or later to descend." It was not only in old age that Jefferson found solace in classical literature, for his *Commonplace Book* is full of quotations from Greek and Latin authors, and his library included an extensive selection from the classical philosophers, moralists and historians. In common with other educated men of the day, Jefferson regarded them as models for style in writing, oratory, law, morals and politics. The founders of the United States were deeply conscious of the influence of republican Rome on the forms of their government, on the virtues of patriotism and civic rectitude and even on the use of such words as *senate, capitol* and *Cin-*

cinnatus. In spite of his insistence on the importance of useful knowledge, Jefferson made no attempt to abolish the professorship of Greek and Latin when he reorganized the College of William and Mary. Indeed, in *Notes on the State of Virginia* he commented: "The learning Greek and Latin, I am told, is going into disuse in Europe. I know not what their manners and occupations may call for; but it would be very ill-judged in us to follow their example in this instance."

Dr. William Small was the professor of natural philosophy, by which was meant science, during Jefferson's stay at the college, and he also taught mathematics. He was clearly the outstanding intellectual figure there at the time and had a great influence on Jefferson, who remembered him gratefully in his *Autobiography*. "It was my great good fortune, and what probably fixed the destinies of my life that Dr. Wm. Small of Scotland was then professor of Mathematics, a man profound in most of the useful branches of science, with a happy talent of communication correct and gentlemanly manners, & an enlarged and liberal mind." Toward the end of his life, when Jefferson had to conduct his grandson through a course of mathematics, he wrote: "I have resumed that study with great avidity. It was ever my favorite one. We have no theories there, no uncertainties remain on the mind: all is demonstration and satisfaction." R.W.

17 Madonna of Saint Jerome

MATTHEW PRATT 1734–1805
Oil on canvas 1764/1766
77.8 x 60.0 (30⅝ x 23⅝)
*National Gallery of Art. Gift of
Clarence Van Dyke Tiers 1945*

16 Lord Dunmore

SIR JOSHUA REYNOLDS 1723–1792
Oil on canvas 1765
236 x 146 (93 x 57½)

Lent by Mrs. E. Murray, Edinburgh

John Murray, fourth Earl of Dunmore (1732–1808), was appointed governor of Virginia in 1771, the last royal governor to hold the office. He had already been governor of New York. His relations with the Virginia Assembly were bad, as he prorogued the assembly in 1772 and dissolved it in 1773 and 1774 for obstructive behavior. Eventually the governor found the situation intolerable, much of the trouble having been caused by his own provocative and high-handed actions, and retired the seat of government to a British man-of-war,

bringing all relations with the assembly to an end. On his return to England he sat in the House of Lords as a representative peer of Scotland, and later was governor of the Bahamas 1787–1796. Lord Dunmore's daughter, Augusta, was illegally married to the Duke of Sussex, son of George III.

Because of his recent marriage, Jefferson did not take an active part in the early sessions of Dunmore's governorship. His relations with the governor were slight except for a request to Jefferson to provide a plan for an extension to the College of William and Mary. From 1773 as the political crisis worsened, Jefferson took his part in the opposition movement, such as participating on the

standing Committee of Correspondence, and was one of the leaders of the Raleigh Tavern meetings. In 1774 Jefferson was chosen as part of the Virginia delegation to the Continental Congress in Philadelphia, and his proposed instructions to the delegates were published under the title of *A Summary View of the Rights of British America*. Both as a writer and a politician Jefferson was gaining in stature and experience in these last years of the colonial period and preparing for his role in the Revolution and the Declaration of Independence. R.W.

During the first two weeks of March 1773, Matthew Pratt was in Williamsburg seeking portrait commissions and advertising for sale "a small but very neat Collection of PAINTINGS, which are now exhibiting at Mrs. Vobe's, near the Capitol; among which are, first, a very good Copy of Correggio's ST. JEROME, esteemed to be one of the best pictures in *Italy*. . . ." Mrs. Vobe ran the King's Arms on the Duke of Gloucester Street, one of the most genteel taverns in Williamsburg, with a clientele that included William Byrd III, George Washington and Thomas Jefferson. The "very good Copy" after Correggio that was on display at the King's Arms had been copied by Pratt from Benjamin West's copy after Correggio's original. Pratt had made his copy while studying with West in London between 1774 and 1776.

While there is no direct evidence that Jefferson visited the King's Arms during the period of Pratt's exhibition, he was in Williamsburg at the time, from March 4 to March 13, meeting with the burgesses at the capitol, a block away. While in town he twice visited the Raleigh Tavern, directly across the Duke of Gloucester Street from the King's Arms, and he did personal errands at a number of shops in the neighborhood.

Considering Jefferson's innate curiosity about things and his keen interest in the arts, it is inconceivable that he did not take advantage of his proximity to the King's Arms to drop in to see Pratt's paintings. They were the first copies after the Old Masters recorded as having been in Virginia—in a day when good copies were considered very respectable substitutes for originals. They would probably have given Jefferson his first opportunity to see, in color, representations of masterpieces he would have known by reputation but, at best, could have seen only through black and white engravings or book illustrations. A final attraction for Jefferson would have been the copy of Correggio's renowned *Madonna of Saint Jerome*, which, according to contemporary reputation, was one of the most perfect pictures ever painted.

All things considered, it can be assumed that Jefferson saw Pratt's *Madonna of Saint Jerome* at the King's Arms. He did not, however, buy it; nor did the subject suit his fancy enough to add to the list of copies of paintings he desired for the decoration of Monticello. Nor did anyone else buy the painting, for it descended in the artist's family until given to the National Gallery by Pratt's great-great-grandson. W.P.C.

18 Nancy Hallam as "Imogen" in "Cymbeline"

CHARLES WILLSON PEALE
1741–1827
Oil on canvas 1770
127 x 102.8 (50 x 40½)
Lent by the Colonial Williamsburg Foundation

By 1770, culture was burgeoning in the small colonial capitals up and down the eastern seaboard, and artists of all sorts, from players to portrait painters, moved from place to place as they could find appreciative patrons.

Nancy Hallam had joined David Douglass' American Company, when they visited London during 1764–1765. The troupe returned to Williamsburg, after a seven-year absence, in time for the June Court in 1770. Staying until August when they went to Annapolis, the company arrived again in Williamsburg for the October General Assembly. On June 14, 1770, the *Virginia Gazette* advertised that "Yesterday Mr. Douglass with his company of comedians, arrived in town from Philadelphia; and, we hear, intend opening the theater in this city, on Saturday, with the Beggar's Opera, and other entertainments."

By 1770, Jefferson had already begun his lifelong habit of regular attendance at the theater, and his account book shows that he bought tickets to performances on nine evenings between June 16 and 28, and that theater going again took many of his evenings in October and November when the players returned. Since *Cymbeline* was part of the company's repertoire at that time, we can almost certainly conclude that Jefferson saw Nancy Hallam as Imogen, a role which was infinitely appealing to eighteenth-century audiences as well as to those of earlier days: that of a girl, disguised as a boy, forlorn among surrounding dangers. In the portrait by Peale, she stands at the dark entrance to the cave of Belarius and her royal brothers, and is as much afraid of the sword she has drawn to protect herself as of the perils within.

One William Eddis praised the play in a letter, noting even that the scenery "reflected great credit on the painter," a statement that lends credence to the supposition that Peale, who was known to have painted stage sets for the company, had been enlisted for that production and that his portrait of Nancy Hallam shows forest and cave as he made them appear on the stage. C.S.

19 An Election Entertainment

WILLIAM HOGARTH 1697–1764
Etching and engraving
1755 Third State
40.3 x 54.1 (15⅞ x 21⅝₆)
Signed bottom left: *Painted and the Whole Engraved by Wm Hogarth.*
Bottom right: *Published 24th Feb^ry 1755, as the Act directs.*
National Gallery of Art, Rosenwald Collection

19a Canvassing for Votes

WILLIAM HOGARTH 1697–1764
Etching and engraving
1757 Third State
40.3 x 54.0 (15⅞ x 21¼)
Signed bottom left: *Painted by W. Hogarth. Engraved by C. Grignion.*
Bottom right: *Published 20th Feb^ry 1757. As the Act directs.*
National Gallery of Art, Rosenwald Collection

19b The Polling

WILLIAM HOGARTH 1697–1764
Etching and engraving
1758 Second State
40.5 x 54.2 (15¹⁵⁄₁₆ x 21⅜)
Signed bottom left: *Engrav'd by W. Hogarth & Le Cave.* Bottom right: *Published 20th Feb^ry 1758. As the Act directs.*
National Gallery of Art, Rosenwald Collection

19c Chairing the Members

WILLIAM HOGARTH 1697–1764
Etching and engraving
1758 Second State
40.1 x 54.4 (15¹³⁄₁₆ x 21⁷⁄₁₆)
Signed bottom left: *Engrav'd by W. Hogarth & F. Aviline.* Bottom right: *Published 1st Jan^ry 1758 as the Act directs.*
National Gallery of Art, Rosenwald Collection

The four prints comprising *An Election*, engraved between 1755 and 1758, are a commentary in Hogarth's pungent style on a process of great interest in the colonies, subject as they were to the British parliament.

An Election Entertainment illustrates the extensive eating and drinking which candidates provided for their supporters, as well as the close and often humiliating contact candidates had to endure with the electorate. This

To the Hon.ble S.r Edward Walpole Knight of the BATH ˰ This Plate ˰ is most humbly Inscrib'd ˰ By ˰ his most Obedient humble Servant ˰ Will.m Hogarth

theme is continued in *Canvassing for Votes*, where the two inns, headquarters of the rival candidates, dispense unlimited hospitality at the candidates' expense, while through competitive bribery they seek to win over the uncommitted. The actual election takes place in *The Polling*. We see the sick and moribund brought to the hustings and the lawyers of the candidates engaged in argument. Finally in a scene full of ironic reference, *Chairing the Members*, the mock heroic triumphal procession degenerates into a free-for-all and celebrates the successfully elected members of parliament.

Hogarth's engravings were well known in colonial America and in Jefferson's Virginia. Newspapers in Boston, Philadelphia and Charleston advertised the sale of prints within

the artist's lifetime. Most popular were the moralizing and didactic *Industry and Idleness* series, but nearly all Hogarth's work was known, and Benjamin Franklin ordered a complete set of prints from Hogarth before his death for the Library Company of Philadelphia. In Williamsburg a set of *An Election* and *A Midnight Modern Conversation* are recorded before the Revolution. Thus while Jefferson did not own any Hogarths at that time, he undoubtedly saw them on his frequent trips to book dealers, who also sold engravings. When his thoughts later turned to securing works of art for himself, in his list dated 1782, the notation "Prints by Hogarth" appears.

Jefferson was certainly aware of Hogarth's aesthetic ideas about the importance of the rococo serpentine

line, a concept which Jefferson used both in the gardens at Monticello and in the serpentine walls at the University of Virginia. Hogarth had published his thoughts in the *Analysis of Beauty*, 1753, a copy of which Jefferson later included, along with the cherished Kames and Burke, in the select library he suggested for John Skipwith in 1771. R.W.

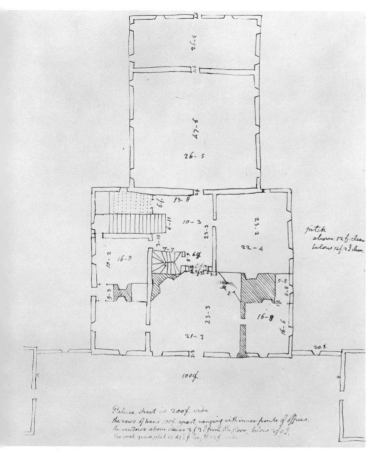

20 Measured plan of the governor's palace, Williamsburg

THOMAS JEFFERSON 1743–1826
Ink on laid paper c. 1768
19 x 24 (7½ x 9½)

*Lent by the Massachusetts Historical
Society, Boston*

This measured plan, presumed to be
of the then existing governor's palace
in Williamsburg, which burned in
1781 and was reconstructed in the
twentieth century, was probably made
to allow Jefferson to study changes
in the design. However, it is not
absolutely certain that this is the original plan of the palace. It has been
suggested that this may be one of
Jefferson's several schemes for
remodeling.

   Jefferson did not like the governor's
palace but wrote in his *Notes on the
State of Virginia* that it was "capable
of being made an elegant seat." The
plan is very similar to one of his
studies for remodeling shown here
at number 21. Already we see Jefferson's love of the octagon shape, which
he admired not only for aesthetic
reasons but also because of its possibilities for introducing maximum
light and air into inner rooms. F.N.

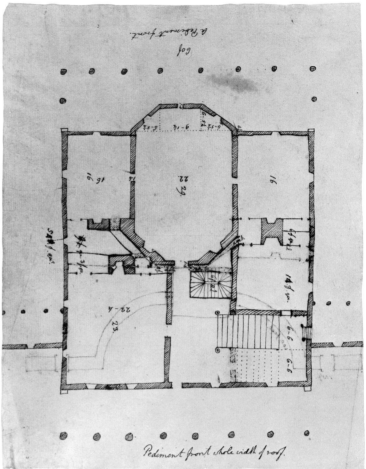

21 Study for remodeling the governor's palace, Williamsburg

THOMAS JEFFERSON 1743–1826
Ink on laid paper 1779–1781
19.5 x 24 (7¾ x 9½)

*Lent by the Massachusetts Historical
Society, Boston*

At the time Jefferson made this drawing, he wrote a letter on the same
paper to Richard Henry Lee dated
January 2, 1780. This is the only other
use of this paper by Jefferson, and
it is the basis for dating this drawing
between 1779 and 1781.

   This neoclassical design is the first
proposal in America or Europe for
a temple-form house. In England, the
temple form had been used previously
for garden structures and churches,
but not for a residence. In the nineteenth century, the style was to become popular in the Greek revival
period and in Jefferson's own Roman
revival. F.N.

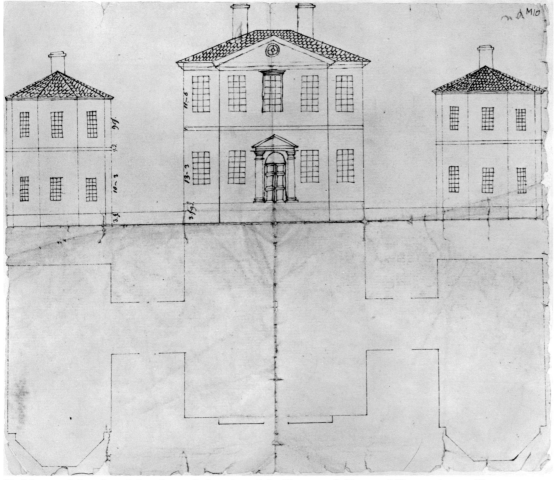

22 Measured drawing of the plan and elevation of the Hammond- Harwood House, Annapolis

THOMAS JEFFERSON 1743–1826
Ink on laid paper 1783–1784
19 x 22.2 (7¼ x 8¾)

Lent by the Massachusetts Historical Society, Boston

Made by Jefferson on a visit to
Annapolis, this drawing indicates his
development as a draftsman as well
as his great interest in the more
up-to-date houses of Annapolis, which
he preferred to Williamsburg. The
octagonal bows at the end of the
wings of this house were a form he
always admired.
    The house is one of the masterpieces
of William Buckland, who represents
the great American success story in
architecture before the Revolution.
Buckland finished Gunston Hall
in Fairfax County, Virginia, and
worked on Sabine Hall and Mount
Airy in Richmond County, Virginia,
before moving to Maryland. Though
he came to America as an indentured
servant, a portrait of him by Charles
Willson Peale shows him dressed
in clothes of the latest fashion and
holding a compass and the plan of this
house. F.N.

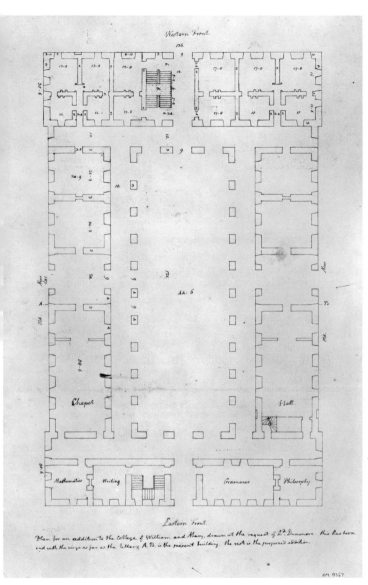

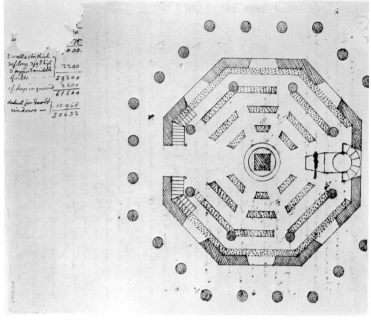

23 Plan for an addition to the College of William and Mary

THOMAS JEFFERSON 1743–1826
Ink on laid paper (facsimile)
1771–1772
23 x 34.5 (9 x 13⅝)
*Original at The Huntington Library,
San Marino, California*

According to Jefferson's notes on
this drawing, he made it "at the
request of Ld. Dunmore," then royal
governor of Virginia. Presumably it
was drawn when Jefferson made two
visits to Williamsburg in 1771–1772.

On September 3, 1772, the
Virginia Gazette announced that the
college intended "to make an additional Building. . . ." Jefferson proposed a rectangular quadrangle, rather
than a square, as originally planned,
and reproduced the general form of the
existing structure, shown on the
lower half of the drawing. The arcade
or piazza, a current term for an

open porch, was to be continued
around the inner courtyard. As
Whiffen has noted, the circulation
system, an arrangement of suites on
corridors, departed from the practice
established at Oxford and Cambridge
Universities and at Morden College,
Blackheath. In 1777, Ebenezer Hazard
noted in his diary that construction
had been halted in its early stages "on
Account of the present Troubles." F.N.

24 Design for an octagonal chapel

THOMAS JEFFERSON 1743–1826
Ink on laid paper (facsimile)
c. 1770
16.5 x 19 (6½ x 7½)
*Original at The Huntington Library,
San Marino, California*

Jefferson frequently consulted Robert
Morris' *Select Architecture*, published in 1755, and Palladio's *Four
Books* for architectural inspiration.
This octagonal chapel with its gallery
and center altar on a circular platform, presumed to be for Williamsburg, claims both as sources. The
octagonal form for a chapel clearly
comes from Morris, but Jefferson tells
us that its exterior with its peristyle
and domed roof derive from the
Temple of Vesta in Rome, reproduced
in Palladio's *Fourth Book*. The
neoclassical chapel with its Tuscan
columns, if built, would have been
in sharp contrast to the other buildings
in the town, since it was stylistically
considerably in advance of the traditional architecture of Williamsburg.

Whiffen noted that the plan's
dimensions are the same as those of
the magazine in Williamsburg, but he
concluded that Jefferson's drawing
was not a plan for remodeling, since
Jefferson specified the number of
bricks he needed to erect the
building. F.N.

25 Harpsichord, London 1772

JACOB KIRCKMAN 1710–1792, and
ABRAHAM KIRCKMAN 1737–1794
Case of burled walnut-veneered panels
with solid walnut lid; brass hinges
and hooks for securing lid; separate
trestle stand.
91.5 x 183 x 122 (36 x 72 x 48)
Single keyboard; three registers:
two at 8' (unison) pitch, one at 4'
(octave) pitch, and a buff stop controlled by four brass knobs at left
and right of nameboard; machine stop
(pedal missing); keyboard range FF
(no FF#) to f′′′.

*Lent by Mrs. Charles F. Willis,
Washington*

This instrument is typical of English
harpsichords of the second half of
the eighteenth century, both as a
musical instrument and as furniture.
The Kirckman family and Burkat
Shudi (Tschudi) were by far the best
known and most prolific makers of
harpsichords in eighteenth-century
England, and instruments by both
makers were exported to colonial
America. Kirckman instruments made
before 1772 were signed by Jacob
alone; beginning in 1772 the name of

his nephew, Abraham, who had become a partner in the firm, was added. After 1789, Abraham's name and occasionally that of his son Joseph appeared on the nameboard. Jefferson ordered two Kirckman instruments in his lifetime, the first in 1786 for his daughter Martha, during their stay in Paris. This harpsichord later crossed the ocean with their baggage, making the last leg of the journey from Richmond in a half-wagonload of hay and arriving safely at Monticello in 1790. It possessed two keyboards and its construction, if typical of Kirckman's usual "double" instruments, would have included three registers: an 8' and 4' on the lower keyboard plus an 8' on the upper, probably with a buff stop acting on the lower 8' and a lute stop acting on the upper 8'. That the 1786 instrument had a machine stop (for changing registers by a pedal) and a Venetian swell (wooden shutters mounted on top of the instrument, making the sound soften when closed) is known from correspondence between Jefferson and the noted London historian of music, Dr. Charles Burney, who watched over the building of the instrument on Jefferson's behalf.

A "celestini" (as Jefferson called it) mechanism, intended to sustain the sound, was added to the instrument by Adam Walker, a London piano maker. This newly patented device was not usual on harpsichords, but Jefferson was fascinated with it and ordered it

installed over Kirckman's objections.

The second harpsichord, for his daughter Maria, was ordered in 1798 and was probably very similar to the first. Jefferson described it as "one of Kirchman's highest priced, and of a fine silver tone; double-keyed, but not with as many pedals as her sister's." The comment about pedals probably implies that this instrument did not possess a machine stop. In 1800 Maria was offered her choice between her harpsichord and the new Hawkins portable grand, which had just arrived at Monticello, but wisely remained loyal to her harpsichord. J.F.

26 English Guitar

JOHN PRESTON, London, late 18th century
Back and sides: curly maple; belly: spruce
76 x 38 (30 x 15)
Lent by the Smithsonian Institution

A typical English guitar, the fingerboard is covered with tortoise shell; tuned c e g c' e' g'; six courses of strings, the top four being double, with a watch-key tuning device. The firm of Preston and Son was established in London in 1774 by John Preston, who in addition to making musical instruments soon began to publish music as well.

The Jefferson family owned a significant number of musical instruments, aside from the two harpsichords given to Martha and Maria by their father. There were several violins, a spinet, a piano forte ordered by Jefferson from London as a wedding present for his future wife, and at least two guitars. The guitar was a popular instrument in Virginia, as the young tutor Fithian's description of the musical education of his charges at Nomini Hall testifies. As early as 1776 Jefferson's account book records a purchase of guitar strings from a Philadelphia merchant, perhaps for Mrs. Jefferson. When his daughter Maria joined him in Paris in 1787, she too began the study of this instrument, and the guitar he purchased for her there returned

with their baggage to Monticello.

Up until about 1825, in both England and America, the term *guitar* referred exclusively to the English guitar, a type of cittern, as opposed to the Spanish guitar, which was normally identified as *Spanish*. Although a "Fingerboard for the Spanish guitar" said to be in Jefferson's own hand has been recorded among the musical literature surviving at Monticello, perhaps intended for his granddaughter, Virginia Randolph, it is extremely likely that his household contained one or more English guitars similar to the Preston instrument displayed here. J.F.

27 Armchair

Mahogany, eastern Virginia
1755–1800
99 x 75 x 43 (39 x 29½ x 17)
Lent by the Mary Washington House, Fredericksburg, Association for the Preservation of Virginia Antiquities

There is evidence of the close cultural ties between England and Tidewater Virginia in this armchair, which dates from the last half of the eighteenth century. Particular construction details and design elements relate this piece to a distinctive group of chairs which are traced to eastern Virginia, a group which is closely English in character.

The outline of the chair relates it

to a pair of side chairs at the Virginia Historical Society as well as a side chair at Colonial Williamsburg. The dog's-head arms are close to those on a pair of armchairs at Shirley Plantation, situated along the James River. The chairs are strikingly English in feeling—sharing with contemporary English chairs an anthropomorphic expression and foreshortened proportions. Dog's-head-carved arms are found on English chairs of the Queen Anne and Chippendale periods, and the stiff, straightened cabriole legs terminating in heavy balls clutched by birdlike claws are typical of the English manner. The outline of the crest rail with scrolled ears and scrolled yoke and of the uppermost splat with vertical ribs ending in rounded arches with scrolls on either side repeats an outline frequently exhibited in English Georgian chairs. The splat might be a variant of a type of English and Irish Chippendale chair which is often seen with vertical ribs in the upper section and an elongated pierced-heart section below. This heart-shaped lower section is surrounded by heavy leaf-carved S-scrolls, with an elongated heart-teardrop opening cut out within. In Virginia this section becomes squatter in shape.

Because of the closeness to English proportions, it seems unlikely that this particular eastern Virginia cabinet-maker based his design for the chairs upon pattern book drawings, but more likely upon actual English chairs with which he was familiar. Certainly English furniture was considered high style by eastern Virginia planters, and this group of chairs points to the planters' political, economic and cultural dependence upon England. That the style appears to be indigenous to Tidewater Virginia suggests the isolationism of the rural South, more easily in communication with England by sea than with their fellow colonists by land. E.G.

28 Cellarette
Walnut and southern hard pine, second half of the 18th century
107 x 80.5 x 47.5 (42¼ x 31¾ x 18¾)
Ink inscription on back of left hand drawer: 22nd August 1797/ 4 ½
$ 10/4 (last word illegible).
Lent by the Colonial Williamsburg Foundation

This substantial cellarette of walnut and southern pine is thought to be of Virginia origin. This example reveals the handsome clarity of form and admirable restraint of decoration displayed in so much southern furniture, which relied on crisp outline, rich graining and simple brasses for effect. The southern cellarette, usually made in two sections, assumed the form of a chest on a stand. The hinged lid of the chest section lifts up to reveal one large and twelve small compartments for the storage of bottles of wine and spirits. The stand contains a mixing slide over two drawers. The plain surface is relieved by simple moldings around the lid and upper edge of the stand and an incised line, which defines the mixing slide, two drawers, skirts and Marlborough legs.

The enormous popularity of the cellarette in the South in the second half of the eighteenth century coincided with the increasing specialization of the use of rooms in the American home, including a room for dining. Perhaps it is also symbolic of the celebrated custom of southern hospitality, a characteristic of plantation society which has been attributed to several factors including the social isolation of agrarian life. E.G.

29 Pair of side chairs
Cherry, eastern Virginia 1755–1800
99.2 x 54.6 x 43.8 (39⅛ x 21½ x 17¼); 99 x 54 x 43.6
(39 x 21¼ x 17⅛)
Lent by the Virginia Historical Society, Richmond

The splats of this pair of cherry wood side chairs are elaborated versions of the Mary Washington chair, with more tightly wound scrolls and crisply carved bellflowers on the ribs. The pair relate in the carving of the crest rails, splats and knees to the pair

of cherry armchairs at Shirley Plantation. The knees are carved with a boldly conceived reversed scallop shell and leafage descending in a V. Much in the English tradition are the flat-arched seat rails. E.G.

30 Side chair
Black cherry and ash, Virginia, probably Williamsburg 1760–1795
99 x 54 x 50.8 (39 x 21¼ x 20)
Roman numeral III in back seat rail, roman numeral VI in slip seat
Lent by the Colonial Williamsburg Foundation

The chair has a history of descent in the Williamsburg family of Benjamin Waller (1716–1786), and the well-articulated overall design, delicate carving and obvious familiarity with fashionable rococo motifs all suggest that the cabinetmaker and his client shared a certain gracious urbanity. The chair's restrained sophistication and simple elegance denote Williamsburg's polite society about which Thomas Jefferson reminisced in 1815, "I have heard [here in Williamsburg] more good sense, more rational and philosophical conversations, than in all my life besides." E.G.

31 Side chair
Mahogany and beech, eastern Virginia 1755–1800
99 x 58.4 x 43.8 (39 x 23 x 17¼)
Roman numeral X in slip seat frame
Lent by the Colonial Williamsburg Foundation

The simplified open splat of this mahogany side chair relates to one on the Mary Washington armchair, and, in a more general way, its unmolded,

tightly scrolled ears bear a marked similarity to the rest of this distinctive group of chairs. The handsomely carved upright scallop shells and bellflowers of the knees suggest English prototypes. The chair has a history of ownership by the descendants of Alexander Spotswood, who was the governor of Virginia from 1710 to 1722. E.G.

32 Coffee pot
JOHN JACOBS
Silver 1734/35
27.9 (11) high
London hallmark, 1734/35; maker's mark of John Jacobs
Lent anonymously

The arms engraved on the side are those of Sir John Randolph (c. 1693–1737), one of the most distinguished Virginia lawyers. He was attorney general of Virginia and speaker of the House of Burgesses. Randolph completed his legal training in London as a member of Gray's Inn and went twice to England on business for the colony. The political eminence of Randolph, in addition to his family's established social position, was enhanced by his knighthood. He was the only Virginian to be so honored during colonial rule. Jefferson was related to the Randolphs through his mother, daughter of Isham Randolph of Dungeness, brother of Sir John. R.W.

35 Chalice, flagon and alms basin

THOMAS HEMING active 1745–1780
Silver 1764–1767
Chalice: 25.4 (10) high; flagon: 27.3 (10¾) high; alms basin: 25.4 (10) diam.
London hallmark, 1764/65 (chalice), 1766/67 (flagon); maker's mark of Thomas Heming (chalice and flagon)

Lent by Bruton Parish Church, Williamsburg, Virginia

The royal arms are those of George III,

thereby indicating that the silver was a gift from the King's Bounty, a fund to help the Anglican Church, although it was Governor Fauquier who made the presentation shortly before he died. Other gifts of Communion plate were made by George III to churches in America partly as an act of generosity and partly to encourage loyalty to church and crown. The rim of the basin is an early nineteenth-century addition, and the flagon has been reduced in height. R.W.

33 Cup and cover

ROBERT TRIMBLE and
BENJAMIN BENTLEY
Silver 1715/16
27 x 26.4 (10⅝ x 10⅜)
London hallmark, 1715/16; maker's mark for Robert Trimble and Benjamin Bentley; Britannia standard mark

Lent by the Colonial Williamsburg Foundation

The cup is part of a collection of silver, belonging to Peyton Randolph, which has returned to his house in Williamsburg. He was a kinsman of Jefferson, who admired him, although their political views differed. After Randolph's death in 1775, Jefferson bought his library.

The decoration was added in the nineteenth century. R.W.

34 Salver

WILLIAM PEASTON
Silver 1753/54
21.6 (8½) diam.
London hallmark, 1753/54; maker's mark of William Peaston

Lent by the Colonial Williamsburg Foundation

This salver is one of a pair and part of a considerable quantity of silver, nearly five hundred ounces in weight, which belonged to Peyton Randolph, king's attorney and speaker of the Virginia House of Burgesses. Much of this plate would have been English, as local silversmiths were unable to satisfy the demand for flatware, drinking vessels, tea and coffee services and all the other necessary table silver in a gentleman's house. The Williamsburg innkeeper, Henry Wetherburn, had an even larger amount of silver, as is revealed in an inventory of 1760, no doubt to serve his more distinguished customers at the annual meeting of the assembly when the gentry came in from their estates. It must also be remembered that in the days before a regular banking system, buying silver was an easy way to save money, as the objects could be quickly converted into ready cash. R.W.

36 Cup and cover

PIERRE HARACHE THE ELDER
active 1675–1700
Silver 1686/87
10.5 (4⅛) high
London hallmark, 1686/87; maker's mark of Pierre Harache the Elder

Lent by the College of William and Mary in Virginia

The cup is a particularly fine example of the work of the Huguenot silversmiths who came to England to escape religious persecution. There appeared to be nothing strange in converting

a posset or caudle cup, originally for spiced drinks, into one for religious use. Many of these cups came to the colonies during the latter part of the seventeenth century and, because of a time lag in fashion, would still have been found in the houses of Virginia gentry during Jefferson's boyhood. Lady Gooch, whose parents' arms are engraved on the side, bequeathed the cup in 1775 to the chapel of William and Mary in memory of her son, who had died in Virginia after being educated at the College of William and Mary. Her husband, Sir William

38 Alms basin
THOMAS FARREN active 1703–1740
Silver 1739/40
24.8 (9¾) diam.
London hallmark, 1739/40; maker's
mark of Thomas Farren
Inscribed: *For the Use of James City
Parish Church*

*Lent by Bruton Parish Church,
Williamsburg, Virginia*

Jamestown, the first English settlement in Virginia, was gradually
abandoned when the capital moved to
Williamsburg in 1699, and the
church had eventually to be closed for
lack of a congregation. The silver,
including the basin, was transferred
to Bruton Parish Church. R.W.

39 Chalice and paten
Silver c. 1660
Chalice: 27 (10⅝) high; paten:
17.5 (6⅞) diam.
London hallmark; maker's mark 1W
within oval
Inscribed: *Mixe not holy things with
profane*; and on base: *Ex dono
Francisci Morrison Armigeri. Anno:
Domi*ⁱ. *1661*

*Lent by Bruton Parish Church,
Williamsburg, Virginia*

The donor of the chalice and paten
was Colonel Francis Morrison, deputy
governor of Virginia. As can be seen
with other pieces in the exhibition,
there was a longstanding tradition
among the official leaders of the colony
to give pieces of plate to Anglican
churches. R.W.

Gooch, was an efficient and popular
governor of Virginia from 1727 to
1749. The college, founded by royal
charter, was staffed mainly by clergymen of the Church of England, and
one of its purposes was "that the
Church of Virginia may be furnished
with a seminary of ministers of the
gospel." The close connection between church and college continued
down to the Revolution, and Jefferson
was a leading force in attempting to
secularize the institution and transform
it into a state university. R.W.

37 Paten
RICHARD GURNEY AND CO.
active after 1739
Silver 1751/52
14 (5½) diam.
London hallmark, 1751/52; maker's
mark of Richard Gurney and Co.

*Lent by the College of William and
Mary in Virginia*

Like the covered cup by Harache, the
paten is engraved with arms of the
parents of Lady Gooch, although it is
not mentioned in her will. R.W.

40 Paten
BENJAMIN PYNE active 1684–1724
Silver 1691/92
7.3 x 27.9 (2⅞ x 11)
London hallmark, 1691/92; maker's
mark of Benjamin Pyne
Inscribed around rim: EX DONO Dⁿⁱ
EDMUNDI ANDROS, EQUITIS, VIRGINIAE
GUBERNATORIS. ANNO DOM. MDCXCIV.

IN USUM ECCLESIAE IACOBIPOLIS.
Inscribed in center: *Presented by
Hugh Munroe of Mobile/to the
DIOCESE of VIRGINIA/through/REV.
B. B. Leacock, 1856*

*Lent by Bruton Parish Church,
Williamsburg, Virginia*

The Anglican Church was the established church in Virginia, and so all
government officials and leading members of the colony would have been
members and given it their financial
support. It is therefore not surprising
that Sir Edmund Andros, governor
of Virginia from 1692 to 1698, should
have presented this piece of Communion plate to Bruton Parish Church,
Williamsburg, although ironically
there were complaints that he did not
uphold the interests of the church
as he should have done. Nevertheless,
his period of rule appears to have been
successful and the College of William and Mary was founded in 1693
during his governorship. R.W.

41 *Plutarchi Chaeronensis Parallela
seu Vitae parallelae* (Geneva: H.
Stephanus, 1572) and *Plutarch's
Lives*, in six volumes, translated
from the Greek . . . to which is
prefixed, *The Life of Plutarch*, by
Mr. Dryden (Edinburgh: printed
by Alexander Donaldson, 1774)
PLUTARCH 46–120 A.D.

Lent by the Library of Congress

The importance of Plutarch's writings
to eighteenth-century thought can
hardly be overestimated, and the
attraction of the great Greek historian
and biographer for Jefferson, as for
many others, must have been his
emphasis on moral concerns, combined
with a preoccupation with historical
accuracy. Jefferson owned several
editions of Plutarch's works, including
his *Lives*. In 1787 while in Paris he
bought a set from Froullé, and after his
return to the United States, bought
a copy from John Pemberton, a
Quaker in Philadelphia, who wrote on
July 16, 1791, "I send the books
thou paid for 2 months past. they are
not in such good order as I could
have wished. they suffered while in the
Bookseller's hands—that if thou does
not approve of them I cannot insist on
thy taking them." A year later, Jefferson
ordered the 1762 edition from Lacking-
ton's catalogue and in 1806 bought
from Roche of Philadelphia Dacier's
French edition in fourteen volumes.

The Geneva and Edinburgh editions, conflated and bound in thirteen
volumes, are bound in calf with gilt
backs. Each is initialed by Jefferson
and has his paragraph numerals in the
margins of the text. The Stephanus, or
Geneva, edition was once in the library
of William Byrd, whose signature is on
the title page of the first volume. J.M.E.

42 *Metamorphoses* (London:
Delphin, 1751)
PUBLIUS OVIDIUS NASO (OVID)
43 B.C.–17 A.D.

Lent by the Library of Congress

Jefferson was probably first introduced
to Ovid, along with other classical
writers, in the school run by the
Reverend James Maury, a classical
scholar with whom the young Jefferson boarded for two years, beginning at age fourteen. At the end of
that time he had begun his lifelong
habit of reading Latin and Greek in
the original and had formed the basis
for a lasting love of the classical writers.

Three works by Ovid were in
Jefferson's library when it was sold to
the Library of Congress in 1815,
including a copy of the *Metamorphoses*
in Latin and one in Old English,
none of which have remained in the
Library of Congress' collections. J.M.E.

43 *Oeuvres de Séneque le philosophe, traduites en Francois par La Grange....* (A Paris: de l'Imprimerie de J. J. Smits et Cⁱᵉ, an III de la République [1795]) and *L Annei Senecae Philosoph Opera ad optimas editiones collata praemittur notitia literaria studiis Societatis Bipontinae* (Biponti: Ex Typographia Societatis, 1782)

SENECA 4 B.C.–65 A.D.
Lent by the Library of Congress

The writings of this Roman philosopher and playwright were an important element in Thomas Jefferson's classical education. As a Roman philosopher, Seneca is second only to Cicero, and like Cicero he was an adherent of the philosophy of Stoicism. His plays had an important influence on the Renaissance drama of France and Italy and on the tragic drama of Elizabethan England.

Jefferson owned a French and a Latin edition of Seneca's works, exhibited here, which he had bound together in ten volumes with straight grain red morocco leather and bordered in gilt. This binding was done by John March in October 1802, just after Jefferson bought the French translation from N. G. Dufief. The Latin edition had been acquired in Paris in 1786 from Gautier.

Writing to William Short in October 1819, Jefferson expressed his opinion that "Seneca is indeed a fine moralist, disfiguring his work at times with some Stoicisms and affecting too much of antithesis and point, yet giving us on the whole a great deal of sound and practical morality." J.M.E.

44 *The Morals* 1744
The Morals of Cicero. Containing, I. His conferences De Finibus: or, concerning the ends of things good and evil. In which, all the principles of the Epicureans, Stoics, and Academics, concerning the Ultimate Point of Happiness and Misery, are fully discussed. II. His Academics.... Translated into English, by William Guthrie, Esq (London: Printed for T. Waller, 1744)

MARCUS TULLIUS CICERO
106–43 B.C.
Lent by the Library of Congress

Cicero was, unquestionably, the most influential of the classical writers, not only in terms of his philosophical content but in also his means of expression. It was Cicero's Latin which was the universal model for style, and when Latin was superseded by the vernacular languages, this influence was transmitted into the new forms. In his letter to John Adams, written from Monticello on July 5, 1814, Jefferson described the great Roman orator and politician as "able, learned, laborious, practised in the business of the world, & honest."

The copy of Cicero's *Morals* in the exhibition was Jefferson's. He initialed the book at signatures I and T. The bookplate is that of the original owner Reuben Skelton, the brother-in-law of Jefferson's wife, Martha Wayles Skelton. J.M.E.

45 *Essays*
The Essays, or Counsels, civil, & moral, of Sir Francis Bacon, Lord Verulam, Viscount St-Alban: whereunto is added by himself A Table of the Colours of Good and Evil. Enlarged in many Places, since the first Edition, by the Honourable Authour himself; and now more exactly published than formerly. To which is prefixed a Preliminary Discourse containing sundry remarkable Memoirs concerning this Noble Authour, his Works, and particularly this of his Essaies (London: Printed by J. Redmayne for Thomas Palmer, 1663)

SIR FRANCIS BACON,
VISCOUNT ST. ALBANS 1561–1626
Lent by the Library of Congress

It would be difficult to pinpoint any single influence on a mind as far ranging as that of Thomas Jefferson; if one were to attempt it, however, Sir Francis Bacon would be an obvious choice. Bacon was a statesman, essayist and philosopher, who studied law and became lord chancellor of England. His motto, "I have taken all knowledge to be my province," could easily have been Jefferson's, and in fact Jefferson included him, with Newton and Locke, in his "trinity of the three greatest men the world has ever produced," as he wrote to Benjamin Rush, January 16, 1811.

When first published in 1597, the work contained only ten essays. The first edition in the form exhibited, with fifty-eight essays, appeared in 1625. The copy exhibited here was Thomas Jefferson's own, with his characteristic initial at signature I and the Library of Congress' 1815 bookplate. The book was bound for Jefferson in Georgetown by John March, in tree calf with gilt back, marbled end papers and sprinkled edges, and is entered in Jefferson's undated manuscript catalogue with the price of 9d. J.M.E.

46 *A Letter Concerning Toleration* (London: J. Crowder, 1800)
JOHN LOCKE 1632–1704
Lent by the Library of Congress

Of all the plain statements on the principles of democracy which influenced Thomas Jefferson's philosophy and language, that of John Locke was preeminent. Locke presupposed an original and necessary law of reason, and he based the constitution of society on it. Consent, for Locke, became a prior condition of the "social contract," not a result of it, so that civil rulers hold their power not absolutely but conditionally. Jefferson and Locke viewed government as a moral trust which lapses if the trustees fail to maintain their side of the contract. The essay on tolerance reinforced Jefferson's liberal opinions and, together with Locke's other writings on government, provided a classic example of the empirical approach to social and political questions which still remains the basis of democratic principles.

The letter, or essay, *On Toleration* was first published in Latin in Gouda, Holland, in 1689. A second edition, in English, appeared the following year in London. Jefferson is known to have bought a copy of the 1790 edition, but it is not in his collection at the Library of Congress. J.M.E.

47 *The Mathematical Principles of Natural Philosophy* (London: Printed for H. D. Symonds, by Knight & Compton, 1803)
SIR ISAAC NEWTON 1642–1727
Lent by the Library of Congress

"Bacon, Locke and Newton," Thomas Jefferson wrote to John Trumbull, on February 15, 1789, "I consider ... as the three greatest men that have ever lived, without any exception...." Newton was well known to Jefferson long before Jefferson bought a 1760 edition of Newton's works in 1814. The *Principia* is generally considered as the greatest work in the history of science; it provided the synthesis of the cosmos and proof of its physical unity. Newton showed that the important and dramatic aspects of nature that were subject to the universal law of gravitation could be explained in mathematical terms within a single physical theory. With Newton the separation of natural and supernatural, of sublunar and superlunar, worlds disappeared. For the first time a single mathematical law could explain the motion of objects on earth as well as the phenomena of the heavens. It was this grand conception that produced a general revolution in human thought, of which the Enlightenment, the French and American revolutions, and Jeffersonian democracy were the social and political counterparts. J.M.E.

48 *The Second Part of the Institutes of the Laws of England: containing the exposition of many ancient, and other statutes.... The sixth edition.... Authore Edw. Coke Milite, J. C....* (London: Printed by W. Rawlins, for Thomas Basset, 1681)
SIR EDWARD COKE 1552–1634
Lent by the Library of Congress

No better appraisal of Coke's *Institutes* can be found than this one by Thomas Jefferson. On January 16, 1814, in a letter to Thomas Cooper, he wrote, "And all these, by the time of Lᵈ Coke, had formed so large a mass of matter as to call for a new digest, to bring it within reasonable compass. this he undertook in his Institutes, harmonising all the decisions and opinions which were reconcilable, and rejecting those not so. This work is executed with so much learning and judgment, that I do not recollect that a single position in it has ever been judicially denied. and altho' the work loses much of it's value by it's chaotic form, it may still be considered as the fundamental code of the English law...."

It is amusing to contrast this opinion with that of the youthful Jefferson who, when a law student at the age of nineteen, wrote to John Page, "And too often I am sure to get through old Cooke [sic] this winter: for God knows I have not seen him since I packed him up in my trunk in Williamsburgh. Well, Page, I do wish the Devil had old Cooke, for I am sure I never was so tired of an old dull scoundrel in my life...."

Coke's *Institutes* are in four parts: the first, "a Commentary upon Littleton," is a reprint of Sir Thomas ittleton's *Tenures*; the second contains the text of various statutes from the Magna Carta to the time of James I, with a full exposition; the third is on criminal law; and the fourth is on the jurisdiction of different courts of law.

Of Jefferson's copies of the various parts and editions of the *Institutes*, only *The Second Part . . . 1681*, shown in the exhibition, is known. In the Library of Congress, it bears Jefferson's initials at signatures I and T and a manuscript note by him on page 148. J.M.E.

49 *The Architecture of A. Palladio; in four Books. Containing a short Treatise of the Five Orders . . . Revis'd, Design'd, and Publish'd by Giacomo Leoni, a Venetian . . . Translated from the Italian Original. The Third Edition*, corrected (London: Printed for A. Ward [and others], 1742)

ANDREA PALLADIO 1508–1580

Lent by the Library of Congress

Palladio, or Palladianism, was the perfect bridge from the classical ideal to Jeffersonian philosophy and style. Palladio's lasting influence was exercised less through his actual buildings than through this textbook. The Palladian style was directly inspired by Roman classical models through the writings of Vitruvius and Alberti. Its characteristics are those of classicism: symmetry, order, fixed mathematical relations of the parts to each other and to the whole, logic and monumentality. Much of Palladio's powerful influence in England was due to his enthusiastic follower Inigo Jones. Jones copiously annotated his copy of the *Architettura*, and these notes were incorporated into the first English translation made by Giacomo Leoni and published in 1715, a copy of which Jefferson owned.

In the first chapter is a sentiment of which Jefferson must have approved and which he remembered as a standard for architectural judgment: "As for the beauty of an edifice, it consists of an exact proportion of the parts within themselves, and of each part with the whole. . . ." J.M.E.

50 *Select Architecture: being regular Designs of Plans and Elevations well suited to both Town and Country; in which the Magnificence and Beauty, the Purity and Simplicity of Designing for every Species of that Noble Art, is accurately treated, and with great Variety exemplified, from the Plain Town-House to the Stately Hotel, and in the Country from the genteel and convenient Farm-House to the Parochial Church. With Suitable Embellishments. Also Bridges, Baths, Summer-Houses, &c. to all which such Remarks, Explanations and Scales are annexed, that the Comprehension is rendered easy, and Subject most agreeable. Illustrated with Fifty Copper Plates, Quarto* (London: Sold by Robert Sayer, 1757, 2nd ed.)

ROBERT MORRIS active 1754

From the Collection of Mr. and Mrs. Paul Mellon

The very first designs of Monticello may have been inspired by Thomas Jefferson's study of Robert Morris' *Select Architecture*. This book, a first edition of which Jefferson owned and which he acquired some time before 1783, is a prime example of the excellence of Jefferson's architectural library. In addition to writing several books, Morris was an English architect who built Wimbledon House and other mansions.

The *Select Architecture* reflected, in Fiske Kimball's words, "the architectural ideas of England, with its Italian background, and its movement towards a return to the picturesque." Thomas Jefferson. The book in the exhibition is a copy of the second edition of 1757. J.M.E.

51 *A Book of Architecture, containing Designs of Buildings and Ornaments* (London: Printed 1728)

JAMES GIBBS 1682–1754

From the Collection of Mr. and Mrs. Paul Mellon

James Gibbs was a Scots architect whose influence on Jefferson was both large and direct. Jefferson was using Gibbs' *A Book of Architecture* in 1770 and 1771, prior to his residence in France, and his tracings of plates 67 and 69 from this book can be seen in his designs for an ice house in the form of a garden temple at Monticello. It is also Fiske Kimball's guess that the octagonal projections to the final plan of Monticello may have come from Jefferson's study of Gibbs' use of the octagon as an interior form.

Gibbs was an enormously popular architect who, in addition to many private homes in England and in Scotland, built the church of St. Martin-in-the-Fields and St. Bartholomew's Hospital in London, the Radcliffe Library in Oxford, and the King's College Fellows' Building and the Senate House in Cambridge. J.M.E.

52 *The Designs of Inigo Jones, consisting of Plans and Elevations for Publick and Private Buildings* (Publish'd by William Kent, with some Additional Designs . . . 1727)

INIGO JONES 1573–1652

From the Collection of Mr. and Mrs. Paul Mellon

Together with his copy of Palladio, this book was one of the most important in influencing Thomas Jefferson's architectural style. In his notes on the decorative structures for Monticello, made in 1779, Jefferson several times refers to the designs of Inigo Jones. Whether he owned a copy of Jones at that time or only had access to one is not certain; by the time he made his manuscript catalogue of his library in 1815, he did own a copy.

Inigo Jones was an English architect and designer of masques who had studied in Italy. During his lifetime he designed many fine buildings in England, including the Banqueting House in Whitehall, the Queen's House, Greenwich, the piazza at Covent Garden and the grand portico at St. Paul's Cathedral. William Kent (1684–1748) was an English painter, designer, architect and landscape gardener; the collection of Jones' drawings which he published were the property of Richard Boyle (1695–1753), third Earl of Burlington, who had lived several years in Italy and was an admirer of Palladio. J.M.E.

53 *The Theory and Practice of Gardening: wherein is fully handled all that relates to Fine Gardens, commonly called Pleasure-Gardens. . . . By Le Sieur Alexander Le Blond. Done from the late Edition printed at Paris, by John James of Greenwich. The Second Edition . . .* (London: Printed for Bernard Lintot, 1728)

ANTOINE JOSEPH DEZALLIER D'ARGENTVILLE 1680–1765, JEAN BAPTISTE ALEXANDRE LE BLOND 1679–1719, and JOHN JAMES d. 1746

Lent by the Library of Congress

In a letter to Charles Willson Peale, dated August 20, 1811, Thomas Jefferson wrote: "I have often thought that if heaven had given me choice of my position & calling, it should have been on a rich spot of earth, well-watered, and near a good market for the production of the garden. no occupation is so delightful to me as the culture of the earth, & no culture comparable to that of the garden. . . ." One of the first books Jefferson bought to satisfy that yearning was that of Dezallier d'Argentville which he entered in the manuscript catalogue of his library as "James on gardening." His own copy of the book, however, is no longer in the Library of Congress collection.

Dezallier d'Argentville was a French artist who studied drawing under Bernard Picard and landscape architecture under Alexandre Le Blond. When *The Theory and Practice of Gardening* was first published, the initials of its author, Dezallier d'Argentville, appeared on the title page. At one point, the French booksellers decided that the book would sell better with the name of an established authority as the author. An edition therefore appeared with the name Alexandre Le Blond, a French architect who was particularly interested in architecture and landscaping as applied to gardens, substituted for the initials of the real author. In the translation by John James, by whose name the book was known to Thomas Jefferson, the "error" was continued. J.M.E.

54 *Elements of Criticism. Volumes I–II. The Third Edition, with additions and Improvements* (Edinburgh: Printed for A. Millar, London; and A. Kincaid & J. Bell, Edinburgh, 1765)

HENRY HOME, LORD KAMES 1696–1782

Lent by the Library of Congress

Perhaps no other writer had as much influence on Thomas Jefferson's philosophy of art as did Lord Kames, the Scottish jurist who was a friend and correspondent of Benjamin Franklin. Through Kames, Jefferson came in contact with the main currents of criticism and aesthetics of his own as well as of earlier times. Kames, as did Jefferson himself, relied heavily on the critical writers of antiquity, and, also like Jefferson, was strongly influenced by John Locke. The Lockeian philosophy which centered around the defense of the dignity of the individual and of intellectual, religious and social freedom has many echoes in Kames' *Elements of Criticism*, sections of which were often quoted by Jefferson.

Jefferson also shared Kames' interest in gardening and was greatly influenced by his treatment of gardening as an art. Jefferson wrote to his granddaughter Ellen Randolph during his second term as president, "To answer your question . . . I must observe that neither the *number* of the fine arts nor the particular arts entitled to that appellation have been fixed by general consent. many. . . . add Gardening as a 7th fine art. not horticulture, but the art of embellishing grounds by fancy. I think L'. Kaims has justly proved this. . . ."

The *Elements of Criticism* was first published in Edinburgh in 1762. Although the copy exhibited is not Jefferson's, he did own a copy of the 1765 edition, which is in the Library of Congress in a modern binding. J.M.E.

55 An Inquiry into the Original of our Ideas of Beauty and Virtue. In Two Treatises. I. Concerning Beauty, Order, Harmony, Design. II. Concerning Moral Good and Evil. The Fifth Edition, Corrected . . . (London: Printed for R. Ware, J. and P. Knapton, T. and T. Longman, C. Hitch [and others], 1753)

FRANCIS HUTCHESON 1694–1746
Lent by the Library of Congress

Francis Hutcheson was a philosopher who taught at Glasgow University. He had a great influence on the "common-sense" school of philosophy. Hutcheson's influence on Thomas Jefferson is particularly noteworthy because of Hutcheson's support of the school of moral utilitarianism as opposed to the egotistic hedonism of the schools of Thomas Hobbes and Bernard de Mandeville.

Thomas Jefferson's copy, exhibited here, is inscribed with his initials at signatures I and T, and has the bookplate of Reuben Skelton inside the front cover, suggesting that Jefferson may have acquired the book through his wife Martha, the widow of Bathurst Skelton. J.M.E.

56 The Book of Common Prayer and Administration of the Sacraments for the Use of the Church of England. (London: Printed by His Majesties Printers, 1662)

Lent by the Library of Congress

The English *Book of Common Prayer*, first published in 1549, was the first single manual of worship in a vernacular language directed to be used universally by, and common to, both priest and people. Its original simplicity has been retained through many revisions and has insured its permanence. The language of the *Book of Common Prayer* is now, and has been for centuries, part of the whole language, often quoted and used even when the original itself is unknown. Thomas Jefferson was raised in the Church of England and was familiar with the *Book of Common Prayer* from his earliest years. His copy, exhibited here, is bound in sheepskin and initialed by him at signatures I and T. The signature of *Richard Harris, 1714*, is at the bottom of a preliminary page.

Jefferson was not conventionally pious, although his father had seen to it that he received the usual instruction in the faith of his ancestors, and it was Jefferson's habit to rely for wisdom more on the classical writers than on Biblical sources. Toward the end of his life, however, he wrote to Samuel Kercheval that the teachings of Jesus were "the purest system of morals ever before preached to man." Though he contributed funds to local churches throughout his life and designed the now destroyed Christ Church in Charlottesville (see no. 452) he believed that "the interests of society require the observation of those moral precepts only in which all religions agree . . . and that we should not intermeddle with the particular dogmas in which all religions differ. . . ." His establishment of religious toleration in Virginia was one of the accomplishments of which he was the most proud. J.M.E.

57 Notes on the state of Virginia; written in the year 1781, somewhat corrected and enlarged in the winter of 1782, for the use of a Foreigner of distinction, in answer to certain queries proposed by him . . . First English edition (London: John Stockdale, 1787)

THOMAS JEFFERSON 1743–1826
From the Collection of Mr. and Mrs. Paul Mellon

Thomas Jefferson's *Notes on the State of Virginia*, the only full-length book he wrote which was published during his lifetime, has been called "one of America's first permanent literary and intellectual landmarks." The *Notes on the State of Virginia* is a book extremely difficult to characterize because of the variety of its subject matter and its origins as an unpublished work mainly for the edification of Jefferson's friends. In Millicent Sowerby's *Catalogue of the Library of Thomas Jefferson*, the description of the book's origins, publishing history and comments about it by Jefferson and by his contemporaries take up thirty double-columned pages.

In his preface to the *Notes*, Jefferson wrote that the book was "written in the year 1781, and somewhat corrected and enlarged in the winter of 1782, in answer to Queries proposed to the Author, by a Foreigner of Distinction, then residing among us." Sometime late in 1780 the secretary of the French legation in America, François, marquis de Barbé-Marbois, prepared a long series of questions at the request of his government and sent them to those men in the several states most likely to know the answers. The set on Virginia was sent to Jefferson for whom it was a perfect assignment and who worked on it with tremendous enthusiasm.

The *Notes* begins with a description of the geography of Virginia—its boundaries, rivers, mountains, waterfalls and caverns—and develops into an abundance of supporting material and curious information. Jefferson wrote of things which interested him deeply and about which he knew a great deal; the *Notes*, therefore, throws a fascinating light on his tastes, curiosities, and political and social opinions.

Phillipe Denis Pierres finished printing the *Notes* in an edition of two hundred copies in Paris on May 10, 1785, and Jefferson immediately began distributing them to friends in the United States and Europe. In most of the copies which he presented, he wrote to the recipients that he was unwilling to expose the book to the public eye and requested the recipient therefore "to put them into the hands of no person on whose care and fidelity he cannot rely to guard them against publication."

In 1786, the Abbé Morellet's French translation of the *Notes* was published in Paris by Barrois; it contained a map of the mid-Atlantic states, with the text in English, on which Jefferson himself had worked. In the next year an English edition with the same map was published in London; and in 1788 a pirated edition, also with the map, appeared in Philadelphia. With additional material in an appendix, a new edition, approved by Jefferson, was published in New York by M. L. & W. A. Davis in 1801. J.M.E.

THE BRITISH CONNECTION: A SUMMARY VIEW

Great Britain was their country as much as America. Many of them had been born there; multitudes of them had been educated there . . . . They were the countrymen . . . of Bacon, Locke, and Newton —of Shakespeare and Milton. . . . The noble benefactions and accumulations of ages in philanthropy and in art, in many a priceless collection, were theirs. The ancient public and private customs— the traditions and prejudices—the social maxims—the bravery and loyalty in man—the stainless faith in woman—the happy and inviolable homes—which were the birthrights of Englishmen, were theirs.

HENRY RANDALL, *Life of Thomas Jefferson*

In his *Essay on the Revolution a History of Virginia*, Edmund Randolph, a member of the Virginia Convention of 1776, identified the historic origins of Virginia's famous pride. "Being the earliest among the British settlements in North America" and "soon withdrawn from the humility of proprietary dependence to the dignity of a government immediately under the crown," the colony's growing wealth had allowed "the sons of the most opulent families" to be sent abroad and "trained by education and habits acquired in England, and hence perhaps arrogating some superiority over the provinces, not so distinguished."

Although Jefferson seems to have been content with his more provincial studies and did not suffer this education in arrogance as did many of his friends and relations, the source of his earliest studies and learning, his introduction to architecture, music and manners as well as philosophy and law derived from the "home" country through books, teachers and close acquaintants coming to the colony from Great Britain.

Jefferson was seventeen when George III came to the throne in 1760. The thirty years between the Peace of Paris in 1763 and the beginning of the French War have been called the Golden Age of Georgian culture, and the fringes of the British Empire along the rivers and bays of the Virginia coast reflected at a distance something of the achievements of the British models of learning and the arts.

Our often narrow focus on the colonial world of Boston, Williamsburg and Philadelphia distorts our perspective of the larger canvas of the British Empire in the eighteenth century. We need to be reminded that Jefferson, Adams, Franklin, Madison and Washington were subjects of the same Georgian society that produced a Johnson, a Reynolds, a Chambers, an Adam, a Gainsborough, a Sterne and a Garrick. This section, then, continues the exploration of the visual and intellectual world in which Jefferson grew up, but the viewer now moves three thousand miles to its political and cultural center in London, the remote source of much that was to inform Jefferson's eye and imagination at an early age on the empire's periphery.

In the early part of the eighteenth century, a revolution in English taste, primarily in architecture but reflected in the other arts as well, was carried out by Lord Burlington and his followers, establishing the earlier work of Andrea Palladio and Inigo Jones as the foundation for reform. The victory of English Palladianism was overwhelming, and by the middle of the century it had, through books, prints and polemics, conquered virtually every aspect of architectural design. Before the "glorious close" of the reign of George II, architecture had been recalled to her "true principles and correct taste," in the words of Horace Walpole. "She found men of genius to execute her rule, and patrons to countenance their labours."

During the decade in which George III succeeded his grandfather, the new wealth introduced by the success of war was brilliantly evident in the imperial magnificence of London drawing rooms and, above all, in country establishments. Works of art collected by Englishmen on the Grand Tour lined halls and stairs of the great Whig piles.

Zoffany, Reynolds and Gainsborough celebrated the new generation in haughty, elegant portraits, and Canaletto followed his English patrons home from their Italian travels to paint Venetian views along the Thames. If he had not seen a Hogarth painting, Jefferson was at least familiar with that artist's popular engravings collected in Williamsburg and with his *Analysis of Beauty* published in London in 1753. If the elegant furnishings of Thomas Chippendale that were beginning to fill the townhouses of Grosvenor Square and the country houses throughout England did not reach Rosewell or Tuckahoe, his followers' productions did, flowing in on tobacco credit. Chippendale's influential guide, *The Gentleman and Cabinet-Maker's Director*, was acquired by Jefferson as part of his fine arts library.

By 1760, London had a population of nearly three-quarters of a million. With its dramatic growth in the decade following the Peace of Paris, a new vitality, confidence and intellectual direction informed cultural and artistic leaders. William Chambers, who had written the classic treatise on architecture of the period, and Robert Adam, who had explored the ruins of antiquity with Piranesi and Clérisseau, were the preeminent architectural lights of the age. Their plans and publications quickly found their way to the growing library of the young farmer and lawyer in Virginia, where they joined the earlier works of Palladio, Kent, Gibbs and Morris.

Indeed, it was almost exclusively through British publications that Jefferson first shared the new ideas of aesthetic and romantic literature that were to transform the arts in the last quarter of the eighteenth century. His enthusiasm in the theory and practice of architecture was very much in the English tradition of the gentleman amateur, a tradition which he shared not only with Lord Burlington's generation but with the new king, as well, who had studied briefly with Chambers. The other profoundly English preoccupation in the arts was the reorganization of the landscape to reflect the elements of design of seventeenth-century painters such as Salvator Rosa and Claude Lorrain. This reorganization was grounded in a complex theory evolved by philosophers and poets who celebrated nature in its wild and natural state. The romantic garden of the eighteenth century is, in many ways, England's most significant contribution to the arts, and Jefferson's own taste was early influenced by the arguments of its chief proponents who sought to overcome the geometric, formal "authoritarian" garden designs laid down by Le Nôtre and his French followers.

Jefferson visited England only once, in 1786, spending six weeks in London and also a week touring the famous English gardens and country seats with John Adams. In order to keep this section in appropriate order, Jefferson's garden tour and the English background of his ideas on landscape design will be included in later sections. Some of the topographical views of London will, however, allude to scenes Jefferson undoubtedly saw or actually commented upon during his brief stay.

High style furniture of the period reflecting Chippendale and Adam inspiration, along with a few exemplary pieces of silver, have been selected to suggest something of the achievements in the decorative arts in England in those creative decades prior to the American Revolution. W.H.A.

58 George III

Studio of ALLAN RAMSAY 1713–1784
Oil on canvas c. 1765
252 x 167.6 (99 x 66)

*Lent by the British Embassy,
Washington*

Very few of George III's subjects in America would ever have seen him, so the painted portrait was the nearest they could come to the reality. Portraits of English monarchs were sent to the capitals of the American colonies as symbols of royal authority and cynosures of loyalty. For this reason the king is here shown as an image of the sovereign, wearing his coronation robes and the Order of the Garter, with the crown as a symbol of his regal position. Portraits of George III and Queen Charlotte by

Ramsay are recorded in the governor's palace at Williamsburg; they must have been the most sophisticated example of painting in the grand manner to be seen in colonial Virginia. Lord Botetourt had the portraits sent from England soon after he arrived in 1768, and they were hung in the ballroom. After his death they are recorded there in an inventory. The Duke of Beaufort, Botetourt's nephew, in accordance with the late governor's intentions, presented the portraits to Virginia. They no longer survive and were perhaps destroyed during the Revolution or when the governor's palace was burnt. After 1775 they would no longer have been welcome objects in the palace.

Jefferson must have been familiar with the pair of paintings as a visitor

to the palace and thus would have had some previous knowledge of the two monarchs' appearance before he was presented to the king and queen in 1786, when he visited London. His reception was ungracious, as George III turned his back on Jefferson to show his displeasure. In spite of their political separation the two men had many interests in common: music, science and the arts, a devotion to their family and a preference for the simple life of a country gentleman.

The original of the present portrait is almost certainly the one in Buckingham Palace dating from 1761–1762. Many versions were painted in Ramsay's studio for official presentation. R.W.

59 Queen Charlotte

Studio of ALLAN RAMSAY 1713–1784
Oil on canvas c. 1765
251.5 x 167.7 (99 x 66)

*Lent by the British Embassy,
Washington*

Charlottesville, Virginia, became the seat of government for Albemarle County in 1761 and was named in honor of Queen Charlotte, who had recently become the wife of George III. It had been a long-established custom, dating back to the beginning of the colonies, to name provinces, counties and towns after English sovereigns and members of their families. Virginia itself was named after the virgin queen, Elizabeth I, and Jamestown after the then reigning monarch James I; and when the

60 Temple Bar from the West

colonial capital moved, it took the name of the king, William III.

Charlotte Sophia of Mecklenburg-Stelitz (1744–1818) was brought up in a small German court. Although the marriage was entirely political, it proved a success, and strong principles and a rigid mind made Queen Charlotte well suited to her husband. The queen played no part in government, confining herself to the care of her fifteen children with whom, as a dutiful husband, George III provided her. She shared the king's taste in music and the arts and patronized Gainsborough (acquiring a collection of his drawings), Beechey and Zoffany. The queen paid for Zoffany's visit to Florence to paint a view of the Tribuna of the Uffizi. Following her husband's example, Queen

Charlotte gave an ungracious reception to Jefferson, when he appeared at court.

Ramsay painted the original portrait of the queen (of which this painting is a copy), who is shown in coronation robes, shortly after her marriage in 1761. Horace Walpole remarked that "it is much flattered, and the hair vastly too light." Like the companion portrait of George III, there are many studio copies of Queen Charlotte's portrait, and one once hung in the governor's palace at Williamsburg. R.W.

JOHN COLLET 1725–1780
Oil on canvas c. 1775
98.4 x 125.7 (38¾ x 49½)

From the Collection of the Earl of Jersey, Island of Jersey, Channel Islands

Temple Bar was built by Wren in 1672 on the site of an earlier gateway that marked the boundary between Westminster and the city of London. This division, which is still commemorated every time a British sovereign enters the city, dates back to the time when London was contained within what has become the financial or commercial center of the City as it is now called, whereas Westminster was a separate district growing up around the king's court.

Over the centuries the people of London had established the right to be self-governing, and were largely independent of royal control. By the eighteenth century, London had spread far outside the old City and included areas that had originally been separate villages.

In the foreground is the Strand, an important street for shops, and through the archway, Fleet Street can be seen, where the scientifically oriented Royal Society had its headquarters, numbering Wren, Newton, Pepys and Boyle among its former members. The iron spikes above the pediment were used to display the heads of executed criminals or traitors, such as those who took part in the Jacobite rebellion of 1745. In the niches are statues of Charles I and

Charles II.

Off the picture plane to the left is Somerset House, designed by Chambers, and to the right the Inns of Court where lawyers were trained for the English bar. Occasionally, Virginians such as Sir John Randolph, a kinsman of Jefferson's, and William Byrd II of Westover, a good friend of Jefferson's grandfather Isham Randolph, went to the Inns of Court to improve their legal knowledge. In this way, as with other forms of education, contact with the mother country was maintained after the first or second generation of settlers. R.W.

61 View of Whitehall Looking North-East

WILLIAM MARLOW 1740–1813
Oil on canvas c. 1765
69.8 x 90.2 (27½ x 35½)
Signed at bottom right: *W Marlow*
From the Collection of Mr. and Mrs. Paul Mellon

Whitehall, leading from Westminster to Charing Cross, was one of the main thoroughfares of London and became the administrative center of Great Britain and her empire. Just as they are today, government offices were housed on the street, and the official residence of the prime minister was on Downing Street to the left just off the picture plane. Also on the left side are the sentry boxes outside the Horse Guards. The building on the right with columns is the Banqueting House by Inigo Jones, built between 1619 and 1622, the only survivor of the old palace of Whitehall, which had been destroyed by fire in 1698, and the first major Palladian building in England. It was the same tradition of Palladianism that was taken up by Lord Burlington and his protégé William Kent, who designed the Horse Guards, in the first half of the eighteenth century and which was to have such an influence on English country houses and eventually colonial Virginia. R.W.

32 St. Paul's from Ludgate Hill

WILLIAM MARLOW 1740–1813
Oil on canvas c. 1775
99 x 78.8 (39 x 31)
Lent by the Governor & Company
of the Bank of England

This view shows the old part of London in the very heart of the city with St. Paul's and shops and offices all round. Visitors to London remarked on the bustle of the streets, and many commercial and trading activities, which would now be only seen indoors, were carried on in the open air. As Samuel Johnson said: "Walking in the streets of London, which is really to me high entertainment of itself, see a vast museum of all objects and think with a kind of wonder that see it for nothing." And again: "No, Sir, when a man is tired of London, he is tired of life; for there is in London all that life can afford."

Wren's masterpiece of St. Paul's Cathedral was built between 1675 and 1709, and the vast scale with dome and towers dominated the London skyline. No such ambitious undertaking had been attempted in England since the building of the medieval cathedrals. With its borrowings from the Italian and French baroque tradition, St. Paul's helped to bring English architecture closer to the European mainstream.

The church with the prominent spire in front of the cathedral dome is St. Martin Ludgate, one of the many churches Wren designed after the Great Fire. His general solution to the problem of church design, a rectangular body with a tower or steeple over the entrance, was to be endlessly repeated in England and the American colonies. Bruton Parish Church in Williamsburg is an example of this export. The so-called Wren Building at the College of William and Mary, while it has nothing to do directly with the English architect, reflects the secular style of the age of Wren. R.W.

63 View through an Arch of Westminster Bridge

GIOVANNI ANTONIO CANAL,
CALLED CANALETTO 1697–1768
Oil on canvas 1747
57.8 x 95.2 (22¾ x 37½)

*Lent by His Grace The Duke of
Northumberland K.G.*

The dating of this view of Westminster Bridge can be narrowed to
between 1746, when Canaletto arrived
in London from Venice, and 1747,
when the supports of the central
arch, shown here still in place, were
removed. A second bridge across the
Thames, the first in many centuries,
was indicative of the increased traffic
in London and the expansion of
the city. The bridge served not only
a growing population but, more
importantly, the richer classes, who
were moving from the old center of
the city to the suburbs, which were

laid out in streets and squares of
dignified houses. The dramatically
framed view of the river looking downstream shows St. Paul's Cathedral
and several spires of churches also
built by Wren. On the left is the
water tower, York Gate and Old
Somerset House. After the Great Fire
of London in 1666, there had inevitably been an extensive rebuilding
program, of which Wren's cathedral
and churches are the most permanent
record. His plan for a redesigned
city, which would have included
advanced Renaissance ideas of urban
development and imposed some order
on the haphazard street patterns,
could not be adopted for economic and
practical reasons, and the lines of
the basically medieval center were
followed when it came to be
rebuilt. R.W.

64 The Lord Mayor's Procession, The Thames at Westminster Bridge

GIOVANNI ANTONIO CANAL,
CALLED CANALETTO 1697–1768
Oil on canvas 1746
96.5 x 127 (38 x 50)

*From the Collection of Mr. and
Mrs. Paul Mellon*

The Thames was still a main artery of
transport in eighteenth-century
London because of the difficulty in
threading the maze of narrow streets,
and the medieval London Bridge
was the only way for road traffic to
cross the river. Westminster Bridge,
begun in 1739 and built by the Swiss
engineer Labelye under the patronage
of the amateur Palladian architect
Lord Pembroke, was thus of great
benefit to the life of London. It combined the skillful engineering necessary
to span twelve hundred feet with a
simple elegance typical of English

Georgian architecture.

This scene shows the magnificent
barges of the Lord Mayor of London
and the major livery companies, whose
ranks supplied the city's government
on the day of the annual swearing
in of the Lord Mayor on October 29.
Canaletto, who had arrived from
Venice in search of commissions, has
taken no account of the season and
has made it summertime, and the
Thames, with all its boats and barges,
is treated like a wider Grand Canal.
Beneath the ceremony lay an important political reality. The rights
and privileges of London were jeal-
ously maintained against all encroach-
ments from the king or Parliament,
and its citizens expressed public
opinion more freely there than anywhere else in England. In the jealous
preservation of their privileges, how-

ever, the authorities of the city of
London could be obstructive to
progress, and their opposition to the
building of the new bridge led to its
construction at Westminster outside
the city limits.

The wide angle of the view gives
a panorama of London with Westminster on the right. The picturesque
medley of roofs and towers includes
the abbey, Westminster Hall, and the
Houses of Parliament with the four
towers of St. John's at Smith Square
in the middle distance. On the left
skyline is Lambeth Palace, the official
residence of the Archbishop of Canter-
bury. Thus we are far removed from
the commercial activity of the old
part of the city, for Westminster was
an area of fine houses and spacious
gardens where many of the members
of Parliament and other important

people connected with church and
state lived. Originally a settlement
around the old royal palace, the district
had grown as the process of government became more elaborate, and
by Canaletto's time there was continuous development between Westminster and the heart of the city. R.W.

65 Death of Wolfe

BENJAMIN WEST 1738–1820
Oil on canvas 1770
165.4 x 245.1 (65⅛ x 96¼)

Lent by the Royal Ontario Museum, Toronto

Born in Swarthmore, Pennsylvania, Benjamin West became president of the Royal Academy, historical painter to His Majesty King George III, and mentor, host and friend to almost all the American artists who traveled in Europe during his lifetime. West started his career as a portrait painter in Philadelphia in 1756. Aided by generous Philadelphians, who believed in his talents, he sought further training in Italy in 1759. Journeying to London for a brief visit in 1763, West spent the remaining sixty years of his life in England. His introduction to George III in 1767 began an association of mutual respect and friendship that lasted almost half a century.

History painting took a new turn with West's *Death of Wolfe*, painted in 1770. He chose the death of General Wolfe, who, in his victory over General Montcalm at Quebec in 1759, secured Canada for Great Britain. By painting General Wolfe and his soldiers in modern dress, West challenged the prominence of Reynolds' grand style, which had previously been used to glorify only the medieval or classical past. West, however, created an imaginary scene utilizing traditional baroque format and poses. The painting revolves around the crumpled figure of Wolfe in the pose of a baroque Pietà, and Wolfe's pale, luminous face is high-lighted. Wolfe's centrality to the composition is emphasized both formally and symbolically by a furled flag and a sky that is divided partially into the light of victory and partially into the darkness of death and defeat. West supplemented the strong three-part structural design created by the figure groupings with a variety of emotions; each face reveals a powerful human response, ranging from the concern of the doctor and the grief of fellow officers to the impassive stare of the "noble savage" and the exuberance of the soldier aware of the victory but unaware of Wolfe's fate.

The exhibition of the painting at the Royal Academy in 1771 coincided with a rising historical consciousness and interest, not only among the English but on the American continent as well. The reception of the painting was overwhelming. An engraving by William Woollett, published by Boydell, added greatly to its celebrated popularity, and at least four copies were commissioned. Most important, George III made West the royal historical painter, an appointment which was decisive in West's career. It promised a sinecure which allowed him to abandon portraiture and pursue history painting, a genre as financially unrewarding in England as in the colonies, though it was a genre granted the highest rank in European art theory.

The great popularity of the *Death of Wolfe* caused George Washington to ponder if his statue by Houdon might be more acceptable in modern dress. Seeking advice, Washington wrote to Jefferson, who responded that not only West, but Copley, Trumbull and Brown all concurred on the choice of modern dress for the statue.

West used a large part of his new financial independence to help American art. There were no art schools in the United States to supply even the basic rudiments of artistic training, and patronage was largely limited to portraiture. West filled this lack by opening his house and studio to any American artist who traveled to London. His protégés included Charles Willson Peale, John Trumbull, Gilbert Stuart, Mather Brown, Matthew Pratt and Henry Benbridge. G.V.

66 The Death of the Earl of Chatham

JOHN SINGLETON COPLEY
1738–1815
Oil on canvas 1779
52.7 x 64.5 (20¾ x 25⅜)
Signed lower right: *J S Copley*/1779
*National Gallery of Art. Gift of
Mrs. Gordon Dexter 1947*

William Pitt the Elder, the "Great Commoner" (1708–1778), was perhaps the greatest statesman in eighteenth-century England. After a disastrous beginning, the eventual triumphs of the Seven Years' War, in Canada, India and on the seas, were largely the result of his inspired leadership. George III and his favorite, Lord Bute, forced Pitt out of office in 1761, because he opposed their desire to make peace with the French. Pitt became prime minister in 1766, but as a result of physical and mental illness his powers were considerably impaired. He also had lost some of his popularity by becoming Earl of Chatham. It was unfortunate that for much of his ministry, which lasted until 1768, Chatham was incapacitated and the government drifted, without

firm control. Although he sympathized with the American colonists and had opposed the Stamp Act (for which statues were put up to him in New York and Charleston), his subordinates were able to impose the Townshend, Declaratory and Mutiny Acts, which further aroused passions in America. When war seemed imminent, Chatham made several attempts to persuade the government to make concessions. Jefferson acknowledged in 1775 that through ". . . Lord Chatham's bill, I entertained high hope that a reconciliation could have been brought about. The difference between his terms and those offered by our Congress might have been accomodated, if entered on by both parties with a disposition to accomodate." Even when the war had started in America, Jefferson recorded the sentiment of the colonies for Chatham in a touching way: "I hope Lord Chatham may live till the fortune of war puts his son into our hands, and enables us by returning him safe to his father, to pay a debt of gratitude." Chatham's last appearance in the House of Lords on April 7,

1778, which this sketch represents, was to oppose complete independence for the colonies as a disaster for England, which could only benefit France. During the debate Chatham collapsed and had to be carried out. He died on May 11 of the same year.

Copley worked on *The Death of the Earl of Chatham* between 1779 and 1781. The finished painting, for which this is a sketch, is in the Tate Gallery, London, and two earlier oil sketches are also in the Tate Gallery. Drawings of the composition and of individual portraits have also survived. The peers are dressed in their parliamentary robes, with the bishops on the left and the Lord Chancellor wearing his hat as the Speaker of the House of Lords. Supporting Chatham on his left is the Duke of Cumberland, brother of George III. Lord Temple, Chatham's brother-in-law, is in the group behind the fainting man's head, and three of the earl's sons, including William Pitt the Younger, are on their father's right.

Copley had moved to London in 1774, following his early success as a portrait painter in his native Boston. In

answer to the comte de Buffon's charge that America had produced no men of genius, Jefferson replied, in his *Notes on the State of Virginia*, with the names of Washington, Franklin and Rittenhouse. Abigail Adams sent word by her husband that she was sorry he had not included Copley and West as well. R.W.

67 The "Out of Town" Party

SIR JOSHUA REYNOLDS 1723–1792
Oil on canvas 1761
53.3 x 82.5 (21 x 32½)

Lent by the City Art Gallery, Bristol

The three men are, from left to right, George Selwyn, George Williams known as "Gilly," and the Honorable Richard Edgcumbe. All three were close friends of Horace Walpole, the youngest son of the prime minister, Sir Robert Walpole, and they met regularly for Christmas and Easter at Strawberry Hill to form the "out of town" party. Strawberry Hill was altered by Horace Walpole beginning in 1748 under the inspiration of medieval art and became one of the best-known examples of "Gothick" architecture. It was a mixture of genuine antiquarianism, for Walpole had an extensive knowledge of English art, especially painting, and a more frivolous delight in novel styles. The result is very different from the serious Gothic revival of the nineteenth century. Nevertheless, the house and its collections became a showpiece, and Walpole was forced to limit the number of visitors who wanted to see it. Gothic architecture, like the fashion for Chinese, or at the end of the century, Egyptian, must have been appealing in its complete break with all the rules of classical architecture accepted since the Renaissance. The conscious and picturesque asymmetry found a parallel in the informal garden, on which Walpole was also an authority. Both George

Selwyn and Gilly Williams were famous wits of the day, and Selwyn had the peculiar reputation of being a regular attender at public executions. Edgcumbe succeeded his father as Lord Edgcumbe and held minor posts in the government. He was a close friend of Sir Joshua Reynolds.

In the painting, the group is sitting in the library at Strawberry Hill. The portrait, which was commissioned by Horace Walpole, used to hang over the chimney piece in the refectory or great parlor. A drawing by John Carter showing it *in situ* is in the W. S. Lewis Collection, Farmington, Connecticut.

Reynolds' sitter book records appointments for the portraits between May 1759 and May 1761. Walpole was pleased with the result, for he wrote in 1761 ". . . it was melancholy the missing poor Edgcumbe [who had died earlier that year], who was constantly of the Christmas and Easter parties. Did you see the charming picture Reynolds painted for me of him, Selwyn and Gilly Williams? It is by far one of the best things he has executed."

Jefferson was in Twickenham on April 2, 1786, and visited Pope's villa and Marble Hill, but although Strawberry Hill was nearby, he did not stop there. He would no doubt have been welcome, for Horace Walpole was pro-American during the Revolutionary War and in a letter of 1774 predicted that "the next Augustan age will dawn on the other

side of the Atlantic. There will, perhaps, be a Thucydides at Boston, a Xenophon at New York . . . and . . . a Newton at Peru." R.W.

68 Sir William Chambers

SIR JOSHUA REYNOLDS 1723–1792
Oil on panel 1780
119.5 x 101.6 (50 x 40)

Lent by the Royal Academy of Arts, London

From the middle of the eighteenth century, English architecture provided some of the most important examples of neoclassicism, and as a school its importance extended far outside its national boundaries. Chambers and Robert Adam were the leading architects of the older generation; George Dance the Younger, Henry Holland, and James Wyatt were their most distinguished successors. There was extensive construction of individual townhouses in London as well as schemes on a larger scale, such as the Adam Brothers' Adelphi and the rebuilding of city halls, prisons, hospitals, schools and other public architecture in towns throughout the country—all of which reflected an increased civic pride, social consciousness and material prosperity. The aristocracy, who benefited through increased incomes from improved agriculture and the beginnings of the Industrial Revolution, built themselves grander country houses, while the newly rich middle classes, ever anxious to establish themselves as landed gentry, also helped to keep architecture flourishing.

His position as architectural tutor to the Prince of Wales, later George III, gave Chambers (1726–1796) an introduction to court and government circles which proved of great advantage to his career, and his influence with the king was crucial to the establishment of the Royal Academy in 1768.

Somerset House is the most important of Chambers' works, and its imposing size and commanding position on the Thames made it one of the most striking buildings in London. The Strand façade of Somerset House appears in the background of the portrait. Having studied under Jefferson's friend Clérisseau in Rome and having spent some time in Paris, Chambers was well aware of the latest developments in architecture, but he also had the unique distinction, for a British architect, of a firsthand knowledge of China. His *Designs for Chinese Buildings*, 1757, a book which Jefferson owned by 1771 when he used it as a source for proposed pavilions at Monticello, appeared at a time when chinoiserie was in favor and drew public attention to Chambers. The Pagoda and other buildings at Kew were built in this style (see no. 357). Thereafter, Chambers confined himself to a combination of the restrained neoclassicism he saw in

France and the English Palladian tradition. His great rival was Robert Adam, who had also worked with Clérisseau, but Chambers was secure in government favor and was the leading establishment architect of his generation, becoming surveyor-general of works. His positions of eminence, his friendship with George III and his knighthood all enhanced the general status of the professional architect, and more and more the amateur country gentleman, rather than relying on treatises and manuals to build his house, turned to those who were professionally qualified. In Virginia, up to the time of the Revolution and for a long time afterward, plantation owners had to follow books on architecture, just as Jefferson, who later did so much to promote professional architecture in the United States, was obliged to do in his early plans for Monticello.

The portrait of Chambers is very much an official one—it shows the president of the Royal Academy painting the treasurer—and fittingly, it was Reynolds' diploma piece. R.W.

69 James Macpherson

SIR JOSHUA REYNOLDS 1723–1792
Oil on canvas 1772
76.2 x 61 (30 x 24)

Lent by the Petworth Collection, England

By the middle of the eighteenth century, there were evident signs that poets were no longer confining themselves to classical themes written in a cool and measured style but were discovering the virtues of the heart and beginning to appreciate the beauties of nature. Antiquarian interest in the distant past also affected writers, and often the public was willing to accept as genuine works that were later exposed as forgeries, such as Macpherson's *Ossian* and Chatterton's Rowley poems.

Encouraged by the publication in translation of genuine Gaelic manuscripts which he had collected, Macpherson (1736–1796) claimed to have found epic poems by Ossian, which he published from 1761 to 1765. In spite of Dr. Johnson's skepticism in the memorable "I hope I shall never be deterred from detecting what I think a cheat by the menaces of a ruffian," it was widely believed to be the product of a Gaelic culture comparable to the world of Homer. In fact Macpherson had composed the poem himself, using some genuine fragments. Nevertheless, the influence of *Ossian* was immense, especially in France and Germany. Goethe and Herder translated his poems, and Napoleon was a great admirer.

The widespread appreciation of *Ossian* can be explained as part of the general phenomenon of early romanticism. It is interesting to note that the poems of Gray, Young and Shenstone, whose famous garden Jefferson was later to visit, were included on the 1771 book list he made for Robert Skipwith, as were Goldsmith's *Vicar of Wakefield* and a translation of Rousseau's *La Nouvelle Héloise.* They show how remarkably advanced was this young Virginian, on the periphery of European culture, and how deep was his early appreciation of the poets of nature and sentiment. The same sensibility later led him to respond enthusiastically to that other manifestation of English romanticism, landscape gardening.

Jefferson became fascinated with the writings of *Ossian*, in which he implicitly believed, and in 1773 corresponded with Charles McPherson of Edinburgh, whom he had met in Virginia and who was a kinsman of the "translator," in an attempt to secure a manuscript copy of the poems in their original tongue regardless of expense. In his letter he said: "These peices [sic] have been, and will I think during my life continue to be to me, the source of daily and exalted pleasure. . . . The tender, and the sublime emotions of the mind were never before so finely wrought up by human hand. I am not ashamed to own that I think this rude bard of the North the greatest Poet that has ever existed." So enthusiastic was he that he wanted to learn the language and asked McPherson to send a dictionary, a grammar and other printed books in Gaelic. The embarrassment to James Macpherson when this request was passed on can be imagined, and he was obliged to make the excuse that even if someone could be found to copy it, he would not permit the unique manuscript to leave his hands. Jefferson had to be content with a New Testament in Gaelic. When the marquis de Chastellux visited Monticello in 1782, he and Jefferson shared their enthusiasm by indulging in an Ossianic evening. And at the end of his life, when the fraud had long been exposed, Jefferson still maintained that *Ossian*, "if not ancient, it is at least equal to the best morsels of antiquity." R.W.

70 Dr. Charles Burney

SIR JOSHUA REYNOLDS 1723–1792
Oil on canvas 1781
75 x 61 (29½ x 24)

*Lent by the Trustees of the
National Portrait Gallery, London*

Charles Burney (1726–1814) was a member of Dr. Johnson's Club, and his sympathetic and attractive nature made him a popular figure in contemporary society. He was more a writer and a critic than a practicing musician, although he had been a pupil of Thomas Arne, and began his career as a most successful teacher of music. The *History of Music* established his reputation as a leading musicologist and, like the accounts of his tours in Europe, which Jefferson owned at least by 1782, is still read today. Jefferson read Burney's musical tours and mentioned in a letter to Burney that they "had prepared me to expect a great deal of pleasure from your acquaintance." Burney's daughter Fanny was the celebrated novelist and diarist.

The portrait was commissioned by Henry Thrale the brewer as part of a series of portraits for the library of his house at Streatham. Mrs. Thrale, like Burney, was a close friend of Samuel Johnson, the writer and lexicographer who, in his famous Club, attracted many of the most celebrated men of the day: Reynolds, Goldsmith, Garrick, Burke, Gibbon and Boswell. Drinking and dining clubs of friends, often meeting at regular intervals in taverns and professional associations, were common in London at that time. Burney is wearing his robes as Doctor of Music, which he received from Oxford in 1769. It is significant that Burney is portrayed as the learned writer on music rather than as a musician. Perhaps this was to establish Burney's enhanced social position, in the same way that the self-portrait by Reynolds, which he gave to the Royal Academy, shows the artist in the robes of Doctor of Civil Law, which Oxford had conferred on him; only the bust of Michelangelo refers to Reynolds' profession as a painter. Copies of this painting made by Burney's relative, Edward Burney, are in the School of Music, Oxford, and the Liceo Musicale, Bologna.

Jefferson had met Dr. Burney briefly when he was in London, and they afterwards corresponded about a Kirckman harpsichord for Martha Jefferson. R.W.

71 David Garrick as "Lord Chalkstone," Ellis Ackman as "Bowman" and Astley Bransby as "Aesop" in "Lethe"

JOHANN ZOFFANY 1734/35–1810
Oil on canvas c. 1766
100.4 x 124.5 (39½ x 49)

Collection of the City Museums and Art Gallery, Birmingham, England

NOT IN EXHIBITION

David Garrick (1717–1779) was the most famous actor of eighteenth-century England. His place in contemporary society did not rest solely on his great acting talent, however, for actors were not then highly regarded socially. Rather, through his charm and ability, Garrick was received in the best company and was much fêted when he visited France. He played in Shakespeare, did much to restore the production of the plays and was the leading figure behind the Jubilee celebrations in Stratford in 1769. Comic parts, however, were more congenial to Garrick. As a close friend of Samuel Johnson, who had taught him at school, he was a prominent member of the Club which was formed around the great writer and conversationalist and counted most of the literary and intellectual men of the day as his friends.

Lethe was one of many plays written

by Garrick. The painting represents those actors who took part in the production at Drury Lane in 1766 by command of George III and Queen Charlotte. From about that time, Garrick gave up acting and concentrated on managing Drury Lane theater, rebuilt by Robert Adam. Another version of this painting is in the Somerset Maugham Theatre Collection. Zoffany painted the actor in character roles several times, including another scene from *Lethe* also at Birmingham. The artist was keenly interested in the theater and was a friend of Garrick's who had helped Zoffany in his earlier career.

Although there was still licensing of plays in London at this time, censorship did not prevent considerable theatrical activity with a varied program, from oratorio and Italian operas to farce. The audience often took an unintended part in the drama by forcefully showing their appreciation or displeasure with the performance, and celebrated actors and actresses had their noisy claques. Sometimes the plays had political overtones, as in Gay's *Beggar's Opera* with its unflattering references to Sir Robert Walpole

the prime minister, or theaters would become caught up in opposition to the government, as when Frederick, Prince of Wales, who had quarreled with his father, patronized "The Opera of the Nobility" in rivalry to Handel, who was supported by George II.

Theater in the American colonies derived most, if not all, of its inspiration from British models, and Jefferson as a young lawyer in Williamsburg saw in 1768 such plays as Addison's *The Drummer*, *The Merchant of Venice*, and *The Beggar's Opera*, performed by the Virginia Company of Comedians, a group which undoubtedly lacked none of the spirit, if a considerable amount of the polish, possessed by Garrick and his contemporaries. R.W.

72 The March to Finchley

WILLIAM HOGARTH 1697–1764
Oil on canvas 1746
100.2 x 133.3 (39½ x 52½)
Signed on inn sign on left: *To*
TENHAM/COURT/NURSERY/1746

*Lent by the Thomas Coram
Foundation for Children, London*

The scene represents the Guards
marching north through Finchley to
Scotland to subdue the Jacobite rebellion under Prince Charles Edward
Stuart. Although Hogarth was strongly
anti-Jacobite and therefore had every
reason to support the government,
he could not resist making fun of its
soldiers, who are portrayed in a most
unmartial condition as they unwill-
ingly abandon the ale houses and their
wives and sweethearts for an un-

certain future in Scotland. There is a
tradition that the dedication of the
engraving was originally offered to
George II, but when he saw the painting, the king was furious at this
insult to his soldiers: "I hate *bainting*
and *boetry* [sic] too! Neither the
one nor the other ever did any good!
Does the fellow mean to laugh at my
guards?" When it was explained that
Hogarth had intended the painting as
a joke, the king replied: "What, a
bainter [sic] burlesque a soldier? he
deserves to be picketed for his in-
solence! Take his trumpery out of my
sight." Comical details and satirical
allusions abound in the composition,
as in so many of Hogarth's paintings,
but even without the arcane knowledge of the specialist, *The March* can
be enjoyed for its obvious humor and

the bursting vitality which so well
mirrors mid-eighteenth-century
England. The Jacobite uprising of
1745 was the last serious internal
threat to the government until the
unrest of the French Revolution.
Many of the rebels and those supporting the Jacobites emigrated to the
colonies, and by the time of the
American Revolution the Stuarts no
longer presented any danger. A feeling
of security and self-confidence after
the defeat of the rebellion no doubt
allowed Hogarth to treat it in such a
lighthearted way, although at the
time there was widespread panic and
a real possibility the government would
be overthrown.

The date on the inn sign must refer
to the painting rather than to the
event depicted which took place in

September 1745. Hogarth in his advertisement for the engraving of 1750
advanced the date of the march to
1746, and various impressions of the
print give the two different dates.
Subscribers to the engraving were also
given the chance to win the painting
of *The March to Finchley* through
a lottery. Two thousand tickets were
issued, and those unsold were given to
the Foundling Hospital, which drew
the winning number.

Jefferson had no sympathy with the
house of Stuart. In the *Rights of
British America* he wrote: "The treasonable crimes [of the Stuarts] against
their people brought on them the
exertion of those sacred and sovereign
rights of punishment, reserved in
the hands of the people for cases of
extreme necessity, and judged by the

73 Chiswick Villa from the North-West

GEORGE LAMBERT 1710–1765
Oil on canvas 1742
88.9 x 105.4 (35 x 41½)
Signed lower right: G. Lambert 1742

*Devonshire Collection, Chatsworth.
Lent by the Trustees of the
Chatsworth Settlement*

constitution unsafe to be delegated
to any other judicature."

Maria Cosway, who played such an
important part in Jefferson's emotional life in Paris, must have seen
Prince Charles Edward, or Charles III
as he styled himself in exile, when
he spent several years in Florence beginning in 1770. Charles Hadfield,
Maria's father, kept a well-known
boarding house and the prince at one
time considered staying there. R.W.

Lord Burlington, who was the leading
supporter of the Palladian movement in eighteenth-century England,
was also a fine amateur architect, and
had studied the works of Palladio
in Italy during his travels, including
the Villa Rotonda near Vicenza.
Between 1725 and 1727, Burlington
added a villa to an earlier house at
Chiswick, outside London, to contain
his library and collections of art and
to entertain his friends. The design was
based mainly on the Villa Rotonda,
with some reference to Palladio's pupil
Scamozzi, and the interior, sumptu-
ously decorated by Kent, with the
sequence of differently shaped rooms,
owes much to the study of Roman
baths. Because of the social distinction
and political importance of Lord

Burlington, who was one of the leading
Whigs, Chiswick became something
of a showpiece for admirers of the
Palladian style in England. Pope, the
friend of Burlington, to whom Pope
wrote his *Epistle on Taste*, was full of
praise: "I assure you Chiswick has
been to me the first thing this glorious
sun has shin'd upon." Lord Hervey,
the diarist, was less complimentary:
"House! Do you call it a house? Why!
it is too little to live in, and too
large to hang on one's watch."

For about thirty-five years Palladian
became the dominant style in English
architecture, especially for country
houses. There was something in the
simple geometry and clear lines that
appealed to the ruling aristocracy,
especially those of Whig politics.
Pope's great couplets summed up Burlington's triumph, linking him
through Jones and Palladio with
Vitruvian antiquity:

> You too proceed! make falling arts
> your care,
> Erect new wonders, and the old
> repair;

Jones and Palladio to themselves
restore,
And he whate'er Vitruvius was
before:
IVth *Epistle*, ll. 191–194

While the rule of common sense in
England in the eighteenth century
must not be exaggerated, it cannot
be accidental that such a rational
style found favor. No doubt for the
same reasons Jefferson approved of
Palladianism.

By the time of Jefferson's visit in
1786 such architecture was quite out
of fashion, and while the dukes of
Devonshire, to whom it had passed by
inheritance, used Chiswick for entertaining, the great days when the
magnificent Burlington received his
guests were a forgotten memory.
Jefferson noted that "the Octagonal
dome has an ill effect, both within and
without," but otherwise was silent
on his reactions to the house, though
it must have made some impression on
his later plans for the renovation of
Monticello (see nos. 476–477).

The view is of the north front of

Chiswick with the main entrance. In the distance is a gateway designed by Inigo Jones, the seventeenth-century originator of English Palladianism. The gateway was given to Lord Burlington in 1736 by Sir Hans Sloane, founder of the British Museum. There are two other views by Lambert, also at Chatsworth, although the figures were probably painted by another artist as was often the case with his pictures. R.W.

74 A Coursing Party

IN THE STYLE OF GEORGE STUBBS
1724–1806
Oil on canvas c. 1765–1770
152.4 x 251.5 (60 x 99)

From the Collection of Mr. and Mrs. Paul Mellon

Horses were naturally of the greatest importance in an age when they were the main means of transport, but they also played a large part in the sporting life of Georgian England through racing and the hunting of foxes and hare. English gentlemen were notorious for their devotion to the chase; for many it was their sole interest. Even the higher levels of government were affected by it, for members of Parliament were usually anxious to return to the country for the hunting season, and Sir Robert Walpole, himself a sporting squire, realized he could not hope to secure a good attendance in the House of Commons after Christmas.

The Virginia gentry, who generally came from a similar social level, felt much the same way about riding and hunting. The earliest settlers noted the great abundance of game and, after satisfying their needs, hunted birds and animals as sport. After about 1730, when the flourishing tobacco trade had

brought prosperity to many landowners, the gentry's style of living became more sophisticated and luxurious, with larger houses and all the appurtenances of their English counterparts. This included foxhunting, with hounds brought over from England. John Clayton, author of *Flora Virginica*, mentions in a letter of 1739 the great variety of game: "Some hunt the fox w'th hounds as you do in England. . . ." In 1742 the Castle Hill hunt was founded by Dr. Thomas Walker, a friend and neighbor of Peter Jefferson's. In 1746 Thomas, sixth Lord Fairfax, came over to Virginia, where his family had estates, and soon he, an enthusiastic foxhunter, established his own pack. He introduced George Washington, whose brother Lawrence had married into the Fairfax family, to foxhunting, and Washington became a keen follower of the hounds as his diary amply reveals. He was occasionally joined by his wife.

Jefferson, too, hunted in his youth, from the time he attended Rev. James Maury's school and took an interest in his horses and was proud of being a good horseman. He continued to ride to the end of his life and traveled much on horseback, whether on busi-

ness or pleasure, or when supervising work on his estate. His fondness for the chase and for racing is brought out in a letter Jefferson wrote in 1808 to his grandson, Thomas Jefferson Randolph, recalling his own youth: "and many a time have I asked myself in the enthusiastic moment of the death of a fox, the victory of a favorite horse, the issue of a question eloquently argued at the bar or in the great council of the nation, well, which of these kinds of reputations should I prefer? That of a horse jockey? a fox hunter? an orator? or the honest advocate of my country's rights?" R.W.

75 The Sharp Family on a Yacht on the Thames

JOHANN ZOFFANY 1734/5–1810
Oil on canvas 1779–1781
115.6 x 125.7 (45½ x 49½)

*Collection of Charles Lloyd-Baker,
Hardwicke Court, Gloucester, England*

NOT IN EXHIBITION

Musical life in eighteenth-century London was full and varied. Groups met in taverns to sing glees and catches, and permanent clubs, such as the Noblemen and Gentlemen's

Catch Club, provided amateur singers with an opportunity to perform. Italian opera was patronized by Lord Burlington and his friends, and Handel wrote many of the operas in vogue at that time before turning to oratorio. Other foreigners, both composers and performers, settled in London, such as Geminiani and Johann Christian Bach, as well as many lesser native composers of whom Arne and Boyce were the most distinguished.

Pleasure boats on the Thames were common during the eighteenth century, and the tradition of playing music on the river had a most distinguished precedent in Handel's Water Music. Zoffany himself used to give concerts on the river, and George III and Queen Charlotte, who were very interested in music, visited the Sharps' yacht and listened to the concerts. Despite this musical activity and interest, it was an age when

music lovers, especially those outside London or the large towns, seldom had an opportunity to hear public concerts, depending instead on available local talent. An accomplished young lady was expected to perform on the harpsichord or pianoforte, and many men also learned to play instruments, so that a family or group of friends could make their own chamber music.

In the same way, Jefferson and his friends performed music at Williamsburg and Monticello. While studying law with George Wythe, he was introduced to Governor Fauquier and took part as a violinist in the chamber concerts at the palace. At Williamsburg, Jefferson also had ample opportunity to hear music publicly performed, ranging from ballad operas to subscription concerts. The performers consisted of visiting musicians, talented amateurs such as Jefferson himself, or resident professionals like Peter Pelham, organist at Bruton Parish Church. Later at Monticello there were concerts drawn from paroled British and German officers. In a letter of 1778 to Giovanni Fabroni, Jefferson expressed his deep love of music. "If there is a gratification which I envy any people in this world it is to your country [Italy] its music. This is the favorite passion of my soul, and fortune has cast my lot in a country where it is in a state of deplorable barbarism." He goes on to wonder if he could import Italian craftsmen who would also be musicians; thus "a passion for music might be reconciled with that oeconomy [sic] which we are obliged to observe." Jefferson listed the musical instruments he wanted for his wind band: "two French horns, two clarinets and hautboys and a bassoon." The mention of clarinets indicates Jefferson was well aware of the latest developments in musical instruments, for they had only recently become an accepted part of an orchestra. Jefferson was by no means alone among Virginians in his devotion to music. St. George Tucker, his family and friends were able to assemble a violin, harpsichord, welsh-harp, flute, drum and timbrels as he recorded in his poem *Musical Evening in the Family.*

This musical group represents the family of William Sharp, surgeon to George III and a friend of Zoffany's, his brothers and sisters with their children. William Sharp is standing with his hat in hand at the top of the composition (a pose Zoffany had already used in his portrait of the third Earl Cowper). The Reverend John Sharp, Archdeacon of Northumberland, is on the right, and their brother, Granville Sharp, is seated in the center behind the harpsichord. Granville Sharp devoted himself to worthy causes and was a sufficiently strong supporter of the American colonies to resign his government position, thereby depriving himself of his income. He made an important contribution to the abolition of slavery and was responsible for bringing before Lord Mansfield the famous Somerset case, which established that a slave became free when he set foot in England. Sharp's interest in America was also shown by his help in establishing the first episcopal bishoprics

in the United States—for which he received honorary degrees from Harvard and William and Mary College. The setting is by the Sharps' house at Fulham. R.W.

76 The Dutton Family

JOHANN ZOFFANY 1734/35–1810
Oil on canvas
100.3 x 124.5 (39½ x 49)

Lent by the Honorable Peter M. Samuel, Farley Hall, Reading, England

The restrained elegance and lack of ostentation in the room shown here were typical of English houses of the eighteenth century. Except in the case of the leading grandees, whose residences were on a palatial scale, the emphasis was on comfort, and as a rule the English aristocracy were not as fashion conscious in architecture or decoration as were their counterparts in France, and did not feel the need to remodel and redecorate in every passing style.

When bad weather prevented visiting, the family had to make their own amusements, the most popular of which were reading, embroidery, and card playing. Though the latter was usually some innocent game, as it is in Zoffany's painting, sometimes more serious gambling led to enormous

losses and ruin for the addict or the inexperienced player. Governor Fauquier of Virginia was a notorious gambler, and his "rage for play introduced it more generally among the People than his more useful and estimable Qualities. . . ." He must have found partners already experienced, for "he visited the most distinguished landholders in the Colonies, and the rage for playing deep, reckless of time, health, or money, spread like a contagion among a class proverbial for their hospitality, their politeness and fondness for expense," wrote a Virginia historian in the early nineteenth century.

Jefferson was aware of the moral and economic dangers of gambling, and kept clear of it. He wrote to his daughter Martha in 1787, "It is our own fault if we ever know what ennui is, or if we are ever driven to the miserable resource of gaming which corrupts our dispositions, and teaches us a habit of hostility against all mankind."

The family portrayed by Zoffany in the drawing room of Sherborne Park, Gloucestershire, are James Naper of Loughcrew, Ireland, who assumed the name Dutton as his mother was the daughter of Sir Ralph Dutton, Baron Sherborne; his second wife, Jane; their eldest son, James, later first Baron Sherborne (born in 1744); and their youngest daughter, Jane, who married Thomas Coke of Holkham, later first Earl of Leicester. While not in the front rank of aristocracy, the Duttons were clearly of considerable social position and not only married into the peerage but eventually achieved that status themselves. The possessor of a title was always treated with the greatest respect in eighteenth-century England, but there was no marked distinction between the titled peerage and the untitled gentry, as there was in the rest of Europe. R.W.

77 A Midsummer Afternoon with a Methodist Preacher

PHILIP JAMES
DE LOUTHERBOURG 1740–1812
Oil on canvas 1777
96.5 x 126.4 (38 x 49¼)
Signed lower left: *P. de Loutherbourg/*
1777

Lent by the National Gallery of
Canada, Ottawa

There is an element of satire in the treatment of both the preacher and his audience. The Methodist might be any traveling showman or salesman setting up his booth, and his listeners' reactions vary from serious meditation, to indifference, to irreverent scoffing. On the right, not mingling with the crowd, are the fashionably dressed gentry, and on the left the incumbent parson with his porcine wife present an amusing contrast. However it might appear to some, Methodism performed lasting

religious and social benefit to those dissatisfied with the Church of England and in need of a more emotional faith or to those who lived in the growing towns of the industrial areas, where the parishes could not absorb the great increase in population.

The Anglican Church was the official state-supported religion, in a privileged position, but tolerating the various dissenting Protestant sects, which were, however, excluded from some aspects of social and political life. The vigor of English religious nonconformity came as a surprise to visitors such as Voltaire, accustomed to the religious persecution by governments on the continent. Even Roman Catholics, now discredited through their support for the exiled Stuart dynasty, were left in peace. Few Englishmen did not belong to one or other of the churches, although there was a group among the intellectuals

who rejected Christianity and subscribed to deism based on reason and a rejection of the supernatural. The eighteenth century in England was not a period of great religious fervor, and "enthusiasm" or fanaticism was discouraged. Yet John Wesley, the founder of Methodism, and his followers must have supplied a great spiritual need for the immense crowds who assembled to hear them preach in the open air, because the churches were closed to them or were incapable of containing such numbers.

John Wesley had visited Georgia with his brother Charles in 1735 and had been greatly impressed with the Moravians who traveled on the same ship to escape persecution. One of his disciples, George Whitefield, visited America several times on missionary tours and was one of the preachers in the spiritual revival known as the Great Awakening from 1740–

1745 in New England. He preached in Bruton Parish Church, Williamsburg, in 1739.

The Anglicans were the established church in Virginia, although with few of the privileges of the Church of England. Other colonies had official churches also. To many colonists any form of support for a particular religion was an infringement on liberty. In Virginia, at the time *A Midsummer Afternoon* was being painted, Jefferson drafted a bill for religious freedom. When the statute was finally passed in 1785, Jefferson was justifiably proud that the Virginia Assembly had been the first in the world to declare complete freedom of religion.

R.W.

78 Warley Camp: The Mock Attack

PHILIP JAMES
DE LOUTHERBOURG 1740–1812
Oil on canvas 1779
121.9 x 184.1 (48 x 72½)
Signed: *P. J. De Loutherbourg 1779*

*Lent by Her Majesty
Queen Elizabeth II*

George III and Queen Charlotte
attended a review at the militia camp
at Warley, Essex, on October 20, 1778.
In the morning the troops marched
past the royal party, which included
Lord Amherst, former commander-in-
chief in North America. Afterwards
". . . many manoeuvres of attack
and defence were performed, with the
continued firing of musquetry and
cannon, to which the situation and
variety of the ground were very favourable and afforded much pleasure to
the numerous spectators." The king
and his suite are stationed in the center
middle distance beside an observatory.

Because of the depletion of men
caused by the fighting in America,
the military establishment in England
was dangerously reduced by 1778,
when France declared war. To meet

the threat of invasion, militia regiments were greatly expanded, their
purpose being to deal with rebellion at
home or to resist foreign attack. Unlike their American counterparts, the
English militia never actually had
to engage the enemy; and a dashing
costume, the attractions of military
life, without any of its dangers and inconveniences, and the convivial
society in camp encouraged the scions
of many leading families to join their
county regiments. Except in time of
grave national emergency, there was,
among the English population, a deep-
rooted suspicion of large professional
armies, going back to the time of the
Stuarts and Cromwell's military rule.
The number of troops in Britain was
never large until the Napoleonic
wars, and these units were used as
much to keep domestic order as to
repel invaders. The royal navy was
always considered the main line of defense. It was customary for some
European powers to use mercenaries,
and the British government relied
on soldiers hired from the smaller German states for service abroad.

The years 1778 and 1779 were a

turning point in the Revolutionary
War. The two opposing forces had
reached a stalemate, for the British had
not followed up their early successes
or made adequate use of their
superiority in matériel. Philadelphia
had been captured and then abandoned, and the grand strategy of sub-
duing the middle colonies had not
been successful. Washington, however, had managed to keep his army
together, even during the hard winter
at Valley Forge, and had shown that
Americans could defeat professional
soldiers at the battles of Trenton and
Princeton. Furthermore, the surrender of Burgoyne at Saratoga in
1777, while not an irreversible blow to
the British, meant their chances of
a quick victory were slight. This defeat
encouraged the French, already un-
officially helping the colonists, to make
a formal treaty of alliance in 1778
and later to fight on their side against
Britain.

Although the British invasion of the
south was successful in 1779 and
1780, there was not the popular support from the colonists that had been
hoped for by the British. On the

British home front, the effects of victories and defeats several thousand
miles away were muted in the time it
took news to arrive. This added to
the government's difficulties in assess-
ing the situation and making sensible
decisions. Land wars had always
seemed remote to the British, and
popular interest was far more concerned with naval battles. In Britain
there was little anti-American sentiment outside official circles, and considerable sympathy was felt among
the Whigs and all who suffered from
the dislocation of trade. To fight
against men of the same national origin
and language seemed like a civil war.
French entry into the war was a
different matter, for France was the
traditional enemy, and even the possibility of invasion aroused patriotic
feeling. R.W.

79 Kneehole writing table

English, c. 1750
Carved mahogany
82.5 (32½) high; 110.5 (43½) long

Lent by The Metropolitan Museum of Art

Rectangular top with broken front and corners, supported by eight full-length cherub terms carved with acanthus on latticework ground. The frieze fitted with three drawers. The apron edged with gadrooned moldings and fitted with one drawer on each side of the arched center. The sides each fitted with three small drawers; the recess with four drawers. On a molded plinth. E.H.

80 Side table

English, c. 1750
Deal with rosewood veneer and mahogany drawer linings; gilt brass handles and escutcheon
77.5 x 95.2 (30½ x 37½)

Lent by The Metropolitan Museum of Art, Bequest of Bernard M. Baruch, 1965

Rectangular top veneered with rosewood, the edge carved with quatrefoils in stippled reserves. The frieze fitted with single drawer, bead and reel edged and mounted with a pair of gilt brass handles and keyhole escutcheon. Projecting apron strip carved with asymmetrical shell flanked by floral sprays. Supported on hipped cabriole legs, the upper parts carved with rosettes in long cartouches surrounded by shell strips and scrolls, with folded leaves below. The brackets carved with scrolls above shell strips. Terminated by hairy claw and ball feet raised on drums carved of separate pieces of wood. One of a pair. E.H.

82 Side chair

English, c. 1750
Carved mahogany
100.6 x 67.3 x 60.7
(39⅝ x 26½ x 23⅞)

Lent by The Metropolitan Museum of Art

Rectangular back carved with flowers, oak leaves and acorns. The top rail with scrolled center and ends. The splat pierced, scrolled, and carved with pendant leaf, drapery swags, and tassels. Supported on cabriole legs with claw and ball feet; the front legs with foliate ornament on the knees. Upholstered in green silk damask. En suite with the settee shown at number 81. E.H.

81 Settee

English, c. 1750
Carved mahogany
104.8 x 208 x 75 (41¼ x 82 x 29½)

Lent by The Metropolitan Museum of Art

The back rectangular with crested corners, framed by carved and pierced scalloped molding. Supported by cabriole legs with claw and ball feet; the three front legs carved at the knees with acorns and oak leaves. Re-upholstered in eighteenth-century Italian green silk damask. One of a pair of settees en suite with sixteen chairs, one of which is shown at number 82. E.H.

83 "Ribband-back" chair

English, Chippendale, c. 1755
Carved mahogany
95.2 x 64.1 x 62.9 (37½ x 25¼ x 24¾)

Lent by The Metropolitan Museum of Art

Pierced "ribband-back" splat; shaped scrolled apron; front legs cabriole with scrollwork on the knees and scrolled feet; back legs plain. Identical, except for the absence of horizontal "ribbands" joining splat to frame, to a design for a "ribband-back" chair published by Chippendale in *The Gentleman and Cabinet-Maker's Director*, 1754, plate 16 center. Seat upholstered in yellow damask. One of a set of four. E.H.

84 Tripod tea table

English, c. 1750
Carved mahogany
71.1 x 87.6 x 76.2 (28 x 34½ x 30)

Lent by The Metropolitan Museum of Art

Rectangular tilt-top with pie-crust edge. The shaft baluster shaped and fluted. The three legs carved with shells and scrolled foliage, terminating in claw feet. E.H.

85 Pair of brackets

English, Chippendale, c. 1755
Carved mahogany
54.6 x 42.5 x 28 (21½ x 16¾ x 11)

Lent by The Metropolitan Museum of Art

Gryphons among foliate scrolls, supporting shaped shelves. From a design by Thomas Chippendale in The Metropolitan Museum of Art, published in *The Director*, 1754, plate 131, figure A. E.H.

86 Fire screen

English, c. 1760
71.1 x 69.8 (28 x 27½); pole: 174 (68½) high, 2.5 (1) diam.

Lent by The Metropolitan Museum of Art

The pole of carved mahogany with spiral turned oval finial and turned base; on three scrolls carved with foliage enclosing an acorn finial on carved foliage and scrolls. The three cabriole legs carved with cartouches on the knees, volutes and pendant acanthus; terminating in flattened volute feet, on casters. Stamped *II* on one leg.

The screen of English tapestry depicting a crimson and blue parrot, and a crested white cockatoo on a brown ground. E.H.

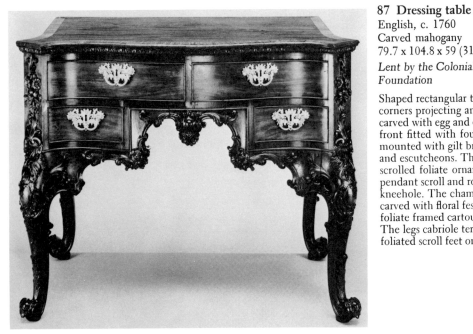

87 Dressing table

English, c. 1760
Carved mahogany
79.7 x 104.8 x 59 (31⅜ x 41¼ x 23⅛)

Lent by the Colonial Williamsburg Foundation

Shaped rectangular top, the front corners projecting and chamfered, carved with egg and dart molding. The front fitted with four drawers, mounted with gilt brass foliate handles and escutcheons. The apron with scrolled foliate ornament centering a pendant scroll and rosette at the kneehole. The chamfered corners carved with floral festoons ending in foliate framed cartouches at the knees. The legs cabriole terminating in foliated scroll feet on low drums. E.H.

88 Armchair

English, c. 1750
Carved mahogany
102.9 x 72.4 x 61.6 (40½ x 28½ x 24¼)

Lent by the Colonial Williamsburg Foundation

Upholstered with original eighteenth-century needlework. Shaped rectangular back and seat. Scrolled arms carved with simple foliate ornament and moldings; the seat rail with cross-hatch and carved rococo ribbon-work centering a trefoil cartouche; cabriole legs with foliate ornament at the knees and scrolled foliate feet on low drums. The back, seat and upper

arms upholstered in needlework depicting, on the back, a parrot in a
landscape surrounded by a scrolled
architectural border centering a grotesque fountainhead at the base; on
the seat, a fruit and floral design in
similar frame. The upholstery is said
to have been drawn and partly executed by Lady Barbara North, daughter of the eighth Earl of Pembroke
and wife of the original owner of the
chairs, Dudley North. Originally
one of a set of twelve. E.H.

90 Sideboard

English, c. 1775
Mahogany and mahogany veneer
with brass rail and curtain
88.3 x 244 x 104.2 (34¾ x 96 x 41)

*Lent by The Metropolitan Museum
of Art*

The frieze and projecting shaped
apron carved with urns, paterae, and
husk swags centering a large urn.
Supported by square tapered legs ornamented in front with husk swags,
terminating in tapered block feet
carved with paterae. En suite with a
pair of pedestals and urns exhibited
here at number 91. E.H.

89 Overmantle mirror

English, Rococo Chinoiserie, c. 1780
233.6 x 181 (92 x 71½)

*From the Collection of Mr. and
Mrs. Paul Mellon*

Gilded pine frame carved with rococo
chinoiserie ornaments in the style
of Thomas Chippendale. At the top,
scrolled corners supporting ho-ho birds,
and in the center a piping Pan seated
beneath a rustic "umbrella" hut, with
an arcade at his side and steps leading
down to an asymmetrical compart-
ment containing a wooded landscape
with grazing sheep. At the base, a
central circular scroll framing a similar
landscape with sheep. The mirror
may be related to a design by Thomas
Johnson published in his *New Book of
Ornaments*, 1760 (plate 2). E.H.

92 Card table

English, c. 1780–1790
Mahogany and satinwood, ebonized
and gilded
75.5 x 49.5 (29¾ x 19½);
97.1 (38¼) long

*Lent by The Metropolitan Museum
of Art*

The shaped rectangular top, when
folded, is ornamented with a fanned
oval in satinwood, the border banded
in green. The frieze channeled with
beaded moldings; supported on slender
fluted legs with calyx-shaped feet.
The channels of the frieze and legs
gilded. The back legs pull out to support the open top leaf. E.H.

91 Pair of sideboard pedestals
and urns

English, c. 1775
Mahogany and mahogany veneer;
the water urn with brass spigot
189.8 x 57.1 x 59.3 (74 x 22½ x 23¼)

*Lent by The Metropolitan Museum
of Art*

The pedestals square with chamfered
corners; the chamfers and frieze
ornamented with urns, husk swags, and
paterae; the front panels with tall
tripod candlestands.
    The urns, one for wine and the
other for water, ornamented with a
wide border of paterae, ribbons, and
husk swags, between a gadrooned base
and a fluted frieze with mask finials.
The foot spiral fluted. The domed
lid with gadrooned cap and fluted urn
finial. En suite with sideboard shown
at number 90. E.H.

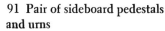

93 Knife box

English, c. 1770–1780
Mahogany inlaid with boxwood
57.8 x 33.6 (22¾ x 13¼)

Lent by The Metropolitan Museum of Art

In the shape of an urn with gadrooned body, inlaid band of floral guilloche, and projecting calyx. The base fluted. The top carved with leaf cap, and surmounted by acorn finial. Carved foliate handles. E.H.

94 Card table

English, c. 1770–1780
Mahogany inlaid with boxwood strings
69.2 (27¼) high; 94 (37) long

Lent by The Metropolitan Museum of Art

The top bowed front and sides, with folding leaf. The frieze edged with carved leaf and husk molding, and with patera blocks at the front angles. Supported by square, tapered legs with foliate capitals and Marlboro feet. E.H.

95 Pair of pedestal candlestands

English, c. 1775
Mahogany and mahogany veneer and ormolu
183.8 (72) high; pedestal:
136 x 30.5 x 30.5 (53½ x 12 x 12)

Lent by The Metropolitan Museum of Art

Pedestals: Square, tapered towards the plinth. The frieze ornamented with paterae and husk swags; the panel with patera.
Candlestands: Each with a single candle socket supported on a scrolled and foliate tripod. E.H.

96 Pair of candlesticks

JOHN CARTER active c. 1767–1789
Silver 1767/68
34.6 (13⅝) high
London hallmark, 1767/68, maker's mark of John Carter

Lent by Leeds City Art Galleries

Three drawings in the Sir John Soane Museum, London, by James or Robert Adam have been used as models for these candlesticks which are part of a more extensive set. The delicacy of the ornament, covering almost the whole surface, is typical of the Adam style in both architecture and decoration and must owe something to Clérisseau, who had been employed by both Robert and James, when they were studying architecture in Italy. R.W.

97 Pair of candelabra

JOHN CARTER active c. 1767–1789
Silver 1774/75
38.1 (15) high
London hallmark 1774/75; maker's mark of John Carter

Lent by Permission of the Committee of Lloyd's, London

Robert Adam provided a drawing, now in the Soane Museum, London, which served as a basis for a set of four candelabra. The drawing is dated 1773, and the candelabra were probably intended for the dining room of 20 St. James' Square, London, the town residence of Sir Watkin Williams Wynn, whose house Adam was then building. Another Adam drawing for the dining room shows differently designed candelabra on tripodal stands, and these pedestals may well have been used for the present pair. Such a combination would have been very popular in the neoclassical period, when the tripod in both England and France was frequently used in furniture and silver. The combination also appeared in paintings of classical subjects to give a correct historical appearance to the setting. In spite of their substantial weight, Adam has

contrived to avoid any feeling of heaviness through the elegant arms of the candleholders, which give a feeling of movement, further increased by the rippling decoration of the surfaces. R.W.

98 Cup

WILLIAM CRIPPS?
Silver 1774/75
42.5 (16¾) high
London hallmark 1774/75; maker's mark W.C. (William Cripps?)

Lent by the Victoria and Albert Museum

Originally a drinking vessel for the rich and powerful, the standing cup had become entirely ornamental by the eighteenth century and looked well on a dining room sideboard. It was a favorite in the neoclassical period and was often used when an official presentation had to be made. The general ovoid form is ultimately based on classical vases, but the severity of the originals, which had been offset by painted decoration, is not copied here. Rather, the cup is decorated with satyrs' masks, swags, palm leaves, paterae and an urn finial, all drawn from the classical repertoire. In the case of the palm leaves, the source may be a plate from Sir William Hamilton's collection of antique vases published in 1766–1767. R.W.

101 Pair of candlesticks

MATTHEW BOULTON 1728–1809,
and JOHN FOTHERGILL
c. 1700–1782
Silver 1774/75
30.5 (12) high
Hallmark of Birmingham 1774/75;
makers' marks of Matthew Boulton
and John Fothergill

Lent by The Museum of Fine Arts, Boston

Boulton and Fothergill were not silversmiths but industrial entrepreneurs engaged in many manufacturing activities connected with metalwork. They were, therefore, constantly looking for designs from engraved sources which would extend their repertoire. In this case, the motif of guilloche and rosettes exactly repeats a border in volume II, plate 106 of d'Hancarville's catalogue of Sir William Hamilton's vases, and was frequently used in silver from Boulton and Fothergill's factory. This is exactly what had been intended by d'Hancarville who wrote in the preface: "[the manufacturers] will be glad to find here more than two hundred forms, the greatest part of which, are absolutely new to them: then, as in a plentiful stream, they may draw ideas which their ability and taste will know how to improve to their advantage, and to that of the public." R.W.

99 Tureen and stand

THOMAS HEMING
active c. 1745–1780
Silver 1776/77
28 x 45.25 x 22.9 (11 x 17¹³⁄₁₆ x 9)
tureen; 49.5 x 29.25 (19½ x 11¼)
stand
London hallmark 1776/77; maker's
mark of Thomas Heming

Lent by the Victoria and Albert Museum

Although tureens were certainly used in the eighteenth-century dining room, their imposing size and weight made them among the grandest pieces on the table or sideboard. Roman vases provided the inspiration for many neoclassical soup or sauce tureens, and such publications as Piranesi's *Vasi* were widely used as sources. The palm leaf decoration and guilloche and paterae frieze were common motifs derived from antiquity.

The matching pair is in the City Art Gallery, Bristol. R.W.

100 Jug

MATTHEW BOULTON 1728–1809,
and JOHN FOTHERGILL
c. 1700–1782
Silver 1776/77
27.3 (10¾) high
Birmingham hallmark for 1776/77;
makers' marks of Matthew Boulton
and John Fothergill

Lent by The Museum of Fine Arts, Boston

The shape of the jug is clearly based on the classical ewer, and the handle may well have come, as has been suggested, from d'Hancarville's catalogue of Sir William Hamilton's vases. The bands of decoration using Greek waves and anthemia and rosettes are also probably based on the same publication. While the jug could well be used for wine, it is more likely that its function was mainly ornamental, that is, it probably served to grace a sideboard. R.W.

102 Pair of sauce tureens

MATTHEW BOULTON 1728–1809,
and JOHN FOTHERGILL
c. 1700–1782
Silver 1776/77
14 x 26.7 (5½ x 10½)
Birmingham hallmark 1776/77;
makers' marks of Matthew Boulton
and John Fothergill

Lent by the Guardians of the Standard of Wrought Plate in Birmingham (The Birmingham Assay Office), England

The original owner of these sauce tureens and their matching soup

tureens, which have also survived, was Mrs. Montagu, the celebrated intellectual and hostess. Her house in Portman Square, built by "Athenian" Stuart in the pure neoclassical style, was a meeting place for some of the most distinguished people of the day: Johnson, Burke, Reynolds, Garrick, Horace Walpole and Fanny Burney. Boulton supplied fittings for Mrs. Montagu's house and silver for her table, for which Mrs. Montagu had precise ideas. "I wish to talk with you on the subject of making me a Service of Plate. I should never invite more than a dozen or thirteen guests, rarely

so many, therefore 9 dishes for each course with Tureens for Soup, and a suitable number of plates would be sufficient. . . . My Tureens must not be very large nor the dishes of the first magnitude."

The oval vase or urn was a popular form in the neoclassical repertoire, ideally suited to tureens. A design for this pair is among a sheet of drawings in Boulton and Fothergill's pattern book now in the Birmingham Reference Library.

Matthew Boulton knew Jefferson, and they had common acquaintances in Benjamin Franklin, Joseph Priestley

and Dr. William Small, Boulton's physician and one-time professor at the College of William and Mary in Jefferson's student days. Jefferson also corresponded with Boulton about a possible order for silver-plated tureens and dishes "plated in the best manner, with a plain bead. . . ."

In 1786, Jefferson and John Adams visited Boulton's industrial mills at Blackfriars Bridge, where Boulton's collaborator, James Watt, had perfected the steam engine. Later Boulton visited Jefferson in Paris, where they further discussed the revolutionary effect of steam power. R.W.

103 Tea urn
THOMAS HEMING active 1745–1780
Silver 1777/78
44.5 (17½) high
London hallmark 1777/78; maker's
mark of Thomas Heming
*Lent by the Cooper-Hewitt Museum
of Design, Smithsonian Institution*

The urn is unusually sculptural for a
piece of silver of the period, and it
seems to relate to baroque and
to Regency designs. Yet the tripodal
base with the acanthus decoration
is characteristically neoclassical. The
feeling of top-heaviness is no doubt
deliberately intended to convey the
burden of the world, which Atlas held
on his shoulders. The globe has allegorical reliefs of the four continents.
Such a distinctive design may have
been specially commissioned. R.W.

THE PROGRESS OF THE HUMAN MIND

But I know also that laws and institutions must go hand in hand with the progress of the human mind. As that becomes more developed, more enlightened, as new discoveries are made, new truths disclosed, and manners and opinions change with the change of circumstances, institutions must advance also, and keep pace with the times.

JEFFERSON to Samuel Kercheval, July 12, 1816

Let me then describe to you a man, not yet forty, tall, and with a mild and pleasing countenance, but whose mind and attainments could serve in lieu of all outward graces; an American, who, without ever having quitted his own country, is Musician, Draftsman, Surveyor, Astronomer, Natural Philosopher, Jurist, and Statesman. . . .

CHASTELLUX, *Travels in North America*

As a son of the Enlightenment, with all of its optimism, curiosity and confidence in the world of experimentation and exploration, and its faith in nature and reason, Jefferson moved quickly and with utter assurance into the intellectual scene of Europe when he arrived in 1784. Something of his own credentials, which secured this impressive intellectual passport placing him on easy terms with the accomplishments and tastes of Europeans, is suggested in the range of interests he shared with the Enlightenment, including his concern with science and exploration and his interest in the classical world of antiquity. The charge by European leaders of the Enlightenment, notably the comte de Buffon and the abbé Raynal, that the American environment was degenerative and unsuitable for man or beast only sharpened Jefferson's own awareness of the cultural and political divisions that separated the New World from the Old.

The Scientific Revolution, ushered in with the publication of Isaac Newton's *Principia* in 1687, was a revolution in man's way of viewing the world. The literature of the Enlightenment is rich with titles beginning with "Observations" and "Views," indicating a heightened visual awareness. The law of optics became an important branch of scientific study after Newton's discoveries, and the iconography of the eye itself, from Masonic ritual to Ledoux's architectural engraving of the Théâtre de Besançon, became a key symbol of the age. The "experimental method" of Newtonian science insisted on the development of keen observation and visual analysis, whether one was identifying plants according to the new Linnaean botanical system, discovering new lands in the American West or the South Pacific, or divining the Golden Mean from antique ruins as a guide to building a capitol for a modern legislature in the wilderness.

The cumulative process of scientific discovery, as it accelerated in the seventeenth century from even before the time of Newton, through the genius of Galileo, Kepler and Harvey, prepared the way for the eighteenth century's new religion, which one might call the Church of the Progress of the Human Mind. It was this intellectual atmosphere that gave the Age of Reason its name and which shaped the imagination and vision of Jefferson. "Nature intended me for the tranquil pursuits of science, by rendering them my supreme delight," he wrote at the close of his second term as president as he prepared to retire with his family and books to Monticello, where his astonishing accomplishments had impressed the marquis de Chastellux almost thirty years earlier.

By the time the young Jefferson had begun to comprehend the laws of the natural world through his "canine appetite" for learning at William and Mary, as well as by following his own "supreme delight" in the practical methods of scientific experiments and observations, the philosophers of the Enlightenment had already extended the "Method of Reasoning," in the words of the Scottish philosopher David Hume, to embrace man himself, his laws, his language, his morals, his history and his political organizations. Extending Newton's discovery of the order of the universe into the daily affairs of men led naturally to the search for the ideal society, of which the American Revolution was to be the great experiment. It was not by chance that Jefferson declared Newton one of the three greatest men of all ages and that the French architect, Etienne Boullée, should design one of his greatest visionary monuments in honor of Newton, whom he believed to be the supreme neoclassical hero.

Paralleling the intellectual ferment in the sciences, leading to the discovery of electricity, oxygen and the reorganization of the study of chemistry, was the seeming paradox of a new interest in the antique world. Political philosophers seeking models for revolution were as avid as sculptors, painters and architects in their detailed explorations of the remains of the antique landscapes scattered about the Mediterranean in France, Italy and Greece. It was an international phenomenon and interest that extended by means of publications and engravings from St. Petersburg to the farms of Albemarle County, Virginia. This paradox, moreover,

was to have a profound impact on the arts. In the neoclassical European vision, the perfect form of antique art embodied the pure, noble, true alternative to the corrupt, jaded excesses of the existing order of the Ancien Régime, manifest in the frivolous productions of rococo court painters and decorators. If the Founding Fathers had no such first-hand decadence to react to in Philadelphia or Williamsburg, they were delighted nevertheless to see themselves wrapped in the neoclassical trappings of the *toga virilis*. The virtue of the New World could have no more appropriate garb as a symbol of the purity of the simple republican society.

The triumph of the American Republic quickly recalled the supposed innocence of antiquity to the imagination of its ambitious leaders, and with his genius for dramatizing that particular moment in history, Jefferson embraced the classical panoply in his own architectural vision, beginning with his designs for the Virginia state capitol. His earliest enthusiasm for classical art had been kindled by the architectural and archaeological publications that were beginning to appear in great profusion, and when he went to Europe, he took every opportunity to study the remains of antiquity first hand. It was in southern France that Jefferson had, in fact, first seen and fallen in love with the little Maison Carrée at Nîmes, an encounter which led to its inspiration for the Richmond capitol.

Whether it was governments, capitols, expeditions, gardens or houses, as Merrill Peterson has pointed out, Jefferson was by instinct a planner. The scientific discoveries of the eighteenth century and the universal curiosity generated by these advances led inevitably to geographic explorations such as the Cook expedition, which opened up undreamed-of worlds of flora and fauna, peopled with societies untouched by the corrupt manners and influences of Western man. Again, acute observation—a keen vision—was essential to the careful recording and assimilation of all this new information, and Jefferson's philosophic and scientific interests and his extraordinary vision as a planner inspired his organization of the Lewis and Clark expedition, one of the great achievements of his first administration.

His *Notes on the State of Virginia*, first published in Paris in 1785, was itself a scientific record and literary exploration of his own native state. This compilation of facts on rivers, climate, population, mountains and aborigines led him inevitably to philosophic speculation on the political and moral implications of a vast continent, conceived as an "empire of liberty," and the American destiny to build there a noble and enlightened society. In the natural sciences, exploration had led to the discovery of thousands of new species of plants and animals. Botany ranked "with the most valuable sciences," as Jefferson put it, and it was this interest that recommended his nomination to the American Philosophical Society, which was considered the headquarters of the Enlightenment in the United States. Jefferson's contribution to this aspect of the widening horizons of the Enlightenment in America and his anxious investigation of the environment is presented in the appropriate setting of the West Garden Court and adjacent galleries on the main floor, under the title "The Pleasures of Nature." W.H.A.

104 Exhuming the First American Mastodon

CHARLES WILLSON PEALE
1741–1827
Oil on canvas 1806
134.6 x 167.6 (53 x 66)
Signed lower right: *C WPeale 1806*
*Lent by The Peale Museum, Balti-
more. Gift of Mrs. Harry White*

From very early in our history gigantic
bones found scattered in the wilderness stirred much conjecture and
scientific inquiry. Legends grew of a
race of giants warring to the death
with immense monsters. Savants from
overseas came searching, and shortly
after Jefferson became president, the

American Philosophical Society listed
the solution of the mystery as a goal
of prime importance. It would finally
refute, as Jefferson's *Notes on the
State of Virginia* had sought to do
some fifteen years earlier, Buffon's
theory that the American climate supported only weak and degenerative
forms of life.

Soon after the *Notes* appeared, discoveries in the marshes and marl
pits of Orange and Ulster Counties,
New York, brought new excitement.
Over the years more fragments
emerged and were passed from hand
to hand. From one site at Shawangunk,
lower and upper jaws with teeth

were sent to Jefferson. This was in
February 1801, when the vote of the
presidential electors, a tie between
Burr and Jefferson, had thrown
Jefferson's public career into the balance, yet he was corresponding with
Dr. Caspar Wistar and others as if "the
great American Incognitum" were
the only issue at stake.

At the same time Charles Willson
Peale, reading of the finds, learned
of a farmer near Newburgh, New York,
who was said to have unearthed a
nearly complete skeleton. He traveled
north at once, found the bones spread
out on John Mastin's granary floor
and was able to purchase all that he

saw there, along with the right to
search the swamp for the remainder.
Here was all that a final solution
required—a skeleton indisputably from
only one animal.

He wrote at once to Jefferson for
help and was immediately granted the
loan of army tents and navy pumps,
while the Philosophical Society, of
which Jefferson was president, advanced money and joined in what was
to become America's first organized
scientific expedition. Peale's great
wheel, dominating the picture, worked
better than the navy pumps, but
the army's tents were used, and one
may be seen pitched in the left back-

ground. The painting dramatizes a crucial moment when a Catskill Mountain storm threatened to undo all that had been accomplished. Peale has depicted lightning ripping the sky and horses galloping in response to a thunderclap, but the labor goes on apace. In contrast to the storm are the scientists, absorbed in their work, as a workman holds up a new-found fragment of bone.

In the crowd scene, Peale amused himself by including portraits of family and friends, many of whom were not actually present at the time. In the group with the life-size drawing, left to right, are the artist, his third wife Hannah in her Quaker cap, Eleanor and Rembrandt Peale, Rubens Peale with his little half-sisters Sybilla and Elizabeth, and next, Patty and Raphaelle Peale. Coleman and Sphonisba Sellers are behind the group, under a prudently raised umbrella. Small Linnaeus and Franklin Peale hold the shaft that keeps the bucket chain in place below. Farther to the left, James Peale, hat on head, gazes into the pit. Betsy, the painter's second wife, who died in 1804, stands just beyond with her young son Titian, a cautionary hand raised toward the storm. Her relatives, Colonel and Mrs. Stagg, are nearby. The ornithologist Alexander Wilson stands alone to the left, arms folded. John Mastin is the man on the foreground ladder.

For Peale, the discovery had raised a bright prospect. He had labored long in an expectation that his Philadelphia Museum must inevitably become, like the great museums of Europe, a national institution. That hope had been rebuffed before, but now, with a friend and a scientist as president, his own political party in power, and with the popular furor that accompanied his discovery, he felt hopeful. It was one of the great disappointments of Peale's life that Jefferson was unwilling to act without the support of a constitutional amendment. However, their mutual interest in the fossils went on as before, the president still finding refreshment from affairs of state in scientific study.

In 1808, when this picture was doing duty both as record of the find and as one of Peale's illustrations of habitat, unfinished rooms in the president's house had become a laboratory in which huge bones from the Lewis and Clark expedition were being assembled. Peale's vision of seeing his museum in Washington had faded, but he still had hopes of its coming into the Jeffersonian orbit as part of the University of Virginia. c.s.

105 Lavoisier and his Wife

JACQUES-LOUIS DAVID 1748–1825
Oil on canvas 1788
286 x 224 (108⅛ x 77)
Signed and dated lower left: L. David Parisïs. Anno 1788

Lent by Rockefeller University, New York

One of the founders of modern chemistry was Antoine-Laurent Lavoisier (1743–1794), who with his revolutionary approach to chemical experiments formed the basis of the science as we know it today. Although Priestley had been the first to isolate dephlogisticated air, it was Lavoisier who gave it the name of oxygen. Later he discovered the composition of water and published his theories in his *Traité élémentaire de chimie* in 1789. He also established and published the chemical terminology still in use.

Lavoisier served as a farmer-general of revenues after 1769 and as general director of the Administration of Gunpowder and Saltpeter after 1771, showing himself to be a capable administrator. He also concerned himself with agriculture and ran a model farm. Although Lavoisier continued in government service in the Treasury after the Revolution and worked on the new system of weights and measures, some of the popular hatred for the farmers-general fell on him. He had already aroused unpopularity by the wall built around Paris in 1787 to collect the customs dues, and many of Ledoux's tollgates were destroyed in the first days of the Revolution. Lavoisier was arrested with the other farmers-general and guillotined in 1794.

David portrayed Lavoisier with his wife and collaborator, Anne-Pierrette Paulze (1756–1836), daughter of a farmer-general. Mme Lavoisier was a painter and skillful engraver; she engraved a number of plates to illustrate her husband's *Traité élémentaire de chimie*. At one time she executed a portrait of *Franklin*, for which the American politician thanked her warmly.

According to tradition David hoped to show his gratitude to Lavoisier by painting this portrait, but no one has yet been able to clarify the nature of the painter's debt to the scientist. Lavoisier was interested in the arts, went to the Salon at the Louvre and noted in the margins of his catalogue of the Salon of 1785 his observations, particularly about the *Oath of the Horatii*.

The portrait was painted in Paris in 1788, and normally it would have been exhibited at the Salon of the following year, but an incident prevented it. On August 6, 1789, Lavoisier, who wanted to exchange some commercial gunpowder for some musket gunpowder, commandeered the gunpowder from the arsenal, which led to a riot in which he almost perished. The directeur des bâtiments du roi, who was in charge of the Salon, felt that it would be better not to exhibit the portrait. Jefferson belonged to the Société de 1789, a club in Paris that also included Lavoisier and David as members. He undoubtedly enjoyed the discussions on art, science and revolution that took place there.

In this portrait, David has emphasized the talents of his models: the chemist's equipment, the balloon flask on the floor, the testing device for gunpowder, all allude to Lavoisier's experiments. He is shown recording the results of his research. The talents of his wife, "depicted as a kind of muse inspiring her husband," are recalled by the drawing portfolio placed on the armchair. A.B. de L.

106 The Astronomer

NICOLAS-BERNARD LÉPICIÉ
1735–1784
Oil on canvas
91.2 x 72.2 (35⅞ x 28⅜)

*Lent by the Museum, Calouste
Gulbenkian Foundation, Lisbon*

Jefferson's interest in astronomy began quite early in his life. There was a telescope on the roof of Rosewell, the home of Jefferson's friend John Page. Jefferson also had a telescope at Monticello and observed the solar eclipse of June 1778, but was handicapped by the lack of an accurate clock. His correspondence over the years frequently mentions astronomy, and among the astronomers to whom he wrote was Jacques Dominique Cassini, the director of the Paris Observatory. Astronomy was included in the list of subjects Jefferson advised Thomas Mann Randolph, Jr., to study, for apart from furthering man's knowledge of the universe, astronomy had a practical use in surveying boundaries, so necessary in a still largely unsettled United States. In the dome room of the rotunda at the University of Virginia, Jefferson de-

signed a planetarium on the ceiling above the library stacks (see 511).

This portrait of an astronomer, whose identity is unfortunately not known, may have been in the Salon of 1777 as number 17. The catalogue entry recorded "Deux autres Portraits sous le même numéro" and from a similar oval format, size and style, the present painting would seem to be a pendant to the *Self-Portrait*, which is also in the Gulbenkian Foundation and which certainly was in the Salon. Saint-Aubin's illustrated catalogue for the 1777 Salon provides additional evidence. *The Astronomer* remains one of the most beautiful of Lépicié's many portraits. The composition is very simple, with a sober background, and the artist has concentrated on a psychological study of the sitter. A sensitive use of light focuses on his head and through highlights defines his hands and clothing and the instruments. A.B. de L.

107 Portrait of Balthazar Sage

JEAN-FRANÇOIS GILLES,
CALLED COLSON 1733–1803
Oil on canvas 1777
100 x 81 (39⅜ x 31⅞)
Signed and dated at lower left:
Colson Pinxit 1777

*Lent by the Musée des Beaux-Arts,
Dijon*

Jefferson's approach to geology was strictly practical. "To learn . . . the ordinary arrangements of the different strata of minerals in the earth, to know from their habitual collocations and proximities where we find one mineral; whether another, for which we are seeking, may be expected to be in its neighborhood, is useful." He realized the importance of coal and metals to the growth of the United States and its economic independence from Europe, and he listed the mineral resources of Virginia in the *Notes on the State of Virginia*.

The portrait of the chemist and mineralogist Balthazar-Georges Sage (1740–1824) is one of Colson's most beautiful paintings in its refinement of coloring, appropriateness of expression and exactness of some of the still-

life details such as the minerals and the jars on the shelves in the background.

At the time of the execution of this portrait in 1777, the sitter was assigned a teaching post at the new school of pharmacy. The following year he was to be awarded a newly created chair in experimental mineralogy at the Hôtel des Monnaies. It was there that the Royal School of Mines was founded at his instigation in 1783, and Sage served as its first director.

Colson portrays Sage in his study, half-length, seated before a Louis XVI style table on which are placed some glass containers, next to an oven used for his demonstrations, with papers in hand. The minerals displayed behind him recall that the scholar, in his home, gave free courses in mineralogy for which he had formed a collection of more than five hundred samples. A.B. de L.

108 Robert Fulton

JEAN-ANTOINE HOUDON
1741–1828
Plaster c. 1803
54.6 x 39.4 x 31.1
(21½ x 15½ x 12⅛)
Signature on right shoulder: *houdon f.*

*Lent by Mrs. Thomas S. Kelly,
New York*

Robert Fulton (1765–1815) began
his career as a portrait painter and
by the age of seventeen was established
successfully in Philadelphia. A few
years later, in 1786, however, he went
to England to improve his health
and, presumably, his prospects as a
portraitist, since the artist Benjamin
West, a family friend, had established
himself there. Fulton was to remain
in Europe twenty years, though his
interests quickly shifted from portrait
painting to engineering, particularly
to the development of canal systems
and naval design. His efforts cul-
minated in his attempt to build a submarine, the design for which he
tried to sell to the French government
with the support of Joel Barlow,
whom he met in Paris in 1797 and in
whose household he lived for a period.
It was through Barlow that Fulton
met Robert Livingston, an association
that was to prove so fruitful that
Fulton's steamboat, built after his
return to the United States in 1807,
was named the Clermont after Livingston's manor on the Hudson. During
his years in France, Fulton tested
wooden models of both the Clermont
and the submarine on the waters
of the Seine, doubtless to the amusement and wonder of passersby.

Jefferson had been fascinated with
the possibilities of steam power,
beginning in about 1786 with his visit
to a steam-powered grist mill in
England. He must have been delighted
to meet his inventive counterpart in
Fulton, and he was fascinated by
Fulton's experiments with the submarine and what Fulton called
"torpedoes." There is an extensive
correspondence between Jefferson and
Fulton on the subject, and in one
letter Jefferson declared that "I am not
afraid of new inventions or improvements, nor bigoted to the practices of
our forefathers. It is that bigotry
which keeps the Indians in a state of
barbarism in the midst of the arts,
would have kept us in the same state
even now, and still keeps Connecticut
where their ancestors were when
they landed on these shores. . . .
Where a new invention is supported
by well-known principles, and promises
to be useful, it ought to be tried.
Your torpedoes will be to cities what
vaccination has been to mankind. It
extinguishes their greatest danger."

The plaster bust of Fulton is a

superb example of Houdon's late style.
The dress of the period is sober and
undecorative, though Fulton's cravat is
somewhat more elaborate than that
of Barlow. His face is serious and
dedicated, combining the sensitivity
and imagination of the artist with a
certain aggressiveness appropriate to his
character as a promoter and man
of affairs.

The relationship of Fulton with his
friend and financial patron Joel
Barlow, whose bust is shown at number 346, is interestingly documented
in an unsigned letter from Fulton to
Ruth Baldwin Barlow in 1813, a year
and a half after Barlow's death:

> Houdon you remember did M. Bar-
> low's Bust, while I was in Paris. I
> wish him to do one for me from it in
> white marble of the best kind and
> in his best style provided it can be
> done for 1000 francs. If so let him
> set about it immediately and I will
> remit the money. Mr. Parker or
> Gregoire will have the goodness to
> execute this commission. I should
> also like to know what M. Houdon
> would charge for a Bust in his best
> style of Franklin, Washington,
> Jefferson, Barlow and Self. This is
> five, if he will do it for 5000 francs
> he may commence and I will remit
> funds. If not, please to let me know
> his price.

[Written vertically on the left margin:
"The bust was executed costing
6000 francs which Barlow now has."]
H.H.A.

109 Experiment with an Air Pump

JOSEPH WRIGHT OF DERBY
1734–1797
Oil on canvas c. 1768
182.9 x 243.8 (72 x 96)

*Lent by the Trustees of the
Tate Gallery, London*

The Industrial Revolution, which
gathered momentum in England from
the middle of the eighteenth century,
changed the history of Europe, the
United States and eventually the whole
world. It was a combination of
scientific discoveries, technological inventions and a new acceptance of
the idea of large-scale industrial production. Perhaps the most important
single development was Watt's improved steam engine which provided
unprecedented power to run machines
and, later, boats and locomotives.
Although admitting that he did not
understand all the technical com-
plexities, Jefferson showed an interest
in the experiments of Fulton and
Rumsey and observed the use of steam
to raise water and to grind corn in
Paris and London. He must have been
reminded of the dangers of relying
on water power to drive grist mills from
his own experience when the Shadwell mill was lost in the flood of 1771.
While he was in Paris, Jefferson
met Boulton, who told him about the

steam engines he made in partner-ship with Watt, and in a typical Jeffer-sonian equation Jefferson compared the efficiency of a steam engine with that of horses: "This makes a peck and a half of coal perform exactly as much as a horse in one day can per-form." He also realized the more general domestic use to which steam could be put and in an 1815 letter to George Fleming, described the way in which "it might perhaps be pos-sible to economize the steam of a com-mon pot kept boiling on the kitchen fire . . . to raise from an adjacent well the water necessary for daily use; to wash the linen, knead the bread, beat the hominy, churn the butter, turn the spit, and do all other house-hold offices which require only a regular mechanical motion." Jefferson paid twelve guineas for "air pumps and apparatus" when he was in London.

Wright lived mainly in Derby in the Midlands of England, which were the industrial center of the country. He knew many of the leading manu-facturers and scientists from the sur-rounding area: Josiah Wedgwood, the potter, Matthew Boulton, the lead-ing industrialist in Birmingham, and Erasmus Darwin, grandfather of Charles Darwin. All these men were members of the Lunar Society, a group concerned with scientific discoveries, which included Dr. Small, Jeffer-son's former teacher in mathematics at the College of William and Mary, Joseph Priestley and Benjamin Franklin. Wright was not himself a member, but he was sufficiently in-terested in science to use it as the subject for his two masterpieces, *A Philosopher Giving a Lecture on the Orrery* and the present painting. The popularity of science and the dif-fusion of specialized knowledge among laymen, which were so widespread in the later eighteenth century, are demonstrated by the large audiences who attended "philosophical lec-tures" or by the interest in watching "drawing room" experiments such as this group of well-dressed people is observing. Air pumps and other scientific instruments were often found in houses as part of the equipment of an educated gentleman and could be of considerable elegance. They were even occasionally found in schools. The demonstration which is being carried out creates a vacuum in the glass and thereby deprives the bird of air. R.W.

110 The Cast Iron Bridge near Coalbrookdale

WILLIAM ELLIS 1747–c. 1805, after Michael "Angelo" Rooker 1743–1801
Engraving 1782
37.5 x 60.3 (14¾ x 23¾)
Signed lower left: *Drawn by M. A. Rooker*, lower right: *Engraved by Wm Ellis.*
Inscribed center: *To George the Third, King of Great Britain &c./This View of the* CAST-IRON BRIDGE, *near* COALBROOK-DALE *in the County of Salop/Is by permission most respect-fully inscribed, by His faithful and dutiful Subjects—The Coalbrook Dale Company—/*LONDON *Published as The Act directs, 4th June 1782, by* Jaˢ. *Phillips, George Yard, Lombard Street*

Lent by the Ironbridge Gorge Museum Collection, Telford, Shropshire, England

The bridge at Coalbrookdale, de-signed by Thomas Pritchard and made at Abraham Darby's works, was opened in 1779 as the first in the world to be made of iron. It has a span of a hundred feet and is still in exist-ence. Together with the iron works in Coalbrookdale (see no. 113), the bridge aroused considerable interest among artists and was engraved several times. Once the practicality of iron had been demonstrated, other more ambitious projects were begun in

England and elsewhere, and the im-provement of road surfaces greatly helped to speed up transportation for both travelers and commerce. When Jefferson was in London in 1786, he apparently purchased an engraving of the bridge, for in his ac-count book, April 11, there is the following entry: "plates of iron bridge 13/ [shillings]." Marie Kimball cites Coalbrookdale bridge as being in Jefferson's collection of prints at the time he finished his second term as president.

Jefferson took an interest in Thomas Paine's bridge-building schemes, which went back to the time Paine lived in Philadelphia. First it was a three-hundred-foot wooden bridge across the Harlem River, though later he planned an iron bridge across the Schuylkill. Paine's inspiration derived from observing organic forms such as the bone structure of animals, tails of birds, reeds and spiders' webs: "When Nature enabled this insect to make a web, she taught it the best method of putting it together." A model in iron was made in 1786 of a single span, which received the ap-proval of Franklin and Rittenhouse. When Paine moved to Paris the model was shown and commended by the Academy of Sciences. Paine wrote to Jefferson: "A Bridge over such a River as the Seine, might be put up in three Months time or less, as all the arches would be begun at once, and the work would admit of as many

hands being employed at the same time as you please." Jefferson was helpful, but in spite of Jefferson's suc-cess in interesting some influential French friends in the idea, Paine's bridge was not built, since Beau-marchais put up a rival scheme. Paine then turned to England and sent an account of his experimental arch to the Royal Society. Sir Joseph Banks wrote of the society's "great satis-faction at the Communication" and added, "I expect many improvements from your Countrymen who think with vigor, and are a great measure free from those shackles of Theory which are imposed on the Minds of our people before they are capable of exerting their Mental faculties to advantage." Walker Brothers of Rotherham agreed to build an arch of ninety feet, and in 1790 it was trans-ported in pieces to London and erected in a field. But Paine's idea of a toll bridge across the Thames remained, like his other building plans, unreal-ized, and after the publication of *The Rights of Man* he had to leave England. There was, however, an indirect progeny of his inventive genius in the iron bridge at Sunderland, designed by Rowland Burdon and made in 1796 by Walker Brothers, who undoubtedly profited from their experience with Paine's experi-ments. R.W.

11 William Hunter Lecturing on Anatomy

JOHANN ZOFFANY 1734/5–1810
Oil on canvas c. 1775
77.5 x 103.5 (30½ x 40¾) oval

*Lent by the Royal College of
Physicians, London*

William Hunter (1718–1783) was
one of the most distinguished
anatomists and surgeons of his day,
specializing in obstetrics. He was
appointed professor of anatomy at the
Royal Academy when it was founded,
where it was standard academic
practice for a young artist to study the
functions of the human body so
that he could draw it correctly. Hunter
is seen here lecturing to students
and members of the Royal Academy,
among whom Sir Joshua Reynolds can
be recognized with his ear trumpet;
Hunter is using as illustrations a live
model, a cast and a skeleton. Another

group by Zoffany, *The Academicians
of the Royal Academy* in the Royal
Collection, treats a similar subject; it
shows a model posing for the life
class and includes a portrait of Hunter.
 Great advances were made in medicine in the eighteenth century. For
the first time, emphasis was placed
more on experimentation and observation than on the repetition of
traditional methods, and thereby a
greater knowledge of the body and
understanding of diseases were established. Hospitals were founded in increasing numbers in Europe and
America and provided a place for the
poor to be treated, though in many
cases they might have survived better
at home. The extension of medical
knowledge and the conquest of disease
and suffering were fundamental ideas
of the Enlightenment.

 Jefferson had an extensive library
on medical subjects. This not only
reflected his interest in the science, but
also gave him some practical knowledge for use in home doctoring, since
a professional medical man would
only be called in for grave cases. At
least one piece of antique sculpture on
his list of desiderata came from
Cheselton's *Anatomy*. Jefferson rated
surgery higher than medicine; he felt
"surgery . . . is a comfortable art
because its operations are freed from
those doubts which must forever haunt
the mind of a conscientious practi-
tioner of the equivocal art of medicine." He also felt there was a danger
of passing fashions in the various
theories propounded and wrote:

 The patient, treated on the fashionable theory, sometimes gets well in
 spite of the medicine. The medicine

therefore restored him, and the
young doctor receives new courage
to proceed in his bold experiments
on the lives of his fellow creatures.
I believe we may safely affirm, that
the inexperienced and presumptuous
band of medical tyros let loose upon
the world, destroys more of human
life in one year, than all the Robin-
hoods, Cartouches & Macheaths
do in a century. . . . The only sure
foundations of medicine are, an
intimate knowledge of the human
body, and observation on the effects
of medicinal substances on that.
The anatomical and clinical schools,
therefore, are those in which the
young physician should be formed.
Jefferson designed an "anatomical
theater" for such study at the University of Virginia (see no. 521). The
theater was destroyed in 1936. R.W.

112 An Inoculation

CONSTANT DESBORDES 1761–1827
Oil on canvas
112 x 147 (44⅛ x 57⅞)

Lent by the Musée de la Chartreuse, Douai

Vaccination as a form of disease prevention had been developed by the English doctor Jenner around 1775 and was used, from the beginning of the nineteenth century, in reducing the danger of smallpox. An earlier form of inoculation against smallpox, actually introducing the virus itself, had been brought to England from Turkey by Lady Mary Wortley-Montague in the 1720s. This was the kind of inoculation that Jefferson received, probably from William Shippen, Jr., in Philadelphia in 1766. Presumably such a novel and still little-practiced technique could only be found in large towns, where there were enough sophisticated and enlightened people to support it. At a time when there was little understanding of diseases, many considered it impious to try to prevent a natural scourge. Jefferson's decision to be inoculated must, therefore, have been a deliberate affirmation of his belief in reason and enlightenment. Smallpox, apart from its lethal effects, could

also disfigure survivors with pock marks. At the time of the Second Continental Congress, Jefferson wrote from Philadelphia about the misfortunes of the American army, half of which was down with "the ravages of the small pox." He welcomed the introduction of the new type of vaccination in a letter to Dr. Benjamin Rush in 1801 and included in his instructions to Meriwether Lewis the need to spread the information among the Indians. "Carry with you some matter of the kine pox; inform those of them with whom you may be, of its efficacy as a preservative from the small pox; and instruct and encourage them in the use of it." His library contained several books on the subject, including those by Drs. Benjamin Waterhouse and John Coxe, pioneers in the introduction of vaccination to America who presented their works to Jefferson. Replying to Waterhouse, Jefferson stated his belief that "every friend of humanity must look with pleasure on this discovery, by which one evil more is withdrawn from the condition of man; and contemplate the possibility, that future improvements & discoveries, may still more & more lessen the catalogue of evils."

Later Jefferson received from Jenner

"evidence at large respecting the discovery of the vaccine inoculation." In his reply he recorded that "having been among the early converts, in this part of the globe to its efficiency, I took an early part in recommending it to my countrymen . . . Medicine has never before produced any single improvement of such utility . . . You have erased from the calendar of human afflictions one of the greatest. Yours is the comfortable reflection that mankind can never forget that you have lived. Future generations will know by history only that the loathsome small-pox has existed and by you has been extirpated."

The painting probably represents Dr. Alibert vaccinating a child, who is held by the artist's niece Marceline Desbordes-Valmore, a poet from Douai. In the background are the cows which no doubt were the source of the vaccine. Dr. Alibert was a noted dermatologist, who became royal physician to Louis XVIII and Charles X and doctor to the Opéra Comique in Paris. A.B. de L.

113 Coalbrookdale by Night

PHILIP JAMES
DE LOUTHERBOURG 1740–1812
Oil on canvas 1801
68.8 x 106.7 (26¾ x 42)
Signed lower right: R. A. 1801/
P. J. de Loutherbourg

Lent by the Science Museum, London

Coalbrookdale in Shropshire became
an attraction to visitors from the
mid-eighteenth century because of its
picturesque scenery. Located where
the river Severn passes through the
Wenlock Hills, the town and surrounding district became the subject of
sketches by several artists such as
Joseph Farington, Cornelius Varley
and Michael "Angelo" Rooker (see
no. 110). In addition to natural beauty
there were the first manifestations
of the Industrial Revolution, which
was to give Britain such economic
power, in the important foundry of
the Abraham Darby family, using coke
for the first time to smelt iron. This
contrast between the beauty of
nature and the devastation of indus-
trialism was strangely attractive to the
eighteenth-century eye. It provided the

emotional distinction between the
beautiful and the sublime in terms of
Burke's aesthetic theories. The agri-
culturist Arthur Young, who visited
Coalbrookdale in 1776, compared the
"romantic spot," the "winding glen"
and "hanging wood" to "that variety
of horrors art has spread at the bottom: the noise of the forges, mills & c.
with all their vast machinery, the
flames bursting from the furnaces with
the burning of the coal and the smoak
of the lime kilns." Except that
Young's visit was by day, the description might well be of de Loutherbourg's painting, but the artist has
chosen the night for dramatic purposes. This gives an almost hellish
aspect to the scene, undoubtedly
stemming from de Loutherbourg's
experience as a theater painter and
the creator of the *Eidophusikon*, a
peep show of contrasting incidents
enhanced by mechanical and optical
effects. R.W.

114 The Ascent of Lunardi's Balloon

JULIUS CAESAR IBBETSON
1759–1817
Oil on canvas c. 1788–1790
50 x 60.6 (20 x 24½)

*Lent by the Trustees of the London
Museum*

The age of ballooning began with the
success of the Montgolfier brothers
in Paris in November 1783, and for the
next few years there were several
flights in hot-air or hydrogen-filled balloons throughout Europe. Jefferson's
letters from Paris make frequent
reference to ballooning. In one he gave
detailed comparative accounts of the
various ascents, the material of the
balloons, the height reached and
distance traveled with drawings of their
shape. Others record the first balloon crossing of the English Channel
by Blanchard and the Massachusetts
Loyalist Dr. Jefferies and an unsuccessful attempt, when an accident
killed "the two first martyrs to the
aeronautical art."

Vincenzo Lunardi, secretary at the
Neapolitan embassy in London, made
the first successful flight from
England in a hydrogen balloon on
September 15, 1784. The scene represented here is his third balloon ascent
of June 29, 1785. On that occasion
George Biggin, who provided the
financial backing for the venture, made
the journey accompanied by a Mrs.
Sage, while Lunardi remained below to
supervise the launching from St.
George's Fields. A great crowd assembled to witness the event, and the
sensational flight brought business
to a standstill, even interrupting the
royal levee at St. James' Palace. The
present painting is a replica, omitting
Mrs. Sage in the basket, of that exhibited at the Royal Academy in 1788
and now in a private English collection.

It is interesting to note that
Trumbull was in London at the time
of Lunardi's first successful attempt
and made a sketch of the event which
he never finished. R.W.

115 The Interior of the Pantheon, Oxford Street

MICHAEL "ANGELO" ROOKER
1743–1801
Watercolor with pen and ink c. 1778
23.5 x 31.1 (9¼ x 12¼)

Lent Anonymously

Benjamin Wilson (1721–1788), painter and scientist, made experiments with electricity and lightning conductors and published several works on the subject. He disagreed with Benjamin Franklin on what type of lightning conductor was most efficient, and his experiment with blunt-ended lightning rods, which is illustrated here, was intended to disprove Franklin's theory, and won the support of George III and the government.

Violent thunderstorms in Virginia made the danger of people and houses being struck by lightning a real one, and Jefferson took an interest in Franklin's research. As a fellow member of the American Philosophical Society, moreover, Jefferson would have been kept informed of Franklin's latest studies. It was these which brought Franklin to the attention of the European scientific world and which justified Jefferson's remarks in the *Notes on the State of Virginia*, that "in physics we have produced a

Franklin, than whom no one of the present age has made more important discoveries, nor has enriched philosophy with more, or more ingenious solutions of the phenomena of nature."

The Pantheon in Oxford Street, London, where Wilson's experiments took place, was built by James Wyatt between 1770 and 1772 and was used first as assembly rooms. Here Lunardi exhibited the balloon in which he made the first ascent in England in 1784 (see no. 114). The great room shown in this painting was based on the Hagia Sophia in Constantinople, though the dome followed that of the Pantheon in Rome. Jefferson must have looked with interest at the architecture of one of the most notable contemporary buildings in London, and from his account book we know that he visited it on March 23, 1786. R.W.

116 Comte de Buffon

JEAN-ANTOINE HOUDON
1741–1828
Terra cotta 1782
59.7 (23½) high
Signed lower front edge: *houdon f. 1782*

Lent by the Fine Arts Museums of San Francisco

George Louis Leclerc, comte de Buffon

(1707–1788), was the director of the Jardin du Roi, later the Jardin des Plantes, when Jefferson arrived in Paris, and was the most eminent naturalist of his time. Jefferson had already in his *Notes on the State of Virginia* taken spirited exception to Buffon's view that both animals and men degenerated in the climate of the New World, and before he sailed for Europe, Jefferson sent to Buffon by his friend the marquis de Chastellux a large panther skin intended to convince him that the panther and the cougar are not identical. In 1787, Jefferson had the skin, skeleton and horns of a moose shipped from New Hampshire for the edification of the French naturalist. Jefferson and Chastellux dined with Buffon at the Jardin du Roi, and their relations remained cordial until Buffon's death in 1788.

In Buffon's respect for evidence obtained through careful observation and experimentation, he was a pioneer of the modern scientific method and anticipated in broad outline the theories of Darwin, in terms of the evolution of plant forms. Houdon executed a marble bust of Buffon in 1782 at the request of Catherine the Great, a passionate admirer who called him "the first mind of the century in his field." The terra-cotta bust exhibited here dates from the same year. At the time of the portrait, Buffon was seventy-four years old, but his strong features make him seem younger. The sharp turn and lift of the head, his slightly parted lips, the heavy compressed brows and the wide, searching eyes all reflect a forceful personality. H.H.A.

117 Telescope

JOHN DOLLOND 1706–1761, and
PETER DOLLOND 1730–1820
Mahogany and brass
103.5 (40¾) long (open); 87.3 (34⅜) long (shut); 48.9 (19⅛) high
Marked: *Dollond-London*

Lent by the University of Virginia, Charlottesville

Used for both terrestrial and celestial observations, this compact telescope is mounted on a collapsible brass stand designed for use on a tabletop. The instrument has an objective lens 2¹⁄₁₆ inches in diameter. When the draw-tube containing the eyepiece was extended, focusing was achieved with the knob visible near the end of the mahogany tube. The tube of the telescope could be unfastened from the brass stand and was cus-

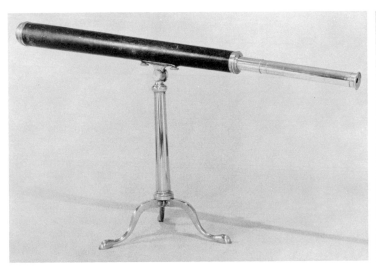

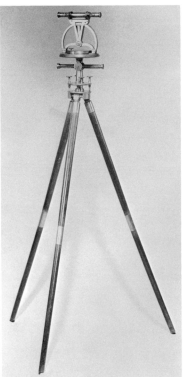

tomarily packed in a mahogany case for traveling. Eyepieces of different powers of magnification were also provided.

This instrument was made and signed by the well-known London firm of Dollond, which produced scientific instruments of outstanding quality and workmanship throughout the second half of the eighteenth century. John Dollond, Sr. (1706–1761), was a Huguenot silk weaver, who in 1752 joined his son, Peter Dollond (1730–1820), in the latter's optical business in London. In 1757 John Dollond reinvented the achromatic lens, which had been first invented in 1733 by Chester More Hall. Dollond's lens was patented, and he produced his first achromatic telescope in 1758. In 1766 Peter Dollond took his younger brother, John Dollond, Jr., into his business and subsequently his nephew, George Dollond, born Huggins. The firm continues under the Dollond name to the present. References to instruments purchased from this firm can be found in Jefferson's account books, and it is possible that this one was bought during his visit to London in 1786, since his account book shows that on March 21 he "pd. Dollond for a telescope £10–10—solar microscope £5–16."

This telescope is typical of several that Thomas Jefferson is known to have owned during his lifetime, and it is likely that in addition to observing distant scenes or arriving visitors, Jefferson used such an instrument for observations of the stars and the planets in the determination of longitude. Jefferson ranked astronomy with the most useful of studies, and in a letter to young Thomas Mann Randolph, Jr., who four years later would marry Jefferson's daughter Patsy, he advised him to study "Astronomy, Natural philosophy (or Physics) Natural history, Anatomy, Botany and

Chemistry. No inquisitive mind will be content to be ignorant of any one of these branches." S.A.B.

118 Theodolite and tripod

JESSE RAMSDEN 1735–1800
Brass and mahogany
Theodolite: 28 x 17.1 x 21
(11 x 6¾ x 8¼); tripod: 106.7 (42) high
Theodolite is marked *Ramsden-London*

Lent by the Thomas Jefferson Memorial Foundation, Charlottesville

Thomas Jefferson's preoccupation with precision measurement may have been inherited from his father, who produced the first accurate map of Virginia (see no. 3) and was one of the Crown commissioners who established the Fairfax line between the source of the Rappahannock River and the Potomac River. In any case, Jefferson purchased for his own use the finest scientific instruments available. This theodolite, made and signed by Jesse Ramsden, is a superb example.

The instrument measures both horizontal and vertical angles by means of the movable upper telescope and the fixed one beneath it. The vertical arc and toothed rack enable the upper telescope to be precisely adjusted to any elevation, while the upper surface of the flat horizontal plate can be rotated to any position around a full 360 degrees simultaneously. A comparison of readings can then be made between the two telescopes.

Thomas Jefferson used this instrument, which represents the most

sophisticated kind of surveying instrument available in his time, and similar ones for surveying his estate and for determining the heights of nearby mountains.

Jesse Ramsden (1735–1800) was an optical instrument-maker in London. He had been trained by a maker of fine scales named Barton and worked for such prominent makers of mathematical instruments as Jeremiah Sisson, George Adams, Peter Dollond, whose sister he married, and Edward Nairne. Between 1768 and 1773 Ramsden devised an engine for graduating mathematical instruments which revolutionized the production of precisely engraved scales. He pioneered in the development of sophisticated astronomical and surveying instruments, and after his death he was succeeded in business by his principal workman, John Berge. S.A.B.

119 Louis XVI, Accompanied by M. the Maréchal de Castries, Ministre de la Marine, Gives His Instructions to M. de La Pérouse for His Trip Around the World

NICOLAS-ANDRÉ MONSIAU
1754–1837
Oil on canvas
172 x 227 (67¾ x 89)
*Lent by the Musée National
du Château de Versailles*

Louis XVI giving instructions to M de La Pérouse was painted by Monsiau in 1816 for the galerie de Diane in the Tuileries, where it was placed as an overdoor. It was part of an important royal commission conceived with the goal of rehabilitating the recently restored monarchy by illustrating events from the lives of former kings. Four paintings were

concerned with Louis XVI, the subjects having been chosen by his brother Louis XVIII.

Jean-François de Galaup, comte de La Pérouse and famous French navigator, was born at Gua, near Albi, in 1741, and died near Vanikoro Island on an unknown date, but probably during the course of the year 1788. In 1785, the French government, wanting to complete the work of Cook, resolved to have the northwest coast of America investigated and to explore the seas around Japan, the Solomon Islands and the southwest of New Holland. La Pérouse was selected as head of this expedition. In order to prepare for the

expedition, memoranda were drawn up by the Académie des Sciences and the Société de Médecine; instructions, outlined by a friend of La Pérouse, captain de Fleurieu, were annotated and completed by Louis XVI. These instructions, in which a noble feeling for humanity is expressed, were too detailed and encompassed too vast a range of projects for a limited stay. As for the rest, the preparations were well made. Two frigates, *La Boussole* and *L'Astrolabe*, took a large number of people on board: scholars, mathematicians, astronomers, naturalists, geologists and physicians. La Pérouse took command of *La Boussole* and gave that of *L'Astrolabe* to

captain de Langle. Leaving from Brest August 1, 1785, the expedition ended in tragic circumstances in about February 1788, when the two frigates and their crews were lost.

Before the departure of the two ships, Louis XVI received La Pérouse in his study at Versailles in the presence of the maréchal de Castries, ministre de la marine, and personally gave him his last instructions. It is this moment that the artist has represented. A.B. de L.

who were given an extensive tour of the capital and other east coast cities and returned to their homes with gifts and messages of peace and friendship (see nos. 126–129).

Sir Joseph Banks did not meet Jefferson when the latter was in London, but they certainly knew of each other, as frequent references are made in Jefferson's correspondence both to Banks and to friends they had in common. One of these was Thomas Paine, author of *The Rights of Man*, in whose project for an iron bridge both Banks and Jefferson took an interest. Another was John Ledyard, the explorer, for whom Banks opened a subscription to further his journey across Russia, and on whose behalf Jefferson spoke to baron de Grimm, Catherine the Great's unofficial ambassador in Paris. It was through Banks that Jefferson heard of Ledyard's death in Cairo. Finally, both men were keenly interested in agriculture and in promoting the introduction of new plants into different parts of the world. Banks inquired about the possibility of growing rice in the West Indies, just as Jefferson investigated the rice production of northern Italy in the hope of improving the American crops. R.W.

120 Sir Joseph Banks, Omai and Dr. Solander

WILLIAM PARRY 1742?–1791
Oil on canvas c. 1775
149 x 149 (59 x 59)

Lent by the Trustees of the Parham Discretionary Settlement, Parham Park, Pulborough, Sussex, England

Sir Joseph Banks (1743–1820), who is the central figure in the painting, was a rich man who devoted himself to natural history and later became president of the Royal Society. He traveled with Captain Cook on his first voyage, 1768 to 1771, which was organized by the admiralty to observe the passing of the planet Venus across the face of the sun. At the same time Cook explored in the South Pacific and along the coasts of Australia and New Zealand. Because of his wealth and influence, Banks was able to take

with him Dr. Daniel Charles Solander (1736–1782), the distinguished Swedish botanist who was a pupil of Linnaeus, and two draftsmen to record the many new species they encountered. It is noteworthy that all three of Cook's voyages included qualified artists, to provide pictorial evidence of the strange lands and peoples they visited (see no. 121). At the time of Cook's second voyage, 1772–1774, Lord Sandwich, First Lord of the Admiralty, suggested that it would be "delightfully instructive to observe how one of the noble savages would conduct himself among people of superior breeding." As a result, when the expedition returned, it brought back a young Tahitian man, called Omai, who had asked to be taken to England. He was made much of by society as, in the words of

Dr. Solander, Omai was "well-behaved, easy in his manners and remarkably complaisant to the ladies." The Tahitian met many famous people of the day, was painted by Reynolds and shown the sights of London. On being presented to George III he greeted him with "how do, King Tosh." De Loutherbourg, the painter and state designer, produced a play at Drury Lane in 1785, based on Captain Cook's last voyage called *Omai, or Obesa Queen of the Sandwich Islands*. Omai returned to Tahiti with Cook on his last voyage, taking back with him an odd assortment of bric-a-brac, representative of western civilization. A somewhat similar experiment was carried out in 1806, when during his second term as president, Jefferson was to receive a delegation of Indians in Washington

121 Matavai Bay, Tahiti

WILLIAM HODGES 1744–1797
Oil on canvas 1776
91.4 x 137.2 (36 x 54)
Signed lower left: Hodges 1776

*From the Collection of Mr. and
Mrs. Paul Mellon*

Hodges was the official artist on
Captain Cook's second voyage to the
Pacific. Zoffany had been the original
choice of the First Lord of the Admiralty, Lord Sandwich; but when Sir
Joseph Banks, who was to finance
the expedition, withdrew, the ship
was declared unseaworthy, and Zoffany
declined to go. The reports on the
ship, *Resolution*, must have been unduly alarmist, because she survived
the voyage satisfactorily and is seen,
together with the *Adventure*, in
another version of the present painting
now in the National Maritime
Museum, Greenwich. The ships were
in Matavai Bay from August 25 to
September 1, 1773. The Mellon version has concentrated instead on
the native craft which would naturally
attract a European artist on account
of their strangeness.

Philosophers in the eighteenth
century were always looking for examples of men who had kept their
original virtue unspoiled by civilization.
For a time the South Sea Islands
were put forward as a latter day Eden.
One of the inhabitants, Omai, was
brought back to England so that
polite society could see a "noble
savage" in the flesh (no. 120). Unfortunately, the paradisaic islands were
soon spoiled by intruders, who
brought disease, alcohol and other un-
desirable effects of European life.

Jefferson's interest in Cook's voyages of discovery is attested to by
several books on the subject in his
library. He also had a personal connection in John Ledyard, a Connecticut man who published an account
of Cook's third and last voyage (1776–
1779) which explored the Northwest Passage and the Pacific. Jefferson
met Ledyard in Paris in 1786 and
became interested in his scheme to find
a way through Siberia to the west
coast of America and then across the
continent. The Empress Catherine

did not approve of the scheme and had
Ledyard arrested and deported.
Later, André Michaux suggested to
the American Philosophical Society
that an expedition should be sent
across the Mississippi in the direction
of the Pacific, an idea which Jefferson
supported and which was to cul-
minate in the Lewis and Clark expedition after the negotiation of the
Louisiana Purchase. R.W.

122 Rhinoceros

GEORGE STUBBS 1724–1806
Oil on canvas c. 1772
69.9 x 92.7 (27½ x 36½)

*Lent by The Royal College of
Surgeons of England, London*

Dürer's engraving in 1515 of a rhinoceros, even though the bizarre armor-plated animal was not done from life, remained the standard image until the eighteenth century. From 1748 to 1751 a rhinoceros traveled through Europe and was recorded by several artists, including Pietro Longhi in Venice. But Stubbs was the first artist to look at the rhinoceros with the eyes of a naturalist and to produce an accurate representation. Apart from Stubbs' profound interest in animals, which would make him view the rhinoceros as more than just a curiosity, the fact that the painting was destined for John Hunter's museum of anatomy and physiology would have demanded particular accuracy. The model was probably a rhinoceros that was exhibited at Pidcock's menagerie in London in 1772. There is a drawing of it in an English private collection, and "nine studies of the Rhinoceros, in different attitudes" were sold at Stubbs' sale after his death. John Hunter commissioned other paintings of exotic animals from Stubbs for his museum as did Sir Joseph Banks and Hunter's brother William, who also formed a museum, now part of Glasgow University.

To Jefferson, "natural history. . . . is my passion," and his observations both in the United States and in Europe, together with books he had read on the subject, gave him an extensive knowledge. The *Notes on the State of Virginia* are full of details about the animals of his native state, and he was constantly championing American fauna against the disparaging opinions of the great naturalist Buffon. In an attempt to disprove the latter's theories that animals in America were smaller because of the climate, Jefferson, after considerable difficulty and expense, had a moose sent over which was stuffed and displayed, and the horns of caribou, elk and deer were also sent to Paris as evidence of the superiority of New World species. In this there was of course an element of propaganda, but Jefferson's genuine interest and curiosity—so typical of his time—in all branches of natural history is shown constantly throughout his career, in his extensive correspondence and in the many specimens sent back by the Lewis and Clark expedition.

In 1787 John Ledyard, the explorer, wrote Jefferson from Siberia providing some descriptions of that distant waste and maintained that he had discovered a fossil of "either the Elephant or Rinoceros bone, for the latter Animal has also been in this country." R.W.

123 Green Monkey

GEORGE STUBBS 1724–1806
Oil on panel 1774
70.5 x 60.3 (27¾ x 23¾)
Signed lower left: G. Stubbs 1774

Lent anonymously

In the eighteenth century, Europeans and Americans, while vaguely aware of countries and even continents waiting to be discovered, still had only the haziest understanding of much of the supposedly known world. Travelers to Africa and Asia were few and were confined to merchants,

soldiers and officials. Rarely, a native from China or the South Seas (see no. 120) might appear to provide concrete evidence of other cultures. From the animal kingdom, foreign potentates sent presents of strange beasts to European rulers, or travelers brought them back as curiosities. George III was presented with a cheetah and a zebra, and the long-established royal menagerie was one of the attractions of the Tower of London. Jefferson must have had some early curiosity about exotic animals, for

at Williamsburg, he paid 7½ pence to see an elk in 1768 and the following year "paid for seeing a tyger ⅓ [one shilling, three pence]." While in Philadelphia for the first Continental Congress he paid a shilling to see a monkey. Meriwether Lewis shipped a live magpie to Jefferson from the upper Missouri during the Lewis and Clark expedition.

The green monkey is of the guenon group of monkeys and a native of Africa. Because of its attractiveness, it is often seen in captivity, and no

doubt Stubbs sketched the animal in a London menagerie. He has painted the monkey's portrait with the sensitivity and sympathy that would normally be given a human sitter. Perhaps it is too much to suggest that the artist has attempted psychological insight, but Stubbs has emancipated himself from viewing a strange animal as a mere curiosity and at the same time avoided any false sentimentality. Another version dated 1798 is in the Walker Art Gallery, Liverpool. R.W.

124 Meriwether Lewis

CHARLES-BALTHAZAR-JULIEN
FEVRET DE SAINT-MÉMIN
1770–1852
Crayon on paper 1803 or 1807
55.8 x 40.6 (22 x 16)

*Lent by the Missouri Historical
Society, St. Louis*

Meriwether Lewis (1774–1809) was
the official leader of the Lewis and
Clark expedition, which traveled
overland to the Pacific Ocean and back
between 1803 and 1806. The successful completion of such an arduous
journey was of great importance to
the history of the United States. Lewis
laid the primary American claim to
the vast northwestern area, established
a route to the Pacific, bringing back
accurate anthropological and geographic data, and helped make feasible
the American fur trade. Mounting
an expedition to the Pacific had been
one of Jefferson's persistent visions
for more than twenty years. Lewis
shared Jefferson's enthusiasm for exploration, and at the age of eighteen
Lewis applied for the post of leader to

the overland expedition proposed
by Jefferson under the auspices of the
American Philosophical Society.
Lewis was turned down, and the
expedition under André Michaux,
which had been turned into a covert
attempt by the French to capture
Spanish New Orleans, was stopped by
the French government before reach-
ing the Mississippi. Eleven years
later, Lewis was Jefferson's undis-
puted first choice. In 1813, four years
after Lewis' death, Jefferson wrote
to Paul Allen, a poet and editor who
supervised the printing of a history of
the expedition,

Of courage undaunted, possessing a
firmness & perseverance of purpose
which nothing but impossibilities
could divert from it's direction,
careful as a father of those committed to his charge, yet steady in
the maintenance of order & discipline, intimate with the Indian
character, customs & principles,
habituated to the hunting life,
guarded by exact observation of the
vegetables & animals of his own

country, . . . honest, disinterested,
liberal, of sound understanding and
a fidelity to truth . . . , I could have
no hesitation in confiding the enter-
prize to him.

Lewis was born at Locust Hill, a
family estate lying within sight of
Monticello. With his father's pre-
mature death in 1779, Lewis was taken
with his mother to the home of his
stepfather, John Marks, on the Broad
River in Georgia. Growing up on
the Georgia frontier, he acquired the
skills of woodsmanship which were to
be so important to him. Tutored in
Virginia, Lewis planned to attend
William and Mary College but was
advised by his guardians to assume the
management of Locust Hill in 1790.
While indifferent to farming as a
life-long occupation, Lewis developed
a familiarity with the land that
played a crucial role in his being chosen
as the expedition leader. His knowledge of the flora of the east enabled
him to differentiate the new species in
the west from those already known.
Volunteering to serve in the militia in
the Whiskey Rebellion in 1794, he
found army life so appealing that
he enlisted in 1795. Serving in the old
Northwest Territory and at Fort
Pickering near present-day Memphis,
Tennessee, Lewis gained further knowledge of the ways of Indians and the
skills needed for wilderness survival.
On February 23, 1801, Jefferson
asked Lewis to become his private
secretary, professing an interest in
Lewis' particular abilities, perhaps with
a thought to the forthcoming expedition: "Your knolege of the
Western country, of the Army, and of
all it's interests & relations has rendered it desireable for public as well as
private purposes that you should be
engaged in that office," he wrote.
While Lewis performed many domestic duties for the widowed president,
he was also privy to affairs of state
and diplomatic maneuverings. In addition, he must have enthusiastically
aided Jefferson's continuing plans for
an expedition to the Pacific.
After Congressional approval had
been obtained in January 1803, Lewis
hurriedly began his preparations.
Tutored in Philadelphia by Caspar
Wistar, Benjamin Smith Barton,
and Benjamin Rush in botany, zoology,
medicine and Indian history, he
traveled to Lancaster to learn about
astronomy from Andrew Ellicott. At
the same time he oversaw the acquisition of necessary supplies and equipment, taking time to modify the size
and action of the standard rifle, to
devise a collapsible iron-frame canoe,
and to concoct a dehydrated soup.
Taking leave of Jefferson on July 4,
1803, Lewis hurried to Pittsburgh
to pick up his fifty-five-foot keelboat.

After traveling down the Ohio River,
he met his friend and fellow-explorer
William Clark, and wintered his
men outside St. Louis. Heading up the
Missouri River on May 14, 1804,
Lewis led the expedition to winter
quarters near a Mandan settlement in
present-day North Dakota. Proceeding again in April 1805, he conducted
his small band through unexplored
and hostile territory across the Rocky
Mountains to the mouth of the
Columbia River. After another winter,
he headed back along much the
same route, arriving in St. Louis on
September 23, 1806, with the loss of
only one man due to sickness.
He reported to Jefferson, "In obedi-
ance to your orders we have peni-
trated the Continent of North America
to the Pacific Ocean, and sufficiantly
explored the interior of the country
to affirm with confidence that we
have discovered the most practicable
rout which dose exist across the
Continent by means of the navigable
branches of the Missouri and Columbia Rivers." As the expedition had
been given up for lost, years later
Jefferson recalled to Paul Allen that
"never did a similar event excite more
joy thro' the United States."
Arriving in Washington with a
group of Indian representatives, Lewis,
along with Clark, to whom he always
gave equal credit, was toasted and
fêted. As a suitable reward for such a
successful mission, Lewis was granted
fifteen hundred acres of western
land and appointed governor of the
Territory of Upper Louisiana.
Upon arriving in St. Louis in March
1808, over a year after his appointment, Lewis found local affairs in
chaos. He soon brought about order by
having the laws codified, establishing a militia, and stabilizing the
frontier. Riding east in 1809 on his
way to Washington to conduct govern-
mental business and oversee the
publication of his journals, Lewis died
in a cabin in Tennessee. While the
evidence strongly points to murder,
Lewis was officially declared a suicide.
By tradition, this portrait was
made by Saint-Mémin, just before
Lewis departed on the expedition, and
was sent to his mother at Locust
Hill. The engraved plate which accompanied all Saint-Mémin portraits was
unfortunately destroyed in a fire at
Locust Hill about 1837. The portrait
could also have been done with the
Indian portraits in 1807, but there is a
second profile by Saint-Mémin lacking the engraved plate which was
more likely to have been done at that
time. Saint-Mémin also drew a rough
full-length sketch of Lewis in buck-
skin and Indian dress. However, the
model for that drawing may have been
Charles Willson Peale's identically
dressed wax effigy in the Philadelphia

Museum, completed after Lewis'
death, since the sketch belonged to
Clark. About 1815 William Strickland
made an aquatint of the full-length
sketch for publication in the
Analectic Magazine. G.V.

125 Thomas Jefferson

CHARLES-BALTHAZAR-JULIEN
FEVRET DE SAINT-MÉMIN
1770–1852
Black and white crayon on paper 1804
60.5 x 43.2 (23¹³⁄₁₆ x 17)
*Lent by The Worcester Art Museum,
Massachusetts*

Jefferson's payment on November 27,
1804, for the original crayon, the
copperplate engraved from this drawing, and forty-eight small engravings
struck from it, was most probably
made, as was customary, on the day of
the sitting. Jefferson, portrayed at
age sixty-one, approaching the end of
his first term as president and already
elected to a second term, must have sat
for the thirty-four-year-old Saint-
Mémin at the artist's rooms in David
Shoemaker's house on F Street in
Washington, where the profilist's
cumbersome physiognotrace was
housed.

Saint-Mémin engraved a second
copper plate of his *Jefferson* and was
striking prints from it for commercial
sale at the time of Jefferson's second
inauguration. That Jefferson's contemporaries found these prints attractive is indicated by the many examples
which have survived. It was this
print, in fact, which Thomas Gimbrede used as the basis for his likeness
of Jefferson in the apotheosis titled
Jefferson the Pride of America, which
he engraved just after Jefferson's
retirement from the presidency. Later
this likeness was copied in Paris in a
lithograph by Langlumé dedicated to
Jefferson's friend David Warden,
"ancien Consul des états Unis à Paris."
Through further copies the Saint-
Mémin portrait, *Jefferson,* became a
widely circulated and familiar image
in France. Cherished by some of
Jefferson's descendants as an especially
characteristic likeness, the Saint-
Mémin portrait was extensively distributed in both America and France
and persistently admired.

Both copperplates still survive: the
original, enclosed in a circle, in
the Princeton University Library; the

replica, bearing the likeness within
an oval, in the Alderman Library of the
University of Virginia. Besides the
original prints taken from the oval
plate early in the nineteenth century,
printings from it have been made

without letters in recent years. The
Langlumé lithograph and its various
derivations survive in the Bibliothèque
nationale. Gimbrede's apotheosis
and a bas-relief by George Miller (in
plaster at the American Philosophical

Society and in bronze at Monticello
and the Henry Francis DuPont
Winterthur Museum) are only the
more notable of the many likenesses
copied from the image engraved from
the oval copperplate. A.B.

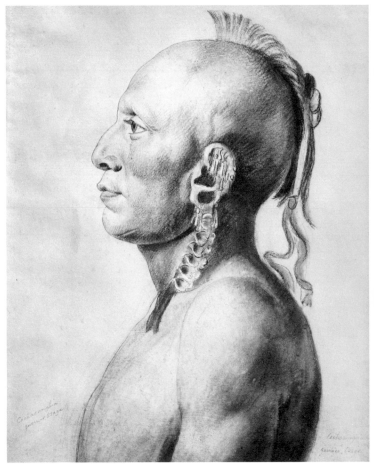

126 Portrait of an Osage Warrior
CHARLES-BALTHAZAR-JULIEN
FEVRET DE SAINT-MÉMIN
1770–1852
Crayon on pink paper c. 1807
53.4 x 38.7 (21¼ x 15¼)
Inscribed: Guerrier/Osage

127 Portrait of Cachasunghia, an Osage Warrior
Crayon on paper c. 1807
54 x 38.7 (21¼ x 15¼)
Inscribed: Cachasunghia/guerrier
Osage

In a secret message to Congress on January 18, 1803, Jefferson officially initiated the expedition of Meriwether Lewis and William Clark some months before the actual signing of the Louisiana Treaty. Jefferson had conceived of an overland expedition to the Pacific Ocean as early as 1783. He hoped to establish trading posts with the Indians and to determine a feasible trade route to the coast; in addition, he wanted to obtain a reliable record and collection of geographical, geological, and botanical data, and an account of the Indian tribes, their history, culture, and language.

Jefferson maintained a life-long interest in the Indians: "A people with whom, in the early part of my life, I was very familiar, and acquired impressions of attachment and commiseration for them which have never been obliterated." In the *Notes on*

the State of Virginia, he defended the Indian from the uninformed disparagement of the French naturalist, Buffon. He also noted, "It is . . . very much to be lamented, that we have suffered so many of the Indian tribes already to extinguish, without our having previously collected and deposited in the records of literature, the general rudiments at least of the languages they spoke." Jefferson began to record the vocabulary of as many different Indian tribes as was possible. In 1801 he wrote to William Dunbar that he had a "tolerably full" collection that included thirty tribal languages. These manuscripts were unfortunately destroyed while being shipped from Washington to Monticello. With this long-standing interest, Jefferson instructed Lewis to invite members of the various Indian tribes to send envoys to Washington. Delegations began arriving

almost continually, beginning in July 1804. Mrs. Margaret Bayard Smith described a group of Mandan, Osage, Delaware, and other Indians from the plains who arrived in Washington in December 1805: "Tall, erect, finely proportioned and majestic in their appearance, dignified, graceful and lofty in their demeanor, they seemed to be nature's own nobility."

In December 1806, Lewis himself returned with members of the Great Osage, Little Osage, and Mandan tribes. On Jefferson's order, Lewis, Clark, and several other members of the expedition kept extensive journals, and Lewis planned to have his published in three volumes by C. and A. Conrad of Philadelphia, the second volume to be entirely devoted to descriptions of the western Indians. While in Philadelphia in May 1807, Lewis recorded in his account book, "paid St. Mémin for like-

nesses of the indians &c necessary to my publication." It is not known if Saint-Mémin made the physiognotraces in Washington or Philadelphia as he and the Indians were in both cities in 1807, but the crayon portraits of the Osage warrior, Cachasunghia, and the chief of the Little Osages are probably among those drawings purchased by Lewis.

The watercolor, reduced from the sketch of the Little Osage chief, is one of five watercolors originally owned by Sir Augustus John Foster, secretary to the British minister in Washington from 1804 to 1807. Fascinated by the plains Indians, Foster wrote extensive notes on the various Indian delegations in Washington, and commissioned paintings from at least two artists. The five highly tinted watercolors, unique in Saint-Mémin's oeuvre, were intended to record the exact dress, ornament and clothing of

128 Portrait of a Chief of the Little Osages
Crayon on paper c. 1807
54 x 38.7 (21¼ x 15¼)
Inscribed: *Indien chef/des petits Osages*

129 Indian Chief of the Little Osages
Watercolor on paper c. 1807
19 x 16.2 (7½ x 6⅜)
Signed: *St. Mémin fecit*
Lent by the New-York Historical Society, New York

the Indians. Historically, these portraits are important, as the physiognotrace technique offered the first ethnological depiction of the American native and introduced a new degree of scientific exactitude in depictions of them.

Jefferson's wish that the Indians appear in their native dress in Washington was a direct indication of his concern for recording and preserving Indian culture. The entrance hall at Monticello he describes as "a kind of Indian Hall" with Indian statuary, weapons, implements, maps, and other paraphernalia arranged on the walls and tables. The crayon portrait of the Little Osage chief in his American military jacket shows how quickly Indian dress was relinquished for that of the white man. G.V.

130 Indian peace medal

ROBERT SCOTT active c. 1800
Silver
10.1 (4) diam.
Inscribed on obverse: TH. JEFFERSON
PRESIDENT OF U.S. A.D. 1801;
on reverse: PEACE AND FRIENDSHIP

*Lent by the National Museum of
History and Technology, Smithsonian
Institution*

It had been the custom for the British,
French and Spanish governments
to present medals bearing the monarch's portrait to friendly Indian chiefs.
The medals were used to establish
authority over the tribes and to sym-
bolize friendship between the Europeans and the Indians. After the
American Revolution, the United
States wished to emphasize that the
government now had legal right to
the territories between the Alleghenies
and the Mississippi and continued
the custom of issuing medals, although
under Washington and Adams none
of these showed the image of the
president. Three of them were designed by Trumbull and struck in
England by Boulton and Watt. Jefferson's peace medal was the first to
show the "Great Father" in the tradition of European monarchs. The
reverse shows the hands of an American officer and an Indian clasped
in friendship. A bracelet worn by the
Indian signifies his loyalty to the
United States government. The medals
were worn around the neck as can
be seen in some of Saint-Mémin's portraits of the Indians who visited
Washington in 1805–1806 and were
received by Jefferson (see nos. 126–
129). On that occasion Jefferson
explained that with the acquisition of
Louisiana, "we are now your fathers;
and you shall not lose by the change."
A Philadelphia newspaper correspondent noted that: "Some had the
likeness of Jefferson, engraved in
silver, I believe, hanging at their
breasts. . . ." Jefferson's interest in
Indians went back to the time when he
was a boy and met the Cherokee chief
"Ontassété" several times at his father's
house. In 1762, while at Williamsburg, the same chief visited the
town before traveling to England
to be received by George III. Many
years later, Jefferson remembered a
moving speech made by "Ontassété"
to his tribe: "His sounding voice,
distinct articulation, animated action,
and the solemn silence of his people
at their several fires, filled one with awe
and veneration, although I did not
understand a word he uttered." He
took his responsibilities toward the
Indians very seriously and on several
occasions made speeches to visiting
groups of chiefs. In one of these
he said:

> We are all now of one family, born
> in the same land, and bound to live
> as brothers, and the strangers from
> beyond the great water are gone from
> among us the great Spirit has given
> you strength, and has given us
> strength; not that we might hurt one
> another, but to do each other all
> the good in our power.

The Jefferson peace medals came
in three sizes: just over four inches,
three inches, and 2⅛ inches in
diameter. They were considered so
handsome that even after Madison became president they continued for
a time to be used. William Thornton,
the architect, who was asked to make
a drawing of Madison, considered
"The Figure of Mr. Jefferson on the
medal is like nothing human or
divine." R.W.

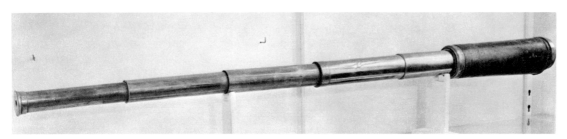

131 Telescope

CARY OF LONDON
Brass and wood with leather wrap
c. 1800
143.8 (56⅝) long

*Lent by the Missouri Historical Society,
St. Louis*

When the party of explorers led by
Lewis and Clark set off up the Missouri
River "under a jentle brease," they
carried in their baggage the Ship's
Master's Telescope. It belonged to
Meriwether Lewis, Jefferson's neighbor
and private secretary, who had been
asked by the president to organize the
expedition with William Clark in
the spring of 1803. Jefferson was concerned that the party be well equipped
and authorized Lewis to secure the
necessary navigation instruments, but
in Lewis' summary of accounts the
large telescope is not mentioned,
although a small pocket glass was purchased in Philadelphia. In all likelihood he had acquired it before em-
barking on preparations for "the dar-
ling project of my heart," as Lewis
called the expedition. W.H.A.

131a Moon Globe

JOHN RUSSELL 1745–1806

Lent by the Science Museum, London

Russell's moon globe was the most
accurate representation of the visible
side of the moon that had yet been
attempted. His careful observations
through a telescope were recorded in
many pencil sketches and used as a
basis for a large pastel map of the
moon in the Radcliffe Observatory,
Oxford. Two maps, known as the
Lunar Planispheres, were also engraved to show the full face of the
moon. Russell also advertised in 1796
a globe or Selenographia made up of
tapering gores, which had details
of the moon's surface engraved on
them. Although the price was a modest
five guineas, the public response was
disappointing and very few examples
were made. R.W.

32 Alexander von Humboldt

FRIEDRICH GEORG WEITSCH
1758–1828
Oil on canvas 1806
125 x 92 (49¾₆ x 36¾₆)
Inscribed lower center: ALEXANDER/
von HUMBOLDT

National-Galerie, Berlin

Alexander von Humboldt (1769–
1859) was one of the most distinguished scientists and most famous
men of his day. He had an interest in
a wide range of subjects including
zoology, geology, botany, and astronomy, but he was most celebrated
for his travels with Aimé Bonpland
between 1799 and 1804 in South and
Central America, territories, which,
until then, had hardly been scientifically explored or surveyed. It was on
his way back to Europe in May and
June 1804 that Humboldt visited the
United States, which he was particularly anxious to see, and met Jefferson, who had not long before sent off
the Lewis and Clark expedition to
the Pacific. In his letter to Jefferson,
announcing his arrival, Humboldt
wrote, "I feel it my pleasant duty to
present my respects and express my
high admiration for your writings, your
actions and the liberalism of your
ideas which have inspired me from my
earliest youth . . . I could not resist
the moral obligation to see the United
States and enjoy the consoling aspects of a people who understand the
precious gift of liberty." Even before
then the two men may have been in
touch, because a twenty-two-page
manuscript in Humboldt's handwriting, now among the Jefferson Papers,
is annotated by the president and
dated April 7, 1804, before Humboldt
even landed in the United States.
The subject was statistical information
on Mexico and Louisiana, one which
naturally greatly interested Jefferson
after his successful Louisiana Purchase
of 1803, especially as he would not
have been able to glean any information from the obstructive Spanish
government.

While staying in Philadelphia,
before going on to Washington, Humboldt was made a member of the
American Philosophical Society. Dr.
Benjamin Rush, the friend and correspondent of Jefferson, Benjamin
Smith Barton, the botanist, and others
took the savant in charge. Charles
Willson Peale showed Humboldt the
curiosities of his museum, including
the celebrated mastodon (see no. 104).
Jefferson's reply to Humboldt's letter
indicated how anxious he was to
meet the traveler. "The countries you
have visited are of those least known
and most interesting, and a lively
desire will be felt generally to receive

the information you will be able to
give. No one will feel it more strongly
than myself, because no one, perhaps, views this new world with more
partial hopes of its exhibiting an
ameliorated state of the human condition." When the two finally met,
Jefferson was able to take advantage
of Humboldt's first-hand knowledge of
Mexico, through political, economic
and geographic statistics together with

an invaluable collection of maps,
to gain more information about the
new southern neighbor of the United
States and establish the proper frontier between them. In the absence of
accurate surveys there were certain
to be disputes over boundaries. Jefferson must have found his visitor, who as
well as meeting the president in
Washington, also visited Monticello,
ready to talk on any subject. Ac-

cording to the president's secretary,
"Jefferson welcomed him with the
greatest cordiality and listened eagerly
to the treasure of information."
Albert Gallatin, who was later to be a
close friend of Humboldt's in Paris,
wrote about him, "He speaks twice as
fast as anyone I know, German,
French, Spanish, and English all
together, but I am really delighted, and
received more information of vari-

ous kinds in less than two hours than I had for two years past in all I read and heard." Humboldt was equally delighted with his impression of Jefferson and in his farewell letter before returning to France wrote of his "good fortune to see the first Magistrate of this great republic living with the simplicity of a philosopher. . . ." Both men had much in common in their boundless curiosity and polymathic approach to knowledge and their liberal politics; support for the French Revolution and detestation of slavery would have been further links.

There were plans for Humboldt to return to the United States and explore the Pacific coast as far as Alaska, continuing, as it were, the work of Lewis and Clark, but his researches and the publication of the monumental *Voyage de Humboldt et Bonpland* kept him in Europe. Humboldt corresponded with his American friends, and the first part of the *Essai politique sur le Royaume de la Nouvelle Espagne* arrived in 1808 and was duly acknowledged just as Jefferson was preparing to leave office and bury himself "in the groves of Monticello and become a mere spectator of the passing events." Later parts of the *Essai* were also sent to Jefferson, and Humboldt recalled his happy memories: "My thoughts dwell often in Monticello, and it is then that I picture the statesman, who established the welfare of an entire continent, among his magnolia trees. Tears come to my eyes when I imagine the most virtuous of men living in such happiness." In his book Humboldt was following Jefferson's idea of a geographic, economic and social survey of a region, the larger area of Mexico being substituted for Virginia. Humboldt had of course read *Notes on the State of Virginia*, and he refers to it in several complimentary remarks on Jefferson. He mentions that the slave trade would have been abolished long before had Jefferson, "a magistrate whose name is dear to all true friends of humanity," been permitted to do so. On the Lewis and Clark expedition, Humboldt explained that "this praiseworthy journey of Captain Lewis was carried out under the patronage of Mr. Jefferson who by this important service to science has added new reasons for the gratitude owed him by scholars of every nation." In return Jefferson sent Humboldt, at his request, a copy of the *Notes*, with a letter expressing diffidence that "they must appear chétif enough to the author of the great work on South America. But from the widow her mite was welcome. . . ."

In this painting, Humboldt has been depicted somewhere on the Orinoco about to put an alstroemeria into his specimen book for pressing. R.W.

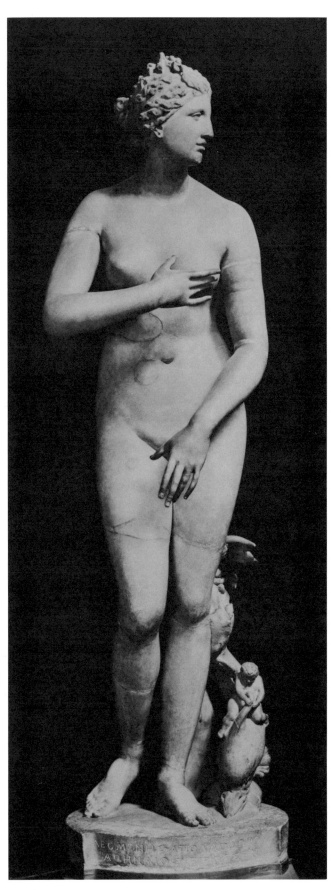

ANTIQUITY

133 The Medici Venus; Aphrodite Rising from the Sea

1st century B.C.–1st century A.D.
Large-grained Greek Island (?) marble
153 (60⅔) high
Signed on the front of the base by the Athenian copyist Kleomenes, son of Apollodoros, as maker: ΚΛΕΟΜΕΝΗΣ ΑπΟΛΛΟΔΩΡΟΥ ΑΘΗΝΑΙΟΣ ΕπΟΩΕΣΕΝ (authenticity of signature contested)
Lent by the Galleria degli Uffizi, Florence

About 1771, when Thomas Jefferson was twenty-eight years old, courting Martha Wayles Skelton and completing designs for the main house of his proposed Palladian villa at Monticello, he composed a list of desiderata for "Statues, Paintings &c" that would have made, had he acquired them, one of the first art galleries of *virtù* in the Western Hemisphere. Heading the list was the "Venus of Medicis. Florence," the best-known image of the goddess of love and of female beauty during his age. Like the rest of Jefferson's selections and their ordering, the choice shows that he was fully aware of the best aesthetic judgments of the cultured and influential English gentleman of taste, long before he arrived in Europe in 1784 as Minister Plenipotentiary to France.

Jefferson's very early humanistic studies in classical languages and literature were further cultivated and refined in the select company of his tutor William Small, his lawyer-mentor George Wythe, and Virginia's governor Francis Fauquier, when Jefferson was a student at William and Mary College and a young lawyer in Williamsburg. But his specific interest in the visual arts probably began in discussions with Dr. John Morgan (1735–1789) of Philadelphia and his circle, with whom Jefferson visited in 1766 (the year before commencing work on Monticello), preceded by recommendations as a "gentleman eminently worthy of your acquaintance." The accomplished physician, who became the founder of the Pennsylvania School of Medicine and who no doubt knew Governor James Hamilton and Captain Charles Cruikshank, both collectors of paintings and antiquities, had visited Scotland for additional medical training, and after that had undertaken a Grand Tour of the continent. There he met many persons of distinction in science, politics, and the arts, including not only such notables as Voltaire but the lesser-known Scottish *émigré* artist, art dealer, and sometime chaeologist-excavator, James Byers, is teacher and guide to the antiquities f Rome. Morgan, who formed a mall art collection and commissioned ppies of famous works, including artoons of Raphael, kept a journal ecording many of the notable sculp- ires and paintings he saw in the manner of Joseph Addison's and, espe- ially, Jonathan Richardson's travel ooks that accompanied touring inglish amateurs. These and other ooks on the *mirabilia* of Italy were lso known to Jefferson, and they were n his well-used library. It is ap- arently on the basis of their descrip- ons and illustrations, as well as rints and other sources, that he made is selections.

Many of the sculptures Jefferson sted were considered by his sources to e the major works of antiquity. And he Medici *Venus* was especially rominent among them. Daniel Webb raised her unsurpassed "beauty nd tenderness," ranking the work ven above the efforts of Raphael. In hatty dialogues where her copy served s a vehicle for long rhapsodic de- criptions of the virtues and seductive harms of the goddess, the antiquarian oseph Spence concluded that "there s nothing in marble equal to the Venus of Medicis for softness and enderness." And, for his part, Addison bserved that "the Softness of the 'lesh, the Delicacy of the Shape, Air, nd Posture, and the Correctness of Design in this Statue are inexplicable."

Of special interest is the account of Richardson:

... the Tribunal. It is octangular, about 25 or 30 foot diameter with windows at the top. . . . The figure fronting the door is the *Venus of Medicis*, of clear white marble . . .: When the sun shines on it, (for I have seen it at all hours of the day, and in all accidents of light) 'tis almost transparent. . . . it has too such a fleshy softness, one would think it would yield to the touch. It has such a beauty, and delicacy; such a lightness. . . . When I had spent above ten hours in this gallery con- sidering the beauty of the statues there [including the *Faun, Knife- Grinder,* and *Wrestlers* of the list; see Note, below] and perpetually found something new to admire 'twas yet impossible to keep my eyes off this [figure] three minutes whilst I was in the room.

Similarities are noteworthy between this description of the Tribune and the proposed plan for the Medici Venus and her companions from the villas and palaces of Florence and Rome, in Jefferson's "Parlour" at Monticello. That central hall—first planned as a solitary rectangular space, then backed by a gallery which was

subsequently incorporated into an enlarged quasi-octagonal room, later meant to be wholly faceted—was designed with two niches for sculptures facing the entry portico. The *Venus* was surely intended by Jefferson for that place, along with a pendant— initially a consort of male beauty, the *Apollo Belvedere,* whose cold and awesome narcissistic perfection was, after consideration, replaced by a more human and sustainedly com- patible example of heroic strength and moral virtue, the Farnese *Hercules* (see Note, below).

Descriptions of Martha Wayles Skelton, the young widow and recent mother whom Jefferson married on New Year's Day 1772, bear a striking resemblance to the youthful and experienced appearance of the Medici Venus. She was reportedly distin- guished for her beauty, was slight and exquisitely formed, had luxuriant hair, a glowing complexion, and large expressive eyes; she was also vivaci- ous, musically gifted, well read, in- telligent, and capable in many practical ways. Jefferson reportedly won her affections over various rivals and after their marriage took her to his solitary mountain, where work had already begun for a house, made after his own ideas and with classical imagination.

Whether the Medici *Venus* in- tended for Monticello was to be an antique version of the statue type, a modern marble copy, a cast, or some other sort of reproduction is not known. Many copies of this statue, and others on the list, were noted by Jefferson's several sources. The observa- tions of Addison are especially informative:

There are many ancient statues of the Venus de Medicis . . . the Her- cules Farnese, the Antinous, and other beautiful originals of the ancients, that are already drawn out of the Rubbish where they lay con- ceal'd for so many ages. I have observed more that are formed after the Venus of Medicis than any other, from whence I believe . . . it was the most celebrated statue among the ancients, as well as among the moderns.

The Venus of the *pudica* type, rep- resented in the Medici statue, had profoundly influenced the designs of Western artists ever since the late Middle Ages. By Jefferson's time, this, its best-known example, had been reproduced in a range of media and sizes. It had become a favorite pur- chase of eighteenth-century antiquarian collectors and amateurs for the art galleries of their palatial homes.

Unfortunately, no version of the Medici Venus statue was ever acquired for Monticello. Jefferson did, how- ever, later own a marble copy of

another famous ancient work described by his sources—the *Sleeping Ariadne* in the Vatican Museum, then popu- larly called a "Nymph" or the "Dying Cleopatra." In 1771 he had con- templated using such a figure in a grotto by a temple and brook in his garden. The scheme and the Latin inscription to accompany it were elements in a venerable classic-roman- tic idyll once realized at the country house of Alexander Pope, whose quatrain-translation Jefferson wished to use.

Like the Venus of Melos, which, since its discovery in the early nine- teenth century, has become a rival in fame, the Medici Venus is a Hel- lenistic-academic improvisation upon several well-known more ancient sculptural motifs. The nude's modest (*pudica*) pose, which ostensibly conceals but also identifies the source of her elemental powers, originates in fertility figures of the ancient Near East; these in turn descend from a Stone Age ancestry. The classical pose was the famous late-fourth-century invention, or revival, by Praxiteles of Athens in the *Bathing Aphrodite* at Knidos, whose beauties reportedly moved its owners to prodigal lust and attracted, for over half a millenium, a ceaseless pilgrimage of admirers to the eastern Greek island. In the Medici Venus, the melting, pulsating, impressionist rendering; the dainty qualities found especially in the head; and much else in the treatment follow directly upon, and amplify, the means of the great Athenian master of sensuality. The body pose is ap- parently still closer to the work of his followers, or a Skopasian rival, known from a more self-covering variant, *Aphrodite Surprised at Her Bath*, best represented by a fine copy in the Capitoline Museum. The youthful, very feminine proportions, the lifelike scale, and the coquettish demeanor of the Medici statue are innovations presenting a more provocative formula than either of its forerunners. The subject, the birth of Venus, is also new, but adds a measure of dignity in its very humanized interpretation. The original version of this Aphrodite has been variously attributed by archae- ologists to naturalistic interpreters from the end of the fourth to the late second century B.C. The Medici Venus was probably made in the same early Roman imperial school as the Louvre *Germanicus*, signed by the Athenian copyist Kleomenes, son of Kleomenes, and the better-known *Augustus Prima Porta*, which has a virtually identical support. Despite its variations from other copies of the same type, an extensively renovated surface, erroneously reset head, and somewhat stiffly restored arms (by

Ercole Ferrata, c. 1680), the Medici Venus is, if not the original com- position, clearly our finest replica. s.h.

NOTE: THOMAS JEFFERSON'S PROJECTED ART GALLERY FOR MONTICELLO
The following list of works intended for Monticello appears in a part of Jefferson's building notebook that has been dated about 1771. The modern identifications of the ancient sculp- tures, their present locations, the probable inspirations for their selec- tion in the library of Jefferson, and one or two recent comprehensive treat- ments are given in the annotations for the numbered entries. It is diffi- cult to assess the identity of item number 8 from Jefferson's known sources; the identities of numbers 4 and 10, though conjectural, seem as- sured; number 13 is probably the famous Renaissance statue group. The paintings whose titles (occasionally amplified) reappear in Jefferson's library notebook, with a list of art books and other paintings that he may have wished to acquired from Europe about 1782, were apparently derived from sources besides books. Addi- tions to the Monticello list, below, like the reference to Bellini, etc., made about 1782, show that the paintings, and perhaps the rest of the works, were probably intended to be copies and have decorative functions; the sculptural groups (11–13) apparently were meant to be duplicated in ceramic figurines. For reproductions of the lists and brief discussions of their date and contents, see Fiske Kim- ball's *Thomas Jefferson, Architect,* p. 136, fig. 79; and his "Jefferson and the Arts," pp. 241f.; and Berman, pp. 77, 96f.
[1] Venus of Medicis. Florence Apollo of Belvedere. Rome [struck] [line division]
[2] Hercules Farnese. Rome [joined to 1 with a bracket]
[3; interlineated] Apollo of Belvedere. Rome
[4] Antinous. Florence [sic] [joined to 3 with a bracket]
[line division]
[5] Dancing Faunus
[6] Messenger Pulling out a thorn
[7] Roman slave whetting his knife
[8] The gladiator at Montalto
[9] Myrmillo expiring. Rome
[10] The Gladiator reposing himself after the engagement. (companion to the former.)
di terra cotta. [written vertically before the next three entries]
[11] Hercules & Antaeus. see Cheselden's anatomy
[12] the two wrestlers
[13] the Rape of the Sabines (3 figures)
[wide space]

Venus de' Medici, *engraving from Perrier (see no. 161)*

[14] St Paul preaching at Athens.
[15] St Ignatius at prayer
[16] Jephtha meeting his dautr.
[17] Sacrifice of Iphigenia.
[18] History of Selencus giving his beloved wife Stra-/-tonice to his only son Selencus who languished/for her. Florence.
[19] Diana Venatrix [sic] (see Spence's Polymetis)
[later addition in another ink]
Bellini tells me that historical paintings on canvas 6.f. by 12 f. will cost £15 sterl. if cop.d by a good hand/
[line division]
Fresco painting of landscape or architecture/cost 4[?]½ the sq. foot.
[line division]
damask silk hangings cost 30/the sq. yard.
[page struck through with diagonal line]

1. Copy by Kleomenes of Athens of Hellenistic *Aphrodite Rising from the Sea*, Tribune, Uffizi, Florence.

2. Copy by Glykon of Athens after Lysippos, *Herakles Resting After His Labors*, National Museum, Naples. Addison, pp. 197, 202, 260; Perrier, pls. 2–4; Richardson, pp. 66, 127f., 130f., 156; Spence, pp. 83, 114f., pl. 16; Webb, p. 46; Johnson, pp. 196ff., 298, no. 51a; A. Reusch, *Guida illustrata del Museo nazionale di Napoli* (Naples, 1909), p. 90, no. 280.

3. Copy after Leochares (?), *Apollo Shooting His Bow* (?), Belvedere Court, Vatican Museum, Rome.

Addison, pp. 202, 260; Perrier, pls. 30–31; Richardson, pp. 126, 156, 275; Spence, pp. 83f. (in a rotunda), pl. 11; Webb, pp. 43, 54, 63, 159, 197. W. Helbig, *Führer durch die öffentlichen Sammlungen klassicher Altertümer in Rom* (Tubingen, 1963–), no. 226; W. Amelung, *Die Sculpturen des vaticanischen Museums* (Berlin, 1903–1908), 2:256, no. 92, pl. 12.

4. (?) Copy after Praxiteles(?), *Hermes Psychopompos* (of Andros type), Belvedere Court, Vatican Museum, Rome. Addison, pp. 197, 203; Perrier, pl. 53; Richardson, pp. 46 ("Bust . . . divine" in "Florence"), 55 ("Florence"), 126, 148, 149, 156, 164, 167, 280 ("Vatican"), 284. Helbig, no. 246; Amelung, 2:132, no. 53, pl. 12.

5. Copy of Hellenistic *Satyr Sounding a Kronpezion* (clapper), from "*Invitation to the Dance*" group, Tribune, Uffizi, Florence. Richardson, p. 57; Spence, p. 253, pl. 35, fig. 8. Mansuelli, no. 51.

6. Copy of Hellenistic *Boy Pulling Thorn from His Foot* ("*Spinario*"), Conservatory Museum, Rome. Perrier, pl. 42; Richardson, p. 115 ("Slave taking a thorn out of his Foot"). Helbig, no. 1448; H. S. Jones, *Sculptures of the Palazzo dei Conservatori* (Oxford, 1926), pp. 43ff., no. 2, pl. 60.

7. Copy of Pergamene(?) *Scythian Sharpening Knife*, from *Flaying of Marsyas* group, Tribune, Uffizi, Florence. Addison, p. 243, "Roman slave whetting knife"; Perrier, pl. 17 "Explorator . . . Hortis Mediceis"; Richardson, p. 57. Mansuelli, no. 55.

8. (?) (a) Copy by Agasias after a Hellenistic follower of Lysippos, *Fighting Warrior* ("*Borghese Gladiator*"), Louvre, Paris. Perrier, pls. 26–29; Richardson, pp. 156, 298. (b) An athletic figure from the Montalto-Negroni-Massimi collection (bought and dispersed by Thomas Jenkins in Rome during the late 18th C.). Cf., e.g., F. de Clarac, *Musée de sculpture antique et moderne . . .* (Paris, 1841–), nos. 2175c (Massimi *Athlete*), 2182 (Negroni *Boxer*), 2196 (Montalto copy of Naukides' *Practicing Discobolos*, illustrated in B. Cavaceppi, *Raccolta d'antiche statue . . .* [Rome, 1769], 2: pl. 42), or D. de Rossi and P. A. Maffei, *Raccolta di statue antiche e moderne . . .* (Rome, 1704), pl. 69 (Kleomenes' pastiche of a *Julio-Claudian Prince* and a 5th century B.C. *Hermes*; "Germanico . . . fù nella villa Montalto, oggi in Francia") and pl. 70 (Lyssipic *Hermes Binding His Sandal*; "Cincinnato . . . fù nella Villa Montalto"). (The rest of the statues on Jefferson's list appear in Rossi and Maffei's popular

picture book [Jefferson list no. 1: Rossi and Maffei pl. 27; 2: 49–50; 3: 2; 4: 3; 5: 35; 6: 23; 7: 41; 8: ?75–76, "Gladiatore . . . Borghesii"; 9: 65; 10: 66, "Marte"; 11: 43; 12: 29]; it was perhaps used by him [cf. further 13].) (c) Other.

9. Copy after Epigonos of Pergamon (?), *Dying Gaul Captain* ("*Dying Gladiator*"), Capitoline Museum, Rome. Perrier, pl. 91, "Mirmillo deficiens . . . Hortis Ludovisianis"; Richardson, p. 301, "Myrmillo dying . . . see print in Perrier"; Spence, p. 83. Helbig, no. 1436; H. S. Jones, *The Sculptures of the Museo Capitolino* (Oxford, 1912), p. 338, no. 1, pl. 85.

10. (?) Copy of Skopaic or Lysippic (?) *Resting Ares with Eros* ("*Ludovisi Ares*"), National Museum, Terme, Rome. Perrier, pl. 38, "Mars quiescens . . . Hortis Ludovisianis." Helbig, no. 2345.

11. Copy of Hellenistic *Wrestlers* ("*Herakles and Antaeus*"), Courtyard, Pitti Palace, Florence. Addison, pp. 178f., 236; W. Cheselden, *The Anatomy of the Human Body*, 5th ed. (London, 1740), p. 131, pl. 120, "after famous statue of Hercules and Antaeus muscles explained . . ."; Spence, pp. 121f., pl. 19, fig. 1, "Palazzo Pitti, Florence." H. Dütschke, *Antiken Bildwerke in Oberitalien* (Leipzig, 1878), 2:18, no. 37; P. B. Bober, *Drawings After the Antique by Amico Aspertini* (London, 1957), pp. 72f., fig. 93; H. H. Brummer, *The Statue Court in the Vatican Belvedere* (Stockholm, 1970), figs. 117ff.

12. Copy of Hellenistic *Wrestlers*, Tribune, Uffizi, Florence. Addison, p. 243; Perrier, pls. 35–36; Richardson, p. 57. Mansuelli, no. 61.

13. (?) Giovanni da Bologna, *Rape of the Sabines*, Loggia dei Lanzi, Florence. Rossi and Maffei, pp. 46f., pl. 47, ". . . Ratto delle Sabine. Opera di Gio Bologna. In Firenze . . ." J. Pope-Hennessey, *Italian High Renaissance and Baroque Sculpture* (London, 1963), 3:82f., pls. 85f. (erected 1583).

14. School of Raphael, cartoon of *St. Paul Preaching at Athens*, Victoria and Albert Museum, London. Jefferson 1782 list, "Paul Preaching at Athens, from a cartoon of Ra. Urbin" (cf. Bridenbaugh, p. 214, Morgan Raphael cartoons). J. Richardson, *An Essay on the Theory of Painting* (London, 1720), pp. 63, 96f., 126ff., 136; Webb, pp. 140, 188. J. Shearman, *Raphael's Cartoons . . .* (London, 1972), pp. 212 and passim, pls. I, 39–46.

15. Esteban Murillo(?), *St. Ignatius*, untraced. Probably a copy of the painting reportedly taken from a captured Spanish ship and in the collec-

tion of James Hamilton, former governor of Pennsylvania, at Bush Hill in the 1760s (cf. Bridenbaugh, pp. 213f.; thence Kimball, "Jefferson and the Arts," pp. 238f.). Jefferson 1782 list, "St Ignatius at Prayer by ." Not listed in the extensive catalogues of C. B. Curtis (*Velasquez and Murillo* [London, 1883], p. 241) or P. Lefert (*Murillo* [Paris, 1892], p. 88).

16. (?) Giuseppe(?) Zocchi, *Jephtha and His Daughter*(?), untraced. Jefferson 1782 list, "Jeptha meeting his daughter by Zocchi." (Reference to a painting by another artist reproduced by this eighteenth-century Florentine painter, etcher, and reproductive printmaker? See, further, lists of the subject in A. Pigler, *Barockthemen*, 2nd ed. [Budapest, 1974], 1:119ff.)

17. Jefferson 1782 list, "The sacrifice of Iphigenia." Reference to some version of (a) Timanthes, *Sacrifice of Iphigenia*, lost in antiquity; Webb, pp. 147, 160, 192; (b) a "vase with the sacrifice of Iphigenia . . . admiranda"; Richardson, *Statues . . . in Italy*, p. 126; or (c) another painting of the subject (cf. lists in Pigler, 2:324ff.).

18. Pietro Berrettini called da Cortona, *Seleucus and Stratonice*, fresco, Salon of Venus, Pitti Palace, Florence. Jefferson 1782 list, "Seleucus giving his wife Stratonice to his son." Known to Jefferson through a reproductive print? (Cf. *Stil und Überlieferung in der Kunst des Abendlandes; Akten des 21. Internationalen Kongresses für Kunstgeschichte in Bonn* [Berlin, 1967], 1: pl. 42, fig. 2.) G. Briganti, *Pietro da Cortona* (Florence, 1962), pp. 142f., 225ff., 322 (G. Zocchi reproduction, "Ceres"), fig. 206; N. Cipriani, *La galleria palatina nel palazzo Pitti a Firenze* (Florence, 1966), p. 98, fig. no. 114584.

19. (?) Gem of Diana as Huntress. Spence, p. 100, pl. 13, fig. 4, "Diana Venatrix [sic]: an Onyx; in Senator Buonaroti's collection, at Florence." (Cf. F. Buonaroti, *Osservazione istoriche sopra alcuni medaglioni antichi* [Rome, 1698] and, further, the copy after Leochares' [?] *Artemis and Stag* ["Versailles *Diana*"], Louvre, for the figure-type.) S.H.

a table in the center, *Clytie*. This last was a particular favorite of Towneley's which he called "his wife." During the Gordon Riots of 1780, when Towneley, as a Roman Catholic, had to leave his house in haste, he took the *Clytie* with him. On the top of the bookcase is the Towneley vase, which is shown in the exhibition at number 135. The *Discobolos* was added to the painting sometime after 1791, as it was only discovered in that year. The other sculpture had been acquired mainly while Towneley was living in Italy, including four years at Rome. This period, 1765–1772, was one of considerable archaeological activity, and there was great competition between Italian and visiting collectors, mainly English, for newly excavated works of art, as well as for those being sold from existing collections.

Towneley is seated on the right, Pierre François Hugues, known as d'Hancarville, is sitting at the table and behind him are Charles Greville and Thomas Astle. D'Hancarville was a well-known antiquary and catalogued the Towneley collection and Sir William Hamilton's collection of vases, *Antiquités étrusques, grecques et romaines*. Jefferson knew him and they both were at the Pavillon de St. Denis to say goodbye to the Cosways when Maria and her husband left Paris. Greville is perhaps known best for sending his cast-off mistress, Emma Lyon, to his uncle, the British envoy at Naples, and so launching the career of Lady Hamilton. Astle was an antiquary and collector. The dog at Towneley's feet had been brought back from Kamchatka in 1780 at the end of Cook's last voyage.

Towneley was famous for his dinner parties, to which many celebrities in the art world came, and it was at his house that Maria Hadfield was introduced to London society by Angelica Kauffmann and met her future husband Richard Cosway (see nos. 340, 341, and 343). Towneley gave away the bride at the Cosways' wedding in 1781, five years before Jefferson met her in Paris. R.W.

134 Charles Towneley in His Gallery

JOHANN ZOFFANY 1734/5–1810
Oil on canvas 1782
127 x 99.06 (50 x 39¼)
Lent by the Burnley Borough Council, Towneley Hall Art Gallery and Museum, England

Charles Towneley (1737–1805) came from a Roman Catholic and Jacobite family and was thereby prevented from taking part in English political life. His collection of classical sculpture was thus a substitute activity and, until the arrival of the Elgin Marbles, was considered the finest in England. Subsequently the government bought the Towneley marbles for £20,000 and presented them to the British Museum.

The painting shows the upstairs library in 7 Park Street, now Queen's Gate, Westminster, with an assemblage of the best of the Towneley collection put in at the wish of the owner. These include the *Venus* found at Ostia, particularly admired by Canova; the *Discobolos* and *A Faun and Nymph*; a statue of *Diana* crouching; a bust of *Homer* excavated at Baiae; statues of a *Youth Silenus* and *Cupid*; busts of *Marcus Aurelius*, *Lucius Verus* and prominently on

135 The Towneley vase

Parian (?) marble 1st century A.D.
93 (36⅜) high, 56 (117) diam.
Lent by the British Museum

The Towneley vase, discovered in
Italy in 1773–1774, found its way
almost immediately to the London
residence of the noted British collector
Charles Towneley, whose portrait
in his gallery by Zoffany is exhibited at
number 134. The stately original
setting was described by the painter
and biographer J.T. Smith:

The dining-parlour looking over
St. James's Park was a room in which
Mr. Towneley has entertained personages of the highest rank in this
kingdom, as well as visitors from all
nations who were eminent for the
brilliancy of their wit or their literary
acquirements; and it contained the
greater part of his statues . . . and one
of the most beautiful vases, perhaps,
in the world: it is embellished with
Bacchanalian figures, and was
brought from the Villa of Antoninus,
where other treasures of art have
been discovered.

The Dionysian orgy depicted around
the vase starts with the goat-legged
Pan clutching a large ritual amphora of
wine and explosively saluting his
master. Beneath his arm, a young and
an old satyr, one dressed and one nude,
embrace and drunkenly reel toward
their god Dionysus. The frenzied procession continues with two dancing
nymphs, or maenads, wearing thin
chitons that slip and lift; one wields a
knife as her partner swings the
severed hindquarter of a kid. They
whirl deliriously around another old
satyr loosely covered by a panther
cloak, with a live beast crouched behind him. He too wildly addresses

and dedicates himself to the wine god.
The diety, mover of libidinous life
forces and rebirth, lets down his torch,
setting the mystery rites in darkness,
and turns his attention to a diaphan-
ously dressed consort, the fertile
priestess Ariadne, who partly supports
him while yielding to his indolence.
The satyr and maenad, who move
away from the royal couple and now
face only each other, are modern
reconstructions except for their lower
extremities. Eight heraldically set
winged and marinelike female creatures
in the decorative frieze below rhyth-
mically face or turn from each other,
holding and sharing libation dishes,
or *phialae*.

From the mid-eighteenth century,
a veritable industry dedicated to the
discovery, repair, manufacture, sale and
advertising of antique decorative
objects had been flourishing in the art
market of Rome. The well-known
antiquities galleries of G.B. Piranesi,
Gavin Hamilton, Thomas Jenkins,
Bartolomeo Cavaceppi, and their con-
freres in Rome were in large part
dedicated to these minor arts. Gavin
Hamilton's letter to Towneley concerning his discovery of the piece tells
something more of its story and
importance:

The vase which I found much broke
[at an imperial villa near Rome]
is restored with great attention, as
the work deserves, being I think in
point of general form and taste of
Sculptor inferior to none extant.

Specialists first renovated, then came
to fabricate, ornamental antiquities
for visiting amateur collectors on tour
and for entrepreneurs like the Adam
brothers, who used them as necessary appointments for the chaste new
antico living spaces which represented
a reaction against the ebullient
rococo decor associated with the dis-
solute French aristocracy. These
ancient works, and soon after, the less
costly and mass-produced translations
from the ceramic factories of Wedgewood, helped to disseminate a
vocabulary for the new classical style.
The licentious mysticism of the
Towneley vase bacchanal may not have
been to the taste of Jefferson; a
more sober decorative classical frieze
of muses from the Wedgewood
works at Etruria ornamented his
dining room fireplace at Monticello.
Versions of sundry decorative classical
reliefs ornament other mantels and
architectural details in Jefferson's villa.
The vase was bequeathed by
Towneley to the British Museum,
where it was prominently displayed
and there apparently seen by Keats
where it helped to inspire various bacchanalian lines in his *Ode to a
Grecian Urn*, which seems also to allude to other classical pieces. The
credo

he memorably expressed in his axiom

'Beauty is truth, truth beauty'—
that is all
Ye know on earth,
and all ye need to know

was supported by a classical imagery
then thoroughly permeating the art
and ethos of contemporary society.

The Towneley vase figures are related to a class of ancient sculptures of
the so-called Neo-Attic school, whose
academic, eclectic, and archaizing
reassessments of masterpieces in the
manner of the Athenian-Periclean
Golden Age flourished through Greco-
Roman times. That ancient neoclassic movement complemented
modern classical revivals and influenced them through many surviving
works. The Towneley vase sculptures
show strong elements of a late baroque antique style that perhaps belongs to a Pergamene tradition prefigur-
ing the more austere, commercial and
decorative mode found in developed
Neo-Atticism, which emerged at
the very end of the Hellenistic Age.
The famous Borghese vase, now in the
Louvre, has a similar bacchanal, of
still more traditional baroque form.
The bronze sepulchral volute crater
found at Dherveni, Yugoslavia, perhaps
from the late fourth century B.C.,
is another Dionysian vessel related in
subject, execution and shape to the
Towneley vase, as are their many forerunners in Athenian ceramics of
the classical age—the so-called
Etruscan painted vases that were also
very popular in Jefferson's time. S.H.

136 The Antique School at Old Somerset House

EDWARD FRANCIS BURNEY
1760–1848
Pen and colored wash 1779
33.6 x 48.9 (13¼ x 19⅝)
Signed middle foreground on sketching
pad: *E.F.B. 1779*. Inscribed on the
verso: *View of the Plaister Room
in the Royal Academy old Somerset
House* with a numbered key identifying
the casts

*Lent by the Royal Academy of Arts,
London*

The scene is the plaster cast room
at the Royal Academy in old Somerset
House, which was replaced by Chambers' imposing new Somerset Room,
begun in 1776 (see no. 356). The
Royal Academy had been given rooms
in Somerset House in 1771 by
George III, three years after its founding. Among the casts of antique
sculpture can be seen *Apollo Belvedere*, *Laocoön*, the *Dying Gaul*,
Antinous, *Meleager* and other pieces
of classical and sixteenth-century
sculpture admired at that time. On the
wall to the right of the door is Leonardo's cartoon of *The Virgin and
Saint Anne with the Infant Christ and
Saint John* now in the National Gallery, London.
Drawing from antique sculpture,
usually in the form of casts because of
the dearth of originals outside Italy,
was an essential part of the training
of an art student until the twentieth
century. Academic theory believed that
by concentrating on and imitating
the most esteemed works of ancient
art, the student would come to have an
ideal of perfection fixed in his mind
and follow it throughout his career.
Unfortunately, little was known
of original Greek sculpture until the
late eighteenth century, when, with
the recovery of genuine pieces from excavations in Italy and Greece, it became obvious that many previously
admired classical marbles were Roman
copies.
For the connoisseur who had
never visited Italy or who could not
buy a piece of original sculpture,
plaster copies were perfectly acceptable
as decoration in entrance halls,
libraries and dining rooms, just as
copies of old master paintings hung on
the walls. About 1771, before he
ever went to Europe, Jefferson made a
list of the pieces of antique sculpture
he would have liked for Monticello. These included some of the most
celebrated pieces of the day: the
Apollo Belvedere, the *Venus
de'Medici*, the *Farnese Hercules*, the
Spinario and *Antinous*. They would,
of course, have been casts or possibly marble copies made in Rome by

a young sculptor glad to earn some extra money. It is most unlikely that Jefferson ever saw any copies, much less originals, of classical sculpture before he went to France, and his knowledge would have been derived from books and engravings, notably Perrier's *Segmenta nobilium signorum e statuaru* (1638–1653), Addison's *Remarks on Several Parts of Italy* (1705) and Richardson's *Account of Paintings, Statues, etc. in Italy* (1722). The first two were in Jefferson's library, and the last he must have known because he included it in a list of desiderata. It may seem surprising that there were no copies of antique sculpture in the large quantity of furnishings Jefferson brought back to Monticello, although he had had several paintings copied. It may be that his close contact with Houdon made him change his mind and decide to have busts of modern heroes instead of antique figures. There was, however, a copy of the famous *Ariadne* from the Vatican in the entrance hall, and this has returned to its original position at Monticello. R.W.

137 Design for the Ruin Room at Santa Trinità dei Monti

CHARLES-LOUIS CLÉRISSEAU
1721–1820
Body color, pen, ink and black chalk on cream paper c. 1765
36.5 x 53.3 (14⅜ x 21)
Inscribed on verso: *Chambre Executé par la Sieur [?] Clérisseau aux Minimes dans l infermerie à la Trinité [obscured] à Rome*

Lent by the Fitzwilliam Museum, Cambridge

This design for a room in ruins was executed shortly after it was designed and still exists (without its original furnishings) in the Convent of Santa Trinità dei Monti. It is one of the most remarkable expressions of the eighteenth century's fascination with classical antiquity. Commissioned by the mathematician Père Le Seur and his associate Père Jacquier, probably upon the recommendation of Johann Winckelmann who wrote about it in a letter of 1767, it was later described by Clérisseau's son-in-law in his biography of Piranesi:

On entering one imagines that one

was seeing the cella of a temple, enriched with antique fragments that had survived the ravages of time; the vault and several parts of the wall, crumbling in places and held up by rotting timbers, allowed daylight to enter and seemed to open a way for the sun's rays. These effects carried out with such knowledge and truthfulness produced a complete illusion. To enhance this effect further, all the furniture was in keeping: the bed was a richly decorated basin, the fireplace a combination of various fragments, the desk a damaged antique sarcophagus, the table and chairs, a fragment of a cornice and inverted capitals respectively. Even the dog, the faithful guardian of this style of furniture, was housed in the remains of an arched niche.

Another version of the Fitzwilliam drawing, together with a view of the other end of the room, is in the Hermitage Museum and includes a description of the project. The actual room was executed in bright flat colors like so many of Clérisseau's gouache pictures, with blues and soft green and various shades of brown for the stonework (see no. 138). Clérisseau, trained as an architect in France and at the French Academy in Rome, was greatly influenced by his teacher Panini in his general conception of ruins, but the more dramatic quality of his vision of antiquity comes from his friend Piranesi, who greatly admired this room and intended to engrave it. The idea of a room in ruins goes back to at least the sixteenth century, and Clérisseau's was to inspire several other ones of the later eighteenth century.

While Jefferson never saw Clérisseau's room it would have appealed to him, for in his travel advice to John Rutledge, Jr., and Thomas Shippen, written shortly after his journey to the Rhineland, he describes the castle at Heidelberg as "the most imposing ruin of modern ages. It's situation is the most romantic and delightful possible. I should have been glad to have passed days at it." Perhaps influenced by his memory of the château, Jefferson later planned to erect a Gothic ruin on the grounds of Monticello, though this was never carried out. T.J.McC.

138 The Triumphal Arch and Tomb of the Julii at St. Rémy

CHARLES-LOUIS CLÉRISSEAU
1721–1820
Gouache on paper 1769
42.5 x 59 (16¾ x 23¼)
Signed lower right: *Arc de Triomphe à St. Rémy en Provence Clérisseau 1769*
Lent by the Victoria and Albert Museum

After spending nearly twenty years in Italy studying and drawing the ancient monuments as well as instructing such men as Robert and James Adam, Clérisseau left the archaeological circle of Winckelmann and his friends to return in 1767 to his native France and, as he told Winckelmann, to undertake a study of the Roman remains in southern France. While only the first volume of the projected study, *Monumens de Nismes*, was published (see no. 158), Clérisseau made countless drawings of the other Roman monuments in France, but very few have survived. The finest of these is this drawing actually dated two years later but undoubtedly based on a drawing done on the spot. (A second signed but undated version is in the collection of J.B. Knapp-Fisher, London.) It is clearly related to the drawings of the arch, which he mentioned in a letter to Winckelmann. Despite Clérisseau's

training as an architect and his archaeological concern, it is interesting to note how he has moved the two monuments together to form a better composition or, as he wrote in another context, "to show each in its most picturesque position." Drawings such as this one continued to provide a major source of income for Clérisseau and to help spread the interest in Roman antiquity. Jefferson's "Notes of a Tour into the Southern Parts of France" mention that he was in St. Rémy on March 24, 1787; he undoubtedly saw the arch and tomb. In his travel advice to John Rutledge, Jr., and Thomas Shippen, written the following year, he notes "St. Remis. Some fine ruins about ¾ of a mile from this place." Jefferson's own copy of *Monumens de Nismes* was bought from Clérisseau himself for seventy-two francs. T.J.McC.

139 Vue A. de quelques unes des Colonnes . . .

GIOVANNI BATTISTA PIRANESI
1720–1778
Etching 1778
50.5 x 69 (19⅞ x 27³⁄₁₆)
National Gallery of Art. Ailsa Mellon Bruce Fund

140 Autre Vue intérieure des restes du College . . .

GIOVANNI BATTISTA PIRANESI
1720–1778
Etching 1778
48 x 68.2 (18¹⁵⁄₁₆ x 26⅞)
National Gallery of Art. Ailsa Mellon Bruce Fund

Striking evidence of the increasing interest in antiquities through the eighteenth century was the sumptuous, illustrated publication of works describing classical architecture. Besides the volumes on Rome, Jefferson owned or wanted a selection of works on Athens, Palmyra, Baalbec, Spalatro, Pompeii, and two works each on Nîmes, Herculaneum, and Greece in general. Perhaps even more exciting than ruins that were already to some extent known was the discovery of Paestum. Paestum struck the imagination not only because of its beautiful temples, but also because, until 1746, it had lain completely unknown, so close to the midst of the furious search for antiquities, no more than sixty miles from Naples. Thus, after their first publication in 1764, the Doric ruins at Paestum were in the next two decades the subject of twice as many major publications as all the ruins of Greece and Sicily combined.

The first serious drawings and engravings of the Paestum temples were sponsored by the Neapolitan antiquary, Conte Gazola; and all but one of the early illustrated publications on Paestum, including the work by Thomas Major which Jefferson owned, go back to that common source. Piranesi's series of twenty large views is the only independent work of the period, the only group clearly made from new on-the-spot drawings by the artist. With his eye for the grandeur of ancient ruins, Piranesi gave these temples a strength and vigor that made other architects' drawings seem dry and schematic. He considered the buildings at Paestum the final demonstration of his lifelong thesis of ancient Italian superiority in architecture:

Les Voyageurs connoisseurs assurent, que par rapport à l'Architecture Grecque des Temples bâtis dans l'Ordre Dorique, ceux de Pesto sont supérieurs en beauté à ceux, qu'on voit en Sicilie et dans la Grèce, et que sans se donner la peine, et la fatigue de longs voyages, ceux ci peuvent suffire pour contenter la curiosité, et qu'enfin cette grande, et majestueuse Architecture donné en son genre l'idée la plus parfait de ce bel Art.

Piranesi completed the Paestum series during the last months of his life, apparently with considerable help from his son Francesco, particularly in the addition of the too large and coarse figures to the noble architecture. It is not even certain that the Paestum series was completely finished and published before Piranesi's death in November 1778, though a contemporary portrait of him holding a dated proof of the title page should be some evidence in support of the traditional assignment of that year for its issue. In any case, the two impressions of plates III and IX here exhibited, as very rare proofs before letters were added, are as close to Piranesi's own hand as the series can ever come. A.R.

Galleria grande di Statue, la cui struttura è con Archi e col lume preso dall' alto. Ella resta nel mezzo di due ampli Cortili, e ad essa si ascende per mezzo di magnifiche Scale. Vi sono Statue, Bassi-rilievi antichi, Iscrizioni, Sepolcri ed altri ornamenti.

141 Galleria grande di Statue

GIOVANNI BATTISTA PIRANESI
1720–1778
Etching 1743
35.6 x 24.9 (14¼/₁₆ x 9¹³/₁₆)
Signed lower left: *Gio. Batta. Piranesi Arch⁰ inv. ed incise in Roma*

Lent anonymously

Designs in unusual perspective were a typically baroque addition to the architectural draftsman's printed repertoire. In the eighteenth century such designs received a new prominence and elegance with publication by the Bibiena family of their extraordinary theatrical sets and decorations. Although Piranesi's first published work, the *Prima Parte di Architetture e Prospettive*, echoes Giuseppe Galli Bibiena's publication three years earlier in its size, its contents, its imaginary compositions, and even its title, Piranesi's designs

nevertheless distinguish themselves by a greater interest in true motifs from classical Roman architecture, set into a cleaner and more monumental frame than the theatrical hodge-podge of Bibiena's work. Thus, Piranesi combines the older baroque tradition of theatrical imagination and magnificence with the newly developing movement toward more accurate, though still imaginative, combinations of ancient Roman motifs in buildings and interior decoration. Piranesi's later works were of great influence on the English and French styles which Jefferson directly experienced in his journeys and reading. Piranesi's use in the *Prima Parte* of ancient Roman motifs within crisper forms would have pleased Jefferson, and Piranesi's style of drawing in this first series—smooth, linear, careful, and balanced—is closer to Jefferson's own clean precision than any of the styles Piranesi

later developed.

The *Prima Parte* was first published between 1743 and 1745, evidenced by six presently known copies, with continual variations, in what thus appears to have been an "umbrella" edition covering Piranesi's various changes in the content of the book. The copy here exhibited shows the series in its finished state, as finally completed and issued in an edition of 1750–1751. It is opened to plate 1, one of the most completely decorated designs in the more "Palladian" of Piranesi's two styles in the volume. Combining and enlarging Roman motifs to form his own view of magnificence, Piranesi provides any Croesus able to afford it with the ultimate hall in which to display those antique statues and inscriptions whose rediscovery was then the rage in Rome. A.R.

142 Varie vedute di Roma antica e moderna

GIOVANNI BATTISTA PIRANESI
1720–1778, et alii
Bound volume of 93 etchings by
various artists, including 47 signed by
Piranesi

*Lent by the University of Virginia,
Alderman Library, Charlottesville*

To determine precisely which works
by Piranesi Thomas Jefferson may
have possessed, or even which works he
may have seen, is extremely difficult.
The disparate and conflicting evidence
consists of items in several catalogue
lists of books, two bills, and two
letters. The only reference in his own
manuscript catalogue of his library,
written 1783–1814, reads: "*Piranesi.
Varie vedute di Roma antica e moderna. fol.*" This reference to the large
size "folio" may be supplemented
with the notation by Jefferson's binder
on his bill that the volume was
"very difficult" to bind. As Jefferson's
title exactly matches the series here
on exhibition, and no other series of
plates by Piranesi, one might hope
for an immediate conclusion; but, unfortunately, it is just as clear that
this series on exhibition is not by any
means folio in size. On the other
hand, Piranesi certainly did etch true
folio size views of Rome, those views

by which he has always been best
known; but the true folio views bear a
very different title from the one
above (*Vedute di Roma disegnate ed
incise da Giambattista Piranesi
Architetto Veneziano*). Besides a virtual repeat of Jefferson's manuscript
catalogue entry in the 1815 printed
catalogue by the Library of Congress,
to whom Jefferson sold his Piranesi
book, very similar contradictory
evidence about Jefferson's copy occurs
in the dealer's original 1805 bill for
it ("*Piranesi, Varie vedute di Roma,
fol.* $13.80") and in Jefferson's 1825
list of books he wanted for the University of Virginia library ("*Vedute
di Roma antica et moderna del
Piranesi . . . f [folio]*").
   Barely in the nick of time, the
answer to our conundrum appeared
only twelve years before the disastrous fire in the capitol destroyed
most of Jefferson's former library,
including his Piranesi. That is, in the
Library of Congress printed catalogue
dated December 1839, which must
have been based on a closer look at the
books themselves, the Jefferson copy
of Piranesi continues to bear precisely the same title Jefferson originally
gave it, but now it is for the first
time dated "1748" and its size is
changed to "4to." The series here on

view is clearly quarto in size; and,
in fact, at least one of its editions is
dated 1748, whereas the early editions
of Piranesi's true folio plates of
Vedute di Roma never bore any date
at all. Thus, we can now feel assured in resolving the earlier conflicting evidence which has stumped
previous authors: what Jefferson knew,
wanted for Virginia, himself possessed and sold to Congress—but
overestimated in size—was indeed this
early series of small views by G. B.
Piranesi, J. L. LeGeay, F. P. Duflos,
P. Anesi, and J. C. Bellicard, an
example of which is on exhibit here.
While these very early works by
Piranesi, his first true views of existent
ruins and modern buildings, show
little of the power and finesse for
which he is justly famous, they still
exemplify an experimental and interesting range from miniature charm to
strident line, from sophisticated compositions to grossly unbalanced ones,
and from successful technique to
unfortunate botch.
   What other works by Giovanni
Battista Piranesi Jefferson may have
known, even if not possessed, is left to
our speculation. Given his acquaintances in London and Paris and his
interests, it seems likely he may have
known quite a few. The only problem

with that speculation is that it leaves
one wondering why—if he knew
them—Jefferson did not acquire or
try to acquire some of Piranesi's more
typical and more mature works.
There are indeed two enthusiastic
letters quoted by Millicent Sowerby,
used by her and others to demonstrate
Jefferson's knowledge and desire.
In both January and March 1791, he
insistently urged his book dealer to
"pray get me by some means or other
a compleat set of Piranesi's drawings of the Pantheon, & especially the
correct design for it's restoration."
Unfortunately, however, so far as we
know, Giovanni Battista Piranesi
never published such a series of designs
of the Pantheon, although Piranesi's
son Francesco certainly did, i.e., in
his *Seconda Parte de'Tempj Antichi
che contiene il celebre Panteon*
(Rome, August 1, 1790). So, Jefferson's letters of desire for "Piranesis"
must refer not to Giovanni Battista
Piranesi but to Francesco Piranesi,
leaving us surprised at his remarkably
quick knowledge of the latter's
publication, and still without hard
evidence of what he may have known
or cared about the former's greatest
works! A.R.

143 Elevation of the reconstructed temple at Palestrina

GEORGE HADFIELD 1763–1826
Pen with sepia and blue washes 1791
102.8 x 392.4 (40½ x 115)
Initialed: *JPB*

*Lent by the Royal Institute of
British Architects, London*

Inspired by his study of ancient classical architecture at the Royal
Academy, George Hadfield returned

in 1790 to Italy, where he had been
born twenty-seven years earlier. He
had moved to London in 1778 with his
talented sister, Maria Cosway, friend
and correspondent of Thomas
Jefferson.
   Hadfield began his studies of
architecture in 1781 and in 1784
received the Royal Academy's gold
medal. Following his apprenticeship in
the office of James Wyatt, he received

the first Traveling Scholarship of
the Academy in 1790 to study in
Rome.
   The year after his arrival, he explored the ancient city of Palestrina
in Latium, where the ruins of the
Roman temple of Fortune (112–70
B.C.) can still be seen.
   The temple fascinated the architects
and artists of the Renaissance. Palladio made studies of it, and later en-

gravings were published by Joseph
Marie Suarès in *Praenestes Antiquae*
(Rome, 1655). John Soane published an elevation of the reconstructed
temple, based on the Suarès plate,
in his *Lectures*, but apparently never
visited the site himself.
   In a series of drawings now in the
collection of the Royal Institute of
British Architects, Hadfield explored
in considerable detail the surviving

fragments of the temple complex, which had been built originally on a series of terraces. On the uppermost platform of the reconstruction, Hadfield shows a small circular temple, which is echoed later in his Van Ness Mausoleum in Oak Hill Cemetery, Washington, D.C.

The drawings of Palestrina were exhibited at the Royal Academy on Hadfield's return to London in 1794 and attracted considerable attention, leading to his invitation to come to the United States. Shortly after the exhibition, John Trumbull, who had met Hadfield's sister with Jefferson in Paris, forwarded his name to the commissioners of Washington recommending Hadfield for the post of superintendent of the capitol, then rising on Jenkins Hill above Tiber Creek. W.H.A.

144 The Remains of the Roof of one of the Arches of the Temple on the 7th Platform

GEORGE HADFIELD 1763–1826
Pen and sepia 1791
54.6 x 81.9 (21½ x 32¼)
Initialed: *JBP*
Lent by the Royal Institute of British Architects, London

Located twenty-four miles to the east of Rome, the ancient city of Palestrina was the site of the Roman temple of Fortuna built by Sulla between 112 and 70 B.C. The Colonna family and later the Barberini family ruled from the Renaissance palaces built on antique foundations. Hadfield, who was assisted in his recording of the ruins by a member of the Colonna family, included views of these buildings in the series of drawings made during his visit to Italy in 1791, after winning the gold medal of the Royal Academy in 1784. His chief interest was in the classical remains of the impressive temple, which with its related buildings rose on a series of terraces nearly three hundred feet to the sanctuary. The arcades enclosing the ascending ramp were vaulted, and it is apparently a fragment of the vault just below the sanctuary of Fortuna that Hadfield recorded here.

Fortuna, however, did not bestow her favors on the young architect's career in the years to follow in Washington. He succeeded Stephen Hallet as supervisor of the building of the capitol, but eventually, like Hallet, was removed because of friction with Dr. William Thornton and the other commissioners. He designed several other public buildings for the new city, including the treasury department (see no. 460) which was burned by the British in 1814, and the city hall (see no. 451). He never attained the reputation that his early abilities had seemed to promise, however, and near the end of his life was forced to pawn the Royal Academy's gold medal, which was later redeemed and returned to Hadfield by his friend Benjamin Latrobe. W.H.A.

145 Further Remains of the Interior of the Temple now converted into a Store House

GEORGE HADFIELD 1763–1826
Pen and sepia washes 1791
55.9 x 84.4 (22 x 33¼)
Initialed: *JBP*

Lent by the Royal Institute of British Architects, London

This drawing from the series of studies of Palestrina is identified by the letter G and is included in the copy of the original list of the drawings which is a part of "Notes on Some Drawings in Illustration of Praneste (Palestrina) Ancient and Modern," a paper prepared by John W. Papworth and presented in 1848 at a meeting of the Royal Institute of British Architects, where the drawings were exhibited. Of those architects who were to contribute to the introduction of the classic revival style in America, only Hadfield and Jefferson had made any serious study of surviving ancient buildings on the site, rather than relying on published sources. W.H.A.

146 The Interior of one of the Square Temples on the 3rd Platform now converted into a cellar

GEORGE HADFIELD 1763–1826
Pen and sepia wash 1791
60.3 x 68.6 (23¾ x 27)

Lent by the Royal Institute of British Architects, London

147 The Triumphal Arch and the Amphitheater in the City of Orange

HUBERT ROBERT 1733–1808
Oil on canvas
242 x 242 (102½ x 102½)
Signed and dated at lower left:
H. Robert 1787

Lent by the Musée du Louvre

This painting is part of a series of four devoted to the classical monuments in Languedoc, commissioned from the artist by d'Angiviller, surintendant général des Bâtiments du Roi, in 1786 for a room in the Château de Fontainebleau. For some unknown reason, this painting and another, *The Maison Carrée, the Arenas and the Magne Tower at Nîmes* exhibited at number 150, stayed in the artist's studio after being exhibited in the Salon of 1787, and did not become a part of the Louvre's collection until the death of the painter's wife in 1822. According to an account written by Robert, he was paid 12,000 livres

for the four paintings.

The choice of subjects is characteristic of the encyclopedic minds of the period and of the men who had a passion for travel and whose interests were stimulated by each new publication. Already under Louis XIV, Colbert had decided to publish representations of the Roman monuments in Provence, but it was not until the time of the antiquarians Caylus and Mariette that this project was realized. During this period a series of large illustrated publications appeared, written by a group of intellectuals interested in restoring ancient monuments. Without attempting to be complete, several French titles can be cited: as early as 1760, the engravings of the *Ports de France* of Joseph Vernet by Cochin fils and Lebas; *Le Voyage pittoresque de Suisse* by Jean Benjamin Delaborde (1777); *Le voyage pittoresque de la France* also by Delaborde (four

volumes published in twelve *prévus*); *Le Voyage d'Italie* or *Voyage pittoresque des royaumes de Naples et de Sicile* by the abbé de Saint-Non (1778–1786); *Le Voyage pittoresque de Grèce* by the comte de Choiseul-Gouffier (1778); and *Les Antiquités de Nismes* by Clérisseau (1778). This movement has its parallel in painting with the series of the *Ports de France* (1754–1765) by Joseph Vernet, as well as the works of Demachy and Clérisseau. In 1772 Natoire, the painter's brother, suggested to Marigny the idea of having painted for the king all the monuments of Provence, as a pendant to the port scenes by Vernet. Concurrently, Clérisseau was commissioned to paint the same monuments for Catherine II.

It was doubtless in Rome, where he stayed eleven years from 1754 to 1765, that Hubert Robert decided to be a painter of ruins. Panini's paintings of ruins had raised the genre

to a more esteemed level than mere landscapes. Hubert Robert proclaimed himself a student of Panini as soon as he arrived in Rome and was grateful for the rest of his life for the advice he was given by the older artist.

Paintings of ruins were admired in the Salons. A painting by Robert in the Salon of 1767, his first Salon, in which he exhibited *Grande Galerie antique, eclairée du fond*, inspired Diderot to write about the poetry of ruins:

> The ideas that the ruins awaken in me are grand. Everything comes to nothing, everything perishes, everything passes, there is nothing but the world that remains, there is nothing but time that endures. How old this world is! I walk between two eternities. No matter where I look, the objects that surround me announce the end and resign me to the one that awaits me. What is my ephemeral existence in comparison with that of this weathered rock, of this deepening valley, of this decaying forest, of these suspended bodies over my head which shake and move? I see the marble of tombs fall into dust, and I don't want to die! . . . A torrent carries nations one after the other to the bottom of a common abyss; I, and I alone, I pretend to stop myself on the edge and rend the flood which flows at my sides! . . . In this deserted refuge, solitary and vast, I hear nothing, I have broken away from all of life's encumbrances, no one harrasses me and no one listens to me; I can talk to myself out loud, afflict myself, cry without constraint.

Another charming aspect of Robert's painting can be found in the animation of the ruins with small figures. He enhances the appreciation of the ruins by this contrast with daily life which still constitutes the charm of Rome and Naples.

It should be noted that an element of fantasy intervenes in the juxtaposition of the classical monuments in this painting, which in reality are separated by several dozen kilometers. Hubert Robert framed the triumphal arch at Orange (placed in the center) with the mausoleum of St. Rémy to the left and the small arch of the same city to the right; in the left background is visible the exterior wall of the amphitheater at Orange.

Hubert Robert traveled in southern France in 1783. Several drawings and paintings from that year have survived, and the artist was able to use them in the execution of his four large canvases. One work relates directly to this painting; it is a drawing, representing the Triumphal Arch at Orange (signed and dated 1783), which is done from the same point of view as the painting. A.B. de L.

148 The Interior of the Temple of Diana at Nîmes

HUBERT ROBERT 1733–1808
Oil on canvas
242 x 242 (102½ x 102½)

Lent by the Musée du Louvre

The Interior of the Temple of Diana at Nîmes is one of a series of four paintings of the antique monuments of Languedoc. Robert skillfully evokes the interior of the temple, which was transformed into a "museum" after 1760 and which was described by Laborde in *Monumens de la France*: "At different times, a great quantity of fragments taken from the ancient baths and other archeological excavations have been arranged in the interior of the temple. This large number of tombstones, altars, friezes, low reliefs, cornices and inscriptions, all in marble, makes of this monument a local museum, perhaps unique in the world." Evidently the work-

ing method of Robert was to paint in Paris what he had seen four years earlier, for during his trip to Provence and Languedoc (about which we know very little), he made a large number of sketches which he used later for his paintings.

The execution of the *Temple of Diana* is exceptionally free; in this regard, Diderot once commented: "I envision de Machy, ruler in hand, drawing the fluting of his columns. Robert threw all of those instruments out the window and only kept his paintbrush." The monument lives, as much perhaps as the figures, through the animation of the back wall, with the passages of light and shade, through the vines that grow over the vault, through the feeling, given by the precarious position of the stones, one on top of the other, of a "house of cards," and through the figures,

philosophers or ridiculously dressed women, who barely emerge from the shadows, like those at the left, or who stand out prominently. At the Salon of 1787, the small scale of the figures was criticized. However, the *premier peintre du roi*, Pierre, spoke in their favor: "I found the figures, with which he has enriched his painting, done with more care than is customary with genre artists. These figures, being in proportion with the scale of the architecture and serving to make the site appear more grand."

A.B. de L.

149 The Pont du Gard

HUBERT ROBERT 1733–1808
Oil on canvas
242 x 242 (102½ x 102½)
Lent by the Musée du Louvre

The Pont du Gard is another in the
series of four paintings representing
the antique monuments of Languedoc,
commissioned from the artist in
1786 for Louis XVI's dining room at
Fontainebleau and exhibited the
following year at the Salon.

The relative indifference of the
critics, usually so fiery, and always
verbose, concerning the paintings by
Hubert Robert is surprising, for the
series he exhibited was very important.
It is safe to say that the reviews
did not reflect the general opinion of
those who saw the paintings and that
the public must have greatly admired
the series.

The format of the canvas, the super-
imposition of the arches, the scale
of the figures in relationship to the
bridge, give the painting a majestic
and monumental feeling, reinforced by
the vastness of the sky above the
bridge, a stormy red which renders
the arches of the Pont du Gard even
more striking. A.B. de L.

150 The Maison Carrée, the Arena and the Tour Magne at Nîmes

HUBERT ROBERT 1733–1808
Oil on canvas
243 x 244 (103 x 103¼)
Lent by the Musée du Louvre

As was his habit, Robert here uses the artifice of grouping together monuments which are actually some distance apart. In fact, the Maison Carrée was built in the center of the city of Nîmes and is several kilometers away from the Tour Magne. Bachaumont expresses his opinion of this method in his *Mémoires Secrets:* "[We are shown] an idealized assemblage of dissimilar buildings which have never been together, a revoltingly strange spectacle for the viewer, in whom is assumed too much ignorance. M. Robert, inventive, filled with resourcefulness in his art, because of his desire to be original, often sins against good taste and common sense." The *veduta ideata*, however, was greatly appreciated in the eighteenth century, and the vogue was established by Panini as early as 1730. Every foreigner passing through Rome tried to bring back, from the hand of Panini if possible, a painting composed of the most famous monuments of antique or modern Rome. In 1756 the duc de Choiseul, French ambassador to Rome, commissioned from Panini a *View of Ancient Rome* and a *View of Modern Rome.*

Jefferson must have admired these paintings in Paris and been happily reminded of his "affair" with the Maison Carrée, the small Roman temple at Nîmes, which he had admired during a trip through the central part of France and northern Italy. He first visited Nîmes in March 1787, and on March 20 wrote to Mme de Tessé from that place: "Here I am, Madam, gazing whole hours at the Maison Quarrée, like a lover at his mistress. The stocking-weavers and silk spinners around consider me as an hypochondriac Englishman, about to write with a pistol the last chapter of his history."

In the explanation of the plans for the capitol building of Virginia at Richmond, on which Jefferson collaborated with the French architect Clérisseau, he praised the charms of the Maison Carrée: "Erected in the time of the Caesars and which is allowed without contradiction to be the most perfect and precious remain of antiquity in existence. . . . I determined, therefore, to adopt this model and to have all its proportions justly drewed." A.B. de L.

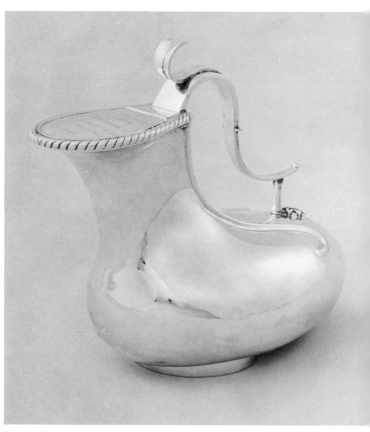

151 Roman askos

Bronze

15.5 x 22 x 18 (6¼ x 8⅝ x 7⅛)

Excavated on the site of the
Maison Carrée in Nîmes, France

*Lent by the Musée des Antiques,
Nîmes*

Used as pouring vessels for oil or wine,
askoi were made from the Bronze
Age down to Roman times. This late
form evolved from earlier askoi which
were in the shape of a wine skin.

Jefferson first saw this bronze askos
in 1787 while visiting the Maison
Carrée in Nîmes, France, where it was
in the collection of Jean-François
Séguier, who had supervised the
restoration of the Maison Carrée. Jefferson had chosen the building as
the model for his designs for the
Virginia state capitol building in Richmond. Because of its association
with the Maison Carrée, Jefferson felt
that a copy of the askos would be a
suitable gift for the French architect
Clérisseau, who had assisted Jefferson
in his designs for the capitol building.

Jefferson had Souche, his former
valet de place in Nîmes, obtain a
wooden model of the bronze askos, but
the first model was lost, and while
waiting for a second model to arrive,
Jefferson decided instead to present
Clérisseau with a coffee urn inspired
by the Greco-Roman vases and urns
discovered at Herculaneum and
Pompeii. c.g.

152 Model of a bronze askos

Mahogany

20.3 x 23.2 x 13 (8 x 9¼ x 5⅛)

*Lent by the Thomas Jefferson
Memorial Foundation, Charlottesville*

This is the second model that Jefferson had his former *valet de
place*, Souche, obtain for him in
Nîmes; the first, made in 1787, was
lost. In 1821, both the silver (see
no. 153) and wooden copies of the
askos were at Monticello, when
Thomas Sully arrived to paint his
famous portrait of Jefferson, now at
the American Philosophical Society in
Philadelphia. As a token of his
appreciation and respect, Jefferson
gave the wooden model to Sully, who
wrote the following inscription on the
base: *Presented/ by Ex-pres. Thos./
Jefferson to Thos./ Sully.* The model
subsequently disappeared until discovered by Mrs. Raymond Porter at
the auction of a country estate in
Bucks County, Pennsylvania, in
1972. c.g.

153 Askos

SIMMONS and ALEXANDER,
Philadelphia

Silver 1801

20.3 x 23.2 x 13 (8 x 9¼ x 5⅛)
Inscribed on the lid: *Copied from a
model/ taken in 1787 by/
Th. Jefferson/ from a Roman Ewer
in the/ Cabinet of Antiquities at/
Nismes*

*Lent by the Thomas Jefferson
Memorial Foundation, Charlottesville*

This silver askos was a product of
Jefferson's search for an appropriate
gift for the distinguished French
architect, Charles-Louis Clérisseau,
detailed in entry number 151. Jefferson
had a wooden model made of the
bronze askos, but the first model was
lost before it could be copied. The
second wooden model of the askos
was brought back to America by
Jefferson and served as the basis for
this silver version.

Several differences exist between
the original bronze askos, the wooden
model and the silver one, notably
the addition of a lid to the silver copy
and a simplified handle which lacks
the floral carving of the wooden model
and the original bronze askos. c.g.

154 Dr. John Morgan

ANGELICA KAUFFMANN 1741–1807
Oil on canvas 1764
152.4 x 110.5 (60 x 43½)

*Lent by the Washington County
Historical Society, Washington,
Pennsylvania*

When Jefferson visited Philadelphia
in 1766 to be inoculated against
smallpox, he carried a letter of introduction to Dr. John Morgan, a rising
young physician in the city. Morgan
set up the first medical school in
America and was later to be director-
general of military hospitals and
physician-in-chief to the American
army, but his importance for Jefferson
lay in his widely cultivated taste and
extensive knowledge of Europe, from
which, after a stay of some years,
he had just returned. Morgan had
visited Rome, Naples, Venice, Florence and many other art centers of
Italy, and his travel diary shows him
to have been an assiduous tourist.
In Rome, as was frequently the case
with visitors from Britain, he was
conducted around the classical sites by
James Byres, soon to be the leading
cicerone to English grand tourists.

155 Winckelmann

ANTON RAPHAEL MENGS
1728–1779
Oil on canvas
63.5 x 49.2 (25 x 19⅜)

Lent by The Metropolitan Museum of Art, Dick Fund, 1948

Later Dr. Morgan wrote a letter of recommendation to Byres on behalf of John Singleton Copley, when that artist visited Rome. Byres' tours included all the main churches and collections of Rome, and Morgan made notes on what he saw. Among the antique sculpture in the Vatican he specially noted the *Apollo Belvedere*, the *Laocoön*, the *Belvedere Torso* and *Meleager* "falsely said to be Antenous." Clearly, classical art made a great impression on the young Philadelphian, for he wrote to a friend while in Rome: "As to the grandeur of the ancients, from what we can see of their remains, it is most extraordinary, Arts with them seem to have been in a perfection which I could not have imagined. Their palaces, temples, acqueducts, baths, theaters, amphitheaters, monuments, statues, sculptures were most amazing. The soul is struck at the review, and the ideas expand."

Morgan, as someone who had traveled widely, had met Voltaire and had been received by the Pope and European royalty, would have seemed unusually sophisticated to Jefferson, who had never before left Virginia.

More important still, perhaps, was the collection of architectural books and art, including copies of old masters and engravings or drawings by Poussin, Titian, Domenichino, Carracci, Le Brun and others, which Dr. Morgan had brought back with him. This, with other collections in Philadelphia, must have been Jefferson's introduction to the world of classical art, sixteenth- and seventeenth-century Italian painting, and the architecture of Palladio and his followers.

The portrait was painted during John Morgan's stay in Rome in 1764. Morgan also acquired a self-portrait by Angelica Kauffmann. It was Angelica Kauffmann who befriended Maria Hadfield, later Mrs. Cosway, encouraged her to go to England, and introduced her into London society. R.W.

Johann Joachim Winckelmann (1717–1768), like Jefferson, was first drawn to classical art through Latin and Greek literature. His first book *Gedanken über die Nachahmung der Griechischen Werke in der Malerey und Bildhauerkunst* (*Reflections on the Imitation of Greek Art in Painting and Sculpture*) was published in 1755, in Dresden, before he had ever been to Rome. His ambition to settle in Rome and become recognized as an antiquarian was eventually achieved and is only one of the many famous examples of a northern European succumbing to the spell of Mediterranean culture. Winckelmann's writings, especially his *History of Ancient Art*, were enormously influential and became key works for the neoclassic movement and the rediscovery of Greek art. His often quoted phrase "noble simplicity and calm grandeur" referring to Greek art, and especially sculpture, was to influence European and American painters and sculptors well into the nineteenth century. Winckelmann was not, however, just an art historian and scholar. His passionate love of Greek sculpture, based on his homosexual attraction to the male nude, inspired him to write lyrical prose-poems in the *History of Ancient Art* on the *Apollo Belvedere*, the *Laocoön* and the *Belvedere Torso*, and so communicate his enthusiasm to contemporaries and to future generations. For him the only way to greatness in art was through imitation of the Greek way of life as well as Greek art. Ironically, Winckelmann never went to Greece, nor, apart from excursions to Naples, did he know collections outside Rome. Yet his writings were enough to make Goethe say "by reading Winckelmann one does not learn anything but one becomes somebody."

While Jefferson's emotional makeup was unlike Winckelmann's, he, too, was possessed by a longing to visit the classical centers of Italy, although he was forced, through lack of time and a scrupulous sense of duty, to turn his back on the temptations of the south when he visited northern Italy: "Milan was the spot at which I turned my back on Rome and Naples. It was a moment of conflict between duty which urged me to return, and inclination urging me forwards" ". . . but I took a peep only into Elysium. I entered it at one door, & came out at another, having seen, as I past, only Turin, Milan, and Genoa. I calculated the hours it would have taken to carry me on to Rome. But they were exactly so many more than I had to spare . . . I am born to lose everything I love." R.W.

156 *Les Édifices Antiques de Rome, mesurés et dessinés tres-exactement sur les lieux par feu M. Desgodets, Architecte du Roi. Nouvelle édition.* (Paris: chez Claude-Antoine Jombert, Fils aîné, de l'Imprimerie de Monsieur, 1779)

ANTOINE BABUTY DESGODETS
1653–1728

From the Collection of Mr. and Mrs. Paul Mellon

The classical influence on Thomas Jefferson which he, in turn, transmitted to his countrymen is nowhere more evident than in architecture. Fiske Kimball wrote, "The sophomoric analogy of the young republic with Rome was on the lips of everyone. Encouraged by Jefferson's example, its builders adopted the temple form not only for their capitols, but for all other government buildings, for banks, and even for dwellings." One of the most important sources for Jefferson's classicism was Desgodets' *Edifices Antiques de Rome.*

The first edition of the work appeared in 1682 after Desgodets, a French architect, had spent sixteen months of study in Rome. The book was published at the expense of Louis XIV and by order of Jean Baptiste Colbert. Jefferson bought his copy of Desgodets from his Paris bookseller, J. F. Froullé, on July 20, 1791, through the agency of William Short, who was in Amsterdam at the time; the price he paid was 72 livres. There are two letters from Jefferson to Short, of January 24, 1791, and March 16, 1791, in which Jefferson repeats his desire for a copy of Desgodets.

The location of Jefferson's copy of Desgodets is not known; it was probably destroyed in the fire of 1851 in the Library of Congress. The copy shown here is a royal folio, made up of seventy-seven leaves of text including the engraved title by Desgodets and 137 plates engraved by various artists after drawings by Desgodets. J.M.E.

157 *Ruins of the Palace of the Emperor Diocletian at Spalatro in Dalmatia* (n.p. [printed for author, 1764])

ROBERT ADAM 1728–1792

From the Collection of Mr. and Mrs. Paul Mellon

In 1757 Robert Adam, Charles-Louis Clérisseau, and two draftsmen went to Spalatro or Spalato (present day Split) in what is now Yugoslavia, where they spent six weeks surveying and drawing the ancient palace, which is now part of the city. The plates for the book that was the result of their efforts were engraved in Venice, and the book appeared in 1764, the first study of a Roman domestic monument. As planned from the first, the book helped to establish Adam as an authority on Roman antiquity, particularly on domestic architecture. Since Clérisseau's name was omitted from all the plates, Adam received full credit for the endeavor. The architectural commissions Adam obtained in England show his knowledge of Roman architectural forms and decorative details, and the varied shapes and sequences of the rooms he created had their source in Roman buildings such as Diocletian's palace. Thus the book not only is a landmark in the archaeological study of antiquity but shows the sources from which Adam derived his style. T.J.McC.

158 *Antiquités de la France. Monumens de Nîmes* (Paris: Phillipe-Denys-Pierres, 1778)

CHARLES-LOUIS CLÉRISSEAU
1721–1820

From the Collection of Mr. and Mrs. Paul Mellon

In 1767, after nearly twenty years in Italy studying the Roman monuments, Charles-Louis Clérisseau returned to his native land to undertake a study of the Roman remains there. He planned a series of volumes and made a great number of drawings which he never used, such as the one of the arch and tomb at St. Rémy, shown here at number 138. Only the first volume, *Monumens de Nîmes,* appeared ten years later. It was the first major archaeological study of Roman France and included the best preserved of all Roman temples, the Maison Carrée. A copy of this book was owned by Jefferson and was probably the reason that Jefferson chose Clérisseau to collaborate on the design of the Virginia state capitol, shown at numbers 394–399. A second enlarged edition of Clérisseau's book was published in collaboration with his son-in-law in 1804. T.J.McC.

159 *Recueil d'antiquités égyptiennes, étrusques, grecques et romaines* (Paris: Desaint & Saillant, 1752–1767), 7 vol.

ANNE CLAUDE PHILIPPE
1692–1765

From the Collection of Mr. and Mrs. Paul Mellon

Almost a personification of the French eighteenth-century *philosophe,* Caylus was an important influence on Jefferson. The *Recueil,* one of Caylus' best-known works, is testimony to the time and attention that he gave to the study and collection of antiquities. Jefferson did not own a copy of the *Recueil,* but Caylus' work was well known to him as an important descriptive interpretation of the works of classical art. J.M.E.

160 *Antiquités étrusques, grecques et romaines gravées par F.A. David. Avec leurs explications; par d'Hancarville . . .* (Paris: L'auteur, 1765–1788), 5 vol.

PIERRE FRANÇOIS HUGHES
D'HANCARVILLE 1719–1805

From the Collection of Mr. and Mrs. Paul Mellon

D'Hancarville was an eminent French antiquarian, whose description of the collection of antiquities belonging to Sir William Hamilton was first published in an English and French edition in Naples in 1766–1767. The copy of d'Hancarville's book in this exhibition was once the property of Charles Towneley (1737–1805) (see no. 134). Towneley, who was an archaeologist and collector of classical antiquities, was a member of the Society of Dilettanti and a friend of Sir William Hamilton. Both Towneley and d'Hancarville were well known to Thomas Jefferson, and Jefferson also knew the Towneley and Hamilton collections, both of which are now in the British Museum. William Short sent a letter to Jefferson on February 17, 1789, describing his recent visit to the Campi Phlegraei near Naples, and noted, "Sir Wm. Hamilton has published a book containing an account of them as well as of Mt. Vesuvius which is on the other side of Naples, with paintings done by the pencil, of different views of that country." J.M.E.

161 *Segmenta nobilium signorum e statuaru, quae temporis dentem inuidium euasere urbis aeternae ruinis erepta typis aeneis ab se commissa perpetuae uenerationis monumentum* (Franciscus Perrier, D.D.D. 1638–1653)

FRANCOIS PERRIER 1590?–1656?

Lent by the Library of Congress

162 *Polymetis: or, An Enquiry concerning the Agreement between the Works of the Roman Poets, and the Remains of the Antient Artists . . .* (London: R. Dodsley, 1747)

JOSEPH SPENCE 1699–1768

Lent by the Library of Congress

Perrier was a French painter and engraver. He spent several years in Rome, and the plates in his book are of the remains of ancient sculpture then still in Rome. Spence's work is a treatise on classical mythology, with lavish illustrations by L.P. Boitard in the form of engravings of ancient works of art and portraits of classical writers.

It was from such works as these that Thomas Jefferson took his concepts of the classical ideal. It was also in these books that Jefferson saw engravings of such works as the Venus de'Medici (see no. 133), which was illustrated in both Perrier and Spence and which headed the list of works that he wanted to have in copy or cast for Monticello. J.M.E.

63 *The Antiquities of Athens measured and delineated by James Stuart F.R.S. and F.S.A. and Nicholas Revett, Painters and Architects. Volume the First* (London: John Haberkorn, 1762)

JAMES STUART 1713–1788, and
NICHOLAS REVETT 1720–1804

From the Collection of Mr. and Mrs. Paul Mellon

Both Stuart and Revett were students of art in Rome, and both were members of the Society of Dilettanti, which supported their plans for publishing accurate descriptions of classical an-

tiquities. Stuart and Revett are credited with being the pioneers of classical archaeology in Europe, and their first volume, published in 1762, had long been on Thomas Jefferson's list of desiderata, until he was able to buy it in Paris. The later volumes published in 1789, 1814, and 1830 were not in his library. J.M.E.

64 *The Ruins of Palmyra, otherwise Telmor, in the desert* (London: printed for the author, 1753)

ROBERT WOOD 1717?–1771

From the Collection of Mr. and Mrs. Paul Mellon

65 *The Ruins of Balbec, otherwise Heliopolis in Coelosyria* (London: printed for the author, 1757)

ROBERT WOOD 1717?–1771

From the Collection of Mr. and Mrs. Paul Mellon

Robert Wood was an Irish traveler and politician who was also an amateur in the field of classical art and architecture. He and his traveling companion and collaborator, James

Dawkins, were members of the Society of Dilettanti, which encouraged their work. Horace Walpole highly praised both these volumes in the preface of his *Anecdotes of Painting* (1762–1771). Although he certainly knew both works, Thomas Jefferson owned only a copy of *The Ruins of Balbec.* J.M.E.

66 *Storia della arti del disegno presso gli antichi* (Milan, 1779)

JOHANN JOACHIM WINCKELMANN 1717–1768

Lent by the Fine Arts Library of the Harvard College Library, Norton Collection

In the same year that Thomas Jefferson became twenty-one, Johann Joachim Winckelmann published his monumental *Geschichte der Kunst des Alterthums.* Of all the celebrations of the "nobility of ancient art," Winckelmann's book was probably the most influential. He was not only the founder of modern archaeology, but he was a moving force in the neoclassical movement during the late

eighteenth century.

Jefferson owned a copy of the first Italian translation of Winckelmann's "History of Ancient Art" (1779), which is now lost. But even without such evidence, it is clear that Jefferson turned to the unquestioned authority which Winckelmann represented concerning the importance of Greek ideals for the eighteenth-century world. Most appealing to Jefferson, of course, was Winckelmann's philosophical approach and his belief that the superiority of Greek art was based in the political institutions which gave rise to it. J.M.E.

OUR
REVOLUTION

You and I, my dear friend, have been sent into life at a time when
the greatest lawgivers of antiquity would have wished to live. How few
of the human race have ever enjoyed an opportunity of making an
election of government. . . .

JOHN ADAMS, *Thoughts on Government
in a Letter from a Gentlemen to his Friend,* Philadelphia, 1776

. . . we utterly dissolve & break off all political·connection which
may have heretofore subsisted between us & the people or parliament
of Great Britain; and finally we do assert and declare these colonies
to be free and independant states, and that as free & independant states
they shall hereafter have power to levy war, conclude peace, contract alliances, establish commerce, & to do all other acts and things
which independant states may of right do. And for the support of this
declaration we mutually pledge to each other our lives, our fortunes, &
our sacred honour.

JEFFERSON, *Declaration of Independence,*
Original Rough Draft, 1776

On June 7, 1776, the Virginia delegation to the Continental
Congress meeting in Philadelphia made an epochal proposition
when it moved "that these United Colonies are, and of right
ought to be, free and independent states." When the vote was
finally taken on July 2, a committee to draft the Declaration had
already been appointed. Thomas Jefferson, who had just turned
thirty-three, was made the chairman.

Nearly ten years later, in the summer of 1785, Jefferson, now
the minister to Paris, was visiting another former member of the
drafting committee, John Adams, who had become the first
American minister in London. During his stay in London, Jefferson met for the first time a young man from Connecticut who had
"pined for the arts" so much that he turned down his family's
offer to go into business or law and instead, moved to Europe to
pursue an uncertain profession as a painter. John Trumbull
had caught the eye of Benjamin West, later president of the Royal
Academy, and was studying in West's London studio when
he first met Jefferson. Trumbull's idealism and dedication appealed
to Jefferson, who "highly approved" of his determination to
prepare himself for "the accomplishment of a national work,"
and invited Trumbull to visit him in Paris where Jefferson had
already established himself in an intimate circle of artists and
connoisseurs.

"I now availed myself of this invitation," Trumbull later wrote in
his *Autobiography,* "and went to his house, at the Grille de
Chaillot, where I was most kindly received by him. My two paintings, the first fruits of my national enterprise, met his warm
approbation, and during my visit, I began the composition of the
Declaration of Independence, with the assistance of his information and advice." The two paintings Trumbull had brought with
him were his *Bunker's Hill* and *Death of Montgomery* which
he had planned to have engraved during his stay.

In a democratic age, Trumbull was concerned about the profession of the artist. Who were to be his patrons without
kings, popes or an aristocracy? What was to be the function of the
artist in a republic, without ducal houses to decorate or field
marshals to memorialize?

Some of these questions were on Trumbull's mind when he told Jefferson that he planned to commemorate "the great events of our Country's revolution" and to pay for it by publishing a series of engravings for subscribers. His concern to free artists from official patronage was shared by Hogarth, who developed a scheme for a lottery to pay for *The March to Finchley* (see no. 72).

Jefferson was immediately sympathetic to Trumbull's efforts and gave him £12 toward a subscription. Jefferson attempted to encourage the artist further by telling Trumbull that he undervalued his own talents but recognized that America "is not yet rich enough to encourage you as you deserve."

In the company of Jefferson and others, including Mr. and Mrs. Richard Cosway who had just been introduced by Trumbull to the minister's circle, Trumbull continued his education, "examining and reviewing whatever relates to the arts." Through Jefferson's introduction, Trumbull met many artists including David and Houdon, whose studios were a regular haunt of the enthusiastic American visitors.

In 1784, the Commonwealth of Virginia had authorized the commission of a statue of Washington "to be erected as a Monument of Affection and Gratitude . . . uniting the Endowments of the Hero the Virtues of the Patriot. . . ." Governor Harrison immediately wrote to Jefferson in Paris and asked him to recommend a sculptor and to supervise the execution. Houdon, possessing "the reputation of being the first sculptor of the world," had already done portrait busts of other Americans including Benjamin Franklin and John Paul Jones and, before he left for America, had completed the bust of the marquis de Lafayette. Jefferson's own admiration for his work made Houdon the "unrivaled" choice for the commission, and he quickly moved to clear the way for Houdon's famous trip to America to obtain a life mask of the general at Mount Vernon.

Through these works of Houdon and Trumbull, the most enduring heroic images of the participants and events of the American Revolution were created, and Jefferson's critical taste and encouragement was central to the production of this legacy. In 1820 Jefferson recalled those earlier days and associations in Paris when in one of his last letters to Maria Cosway he wrote that their mutual "friend Trumbull is well, and profitably and honorably employed by his country in commemorating with his pencil [for the capitol at Washington] some of its Revolutionary honors. . . ." W.H.A.

167 The Declaration of Independence, 4 July 1776

JOHN TRUMBULL 1756–1843
Oil on canvas 1787–1820
53.6 x 79.1 (21⅛ x 31⅛)

*Lent by the Yale University
Art Gallery, New Haven,
Trumbull Collection*

Jefferson's portrait was the second (after that of John Adams) to be painted into *The Declaration of Independence*. Trumbull executed it during the winter of 1787–1788 when he stayed at the Hôtel de Langeac for the second time as guest of the American minister to France. When Jefferson's good friend Maria Cosway saw it, at Trumbull's return to London, she teased the artist constantly for a copy. He eventually made one for her (see no. 339), together with two others, one of which he gave to another of Jefferson's great admirers, Angelica Schuyler Church, the other to Jefferson's daughter, Martha. "Wish me joy," Maria Cosway wrote Jefferson, "for I possess your Picture. Trumbull has procured me this

happiness which I shall ever be grateful for."

Jefferson is clearly the hero of the scene, standing at the center of the group in the *ad locutio* pose traditional for statesmen ever since the *Augustus Primaporta*. He holds in his right hand the astounding document he had largely drafted. John Adams' importance is stressed by his position on the central axis of the composition, while Franklin is emphasized by his bulk and set off by the door behind him. Roger Sherman and Robert Livingston are secondary figures in this principal group.

Jefferson and Trumbull, together with Adams, whom the artist also consulted, agreed that authenticity must be a major concern in the *Declaration*; no idealized portraits were to be introduced "lest it being known that some were to be found in the painting, a doubt of the truth of others should be excited in the minds of posterity." Jefferson collaborated with Trumbull on the preliminary sketch ". . . to convey an

idea of the room in which the congress sat. . . ." When Trumbull returned to the United States at the end of 1789, and for the following four years, he traveled up and down the eastern seaboard collecting portraits, sometimes with his canvas at hand onto which he painted his sitters, sometimes making miniature oil and pencil sketches to serve as models from which he would later work.

The Declaration of Independence is a remarkable painting in which ordinary men in simple everyday garb, seated on plain windsor chairs, at desks covered with dull green baize, watching their committee present a report to the president, distill a sense of historic undertaking. Without flourish, without heroic gestures, the *Declaration* is not grand, and yet it achieves grandeur. The immobility of the figures and the airlessness of the room suggest the calm center of the struggle that the act of independence now made inevitable. The newborn state was in the hands of republicans driven at least in theory by the

dictates of republican Reason. The painting, like Jefferson's Declaration itself, American to the core, may be said at the same time to be an ultimate statement of the European Enlightenment: in visual form it expresses the clear, direct rhetoric of the document those men laid on the desk of John Hancock on July 4, 1776.

A large version of the *Declaration*, with life-size figures, is in the rotunda of the United States capitol. I.B.J.

168 The Death of General Mercer at the Battle of Princeton, 3 January 1777

JOHN TRUMBULL 1756–1843
Oil on canvas 1787–1831
52.8 x 75.9 (20½ x 29⅞)

*Lent by the Yale University
Art Gallery, New Haven,
Trumbull Collection*

Standing before *Princeton* in the
Trumbull Gallery one day, Benjamin
Silliman asked Trumbull, his nephew-
in-law, "Suppose Sir that your paintings in the Gallery were doomed
to destruction and you were allowed to
save only one, which should it be?"
The artist answered, "This painting of
Princeton."

The Death of General Mercer at
Princeton was begun in London in
1787 and finished in 1831, according
to Trumbull's notation of a draft
list of paintings drawn up that year. A
series of drawings for the work, which
the artist signed and numbered on
the back, one through five (now at
Princeton University), shows the
development of the composition,
whose principal motif of General

Mercer leaning against his fallen horse
seems to have been inspired by
Benjamin West's *Edward III Crossing
the Somme*, executed in 1788 with
Trumbull as his assistant.

General Mercer was portrayed from
a sketch Trumbull made of Mercer's
son, in 1791, although the artist
did not execute the portrait in the
painting until 1827 when the seventy-
one-year-old artist wrote Mercer,
"My success in your portrait . . . has
convinced me that . . . with the aid of
the Optician I can still execute such
small work as well as formerly. . . ."
General George Washington had
favored Trumbull with a special sitting,
on horseback, so that the artist could
study him mounted for this painting
and others in the American history
series. I.B.J.

169 The Surrender of General Burgoyne at Saratoga, 16 October 1777

JOHN TRUMBULL 1756–1843
Oil on canvas c. 1822–1831
54.6 x 78.8 (21½ x 31)

Lent by the Yale University Art Gallery, New Haven, Trumbull Collection

Although Trumbull had planned *Saratoga* between 1787 and 1793, along with his other American history paintings, and had made sketches for it, he had at that time composed only an outline sketch partly filled in with India ink (unlocated). This small oil was executed after he had finished the large rotunda painting in the capitol, of which it is a copy. A draft list of paintings drawn up by Trumbull c. 1831 included "no. 9. The Surrender of Gen. Burgoyne unfinished Copy of the large picture in the Capitol of Washington, which was composed & painted in this City [New York] in 1822." Actually the rotunda *Saratoga* was completed in December 1821.

The portraits in *Saratoga* of Greaton, Scammell, Phillips, and Whipple are posthumous. The sources for Burgoyne, Riedesel, and Armstrong are not known, but the remaining nineteen were probably all painted from life.

The painting shows General Horatio Gates at the center, with his chief-of-staff Colonel Morgan Lewis prominent to his left, receiving General Burgoyne attended by General William Phillips. Burgoyne has dismounted, his horse held by a groom behind him, and offers his sword which Gates magnanimously refuses, inviting his captive into the tent to partake of refreshments. According to Trumbull, both *Yorktown* and *Saratoga* portray "men of the same race as those of the 4th of July—men who can conquer but [are] too high minded to wound the feelings of a fallen enemy."

The grouping of the principal figures was probably suggested by Benjamin West's *Edward the Black Prince Receiving John, King of France,* which West painted for the audience chamber of George III at Windsor Castle before 1787–1789 with Trumbull as his assistant.

In December 1816, Trumbull wrote to Jefferson asking for his support in obtaining the commission to do the four paintings for the capitol:

Twenty eight years have elapsed, since under the kind protection of your hospitable roof at Chaillot, I painted your portrait in my picture of the Declaration of Independence. ... The Government of the U.S. are restoring to more than their usual Splender the Buildings devoted to National purposes at Washington. ... I have thought this a proper opportunity to make first application for public patronage, and to request to be employed in decorating the walls of their buildings with the paintings which have employed so many [years] of my life.... future artists may arise with far Superior Talents, but time has already withdrawn almost all their Models; and I who was one of the youngest Actors in the early scenes of the War, passed the Age of Sixty.... I.B.J.

170 Surrender of Lord Cornwallis at Yorktown, 19 October 1781

JOHN TRUMBULL 1756–1843
Oil on canvas 1787–c. 1828
53 x 77.8 (20⅞ x 30⅝)

*Lent by the Yale University
Art Gallery, New Haven,
Trumbull Collection*

Following Trumbull's stay with him
in 1786, Jefferson had invited the
artist repeatedly during 1787 to return
to Paris and the Hôtel de Langeac
for another visit, but it was December
before the artist was able to leave
London. He brought with him the
prepared canvas for *Yorktown*, and in
Jefferson's home painted fifteen portraits of French officers who participated in the battle of Yorktown or
were present at the surrender. "I have
been in this capitol of dissipation
& nonsense near six weeks," the Connecticut Yankee artist wrote home
to his strait-laced family in Lebanon,
"getting the portraits of the French
officers who were at Yorktown . . .
I have almost finished them [Febru-
ary 6, 1788] . . . Rochambeau—

DeGrasse—DeBarras—Viomenil—
Choisy—Lausun—deCustine—
DeLaval—Deux Ponts—Pherson [*sic*]
—& Dumas—besides the Marquis
de Lafayette." Most of the portraits
of Americans were probably done from
life between 1790 and 1793; the
only posthumous one is that of Lieutenant Colonel John Laurens.

A draft list of paintings drawn up by
Trumbull c. 1831 included *Yorktown*
with the notation, "Composed in
London 1787 . . . finished since in
America." He wrote Alexander Robert-
son on March 2, 1828, "I have . . .
worked on various unfinished parts of
Yorktown. . . ."

Trumbull had originally keyed the
new unnumbered British officer standing beside the mounted General
Lincoln as Lord Cornwallis. Jefferson,
in a letter to Samuel Adams Wells
(June 23, 1819), commenting on in-
accuracies in *The Declaration of
Independence*, remarked, "But as far
back as the days of Horace at least we
are told that *pictoribus atque poetis;
Quidlibet audendi semper fuit aequa*

potestas [painters and poets always had
the right to attempt anything].
[Trumbull] has exercised this licentia
pictoris in like manner in the surrender of York, where he has placed
Ld Cornwallis at the head of the
surrender altho' it is well known that
he was excused by General Washington from appearing." As a result of
public criticism, however, Trumbull
removed the name from his *Yorktown Key*.

The painting represents the moment
when General O'Hara, acting for
Cornwallis, stands between the lines
of the mounted American and French
officers at the head of the British
surrender party. "Not an Eye or a
Movement is . . . expressive of Exuda-
tion," the artist wrote. War in the
eighteenth century, for officers, was
still a gentleman's occupation.

A large version of *Yorktown* with
life-sized figures is in the United States
capitol rotunda. I.B.J.

171 The Resignation of General Washington, 23 December 1783

JOHN TRUMBULL 1756–1843
Oil on canvas c. 1824–1828
50.8 x 76.2 (20 x 30)

*Lent by the Yale University
Art Gallery, New Haven,
Trumbull Collection*

Trumbull's first ambitious painting
(now lost), executed in Benjamin
West's painting room for exhibition
at the British Royal Academy (1784,
no. 153), was based on the story of
Cincinnatus, the Roman general who
after saving Rome went back to his
farm to live in peaceful retirement. The
work was begun shortly after General
Washington's resignation, which
deeply stirred Trumbull's imagination
and "excited the astonishment and
admiration of [Europe]," the artist
wrote his brother. He gave his Cincinnatus the features of Washington,
whom he referred to as the "American
Cincinnatus."

While Trumbull was in America
during 1789–1794, he painted a large
number of miniatures for future

use in his planned series of American
history paintings. It was not until
1822 that he began work on the *Resignation*, one of the four paintings
commissioned by the United States
government for the capitol rotunda,
and by that time many of the sitters
were dead, so that only the early
miniatures could serve as authentic
models. New portraits were also added,
for example that of President James
Madison, to whom Trumbull wrote on
October 1, 1823, "[At the resignation,
Mr. Jefferson] and Mr. Munro [sic]
were . . . present—their portraits are introduced of course in the picture.
And that I may have all the *Virginia
Presidents*, I have taken the liberty . . .
of placing you among the Spectators:—it is a Painter's licence, which I
think the occasion may well justify."

The small painting that completes
the series of eight, at Yale, is a copy
of the rotunda work, probably begun
while he was finishing the large
one, and completed in 1828, since he
wrote a friend on March 2, 1828,
"I have nearly finished my small copy

of the Resignation of Washington."
The *Resignation* is conceived in
terms of *The Declaration of Independence* (see no. 167). Like the latter,
it takes up the theme of lofty-
minded dedication to republican principles. Its muted colors, contrasting
with the bright hues of the military
scenes in the series, emphasize the significant anti-militarism of Washington's resignation. "Beloved by the
military, venerated by the people, who
was there to oppose the victorious
chief, if he had chosen to retain that
power," Trumbull wrote. "The
Caesars—the Cromwells, the Napo-
leons—yielded to the charm of earthly
ambition, and betrayed their country
. . . Washington alone aspired to
loftier, imperishable glory—to that
glory which virtue alone can give."

The scene represents Washington
at Annapolis where Congress was
then sitting, holding in his right hand
the resignation. By pairing Washington in the *Resignation* with Jefferson in the *Declaration* in position
and pose, Trumbull underlined the

meaning of Washington's action as a
reaffirmation of the Declaration of
Independence; at issue in both events
was the commitment to republican
government. I.B.J.

172 George Washington

JEAN-ANTOINE HOUDON
1741–1828
Marble c. 1785
59.7 (23½) high

*Lent by Mrs. Thomas S. Kelly,
New York*

The story of Houdon's visit to the United States to make a bust of Washington as the basis for the statue now in the rotunda of the capitol in Richmond, Virginia, is well known and need only be summarized here. Jefferson was the principal figure in achieving the commission for Houdon after the Virginia Assembly in June 1784 had voted the commission of a marble statue of General Washington. It was assumed that the statue must be made in Europe, since there was then no sculptor in the United States capable of carrying out the commission.

On receiving Governor Harrison's request to supervise the execution of the commission, Jefferson immediately wrote to him from Paris in January 1785: "There could be no question raised as to the sculptor who should be employed, the reputation of Mons. Houdon, of this city, being unrivaled in Europe. . . ." Jefferson further emphasized that studies must be made from Washington himself and that Houdon, anxious for this notable commission, had expressed a willingness to go to America by the April packet. Jefferson also wrote to the same effect to Washington himself, referring to Houdon as having the reputation of being "the first statuary

in the world. . . . [who] is so enthusiastically fond of being the executor of this work, that he offers to go to America for the purpose of forming your bust from the life. . . . A bust of Voltaire executed by him," Jefferson continued, "is said to be the finest in the world" (see no. 334). There were extensive discussions concerning Houdon's fees, and in fact the matter of payment dragged on for many years before the sculptor finally received his full compensation. Houdon agreed to modest terms, in the hope that this statue would lead to the commission for a great equestrian statue, a hope which was never realized. As the result of a serious illness the sculptor's sailing was delayed until July 20, when he left with Benjamin Franklin, who was returning to the United States. He arrived at Mount Vernon on October 2 and, working with great rapidity, completed a life mask, a terra cotta, and one or more plasters before October 7, when he departed for Philadelphia. Houdon returned to Paris on Christmas day 1785, and a bust of Washington, presumably a plaster, which had been shipped separately, arrived in May 1786.

Washington had rather diffidently expressed a preference for modern dress, and although in sketches Houdon seems to have experimented with classical draperies and an allegorical concept of Washington as the protector of agriculture, it was in his uniform as commander in chief that he was finally portrayed. This agreed completely with the opinions of Jefferson and other expatriate Americans on the subject. Jefferson wrote to Washington in August 1787, "I found it strongly the sentiment of West, Copley, Trumbull, and Brown, in London; after which it would be ridiculous to add that it was my own. I think a modern in an antique dress as just an object of ridicule as a Hercules or Marius with a periwig and a *chapeau bras.*" The fasces and the plow, the symbols of authority and agriculture, remained in the final statue as support for the figure. There was extensive argument between Houdon, Jefferson and others concerning the form of the inscription, but in 1814, when it was finally carved upon the pedestal, it followed the elaborate original text written by James Madison. The statue was shipped to the United States in January 1796.

As might be expected, Houdon made many busts in terra cotta, plaster, and probably in bronze. The original terra cotta, left with Washington, is believed to be the one still at Mount Vernon. The fine terra cotta in the Louvre could not be the original, since it clearly shows the ridges of a piece mold.

Houdon showed a bust in the Salon of 1787 labelled "no. 259—Le général Washington, fait par l'auteur dans la terre de ce general en Virginie." In the Salon of 1793, there appeared a model of the statue, "No. 122—Le général Washington, statue esquisse en plâtre, d'environ I pied." Another version of the Washington bust at Versailles is quite different in concept from the earlier one and was, according to Giacometti, made for the Gallery of the Consuls at the Tuileries. It is signed on the right shoulder "houdon an 9" (1800). In the neoclassic mode, the torso is squared off to form its own base and the name WASHINGTON is carved across the front. Washington is in classic dress with a wide riband arranged diagonally across the right shoulder, which is delicately ornamented with a sword, fasces and his monogram set within oval wreaths. In this version, with its somewhat narrowed eyes and compressed mouth, Houdon, possibly because of the proposed location within an assembly of great leaders, recast his original concept to emphasize Washington as a wise and noble, yet imperial, ruler.

In the many surviving busts made after the original modeled at Mount Vernon, there is a curiously reflective and inward quality in the personification of Washington. It is interesting to note that among the surviving Washington busts by Houdon, there is not a single one, as far as can be determined, in modern dress. All are à *l'antique,* either draped or undraped, as though Houdon in this manner were having a quiet revenge for being unable to present Washington in his statue as a Roman emperor. The marble bust in the present exhibition is the finest example of the draped variant, while the plaster bust in the Boston Athenaeum is a superb presentation of the undraped classical version which has historic associations. It is one of the busts that Jefferson purchased from Houdon and brought back to decorate the "tea room" at Monticello.

There survive more than twenty Washingtons attributed to Houdon. Of the undraped versions, the original terra cotta is at Mount Vernon, and the original marble, a work very close to the Athenaeum plaster, is in the National museum in Stockholm. The draped marble Washington shown here is very similar to the terra cotta in the Louvre, except for slight variations in the drapery and the treatment of the hair at the back. In these classical busts, Washington's hair is rather long and brushed out at the sides, although the ribbon which gathered the hair together with a long lock at the back is eliminated, and the hair is cut raggedly at the neck. H.H.A.

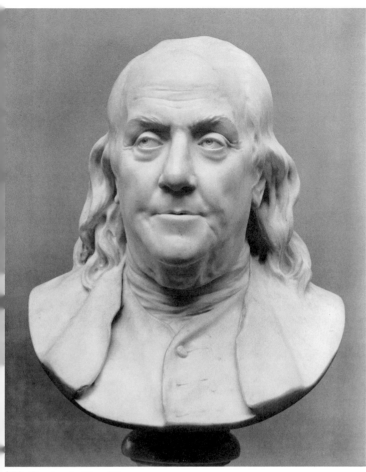

173 Benjamin Franklin

JEAN-ANTOINE HOUDON
1741–1828
Marble 1778
57.1 (22½) high
Signed: *houdon f. 1778*
Lent by The Metropolitan Museum of Art

Franklin went to Paris in 1776 to negotiate a treaty of alliance between France and the United States and remained as minister to France until he returned to America with Houdon in 1785. During this period he became to French intellectuals of the liberal wing a symbol of democratic ideals and of the American Enlightenment. His homely wit and simple manners, perhaps somewhat played up for the French court, his Quaker dress and his delight in the company of lovely ladies, made him immensely popular in the salons of Paris.

Houdon's portrait of Franklin has become so much a part of the iconography of America that it is difficult to analyze it objectively. It has appeared for generations on American currency, stamps and national memorials of every description as a symbol of thrift and economic wisdom for

banks and other financial institutions.

The basic type of *Franklin* bust by Houdon shows him in plain, modern dress, without shoulders and, as is customary with the abbreviated type, rounded at the bottom.

The fine marble in the Metropolitan Museum, signed and dated *Houdon f. 1778*, was left behind in Philadelphia, when Houdon returned to Paris from the United States in November 1785 after having visited George Washington at Mount Vernon. He had left a number of sculptures in the care of Robert Edge Pine, the painter, hoping that they might be sold. Pine died in 1788 and others took up the task of disposing of them. On January 20, 1802, Pierre Samuel du Pont de Nemours, who was friendly with Houdon and his wife, wrote to Thomas Jefferson, soliciting his interest in selling to the Virginia congress the bust of *Franklin* then in du Pont de Nemours' collection. But there was little money available and not enough interest in buying works of art so soon after the Revolutionary War. Du Pont de Nemours' son finally sold the bust to John Church Cruger about 1836. From Cruger it passed to his daughter and

son-in-law, Dr. Samuel Bard, and then to their son, John Bard, who presented it to the Metropolitan Museum in 1882. The marble bust of Franklin in contemporary dress, simple and puritanical, has a somewhat rigid frontality suggesting his qualities of forthrightness. The eyes look up into the distance. He wears his own hair, thin on top and flowing down over his ears and shoulders. The wrinkles at the corners of the eyes are emphasized, the lips are slightly parted in what might be the beginning of a smile. The entire expression is one of benevolence, wisdom and humor, as appropriately it should be. Curiously, if viewed from certain angles, these characteristics are replaced by an expression that can only be described as somewhat weary and apprehensive. The bust exists in innumerable examples of varying qualities. There are fine plasters at Gotha in Germany and in the St. Louis and Toledo museums, as well as an excellent terra cotta in the Louvre. The only bronze known that could be an original is in the Middendorf Collection, Washington.

The subject of Franklin interested Houdon sufficiently that he later made a variant more monumental in scale showing him in a sort of toga, presumably to suggest the qualities of an ancient philosopher. This is possibly the *Franklin* listed in the catalogue for the Salon of 1791 (Franklin died in 1790), one plaster of which is in the Boston Athenaeum and another in the Musée des Beaux-Arts at Angers, both of good quality but neither signed nor dated.

The Boston Athenaeum owns three plaster busts by Houdon, this large Franklin and portraits of Washington and Lafayette. It originally owned four, the fourth being a bust of John Paul Jones, perhaps that now in the Boston Museum of Fine Arts (see no. 175). There is also a second bust of Franklin in modern dress on loan to the Athenaeum from the American Academy of Arts and Sciences which was conceivably at one time the property of the Athenaeum. The *Washington, Lafayette, John Paul Jones,* and a *Franklin* came originally from the collection of Thomas Jefferson. They were willed to Jefferson's granddaughter, the wife of Joseph Coolidge, Jr., of Boston, and were deposited by Mr. Coolidge in the Athenaeum in 1828. The trustees' record at the Athenaeum from March 11, 1828, notes that it was voted that busts of Jones, Franklin and General Washington belonging to Joseph Coolidge, Jr., be received as a deposit. The treasurer's journal for October 1828 holds that Mr. Cope Coolidge had been paid $100 for the bust of Lafayette.

There is some question as to which

of the two *Franklins* came from Jefferson, but the probability is that it was the earlier version in modern dress. The scale and format of the *Franklin* is comparable to that of the other three busts and all four were supposed to have been on display in the "tea room" of Monticello. H.H.A.

174 Marquis de Lafayette

JEAN-ANTOINE HOUDON
1741–1828
Plaster c. 1785
73.7 (29) high
Lent by the Boston Athenaeum

The marquis de Lafayette, a hero on both sides of the Atlantic for his role in the American Revolution, was only twenty-nine years old when Houdon portrayed him from life in 1785. The plaster bust shown here was in Jefferson's collection at Monticello along with Houdon's representations of Franklin, Washington and John Paul Jones (see nos. 172, 173, and 175).

In December 1781, the Virginia legislature had voted to commission a bust of Lafayette and present it to him in gratitude for his military services. Though Lafayette was sent a copy of the resolution, the project lagged until the marquis complained to Washington in 1784. Shortly thereafter, Benjamin Harrison, governor of Virginia, instructed Thomas Barclay, consul at Nantes, to arrange for a sculptor to execute the commission.

In December of that year, the Virginia Assembly voted to present the bust not to Lafayette but to the city of Paris, with a second bust to be installed in Richmond. Barclay had meanwhile chosen Houdon as the sculptor, and Jefferson, who must have been pleased with the choice, wrote to the Virginia governor, "I shall render chearfully any services I can in aid of Mr. Barclay. . . . The Marquis de Lafayette being to pass into Germany and Prussia it was thought proper to take the model of his bust in plaister before his departure. Monsieur Houdon was engaged to do it,

and did it accordingly."

The first marble, that to be presented to the city of Paris, was completed early in 1786 and the marble for Virginia a short time later. Jefferson undertook the complicated arrangements for the presentation of the bust in Paris. It was duly installed in the great hall of the Hôtel de Ville in an elaborate ceremony but was destroyed soon afterward in the upheaval of the French Revolution.

The plaster from the Boston Athenaeum shows the marquis in modern uniform without the elaboration of classicizing drapery found in the marble executed by Houdon which was in the Salon of 1787 and is now, as voted by the Virginia Assembly, in the capitol at Richmond. Of the Boston Athenaeum version, there is at Girard College in Philadelphia another plaster which has been painted bronze color. A marble *Lafayette* at Versailles shows him with a wig and is signed and dated "houdon an 1790" over an earlier signature, "houdon fecit." Other signed busts of this type support the 1790 date, and the Versailles bust would be the one exhibited in the Salon of 1791. Several porcelain versions of the later *Lafayette* exist: one in the Fogg Art Museum in Cambridge is decorated across the base with a leafy branch and the name *Lafayette*, and another is in the collection of Mr. Samuel Barlow, a descendant of Joel Barlow, who was also portrayed by Houdon (see no. 346). The Musée de Mans possesses a signed and dated plaster of the Versailles type with perruque.

Jefferson valued Lafayette highly, though in coded letters to Madison he sounds wary of the marquis' love of the spotlight; in 1785 he wrote, "I take him to be of unmeasured ambition but that the means he uses are virtuous," and two years later, "The Marquis de Lafayette is a most valuable auxiliary to me. His zeal is unbounded. . . . He has a great deal of sound genius, is well remarked by the king. . . . His foible is a canine appetite for popularity and fame." H.H.A.

175 John Paul Jones

JEAN-ANTOINE HOUDON
1741–1828
Marble 1781
69.8 (27½) high
Signed on back of collar: *Houdon 1781*
Lent by the United States Naval
Academy, Annapolis, Maryland

John Paul Jones first came to Paris
in 1780 and was lionized as the
triumphant hero of a series of notable
battles in 1778 and 1779 as commander of the French ship *Bon
Homme Richard*. The Masonic Lodge
of the Nine Sisters ordered a bust of
him to be executed by Houdon and
presented at a court festival in Jones'
honor. A plaster bust of Jones, painted
the color of terra cotta, was exhibited

in the Salon of 1781 as "no. 261—
Paul Jones."

When he returned to Paris four
years later, John Paul Jones ordered
at least eight plaster copies for his
friends, including Washington, Jefferson and Lafayette. Although made
later, these have retained the original
date of 1780. Jones asked Jefferson
to make the arrangements with
Houdon for the plaster replicas and to
arrange for their shipment to the
United States, where they arrived in
January 1790. Jefferson's copy of the
bust went to Monticello, where it
remained until his death.

Abigail Adams wrote of Jones in
1784, "From the intrepid character he
justly supported in the American
Navy, I expected to have seen a rough,

stout, warlike Roman—instead of
that I should sooner think of wrapping
him up in cotton wool, and putting
him into my pocket, than sending him
to contend with cannon balls. He is
small of stature, well proportioned, soft
in his speech, easy in his address,
polite in his manners, vastly civil,
understands all the etiquette of a
lady's toilette as perfectly as he does
the masts, sails and rigging of his ship."

Jefferson valued Jones' skills as a
commander to such a degree that he
wrote to Monroe about the Barbary
pirates, "I am of opinion Paul Jones
with half a dozen frigates would totally
destroy their commerce. . . ."

The splendid marble exhibited here
shows Jones in his admiral's uniform
decorated with the cross of Military
Merit received from Louis XVI.
Although in the salons of Paris he
obviously subordinated those qualities
which made him a great naval hero,
they shine forth from the portrait by
Houdon, which shows a strong,
resolute face, suggestive of a keen intelligence and an ability to act quickly
and decisively. Pudelko draws an
interesting comparison between the
face of Jones in this bust and the face
of Donatello's condottiere *Gatte-
malata*. Seen in profile, the resemblance between the two is striking. The
face of Jones also illustrates superbly
the powerful sense of structure which
in Houdon's busts reflects both his
intense study of anatomy and his control of sculptural form.

Aside from the marble, a number
of plasters with long histories exist.
In the Pennsylvania Academy, there is
a plaster painted the color of bronze,
which has been there since approximately 1800, and there is, in the
Museum of Fine Arts, Boston, a fine
plaster which may be the same one
that disappeared from the Boston
Athenaeum during the nineteenth
century. Presumably the bust was
loaned to the "Boston Museum"
(which was actually a theater, not a
museum) to be used as a stage effect
in a play. The Boston Museum was
torn down around 1900 and its contents were sold. Charles W. Taylor,
one of the editors of the *Boston Globe*,
bought the bust of Jones at the sale
and later presented it to the Museum
of Fine Arts.

If this sequence of events is accurate, then the Boston plaster is that
which originally belonged to Thomas
Jefferson (presumably the one which
was given to him by Jones himself).
This, like the *Franklin*, *Washington*,
and *Lafayette*, came to the Boston
Athenaeum from Jefferson's heirs. The
National Academy of Design in
New York also owns two plasters
which have been in its possession since
at least 1852.

There is a somewhat macabre post-

script to the story of the *John Paul
Jones* bust which nevertheless is of interest as evidence of the remarkable
precision in Houdon's rendition of his
portraits. Jones died in Paris in 1792
and was buried in the St. Louis
Cemetery for Foreigners. In 1899 the
grave was discovered and in 1905
the body was transferred to the Naval
Academy at Annapolis. In the identification of the body the head measurements of Houdon's bust were used
for comparison and were found to
conform exactly. H.H.A.

SET OF AMERICAN REVOLUTIONARY WAR MEDALS

One of the tasks that Jefferson inherited as American minister to France was the supervision of the work on the various medals voted by Congress to victorious officers in the Revolution. Franklin had already engaged Duvivier to provide the silver medal for François de Fleury, a French volunteer, and David Humphreys, the secretary of the American commissioners sent to Europe to negotiate treaties of commerce, was instructed to arrange for the making of the medals and swords awarded by Congress. By the time of Humphreys' return to the United States in 1785 he had arranged for Dupré and Gatteaux to provide dies for the

medals to be awarded General Horatio Gates and General Nathaniel Greene. The Académie Royale des Inscriptions et Belles-Lettres had composed designs for the medals for General Washington, General Morgan, Colonel Howard and Colonel William Washington, though none had yet been struck. The Gates and Greene medals were completed in the first half of 1787, and acting on a suggestion of Jefferson's, Congress directed Jefferson to prepare sets for presentation to the sovereigns and states of Europe and leading universities, as well as for distribution within the United States. Jefferson's task was thus greatly magnified, but in his usual methodical way he arranged for designs

the remaining medals for Wayne, Stewart and, as a belated recognition by Congress, to John Paul Jones. Descriptions of the medals in English and French were prepared and boxes to contain them were made. Most important, Duvivier was engaged to cut the dies for the General Washington, Colonel Howard and Colonel Washington medals; Dupré did those for General Morgan and Commander Jones; and Gatteaux for Wayne and Stewart. All, with the exception of the Jones medal, were ready by the time Jefferson left France in 1789, and he was able to take a set of proofs in tin, "in fact more delicate than the medals themselves," which was hung at Monticello in the parlor. Jefferson's responsibility for the series appeared to be completed when he handed over the medals for presentation to Washington in 1790, but by a curious oversight the award to Colonel Henry Lee, "Light-Horse Harry," had been forgotten and Jefferson, on being told of this, supervised the production of a medal by Joseph Wright.

The present set belonged to George Washington and had been authorized by Congress. Jefferson presented the medals to the president immediately after his arrival in New York on March 21, 1790. R.W.

176 De Fleury medal

PIERRE SIMON BENJAMIN
DUVIVIER 1730–1819
Silver 1780
Obverse, signed lower left: DUVIVIER S.
Inscribed: VIRTUTIS ET AUDACIÆ
MONUMET PRÆMIUM exergue:
D. DE FLEURY EQUITI GALLO/PRIMO
SUPER MUROS/RESP. AMERIC. D.D.
Reverse, inscribed: AGGERES PALUDES
HOSTES VICTI exergue: STONY-PT.
EXPUGN./XV JUL. MDCCLXXIX
*Lent by the Massachusetts Historical
Society, Boston*

For his part in the battle of Stony
Point the French colonel de Fleury
was awarded a silver medal. It was
the first medal to be executed and
Franklin, still American minister to
France, engaged Duvivier to cut the
dies. R.W.

177 Libertas Americana medal

AUGUSTIN DUPRÉ 1748–1833
Silver 1783
4.6 (1¹³⁄₁₆) diam.
Obverse, signed at truncation of neck:
Dupre F. Inscribed: LIBERTAS'
AMERICANA exergue: 4 JUL. 1776.
Reverse, signed lower right: DUPRE F.
Inscribed: NON SINE DIIS ANIMOSUS
17 OCT. 1777.
INFANS. exergue: 19   1781.
*Lent by the Massachusetts Historical
Society, Boston*

On hearing of the news of the surrender of Yorktown, Franklin, then in
Paris, wrote to Secretary of State
Robert Livingston in March 1782:
"This puts me in mind of a medal I
have had a mind to strike since the late
great event you gave me an account of,
representing the United States by the
figure of an infant Hercules in his
creadle, strangling the two serpents;
and France by that of Minverva, sitting
by as his nurse, with her spear and
helmet, and her robe specked with a
few 'fleur de lis.' The extinguishing of
two entire armies in one war is what
has rarely happened, and it gives
a presage of the future force of our
growing empire. . . ." France played a
more active part in the final composition by warding off the attack of a
lion or leopard, representing England.
The inscription on the reverse comes
from Horace and reads in translation,
"The Courageous child helped by
the Gods." The head of Liberty on
the obverse later served as a model for
some of the early American coins.
    Franklin used the medals as propa-
ganda and gave copies to the king
and queen and the French ministers.
He also had printed a descriptive
pamphlet with an engraving of both

sides of the medal and an explanation
in English and French so that the
meaning would be quite clear.
    Although Franklin had the *Libertas
Americana* medal struck on his own
initiative, his contacts with Dupré
must have been useful to his successor
Jefferson, when the latter had to
carry out Congress' order for medals
to military leaders. R.W.

178 Benjamin Franklin medal

AUGUSTIN DUPRÉ 1748–1833
Silver 1786
4.6 (1¹³⁄₁₆) diam.
Obverse, inscribed: BENJ. FRANKLIN
NATUS BOSTON. XVII JAN. MDCCVI.
Reverse, inscribed: ERIPUIT COELO/
FULMEN/SCEPTRUM QUE/TYRANNIS
exergue: SCULPSIT ET LIGAVIT/AUG.
DUPRE ANNO/MDCCLXXXVI
*Lent by the Massachusetts Historical
Society, Boston*

As Franklin's mission to France drew
to a close, a medal was commissioned
by one or more of his friends and
admirers. Dupré, who was a friend of
the American minister and lived quite
close to him, prepared several designs before the final one was chosen.
The portrait, while close to Houdon's
bust, could well have been based
on a sketch from life. There were two
separate issues of the medal, one,
in 1784, with a winged genius on the
reverse, the other, in 1786, with the
same reverse as the example exhibited
here. R.W.

179 General George Washington medal

PIERRE SIMON BENJAMIN
DUVIVIER 1730–1819
Silver 1789
6.8 (2⅝) diam.
Obverse, signed below bust: DU VIVIER/
PARIS. F. Inscribed: GEORGIO WASH-
INGTON SUPREMO DUCI EXERCITUUM
ADSERTORI LIBERTATIS exergue:
COMITIA AMERICANA. Reverse, in-
scribed: HOSTIBUS PRIMO FUGATIS
exergue: BOSTONIUM RECUPERATUM/
XVII. MARTII/MDCCLXXVI.
*Lent by the Massachusetts Historical
Society, Boston*

This medal, which was the first in the
series to be voted by Congress, only
eight days after the event celebrated,
was among the last to be completed.
Washington was awarded a gold medal
to commemorate the evacuation of
Boston by the British on March 17,
1776, the event shown on the reverse.
Although Humphreys had applied
to the Académie Royale des Inscriptions et Belles-Lettres as early as the
spring of 1785 for advice on the

design of the medal, nothing further
had been done by the beginning of
1786. The delay is partly explained by
the need to wait for Houdon's return with the life mask of Washington,
which formed the basis for the busts
of the commander in chief, which were
used in turn for the profile on the
medal. Washington received his
award together with the medals voted
to the other officers in New York,
when Jefferson arrived in March 1790.
By that time public interest in the
medals had subsided, and there was no
comment in the press. Neither did
Washington make any mention of it
in his diary. R.W.

180 Lieutenant-Colonel John E. Howard medal

PIERRE SIMON BENJAMIN
DUVIVIER 1730–1819
Silver 1789
4.6 (1¹³⁄₁₆) diam.
Obverse, signed lower left: DUVIV.
Inscribed: JOH. EGAR. HOWARD
LEGIONIS PEDITUM PRÆFECTO exergue:
COMITIA AMERICANA. Reverse, in-
scribed: QUOD/IN NUTANTEM HOSTIUM
ACIEM/SUBITO IRRUENS/PRÆCLARUM
BELLICÆ VIRTUTIS/SPECIMEN DEDIT/
IN PUGNA AD COWPENS/XVII. JAN.
MDCCLXXXI
*Lent by the Massachusetts Historical
Society, Boston*

Howard was awarded a silver medal
for his part in the battle of Cowpens,
when he led the third and main line of
militia, which trapped the British
forces. The history of the medal is the
same as General Morgan's. R.W.

181 General Daniel Morgan medal

AUGUSTIN DUPRÉ 1748–1833
Silver 1789
5.6 (2³⁄₁₆) diam.
Obverse, inscribed: DANIELI MORGAN
DUCI EXERCITUS exergue: COMITIA
AMERICANA. Reverse, signed in exergue:
DUPRÉ INV ET F. Inscribed: VICTORIA
LIBERTATIS VINDEX. exergue: FUGATIS
CAPTIS AVT CAESIS/AD COWPENS
HOSTIBUS/XVII. JAN. MDCCLXXXI.
*Lent by the Massachusetts Historical
Society, Boston*

In January 1781 Morgan defeated a
British force under Colonel Banastre
Tarleton at Cowpens, South Carolina,
and helped to counteract the almost
continuous successes of the British
in the southern colonies. Tarleton led
a raid on Monticello in June of the
same year which just failed to capture
Jefferson, who had fled with his
family to Poplar Forest. The scene on

the medal records Morgan's victorious attack and shows him crown
with a laurel wreath by an American
Indian. Congress awarded a gold me
to Morgan.
    Humphreys requested a design
from the Académie Royale in Noven
ber 1785 but kept insisting that
nothing further could be done until
more information was available on t
details of the battle. The matter thus
hung fire until after Humphreys left
Paris in 1786 and Jefferson succeed
to his responsibility. The dies were
cut in mid-1789 and the medal finall
presented after Jefferson's return. R.

182 General Nathaniel Greene medal

AUGUSTIN DUPRÉ 1748–1833
Silver 1787
5.5 (2³⁄₁₆) diam.
Obverse, inscribed: NATHANIELI
GREENE E GREGIO DUCI COMITIA
AMERICANA. Reverse, signed lower le
DUPRE. Inscribed: SALUS REGIONUM
AUSTRALIUM. exergue: HOSTIBUS AD
EUTAW/DEBELLATIS DIE VIII SEPT/
MDCCLXXXI
*Lent by the Massachusetts Historica
Society, Boston*

Greene's victory at Eutaw Springs
would hardly have merited special
recognition by Congress, indeed it w
doubtful if it could be counted a
victory at all. Nonetheless in the long
run it provided a tactical check to
British forces in the south, and in the
euphoria after the surrender of Yor
town Congress voted a gold medal
to Greene for his "wise, decisive an
magnanimous conduct in the action
Greene came from Rhode Island and
may have benefited from a desire
to balance the heavy preponderance
southern officers who received re-
wards. The Greene medal was one of
the two struck in 1787, and in the
letter to Jay informing him of its co
pletion, Jefferson first suggested
presenting sets to all the universities
of America and the sovereigns of
Europe. Greene was unable to receiv
the medal as he had died the year
before. R.W.

3 General Horatio Gates medal

COLAS-MARIE GATTEAUX
51–1832
lver 1787
5 (2³⁄₁₆) diam.
bverse, signed below bust:
GATTEAUX. Inscribed: HORATIO
.TES DUCI STRENUO exergue: COMITIA
MERICANA. Reverse, inscribed: SALUS
GIONUM SEPTENTRIONAL. exergue:
)STE AD SARATOGAM/IN DEDITION.
:CEPTO/DIE XVII OCT. MDCCLXXVII

*ent by the Massachusetts Historical
ciety, Boston*

he scene represents the surrender of
e British forces at Saratoga in
'77 by General Burgoyne to General
ates. Saratoga was a signal defeat
r the British plan to subdue New
ngland and contributed to France's
cision to enter the war openly on
e American side. Congress voted a
)ld medal in the same year. As
ith the other medals, there was a con-
derable delay before it was finally
elivered, and the die was not ready
ntil 1787. William Short sent the
edal to the United States in the
ring of that year, while Jefferson was
1 his trip to Italy and the south of
rance. R.W.

**84 General Anthony Wayne
edal**

ICOLAS-MARIE GATTEAUX
757–1832
ilver 1789
3 (2⅛) diam.
bverse, signed lower right: GATTEAUX.
nscribed: ANTONIO WAYNE DUCI
XERCITUS exergue: COMITIA AMERI-
ANA. Reverse, inscribed: STONEY-
OINT EXPUGNATUM exergue: XV JUL.
IDCCLXXIX

*.ent by the Massachusetts Historical
'ociety, Boston*

The reverse of this medal represents
he site of Wayne's victory on the
Iudson River in July 1779, which
telped to end the war in the northern
ection of the colonies. Humphreys
ieglected to inform Jefferson that
ieither the gold medal awarded by
Congress to Wayne, nor the silver
nedal awarded to Stewart for Stony
'oint had been executed, so they were
ncluded in the last batch struck in
.789. R.W.

185 Major John Stewart medal

NICOLAS-MARIE GATTEAUX
1757–1832
Silver 1789
4.6 (1¹³⁄₁₆) diam.
Obverse, signed lower left: GATTEAUX.
Inscribed: JOANNI STEWART COHORTIS
PRÆFECTO exergue: COMITIA AMERI-
CANA. Reverse, inscribed: STONEY-
POINT OPPUGNATUM exergue: XV JUL.
MDCCLXXIX

*Lent by the Massachusetts Historical
Society, Boston*

Stewart was awarded a silver medal for
his part in the battle of Stony Point.
The reverse shows him leading his
troops into the ramparts of the
fort. R.W.

**186 Lieutenant Colonel William
Washington medal**

PIERRE SIMON BENJAMIN
DUVIVIER 1730–1819
Silver 1789
4.5 (1¾) diam.
Obverse, signed lower right: DUV.
Inscribed: GUILIELMO WASHINGTON
LEGIONIS EQUIT. PRÆFECTO exergue:
COMITIA AMERICAN. Reverse: QUOD/
PARVA MILITUM MANU/STRENUE
PROSECUTUS HOSTES/VIRTUTIS IN-
GENITÆ/PRÆCLARUM SPECIMEN
DEDIT/IN PUGNA AD COWPENS/XVII.
JAN. MDCCLXXXI

*Lent by the Massachusetts Historical
Society, Boston*

Colonel Washington, who was a distant kinsman of the president's, led
the cavalry reserve at the battle of
Cowpens. For his distinguished conduct he was awarded a silver medal,
and its history is similar to the other
Cowpens medals. R.W.

187 John Paul Jones medal

AUGUSTIN DUPRÉ 1748–1833
Silver 1789
5.6 (2⁷⁄₃₂)
Obverse, signed on truncation of
shoulder: DUPRÉ F. Inscribed: JOANNI
PAULO JONES CLASSIS PRAEFECTO.
exergue: COMITIA AMERICANA. Reverse,
signed: exergue DUPRÉ. F. Inscribed:
HOSTIUM NAVIBUS CAPTISUAT FUGATIS.
exergue: AD ORAM SCOTIAE XXIII. SEPT.
M. DCCLXXVIIII.

*Lent by the Massachusetts Historical
Society, Boston*

There was a surprising delay between
Jones' famous victory off Flamborough
Head in 1779, when the *Bon Homme
Richard* defeated H.M.S. *Serapis* in a
hard-fought battle, and the vote of

a gold medal in 1787. It may be that
Jones' enemies in America had prevented such a move, and he was out of
the country for much of the time
before then. Although it was the latest
in the series, his medal was ready
by 1789. Jones, in a letter to Jefferson
of August 1788, ordered four gold
medals and planned to have more
struck. He also suggested that Dupré

should study the wax medals of
Renaud, who had made them for
Jones, taking care to avoid any mistakes. Jefferson replied that he had sent
an example of the Renaud to Dupré,
who used it, together with an engraving by Lerprinière and Fittler, as
the basis for the reverse. The obverse
profile derives from Houdon's bust
of Jones (see no. 175). R.W.

188 Diplomatic medal

AUGUSTIN DUPRÉ 1748–1833
Bronze 1791
6 (2⅜) diam.
Obverse, signed lower right: DUPRÉ.F.
Inscribed: TO PEACE AND COMMERCE
exergue: IV JUL. MDCCLXXVI. Reverse,
inscribed: THE UNITED STATES OF
AMERICA

Lent by the Smithsonian Institution

Although Jefferson had already returned to America to become secretary
of state, he played an important part
in the design of the diplomatic medal.
Its genesis goes back to April 30,
1790, when the former French
minister, marquis de la Luzerne, was
offered a gold medal and chain by
the former French minister. On the
same day Jefferson wrote to William
Short: "It has become necessary to
determine on a present proper to
be given to Diplomatic Characters on
their taking leave of us; and it is

concluded that a medal and chain of
gold will be the most convenient. . . .
On one side must be the Arms of
the United States, of which I send you
a written description. . . . The device
on the other side we do not decide on
One suggestion has been Columbia
(a fine female figure) delivering the
emblems of peace and commerce to a
Mercury, with the Legend 'Peace
and Commerce' circumscribed, and
the date of our Republic, to wit, IV
Jul. MDCCLXXVI, subscribed as an
Exergum." Whether the ideas were
Jefferson's or someone else's, they were
almost completely adopted by
Dupré. There was a considerable delay
in executing this medal and a second
one for comte de Moustier in 1791,
because Dupré was also working on the
new French coinage. The two medals
were ready by February 1792. No
further examples were struck for
presentation. R.W.

EUROPE: THE VAUNTED SCENE

*Behold me at length on the vaunted scene of Europe! It is not neces-
sary for your information that I should enter into details concerning
it. But you are, perhaps, curious to know how this new scene has
struck a savage of the mountains of America.*

JEFFERSON to BELLINI, September 30, 1785

PARIS

In the spring of 1784, Thomas Jefferson was appointed by Congress
to join Benjamin Franklin and John Adams as commissioners
in Paris to negotiate treaties of friendship and trade on behalf of
the American Republic. Jefferson and his daughter arrived in
Paris on August 6, 1784, from Boston, where they had sailed on
the *Ceres* the month before.

For the next five years, "the vaunted scene of Europe," with
all of its rich texture of art, architecture and antiquity, was to
absorb the critical eye and finely tuned curiosity of the new American diplomat. It was an opportunity to indulge his consuming
interest in the arts with an enthusiasm that had been growing since
his earliest studies. "It seems that in France," Dumas Malone has
written, "Jefferson was better able to do the sort of things he

wanted to do, and to be the sort of man he wanted to be," than
ever again in his life. However much he was devoted to the secluded
rural life of Monticello and his native Virginia, Jefferson was
captivated by the aesthetic and intellectual atmosphere of Paris,
its cultivated drawing rooms, its artists, its exhibitions, its architects, the civilities of its citizens. Next to Virginia, he was later
to confess, the place of his greatest affections on earth was France.

When Jefferson arrived in Paris, his old friend Doctor Franklin
was nearing the end of his long career as the beloved American
minister to the court of Versailles. John and Abigail Adams who
had been at The Hague returned to Paris a week after Jefferson's
arrival to join the other commissioners.

Beyond the small group of Americans in Paris, including David
Humphreys, secretary to the delegation, and William Short,
Jefferson's protégé and private secretary, there were a number of
old friends and leading French figures, whom he had met during
the Revolution. The marquis de Chastellux arranged for Martha
to attend the fashionable school for young ladies in the Abbaye
de Panthemont. When the marquis de Lafayette returned from
America, he immediately introduced the Virginian into his own
family circle, which included the comtesse de Tessé, a member of
the renowned Noailles family. Mme de Tessé, perhaps more than
anyone else Jefferson was to meet during his Paris years, shared
with him his deep and far-ranging passion for art, architecture
and landscape gardening. Their correspondence during the period
is a marvelous confection of exchanges on everything from the
merits of the painter David to the correct method of propagating
the seeds of the *Juniperus virginiana*, which Jefferson had secured
from Virginia for the comtesse's extensive gardens at the Château
de Chaville outside of Paris.

In July 1785, Jefferson succeeded Franklin as minister, but his
duties were almost entirely limited to commercial negotiations
and attempts to establish a secure trade arrangement for American
products, so that he had ample time to explore the artists' studios,
the bookstalls and particularly the new neoclassical buildings that
were then beginning to appear in and around Paris. During the
decade of 1780–1790, before the convulsions of the French Revolution, the strong links between the Enlightenment and the leading artists dedicated to advancing a new style out of a renewed
vision of antiquity, were carrying forward an aesthetic revolution
quite independent from the new political ideas that would cul-
minate in the Revolution. Jefferson's response to the new art was
immediate and complete. "I do not feel an interest in any pencil
but that of David," he wrote of the creator of *The Oath of the
Horatii.* "Were I to proceed to tell you how much I enjoy their
architecture, sculpture, painting and music, I should want words,"
he confessed to his friend Charles Bellini. Among those artists
he admired, besides David, there were Houdon and Drouais and
the architects of the most visionary direction such as Ledoux and
Boullée, whose works were to influence Jefferson's own architectural creation when he returned to America.

The Paris Salons during the decade of the 1780s were major
events, attracting hundreds of visitors each day to the galleries in
the Louvre where the biennial exhibitions were held. Jefferson

attended the Salons of 1785, 1787 and 1789 and had the pleasure of seeing his own bust by Houdon, titled *M. Sefferson, envoye des Etats de la Virginie*, in the Salon of 1789, just before he returned to America.

The new buildings that were going up in and around Paris immediately drew Jefferson's interest. Not only was he entranced by the new designs—"While I was in Paris I was violently smitten with the Hôtel de Salm"—he was equally drawn to new examples of architectural technology. His memory of the revolutionary glass dome of the Halle aux Bleds was later reflected in his directions to Benjamin Latrobe in his work on the capitol building in Washington. When plans were being considered for a president's house in Washington in 1792, Jefferson wrote Washington that he preferred the models of "the celebrated fronts of modern buildings which have already received the approbation of all good judges. Such are the Galerie du Louvre, the Gardes Meubles, and the two fronts of the Hôtel de Salm."

Jefferson's house on the Champs Elysées became the center of life for Americans visiting Paris; there he introduced his countrymen to his own cultural and intellectual circle of French luminaries. He particularly enjoyed laying out an itinerary for young American visitors, which always included extensive references to architecture, antique ruins and notable gardens. He saw these young men as future leaders, dedicated to public service in their own country when they returned, and believed that it was important for them to absorb and learn from the best that was available to them in Europe. Young John Quincy Adams recorded in his diary his devotion to "Mr. Jefferson a man of universal learning . . . whom I love to be with."

During the last two years of his stay in Paris, the domestic political situation continued to deteriorate. Finally the king's position collapsed with the calling of the Etats-Généraux in May 1789. From their first meeting, Jefferson drove "daily from Paris to Versailles and attended their debates . . ." not realizing that events were moving faster than the deliberations of the politicians.

On June 1, Jefferson wrote to young John Trumbull in London, urging him to continue his studies in Paris while serving as the minister's private secretary. As late as June 29, in a brief note to Trumbull asking him to deliver to John Jay Jefferson's extensive account of the crisis, he noted that "all danger of civil commotion here is at an end, and it is probable they will settle to themselves a good constitution." On July 14, while visiting his friend, Louis-Dominique Ethis de Corny, word came that the ancient fortress of the Bastille had surrendered and its demolition had begun.

Still the atmosphere during the summer of 1789 was not so desperate as to interrupt those amenities and exchanges with his friends which Jefferson so valued, and which stood outside the preoccupation with political upheavals and intrigue.

In early June, Jefferson received from Odiot, the silversmith, the handsome neoclassical coffee urn executed from Jefferson's own design (see no. 527). He had commissioned it for his friend Clérisseau as a gift for his collaboration on the plans and model of the Virginia capitol (see nos. 393–399). On the day before the Bastille fell, Jefferson sent a charming note to Mme Denise Broutin, enclosing a copy of Thomas Whately's *Observations on Modern Gardening*, a book that was to advance French interest in English landscape design. Among the plaster busts for which Jefferson paid Houdon 1000 livres in July of that fateful year was probably a copy of his own that had been in the Salon.

"Tumult and violence" continued to hang over Paris and on July 25 he wrote Maria Cosway, "The cutting off heads is become so much á la mode, that one is apt to feel of a morning whether their own is on their shoulders." But on August 5, detached heads were sufficiently removed from the minister's mind to enable him to write again to John Trumbull that "tranquility here is pretty well restored" and ask the artist to secure four pairs of plated silver candlesticks (see no. 538) that had been stolen from his house. In the margin of the letter Jefferson sketched the design in the form of a Corinthian column and noted that he thought no other "form is so handsome."

Three weeks later Jefferson finally received word that he was to be allowed to return to the United States on a temporary leave of absence. On September 26, however, while Jefferson was still en route, the Congress confirmed his nomination as Washington's secretary of state, and he was hailed on his arrival as an official of the new government.

On leaving the rarified and congenial intellectual atmosphere that he had loved with both his "head and his heart," Jefferson paid tribute to his extraordinary experiences there and to the people who had completely captivated him. He wrote many years later in his *Autobiography*, "A more benevolent people I have never known, nor greater warmth and devotedness in their select friendships. Their kindness and accommodation to strangers is unparalleled, and the hospitality of Paris is beyond anything I had conceived to be practicable in a large city. Their eminence, too, in science, the communicative dispositions of their scientific men, the politeness of the general manners, the ease and vivacity of their conversation, give a charm to their society to be found nowhere else."

Shortly before he left Paris, Mme de Tessé sent around to the Hôtel de Langeac a parting gift of a pedestal in the form of a classical column, which Jefferson took back to Virginia and placed in the front hall at Monticello. On it in Latin was inscribed:

To the Supreme Ruler of the Universe, under whose watchful care the liberties of N. America were finally achieved and under whose tutelage the name of Thomas Jefferson will descend forever blessed to posterity.

W.H.A.

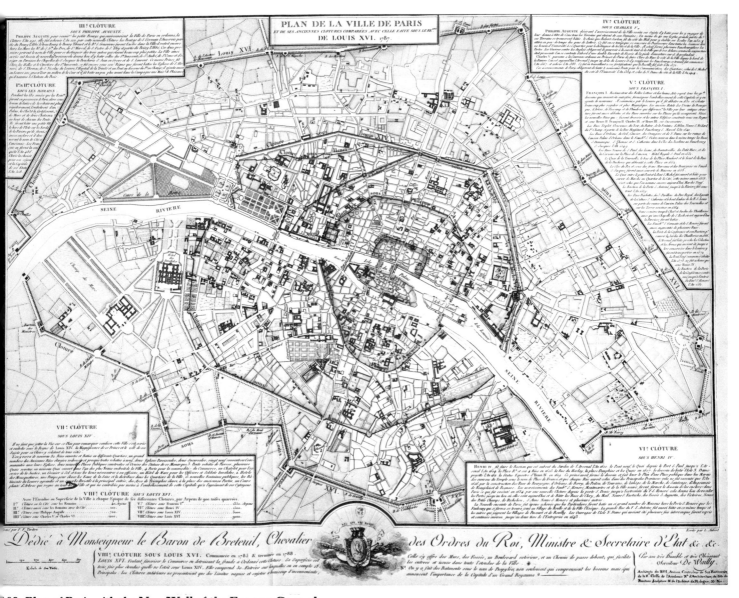

189 Plan of Paris with the New Wall of the Farmers-General

PIERRE-FRANÇOIS TARDIEU
1714–c. 1774
Engraving 1787 (facsimile)
Signed lower left: *Gravé par P.F. Tardieu, Place de l'Estrapade Nº 18*

Original at the Bibliothèque nationale

This map of Paris showing the successive walls that had encircled the city since Roman times was published in 1787 and thus includes the new farmers-general wall ("Clôture sous Louis XVI") under construction when Jefferson was living in Paris. "The wall of circumvallation round Paris and the palaces by which we are to be let in and out are nearly completed," he could report in August 1787 to David Humphreys, who had himself recently resided in Paris. This new wall, which considerably extended the city limits, was designed as a barrier to facilitate collection of municipal customs duties. As such it was not popular and increased public criticism of the farmers-general, the forty financiers to whom the king entrusted the gathering of taxes.

The palaces mentioned by Jefferson were the tollhouses (*bureaux*) at each of the forty-seven gates (*barrières*) designed by the architect Claude-Nicolas Ledoux (1756–1806), who conceived them as *propylaea*, a garland of gateways worthy of the great city. The wall was authorized in 1782, Ledoux's plans approved, and the work begun in January 1785. The architect's fortunes suffered an eclipse when his patron the Minister of Finance Calonne was dismissed in 1787. Though eventually reinstated in his functions, Ledoux was again retired in 1789 by Necker. In July of that year, while Jefferson was still in Paris, the colonnaded palaces—*calonnades* as they came to be derisively called in reference to the unpopular Calonne—were sacked and blackened by incendiaries. Most of them, nevertheless, survived into the mid-nineteenth century. Four of them exist today: the Rotonde de Monceau in the Parc Monceau, the Rotonde de la Villette in the Place Stalingrad, the Barrière du Trône in the Place de la Nation, and the Barrière d'Enfer in the Place Denfert-Rochereau. Standing along the line of the old *Clôture sous Louis XVI*—the *boulevards extérieurs* as they are still anachronistically called—these surviving little palaces can serve as points of reference for delimiting the Paris in which Jefferson resided for five years. H.C.R.

190 Proclamation of the Versailles Peace Treaty between France and England on November 25, 1783

ANTOINE VAN YSENDICH
1801–1875
Oil on canvas
40 x 73 (28¾ x 55)
Signed at lower right: *Ant. van Ysendy*

*Lent by the Musée National du
Château de Versailles*

This painting is not an eye witness
account of the proclamation of peace,
because it was painted many years
later, but there is every reason to
suppose that the scene has been
accurately recorded. The peace between France and Great Britain was
signed on September 3, 1783, at
Versailles and proclaimed on November 25. It is this event which the
painting depicts. The chief magistrates
of Paris with their escort, the king of
arms, and heralds paraded through
the city stopping at all the main
squares to read the proclamation.
Here, they are outside the Palais des
Tuileries. Although the involvement
of France in the American war with
Britain had been popular in France as
a means of revenge for earlier defeats
at the hands of the British, in the
end there was nothing to show for it.
The French government moved closer
to bankruptcy, and liberal nobles, such
as Lafayette, who had volunteered to
fight on the American side, returned
determined to bring about social and
political change in their own country.

The Treaty of Paris, also signed on
September 3, 1783, between the
United States and Great Britain,
formally recognized the independence
of the thirteen colonies by the mother
country. Jefferson had been elected
one of the American commissioners to
negotiate preliminaries of the peace in
1781, but he declined with regret: "I
lose an opportunity, the only one I
ever had and perhaps ever shall have
of combining public service with
private gratification, of seeing
count[ries] whose improvements in
science, in arts, and in civilization it
has been my fortune to [ad]mire at a
distance but never to see. . . ." He
had in fact been asked to go to France
with Franklin and Dean in 1776 as
one of the three commissioners to
the court of France, but family
circumstances prevented his leaving
Virginia. In 1782 the appointment as
peace commissioner was renewed and
Jefferson prepared to leave for France,
glad to have a distraction after the
death of his wife, but the British
blockade delayed his departure so long
that his presence at the conference
became unnecessary. His ultimately
successful mission to France in 1784
was as one of the plenipotentiaries
to negotiate treaties of friendship
and commerce. A.B. de L.

191 Cul-de-sac Taitbout

RITTMAN active 1780, and
JEAN JUNIÉ active 1780
Replica of original 1786 pen and
watercolor drawing, reprinted in 1906
60 x 96 (23⅝ x 37¾)

*Collection of the Bibliothèque
nationale*

NOT IN EXHIBITION

On October 16, 1784, after two
months in temporary lodgings, Jefferson signed a lease for "*un hôtel sis à
Paris rue et Cul de sac Taitbout
Chaussée d'antin.*" The lessor, M
François Guireaud de Talairac, who
lived near the Church of Saint-
Eustache, held the minor office of
*conseiller du Roy, juge rapporteur
du point d'honneur,* and was a building
contractor owning other property in
the newly developed Chaussée d'Antin
quarter of the city. No picture of the
house has survived, but its outlines
can be discerned on this sheet from an
atlas of plans completed in 1786 by
Rittman and Junié for the Arch-
bishopric of Paris. M "Guereau's"
property on the western side of the
Cul-de-sac Taitbout is here numbered
"5." The house, as described in the
lease, consisted of three *corps de logis,*
forming a letter E joined to the
adjacent house of similar form. The
entrance from the street opened into
a first courtyard, at the far side of
which were steps and some sort of

portico leading into the main wing of the house. Beyond this was another courtyard and a small triangular plot in the rear.

Compared with the more spacious mansions in the neighborhood, such as those in the Chaussée d'Antin itself (designed by architects like Ledoux and Brongniart), Jefferson's *hôtel* was a relatively small townhouse without grounds or a view. It must have been of very recent construction, as the Cul-de-sac Taitbout had been opened up only about 1775. As the house was rented unfurnished, Jefferson made extensive purchases of household furnishings, pictures and books, many of which eventually followed him back to the United States. He lived in the Cul-de-sac Taitbout for only one year. After learning of his appointment as minister to the French court to succeed Franklin and thus foreseeing a longer residence in Paris than originally expected, Jefferson again set about house hunting and eventually found one "in a situation much more pleasing to me than my present," as he wrote to Mrs. Adams in London. In mid-October 1785 he moved to the Hôtel de Langeac at the Grille de Chaillot, where he would live for the four remaining years of his sojourn in Paris (see nos. 202–204).

In 1799 the Cul-de-sac Taitbout was extended southward to the boulevard des Italiens and renamed rue du Helder after the French victory in the Netherlands. Still later, the final extension of the boulevard Haussmann left a small triangle now called Place Adrien Oudin to mark the spot where the Cul-de-sac Taitbout once branched off from the street of that name. Jefferson's residence, no longer standing, would have been on the southern side of the boulevard Haussmann at or near the corner of rue du Helder in the present Ninth Arrondissement. H.C.R.

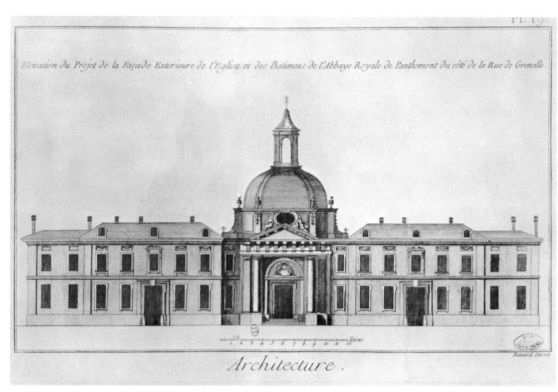

192 Project for the Façade of the Church and Buildings of the Royal Abbey of Panthemont: Elevation, Rue de Grenelle

ROBERT BENARD b. 1734, after
François Franque 1710-after 1792
Engraving c. 1755
Signed lower left: *Benard direx.*

Lent by the Bibliothèque nationale

The Abbaye Royale de Panthemont occupies a special place in the chronicle of Jefferson's Paris years. His daughters Martha ("Patsy") and Mary ("Polly"), who joined her older sister in 1787, were boarding pupils in this Faubourg Saint-Germain convent until the last summer before their return to the United States. Their lessons included French (which they learned to speak fluently), a bit of Latin and Spanish, and such genteel arts as needlework, drawing, dancing, and the harpsichord. As the convent was also a select residence for aristocratic spinsters, widows, and those seeking refuge for other reasons, the proximity of these *dames en chambre* contributed to the worldly education of the younger schoolgirls like *les Demoiselles Jefferson*. Martha's letters to her father (written when he was absent from Paris) provide a delightful glimpse of life at Panthemont. Upon one occasion she reported that Madame l'Abbesse "has visited almost a quarter of the new building, a thing she has not done for two or three years before now."

Panthemont and its buildings were in large measure the creation of the enterprising Abbess, Mme Béthisy de Mézières (related through her mother to the Jacobite family of Sutton D'Oglethorpe). Soon after assuming her duties in 1743 she inaugurated an ambitious building program. The cornerstone of the new church was laid by Cardinal Rohan in 1747, and the building, serving as the convent chapel, was dedicated by the dauphin in 1753 and completed in 1756. The engraving exhibited here is one of a series of six engraved by Benard from projects drawn by the architect François Franque, a collaborator of Pierre Contant d'Ivry (1698–1777). Benard's engravings were published in the first volume of Diderot & D'Alembert's *Encyclopédie, Recueil de Planches* (1762), in the section devoted to "Architecture," where it is noted that the Panthemont buildings, as finally built by Contant d'Ivry, did not conform in all particulars to the more extensive Franque projects. Jefferson might well have seen the engravings in the *Encyclopédie*, a set of which he had acquired for the state of Virginia prior to his departure for France.

The entrance to the Panthemont church was from the rue de Grenelle. Other buildings, those of the convent proper, faced gardens which then extended halfway back to the rue Saint-Dominique. With the advent of the French Revolution, Panthemont suffered the fate of other such ecclesiastical properties and was confiscated in 1790. Contant d'Ivry's chapel was eventually ceded, in 1846, to the Eglise Réformée de France. Since that time Protestant services have been held in the former convent church, now known as the Temple de Pentemont at 106 rue de Grenelle. The other convent buildings, now entered from the rue de Bellechasse, serve as the Ministry of War Veterans. H.C.R.

193 Public Sale in the Auction Room of the Hôtel Bullion

PIERRE-ANTOINE DE MACHY
1723–1807
Oil on canvas
22 x 33 (8⅝ x 13)

Lent by the Musée Carnavalet, Paris

Jefferson frequented auction rooms in
Paris, while he was minister there
from 1785 until 1789, and the
paintings he bought at the sales—for
example, a *Daughter of Herodias with
the Head of Saint John the Baptist*
attributed to Simon Vouet and a
Saint Peter by Guido Reni—later
adorned Monticello.

The scene represented here is an
evening auction. Two auctioneers
walk back and forth on a platform
lighted by chandeliers, presenting the
paintings to a large audience who are
either seated or standing on chairs.
The paintings are hung on the walls.
In the background four stone columns
define the limits of a storeroom,
where paintings are stacked.

The identification of the room
poses some problems, as auction
rooms were numerous in Paris at the
end of the eighteenth century.
According to tradition, the room
represented here is that of Paillet
established about 1780 in the former
Hôtel Bullion, but the auction room
installed under the galleries of the
Palais Royal at numbers 72 to 75
could have had the same appearance.
The auction room of the dealer
Lebrun, husband of Mme Vigée-

Lebrun, rue de Cléry, was, like the
room in the Hôtel Bullion, monumental in scale but without columns.

A.B. de L.

194 Place Louis XV, Paris

JOHN TRUMBULL 1756–1843
Pencil 1786
11.5 x 18 (4½ x 7⁷⁄₁₆)
Inscribed across top: *Place de Louis
15ᶻᵉ d'au travers la Rivière près
des Invalides—at Paris 6ᵐᵉ Août—
1786*

*Lent by Mrs. Norman Holmes
Pearson and the late Mr. Pearson,
Hampden, Connecticut*

The Place Louis XV, described by
Arthur Young as "not properly a
square, but a very noble entrance to a
great city," was barely completed,
when Jefferson arrived in Paris. Begun
in 1757, it was designed by Ange-
Jacques Gabriel (the architect of the
Ecole Militaire) as a grandiose setting
for Edmé Bouchardon's equestrian
statue of Louis XV, *le bien aimé*,
commissioned by the city of Paris to
commemorate popular rejoicing over
the reputedly miraculous recovery
of the monarch. Jefferson had a distant
view of the statue from his Hôtel de
Langeac residence halfway up the
Champs Elysées and came to know
the square better perhaps than any
other spot in Paris. He especially
admired Bouchardon's statue and
Gabriel's façade of the Garde
Meubles, which he ranked among the
"celebrated fronts of modern buildings" worthy of emulation in America.

John Trumbull's view, sketched in
August 1786, is taken from the Left
Bank of the Seine looking diagonally
across the square. There was then no
bridge at this point connecting the
square with the Left Bank. Perronet's
Pont Louis XVI (later known as the
Pont de la Concorde), though begun
in 1787, was not completed until
after Jefferson's return to the United
States. Trumbull's sketch shows the
colonnaded front of the Garde
Meubles (now the Ministère de la
Marine), behind which rises the dome
of the Church of the Assumption.
To the right of the Garde Meubles
is the Hôtel de La Vrillière and still
farther to the right, the entrance to
the Tuileries Gardens. Bouchardon's
statue of Louis XV, also discernible
in the sketch, was pulled down during
the French Revolution, replaced by
the guillotine, and still later by the
familiar Egyptian obelisk of the
present Place de la Concorde.

Save for "the architecture of the
Garde Meubles du Roi," which he considered "good," Trumbull himself
thought the effect of the square
was destroyed "by being cut into
numberless small parts, divided by
heavy balustrades of stone and deep
trenches; the little abominable

buildings, like warehouses, are vile, and the statue itself, with its accompaniments, bad. . . ." Only the horse escaped his strictures.

This unpretentious sketch, which has the distinction of being one of the earliest extant views of Paris by an American artist, was selected by Trumbull to illustrate the *Autobiography* compiled in his old age and published in 1841. It appears as plate 6 with the legend: "The Square of Louis 15th at Paris—the Gardemeubles & entrance of the Tuilleries & Champes Elysees— afterward the Square of the Revolution." H.C.R.

195 The Ditches around the Place Louis XV

HUBERT ROBERT 1733–1808
Red chalk
37 x 48 (14$\frac{9}{16}$ x 18$\frac{7}{8}$)
Signed at lower right: *Robert*
Lent by the Musée Carnavalet, Paris

Hubert Robert, the painter of imaginary visions, could not prevent himself from transforming reality. It is revealing to compare his drawing of the Place Louis XV (now called Place de la Concorde) with the *Elevation of the Buildings on the Place-Louis XV* by Jacques-Ange Gabriel (see no. 305), in order to measure the extent of Robert's invention. The terrace with the sentry box standing at right angles, the blocks of stone which obstruct the ground in the square, and the pile of hay visible at the back of the ditch are all products of his fantasy, of the artist's imagination. But Robert also respected the essence of Gabriel's masterpiece and copied the beautiful, receding perspective view of the building, which was used by Gabriel and which lowers the viewpoint of the drawing.

As usual, the composition is original, the strokes nervous and sensitive, the drawing of varied density, the red chalk selectively applied. There is an almost identical drawing in the Musée de Valence. A.B. de L.

196 Paris seen from Franklin's former House at Passy

JOHN TRUMBULL 1756–1843
Ink 1786
11 x 18 (4⅜ x 7⅛)
Inscribed on verso: *Vue de Paris prise du Maison cidevant du Francklin a Passy*
Lent by Mrs. Norman Holmes Pearson and the late Mr. Pearson, Hampden, Connecticut

Trumbull's sketch was probably made on August 13, 1786, the day he "dined, in company with Mr. Jefferson, at the Abbés Chalut and Arnoux in Passy." It was, he noted in his diary, "a *jour maigre*, or fast day, but the luxury of the table in soups, fish and fruits, truly characteristic of the opulent clergy of the times." The two abbés, whose friendship Jefferson had inherited from Franklin and the Adamses, lived in Passy, then a village beyond the city limits, on the heights overlooking the Seine. Their residence was along the rue Basse de Passy (present rue Raynouard), not far from Leray de Chaumont's Hôtel de Valentinois, where Franklin had lived during his years in France.

Several of the landmarks that punctuated the Paris skyline of Jefferson's day appear in Trumbull's rapid but vigorous sketch. At the left is the dome of the Invalides, beyond and to the right of which rise the two towers of Notre-Dame. In the middle distance stands Gabriel's Ecole Militaire facing the tree-lined champ de Mars, as yet unencumbered by the Eiffel Tower. In the distance at the left of the Ecole Militaire are the two towers of the Church of Saint-Sulpice, then being rebuilt under the direction of the architect Chalgrin, one of them encased by scaffolding. Another reminder of current building activity can be discerned on the far horizon to the right of the Ecole Militaire. This pile of "sticks and chips," to borrow a phrase from Jefferson, represents the unfinished dome of the Church of Sainte-Geneviève (subsequently known as the Panthéon), then nearing completion according to Soufflot's design (see nos. 198, 306). Only a few days before dining at Passy, Trumbull had gone through every part of the building "to the highest scaffolding of the dome." The inner columns, he noted, "seemed just carried up to their height and the workmen laying up the arches of the intercolumniations, which are to form the windows; the external colonnade was carried to about half its height." The view of Paris from the highest scaffolding—

"the extent of the city, the vast and opulent country terminating partly in rough and broken hills, partly in a fine champaign"—formed "a coup-d'oeil entirely superior to anything I have hitherto seen."

Another view presumably drawn at the same time as this one, but in pencil and from a different vantage point, was published by Trumbull as plate 7 in his *Autobiography* (1841) with the legend: "Paris, as seen from the house of the Abbés Chassé & Arnout at Passy—J.T—1786." H.C.R.

97 The Construction of the Hôtel de Salm

Oil on canvas c. 1784
56.5 x 101 (22¼ x 39¾)
Signed at the bottom right on a rock,
Jaldot, Jaldot, or Jallot
Lent by the Musée Carnavalet, Paris

The details of the construction of the
Hôtel de Salm will be found in the
entry for the model (see no. 288). The
painting shows the *hôtel* in the course
of construction and must date from
about 1784. Unfortunately, the artist
remains unknown, as the signature is
impossible to interpret clearly. There
are, however, reminiscences of Lépicié
and Vernet in the picturesque
arrangement of figures in the foreground and the attention to anecdotal
detail.

Jefferson's fascination with the
Hôtel de Salm is amply documented
in a letter to Mme de Tessé in 1787:

While at Paris, I was violently
smitten with the hôtel de Salm, and
used to go to the Thuileries almost
daily to look at it. The Loueuse des
chaises, inattentive to my passion
never had the complaisance to place
a chair there; so that, sitting on the
parapet and twisting my neck round
to see the object of my admiration,
I generally left it with torticollis.

A.B. de L.

198 Procession in Front of the Church of Sainte-Geneviève

FRANÇOIS-DENIS NÉE 1732–1818,
after Meunier active 1780
Engraving, 1788, from Voyage
pittoresque de la France, Dépt. de
Paris, No. 85
26 x 20 (10¼ x 8)
Signed lower left: Dessiné par
Meunier; lower right: Gravé par Née
Lent by the Musée Carnavalet, Paris

The Church of Sainte-Geneviève,
crowning the Montagne Sainte-
Geneviève in the Latin Quarter of
Paris, ranks among the outstanding
neoclassic monuments of the
eighteenth century. The idea of a
new church honoring the patron
saint of Paris originated in a vow made
by Louis XV at the time of his near-
fatal illness in 1744. The realization
of the project became the responsibility of the king's surintendant des
bâtiments, the marquis de Marigny,
who entrusted the plans to the
architect Jacques-Germain Soufflot
(1713–1780). A symbolic first stone
was laid in 1764 with a life-size
backdrop painted by de Machy in
trompe l'oeil to represent the projected

classic portico. Work continued
slowly under Soufflot's supervision
until his death in 1780 and thereafter, according to his plans, under
Rondelet and others. The church
reached completion only in 1788.

Sainte-Geneviève was thus one of
the several important construction
sites to meet Jefferson's eye upon his
arrival in Paris in 1784. He acquired a
set of the engraved plans published in
1757 (one of these engravings by
Charpentier after Soufflot has survived
at Monticello) and by comparing
them with the current work in
progress could note the architect's
modifications of his original concept,
notably in the imposing dome.
Glimpses of the still unfinished dome
are found in such Paris views as
Lespinasse's panorama from the lower
slopes of the Montagne Sainte-
Geneviève (1786) and John Trumbull's sketch, also 1786, from the
distant heights of Passy (see no. 196).
Trumbull, furthermore, describes in
his diary his tour of the uncompleted
dome. A small drawing by Jefferson
of a cruciform building crowned by a
central dome is supposed by Fiske

Kimball to be a rough sketch of the
Eglise Sainte-Geneviève made in 1792,
when Jefferson was discussing plans
for the capitol in Washington with
the architect Stephen Hallet.

The scene depicted by Meunier
shows the church, by then virtually
completed, with a procession bearing
the châsse containing the miraculous
relics of the saint, whose prayers
once saved Paris from Attila the Hun.
During the Revolution the Sainte-
Geneviève became the Panthéon
where distinguished Frenchmen were
either buried or commemorated. H.C.R.

199 Le Guichet du Louvre

FRANÇOIS-DENIS NÉE 1732–1818
after Meunier active 1780
Engraving
20 x 26 (7⅞ x 10¼)
Signed lower left: Dessiné par
Meunier; lower right: Gravé par Née
Lent by the Musée Carnavalet, Paris

Meunier's view of the entrance ("the
wicket") into the Cour Carrée of
the Louvre shows printsellers' wares
on display there; the words "Marchan
d'Estampes" can be discerned above
the pictures on the wall at the left.
In the course of his walks in Paris,
Jefferson must have paused more
than once to scrutinize displays like
this. Since the subject in works of art
was of primary interest to him, prints,
as distinguished from paintings on
canvas, had the advantage, he once
told John Trumbull, of being "good
things at a small price." Additions to
his portfolio of prints, several of whic
he later had framed and hung at
Monticello, included architectural
plates, city plans and views, engraved
portraits, and occasional genre scenes.
Among the prints that have returned
to Monticello in recent years are
several characteristic products of the
eighteenth-century Paris print trade,
such as Le Déjeuné de Ferney
depicting Voltaire breakfasting in
bed, engraved by Née and Masquelier
or the pair entitled Aglae Sauvée and
Nanette Effrayée that once belonged
to Jefferson's daughter Martha.

The scene sketched by Meunier an
engraved by Née met the stroller's
eye as he entered the Cour Carrée
through the guichet on its eastern
side. This wing of the Louvre, facing
the Church of Saint-Germain-
l'Auxerrois and then but recently
"disengaged" from the adjoining
houses obscuring it, was fronted by
the great colonnade designed in the
seventeenth century by Le Vau,
Perrault, and Lebrun. Jefferson ranke
it with the "celebrated fronts of
modern buildings" that had "already
received the approbation of all good
judges." The design of the colonnade
façade was carried into the vaulted
entranceway, as can be seen here in
Née's engraving. Across the courtyard is Lemercier's Pavillon de
l'Horloge (also known as the Pavillon
de Sully), dating from the seventeenth
century and still familiar today despite
its Second Empire furbelows.

It was only a few years before
Meunier recorded its appearance that
the Cour Carrée was cleared of the
small houses that had long cluttered
it. The Louvre of the 1780s had not
yet become an integrated museum
(which dates officially from a decree
of the National Convention in 1793)
though various royal collections were

cattered throughout the rambling palace. The Academy of Painting and Sculpture (which held its biennial exhibition in the Salon Carré), the Academy of Architecture, and the other royal academies had their headquarters in the Louvre, while painters, sculptors, and architects enjoyed the much-prized privilege of lodgings and studios. Several of the painters represented in the present exhibition—Hubert Robert, David, and de Machy, for example—had quarters in the Cour du Louvre, as did Jefferson's good friend, the architect Clérisseau. H.C.R.

100 Interior View of the New Circus in the Palais Royal and of the Ambassadors of Tipoo-Sahib received there by the Duchess of Orleans

CHARLES-FRANÇOIS-GABRIEL LE VACHEZ et fils active 1760–1820
Aquatint 1788
27.5 x 35.5 (10⅞ x 14)
Signed below border, left: *Le Vachez fil. del. et sculp.* At bottom of sheet: *A Paris chez Le Vachez M[archan]d de Tableaux au Palais Royal, sous les Colonnades, No. 258.*

Lent by the Musée Carnavalet, Paris

In a letter summarizing the latest happenings and "wonderful Improvements" taking place in Paris, written to David Humphreys in August 1787, Jefferson reported that "The Palais Royal is gutted, a considerable part in the center of the garden being dug out, and a subterranean circus begun wherein will be equestrian exhibitions &c." This subterranean circus was the latest in a series of improvements made by the duc d'Orléans in his new Palais Royal gardens, which had

been opened to the public in 1784 and which were already, as Sébastien Mercier phrased it, "the capital of Paris."

The latest digging in the garden set Paris tongues wagging. What was the duc d'Orléans up to now? Some imagined that it was to be a garden *à la Babylonienne*, others thought it was a vast ballroom, while still others surmised that Astley's equestrian spectacles would be transferred there from the boulevard du Temple. Those haunted by antiquity decided that it would be "something like an ancient hippodrome." The completed circus designed by Victor Louis, was not completely subterranean, as can be seen in Le Vachez's view. The balconies overlooking the colonnaded area were at ground level. The portion above ground was masked on the outside by trellised greenery and decorated with statues. The glassed roof, according to a contemporary description, was ribbed with strips of "laminated copper," a new invention combining "solidity, lightness, and economy." Mercier, generally a carping critic, who fumed at the current craze for colonnades, had only praise for this latest example of Victor Louis' work: "the most beautiful, the most graceful, most original architectural monument, dare we say, to be found in Paris."

The new circus thus ranked among the sights to be seen by tourists and state visitors alike. Le Vachez's topical print shows the ambassadors of Tipoo-Sahib being received there by the duchesse d'Orléans on September 13, 1788. These exotic envoys from the sultan of Mysore (who was courting French support in his struggle with the English) inevitably titillated the curiosity of the Parisians (like the fictitious Oriental visitors of Montesquieu's *Persian Letters*) and were for a brief span the talk of the town. Jefferson, who was present at their official reception by the king at Versailles on August 10, dismissed the "unusual pomp" as a mere "*jeu d'enfants*." His eye, nevertheless, caught the picturesque details of the scene and he regretted that his friend Mme de Bréhan (then absent in America) was not present with her pencil and sketchbook. Mme Vigée-Lebrun, as she relates in her memoirs, painted from life a portrait of the first ambassador ("Davich Khan") and of the second ("Acbar Ally Khan") with his son. The portraits were shown at the Salon of 1789 (catalogue nos. 79, 80), where Houdon's bust of Jefferson was first exhibited.

The circus, controversial from the start, turned out to be the most ephemeral of the Palais Royal improvements. After serving during the Revolution as a ballroom or concert hall, a political assembly room, even as an educational institute called the Lycée des Arts, it was consumed by fire in 1798 and the pit of ruins was eventually filled in. Flowerbeds and reflecting pools now cover the site. H.C.R.

201 Place Louis XV at the Launching of the Balloon of MM Charle and Robert, December 1, 1783

Attributed to PIERRE-ANTOINE DEMACHY 1723–1807
Pen and watercolor
42.3 x 62.6 (16⅝ x 24⅝)

Lent by the Musée Carnavalet, Paris

This drawing was once believed to represent the ascent of the balloonists Robert and Hullin in September 1784, but the correct identification has now been made on the basis of the balloon's shape, which was different from that shown in this painting. The Montgolfier brothers' successful launching of a balloon in June 1783, followed by the first manned free flight in November of the same year, and led to many imitators. Charles, who was a medical doctor, and his friend Robert flew their hydrogen balloon on December 1, 1783, a distance of thirty-six kilometers in a flight of just over two hours. Several artists recorded the new craze, and de Machy exhibited two paintings at the Salon of 1785, both of which showed Charles and Robert's ascent. Their exploit appears also as a subject in the decorative arts.

Ballooning soon spread outside France, and Jefferson mentions it several times in his letters. He sent copies of "an account of Robert's last voiage thro' the air" on November 11, 1784, to Madison, John Page, David Rittenhouse, Charles Thomson and James Currie. Madison had earlier asked Jefferson for information on the means of creating enough warm air to achieve "that extreme Levity, which must be necessary for the Purposes of a Balloon." Even before his departure for France, Jefferson was well informed of the relative merits of the various methods used by different aeronauts and tabulated the sizes of different balloons, the means used to create hot air or gas, the distance and height traveled, and the profiles of the variou balloons. A.B. de L.

202 Plan for remodeling the Hôtel de Langeac. Circular room of mezzanine

THOMAS JEFFERSON 1743–1826
Pencil on coordinate paper (facsimile)

Original at the Huntington Library, San Marino, California

Jefferson made these drawings to study possible changes in the room arrangement on the mezzanine of his rented Paris house. Since no floor plan exists of this intermediate level situated between the main ground floor reception area and the elegant first floor private apartments above, it is difficult to know exactly what changes he is proposing. This mansion had been begun some years earlier by the famous Parisian architect Chalgrin for a French noblewoman and was designed in the latest style, with all the newest conveniences, including water closets.

Though he thoroughly enjoyed his sojourn in Europe, Jefferson never forgot the attractions of his own home, saying, "I am savage enough to prefer the woods, the wilds, and the independence of Monticello to all the brilliant pleasures of this gay capital." F.N.

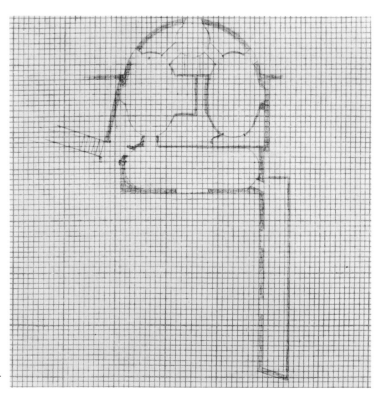

203 Hôtel de Langeac. Study for changes

THOMAS JEFFERSON 1743–1826
Pencil on wove paper 1785
23.5 x 28.5 (9¼ x 11¼)

Lent by the Massachusetts Historical Society, Boston

Jefferson made plans for modifying practically every house he ever lived in. The Hôtel de Langeac, his principal residence in Paris, was no exception. Jefferson moved into the rented mansion on October 17, 1785, and soon after that date his account book records sums paid to workmen and carpenters, undoubtedly for modifications to the interior. The plan of the mansion is defined by acute angles, necessitated by the intersection of the Champs Elysées and the rue de Berry, and has numerous oval salons and a large service court.

The two sketches to the left and below the large existing ground floor plan show a pair of schemes for combining two small rooms into one large room. The upper drawing to the left of the plan is probably the later design and features a large room with a curved end facing on the Champs Elysées. F.N.

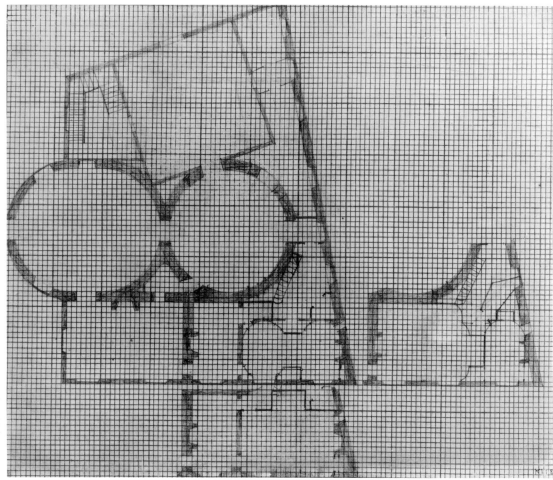

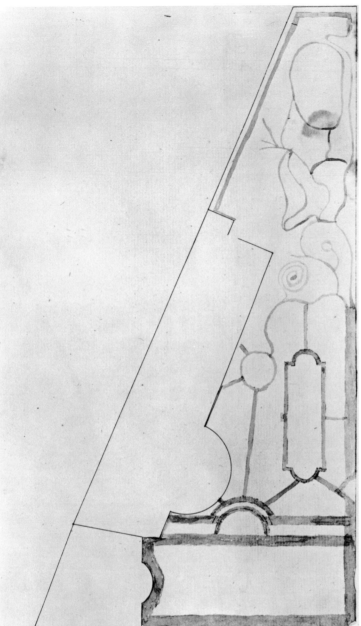

204 Plan for the garden of the Hôtel de Langeac

THOMAS JEFFERSON 1743–1826

Pen and wash on laid paper (facsimile)

Original at the Huntington Library,
San Marino, California

This is a good example of Jefferson's
interest in the English style garden,
or *jardin anglais*. Apparently the
garden, as he designed it, has a berm,
or built-up ledge or shoulder, to
increase the apparent scale of the
design. Though the exact date of this
plan is not known, Jefferson may very
well have executed it after his return
from touring English gardens in the
spring of 1786, though his predilection
for the English style antedated his
trip. F.N.

**205 The Rising of the Sun with
Aurora's Chariot**

JEAN-SIMON BERTHÉLEMY
1743–1811

Oil sketch

*Lent by the Musée Municipal,
Quimper*

Berthélemy painted a ceiling with the
subject of the rising sun in the oval
salon of the Hôtel de Langeac where
Jefferson lived for four years. This is
most probably the sketch for the now
destroyed painting. R.W.

**206 A Cloister of the Hermits at
Mont Valérien A Monks Cell,
Mont Valérien**

Gouache on paper, 1804

Lent by the Bibliothèque nationale

Speaking of the years in France with
her father, Martha Jefferson Randolph
recalled that "whenever he had a
press of business, he was in the habit
of taking his papers and going to the
hermitage, where he spent sometimes
a week or more till he had finished
his work. The hermits visited him
occasionally in Paris and the
Superior made him a present of an
ivory broom that was turned by one
of the brothers."

Jefferson's hermitage was atop
Mont Valérien, or Mont Calvaire,
west of Paris, across the Seine from
the Bois de Boulogne. Since the early
seventeenth century, pilgrims and
penitents had followed the Stations
of the Cross up the slopes of the hill
to the Calvary set on its summit. As
distinguished from the Prêtres du
Calvaire—a religious order serving the
pilgrimage church—a community of
lay brothers, known as the Hermits,
sold *vin de Suresnes* from their vineyards, fine quality silk stockings from
their manufactory, and kept a board-
inghouse for paying guests. The latter,
wrote Sébastien Mercier in his
Tableau de Paris, "enjoyed good air,
a magnificent view, and found comfort
for body as well as for soul." The
sightly hermitage was something like
a gentlemen's club, where the guests
found agreeable table companions,
exchanged reading matter, and kept
abreast of the latest gossip of court
and town. "If you plan to go to the
Hermit brothers tomorrow," one of
the habitués (M Frémyn de
Fontenille) reminded Jefferson,
"please pay my respects to the
gentlemen of our table. . . . tell good
brother Joseph to tell the cook to
have something good for you. If
they're not forewarned, the cuisine
lacks variety and is very lean."

"The sky is clearing and I shall
away to my hermitage!" Jefferson
wrote to a friend one October
morning in 1787, as he set out from
his Champs Elysées residence. Jefferson's Account Book records payments
chiefly in the autumn of 1787, for
"ferriage to Mont Calvaire," for
room and board for himself and horse
(confirmed by the Hermits' own
accounts), as well as for silk stockings
bought for John Adams.

The hermits of Mont Calvaire
survived the early years of the French
Revolution, thanks to their agricultural
labors and stocking manufactory,
adjudged "useful to society," but
the priests were dispersed in 1792.
After serving for a time as Merlin
de Thionville's country estate, the
hill resumed its role as a place of
pilgrimage during the Empire and
Restoration. Since 1840, when
fortifications were built there, the
summit has been under military
jurisdiction. H.C.R.

107 Château de Marly

PIERRE-DENIS MARTIN, le Jeune
1663–1742
Oil on canvas 1724
296 x 224 (116 x 88½)
Signed lower left: *Martin le Jeune
peintre ordinaire du Roy 1724*
*Lent by the Musée National du
Château de Versailles*

The Château de Marly was built for
Louis XIV by Jules-Hardouin Mansart
in 1679. The main building housed
the king, and twelve pavilions in two
lines of six were for the courtiers.
Together, the buildings formed a
conceit of the sun, Louis XIV's
emblem, governing the twelve months
or signs of the zodiac transformed
into architectural terms. The elaborate
gardens with terraces, canals and
sculpture were an integral part of
the overall design and the château
has been called "a colony of gazebos
rather than a palace." Jefferson visited
Marly with Maria Cosway in 1786,
as he recalled in a letter: "the
rainbows of the machine of Marly . . .
the châteaux, the gardens, the
statues of Marly. . . ." The singular
arrangement of the buildings at Marly
may well have stayed at the back of
Jefferson's mind and influenced him
when he designed the rotunda and
pavilions at the University of
Virginia. R.W.

208 The Terrace of the Château at Marly

HUBERT ROBERT 1733–1808
Oil on canvas
90.2 x 132 (35½ x 52⅛)

*Lent by the William Rockhill Nelson
Gallery of Art, Atkins Museum of
Fine Arts, Kansas City (Nelson Fund)*

Marly, like many other châteaux in
the Ile-de-France, was a subject which
often tempted Hubert Robert. The
estate, composed of a château, twelve
pavilions and extensive gardens
(groves, forests, formal flower
gardens), frequented by the court of
Louis XV and that of Louis XVI,
was demolished during the French
Revolution. Hubert Robert depicted
one of the terraces at Marly which
borders the château and offers an
admirable view of the forest of
Saint-Germain-en-Laye and its
château, which can be seen in the
middle distance of the painting. The
elegant woman in the center points it
out to her companions.

There are several known paintings of
Marly by Robert. Some paintings
relating to Marly were exhibited in
the Salons (for example, in the Salon
of 1783 under no. 66, *Two pictures
painted from nature in the gardens at
Marly*), but there are no records that
indicate the Kansas City painting
figured in a Salon.

The work is fascinating in its
freedom of execution (the rendering
of the earth in the foreground),
the feathery pictorial treatment (the

grass and the tree at the right), the
vivid coloring, and the transparency of
the light. It is reminiscent of Diderot's
critique: "C'est un peintre assurément
que ce Robert; mais il fait trop
facilement, ses morceaux sentent la
détrempe. . . ."

The statue on a pedestal to the
right represents Mercury attaching
wings to his heels (1748) by Jean-
Baptiste Pigalle. This celebrated
statue, which established Pigalle's
reputation, was copied in many
different sizes and media; however,
neither the original statue nor a
replica of it was ever in the gardens
at Marly. Robert has painted an
imaginary scene, including a marble
version of the statue, perhaps as
homage to the talent of the sculptor,
who was a personal friend.

The beautiful grounds of Marly
were close enough to Paris for visitors
from the city to make excursions there,
and the château was included in the
celebrated tour Jefferson made with
Mrs. Cosway in 1786.

Trumbull, who had introduced
Jefferson to Maria Cosway and who
may have accompanied them on some
of their expeditions around Paris, met
Robert during a Paris visit in 1786.
He admired a painting in the comte
de Vaudreuil's collection ("architecture and figures, by Mr. Robert, is a
fine picture, in which the aerial
perspective is beautiful") and
later dined there in the artist's
company. A.B. de L.

09 Perspective View of the Machine de Marly

IERRE AVELINE, le vieux
656–1722
ngraving
1.7 x 31.6 (8½ x 12½)
igned, bottom line of legend:
it par Aveline
ent by the Bibliothèque nationale

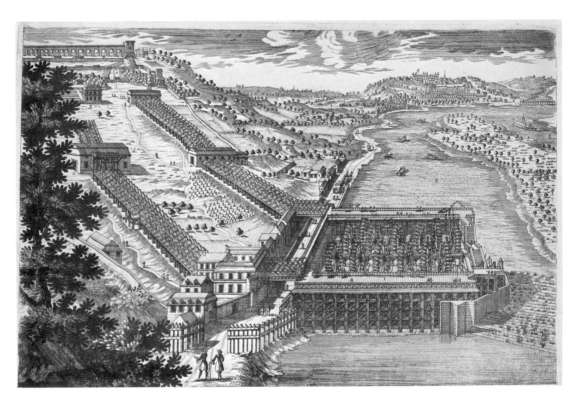

When on the last lap of his journey
rom Le Havre to Paris, on August 6,
784, Jefferson paused beside the
eine at Marly and paid 2f.8 "for
eeing works." The "works" he saw
/as the celebrated Machine de
Marly, whose great wooden wheels
aised river water through a series of
umping stations to an aqueduct and
eservoirs situated on the heights
bove Louveciennes. The machine,
ong considered a hydraulic wonder,
/as constructed between 1681 and
684 by the Belgian engineer from
iège, Arnod de Ville, with the
ssistance of his compatriot,
Rennequin Sualem, a master
arpenter. The machine was a
orollary of the Château de Marly,
he royal pleasure ground then being
uilt for Louis XIV as a "hermitage"
r retreat from the greater splendors
f Versailles.

Water was an important decorative
element in the design of the Marly
grounds, which were laid out on slopes
and ravines above the Seine. Cascades,
asins, *pièces d'eau* and *jets d'eau*,
contributed greatly to Marly's
distinctive charm. Though the
machine was initially built to fill the
eservoirs that fed Marly, water was
eventually piped from them over the
plateau to Versailles.

The machine and related waterworks that Jefferson saw were replaced
after the French Revolution by others
tilizing steam engines, artesian wells
and other methods. The aqueduct of
Marly—shown on the horizon in
the upper left corner of Aveline's
somewhat stylized and stiff engravings
—though no longer serving its
original purpose, is still standing, a
classic landmark visible from the
western suburbs of Paris.

Whenever Jefferson took the
road from Paris out to Saint-Germain-
en-Laye ("5" on the Aveline engraving), he passed close by the Machine
de Marly. Useful inventions, such as
those for raising water to high ground,
a lifelong preoccupation at Monticello,
inevitably challenged his wits. H.C.R.

210 Halle aux Bleds, exterior

JEAN-BAPTISTE MARÉCHAL
active 1780
Pen and wash 1786
Signed lower left: *Maréchal en 1786*

*Collection of the Bibliothèque
nationale, Cabinet des Estampes*
NOT IN EXHIBITION

The Halle aux Bleds, the Paris grain
market, standing on the site of the
former Hôtel de Soissons near the
Church of Saint-Eustache, formed
the centerpiece of a planned urban
landscape. The circular edifice built
around an open court, designed by
Nicolas Le Camus de Mézières
(1721–1789), was completed in
1767, whereas the dome, finished
some ten years later, was the work of
J. G. Legrand (1753–1809) and
Jacques Molinos (1743–1831), who
revived a method of construction
described by the Renaissance architect
Philibert Delorme in his *Inventions
pour bien bastir*. The light weight of
the structure enabled the builders to
insert in the space between the ribs
twenty-five windows radiating from
the central lantern and flooding the
interior with daylight.

Thiéry's detailed description of the
new market in his *Guide des Amateurs*
is a measure of its prestige among
connoisseurs of the time. Arthur
Young described it as "by far the finest
thing" he had seen in Paris: "A vast
rotunda, the roof entirely of wood,
upon a new principle of carpentry . . .
so well planned and so admirably
executed that I know of no public
building that exceeds it in either
France or England." Jefferson, with
the public buildings of Richmond in
mind, inevitably cast his eye on this
Paris market. When visiting it in
August 1786 in the company of John
Trumbull, he soon found, however,
that the latter's London friends,
Richard and Maria Cosway, were
competing with the "sticks and chips"
of the market for his attention. H.C.R.

Pavillion of Lusienne

Bahilee Chartreus pavillion francilivega Flevire

211 Pavilion of Louveciennes

SIR WILLIAM CHAMBERS
1726–1796
Drawing 1774
36.5 x 23.5 (14⅜ x 9¼)
Lent by the Royal Institute of British Architects, London

In May 1774, ten years before Jefferson's arrival, Sir William Chambers visited Paris with his brother John, a Swedish East India Company merchant. As he wrote, "Many great things have been done since I last saw Paris, which I must examine with Care and make Proper remarks upon." It was a long anticipated visit, for Chambers had been engaged in machinations to gain the project for building new public offices next to Old Somerset House in London. He had last been in Paris in 1754 and was anxious to acquaint himself with the latest French public buildings. His *Paris Album* is a record of what he saw and what was then being built in the neoclassic style by friends like Antoine, Peyre, de Wailly and Soufflot. Chambers' drawings of the work of Ledoux are interesting in that they are a contemporary record. It is not at all impossible that Chambers met Ledoux in Paris. The pavilion at Louveciennes, designed for Mme du Barry in 1771, is also shown here at numbers 296–298; it was the object of one of Jefferson's excursions with Maria Cosway in 1786. J.H.

212 The Pavilion of Bagatelle, three views

FRANÇOIS-DENIS NÉE 1732–1818, after L. Bélanger active late 18th century
Engraving, from Laborde, et al., *Voyage pittoresque de la France: Isle de France*, no. 82
Signed lower right, *Dirigé par Nee*; lower left, *L. Bellanger pinxit*
Collection of the Bibliothèque nationale, Cabinet des Estampes
NOT IN EXHIBITION

213 Gardens of Bagatelle, showing Philosopher's Grotto

FRANÇOIS-JOSEPH BÉLANGER
1744–1818
Pen and watercolor
24.6 x 37 (9¾ x 14⅝)
Collection of the Bibliothèque nationale, Cabinet des Estampes
NOT IN EXHIBITION

Bagatelle, said the eighteenth-century connoisseur the prince de Ligne, "is the prettiest bagatelle in the world." No other creation of the Louis XVI period better epitomizes the taste of the times in architecture and landscape gardening (see also nos. 212, 293–295). When walking in the Bois de Boulogne or when crossing it on his way to his Mont Calvaire retreat, Jefferson often passed by Bagatelle and no doubt took note of the words above the entrance gates: PARVA SED APTA. On one occasion he

wrote to his friend Trumbull, "I am just come in from a tour made with the girls [his daughters] to Bagatelle, etc." His Account Book for that day (August 24, 1788) duly records his payment of 4 -4 for "seein Bagatelle."

The pavilion at Bagatelle was built in the autumn of 1777 for the comte d'Artois in sixty-four days on a wager with Queen Marie-Antoinette, his sister-in-law. Both the pavilion with its domed round salon and the adjacent grounds were designed by the comte's architect François-Joseph Bélanger (1744–1818), who had earlier traveled in England and acquired a taste for "picturesque" landscapes. The planting of the gardens, under the supervision of a Scottish gardener, William Blaikie, extended over several years. Bagatelle, now the property of the city of Paris, was owned in the course of the nineteenth century by the fourth Marquess of Hertford and by Sir Richard Wallace, the well-known collectors. Bélanger's pavilion, though coiffed with an inappropriate bonnet that distorts the original design, still stands, but only vestiges of his picturesque park, now eclipsed by rosaries and other horticultural attractions, remain today.

Paintings or engravings provide glimpses of the gardens *dans le genre pittoresque* that caught the eye of Jefferson and his contemporaries. Le Rouge's albums include a complete plan while Thiéry's *Guide des amateurs* (1787) describes them in elaborate detail. The Bagatelle gardens, like others that Jefferson visited in France and England, were designed to confront the stroller with a series of pictures, of surprises at every turn of the sinuous paths. Bagatelle boasted cascades, islets, a Chinese bridge and a *pont de Palladio*, a Diana in marble, an Egyptian obelisk, as well as such *fabriques* as a subterranean Gothic cloister, a paladin's tower, a hermitage, and a philosopher's house. When Thiéry penned his description, an "isle of tombs" was being laid out. Moss, reeds, gnarled roots, exotic shrubs and trees, completed the scene.

Jefferson was preconditioned to appreciate the "modern style" of such gardens. As a young man in his twenties, he had included Thomas Whately's *Observations on Modern Gardening* (1770) (see no. 606) in a list of books for a gentleman's library compiled in 1771, and when planning the grounds at Monticello, he had dreamed of a scheme embracing a deer park, cascades, a Grecian or Chinese temple, as well as a "Burying place" in "some unfrequented vale" set among "antient and venerable oaks" interspersed with "gloomy evergreens." H.C.R.

214 View of the Column House and Temple of Pan

Attributed to LOUIS CARROGIS, CALLED CARMONTELLE 1717–1806
Pen and brown wash 1785
50.3 x 35.4 (19¾ x 14)

Lent by the Nationalmuseum, Stockholm

"Go on then, like a kind comforter," says Jefferson's Heart in the dialogue with his Head, "and paint to me the day we went to St. Germains. How beautiful was every object! . . . Recollect too Madrid, Bagatelle, the King's garden, the Dessert. How grand the idea excited by the remains of such a Column! The spiral staircase too was beautiful. . . ."

The "Dessert" that Jefferson and Mrs. Cosway visited on that memorable summer day in 1786 was Le Désert de Retz, the country estate of M de Monville, situated some four miles from Saint-Germain-en-Laye on the edge of the Forest of Marly near the village of Chambourcy. In the heart of M de Monville's wilderness, designed by him with the assistance of the architect François Barbier, was a huge "ruined" column, inside which living quarters were ingeniously disposed around a central spiral staircase. Strolling through the grounds the sightseer could also discover a Chinese house (which, said the prince de Ligne, the emperor of China himself would not disown),

a temple to the god Pan, an obelisk, a pyramid (serving as an ice-house), a Gothic ruin, and even an "Almost Ruined Little Altar."

One of Le Rouge's albums depicting the fashionable gardens of the period (*Jardins Anglo-Chinois*, bk. 12, 1785) includes engraved plans and views of M de Monville's Désert. See also number 299. A somewhat similar series, from which the drawing exhibited has been taken, is preserved in Sweden. These drawings were probably commissioned by King Gustavus III, who was in close touch with the latest fashions in France when making improvements at Drottningholm and at his Château de Haga. Traveling as the "Comte de Haga," Gustavus visited France in 1784 (a few weeks before Jefferson's arrival there) and was fêted at Versailles, Trianon, and Chantilly. The unsigned drawings have been variously attributed to Louis-Jean Desprez, to François Barbier, and more recently, to Carmontelle.

M de Monville, himself almost ruined by his extravagances, was forced in 1792 to sell his Désert to an Englishman by the improbable but somehow appropriate name of Louis Disney Ffytche. By the mid-twentieth century Jefferson's "Dessert" had become a weedy jungle. Despite the cries raised by modern connoisseurs of the neoclassic, pre-romantic, and

surreal, and its classification as an historic monument, the Column House now seems threatened by genuine ruin. H.C.R.

215 The Studio of Houdon

LOUIS-LÉOPOLD BOILLY
1761–1845
Oil on canvas
85 x 105 (33½ x 41⅜)

Lent by the Musée Thomas Henry, Cherbourg

In this representation of the artist Houdon's studio, busts of Jefferson and Franklin can be seen on the shelves, together with some of Houdon's famous pieces. Jefferson was of course familiar with Houdon's studio which he visited because of the artist's important role in obtaining the statue of Washington for Richmond, Virginia. Jefferson also was to have presented Houdon's bust of Lafayette to the city of Paris, but ill health prevented him at the last minute from attending. In addition to his own bust Jefferson owned plasters by Houdon of Washington, Franklin, John Paul Jones, Turgot, Voltaire and Lafayette. He admired and hoped to obtain plasters of *L'Ecorché, La Frileuse* and the *Diana* seen in the background (see no. 335). Trumbull in his *Autobiography*

mentions looking at a "little Diana in marble, a very beautiful figure—an honor not only to the artist, but to the country and age in which he lives."

The neoclassical painters of the early nineteenth century liked to depict the studios of artists. Boilly often used this theme, for example, in the *Studio of Isabey* in the Louvre, or the *Studio of a Young Artist* in the Pushkin Museum, Moscow. He painted the *Studio of Houdon* twice, the second version being in the Musée des Arts Décoratifs, Paris. The Paris version, which was painted in 1803, has almost the same composition as the Cherbourg painting which dates from sometime later. Both show Houdon's studio at the Collège des Quatre-Nations, and in this case the artist is correcting an academic study of a nude model made by one of his pupils. It has been observed that this academic study seems to be a copy of a traditional eighteenth-century pose, perhaps inspired by the *Shepherd*, Mouchy's reception piece for admission to the Academy in 1768. The man standing behind Houdon is Vivant-Denon,

the director of the Louvre.

There are several preparatory drawings for this painting in a French private collection.

Boilly painted this work with a highly finished surface, a smooth and brilliant technique inspired by Dutch artists of the seventeenth century (Ter Borch, Gerard Dou, Metsu and their followers). He had several examples of paintings by these artists in his private collection. A.B. de L.

216 Marquis de Condorcet

JEAN-ANTOINE HOUDON
1741–1828
Plaster 1785
69 x 49 x 32 (27⅛ x 19¼ x 12⅝)

Collection of the Musée du Louvre

NOT IN EXHIBITION

The marquis de Condorcet (1743–1794), mathematician, philosopher, and political leader, belonged to the liberal wing of the Encyclopédistes. He was elected to the Academy of Science in 1769 and to the French Academy in 1782. On the side of the Revolution, Condorcet was

elected a deputy from Paris, but he opposed the excesses of the Jacobins under the Terror and was condemned to death. He remained in hiding for eight months during 1794 and at the time wrote his *Esquisses d'un tableau historique des progrès de l'esprit humain*, a work in which he still saw the Revolution as the gateway to a utopian society. Emerging from hiding to protect his helpers, he was captured, imprisoned, and according to tradition, committed suicide.

Condorcet was a distinguished representative, with the duc de la Rochefoucauld, of the Society of the Literati, into which Jefferson was admitted upon his arrival in Paris, and which he found so congenial. A strong friendship developed between Jefferson and Condorcet. The latter was present with Lafayette and la Rochefoucauld at the dinner given on Jefferson's departure, September 25, 1789.

Houdon's portrait, created in 1785, shows the marquis with his head sharply turned to his left, his eyes fixed on a distant point. The expression is aloof, withdrawn, seeming almost disdainful, despite the fact that he was a noted champion of human rights against tyrany.

There is also a marble of Condorcet in the American Philosophical Society, Philadelphia. There can be no doubt that the marble in Philadelphia and the plaster here represent the same man and that the man is Condorcet. He is shown in modern dress with perruque, the sober dress of scholars or professional men at the end of the eighteenth century. The history of the marble in the American Philosophical Society, Philadelphia, is impeccable. It has been in the Philosophical Society continuously since it was deposited there in 1819 by William Short, earlier Thomas Jefferson's secretary. Short's letter to Thomas Jefferson dated from Philadelphia, October 21, 1819, recounting the circumstances of his acquiring the *Condorcet* bust is published in the catalogue of the Philosophical Society:

Apropos of philosophers; you recollect without doubt the marble bust of Condorcet, which stood on a marble table in the Salon of the Hôtel de la Rochefoucauld. When it was determined no longer to receive him in the house [for his revolutionary leanings], it was thought *inconvenient* to keep the bust there. The grandchildren, who never liked him, availed themselves of this to have the bust transported to the *garde meuble* without consulting the old lady, whose leave was generally asked on every occasion. She passed over this in silence, however, & never made a remark or enquiry as to the disappearance of the bust. It had cost her a great effort to signify to the original that his presence had become disagreeable; she had really a parental affection for him, & had given a remarkable proof of this at the time of his marriage. On her death I asked this bust of the granddaughter, who gave it to me with great pleasure. It has been on its way here ever since I left France, & has passed through as many cases & *discrimina rerum* as Eneas himself (or perhaps it was Ulysses) on its way. It has finally arrived & is at present placed in the Philosophical hall in the most suitable company, the busts of Franklin, yourself, Turgot.

H.H.A.

217 Christoph Willibald von Glück

JEAN-ANTOINE HOUDON
1741–1828
Terra cotta c. 1775
49 x 35 x 28 (19¼ x 13¾ x 11)
Lent by Michael Hall

The Salon of 1775 included portraits of several distinguished men and women. Among these was Christoph Willibald von Glück (1714–1787), one of the founders of modern opera. Glück had made his principal reputation in Vienna, and, therefore, when he visited Paris in 1773–1774 to present his opera *Iphigenia in Aulis*, he enjoyed the patronage of the Austrian dauphine, Marie-Antoinette. The opera was an enormous success both for the composer and for the singer Sophie Arnould in the title role. Houdon, with his rapidly developing talent for seeking out celebrities,

commemorated both.

Jefferson arrived in Paris shortly after the quarrel between supporters of the classic French opera of Glück and those who espoused the more informal *opéra-comique* imported from Italy, whose leading representative in Paris at that time was Piccini. Jefferson had been introduced to Piccini by Mazzei and was no doubt greatly interested in the debate, in which many of his friends such as Mme d'Houdetot, Marmontel and Chastellux were involved as supporters of Piccini. Benjamin Franklin wrote about the fracas in 1778 in "The Ephemera," a "bagatelle":

We had been shown numberless skeletons of a kind of little fly, called an ephemera, whose successive generations, we were told, were bred and expired within the day. I happened to see a living company of them on a leaf, who appeared to be engaged in conversation . . . but as they, in their natural vivacity, spoke three or four together, I could make but little of their conversation. I found, however, by some broken expressions that I heard now and then, they were disputing warmly on the merit of two foreign musicians, one a *cousin*, the other a *moscheto*, in which dispute they spent their time, seemingly as regardless of the shortness of life as if they had been sure of living a month. Happy people! thought I, you live certainly under a wise, just, and mild government, since you have no public grievance to complain of, nor any subject of contention but the perfections and imperfections of foreign musicians.

Houdon's concern for making the portrait bust a unity, for relating the design of the torso and accessories of dress to the individual portrayed, is to be seen in the *Glück* presented in the Salon of 1775. Glück was an artist, a great musician, and Houdon gave him the attributes of genius. His face was deeply pockmarked, and the sculptor used this fact to establish his theme. He clothed him in a heavy coat, whose texture is an overall pattern of slashed grooves, free and direct in their expressive impact. Here there was no attempt to simulate the appearance of the actual material, but rather, in a manner almost Rodinesque, to bring out the quality of the clay. The open shirt, the unbuttoned vest, the short, dishevelled hair, and the alert, tilted pose of the head all emphasize the impact of genius. Surviving examples of the bust exist in two versions, one with truncated shoulders and one with full shoulders and indications of the upper arms. H.H.A.

218 Madame de Wailly

AUGUSTIN PAJOU 1730–1809
Marble 1789
62.2 (24½) high
Signed and dated on the back:
Pajou F. 1789

Lent by The Metropolitan Museum of Art

Throughout the seventeenth century in France, the honor of being portrayed in a sculptured bust was generally reserved for the nobility or important church and government officials. During the first two decades of the eighteenth century, the sculptor Antoine Coysevox executed a number of busts of his artist-friends and, thereafter, a wider range of sitters began to be portrayed in bust form. Expanding upon the tradition established by Coysevox, Pajou portrayed not only many of his artist-friends but also their wives. For example, in addition to a portrait of his own wife, Pajou did busts of Mme Aved, Mme Hall, Mme N.-S. Adam, Mme Le Comte, and the bust exhibited here of Mme de Wailly.

Pajou and the architect Charles de Wailly were students together at the French Academy in Rome during the years 1752–1756. They evidently became close friends, and during the 1770s, when both had become established artists, Pajou acquired a portion of some land owned by de Wailly, who then built contiguous houses for the sculptor and himself. In 1789 Pajou executed busts of both Charles de Wailly and his wife which were exhibited in the Salon where Jefferson admired them.

Henri Stein lists two examples of the *Bust of Monsieur de Wailly*: one, a plaster which had been in the Musée de Versailles and was then lost; and

the other, belonging to the baron Bethmann in Paris, which Stein confusingly refers to as a plaster in his text but the illustration of which he labels as a terra cotta. The Bethmann bust was listed as a plaster when sold in 1923 and now also seems to be lost.

Pajou's busts of M and Mme de Wailly seem to have been conceived as pendants. He is shown with the head turned slightly to his left, and she appears with her head turned to the left. Both portraits share in common an idiosyncrasy found in many of Pajou's busts: in each the sitter's head is inclined slightly forward.

Pajou's *Bust of Madame de Wailly* is one of his most unusual and interesting portraits. It is a classicizing bust, which does not seem to be based upon any specific classical prototype. The sitter appears in a simple togalike garment, which rather daringly reveals not only her left shoulder but also the side of her left breast. While a number of eighteenth-century busts of women go so far as to completely reveal one breast, they are generally portraits of actresses, and the nudity is usually sanctioned by the artistic conceit of portraying these women as they appeared in their most famous stage roles. In addition to actress portraits, one usually associates *decollétage* with busts done in a lively rococo style and depicting the sitter in contemporary dress, often bordered by fancy lace. Pajou's portrait of Mme de Wailly is unusual in its incorporation of the partially revealed breast within a sober, classicizing work. It would be interesting to be able to compare Pajou's portrait of Mme de Wailly with the bust of the same sitter (done when she had remarried and become Mme Fourcroy) which was exhibited by Houdon at the Salon of 1806.

Although a total of over thirty-five portrait busts were exhibited at the Salon of 1789, Pajou's gifts as a portraitist—generally ranked below those of Houdon and Caffieri— had probably never appeared better in relation to the competition from other sculptors. For in the Salon of that year he exhibited three of his most beautiful portraits: a marble bust of his teacher J.-B. Lemoyne, a terra cotta bust of his friend the painter Hubert Robert, and this bust of Mme de Wailly. P.F.

219 The comte d'Angiviller

JOSEPH-SIFFRED DUPLESSIS
1725–1802
Oil on canvas c. 1779
129.5 x 107 (51 x 42⅛)

*Lent by Mr. John V. Sheffield,
Whitchurch, Hampshire*

Charles-Claude de la Billardie, comte d'Angiviller (1730–1810) was appointed *directeur des bâtiments du roi* in 1774 by his friend Louis XVI. The *directeur*, of which d'Angiviller was perhaps the greatest in the eighteenth century, was in charge of the architecture and decoration of the royal palaces and held a position of great power through the commissions he gave to architects, painters and sculptors. D'Angiviller reorganized the administration of his department, founded a free drawing school, and commissioned a series of paintings from leading artists of subjects taken from French history. His most original idea was to found a national museum, the ancestor of the modern Louvre. The Grande Galerie of the Louvre was to be remodeled, and in this portrait d'Angiviller is holding a plan for the remodeling. Although the royal collections were opened to

the public in various palaces, the more grandiose scheme of gathering them together in the Louvre came to an end with the outbreak of the French Revolution. It was, however, taken up and vastly expanded under the Revolution and Napoleon. Duplessis approved of d'Angiviller's idea, and the inclusion of the Grande Galerie plan in the painting reflects his support for the *directeur*. This was noted by Dupont de Nemours who wrote: "There is still another portrait I want to tell you about because it is very well painted and I like the man it represents. . . . He holds the plan of the gallery in which the statues of great men are to be placed. It was a happy idea on the part of the painter, a subtle eulogy, an ingenious was to sign the painting . . . the accessories are superb." D'Angiviller is wearing the star and cross of the order of Saint Lazarus and Mount Carmel and the cross of the order of Saint Louis.

Besides their common interest in the arts Jefferson and d'Angiviller would also have had a link in their love of gardens. Richard Cary, one of Jefferson's neighbors in Virginia, corresponded with d'Angiviller on the subject of plants, and Fiske Kimball

cites d'Angiviller as one of Jefferson's circle of associates in Paris. Their paths would have crossed if only through the circumstance that the comtesse de Flahault, d'Angiviller's sister-in-law, was the mistress of Gouverneur Morris, Jefferson's successor as American minister to France. A.B. de L.

220 Portrait of Architect Ledoux and His Family

MARGUÉRITE GÉRARD 1761–1837
Oil on panel
30.5 x 24.1 (12 x 9½)

Lent by the Baltimore Museum of Art, Mary Frick Jacobs Collection

Claude-Nicolas Ledoux (1736–1806) was perhaps the most original of the neoclassical architects in France. His ideas transcended his age and have been appreciated only in our day. The destruction of many of his finest works kept him from being widely known, and his astonishingly imaginative schemes for buildings, which were never realized, were dismissed as the impractical visions of an eccentric. Ledoux's career up to the French Revolution was successful and he had commissions both in Paris and the provinces. He built several *hôtels* of great originality in the capital: the Hôtel de Thélusson, the Hôtel de Montmorency, the Pavillon Guimard, the Maisons Saiseval and the Maisons Hosten. He obtained official favor with his commission for Mme du Barry of the Pavillon at Louveciennes, but nothing came of the plan to build a much larger château. In the same way his grandiose ideas for the *salines* or saltworks at Chaux were only partially fulfilled (and, indeed, he had exceeded his original commission by planning a whole town). Ledoux's most ambitious undertaking, the tollhouses or *barrières* around Paris, built from 1785 up to the time of the Revolution should have been the apex of his career. They showed great imagination, in providing architectural variety for more than fifty structures, but their aesthetic daring was lost on the Parisians, with whom they were most unpopular and gave rise to a witticism "ce mur murant Paris rend Paris murmurant." They also proved expensive to build. Many were destroyed by the mob at the beginning of the Revolution. Ledoux himself was imprisoned during the Terror and barely escaped with his life. His last years were devoted to producing *L'architecture considérée sous le rapport de l'art, des moeurs et de la législation*, but only two-thirds had been published by the time of his death and the rest was published in 1847.

The characteristics of Ledoux's architecture are simplicity and grandeur. The scale was often immense, although he seldom, even in his imaginary schemes, indulged in the megalomanic scale of some of his Romantic contemporaries. He could also handle small works with the greatest refinement. His aim was to reduce architecture to its simplest shapes, the circle and square, sphere

and cube, and the importance he gave to light and shade in the massing of the component parts, reveals a pictorial approach to his creativity.

Jefferson was certainly aware of Ledoux's work. He visited Louveciennes, used the Pavillon Guimard as the basis for one of the pavilions in the University of Virginia, and referred in a letter of 1787 to "the wall of circumvallation around Paris and the palaces by which we are to be let in and out are nearly completed." R.W.

221 Jacques-François Desmaisons

JACQUES-LOUIS DAVID 1748–1825
Oil on canvas 1782
90.1 x 70.2 (36 x 28½)
Signed and dated lower left of center:
J L David f/ 1782

Lent by the Albright-Knox Art Gallery, Buffalo

Jacques-François Desmaisons (1711–1800), architect to the king, was David's uncle; he was married to one of the sisters of Marie-Geneviève Buron, mother of the artist. Two circumstances favored a close relationship between uncle and nephew. David, having lost his father at the age of nine, was taken in and educated in part by his uncle François Buron (brother of his mother) and in part by the architect Desmaisons (an uncle by marriage). Secondly, Desmaisons constantly encouraged his nephew in the study of fine arts at the very time when his mother wished to destine her son for a military career.

Desmaisons was a well-known architect. In 1758 the Academy of Architecture presented his name to the king, and he became a member in 1762. He was ennobled in 1769, when he was named knight and royal architect. After the fire of 1776, which devastated a part of the Palais de Justice, he was commissioned to reconstruct the buildings in the Cour de Mai. The façade was regarded as a masterpiece. At the time David was painting the portrait, Desmaisons had just published, to the commendation of the experts, drawings for the grand staircase of honor with two ramps for the archdiocese of Paris (*Mercure de France*, January 1782).

The attributes of Desmaisons' profession, architectural drawings, a ruler, compasses and books on architecture including one by Palladio, lie scattered on the table. The elegant clothes and confident air of Desmaisons indicate a highly successful architect. A.B. de L.

222 Joseph-Marie Vien

JOSEPH-SIFFRED DUPLESSIS
1725–1802
Oil on canvas 1784
133 x 100 (52¼ x 39⅜)
Signed and dated lower right:
J. S. DUPLESSIS pinx. 1784

Lent by the Musée du Louvre

The painter portrayed here is
Joseph-Marie Vien (1716–1809),
director of the French Academy at
Rome from 1775 until 1781 and
subsequently a professor at the French
Royal Academy of Painting. He
played a central role in the formation
of French neoclassicism with his
painting *Selling of Cupids*, which
appeared in the Salon of 1763 and
enjoyed much fame as a result; he is
the only painter to have been buried
at the Panthéon. Vien had a profound
influence on several generations of
French painters; he was called the
"restorer of the French school," and
David declared in his funerary elegy,
"Our father has ceased to live."
   The painting of Vien was exhibited
at the Salon of 1785, together with

the *Portrait of Chabanon* (see no.
240). They are the only portraits of
the five shown in the Salon of 1785
to have been rediscovered. This
portrait was commissioned from
Duplessis fourteen years earlier, in
1771, as a requirement for his
admission to the Academy, but he was
unable to execute the portrait because
of Vien's departure for Rome. Vien
reappeared at the meetings of the
Academy on November 24, 1781, but
Duplessis, who had not forgotten the
commission of the portrait for his
admission, only finished the painting
in time for the Salon of 1785. Many
portraits were made of Vien. An oil
sketch for this painting is in the
Museum of Fine Arts, Boston.
   The portrait is an ambitious work
in its monumentality and the life-size
representation of the sitter in three-
quarter view, in the treatment of the
background and the theatrical curtain
which frames the model and in its
careful execution. There is great
attention to detail in the clothing and
the chair; the rather sculptural
rendering of the face is done with

psychological sensitivity. The
coloring is subdued, sober, with a
yellow-bronze hue for the curtain and
a mauve-purplish red for the dressing
gown, and patches of color on the
palette. A.B. de L.

POLITICAL AND SOCIAL LIFE

223 Thomas Jefferson

MATHER BROWN 1761–1831
Oil on canvas 1786
82.1 x 64.4 (35 x 28)
Signed lower right: *M Brown pt 1786*

Lent by Mr. Charles Francis Adams

The life portrait, now lost, of which
this is a replica, was painted at
Mather Brown's studio in Cavendish
Square during Jefferson's London
visit in March and April of 1786. The
portrait depicts Jefferson at forty-three
as America's minister plenipotentiary
to the court of Versailles, "the
engaging and intelligent favorite of
the Paris salons." The American-born
Brown, in his sixth year of painting in
England and among the more
fashionable of London's portraitists,
was himself only twenty-four at the
time.
   As the earliest of the identified
portraits of Jefferson, it is unfortunate
that it was not considered by
Jefferson's friends to be a good likeness of the subject. John Trumbull
wrote Jefferson in March 1788, after
seeing Brown's portraits of both
Adams and Jefferson: "Mr. Adams is
like. Yours I do not think so well of."
And William Short reported that
while the "picture by Brown of Mr.
Adams is an excellent likeness; that of
Jefferson is supposed by every body
here to be an étude. It has no feature
like him." It was undoubtedly because
of this reaction that Mather Brown's
portrait has come to play only a
peripheral role in shaping our image
of Jefferson.
   The figure in the background
carrying a Phrygian cap on a pole
represents Liberty. A.B.

224 Martha Jefferson

JOSEPH BOZE 1744–1826
Oil on ivory 1789
8.9 x 6.4 (3½ x 2½)

Lent by the Department of State, Washington, D.C.

Martha Jefferson, called Patsy by her family, was born in 1772, the eldest of Jefferson's six children and one of two, both daughters, who survived to adulthood. She married Thomas Mann Randolph, Jr., in 1790 and died in 1836. The miniature was painted in 1789, just about the time Martha left her convent school at Panthemont, and it has been suggested that the portrait may have been a parting present to the head-mistress. We have a contemporary description by Nathaniel Cutting of Martha: ". . . tall and genteel . . . and though she has been so long resident in a Country remarkable for its Levity and the forward indelicacy of its manners, yet she retains all that winning simplicity, and good humour'd reserve that are evident proofs of innate Virtue and an happy disposition.—Characteristicks which eminently distinguish the Women of America from those of any other Country."

Martha accompanied her father to France, and although only twelve and away at her boarding school for long periods, she helped to brighten Jefferson's domestic life, at that time so bleak because of his wife's recent death. There were frequent letters between the two, and the subjects were very much the same as in the correspondence of any father and daughter. Language was no difficulty, as Martha soon learned French and settled down happily in her new ambience. Jefferson confessed ruefully that "she speaks French as easily as English, while Humphries, Short and myself are scarcely better at it than when we landed. . . ." Martha's letters are full of schoolgirl gossip, mixed sometimes rather incongruously with political news. "I have another landscape since I wrote to you last and begun with another piece of music." Jefferson's liberal views must clearly have been absorbed by his daughter, because she wrote in the same letter: "I wish with all my soul that the poor negroes were all freed. It greives my heart when I think that these our fellow creatures should be treated so terribly as they are by many of our country men."

Jefferson was most interested in his daughter's progress in music, then considered an essential accomplishment for young ladies, and ordered a harpsichord for her. "I forgot in my last letter to desire you to learn all your old tunes over again perfectly, that I may hear them on your harpsicord on it's arrival." He was anxious that she should persevere with subjects, even when they were difficult. "I do not like your saying that you are unable to read the antient print of your Livy, but with the aid of your master. We are always equal to what we undertake with resolution. A little degree of this will enable you to decypher your Livy." Advice flowed from Jefferson's pen on the formation of moral principles and the correction of faults. Laziness he regarded as a sin, and being a constantly active man himself, he could not understand how others wasted their days in idleness. "A mind always employed is always happy. This is the true secret, the grand recipe for felicity." And in a long admonition he wrote: "It is your future happiness which interests me, and nothing can contribute more to it (moral rectitude always excepted) than the contracting a habit of industry and activity. Of all the cankers of human happiness, none corrodes it with so silent, yet so baneful a tooth, as indolence. Body and mind both unemployed, our body becomes a burthen, and every object about us loathsome, even the dearest. Idleness begets ennui, ennui the hypochrondia, and that a diseased body. . . ." On one occasion Martha wanted to anticipate her allowance to buy some clothes, and while Jefferson complied, he used the occasion to give a lecture on debt, a subject on which he could speak from his own experience. "But do you not see my dear how imprudent it is to lay out in one moment what should accommodate you for five weeks? That this is a departure

from that rule which I wish to see you governed by, thro' your whole life, of never buying any thing which you have not money in your pocket to pay for? Be assured that it gives much more pain to the mind to be in debt, than to do without any article whatever which we may seem to want." Jefferson's affectionate concern for his children comes through in another letter. "I need not tell you what pleasure it gives me to see you improve in every thing agreeable and useful. The more you learn the more I love you, and I rest the happiness of my life on seeing you beloved by all the world, which you will be sure to be if to a good heart you join those accomplishments so peculiarly pleasing in your sex. Adieu my dear child; lose no moment in improving your head, nor any opportunity of exercising your heart in benvolence."

At seventeen when this portrait was painted, Martha Jefferson had reached marriageable age, and no doubt Jefferson was already thinking about her future. Abigail Adams had writen facetiously three years earlier: "Suppose you give me Miss Jefferson and in some future day take a Son in lieu for her. I am for Strengthening the federal union." R.W.

225 Louis XVI

JOSEPH-SIFFRED DUPLESSIS
1725–1802
Oil on canvas
80 x 62 (31½ x 24⅜)
Lent by the Musée National du Château de Versailles

Louis XVI (1754–1793) succeeded his grandfather, Louis XV, in 1774. As a man, he was well-meaning, and his blameless domestic life showed a marked contrast to the promiscuity of Louis XV. However, as a monarch, his idolence and irresolution were great handicaps in trying to deal with the crises that overtook France during his reign. The national finances were in a perilous state following France's entrance into the American war against Great Britain, and quarrels between the king and the Parlements or privileged courts almost brought the country to an administrative impasse. As the existing government machinery was incapable of solving these problems, the Etats-Généraux were summoned. With the advent of revolution, whatever efforts Louis XVI might have made to cope with the situation were curbed under the influence of his wife Marie-

Antoinette and his reactionary brothers. The dignity and courage of the king at his trial and execution helped, to a limited extent, to redeem the mistakes of his rule.

Jefferson presented his credentials to Louis XVI at Versailles in May 1785, and as he reported to Jay, "I . . . delivered my letter of credence to the king at a private audience and went through the other ceremonies usual on such occasions." Jefferson's early feelings about Louis were quite warm. He mentioned in 1786 his general popularity: "When our king goes out, they fall down and kiss the earth where he has trodden; and then they go to kissing one another. And this is the truest wisdom." Later Jefferson revised his opinion: "The king goes for nothing. He hunts one half of the day, is drunk the other, and signs whatever he is bid." After the outbreak of the French Revolution, Jefferson, aware of the king's shortcomings, still felt that Louis, given the opportunity, would have tried to keep within the constitution, and while neither approving nor condemning Louis XVI's execution, Jefferson wrote in his *Autobiography* that he would not have voted for the penalty

226 Marie-Antoinette

MARIE-LOUISE-ELISABETH
VIGÉE-LEBRUN 1755–1842
Oil on canvas
271 x 195 (106⅜ x 76⅜)
Lent by the Musée National du Château de Versailles

of death. Reviewing these events from the distance of over thirty years while in retirement at Monticello, Jefferson judged Louis XVI fairly: 'He had not a wish but for the good of the nation, and for that object, no personal sacrifice would ever have cost him a moment's regret. But his mind was weakness itself, his constitution timid, his judgment null, and without sufficient firmness even to stand by the faith of his word." A.B. de L.

Mme Vigée-Lebrun was, pre-eminently, the painter of Marie-Antoinette and did many portraits of the queen. The artist wrote in her *Souvenirs*: "It was in the year 1779 . . . that I first painted a portrait of the queen, who was then in the full bloom of her youth and beauty. Marie-Antoinette was tall, admirably well built, rather heavy without being too much so. . . . In all of France she was the woman who walked best. It is very difficult to describe to someone who has not seen the queen such a blending of grace and mobility. It was then that I did the portrait which shows her with a large basket, wearing a satin dress and holding a rose in her hand." The original painting was sent to Marie-

Antoinette's mother Maria Theresa and is still in Vienna. Several copies were made, of which this is one.

Jefferson's comments on Marie-Antoinette were not flattering. Her extravagance and frivolity met with his disapproval, and later he felt she had a harmful influence on the king. In his *Autobiography*, Jefferson passed judgment on the queen, writing,

This angel, as gaudily painted in the rhapsodies of the Rhetor Burke, with some smartness of fancy, but no sound sense was proud, disdainful of restraint, indignant at all obstacles to her will, eager in the pursuit of pleasure, and firm enough to hold to her desires, or perish in their wreck. Her inordinate gambling and dissipations, with those of the Count d'Artois and others of her clique, had been a sensible item in the exhaustion of the treasury, which called into action the reforming hand of the nation; and her opposition to it her inflexible

perverseness, and dauntless spirit, led herself to the Guillotine, & drew the king on with her, and plunged the world into crimes & calamities which will forever stain the pages of modern history. I have ever believed that had there been no queen, there would have been no revolution.
A.B. de L.

227 Charles-Alexandre de Calonne

MARIE-LOUISE-ELISABETH
VIGÉE-LEBRUN 1755–1842
Oil on canvas 1784
149 x 128 (58⅝ x 50½)
Signed and dated at the lower right:
Le Brun fe 1784

Lent by Her Majesty
Queen Elizabeth II

Calonne (1734–1802) was appointed comptroller general in 1783, at a time when the French finances were in a critical state, with an increasing deficit after the war with Great Britain on behalf of the United States. He realized that the only way to put the budget on a sound basis was by abolishing the many restrictive taxes and internal customs barriers which impeded trade and bore heavily on the middle and lower classes, who had to pay most of the taxes from which the nobility and clergy were exempt. These privileges Calonne proposed to abolish. Inevitably he met strong opposition from vested interests and the Assembly of Notables, which met in 1787, was adamant in refusing to accept his proposals. Shortly afterwards he was dismissed. Calonne was French finance minister for about half the period of Jefferson's time in

Paris, and the two men were frequently in touch on the subject of American trade. Jefferson was anxious to reduce American reliance on the British near monopoly of imports and exports. Tobacco, as well as being the main production of his native Virginia, was the most important item traded with France, but Jefferson also concerned himself with obtaining concessions for rice and fish oils, two main American exports. After Calonne's fall from power, he wrote an address to the king in justification of his conduct. In a letter to Mme de Corny, Jefferson considered that, "Tho it does not prove M. de Calonne to be more innocent than his predecessors, it shows him not to have been that exaggerated scoundrel which the calculations and the clamours of the public have supposed . . . In fine, it shows him less wicked, and France less badly governed, than I had feared."

The portrait of Calonne is one of the best-documented paintings in the oeuvre of Vigée-Lebrun. In fact, she wrote at great length about it in her *Souvenirs*:

Shortly before the Revolution, I did the portrait of M. de Calonne, and I exhibited it at the Salon; I

painted this minister seated, three-quarter length which prompted Mademoiselle Arnoult to say when she saw it: 'Madame Lebrun has cut off his legs in order to make him sit still.' Unfortunately, this witty remark was not the only one inspired by my painting. At that time I was faced with the most odious slanders. First of all, there were a thousand rumors circulating about the payment for the portrait . . . , I was harassed with libelous stories; everyone accused me of living in intimacy with M. de Calonne . . . M. de Calonne never seemed very attractive to me, for he wore a banker's wig. A wig! Judge for yourself how, with my love of the romantic, I could have accustomed myself to a wig! . . . Finally, I remember having rushed his portrait to the point of not painting the hands from life, even though it was my practice to always paint them from the model.

The portrait was exhibited at the Salon of 1785, where the artist showed at least ten other pictures, among them the *Bacchante* from the Musée Nissim de Camondo (a replica is shown here at no. 246) and the *Portrait of Madame de Ségur* (exhibited here at no. 247). In the years preceding the Revolution, Mme Vigée-Lebrun, at the height of her talents, painted a number of masterpieces.

Calonne is shown seated in a Louis XV style armchair, wearing the order of the Saint-Esprit, and holding a letter addressed *au Roi*. This state portrait was well received by the critics. "From the midst of all of those beautiful women M. le Contrôleur général stands out, and, since he is not an enemy of the feminine sex, the good viewers wish to see him attended by his harem. . . ." A.B. de L.

228 Alessandro, Conte Cagliostro

JEAN-ANTOINE HOUDON
1741–1828
Marble 1786
78.1 x 58.6 x 34.5 (30¾ x 23¹/₁₆ x 13⁹/₁₆)
Signed and dated 1786
National Gallery of Art

The Salon of 1787 included a remarkable number of individuals who might be called members of the aristocracy. It was in this Salon that Houdon was able to exhibit a marble bust of *Louis XVI* as well as the magnificent *Baillé de Suffren*, now in the Mauritshuis, The Hague. There were, as well, the superb busts of the *Marquis de Bouillé*, the *Duc de Nivernais*, and the *Marquis de Méjanes*. The Salon also included the marble of the *Marquis de Lafayette* "pour les États de la Virginie" (see no. 174). All of these gentlemen were portrayed with a baroque splendor that reveals the continuing technical powers of the artists, even as the prevailing style in art, as in politics, was changing dramatically on the eve of the French Revolution.

Although not included in the Salon, and never a member of the aristocracy, Giuseppe Balsamo, better known under his alias, Alessandro, Conte Cagliostro, was by no means the least interesting of the individuals portrayed. He was a Sicilian adventurer who, together with Casanova, ranked as a leading charlatan of the eighteenth century. After various adventures in Italy and extensive travels in the Near East, Cagliostro embarked on a full-scale European career as alchemist, physician, mesmerist, astrologer and necromancer. In France between 1780 and 1786, he had a great success at the court of Versailles until finally banished. Returning to Rome in 1789, he was condemned by the Inquisition for heresy and sorcery and died in prison.

Cagliostro was a Freemason and used his actual or pretended knowledge of the Oriental mysteries of Freemasonry as a cover for other activities. It was probably through Houdon's membership in the Lodge of the Nine Sisters that he met Cagliostro, then at the height of his fame in Paris, and did his portrait. The marble bust is a masterpiece of interpretation. Although Cagliostro habitually wore a strange, intricately arranged perruque and was extravagantly dressed, covered with large diamonds which he contended he had made himself through his control of the philosopher's stone, the sculptor chose to subordinate the accessories. Cagliostro is shown informally dressed, his frilled shirt open, his waistcoat partly unbuttoned, with no wig covering his bald head. The charlatan, not yet revealed as such, is presented as the poet, the man of imagination. As in his great portraits of the *philosophes*, the men of the Enlightenment, Houdon concentrates on the face and head in an effect that can only be described as hypnotic. Cagliostro's head is turned sharply to his left and lifted high, as though he were seated and had turned to look at someone who had approached him from the side. All who had met the magician in Paris seem to have commented on the power and intensity of his gaze, and it is on this that Houdon focuses. The face is fat and undistinguished; the slightly open mouth rather unpleasantly sensual. The eyes are large and somewhat protuberant, fixed exactly on some specific object or person; and the artist has managed to convey a sense of absolute concentration. It is a strange and disturbing characterization. Cagliostro gives the impression of being not just a clever trickster, but a sinister and possibly dangerous individual. In looking for comparable studies among Houdon's portraits, one is reminded perhaps of the actor Larive. There is the same sharp turn of the head, the same wide and staring eyes. But while Cagliostro is also obviously an actor, he is acting his part much more convincingly than Larive. Cagliostro was involved in the famous affair of the diamond necklace, and it was this that led to his expulsion from France. Jefferson was in Paris during the period of the scandal and, like everyone else, was fascinated by it. Briefly, the affair had to do with an attempt on the part of comtesse de La Motte to acquire an enormously expensive diamond necklace for herself, pretending it to be for the queen,

Marie-Antoinette. Aside from Cagliostro, the Cardinal de Rohan and many others were involved. When the intrigue was exposed and the intriguers punished, there still remained a stigma on the guiltless Marie-Antoinette. The scandal was used by opponents of the crown to point out the queen's moral laxness and frivolity. The clumsy manner in which the affair was handled increased antagonism to the monarch, to the point that Napoleon regarded it as one of the causes of the French Revolution.

H.H.A.

229 Madame de Tott Painting the Portrait of the Comtesse de Tessé
Miniature on ivory
7 (2¾) diam.
Lent by the comte de Pusy La Fayette, Paris

Among the circle of Jefferson's closest friends in Paris, Mme de Tessé (1741–1814), born Adrienne-Catherine de Noailles, was one with whom he had many interests in common: gardening, the arts and a liberal view of politics. According to her niece the marquise de Montagu, sister of Mme de Lafayette,

Madame de Tessé was in every respect a remarkable person: small, piercing eyes, a pretty face marred at the age of twenty by small pox, which, it is said, was no worry to her, thanks to her precocious mind . . . an imposing air, grace and dignity in all her movements, and above all infinitely witty. She was one of those ladies of the Old Régime, captivated by the philosophical ideas of the century, and intoxicated by the seductive innovations which were to bring about, in their eyes, the regeneration and happiness of our country. In a word she was a liberal and a philosopher. In philosophy, Voltaire, with whom she was closely connected, was her master; in politics, M. de la Fayette, her nephew, was her hero.

The comtesse de Tessé's garden at

Chaville was well known to Jefferson, and he contributed seeds and plants from America, often of species then unknown in Europe. Their correspondence frequently refers to shipments from Virginia, and even after Jefferson left France, William Short was instructed to send plants to her. The countess was also happy to return Jefferson's generosity and sent trees to be planted at Monticello. A mutual interest in the arts must have often been the topic of conversation, as it was frequently the subject of their letters. Jefferson wrote his famous letter from Nîmes to her: "Here I am, Madam, gazing at the Maison quarrée, like a lover at his mistress." One of the most elegant furnishings at Monticello, where it stood in the entrance hall surmounted by Ceracchi's bust of Jefferson, was a gift from Mme de Tessé: a "fluted column of dark variegated marble which is supported by a pedestal of snow white marble" and ornamented with the twelve signs of the zodiac. A Latin inscription in praise of Jefferson on it can be translated: "To the Supreme Ruler of the Universe, under whose watchful care the liberties of North America were finally achieved, and under whose tutelage the name of Thomas Jefferson will descend forever blessed to posterity." It was probably Mme de Tessé's intention that the pedestal should be outside "in the woods of Monticello." Jefferson, in thanking her for the present, modestly deprecated the eulogistic inscription. "I was never so conscious of my littleness as when praises are bestowed on me which I do not merit. I have the feelings of a thief running away with the property of others."

Her admiration of Lafayette and her liberal views made Mme de Tessé a supporter of the French Revolution. Gouverneur Morris records in his diary going with Jefferson to dinner at Mme de Tessé's house and being somewhat taken aback at finding himself in an uncongenial political atmosphere. "Republicans of the first Feather. The Countess, who is a very sensible Woman, has formed her Ideas of Government in a Manner not suited (I think) either to the Situation, the Circumstances or the Dispositions of France. . . ." The excesses of the Revolution, however, drove Mme de Tessé and her family into exile in Switzerland, and Short mentioned to Jefferson: "Mde de Tessé is still in Switzerland with Mde de Tott . . . She writes me that her occupations are sewing coarse cloth and attending to the most common domestic operations . . . she thinks herself worthy of being an American wife."

Sophie Ernestine de Tott (c. 1759–c. 1840), always called Mme de Tott, although in fact she was not married, had become the protégée of the comtesse de Tessé, who treated her as a daughter. Consequently Jefferson would have seen her on his visits to the older woman. He gave Mme de Tott presents of books and helped her with her studies in Homer, whom he referred to facetiously as "your divine countryman Homer," because he thought Mme de Tott to be of Greek birth. Their correspondence took on a tone of affectionate badinage and is reminiscent of the playful letters to Maria Cosway, who was almost the same age. Jefferson appears to have been particularly susceptible to the attractions of pretty women. But the letters between the two were sometimes on more serious subjects. While he was traveling in the south of France, Jefferson wrote such a vivid description of Marseilles that Mme de Tott wrote: "I have had a great interest in reading and rereading all the scenes you have sketched with a pencil worthy of Teniers and sometimes worthy of Raphael." Earlier Jefferson had asked her opinion about a painting by Drouais, *Maurius at Minturnae* (see no. 333), which he greatly admired. Mme de Tott, however, was much less enthusiastic, and Jefferson obediently modified his opinions.

The miniature of Mme de Tott painting the comtesse de Tessé was perhaps painted by Mme de Tott's father, the baron de Tott, an amateur artist who had traveled extensively in the Near East. A.B. de L.

230 Madame d'Houdetot
VALLIÈRES active late 18th century
Oil on canvas
Lent anonymously

Comtesse d'Houdetot, born Elisabeth-Françoise-Sophie de LaLive de Bellegarde (1730–1813) was one of Jefferson's close friends in Paris. She had one of the leading salons and although not a beauty, her great charm and amiability attracted many people besides Jefferson. Rousseau fell in love with her, as he records in his *Confessions* and he made her the heroïne Julie in *La Nouvelle Héloïse*. The passion was not reciprocated. Instead, she had a lifelong attachment to Charles-François Saint-Lambert, the poet and philosopher, and lived at times in a happy ménage à trois with her husband and lover. To Jefferson she was "the good Countess d'Houdetot" and he often visited her house at Sannois. Mme d'Houdetot was a great admirer of Franklin and constantly passed on messages to him through Jefferson. Saint John de

Crèvecoeur was another friend in common, and both the countess and Jefferson took an interest in de Crèvecoeur's sons when he went to America. All things connected with America interested Mme d'Houdetot, who was a strong supporter of the American Revolution and wrote to congratulate Jefferson when Virginia ratified the Constitution. She called herself a fellow citizen because Saint John de Crèvecoeur had arranged for New Haven, Connecticut, to bestow citizenship on her and a group of French sympathizers of America. Jefferson wrote a farewell letter to the countess just before leaving France, in which he expressed the hope that he would find Franklin still alive by the time he reached America. In her reply she said, "I lose in you the person whose wisdom and temperament give me most confidence when mine begin to be unsettled." She continued to miss his company, and wrote, "The regrets which you left behind on leaving France are greatly increased now that we have lost the hope of seeing you again. I very much miss the consolations I received from your intelligence." Like so many of Jefferson's friends such as Mme de Corny, comtesse d'Houdetot quickly became disillusioned with the French Revolution and contrasted the peace of America with the confusion of France: "I believe before your departure you knew of the horrid outrages of the sixth of October [when the Royal Family had been forced to leave Versailles for Paris]. This storm so far from producing a calm, leaves us the fear that we shall be for a long time the victims of the errors of our Legislators and of the ill intentions of some of them. . . . The effects of anarchy are experienced in every part of the kingdom. . . . The characteristic difference between your revolution, and ours, is that having nothing to destroy, you had nothing to injure, and labouring for a people, few in number, uncorrupted, and extended over a large tract of country, you have avoided all the inconveniences of a situation contrary in every respect." R.W.

231 Tea in the Salon des Quatre Glaces of the Hôtel du Temple, with the Court of the Prince de Conti listening to the young Mozart

MICHEL-BARTHÉLÉMY
OLLIVIER 1712–1784
Oil on canvas 1777
54 x 70 (21¼ x 27½)

Lent by the Musée National du Château de Versailles

Though this painting was executed several years before Jefferson's arrival in Paris, it portrays the type of salon gathering in which he would often have taken part during his years there. This particular scene represents the elegant Salon des Quatre Glaces at the Temple, the residence of the prince de Conti, who was a member of the French royal family and a patron of writers and philosophers, including Rousseau. The combination of aristocrats and intellectuals taking tea, while they listen to Mozart playing, is typical of the salon, where wit and sprightly intelligence gave the entrée to those not of noble birth. Such distinguished names as the maréchale de Luxembourg, the maréchale de Mirepoux, the princesse de Beauveau and comtesse de Boufflers, who acted as hostess in the prince de Conti's salon, mix with president Hérault, who as well as holding an important legal position, was a popular historian, and Dortous de Mairan, the distinguished physician and astronomer and a protégé of the prince. The salon atmosphere was informal and relaxed, in contrast to the rigid etiquette of the court at Versailles. It was indeed this blending of elegance, informality, and intellectual conversation which appealed to Jefferson, at least in moderation, and provided the unique combination for the salon, France's most original contribution to eighteenth-century culture.

The Temple was later to have less happy associations. During the Revolution it was used as a prison for, among others, the French royal family.

A notebook at the lower left corner of the painting bears the following verses, attributed to Pont de Veyle: "Of sweet and lively cheer/ each one here is an example/ altars are prepared for the tea/ it deserves to have a temple!"

The concerts given at the home of the prince de Conti, whose back is inexplicably to the viewer, were the most famous in Paris. The "salon of four mirrors" was also the music room, as can be seen by the trophy of musical instruments on the panel above one mirror. The young Mozart is portrayed on his second visit to Paris at ten years old; seated before the harpsichord, he gives a note to Geliotte, who is tuning his guitar. Music was, of course, one of Jefferson's chief loves, and among his extensive music library were works by Mozart, perhaps meant by Jefferson to be played in company with his daughter Patsy, since they were arranged for more than one instrument. A.B. de L.

232 Saint John de Crèvecoeur

VALLIÈRES, active late 18th century
Lent anonymously

Michael Guillaume Jean de Crèvecoeur (1735–1813), better known as Saint John de Crèvecoeur, achieved great success with his *Letters of an American Farmer* published under the name of J. Hector St. John in 1782. They were based on his own experience and observations as a farmer in New York and helped to give a picture of the American pioneer to a European audience. De Crèvecoeur spent much of his life acting as a link between the country of his birth, France, and the United States, where he settled when it was still under British rule, after spending some years in Canada. He arrived in New York in 1759 and became naturalized in 1765. His divided sympathies and the dislocation of his peaceful life forced him to leave America at the time of the Revolution, but he returned afterwards as French consul in New York, where he remained until 1790.

De Crèvecoeur had an introduction to Jefferson from Chastellux and first wrote to him in 1784 for information on the distillation of brandy from potatoes. The two men were keen naturalists and farmers and had an equal desire to exchange the plants of the old and the new worlds. Jefferson sent him a copy of his *Notes on the State of Virginia* and de Crèvecoeur reciprocated with his *Letters*. De Crèvecoeur helped to popularize potatoes in Normandy, where he had grown up, and claimed to have introduced alfalfa, sainfoin and other fodder crops into the United States. Jefferson kept up a long correspondence with de Crèvecoeur, and they exchanged political news, notes on plants and gossip about their mutual friends, like Mme d'Houdetot, to whom, with Franklin, Buffon and other leading figures in the Parisian world, the writer had been introduced after the success of his *Letters of an American Farmer*. An unusual criticism of these was made later by Moustier, the French minister to the United States, in a confidential memorandum on the consuls of Crèvecoeur's accounts of the life of a pioneer farmer had led many French immigrants to settle in the United States, and instead of making their fortunes they had found only misery. Jefferson's close relations with de Crèvecoeur extended to his family, and the American minister attended the wedding of the Frenchman's daughter and also interested himself in de Crèvecoeur's two sons, who were left behind in a pension near the Hôtel de Langeac, when their father went as consul to New York. R.W.

233 Thomas Jefferson

EDMÉ QUENEDEY 1756–1830
Aquatint proof (before letters engraved about 1801; an example at the Bibliothèque nationale from the same plate is inscribed: *Quenedey del. ad vivum et Sculp.*) 1789
52.4 x 39.5 (20⅝ x 15⅝)

Lent by The Yale University Art Gallery, New Haven

Quenedey's original life-sized portrait of Jefferson, done in 1789, was drawn in crayon on paper, as are the few surviving examples of his original physiognotrace delineations. But unlike Saint-Mémin, whose later physiognotrace drawings were sold as finished portraits along with the small engravings made from them, Quenedey regarded the large drawings only as a preliminary step to the final product: the engraved miniature profiles printed from the copper plate onto which Quenedey's partner, Gilles-Louis Chrétien, transferred the original drawing by means of a pantograph.

Jefferson sat for the portrait in Paris at the Quenedey-Chrétien establishment in the rue Croix des Petits Champs just east of the Palais Royal on April 23, 1789. Six days later Jefferson called for the copper plate, upon which Chrétien had engraved Quenedey's delineation, and twelve prints struck from it.

The fact that examples of the engravings of this portrait are not mentioned as enclosures in any of Jefferson's letters to friends in America in the months immediately after their execution and that none are known to survive among the effects of Jefferson's friends in France, suggests that Jefferson was more interested in the mechanical aspects of the physiognotrace than he was pleased with the likeness which resulted from his first contact with it. It is very probably the first portrait of an American taken by means of this invention, and it draws our attention as a very exact outline of Jefferson's profile, rather than as a portrayal of the inner character.

It has been plausibly suggested that the drawing may still have been in the artist's possession at the time of Jefferson's election to the presidency and that it was from this that Quenedey reengraved the portrait shown here, perhaps with the intention of commercial distribution. It is also possible that this version of the portrait may have been engraved by Quenedey not from the original drawing, but from a proof of the 1789 Chrétien likeness, retained for the artist's collection. Since even the engravings struck about 1801 survive only in rare instances, the portrait, doubtless, had a limited circulation. A.B.

234 Gouverneur Morris

GILLES-LOUIS CHRÉTIEN
1754–1811, after Edmé Quenedey
1756–1830
Engraving from physiognotrace portrait 1789
5.1 (2) diam.
Signed beneath circular borderline: *Dess. p. Quenedey gr. p. Chretien inv. du phys.*

Lent by the Prints Division, the New York Public Library

Gouverneur Morris (1752–1816), who had arrived in Paris earlier that year, was incompatible with his countryman Jefferson in personal style, and noted in his diary that "he and I differ in our Systems of Politics." However, on April 22, 1789, he recorded that he and Jefferson "went to the Palais Royal to get our Profiles taken, but it is too late for this Day and he is to call on me some Morning for the Purpose."

Jefferson called next morning at Morris' hotel in the rue de Richelieu and the two walked over to the Palais Royal, where tickets for sittings could be obtained. They could get but a single ticket, which Jefferson used for having his profile taken in Quenedey's studio in the rue Croix des Petits Champs (see no. 233). It was nearly a month later before Morris had his own sitting and not until June 7 that he could "call for my Profile Plate."

Morris' profile was taken by means of the physiognotrace (*physionotrace*) invented by Gilles-Louis Chrétien and then being exploited commercially by him in partnership with Edmé Quenedey. This mechanical tracing device, guided by the operator's eye, produced a life-size profile of the sitter's head, from which a reduction was engraved on copper. Prints were then struck in the traditional manner from the small copper plate, which the customer generally received along with a dozen or so small prints. Further prints could eventually be struck, as with a calling card. The physiognotrace, a great novelty when Morris and Jefferson were in Paris, has sometimes been called a "precursor of photography," but this is true only in the sense that it made available in quantity relatively inexpensive personal portraits and thus created a fashion and a demand that daguerreotypes, carte-de-visite photographs, and other forms would later meet.

A physiognotrace similar to Chrétien's invention was subsequently employed in the United States by the French émigré artist Févret de Saint-Mémin. When President Jefferson sat for Saint-Mémin at Washington in November 1804, he was thus resuming acquaintance with an ingenious invention he had first seen in Paris in 1789. H.C.R.

235 Meeting of the Assemblée des Notables Presided Over by Louis XVI and Held in the Hôtel des Menus Plaisirs at Versailles

JEAN-MICHEL MOREAU, CALLED MOREAU LE JEUNE 1741–1814
Pen and ink with wash 1787
50.4 x 80 (21¼ x 31½)
Inscribed, lower right on the mount: *J.M. Moreau le J^ne 1787*
Lent by the Musée National du Château de Versailles

Writing years later in his *Autobiography*, Jefferson sketched the events that led to the convening of the Assembly of Notables, shown here:

> The dissipations of the Queen and court, the abuses of the pension-list, and dilapidations in the administration of every branch of the finances, had exhausted the treasures and credit of the nation, insomuch that it's most necessary functions were paralyzed. . . . the King . . . advised therefore the call of an assembly of the most distinguished characters of the nation, in the hope that they would be induced to authorize new taxes, to controul the opposition of the parliament, and to raise the annual revenue to the level of expenditures. An Assembly of Notables, therefore, about 150. in number named by the King, convened on the 22d of Feb.

This drawing, ordered by the king, was shown in the Salon of 1787 where Jefferson saw it.

Moreau had succeeded Cochin in the official position of *dessinateur des Menus Plaisirs du roi*. Essentially an illustrator, the author of historical and allegorical compositions, of costume design and moralizing scenes, Moreau le Jeune is the personification of eclecticism. The drawings that he exhibited at the Salon of 1787 illustrate his versatility and include one history drawing, called *Tullia Running Her Chariot Over Her Father's Body*, seven drawings intended to embellish an edition of Voltaire, and the drawing exhibited here. A.B. de L.

236 Meeting of the Etats-Généraux in the Room of the Menus Plaisirs at Versailles

JEAN-MICHEL MOREAU, CALLED
MOREAU LE JEUNE 1741–1814
Pen and ink with wash 1789
29.2 x 40.2 (11½ x 15⅞)
Signed and dated at center bottom:
J.M. Moreau le j^{ne} 1789. Inscribed
on the mount: *Ouverture des Etats
g^{aux}/à Versailles le 5 Mai 1789*
*Lent by the Musée National du
Château de Versailles*

Jefferson followed minutely the events
leading to what he hoped would be
the establishment of a republican
government in France. He described
the meetings of the Etats-Généraux
in 1789, the first in more than 170
years, in his *Autobiography*:

The States General were opened on
the 5th of May 89. by speeches from
the King, the Garde des Sceaux
Lamoignon, and Mr. Necker. . . . I
felt it very interesting to understand
the views of the parties of which
it was composed. . . . I went therefore
daily from Paris to Versailles, and
attended their debates, generally
till the hour of adjournment. Those
of the Noblesse were impassioned
and tempestuous. . . . The debates of
the Commons were temperate,
rational and inflexibly firm.

The first meeting took place on
May 5, 1789, in the Menus Plaisirs
at Versailles, which had been
especially decorated for the occasion.
The king can be seen on a platform
sitting on his throne, with the queen
on his left. At the foot of the platform,

the ministers are seated at a table.
Facing them are the delegates of
the three estates, nobility, clergy and
the third estate, which was equal in
number to the other two. Guards and
spectators fill up the sides.

The significance of the event was
fully appreciated at the time, even
though the revolution had not yet
begun. It was the first of a long series
of events leading up to and changing
the course of the French Revolution.
These events included the Oath of the
Tennis Court, the fall of the Bastille,
and the various *journées* that brought
about an acceleration in the pace of
change and were eventually recorded
by artists like David, Robert, and a
host of draftsmen, in paintings, drawings, and engravings, leaving posterity
a unique fund of graphic illustration
of which Moreau's drawing is a
valuable part. A.B. de L.

237 The Oath of the Tennis Court

JACQUES-LOUIS DAVID 1748–1825
Ink and wash 1791
66 x 101 (26 x 39¾)
Signed and dated at bottom right:
J.L. David faciebat, anno 1791
*Lent by the Musée National du
Château de Versailles*

Jefferson saw the events of the
French Revolution to some extent
as the inevitable downfall of the
decadent European society from
which inhabitants of the New World
were fortunate enough to have
escaped. He also, however, imagined
that each tumultous event was to be
the final one and constantly expressed
the belief in his letters that the
difficulties would soon be resolved.
He reported on the event commemorated here, the Oath of the Tennis
Court, which took place June 20,
1789 (six weeks after the first meeting
of the Etats-Généraux and three weeks
before the fall of the Bastille), in a
letter to John Jay:

My letter gave you the progress of
the States General to the 17th,

when the Tiers had declared the
illegality of all the existing taxes,
and their discontinuance from the
end of their present session. . . . On
the 19th, a Council was held at
Marly, in the afternoon. It was there
proposed, that the King should
interpose by a declaration of his
sentiments in a *séance royale*. The
declaration . . . announced the
King's views, such as substantially
to coincide with the Commons. It
was agreed to in Council, as also
that the *séance royale* should be held
on the 22d, and the meetings till
then be suspended. While the
Council was engaged in this
deliberation at Marly, the Chamber
of the Clergy was in debate . . . and
it was determined . . . that their
body should join the Tiers. These
proceedings of the Clergy were
unknown to the Council at Marly,
and those of the Council were kept
secret from everybody. The next
morning (the 20th), the members
repaired to the House as usual, found
the doors shut and guarded. . . . They
presumed . . . that their dissolution

was decided, and repaired to
another place, where . . . they bound
themselves to each other by an oath,
never to separate of their own
accord, till they had settled a
constitution for the nation on a
solid basis.

The location of the group's meeting
and oath-taking was an indoor tennis
court. David's drawing, which, though
unfinished, was shown in the Salon
of 1791, makes many of the participants easily recognizable, and all of
them must have been known at least
by reputation to Jefferson. Bailly, the
president of the Third Estate, is
standing on a table, raising his hand
to swear, having just read the text of
the oath. In front of him three
clergymen, the abbé Gregoire, the
Protestant pastor Rabaut de Saint-
Etienne and the Carthusian monk
Dom Gerlé embrace as they swear
the oath. Sieyès is to the left of Bailly
near the table, while Robespierre on
the other side seems to be about to
burst with pent up emotion. Other
well-known political figures who can
be recognized are Mirabeau and

Barnave on the right and Barère on
the left, writing a record of the
historic meeting. In the right-hand
corner is the only deputy who refused
to swear, obstinately keeping his
hands tightly to his chest. The
tremendous enthusiasm has been
admirably conveyed in the vehement
gestures, emotional embraces and the
touching group supporting an old
man while he too takes part in the
oath.

David painted several of the
revolutionary heroes and martyrs, such
as Marat and Lepelletier, and took an
active part in politics. It may be that as
a painter of contemporary history,
which he continued to record in the
enormous canvases of Napoleon's
achievements, he felt the need to be
topical. The Oath of the Tennis
Court, while of great importance in
the history of the French Revolution,
was soon overtaken by more stirring
events, the fall of the Bastille, the
march on Versailles and the destruction of the Ancien Régime. A.B. de L.

238 The Bastille During the First Days of Its Demolition

HUBERT ROBERT 1733–1808
Oil on canvas 1789
77 x 114 (30⅜ x 44⅞)
Signed and dated at lower right:
*démolition de la Bastille le 20 juillet
1789, H. Robert pinxit*
Lent by the Musée Carnavalet, Paris

"As Mme Broutin cares for an English garden, Mr. Jefferson thought she might find pleasure in a book translated from the English in which this subject is treated superbly," wrote Jefferson to a Frenchwoman of his acquaintance the day before the fall of the Bastille. "If by chance she finds something to help her in the enhancement of her lovely countryside, he will be enchanted to have been able to make even this small contribution." Earlier that morning, however, he had expressed concern for the explosive situation in Paris in a letter to Thomas Paine:

Mr. Necker was dismissed from office the evening of the 11th. . . . this was not generally known in Paris until yesterday afternoon. The mobs immediately shut up all the playhouses. The foreign troops were advanced into the city. Engagements took place between some of them and the people. The first was in the place Louis XV, where a body of German cavalry being drawn up, the people posted themselves upon and behind the piles of stones collected there for the bridge, attacked and drove off the cavalry with stones. . . . This was a little before dusk, and it is now early in the morning: so I have not ascertained any particulars.

Two days after the demolition shown in this painting, Jefferson expressed hope that the violence had ended: "Great events have taken place here within these few days," he wrote to John Mason, "Yesterday the king went without any cortege but his two brothers to the States general and spoke to them in very honest and conciliatory terms; such as in my opinion amount to a surrender at discretion."

Bitter skirmishes and bloodshed continued, however, and he wrote to Maria Cosway on July 25 that "In the mean time we have been here in the midst of tumult and violence. The cutting off heads is become so much à la mode, that one is apt to feel of a morning whether their own is on their shoulders."

A sketch of the demolition of the Bastille was shown in the Salon of 1789 and may be a study for the present painting. A story told about the painting in the Salon relates that Lafayette was admiring it with one of his friends and said aloud that "the man who owned it would be very happy," whereupon the artist, standing nearby, approached the general and gave him the painting. A note in the files of the Musée Carnavalet, however, says that the *Demolition of the Bastille* was one of four paintings commissioned from Robert from M de Vergennes, who was imprisoned at the time and, in fact, was guillotined before he saw them.

The royal prison is seen from the intersection of the rue Saint-Antoine and the rue des Tournelles. This angular presentation of the fortress shows its imposing mass and projecting towers, on the rim of which can be seen a swarm of volunteer wreckers throwing the stones into the moats, while in the foreground other wreckers are demolishing the lower parts of the building. In the background is the burning governor's house. A.B. de L.

LAUDA-CONATUM

EXPOSITION au SALON du LOUVRE En 1787.

SALONS: 1785, 1787, 1789

In the eighteenth century, artists rarely had opportunities to make themselves known to the public, to connoisseurs, or to their colleagues. Royal commissions were intended for buildings which were practically inaccessible to the general public; rich noblemen and members of the wealthy upper middle class did not always open their doors freely. Only churches were public, and as a result, the paintings which decorated them were easy to see (which doubtless explains why artists were paid less for them, since they hoped to recover what they lost in the price by the reputation that would result from this exposure). In fact, the only real opportunity that the artist had to make himself known, to compare his most recent creations with those of his colleagues, and to make an attentive critic appreciate the progress made from one exhibition to the next, was to exhibit at the Salon.

During Jefferson's years in Paris there were three Salons, one each in 1785, 1787, and 1789. Like most Parisians he could not have missed visiting these exhibitions. On August 30, 1787, he wrote to John Trumbull who was then in London,

The Salon has been open four or five days. . . . Upon the whole it is well worth your coming to see. . . . The whole will be an affair of 12. or 14. days only . . . and as it happens but once in two years, you should not miss it.

From 1737 on, the Salon was held in the large salon of the Louvre, the Salon Carré. The word *salon*, which we use today for all kinds of more or less artistic exhibitions, comes from that room in the Louvre where the masterpieces of French painting from the fifteenth and the sixteenth centuries are now exhibited, including the Avignon *Pietà*, the *Diana the Huntress* from the School of Fontainebleau, and others. Before 1737, some exhibitions most certainly were held—the first Salon took place in 1673—but it was not until after 1737 that it became a regular institution with its own rules and customs, and was held at regular intervals. Between 1673 and 1791, the date of the last Salon in its classical form, there were thirty-six exhibitions held, or at least thirty-six

hich were accompanied by a *livret*, or catalogue. During Jeffer-
on's time in Paris, the Salon was biennial; it opened its doors on
ne day of Saint Louis, the king's feast day, August 25, and lasted
bout one month. The king himself and the royal family came to
ee it, usually, before the opening. Admission was free; people came
om all over Europe to admire the latest works of the most cele-
rated artists of the time. Some of those artists who were then
mong the most famous are forgotten today. It is known through
contemporary, Mathon de la Cour, that during the Salon of 1763
every day seven or eight hundred people from all the provinces
nd almost all nations" visited it.

The Salon included paintings, drawings, sculpture, and en-
ravings. In order to exhibit, an artist had to be a member of the
cadémie Royale de peinture et de sculpture or at least a candi-
ate for membership (*agréé*). This body, which included, almost
ithout exception, the best French artists or artists living in France
t that time, played a primary role in the formation and orientation
f aspiring artists. It not only taught the basic techniques of the
rofession, which were still those of craftsmen, but also gave a
eneral education to young artists, literary as well as scientific,
eligious as well as historical. The Académie selected the most
rilliant students through a series of competitive examinations in
rawing and sketching, awarded medals and prizes, and gave these
oung artists a carefully supervised course of study at the Ecole
Royale des élèves protégés. For those who won what was later to
e called the "prix de Rome," there was the opportunity to study
t the Académie de France à Rome, which was then installed in
he Palazzo Mancini and directed by artists of the first rank. In
efferson's time the director of the Académie was Menageot, whom
'Angiviller, the *surintendant des bâtiments*, preferred to David.
Upon the return of the prize-winning students from Rome (there
re exhibited here several paintings which were executed by *pen-
ionnaires* at the Palazzo Mancini: *Marius at Minturnae* by Drouais
nd *Jacob Coming to Find the Daughters of Laban* by Gauffier)
nd at the end of the study period for students in Paris, the young
rtists presented themselves as candidates for membership (*agréés*)
n the Académie. Before being admitted, each artist presented one
r two reception pieces (*morceaux de réception*). Very often the
quality of these works was such that they were considered master-
ieces, and became part of the Académie's collection. Watteau's
The Journey to the Island of Cythera, the *Skate* and the *Buffet* by
Chardin, and *Hector and Andromaque* by David are a few notable
examples. There are several such reception pieces in this exhibition,
ncluding *Cicero Discovering the Tomb of Archimedes at Syracuse*
oy Valenciennes, *Vien* by Duplessis, *Lagrenée l'aîné* by Mosnier,
nd *Charles-Amédée Van Loo* by Labille Guiard. There were
approximately one hundred *académiciens* between 1785 and 1789,
and forty candidates, not including the *honoraires amateurs* and
the *associés libres*, the rich collectors, the influential critics, and
the theorists.

It is useful to remember that, according to the subject chosen
for a reception piece, the artist was categorized as a history painter,
a portraitist, a genre painter, a still-life painter or a landscape artist.
This classification represented a hierarchy of genres in which
history painting was held in the highest esteem. The eighteenth
century—and Jefferson in admiring the *Marius at Minturnae* by
Drouais was no exception—placed primary emphasis on the subject,
or the way in which the subject could fire the imagination and stir
the soul, or could serve as an example of virtue. And it is true that
no matter how perfect a still-life by Chardin was, it could not, even
for Diderot, the most audacious and liberal of the critics of the
period, convey the moral lesson of a history composition by
Greuze. In a word, to paint man with his psychological complexity,
man as hero or coward, saint or tyrant, was seen as the most noble
task of the artist. And to do this, he had to prove himself endowed
with that supreme quality of the creative artist: invention.

The hierarchy of subject matter also explains another hierarchy,
that of the academicians among themselves. Between Jean-Baptiste-
Marie Pierre, the first painter to the king (*premier peintre du
Roi*) from 1770 to 1789, and the most recent *agréé*, there was a
whole scale of ranks: *recteur, professeur, adjoint à professeur,
conseiller*, and *académicien*. On the first page of the Salon catalogue of 1789, Vien, who became *premier peintre du Roi* at Pierre's
death, enumerated his titles: "Chevalier de l'Ordre du Roi [he
was ennobled], Premier Peintre de sa Majesté, ancien Directeur
de l'Académie de France à Rome, Honoraire de l'Académie Royale
d'Architecture, etc . . . Directeur, Chancelier et Recteur." Of the
artists whose works are shown here, Brenet and Lépicié were
professeurs, Vincent was an *adjoint*, and Joseph Vernet and
Duplessis, the portraitist of Franklin, were *conseillers*. Among the
académiciens were Berthélemy who had decorated the ceiling of
the Hôtel de Langeac, Regnault, Peyron, Perrin, and David who
triumphed at the Salon of 1785 with his *Oath of the Horatii*.
Women were not excluded from the Académie: Mmes Vallayer-
Coster, Vigée-Lebrun and Labille Guiard were also members.

In these Salons about 350 paintings, engravings and drawings
were exhibited. Upon looking at the large numbers of drawings
and engravings shown in each Salon, often as many as five or ten
by each artist, it is easy to understand how crowded the walls of
the exhibition were, and how little coveted was the thankless task
of the *tapissier*, or picture hanger. This person, who was chosen by
the academicians from their own ranks, had the delicate job of
hanging art works in a place where space was tight, where the light
was mediocre or at least unevenly distributed (in 1789 they experimented for the first time with skylights) and where each artist
wanted his works to be shown to best advantage. The position of
tapissier, which Chardin had held for years beginning in 1755
to the general satisfaction of the academicians, was not greatly
sought after; Amédée Van Loo, whose portrait by Labille Guiard
is exhibited here at number 242, held it in 1785, but was probably
replaced in 1787 and 1789 by Durameau. There were countless
small details to be attended to in the preparations for the Salon:
in 1783, for example, among the bills is one for the purchase of
gloves for the workmen who handled the paintings, the frames
of which had often been newly gilded. Because of the throngs who
visited the Salon daily, it was decided in 1787 that the Swiss guards
in the Louvre needed special assistance for the duration of the
exhibition, and they were supplemented by six retired soldiers who

were paid a total of 30 livres. In 1789, the students at the Académie took responsibility for guarding the exhibition rooms.

Prior to their display in the Salons, works by the *agréés* and the *académiciens* alike (but not those by the officials) had to be submitted to a jury, a custom which was begun in the mid-eighteenth century. This jury seems to have been liberal in its selections, though there is very little information about its role. Its main function appears to have been to eliminate works with licentious subjects or works which could lead to scandal. Thus on August 9, 1785, the *premier peintre* Pierre wrote to d'Angiviller,

Tomorrow, the works which will be admitted for the Salon will be examined; two little figures by Houdon have been proposed . . . one of them . . . is not so wonderful; the other could very well not be accepted because of its type of nudity; a completely nude figure is not as indecent as those which are draped with false modesty.

One of the most interesting aspects of the Salon was its catalogue, or *livret*. Of the Salons held between 1673 and 1791, thirty-six had published catalogues, one of which Jefferson bought and sent to Trumbull in 1787. The number of copies printed in 1791 was 20,000 and sold for twelve sols. The profits from its sale went to the Académie and paid for its caretaker and the artists' models. The catalogue's editor, the painter Renou, who had served for many years by the time of Jefferson's stay in Paris, had at the beginning of his career received a fixed sum of 300 livres, which was later increased to 600 livres. The 1789 catalogue incorporated 350 entries, with one section for paintings and drawings, one for sculpture, and a third for engravings. History, portraits, allegories, landscapes, still lifes, and trompe l'oeil all had their place in the catalogue (in 1787, Pierre complained that in that year "portraits and genre somewhat smother history"). Paintings were categorized in descending order of importance, their table of contents numbered. Some of the paintings were enormous (the *Combat of Entellus and Dares* by Durameau, today at Riom, measures thirteen feet wide and ten feet high), and many artists were represented by more than one work. In the Salon of 1789, Vernet exhibited twelve paintings, and he was outdone by de Marne, who had seventeen in the exhibition that year. Rank was strictly adhered to: the *Portrait of the King* (Louis XVI) by Callet was number 63 in the catalogue of 1789, the low standing of the painter outweighing the importance of the sitter, even though at the Salon the place of honor was given to this official portrait of the king.

One essential aspect of the life of the Salons remains to be explained, that of the critics. It would be incorrect to believe that Diderot and Bachaumont were the only ones to have given an opinion about the works exhibited. Every newspaper of the period and every gazette, of which there were hundreds, printed the opinions of the critics, called *Salonniers*, who often hid behind pseudonyms such as *Ah! Ah! Encore une critique du Sallon* ("Ah! Ah! Yet another Salon critic"), *Coup de patte sur le Sallon* ("A sarcastic view of the Salon"), *L'espion du Sallon de peinture* ("The spy at the paintings Salon") and *Jugement d'une demoiselle de quatorze ans* ("Opinion of a fourteen-year-old girl"). Sometimes in verse, often malicious or even slanderous when they referred to the private lives of the artists, these observations were nevertheless of an alarming monotony in their remarks about the works exhibited. Aside from long descriptions of the subjects, given for the benefit of readers who could not come to Paris, they untiringly used the same adjectives and the same standards of judgment. Rarely could one find an original sentence, an audacious comparison, or a digression which contained a valid aesthetic opinion.

The few lines written by Jefferson about the Salon of 1787 are of interest for their simplicity. "The best thing is the *Death of Socrates* by David," he wrote to John Trumbull about the painting exhibited here at number 331. He then went on to praise a trompe l'oeil by Roland de La Porte ("in imitation of Relief as perfect as it can be"), the works of Hubert Robert, and the portraits of Vigée-Lebrun. Certainly the Salon of 1787 had more noteworthy works displayed than these few, but the future American president singled out the essential, recognized the greatest painter of the century at a time when the critics still hesitated, and indicated his admiration of that series of depictions of Roman monuments in the south of France which he had visited six months before.

In the presentation of this exhibition, it seemed desirable to us to present to the American public a kind of reconstruction of a Salon. The location is not the same, the lighting is entirely different, and we were unable to include as many large paintings as we would have liked. The works presented, even though they were all exhibited in one of the three Salons that Jefferson visited during his stay in Paris, are displayed differently. The room, where the paintings are hung frame to frame, as they should be, shows a choice, without prejudice, of what a Salon visitor could have admired, evoking in its variety the essence of French painting on the eve of the Revolution. Let us hope that this room will give many visitors the desire to know better the works of art from a period in the history of French art which is little known, because the great masters have obscured the less gifted artists, and because the ambitions and goals of some of these artists are completely misunderstood today. Let us also hope that an attempt will one day be made to create a detailed reconstruction of these three Salons and that, as a result, works like the Roland de La Porte *Crucifix* which was admired by Jefferson will reappear. P.R.

39 Belisarius

ACQUES-LOUIS DAVID 1748–1825
il on canvas 1784
01 x 115 (39¾ x 45¼)
ent by the Musée du Louvre

his is a reduced replica of the
Belisarius, which was exhibited at the
lon of 1781, now at the Musée de
lle; the replica was shown at the
lon of 1785, number 104. Although
is signed by David, there is early
ocumentary evidence that his pupil
bre painted much of the picture,
d some scholars believe that Girodet
so helped in its production. Most of
e critics favorably compare the
duction to the larger painting.
ne anonymous critic wrote, "His
Belisarius is in miniature the
autiful painting which we have
ready seen by this artist. It is of a
zzling beauty, simple, noble and
nders the scene most tenderly; the
odeling and the color here are of an
tonishing superiority; one walks
ound each figure, and one could
en calculate the distance between
em. In a word it is a charming
ork which cannot be praised too
uch."
There are significant changes
tween the two paintings. Whereas
e Lille Belisarius is almost square,
e Louvre reduction is more
rizontal, giving the composition
ore extension on the left with
eater space between the soldier and
e woman   hence, no doubt, the
itic's praise, "One walks around
ch figure." Moreover, the two men
the background have been moved

more into the center, away from the
left edge. The backgrounds also vary.
In general the composition of the
smaller Belisarius is clearly more
Poussinesque than the earlier
painting.
    The story of Belisarius, the sixth-
century Byzantine general, who after
spectacular victories on behalf of the
empire was accused of conspiracy,
disgraced and blinded, was painted
several times in the second half of the
eighteenth century. Peyron, Vincent
and Durameau all used the story in
paintings in the 1770s. For the
eighteenth-century artist, the subject
illustrated fortitude under adversity,
the virtues of charity and the reverses
of fortune that could overtake even
the most powerful. This provided
matcrial for the moralizing which was
so popular at the time, even though
the incident was legendary, the
historical truth being that Belisarius'
disgrace lasted only a short while.
The source is probably to be found
in literature, such as Marmontel's
Bélisaire of 1767.
    When John Trumbull, who was on
friendly terms with David, visited the
artist's studio on August 9, 1786, he
saw among the paintings there
"Belisarius receiving alms, likewise
large as life—as well composed and
drawn as the other [Oath of the
Horatii], and better colored." Trumbull had painted the same subject
himself, while still in the United
States, by copying an engraving after
Salvator Rosa. A.B. de L.

240 M. de Chabanon

JOSEPH-SIFFRED DUPLESSIS
1725–1802
Oil on canvas
81 x 64.5 (31⅞ x 25⅜)

Lent by the Musée des Beaux-Arts,
Orléans

Michel-Paul Guillaume de Chabanon,
who was born in the French colony of
Saint-Dominique in 1730 and died in
Paris in 1792, was almost as famous
a musician as he was a writer.
Duplessis refers to both of his
model's talents in the still-life
arrangement on the table in the
background of the portrait which
includes books, a violin and some
musical scores. An erudite poet,
translator of Pindar and Theocritus,
author of tragedies and of essays,
Chabanon was elected to the French
Academy in 1780. He also had a
reputation as a violinist. The biographers of Chabanon all refer to his
brilliant playing of the violin part in
the concert des amateurs, which was
directed by the chevalier de Saint-
Georges, a Negro composer from
Guadeloupe, at the Hôtel Soubise.
He combined his diverse talents in
his musical writings: Eloge de
Rameau was published in 1764, and
De la musique, considérée en elle-même
et dans ses rapports avec la parole, les
langues, la poésie et le théâtre, a
two-volume work, appeared in 1785.
    This portrait was exhibited at the
Salon of 1785, number 45, along with
several others by Duplessis. Among
them were the Portrait of Vien (here
exhibited at no. 222). The critics,
always favorable to Duplessis, consistently praised his portraits,
especially that of Chabanon.
    The brushwork in the painting is
light and fluid, supple and free,
particularly in the subtle gray
tonalities. There is a replica at
Versailles. A.B. de L.

241 Self-Portrait with Two Pupils

Un Tableau (Portrait) de trois Figures
en pied, représentant une Femme
occupée à peindre & deux Elèves la
regardant
ADÉLAÏDE LABILLE-GUIARD
1749–1803
Oil on canvas 1785
210 x 152 (83 x 59½)
Signed and dated lower left:
Labille fme Guiard 1785

Lent by The Metropolitan Museum
of Art

The Self-Portrait with Two Pupils
was exhibited at the Salon of 1785,
number 101, under the title: "A
painting of three full-length figures
representing a woman painting and
two students watching her." The
thirty-six-year-old artist here appears
in full possession of her talents and
charm. The Salon critics identified the
two students as Mlle Marie-Gabrielle
Capet (1761–1818), looking at the
canvas, and Mlle de Carreaux de
Rosemond (?–1788). The first
was a favorite of Mme Labille's,
with whom she shared a house. After
Mme Labille's death, Mlle Capet
stayed on as housekeeper to the artist's
husband. However, very little is known
about the second student. A bust of the
artist's father, Claude-Edmé Labille, is
visible in the background. Executed by
Pajou, it was shown in the same Salon
(no. 198) and is now in the Louvre.
    This very ambitious painting caused
a sensation, and its triumphant success
established the artist's reputation. The
critics reviewed it enthusiastically.
Several of them judged it to be one of
the best paintings in the exhibition,
even worthy of comparison with the
works of the great masters on the level
of David or at least Vigée-Lebrun,
Labille-Guiard's rival. A.B. de L.

242 The Painter Charles-Amédée van Loo

M. Amédée Wanloo, Peintre du Roi,
Professeur de son Académie
ADÉLAÏDE LABILLE-GUIARD
1749–1803
Oil on canvas 1785
130 x 98 (51¼ x 38½)
Signed and dated: *Labille f Guiard*
1785

Lent by the Musée National du
Château de Versailles

Charles-Amédée van Loo (1718–
1795), depicted here by Adélaïde
Labille-Guiard, belonged to a large
family of painters, a circumstance
typical of eighteenth-century France,
in which there was a strong dynastic
tradition among artists. After studying
with his father, he became a member
of the Académie Royale in 1746.
Later he moved to Berlin and became
principal painter to Frederick II, a
great admirer of French art. On
returning to France, Van Loo became
professor and eventually associate
director of the Academy. It was his
responsibility to hang the Salon of
1785 in which his portrait was
number 98. Labille, who was a friend
of Van Loo's, presented the portrait
as her *morceau de réception* to the
Academy. Several other portraits by
her were also in the exhibition,
including her *Self-Portrait with Two
Pupils* (no. 241). The critics received
her work favorably. A.B. de L.

243 The Farmyard

Autre intérieur de ferme, appartenant
à M. le Duc de***
NICOLAS-BERNARD LÉPICIÉ
1735–1784
Oil on canvas 1784
64 x 77 (24¼ x 30⅝₆)
Signed and dated at upper left:
N.B. Lépicié 1784

Lent by the Musée du Louvre

The Farmyard that Nicolas-Bernard
Lépicié painted in 1784 reveals the
artist's preoccupation during the last
years of his life. In about 1783 he
underwent a moral crisis and completely renounced his career as a
history painter, to devote himself
to subjects taken from rustic life in
the manner of Teniers. His decision
was influenced by Diderot and other
critics, though it was not the first
time that he had painted country
scenes.
   The author of the review in the
Journal de Paris (1785) relates that
one of the country parties that took
place "last year inspired in him
[Lépicié] an interest in animals, of
which he made a quantity of studies
on the spot. . . ." Three paintings of
farmyards by Lépicié appeared in the
Salon of 1785, one of which, number
6, may be the present painting.
   The innovation in these works is
found in their combination of naïveté
and refinement, the careful attention
to the various simple, daily tasks of the
farm, interpreted through exact
drawing and a bright palette. His figure
style is halfway between the realism
of Chardin and the naturalism of
Greuze.
   The critics of the period were

unanimous for once in congratulating
Lépicié on having abandoned history
painting in favor of genre painting:
"He did not cover himself with glory
in his large projects; only those on a
small scale are suitable for him. Several
intimate paintings by this charming
artist were just exhibited . . . the
choice of subjects, the meticulous
rendering of all the objects, the fresh
coloring, the light and witty brush
work make these paintings worthy of
the most refined collections. M.
Lepicié is truly the Teniers *par
excellence* of France. What inexplicable madness always drove him to
solicit large works, subjects from
history?" A.B. de L.

244 The Body of his Son Lausus being Brought to the Wounded Mezentius

Mézence blessé à qui l'on porte le
corps de son fils, Lauzus
JEAN-JOSEPH TAILLASSON
1745–1809
Gray wash over black pencil sketch
(two joined sheets) 1785
48.7 x 77.7 (19⅛ x 30¼)
Signed at lower left: *Taillasson*

Lent by the Musée des Beaux-Arts,
Nancy

The drawing is presumably not a
drawing for the painting of the same
subject exhibited in the Salon of
1783, but may well be a reworking
of the composition. However, the
painting is now lost. Two other
drawings by Taillasson were also
exhibited in 1785 under the same
number, 118, *Panthea and Abradatas
receiving gifts from Cyrus* and
*Autolion, General of the Crotonians,
Wounded by the Ghost of Ajax,*
exhibited here at number 245. The
composition and the spirited style of
the drawing recall Vigée-Lebrun rather
than David and suggest the inspiration
was more seventeenth-century
classicism than later eighteenth-
century neoclassicism. The wash is
broadly handled, and light and shade
are contrasted with great subtlety.
   Virgil in Book 10 of the *Aeneid*
describes the combat between
Mezentius, the king of the Estruscan
city of Caere, and Aeneas. Mezentius
was a tyrant who had been banished
by his people. Aeneas killed him, along
with his son, who had attempted to
save Mezentius. A.B. de L.

245 Autolion, General of the Crotonians, Wounded by the Ghost of Ajax

Autoleon, Général des Crotoniates, blessé par l'ombre d'Ajax
JEAN-JOSEPH TAILLASSON
1745–1809
Black pencil and wash
37 x 49 (14½ x 19¼)
Signed at lower left: *Taillasson*
Lent by the Musée Fabre, Montpellier

The Locrians usually left a space in front of their battle line in memory of Ajax, son of Oileus, their national hero. In a war waged by the Crotonians against the inhabitants of Locri, their general, Autolion, charged into this space and was wounded in the thigh by the ghost of Ajax. Since the wound did not heal, he spoke to an oracle, who ordered him to go to the island of Leuce and to appease the spirit of the dead hero by making a sacrifice. Autolion obeyed and was healed.

This drawing was exhibited in the same Salon, at number 118, as *The Wounded Mezentius*, exhibited here under number 244. It is striking to see how Taillasson's work differs according to which medium, painting or drawing, he uses. His paintings are highly finished, cold, precise, and meticulous, with an elegant and calculated refinement, in a word, neoclassical. His drawings, by contrast, are impetuous, nervous, free, and executed in a manner which recalls at the same time Vigée-Lebrun and Doyen. Although the drawing was called an *esquisse dessinée*, there is no evidence that a finished painting was ever completed from it or that a painting was intended.

In the drawing, Autolion is at the right, rushing into the void, while an allegorical figure tries in vain to hold him back. A.B. de L.

246 Seated Bacchante

Bacchante assise, de grandeur naturelle, & vue jusqu'aux genoux
MARIE-LOUISE-ELISABETH
VIGÉE-LEBRUN 1755–1842
Oil on canvas 1785
111.8 x 88.9 (44 x 35)

Lent by the Fine Arts Museums of San Francisco

This *Seated Bacchante* is a faithful replica of the painting in the Musée Nissim de Camondo, Paris, and was exhibited at the Salon of 1785, as number 86. This bacchante is sometimes published as *Self-Portrait as a Bacchante*, but there is nothing to justify the identification of the features of the artist with those of the bacchante.

The painting was an enormous success at the Salon. There is hardly a critic who did not discuss it in his review. The opinions, as always, are at opposite extremes, from the highest praise: "One sees again from Madame Lebrun a magnificent Bacchante whose pose and coloring are enchanting. There is great variety in the natural talent of Madame Lebrun"; to the most severe criticism: "The expression of the Bacchante, which should be masculine and savage, is here silly and unpleasant, the heavy knees are of a disgusting shape . . . ." Several critics testify to the extraordinary success of the painting: "Our admiration for her [Vigée-Lebrun] is not, however, unique, but we do not sound like those enthusiasts who shout in the Salon, in the public gardens, in the cafés, that Madame Lebrun has crushed Roslin; she is a thousand times better than Duplessis; Vestier does not approach her; she triumphs over Madame Guiard."

There were, however, criticisms that the woman looked more like one of the graces than a bacchante. If it were not for the presence of the panther skin and the bunches of grapes, it would indeed be difficult to see the model as a bacchante. While the subject of a bacchante is common in French eighteenth-century painting, mythological paintings are rare in the oeuvre of Vigée-Lebrun; in the catalogue of her works which she gives at the end of her *Souvenirs*, ten history paintings (more exactly, mythological) are listed among 660 portraits.

Mme Vigée-Lebrun was one of the artists John Trumbull met when he stayed with Jefferson in 1786. He saw and admired many of her works in private and public collections, as, for example, a *Self-Portrait* at the comte de Vaudreuil's. At the Royal Academy, "Madame Le Brun's Peace and Plenty holds a conspicuous rank; the coloring is very brilliant and pleasing." Trumbull also dined with the Lebruns and was full of praise: "Madame Le Brun is one of the most charming women I ever saw; her pictures have great merit, particularly a portrait of herself and her daughter, which is not yet finished; in the composition of this picture there is a simplicity and sweetness worthy of any artist, and a brilliance of coloring quite charming." A.B. de L.

247 The Countess de Ségur

MARIE-LOUISE-ELISABETH
VIGÉE-LEBRUN 1755–1842
Oil on canvas 1785
92 x 73 (36¼ x 28¾)
Signed and dated at upper right:
L^{se} V^e LeBrun/f. 1785

Lent by the Musée National du Château de Versailles

Mme Vigée-Lebrun in her *Souvenirs* speaks several times of the comtesse de Ségur (1756–1828), who was among her most faithful friends. The comte de Ségur was an active supporter of the American Revolutionary War and was a member of the corps of volunteers led by Rochambeau, winning the rank of colonel in a naval battle. Later he became French ambassador to Catherine II of Russia and achieved high rank under Napoleon. The *Countess de Ségur* was number 88 in the Salon of 1785.

According to the list of paintings executed before 1789, Mme Lebrun recorded a portrait of "Madame la comtesse de Ségur" together with a copy, and she also painted the comte de Ségur and his father. The artist has painted the countess in simple, almost country costume, the informality emphasized by the flowers scattered casually on the table and by the whimsical hat. It was not unknown for French ladies to dress up as peasants, and the cult of simplicity became fashionable through the writings of Rousseau and the arcadian writings of Solomon Gessner. Mme de Pompadour had been painted as a shepherdess, and Marie-Antoinette and her friends played at being dairy maids in the *Laiterie* at Versailles.

A note of sentimentality is also present, and the admirer of Richardson's *Pamela* cannot resist making her model slightly mannered and affected. The teeth are shown in an artificial smile, the gaze is languid and seems to be lost in space, while the pathetic expression is a deliberate attempt to touch our feelings in the manner of Greuze. But as always in Mme Lebrun's work, the smallest details are beautifully executed. The pose is elegant and graceful, while light is admirably controlled and plays an important part in unifying the composition. A.B. de L.

248 Tithonus and Aurora

L'Etude répand des fleurs sur le Tems
SIMON JULIEN 1735–1800

*Lent by the Musée des Beaux-Arts,
Caen*
In Salon of 1785, as no. 160

**249 Psyche Looking at the
Sleeping Cupid**

*Psiche venant à la faveur d'une
lampe, pour poignarder son amant
qu'elle croit un monstre: elle
reconnoît l'Amour*
JEAN-BAPTISTE REGNAULT
1754–1829

*Lent by the Musée des Beaux-Arts,
Angers*
In Salon of 1785, as no. 108

250 Monsieur Pécoul

M.P***
JACQUES-LOUIS DAVID
1748–1825

Lent by the Musée du Louvre
In Salon of 1785, as no. 105

**251 Coriolanus among the Volscians, Ceding to the Pleas of
His Mother, His Wife and the Roman Women, Renounces
Avenging Himself Against Rome**

*Coriolan chez les Volsques, cédant
aux prières de sa mère, de sa femme
& aux larmes des Dames Romaines,
renonce à se venger de Rome*
JEAN-JACQUES-FRANÇOIS
LE BARBIER THE ELDER, CALLED
LE BARBIER L'AÎNÉ 1738–1826
Lead pencil, pen and black ink, gray
wash 1788
50.8 x 68.7 (20 x 27)
Signed and dated at lower left:
Le Barbier l'ainé in. 1788

*Lent by the Musée Tavet-Delacour,
Pontoise*

The story of Coriolanus among the
Volscians illustrates a decision made
with great courage. Condemned to
exile in 490 B.C. by the Roman
people, who refused to accept his
oligarchical politics, Gaius Marcius
Coriolanus, a general, found refuge
among the Volscians, against whom
he had formerly fought. Driven by a
desire to avenge himself, he encouraged Volscians to go to war against
the Romans and took command of
the army himself. After the Senate
pleaded with him in vain not to bear
arms against his country, his mother,
Veturia, and his wife, Volumnia, came
to beg him for mercy. Coriolanus,
won over by their entreaties, ordered
his troops to withdraw, but the
Volscians would not forgive him for
his decision and condemned him to
death. The subject was a popular one
with artists, for its dramatic and moral
message, especially in the neoclassic
period. It illustrated that the ties of
family affection were stronger than

hatred and that ultimately patriotism
would triumph over a desire for
revenge. As in many other paintings
of the French Revolutionary
period, moral courage and virtue are
here depicted to serve as an example
to contemporaries.

It is interesting to note that Le
Barbier in this drawing, exhibited as
number 100 in the Salon of 1789,
draws on the compositions of Nicolas
Poussin; the hanging drapery at the
left, the group of women at the right,
and the relationship between the
figures and the landscape are identical
to those found in the works of
Poussin. A.B. de L.

**252 View of the Cascades at
Tivoli and the Temple of the Sibyl**

*Vue des cascatelles de Tivoli &
du Temple de la Sibylle: la figure
que l'on y voit est Horace méditant*
JEAN-FRANÇOIS HUE 1751–1823
Oil on canvas 1786
128 x 188 (50⅜ x 74)
Signed and dated at lower left:
J.F. Hue. Rome 1786

*Lent by the Musée des Beaux-Arts,
Tours*

Hue continued to exhibit landscapes,
inspired by sites in Italy, for many
years after he had traveled there in
1785–1786. The 1787 Salon
catalogue number 86 provides some
information: "The figure seen in the
picture is Horace meditating." In the
foreground the artist has added an
historical scene, in the manner of
Valenciennes and Claude, which
serves as a justification for the
landscape. Hue knew that the site of
Tivoli could not be represented
without the figure of Horace, the
famous Roman poet who had a house
there.

Tivoli was, moreover, a "required"
site at this period for all landscape
artists who went to Italy. The picturesqueness of the cascades, combined
with the reference to antiquity in the
Temple of the Sibyl, which can be
seen at the upper right, and the
numerous literary associations of
Tivoli, contributed to the celebrity
of the place both for tourists and
artists. Hubert Robert and
Fragonard are among those who
painted views of Tivoli.

The site here has been rearranged
by the artist, which suggests that in
spite of the signature and date, the
View of the Cascades of Tivoli was
probably painted from memory, based

n studies made from nature. An
ngraving could also have aided Hue
n his work. All of the left side of the
omposition has been invented by the
ainter, since the closest lake or
ortion of the sea was at least twenty
ilometers away. Also, the moun-
ainous horizon is imaginary.
ictorially, the work is reminiscent
f the style of Vernet, an artist under
hom Hue studied.

Hue exhibited four other
Italian" landscapes at the same
alon of 1787; among them *The
emple of the Sibyl and the Country-
de at Tivoli, Illuminated by the
etting Sun.* A.B. de L.

53 Madame Adélaïde

DÉLAÏDE LABILLE-GUIARD
749–1803
Oil on canvas
11 x 153 (83 x 60½)
*Lent by the Phoenix Art Museum,
Arizona*

This portrait of Mme Adélaïde is a
maller version, with some differences,
f the larger portrait in the collections
t Versailles. Labille-Guiard made
wo replicas of the painting, the
irst, now lost, was painted for the
omtesse de Chastellux, the second
s in a collection in Paris. It is not
known for whom the Phoenix
picture was painted.

Mme Adélaïde, born at Versailles
March 23, 1732, was the sixth child
of Louis XV and Marie Leczinska.
She took the title of madame upon the
death of her elder sister Mme
Henriette. Mme Campan, reader to
mesdames, described her as follows:
"Madame Adélaïde was wittier than
Madame Victoire, but she lacked
completely the kindness which alone
inspires affection in adults: brusque
manners, a harsh voice, a clipped
pronunciation made her overbearing."

The Versailles painting, a great
state portrait, was exhibited at the
Salon of 1787, number 110. The
entry in the Salon catalogue is
instructive: "At the foot of a
medallion containing low relief
portraits of the late King, the late
Queen, and the late Dauphin, the
princess, who is supposed to have
painted them herself, has just written
these words 'leur image est encore
le charme de ma vie.' On a folding
stool trails a roll of paper, on which
is drawn the plan for the convent
founded at Versailles by the late
Queen and of which Madame
Adélaïde is the directress."

The gilt armchair which is identical
to one in the Metropolitan Museum
of Art, New York, the folding stool,
and the easel are examples of the
magnificent furniture with which she
liked to surround herself.

Mme Labille-Guiard was the
painter patronized by the king's
aunts, while her great rival Mme
Vigée-Lebrun was the favorite of
the queen. This reflected more than
just a personal preference, for the
deeply religious princesses disap-
proved of Marie-Antoinette and the
frivolous atmosphere of the court at
Versailles. The portrait of Mme
Adélaïde was hung in conscious
rivalry almost next to that of
Marie-Antoinette in the Salon of
1787. A.B. de L.

254 View of the Port-au-Bled, Taken from the Far Side of the Old Cattle Market

*Vue du Port-au-Bled, prise à
l'extrémité de l'ancien Marché-aux-
Veaux*
LOUIS-NICHOLAS DE LESPINASSE
1734–1803
Pen and watercolor heightened with
gouache
32 x 63.2 (12⅝ x 24⅞)
Old inscription at the bottom of the
mounting: *Dessiné par le chevalier
de l'Espinasse en 1782 et Troisième
vue intérieure de Paris. Vue du Port
au Blé pris à l'extrémité de l'ancien
marché aux Veaux regardant le Pont
Notre-Dame*

Lent by the Musée Carnavalet, Paris

The chevalier de Lespinasse, who had
been a professional soldier, exhibited
nine topographical watercolors at the
Salon of 1787, seven of them views
of Paris. The *Port-au-Bled* was number
157. One of them was the artist's
reception piece for admission to the
Royal Academy. As records of a Paris
that has now disappeared, the views
are of the greatest interest to historians. The *port-au-bled* stood on the side
of the Seine where the present *hôtel
de ville* is now situated. Four years
after the drawing was made, the
houses on the pont Notre-Dame were
demolished and this provided the
subject for one of Hubert Robert's
paintings. A.B. de L.

255 View of Port Saint-Paul, taken from the Quay facing the Passenger Boat Office

*Vue du Port S. Paul, prise sur le quai,
vis-à-vis le Bureau des Coches d'eau*
LOUIS-NICHOLAS LESPINASSE
1734–1803
Pen and watercolor heightened with
gouache 1782
29 x 62.5 (11⅜ x 24⅝)
Signed and dated at lower left:
d.L. 1782. Monogram A.R.D. on the
mounting

Lent by the Musée Carnavalet, Paris

The *View of Port Saint-Paul* was

number 159 in the Salon of 1787,
where Lespinasse exhibited seven
views of Paris. The Port Saint-Paul
bordered the Seine on a slope in
front of the quay des Celestins, the
houses of which can be seen from
the opening of the rue Saint-Paul to
the convent of the Celestins and the
Arsenal. The wooden Pont de
Grammont crossed over a branch of
the Seine (today it is filled in and has
become the boulevard Morland)
separating the right bank from
Louviers island, which was covered
with enormous piles of timber.

Standing before this fantastic topographical document, one cannot help
but admire the exceptional quality
and the extraordinary freshness of the
watercolor, which allows an
appreciation of the smallest details
of the landscape represented. It was
one of the most picturesque sights
in Paris, with constant activity in the
passenger boats which called there
and in the corn market, the fish
auction and the stacks of wood floated
down the river to be sold as
firewood. A.B. de L.

256 View of the Demolition of the Church of the Saints-Innocents, Taken from the rue Saint-Denis

Vue de la démolition de l'église des Saints-Innocents, prise de la rue Saint-Denys
PIERRE-ANTOINE DE MACHY
1723–1807
Oil on canvas 1787
50 x 77.5 (19¾ x 30½)

Lent by the Musée Carnavalet, Paris

Pierre-Antoine de Machy, "Professor of Perspective" at the Académie Royale de peinture, exhibited at the Salon of 1787, number 25, this *Demolition of the Church of the Saints-Innocents* with two other paintings of the same church, *Another Interior View of the Church of the Saints-Innocents, Illuminated by the Light of a Fire* and *Another View of the Same Building*, also in the Musée Carnavalet.

Like his contemporary, Hubert Robert, de Machy was a painter with a passion for ruins. If the urban demolitions, numerous in Paris at the end of the eighteenth century, no longer provided him with a subject to paint, he imagined structures to satisfy his taste for the picturesqueness of ruins.

At the beginning of the year 1787 the Church of the Saints-Innocents, as well as the cemetery next to it, was demolished as a sacrifice to the demands of town planning. The demolition work of the cemetery and the church took place under the direction of the architects Legrand and Molinos and the engineer Six. The church stood at the angle of the rue aux Fers (today the rue Berger) and the rue Saint-Denis; the apse (seen at the left in the painting) opened onto the latter street. The artist placed his easel on the side of the rue Saint-Denis, which allows the viewer to see a large part of the street, the apse and radiating chapels under demolition, and a part of the nave.

To the right of the church being demolished and next to the narrow façade of a house across from it, the famous fountain of the Saints-Innocents with sculptures by Goujon can be seen in its original location at the southwest angle of the rue Saint-Denis and the rue aux Fers. It was transferred to a new site in 1788. A.B. de L.

257 Electra at the Tomb of Agamemnon

Electre. Cette Princesse, mise par Egiste au rang des Esclaves, va faire des libations au tombeau d'Agamemnon
JEAN-JOSEPH TAILLASSON
1745–1809
Oil on canvas 1785
71 x 58 (28 x 23)
Signed and dated at bottom left:
Taillasson, 1785

Lent by Professor Robert Rosenblum, New York

Electra at the Tomb of Agamemnon is certainly the painting exhibited at the Salon of 1787 as number 123. The catalogue note reads, "This Princess, placed by Aegisthus among the slaves, goes to make libations on the tomb of Agamemnon; there she sees some hair, flowers and a sword. She thinks that only Orestes could have made these offerings; she hopes to see her brother again, whom she loves, and to find in him the avenger of her family." If we assume that the dimensions have been reversed, and such mistakes were frequent in the Salon catalogue, then *"deux pieds deux pouces de haut"* and *"deux pieds neuf pouces de large"* corresponds to the size of the present painting.

Taillasson was the pupil of Vien, and his paintings are among the purest expressions of neoclassicism, with their subtle elegance and careful construction. The influence of Vien can perhaps be seen in the background of trees and in the temple, recalling the *Marchande d'amours*. Electra's rather theatrical gesture appears in several of Taillasson's compositions, so it was obviously a favorite of his.

It is revealing to reproduce some of the criticisms of the *Salonniers*, the numerous band of critics who published their comments, usually not very perceptive, on the works of art. In the Salon of 1787, *Electra* was largely overlooked in favor of Taillasson's reception piece, *Philoctetes*. One critic wrote, "The painting which represents *Electra* has considerable character, but it lacks both feeling in drawing and in color." Another felt that *Electra* was not the heroine of Euripides: "She has neither her character, nor her sorrow, nor her pride." A third critic found that the painting was rather dark. A.B. de L.

258 Cicero Discovering the Tomb of Archimedes at Syracuse

Cicéron decouvrant à Syracuse le tombeau d'Archimède
PIERRE-HENRI DE VALENCIENNES
1750–1819
Oil on canvas 1787
119 x 162 (46⅞ x 63¾)
Signed at lower right:
P. DEVALENCIENNES, 1787

Lent by the Musée des Augustins, Toulouse

Cicero Discovering the Tomb of Archimedes is Valenciennes' reception piece for the Royal Academy in Paris. The 1787 Salon catalogue number 171 gives an explanation of the subject:

Archimedes having been killed during the sack of Syracuse, the city which he had defended for three years solely through the efforts of his own genius, against the Romans commanded by Marcellus, was so completely forgotten by his fellow citizens that when Cicero was elected Quaestor of Sicily, one hundred and thirty-seven years after the ruin of Syracuse, no one was able to indicate the location of the tomb of this great man. They even denied that it was in their city. But Cicero, having good directions and knowing that Archimedes had requested before dying that this tomb should have as its only ornament the beautiful geometrical figure of a sphere circumscribed by a cylinder, discovered the tomb by that sign. It was buried in undergrowth; he had all that covered it cut away, and showed it to the people of Syracuse.

Valenciennes had visited Sicily in 1779 and speaks at length about this country in his *Eléments de perspective pratique à l'usage des artistes, suivis de*

eflections et conseils à un élève sur la einture, 1799. He even gives a description of the site of Syracuse, and what he says in general about Sicily is informative, in relation to his ambitions for his own art:

Sicily is one of the most beautiful countries and the most useful for doing great and majestic studies of all kinds. We counsel the landscape painter to travel through it in every direction, and to contemplate all the imposing objects which present themselves to view. He often will find there models for some of Poussin's superb compositions, and the grandiose style which characterizes his immortal works. In reading the descriptions of Diodorus and Theocritus, of the same places, the artist's imagination is exalted, and the appearance of the sites that he will encounter can inspire his genius and establish, forever, the talent with which nature will have favored him.

What interests Valenciennes is to apture the disappearance and detruction, by the erosion of time, of he legendary sites of pastoral bliss. Rather than try to evoke the desolaion of these ruins through his art, Valenciennes hopes that the viewer's magination, guided by literary feeling and archaeological erudition, will be used to reconstruct the actual appearance of the past and its poetic side: 'Since the artist no longer finds, in he actual site nature as his imaginition conceived it, he must recreate t according to the description of he poets who depicted it with the nost grandeur and elegance." A.B. de L.

259 The Ancient City of Agrigento, Imaginary Reconstruction

L'ancienne Ville d'Agrigente

PIERRE-HENRI DE VALENCIENNES
1750–1819
Oil on canvas
110 x 164 (43¼ x 64⁹⁄₁₆)
Lent by the Musée du Louvre

The Ancient City of Agrigento is the second landscape of Sicily that Valenciennes exhibited at the Salon of 1787, number 172, the first being *Cicero Discovering the Tomb of Archimedes at Syracuse,* here exhibited at number 258. As the Salon catalogue explained the subject: "The custom of the people of Agrigento was to have stationed in front of the door of their house and at the city gates, slaves who were to entice strangers to take lodging in their master's house. Gellias, who was a very rich private citizen, even sent his slaves out onto the main roads with the same objective. And it is this moment that the artist has chosen to illustrate in the foreground of his painting." The stele at the left, which bears the Greek inscription ΑΓΡΑΓΑΣ, designates the entrance to the city. Agrigento was famous for its sumptuous houses, and it is in speaking of the people of Agrigento that a writer says: "They built as though they would live forever." Valenciennes gives in his *Eléments de perspective pratique à l'usage des artistes . . .* (1798–1799), as in his painting, a detailed description of the city:

The ancient city is almost at the base of the hillside where it meets the sea: its superb ruins can be seen from a great distance. Its temples are all located on promontories and blend perfectly with their surroundings. The Temple of Concord is the first one to come into sight, no matter from what direction one approaches the city. It is, without question, one of the most beautiful ones known, in its proportions, its purity, its elegance, its severe style and its state of preservation. The temple of the giants is completely in ruins . . . ."

The painting, a masterpiece of balanced composition, is strongly influenced by Claude Lorrain. The use of light, the foreground scene, the little figures in the middle distance, the importance given to the architecture, the sense of proportion, all recall his majestic, idyllic, serene landscapes. It illustrates what Valenciennes wrote about the two ways for an artist to paint nature: "The first is that which makes us see nature as it is, and represents it as faithfully as possible. The second is that which makes us see nature as it could be, and as the fanciful imagination represents it to the eyes." It is clear that "to see nature as it could be" is what interested Valenciennes, and this search for ideal nature was achieved through his careful study of the work of Lorrain. A.B. de L.

260 Eugène-Joseph-Stanislas Foulon d'Ecotier

M.*** en habit de satin noir, tenant en sa main la carte des Isles de la Guadeloupe

ANTOINE VESTIER 1740–1824
Oil on canvas, oval format 1785
80.3 x 63.8 (31⅝ x 25⅛)
Signed and dated at lower center:
Vestier pinxit 1785

Lent anonymously

This portrait was exhibited at the Salon of 1787, number 148, without naming the sitter, but modern scholars have identified the person represented as Eugène-Joseph-Stanislas Foulon d'Ecotier, born in 1753. In 1785 Stanislas was named *intendant* of Guadeloupe, which was then under the jurisdiction of the Ministère de la Marine, and presumably this portrait shows him, at age thirty-two, about to leave France for his assigned post. The map which d'Ecotier holds, "Carte reduite des isles de la Guadeloupe Marie Galante et les Sainte," indicates his new position. The books on the shelf also refer to the administration of the French colony.

The style of the portrait is very close to that of the paintings by Duplessis, especially the *Portrait said to be of Andre Dupré de Billy,* at the California Palace of the Legion of Honor, San Francisco, which shows an identical refinement and elegance, the same palette dominated by whites, blacks and grays, a similar porcelainlike quality of the paint surface which prefigured portraits by Ingres, and an identical technical perfection. There is a close stylistic parallel with the portrait of Jean-Henry Riesner also by Vestier, at the Musée de Versailles. A.B. de L.

261 The Marquise de Pezé and the Marquise de Rouget with Her Two Children

Mde la Marquise de Pézé & Mde la Marquise de Rouget, avec ses deux enfans
MARIE-LOUISE-ELISABETH
VIGÉE-LEBRUN 1755–1842
Oil on canvas
123.5 x 155.7 (48⅝ x 61⅜)
National Gallery of Art

The Marquise de Pezé and the Marquise de Rouget with Her Two Children is one of many portraits exhibited by Vigée-Lebrun at the Salon of 1787, number 98. Noticed by critics and amateurs alike, it was very well received, and one writer wrote, "The . . . painting is outstanding in the freshness of the flesh tones, by the exquisite taste shown in the composition of the figures, and in the inimitable grace of the poses."

The two women were friends of Mme Vigée-Lebrun, who speaks of them in her *Souvenirs* during the period before the Revolution. They were frequently included in the receptions the painter gave at her home, and she recalled the pleasure of entertaining her friends, "The easiness, the gentle gaiety which reigned at those light evening meals giving them a charm that dinners will never have again."

As Vigée-Lebrun liked to do, the portrait has an informal, almost rustic character, which we have also noted in her *Countess de Ségur* (here exhibited at number 247). The landscape, with a balustrade at the right, is rarely given such importance in Vigée-Lebrun's other paintings. Perhaps there is an added influence in this portrait of Domenichino. A passage in the *Souvenirs* refers to the

Bolognese painter: "How I hated women's dress then; I did everything possible to make it more picturesque, and I was delighted, when I won the confidence of my models, to be able to dress them according to my fancy; shawls were not yet in fashion, but I placed filmy scarves lightly entwined around the body and over the arms, with which I tried to imitate the beautiful style of the draperies of Raphael and Domenichino." Actually, the chiffon turbans placed on the heads of the two women seem by their roundness to lighten the mass of hair and to elongate the oval of their faces, just as in the works of the Bolognese painter. The painting, in the grace of the poses, the amiable beauty of the four models, the combination of naturalness with coquettishness, the superb play of light on the watered silk of the marquise de Pezé's dress, the contrasting colors, dark in the landscape, light in the faces, constitutes one of the masterpieces in the arts of Mme Vigée-Lebrun.

It is paradoxical that although Mme Vigée-Lebrun did not like English painting, the children here have a similar sentimental charm to those in the paintings of Romney and Hoppner. A.B. de L.

262 Aesculapius Receiving from Venus the Healing Herbs for Aeneas

Esculape reçoit des mains de Vénus les herbes et simples nécessaires à la guérison d'Enée
JEAN-CHARLES-NICAISE PERRIN
1754–1831
Lent by the Ecole des Beaux-Arts, Paris
In Salon of 1787, as no. 166

263 M. Bridan

M. Bridan. Sculpteur du Roi & Professeur de l'Académie
JEAN-LAURENT MOSNIER
1743/44?–1808
Lent by the Ecole des Beaux-Arts, Paris
In Salon of 1787, as no. 224

264 Curius Dentatus Refusing the Presents of the Samnites

Curius refusant les présens des Samnites
JEAN-FRANÇOIS-PIERRE
PEYRON 1744–1814
Lent by the Musée Calvet, Avignon
In Salon of 1787, as no. 153

265 Sophonisba Receiving the Poisoned Cup

Autre Esquisse, dessinée & lavée sur papier bleu, représentant Sophonisbe, recevant la coupe empoisonnée que Massinissa est forcé de lui envoyer
JEAN-CHARLES-NICAISE
PERRIN 1754–1831
Lent by Germain Seligman, New York
In Salon of 1787, as no. 168

266 Sketch for an Allegorical Painting in the Chamber of Commerce, Rouen

Grande esquisse d'un Tableau allégorique qui doit être exécuté pour la Chambre du Commerce de Rouen
ANICET-CHARLES-GABRIEL
LE MONNIER 1743–1824
NOT IN EXHIBITION
Collection of the Musée des Beaux-Arts, Rouen
In Salon of 1787, as no. 216

SALON OF 1789

267 M. Sue

Portrait de M. Sue, Professeur Royal en Anatomie aux Ecoles de Chirurgie, de la Société des Londres & d'Edimbourg, &c., Professeur pour l'Anatomie à l'Académie Royale de Peinture
GUILLAUME VOIRIOT 1713–1799
Oil on canvas
127 x 96 (50 x 37¾)
Lent by the Musée National du Château de Versailles

Pierre Sue (1739–1816) had a distinguished career in both medical practice and research and was official surgeon to the city of Paris. He also became an important official in the college of surgeons and was professor of anatomy at the Royal Academy of Painting. Sue is dressed soberly in black to emphasize his professional position, and there is further reference to his skills in the *écorché* model. Voiriot exhibited several other portraits in 1789. This was number 336.
A.B. de L.

268 Drawing for the Pulpit of Saint-Sulpice

Dessin d'une Chaire pour l'Eglise de Saint-Sulpice

CHARLES DE WAILLY 1729–1798
Pen and ink and watercolor
67.8 x 47.3 (26¾ x 18⅝)

Lent by the Cooper-Hewitt Museum of Decorative Arts and Design, Smithsonian Institution

De Wailly, a member of the Royal Academy, was the only architect to exhibit his drawings regularly at the Salon. The present drawing, one of two by him in the exhibition, was shown in the Salon of 1789, number 314. De Wailly was with Chalgrin one of the architects responsible for the maintenance of Saint-Sulpice. Servandoni, the original architect of the church, had provided the design for a pulpit, and there had been schemes by later artists to provide something more permanent. In the Salon of 1781, de Wailly had shown a drawing for the pulpit of Saint Sulpice, but the final and present structure was not completed until 1788. Several other drawings give the genesis of de Wailly's ideas, and the Musée Carnavalet has a counterproof of the drawing with autograph details and some slight variations from the Cooper-Hewitt version. While the architectural setting is accurate, de Wailly has created more than a mere topographical rendering, and by the expressive use of shadows and by placing his figures as if they were on a stage, he has achieved a dramatic representation. A.B. de L.

269 The Deluge

Le Déluge

JEAN-BAPTISTE REGNAULT
1754–1829
Oil on canvas
89 x 71 (35 x 27.9)

Lent by the Musée du Louvre

The theme of the deluge inspired many French painters, including Gamelin, Hue, Danloux and Girodet, at the end of the eighteenth century and at the beginning of the nineteenth century. The sources from which French artists of the period drew this subject were various. The most obvious is the flood in the Bible, but there is also a literary source in the loves of Phanon and Semive in Gessner's poem, and a pictorial reference to Poussin's *Winter* (sometimes called the *Deluge*) in the Louvre. It would seem, however, that Regnault's painting is based on none of these, but on a drawing by the artist himself used for an illustration to Ovid's *Metamorphoses*, translated by abbé Banier and published in 1787.

Regnault chose to represent, in the words of a contemporary writer, "the most beautiful thought that the deluge has to offer." The critics were unanimous in their praise of the sense of pathos with which Regnault expressed the theme of the *Deluge*, number 91 in the Salon of 1789: "[the man] finds himself forced either to give up his father to the torrent, or to abandon his wife there . . . What a deplorable situation! what morbid anxiety! . . . the soul is moved, the heart is torn and tears [are] ready to fall from all eyes. . . ."

Regnault also exhibited in the same Salon a *Descent from the Cross*, which is in marked contrast in style to *The Deluge*. A.B. de L.

270 The Lictors Returning to Brutus the Bodies of his Sons

J. Brutus, premier Consul, de retour en sa maison, après avoir condamné ses deux fils, qui s'étoient unis aux Tarquins & avoient conspiré contre la Liberté Romaine, des Licteurs rapportent leurs corps pour qu'on leur donne la Sépulture

JACQUES-LOUIS DAVID 1748–1825
Oil on canvas 1789
70.07 x 90.08 (27¹³⁄₁₆ x 35¾)
Signed and dated lower left:

Lent by The Wadsworth Atheneum, Hartford. Ella Gallup Sumner and Mary Catlin Sumner Collection

The superintendent of royal buildings, M d'Angiviller, perhaps as a consolation to David for not having been named director of the French Academy in Rome after the extraordinary success of *The Oath of the Horatii* and *The Death of Socrates*, commissioned a new painting from him in 1787. David proposed two subjects: "Coriolanus, after having taken refuge with and been given help by the Volscians, decides to seek revenge against his country," and "The departure of Atilius Regulus who preferred to expose himself to the worst tortures and to the death that awaited him at Carthage rather than consent to the negotiations proposed by the Africans." D'Angiviller chose the first subject. When the time came, David was not ready for the Salon of 1787; therefore, the same painting was recommissioned from him for the Salon of 1789. Contrary to all custom, David, on his own decision, abandoned the subject agreed upon and painted that of Brutus: "Junius Brutus, first consul, returned to his home, after having condemned his two sons who had joined the Tarquins and had conspired against the freedom of Rome. The lictors bring back their bodies to be buried." Reading Plutarch must have given him the idea for the subject.

With the *Paris and Helen*, commissioned by the comte d'Artois, brother of Louis XVI and the future Charles X, the *Brutus* was exhibited in the Salon of 1789 as number 88 in spite of d'Angiviller's order forbidding it. Like the *Oath of the Horatii* and the *Socrates*, the work celebrates patriotism and contempt of death, and exalts superhuman greatness and sacrifice of the family for the state. In such an important political year, when France was reverberating with new words such as *virtue, country, devotion,* and *sacrifice*, Brutus, defender of the republic, conquerer of the Tarquins, represents a kind of hero, and David's painting, a political manifesto. The subject, which shows the virtue of a Roman of the republic, was felt by many contemporaries to be in sharp contrast with the conduct of their own king. The work was an enormous success at the Salon, as evidenced in a letter that David wrote to Wicar dated September 17, 1789: "I have just exhibited my Brutus at the Salon. It seems to me that among my paintings it is the one that has caused the greatest stir. They are heaping praise on me, and I am careful to only accept what is proper. In general I do not allow myself to be taken in too much by this talk, it encourages me and that is all. Primarily they praise the thought and above all that it has been expressed in a subtle way. There is something Florentine in the appearance of my

Brutus: you will see it some day; let no more be said, I did what I could, of that I can assure you."

The painting in the Wadsworth Atheneum is a small version of the Louvre painting, executed the same year, and follows the original exactly.

Trumbull, with whom Jefferson discussed paintings while the artist stayed with him in Paris, knew David, "my warm and efficient friend," and visited his studio where he saw the *Oath of the Horatii*, "figures large as life, the story well told, drawing pretty good, coloring cold." Also in the studio was *Belisarius* (see no. 239). David, to whom Trumbull had introduced himself and whom Trumbull found "a pleasant plain, sensible man," returned the compliment and called on the young American soon afterwards. "[He] did me the honor to visit my pictures; his commendation, I fear, was too much dictated by politeness." A.B. de L.

271 Jacob Coming to Find the Daughters of Laban
Jacob venant trouver les filles de Laban

LOUIS GAUFFIER 1762–1801
Oil on canvas 1787
100 x 138 (39⅜ x 54⅝₁₆)
Signed and dated at lower left:
Gauffier Romae 1787

Lent by the Musée du Louvre

The painting *Jacob and the Daughters of Laban*, exhibited in the Salon of 1789 as number 346, was executed by Gauffier in Rome in 1787, when he was a *pensionnaire* at the French Academy (he won the first prize in 1784, dividing it equally with Germain Drouais), and it is partly for that reason that the work is fairly well known. It is also mentioned in the correspondence of Lagrenée l'aîné, who never failed to keep the superintendent d'Angiviller regularly informed of the work of the *pensionnaires*, and in a series of letters by Drouais to David. Lagrenée wrote the following to d'Angiviller about the Louvre painting on May 16, 1787: "The young Gauffier has just created a delectable painting, even better than the one of last year. The painting is intended for M. le président Bernard. Tell me, I beg of you, if after the feast day of Saint Louis, I can send it to you by mail." Apparently Gauffier was a slow worker because of ill health.

Elsewhere Drouais, Gauffier's rival, wrote to David in a letter dated October 4, 1786: "I must be very alert this year since it is said that Gauffier is sketching a painting which is charming and already much better than the other one. The subject is Rebecca. You know the one done by Raphael in the Loggia in which a man arrives holding a crooked staff, and who is stunned by the beauty of Rebecca who holds another woman by the shoulder. The scene takes place

at the edge of a fountain where some sheep are drinking. Unless he does not carry it out as conceived, it would be difficult to do better." On June 13, 1787, he wrote to David that the painting had been completed and was much admired by the connoisseurs. And finally in a last letter (undated): "I must tell you about the Salon. Gauffier exhibited a little painting that is charming and above all impressive in its finish, it is like a miniature. It is maddening that with the great merit of his painting he should have pillaged and flayed Raphael, it is an unforgivable thing. The landscape is beautifully painted, and to be honest, it is a charming painting."

Drouais was mistaken when he wrote that the subject of the painting was the story of Rebecca; it is Jacob, Rebecca's son, who arrives at the home of Laban where he meets Laban's two daughters, Rachel and Leah (Genesis 29:1–14). But Drouais' letters are fascinating for their revelation of the relationship between the two *pensionnaires*, both students of David, and for the evocation of the artistic climate of the period.

Gauffier's painting caused such a sensation that one can find a third echo of it in a letter from the Swiss, Conrad Gessner, to his father Salomon Gessner. "The French *pensionnaires* have just exhibited their paintings. There are among them this year, some young people of marked talent . . . I noticed among others, a small painting, the subject of which is *Jacob and Rachel* by a young artist named Gauffier. The figures are six *pouces* high: they are grouped with taste, well drawn, and of the most beautiful coloring. The landscape

seems to have been painted by a professional artist: no history painting was comparable to it; the sheep would be worthy of the brush of Roos. In general, this painting is distinguished by an attractive organization, a beautiful composition, and a very pure taste."

Certainly Gauffier has borrowed from Raphael's fresco in the Loggia, and he has also taken poses from compositions by Poussin.

In the movement of French neoclassical painting at the end of the eighteenth century, Gauffier was the one whose neoclassicism was most directly nourished by classical French painting of the mid-seventeenth century. Gauffier retained from painters like Stella, Lesueur, or Nicolas Poussin a sense of refinement, as well as their use of clarity, as can be seen in the low relief composition, the cold correctness in the drawing, and the frigid aspect of the whole. A.B. de L

72 Naval Battle off the Island of Grenada, July 6, 1779

*Combat naval qui a assuré la conquête
de la Grenade, sous les ordres de
M. le Comte d'Estaing, Vice-Amiral
de France, contre l'Amiral Byron*

JEAN-FRANÇOIS HUE 1751–1823

Oil on canvas

128 x 217 (50½ x 86)

*Lent by the Musée National du
Château de Versailles*

There are two paintings by Hue with
the subject of the battles for Grenada:
*The Taking of the Island of Grenada,
July 4, 1779* in the Musée de Ver-
sailles, and the *Naval Battle off the
Island of Grenada* exhibited here.
Both of them were commissioned
from the artist by Louis XVI, but only
the second one was shown in the
Salon, as number 69. They recreate one
of the brilliant naval victories of the
comte d'Estaing, vice admiral of the
Asian and American seas, against the
British in the American Revolutionary
War. The British naval force under
Admiral Byron arrived the day after
the French capture of the island. The
battle was fought vigorously by both
sides and lasted all day, the British
numbering twenty-one ships and the
French twenty-five. Towards evening
the disabled English squadron beat a
retreat and took refuge on the island
of Saint Christopher, where d'Estaing
pursued them without being able to
induce them to continue the battle.

The Salon critics were more responsive to the *Cascades at Tivoli* or the
landscapes of Hue than to these scenes
of naval battles and make no mention
of this painting or its companion.
A.B. de L.

273 The Death of Cleopatra

La Mort de Cléopâtre

NICOLAS-ANDRÉ MONSIAU
1754–1837

Brown wash heightened with gouache
1791

43 x 53 (17 x 20⅞)

Signed and dated at lower left:
Monsiau 1791

Lent by the Musée Rolin, Autun

Poussin as much as David is the source
for this beautiful neoclassical drawing.
Although it is dated 1791, a *Death of
Cleopatra* was exhibited in the Salon
of 1789, number 194. The drawing
exhibited here is linked through its
composition to the heroic tradition
of the seventeenth century and more
specifically to the *Death of Germanicus* by Poussin. In addition to
the arrangement of the figures being
borrowed by Monsiau from Poussin's
painting, several details are identical to
Poussin as, for example, that of the
drapery placed near the middle of the
composition. This was regarded as
characteristic of Poussin, and Mme
Vigée-Lebrun mentions in her *Souvenirs* that when she gave a "Greek
supper" she arranged the drapery "like
those one sees in the paintings of
Poussin."

The debt to David is equally important, from the general neoclassic
style to several precise details. The
two soldiers entering at the left, while
they are reminiscent of Poussin's *Rape
of the Sabines*, recall the soldier in
the background of David's *Belisarius*.
Monsiau, in Rome from 1776 until
1780, knew David well. The refinement and quality of execution and the
white gouache highlights can be found
in a number of other neoclassical
drawings, such as those by Perrin. A.B. de L.

274 Louis-Jean-François Lagrenée, called l'Aîné

Portrait de M. de Lagrenée l'aîné, ancien Directeur de l'Académie de France à Rome
JEAN-LAURENT MOSNIER
1746–1808
Oil on canvas 1788
133 x 100 (52⅜ x 39⅜)

Lent by the Musée National du Château de Versailles

Accepted as a candidate (agréé) for membership in the Academy on July 29, 1786, Mosnier was received as an academician on May 31, 1788, with his portraits of Bridan and of Lagrenée l'aîné. The portrait of Charles-Antoine Bridan, professor at the Académie Royale de peinture, was exhibited at the Salon of 1787, see number 263. Mosnier received the commission for the second portrait, because Lenoir had not undertaken the project as he was ordered to do, on January 26, 1788. By the end of May the portrait of Lagrenée was ready, and was exhibited in the Salon of 1789, number 125.

The artist represented Lagrenée standing, three-quarter length, facing the viewer, turned slightly to the right, draped in an ample red cloak lined in black. At the left there is a chest on which a palette and brushes are placed. Behind him, on an easel, is a canvas, on which two helmeted figures are sketched, one holding a sword and a shield, the other a lance. This painting has not been identified.

One of the salon critics wrote of Mosnier: "Let us come to the portraits. The one which, in my judgement, bears away the palm, is M. Mosnier. There are several portraits, about which I believe I can say that, according to what I have seen of our modern painters, I have very rarely seen anything as beautiful. . . ." A.B. de L.

275 Project for the Remodeling of the Salon of the Louvre in 1789

Projet pour l'aménagement du Salon du Louvre en 1789
CHARLES DE WAILLY 1728–1798
Black and red chalk 1789
33.2 x 37.5 (13¼ x 14¾)
Signed and dated at lower right:
De Wailly, 1789

Lent by the Musée Carnavalet, Paris

This drawing is a project for the remodeling of the Salon Carré in the Louvre, where every two years the Académie Royale de peinture et de sculpture presented an exhibition, known as the Salon, of the works of its members. It should be remembered that when Thomas Jefferson was ambassador in Paris, he visited with great interest the Salons of 1785, 1787 and 1789.

The inscription, probably an autograph, at the bottom of the old mount is explicit. The Salon Carré had recently undergone some modifications, when in 1789, the architect Guillaumot, who had written a *Mémoire sur la manière d'éclairer la galérie du Louvre*, had had the ceiling pierced and a lantern installed in order to assure overhead lighting in the room and, to increase the wall surface for hanging pictures, had blocked up the windows. Charles de Wailly's drawing is a protest against Guillaumot's modifications. De Wailly proposes the reopening of the windows and the building of a gallery supported by columns. That is what is explained at length in the inscription. Despite this justification of his ideas, the project by de Wailly was rejected.

De Wailly combined this project for the remodeling of the Salon Carré with the depiction of the Salon of 1789; this drawing is all the more precious since it is the only representation of the last Salon of the Ancien Régime. The drawings by Gabriel de Saint-Aubin of the Salons of 1757, 1765, 1767 and 1769, two engravings by Martini showing the Salons of 1785 and 1787 and this drawing are the only graphic documents of these great artistic manifestations.

The approximately seventy-five drawings, paintings and sculptures rapidly sketched by de Wailly in this drawing are actually only a small percentage of the 350 entries in the Salon of 1789. In spite of their greatly reduced size, the architect's sketches are extremely legible. One recognizes, for example, in the upper row of the central section from left to right, *The Death of Socrates* by Peyron (now in the Louvre), *The Death of Seneca* by Perrin in the middle (now at the Musée de Dijon), and at the right *The Lictors Returning to Brutus the Bodies of His Sons* by David (now in the Louvre; a replica is here exhibited under no. 270). De Wailly includes his own drawing of the *Pulpit at Saint-Sulpice* at the lower left. A.B. de L.

276 The Triumph of Paulus Aemilius

Triomphe de Paul Emile. Paul Emile triomphant de Persée, dernier Roi de Macédoine, qui fuit avec sa famille le char du vainqueur
ANTOINE-CHARLES-HORACE, CALLED CARLE VERNET 1758–1836
Lent by The Metropolitan Museum of Art
In Salon of 1789, as no. 342

277 The Continence of Scipio

La Continence de Scipion
NICOLAS-GUY BRENET 1728–1792
Lent by the Musée des Beaux-Arts, Strasbourg
In Salon of 1789, as no. 4

278 Jean Theurel

Portrait de Jean Theurel, Doyen des Vétérans pensionnés du Roi au Régiment de Touraine, né le 8 Septembre 1698, à Orrain, en Bourgogne; il a monté trois gardes audit Régiment, sous Louis XIV, au siège de Kell; à la tranchée il reçut une balle qui lui traversa le corps, à la bataille de Minden il eut dix-sept coups de sabre, dont sept sont marqués sur sa tête.
ANTOINE VESTIER 1740–1824
NOT IN EXHIBITION
Collection of the Musée des Beaux-Arts, Tours
In Salon of 1789, as no. 105

279 Not in Exhibition

280 A Ruined Barn

Une Grange ruinée que le Soleil éclaire à travers plusieurs solives; on y voit des femmes & différens animaux
JEAN-FRANÇOIS LÉGILLION 1739–1797
Lent by the Musée du Louvre
In Salon of 1789, as no. 139

JEFFERSON AND FRENCH ARCHITECTURE IN THE SECOND HALF OF THE EIGHTEENTH CENTURY

The second half of the eighteenth century was a critical period for the influence of French art on the western world. French artists were deluged with commissions from abroad, while foreign artists flocked to work and study in France as never before. In the United States, in particular, there was an architect of French origin or training in all the most important workshops: Major L'Enfant, Etienne-Sulpice Hallet, Benjamin Latrobe, Joseph Fr. Mangin, Maximilien Godefroy, Joseph-Jacques Ramée. The young Charles Bulfinch spent four months in Paris in 1786, absorbing what he could of French art and architecture under the benevolent guidance of his countryman Thomas Jefferson.

However, it was at that time also that French artistic hegemony began to be strongly contested, beginning with the rediscovery of antique remains in Italy in the 1750s which made Rome a new magnet for European and American artists and scholars. Greco-Roman art, monumental and virile, was unalterably opposed to the *petite manière française*. From the antique example, the French classicists had retained no more than a few principles of order, harmony and equilibrium. France did not open itself to the new style until the 1770s, somewhat after it had become an important influence in the England of Burlington, Kent and Adam.

Jefferson used his sojourn in Europe between 1784 and 1789 to deepen his knowledge of French as well as English art and architecture. One may think that he would clearly have preferred the latter. However, of the English he wrote to his friend John Page, "Their architecture is the most wretched style I ever saw." Of the French, "Were I to proceed to tell you how much I enjoy their architecture, sculpture, painting, music, I should want words," he wrote to Charles Bellini in 1785.

Among the buildings which aroused Jefferson's admiration were some works of the seventeenth century, including the *grande galérie* and colonnade of the Louvre, as well as Versailles and Marly, but he was attracted primarily to the work done after 1760. Unfortunately, Jefferson too seldom recorded his judgments of the contemporary buildings which he must have seen. We are familiar with his admiration for the Hôtel de Salm, the Désert de Retz, and the Halle aux Bleds, while he cast a critical eye on the walls of the farmers general. However, it is interesting to consider some of the buildings which seem to have escaped his notice. He did not, for instance, take advantage of his trip to eastern France to see Ledoux's Saline de Chaux, though it may have been unknown to him since the project at Chaux was not published until 1804.

Reticence in the case of the walls of the farmers-general (which, however, he included in a list of "wonderful improvements") and his apparent ignorance of the *saline* characterized Jefferson's attitude toward these important works of Ledoux, who was perhaps the greatest architect of the century. It is necessary to view French architecture as a whole to understand the significance of the rather circumscribed area of Jefferson's enthusiasms.

Before the 1770s, French architects had delighted in following the traditions laid down by the great creators of the century of Louis XIV. Despite his taste for Greco-Roman architecture, Jefferson did not follow the most intransigent antiquarians in their wholesale condemnation of the *manière française*. For the construction of the president's house in Washington, more than a decade later, he suggested an imitation of the Garde-Meubles by Gabriel on the Place de la Concorde, which exemplified the most traditional French style, with a strong resemblance to the Louvre colonnade and the public squares built for Louis XVI.

The Hôtel de Salm, another model proposed by Jefferson for the president's house, was built in 1782 as a relatively late manifestation of the antique style. If it represents the architectural ideal of Jefferson, it does so by associating all the elegance of a traditional French *hôtel* with the monumental grandeur of antique architecture. In this blending of styles the French were perhaps able to create a more successful whole than were English architects who, faithful to every detail set forth by Palladio, often sacrificed comfort to authenticity. In the area of picturesque ruins, there is little in England to compare with the Désert de Retz, an enormous broken column inside which was an ingeniously planned private dwelling. However, the most original contribution of the French to the antique style was neither the Hôtel de Salm nor the Désert de Retz. Next to the Hôtel de Salm were the curious Maisons Saiseval by Ledoux, built during Jefferson's stay in Paris, in which could be seen under cover of antique details the emergence of a new style. Jefferson, however, was primarily attracted by Ledoux's small Château de Louveciennes, which is scarcely distinguishable from the works of Gabriel, and by the neoclassical Hôtel Guimard, the façade of which was later echoed in Pavilion IX of the University of Virginia.

During the years that Jefferson was in Paris, the forces leading to the French Revolution were rapidly gathering momentum. Jefferson, acutely aware of political developments, did not fully discern that at the same time, a similar movement was taking place in the studios of artists. Attached to a certain form of architecture based on antique Greek and Roman styles, he did not appreciate the masters who strove to incorporate elements of all known architectural styles into a primitive, natural architecture, reduced to elementary forms.

Three styles of architecture coexisted in Paris in Jefferson's day: the French, the antique and the revolutionary. These found expression in three genres: private, public and theoretical. Private architecture was the genre of choice of the French style, since two centuries of tradition had formed the French model of a dwelling, while public architecture was open to a Greek or Roman treatment. Jefferson himself made this distinction, when for the president's house he proposed the imitation of French models, while for the capitol he preferred "the adoption of some one of the models of antiquity, which have had the approbation of thousands of years." Before the 1770s there were in fact few public buildings in France, and an example of their development can be seen in the evolution of theaters, which had been incorporated into private dwellings until, in the late eighteenth century, they became separate buildings, often in the form of antique temples around which other public buildings were grouped.

Revolutionary architecture manifested itself most often in theoretical architecture; its originality condemned it to be a style confined to paper. It was taught by the most influential masters in the Académie d'architecture, however, and the Grand Prix competition, which opened an official career to the winners, was crowded with entries illustrating the principles of the new architecture. Even if Jefferson did not follow the work at the Academy while he was in Paris, he may have learned about the new style by looking at the published engravings of the Grand Prix winners' projects, which were circulated internationally. One might conclude, however, that his silence represented some reservations about the new style, an opinion held by most of the architects who began to work in the first years of the nineteenth century.

Revolutionary architecture, indeed, had only an ephemeral existence. Napoleon, in his desire to create an official architecture for the Empire, turned instinctively back to the style of the Hôtel de Salm, and Jefferson was perhaps also more concerned about giving a Roman ancestry to the architecture of the new American republic than about venturing down the unknown paths of the more theoretical Revolutionary style. P. DE M.

LITERATURE: Louis Réau, *Histoire de l'expansion de l'art français* (Paris: H. Laurens, 1924–1933); Thomas J. Watermann, "French Influence on Early American Architecture," *GBA*, 28 (Aug. 1945), 87–112; Kimball, *Jefferson: The Scene of Europe*; Louis Hautecoeur, *Histoire de l'architecture classique en France*, 4 (Paris: A. Picard, 1952); Emil Kaufmann, *Architecture in the Age of Reason; Baroque and Post-Baroque in England, Italy, and France* (Cambridge: Harvard University Press, 1955); Michel Benisovich, "Thomas Jefferson, amateur d'art à Paris," *Archives de l'art français* (1959), pp. 237–239; Michel Gallet, *Demeures parisiennes: l'époque de Louis XVI* (Paris: Le Temps, 1964); Robert Rosenblum, *Transformations in Late Eighteenth Century Art* (Princeton: Princeton University Press, 1967); Kimball, *Thomas Jefferson, Architect*; Michel Gallet, "Paris in the Neoclassical Period," *Apollo*, 101 (Apr. 1975), 312–314; Jefferson to Charles Bellini, Sept. 30, 1785; Jefferson to John Page, May 4, 1786; Jefferson to Pierre L'Enfant, Apr. 10, 1791.

281 The Discovery of the Laocoön

HUBERT ROBERT 1733–1808
Oil on canvas 1773
119.4 x 142.6 (47 x 64)
Signed and dated at bottom right:
H. Robert 1773

*Lent by the Virginia Museum of
Fine Arts, Richmond*

There is no study of architecture
which does not owe a certain place to
painting, but the eighteenth century
marked the beginning of professional
specialization. To be sure, painters
often chose architecture as a subject,
and architects, who still studied drawing in depth, were generally capable of
sketching a history painting; but, it
is nonetheless true that the race of
great artists, knowing how to carry
out from beginning to end the creation
of a history painting as well as that
of a building, was disappearing. It was

at the moment when practice tended
to separate the two arts that theory
reunited them more than ever. Architectural theoreticians contended that
during the period of conception, there
was always painting; that the construction was the realization of the
painted idea. What architects called
"picturesque" was, of course, the
best illustration of that principle.
  The inspiration for the new gardens,
with their picturesque vistas and
"antique" ruins, came from classical
landscape paintings, such as those
of Lorrain, and the working sketch
itself was a painting through which a
Hubert Robert or a Carmontelle foreshadowed the finished work. For every
design, no matter what kind, the
custom had been established since the
middle of the century to present the
proposed project in a drawing making
use of all the illusionistic resources

of perspective and shading. "You want
to become an architect, begin by
becoming a painter," wrote Ledoux,
and many shared his view. The theoreticians of the new architectural
aesthetic, called *naturelle* because its
basic concept was the imitation of
nature, believed that architecture was
a superior art, and that construction
was needed to add the third dimension
which was missing from the painted
design.
  The work of Hubert Robert illustrates particularly well the complex
and reciprocal relationship which
existed between painter and architect.
The composition of the *Laocoön* may
have been the source of inspiration
for the *tableaux* drawn by Boullée
for his project for a metropolitan
cathedral (see no. 319). As for the
subject of Robert's painting, it was
clearly related to the project to

redesign the *grande galérie* in the
Louvre to house the royal collections,
an idea which was studied by several
architects. While with his museum
project (here under nos. 320–323)
Boullée raises the subject to the
highest plane of architectural expression, Hubert Robert takes the *grande
galérie* of the Louvre itself as a motif
and treats the theme several times,
going so far as to imagine what it
would look like in ruins. The cycle was
thus completed; through the artifice of
painting, the modern building became
indistinguishable from the antique
ruin which was its inspiration.
  In the *Discovery of the Laocoön*,
signed and dated 1773, eight years
after his return from Italy, Robert has
combined his fondness for painting
classical architectural subjects with
the popularity of the sculpture
Laocoön, which was discovered in

Rome in 1506 and by the end of the eighteenth century was a standard work in every anthology of antique sculpture. The *Laocoön* captured the imagination of such eminent minds as Diderot, who wrote, "What touches me most in this famous group is the maintenance of man's dignity in the midst of the most profound suffering. The less the anguished man complains, the more he arouses my compassion. . . . the sculpture is deeply moving without inspiring horror." When, for his friend Beaumarchais, Robert decorated eight vertical wall panels for a neo-Greek *salon* dedicated to the glory of antique sculpture, he chose to represent the *Venus de' Medici,* the *Farnese Hercules,* the *Farnese Flora,* the *Apollo Belvedere,* the *Bathing Nymph,* the *Capitoline Gladiator,* the *Laocoön* and the *Marcus Aurelius.*

Jefferson certainly saw pictures and copies of the *Laocoön,* though he did not include it in the list of sculpture of which he desired casts or copies for Monticello. His predilection for the classical style in architecture, however, represented by this painting, is well known, and he later suggested in a letter to L'Enfant that the Louvre's *grande galérie* be used as a model for the capitol in Washington.

A.B. de L. and P. de M.

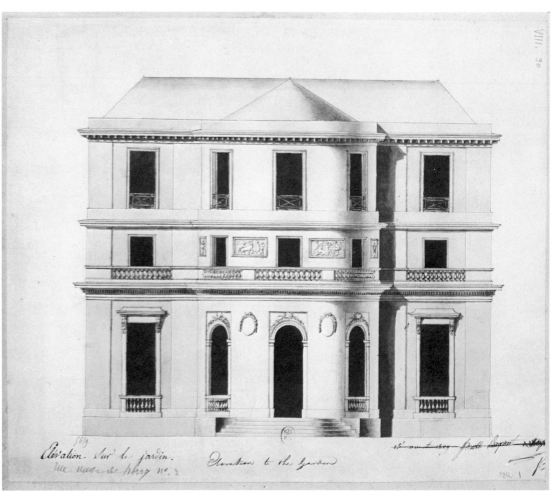

282 Hôtel de Langeac, elevation

Pen
33.7 x 27.5 (13¼ x 10⅞)
Inscribed below: *Elevation sur le jardin.* Crossed-out inscriptions, lower right: *15 Aôut 1809* and two illegible signatures
Lent by the Bibliothèque nationale

Named to replace Franklin as foreign minister for the United States, Jefferson left his lodging at the cul-de-sac Taitbout and, on October 17, 1785, installed himself in the more comfortable and elaborate residence, the Hôtel de Langeac, where he remained until his return to America in 1789.

He could not have made a choice better suited to his taste. The house occupied the angle of the Champs Elysées and the new rue de Berri, at the western limit of Paris. Beyond were the villages of Chaillot, Passy, and Auteuil which, at the time of Jefferson's stay, were united by the creation of the encircling wall of the farmers-general. The Grille de Chaillot, adjoining Jefferson's new residence, was torn down at this time. The house was in "une heureuse situation," noted

Thiéry in his *Guide des amateurs et des étrangers voyageurs à Paris,* which was published shortly afterward; it had gardens looking out on the Champs Elysées, one of the most agreeable and frequented promenades in Paris.

Besides its convenient location, the townhouse had the advantage of a design which was perfectly in accord with the most enlightened taste of the day. Its construction had been begun in 1768 according to the plan of the architect Jean-François-Thérèse Chalgrin. According to Thiéry, especially notable were the layout of the rooms and the salon ceiling painted by Berthélemy. For Jefferson, the introduction to contemporary French architecture began at home.

During his stay, Jefferson modified the residence to some extent, and furnished it (some of the furniture he bought for this purpose is now at Monticello) and redesigned the garden with plantings of species imported from America. Three drawings by Jefferson are shown at numbers 202–204 which detail his planned modifications of the house and garden. The ele-

vation by an unknown artist shown here is part of a group of drawings including a plan and two other elevations, executed for a later resident, as part of a project for raising the attic. In order to see the building as it was in Jefferson's time, it is necessary to block out the last story. P. de M.

283 Nouvelle Amérique project, plan

FRANÇOIS-JOSEPH BÉLANGER
1744–1818
Pen and wash
60 x 90 (23⅝ x 35⁷⁄₁₆)
Inscribed in center: *Plan de la nouvelle Amérique à construire dans une partie de l'emplacement du fief d'Artois*
Lent by the Bibliothèque nationale

This Nouvelle Amérique project was conceived about 1778 by Bélanger for the king's brother, the comte d'Artois, who had acquired a vast tract of land located between the Champs Elysées, the rue du Faubourg Saint-Honoré, the rue de Berri and the rue de la Boëtie. The comte d'Artois intended to construct his stables there and to create a new *quartier*. It was to bear the name of "Nouvelle Amérique" in honor of Benjamin Franklin who, at that time, was gaining the respect and affection of all of Paris. Thus, Jefferson's residence, the Hôtel de Langeac, would have been encircled by a small town with streets named after the heroes of the new American nation.

The idea of dividing the land was never carried out. Nevertheless, this witness to Franco-American friendship was indicative of the times; in 1784, the architect Victor Louis projected a square for the city of Bordeaux upon which, through triumphal arches, were to open thirteen streets bearing the names of American states; on a central column were to be bas-reliefs representing "the principal acts of Louis XVI's reign which brought about the independence of America." A project by de Wailly for the reorganization of Port-Vendres in honor of the new American nation resulted in the completion of only one element: an obelisk decorated with bas-reliefs relating to the history of the movement for independence. P. de M.

284 Hôtel d'Argenson
Photograph

This house, built by Jean-Philippe Lemoine de Couzon at number 38, avenue Gabriel between 1780 and 1787, is the only vestige of the Champs Elysées buildings which were contemporary with Jefferson's sojourn in Europe. The building enjoyed a certain esteem; it was included in Krafft and Ransonnette's book, an assemblage of the most important creations of Parisian private architecture from the last years of the eighteenth century. Its principal façade, preceded by a small garden, looks out on the promenade of the Champs Elysées. P. de M.

285 Vue de la Maison de Mme Brunoy

J.A. LE CAMPION active late 18th century, after Antoine Louis François Sergent 1751–1847
Collection of the Bibliothèque nationale
NOT IN EXHIBITION

286 Hôtel de Brunoy
Watercolor

Lent by the Bibliothèque nationale

The *hôtel*, built by Boullée from 1775 to 1779 for the marquise de Brunoy, was almost unanimously considered to be the most important architectural curiosity of the Champs Elysées and

one of the most significant creations of the 1770s. Destroyed in 1930, the *hôtel* extended from the rue du Faubourg Saint-Honoré, where it had its entrance (at present, no. 45), to the Champs Elysées which bordered its garden.

The declared ambition of contemporary French architects was to combine the traditional French townhouse room arrangements, which were recognized as exemplary by all of Europe, with the monumental spaces of an antique temple. Since the sixteenth century, Palladio had provided examples of house-temples. However, the great spaces of Venetian villas could not be adapted to the new requirements of comfort and convenience. In plan, the Hôtel de Brunoy was not particularly different from other neighborhood residences which were almost all built in the first half of the century. The main building, or *corps-de-logis*, had offices in the basement and on the main floor contained reception rooms, notably a *grand salon* whose false vault was decorated with a large painting by François-André Vincent. In the wings were entrances, vestibules, staircases and smaller, more intimate rooms than those in the main building. The interior decoration of the *hôtel* was done by the sculptor Gilles-Paul Gauvet.

In the composition of the garden, Boullée had rediscovered the advantages of Palladio's "massed plan," in which the wings and a part of the *corps-de-logis*, covered by a trellis, merged with the greenery of the garden. The central portion of the *corps-de-logis*, comprised of only a single story which was lit solely on the court side, was dominated by a colossal order of columns and crowned by a false, stepped pyramid, which served as a support for a statue of the goddess Flora. In his desire to create a building on a grand scale, Boullée chose for his model one of the seven wonders of the antique world, the mausoleum of Halicarnassus. The "Temple de Flore" (the contemporary name for the *hôtel*) was placed within a green framework, specially planned to charm the passerby. The public promenade of the Champs Elysées was, in effect, only separated from the garden of the *hôtel* by a low barrier (the present avenue Gabriel was cut through in 1818).

"How you would have been enchanted, dear friend," wrote one observer in 1782, "if, witness of our surprise, you had seen, like us, the *hôtels* between the Tuileries and the Champs-Elysées. The small hôtel de Brunoy . . . offers to the eye a very pretty garden where one perceives two subterranean promenades with plantings of honeysuckle, rose bushes, and

other fragrant shrubs." The author of the article on Boullée in the *Biographie universelle* (1834) wrote: "This composition, of a completely new type at the time it appeared, marks an epoch by being the first work which brought back the beautiful style" (that is, the antique style).

Proof of the Hôtel de Brunoy's celebrity is found in all the guides of Paris and in the important compendium of Krafft and Ransonnette, a copy of which Jefferson acquired during his years in Paris. P. de M.

287 Reconstruction of the Salon, Hôtel Grimod de la Reynière

JEAN-CHRISTIAN KAMSETZER 1753–1795
Pen and wash 1782

Lent by the Biblioteka Universyteckiej, Warsaw

During Jefferson's time, there was constructed at the entrance to the Champs Elysées, next to the buildings conceived by Gabriel for the Place Louis XV (Place de la Concorde), the *hôtel* that had been designed for the farmer-general Grimod de la Reynière in 1769 by the architect Barré. Purchased by the United States government in 1928, it was destroyed in 1931 to make room for the present embassy.

The *hôtel* had a salon decorated by Clérisseau, whom Jefferson took as his advisor for the planning of the capitol at Richmond. Clérisseau was widely known as an informed archaeologist and a brilliant designer; in 1778 he had published the first volume, *Monumens de Nismes*, of what was to be a series on French antiquities. This work included Jefferson's favorite, the Maison Carrée (see no. 150). It is possible that de la Reynière's *salon*, one of the few works by Clérisseau in Paris, played some role in the contact between Jefferson and Clérisseau, especially since it was one of the most important French examples of the fashionable "grotesque" style, which imitated ancient Roman painting and was characterized by figures and floral designs interwoven, the figures often having comically distorted features. Though there had been a long tradition of this type of decoration, the "grotesque" took on a distinctly archaeological character in the second half of the eighteenth century due to the influence of Clérisseau and Robert Adam, who gave his name to that style of decoration in England.

Unfortunately, Clérisseau's decoration cannot be precisely dated. He returned from Rome the year before the construction of the *hôtel* began. However, the decoration of the *salon*

does not seem to be contemporary with the *hôtel* itself. In fact, the overdoors were commissioned from Lavallée-Poussin, who was in Rome from 1759 to 1775. Yet the presence in Paris of Lavallée-Poussin, or even of Clérisseau, was not necessary for the execution of the work. As a result, it is generally agreed, that the *salon* should be dated to the years around 1775. Svend Eriksen dates it between 1772 and 1775. The *salon* is known through the reconstruction by the architect Kamsetzer, shown here. Four panels from the *salon* of the Hôtel Grimod de la Reynière are in the Victoria and Albert Museum. P. de M.

288 Model of the Hôtel de Salm
Made by THEODORE CONRAD, Jersey City, New Jersey, from drawings prepared by the School of Architecture, University of Virginia, under the supervision of Professor FREDERICK DOVETON NICHOLS

The construction of the Hôtel de Salm (actually the Palais de la Légion d'Honneur) is virtually contemporary with Jefferson's sojourn in Europe. Begun in 1782 following the plans of Rousseau, construction lasted five years due to the financial difficulties of the work's patron, the prince de Salm-Kyrborg. A painting showing the building under construction is shown at number 197.

Jefferson followed the *hôtel's* building with great interest. It responded admirably to the definition of the ideal residence: distribution of space *à la française* and elevations *à l'antique*. It had the general plan of a French *hôtel*: a large court of honor opening through a portal onto the street, with service courts on each side and a circular salon forming the avant-corps of the rear façade. The crowded plan of the *corps-de-logis*, or main building, conformed less to French conventions. However, in the second half of the eighteenth century, the fashion for rooms lit solely by vaults often led to the use of this kind of plan.

As far as the elevations *à l'antique* are concerned, they had already appeared in French architecture of the 1760s: in Gabriel's Château de Compiègne with an entrance colonnade and Ledoux's Hôtel d'Uzès, with a colossal portico before the *corps-de-logis*. Yet, these constructions did not present a very marked archaeological character, as was the case with the project for the Hôtel de Condé, drawn in 1763 by Marie-Joseph Peyre and published in his *Oeuvres d'architecture* of 1765. The wide readership of this publication explains the great similarities between Rousseau's drawing and Peyre's project.

289 Hôtel de Mlle Guimard

FRANÇOIS-JOSEPH BÉLANGER
1744–1818
Gouache

Lent by the Bibliothèque nationale

If Rousseau was not totally original, he nevertheless had the opportunity to oversee the building of one of those *hôtels* of grandiose dimensions which generally remained limited to the speculations of theoreticians. Jefferson's admiration was justified, and it was, moreover, shared by many, as it still is today. Salm is one of the rare neoclassic buildings which has been imitated in the twentieth century. We find nearly identical reproductions of it at the Château de Rochefort-en-Yvelines, built in 1896, and in the California Palace of the Legion of Honor, built after World War I. The French pavilion at the 1915 international exhibition in San Francisco was also a reproduction of the Parisian *hôtel*. The Hôtel de Salm can be seen as a kind of symbol of Franco-American relations. P. de M.

The house built between 1770 and 1774 for Marie-Madeleine Guimard, a dancer at the Opéra, is one of the rare buildings by Ledoux that brought its creator nothing but praise. The massive house plan for the Hôtel Guimard had been made fashionable in the 1760s by the construction of the Petit Trianon. The apsidal porch covered by a semidomed roof and closed by a colonnade was inspired by Roman models and, perhaps, more directly by a 1767 composition by Neufforge. The plan of the Hôtel Guimard was adopted by Jefferson in Pavilion IX at the University of Virginia (see no. 502), and was Ledoux's only concession to the prevailing fashion for elevations *à l'antique*. The building was cited by the guide books as the Temple of Terpsichore, a reference to the entrance colonnade, which supported a sculpted group by Merchi representing Apollo crowning the muse of the dance. On the apse was a relief by Lecomte on the same theme.

Today, nothing remains of this pavilion except the ingenious little theater that Ledoux had built in the servants' quarters facing the street. The *hôtel* was destroyed in 1862 along with all the houses in the Chaussée d'Antin quarter, which constituted one of the most remarkable architectural ensembles of the end of the eighteenth century. P. de M.

290 Perspective View of the Hôtel de Thélusson

CLAUDE-NICOLAS LEDOUX
1736–1806
Engraving (facsimile)
Inscription at lower left: *Le Doux Architecte du Roi delin*. In the center: *Vue perspective de l'entrée de la maison de Madame de Thélusson*

The Hôtel de Thélusson was one of the most talked-about buildings in Paris during the 1780s. Its construction caused a sensation, and people thronged to see it. Ledoux had finally met in Mme de Thélusson, heiress to her husband's immense fortune, a client whose extravagance was equalled by his genius.

The *hôtel*, built from 1778 to 1781, was situated between rue de Provence and rue de la Victoire, with the principal entrance in the form of a triumphal arch on the rue de Provence. An underground passageway led from the entrance up to the first floor of the house. The reception rooms were on the second floor. The servants' courtyard opened in the back onto the rue de la Victoire. The main house was framed by two isolated and more modest houses, intended for Mme de Thélusson's sons. The entire estate was destroyed in 1824.

In the amplitude of its plan, the Hôtel de Thélusson was the precursor of the Hôtel de Salm, the construction of which began just as the Hôtel de Thélusson was being completed. But Rousseau, a man of respectable and consistent talent, produced nothing that had the audacious and controver-

sial qualities of Ledoux's production. One has only to compare the monumental entrance arches of these two *hôtels*: at Salm, the volume and design were those of a traditional main gate; its antiquarian character was indicated only by the figures of fame which decorated the cornerstones. It was done in a style which would reappear thirty years later as Napoleonic classicism. At Thélusson, however, the gate's classical inspiration completely transformed the genre: the entrance

archway, the proportions of which surprised and sometimes shocked Ledoux's contemporaries, imitated the arches of antiquity as they appeared in the engravings of Piranesi, partially buried in the ruins of ancient Rome. The entrance gate at Thélusson is one of the first constructions of "buried architecture," a style which was to be fashionable for half a century. Thereafter, many works would have arched bays with springing points almost at ground level. P. de M.

292 Perspective view of the houses of M. Saiseval

Engraving (facsimile), 1847
Inscribed at top: *Vue perspective des Maisons de M. de Saiseval*. At lower left: *Le Doux Architecte*

The group of houses built in 1786 or 1788 by Ledoux for the marquis de Saiseval (or de Saisseval) occupied a position on the left bank of the Seine next to the Hôtel de Salm.

It was not a question here of constructing a palace; the owner of the property wanted a house for himself surrounded by houses to be rented. The eight buildings are arranged in a checkered pattern; the open spaces, designed as gardens, are equivalent to the building spaces.

The composition of this group, today destroyed, is only known through an engraving, published in 1847, which may not accurately reproduce the original plan. However, it conforms well with what is known about Ledoux's style on the eve of the French Revolution: the general organization was in the manner of Palladio; a semicircular colonnade formed a porch, the pediment was flattened to correspond to the gable ends of a saddleback roof, and the whole was crowned with a cylindrical top. P. de M.

293 Proposed plan for execution. Front elevation of the Château de Bagatelle

FRANÇOIS-JOSEPH BÉLANGER
1744–1818
Pen and wash
49.3 x 31.6 (19⅜ x 12⁷⁄₁₆)
Inscribed at bottom: *Bon Elévation de Bagatelle du côté de la Cour d'honneur*
Lent by the Bibliothèque nationale

294 Proposed plan for execution. Elevation from the Courtyard of the Château de Bagatelle

FRANÇOIS-JOSEPH BÉLANGER
1744–1818
Pen and wash
49.5 x 40.2 (19½ x 15⅞)
Inscribed at bottom: *Bon Elévation du pavillon de Bagatelle du côté du chemin qui conduit de Saint-Denis à Saint-Cloud*
Lent by the Bibliothèque nationale

295 Proposed plan for execution. Cross section of the Château de Bagatelle

FRANÇOIS-JOSEPH BÉLANGER
1744–1818
Pen and wash
49.7 x 31.5 (19⅝ x 12⁷⁄₁₆)
Inscribed at bottom: *Bon Coupe du pavillon de Bagatelle du levant au couchant sur le vestibule*
Lent by the Bibliothèque nationale

On the road that led from his *hôtel* on the Champs Elysées to the convent of Mont-Valérien where he liked to retreat, Jefferson passed the small Château de Bagatelle, a building made famous by the bet that the comte d'Artois, brother of the king, had to build it during the time of one of the court's trips to Fountainebleau.

Bélanger's proposed plan, approved by the comte d'Artois on September 1, 1777 (the word *Bon* inscribed on the drawings is the mark of that approbation), had been completed in forty-eight hours. The construction was finished on November 26, 1777, after sixty-four days of work.

It was not a question of a modest garden building, as its name might lead one to believe; it was a small château with outbuildings and a garden, which was laid out by the English gardener Thomas Blaikie. The decorations were commissioned from the most able craftsmen and artists of the period, who continued to work on it until 1781.

The house itself, separate from the other buildings, was one of those pavilions with a blocklike plan which had been made fashionable in the 1760s by the construction of the celebrated Petit Trianon at Versailles. At Bagatelle, no feature was novel, but at the same time it was "one of the great successes of French architecture in modern times," wrote the German architect Friedrich Gilly, who left an important description of Bagatelle, illustrated with sketches. Bagatelle was indeed one of the major steps in the development of French architecture. One of Jefferson's excursions with Maria Cosway included a visit there, as he wrote in his famous "head and heart" dialogue, "Recollect too

Madrid, Bagatelle . . . every moment was filled with something agreeable."

The pavilion at Bagatelle was greatly altered during the nineteenth century, and the outbuildings were destroyed.

P. de M

296 Plan for the pavilion at Louveciennes

CLAUDE-NICOLAS LEDOUX
1736–1806
Engraving (facsimile)
Inscribed at top: *pl. 270 bis.* At bottom left: *Le Doux Architecte du Roi.* In center: *Plan du rez-de chaussée du pavillon de Louveciennes*

297 Front elevation of the pavilion at Louveciennes

CLAUDE-NICOLAS LEDOUX
1736–1806
Engraving (facsimile)
Inscribed at lower left: *Le Doux Architecte du Roi.* In center: *Elevation du Pavillon de Louveciennes du cote des jardins*

Elévation du côté de l'Entrée, du projet d'extension du Pavillon de Louvecienne.

298 Project for the château at Louveciennes: front elevation

CLAUDE-NICOLAS LEDOUX
1736–1806
Pen and wash
92 x 24 (36¼ x 9⁷⁄₁₆)
Inscribed at bottom: *Elévation du côté de l'Entrée, du projet d'extension du Pavillon de Louvecienne*
Lent by the Musée de l'Ile de France, Sceaux

Built between December 1770 and December 1771, the pavilion at Louveciennes is a kind of rural counterpart to the contemporary *hôtel* designed by Ledoux for the famous dancer Mlle Guimard at Chaussée d'Antin. And the gallant love affairs of the dancer find their complement here in the romances of the king, who met the comtesse du Barry in this new

"temple of Venus."

"The curious flock to Luciennes [Louveciennes] to see the pavilion of Mme la comtesse du Barry . . . that sanctuary of sensual pleasure," wrote Bachaumont. Jefferson was among the inquisitive crowd, as were some architects such as Chambers and Quarenghi both of whom made sketches of it.

The greatest interest is generated by the interior decoration, which was of exceptional refinement and which was painted by eminent artists such as Fragonard, Drouais, and Vien. As for the architectural aspect, it was not brilliantly original, since it was inspired, even more than the Hôtel Guimard, by Gabriel's Petit Trianon which was built between 1764 and 1768. The apse-shaped porch here again was Ledoux's primary innovation,

but it does not have the semidomed roof of the Hôtel Guimard. In the first years of the eighteenth century, Boffrand, one of Ledoux's teachers, designed a similar entrance for the château at Saint-Ouen.

Meanwhile, the comtesse du Barry had conceived a project to construct a large château which was to incorporate the pavilion. The layout of the foundation was begun in 1773. The death of the king on May 10, 1774, interrupted work on the château and saved the pavilion, which has survived, with some alterations, to the present day. The pavilion, whose rear façade and floor plan would have been left intact, would have formed no more than the end of the left wing of the château. The front façade would have been destroyed in order to make it deeper,

and the new façade would have retained the four-columned portico, but without the apse.

Fortunately, the proposed plan for the château has survived. It is one of the rare drawings by Ledoux (or from his workshop) known. It was engraved according to the author's instructions and published posthumously in a portfolio in 1847. The engraving shows an important change: The slanted roof of the pavilion in the drawing was replaced by a flat roof which was completely hidden by the crowning balustrade. This indicates that during the 1770s Ledoux made a clear distinction between the alternatives of using a style à *l'italienne,* which associates the flat roof with a closed plan, and the style à *la française,* traditionally distinguished by an open, long plan and by

slanted roof, the invention of which
attributed to François Mansart.
arlier, he systematically sacrificed the
icturesque aspect of roofs to the
urity of geometric forms. As has been
marked by Ledoux specialists, the
ngraved work published in 1804 and
847 gives an amended version of the
ctual constructed buildings which
ave today been largely destroyed.
. de M.

99 Plans and elevation of the
olumn house, Désert de Retz

EAN-CHARLES KRAFFT
764–1833, after Boullay, active late
8th and early 19th century
ngraving
2.8 x 36 (9 x 14⅛)
ollection of the Bibliothèque
ationale
OT IN EXHIBITION

o the Désert de Retz is attached the
iemory of one of Jefferson's outings
i the company of Maria Cosway. The
ost of this isolated park was anything
ut a hermit, and his columnar house
eflected only one of his many inter-
sts. That M de Monville, the owner
f the property, should have been
mong other things experienced in the
rt of love, the most elegant dancer
i Paris, an accomplished horseman, a
alented musician, and an outstanding
rcher, makes paradoxical his prefer-
nce for mysterious, bizarre surround-
igs. However, de Monville was also
botanist and an amateur architect,
vo interests which would have excited
efferson's interest. De Monville can
e considered the true creator of the
Désert, which was admired as much
or the diversity of its botanical species
s for the ingenuity of its buildings.
There is no reason to doubt contem-
orary accounts which attribute to him
he conception of the house in the form
f a column in ruins. De Monville
nly enlisted the help of a draftsman,
rançois Barbier, to realize his plan.
"How grand the idea excited by the
emains of such a column! The spiral
taircase too was beautiful," wrote
efferson to Maria Cosway. The very
nusual ground plan was to remain in
is mind and formed the basis for the
round floor plan of the rotunda at
he University of Virginia. Most of
he buildings were constructed be-
ween 1774 and 1785. Only a few
estiges survive, and the column house
as lost all of its interior partitions.
. de M.

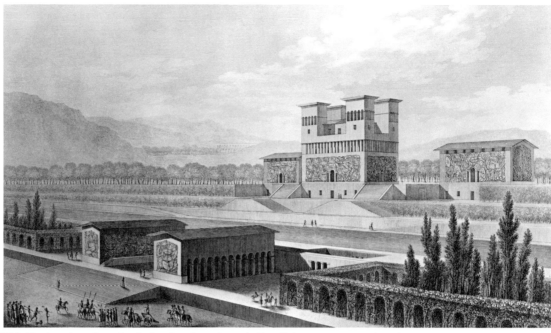

300 Project for a hunting lodge for the prince de Bauffremont, perspective view

CLAUDE-NICOLAS LEDOUX
1736–1806
Engraving (facsimile)
Inscribed below to the left:
Le Doux Architecte du Roi 1778.
In the middle: *Vue perspective,*
and to the right: *gravé par van Maelle*
and *pl. 110.*

This project was published in 1804
by Ledoux in his *Architecture considérée sous le rapport de l'art,* along
with the designs for an ideal town that
he wanted to construct around the salt
factory at Chaux, in the Franche-
Comté (see no. 318).
The prince de Bauffremont had
approached Ledoux, perhaps as early
as the 1770s, with a commission to
design a lodge for gatherings of provincial nobility during hunting parties.
The insertion of this edifice in the
project for an ideal town was doubtless
due to the artist's desire to reuse a
project which was never realized. The
design was probably somewhat modernized for its inclusion in the town
at Chaux: though the engraving is
dated 1778, the style is that practiced
by the imitators of Ledoux in the early
nineteenth century. The prince de
Bauffremont "wants a salon, corridors,
courts, stables, a kennel, and since
everyone will return to his own home
at night, the permanent living areas
will not be very considerable," wrote
Ledoux describing the project.
In stressing Ledoux's astonishing
originality, it is well to remember that
one of the most important changes
in the history of architecture came
within the period of Jefferson's stay
in Europe. The historical references,

without which architects in the second
half of the eighteenth century seemed
unable to compose, are almost completely absent in this drawing. The
building's novelty, which places it
closer to modern architecture than to
the Renaissance-based architecture
that had come before it, lies not only
in the play of solids and voids, but in
the revolutionary absence of moldings, which had, until the appearance
of Ledoux, been considered the essence
of architectural expression. P. de M.

301 Barrière de l'étoile
Lent by the Bibliothèque nationale

302 Tollgate at the Etoile in 1859
MARVILLE, active mid-19th century
Photograph
Lent by the Musée Carnavalet, Paris

303 Loursine tollgate, elevation

CLAUDE-NICOLAS LEDOUX
1736–1806
Pen and wash
60 x 41 (23⅝ x 16⅛)
Lent by the Musée Carnavalet, Paris

One of the principal sources of income for the farmers-general (*fermiers-généraux*) came from their right to collect a toll or tax on all commodities entering Paris. To facilitate the collection of these taxes, the decision was made in January 23, 1785, to build a wall around Paris. It was to be twenty-three kilometers long and would incorporate forty-seven tollgates (*barrières*) and a certain number of observation posts. Ledoux, already selected to direct this work, had prepared his first plans in 1783.

The construction of a wall which "put Paris in prison" could not help but be unpopular. Also, since the expense was considerable and Ledoux's megalomania lent itself to criticism, public opinion accused the architect of being an accomplice in a vast swindle. By the spring of 1787, the scandal had become so great that Ledoux was removed as director of the project. After some modifications, however, his designs were carried out under the supervision of the architects Antoine, Raymond and Brébion.

The controversy created by this major enterprise of Ledoux is particularly instructive. The critics took exception to the buildings of temples to house modest clerks. "How M. Ledoux likes columns and puts them everywhere; he has squandered them, which gives a luxurious appearance to these tax collectors' lairs," wrote Bachaumont, one of his most acerbic critics. There was, in fact, a fundamental misunderstanding about the project. Encouraged at the beginning by the king himself, and more consistently by Calonne, the general comptroller of finances, Ledoux ignored the commercial nature of the wall and believed himself authorized to follow the example of the architects to Louis XIV, who had built superb gateways along the old fortified walls. Could not Mercury lay claim to the same privileges as Mars? "The minister desired," wrote Ledoux, "that the gateways to the capital of the world announce to the foreigner the grandeur of an opulent city." During the days of July 10–14, 1789, the people physically attacked this monument built to cupidity; but, as soon as the toll taxes were abolished, the revolutionary government decided that the gates would be "erected as public monuments" and that there would be graven on them in bronze letters, "the victories of the Republican armies over the tyrants." The architect Jacques-Guillaume Legrand, a discerning critic of contemporary artistic productions, wrote in the early days of the Republic: "The idle . . . have repeated to satiety that it was too great an outpouring of money for the housing of clerks. Did they not realize that it was not a question of such a niggardly detail . . . and that the gateway into Paris . . . should not present itself to the stranger like the entrance to a village or a wretched inn on a cross road?"

However, it is apparent that it was actually Ledoux's originality that motivated these criticisms. There is an echo of it in a report of 1813 made to Napoleon by Fontaine, his *architecte ordinaire*: "The tollgate buildings of Paris, executed at a time when a mania for innovation occupied all minds, were then regarded by many people as the creations of a genius. Their oddness was taken for innovation." In his commentaries on French architecture, Jefferson reserved his only known unfavorable judgment for the tollgates which may have been as much politically motivated as aesthetic: "Paris is everyday enlarging and beautifying. . . . I do not count among its beauties the wall with which they have enclosed us."

Was he not, however, touched by the pure, classical beauty of the Etoile tollgate, which was in a way "his" gate since he had to pass through it when, coming from Bagatelle, Longchamp, Madrid or from Mont-Valérien, he returned to the Hôtel de Langeac via the avenue de Neuilly? That tollgate replaced, moreover, the Chaillot gate which, situated on the Champs Elysées just at the level of the Hôtel de Langeac, had marked since 1732 the western city limits of Paris. The king had wanted the design of the Etoile gate to be particularly imposing since it would serve as a monumental gateway on the main road leading to the Louvre. Napoleon, who well understood this clever idea of the monarchy but who shared his architect's opinion of Ledoux's work, had built in 1806, between the two pavilions of the tollgate, his celebrated triumphal arch, an architectural redundancy which Napoleon III took upon himself to correct by having the tollgate destroyed in 1860.

Other than the Monceau rotunda, three tollgates have been preserved: the Grille de la Villette to the north, the Trône gate to the east and the Grille d'Enfers to the south.

The Loursine tollgate (also called gate of the Chemin de la Santé, or of Gentilly or de la Glacière), close to the Grille d'Enfer, was a temple without wings. Jefferson adopted a similar design for the capitol at Richmond. P. de M.

304 Tollgate at la Villette

Photograph
NOT IN EXHIBITION

305 Elevation of the buildings on the Place Louis XV [Place de la Concorde]

JACQUES-ANGES GABRIEL
1698–1788
Pen and wash
131.8 x 37 (51⅞ x 14⁹⁄₁₆)
Lent by the Archives nationales, Paris

The decision to create a public square at the junction of the Tuileries and the beginning of the Champs Elysées dates from 1750. At that time the avenue was bordered by gardens of the *hôtels* which faced the rue du Faubourg Saint-Honoré. The creation of the square was to give a new impetus to the growth of the western sectors of Paris. Gabriel, first architect to the king, presented his first plans for the project in 1753, and work began on it the following year. In 1763, on the occasion of the inauguration of the equestrian statue of Louis XV by Bouchardon, which was to ornament the center of the square (destroyed during the Revolution), the façades were finished.

In fact, Gabriel's plan was only for the façades. It was not until later that the use and disposition of the building to be constructed behind them were determined. Buildings were erected only on the north side of the square, facing the river Seine, which marked its southern boundary. Three parallel streets originated from its center and from the extremities of the north side. The drawing exhibited here only shows the left half of the composition; the right half is identical to it. The two main façades, separated by the middle street (rue Royale), were supposed to be framed by two secondary façades situated on the far side of the lateral streets and therefore beyond the boundaries of the square. The secondary façade on the right was constructed closely following Gabriel's plan (Hôtel Saint-Florentin), but to the left, the farmer-general Grimod de la Reynière, owner of the land, obtained permission to build without taking into consideration Gabriel's plan for the ensemble. It has already been mentioned (see no. 287 on the salon de la Reynière) that the Hôtel de la Reynière was destroyed in 1931 to make way for the present United States embassy, which is itself more in keeping with the symmetry envisioned by Gabriel. Among the buildings which were constructed in the space behind the principal façades were the furniture storerooms of the king (*garde-meubles du Roi*) on the right (Jefferson refers to the work of Gabriel as the "garde-meubles"), and on the left at the corner of the rue Royale, the Hôtel de Coislin, which was rented by Silas Dean, a representative in the United States Congress, and where the treaty of alliance of 1778 recognizing the independence of the United States was probably signed.

In this work, Gabriel seems to be the faithful heir to the architects of the preceding century. The two main façades have the same basic composition as Jules Hardouin-Mansart's façades in the Place des Victoires and in the Place Vendôme: a ground floor with smoothly rusticated masonry and semicircular arched bays forming the base for a colossal order of columns which rises in front of the two upper floors. The use of columns and the proportions of the base to the height of each column resembles the colonnade of the Louvre. As for the general cheme, it recalls again the public quares by Mansart, which were themselves only a decoration of façades, ehind which construction was left o private initiative. Up until the time f Gabriel, public architecture was erceived as the art of organizing rban space. It is still a long way from nose isolated, completely conceived nonuments, preceded by a portico *l'antique*, which became increasingly opular and established the kind of ublic edifice as Jefferson himself onceived it should be. Jefferson ecommended to the architects work- ıg in Washington to imitate the *ırde-meubles* in their designs for the resident's house. P. de M.

06 The Church of Sainte-Geneviève (now called the Panthéon), Paris

Photograph

n 1756 work began on what was to ecome one of the largest churches n Paris and one of the most important European architectural creations of the econd half of the eighteenth century: acques-Germain Soufflot (1713– 780) was commissioned to rebuild he abbey church of Sainte-Geneviève. ince construction moved ahead lowly, Soufflot had the time to rework is designs several times, and it was ot until 1777 that he submitted the lefinitive plan for the lantern tower, he construction of which was com- leted in 1790, ten years after the rchitect's death. Thiéry, in his *Guide les amateurs . . . à Paris* (1787) lescribes the state of the building at bout the same time Jefferson visited he work site. "This edifice is now ompletely covered. Of the heavy onstruction only the cupola of the lome remains to be done [that is, the antern tower]. The entablature above he interior columns of the dome is urrently being set in place, the ex- erior columns [of the lantern tower] ıre also being erected." This descrip- ion suggests that Jefferson could visualize rather precisely what the inished building would look like. Soufflot's plan was slightly modified ater. In 1791, the church having become the "Panthéon" destined to iouse the tombs of great men (*Grands Hommes*), it was judged necessary to darken the interior by blocking out all of the lower windows con- structed by Soufflot, to give the build- ing a character more in keeping with its new funerary role. In 1806, the four crossing pillars were reinforced: Soufflot had constructed them from a triangular center shaft with an en- gaged column at each angle. When reinforced, the columns were ab-

sorbed into the mass of the pillars, the angles of which were decorated with pilasters.

At Sainte-Geneviève, ambition was to synthesize Greek decoration with Gothic structure and a Renaissance dome. Upon analysis, the work indeed seems to be a synthesis of historic references. Nothing is entirely new; the ensemble is, nonetheless, of a remarkable originality. Greek decor- ation, in Soufflot's mind, meant the use of the column. For the classical portico, Soufflot could find in Paris itself two examples dating from the seventeenth century: the church of the Sorbonne, and the church of the Assumption. For several years already, the theoreticians, who condemned the heavy effect of the massive arcades traditionally used in churches since the time of the Renaissance, had recommended instead the use of in- terior colonnades under an entablature. In that respect, Soufflot had been preceded by Contant d'Ivry, the archi- tect of the church of Saint-Vaast d'Arras and, even earlier, by Perrault, who was responsible for the project for the church of Sainte-Geneviève, and Mansart the designer of the chapel of the Château de Versailles. P. de M.

307 Ecole de Chirurgie, plan of the ground floor

JACQUES GONDOIN 1737–1818, and CLAUDE-RENÉ-GABRIEL POULLEAU, b. 1749
Etching
49.7 x 41.8 (19⅝ x 16⅜)
Inscribed above: *Plan du Rez de chaussée des Ecoles de Chirurgie. pl. VI.* Below: *C.R.G. Polleau Sculp.*
Collection of the Bibliothèque nationale
NOT IN EXHIBITION

308 Ecole de Chirurgie, street elevation

JACQUES GONDOIN 1737–1818, and CLAUDE-RENÉ-GABRIEL POULLEAU, b. 1749
Etching
52.5 x 33.5 (20⅝ x 13³⁄₁₆)
Inscribed above: *pl. VIII.* Below: *C.R.G. Poulleau Sculp.*
Collection of the Bibliothèque nationale
NOT IN EXHIBITION

309 Ecole de Chirurgie, interior view of the amphitheater

JACQUES GONDOIN 1737–1818, and CLAUDE-RENÉ-GABRIEL POULLEAU, b. 1749
Etching, in Gondouin, *Descriptions des Ecole de chirurgie* (Paris, 1780)
35.5 x 54 (14 x 21¼)
Inscribed above: *Pl. XXIX.* Below: *C.R.G. Poulleau Sculp.*
Lent by the Boston Athenaeum

The Académie de Chirurgie (Academy of Surgery) received its statutes and the right to teach in 1750, and Gon- doin was commissioned in 1769 to construct the Ecole de Chirurgie (today the Faculté de Médecine). The first stone was officially placed on December 14, 1774, although the building was nearly completed by then.

At the back of a colonnaded court, closed to the street by a portico, Gondoin raised a colossal order of

columns under a pediment which marked the entrance to the amphi- theater. It was a sort of temple with *peribolus*.

The Ecole de Chirurgie was the first *à l'antique* public edifice in Paris. "The whole system of old French architecture was turned upside down by this unexpected work and the partisans of the establishment were stupefied at the sight of a façade with- out a pavilion, without an *avant-corps* in the middle, without an *arrière- corps*, and in which the cornice con- tinued from one end to the other without projection or profile, in con- trast to the normal usage in France," wrote Charles-Paul Landon in the *Annales du Musée* in 1803. He saw the true character of the novelty of the building. We have already cited, in reference to the Hôtel de Salm, several works which preceded the Ecole de Chirurgie and presented the same general approach. But the street façade, rectangular and without any relief, was a prototype of the new architecture. Moreover, it could well have been inspired by *The Ruins of Balbec* (Baalbek), published in 1757 by Robert Wood. The amphitheater's large vault with zenithal lighting is one of the most monumental imitations of a Roman cupola.

Jefferson could not have been insensitive to a monument influenced by antiquity which was also so close to his "cher" Hôtel de Salm. The surveys of Chambers and Quarenghi bear witness to the interest which the Ecole de Chirurgie had for foreign architects. P. de M.

310 Halle aux Bleds, project section

JACQUES MOLINOS 1743–1831
Pen and wash
55 x 37.2 (21⅝ x 14⅝)
Signed below to the right: *Molinos, architecte de la ville de Paris*

Lent by the Musée Carnavalet, Paris

The new Halle aux Bleds of Paris was constructed between 1763 and 1766 by Nicolas Le Camus de Mézières. It was a ring-shaped building enveloping a circular court. Originally, the court was to serve only for the circulation of wagons bringing grain; but the covered areas of the hall not being large enough, the court was soon used for the storage of merchandise. Le Camus proposed to cover it with a cupola, the design for which was published in 1769, but this idea was not carried out until 1783 by Legrand and Molinos.

The striking design and the comment it aroused inevitably attracted the attention of Jefferson, for whom the Halle aux Bleds was "the most superb thing on earth." The building of Le Camus had been compared to Roman amphitheaters, and the cupola of Le Grand and Molinos to that of the Pantheon. However, in this work, structural achievements overshadowed the classical details. Jefferson and his contemporaries admired the stone and brick vaulting of the circular galleries

and, even more, the framework of the false cupola in wood. In order to construct it, Legrand and Molinos had had the idea of returning to a technique invented by Philibert Delorme in the second half of the sixteenth century. Delorme had replaced all the large pieces of wood by small boards assembled in two parallel courses with alternated joints, thus permitting the coverage of large spaces. This was demonstrated by Delorme himself in his project for the convent of the Dames de Montmartre; his solution worked well in the Halle aux Bleds, since it had been evolved for a ring structure forming a sort of hollow tower, the empty center of which was covered by a timber-work cupola. This technique "à la Philibert Delorme" had often been used by French architects in the last quarter of the eighteenth century; it disappeared only with the development of an iron framework technique, which, in fact, owed much to the older method and helps to explain the renewed interest in it. In the meantime, since 1782, Bélanger had indicated the way toward modern solutions by proposing an iron cupola for the Halle aux Bleds. He was able to realize his project in 1808, the cupola of Legrand and Molinos having been destroyed by fire in 1802.

The Halle aux Bleds has completely disappeared today; in its place is the

Bourse de Commerce (stock exchange).

The drawing by Molinos exhibited here should be dated slightly prior to 1783. It shows exactly the disposition of Le Camus' construction with its circular double gallery, granary, and central space with arcades. However, the drawing of the cupola projected above the building's cornice does not conform to the one which was executed; in the latter, the timberwork spindles alternate with the window spindles, giving more abundant light than the originally planned zenithal glass opening. P. de M.

311 Halle aux Bleds, plan

NICOLAS LE CAMUS DE MÉZIÈRES
1721–1789
Engraving

Collection of the Bibliothèque nationale
NOT IN EXHIBITION

INTÉRIEUR DE LA NOUVELLE SALLE DE COMÉDIE FRANÇAISE DE L'ANCIEN PROJET.

312 Théâtre de l'Odéon, section

CHARLES DE WAILLY 1730–1798
Pen and wash   1776
93 x 59 (36⅝ x 23¼)
Signed and dated below on the right:
De Wailly faicit 1776. Inscribed
below, center: Intérieur de la nouvelle
salle de Comédie française de l'Ancien
Port.

Lent by the Musée Carnavalet, Paris

In 1767, the architects Peyre and
de Wailly were commissioned to
reconstruct the Comédie Française.
Work only truly began in May 1779,
and the theater was opened on April
9, 1782. Still standing today, though
very much changed, it is known under
the name, which it took in 1796, of
Odéon.

Scholars, who have studied the
complex genesis of this building, relate
the drawing exhibited here to the
so-called third project of 1771 which
was taken up again, with modifications,
in the completed project of 1778. The
present drawing has been identified as
one of two exhibited by de Wailly in
the Salon of 1781. However, this identification does not seem convincing.
Why should de Wailly have presented,
at this Salon, drawings which were
already superceded and different from
those upon which the construction was
being based?

Moreover, the dating of these drawings is open to discussion. The elevation, not shown here, bears the date
of 1771 next to the signature; but we
also find the date of 1770 on the bas-

relief of the central portico and in the
dedication. The double-arcaded
porticos connecting the theater to
neighboring buildings may well have
been added as an afterthought. The
conception of this façade, judged by
contemporaries as too austere for a
theater, must be, for the most part,
the work of Peyre.

The perspective section shown here
is not dependent upon the elevation
of 1770–1771. To realize this, it is
sufficient to note that the sculpted
group of the two muses has disappeared and the attic is pierced by the
central, semicircular bay which appears
in the final project of 1778. The perspective section is, moreover, dated
1776. However, the layout of the
entrance vestibule already appears in
a drawing in the Louvre which would
be de Wailly's 1771 morceau de
réception for his entrance into the
French Royal Academy of Painting
and Sculpture.

De Wailly was not only a member
of the Academy of Architecture but
of the Academy of Painting as well.
This is not surprising considering the
quality of the small figures which
animate the composition and which
are certainly by his hand. It is to him,
rather than to Peyre, that one should
attribute the interior decoration. The
scene which is playing on stage, a
passage from the fifth act of Racine's
Athalie, is, indeed, characteristic of
the style of this artist who was influenced by his master Servandoni.

In response to criticism, the interior

was modified in its execution: the
opening of the stage was reduced and
the columns, which divided it in three
parts, were suppressed. With them
disappeared the interesting device
which permitted the construction of
three sets, each with its own perspective system, simultaneously representing three distinct places. It was at the
expense of the stage opening that
stage boxes were created. These boxes
were, in the distribution of seats,
traditionally reserved for important
spectators—a hierarchy which the
architect had at first thought to sup-
press in order to give more unity to
the room. Finally, the grand staircase,
judged too expensive, was shortened

by one floor and was terminated at the
first balcony.

The finished building was thus one
of the first modern theaters in France.
Without bringing in any really new
ideas, the authors had the merit of
realizing the conceptions of theoreticians who, for nearly half a century, had
been arguing about the ideal form for
a theater. The circular plan of the room
was particularly admired, as well as
the unusual development of the reception areas (vestibule, staircase, foyers),
and, finally, the monumental quality
of mass, the edifice being entirely
isolated by surrounding streets and
fronted, like an antique temple, by a
portico. Until then, Paris had, instead
of theaters, spectacle rooms integrated
into the layout of a palace like the
Tuileries or the Palais-Royal, or arranged, in an improvised fashion,
within a block of houses. P. de M.

313 Plan of the level of the first tier of boxes of the Bordeaux Theater

NICOLAS (CALLED VICTOR)
LOUIS 1731–1800
Engraving
34 x 60 (13⅜ x 23⅝)
Inscribed at top: plan au niveau des
Ières loges, pl. V

Collection of the Bibliothèque
nationale
NOT IN EXHIBITION

314 Front elevation of the Bordeaux Theater

NICOLAS (CALLED VICTOR)
LOUIS 1731–1800
Pen and wash
62.7 x 41.5 (24⅝ x 16⅜)
Inscribed at top: Elévation géométrale
de la principale entrée

Lent by the Archives municipales,
Bordeaux

Élévation Géométrale de la principale Entrée

315 Cross section facing the stage
Bordeaux Theater

NICOLAS (CALLED VICTOR)
LOUIS 1731–1800
Pen and wash
70.4 x 52.7 (27¾ x 20¾)
Lent by the Archives municipales,
Bordeaux

316 Cross section of the
auditorium of the Bordeaux
Theater

NICOLAS (CALLED VICTOR)
LOUIS 1731–1800
Pen and wash
74.4 x 53.2 (29⁵⁄₁₆ x 20¹⁵⁄₁₆)
Lent by the Archives municipales,
Bordeaux

Could Jefferson have visited Bordeaux
in 1787 without going to see the
largest theater in France, which had
opened seven years earlier? It is true
that there was nothing new to discover
there in comparison with what he
could see at the Odéon Theater in
Paris. In fact, Louis' first projected
plan for the theater was executed in
Paris in 1772 before his departure for
Bordeaux. The 1774 plan, which is
exhibited here, is quite close to the
finished building and incorporates the
basic layout of Peyre and de Wailly's
plan for the Odéon, but considerably
enlarged, especially in the entrance
and exit areas. The entrance lobby
contains on its upper level a concert
hall framed by two statues, and features a grand staircase, the most
remarkable aspect of this unusual
building. The entrance lobby by itself
forms a separate entity. P. de M.

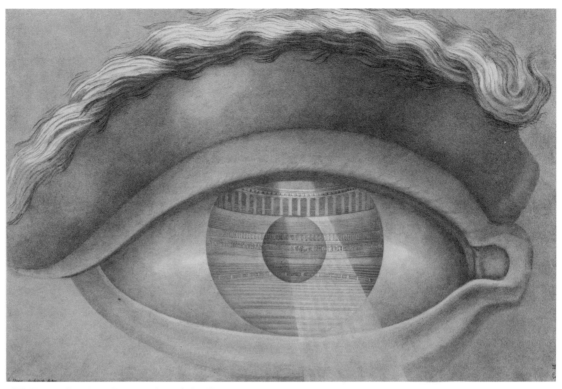

317 Eye reflecting the interior of the Besançon Theater

CLAUDE-NICOLAS LEDOUX
1736–1806
Engraving (facsimile)
Inscribed at lower left: *Le Doux,
Architecte du Roi.* At right: *pl. 113*

The theater at Besançon was built between 1778 and 1784. Ledoux's first drawings for it date from 1775. It is, along with the Odéon in Paris and the Bordeaux Theater, the most representative example of a modern theater, with its isolated building, classical entrance portico, seats on the ground floor, balconies in semicircular tiers, dividers between boxes no higher than the railing, an orchestra pit, a wide stage, and large exits and lobbies.

In the publication of his works in 1804, Ledoux introduced this enigmatic drawing entitled *Coup d'oeil du théâtre de Besançon*, accompanied by a rambling commentary, which is open to interpretation.

First of all, this eye is that of the architect himself. The eye of the creator open on the world, the eye in which the first image of creation is formed. It is the eye of the spectator as well. Optical laws define the shape of the auditorium; in order that all of the spectators be equidistant from the center of the stage, the room must be semicircular. But "everything in nature is a circle." In the eye, "transparent mirror of nature," the semicircle of the auditorium is completed by its reflection. Looking for an all-encompassing optical system, Ledoux

asked himself: "Why did God, architect of the world, who left nothing to be desired in all creation, not put eyes in the back of man's head?" The eye is the image of the theater and of the universe: globe and pupil correspond to auditorium and stage.

The major theater projects by contemporary architects always included a perspective view showing the stage seen from the auditorium; the scenery, shown in place of the action on stage, usually represented another of the architect's projects. It was a play within a play, architecture within architecture. Ledoux's eye is based on the same principle of composition. But, by a curious inversion, it is the view of the auditorium which appears in the background. The eye of the spectator therefore reflects nothing but himself. The spectator is made the spectacle. Ledoux insists on the fact that the spectators themselves must form the main scenery in the auditorium. It is what the architect Boullée, who had the same preoccupations, concludes from this strong image: "The assemblage of the fair sex arranged so as to take the place of a bas-relief" must characterize the theater, which is the temple of Venus.

The eye, source of pleasure, is compared by Ledoux to the round frame in which "one inserts the portrait of the woman one loves." The eye "receives the divine influences which fill our senses . . . with nothing but pleasures and delights, it prepares us!"

To the eye of the voyeur, to whom the architect Jean-Jacques Lequeu devoted literary and theoretical architectural studies, the erotic meaning is even more explicit. If Ledoux's inuendoes are more veiled, the veil is nonetheless transparent. Ledoux fought against those stages which were too narrow and "only offer to the desirous eye a narrow slot." Cosmic side, erotic side, the metaphor turns without the artist ever losing the feeling of the unity of his subject. He identifies the attraction, feminine magnetism, with the principle of universal gravitation.

This text is one of the rare passages in Ledoux's publication that can be precisely dated. In 1794 the artist, discouraged by the lack of comprehension and by the malice of his fellow man, his mind deranged by his fantasies, was in the de la Force prison and in fear of the guillotine. The drawing itself must have been executed at the same time as the text. P. de M.

318 Perspective view of the city of Chaux

CLAUDE-NICOLAS LEDOUX
1736–1806
Engraving (facsimile)
Inscribed at bottom: *Le Doux Arch^te du Roy; Vue perspective de la Ville de Chaux; pl. 15*

Jefferson left France without having seen the most important architectural creation of the second half of the eighteenth century, the salt factory at Chaux. However, it is possible that he knew the work, published in 1804 and entitled *L'Architecture considerée sous le rapport de l'art, des moeurs et de la législation*, in which Ledoux illustrated an idealized version of the salt factory.

In 1773 the decision was made to create a factory to exploit the salt waters near the forest of Chaux, and in the same year Ledoux presented his designs for the project, which was begun in 1775. The salt factory, which has survived until today without much damage, has a semicircular plan; the

main entrance is in the middle of the arc of the circle and the director's house, in the center, aligns with other buildings to form the diameter. These are the building arrangements which appear on the lower part of the *Vue perspective de la ville de Chaux*.

This view, published in 1804, was considered for a long time to be a construction project that had only been partially realized. It is accompanied by several highly original designs for public and private buildings. The commission of 1773 was of great importance, since, in addition to the already considerable number of buildings for the factory, it was necessary to build a courthouse, a prison, a chapel, and housing for the workers: "All of these buildings will be solidly constructed and laid out according to their purpose, but without decoration and with a simplicity appropriate to a factory," wrote a contemporary source. Since critics reproached Ledoux for once again exceeding the limits of the proposed scheme, it is

tempting to date the whole group of designs published in 1804 to the 1770s, without taking into consideration the fact that Ledoux would not have been so impractical as to propose buildings unsuitable to the plan, and that if he had he would not have been taken seriously. Moreover, the engraved plan for a monumental church, for example, cannot be the chapel proposed in the original commission, since the chapel was actually built and consisted of nothing more than a large room incorporated into the mass of the director's house. The constructed ensemble offered, however, ample material for the critics, who could not accept Ledoux's use of the most noble order of architecture to ornament a simple factory. The same criticism was made of his Paris tollgates.

Ledoux then little by little surrounded the original nucleus of the factory with a rich overlay of buildings in accordance with his conception of an ideal city. For the most part, they must have been designed in the 1780s.

In 1794, in his poem *De l'Imagination*, the abbot Delille described this "generous project" where one finds "All that, in the heart of a vast city,/ Pleasure or necessity demands;/ Everything that which, for men developing industry;/ Ornaments, enriches, enlightens, and defends the country."

What an example to contemplate for Jefferson, who was to guide the creation of the capitol of the new United States of America. P. de M.

319 Project for a large metropolitan church, interior view

ETIENNE-LOUIS BOULLÉE
1728–1799
Pen and wash
61 x 33 (24 x 13)
Signed and dated below to the left:
1782 Boulée invenit
Lent by the Royal Institute of British Architects, London

This project is typical of the works which were being executed in the 1780s in the studios of the professors of the Academy of Architecture, and comes directly from one of the most influential of them. The subject of the competition for the Grand Prix of 1781 was a cathedral, and the drawings presented by the students are extremely close to those which Boullée produced as teaching examples in 1781 and 1782.

The architect of the Church of Sainte-Geneviève (see no. 306), Jacques-Germain Soufflot, had died the year before with the church still far from completion, and Boullée's project may be seen as an attempt to improve on Soufflot's solutions to the problems posed in the design of a large church. The construction of Sainte-Geneviève was too far advanced to be modified in any major ways, however, and the theoreticians of the academy in any case preferred the creation of prototypes to the modification of existing plans.

Where Soufflot's spaces were highly structured, Boullée's were continuous, evocative of infinity and divinity. In place of the front and rear projections of the building, which break the orders of columns at Sainte-Geneviève, Boullée substituted several files of colonnades in long alignments; for the domes and cupolas, he substituted cylindrical vaults.

Doubtless, he found in the reproductions of the *Ruins of Balbec*, the model for this tri-structural idea with porticos and cylindrical vaults. But, he must also have had other works of reference in mind; perhaps even the *Discovery of the Laocoön* by Hubert Robert (see no. 281). Most of the great theoretical projects of Boullée may, in fact, be seen to parallel the productions of contemporary painters, especially those of Hubert Robert. Particularly notable is the contrast between dark structures and luminous crossings. "If I can avoid direct lighting, and make it penetrate without the spectator perceiving where it comes from, the effects resulting from a mysterious light will produce a truly enchanting magic," wrote Boullée, for whom architecture and painting were a single art.

When the hope of realizing the most utopian projects appeared after the Revolution, Boullée, yielding to the illusion that he would be able to construct his immense temple to the supreme being, proposed to build it on the summit of Mont Valérien, in the very place where Jefferson often retreated. Boullée and Jefferson shared an attraction for elevated sites, to which they attached an architectural and spiritual function. P. de M.

320 Project for a museum, plan
ETIENNE-LOUIS BOULLÉE
1728–1799
Pen and wash
110.3 x 110.3 (43⅜ x 43⅜)
Inscribed below: *plan d'un Muséum Au centre duquel est un Temple à la Renomée*
Lent by the Bibliothèque nationale

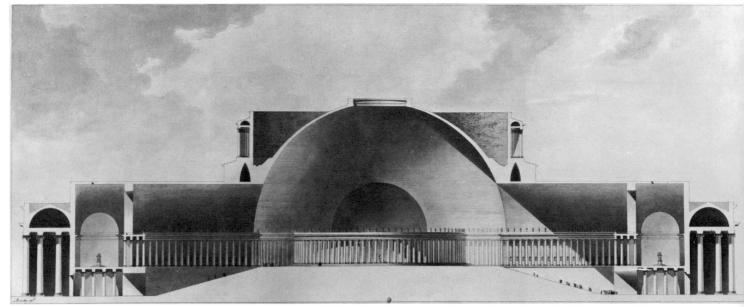

321 Project for a museum, section

ETIENNE-LOUIS BOULLÉE
1728–1799
Pen and wash
94.5 x 37 (37³⁄₁₆ x 14⁹⁄₁₆)
Signed below to the left: *Boullée in^{it}*.
Inscribed below in the middle:
Coupe du Musaeum.

Lent by the Bibliothèque nationale

Because of the interest of the subject and the audacity of Boullée's conception, this project for a museum must be considered one of the most important creations of revolutionary architecture.

To assemble all the productions of human genius was one of the preoccupations of the eighteenth century. The competition subject for the 1779 Grand Prix, won by Boullée's pupil, had been defined by the Academy of Architecture in the following manner: "The Academy calls for a museum to contain the productions of the sciences, the liberal arts, and natural history. The depot of the sciences will include a library, a medal cabinet, several rooms for geography and prints; the depot for natural history will include rooms for anatomy, injection, animal preservation, plants and shells. . . ." Architecture offers a common ground where the sciences and the arts can meet. A philosophical architect like Boullée had a great interest in the natural sciences, though it is apparent in his project that little space was reserved for permanent exhibitions. Only the portion constructed on a square plan would have a functional end; the semicircular porticos are nothing more than sumptuous *avant-corps* announcing the entrances, while the building, shaped

like a Greek cross which cuts the interior court, is a temple of fame. The latter is, in fact, the essential part of the edifice which is, above all else, a secular cathedral, the Pantheon of great men. At the opened crossing of an immense dome is the temple proper, formed by a circular colonnade; the four arms of the cross are filled with monumental staircases which climb to the crossing. This temple was to have four entrances directed toward the cardinal points of the compass to show that all nations were welcome. In the project of Jacques-Pierre Gisors, Boullée's pupil and winner of the 1779 Grand Prix, one finds a first expression of his teacher's idea, with the same plan, and the same exterior crowning element in the form of a columniated drum without dome. It is known that Boullée strongly inspired the competition projects of the Academy and that his own projects often may best be considered as masterly corrected exercises. In Boullée's project, dated 1783, the essential contribution of the master was the treatment of the interior space. There were, in reality, two fitted interior spaces. The one, limited by the colonnades and given measure by their rhythm, was the space controlled by man, that of knowledge. The other, domain of the supreme being, was unconquered space, evoked by the vaults which appeared to be built up to the sun, behind the colonnades.

The directness with which the cylindrical vaults penetrated into the dome—no decoration, no moldings to ease the brutal encounter—had an accent of startling modernity.

The two beautiful interior views were, however, characteristic of their time. They summarized a century of

research on the pictorial effects of architecture. For Boullée, a painter by vocation, nourished by the inventions of Piranesi and his followers, architecture was the art of presenting great ideas. P. de M.

322 Project for a museum, interior view

ETIENNE-LOUIS BOULLÉE
1728–1799
Pen and wash
85 x 47 (33½ x 18½)
Signed below to the left: *Boullée invenit*. Inscribed below in the middle:
Vue intérieure d'un museum. Prise au niveau du Temple de la Renomée.

Lent by the Bibliothèque nationale

323 Project for a museum, interior view

ETIENNE-LOUIS BOULLÉE
1728–1799
Pen and wash
84 x 46.3 (33¹⁄₁₆ x 18¼)
Signed and dated below to the right:
Boullée 1783

Lent by the Bibliothèque nationale

185 EUROPE: THE VAUNTED SCENE

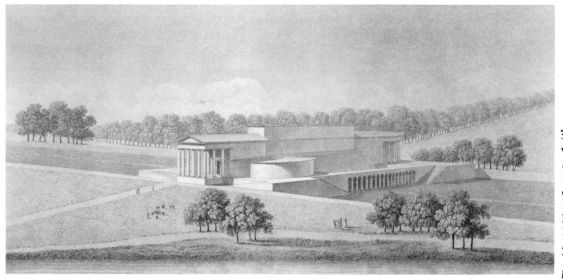

324 Oi'kema project, perspective view

COQUET and BOVINET active late
18th century, after
CLAUDE-NICOLAS LEDOUX
1736–1806
Engraving (facsimile)
Inscribed below to the left: *Le Doux
Architecte du Roi.* In the center:
Vue perspective, to the right: *gravé
par Coquet et Bovinet, pl. 103*

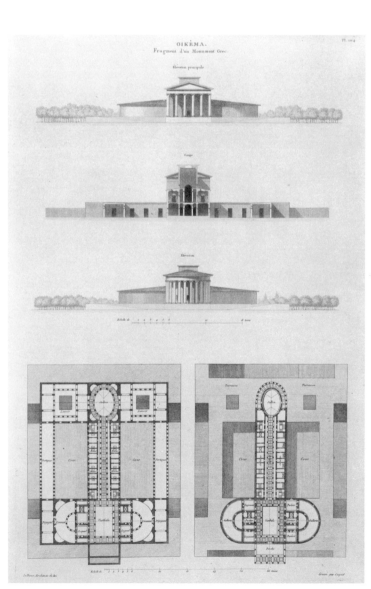

OIKEMA.
Fragment d'un Monument Grec.

325 Oi'kema project, plans, section, elevations

COQUET active late 18th century,
after CLAUDE-NICOLAS LEDOUX
1736–1806
Engraving (facsimile)
Inscribed above: *Oi'kema. Fragment
d'un Monument grec, pl. 104.*
Inscribed below to the left: *Ledoux,
Architecte du Roi.* Inscribed below
to the right: *Gravé par Coquet*

Under this ambiguous title (*Oi'kema*
signifies "habitation" as well as "place
of debauchery" in Greek), Ledoux
presents a building with a provocative
and obscure symbolism of which he
alone possessed the secret.

This house of pleasure has a moralizing function. On the façade is inscribed "Here one captivates the
changing graces to eternalize virtue."
It is a prison of venal love. Virtue
"exists that the names of those who
frequent these haunts be inscribed in
ineffaceable letters on the surfaces that
art . . . has taken the pleasure to
purify." The artist enjoys playing with
words just as he does with forms. By
the nudity and purity of its volumes,
the supervised house of pleasure is an
homage to "Virtuous Hymen" just as
the house of detention pays tribute to
justice.

The Oi'kema project should, doubtless, be included in the program ensemble for the ideal town at Chaux.
A second project, of rather close conception, bears the title "maison de
plaisir." The description of the site
planned for this building is very
characteristic of the revolutionary
architects who sought to bring their
creations into accord with those of
nature. "The small valley which supports this edifice is surrounded by

marvelous enticements; a gentle wind
caresses the atmosphere; the fragrant
varieties of the forest—thyme, iris,
violet, mint—blow their perfumes on
these walls; the foliage which shelters
them spreads freshness and rustles in
murmurs. The loving wave trembles
on the bank which confines it; its
actions whet the air, and the echo
breaks out in delicious sounds," wrote
Ledoux.

As original as the conception may
appear, it is not without precedent.
The plan of the Porticus lugentium
of the Campo Marzio in Rome, as it
appeared in the rendering by Piranesi,
also had a phallic form. P. de M.

326 Elevation, Newton's cenotaph, exterior by night

ETIENNE-LOUIS BOULLÉE
1728–1799
Pen and wash
65.3 x 40.2 (25⅝ x 15⅞)
Signed and dated below to the right:
Boullée 1784. Inscribed in middle,
below: *A Newton.*
Lent by the Bibliothèque nationale

327 Section, Newton's cenotaph, interior by day

ETIENNE-LOUIS BOULLÉE
1728–1799
Pen and wash
65 x 39.8 (25⅞₁₆ x 15⅞₁₆)
Signed below to the left: *Boullée.*
Inscribed in middle, below:
Coupe du cenotaph de Newton.
Lent by the Bibliothèque nationale

In 1784, with his project of a cenotaph for Newton, Boullée found a radically new solution to the problems that he had already tackled the preceding year with his project for a museum (see nos. 320–323), the metaphorical representation of knowledge and the creation of an architectural space giving the illusion of infinity and of nature.

Newton, whose portrait ornamented Boullée's study, was viewed as the eminent "inventor" of the laws of the universe. "Sublime spirit! Vast and profound genius! Divine being! O Newton!" cried Boullée. "If by the extent of your insights and the sublimity of your genius, you determined the shape of the earth, I have conceived the project of enveloping you with your own discovery." In this curious apostrophe Boullée would not appear to be very familiar with the works of Newton although we know from other sources that he had solid training in astronomy, the science of the architecture of the universe. His archaeological knowledge also enabled him to consider the many illustrations that antiquity had given of the relationships between architecture and astronomy.

The sphere, both a cosmic and a Christian symbol, was seen as the perfect representation of infinite space. The spectator who entered the cenotaph was to be "obligated, as by a hundred major forces, to hold himself in the place which is assigned to him," that is to say, at the inferior pole.

In a drawing not exhibited here, Boullée shows the effect of this space when it is filled by the darkness of night. The vault is pierced by small apertures which are distributed according to the map of the heavens. The effect of the light is even more curious, since Boullée illuminates the interior of the cenotaph by a mysteriously luminous astrolabe.

Boullée states that he is the first to have given a spherical form to a building. In truth, during the last years of the eighteenth century, there was a proliferation of projects on this theme. Although certain of these are not dated exactly, scarcely anyone but Ledoux could presume to dispute Boullée's claim. Jefferson's own plan for the rotunda at the University of Virginia is described with a sphere (see nos. 506, 508, 509) and he projected a scheme for a planetarium on the ceiling of its dome. P. de M.

328 Vision inspired by the cemetery at Chaux

EDME BOVINET 1767–1832,
after CLAUDE-NICOLAS LEDOUX
1736–1806
Engraving (facsimile)
Inscribed below to the left: *Le Doux Architecte du Roi.* In the center: *Elevation du Cimetière de la ville de Chaux.* To the right: *Bovinet Sculp, pl. 100.*

The projected cemetery for the town of Chaux is a sort of columbarium formed by circular corridors tied to a central sphere by radiating galleries. It is completed by a *tableau* of the heavens, curiously called *Elévation du Cimitère de la Ville de Chaux.* In the commentary that Ledoux makes about the cemetery, we may discern a critique of Boullée's project for a cenotaph for Newton. "Confident of the secrets of the heavens, Copernicus, Kepler, Tyco Brahé, Descartes, Newton, Herschel, . . . you can do without that perishable vault which covers ostentatious epitaphs; your glory will remain longer than them; were that the planets you see more numerous, they could not contain your tombs." If our interpretation is correct, Ledoux's fantasy would be after 1784, the date of Boullée's project. Convinced that the amplitude of his vision went beyond the limits of architectural construction, Ledoux abandoned traditional architectural drawing methods and dedicated an image of the planets to the great men of astronomy.
    Nevertheless, he utilized the great hollow sphere in his cemetery project, which has long been dated 1773 on

the basis of a note by Ledoux. W. Herrman has shown that this note concerned a project for a salt factory and not the cemetery project: the ensemble of projects for an ideal town would clearly be later. P. de M.

329 Project for a sepulchral monument for the sovereigns of a great empire, elevation

PIERRE-LÉONARD FONTAINE
1762–1853
Pen and wash
268.9 x 69.2 (105⅞ x 27¼)
Lent by the Ecole des Beaux-Arts,
Paris

It was as a student that Fontaine, the future architect of Napoleon, presented this project in 1785 at the Prix de Rome competition for which the assigned subject was "a sepulchral monument for the sovereigns of a great empire, placed in an enclosure in which one will lay-out the spectral sepulchres for men of the nation."

Fontaine won only the second prize, although his project had been found "supérieurement dessiné"; the Academy had thought it well to show its disapproval of that tendency among students to create architectural *tableaux* at the expense of their trade. It seems likely that certain masters did not share this judgment, especially Boullée, who had himself provided several examples which directly inspired Fontaine.

The theme, as surprising as it may appear, was not completely novel in 1785. The cult of great men, restored by the Enlightenment, and a better knowledge of antique funerary monu-ments led architects to reconsider the rather neglected theme of the mauso-leum, a theme particularly favorable to the development of a purely specu-lative architecture. Already in 1766, Desprez had proposed a monument to Voltaire which included a central mausoleum, obelisks, and an enclosure. But a comparison of the two projects indicates very well the road traveled: the abstraction of volumes, accentu-ation of the scale by the monumental relation of the porticos and pyramids and dramatization of the lighting effects.

All of that precisely summarizes the contributions of Boullée. However, Fontaine's project is the bearer of a supplementary import. Once having become the official creator of the *style Empire*, Fontaine spoke of his 1785 project as a youthful error. In effect, with the restoration of public order, the lyricism which animated the architecture—as it did the politics—of the Revolution had become charged with pomposity. And in the new age, the prevailing wish was to forget the earlier architecture—so modern in many ways—by the last creators of the eighteenth century. P. de M.

330 Shelter for the Poor

CLAUDE-NICOLAS LEDOUX
1736–1806
Engraving (facsimile)
Inscribed below: *L'Abri du Pauvre, pl. 33*

The Napoleonic reaction does not entirely explain the disappearance of revolutionary architecture. In its quest for the most basic sources of archi-tecture, Ledoux and his contempo-raries progressively stripped their designs of what they considered the ephemeral ornaments accumulated over the centuries, and at the end found themselves with nothing. Per-haps Ledoux may have come to see that pushed to this extreme, archi-tecture ceased to exist, and merged with nature, a feeling expressed by him in describing this project for a shelter for the poor: "The vast uni-verse . . . is the house of the poor. . . . It has the azure vault for a dome." P. de M.

331 The Death of Socrates

JACQUES-LOUIS DAVID 1748–1825
Oil on canvas 1787
130 x 196 (51 x 77¼)
Signed and dated at left:
LD.MDCCLXXXVII. Signed at right:
L. David

*Lent by The Metropolitan Museum
of Art*

Charles-Michel Trudaine de la Sablière commissioned this painting in April 1786. David's main source was his earlier painting, *Phaedo*, and for specific details he turned to the Oratorian scholar Adry, who gave him information on the correct poses for Plato at the foot of the bed, for Crito seated in the right foreground and for Apollodorus at the edge of the composition raising his arms. From the middle of the century, beginning with Lafont de Saint-Yenne's recommendation in *Sentiments sur quelques ouvrages du Salon*, and taken up by Diderot, the death of Socrates became a popular subject with artists. The Académie set it as the subject for the Prix de Rome in 1762, and several versions appeared in the 1780s, including one by Peyron which was also exhibited in the Salon of 1787.

The painting is composed in low relief, with all the figures arranged on the same plane. Profiting from the criticisms made against the *Oath of the Horatii*, David was careful to link the various individuals and groups together. Similarly he avoided a completely flat background and used perspective to lead the eye through a barrel-vaulted passageway to the stairs in the distance, a conceit similar to those in some of the fantastic projects of the architect Desprez. The poses are arbitrary and theatrical, conferring grandeur, in their antique nobility and simplicity, upon the drama played before the spectator.

Among the many critics who praised the work, Sir Joshua Reynolds singled it out for particular notice, comparing it to the Sistine Chapel and Raphael's *Stanze*, and recorded his belief that "ten days of examination only confirmed the general impression which I had formed, which is that it is perfect in every way." Another visitor to the Salon was Jefferson, who wrote on August 30, 1784, to Trumbull, "The best thing is the *Death of Socrates* by David, and a superb one it is." Thus the taste of the leading English painter and writer on aesthetics was in agreement with the relatively untutored opinion of a Virginian, who had been exposed to serious art at first hand only since his arrival in Europe three years before. A.B. de L.

332 The Oath of the Horatii

JACQUES-LOUIS DAVID 1748–1825
Pencil, pen and wash with some heightening in white 1784
229 x 333 (89¾ x 131)
Signed and dated at lower right:
L. David inv, 1782 (signature apocryphal)

Lent by the Musée des Beaux-Arts, Lille

"I do not feel an interest in any pencil but that of David," wrote Jefferson to Mme de Brehan in 1789. Jefferson admired his *Death of Socrates* (see no. 331) and he could have seen the painting, for which this sketch was made, at the Salon of 1785. *The Oath of the Horatii* was commissioned by the king through comte d'Angiville in 1783, David's idea of a painting on the story of the victory of the Horatii over the Curiatii went back to 1781, and at least two of his drawings indicate his changing views on what point in the drama he would choose as his subject: Horatius returning to Rome having killed his sister Camilla for mourning her lover (one of the Curiatii), or the father of Horatius defending him before the Roman people. Having settled, in discussion with his friends, what incident he would paint, David went to Rome in 1784 and there found the artistic atmosphere which helped him evolve his ideas for the composition. The present drawing was almost certainly done in Rome, as an old inscription on the mount, now lost but recorded, confirms. There were still to be some changes in the completed painting, in which David omitted some details and introduced a more sober background. The mother, instead of lamenting, protects her grandchildren in a restrained enclosing gesture.

The influences on David were various. In Italy he studied antiquity, Raphael and the Bolognese school, and the contemporary work of Gavin Hamilton. There was also the influence of Poussin, whose *Rape of the Sabines* inspired the pose of the three brothers, and of Beaufort's *Brutus*. Literary sources include Livy and Corneille's *Horace*. But from all these, David has created an entirely original work, the aesthetic manifesto of a new style in French painting. A.B. de L.

33 Marius Imprisoned at Minturnae

JEAN-GERMAIN DROUAIS
1763–1788

Oil on canvas 1786
271 x 365 (106¾ x 143¾)

Lent by the Musée du Louvre

Marius at Minturnae was painted in Rome in 1786, when Drouais was still a *pensionnaire* at the French Academy. It is an extraordinarily precocious work for one so young and reveals Drouais' talents, which, unfortunately, were cut short by his early death. The artistic climate of Rome at that time was very competitive. David had exhibited his *Oath of the Horatii* to tremendous acclaim. Gauffier and Wicar were also studying here, while the resident painters, Batoni, Tischbein and their pupils, watched closely what went on at the French Academy. The influence of the German neoclassical painter, Mengs, and his mentor, Winckelmann, was paramount, and through the new Museo Pio-Clementino and recent archaeological excavations, interest in classical antiquity revived and contributed to the prevailing neoclassical style in art.

Drouais' masterpiece invited immediate comparison with David and was indeed created in conscious imitation of and rivalry with the *Oath of the Horatii*. The first and obvious quality the two paintings have in common is the ambitious size and format. In the choice of subjects both paintings show men of exceptional character. In the *Oath*, the theme is patriotic self-sacrifice; in the *Marius* is shown the reaction of an enemy soldier, when confronted with the power of a former conqueror, on whom the soldier can revenge himself. The distribution of the figures and the empty spaces, like pauses in music, are carefully thought out, and a severe architectural decoration is common to both. The dynamic gestures of the three Horatii is recalled in Marius' dramatically extended right arm. His forceful profile also finds precedent in the profiles of the Horatii in the best classical tradition. Contemporaries were not always prepared to give the palm to David, and a near contemporary writer, Chaussard, recorded that "the young Drouais taking an even more daring step created a painting of Marius alone and without advice, which he timidly exhibited to the Roman public. This work had the greatest possible success there and was equally praised by artists and connoisseurs. All of Paris rushed to see this painting." Proud'hon was in Rome when the painting was exhibited and wrote to a friend: "You tell me, my friend, that the painting by M. Drouais is preferred to that by M. David. If one only looked at the facility of the brushwork in the painting by Drouais, one would be right."

Jefferson also admired the *Marius* and wrote to Mme de Tott on February 28, 1787, about the painting:

Have you been Madam, to see the superb picture now exhibiting in the rue Ste. Nicaise, No. 9. chez Mde. Drouay? It is that of Marius in the moment when the souldier enters to assassinate him. It is made by her son, a student at Rome under the care of David, and is much in David's manner. All Paris is running to see it; and really it appears to me to have extraordinary merit. It fixed me like a statue a quarter of an hour, or half an hour, I do not know which, for I lost all ideas of time, even the consciousness of my existence. If you have not been, let me engage you to go. for I think it will give you great pleasure. Write me your judgment on it: it will serve to rectify my own, which as I have told you is a bad one, and needs a guide.

Her reaction was cooler; and although acknowledging that she had been astonished by it and that she admired the painting of the soldier, in whom "the tone of his coloring is harmonious and strong, his pose is perfectly beautiful, perfectly natural," she found fault with Marius. She criticized "the deliate, almost puny face," found fault with the coloring, and objected to his "too nonchalant" arm on which he is leaning. Yet she conceded that the painting "is, nevertheless, made to produce the greatest sensation, and announces the greatest talent in its creator." Jefferson accepted her objections in good part and wrote that her letter "has confirmed a part of my own ideas, given some which escaped me, and corrected others wherein I had been wrong."

Gaius Marius was a distinguished Roman general, who had many successful campaigns against the Numidians and later the Cimbri and Teutones at the end of the second century B.C. His military achievements gave him a powerful position in the state, but his rival, Sulla, succeeded in defeating him outside Rome, and Marius was forced to flee to Minturnae. The soldier ordered to kill him was unable to carry out the task, and Marius eventually returned to Rome and exacted vengeance on his enemies. He died shortly after he became consul for the seventh time. A.B. de L.

334 Voltaire

JEAN-ANTOINE HOUDON
1741–1828
Marble 1778
52.7 (20¾) high
Inscribed on back in center: *Arouet de Voltaire né à Paris en 1694, et mort en 1778. Houdon f. 1778.*
National Gallery of Art

Since Voltaire died in 1778 and Jefferson did not arrive in France until 1784, the two never met. But the Paris that Jefferson encountered during his stay between 1784 and 1789 was permeated with the tradition and legend of Voltaire. As one of the major American representatives of the Enlightenment, Jefferson was well acquainted with Voltaire's writings and was unquestionably sympathetic to most of the positions taken by the French philosopher. We know that he frequented the society of the *philosophes*; the marquis de Condorcet was a particular friend of his. The portrait busts which Jefferson ordered from Houdon to take back with him to America included a plaster of Voltaire as well as busts of Lafayette and of the distinguished economist and *philosophe* the marquis de Turgot.

Houdon made many busts of Voltaire as a result of the aged philosopher's immense popularity, including versions in terra cotta, plaster, marble, and bronze, with perruque in modern dress and without perruque in classical garb, draped and undraped. The marble shown here was executed in modern dress with perruque. A similar bust, with the addition of a cloak or swag of drapery over the right shoulder, was presented on the stage of the Comédie Française in March 1778, at the sixth performance of Voltaire's play, *Irène*, at which Voltaire received a laurel wreath from the Comédiens. A number of other busts, including a marble at the Louvre and another at Versailles, also exist.

Houdon's portrait of *Voltaire* is one of the most famous portrait sculptures in history. The artist's genius for suggesting a living personality through the transitory expression is here exemplified. Although this is the face of a very old man, close to death, there shines forth the vitality and indestructible spirit of the philosopher. It is almost impossible to define his expression. He is not exactly smiling or frowning, and certainly he is not posing for his portrait. He is caught at a moment of transition, and it is this that imbues the face and, in the case of the statue, the entire figure with the intense sense of an inner life. H.H.A.

335 Diana

JEAN-ANTOINE HOUDON
1741–1828
Marble 1778
63 x 45 (24¾ x 17¾)
Signed: *Houdon f. 1778*
National Gallery of Art

In 1775 the Duke of Saxe-Gotha ordered from Houdon a statue of *Diana* for his gardens. When completed in 1780, Houdon's statue embodied two elements which, if not unique, were at least unusual in the tradition of Diana Huntress: those of rapid movement and complete nudity. A bust of the work, which Houdon executed at the same time, shown here, was received with admiration in the Salon of 1777. The fact that the bust was exhibited in the Salon of 1777 and is dated 1778 is in accord with Houdon's practice. Aside from commissioned marbles, which might be dated when the artist finished them, it was his custom to date his busts when they had been purchased and had actually left his studio.

Jefferson's admiration for Houdon's work is well known, and he contemplated acquiring a plaster of the *Diana* statue, though as far as we know she did not join the busts of Washington, Franklin and many other eminent acquaintances, which made up Jefferson's collection of Houdon's sculpture.

Another marble bust of Diana is recorded in the collection of the comte Mansard de Sagonne. This bust does not include the quiver strap between the breasts as recorded in Saint-Aubin's drawing. A third marble bust, formerly in the collection of King Stanislas-Auguste Poniatowski of Poland, disappeared during World War II. The bust of Diana has been reproduced many times after Houdon's death, in bronze, terra cotta, marble, and porcelain. In a number of these the breasts have been chastely draped.

In quality, the marble bust in Washington is certainly closest to the marble statue, now in the Gulbenkian collection in Lisbon, which constitutes the definitive version. The bust is a superb example of the artist's mastery of marble carving during the period when he was at the height of his powers. H.H.A.

336 Jacob Blessing the Sons of Joseph

ADRIAEN VAN DER WERFF
1695–1722
Oil on panel c. 1710–1720
61.1 x 47.5 (24⅟₁₆ x 18¹¹⁄₁₆)

Lent by the Allen Memorial Art Museum, Oberlin College

A taste for the *petit maîtres* of the seventeenth-century Dutch schools was fashionable among connoisseurs in the eighteenth century. The highly finished and usually small-scale works of such artists as van Mieris, Dou and van der Werff were much admired, perhaps more so even than Rembrandt, and they fetched high prices in the sale room. Such an avid collector of Dutch paintings as the duc de Choiseul, whose country estate, Chanteloup, Jefferson was later to visit (see no. 355), had many examples of these cabinet pictures, including examples by van der Werff. It was, therefore, quite in keeping with contemporary aesthetics that Jefferson singled out the works of van der Werff when he visited the Electoral Gallery at Düsseldorf on April 3, 1787: "The gallery of paintings is sublime, particularly the room of Vanderwerff." Trumbull had visited the gallery earlier and recommended a visit to Jefferson, although his view of van der Werff differed markedly from Jefferson's. "Of all the celebrated pictures I have ever seen [these] appear to me to be the very worst— mere monuments of labor, patience, and want of genius." This in no way refutes Jefferson's opinion, but rather reflects the difference in age between the two men, the older man still appreciating the baroque, while the young Trumbull, as a painter, was caught up in the neoclassical movement in Paris through his friendship with David, Hubert Robert, Ména-

geot, Vincent, Mme Vigée-Lebrun, and other artists. He would have, therefore, been less sympathetic to a style against which neoclassicism was reacting. Jefferson, however, was quite capable of appreciating David also, and it may have been the smooth surfaces and detailed care of their execution that gave David's paintings an appeal in common with van der Werff's. R.W.

337 Hercules and Lichas

ANTONIO CANOVA 1757–1822
Bronze, after 1796
41.9 x 25.4 (16½ x 10)
Inscribed on the base: *Canova f.*

Lent by the Collection of the North Carolina Museum of Art, Raleigh

Antonio Canova was probably as famous in his own day as any other sculptor in history. It is, therefore, no surprise that when Jefferson was asked by Nathaniel Macon on behalf of the state of North Carolina for advice about a sculptor to execute a statue of George Washington, he responded as follows: "Who should make it? There can be but one answer to this. Old Canova, of Rome. No artist in Europe would place himself in a line with him; and for thirty years, within my own knowledge, he has been considered by all Europe, as without a rival." Jefferson's advice was sound, and it was followed (the statue of Washington was commissioned from Canova in 1818, delivered in 1821, and mutilated by a fire in 1831). It seems probable that, to a great extent, his knowledge of Canova's work—like his knowledge of some of the famous antique sculptures which he admired but had never seen —was based upon hearsay, literary accounts and reproductions in engravings and in small bronzes such as the present group, although his friend David who had known Canova in Rome may have first alerted Jefferson to the talented sculptor.

Canova initially received a commission for a colossal group of *Hercules and Lichas* in 1795 from Onoratio Gaetani, the major domo of the king of Naples. The earliest record of the composition is in a drawing, dated October 19, 1795, which is in the Museo Civico at Bassano. A full-scale plaster model was completed

by April 2, 1796, and is now in the Accademia in Venice. Another, nearly identical, large plaster cast is in the Gipsoteca di Possagno. Due to the financial difficulties of the original patron, Canova's large group was not transferred into marble until 1811–1815, when he received another commission for the work from a new patron, the Marchese Torlonia; the over-life-size marble is now in the Museo Nazionale d'Arte Moderna, Rome.

The story upon which this work is based appears in Sophocles' *Trachinae* and Ovid's *Metamorphoses*. Lichas, the messenger of Hercules, has just returned bearing a shirt, which has been soaked in the blood of the dying centaur Nessus. The shirt has been sent as a gift to Hercules from his wife, Deianira, who mistakenly believed that the centaur's blood would rekindle Hercules' wandering affection for her. Canova has depicted the moment when Hercules, after putting on the shirt, immediately feels excruciating pain and realizes that the garment has poisoned him and he is going to die. In his fury and anguish, Hercules picks up the helpless Lichas and flings him into the sea.

In his earlier works (such as the *Theseus and Minotaur*, 1781–1782), Canova often consciously selected a calm or inactive pose, concentrating upon the creation of a new kind of classical beauty and on purity of form. In contrast, with the *Hercules and Lichas*, it seems possible that he chose the rather *recherché* subject precisely because it provided him with the opportunity to depict an extremely intense and dramatic action. In fact, the *Hercules and Lichas* may have been intended to form an active counterpart to the famous resting figure of the *Hercules Farnese*— located in Naples, where Canova's work was originally to be placed— upon which, in part, it seems to be based. It has also been suggested that in the *Hercules and Lichas*, Canova's choice of treatment of his subject was intended as a commentary upon contemporary political strife. Retrospectively, if Canova's famous *Perseus* may be seen as an attempt to equal the classical repose and ideal forms of the *Apollo Belvedere*, the *Hercules and Lichas* may, in terms of theme and expression of emotion, be seen as Canova's answer to the *Laocoön*.

Canova's *Hercules and Lichas* was not only novel and interesting to other artists, it was, apparently, very popular. In 1823, one of Canova's friends and biographers wrote of the *Hercules and Lichas*: "There is in Paris a sketch, one foot high, which was the first idea for this group, and this sketch has elicited such admiration that a great number of reproductions have been cast in bronze."

The present bronze is not a reduction of the finished marble, from which it varies in many respects, and it may possibly be one of the casts made from the lost original sketch to which Quatremère de Quincy referred. Other small bronzes made from the same sketch are in Bremen (Kunsthalle) and Leningrad (Hermitage). These small bronzes, aside from their intrinsic beauty, help to give some idea of how Canova's reputation was spread and how an interested amateur like Jefferson may have kept in touch with the European art scene. P.F.

338 Thomas Jefferson

REMBRANDT PEALE 1778–1860
Oil on canvas 1800
87 x 65 (34¼ x 30⅛)
Lent by The White House

Painted sometime after Jefferson's arrival in Philadelphia in late December 1799 and before his departure for Monticello in the middle of May 1800, the portrait depicts the fifty-seven-year-old vice president on the threshold of the presidency of the United States. Though Rembrandt Peale himself had just turned twenty-two, he was an experienced portraitist, having painted Washington five years earlier. The young painter was at the zenith of his native style, a style which was to undergo what was not a thoroughly happy sophistication during his study in Europe two years later.

Among the earliest and most penetrating likenesses of Jefferson, this portrait played a more significant iconographic role during Jefferson's lifetime than any other portrait. Shortly after its completion, it became the prototype of a widely distributed series of American and European engravings. The American public received its first visual image through these engravings of the man they were twice to choose as president.

Peale's arresting portrait thus served as an important and convincing piece of political propaganda. No portrait of Jefferson, with the exception of that painted in 1805 by Gilbert Stuart (which later eclipsed that of Peale in the public mind) seems to have been so frequently copied. This was, in fact, so thoroughly the image of Jefferson impressed upon the senses of the American people

during his lifetime that political cartoonists copied its lineaments in order to make the Jefferson of their satires immediately recognizable. It was the ultimate source of the French and English image of the man who, next to Franklin, most nearly symbolized the New World in the eyes of the Old.

While the image proliferated and persisted, the original portrait was

neglected. After the holdings of the Peale Museum in Baltimore were dispersed, its location and identity became hazy. By the late nineteenth century, scholars began a search for the original which was not successful until 1959, when the portrait discovered as the property of the Peabody Institute of the city of Baltimore was recognized as the long sought-after life portrait of 1800. A.B.

JEFFERSON, TOURIST

While Jefferson lived in Paris as minister plenipotentiary to the court of Louis XVI, he made three notable trips. In 1786, John Adams invited him to England on diplomatic affairs. The following year he made a tour of southern France and northern Italy. In 1788, the year before he returned to the United States, he again joined Adams in The Hague to participate in negotiations for a loan from Dutch bankers to underwrite the new American government, returning to Paris by way of Germany.

The environs of Paris itself provided almost daily opportunities and temptations for Jefferson's boundless curiosity. The steady stream of American visitors—John Trumbull, Charles Bulfinch, the William Binghams from Philadelphia, young Thomas Shippen and John Rutledge, Jr., to whom he sent his famous "Hints to Americans Travelling in Europe"—all record their gratitude for the enthusiastic help their knowledgeable and sophisticated guide provided.

In the summer of 1786, Richard Cosway, the fashionable English portrait painter, and his beautiful artist wife arrived in Paris about the same time that Trumbull made his first visit. The Cosways were introduced into the Jefferson circle, and with the painter, Mme Vigée-Lebrun, M d'Hancarville, the archaeologist, and various other French friends, the group orbited through the city and countryside. "I distinctly recollect," Trumbull later wrote, "that this time was occupied with the same industry in examining and reviewing whatever related to the arts, and that Mr. Jefferson joined our party almost daily and here commenced his acquaintance with Mrs. Cosway."

Jefferson's famous and remarkable love letter "Head and Heart" records the depth of Jefferson's entanglement with the "golden-haired, languishing beauty" Maria Cosway, who adored the excursions Jefferson mapped out to romantic spots such as royal parks, "the bowers of Marly" and the folly of the Désert de Retz. "The wheels of time moved on with a rapidity, of which those of our carriage gave but a faint idea," Jefferson recalled, and begged his heart to "paint to me the day we went to St. Germains. How beautiful was every object."

On September 18, 1786, Jefferson dislocated his wrist, "trying to leap over a large kettle in a small courtyard," bringing to an end the romantic travels. The trip to southern France the following spring in fact was made on the advice of doctors who recommended the waters of Aix-en-Provence as a cure for the injured arm. Jefferson and Mrs. Cosway continued to correspond after she and her husband returned to London, and the following year she came once again to Paris but the idyll of the previous year was not recaptured.

The trip to southern France and Italy was one of the great experiences of Jefferson's five years in Europe. Through Burgundy, along the Languedoc Canal and in the ports of Bordeaux and Marseilles, he studied and noted endless details of farming, wine production, commerce and transportation systems, with an eye toward their practical application in America.

At the Château de L'Aye-Epinaye he saw that "delicious morsel of sculpture" the Diana and Endymion group by M. A. Slodtz. And as he moved further south, the array of antique ruins at Orange and Nîmes caught his enthusiastic eye. "I am immersed in antiquities from morning to night," he wrote Mme de Tessé. "Here I sit, Madame," he continued, "gazing whole hours at the Maison Carrée, like a lover at his mistress . . . I have been nourished on the remains of Roman grandeur."

On April 13, 1787, Jefferson crossed the Alps from Nice into Italy for "a peep into Eylisium." It was a short visit, limited to the north and including the major cities of, Turin, Milan and Genoa. "In architecture, painting and sculpture, I found much amusement," he wrote to George Wythe, but the primary objective was to study the methods of rice production for possible use in South Carolina.

Beginning with his first youthful fantasies on laying out the grounds of Monticello, Jefferson had developed an abiding interest in gardening and landscape design. Thomas Whately's *Observations on Modern Gardening* was one of the first books he acquired on the subject. In the company of John Adams and with Whately's work as a guide, the two future presidents decided to travel "into the country of some of the most celebrated gardens" during Jefferson's brief visit to England in 1786. Chiswick, Stowe, Painshill, Moor Park, Blenheim and William Shenstone's famous Leasowes were some of the high points. "The gardening in that country," Jefferson later wrote to his old classmate, John Page, of Rosewell, "is the article in which it surpasses all the earth."

The memories and inspirations of Jefferson's European travels constantly recurred to him when he returned to America, and influenced his plans for the new federal city of Washington, the public buildings of Richmond, the remodeling of Monticello and finally the building of his greatest masterpiece, the University of Virginia. The experience of the eye and of the heart during those five years were to profoundly shape his vision of what he hoped the New Republic would demonstrate in its public buildings, monuments, cities and universities, transforming the best that Europe had to offer to serve the ideals of the American experiment. w.h.a.

339 Thomas Jefferson

JOHN TRUMBULL 1756–1843
Miniature in oil on board 1788

Lent by the Instituto "Maria SS. Bambina," Lodi

John Trumbull spent two months of the winter of 1787–1788 as a guest in Jefferson's Paris residence, the Hôtel de Langeac, painting portraits of the French officers for his depiction of the surrender at Yorktown, and also the portrait of his host onto the canvas of the original version of his *Declaration of Independence*. It was early in this Paris stay that Trumbull introduced Jefferson to two painters from London, Richard and Maria Cosway, and thus set in motion the celebrated struggle between Jefferson's "Head and . . . Heart." The Lodi miniature is a replica painted expressly for Maria Cosway from the life portrait in Trumbull's *Declaration*. Mrs. Cosway had asked Jefferson, just after Trumbull's return to London early in March 1788, to give the painter "leave to make a Coppy." This miniature and another taken from the original by Angelica Schuyler Church were in their hands by July 1788. That September William Short, knowing of these two replicas, suggested that Trumbull "do a very clever gallant thing": *"Send a copy of the same to Miss Jefferson."* Thus three replicas of the miniature were made that year. But the earliest of these, the Lodi miniature, is painted with a freedom granted only a confident painter while executing a commission for another artist whose work he admired. It is also the work of a painter clearly aware of the remarkable attachments between Jefferson and Mrs. Cosway.

Not only does this miniature commemorate the most extraordinary friendship of Jefferson's life, it also immediately brings to mind the familiar life portrait—Jefferson with unpowdered hair, in the costume of the earlier decade, towering above his associates in the presentation of the Declaration of Independence—the preeminent icon of Jefferson's imposing position in the birth of the nation. A.B.

40 Maria Cosway

RICHARD COSWAY 1742–1821
oil on canvas
74.9 x 47 (29½ x 18½)
Lent by the Cincinnati Art Museum

Jefferson's close friendship with Maria Cosway is one of the most charming and yet strangest episodes of his Parisian years and indeed of his entire life. True, he was clearly susceptible to youth and beauty, and his friends in Paris must have included many pretty women like Mme de Tott and Angelica Schuyler Church, yet for none did he show the intensity of feeling contained in his famous letter to Maria Cosway, a dialogue between the "Head" and the "Heart." Nothing in Jefferson's past prepares us for this romantic incident in his career.

In August 1786 Jefferson met Maria Cosway and her husband through John Trumbull at the Halle aux Bleds which he visited to gather ideas for a public market in Richmond. The attraction must have been immediate, a combination of Maria's golden hair, slender figure, musical voice, intelligence and sophistication, for Jefferson immediately canceled a dinner engagement, pleading the sudden arrival of some urgent dispatches. Instead, he went with his new friends to St. Cloud and then to Ruggieri's pleasure garden, "and if the day had been as long as a Lapland summer day . . . we would still have found means . . . to have filled it." There followed an idyllic interlude in Jefferson's life when he saw the Cosways, and especially Maria, nearly every day, and they made excursions to places near Paris: "St. Germain. How beautiful was every object! the Port de Neuilly, the hills along the Seine, the rainbows of the machine de Marly, the terras of St. Germains, the chateaux, the gardens, the statues of Marly, the pavillon of Lucienne. Recollect too Madrid, the Bagetelle, the King's garden, the Dessert . . . every object wore it's liveliest hue!" Unfortunately these pleasure trips were interrupted when Jefferson fell and dislocated his wrist and was confined indoors. Shortly afterward, the Cosways left for Brussels, and in spite of his pain Jefferson insisted on going to say goodbye. A few days later he wrote that extraordinary letter to Maria Cosway, a "Dialogue between my Head and my Heart." It is written in an exalted mood, almost as if Jefferson were "high," and it probably tells as much as we shall ever know about the relationship between the two, as well as providing fascinating insights to Jefferson's personality. The attraction of a younger woman to a middle-aged

man, and Jefferson was then forty-three, is of course not surprising, and Maria Cosway's looks and accomplishments had already gathered many admirers around her. The underlying passion Jefferson felt comes through in his grief at their parting: "I am indeed the most wretched of all earthly beings. Overwhelmed with grief, every fibre of my frame distended beyond it's natural powers to bear, I would willingly meet whatever catastrophe should leave me no more to feel or to fear." The pleasure of her company is evoked: "In the evening, when one took a retrospect of the day, what a mass of happiness had we travelled over!" Yet there is no hint of impropriety or shared complicity. As a gentleman, Jefferson's sense of honor would have prevented him from deceiving the lady's husband, who in any case must have sometimes chaperoned them, or they would have had Trumbull's company. The tone of Parisian society would not have been any bar to such a liaison, quite the contrary, but Jefferson carried with him when he crossed the Atlantic a more rigorous code of conduct, and he often contrasted unfavorably the morals of the French with those in America.

Even had he been tempted, it is unlikely he would have met with much response, because Maria, although no doubt flattered by the obvious admiration of such a distinguished man, had already survived several London seasons and knew how to keep her heart to herself. Her religious nature, which eventually led her to settle in a convent, would also have been a check to anything more serious than a mild flirtation. At the end of the letter we are still left wondering which speaker represents Jefferson's true thought and feelings. Is it the man of reason extolling the intellectual pleasure and maintaining that "the most effectual means of being secure against pain is to retire within ourselves, and to suffice for our own happiness. Those, which depend on ourselves, are the only pleasures a wise man will count on"? Or is it the man of sensibility: "And what more sublime delight than to mingle tears with one whom the hand of heaven hath smitten! To watch over the bed of sickness, and to beguile it's tedious and it's painful moments"? In this dichotomy between thought and feeling, head and heart, Jefferson shows himself to be a man of his time, when the age of reason merged with the romantic movement. On balance, the argument seems to come down on the side of the heart which has the last word. That can be explained by the emotional shock of falling in love, which jolted this normally rational man out of his habitual reliance on

his intellect alone.

Maria Cosway, to judge from the many portraits of her, was a very beautiful woman, and with her looks were united artistic and musical talents. Her paintings and drawings were exhibited at the Royal Academy, and she gave concerts at her London house. She was born in Florence in 1759 of English Roman Catholic parents and came to London after studying art in Italy. Soon afterward in 1781 she married Richard Cosway, the fashionable miniaturist, and while it was probably a marriage of convenience, Maria made him a good wife. In her later years she lived abroad, first in Lyon and then in Lodi, where she died in 1838, superintending a school for girls.

Jefferson was to see Maria Cosway again in Paris in 1787, and they corresponded intermittently for many years; but the great warmth of their first meeting was never recaptured and their friendship declined into pleasant memories of the past. R.W.

Merit" to the success of her art. "Had Mr. C. [Cosway] permitted me to rank professionally I should have made a better painter but left to myself by degrees instead of improving I lost what I had brought from Italy of my early studies."

It is interesting that both Jefferson and Maria Cosway should end their days supervising the educational establishments they had founded. He wrote to her in 1822: "The sympathies of our earlier days harmonize, it seems, in age also. You retire to your college of Lodi and nourish the natural benevolence of your excellent heart by communicating your own virtues to the young of your sex . . . I am laying the foundation of an University in my native state, which I hope will repay the liberalities of its legislature by improving the virtue and science of their country, already blest with a soil and climate emulating those of your favorite Lodi." R.W.

341 Maria Cosway

RICHARD COSWAY 1742–1821
Pen c. 1785
30.5 x 22 (13¾ x 8⅝)

Lent by the Instituto "Maria SS. Bambina," Lodi

As with the portrait of her husband (no. 343), the drawing of Maria Cosway would seem to be preparatory to an engraving. She is shown with the attributes of her art, the palette and brushes, a book of drawings and a statue of Minerva, while the organ makes a reference to her musical talents. Both portraits date from about 1785, when the Cosways' house in Pall Mall was a fashionable center and Maria was described as a "golden-haired, languishing Anglo-Italian, graceful to affectation, and highly accomplished, especially in music." Growing up in Florence, she had the advantage of studying major

collections of paintings, and according to herself, Zoffany, who was then working on his view of the *Tribuna*, gave her instruction. She also visited Rome and knew Batoni, Mengs, Fuseli and other leading artists. From the time of her marriage in 1781 until 1789, Maria Cosway exhibited almost every year at the Royal Academy, her subjects usually being portraits or illustrations to literature. After the birth of her child she spent long periods on the continent because of declining health, and while in Paris worked on *A Description of the Louvre*. Mrs. Cosway was never a professional artist, and she looked on her talent as a graceful social accomplishment which could be used to advance her position in the world and her husband's career. As she said herself, "the novelty and my Age Contributed more than the real

342 Mrs. Cosway and Her Daughter

JOHN RAPHAEL SMITH 1752–1812
Black chalk with touches of red chalk
26.7 x 21.6 (10½ x 8½)

From the Collection of Mr. and Mrs. Paul Mellon

The Cosways' only child, Louisa Paolina Angelica, was born in 1789 and died in 1796. From the age of the child in the drawing, the portrait must have been done shortly before her death. Her mother spent much of her time on the continent, so Smith must have taken the opportunity of one of her infrequent visits to England. The child was regarded as something of a prodigy and could read Hebrew before she read English. Her mother took the girl's death badly and according to Horace Walpole was "so afflicted that she shut herself up in her chamber and would not be seen." While the identification of the subjects is not documented, the features of the woman sewing agree with undoubted portraits of Mrs. Cosway.

In 1794, when Maria Cosway returned to London, she wrote to Jefferson after a lapse of some years, "I have found a pretty little girl, I hope she will make some comfort, she shows natural talent & a good soft disposition." If Jefferson heard of the child's death from her mother, the letter has been lost, and it was in a letter to Angelica Church that he wrote: "We have with us a Mr. Niemcewitz, a Polish gentleman who was with us in Paris when Mrs. Cosway was and who was of her society in London last summer. He mentions the loss of her daughter, and the gloom which that and other circumstances had thrown her, that it has taken the hue of religion, that she is solely devoted to religious exercises and superintendent of a school she has instituted for Catholic children, but that she still speaks of her friends here with tenderness and desire. Our letters have been rare but they have let me see that her gayety was gone and her mind entirely placed on the world to come." R.W.

343 Self-Portrait

RICHARD COSWAY 1742–1821
Pen c. 1785
27 x 18 (10⅝ x 7⅛)

Lent by the Instituto "Maria SS. Bambina," Lodi

This carefully done drawing was presumably made for an engraving, but no example has survived. The similarity in size and style would suggest that it is a companion to the drawing of Maria Cosway (no. 341). Richard Cosway, although small and ugly, was extremely vain and always dressed in the height of fashion. He was fond of portraying himself in romantic costume based on the self-portrait of Rubens, whose bust, together with that of Michaelangelo, has been placed on the balustrade. It is not perhaps accidental that the same costume is used in a miniature of the Prince of Wales, Cosway's chief patron.

Although Cosway accompanied his wife to Paris in 1786, when they met Jefferson, he was too busy with his own business to do much sightseeing, and he seems to have accepted the admiration the American minister showed for Maria Cosway with complacence, no doubt understanding the innocent nature of the romance. Jefferson always treated him with politeness, and Cosway's name appears in the formal greetings of the letters between Maria and her admirer. R.W.

344 Self-Portrait

JOHN TRUMBULL 1756–1843
Oil on canvas 1777
75.5 x 60.3 (29¾ x 23¾)
Inscribed on back: *John Trumbull Ipse pinxit aestat 21*

Lent by the Museum of Fine Arts, Boston, Bequest of George Nixon Black

In the artist's manuscript "Account of Paintings," this *Self-Portrait* is listed under the heading of "Lebanon" as number 28, "Portrait of myself, headsize, July 1777, given to Miss Tyler."

Trumbull, the first college graduate in America to become a professional artist, had charged out William Hogarth's *Analysis of Beauty* from the Harvard library when he attended the college during 1772–1773. In this early *Self-Portrait* he pays homage to the artist on whom he "leaned"; seated as if before an easel, Trumbull portrays himself with his palette not only arranged according to Hogarth's recommendation (pl. 24, fig. 1) but actually resting on Hogarth's book.

Trumbull's Harvard days had also brought him in touch with John Singleton Copley and his paintings.

The *Self-Portrait* shows the influence of Copley in the conception and placement of the figure: as in Copley's *Paul Revere*, also a half-length, the subject is linked with his métier. The light comes from the left, casting the right side in shadow. Trumbull, like Revere, glances straight out, the direction of his gaze at an angle from the set of his head; a half-smile lurks around the mouth and the expression in each face is ambiguous and introspective. Trumbull did not have Copley's command of tonal subtleties, however, and a certain archaic hardness is thus evident in this work, painted before the artist's first trip to England, where under the tutelage of Benjamin West, he would learn to loosen his brushstroke and soften his contours. I.B.J.

and then, after the wars, to Italy—a tour recorded with a Jeffersonian precision of observation, feeling, and title in his *Notes on Italy*, 1831. C.S.

346 Joel Barlow

JEAN-ANTOINE HOUDON
1741–1828
Plaster 1803
58.4 (23) high
Signed under right shoulder: *houdon an XII*. Inscribed under left shoulder: *J. Barlow 50 ans*

Lent by the Pennsylvania Academy of Fine Arts, Philadelphia

345 William Short with the Temple of Paestum in the Background

REMBRANDT PEALE 1778–1860
Oil on canvas 1806
77.5 x 63.8 (30½ x 25⅛)

Lent by The College of William and Mary in Virginia

William Short, Jefferson's young kinsman and informally adopted son, had returned to Philadelphia in 1804. Soon after his arrival he was elected a member of the American Philosophical Society, a recognition of scholarly interests and achievement which was accorded at the same time to the young Prussian nobleman, Alexander von Humboldt, also home-bound from travels abroad.

Rembrandt Peale's portrait of Short shows him at forty-seven years of age, a gentleman of leisure and charm, retired from diplomatic honors won in France, the Netherlands and Spain. Rembrandt Peale, who had painted Jefferson the year before, was twenty-eight, still dreaming of conquests in art. He had been in England five years before, but the outbreak of war had prevented his crossing to France. One can imagine the conversation between painter and subject, Short responding to the younger man's enthusiasm as,

years before, he had responded to Jefferson's. Traveling farther than Jefferson was able to do, Short had written back to Paris in detail on matters as wide-ranging as the manufacture of macaroni, the excavation of ancient ruins, or what he had called "that chef d'oeuvre of modern architecture," Saint Peter's at Rome where he "felt then if I ever did the force of the true sublime."

Behind Jefferson's studies of nature and history lay the sturdy rationalism of the eighteenth century, but in these younger men romanticism was the stronger element, and it fills this portrait. The background reflects the conversation and the mood of the work, with the great temple at Paestum, filling the whole, not as an architectural study but as an expression of the awesome presence of the past. The little figure, gesturing wildly at the right, strikes an accent to the temple's enormous size, and at left another small figure of a man seated on a fallen block of stone speaks for contemplation. That block is still there today.

Certainly, Rembrandt Peale's longing to return to Europe had much stimulation here. He did, in fact, return three times, twice to France

Joel Barlow, who was a poet as well as a statesman and liberal thinker, lived in Europe for seventeen years between 1788 and 1805. During the years 1790 to 1792 he resided in London, where he was a friend of Thomas Paine. In 1792 he moved to Paris and in 1795 was appointed the American consul to Algiers. In 1805 he returned to America but returned to France as American minister in 1811. He died suddenly in 1812 while on a trip to Poland.

As soon as Barlow arrived in Paris in 1788, he called on Jefferson and spent the fourth of July with him. He left on a trip to England nine days later and made a point of visiting Pope's garden, which Jefferson had seen on his tour with John Adams in April 1786 and about which Barlow had a great deal to say in his Journal: "[It] is in the truest English style of gardening, rather more solemn and gloomy than what is common, but perfectly in harmony with the turn of mind that most distinguishes the planter" and "There is as much real taste discovered here as in any of his [Pope's] writings." On the following fourth of July 1789, ten days before the fall of the Bastille, Barlow was present at the farewell dinner marking the approaching end of Jefferson's term as minister. And it was probably Barlow who authored the congratulatory address offered the host: "As this is the anniversary of our Independence, our sensations of pleasure are much increased from the idea that we are addressing ourselves to a man who sustained so conspicuous a part in the immortal transactions of that day—."

Barlow kept in touch with Jefferson and in 1801 wrote him of his intention to devote his life to the improvement of America. Jefferson wrote back that, "Mr. Madison and myself have cut out a piece of work for you, which is to write the history of the United States, from the close of the war downwards. We are rich ourselves in materials and can open all the public archives to you; but your residence

here is essential because a great deal of the knowledge of things is not on paper but only within ourselves." He even had singled out a house for Barlow in Washington: "a lovely seat . . . on a high hill commanding a most extensive view of the Potomac." This was Kalorama, which Barlow later bought.

When the Barlows finally arrived in New York in August 1805, Jefferson urged them to come directly to Virginia: "The mountains among which I live will offer you as cool a retreat as can anywhere be found." But it was not until 1808 that Barlow visited Monticello.

Barlow was greatly interested in education. In September 1800 he wrote to Jefferson proposing that a national university, for which Washington had left a bequest, be put in motion. Jefferson was enthusiastic and Barlow produced his innovative *Prospectus of a National Institution*, with features far ahead of its time.

Barlow was a man of parts, interested also in science, as his long friendship with Fulton (see no. 108) and his involvement with Fulton's experiments indicate. He was elected to the American Philosophical Society in 1809, and he was a friend of Charles Willson Peale, who painted Barlow's portrait for his painting *Temple of Wisdom* and displayed a copy of the *Columbiad* in the Peale Museum.

In the Salon of 1804, Year 13 of the Republic, Houdon exhibited plasters of Joel Barlow and Robert Fulton, designated simply as "Monsieurs Barlow et Fulton." A plaster of Barlow was in the sale of Houdon's estate in 1828. The Pennsylvania Academy plaster exhibited here appeared in the supplement to the catalogue of the Academy's exhibition of 1812 as "a ust of Joel Barlow, Esquire, done in Paris by Houdon." It has been in the academy ever since, though there is no information concerning the donor of the bust. Coincidentally, Barlow died on December 24, 1812. The inclusion by Houdon of Barlow's name and age in the form on this bust is most unusual and might have been done at the request of the subject.

There is a cliché in Houdon scholarship that his portraits declined in quality during his later years. This is negated by the late, great portraits of Necker, Mirabeau, Barthélémy and Napoleon. The portrait of Joel Barlow is one of the finest of the late studies. Barlow is portrayed as a massive, powerful and even belligerent individual with frowning eyes, compressed mouth and jutting chin. The severe cut of his coat and simple cravat suggest the new democratic ideal, in which America had, since the accession of Napoleon, taken the leadership.

A marble bust of Barlow by Houdon has been in the Barlow family continuously until it was recently acquired by the White House. This bust has no signature date but is of extremely high quality. Ten plasters were made from it in 1912 and given to different museums, both in the United States and in Europe. H.H.A.

347 John Adams
MATHER BROWN 1761–1831
Oil on canvas 1788
95.2 x 69.2 (34½ x 27¼)

Lent by the Boston Athenaeum

John Adams and Jefferson first met in Philadelphia at the Continental Congress in 1775, where they developed mutual respect for each other's aims and intellect. This friendship was renewed and greatly strengthened in the summer of 1784, when Jefferson joined Adams and Franklin in Paris to negotiate treaties of amity and commerce with various European countries. After more than seven months of work and sociability, Jefferson gave a candid but affectionate assessment of his friend to James Madison: "He is vain, irritable and a bad calculator of the force and probable effect of the motives which govern men. This is all the ill which can possibly be said of him: he is profound in his views: and accurate in his judgment except where knowledge of the world is necessary to form a judgment. He is so amiable, that I pronounce that you will love him if ever you become acquainted with him."

When Adams, as minister to the court of St. James, pressed Jefferson to come to London in the spring of 1786 to negotiate with the ambassador to Tripoli, Jefferson took the opportunity to travel through parts of England. After spending two days seeing nearby sights at Twickenham, Painshill, Woburn Farm, and Hampton Court, Jefferson joined Adams on April 4 for an extended tour of English gardens—Chiswick, the Leasowes, Stowe, Caversham and Blenheim—with a sampling of towns such as Birmingham, Worcester and Stratford-on-Avon. While Jefferson compared what he saw to Thomas Whatley's descriptions in *Observations on Modern Gardening*, Adams reserved his pen for historic sites and examples of ostentation. At Worcester Adams found the people appearing "so ignorant and careless" that he was provoked to ask, "And do Englishmen so soon forget the ground where liberty was fought for?" While aware of the elegance and beauty in architecture, painting and sculpture exhibited in the various private estates, Adams commented sardonically on its cause and cost: "A national debt of two hundred and

seventy-four millions sterling accumulated by jobs, contracts, salaries, and pensions in the course of a century might easily produce all this magnificence. The pillars, obelisks, &c., erected in honor of kings, queens and princesses might procure the means."

Back in London, Jefferson continued his sightseeing at the Tower of London and such gardens as those of Moor Park and Kew. On April 20, he accompanied the Adams family on a trip to Osterley and Syon House. Jefferson was impressed by his English travels, noting that "the gardening in England is the article in which it surpasses all the earth."

While in London, Jefferson commissioned his own portrait from Mather Brown, perhaps at Adams' suggestion. By the fall, when he had determined on a portrait of Adams for his collection of "principal American characters," he again chose to commission Brown. Adams was not able to sit for the second portrait until the spring of 1788. In this portrait Adams is depicted in the style of a *portrait d'apparat*, in which he is shown poised with pen and paper, Jefferson's *Notes on the State of Virginia* prominently displayed on his left. Brown shows a somewhat serious and formal Adams at the close of his difficult but important years in Europe. The Adams family as well as the painter John Trumbull considered it an excellent likeness. The finished painting was sent to Jefferson in Paris.

The friendship between Jefferson and Adams, strained to the point of silence by the political rivalries of the 1790s, was not resumed until Dr. Benjamin Rush of Philadelphia effected a reconciliation in 1812. Jefferson reported to Rush that discovering that Adams still maintained a great affection for him was all he needed to "revive towards him all the affections of the most cordial moment of our lives." From that date a rich, profound and unique corrrespondence developed between the two aging statesmen as they pondered past history and the role they had played in it.

A letter from you calls up recollections very dear to my mind. It carries me back to the times when, beset with difficulties and dangers, we were fellow-laborers in the same cause, struggling for what is the most valuable to man, his right of self-government. Laboring always at the same oar, with some wave ever ahead threatening to overwhelm us, and yet passing harmless under our bark, we knew not how we rode through the storm with heart and hand, and made a happy port,

wrote Jefferson to Adams in 1812. G.V.

348 Abigail Adams

RALPH EARLE? 1751–1801
Oil on canvas c. 1785
85.1 x 73 (33½ x 28¾)

*Lent by the New York State Historical
Association, Cooperstown*

Abigail Adams (1744–1818) was the
wife of John Adams and the mother
of John Quincy Adams. A remarkable
and resolute woman, she maintained
a correspondence throughout her life
that gives a continuous view of her
convictions and principles as well as a
vivid description of day-to-day living
during the American Revolution and
the early years of the United States.
Born in Weymouth, Massachusetts,
where her father, the Reverend
William Smith, was the minister of
the Congregational Church, Abigail
married Adams in 1764. She remained
in Massachusetts during the
Revolution, while her husband was
first in Philadelphia, then in Europe.
Traveling to join him in the summer
of 1784, she settled into a large and
elegant house in Auteuil, a small
village outside Paris near Passy where
Franklin lived. Jefferson was to be
a frequent visitor and became a close
friend of Abigail's. In a letter to a
friend in 1785, she pronounced him
to be "one of the choice ones of the
earth."

Together the two Adamses and
Jefferson explored and experienced
Paris in the final days of the Ancien
Régime. They dined together weekly,
often including a small, select circle of
acquaintances comprising members of
the American legation, the abbés de
Mably, Arnoux and Chalut, and the
marquis and marquise de Lafayette.
The three also went to the theater
and opera, while Jefferson invited the
Adamses on at least one occasion to
dine with him and attended a masked
ball lasting all night. In addition he
introduced them to his beloved
concerts spirituel, given in the magnificent Hall of the French Comedians
in the northern pavilion of the
Tuileries. In March 1785 Jefferson
and the entire Adams family were
invited by the marquise de Lafayette
to sit in her family tribune above
the choir in the great cathedral of
Notre Dame, to witness the rare
ceremony of the king assisting in a
Te Deum sung in celebration of the
birth of a royal prince.

With Adams' appointment as
minister to the court of St. James
and the family's removal to London
in May 1785, Jefferson initiated a
correspondence with Abigail. At
times light and bantering, at times
somewhat philosophical, the letters
show the sincere affection and friendship that developed between them
over the months in Paris.

The reunion of the Adamses and
Jefferson in New York in 1790 made
correspondence unnecessary, but
unlike the wealth of details available
on their earlier association, information on their friendship does not exist
after this date. Growing political
differences climaxing in Jefferson's
election to the presidency ended all
contact with Abigail until she was
moved to break the silence following
the death of Jefferson's daughter,
Maria Eppes, in 1804. As a child,
Polly, as Maria was then called, had
been confided to Abigail's care in
London on her way from America to
join Jefferson in Paris. Following
her death, there followed a candid
exchange between Abigail and
Jefferson, unknown to Adams,
explaining and justifying much of the
mutual distrust. Abigail ended the
correspondence after an exchange of
seven letters and never seems to have
forgiven Jefferson in the manner that
her husband was to do eight years
later.

In 1784 Mather Brown wrote with
youthful exuberance about his newly
launched painting career in England:
"I will let them see if an obscure
Yankey Boy cannot shine as great as
any of them." He added that his
main objective would be "to get my
name established and to get Commissions from America, to paint their
Friends and Relations here." With
this in mind, he asked Adams for
permission to paint his portrait.
Adams agreed, and writing to her
brother, John Quincy Adams, young
Abigail reported on three family
portraits recently completed by
Brown: "By the way, I must not omit
to tell you, that a rage for Painting
has taken Possession of the Whole
family, one of our rooms has been
occupied by a Gentleman of this
profession, for near a fortnight, and
we have the extreme felicity of
looking at ourselves upon Canvass."
After discussing the portrait of her
father (now lost) and herself (now in
the Adams National Historic Site,
Quincy), she added that Brown had
taken "a good likeness of Mamma,
too."

Identified as Abigail Adams in 1948,
this portrait bears little stylistic
similarity to Brown's work. The
signature "R. Earl Pinxit" appears to
be of doubtful authenticity, as it was
added on top of the varnish, probably
at a later date. Stylistically, however,
the attribution to Earle seems plausible,
although historically it is difficult to
prove. An American loyalist banished
from Connecticut during the Revolution, Earle was in England from
1776, but returned to the United
States in May 1785, the month

Abigail arrived in London from Paris.
Abigail makes no mention of having
her portrait painted during her brief
stay in London in 1784, when she
visited Copley to see the portrait of
her husband. Earle had settled in
northwestern Connecticut by 1788,
when the Adams returned to Massachusetts. As there is no known
opportunity for Earle to have painted
the portrait from life, and no mention
of Earle or a portrait by him in the
Adams family correspondence, the
portrait may be a copy of Brown's
lost original. The identity of the
painter must remain unknown at
present. However, it seems fairly
indisputable that the portrait
represents Abigail as a mature woman
about the time of her stay in
Europe. G.V.

349 The Amphitheater at Nîmes

WILLIAM MARLOW 1740–1813
Watercolor
33.6 x 51.4 (13¼ x 20¼)
Signed bottom left: W. M.

From the Collection of Mr. and Mrs. Paul Mellon

In February 1787, Jefferson, who the previous fall had dislocated his wrist, "by the advice of my Surgeons set out . . . for the waters of Aix-en-Provence. I chose these out of several proposed to me, because if they fail to be effectual, my journey will not be useless altogether. It will give me an opportunity of examining the canal of Languedoc and acquiring knowledge of that species of navigation which may be useful hereafter: but more immediately it will enable me to take the tour of the ports concerned in commerce with us, to examine on the spot the defects of the late regulations respecting our commerce, to learn the further improvements which may be made in it. . . ." There was also the attraction of the Roman remains in Provence, and on March 19, 1787, Jefferson found himself at Nîmes, where he spent four days. His journey gave him the first opportunity to see classical architecture, and the effect of being "nourished with the remains of Roman grandeur" was like heady wine. In his well-known letter to the comtesse de Tessé, Jefferson wrote: "From a correspondent at Nismes, you will not expect news. Were I to attempt to give you news, I should tell stories one thousand years old. I should detail to you the intrigues of the courts of the Caesars, how they affect us here, the oppressiveness of their praetors, prefects &c. I am immersed in antiquities from morning to night. For me the city of Rome is actually existing in all the splendors of it's empire."

The amphitheater at Nîmes dates from the second half of the first century A.D. and is particularly well preserved. Other views of Nîmes are to be found in the exhibition (see nos. 148, 350). R.W.

350 Nîmes from the Tour Magne

WILLIAM MARLOW 1740–1813
Pen, brown and gray ink, and watercolor
36.8 x 53.7 (14½ x 21⅛)
Signed lower left: W. Marlow.
Inscribed in center of contemporary wash-line mount: Nîmes

From the Collection of Mr. and Mrs. Paul Mellon

Jefferson's four days at Nîmes were among the most enjoyable of his tour

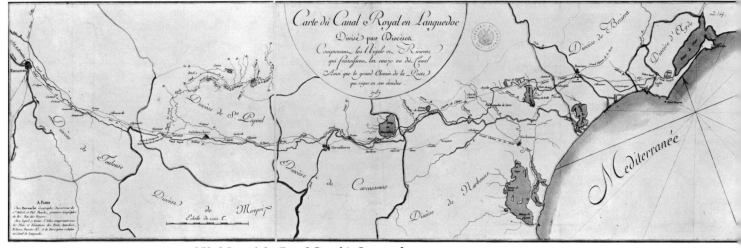

351 Map of the Royal Canal in Languedoc

of southern France, for the town was rich in Roman remains. "In Architecture nothing anywhere except the remains of antiquity. These are more in number, and less injured by time than I expected, and have been to me a great treat. Those at Nismes, both in dignity and preservation stand first," he wrote. This view of the Tour Magne or Turis Magna, which probably dates from the end of the second century B.C., also gives a good general picture of Nîmes with the Maison Carrée and the Amphitheater, in Jefferson's words "two of the most superb remains of the antiquity which exist. They deserve to be studied." However, antiquities did not take up all his time and attention. Always interested in agricultural details, and looking out for technical advances, he noted that the earth was full of limestone and that a grist mill worked by a steam engine was being built. In the advice he later gave to Shippen and Rutledge, Jefferson remembered "the name of the hotel I lodged at the first time I was there was, I think, le petit Louvre, a very good inn—the 2ᵈ time [May 9, on the way to Montpellier] I lodged at the Luxembourg, not so good.— The vin ordinaire here is excellent and costs but 2 or 3 sous a bottle. This is the cheapest place in France to buy silk stockings." Jefferson also found time to engage in political intrigue. He was asked by José de la Maia, a Brazilian, for help in a revolt against the Portuguese, but Jefferson gave only a cautious answer. He was generally sympathetic to the independence of South America from European rule but also realized the importance of Portuguese trade to the United States. R.W.

DEZAUCHE active late 18th century
Engraving 1787
Signed lower left: *A Paris. Chez Dezauche Géographe Successeur des Srs. Delisle et Phil. Ruache premiers Géographes du Roi, Rue des Noyers. Chez lequel se trouve l'Atlas comprenant tous les Plans et Elévations des Ponts, Aqueducs, Ecluses, Bassins &c et la Description relative au Canal de Languedoc*

Lent by the Library of Congress, Washington Papers

"I write to you, my dear Patsy, from the Canal of Languedoc, on which I am at present sailing, as I have been for a week past, cloudless skies above, limpid waters below, and on each hand a row of nightingales in full chorus. . . ." On the same day (May 21, 1787) that Jefferson penned these lines to his daughter, he assured William Short that of all the methods of traveling he had tried, this was the pleasantest. He had had his carriage dismounted from its wheels and placed on the deck of a light bark, and he was thus towed on the canal instead of the post road. "I walk the greater part of the way along the banks of the canal, level and lined with a double row of trees which furnish shade. When fatigued I take seat in my carriage where, as much at ease as in my study, I read, write, or observe. My carriage being of glass all round, admits a full view of all the varying scenes thro' which I am shifted, olives, figs, mulberries, vines, corn and pasture, villages and farms."

The Canal de Languedoc, or Canal du Midi, an inland waterway connecting France's Mediterranean and Atlantic ports, famed as a great feat of engineering, was built during the reign of Louis XIV by Pierre-Paul de Riquet (1604–1680), who died the year before its completion. It took

Jefferson nine days to cover the whole distance—"200 American miles, by water," as he estimated it—from Cette on the Mediterranean to Toulouse on the Garonne River, with a day's side trip on horseback into the Montagnes Noires to inspect the Bassin de Saint-Ferréol, one of the series of reservoirs that fed the main canal. While dreaming of naturalizing nightingales in Virginia, Jefferson made statistical memoranda on the canal: distances, depths, altitudes, traffic, vessels, bridges and locks. At Toulouse he gathered more data and discussed with M Pin his own idea for an improved lock gate: "a quadrantal gate turning on a pivot, and lifted like a pump handle, aided by a windlass and cord, if necessary."

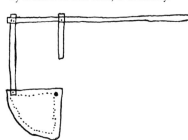

Canal navigation was a subject Jefferson had "much at heart." Even before leaving for Europe he had discussed with Washington, among others, the possibility of opening water communication between the Potomac, the Ohio, and Lake Erie. With this in mind Jefferson sent Washington copies of the memoranda he had compiled when proceeding along the Canal de Languedoc, with a copy of the Dezauche map—the same copy on display in the exhibition. In acknowledging Jefferson's "satisfactory account of the Canal of Languedoc," Washington added: "It gives me pleasure to be made acquainted with

the particulars of that stupendous work, tho' I do not expect to derive any but speculative advantages from it. When America will be able to embark in projects of such pecuniary extent, I know not; probably not for very many years to come—but it will be a good example and not without its uses, if we can carry our present undertakings happily into effect." H.C.R.

352 *Voyage pittoresque de la France: Description générale et particulière de la France* and *Ouvrage enrichi d'estampes* (Paris P.-D. Pierres, et al., 1781–1800)

JEAN-BENJAMIN DE LABORDE, et al.
Two of twelve volumes, text and plates
Lent by the Boston Athenaeum

The *Voyage pittoresque de la France,* planned and initiated by Jean-Benjamin de Laborde and pursued by such collaborators as Béguillet and Jean-Etienne Guettard, ranks with the abbé Saint-Non's *Voyage pittoresque . . . du Royaume de Naples et de* abbé Saint-Non's *Voyage pittoresque Sicile* and Choiseul-Gouffier's *Voyage pittoresque de la Grèce* as one of the great illustrated French books of the late eighteenth century. It was issued to subscribers in parts, the first *livraisons* appearing in 1781. The initial success of the enterprise depended to a great extent upon the wealthy bibliophiles and *amateurs* who were fated to be ruined or dispersed by the French Revolution. Publication thus lapsed in the 1790s, but a final attempt to revive and ontinue it was made c. 1800. As originally planned, it was to have been an encyclopedia and artistic inventory of all the French provinces. Though it never reached this goal, the twelve volumes and 450 or more plates faithfully mirror the appearance of the country, especially its architectural monuments, at the time of Jefferson's residence and travels in France. Paris, Ile-de-France, Normandy, Burgundy, Provence, are all well represented. Among the *lacunae* are Alsace, Brittany, and the châteaux de la Loire.

The drawings for the plates, executed for the most part in the 1780s, reveal the talents of such "little masters" as the Chevalier de Lespinasse, Jean-Baptiste Lallemand, Meunier, J.-J. Le Veau, and many others. Examples of these original drawings, generally done with the plan that an engraving would be made, have survived in such collections as the Musée Carnavalet and the Bibliothèque nationale's Cabinet des Estampes. Separate plates from the *Voyage* by such skillful engravers as Née, Masquelier and others, have long been part of the printsellers' stock-in-trade. Complete sets of the *Voyage pittoresque* are bound up in various sequences, some in order of the publication of the parts, others methodically rearranged according to the regions described and depicted.

Two volumes from the Boston Athenaeum copy are exhibited. Volume 8 is opened to the *Vue de la Fontaine de Vaucluse et des Environs,* engraved under Née's direction after a drawing by Genillion. Jefferson visited Vaucluse on May 8, 1787, during his tour in southern France, and noted in his diary: "The stream issuing from the fountain of Vaucluse is about 20. yards wide, 4. or 5. deep and of such rapidity that it could not be stemmed by a canoe. They are now mowing hay, and gathering mulberry leaves. The high mountains, just back of Vaucluse, are covered with snow. Fine trout in the stream of Vaucluse, and the valley abounds peculiarly with nightingales." "After visiting the tomb of Laura at Avignon," he wrote to his daughter Martha, "I went to see this fountain, a noble one of itself, and rendered forever famous by the songs of Petrarch who lived near it. I arrived there somewhat fatigued, and sat down by the fountain to repose myself. It gushes, of the size of a river, from a secluded valley of the mountain, the ruins of Petrarch's château being perched on a rock 200 feet perpendicular above. To add to the enchantment of the scene, every tree and bush was filled with nightingale's in full song."

353 The Interior of the Port of Marseilles, Seen from the Clock Tower in the Park

Volume 12 is opened to the *Vue de la Principale Entrée de la Ville d'Aix,* engraved by Née after a drawing by Meunier. A visit to Aix-en-Provence, in the hope that the mineral waters there might restore his dislocated wrist, was the ostensible reason for Jefferson's journey to southern France. But, after four days there (March 25–28, 1787) and "having taken 40. douches, without any sensible benefit," as he told William Short, "I thought it useless to continue them. My wrist strengthens slowly: it is to time I look as the surest remedy, and that I believe will restore it at length." Nevertheless, Jefferson found the town itself most attractive.

The man who shoots himself in the climate of Aix must be a bloody-minded fellow indeed.—I am now in the land of corn, wine, oil, and sunshine. What more can man ask of heaven? If I should happen to die in Paris I will beg of you to send me here, and have me exposed to the sun. . . . This city is one of the cleanest and neatest I have ever seen in any country. The streets are straight, from 20. to 100. feet wide, and as clean as a parlour floor. Where they are of width sufficient they have 1. 2. or 4. rows of elms from 100 to 150 years old, which make delicious walks.

H.C.R.

JOSEPH VERNET 1714–1789
Oil on canvas 1754
165 x 263 (65 x 103⅛)
Signed and dated at lower center:
peint par Joseph/ Vernet à Marseille/ en 1754

Lent by the Musée de la Marine, Paris

During his tour of southern France in 1787, Jefferson visited Marseilles from March 29 to April 6 and stopped there again on his return from Italy in May. His extended stay is explained by his desire to gather information on American trade while in this important trading port. He also hoped to find out more about the production of rice, much of which was shipped from Marseilles, and to see the machine used for husking, but in this he was disappointed and had to go on to Italy. Meanwhile he had made observations in his notebook on olives, figs, grapes and other useful plants, and hoped to become "acquainted with a well-informed gardener whom I expect to find among the most precious of my acquaintance. From men of that class I have derived the most satisfying information in the course of my journey and have sought their acquaintance with as much industry as I have avoided that of others who would have made me waste my time on good dinners and good society."

In 1753 Louis XV ordered Joseph Vernet, who had returned from Italy the preceding year, to paint views of the principal seaports of France. In October of the same year, M de Marigny, *surintendent des bâtiments,* drew up the "*projet d'itineraire pour M. Vernet, peintre du Roi, pour les Marines,*" an itinerary for the artist to follow which specified the points of view and the compositions of the paintings, and stipulated that these paintings should be executed on the site.

The series of French ports was to include twenty-four paintings, each measuring 165 x 263 cm. and depicting Monaco, Antibes, Toulon (three views), Marseilles (two views), Bandol, Cette, Bayonne, Bordeaux (two views, see no. 354), Rochefort, Aix-en-Provence (two views), Saint-Malo, le Havre, Calais and Dunkerque. But at the request of the painter, tired of the constant travel and unhappy with the remunerations which he found to be insufficient, this number was reduced to fifteen. The artist was paid 6000 livres for each of these paintings, the dates of which fall between 1753 and 1765. As they were completed, the Ports of France were exhibited at the Salons where they were enormously popular with the public as well as the critics.

Vernet began his series with Marseilles, his preferred city; he stayed

354 View of the City and the Port of Bordeaux Taken from the Side of the Saltworks

JOSEPH VERNET 1714–1789
Oil on canvas 1758
165 x 263 (65 x 103⅛)
Signed at lower left: *peint par Joseph Vernet à Bordeaux*

Lent by the Musée de la Marine, Paris

there from October 1753 until September 1754 to paint (as his contract stipulated) one exterior view and one interior view of this port. *The Interior of the Port of Marseilles* is the second painting of the series. It was executed as a pendant to the *View of the Entrance to the Port of Marseilles, Taken from the Mountain Called Tête de More*. The Salon catalogue gives some explanation of what the artist was trying to achieve: "Since it is in this port that the greatest commerce with the East and Italy is carried on, the author has enriched this painting with figures from different seafaring nations of the East, Barbary, Africa and others. All the characteristics of a merchant port with far-reaching commercial trade are gathered together." It is interesting to examine the anecdotes painted by Vernet in the foreground of the painting: along the wharf, where the merchandise is stacked, walks a motley crowd in which one recognizes the governor himself, accompanied by ladies and by *abbés*, who served as a guide to the artist and identified for him the different nationalities, foreign costumes and other details. It might be said that the *Interior of the Port of Marseilles* is not so much a marine painting as it is a genre scene. A.B. de L.

The agriculture practised in the neighborhood of Bordeaux, particularly that of the vineyards, was of primary interest to Jefferson during his visit in May 1787. American trading considerations were undoubtedly one reason for his copious notes on the produce of the area, but as always Jefferson had a keen eye out for techniques which could be imported with benefit to the New World.

"The celebrated vineyards . . . are plains," he wrote in his "Notes of a Tour into the Southern Parts of France." "The soil of Hautbrion particularly, which I examined, is a sand, in which is near as much round gravel . . . and a very little loam: and this is the general soil of Medoc." Almost a quarter of a century later, on the eve of the War of 1812, Jefferson must have remembered his visit to the Bordeaux wine country as he wrote to a fellow Virginian interested in viticulture:

I formerly believed it was best for every country to make what it could make to best advantage, and to exchange it with others for those articles which it could not so well make. I did not then suppose that a whole quarter of the globe could within the short space of a dozen years, from being the most civilized, become the most savage portion of the human race. . . . We must endeavor to make every thing we want within ourselves, and have as little intercourse as possible with Europe in it's present demoralized state. wine being among the earliest luxuries in which we indulge ourselves, it is desirable that it should be made here and . . . I have myself drank wines made in this state & in Maryland, of the quality of the best Burgundy.

The view of Bordeaux exhibited here was one of a series commissioned by Louis XV from Joseph Vernet, of which another is exhibited at number 353. Painted a generation before Jefferson visited the city, the painting is described in the catalogue of the Salon of 1759, in which it was exhibited:

This view is taken from the side of the Saltworks, where one sees the two pavilions at the end of the Place Royale, in one of which is housed the *hôtel des Fermes*, and in the other the *Bourse*, a part of the château Trompette, beyond it is the suburb called Chartrons, and Palue in the distance. In the far background is Lormon, a village about four kilometers below Bordeaux at the foot of a mountain which is the furthest point at the edge of the painting.

A.B. de L

355 View of the Pagoda of Chanteloup taken from the grand Salon

[pe]ncil
[in]scribed in ink, lower center recto:
[v]ue de la Pagode de Chanteloup
[pri]se du grand Salon

[C]ollection of the Bibliothèque
[Na]tionale, Cabinet des Estampes
[N]OT IN EXHIBITION

[In] the itinerary and travel advice that
[Je]fferson prepared in 1788 for his
[yo]ung compatriots Shippen and
[R]utledge, he included the recommen-
[da]tion: "Chanteloup: Well worth
[s]eeing and examining." He himself
[h]ad visited Chanteloup the previous
[ye]ar on his return from his tour in
[so]uthern France. At Tours he had
[re]ceived a letter from his friend the
[m]arquis de Chastellux urging him,
[a]mong other things, to see Chanteloup
[o]n his way back to Paris. Jefferson
[to]ok the hint and thus turned off the
[m]ain road at Amboise on June 8,
[1]787, and paid his seven francs and
[fo]ur sous for "seeing Chanteloupe." In
[th]e course of what must have been a
[ra]ther brief visit, he noted that he
[']heard a nightingale to-day at
[C]hanteloup" and discussed its nesting
[h]abits with the gardener, he drew
[di]agrams of a device enabling one
[h]orse to work three pumps in the
[ki]tchen garden, and he took notes
[o]n "an ingenious contrivance to hide
[th]e projecting steps of a stair-case"
[th]at he saw in the boudoir. Jefferson's
[tr]avel notes, it should be emphasized,
[c]onsist largely of jottings, of
[m]emoranda filed for future reference,
[a]nd rarely include purely descriptive
[p]assages. The harmonious ensemble
[f]ormed by the château, its gardens,
[a]nd the Chinese pagoda closing the
[v]ista, must nevertheless have
[im]pressed him.

The Chanteloup that Jefferson saw
[w]as the creation of the duc de
[C]hoiseul, who had acquired the
[e]state in 1761. He enlarged and
[t]ransformed the old château with the
[a]ssistance of his architect Louis-Denis
[L]e Camus (sometimes referred to as
[L]e Camus-Choiseul to distinguish him
[f]rom the better-known Le Camus de
[M]ézières) and continued embellishing
[i]t after his exile there in 1770.
[C]hanteloup became famous as a
[c]enter for the liberal literati as well as
[f]or artists. The Chinese pagoda was
[e]rected by Choiseul as a monument
[t]o the friends who had remained
[f]aithful to him despite his official
[d]isgrace. Abbé Barthélemy, the author
[o]f Le Jeune Anarchasis, devised the
[in]scriptions placed in this temple of
[f]riendship.

"This country has just lost a great
[s]tatesman in the duke de Choiseul,"
[J]efferson reported to an American
[c]orrespondent in May 1785.
["]Though out of the administration,

he was universally esteemed, and always supposed to be in the way of entering into it again. He died two days ago." When Jefferson stopped at Chanteloup in June 1787, it had already been purchased from Choiseul's debt-ridden heirs by the duc de Penthièvre. Arthur Young, who visited Chanteloup that same year, penned in his Travels an extensive description which supplements Jefferson's succinct memoranda. Chanteloup survived the Revolution and Empire under successive owners but was demolished in 1823 for the salvage value of the stone. Only the Chinese pagoda and a few small pavilions remain today as mementoes of what Young called "the magnificent seat of the late Duke de Choiseul."

H.C.R.

356 Somerset House, St. Paul's Cathedral and Blackfriar's Bridge

JEAN-LOUIS DESPREZ 1743–1804
Pen and watercolor
57.8 x 177.2 (22¾ x 69¾)

From the Collection of Mr. and Mrs. Paul Mellon

Work on Somerset House, Chambers' masterpiece, began in 1776 and continued after his death. It was built on the site of old Somerset House, which dated from the sixteenth century, and the purpose was to provide offices for several government departments. Such a move was unprecedented in England, although not in France, and can be regarded as an attempt to rationalize govern-ment bureaucracy. A building operation of this size had not taken place in London since the time of Wren.

Desprez's watercolor gives a good impression of Somerset House before a later embankment removed the Thames from the basement arcade, thereby destroying much of the dramatic setting. Chambers' insignificant pediment and dome, which were much criticized, have here been greatly enlarged as more fitting to the scale of the building. Although the river front was not finished in the eastern or right portion by Chambers' death in 1796, it is shown complete. Jefferson must certainly have visited this, the most notable public building then in con-struction, while he stayed in London. He was already familiar with Chambers through his writings and saw examples of his architecture at Kew and at Osterley where Chambers had added the gallery. R.W.

357 Kew Gardens with the Pagoda and Bridge

RICHARD WILSON 1713–1782
Oil on canvas 1762
47.6 x 73 (18¾ x 28¾)

From the Collection of Mr. and Mrs. Paul Mellon

Kew was the country residence of Frederick, Prince of Wales, and after his death in 1751, of his widow and son, later George III. Chambers was employed as the architectural tutor to the young prince and architect to the princess dowager of Wales, who took a keen interest in gardening. For her

Chambers built a medley of exotic buildings in Moorish, Chinese, or antique styles which were scattered about the grounds at Kew, also laid out by him. Chambers published these in *Plans, Elevations, Sections, and Perspective Views of the Gardens and Buildings at Kew* in 1763, and Jefferson had a copy in his library.

The view of the pagoda is seen across the lake. It was completed in the spring of 1762, so Wilson may have relied partly on a drawing of it lent to him by his friend Chambers. The architect had a direct knowledge

of Chinese buildings from a visit he had made to Canton, but the pagoda, while based on Chinese originals, is very much in the fanciful tradition of chinoiserie. It is one of the few buildings at Kew which still survives. R.W.

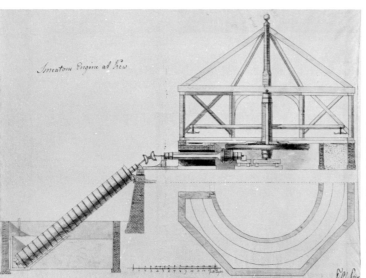

358 Smeaton's Engine at Kew

FREDERIK MAGNUS PIPER
1746–1824
Pen and wash
50 x 70 (19¹¹⁄₁₆ x 27⁹⁄₁₆)
Signed lower right: *F:M: Piper.*
Upper left: *Smeaton's Engine at Kew*

Lent by the Royal Academy of Fine Arts, Stockholm

Piper was twice in England to study landscape gardening, once from 1772 to 1776 and again from 1778 to 1780. He toured the famous gardens at Stourhead, Stowe, Painshill and Kew using Whately's *Observations on Modern Gardening* as his guide. It is likely that this view of Smeaton's engine for raising water dates from the first visit, as Piper made other drawings of Kew in that period.

Jefferson also went on a tour of

English gardens with Whately's book in hand. He visited Kew on April 14, 1786, and makes no comment on the assortment of buildings in various styles built by Chambers for the mother of George III. Instead with his eye for the practical he noted "Archimedes' screw for raising water," and drew a diagram of it with a description. R.W.

359 Pope's Villa, Twickenham

JOSEPH NICKOLLS
Active 1726–1748
Oil on canvas c. 1726
44.5 x 81.3 (17½ x 32)

From the Collection of Mr. and Mrs. Paul Mellon

Alexander Pope, the great English poet of the first half of the eighteenth century, moved to Twickenham in 1719 and began to develop his garden in a new and more informal manner than had been customary. Charles Bridgeman, who worked on Stowe, and William Kent, who designed the garden at Chiswick, were friends of Pope and may have given him advice, but much of the planning was his own. By the time of his death in 1744, Pope's grounds contained a grotto, connecting, under a road, the house with the main part of the garden, a quincunx, an obelisk, a shell temple, a mound, a wilderness, a grove, an orangery, a vinery and a garden house and the usual kitchen garden. The poetic and evocative approach to gardening, an early example of romanticism, was much imitated through the celebrity of Pope and his garden, and as early as 1766 Richard Stockton of Morven, Pennsylvania, thought of using the garden at Twickenham as a model. In a small area Pope managed to achieve great variety and so in his own words:

> He gains all ends who pleasingly confounds
> Surprises, varies and conceals the bounds . . .

Jefferson went to Twickenham on April 2, 1786, the same day he visited Hampton Court, Esher Place and Chiswick (see no. 73) on a short tour of places near London in company with John Adams and Colonel Smith, Adams' future son-in-law. Jefferson records in his memorandum a bare account of the size of the garden and the house, only mentioning "in the centre of the garden a mound with a spiral walk around it. A rookery" and transcribing Pope's inscription to his mother on the obelisk: "Ah! Editha, matrum optima, mulierum amantissima, Vale." Jefferson had composed an epitaph for his sister Jane in 1765 beginning : "Ah, Joanna, puellanum optima." The villa had been extensively altered by the time of Jefferson's visit.

A companion view of Twickenham, by Nickolls, also in the Mellon collection, is dated 1726, but it has been suggested that both are in fact later copies of drawings done by A. Heckell in 1748 and engraved in 1749. R.W.

360 The North Terrace of Windsor Castle, Looking West

PAUL SANDBY 1730–1809
Watercolor c. 1768
38.1 x 54.6 (15 x 21½)

From the Collection of Mr. and Mrs. Paul Mellon

Among the places outside London that Jefferson visited in 1786 was Windsor, where on March 22 he toured the castle and paid five shillings presumably to whomever showed him around. George III and his family were often at Windsor, as the king preferred to live outside London, but there was little restriction on public entry to the grounds, and when the royal family walked on the terrace they sometimes had difficulty getting through the crowds. Jefferson's comments on the castle, the oldest surviving residence of the English sovereigns, are unrecorded. It would have been both more picturesque and less palatial than it was after George IV's extensive renovations. R.W.

361 View of Painshill

FREDERIK MAGNUS PIPER
1746–1824
Pencil 1779–1780
50 x 70 (19¹¹⁄₁₆ x 27⁹⁄₁₆)
Signed lower left: *View at Paynes-hill/
drawn 1789. by F:M: Piper————/
Shews the arrival of the/ water from
the great/ wheel, that winds it up/
from a neighbouring rivulet; It
represents/ a kind of Grotto over/
arched by great trunks/ of oak ————*

*Lent by the Royal Academy of
Fine Arts, Stockholm*

Water was an essential part of
eighteenth-century gardens. In the
earlier, formal arrangements the
water was static in lakes and pools,
with fountains providing the only
movement, but romantic gardens
made more use of moving water,
especially streams and cascades. At
Painshill a giant wheel carried up
the water of the river Mole, which
then fell through a grottolike opening
into an artificial lake. Dense planting
of trees added to the simulated
naturalism of the design. R.W.

362 Plan of the Grotto at Painshill

FREDERIK MAGNUS PIPER
1746–1824
Pen and wash 1780
50 x 70 (19¹¹⁄₁₆ x 27⁹⁄₁₆)
Signed lower right: *Fred. M. Piper
delin ᵗ 1780.* Lower margin: *Plan de la
Grotte des Jardins de Painshill dans
le Comté de Surry prés de Londres/
construite par mr Hammilton*

*Lent by the Royal Academy of
Fine Arts, Stockholm*

Painshill, south of London, in Surrey
was created by the Honorable William
Hamilton in the 1740s. It became one
of the most celebrated landscape
gardens, and Whately praised it for
the consistency "preserved in the
midst of variety; all the parts unite
easily." Painshill, like other English
gardens, was composed on painterly
principles, based on a study of the
landscapes of Claude Lorrain and
Gaspar Poussin.
    Jefferson visited Painshill on April
2, 1786, during his garden tour of
England. He remarked that the
"Grotto [was] said to have cost
£7000," which was an enormous sum
to spend on just one item, and
approved of Whately's comments.
Grottoes were popular in gardens, the

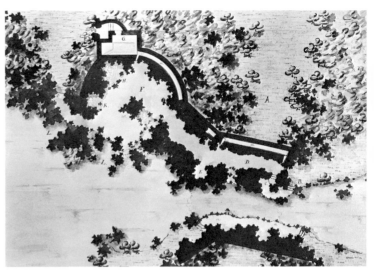

fashion probably being set by Pope's
at Twickenham or, perhaps, by the
famous grotto at Stourhead, for which
the poet wrote some verses. In classical
times natural grottoes were associated
with oracles and religious mysteries.
Eighteenth-century artificial grottoes
were romantic and evocative, often
with water dripping down the walls, as
at Painshill, and the sound echoing
in the dimly lit chamber must have

filled visitors with a pleasing sense
of being in an underground cave.
The grotto at Painshill was one of the
most elaborate and admired; it had
feldspar chips on the ceiling which
sparkled in the half-light, and with
the stalactites, minerals and fossils
created an atmosphere of enchantment. R.W.

363 Merton College, Oxford

MICHAEL "ANGELO" ROOKER
1743–1801
Oil on canvas 1771
71.1 x 91.4 (28 x 36)
Signed lower left: *MARooker/
Pinx/[?]*

*From the Collection of Mr. and Mrs.
Paul Mellon*

At the end of his tour of country
houses and gardens, and after visiting
Blenheim on April 9, 1786, Jefferson
passed through Oxford. His account
book records a payment of five
shillings for "doorkeeps of colleges,"
so he must have found time to do some
sightseeing; but no Jeffersonian
comment on this ancient seat of
learning has survived. Tory, Anglican
Oxford would not have had much
attraction for the would-be reformer
of William and Mary College,
Virginia, but it may be that the
cloistered quadrangles of the English
university gave him some ideas much
later for the planning of the University
of Virginia. While much of the
architecture of the colleges was
medieval, there were a considerable
number of eighteenth-century buildings
in the classical may have influenced
Jefferson's decision to have the rotunda
as the library for his university. R.W.

364 Turin with the Palazzo Reale

BERNARDO BELLOTTO 1720–1780
Oil on canvas c. 1745
124.4 x 172.7 (49 x 68)
Signed lower right: BERNARDO
BELLOTTO./Dt. IL CANALETTO./f!

*Lent by Mr. and Mrs. John Koch,
New York*

A visit to Italy had been in
Jefferson's mind at least since 1763,
when he wrote to his great friend
John Page that he planned a long
trip to Europe, including Italy "where
I would buy me a fiddle." It would
indeed have been surprising if a
well-to-do Virginia gentleman with a
taste for the arts had not contemplated
making a Grand Tour like that made
by the English upper classes. When
he went to Philadelphia to be
inoculated in 1766, Jefferson met Dr.
John Morgan who had only just
returned from several years in Europe,
passing considerable time in Italy
where he had amassed an art collection in the best tradition of the
eighteenth-century *cognoscenti*. The
list of antique sculpture which
Jefferson considered ordering for
Monticello around 1771 were all
based on originals in Italy, and his
desire to see the sculpture first-hand,
united with his admiration for classical
architecture and his delight in the
Latin and Greek classics, would have
been a powerful motive for visiting

Rome, Naples, Florence and other
major centers of art.

Unfortunately, his brief stay in
northern Italy, partly to regain his
health and partly to gather information for American agriculture and
trade, left him no time for going to
Florence or Rome. Even then, his
journey, which was part of an
extended tour of southern and western
France, was largely inspired by a
desire for information on the growing
of rice. It had not been his original
intention to travel to Turin "having
no object further eastward except
the rice." But at Nice he discovered
that the ricefields were more distant
than he had earlier been led to believe
and "they tell me there are none
nearer than Vercelli and Novarra,
which is carrying me almost to Milan. I
fear that this circumstance will
occasion me a greater delay than I had
calculated on." Willingly, or unwill-
ingly, therefore, Jefferson found
himself crossing the Po valley on
April 16 on his way to Turin, where
he stayed for four days. During that
time he had talks on possible trade
between the kingdom of Sardinia and
the United States, but the main
purpose of his journey, information
on rice production, still eluded him
and he was forced to travel to Milan.
In Turin he went twice to the theater
and sampled some of the "red wine
of Nebule made in this neighborhood

which is very singular. It is about as
sweet as the silky Madeira, as
astringent on the palate as Bordeaux,
and as brisk as Champagne. It is a
pleasing wine." He noted hearing the
first nightingale of the year and made
two sketches of wheels used to transport long pieces of timber. A map,
presumably one of those he bought
with guide books on his second day
in Turin, was in the group he later
lent to L'Enfant when the planning
of Washington was being considered.
The streets of Turin were laid out on
a grid system, which must have
appealed to Jefferson as it did to
William Short, who considered it "the
handsomest city . . . in Europe on
account of its regularity." The
architecture, however, being generally
baroque, may have been less attractive
to a lover of Palladio and the antique.
Jefferson's account book records a
visit to the stupendous basilica of
Superga, and the classicizing baroque
of Juvarra's masterpiece might have
met with his cool approval. He also
visited Stupinigi, the royal hunting
lodge, and another royal palace at
Moncalieri. Within the city,
Guarini's chapel of the Holy Shroud
might well have attracted his attention with its idiosyncratic spire, but
such an exaggerated style would not
have been to Jefferson's taste. The
spire of the Santa Sindone together
with the cathedral campanile can be

seen in the middle distance of
Bellotto's view, one of several
versions. The royal palace and old
city walls were on the left and the
Alps appear on the skyline.

It was obviously with real regret
that Jefferson turned his back on his
only chance to see Rome. A less
public-spirited man could have
justified the extra time, but Jefferson
obviously felt he had been away from
Paris long enough and that duty must
come before pleasure. He wrote to
Maria Cosway: "But I took a peep
only into Elysium. I entered it at one
door, and came out at another,
having seen, as I past only Turin,
Milan and Genoa. I calculated the
hours it would have taken to carry
me on to Rome. But they were
exactly so many more than I had to
spare. Was not this provoking? In
thirty hours from Milan I could have
been at the espousals of the Doge and
Adriatic. But I am born to lose
everything I love." And to another
friend he wrote "Milan was the spot
at which I turned my back on Rome
and Naples. It was a moment of
conflict between my duty which urged
me to return, and inclination urging
me forward." R.W.

365 View of the Façade of the Country House Called Welgelegen in the Harlem Wood, belonging to Mr. Henry Hope of Amsterdam

H.P. SCHOUTEN 1747–1822
Drawing 1791
35.5 x 54.5 (14 x 21½)

*Lent by the Gemeentearchief,
Haarlem*

When passing through Utrecht during his tour in Holland in March 1788, Jefferson noted that the canal there was lined with country houses "which bespeak the wealth and cleanliness of the country, but generally in an uncouth taste and exhibiting no regular architecture." By this he presumably meant that they were not built according to the rules set forth in his architectural books. He did, however, find one Dutch country house of refined taste worth his notice and, furthermore, worth sketching in his notebook:

The country house of Henry Hope (1736–1811), the Amsterdam banker and art collector, was nearing completion when Jefferson saw it on March 20, 1788. "It is said this house will cost four tons of silver, or forty thousand pounds sterling," he wrote. "The separation between the middle building and wings in the upper story has a capricious appearance, yet a pleasing one. The right wing of the house (which is the left in the plan) extends back to a great length, so as to make the ground plan in the form of an L. The parapet has a panel of wall, and a panel of

balusters alternately, which lighten it. There is no portico, the columns being backed against the wall of the front."

Hope's "Welgelegen" was built for him on the edge of the Haarlem Wood by the Flemish-born master builder Jean-Baptiste Dubois (b. 1762) from plans drawn by the Dutch architect Leendert Viervant, Jr., from Amsterdam (1752–1801). The house was thus a characteristic creation in the international neoclassic manner. Schouten's view, drawn in 1791, some three years after Jefferson's sketch, shows the finished mansion with bas-

reliefs and statues (including the *Laocoön*) ornamenting the front. Hope enjoyed his country seat only for a brief period. With the arrival in 1795 of the French Republican army under Pichegru and the formation of the Batavian Republic, he removed himself and his renowned art collection to London. The "Paviljoen," as it came to be generally called, was sold in 1808 to His Majesty Louis Napoléon, king of Holland, who subsequently signed his act of abdication there in 1810. With the restoration of the House of Orange the estate became national

property and is now the seat of the provincial government of North Holland. H.C.R.

366 View of the Westerkerk, Amsterdam

ISAAK OUWATER 1750–1793
Oil on canvas 1778
53.34 x 63.50 (21 x 25)
Signed lower right on boat:
Ik OUWATER *1778*

*Lent by The National Gallery of
Canada, Ottawa*

The Westerkerk, dating from the first
half of the seventeenth century, is one
of the most important churches in
Amsterdam, with a particularly
conspicuous tower. Rembrandt is
buried there. The chimes were
famous, even in Jefferson's time, and
he made a musical annotation of them
while he was there between March
10 and March 30, 1788. With John
Adams, who was about to return to
the United States, Jefferson went to
Amsterdam to negotiate a new loan
with the Dutch bankers for the
United States. Jefferson's time was
not entirely taken up with this
financial business, for he was able to
indulge in ample sightseeing, noting
the principal buildings and anything
strange or potentially useful. He
observed the way windows were
opened so that they let in air but not
the rain, how an empty boat was
pulled over a dam, the swivel bridge
across a canal, and wind sawmills.
Jefferson bought books from Van
Damme, Amsterdam being a noted
publishing center, and ordered
ironware, tea, coffee, and chocolate
cups of East Indian porcelain. His
curiosity led him to write down how
the coops were arranged in the large
aviary of a Mr. Ameshoff. Such a
variety of activities is typical of
Jefferson's practice when traveling in
unknown country. His quick mind,
interested in so many subjects, was
forever observing and recording for
future use curious and unfamiliar
sights. R.W.

367 Court Pond at The Hague, near the "Binnenhof"

PAULUS CONSTANTIJN
LA FARGUE 1729–1782
Oil on canvas 1762
93.5 x 124 (36¹³⁄₁₆ x 48¹³⁄₁₆)
Signed lower left: *P.C. La Fargue/*
Pinx 1762

Lent by the Haags Gemeentemuseum,
The Hague

Jefferson records in his *Autobiography* how in March 1788 he left Paris to meet John Adams at The Hague. Adams was about to return to the United States as vice president and so had to take leave of the Dutch government to which, in addition to being minister in London, he had also been accredited. The financial affairs of the United States were at a low ebb, and at this particular juncture the recently adopted American constitution added to the uncertainties of raising more money, because there would be a delay before the new government could make the necessary arrangements. "I was daily dunned by a company who had formerly made a small loan to the U.S. the principal of which was now become due; and bankers in Amsterdam had notified me that the interest on our general debt would be expected in June; that if we failed to pay it, it would be deemed an act of

bankruptcy and would effectually destroy the credit of the U.S. and all future prospect of obtaining money there . . . I saw that there was not a moment to lose, and set out for the Hague on the 2d. morning after receiving the information of Mr. Adams' journey." Jefferson was afraid he might miss Adams, so it was a relief when he found him there on the ninth of March, and they continued their journey to Amsterdam to reestablish American financial credit on a surer footing.

Jefferson could not fail to be reminded of the recent constitutional revolution in the Netherlands, where the Patriots supported by France had been defeated by the Orange party with the help of British diplomacy and Prussian arms. Jefferson's account of the crisis in his *Autobiography* is certainly not objective, but it reveals his strong support for the Patriots, whom he regarded as taking a similar stance to the American colonists against their sovereign. The virtuous Patriots whose "object . . . was to establish a representative and republican government" are contrasted with "the treasonable perfidy of the Prince of Orange."

The collection of buildings called the Binnenhof was the center of government and formerly of the

court, and was a fashionable area in the eighteenth century. A corner of the Mauritshuis, a famous piece of seventeenth-century architecture, can be seen at the extreme left of the painting. R.W.

368 Main Square at Düsseldorf
THOMAS ROWLANDSON 1757–1827
Pen and watercolor 1791
27.4 x 42 (10¹³⁄₁₆ x 16⁹⁄₁₆)
Signed lower left: *The Palace and*

Picture Gallery at Düsseldorff. Lower right: *Rowlandson del 1791*

Lent by the Stadtgeschichtliches Museum, Düsseldorf

On his tour of the Rhineland in April 1788 Jefferson stopped at Düsseldorf. He enjoyed his stay at Zimmerman's, and he recommended this inn "Zweig brudder Hoff" to Shippen and Rutledge as "the best tavern I saw in my whole journey, in the palace is a collection of paintings equal in merit to anything in the world . . . this will be worth repeated examination." On the back of the drawing Rowlandson has written a description of the collection. "This gallery is divided into five classes. The first consists of pictures done by Rubens. The second by such as were drawn by some of the most eminent Flemish painters, particularly those of Vandyck. The third contains some pieces done by the ablest painters of Italy. The fourth is adorned with the Works of Chevalier Van der Werf, a Dutch painter, who has equalled all the Flemish painters in beauty of design and colouring. The fifth, which is the richest, consists of choice pieces done by Raphael, Julio Romano, Guido, Titian, Paul Veronese, Corregio, Albano, Rubens, Vandyke, Rembrandt and several others."

Rowlandson's inscription is mistaken, for it is not the picture gallery that is in the background but the town hall. Perhaps he was misled by the statue of the elector Johann Wilhelm, who did so much to build up the celebrated collection of paintings. As always with Rowlandson, the borderline between factual reporting and caricature is hard to place, especially in the equestrian statue. R.W.

FRENCH DECORATIVE ARTS

369 Canapé
Beechwood
96 x 171 x 70.5 (37¾ x 51½ x 29½)
Lent anonymously

370 Fauteuil à la Reine
Beechwood
96.5 x 65 x 49.5 (38 x 22 x 25½)
Lent anonymously

371 Bergère
Beechwood
226 x 165 x 178 (89 x 64.8 x 70)
Lent by Mr. and Mrs. Philip W. Bonsal, Washington

From a set made for Queen Marie-Antoinette in 1779, the pieces are richly carved around the back and seat rail with repeating floral motifs, and gilt. The bergère is upholstered with blue brocade. The padded arm supports are in the form of inverted

cornucopias, from which flowers emerge. The straight legs are tapering and carved with twisted flutes and surmounted by foliated capitals.

The top rail of the back of the sofa is straight and the uprights at each end are surmounted by fluted balls. The top rails of the backs of the two chairs are each curved, the back of the *fauteuil* being flat and that of the *bergère* coved to fit the human body and entirely upholstered except for two supporting members at the back, which are carved with fluting and floral motifs.

All the pieces exhibited here have been reupholstered (a fragment of the original upholstery is exhibited at no. 376), but the webbing beneath the seat of another chair from the same set now in the Metropolitan Museum of Art bears the stenciled mark W, surmounted with a closed crown for the palace of Versailles and the inventory number 4499. M Verlet has shown that all three pieces came from a large suite of seat furniture including (among other pieces) six *fauteuils*, one sofa, one *bergère*, and several screens and stools. They were delivered by Capin, the principal court upholsterer, on October 20, 1779, for use in the Cabinet de la Reine at Versailles.

For the design of the *fauteuils* and the *bergère*, Jacques Gondoin (1737–1818), the principal *dessinateur du mobilier de la Couronne*, was paid 300 livres each and 400 livres for the design of the *canapé*. The carving by the Babel workshop of the set of six *fauteuils* cost 2880 livres, and the gilding by "la veuve Bardou, peintre et doreur ordinaire due Garde meuble de la Couronne" of the entire suite of furniture, 5832 livres. Although Capin was paid 841 livres for upholstering the six *fauteuils*, by far the most costly item in the account was for the upholstery material itself, which cost some 121,000 livres.

A second inventory number stenciled on the webbing of the chair in the Metropolitan Museum suggests that part of the suite was removed from the queen's apartments shortly before the Revolution to the Appartements des Mesdames, perhaps for the use of Mme Elizabeth.

Part of the set was purchased in 1793–1794 by Gouverneur Morris probably at, or immediately after, the sale of the contents of Versailles, which continued for over three hundred days, from August 25, 1793 to August 11, 1794. The descriptions in the sales lists are, however, far too abbreviated to enable this set to be identified.

Gouverneur Morris had come to Paris in 1789 primarily to negotiate the sale of tobacco through the French tax farm, but he remained there throughout the Revolution, eventually being asked by Jefferson to undertake the negotiations for the settlement of the American debt to France. It was Morris who stood for Houdon for the modeling of the body of the sculptor's statue of Washington. F.W.

372 Bergère à la Reine
88.3 x 56 x 48.3 (34¾ x 22 x 19); height at seat: 38 (15)
Wood, painted gray, upholstered with gold silk
Lent by The White House

This chair in the Louis XVI style was presented by Lafayette to Dolley Madison, a great lover of French furniture, who ordered a quantity of it from Paris for the decoration of the president's house. Later she gave this chair to Mrs. William Thornton, wife of the architect.

The frame of the trapezoidal back is carved all around with a simple repeating leaf motif and with beading. It is flanked at each side with a fluted column surmounted with a finial carved to resemble a feather *panache*. The top rail is arched in the center *en anse de panier*.

The curving and padded arms are carved at the sides with a simple molding and terminate above the arm supports in an acanthus scroll. The arm supports themselves are baluster-shaped and fluted and rest in leaf-cups, set well back behind the forelegs. The seat rail is richly carved in front and at the sides with dentils and leaf motifs. The legs are circular,

tapering and fluted and terminate in ball feet. The rear legs are slightly canted.

A very similar chair, with a top rail of a slightly different design, was given to Jefferson by President Monroe, who had purchased it in France.

The arm supports are set back behind the forelegs in order to accommodate the wide skirts worn by ladies in the early 1780s. This suggests that the chair dates from a rather later period than, for example, numbers 369–371. F.W.

373 Fauteuil en Cabriolet
Painted beechwood, upholstered with gold silk
86.4 x 56.5 x 49.5 (34 x 22¼ x 19½)
Lent by The White House

This Louis XVI style chair was purchased by Washington from the comte de Moustier (1751–1817), French representative in America 1787–1790. Presumably the president acquired this chair in 1790, when de Moustier returned to France.

The coved, trapezoidal back is flanked at each side by a detached fluted column carved on the square base and above the capital with a rosette. The downward curving arms are likewise fluted and padded. They

rest on fluted baluster-shaped arm supports. It is carved around the seat rail at front and sides with a beading between simple moldings.

The legs, circular and tapering, have peg-top feet and are carved on two sides above the capital with a rosette within a lozenge beneath a panel of ribbing. The rear legs are slightly canted.

It seems likely that there formerly were finials above the side members of the back, but these have disappeared. A very similar but rather simpler chair, the frame of which was once painted white and gold, was given to Jefferson by President Monroe and is now at Monticello. F.W.

374 Fauteuil à la Reine
Beechwood, upholstered in brown leather
82.5 x 54.6 x 52 (34½ x 21½ x 20½)
Lent by the Thomas Jefferson Memorial Foundation, Charlottesville

This chair is thought to have been purchased by James Monroe during his stay in France from 1794 to 1796, at which time he attended the Revolutionary sales. Upon his return to America, Monroe is said to have sold the chair to Thomas Jefferson, who used it at Monticello. C.G.

375 Boiseries
CLAUDE-NICOLAS LEDOUX
1736–1806
Oak
365 x 81.3 (143¾ x 32) each
Lent by The Museum of Fine Arts, Boston

These four panels formed part of the decorations designed by Claude-Nicolas Ledoux (1736–1806) for the Hôtel de Montmorency in Paris, which he built for the *fermier-général* Bouvet de Vezelay at the corner of the rue Basse-du-Rempart and the rue Chausée d'Antin between 1770 and 1772. One of the Boston panels, not shown here, is carved with the monogram of the Montmorency family. A drawing by Ledoux in the Archives Nationales, reproduced in Michel Gallet's *Stately Mansions*,

shows the disposition of four of the panels on the window side of the room. The hotel was demolished in 1848, and the panels were acquired at that time by Edward Preble Deacon, who was in Paris at that moment, for installation in the house which his father-in-law Peter Parker was building for him on Washington Street in Boston. The contents of this house, called Deacon House, were dispersed at a sale held on February 1–3, 1871, and presumably the panels were removed from the house at that time. They were bought by the Boston Athenaeum in 1879.

Carved in full relief and partly gilded on a ground painted white, each panel is carved with a Renaissance style candelabrum. On two of them, a trophy is supported by a half-draped female figure standing on a rectangular platform. On the third, the trophy is supported by a putto standing on an inverted capital.

In the one case, the female figure clasps a lyre and perhaps represents the muse Erato. She supports a trophy of musical instruments and emblems of architecture. In the second, the figure represents Diana with an unstrung bow and supports a trophy, which emerges from a basket resting on a flaming tripod supported on her head and which represents the chase. The putto also supports a trophy of the chase, which emerges from a tall three-legged vase resting on his head. Hymeneal crowns linked by floral pendants are suspended at each side of all the trophies.

Jefferson admired Ledoux's work, especially the Hôtel Guimard (see no. 503) and the Pavilion of Louveciennes (see nos. 296–298), the latter of which was built for Mme du Barry during the same years as the Hôtel de Montmorency. Both these buildings, and the wall panels exhibited here, would have been representative of the most avant-garde style when Jefferson arrived in Paris in 1784. F.W.

376 Framed panel of embroidery
81.3 x 61 (32 x 24)

Lent by Mr. and Mrs. Philip W. Bonsal, Washington

In the accounts for the suite of furniture which included the three pieces described at numbers 369–371, the upholstery, a fragment of which is shown here, is described as "satin broché de soye et chenille, orné de médaillons et bordures, dessins arabesques." It was embroidered at Lyon after designs by Jacques Gondoin and was furnished by "J.n Charton fabricant du Roy à Lyon." A part of the embroidery was carried out by "la veuve Tremeau, brodeuse du Roy. . . ." It was enriched with very elaborate *passementerie* consisting of tassels "en choux pour carreaux . . . garni de jassemins et torsade de soie nuée," which were supplied by the widow Saporito. Altogether the upholstery material was by far the most considerable item in the cost of this set of furniture. F.W.

377 Bureau à Cylindre
Bird's-eye mahogany veneer (acajou moucheté) on an oak carcass. Mounts of bronze, chased and gilt.
127 x 146 x 76.5 (50 x 57½ x 30⅛)
Lent anonymously

Cylinder-topped writing desks of this type first appeared in Paris in the late 1750s and were then known as *bureaux à la Kaunitz* (presumably because the Russian prince of that name bought an early example). The desk exhibited here must, however, date from sometime during the late 1780s.

Of rectangular neoclassic design, the writing top is closed by a quarter-cylindrical cover, which may be turned back by means of two square drop handles at the front to disappear into the interior of the desk at the back. Above the cylinder is a shallow rectangular podium, fitted with three shallow drawers and surmounted by a marble top surrounded on three sides by a pierced brass gallery. The interior, within the cylinder, is fitted with pigeon holes and drawers. The kneehole below the cylinder is flanked at each side by two shallow drawers and surmounted by a longer drawer above the recess. A slide for books, at which a secretary may also take dictation, may be pulled out from the top of the writing table at the left. The whole rests on four square tapering legs with chamfered corners and mounted with simple capitals and feet of gilt bronze. The drawer fronts, the cylinder top, and the panels at each side are framed in a simple molding of gilt bronze. Small panels of decorative gilt bronze separate the drawers above the cylinders and the keyhole escutcheons are of simple rectangular design. F.W.

78 Commode

JEAN FERDINAND
SCHWERDFEGER active 1786—
after 1799
Cuban mahogany veneered on oak;
mounts of bronze chased and gilt;
top surmounted by white statuary
marble
90.2 x 124 x 54.6 (35½ x 48⅞ x
21½)

*Lent by The Museum of Fine Arts,
Boston*

The chest contains two principal
drawers in front with no division
between them, beneath two shallow
drawers in the frieze. The sides splay
slightly outward towards the rear.
A mahogany column with a
Corinthian capital and a base of
basketwork design is set into a recess
at each forecorner. The whole rests
on four short thick feet tapering and

fluted with basketwork capitals and
shoes of gilt bronze. The frieze is
mounted with a continuous leaf scroll
enclosing sunflowers; a band of basketwork runs around the base above the
feet, and the four drawer-handles are
in the form of laurel wreaths
surrounding lion's masks.

The *commode* is unstamped but
bears so close a resemblance to the
work of Jean Ferdinand Schwerdfeger,
whose style is highly idiosyncratic,
that it may be attributed to him with
some confidence. A small table in the
Louvre (Schlichting Collection, cat.
no. 82) which bears his label, for
example, has similar columns, legs,
and frieze mounts. These last also
appear on the celebrated jewel cabinet
by Schwerdfeger, which was
presented to Queen Marie-Antoinette
by the city of Paris in 1787, now in
the Musée de Versailles. F.W.

379 Console

ADAM WEISWEILER active 1778—
after 1810
Mahogany mounted with bronze
chased and gilt; top of white statuary
marble
92.7 x 181 (36½ x 46½)

*Lent by The Museum of Fine Arts,
Boston*

This side table is characteristic of the
style of Adam Weisweiler, its bulbous
columns and tall peg-top feet
appearing, for example, on a *vuide-
poche* or work table from the Tuileries
stamped by Weisweiler, which is now
in the Wallace Collection, London
(cat. no. F 325). The frieze mounts,
which may possibly be by Pierre
Gouthière, are found on a cabinet
stamped by the same *ébéniste* in the
English Royal Collection at Windsor
Castle and the interlacing stretcher
on a small *sécrétaire à abattant* in the

Wallace Collection (cat. no. F 308).
There are many other instances of
Weisweiler's use of these features as
well.

The table top is trapezoidal in
shape, with incurving sides splaying
outward toward the back. It is
supported on four legs, bulbous at
the top and tapering toward the lower
end. Their flutes are filled with filets
of gilt bronze. The legs are linked by
a stretcher of complex interlacing
design and supported on tall, peg-top
feet. A complex boss depends
beneath the center of the stretcher.

The frieze is mounted in the
center of the front with a Medusa
mask flanked with cornucopiae and
confronted goats. A band of floral
and foliated volutes is entwined
around the goats and extends across
the lower front. The friezes at the
sides are similar but entwine around
playing putti. F.W.

380 Fauteuils en cabriolet

Beechwood, carved and gilt. Nineteenth-century upholstery
95.2 (37½) high; 57.1 (22½) deep; height of seat rail: 30.5 (12). (Note: there is a small discrepancy between the dimensions of the two chairs. Maximum dimensions have been given)

Lent by The Museum of Fine Arts, Boston

381 Firescreen

Beechwood, carved and gilt, with a panel of the original blue and white damask upholstery
105.5 x 72.2 x 40.6 (41⅝ x 28⅜ x 16)

Lent by The Museum of Fine Arts, Boston

The square-backed chairs are carved around the back and the seat rail with a repeating leaf motif, framed between moldings with pearling along the outer edge. The arms are padded and each is supported on an armrest carved with imbricated medallions

and terminating in a large acanthus leaf. The legs are tapering and fluted with *chandelles*. They are surmounted with plain capitals and terminate in simple flattened ball feet.

The frame of the screen is similarly carved and the splayed feet end in large scrolls carved at the upper end with a prominent acanthus leaf. The upholstered panel may be raised and lowered by means of a knob at the top and counterweights.

A fragmentary label beneath one of the chairs at number 380 (and on other pieces from the same set) can be reconstructed to provide the name of the gilder, Chatard, the date, 1787, and the words *Thierry, Commissaire, Chambre à coucher, à Paris juillet No. 181*.

From these labels and other documents, Mr. Howard C. Rice, Jr., and M Pierre Verlet have been able to reconstruct the history of these three pieces which formed part of a suite of a bed, two armchairs, four chairs, a *bergère* armchair, a firescreen and a *prie-dieu* ordered on July 17, 1787, for the use of Thierry de Ville d'Avray in his apartment in the Hôtel du Garde Meuble, which still stands at the corner of the Place de la Concorde (then called Place Louis XV) and the rue Saint-Florentin. Thierry de Ville d'Avray was *commissaire-général de la maison du Roi au département des meubles de la couronne*, which is to say that he was the official finally responsible for the furnishing of all the royal establishments. He was an able administrator and introduced important reforms in his department on the eve of the Revolution. His own apartment in the Hôtel du Garde Meuble was furnished with great magnificence.

From the numerous surviving documents relating to this furniture, we learn that the set was made by the chairmaker J. Séné (active 1769–1803), that the carving for which Jean Hauré (working 1774–1796), the principal *fournisseur de la Cour*, was paid was, in fact, undertaken by Vallois, and the gilding by Chatard, who was the chief gilder employed by the court in the years before the Revolution. The upholstery was undertaken by the court *tapissier*, Capin.

Séné was paid 21 livres for supplying the frame of the screen, and Hauré received 84 livres for the carving. The payment to Séné for the frames of the armchairs is not mentioned separately, but Vallois charged 72 livres for carving them. Chatard was paid 1543 livres for gilding the entire suite *en or bruni* or *mat* (there is no trace of these contrasting types of gilding on the chairs or the rest of the set today).

The upholstery, a damask woven

with a "grand dessin arabesque . . . cariatides, tetes de lions [*sic*], bordures . . .," was supplied by Reboul and Fontebrune and applied to the frames by Capin. The blue and white material, which had already been used for the upholstery of the chairs in the Salon des Jeux du Roy at Fontainebleau, survives in a fragmentary state on the screen and on a bed not exhibited here.

During the Revolution, Thierry's furniture was confiscated, and he himself lost his life in the September Massacres. Although documents do not exist to prove it, it seems as certain as possible that this set of furniture and other works of art from the Museum of Fine Arts, Boston, exhibited here (nos. 382–384) were acquired immediately after the Revolution by James Swan, a highly successful Boston merchant who had extensive dealings with the Revolutionary government in France. In 1794, at a time when the infant French republic was in great need of

certain commodities from abroad to pursue the wars in which it was engaged, Swan was appointed the American agent of the Commission des Subsistences, set up to obtain these commodities from abroad. A number of other agents were appointed for the same purpose in neutral European countries. Swan supplied such things as wheat, rice, potash (for making gunpowder), whale oil, and dried beans and meats. Like his fellow agents, Swan found it uneconomic to be paid in the constantly devalued French currency and, therefore, arranged to be paid in kind with goods which could be sold abroad. His importations to America included wine, mirrors, textiles, and, in addition, fine furniture selected from that seized from the royal palaces, from *emigrés* and from other enemies of the republic. Much of the furniture descended in his family until it was presented at various times to the Museum of Fine Arts, Boston. F.W.

382 Pair of Firedogs (Feux)

Bronze, chased and gilt
48.3 x 45.4 (19 x 7⅞)

Lent by The Museum of Fine Arts, Boston

On a rectangular base with rounded ends, chased with twisted flutes and supported on peg-top feet, stand two confronted goats, their forefeet resting on a basket of grapes, which they are devouring. A thyrsus rises from the center of each basket, which is supported on a leaf cup.

Generally attributed to Pierre Gouthière (1732–1813/14) like so much gilt bronze of fine quality and late Louis XVI date, these firedogs are more likely to be by Pierre-Philippe Thomire (1751–1843). They accord with what is known of his pre-Revolutionary style and may be compared, for instance, with the goat handles, documented as made

by Thomire, of the pair of Sèvres vases made in 1784 and purchased by Louis XVI, who installed them on the chimneypiece of the *Ancien pièce de café* in his private apartments on the first floor of the palace of Versailles. They are now in the English Royal Collection.

The goats are also found on another pair of Sèvres vases in the Walters Collection, Baltimore. The design of the goats was perhaps taken from an engraved design for a vase by de Wailly (1730–1798), published in 1760. F.W.

384 Mantle clock
White statuary marble and bronze, chased, partly gilt and partly patinated
73.7 x 50.8 (29 x 20)

Lent by The Museum of Fine Arts, Boston

83 Pair of vases

vres porcelain

1.1 (28) high; 33 (13) diam.

ent by The Museum of Fine Arts, oston

hese vases are of the type known as ses *Bachelier* after Jean-Jacques achelier, who was appointed *irecteur artistique* at Vincennes in 748 and continued working at the vres factory until 1793. This design as introduced at the factory about 770, though the plaster model, ntitled *vase Bachelier rectifié*, still reserved in the Musée Céramique at vres, lacks the handles.

The ground color is dark cobalt lue (*bleu du Roy*) extensively nriched with gilding. There is a attened oval reserve at each side of e body, painted with scenes from e life of the Roman general elisarius in the front and with a ilitary trophy at the back. One ows *Belisarius Unfettering Justinian* nd the other shows *Belisarius Leaving rison*.

The vases bear no marks but can be entified from two entries in one of e work ledgers at Sèvres under the ame of the painter Antoine Caton, ho worked at the factory as a figure ainter from 1749 to 1786, and fterward served as foreman of ainters until 1798: "12 janvier 1779: Vase Bachelier 1ère grandeur. Beau leu. Sujet de Belisaire. Vu." and "21 nai 1779: 1 Vase Bachelier 1ère randeur. Sujet de Belisaire. Vu."

The trophies were painted by Charles Butteux or Buteau, who was working at the factory as a painter of trophies, flowers and freizes from 1756 to 1782. In the same ledger, this is recorded in another entry, dated July 1779, which reads as follows under the heading Butteaux *père*: "2 vases Bachelier 1ère grandeur de M. Caton, beau bleu, attributs. Vu."

The vases appear to have been purchased for the French crown. An entry in an inventory of the porcelains in the palace of Versailles, drawn up on the eve of the French Revolution either in 1778 or 1779, reveals that they were among the porcelains in the Cabinet de Conseil where they stood on the chimney-piece:

2 autres vases en porcelaine fond bleu à ornemens dorés, garnis chacun de médaillions dont 2 représentent différens personnages et les 2 autres des attributs militaires, garnis chacun de leurs couvercles à pomme de pin, Hauteur total 25 pouces sur 12 pouces de large, à 2.400 1 . . . 4.800 1.

F.W.

The movement, signed *Caillouet à Paris* on the enamel dial, is supported between two marble brackets resting on a shaped plinth of the same material, both lavishly mounted with gilt bronze.

Against the front of each bracket stands an Egyptian caryatid terminal figure of gilt bronze in the form of a tapering pilaster with human head and feet resting on a cinerary urn. Above the brackets are seated female winged sphinxes addorsed at each side of the cylinder containing the move-ment. They are of patinated bronze and support a panache of feathers of gilt bronze on their heads. Above the movement is a marble urn, supported on a high base and sur-mounted by a gilt bronze eagle poised for flight.

Floral enrichments of great complexity are mounted at each side of the brackets and above the dial. The front of the plinth is inset with three rectangular panels of gilt bronze chased in relief with putti engaged in various playful activities. The clock is of a type sometimes known as *squelette*, and became popular in Paris in the latter part of the reign of Louis XVI. A somewhat similar clock, clearly by the same casemaker, is in the Musée des Arts Décoratifs in Paris. F.W.

385 Aristotle surprised by Alexander while pulling the Chariot of Aspasia

Silk and wool, c. 1792
285 x 247 (112½ x 97)

Lent anonymously

386 Alcibiades surprised by Socrates playing among the Women

Silk and wool, c. 1792
285 x 247 (112½ x 97)

Lent anonymously

These two tapestries, in the extreme neoclassic style, were woven at the Beauvais tapestry factory after cartoons by the painter Monsiau (1755–1837).

Two sets were woven, one in 1792 and a second in 1793, in a last effort by the *directeur* M de Menou, before his retirement, to combat the difficult situation into which the Revolution had thrown the Beauvais factory and its workers. A second set is still to be found in the Ministère des Affaires Etrangères in Paris. It is impossible to say from which weaving the present tapestries come, but it seems likely that the set woven in 1792 is the one now in the possession of the French government.

Gouverneur Morris presumably acquired the tapestries during the course of the French Revolution, when he bought a considerable quantity of such things and when he was given silver and other objects for safekeeping by his friends among the nobility. F.W.

387 Long case clock

Mahogany veneer mounted with gilt bronze
188 x 57 x 29 (74 x 22½ x 11⅜)

Lent anonymously

The clock rests on a tall, square base supported on a low plinth. Beneath the dial, which is surmounted by pendant laurel sprays tied by a ribbon bow to a feigned nail, is a trapezoidally shaped window, framed with a gilt bronze molding, through which the pendulum can be seen. A similar horizontal oval window in the base allows the pendulum bob to be seen as it swings. Around the body of the case, immediately above the base, is a thick molding of gilt bronze in the form of reeding bound with ribbon.

The case is surmounted with a bust of a Roman, perhaps Brutus, in patinated bronze, supported on a circular and tapering plinth of gilt bronze.

A very similar clock, the case stamped by Nicolas Petit (active 1761–after 1789), is in the Wallace Collection, and it is likely that the present clock case is by him also. The bust surmounting the clock is probably a later addition. F.W.

THE
JEFFERSONIAN
CREATION

It is not flattering to say that you have planted the arts in your country. The works already created are the monuments of your judgment and your zeal and of your taste. The first sculpture that adorns an American public building perpetuates your love and your protection of the fine arts.

LATROBE *to Jefferson August 13, 1807*

You see I am an enthusiast on the subject of the arts. But it is an enthusiasm of which I am not ashamed, as it's object is to improve the taste of my countrymen, to increase their reputation, to reconcile to them the respect of the world, and to procure them it's praise.

JEFFERSON *to Madison September 20, 1785*

The legacy of Thomas Jefferson's creative genius survives in the buildings he planned, the grounds that he laid out, the few elegant pieces of furniture and silver produced from his designs and the 520 drawings that document his devotion to the eye and the imagination. In his lifetime, he had not only played a major role in the creation of a new and untested form of government, bringing it through the dangerous, formative years of political organization, but had given it a style as well. His judgment, zeal and taste, as Benjamin Latrobe declared, set the direction for the architecture of the new Republic, and his determination to uphold the highest standards in architecture, landscape design and city planning remains an unprecedented example of national leadership.

As a young man, he was struck by the shortcomings of Colonial architecture and deplored the fact that government itself set no example to improve the general level of public taste. "The first principles of the art are unknown, and there exists scarcely a model among us sufficiently chaste to give an idea of them," he wrote in his *Notes on the State of Virginia*. Yet he was optimistic that perhaps the new experiment in government would somehow generate the right atmosphere to attract a 'spark' to fall "on some young subjects of natural taste, kindle up their genius, and produce a reformation. . . ." Certainly such a spark did somehow ignite his own combustible talents, enabling him to grow from a gentleman-amateur to the stature of a genuine artist, creating new forms out of the ancient tradition of building, to serve the needs of the young democracy.

From the first tentative plans for Monticello to the crowning dome of the rotunda at the University of Virginia, the influence of the great architectural books of the sixteenth, seventeenth and eighteenth centuries on Jefferson's work is well documented. His own building notes and specifications for cornices, columns and pediments are always clear and concise about historic precedents and sources, like a good legal brief. No other American architect had made such a thorough study of the basic published material of architectural design and techniques then available.

Jefferson combined his intellectual preoccupation with these fundamentals with a practical experience in building, which he had gained in the many construction projects at Monticello and his other Virginia property. From the beginning of work on Monticello in 1769 through all of its changes and alterations, it was a virtual laboratory for his endless architectural experiments and ideas.

His friends and neighbors quickly recognized his ability and over the years he produced designs for their houses, including Edgemont, Barboursville and Farmington.

The removal of the capital of Virginia from Williamsburg to Richmond, a move that Jefferson had long advocated, presented him with the opportunity to guide the commissioners in the design of the capitol buildings. He was in Paris at the time, and his recent exposure to the neoclassical developments there and his study of ancient ruins prompted him to propose that the plans for the new capitol building follow the Roman Maison Carrée at Nîmes. The completed structure was a landmark in American architecture, becoming the first important temple-form structure of modern times, announcing the reign of neoclassicism in post-Revolutionary America.

When Jefferson returned to America from France as secretary of state, Washington's administration was engaged in the plans for the permanent seat of the new government on the site that Washington himself had chosen along the Potomac. As Harold Dickson has pointed out in his *Arts of the Young Republic*, the trio of the president, Major L'Enfant and Thomas Jefferson combined those remarkable talents that enabled them to develop with such consumate skill, judgment and taste the basic elements of the new seat of government—an overall city plan, an executive residence and a legislative complex that has survived and functioned through all the changes and growth of the Republic down to the present time.

Jefferson was particularly keen on the style and appearance the public buildings would take and quickly proposed a design competition for the capitol and the president's house. His other concern was to attract and encourage trained architects from abroad to work for the new government and to assist in developing native talent as well. Dr. William Thornton from the West Indies, the Frenchman Stephen Hallet, and George Hadfield and Benjamin H. Latrobe, both from England, all worked with Jefferson and were encouraged by him in his efforts to enlist the best and most competent professional services in such an important project. Later, the young American Robert Mills would study under his tutelage, leaving us renderings of Jefferson's designs that surpassed the draftsmanship of Mills' self-taught tutor.

Jefferson's own abilities as an architect were early recognized not only by his Albemarle neighbors but by foreign travelers such as the marquis de Chastellux and La Rochefoucauld-Lianecourt, who both commented on the impressive artistic achievement of the first version of Monticello. Chastellux's famous observation that Jefferson was the first American to study the fine arts "to learn how to shelter himself from the weather," is accurate in detail and symbolically appropriate. But opinions of Jefferson's attainments as an architect were not so generous in succeeding generations, partly because his political achievements overshadowed his creative side, but chiefly because his drawings were not collected together or published for any organized study. Through the efforts of his great-grandson, Thomas Jefferson Coolidge of Boston, who traveled widely in Virginia collecting the drawings from other descendants, the great body of the third president's architectural papers were deposited in the Massachusetts Historical Society where they have been carefully preserved. In 1916, Fiske Kimball published these drawings in his milestone study, which was later reissued under the editorial supervision of Professor Frederick Doveton Nichols of the University of Virginia, thus marking the beginning of contemporary scholarly reappraisal. Professor Nichols in 1960 (revised 1961) compiled for the first time the definitive checklist of all the Jefferson drawings from various collections around the country, providing an essential research tool.

Among the surviving drawings are sketches and plans for a variety of objects which Jefferson made to guide craftsmen in their production. Ranging from window curtains, coffee urns, and goblets to parquet floors and garden gates, it is an astonishing record of how his visual imagination was directed to perfecting the everyday details of his surroundings. When the artist John Trumbull offered him one of his engravings, Jefferson immediately wrote back to acknowledge the gift and give his precise thoughts on how it should be framed. Proportion, balance and simplicity were uppermost in his mind when ordering table silver

either for his friends or for Monticello. Two surviving drawings in Jefferson's hand for a silver tea urn and a pair of goblets are related to similar pieces that have also survived.

Jefferson ordered a number of pieces of silver while he was in Paris, where he found the neoclassic designs very much to his taste. Indeed, the design of the "coffee pot" as he called it, now in the Massachusetts Historical Society, is very close to the designs of urns which were produced by Odiot, the silver firm that Jefferson frequently patronized in the 1780s. Both French and English silver pieces were undoubtedly packed in the numerous crates which he shipped back to Monticello, when he returned to the United States in 1789.

It was on the building of the University of Virginia that he was to concentrate all of his creative energy during the last years of his life. The development of his achievement can be traced from the first preliminary sketches to the final volutes on the columns of the rotunda, and it is through an examination of these drawings and plans as well as the completed work, that one can see Jefferson's final achievement as an artist in all of its dimensions. Here again, the extraordinary range of his creative powers, his grasp of the central functions of an institution of higher learning, the preeminent place of the library, the close living relationship of students to faculty with the whole complex set out on the plain below Monticello, sited so that the Lawn of th university would be a platform to view the mountains beyond, is a monument to his lifelong commitment to the eye and the mind.

The University of Virginia, like all of his surviving creations, must be experienced through an actual visit, but the documents and designs that flowed from his pen again and again demonstrat his "wisdom and taste," as one of his cosponsors of the university project succinctly put it. Even though Jefferson had frequently pointed out the unwarranted extravagance of an uncontrolled passion for painting and sculpture, architecture, being his own mania, was exempt. Wisdom and taste cost money where buildings were concerned and his plans for the university were no exception, the estimates doubling and tripling in the face of an alarmed legislature. His insistence on "correct" classical details drawn from ancient sources in rich profusion of each façade was intended as a didactic element for the education of the students, and this, coupled with the separate housing of students and departments in a monumental design, was unique in American university experience. His artistic impulses, followed to their logical consequences, united art and life into something new, something revolutionary and something uniquely Jeffersonian. The political philosopher, the statesman, the educator, the architect, the builder and the visionary continue to speak to us across the years, and nowhere more clearly than throug his last creation.

While Jefferson is best known for his design of Monticello and the University of Virginia, the range of his creative originality extends over many other works, large and small. This part of the exhibition has been divided into sections which explore his interes and contributions to domestic architecture, public buildings, and the decorative arts. The university, because of its complexity and its importance, will be dealt with in a separate note. w.h.a.

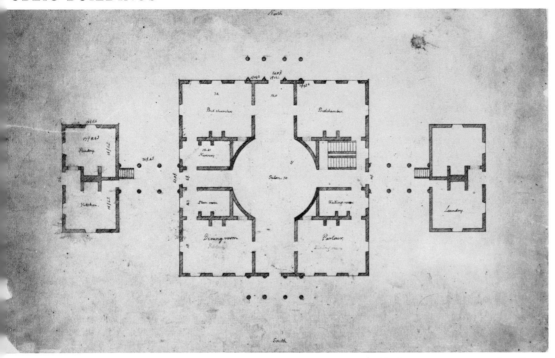

388 Governor's House, first floor plan
THOMAS JEFFERSON 1743–1826
Ink on laid paper c. 1780
49.9 x 29.9 (19½ x 11¾)
Lent by the University of Virginia, Alderman Library, Charlottesville

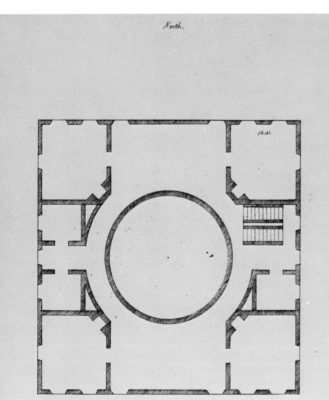

389 Governor's House, second floor plan
THOMAS JEFFERSON 1743–1826
Ink on laid paper c. 1780
48.9 x 30.5 (19¼ x 12)
Lent by the University of Virginia, Alderman Library, Charlottesville

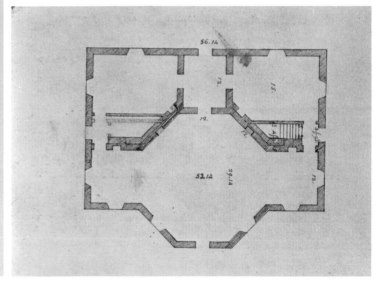

390 Study for Governor's House
THOMAS JEFFERSON 1743–1826
Ink on laid paper 1780
15.2 x 19.4 (6 x 7⅝)
Lent by the Massachusetts Historical Society, Boston

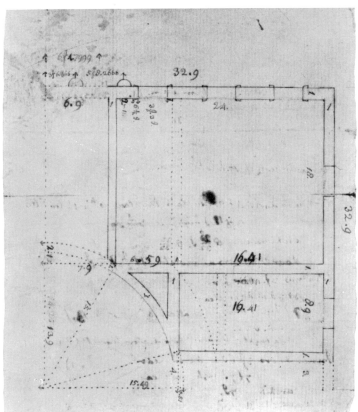

391 Study for Governor's House
THOMAS JEFFERSON 1743–1826
Ink on laid paper c. 1780
10.2 x 12.1 (4 x 4¾)
*Lent by the Massachusetts Historical
Society, Boston*

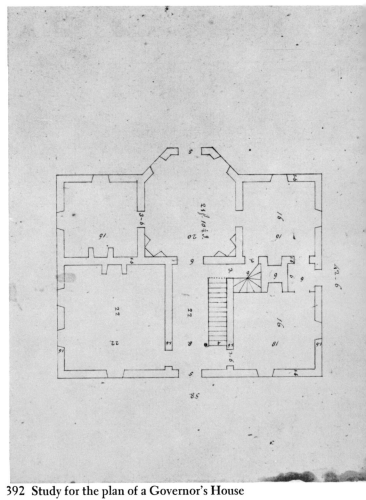

392 Study for the plan of a Governor's House
THOMAS JEFFERSON 1743–1826
Ink on laid paper c. 1779
69.9 x 38.1
*Lent by the Massachusetts Historical
Society, Boston*

Even before 1780, when he was appointed head of a committee to erect public buildings for the new Virginia capital at Richmond, Jefferson had made studies for a governor's house to be built there, using the idea of a temple form, which had also dominated his plans for remodeling the governor's palace in Williamsburg (see nos. 20, 21). Both of these forays into designs for a residence of a public figure show that Jefferson's taste for classicism in architecture was developed long before his exposure to antique ruins in Italy and France or his friendship with the architect Clérisseau, who was to be instrumental in the design of the Richmond capitol (see nos. 394–399).

Five drawings for the governor's house are shown here. One, which may have been the earliest drawing, shows the same plan that Jefferson proposed for Williamsburg, except for the inclusion of a central stair hall. An octagonal room is the most important feature of this design. Another, more developed plan shows a small compact design, along the lines of a pavilion, and could be regarded as half of a *villa rotonda*. This is similar to plate 12 in Morris' *Select Architecture*, a book frequently used by Jefferson. The octagonal room is featured again in this plan, with the adjoining rooms opening directly into it.

Yet another drawing shows one quarter of the scheme for a *villa rotonda*. In this final design for the governor's house, Jefferson repeated the idea he had proposed years before for the governor's palace in Williamsburg, and was later to propose for the president's house in Washington (see nos. 410–415). This design for Richmond is smaller than either the Williamsburg or Washington schemes, which undoubtedly reflects the finances of the state during the early days of the republic. The plan has only one portico, four columns wide instead of the four six-column porticoes in Palladio's design for the Villa Rotonda, after which this is modeled, or the four porticoes in Jefferson's later plan for the president's house. Jefferson's debt to Palladio is further acknowledged by the similarity of the exterior to the original. It should be remembered that a general borrowing of aesthetic ideas was not regarded as plagiarism in Jefferson's day. This drawing is executed on the same paper as Jefferson's three plates for the extension of Richmond, and thus dates from about 1780.

The two floor plans, one for the first and one for the second floor, give the arrangement and dimensions of the final design, showing a rotunda house adapted to the traditional Virginia plantation house design, with wings connected by short colonnades. The circle in the center of the second floor is the upper part of a two-story high salon, which is closed off from the rest of the second floor, making the plan rather awkward. F.N.

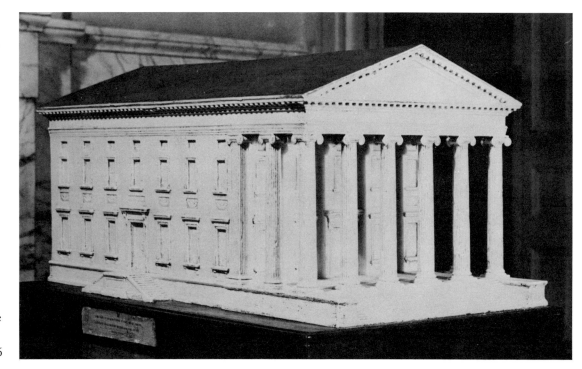

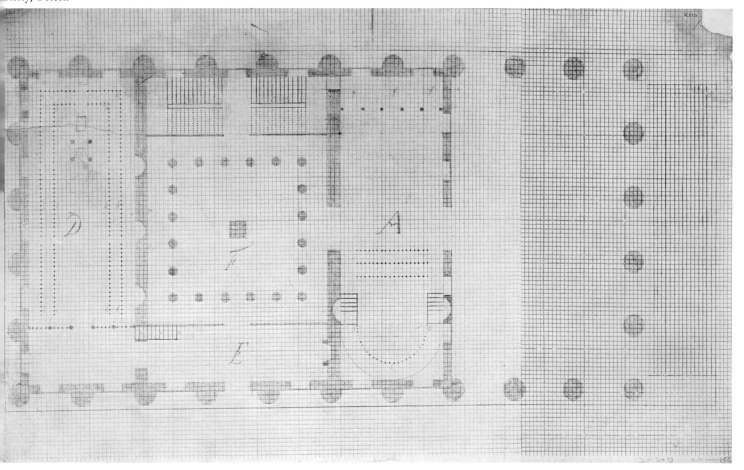

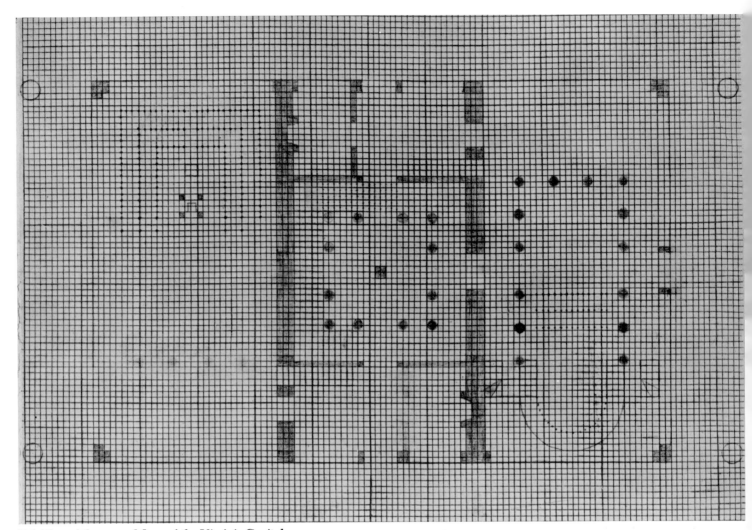

395 Plan of the second floor of the Virginia Capitol

THOMAS JEFFERSON 1743–1826
Pencil on wove paper
26.6 x 44.4 (10½ x 17½)

*Lent by the Massachusetts Historical
Society, Boston*

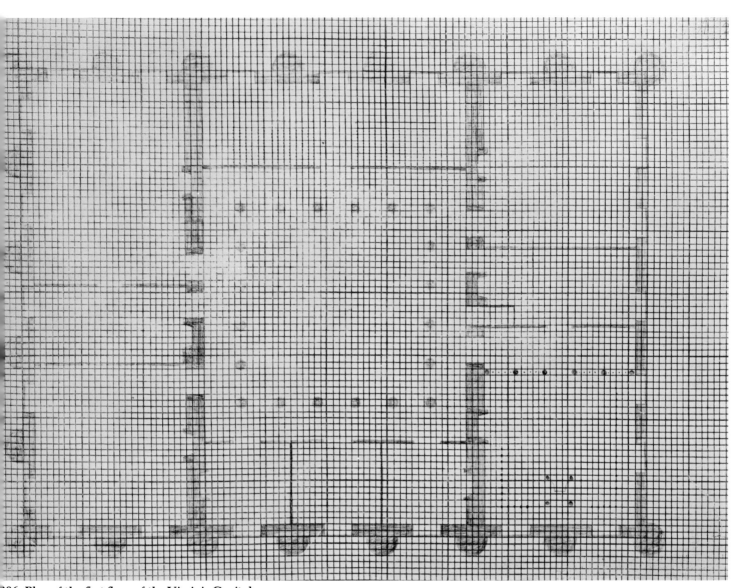

396 Plan of the first floor of the Virginia Capitol

THOMAS JEFFERSON 1743–1826
Pencil on wove paper
38.1 x 26.6 (15 x 10½)
Lent by the Massachusetts Historical
Society, Boston

397 Side elevation of the Virginia Capitol
THOMAS JEFFERSON 1743–1826
Pencil on wove paper
37.5 x 27.9 (14¾ x 11)
*Lent by the Massachusetts Historical
Society, Boston*

398 Side elevation of the Virginia Capitol
THOMAS JEFFERSON 1743–1826
Pencil on wove paper
49.5 x 65.4 (19½ x 25¾)
*Lent by the Massachusetts Historical
Society, Boston*

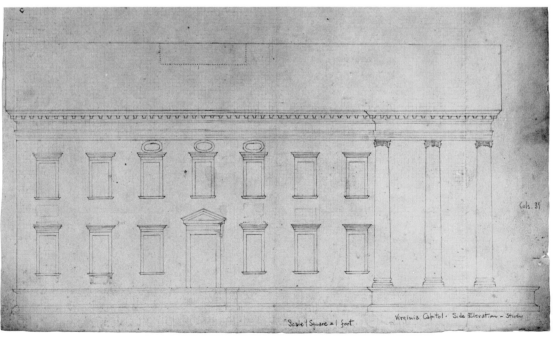

Jefferson made his first studies for the new capitol building in 1780, the year the capital was moved to Richmond from Williamsburg. He envisioned it as a templelike structure with porticoes at each end. In 1784 Jefferson went to France as minister and in August of the following year wrote to James Buchanan and William Hay that he had found an architect "whose taste has been beformed on a study of antient models. . . . He has studied 20 years in Rome and has given proofs of his skill and taste by a publication of some antiquities of this country." This architect was Charles-Louis Clérisseau and the "publication of some antiquities" was his book on the monuments of Nîmes exhibited here at number 158. In September Jefferson wrote to James Madison that the external form and plan had been agreed upon and "we took for our model what is called the Maison Quarrée. . . ." Later he wrote that he himself had undertaken the number and sizes of the rooms and their relationship to one another, as it was impossible for a foreign architect to know about these matters. Jefferson's drawings are studies relating to this. Three elevations by Jefferson show studies for the exterior and demonstrate the close relationship to the Maison Carrée model. In two of these the additions in soft pencil suggesting changes in the roof pitch, the addition of consoles, window enframements and panels are Clérisseau's; the single portico is probably also his. The final drawings, which are now probably lost, were sent to Richmond in January of 1786. The model by Bloquet shown at number 393 was not ready until June and did not leave Le Havre until December. It most nearly represents the building's final design, with Clérisseau's suggested reduction of the depth of the portico; the change to Ionic from Corinthian capitals and the addition of inset panels with garlands were also due to him.

As executed the capitol was much simpler. The inset panels and garlands were left out, the columns were not fluted, the stairs were originally not built, different materials were used and pilasters were added to the side walls. Most, if not all, of these things were done for financial reasons and were probably decided by the builder.

It is not possible to decide definitively on what parts Clérisseau and Jefferson each played in the design for the capitol. Clérisseau certainly knew more about the Roman original than Jefferson and was a skilled professional architect but Jefferson as early as 1780 was thinking of a templelike structure. The two undoubtedly collaborated on a project of interest

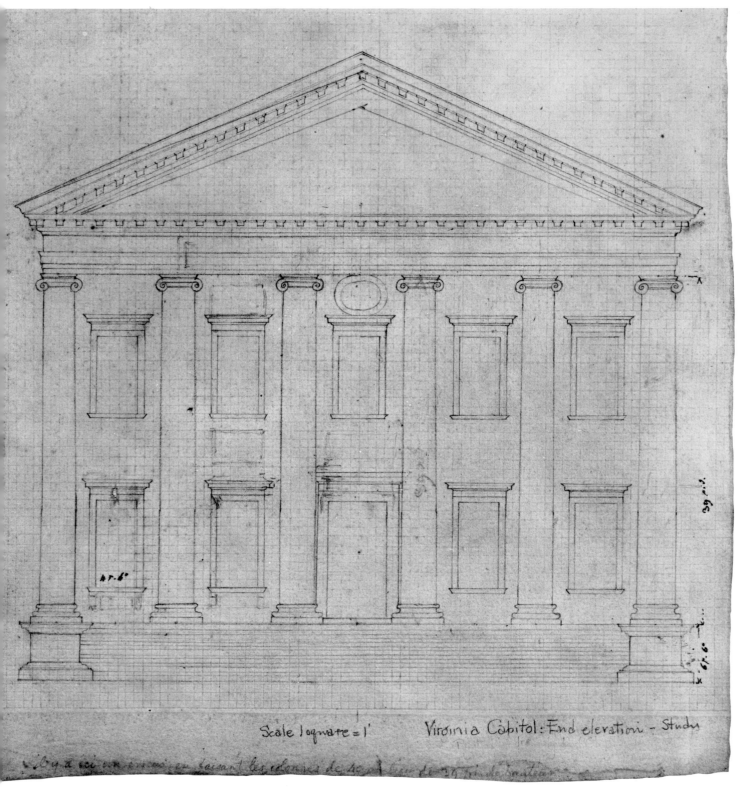

Scale 1 square = 1'   Virginia Capitol: End elevation - Study

399 Front elevation of the Virginia Capitol

o both of them, a building which
as been called "The First Monument
of the Classical Revival." T.J.MCC.

THOMAS JEFFERSON 1743–1826
Pencil on wove paper
41.9 x 26 (16½ x 10¼)
*Lent by the Massachusetts Historical
Society, Boston*

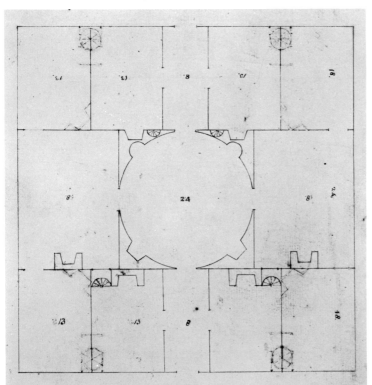

400 Study for the plan of a rotunda house, probably a new governor's palace for Williamsburg

THOMAS JEFFERSON 1743–1826
Ink on laid paper (facsimile)
1772–1773

Original at the Huntington Library, San Marino, California

The rotunda house was a design that Jefferson returned to again and again in his plans for residences, not only in the early study for the governor's palace in Williamsburg, shown here, but for the governor's house in Richmond (see nos. 388–392) and in his anonymous entry in the president's house competition (see nos. 410–415). Only at Monticello, however, was his domed plan actually constructed. Toward the end of his life, he succeeded in constructing a rotunda in its purest form at the University of Virginia.

Jefferson's first book on architecture was probably Leoni's translation of Andrea Palladio's *Quattro Libri*. It was purchased from an old cabinetmaker who lived near the college gate in Williamsburg, as Jefferson said, and this was the catalyst that stimulated his interest in architecture.

In this book he found the illustrations for one of the most famous houses in the world, a building Jefferson admired intensely: the *Villa Rotonda* near Vicenza, Italy. Even as his technical abilities in design increased, he never lost his admiration for the villa of Palladio, though he was unable to take the time to go to Vicenza to see it when he made a trip to southern France and Italy in 1787.

Editions of Palladio were scarce in early Virginia, as Jefferson wrote in a December 24, 1804, letter to James Oldham, a Virginia builder:

In answer to your's of the 17th desiring me to procure a Palladio for you either here or at Philadelphia, there never was a Palladio here even in private hands till I brought one; and I scarcely expect it is to be had in Philadelphia; but I will try both there and at Baltimore. The late Mr. Ryland Randolph of Turkey Island had one, which is probably out of use. Mr. David Randolph could probably give you information respecting it, and whether it can be bought. The chance of getting one in America is slender. In the mean time, as you may be distressed for present use, I send you my portable edition, which I value because it is portable; you will return it at your own convenience. It contains only the 1st book on the orders, which is the essential part. The remaining books contain only plans of great buildings, temples, etc. Accept my salutations.

F.N.

401 Plan of a prison, description

FRANÇOIS-PHILIPPE CHARPENTIER 1734–1817, after Pierre-Gabriel Bugniet d. 1806
Engraving (facsimile)

402 First floor plan of a prison

FRANÇOIS-PHILIPPE CHARPENTIER 1734–1817, after Pierre-Gabriel Bugniet d. 1806
Engraving (facsimile)

When asking Jefferson to have a plan drawn in Paris for the capitol at Richmond, the directors of public buildings also requested "a draught for the Governor's house and prison." In his reply dated August 13, 1785, Jefferson wrote: "Having heard high commendations of a plan of a prison drawn by an architect at Lyons I sent there for it. The architect furnished me with it. It is certainly the best plan I ever saw. It unites in the most perfect manner the objects of security and health, and has moreover the advantage, valuable to us, of being capable of being adjusted to any number of prisoners, small or great and admitting of execution from time to time, as it may be convenient." Jefferson thereupon proceeded to have a plan drawn, designed for forty prisoners instead of the nine hundred "cells or chambers" envisaged in the Lyonnaise architect's scheme. On January 26, 1786, he sent to Virginia the plans for the Richmond prison, and with it "the plan of the prison proposed at Lyons which was sent me by the architect, and to which we are indebted for the fundamental idea of ours."

In later correspondence Jefferson identified the Lyonnaise architect as Bugniet and further specified that the latter had prepared an engraved plan of a prison. The engraved plan sent by Jefferson has been lost, as has his own plan for Richmond. Another example of the Bugniet plan, exhibited here, is similar to the scheme that excited Jefferson's interest and inspired his own plan. These four engravings by F. P. Charpentier were published in 1765 according to a notice in the July issue of the *Mercure de France* for that year. The first is a descriptive text outlining Bugniet's concept, while the plans themselves show a floor plan, an elevation, and a cross-section. Although the *Mercure* headed its notice "Plan d'une prison pour la Ville de Paris, inventé et dessiné par le sieur P. G. Bugniet, architecte," Bugniet's own description refers to the prison only as one that "might serve as a central prison for a Capital, even for Paris." It might therefore be better described as a plan for an ideal prison. Bugniet later built the Prison de Roanne at Lyons (1785, demolished 1837), but this apparently bore little relationship to his earlier ideal scheme.

At the time Jefferson sent his plan

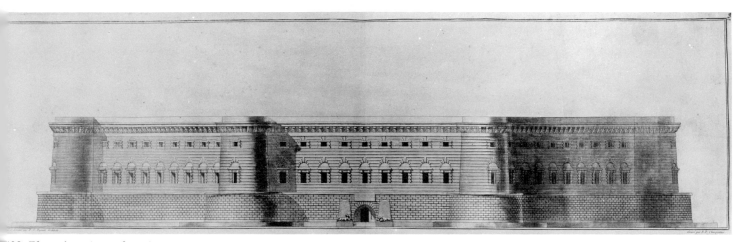

403 Plan of a prison, elevation
FRANÇOIS-PHILIPPE
CHARPENTIER 1734–1817, after
Pierre-Gabriel Bugniet d. 1806
Engraving (facsimile)

404 Plan of a prison, cross-section
FRANÇOIS-PHILIPPE
CHARPENTIER 1734–1817, after
Pierre-Gabriel Bugniet d. 1806
Engraving (facsimile)

to Richmond no immediate action
was taken on building a prison there.
When the business was resumed in
1797, the Virginia authorities turned
to Benjamin Latrobe. The principle
but not the exact form of his own
plan, Jefferson wrote in his *Autobiography*, "was adopted by Latrobe
in carrying the plan into execution,
by the erection of what is now called
the Penitentiary, built under his
direction." The Penitentiary (which
burned in 1823), Fiske Kimball has
said, "is not to be counted among
Jefferson's works, though the fruitful
idea which it embodied had come
from him" (see no. 405). Tracing the
genetic process a step farther back,
a share in the fruitful idea can be
attributed to Pierre-Gabriel Bugniet
and his plan for an ideal prison. H.C.R.

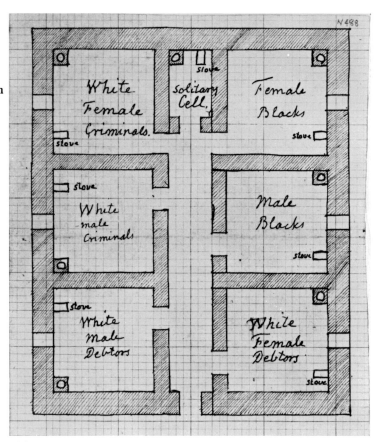

405 A prison with a cell for solitary confinement

THOMAS JEFFERSON 1743–1826
Ink on laid paper
12.3 x 23.2 (4⅞ x 9⅛)
*Lent by the Massachusetts Historical
Society, Boston*

Jefferson was much interested in the
new social theories for the rehabilitation of criminals in which solitary
confinement played a prominent part.
His involvement with prison design
began when, during his stay in Paris,
he was asked for advice on the

building of a new capitol and a penitentiary for Richmond (see nos. 401–
404 for details on Jefferson's role
in the development of the prison
plans). Jefferson recalled in his *Autobiography*, "With respect to the plan
of a prison . . . I had heard of a benevolent society, in England, which
had been indulged by the government,
in an experiment of the effect of
labor, in *solitary confinement*, on
some of their criminals; which experiment had succeeded beyond
expectation."

When the prison was finally begun
ten years later under the supervision
of Benjamin Latrobe, Jefferson corresponded with Latrobe and Governor
James Wood about its design. This
undated sketch shows the solitary
confinement facilities which he
thought so important in keeping
youthful offenders from contact with
hardened criminals. F.N.

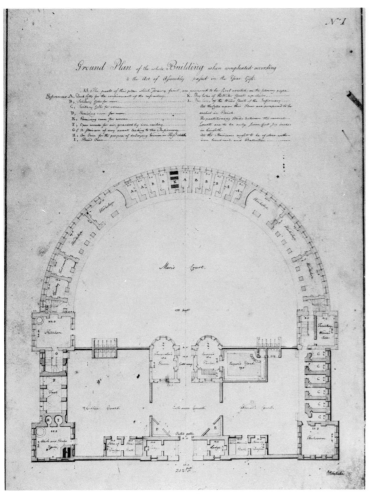

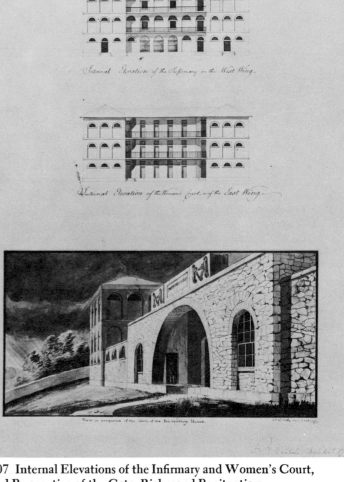

406 Ground Plan of the Richmond Penitentiary

BENJAMIN HENRY LATROBE
1764–1820
Pen and ink 1797
51.5 x 38.1 (20¼ x 15)
Signed lower right: *BHLatrobe. 1797*
*Lent by the Virginia State Library,
Richmond*

Influenced by Jefferson's longstanding concern for greater humanity within penal systems, the state of Virginia in 1796 sponsored a competition for the design of a new penitentiary appropriate to the reforms enacted in that same year. Benjamin Henry Latrobe was awarded the commission and appointed to direct the work. A prominent feature of his design is the semicircular court around which the cells are placed. This plan affords the keeper, whose watch is located at bottom center of the men's court, maximum visibility of the cells and exercise area. It has been pointed out by Hamlin that Latrobe does not indicate segregation of prisoners on the basis of race, a rather unusual attitude for the period.

As early as March 1785, the directors in charge of public building in the young city of Richmond had turned to Jefferson, then in France, with a request for plans for a capitol and—less urgently—a governor's house and a prison. Jefferson had heard "high commendations" of the plans of a new prison at Lyons by Pierre-Gabriel Bugniet (see nos. 401–404). B.S.

407 Internal Elevations of the Infirmary and Women's Court, and Perspective of the Gate, Richmond Penitentiary

BENJAMIN HENRY LATROBE
1764–1820
Pen and ink, watercolor 1797
50.9 x 36.2 (20 x 14¼)
Signed twice in lower right:
B. H. Latrobe Archt. del. 1797
B. H. Latrobe Architect 1797
*Lent by the Virginia State Library,
Richmond*

An example of Latrobe's use of vaulted masonry for fire resistance in public buildings can be seen in his perspective view of the gate of the Virginia penitentiary, the first large prison in America to be conceived architecturally. Although in this watercolor Latrobe depicts a stormy sky, setting the conventional gloomy tone of prison life, the building itself incorporated ideas which were well in advance of their time. The corner-stone inscription, written by Latrobe, projects a sense of hope, through rehabilitation, for the incarcerated:

The Legislature
of the Commonwealth of Virginia
having abolished the antient
sanguinary criminal code
The first stone of an Edifice
The Monument of that Wisdom
which should reform while it
punishes the Criminal
was laid on the 7th day of August
in the year 1797, and of
American Independence the 22nd
by Jⁿ Wood Esq., Governor
Gr. Master of Masons

The prison, whose ground plan is shown at number 406, was Latrobe's major commission during his years in Virginia. B.S.

408 View of the City of Richmond from the South side of the James River

BENJAMIN HENRY LATROBE
1764–1820
Watercolor, pencil, pen and ink 1798
17.8 x 26 (7 x 10¼)

Lent by the Maryland Historical Society, Baltimore

In this view of Richmond, the former Bushrod Washington house, by 1798 the residence of Colonel Harvie, is located on the summit of the hill above the letter a which appears in the lower left of the drawing. At the center are two trees between which can be seen the "Backstreet" of Richmond. The capitol is at the center; the large house immediately to the right is that of the governor. "The Houses in the foreground are part of the City, now much neglected, East of Shockoe Creek, Schockoe Creek now discharges itself into the James River at the Rocks over [letter] c. Formerly it ran close under the Bank . . . and had a channel deep enough for any Vessels which could pass Harrison's bar. It is now choaked up to the great injury of Richmond," wrote Latrobe in his *Sketchbook*.

Jefferson lived in the governor's house in 1780, when the assembly first met in Richmond. He had first introduced a bill to move the capital from Williamsburg in 1776, motivated not only by the old capital's vulnerability to attack from the sea, but by a desire to place the capital more centrally between the Tidewater and the frontier portion of Virginia, which was rapidly growing in population. B.S.

409 View of Richmond from Bushrod Washington's Island

BENJAMIN HENRY LATROBE
1764–1820
Watercolor, pencil, pen and ink 1796
17.8 x 26.2 (7 x 10⁵⁄₁₆)

Lent by the Maryland Historical Society, Baltimore

Newly arrived from England, the architect Latrobe entered Richmond for the first time in early April 1796. In his journal entry for April 7, he discusses the "general similarity" between the settings of the English town of Richmond and its American namesake, noting that the "hills are so similar in their great features, that at first sight the likeness is most striking. The detail of course must be extremely different. But the windings of James river have so much the same cast with those of the Thames, the amphitheatre of hills covered partly with wood, partly with buildings . . . are so like the hills on the South bank of the Thames . . . that if a man could be imperceptibly & in an instant conveyed from one side of the Atlantic to the other he might hesitate for Some minutes before he could discover the difference."

These hills, as recorded by Latrobe, were already occupied by a city of some size and dignity, quite changed from the scene presented to Jefferson as he frequently passed through in his early travels between Shadwell or Tuckahoe and Williamsburg. As a young lawyer he practiced at the Richmond courthouse, and it was his Bill for the Removal of the Seat of Government of Virginia, first prepared in 1776 and at length passed by the General Assembly in 1779, which finally settled the capital at Richmond. Its most radical provision called for separate buildings for the legislative, judicial and executive branches, a plan later abandoned for economic reasons.

Fiske Kimball has identified drawings of a temple structure in the Massachusetts Historical Society (see nos. 394–399) as Jefferson's first plans for this revolutionary concept for housing a republican government, dating them 1780, five years before Jefferson finally adopted the Maison Carrée as a model for the capitol. B.S.

THE COMPETITION FOR THE DESIGN OF THE PRESIDENT'S HOUSE (now White House) IN WASHINGTON, D.C., IN 1792

The two competitions established in 1792 for the design of the president's house and the capitol in Washington constitute the first important architectural competitions in the United States. They mark the transition from the work of builders and amateurs, who had so far dominated American architecture, to that of the professional architects who were henceforth to assume the leading role. Although the competition for the capitol was beset with various difficulties that delayed the controversial outcome for more than a year, the one for the president's house proved relatively free of any controversies or complications. First and second prizes were awarded on the day following the judging of the entries, at which time the winner, James Hoban, was also engaged to supervise construction work.

In his monumental work on *Thomas Jefferson, Architect* (1916) and in a series of articles published in 1918–1919 on the competition, Fiske Kimball reproduced and discussed several of the design submissions for the president's house. Further study of the drawings in possession of the Maryland Historical Society, the Massachusetts Historical Society, and the University of Virginia and of attendant documents assembled at the National Archives and the Library of Congress, together with examination of material unearthed in various regional archives, now make it possible to shed further light on the competition. This new information is contained in the present essay and in the entries accompanying the surviving competition and related drawings, which are exhibited together here for the first time.

By passage of the Residence Act on July 9, 1790, the seat of government of the United States was permanently established within a district ten miles square situated on the banks of the Potomac. By this act President Washington was likewise authorized to appoint three commissioners of the federal city to survey and lay out the new federal capital and to "provide suitable buildings for the accomodation of Congress and of the President and for the public offices of the United States." Daniel Carroll of Rock Creek, Thomas Johnson of Maryland, and David Stuart of Alexandria, Virginia, were appointed to undertake the task. The exact boundaries of the federal district and the location of buildings within it were left to the president to decide. His most trusted advisor in this matter was Thomas Jefferson, secretary of state in Washington's administration, who took a deep and personal interest both in the competitions and in the planning and building of the capital city.

In 1791 Washington appointed a French engineer-architect, Pierre-Charles L'Enfant, to plan the new capital. L'Enfant based his scheme on the broad radiating avenues of the typical baroque city plan. Working with the triangle between the Potomac and Anacostia rivers, he established two focal points, one on the east side centered on the capitol building, the other to the northwest centered on the president's house. Although L'Enfant had likewise been expected to design the principal government buildings, his dismissal in 1792 as a result of conflict with he commissioners raised the question of obtaining the services of suitable architects for the task. The idea of holding a competition to seek the best designs for the president's house and capitol, which had first been suggested by Jefferson in a memorandum of September 8, 1791, was adopted by Washington and the commissioners at this time. Jefferson's "sketch of an advertisement," located among his papers (Series 3) in the Manuscripts Division of the Library of Congress, shows that the official announcement of the competition for the president's house was essentially his work. It stipulated a premium of five hundred dollars or a medal of equal value for the best design and set forth general requirements for the mansion. A suggestion from Washington that the site be taken into account in the design was penciled in at the bottom of Jefferson's draft that was enclosed in a letter of March 6, 1792, from the secretary of state to the commissioners. The final advertisement, issued by the commissioners on March 14, followed the draft with negligible changes:

Washington in the Territory of Columbia
A Premium
of 500 dollars or a medal of that value at the option of the party will be given by the Commissioners of the federal buildings to the person who before the fifteenth day of July next shall produce to them the most approved plan, if adopted by them for a Presidents house to be erected in this City. The site of the building, if the artist will attend to it, will of course influence the aspect and outline of his plan and its destination will point out to him the number, size and distribution of the apartments. It will be a recommendation of any plan if the Central part of it may be detached and erected for the present with the appearance of a complete whole and be capable of admitting the additional parts in the future, if they shall be wanting. Drawings will be expected of the ground plats, elevations of each front and sections through the building in such directions as may be necessary to explain the internal structure, and an estimate of the Cubic feet of brickwork composing the whole mass of the walls.

March 14,th 1792. The Commissioners

This advertisement, which the commissioners "ordered to be published in the principal Towns in the United States," appeared in the April 3, 1792, edition of the *Maryland Journal and Baltimore Advertiser*.

Although the program did not suggest it, the character deemed appropriate for the president's house was a matter of some concern for both Jefferson and Washington. In a letter to L'Enfant of April 10, 1791, Jefferson had indicated that, "for the President's house, I should prefer the celebrated fronts of modern buildings, which have already received the approbation of all good judges. Such are the Galerie du Louvre, the Garde meubles, and two fronts of the Hotel de Salm." Although elements from these "modern buildings" were incorporated in a supposed preliminary study by Jefferson, the design which he subsequently submitted anonymously in the competition was modeled instead after Palladio's famous sixteenth-century *Villa Rotonda* near Vicenza.

Unlike his enterprising secretary of state, Washington was less aesthetically inclined and professed, in a letter to the commissioners dated July 23, 1792, "to have no knowledge in

Architecture." His concern for the more practical aspects of the program is seen in the reference to the president's house contained in his letter of March 8, 1792, to David Stuart, one of the commissioners. "For the President's house," he wrote, "I would design a building which should also look forward but execute no more of it at present than might suit the circumstances of this country, when it shall first be wanted. A Plan comprehending more may be executed at a future period when the wealth, population and importance of it shall stand upon much higher ground than they do at present." Apart from revealing his concern for avoiding undue ostentation, Washington's remarks advance the concept of building, or at least designing, the president's house in stages. This concept was incorporated in the final announcement of the competition for the president's house, and was subsequently reflected in several of the designs submitted.

The commissioners themselves appear largely to have remained silent on the subject of the character of the president's house. However, a rare passage in their letter of January 4, 1793, to the municipal authorities of Bordeaux requesting permission to recruit craftsmen in the French city supplies an effusive characterization of that architectural style which the commissioners expressed ambition to promote in the new federal district. "We wish," they wrote to their French colleagues, "to exhibit a grandeur of conception, a Republican simplicity, and that true Elegance of proportion which corresponds to a tempered freedom excluding Frivolity, the food of little minds." As may be seen from the surviving competition drawings exhibited here, however, the commissioners' ebullient expectations—expressed well after the fact—far exceeded the caliber of most of the results obtained.

The evidence needed for a full knowledge of the competition and the competitors for the president's house is widely dispersed and, in some instances, either lost or yet to be discovered. The absence in the records of the commissioners, presently deposited in the National Archives, of anything like an inventory of drawings submitted in the competition now makes it impossible to be sure of the total number of entries or drawings originally submitted. Of the competition drawings themselves, the greater number evidently passed from the possession of the commissioners to Benjamin H. Latrobe some time during his tenure as surveyor of the public buildings from 1803 to 1811. A folio scrapbook containing competition drawings for the capitol and president's house was presented on October 12, 1865, by a son, John H. B. Latrobe, to the Maryland Historical Society, which retains possession of them. Among the entries for the president's house included in this collection are those of James Hoban, James Diamond, Jacob Small, and Andrew Mayfield Carshore, together with that of Thomas Jefferson signed with the pseudonymous initials A. Z. Hoban's plan for the president's house was discovered amid the great collection of Jefferson drawings brought together early in this century at the Massachusetts Historical Society in Boston by Thomas Jefferson Coolidge, Jr. These constitute all the extant competition drawings for the president's house, exhibited here, of which the whereabouts are known today.

Designs known to have been submitted but which are neither included in the above collections nor have yet been located elsewhere are those by John Collins, Stephen (Etienne Sulpice) Hallet, and Collen Williamson. Persuasive evidence of the existence of Collins' submission comes from the resolution passed on July 17, 1792, by the commissioners, citing his entry for being "scientific and the second in merit which has been laid before them," and directing payment of $150 to Collins "as a Token of their sense of the merit of his Essay." Evidence of the existence of the entries by Hallet and Williamson is less conclusive. It is restricted to passing references in letters, which have been found in other instances to be occasionally in error. Knowledge of Hallet's submission comes from a single reference in Jefferson's letter of July 11, 1792, to the commissioners. In it, he advises them that he is forwarding them "a plan of a Capitol and another of a President's House by a Mr. Hallet." The existence of Williamson's drawings is indicated in the concluding sentence of a letter to him from the commissioners on July 19, 1792, which reads: "Yr. favor with a plan for the President's pallace not come to hand until the 16th Instant," or the day after the announced deadline.

Absence of Williamson's drawings, though regrettable, is not likely to alter significantly our picture of the character of the competition. A master mason and builder who was for a time superintendent of stonecutters for the capitol, Williamson probably would not have produced drawings of any conspicuous architectural merit. Given the special consideration accorded Dr. William Thornton's late submission to the competition for the capitol, it is likely that similar concessions might well have been made for Williamson's design for the president's house, had it been deemed deserving of such consideration by Washington and the commissioners. It is most unfortunate, on the other hand, that the missing drawings include those by Collins and Hallet. In view of its having been awarded the second premium, the loss of Collins' entry and, for that matter, the absence of any certain knowledge of the man makes the record of so important a competition sadly incomplete. Given the caliber of Hoban's design on the one hand, and that of the known rejected entries—especially Jefferson's—on the other, discovery of Collins' submission would do much to further our knowledge not only of the competition, but also of the state of American architecture during this crucial period of its development. The apparent loss of Hallet's supposed design for the president's house is perhaps even more regrettable. A French architect who was of more established training than any of the other known entrants in the competition, Hallet might have been expected to produce a design whose caliber would surely have been at least equal to that of Hoban's winning submission. Jefferson's reference to it in his letter might conceivably have been based on a mistaken impression, stemming from a hurried glance through Hallet's drawings, that they contained designs for the president's house as well as for the capitol. No other documentary reference to Hallet's drawings for the president's house has been uncovered, however. The other possibility may be that Hallet's drawings for the president's house—if they did, in fact, exist—could have been lost prior to the final judging on July 16–17, 1792, and so escaped the notice of Washington and the commissioners. Yet that prospect, of which no mention is made anywhere in the known records, seems somehow unlikely.

There is, finally, the question of one other possible entry for the president's house. In his fourth article on the "Competition for the Federal Buildings, 1792–1793" published in the August 1919 issue of the *Journal of the American Institute of Architects*, Fiske Kimball alludes to a design by Philip Hart for the president's house. The only known reference to Hart's drawings, however, and the one cited in Kimball's article, is a letter of June 6, 1792, to Jefferson from the commissioners. In it, they advise the secretary of state that "We hand, through Maj^r Ellicott for the Presidents view, a Draft for the Capitol by Wm Hart of Taney Town." No mention is made in that letter, however, of any "draft" by Hart for the president's house. Moreover, a thorough restudy of Hart's competition drawings in possession of the Maryland Historical Society indicates that the Hart design identified by Kimball as being for the president's house is, in all probability, a variation of the other Hart design for the capitol contained in the collection. Though none of the drawings is identified as being for either the capitol or the president's house—a frequent failing of the entries in the Maryland collection—the disposition of all of Hart's plans suggests rooms and facilities geared more for a capitol building than for a presidential residence.

Mention should also be made here of two elevations executed by Dr. William Thornton and preserved by the American Institute of Architects, which were suggested by Glenn Brown in 1896 as ones that Thornton might have proposed for the president's house. However, in an article entitled "William Thornton and the Design of the United States Capitol" published in 1923, Fiske Kimball and Wells Bennett pointed out that these elevations were in exact agreement with one of Thornton's known plan studies for the Capitol, and therefore could not have been intended by him for the president's house. Indeed, although Thornton had at the outset expressed his intention to submit drawings for both the Capitol and the president's house, there is no evidence to indicate that the latter was ever submitted or even developed by Thornton. He was advised in a letter from the Commissioners dated November 15, 1792, that "a choice has been made for the President's House"; they informed him that "We shall be glad however to receive your plan for the Capitol." Thornton's two elevations in question, together with the corresponding plans, clearly were aimed for the more expansive Capitol building.

Drawings due on July 15 were reviewed by President Washington and the three commissioners on the following two days. Jefferson's absence from so momentous a proceeding, highly unusual under ordinary circumstances, may doubtless be explained by the fact that he was himself an anonymous entrant in the competition and so reluctant to impose his views directly on this particular deliberation. On July 17, the commissioners declared the entry by James Hoban "the best plan of a President's house" and the one by John Collins, "the second in merit." The ollowing day, they issued a certificate to Hoban indicating that he "chuses a Gold medal of 10 Guineas value—the Ballance in money," as well as confirming his retention for three hundred guineas a year "to make the drawings and superintend the execution of his plan of the Palace and such other work of that kind as may be in execution."

The apparent failure of Washington or the commissioners to discuss the merits of any of the entries save Hoban's is doubtless indicative of their disappointment in the caliber of the other submissions. In a letter of July 9 to David Stuart, one of the commissioners, Washington openly lamented the mediocre quality of the drawings at hand, complaining that "if none more elegant than these should appear on or before the 10th. instant, the exhibition of architecture will be a very dull one indeed." It is difficult, of course, to ascertain precisely which drawings proved the object of Washington's unflattering remarks. Nevertheless, the ebullient sentiments expressed by the commissioners to the counterparts in Bordeaux notwithstanding, the surviving competition drawings here exhibited amply illustrate the applicability of Washington's assessment to the vast majority of designs submitted in the competitions for both the president's house and the capitol.

Although all represent inspired efforts to surpass the ordinary buildings of the American colonies and so express in architectural terms the noble ideals embraced by the new republic, none of the entries for the president's house save those of Hoban and Jefferson displays anything more than, at best, a provincial sense of composition and scale or the most rudimentary grasp of building technique. It was doubtless this fact that inspired John H. B. Latrobe to characterize these designs, in his essay accompanying the competition drawings presented in 1865 to the Maryland Historical Society, as being "below criticism" and to assert, in a moment of unmitigated candor, that "the poorest carpenter's apprentice of the present day, who aimed at architectural construction, would be ashamed of the most of them." No less striking is the fact that few native-born designers in the United States elected to enter the competition. Of the known competitors, only Jefferson and Jacob Small fall into that category. James Hoban, Andrew Mayfield Carshore, and evidently James Diamond were all born in Ireland, while Hallet was a native of France; nothing is known of the background or whereabouts of John Collins, who won second prize in the competition. Of these, moreover, only Hoban and Hallet—if, indeed, the latter was a participant in the competition—could be considered what we today would regard a professional architect. To be sure, Jefferson, the enlightened amateur, was in many significant ways an architect in conception if not in fact. The other entrants, judging by their drawings displayed here and by what information about them could be uncovered to date, encompass the full range of backgrounds typical of amateur architects in Colonial America. Though advertising himself as an architect, James Diamond doubtless was of the builder variety; Jacob Small, though assuming the title of architect, was evidently never more than a carpenter; Andrew Mayfield Carshore was a distinguished teacher whose entry in the competition appears to have been his only excursion into the realm of architectural design. In all instances, these competitors continued the widespread practice in eighteenth-century America of relying heavily on the architectural books proliferating in the period for inspiration and technique. The best designs in the competition, those of Hoban and Jefferson, relied most closely upon an academic imitation of known prototypes. The others, though obviously without much tutored skill in design or building, departed more freely and with varying degrees of success from their sources, altering both detail and *parti* in accordance with their sense of appropriateness, invention, and taste.

On the whole, the designs for the president's house are rather uninspired, bookish performances that looked to traditional sources of older styles—even if ones generally untypical of the contemporary American scene—rather than pointed the way to any new trends, such as the neoclassical style that was to flourish in American architecture only with the full-fledged work of Jefferson, Bulfinch, and especially Latrobe and his pupils. Still, even if those entering the competition proved for the most part incapable of responding, either conceptually or technically, to the monumental task at hand, then final judgment on the competition drawings, especially those of the minor competitors, should not be passed without appreciation of their historical importance or, in Kimball's words, "their novelty and merit for their own time." A.S.

THOMAS JEFFERSON'S DESIGNS FOR THE PRESIDENT'S HOUSE

As Thomas Jefferson's life and architectural development is treated in considerable detail elsewhere, discussion here will be limited to the circumstances surrounding his involvement with the competition for the president's house. Suffice it to say that, although naturally obscured by his better-known accomplishments in statesmanship, Thomas Jefferson's architectural achievement is one of the more-remarkable aspects not only in his career but also in the history of American architecture, in view of his leading role in helping shape a new national style.

It has long been known that Jefferson, as secretary of state during President Washington's administration, took a deep interest in the building of the new capital city, and that he drafted the advertisement and program for the competition for the president's house. However, it remained for Fiske Kimball to discover, in the course of preparing his monumental opus on Jefferson's architectural work, that Jefferson had also submitted a design anonymously in that competition. The great collection of Jefferson architectural drawings at the Massachusetts Historical Society, on which Kimball's monograph concentrated, includes a series of studies by Jefferson for a rotunda house with dome and four porticos, modeled after Palladio's famous sixteenth-century Villa Rotonda. These drawings proved to duplicate in every aspect a similar set of drawings among the competition designs for the president's house preserved at the Maryland Historical Society; the only unsigned set, identified simply by the initials A.Z., it had previously been attributed to the Maryland builder Abram Faws, even though the writing and numbering in the notations on the various drawings are unmistakably in Jefferson's hand.

The advertised program for the president's house left almost everything to the designer's judgment. Unlike the program developed for the capitol, there was no stipulation of the number, type, or size of rooms to be provided, an omission which doubtless accounted for the diversity among entries. However, a personal memorandum of Jefferson's, produced for one of the commissioners' meetings some time in March 1792 and located among his papers (Series 3) in the Manuscripts Division of the Library of Congress, reveals his thinking about the kind and size of accommodations needed for the president's house. The draft, in which floor areas were estimated "in Squares of 10 f. or 100 square feet," reads as

follows:

President's house.

Antichamber	10.	
	Squares of full elevation	
Audience room	15	
Parlours. 1 of	15	
" 1 of	10	
Dining Room. 1 of	10	60
Parlours. 1 of	7½	
" 1 of	5	
Dining room. 1 of	5	
Study	5	
Library	10	
Clerks rooms 2	10	
Bedrooms with antichamb. & Dressing room to each.		
4 of	32	
Bedrooms single. 6	24	
making altogether	98½	
squares of half elevation,		
to be counted as		49½
109 squares or 105 f. square		

Servants apartments, the kitchen & its appurtenances to be in an interval of 7 f. pitch between the floor of the house & cellars, consequently to be sunk a foot or two below the surface of the earth.

There is no evidence to indicate whether this information was supplied to the other competitors, although Jefferson doubtless applied it in developing his own design for the competition.

Bolstered by a first-hand knowledge of architecture and architects on the continent, Jefferson's cosmopolitan opinions on the character of the proposed executive mansion—as, indeed, of the architecture he believed suitable for the emerging republic—were decidedly in favor of casting aside the mainstream of provincial building that had prevailed in colonial America. Jefferson evidently feared, in view of the weakness of the plans first submitted and of the dearth of trained architects in America, that none of the designs submitted would conform to his expectations, much less command respect abroad; whether Jefferson was aware of the designs by Hoban and Collins prior to preparing his own is unknown, but doubtful. In any event, his concern for the results of the competition obviously combined with his architectural self-confidence to induce Jefferson to undertake preparation of two designs himself and to submit one of them anonymously in the competition.

In 1791 Jefferson had suggested to L'Enfant the façades of three buildings in Paris as models for the presi-

dent's house: the Galérie du Louvre, the palace in the Place de la Concorde, and the striking Hôtel de Salm. In an interesting sketch thought by Kimball to represent his first study, Jefferson attempted roughly to combine all three as the entrance front, the flanks, and the river front of the projected building. For unknown reasons, he did not complete the design but turned instead in his second effort to a more compact and coherent model—Palladio's elegant Villa Rotonda. It is this design that was submitted by him in the competition. Despite the meagerness of his draftsmanship—which nonetheless far surpassed that of most other entries—Jefferson's design gives a suggestion of the unity and dignity distinguishing the Palladian model that, given his realized projects, would surely have characterized the building he proposed as well. How eminently fitting it would have been if he had won the competition and ten years later moved, as president, into a house of his own design.

In turning to Palladio's Villa Rotonda for his anonymous entry, Jefferson returned, albeit in more pristine fashion, to the model he had considered in about 1780 for the governor's house in Richmond. He was to return once more to the rotunda form in 1803, when Robert Mills, then at Monticello as an architectural student, executed some handsome drawings of designs by Jefferson for a modified rotunda house in which two of the porticos on opposite sides were replaced with octagonal bays. It is conceivable that these exercises, the freest version and most practical of Jefferson's essays in the rotunda form, employed his earlier design for the president's house as a point of departure, perhaps in an attempt to domesticate the monumental Palladian prototype for American living.

Following the selection by Washington and the commissioners of Hoban's as the winning design, Jefferson's involvement with the president's house diminished appreciably, perhaps coincidentally, and resumed only after his occupation of the mansion as president in 1801. Although the exterior had been completed largely according to Hoban's plans, the interiors had progressed far more slowly; many of the rooms still had to be plastered, and the grand staircase had not even been erected. The task was completed under Jefferson's guidance. To provide space for household and official work, Jefferson designed low-lying pavilions east and west of the mansion, connected by colonnades surmounted by a promenade, as at Monticello; Latrobe completed these

three years later, building a fireproof vault in the east colonnade for the treasury. The same year, in close consultation with Jefferson, Latrobe laid out the grounds and planned a semicircular portico for the south front, recalling the one in Hoban's original design, and a larger one with a *porte cochère* for the north; these were not completed until 1824 and 1829, respectively. Although Jefferson's modifications to the president's house progressed slowly, they nonetheless allowed him to put his personal stamp on the new executive mansion.

Doubtless because of the anonymity of his submission, Jefferson not only absented himself from the final judging of the entries, but also remained uncharacteristically silent about so important an undertaking. Given his inclination to articulate various conceptions that he sought to transform into architectural realities, the apparent absence in his writings of references both to his and to the other designs for the president's house is both disappointing and regrettable. Nor has any other evidence been discovered thus far that could shed any specific light on the views of these designs held by Washington or the commissioners or, for that matter, any other contemporary. Thus, there is much about the circumstances that led Jefferson to enter the competition that is still unknown. It remains to be discovered, for example, whether his design was a result of spontaneous effort, or grew out of an early, deliberate attempt to tackle the problem. Nor is it known if Jefferson ever had occasion to see either Hoban's or Collins' entries before the deadline, much less whether he approved of their being awarded the first and second premiums. The absence of any certain answers to these and other similar questions, however, should not obscure the significance of Jefferson's having entered the competition or cloud his lucid and forward-looking conception of neo-classical directions for channeling the growth and development of American architecture. The simple, clear-cut lines and unity of his competition entry is a significant embodiment of such a conception. Not least, its relative coherence suggests that Jefferson, as much as any of the other competitors, fully comprehended the art of architectural form. A.S.

410 Preliminary study for the competition design. Elevation

THOMAS JEFFERSON 1743–1826
Pencil on coordinate paper 1792
54 x 37 (21¼ x 14½)

Lent by the Massachusetts Historical Society, Boston

411 Preliminary study for the competition design. Plans

THOMAS JEFFERSON 1743–1826
Pencil on joined coordinate paper 1792
53 x 71 (20¾ x 27½)

Lent by the Massachusetts Historical Society, Boston

These two sheets of drawings were discovered by Kimball in the Coolidge Collection of the Massachusetts Historical Society. That they were drawn by Jefferson is indicated by the technique, similar to that in his other known drawings, and the coordinate paper, one which he used most frequently at this time. This set of drawings coincides exactly in line and dimension to the set submitted in the competition for the president's house, which is preserved by the Maryland Historical Society and on display here (nos. 412–415). That the drawings are preliminary studies for the competition design in question is suggested by the tentative and incomplete rendering of all non-essential elements.

Jefferson appears to have been the first American architect to use coordinate paper. He did so to work out his proportions mathematically before drawing his final plans in ink. The use of coordinate, or graph, paper constituted the origin of what is now termed the "modular" system of design, by which is meant the sizing of building elements and components as multiples of a common denominator.

A.S.

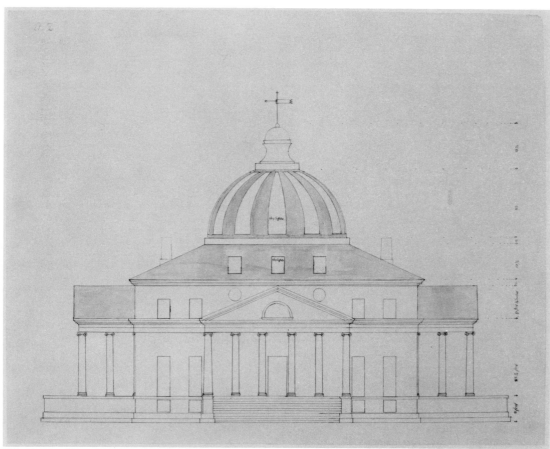

412 Original competition drawing. Elevation

THOMAS JEFFERSON 1743–1826
Pen and ink with gray wash 1792
32.7 x 42.4 (12⅞ x 16¹¹⁄₁₆)
Signed upper left: A.Z. Later inscribed in pencil on upper right: *Abram Faws.*
Notation on central panel of dome: *skylights.* Notation on central panel on roof below dome: *skylights.*

Lent by the Maryland Historical Society, Baltimore

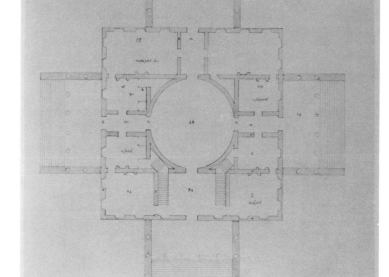

413 Original competition drawing. First floor plan

THOMAS JEFFERSON 1743–1826
Pen and ink with gray wash 1792
40.5 x 42.4 (15¹⁵⁄₁₆ x 16¹¹⁄₁₆)
Inscribed in ink on verso: *Faws*

Lent by the Maryland Historical Society, Baltimore

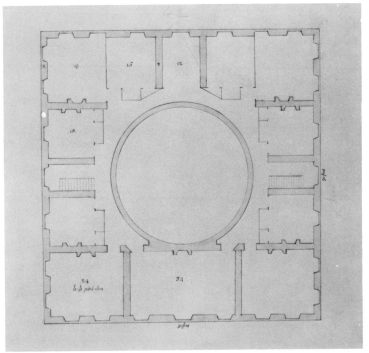

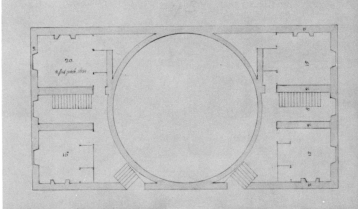

414 Original competition drawing. Second floor plan
THOMAS JEFFERSON 1743–1826
Pen and ink with gray wash 1792
27 x 41.3 (10⅝ x 16¼)
Lent by the Maryland Historical
Society, Baltimore

415 Original competition drawing. Third floor plan
THOMAS JEFFERSON 1743–1826
Pen and ink with gray wash 1792
27 x 41.3 (10⅝ x 16¼)
Lent by the Maryland Historical
Society, Baltimore

The unsigned set of competition drawings is identified only by the initials A.Z. on the elevation. These drawings were subsequently determined by Kimball to be the work of Jefferson on the basis of their matching in every aspect the studies in the Coolidge Collection at the Massachusetts Historical Society, their displaying a drawing technique identical to Jefferson's, and their containing notes and figures rendered in Jefferson's unmistakable hand. Significantly, the handwriting of the inscriptions *Abram Faws* in pencil on the elevation and *Faws* in ink on the first floor plan does not correspond to the script in which the notes and figures are rendered on the actual drawings. Kimball's suspicion that the mistaken attribution to Faws, made without knowledge of the actual designer, grew out of a subsequent misreading of Z as F for the last letter of the initials is plausible.

The model for Jefferson's design is the Villa Rotonda, as depicted in Giacomo Leoni's first edition of *The Architecture of A. Palladio* (London, 1715), which Jefferson had acquired before 1769. Though increasing the dimensions of the Palladian model (about ninety feet square as compared to seventy), rather than reducing

them as he had in his study for the governor's house at Richmond, Jefferson retained its essential format. The form of the dome and its termination, the subdivision of the stories, and the proportions of the four hexastyle Ionic porticos are all identical to those rendered in Leoni's plates. Yet there are certain exterior modifications that are uniquely Jefferson's. The portico has been altered by substituting an inner column for each of the side walls and adding a lunette in the pediment, thereby recreating a hallmark of Jefferson's work and reducing by almost half the number of steps and, hence, the podium height. The fenestration has been modified in a manner resembling the later pattern at Monticello: a window bay has been added on each side of the portico, while the windows inside the latter have been eliminated; in addition, all windows have been elongated by extending those on the second story down to the cornice below, those on the first floor down to the floor, and those set in the basement both up to the stringcourse above and down to the building base below. A more radical and purely Jeffersonian departure is the addition of skylights to the dome, extending in alternate panels from the crowning element

to the base, and to the hipped roof below, employing three over the center. Here, Jefferson doubtless borrowed from his highly innovative and dramatic use of skylighted illumination at Monticello.

The interior likewise underwent a modification that is, however, more difficult to discern in any detail. Providing three floor plans, two more than appear in Leoni's plates, on the whole Jefferson adapted the original model very well to the requirements as he had specified them without disrupting the unity of expression. That he attempted to counteract the natural de-emphasis of axis in a rotunda plan by creating one principal entrance is indicated by the location at one end of a large hall with two open flights of stairs; these stairs—which are a rare gesture for someone who believed them to be an extravagant use of space—are, perhaps for this reason, terminated awkwardly at the second story, suffering from an apparent lack of the requisite circular balcony in the original model. The striking alcove bedrooms, which Jefferson introduced in this country, are identical in general arrangement to the bedroom in his Paris hotel and especially to the bedrooms he subsequently installed in Monticello. A.S.

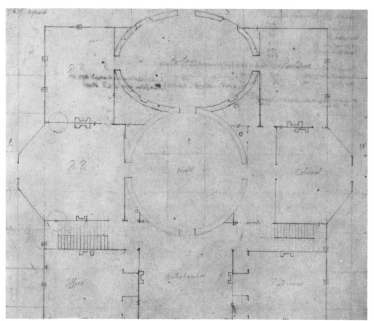

416 Study for a rotunda plan house. Plan

THOMAS JEFFERSON 1743–1826
Pencil on wove paper c. 1801–1803
20.5 x 24.3 (8¹⁄₁₆ x 9½)
Inscribed upper left: 76. f. square.
Notes in ink on verso: *quantity of
wall running measure/feet/Elliptical
room 95/Circular d° 95/external walls
272/partition walls 104/[total] 566/
Basement story 12. f. pitch. 2½ f.
thick = 30 cub. feet for each foot
running measure/Principal story 19.
2.f = 38/Attic story 10. 1½ = 15/
[total] 83. x 566 = 46,978 cub. feet =
{ brick 2½ I. thick 19. br. to the cub.
foot 892,582/perch of stone 1880 @
3.D 5640. D/61 squares of iron
sheeting @ 25.D. = 1525 D./17 d°
for dome 425.*

*Lent by the University of Virginia,
Alderman Library, Charlottesville*

Though Kimball suggested in 1916
that this preliminary study for a modified rotunda plan house might be
for Shadwell, this does not appear very
likely. On the other hand, there is
reason to suspect that, in its development, Jefferson might well have used
his anonymous entry in the president's
house competition as a point of departure either for the design of a
later unrealized residence or for a
purely personal study of ways to improve various shortcomings of his
earlier competition design. Even
though the calculations on the reverse
of the drawing suggest a more concrete undertaking, the latter alternative
seems more likely. His moving into

the unfinished president's house in
March 1801 would have placed Jefferson in a compelling situation to
contemplate anew his earlier design
for the mansion. It is well known that
he never occupied any house for long
without making plans to modify it.
This was the case not only with his
beloved and ever-changing Monticello,
but with his houses in Paris, New
York, and Philadelphia as well. It
was to prove no less the case with the
presidential mansion.

Though smaller than his competition entry and more the size of his
proposed design for the governor's
house at Richmond, this plan bears a
striking resemblance to certain aspects
peculiar to the president's house. Its
orientation is identical to that of the
executive mansion: the elliptical room,
resembling Hoban's but turned on
its side, faces south, and the north
front is obviously intended as the
entrance façade. There is also a general
similarity between the rooms indicated on Jefferson's plan and those
identified on Latrobe's inventory
plan in 1803 of Hoban's structure. To
be sure, the grand audience receiving
room is absent, and a bedroom now
appears in this plan—doubtless reflecting Jefferson's propensity, so well
expressed at Monticello, for having
his sleeping quarters adjoin his cabinet
and library. Otherwise, Jefferson's
plan provides for two dining rooms
and two parlors—a more formal
dining room obviously intended in the
west octagonal bay and a grand
parlor in the elliptical room just south

of the circular rotunda hall—surely
more than a more conventional residence would require, but equal to the
number indicated in Latrobe's depiction of Hoban's scheme.

Jefferson's modified plan also suggests several improvements over his
anonymous entry in 1792. That
scheme, which Ackerman characterized
in his study of Palladio as having
been "all too literally stolen from the
illustrations of the Villa Rotonda,"
was far less suited in reality to the
site and function of the executive
mansion in Washington. Though its
dome and pedimented columnar porticos made it an admirable symbol
of grandeur, its symmetry about two
axes allowed too little flexibility. The
resulting de-emphasis of axis likewise
complicated the problem of creating
an identifiable principal entrance, the
problem being one of symbolic
orientation as well as practical function. In Jefferson's later scheme, that
problem was happily resolved by
retaining only one of the four porticos
on the north entrance front and
transforming the other three into
functional extensions of interior space:
his favorite octagonal bays were employed on the east and west sides,
while the grand elliptical room projected laterally on the south front.
The earlier problem of awkward termination of the two principal staircases in the entry hall was likewise
resolved; both were inserted decisively
on the east and west ends of the block,
just off the hall, with no other stairs
provided.

The resulting scheme is more compact and efficient than the competition design, and surely the freest and
most lucid of Jefferson's attempts
to render a rotunda plan. A set of
drawings executed for Jefferson by
Robert Mills in 1803—the same year
in which Latrobe produced his inventory plan of the mansion—provides
an accurate and impeccably executed
rendering of the envisioned architectural embodiment of such a plan.
That Jefferson's sketch formed the
basis for Mills' effort, and so dates
from before that time, is indicated by
the striking similarity, in virtually
every aspect, of the two plans. Had
such a scheme—especially one so well
rendered—been submitted in the
competition for the president's house,
the results might well have proven
different. A.S.

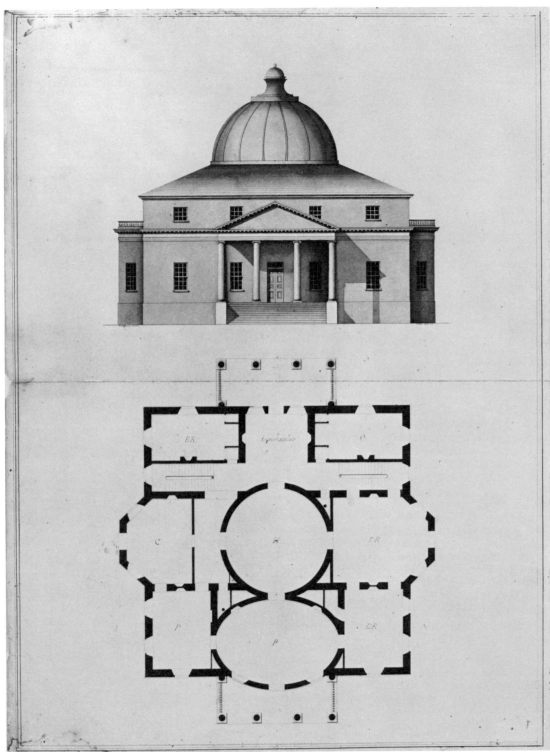

417 A rotunda house. Drawing exercise. Elevation and plan

ROBERT MILLS 1781–1855
Ink and wash 1803
53 x 40 (20⅞ x 15¾)
Signed lower right below elevation:
R. Mills Del! 1803. Inscribed lower
left below elevation: *T. Jefferson,
Arch!*

*Lent by the Massachusetts Historical
Society, Boston*

This is a set of three drawings executed by Robert Mills in 1803, while he was an architectural pupil of Jefferson at Monticello. The close correspondence of the plan with Jefferson's study (no. 416) indicates the source of Mills' stunning renderings, which no doubt constitute a drawing exercise assigned by Jefferson.

Robert Mills (1781–1855), architect and engineer, was born in Charleston, South Carolina. He was the first American to seek regular training for an architectural career. He began in 1800 by studying with James Hoban, architect of the president's house and a former resident of Charleston, from whom he learned the rudiments of draftsmanship, rendering, and construction. Anxious to go beyond the somewhat obsolete academism of the Irish builder-architect, Mills became a pupil of Jefferson, who took him into Monticello in 1803. It was in those months that these drawings were executed. Later in that year, Jefferson advised Mills to attach himself to Benjamin Latrobe; Mills did so, remaining as a draftsman and clerk in Latrobe's office until 1808. From that time until 1820, he worked as an architect in Philadelphia, Washington, and Baltimore. He then returned to Charleston as state engineer and architect. In 1836 President Jackson appointed Mills architect of public buildings in Washington. In this post he was responsible for designing and supervising the construction of the treasury building in 1836 and the patent office and the old post office, both begun in 1839. He designed numerous other important landmarks as well, including the Washington Monuments in Baltimore and Washington. Seeking to create a truly American architecture, Mills devised plans for public buildings that were highly practical. His buildings, like Latrobe's the epitome of American classical rationalism, give the effect of great dignity and solidity.

An obvious version of the Villa Rotonda, Mills' rendering of the façade resembles more the original model than Jefferson's competition entry. The portico, reduced to four columns, together with the projecting octagonal bays and oval room, represents the most conspicuous exterior departure from the Palladian model. On the interior, the modifications are more considerable, especially in the latent neoclassical room arrangement. The section and second floor plan, however, show that the circular balcony within the rotunda, absent from Jefferson's 1792 design, has been reinstated here. Though it may have lost something of the innate cross-axial formal balance of the Villa Rotonda, the design rendered by Mills became more flexible, less doctrinaire, and infinitely more practical than Jefferson's anonymous entry in the competition for the president's house.

That these drawings, however impeccable, were "student exercises" is suggested by the introduction of certain naive conditions. These include the setting of back-to-back fireplaces *within* a two-foot wall thickness—a constructional impossibility—and the apparent failure to reflect the oval room below on the second floor plan; the latter plan seems the least well executed of the three drawings. Nonetheless, these magnificent renderings already make clear the enormous drafting talents possessed by the young Mills. The section and elevation, evidently most free of Jefferson's preliminary and thus restrictive schemes, likewise display an unerring eye for composition. A.S.

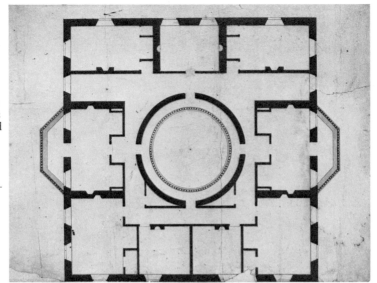

418 A rotunda house. Drawing exercise. Second floor plan
ROBERT MILLS 1781–1855
Ink and wash 1803
20.5 x 27.9 (8¹⁄₁₆ x 11)
Lent by the University of Virginia,
Alderman Library, Charlottesville

419 A rotunda house. Drawing exercise. Section
ROBERT MILLS 1781–1855
Ink and wash 1803
20.5 x 27.7 (8¹⁄₁₆ x 10⅞)
Signed lower right: *Rob.ᵗ Mills Del.ᵗ*
Inscribed lower left: *Tho.ˢ Jefferson Arch.ᵗ* Inscribed lower center: *Longitudinal Section.*

Lent by the University of Virginia,
Alderman Library, Charlottesville

JAMES HOBAN'S DESIGN FOR THE PRESIDENT'S HOUSE

Architect and builder, James Hoban was born about 1762 near Callan, County Kilkenny, Ireland, the son of Edward and Martha Bayne Hoban. He studied in the schools of The Dublin Society and was a pupil in the architectural drawing class taught by Thomas Ivory, architect of numerous important buildings in Ireland. On November 23, 1780, Hoban was awarded the second premium for his drawings of "brackets, stairs, roofs, &c." He worked on several buildings in Dublin, including the Royal Exchange and the customs house, begun in 1781.

After the American Revolution, young Hoban emigrated to this country, where he evidently first went to Philadelphia. On May 25, 1785, he advertised in the *Pennsylvania Evening Herald* that "Any Gentleman Who wishes to build in an elegant style, may hear of a person properly calculated for that purpose, who can execute the Joining and Carpenter's business in the modern taste, equal to any now done in the city of Dublin." Within two years, Hoban settled in Charleston, South Carolina, where he remained until 1792.

Little is known of Hoban's years in Charleston, although the period seems to have been at least moderately productive. By 1789 he had entered into a partnership with Pierce Purcell, setting up a design and carpentry practice. Their advertisement in the May 4, 1790, issue of the *Charleston City Gazette and Daily Advertiser* reads: "Plans, elevations, sections of buildings, &c., drawn at a short notice, and the different branches of carpentry executed on the lowest terms and most approved manner by Hoban & Purcell." Significantly, the same advertisement began with Hoban's announcement of the creation of an evening architectural school: "Several applications being made to the subscriber, has induced him to establish an evening school, for the instruction of young men in Architecture, to commence on the 3rd day May next. From the experience he has had, and the testimonial approbation of one of the first academies of arts and sciences in Europe, he hopes to merit the sanction of the public, and give satisfaction to his employers." Doubtless the most important of Hoban's commissions while in Charleston was the design of the state capitol at Columbia. Completed in 1791, its front with central portico and high basement followed L'Enfant's design for the Federal Hall in New York; the building was destroyed in 1865, when the city was burned by Sherman's army. In 1792 Hoban was mentioned

in the *Charleston Post and Daily Advertiser* as architect of a theater. In early June of that year, intent on entering the announced competition for the federal buildings in the new federal district, he set out for Philadelphia with a letter of introduction to President Washington from Colonel Henry Laurens, a prominent Charlestonian who had been a member of the Congress of 1775 and one of the negotiators of the peace with Great Britain.

Hoban took part in the competition following his arrival in Washington later that month. There is no record of his having submitted a design for the capitol; no drawings by him for that building are preserved. His design for the president's house was awarded the first premium on July 17, for which Hoban received a building lot in the city, a medal worth ten guineas, and the balance of the stipulated $500 award in cash. He was also retained to supervise construction of the building according to his plans for a fee of three hundred guineas a year. Hoban assisted the commissioners in laying the cornerstone on October 13, 1793, as master of the Federal Masonic Lodge, which he had helped organize on September 6. He continued in charge of the construction until the president's house was occupied, still unfinished, by Adams in 1800 and then by Jefferson in 1801. After the destruction of the public buildings by the British in 1814, Hoban rebuilt the White House, incorporating certain changes on the exterior by Latrobe; the south portico was finished in 1824, the north portico in 1829.

Hoban was the only person connected with the new federal capital who remained continuously identified with it from its inception until his death in 1831, attesting to his recognized knowledge, competence, and probity. He was almost continuously employed in superintending work for the government, such work extending to roadways and bridges as well as buildings. Though not one of the architects for the capitol, Hoban was employed as one of the superintendents of the building, where he was active at intervals until the appointment of Latrobe in 1803 as surveyor of public buildings. Among Hoban's other projects in Washington were the Great Hotel (1793–1795) and the Little Hotel (1795). In 1798 he was one of the bidders for the construction of the first executive office building. Although a lower bid was accepted, Hoban was entrusted by the commissioners with superintending the work. The first state and war offices,

begun in 1818, were both designed and erected by him. On the incorporation of Washington in 1802, Hoban became a member of the city council and remained in that post until his death. In January 1799, Hoban married Susannah Sewell and subsequently had ten children.

The great achievement of Hoban's career was undoubtedly winning the competition for the design of the president's house. That he favorably impressed all officials with whom he came into contact in the course of the competition is clearly indicated by available evidence. After presenting himself to President Washington in Philadelphia and making known his intention to enter the competition, Hoban was given a letter of introduction to the commissioners. In that letter, dated June 18, 1792, Washington informed the commissioners that the Charleston architect had been strongly recommended to him by Colonel Laurens and others in South Carolina "as a person who had made Architecture his study, and was well qualified, not only for Planning or designing buildings, but to superintend the execution of them." Citing Hoban's interest in the competition, Washington continued: "I have given him this letter of introduction in order that he might have an opportunity of communicating his views and wishes to you, or obtaining any information necessary for completing of the Plans." Although Washington emphasized that his letter was not to be taken as an endorsement of Hoban's qualifications, of which he had no personal knowledge, two other letters addressed to Commissioner Daniel Carroll by Jacob Read and E. A. Burke of Charleston affirmed Laurens' high praise of Hoban's professional abilities and experience. In his letter of May 12, Burke described Hoban as "a man of serious and considerable talents in his Profession both for design and execution," and indicated that "He wishes to be made known to one of the Commissioners as a candidate in the business of the Federal buildings, resting on his own abilities for the event." Read's letter of May 24 likewise referred to Hoban as "a very ingenious Mechanic & draftsman," concluding: "From what I have seen of Mr. Hobans Drafts, I think he will stand a fair Chance to get some one of the Premiums offered for Drafts." That the commissioners were early impressed with Hoban's work is indicated by their letter to Jefferson on July 5, some ten days prior to the competition deadline. In it, they informed the secretary of state that "Mʳ Hoben applies himself closely

to a Draft of the Presidents House," and confided that "he has made very favourable Impression on us." On the day after awarding Hoban the first premium, the commissioners wrote Samuel Blodgett in Boston, "That the President has approved the Plan [by Hoban] for a Palace, which we think convenient, elegant, and within a moderate Expence." Washington's letter of July 23 to the commissioners expressed obvious approval of Hoban's design and retention to supervise its execution. "If his industry and honesty are of a piece with the specimen he has given of his abilities," Washington wrote of Hoban, "he will prove a useful man & a considerable acquisition."

It appears as if Jefferson did not see, and may perhaps have refrained from seeing, Hoban's design prior to the deadline for the competition. For, in replying on July 11 to the aforementioned letter in which the commissioners conveyed their favorable response to Hoban's emerging design for the president's house, Jefferson failed even to acknowledge their reference to Hoban—a highly uncharacteristic omission on his part. Although lacking Jefferson's much-favored architectural features of a true temple portico with free-standing colonnade and dome, Hoban's design for the president's house was unlike anything in the United States at the time. If not from one of the more "celebrated fronts of modern buildings," it was still taken from a respectable academic precedent, being derived from designs for a typical eighteenth-century "Gentleman's Mansion" in Great Britain such as those so generously illustrated in James Gibbs' *Book of Architecture* (1728) and embodied in such buildings as Leinster House in the capital, Dublin (1745–1747). For a new national architecture, striving to discard the provincial vagaries of the American Georgian style, Hoban's simple design of correct academic forms and details combined restrained overtones of European grandeur with an appropriately classical base to create a building both handsome and well-proportioned. Not least, it doubtless conformed in both expression and scope to Washington's austere image of an appropriate executive mansion for the new federal republic. A.S.

420 Original competition drawing. Elevation

JAMES HOBAN C. 1762–1831
Pen and ink with gray wash and
green compound border 1792
25.3 x 45.3 (9¹⁵⁄₁₆ x 17⅞)
*Lent by the Maryland Historical
Society, Baltimore*

Hoban's design is essentially a variation of plate 53 of James Gibbs' *Book
of Architecture* (1728), a favorite
resource of early American builders
as well as of students in the Dublin
Society. The central tetrastyle Ionic
pedimented pavilion, the low basement, the general type of window
frames in both upper and lower stories,
the stepped entrance to the first story,
and the general proportional relationships of part to the whole leave
little doubt that Hoban modeled
his elevation closely after Gibbs' plate
for a "Gentleman's house" in
Hertfordshire.

There are notable departures from
Gibbs' façade, however. These include
elimination both of quoining at the
corners of the building and of the
rustication on the basement save for
the window treatment, addition of an
attic balustrade, and the superposition
of alternating angular and segmental
pediments on the window frames of
the first story. Some of these depar-

tures, which appear in other designs
illustrated in Gibbs' book, proceed in
the general direction of the façade
of Leinster House in Dublin, which
popular tradition holds to be the
source for Hoban's design.

Despite general similarities in the
eleven-bay entrance façades, some of
them common to many buildings of
the eighteenth century, Leinster House
differs appreciably from the format
of Hoban's design in its use of the
taller Corinthian order and of a high
basement with the principal entrance
and articulated window frames. Apart
from the façade, moreover, Leinster
House has no resemblance to Hoban's
design in its other façades or in its
interior arrangement.

An element of originality in Hoban's
design is conveyed by the addition
of two innately native features: an
American eagle in the pediment surmounting the Ionic pavilion, which
was never applied, and a garland of
American roses fashioned over the
shortened entrance doorway. A.S.

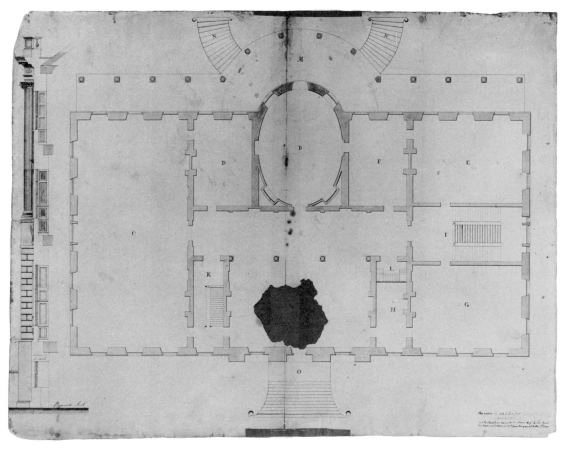

421 Original competition drawing. Principal floor plan and section

JAMES HOBAN C. 1762–1831
Pen and ink with gray wash on joined
paper with light pencil sketching 1792
53.5 x 72 (21¹⁄₁₆ x 28⅜)
Inscribed lower left by Jefferson in ink:
*the scale is .137 I. to a foot (i.e. 2 Fr.
ligues?)/or 7.29 feet to the Inch/but
the elevation seems to be about 4.f.
to the Inch/the basement story is
13.f. from the ground floor to the 1ˢᵗ
floor.* Notation lower left: *Section of
the Wall.* Notation left of section:
1ˢᵗ Story/Surface. Notation right of
section: *Basement Level.*

*Lent by the Massachusetts Historical
Society, Boston*

This sheet includes two drawings: a
section through the north façade and
a plan of the principal story. The
plan which Latrobe prepared for
Jefferson, recording the state of the
president's house in 1803, does not
depart appreciably from Hoban's competition drawing exhibited here, save
in the elimination of the south Ionic
colonnade across the entire façade,
which was not built. According to
Latrobe's plan, the rooms identified
by capital letters on the Hoban
drawing include the hall off the north
entrance (A), the "Public" or state
dining room in the southwest corner

(G), the library and cabinet room
in the southwest corner (E), the
president's antechamber (F), the
oval drawing room on the south or
garden side (B), the "Common" or
family dining room (D), and the great
public audience chamber to the
east (C).

The plan, which shows that the
great portico to the north added by
Latrobe was not a feature of the
original scheme, has many aspects in
common with plate 52, the companion
to the aforementioned Gibbs plate
for the façade. In each case there is a
division into three main parts by
transverse walls in identical positions,
and the entrance hall is flanked by
stairs of similar arrangement and subdivided by columns and niches quite
similar in location and detail. Even
the methods of indicating windows
and fireplaces are identical.

Significant changes from the Gibbs
model include an appreciable enlargement of the plan (about 170 x 85
feet versus 136 x 72 feet), the different subdivision of the east and west
ends, and the introduction of the
distinctive projecting oval drawing
room on the south or garden side,
thereby making three rooms instead
of the long gallery. It is difficult to
ascertain the source for Hoban's projecting oval room, a feature not em-

ployed in any of the plans illustrated
in Gibbs' book. Perhaps in his dealings
with the commissioners and others
in their office, Hoban might have
come across Jefferson's letter to
L'Enfant which included mention of
a comparable façade on the Hôtel
de Salm in Paris.

Kimball's suggestion that Hoban
prepared the plan prior to the elevation is probably correct. Although
there is a general correspondence
between Hoban's plan and Latrobe's
of 1803, the section accompanying
the former indicates rustication of a
rather taller basement story and, even
more striking, the addition of a third
story. It thus resembles more the
Gibbs and even Leinster House prototypes than Hoban's elevation and
executed building, with only two
stories in addition to the shorter
unrusticated basement and more simplified plinth block, sill, and stringcourse profiles.

Because Hoban did not indicate any
measurements on the drawing, it is
extremely difficult to be certain of
the actual scale of the plan and section. Kimball's suggestion that the
scale for the plan was originally six
feet to the inch but later taken by
Jefferson to be the more complicated
7.29, when it was briefly proposed to
increase the original dimensions by

one fifth, is problematical. The original scale proposed by Kimball would
make the building length in the plan
about five sixths shorter than the
one in Hoban's elevation, which most
approximates the executed building.
Examination of the elevation, on
which the scale is noted, and the plan
indicates that, if the building length
in both drawings is taken to be identical, as seems likely, the scale noted
by Jefferson, however unconventional,
reflects fairly accurately the building
length in Hoban's elevation.

The assertion, first made by Glenn
Brown in 1903 and later perpetuated
by other writers that Hoban's plan
contemplated a building with wings,
is not supported by available evidence,
much less by any reference to such a
scheme in Hoban's drawings. The
only apparent possibility for development of Hoban's plan in stages, which
likewise is neither mentioned in the
records nor indicated in Hoban's
plan or executed building, would
have been the initial reduction of the
building by omitting the rooms
marked C, E, I, and G. A.S.

The entry by Jacob Small is symptomatic of the difficulties still encountered in attempts to document the competition for the president's house. Only the name "Jacob Small" appears in the competition drawings. Yet there is still no documentary evidence to determine conclusively whether this entrant from Baltimore is the elder Jacob Small, who designed and built the still-standing Old Otterbein Church (née the Evangelical Reformed Church) and a wooden bridge over Jones Falls at Baltimore Street, or his son, the younger Jacob Small, who amassed a fortune as builder and lumber dealer in Baltimore, served that city's mayor from 1826 to 1831, and late in life assumed the title "architect." In his May 1919, article in the *American Institute of Architects Journal*, Fiske Kimball assumed that the elder Small was the entrant, but included biographical information that obviously relates to his son. The difficulty, exacerbated by the fact that both father and son evidently used the same name without any other distinguishing designations, stems from the lack of certain knowledge about the date of the elder Small's death. Legal and genealogical references recently uncovered, though still inconclusive, suggest that the year of Jacob Sr.'s death may have been 1794—some two years after the competition. Yet, at the same time, the pedestal gravestone in St. Paul's Cemetery in Baltimore, examined by the present writer, indicates that the elder Small died on September 27, 1791, or some six months *before* the competition; although the "1" in the year of death is now somewhat weathered, it nonetheless appears to correspond closely in spacing and design to the equivalent digit in the clearly legible death date—September 29, 1791—given for his wife Ann Barbara on the adjoining side of the same gravestone.

Thus, it is difficult to be sure whether Jacob Sr. was, in fact, alive or not at the time of the competition 1792. Even if he were, however, that fact alone could offer no conclusive proof that it was he and not his twenty-year-old son who had actually executed the competition drawings. Nor, under the present circumstances, can the possibility be overlooked that the younger Small might either have collaborated with, or have worked independently of, his father in the event of the latter's being alive at the time. The Small competition drawings reveal a certain rudimentary level of draftsmanship that might as easily have come from a young and inexperienced hand as from the hand of an older, more experienced builder.

That the Small family became an established line of builders and architects in Baltimore is seen in the work not only of the elder Jacob and his son, but also in the work of Jacob Jr.'s son, William F. (1798–1832), who studied with Latrobe in Washington before striking out on his own. William became the established architect of the family. His most important buildings in Baltimore are the Athenaeum (1824–1826), Barnum's City Hotel (1825–1826), the First English Lutheran Church (1825–1826), and numerous schools and residences.

Jacob Small, Jr. (1772–1851), perhaps the more plausible entrant in the competition for the president's house, assisted in the construction of many of the larger buildings in Baltimore. Among the buildings for which he was identified by various sources as being the carpenter-builder are the Baltimore Cathedral (1808–1821) and the Baltimore Exchange (1816–1820) which Latrobe had designed (the latter with Maximilian Godefroy), and the old Masonic Hall (1812–1822), designed by Godefroy and William Small. His lumber dealership likewise flourished in Baltimore; he is known to have supplied mahogany for the capitol building in Washington.

Small was elected mayor in 1826 and again in 1828 and 1830, resigning in 1831. It was during his administration that the construction of the Baltimore and Ohio Railroad was begun, the nucleus of Patterson Park was accepted, the first public school was erected, and the Washington Monument designed by Robert Mills was completed.

Some indication of the scope of Small's building career is given by several advertisements in Baltimore newspapers and directories. As early as 1812, Small was referring to himself as "Architect and House Carpenter," as noted in the advertisement he placed in the July 23 issue of the *American and Commercial Daily Advertiser* to sell his house on Hanover Street. An unidentified original advertisement by Small located in the Dielman and Hayward files at the Maryland Historical Society Library, noted as dating from some time in May 1833, declared: "The undersigned having retired from the services of the Baltimore and Ohio Railroad Company, will resume his profession of ARCHITECT and PRACTICAL BUILDER." The same advertisement also informed the public that his office was located "in the south west Room, on the principal floor of the Baltimore Exchange." That he was able to maintain an office in so prominent a building speaks well of Small's standing in the community, although not necessarily of his capacity as architect. Yet by 1838, his listing in *Matchett's Baltimore Directory* identified Small simply as "architect"; all references to carpenter or builder had now been dropped entirely. There is some indication that Small may have designed and built numerous residences in Baltimore, although no material has yet been uncovered to shed any light on this aspect of his career.

His later calling himself an architect notwithstanding, Jacob Small, like his father, doubtless emerged out of the mainstream of early Colonial carpenters and builders whose continual use of architectural texts and handbooks must have served to bridge, at least in their minds, the distance between carpenter and architect. These craftsmen, who today would be regarded more as builders and contractors, are to be distinguished from genuine architects-builders, such as James Hoban, who possessed a more sophisticated European training and credentials, advertised for apprentices, and included the teaching of architecture as a sideline in their careers. It is apparent that many of the carpenters and builders of this period were setting themselves up as architects with rather flimsy credentials. Small's son William, on the other hand, emerged more credibly as a full-fledged architect on the strength of his training in Latrobe's office.

That Small would have been only twenty at the time he entered the competition for the president's house accounts to a great extent for the spareness of his drawing and compositional skills. On the other hand, his father's design for the Otterbein Church and the executed building itself had not exhibited anything more than an uninspired, conventional Colonial scheme for a simple church with galleries and a west tower, the only distinguishing feature of the building. As depicted in the view on the 1822 Poppleton plat of Baltimore and evidenced in the actual building, the squat brick tower, with pilaster strips at the corners and a kind of attick story with circular openings on each face, is surmounted by a large octagonal belfry with a domical roof, crowned by a small lantern of similar form. Devoid of any rich detail, the whole suggests a marginal command of proportion and scale on the elder Small's part. Something of the same difficulties must have beset the younger Small as well in his designs for the president's house, whose elevations applied many of the features used in his father's church.

The basic form employed by Small for all four of his designs for the presidential mansion was that of an elongated two-story block, with hipped roof and pedimented entrance pavilion; the more elaborate variants have a shallow basement and two end pavilions connected to the central block by open arcades. Reminiscent of certain aspects in plates illustrated in Gibbs' *Book of Architecture* (1728) and in the *Modern Builder's Assistant* (1747) by the Halfpennys, Morris, and Lightoler, this scheme does not differ essentially from that of many late Colonial houses save for its enlarged size. In all but one of these variants, Small used the same belfry featured in his father's church to crown the roof. The only ornamentation employed was a colossal order of Tuscan pilasters, again reminiscent of those used by his father and likewise evoking the only sense of classical detail, to subdivide the façades.

Small was the only entrant to provide four separate designs. Proceeding generally from the smallest and most austere to the largest and most expressive, they appear to be a direct response to that provision in the advertisement, of such concern to Washington, which called for the possible enlargement of the building in stages. However, rather than provide for the expansion of a single basic plan, Small elected instead to render four different buildings. Although each design could be either expanded or reduced, the provision of four designs which do not differ appreciably in style—and so do not offer any stylistic choices—but which do differ significantly in size and scope suggests the mind of an inexperienced designer. Nor do they represent any significant departure from the more pedestrian directions in Colonial American architecture. A.S.

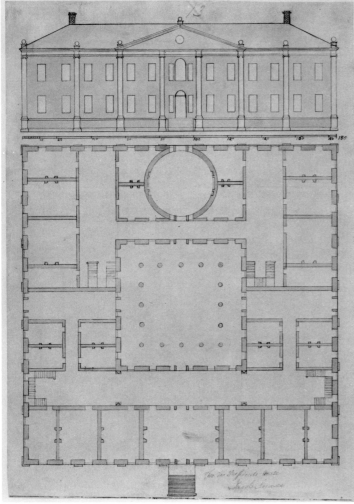

**422 Original competition drawing. Front elevation and
principal floor plan, scheme A**

JACOB SMALL, JR. 1772–1851
Pen and ink with gray wash 1792
36.1 x 25.6 (14³⁄₁₆ x 10⅛)
Signed lower right: *Jacob Small.*
Inscribed lower right: *For the
Presidents House*

*Lent by the Maryland Historical
Society, Baltimore*

The only Small variant without a
lantern, although equal in size to the
largest of his four designs (scheme D),
this plan reflects an attempt to create
a rotunda and monumental colonnaded hall, as well as to vary the shape
of the rooms. The resulting circulation patterns, however, are unduly
complicated and wasteful of space.
In the façade, also similar to the one
in Small's fourth variant, the pilasters
occur at equal intervals of two window
bays; they rest on pedestals, whose
height determines the building
podium, and are crowned by a curious
motif consisting of a sphere resting
on a stubby base. The central pedi-

mented pavilion, though likewise
articulated every two bays, departs
somewhat from the norm: the two
interior pilasters are without the
crowning feature, while the central bay
is composed of a round-arched opening at each level flanked by smaller
rectangular windows to simulate a
Palladian motif, Small's only attempt
to enliven the fenestration. On the
whole, the results are far from convincing from either a practical or an
aesthetic standpoint. A.S.

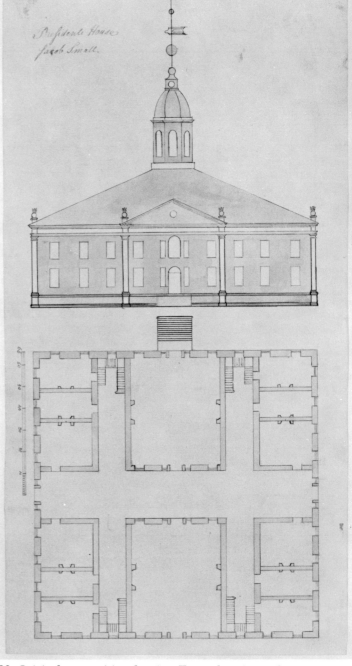

**423 Original competition drawing. Front elevation and
principal floor plan, scheme B**

JACOB SMALL, JR. 1772–1851
Pen and ink with gray wash 1792
38 x 20.2 (14¹⁵⁄₁₆ x 7¹⁵⁄₁₆)
Signed upper left: *Jacob Small.*
Inscribed upper left: *Presidents House*

*Lent by the Maryland Historical
Society, Baltimore*

Although this plan, the smallest of
Small's four schemes for the president's house, is perhaps the most
straightforward, the elevation is also

the most primitive of the four. The
pilasters are applied at the corners
of the building and of the central
pavilion. The fenestration is rendered
most unevenly. Moreover, the lantern, which actually is about the same
size as those indicated on the other
two schemes, is poorly proportioned
for this particular building: it is too
large to be a lantern, yet too small
to be a dome. A.S.

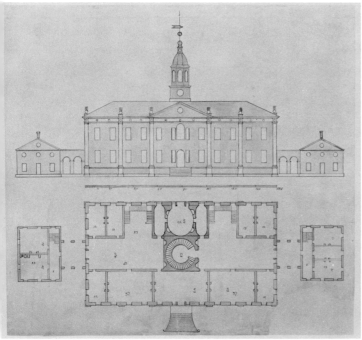

424 Original competition drawing. Front elevation and principal floor plan, scheme C

JACOB SMALL, JR. 1772–1851
Pen and ink with gray wash 1792
32.7 x 36.3 (12⅞ x 14¼)

Lent by the Maryland Historical Society, Baltimore

One of Small's five-part schemes, this plan, perhaps more than any other, demonstrates Small's inability to manipulate the size or arrangement of rooms with any degree of authority or skill. In addition to providing an excessive amount of circulation area at the expense of useful space, he failed to orient the grand, circular staircase to a more centralized access. Also, his three oval rooms, potentially the most stylish features of this plan, are underscaled and effectively disconnected from the rest of the building. The two end pavilions, connected to the central block by two open arcades, no doubt were intended to afford some provision for the future expansion of the building, as mentioned in the advertisement; however, the shallow two-bay arcades would surely have needed to be lengthened in order to accomodate the stairs—which Small overlooked—from the first level of the central block down to the floor level of the arcade.

Although the façade and particularly the lantern is generally of pleasing proportions, the whole suffers from a great disparity of scale between the connecting arcades and central block on the one hand, and the same arcades and the end pavilions on the other. A.S.

425 Original competition drawing. Front elevation and principal floor plan, scheme D

JACOB SMALL, JR. 1772–1851
Pen and ink with gray wash 1792
45 x 45.1 (17¹¹⁄₁₆ x 17¾)
Signed upper left: *Jacob Small.*
Inscribed upper left: *plan of the Presidents house*

Lent by the Maryland Historical Society, Baltimore

The façade of the central block in this, the most elaborate of Small's schemes in terms of both size and expression, is similar to the one in his first scheme. Here, however, a lantern, basement windows, and circle templates in the frieze have all been added; it is essentially the same plan, with certain minor improvements. The tripartite end pavilions, vaguely reminiscent of those at Holkham Hall, are more elaborate than the ones detailed in scheme C; the pavilion on the left evidently was intended to accomodate stables on the ground floor.

The floor area of the central block alone is more than twice that of Hoban's design and executed building. A.S.

JAMES DIAMOND'S DESIGN FOR THE PRESIDENT'S HOUSE

Very little is known about James Diamond beyond the information supplied on his competition drawings, indicating that he was, at the time, from Somerset County, Maryland. None of the county histories or publications on the architecture of the region make any reference to him. A land deed recently located in Somerset County reveals that a James Diamond purchased a three-hundred-acre tract of land there on May 6, 1794. Also located was Diamond's will, dated October 18, 1794, and probated on May 23, 1797, dividing his estate between his wife Ann and three sons in Ireland, John, Thomas, and James. This may suggest that Diamond was born in Ireland.

The one remaining reference to Diamond is an unusual advertisement that appeared in the April 29, 1785, issue of the *Maryland Gazette or the Baltimore General Advertiser*. "By a gentleman from Somerset-county," the advertisement begins, "we are informed, that the ingenious Mr. James Diamond, architect, in the county aforesaid, has invented and brought into practice, an instrument so curiously calculated, as to determine the right line, distance, bearing, and magnitude of any object by sight only, whether accessible or inaccessible, without change of place or station, by a method entirely new." Its most extraordinary aspect, according to the advertisement, was that "the most distant hint of the principles on which it is calculated, is not to be met with in Euclid, or any other ancient or modern author, which is no small honour to the inventor, and to this country in general." Apart from referring to Diamond as an architect, the advertisement made no mention of that aspect of his work. Judging by the fact that this exceptional instrument was deemed suitable for such undertakings as "gunnery, navigation, and surveying," the latter activity might have prompted Diamond's invention. No patent for it has been located; apparently one was never issued.

Despite such obvious *retardataire* features as the overscaled eagle crowning the building, Diamond's design for the president's house possesses a sufficient degree of coherence and organization to suggest a certain acquaintance with academic forms and details. Its use of a two-story façade set on a tall basement, with a pedimented columnar portico and two pedimented end pavilions, each highlighted by a Palladian window, all suggest elements prominently depicted

in several façades illustrated in Campbell's *Vitruvius Britannicus* (1715–1725) and *The Modern Builder's Assistant* (1742) by Halfpenny, Morris, and Lightoler. At the same time, treatment of the articulated door and window frames and especially of the Ionic capitals on the portico columns, though obviously of academic derivation, is sufficiently naive to indicate that Diamond's command of such details was nowhere near as authoritative and refined as was Hoban's.

Significantly, among the entrants whose drawings are preserved, Diamond was the only one to provide for the expansion of his designed building by supplying "Arcades leading to the Wings if necessary"; the wings themselves were not indicated on his plans. He also provided for a modicum of flexibility by stipulating that the open court in the center could be "chang'd to a Picture gallery and Lighted from the Top," presumably by skylights; the result, in his words, "would have a grand Effect." Yet, despite its relative coherence and his attempts to introduce innovative forms, there is still something too whimsical and contrived about the whole for Diamond's design to appear fully convincing. A.S.

426 Original competition drawing. Front elevation and principal floor plan

JAMES DIAMOND died c. 1797
Pen and ink with gray and brown wash
1792
48.6 x 37.4 (19⅛ x 14¾)
Signed lower center: *By James Diamond of Sommerset* [sic] *C: State of Maryland.* Inscribed lower center: *To the Honble Commissioner's* [sic] *of the* FEDERAL *Building's* [sic] *&c. a* PLAN *and* ELEVATION *of a* PRESIDENT'S HOUSE. Notation bottom center:
A. Saloon, B. Withdrawing room, C. Dining Room, D. Breakfast parlour E. Private drawing-room,/F. Gallery round the Court, G. Court. H. Staircase, I. Library, K. Anti room, L. Hall,/ M. Anti room, N. Conference room.— Note this Plan is the Principal floor— the Open Court/G. may be chang'd to a Picture-gallery and Lighted from the Top, which would have a grand Effect.
Inscribed in ink on verso: *James Diamond*

Lent by the Maryland Historical Society, Baltimore

The principal façade in this drawing, the first of three surviving ones by Diamond, appears to be a composite of several reproduced in Colen Campbell's *Vitruvius Britannicus*, although it lacks the incisiveness and precision of Campbell's details. The general format of a two-story tetrastyle portico over basement, six bays in the intervening curtain walls, end pavilions featuring Palladian windows, and stringcourses separating each story is strongly reminiscent of the façade for Grimsthorp in Lincolnshire, depicted in plate 13 of volume 3. Significant differences center on the use in Grimsthorp of rustication and quoining, a treatment absent in Diamond's design; the use of the Corinthian order in the portico of the former, and of the Ionic in that of the latter; and, finally, the rise of squared end pavilions above the main cornice in Grimsthorp, with the same pavilions being shortened by a story and crowned by pediments in Diamond's variant. Certain other differences, including the use of the Ionic order, of balustrades at the bottom of all first-story window openings, and of

round-arched openings in the basement, all suggest Diamond's reference to another building, Woburn Abbey in Bedfordshire, depicted in plates 22–23 of volume 4, *Vitruvius Britannicus*. From the latter building Diamond appropriated compound openings, consisting of a shorter round-arched window set into a full-length round-arched opening, for all the openings in the basement level of his façade; the same full-length round-arched openings, but without the shorter inset windows, appear on the first-story level of his portico. Unlike the conventional basement entrances indicated for Grimsthorp and Woburn Abbey, Diamond attached a set of winding stairs to both sides of the portico at the parlor level, a more provincial treatment suggested in plate 49 of *The Modern Builder's Assistant* by Halfpenny, Morris, and Lightoler.

The use of a central open court, for which no precedent can be found in *Vitruvius Britannicus*, might have been appropriated by Diamond from plate 19 in Halfpenny's *Art of Sound Building* (1725). A.S.

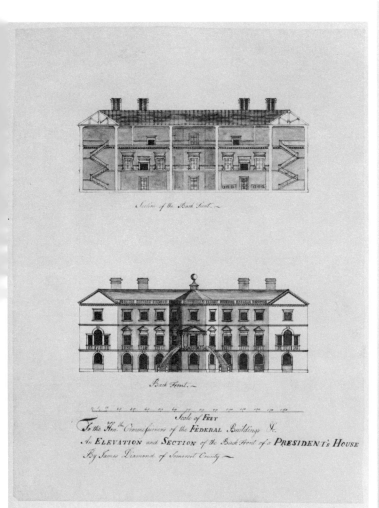

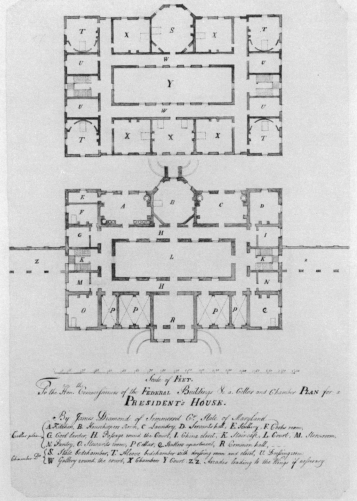

427 Original competition drawing. Section and rear elevation

JAMES DIAMOND died c. 1797
Pen and ink with gray and brown wash
1792
49 x 37 (19⅝₁₆ x 14⁹⁄₁₆)
Signed lower left: *By James Diamond
of Somerset County—*. Inscribed
upper center: *Section of the Back
Front*. Inscribed lower center: *Back
Front—/Scale of* FEET/*To the Honble
Commissioners of the* FEDERAL
Buildings &c./An ELEVATION *and*
SECTION *of the Back Front of a*
PRESIDENT'S HOUSE

*Lent by the Maryland Historical
Society, Baltimore*

This rather crudely drawn section,
which unfortunately does not show the
interior courtyard, reveals an erratic
handling of stairs and suggests highly
ornate door frames and mantlepieces,
perhaps with pulvinated friezes, for
the first or parlor floor.

The central projecting octagonal
bay, a feature which this elevation has
in common with the interior courtyard elevation in Diamond's design

for the capitol, recalls the elevation
illustrated in plate 47 of *The Modern
Builder's Assistant*, down to the
pyramidal roof form rising behind a
similar attick balustrade. The awkwardly framed tetrastyle Ionic portico
across the front face of the bay at the
first story has a pair of winding stairs,
similar to those at the front, attached
at either side. A.S.

428 Original competition drawing. Ground and second floor plans

JAMES DIAMOND died c. 1797
Pen and ink with gray wash 1792
53.2 x 37.5 (20¹⁵⁄₁₆ x 14¾)
Signed lower center: *By James Dia-
mond of Sommerset* [sic] *C?. State of
Maryland*. Inscribed lower center:
Scale of FEET/*To the Honble Com-
missioners of the* FEDERAL *Buildings,
&c. a Cellar and Chamber* PLAN *for a/*
PRESIDENT'S HOUSE.
Notation on bottom center:
CELLAR PLAN
A. Kitchen, B. Housekeepers Room,
C. Laundry, D. Servants hall, E.
Scullery, F. Cooks room,/G. Cool
larder, H. Passage round the Court,
I. China closet, K. Stair-case, L. Court,
M. Store-room,/N. Pantry, O.
Stewards room, P. Cellar, Q. Butlers
apartment, R. Common hall,
CHAMBER D°
S. State bedchamber, T. Alcove bed-
chamber with dressing room and
closet, U. Dressing room/W. Gallery
round the court, X Chambers Y

Court ZZ. Arcades leading to the
Wings if necessary

*Lent by the Maryland Historical
Society, Baltimore*

The most distinctive feature of this
plan is the alcove bedrooms provided
at the four corners of the second
story or chamber plan. Provision of
the arcades for additional wings is
doubtless in response to suggestions
for possible expansion of building
contained in the advertisement for the
competition for the president's house.
A.S.

ANDREW MAYFIELD CARSHORE'S DESIGN FOR THE PRESIDENT'S HOUSE

Surely the most enigmatic of the known entrants in the competition for the president's house, Andrew Mayfield Carshore is the only one among them who evidently was not otherwise occupied as an architect or builder. An acclaimed linguist, teacher, and poet in the Hudson River area of New York, Carshore had come to this country with General Burgoyne's army as an impressed young British soldier from Ireland. After the surrender at Saratoga in October 1777, he proceeded to Kinderhook, where he opened and operated an English school for a period of time. He then went to Claverack, where he moved in with the family of Dr. Gebhard, founder and superintendent of the Washington Seminary. While residing with Dr. Gebhard, Carshore acquired a knowledge of Greek and Latin, which he turned to good advantage by being appointed a professor at the seminary. He was, by all accounts, a man of unusual genius and possessed great aptitude as a teacher, succeeding N. Meigs as principal of the seminary. Under his direction, Washington Seminary achieved a reputation as a seat of classical learning, at times drawing more than a hundred students from the surrounding area, Albany, and New York. In 1805, Carshore left to become principal of the newly formed Hudson Academy. After serving in that position for five years, he moved to Old Saratoga, where he resided for the rest of his life. In addition to his teaching responsibilities, Carshore also took part in the organization of Columbia County after the Revolution and was clerk of its first board of supervisors.

That Carshore was a rank amateur in architectural matters, with no professional qualifications whatever to undertake preparation of a competition design for the president's house, appears to be borne out by his drawings; they are the least authoritative and convincing of all the surviving competition drawings. Given his stature as educator, it would not have been at all unlikely for Carshore to have had access to architectural books. Yet it is difficult to discern the impact of any specific book on Carshore's design. The only distinctive aspect of his drawings is the striking script in which the notes and especially the titles are rendered, affirming Carshore's wide acclaim in the Claverack and Hudson areas for his impeccable penmanship.

It is difficult to know precisely what might have motivated someone like Carshore to enter the competition. Perhaps it was a feeling of pride in his new-found home and a corresponding desire to contribute in some appropriately symbolic way to its formal establishment. In any event, however noble his intentions, the results represent little more than a parody of Colonial American architecture. His design evokes an image of a late pre-Revolutionary New England townhouse in the manner of Lee Mansion in Marblehead, Massachusetts (1768). It appropriated the features of a three-story front with characteristic fenestration, pedimented central pavilion with an Ionic doorway, and a hipped roof with modillion cornice surmounted by two simple cupolas, devices found frequently, though not in pairs, on New England houses of the period. The end pavilions, which Carshore obviously envisioned as subsequent additions to the mansion, expand the typical New England form into a less characteristic five-part front. Unlike the exquisitely and correctly proportioned Lee Mansion or any comparable New England prototype, however, Carshore's essay is at once more whimsical and awkward, its parts fragmented rather than integrated into a unified, classical whole. Still less can such exotic details as Carshore's fanciful provision for the front door of the mansion be viewed as the work of a disciplined designer.

A feature that made Carshore's design unique among the known competition entries was what he termed "the Canopy over the President's Chair." This, the only known instance in which a virtual throne was provided for the president, must have surely seemed rather disconcerting to Washington, who sought consciously to avoid the slightest pretense of regal trappings in his life, much less in the new executive mansion. A.S.

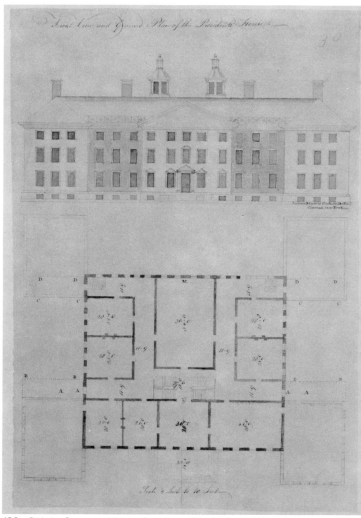

429 Original competition drawing. Front elevation and principal floor plan

ANDREW MAYFIELD CARSHORE
active late 18th century
Pen and ink with gray wash 1792
38.9 x 27.3 (15⅝ x 10¾)
Signed upper right: *Andrew Mayfield Carshore, Deltn./Claverack State New York.* Inscribed upper center: *Front View and Ground Plan of the President's House.* Inscribed lower center: *Scale ½ Inch to 10 Feet*

Lent by the Maryland Historical Society, Baltimore

The arrangement of rooms, circulation spaces, and stairways in the plan is awkward. Likewise, the four corner pavilions, here lightly indicated doubtless as a provision for subsequent expansion of the building, could hardly function as integral components of an expanded whole.

The erratic spacing of the bays prevents the simple façade from assuming a more vigorous aspect. The naive, wider spacing of the bays combines with the crudely articulated Ionic doorframe to emphasize the centrality of the pedimental pavilion. Angular pediments are placed on the first-story windows of the pavilion and nowhere else; these pediments are not noted on the perspective drawing. A.S.

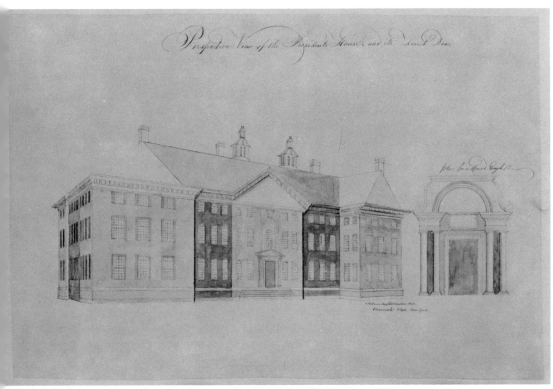

430 Original competition drawing. Perspective drawing and elevation of front door

ANDREW MAYFIELD CARSHORE
active late 18th century
Pen and ink with gray and brown wash
1792
25.3 x 38.4 (9 15/16 x 15 1/8)
Signed lower left: *Andrew Mayfield Carshore, Fecit/Claverack, State New York.* Inscribed upper center: *Perspective View of the Presidents House and its Front Door.* Notation above the front door elevation: *Place for a spread Eagle*

Lent by the Maryland Historical Society, Baltimore

The amateurish method and quality of the perspective drawing and the remarkable naiveté of the front door motif attest vividly to the thoroughly unschooled nature of Carshore's architectural background. A.S.

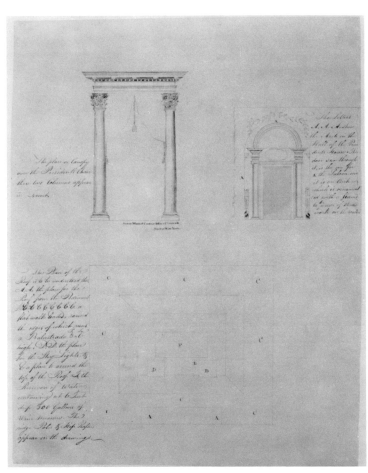

431 Original competition drawing. Roof plan and elevations of canopy and hall doorway

ANDREW MAYFIELD CARSHORE
active late 18th century
Pen and ink with gray wash 1792
38.1 x 30.2 (15 x 11 7/8)
Signed upper left: *Andrew Mayfield Carshore Delin: Claverack/State of New York.* Notation below elevation of canopy: *The place or Canopy/over the Presidents' [sic] Chair/these two Columns appear/in Front.* Notation to right of hall doorway elevation: *The Letters/A, A, A, show/the Arch in the/Hall of the Presi/dents House. The/door seen through/it, is the one for/the Saloon, over/it is an Arch—/which is ornament/=ed with leaves/ to be made of stucco/work on the wall.* Notation left of roof plan: *This Plan of the/Roof is to be understood thus,/ A, A, the place for the/Roof from the Pediment/C C C C C C C C, a/ flat walk leaded, round/the edges of*
                    Ft. In.
which runs/a Balustrade 3 " 6 / high; D, D, the place/for the Sky Lights, & /E a place to ascend the/top of the Roof; F, the/Reservoir of Water/ containing at 6 Feet/deep 300 gallons of/Wine Measure. The/ ridge Poles of High Rafters/appear on the drawings.

Judging by the drawing and notations, Carshore intended his striking "Canopy over the President's Chair" to simulate a portico consisting of a pair of Corinthian columns standing some feet from the wall and supporting a flat deck, whose ends would be expressed in the form of the entablature shown in the drawing. Scooped drapes would be employed in the manner suggested in the drawing, most likely intended for the sides as well as the front of the canopy. Though somewhat more severe than the other of Carshore's features, this canopy represents the only attempt among the known entries to provide what in effect is a throne for the president.

Far more in keeping with Carshore's apparent fanciful predilections is the hall doorway elevation, with plaster swags over an articulated arch that rests on a pair of Ionic pilasters crowned by a turned entablature with pulvinated frieze.

Significantly, Carshore is the only one of the entrants to provide any architectural details or roof plan. The latter, not surprisingly, does not correspond to the rendering of the roof in the perspective drawing of the building. A.S.

View of the East front of the Presidents House with the addition of the North & South Porticos.

432 East Front of the President's House

BENJAMIN HENRY LATROBE
1764–1820
Watercolor, pen and ink 1807
39.1 x 50.3 (15⅜ x 19¹³⁄₁₆)
Signed lower right:
BHLatrobe 1807
S.P.B. UStates

Lent by the Library of Congress

Latrobe did not favor Hoban's plan for the president's house, a design dependent on the architectural style of eighteenth-century England rather than the neoclassical style he preferred. To Latrobe, Hoban's structure lacked importance, and as Hamlin points out, he found the south entrance "disproportioned" and the north entrance portico pavilion "undistinguished." In 1807 Latrobe developed a new design for the building, both interior and exterior adding a semicircular portico on the south side (see no. 433), and a prominent entrance portico at the north, seen at the right in this drawing. Though the suggested interior alterations were not made, stone foundations, platforms and steps for both porticos were completed during Jefferson's administration and were surely, to Latrobe and Jefferson, more appropriate than "the wooden stairs and platform [which] were the usual entrance to the house," as Latrobe noted during the Adams administration.

During Madison's presidency, Latrobe served as Dolley Madison's consultant in the decoration of the president's house. Between 1809 and 1811 he furnished and fitted the house in the fashionable classical revival style, all of which was lost in the burning of the president's house by the British in 1814.

James Hoban, the original architect, was appointed to restore the president's house after the fire, and in 1824 he built Latrobe's porticos on the foundations laid during Jefferson's years as president. B.S.

Elevation of the South front of the President's house, copied from the ... as proposed to be altered in 1807. Jan. 1817. B. Latrobe

433 South Elevation of the President's House

BENJAMIN HENRY LATROBE
1764–1820
Watercolor, pen and ink 1817
40 x 53.5 (15¾ x 21¹⁄₁₆)
Signed lower right: *BHLatrobe*
Lent by the Library of Congress

During his administration, Jefferson took an active interest in the completion of the president's house, though first priority financially was given to work on the capitol. With Latrobe's appointment by Jefferson as the surveyor of public buildings, the design of the president's house changed. Among the alterations Latrobe made in Hoban's plan was the addition of colonnades, seen to the left and right in this drawing, and the south portico, seen at the center. As early as 1804, Jefferson suggested the use of the colonnades to connect the president's house to the executive offices. To the east colonnade wing, at the right in the drawing, Latrobe added a fireproof section for the treasury department. In 1810 a fireproof section was added to the west colonnade wing to house the post office department.

Latrobe's drawing, dated 1817, was made after the original of 1807. In the right rear can be seen St. John's Church, designed by Latrobe and not completed until 1816. B.S.

THE BUILDING OF THE CAPITOL IN WASHINGTON

When Pierre L'Enfant laid out the new city of Washington, he worked on tentative plans for a capitol, but they were still unfinished when he was dismissed by the commissioners in 1792. Jefferson had earlier proposed a competition for the best designs for a president's house and a capitol, and this plan was adopted, the capitol competition being won by William Thornton, a gifted amateur architect. Another more architecturally experienced contestant, Stephen Hallet, was appointed to supervise the construction of the building, and on September 18, 1793, its cornerstone was laid by Washington.

Hallet, however, had discovered serious flaws in Thornton's design, and with the approval of Jefferson and others, was authorized to modify the plan. He was dismissed in June 1794, after a disagreement with the commissioners, and was succeeded by George Hadfield. A few months after Hallet's departure, William Thornton was appointed to the board of commissioners, where he remained closely involved with the progress of construction. Hadfield served as supervisor until 1798, when he, too, was replaced on the grounds of friction with Thornton and the other commis-

sioners. James Hoban, architect of the president's house who had been supervising its construction, then took over the job until in 1803 Jefferson, as president, created the post of surveyor of the public buildings, to which he appointed Benjamin Latrobe, already well known for his design for the Richmond penitentiary. Latrobe made changes in the north wing of the capitol, which had been externally completed in 1800, to unite the chambers for the Senate, the Supreme Court, and the Library of Congress. In 1807 the south wing was ready for use by the House of Representatives.

By 1811, with war expenditures increasing, Congress refused to authorize any new construction on the capitol and in 1812, to Latrobe's disappointment, voted a final appropriation to settle outstanding debts. After its burning by the British in August 1814, however, Latrobe was put in charge of the reconstruction of the building, though he resigned in 1817 due to disagreements with public officials. Though still incomplete, the capitol was ready to be reoccupied in 1819, two years after Latrobe had been succeeded by Charles Bulfinch, who was to carry the project to its final completion in 1828. s.h.b.

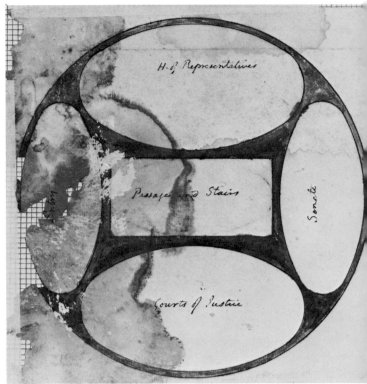

434 Study for the capitol building, Washington

THOMAS JEFFERSON 1743–1826
Laid paper 1792
18.1 x 17.8 (7¼ x 7)
Lent by the Massachusetts Historical Society, Boston

After Jefferson returned from France in 1789 and took the position of secretary of state under Washington, he became involved in plans for the location and design of the new federal city and was in effect Washington's liaison with the three appointed commissioners and with Major Pierre Charles L'Enfant, who had asked to be allowed to design a plan for the city. Jefferson supplied L'Enfant with various plans of European cities and characteristically began to sketch out ideas for the plans of the new public buildings.

This drawing indicates that in 1792 Jefferson was already thinking about the possibilities of using a rotunda form for the capitol, no doubt inspired by the Pantheon. "Whenever it is proposed to prepare plans for the Capitol, I should prefer the adoption of some one of the models of antiquity, which have had the approbation of thousands of years," he wrote to L'Enfant in 1791. F.N.

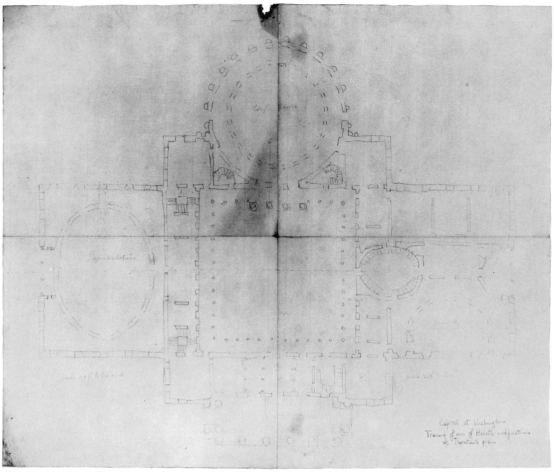

435 Tracing by Jefferson of Hallet's modifications of Thornton's design of the capitol, Washington

THOMAS JEFFERSON 1743–1826
Pencil on laid paper 1796–1803
50.1 x 41.2 (19¾ x 16¼)

Lent by the Massachusetts Historical Society, Boston

Though Jefferson did not submit a plan of his own in the competition for the design of the capitol, his suggestions for a rotunda plan on the order of the Pantheon were adopted by Stephen Hallet, whose finished design, however, was overshadowed by the similar but more impressive contribution of Dr. William Thornton.

"Doctor Thornton's plan of a capitol has been produced, and has so captivated the eyes and judgment of all as to leave no doubt you will prefer it when it shall be exhibited to you," wrote Jefferson to Daniel Carroll, one of the three commissioners. "It is simple, noble, beautiful, excellently distributed, and moderate in size."

Hallet was given the job of drawing working plans and supervising the construction of Thornton's design, and he soon found that the plan could

be carried out only after alterations had been made. This tracing by Jefferson of Hallet's proposed modifications was probably done about this time. Jefferson's report on Hallet's findings, setting forth the objections to Thornton's plan, was sent to Washington in July 1793:

The intercolonnations of the western and central peristyles are too wide for the support of their architraves of stone; so are those of the doors in the wings. . . . The colonnade passing through the middle of the Conference room has an ill effect to the eye, and will obstruct the view of the members; and if taken away, the ceiling is too wide to support itself. . . . The stairways on each side of the Conference room want head room. . . . The windows are in some important instances masked by the galleries. . . . Many parts of the building want light and air in a degree which renders them unfit for their purposes. . . . Other objections were made which were surmountable, but those preceding were thought not so, without an alteration

of the plan. This alteration has in fact been made by Mr. Hallet in the plan drawn by him, wherein he has preserved the most valuable ideas of the original and rendered them susceptible of execution, so that it is considered as Dr. Thornton's plan reduced into practicable form . . . in removing one of the objections, that is to say, the want of light and air to the Executive and Senate chambers, a very capital beauty in the original plan, to wit, the Portico of the Eastern front, was suppressed, and ought to be restored; as the recess proposed in the middle of that front instead of the Portico projecting from it, would probably have an extreme ill effect. . . . By advancing the Executive chamber, with the two rooms on its flanks, into a line with the Eastern front, or a little projecting or receding from it, the Portico might be re-established, and a valuable passage be gained in the center of the edifice, lighted from above, and serving as a common disengagement to the four capital apartments. F.N.

436 Elevation of the North Wing of the Capitol

WILLIAM THORNTON 1759–1828
Ink and wash 1795–1796
44.4 x 60.5 (17½ x 23⅞)

Lent by the Library of Congress

Though Thornton's design for the capitol had great interest and variety, it lacked professional finish in many minor ways. Hallet, therefore, was retained to modify the design, and it was he who first utilized the low, saucerlike dome, similar to the Roman Pantheon. Many other of his suggestions were eventually adopted. Neither Jefferson nor Latrobe was completely satisfied with Thornton's scheme. Latrobe's criticisms, particularly of the exterior massing of dissimilar domes, led to violent and public controversy between him and Thornton. Latrobe classed Thornton as being a man "having brilliant ideas, but possessing neither the knowledge necessary for the execution nor the capacity to methodize and combine the various parts of a public work." Thornton's contribution shrinks to an attractive combination of elements chosen for individual magnificence. He displayed an amateur's indecision before alternatives in design, a vagueness in structural matters, and a dependence on academic rule. Yet the building showed much grandeur in conception and had great masses and interior spaces. As Latrobe also said, "It is one of the first designs of modern times." F.N.

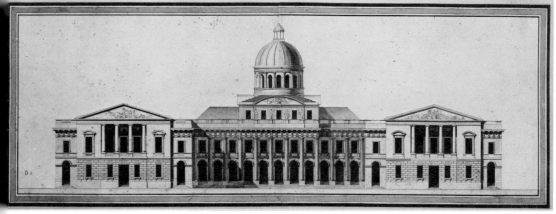

37 West Elevation of the Capitol at Washington

STEPHEN HALLET active 1789–1796
Watercolor
6.8 x 101.6 (14½ x 40)
Lent by the Library of Congress

Stephen Hallet conferred with Jefferson as early as 1791 on an appropriate design for the capitol, and following Jefferson's stated preference for a temple form, Hallet produced an octastyle peripteral temple with similarities in plan to the Pantheon in Paris. Though his design underwent many modifications, it was superseded by the plan of Dr. William Thornton, shown here at number 436. Jefferson wrote to the commissioners on Hallet's behalf, after it had become clear that Thornton's design would be chosen,

Some difficulty arises with respect to Mr. Hallet, who you know was in some degree led into his plan by ideas we all expressed to him. This ought not to induce us to prefer it to a better; but while he is liberally rewarded for the time and labor he has expended on it, his feelings should be saved and soothed as much as possible. I leave it to yourselves how best to prepare him for the possibility that the Doctor's plan may be preferred to his. Some ground for this will be furnished you by the occasion you will have for recourse to him, as to the interior of the apartments, and the taking of him into service at a fixed allowance. . . .

F.N.

438 U.S. capitol in the course of construction

BENJAMIN HENRY LATROBE
1764–1820
Pencil, pen and ink 1806
20.3 x 32.4 (8 x 12¾)
Lent by the Maryland Historical Society, Baltimore, Papers of Benjamin H. Latrobe

When in March 1803 Congress appropriated funds for the completion of the south wing of the capitol, Jefferson unhesitatingly wrote to offer the position of the first surveyor of the public buildings of the United States to Benjamin Henry Latrobe. In his seven years in America the young architect had already left his mark on the public buildings of the country through his bold design for the Richmond penitentiary and two important Philadelphia commissions, the ingenious waterworks and the Bank of Philadelphia. Further, he had impressed and delighted Jefferson with his design for a dry dock for the navy's great frigates, which the president had stipulated must have a roof "like that of the Halle of Blés in Paris."

The new surveyor faced a delicate and challenging situation. Thornton, whose brilliant but untutored design for the capitol had carried the day in President Washington's and Secretary of State Jefferson's competition, had managed thus far to put to rout every professional architect engaged to execute it—Hallet, Hadfield, and Hoban in turn—and to bring the work almost to a standstill.

Latrobe's sketch shows clearly his success in pushing forward the work on the south wing, which stands enclosed in scaffolding, its walls risen almost to their full height. As the time approached to enclose the House of Representatives, the partnership between architect and president was tried to the utmost in the battle of the ceiling. Jefferson, again recalling the magnificence of the Halle aux Bleds, wanted to repeat its wedge-shaped skylights. Latrobe feared that dazzling light, leakage and condensation of moisture would pose insoluble problems.

To the right stands the north wing, in which the Senate was already housed, the crisp lines of its completed façade standing out against the sky. B.S.

joint," he maintained, "dropping upon the head or desk of a member will disturb the whole house." Jefferson eventually deferred to Latrobe's judgment, but with the rejoinder: "I cannot express to you the regret I feel on the subject of renouncing the Halle aux Bleds lights of the Capitol dome. That single circumstance was to constitute the distinguished merit of the room, and would solely have made it the handsomest room in the world, without a single exception. Take that away, it becomes a common thing exceeded by many."

By the time Jefferson paid this tribute to it, the Legrand and Molinos dome he had known in Paris was already a memory. In the course of repair work undertaken in 1802, a soldering stove set fire to the wooden frame and the entire dome collapsed. It was rebuilt in 1809–1811 by Bélanger with the assistance of the engineer Brunet, who replaced the "sticks and chips" with iron ribs—an early use of structural iron foreshadowing later architectural developments. The entire building was eventually demolished to make way for the Bourse du Commerce in 1889, which is still standing, albeit precariously, on the circular site of the old Halle aux Bleds. H.C.R.

439 View of the Capitol

WILLIAM BIRCH 1755–1834
Watercolor 1800
22 x 28.7 (8⅝ x 11¼)

Lent by the Library of Congress

William Birch was an enamel painter and engraver, from Warwickshire, England, who came to Philadelphia in 1794 with a letter of introduction from Benjamin West. He became well known for his landscapes in watercolor and his miniatures in enamel. His most famous works were a series of views of Philadelphia, produced from 1798 to 1800 with the aid of his son Thomas (1779–1851), who later became famous as a landscape and marine artist.

This view of the north, or Senate, wing of the capitol illustrates the similarity to Wanstead House, England. Nonetheless, there is a French character to the design which is most pronounced in the carved consoles, which are used on either side of the central opening on the ground floor. These are also used to support the segmental pediments and the arch on the first floor. Perhaps they indicate the influence of the French architect, Stephen Hallet, who was the original supervisor of the capitol construction.

F.N.

440 Interior view of the Halle aux Bleds

Lent by the Bibliothèque nationale

The Halle aux Bleds, or grain market, was completed in 1769, though the dome, designed by J. G. Legrand and Jacques Molinos, was not completed until over ten years later. The architects employed a Renaissance method of construction which enabled them to construct a dome so lightweight that glass windows could be inserted between the ribs, letting daylight into the vast interior.

The Halle aux Bleds came to occupy a special place in Jefferson's memories of Paris, and he was often to recall in his mind's eye the Legrand and Molinos dome. In 1802, for example, when unsuccessfully proposing to Congress a plan for a dry-dock, he suggested a "roof of the construction of that over the meal market in Paris, except that it is hemispherical, this semi-cylindrical." Again, in 1805, when discussing with Benjamin Latrobe the dome covering the House of Representatives in the capitol at Washington (see nos. 441–443), he proposed the Halle aux Bleds as a model. Latrobe saw many disadvantages, such as troublesome sunlight and possible leakage. "A single leaky

441 Preliminary section of the House of Representatives

BENJAMIN HENRY LATROBE 1764–1820
Watercolor, ink, pencil 1804
34 x 55.6 (14⅜ x 21⅞)

Lent by the Library of Congress

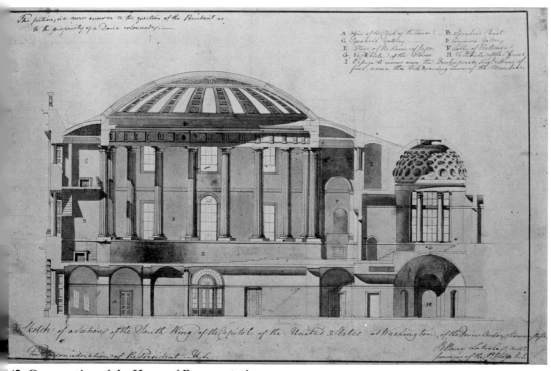

This section is a mere answer to the question of the President as to the propriety of a Doric colonnade.

A *Office of the Clerk of the House.*   B *Speaker's Closet*
C *Speaker's Gallery*   D *Common Gallery*
E *Floor of the House of Repr.*   F *Gallery of Visiters*
G *Vestibule of the House*   H *Vestibule unter floor*
I *Offices to rooms over the Doric portch, sing'g rooms of fire's sewer than withdrawing rooms of the Members.*

Sketch of a Section of the South Wing of the Capitol of the United States at Washington, of the Doric Order of Roman style

For the consideration of the President U.S.   B Henry Latrobe archit, Surveyor of the P. bldgs U.S.

442 Cross section of the House of Representatives

BENJAMIN HENRY LATROBE
1764–1820
Watercolor 1804
34.6 x 55.8 (13⅝ x 22)

Lent by the Library of Congress

The design for the ceiling of the House of Representatives initiated a battle between Latrobe and Jefferson detailed at nos. 440 and 443 which, on Latrobe's part, did not end until the Capitol was rebuilt after its burning by the British in 1814. In this drawing, Latrobe demonstrated how the light, being far too bright in summer, would fall in the chamber. At the same time, perhaps aware of Jefferson's steadfastness in this matter, Latrobe provided a design for venetian blinds in an attempt to control the problem of the light. Latrobe also believed that leakage from the skylights was certain, and as he wrote in May 1807, 'condensed vapor would shower down upon the heads of the members from the 100 lights." Latrobe suggested instead a dome topped by a lantern, which he had used in the Bank of Pennsylvania. Vertical glass panes would be easier to waterproof, and a dome with a lantern would eliminate the problem of moisture condensation and would provide more even and diffused light in the chamber. Jefferson found the plan unacceptable, saying that he could find no prototype for it in ancient classical architecture. B.S.

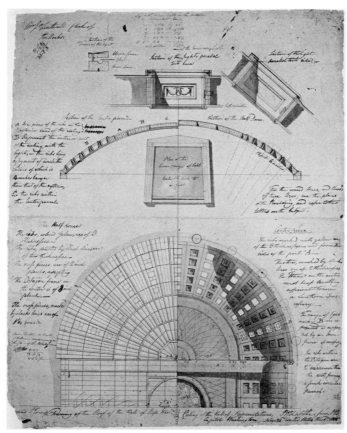

443 Ceiling of the House of Representatives

BENJAMIN HENRY LATROBE
1764–1820
Pen and ink, watercolor, pencil 1805
68.6 x 56.2 (27 x 22⅛)
Signed lower right: *BHLatrobe, Surv. PB*

Lent by the Library of Congress

In this drawing Latrobe answered Jefferson's challenge with regard to the problem of leakage of the ceiling of the House of Representatives. Each ribbed, wedge-shaped window was to have been replaced by five square ones, each framed on three sides, the fourth open for drainage, thus reducing the number of joints and therefore the potential amount of leakage. Jefferson was satisfied with the compromise plan; however, in the summer of 1806 Latrobe informed Jefferson that he had framed a lantern in the event that the glass, ordered from Germany, did not arrive in time. Latrobe was still attempting to convince Jefferson to approve a dome with a lantern rather than skylights. Jefferson, however, would not be swayed. On May 21, 1807, Latrobe wrote to Jefferson again trying to influence the president, largely in response to Jefferson's concern at not finding an ancient classical prototype for the lantern design, saying,

My principles of good taste are rigid in Grecian architecture. I am a bigoted Greek in the condemnation of the Roman architecture of Baalbec, Palmyra, and Spalatro. . . . Wherever, therefore the Grecian style can be copied without impropriety I love to be a mere, I would say a slavish copyist, but the forms of the distribution of the Roman and Greek buildings which remain, are in general, inapplicable to the objects uses of our public buildings. Our religion requires a church wholly different from the temples, our legislative assemblies and our courts of justice, buildings of entirely different principles from their basilicas; and our amusements could not possibly be performed in their amphitheatres. . . . It is not the *ornament*, it is the use of it that I want.

In August 1807 the glass began to be set in place. As Latrobe had foreseen, there was leakage. Once again he suggested abandoning the plan; Jefferson held fast. In an attempt, therefore, to control the leakage and condensation Latrobe installed sheets of glass larger than the openings and adapted some of the lower skylights to allow circulation of air in the ceiling area. The lighting conditions were modified by permanently covering all of the skylights in the western portion of the dome.

After the burning of the capitol in 1814, however, Latrobe, no longer under Jefferson's control, installed his original lantern design. B.S.

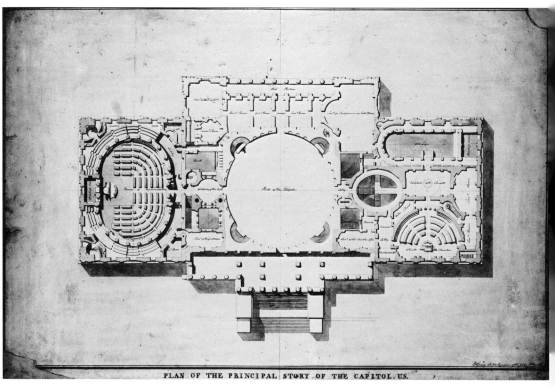

PLAN OF THE PRINCIPAL STORY OF THE CAPITOL. US.

444 Principal story of the United States capitol

BENJAMIN HENRY LATROBE
1764–1820
Watercolor, pencil, pen and ink 1806
49.1 x 75.9 (19�5/₁₆ x 29⅞)
Signed lower right: *B. Henry Latrobe surv. of the pblic Bldgs US 1806*
Lent by the Library of Congress

The circumstances surrounding Latrobe's resignation of the office of surveyor of the public buildings were those of sabotage, in which Colonel Samuel Lane maligned Latrobe to President Monroe. Being far less responsive than his predecessors Jefferson and Madison to the problems of building so great a structure as the capitol, Monroe was unable to appreciate the extent of Latrobe's achievements, aesthetic and mechanical, in the project and assumed Lane's self-righteous and unenlightened position. Monroe did not realize that between 1815 and 1817, as Hamlin points out, Latrobe had removed all of the damaged structure that remained standing after the fire, designed a new, improved plan for the south wing, revised the plan for the north wing so as to enlarge the Senate chamber, as had been requested, and designed the plan of the central rotunda and the library wing to the west. In addition to removing that part of the building damaged by fire, in two and a half years Latrobe had also directed the building of what had previously taken six years to construct. Under his successor Bulfinch's direction, the project required eleven more years before completion. Bulfinch, acknowledging his dependence on Latrobe's designs, largely followed the aesthetic of Latrobe's plans for the north and south wings, though he modified the design for the exterior dome and the details of the west front. B.S.

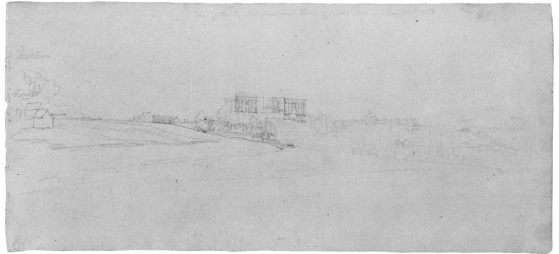

445 View of the capitol from my shop

BENJAMIN HENRY LATROBE
1764–1820
Pencil, pen and ink 1813
21.3 x 48.9 (8⅜ x 19¼)
Lent by the Maryland Historical Society, Baltimore, Papers of Benjamin H. Latrobe

In his work as surveyor of the public buildings, Latrobe was constantly under attack by those who objected to the expenses incurred in the erection of a suitable new capitol. Latrobe, surveyor of the public buildings since March 1803, was by 1811 referred to as "the late Surveyor of the Public Buildings."

Jefferson, realizing Latrobe's disppointment, attempted to console ıim in a letter of July 12, 1812:

> With respect to yourself, the little disquietudes from individuals not chosen for their taste in art, will be sunk into oblivions, while the Representative Chamber will remain a durable monument of your taste as an architect. . . . I shall live in hope that the day will come when an opportunity will be given you of finishing the middle building in a style worthy of the two wings, and worthy of the first temple dedicated to the sovereignty of the people, embellishing with Athenian taste the course of a nation looking far beyond the range of Athenian destinies.

In the months following the burning of the capitol in August 1814, a sum was appropriated for its rebuilding, and Latrobe, who had previously been refused employment by President Madison on account of his being "unpopular," offered his services in the capitol project. He was appointed and served until November 20, 1817, when he resigned as a result of an incompatibility between the commissioner of public buildings, Colonel Samuel Lane, and himself. Charles Bulfinch, the Boston architect, was appointed to succeed Latrobe. B.S.

446 Letter concerning the tobacco plant and the capital derived from it. November 5, 1816

BENJAMIN HENRY LATROBE
1764–1820
(facsimile)
Signed: *From Benjamin Henry Latrobe to Thomas Jefferson.*
Original at the Library of Congress

Among Latrobe's contributions to the architecture of the capitol was the development of an American iconography in the use of decorative motifs,

based on plants indigenous to the country and important to it economically, on capitals in the north wing. The cotton capital of 1809, designed for a cupola over the Senate lobby, was executed but it is not known whether it was ever put in place. In the same year Giovanni Andrei finished for use in the Senate rotunda the corn capital, a model of which Latrobe sent to Jefferson. In a letter of August 28, 1809, Latrobe wrote to Jefferson: "This capital, during the summer session obtained me more applause from the members of Congress than all the Works of Magnitude." Jefferson, as Latrobe had suggested, subsequently used the capital as the base for a sundial. After the fire, which the corn capitals survived, Latrobe designed and Iardella executed the tobacco capitals for the oval lobby on the upper floor of the north wing. In this letter, dated November 5, 1816, Latrobe explains to Jefferson, making use of a "hasty and imperfect sketch," "I have therefore composed a capital of leaves and flowers of the tobacco plant which has an intermediate effect approaching a Corinthian order and retaining the simplicity of the Clepsydra or Temple of the Winds. Iardella a sculptor who has just arrived, has made an admirable model for execution in which he has well preserved the botanical character of the plant, although it has been necessary to enlarge the proportion of the flowers to the leaves, and to arrange them in clusters of three." Latrobe never felt that the tobacco capital equalled the corn capital, and on June 28, 1817, wrote to Jefferson regarding a tobacco capital he presented to the former president: "If you can find a place for it, I would recommend that it be painted, that the leaves of the upper tier, be colored in the lower part with a faint brown (umber), as I shall do in the rotunda of 16 columns in the North wing of the Capitol, in which I have applied them. Otherwise they do not sufficiently distinguish themselves." B.S.

447 Sketch for a classical figure

BENJAMIN HENRY LATROBE
1764–1820
Watercolor and pencil
70.3 x 47.4 (27¹¹⁄₁₆ x 18¹¹⁄₁₆)
Lent by the Library of Congress

Little is known of the projected placement of this sculpture of a classical figure, although Latrobe called for dramatic sculpture decoration in the House of Representatives, with Jefferson's enthusiastic backing. Such elaborate use of sculpture had never before been attempted in America. At the president's direction, two Italian sculptors were recruited and arrived in February 1806. Giuseppe Franzoni (1786–1816) completed a seven-foot seated figure of Liberty to be placed behind the Speaker's chair. Liberty's handmaidens, Art, Science, Agriculture, and Commerce, adorned the entrance. Above it all was a colossal American eagle with a wingspread of more than twelve feet, for which Charles Willson Peale provided from his Philadelphia museum not only drawings but an eagle's head and claw to guide the sculptor. All was destroyed when the capitol was burned in 1814.

Talbot Hamlin attributes this drawing to Franzoni, and suggests that it represents the Athena designed for the Supreme Court chamber in the capitol building. B.S.

448 Egyptian Design of the Library of Congress

BENJAMIN HENRY LATROBE
1764–1820
Ink, watercolor, pencil
50.2 x 61.9 (20¾ x 24⁵⁄₁₆)
Signed lower left: *By BHenry Latrobe Surveyor of the Public Bldgs UsStates*
Lent by the Library of Congress

As the south wing with its magnificent chamber for the deliberations of the Representatives neared completion in 1807, Latrobe was able to turn his attention to the north wing. Substantially completed upon Thornton's plans before Latrobe received his appointment, it now required extensive changes and a new, comprehensive design which would unite rooms for the Senate, the Supreme Court, and the Library of Congress in a harmonious and convenient whole. Latrobe's elegant Egyptian design for the Library in the western half of the wing was part of this scheme, but with the approach of war, funds became scarce and he was able to make only a few necessary repairs. A later plan for the Library, also in the Egyptian mode, proposed a bold projection on the west with a spacious library room stretching its entire length, leaving the whole of the main floor of the wing for the Senate chamber.

When the Library and its contents burned in the War of 1812, Jefferson wrote immediately from Monticello: "I learn from the newspapers that the vandalism of our enemy has triumphed at Washington . . . by the destruction of the public library with the noble edifice in which it was deposited. . . . I presume it will be among the early objects of Congress to re-commence their collection." He went on to offer to the country his own library of between nine and ten thousand volumes, gathered steadily over fifty years in America and abroad. B.S.

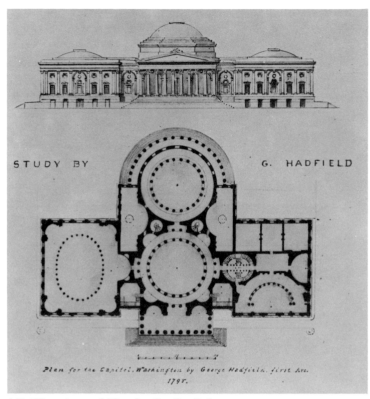

STUDY BY   G. HADFIELD

Plan for the Capitol. Washington by George Hadfield. first Arc.
1795.

449 Elevation and Plan for the Capitol

ANDREW JACKSON DAVIS
1803–1892, after George Hadfield
1763–1826
Ink and wash 1832
36.5 x 26 (14⅜ x 10¼)
*Lent by the Columbia Historical
Society, Washington*

After consulting his friends Benjamin West and James Wyatt in London, John Trumbull answered William Thornton's request for a superintendent of construction of the U.S. capitol by recommending the young architect, George Hadfield. Hadfield had studied at the Royal Academy, where he received a gold medal in 1784, and after working under Wyatt, surveyor general of the Board of Works, he spent several years in Italy where he studied Roman archaeological sites.

He was appointed to the job in Washington in 1795, shortly after his return to London, where he had exhibited his drawings of the Temple of Fortune at Palestrina.

Work on the capitol was complicated by the fact that the foundations laid by Stephen Hallet, the first superintendent, were on a plan different from that originally designed by Thornton. As Jefferson, then secretary of state, put it after a conference with the president in an attempt to mollify both architects, Hallet's plan would be "considered as Dr. Thorn-

ton's plans rendered into practical form." Hadfield liked neither Thornton's design nor Hallet's execution and so proposed yet another scheme. Hadfield's plan for a lower basement, a colossal order for the portico and the low and simple domes was rejected by the commissioners, precipitating his resignation, "not because his knowledge was not eminent," Trumbull later wrote, "but because his integrity compelled him to say that part of the original plan *could not be executed.*"

Latrobe's tribute to Hadfield written some years before his death sums up his professional frustrations and defeats: "He loiters here, ruined in fortune, temper and reputation, nor will his irritable pride and neglected study ever permit him to take the station in the art which his elegant taste and excellent talent ought to have obtained." w.h.a.

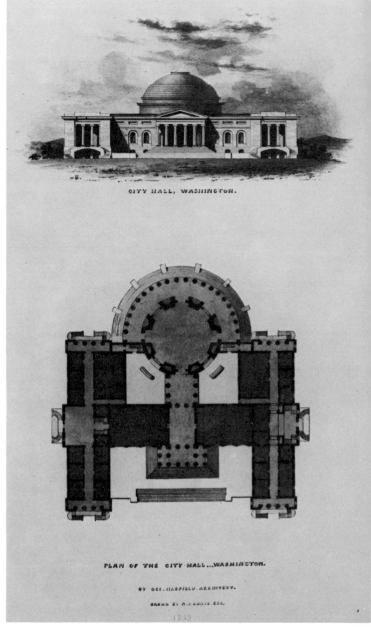

CITY HALL, WASHINGTON.

PLAN OF THE CITY HALL...WASHINGTON.

BY GEO. HADFIELD, ARCHITECT.

DRAWN BY A.J.DAVIS ESQ.

1832

450 Elevation and Plan of the City Hall, Washington

ANDREW JACKSON DAVIS
1803–1892, after George Hadfield
1763–1826
Ink and wash 1832
36.2 x 21.6 (14¼ x 8½)
*Lent by the Columbia Historical
Society, Washington*

When the commissioners of the city of Washington refused to allow George Hadfield to supervise the execution of his design for the Treasury executive office in 1798, he resigned in professional indignation. He remained in Washington, however, and on Jefferson's recommendation designed several public buildings

including the Washington County Jail in 1802 and the Arsenal in 1803. In 1820 he produced the plans for the City Hall in Judiciary Square, now the District Court Building. These plans along with Hadfield's plan for the capitol were in the possession of William Elliott, United States city surveyor, in 1832, when they were copied by the young architect A. J. Davis. The date of 1833 on the mount does not correspond to Davis' journal entry, however, which records the work a year earlier.

The south front of the building (refaced in 1917) follows Hadfield's design, which included the Ionic portico, but the plans for the dome

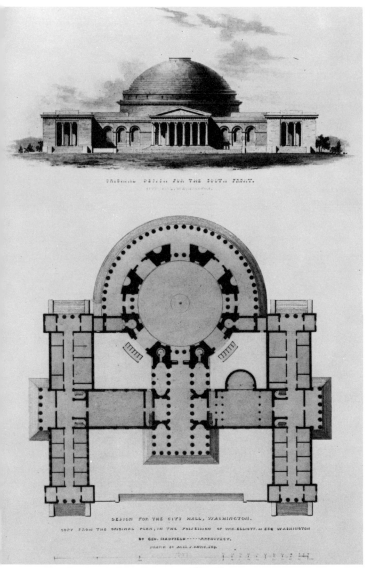

451 Elevation and Plan of the City Hall (Corinthian Order)

ANDREW JACKSON DAVIS
1803–1892, after George Hadfield
1763–1826
Ink and wash 1832
36.5 x 24.1 (14⅜ x 9½)

Lent by the Columbia Historical Society, Washington

This more imposing scheme for the projected city hall contains echoes of the French architects Boullée and Ledoux in the mass of the dome and monumental colonnade on the west front.

In the years prior to the commission of the city hall, Hadfield had designed Arlington, the house of G. W. Parke Custis, as well as that of Commodore Porter and John Mason on Mason's (now Roosevelt) Island in the Potomac.

Jefferson's admiration and support

and elaborate north façade were not carried out when the building was finally completely in 1849. Before Hadfield died in obscurity, "he had the opportunity of erecting a noble monument to himself in the city hall, a beautiful building, in which is no waste of space or materials," noted John Trumbull, who had known Hadfield, the brother of Maria Cosway, in happier days when they were both students in London at the Royal Academy. W.H.A.

for Hadfield continued after he had retired from the presidency. In 1822 he forwarded a letter of Hadfield's to his sister, Maria Cosway, with the report that her brother was "much respected in Washington, and since the death of Latrobe, our first architect, I consider him as standing foremost in the correct principles of that art." W.H.A.

452 Christ Church, Charlottesville

Photograph, 19th century
10.1 x 14 (4 x 5½)

Lent by the University of Virginia, Alderman Library, Charlottesville

Christ Episcopal Church in Charlottesville was the only ecclesiastical design by Jefferson that was ever constructed. During most of Jefferson's life, there was no church in Charlottesville, and during the early 1820s a plan to build a church for all denominations failed to be realized. In 1824, a church specifically for Episcopalians was proposed, and the Reverend F. W. Hatch, Christ Church's first minister, wrote to Jefferson, "I will forward to you a plan for the building for your approbation as soon as it comes to hand, but would prefer receiving from you a draft which our means would justify us in adopting." A little later his request was more specific, asking for "a plan of a church that might be built for $2,500, we would be much obliged to you."

Jefferson not only designed the church, but was one of the largest contributors to its building and to the support of its minister. The exterior was based on Chalgrin's Saint-Philippe du Roule (see nos. 453, 454), which was only a few blocks from Jefferson's residence in Paris. In turn, Christ Church influenced the design of many Virginia churches, including St. Thomas' Church in Orange and the Presbyterian church in Fredericksburg. Christ Church was torn down in 1895 to make way for a larger structure. F.N.

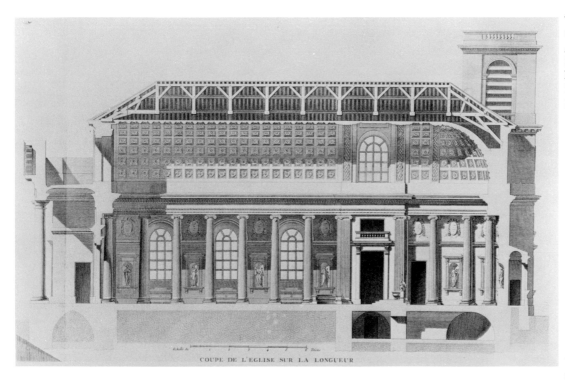

Echelle de ... Toise

COUPE DE L'EGLISE SUR LA LONGUEUR

453 The Church of Saint-Philippe du Roule, longitudinal section

After JEAN-FRANÇOIS CHALGRIN
1739–1811
Etching
31.8 x 56.5 (12½ x 22¼)
Lent by the Musée Carnavalet, Paris

454 The Church of Saint-Philippe du Roule, latitudinal section

After JEAN-FRANÇOIS CHALGRIN
1739–1811
Etching
31.9 x 49.4 (12½ x 19½)
Lent by the Musée Carnavalet, Paris

The Church of Saint-Philippe du Roule, which is usually cited as the model rather freely imitated by Jefferson in his design for Christ Church in Charlottesville (no. 452), was opened to the public in 1784, the year of Jefferson's arrival in Paris. Jefferson's Paris residence, the Hôtel de Langeac, also designed by Chalgrin, was near the church; and Jefferson, with his admiration for Chalgrin and interest in all things architectural, must have frequently had his attention drawn to the new building.

The use of the basilican design of the church marked a return to the tradition of early Christian basilicas, which were, in turn, imitations of Roman basilicas. As early as 1764 at St. Symphorien at Versailles, Trouard had used this design, which the antiquarians preferred to the more eclectic solution offered by Soufflot for the Church of Sainte-Geneviève. At Saint-Philippe du Roule there were no Gothic or Renaissance elements such as a dome with a lantern tower or pierced vaults; rather, the large barrel vault which covered the central nave was made of paneled wood supported by a framework in the style of Philibert Delorme, whose system Jefferson greatly admired in the sky-lighted ceiling of the Halle aux Bleds, shown here at number 440. P. de M.

CHŒUR

Echelle de ... Toise

DEUXIEME COUPE DE L'EGLISE SUR LA LARGEUR

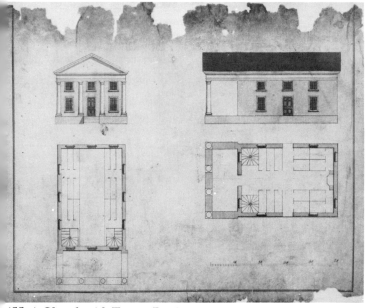

455 A Church with Tuscan Portico

CORNELIA JEFFERSON
RANDOLPH (?) 1799–1871
Ink and watercolor on wove paper
c. 1820
35.5 x 28 (14 x 11)
*Lent by the University of Virginia,
Alderman Library, Charlottesville*

Jefferson carefully oversaw the progress
in drawing skills made by his granddaughter, Cornelia Jefferson Randolph,
who spent much of her childhood
at Monticello. This seems to have
been an exercise done by her, under
her grandfather's eye.

Jefferson attended church in Charlottesville, where each week a different
group held services in the courthouse. He may at this time already
have been considering the need for a
church building, and four years later
designed Christ Church, shown here
at number 452. F.N.

456 Thomas Jefferson

BENJAMIN HENRY LATROBE (?)
1764–1820
Pencil c. 1799
38.7 x 31.1 (15¼ x 12¼)
*Lent by the Maryland Historical
Society, Baltimore, Papers of
Benjamin H. Latrobe*

No documentary evidence has been
uncovered to establish Latrobe's
authorship of this drawing or the fact
that Jefferson sat for such a sketch.
The discovery of the portrait in the
Latrobe papers, however, and its similarity, in the eyes of such scholars as
Fiske Kimball and Talbot Hamlin,
to other signed drawings by Latrobe
led to its attribution to the architect.
That the portrait was taken from
life is suggested not only by the many
opportunities which the artist was
given to observe Jefferson, but most
especially by the fact that no likeness
survives from which it indisputably
derives.

In the absence of documents,
scholars have dated the portrait solely
on the basis of their impression of
the age it depicts, within the limita-
tion of Latrobe's association with
Jefferson, and have offered various
dates from 1799 to 1802.

The portrait is clearly problematic;
but until someone comes forth with a
Jefferson from which this image is
unquestionably derived or until
evidence emerges to offer a more
plausible attribution than Latrobe, it
seems reasonable to sustain the suggestions about the drawing offered in
the past. Happily it is an arresting
and fresh likeness that awaits further
study. A.B.

457 Benjamin Henry Latrobe

CHARLES WILLSON PEALE
1741–1827
Oil on canvas c. 1804
57.1 x 49.5 (22½ x 19½)

Lent by The White House

This canvas is typical of those painted
for the gallery of Charles Willson
Peale's museum of natural history,
where *homo sapiens* was represented
by portraits of the heroes of liberty
and knowledge. For the first twenty
years of its history, the artist firmly
believed that his museum must inevitably become "the foundation" of a
national institute of science and art,
and Latrobe was included in its gallery not only as America's most
eminent architect and engineer, but
as one who shared and promoted
Peale's objective. Long a personal
friend of Peale and a fellow member
of the American Philosophical Society,
Latrobe in 1801 designed a huge
museum building, a drawing which
was exhibited for many years as the
ultimate ideal.

Latrobe's residence in Washington
as superintendent of public buildings kept him close to Jefferson and
helped to keep alive Peale's hope that
a great museum might be built there.
A new proponent appeared in 1804:
the young Prussian nobleman Alex-

ander von Humboldt, fresh from his
South American explorations, who
produced maps and statistics for Jefferson on the new Louisiana territory.
Peale would always remember their
state dinner at the president's house,
when "not a single toast was given or
called for, or politics touched on, but
the subjects of Natural History, and
improvements of the conveniences of
life, manners of different nations
described, or other agreeable conversation animated the whole company."
Humboldt made his plea for a national
museum but could not overcome
the president's reluctance to propose
it without a supporting constitutional
amendment. Humboldt's portrait,
beside Latrobe's in the museum, attested to Peale's gratitude. C.S.

458 James Hoban

Wax

*Lent by Mrs. John M. Carter,
Wayne, Pennsylvania*

James Hoban (1762?–1831) studied
architecture in Ireland at the
Dublin Society, whose later headquarters, Leinster House, may have
been at the back of Hoban's mind
when he designed the president's
house in Washington. He emigrated to
the United States, settling first in
Philadelphia and then moving to
South Carolina, where he built the
state capitol at Columbia. Hoban's
drawing won the competition for the
president's house in July 1792, and
the architect supervised the construction of the house until Jefferson became president in 1801 and at the
same time worked on the capitol. After
the burning of the president's house in
1814, Hoban was engaged on its rebuilding, and he also designed and
built the state and war offices. By the
time of his death, Hoban had acquired
a substantial fortune through his real
estate holdings in Washington. R.W.

459 William Thornton

CHARLES-BALTHAZAR-JULIEN
FÉVRET DE SAINT-MÉMIN
1770–1852
Charcoal and white chalk on pink
paper c. 1799 or 1804
66 x 50.8 (26 x 20)

*Lent by The American Institute of
Architects, on permanent loan from the
American Colonization Society*

Born in a Quaker settlement in the
British Virgin Islands, William
Thornton was sent to England for his
education and toured the continent
after receiving his medical degree. He
became a United States citizen in
1788, because of his admiration for
the democratic system, and lived in
Philadelphia until his involvement in
the design of public buildings for the
new capitol took him to Washington.

A contemporary view of Thornton,
quoted by William Dunlap in 1834,
describes him as "a scholar and a
gentleman—full of talent and eccen-
tricity—a Quaker by profession, a
painter, poet, and a horse racer. . . .
human and generous . . . his company
was a complete antidote to dullness."
Thornton apparently never practiced
medicine, though his interests extended to the sciences as well as the
arts; he supported Fitch's experiments
with the steamboat, produced a
widely read essay on the teaching of
deaf-mutes, and was an active member
of several learned societies.

In the same year that he became a
citizen, Thornton won his first architectural competition: that for a design
for a public library in Philadelphia.
He later wrote that he "got some
books and worked a few days, then
gave a plan in the ancient Ionic order
which carried the day." In 1793,
Thornton's design for the United
States capitol building was chosen over
that of the more experienced architect, Stephen Hallet, who was, nevertheless, appointed to draw working
plans and oversee the construction of
Thornton's design. It soon became
clear that the plan would need extensive revisions in order to be made
practicable, and Hallet made these
with Jefferson acting as advisor and
intermediary (see Hallet's changes,
exhibited at no. 435). Thornton, appointed one of the commissioners of
the city of Washington in 1794,
remained closely involved with the fate
of his plan.

In 1802, he was named head of
the Patent Office and single-handedly
saved it from British attack in 1814
by insisting that it contained private
property, which the British had
promised not to destroy.

Thornton maintained his interest
in architecture throughout his life.

His other architectural designs include the Octagon House in Washington for Colonel John Tayloe, Tudor Place in Georgetown for the Peter family, and Woodlawn for Washington's step-daughter, Eleanor Custis Lewis. Jefferson sought Thornton's advice for the plan of the University of Virginia, which Thornton praised as "admirably calculated for almost indefinite extension."

Saint-Mémin, whose portraits of members of the Osage tribe and of Meriwether Lewis are exhibited at numbers 124 and 129, could have drawn this portrait of Thornton on one of several visits to Washington.

G.V.

460 Elevation of the first executive office for the Treasury Department, Washington

GEORGE HADFIELD 1763–1826
Ink and wash 1796–1797
31.7 x 62.2 (12½ x 24½)

Lent by the Massachusetts Historical Society, Boston

When the seat of government was transferred from Philadelphia to Washington in 1800, the Treasury Department moved into new executive quarters which stood at the south-west corner of Pennsylvania Avenue and Fifteenth Street. It was destroyed by the British in 1814. Hadfield sub-mitted the design for the Treasury to the commissioner of the city of Washington in 1798, while serving as superintendent of the capitol.

Hadfield had come to Washington from London in 1795 on the recom-mendation of John Trumbull, whom he had met when they both were studying at the Royal Academy. Six years earlier, Hadfield had carried a letter of introduction from his sister, Maria Cosway, to Jefferson in Paris but the minister was unable to meet him at the appointed time because of illness.

As a professionally trained architect of obvious talent and promise, he was encouraged, upon his arrival in Washington, in his work by his sister's friend, who was actively engaged in planning the new city and its public buildings. Hadfield's contemporary, Benjamin H. Latrobe, also recognized the ability of the young architect: "All that he proposed . . . proved him a man of correct tastes, of perfect theoretic knowledge and of bold integrity."

Hadfield's study of Stuart and Revett's *Antiquities of Athens*, pub-lished in 1787, is evident in the design of the portico, which is adapted from the north porch of the Erech-theum and illustrated in that impor-tant book. Jefferson himself had purchased the first volume of *Anti-quities* when he was in Paris.

On the front of the drawing are written the general dimensions of the building, *148. by 57-6;* on the back is the following inscription:

Elevation of the Executive Office referred to in the agreement of 23ᵈ. June 1798 with Leonard Harbaugh. Test Elisha D. Williams
W. Brent
Leonard Harbaugh
Gust S. Scott
William Thornton
Alex. White

The drawing is from the Coolidge Collection of Jefferson's architectural drawings in the Massachusetts His-torical Society and was acquired from Jefferson descendants by Thomas Jefferson Coolidge, also a kinsman. When or how it came into the pos-session of Jefferson is not known.

W.H.A.

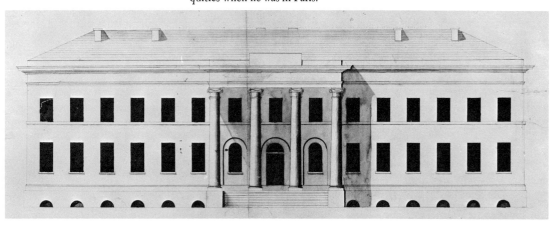

DOMESTIC ARCHITECTURE

MONTICELLO

In 1757 Peter Jefferson died, leaving his land on the Rivanna and Fluvanna rivers to be divided between his sons Thomas and Randolph. When Thomas Jefferson reached his majority, he chose the acres on the Rivanna, which included the future site of Monticello. Only a few years later, in1767, Jefferson had already begun his first tentative drawings for a mountaintop house. By 1771 he had begun construction, and on a snowy night in January 1772 he brought his bride to live in the southeast pavilion, the only completed segment of his grand plan.

Over the next ten years, the main house was slowly completed, though no dependencies beyond the initial pavilion had taken form, when the death of his wife, followed by Jefferson's five years in Paris, brought a halt to construction.

In 1789 Jefferson returned from abroad, his architectural tastes profoundly influenced by the new neoclassical architecture of Paris and the ruins of classical antiquity that he had inspected in the south of France. His plans for the renovation of Monticello, however, did not begin to bear fruit until 1796, when work began that would extend over the next twelve years. In his desire to approximate the one-story domed effect which he so admired in the Hôtel de Salm, Jefferson doubled the width of his house, lowered the second story which had been projected in his early designs, and placed an octagonal dome over the salon. Dependencies were also constructed during this period.

About 1804, Jefferson proposed extensive changes for the grounds of Monticello, in accordance with his knowledge of English landscape design. His retirement from public life in 1809 gave him increased opportunities for the "putting up and pulling down" that he loved, and small changes and improvements continued until his death in 1826. s.h.b.

461 Model of Monticello

Made by THEODORE CONRAD, Jersey City, New Jersey, from drawings prepared by the School of Architecture, University of Virginia, under the supervision of PROFESSOR FREDERICK DOVETON NICHOLS. See numbers 462–465.

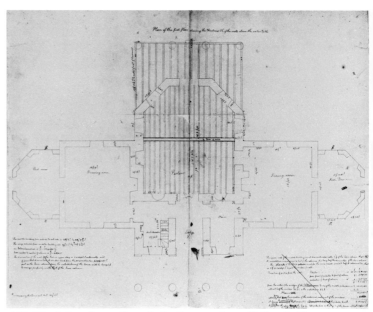

462 Final first-floor plan of the first version of Monticello

THOMAS JEFFERSON 1743–1826
Ink on laid paper after April 1771
60.5 x 49.5 (23¾ x 19½)

Lent by the Massachusetts Historical Society, Boston

Jefferson made substantial changes in this plan at a later date, adding octagonal projections to the parlor and wings. The line of the earlier walls of the parlor and the portico columns can still be seen where they were not erased completely. The drawing in its original state was a refinement of an earlier study, not shown here, in which door and window openings were wider than they are in the final version, and engaged columns took the place of the pilasters. F.N.

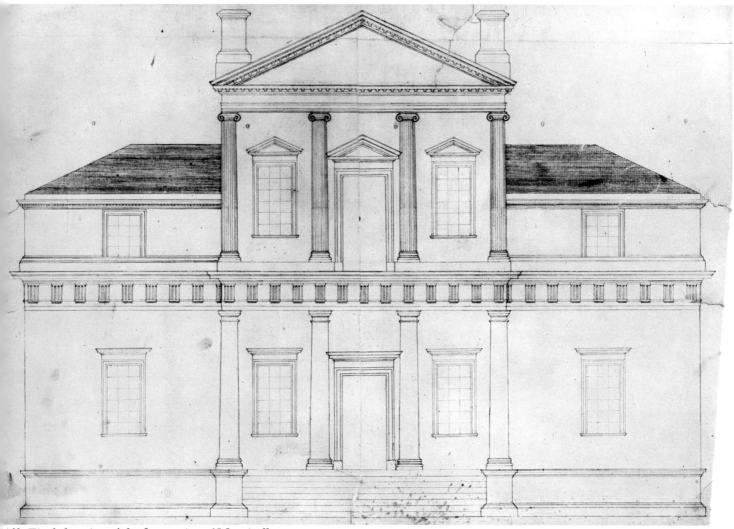

463 Final elevation of the first version of Monticello

THOMAS JEFFERSON 1743–1826
Ink on laid paper after April 1771
51 x 34.2 (20 x 13½)

*Lent by the Massachusetts Historical
Society, Boston*

Except for the absence of the one-
story octagonal bows terminating the
wings which were added later to the
plan, this drawing represents the final
design for the elevation of the first
version of Monticello. The superimposed porticos proportioned after
Palladio's Doric and Ionic orders, the
entablature of the first-story order
carried around the flanks of the house
and the lines of the pedimented roof
carried the depth of the central block
are classical features which, in combination, were unique in the domestic
architecture of the American colonies.

F.N.

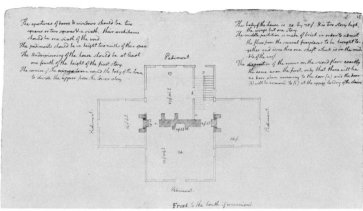

464 Early plan for Monticello

THOMAS JEFFERSON 1743–1826
Ink on laid paper 1768–1770
18.5 x 23 (7¼ x 9)

*Collection of the Massachusetts
Historical Society, Boston*

NOT IN EXHIBITION

This drawing, presumed to be a study
for Monticello, relates to the similar
study exhibited here at number 462.

465 Early plan for Monticello

THOMAS JEFFERSON 1743–1826
Ink on laid paper 1768–1770
31 x 19 (12¼ x 7½)

*Lent by the Massachusetts Historical
Society, Boston*

Jefferson began his plans for a mountaintop house as early as 1768, and
this is one of his earliest known drawings presumed to be for Monticello.
The cruciform plan with a two-story
central block, flanked by one-story
wings, is typical of a late Georgian
Virginia farmhouse and is admirably suited to the climate, as most of
the rooms have windows on three
sides. The construction was to be
wood, except for an inner masonry

wall, which was planned to conduct
all the fireplace flues to a single
chimney rising from the middle of th
roof. The classical features noted by
Jefferson in the margin are the pedimented roofs and cornice carried
around the body of the house. His
note that "the pediments should be
height two ninths of their span"
and the apertures of doors and windows, "two squares or two squares &
a sixth," indicates that he had access
to Palladio's *Four Books of Architecture,* which cites these proportion
The plan relates in many ways to
plate 37 in Robert Morris' *Select
Architecture,* which had been published in London in 1755 and leads
one to believe that Jefferson may hav
acquired his copy by this time. F.N.

The cruciform plan and the disposition
of rooms in number 465 have been
retained. However, the building material has been changed from wood
to brick, and an arcade with a portico
above has been added to the front
of the central block. This feature reappeared more than fifty years later
in the design for Pavilion VII at the
University of Virginia. F.N.

466 West elevation of the final version of Monticello

Attributed to ROBERT MILLS
1781–1855
Ink and wash 1803?
36.8 x 21 (14½ x 8¼)

*Lent by the Massachusetts Historical
Society, Boston*

After learning the fundamentals of
draftsmanship and building with
James Hoban in Washington, Robert
Mills studied architecture with Jef-

ferson at Monticello, where he had
access to Jefferson's superb collection
of architectural books. Later Mills
went on to a distinguished architectural career of his own and is most
famous for his design for the United
States treasury building and the Washington Monument.

This rendering of the west front of
Monticello was made while Mills
was in residence there in or before
1803. Though the house was not com-

plete at the time, the exterior must
have been essentially finished by then,
because the only differences between
Mills' rendering and the finished
building are differences in detail.

Mills did not sign this rendering, but
the technique is the same as two others
for Monticello which he did sign.

In letters to William B. Giles on
March 19, 1796, and to C.F.C. de
Volney on January 8, 1797, Jefferson
described the ongoing construction

on the house: "I have begun the
demolition of my house, and hope to
get through its re-edification in the
course of the summer." "I had hoped
. . . to have finished the walls of my
house in the autumn, and to have
covered it early in winter. But we did
not finish them at all. I have to resume the work, therefore, in the
spring, and to take off the roof of the
old part during the summer, to cover
the whole." F.N.

467 Chiswick Villa from the southeast

WILLIAM KENT 1685–1748
Pen and ink with brown wash over
pencil c. 1730
29.2 x 37.1 (11½ x 14⅝)
Devonshire Collection, Chatsworth.
Lent by the Trustees of the Chatsworth Settlement

Chiswick Villa was begun in 1725 by
Lord Burlington as part of his estate
outside London. He added to the
existing Jacobean house a villa for
entertaining his friends and housing
his collection of books and art. The
idea of a *villa suburbana*, situated on
the outskirts of a town, rather than in
the country, goes back to Roman
times and was revived in Italy during
the Renaissance. Burlington's models
were buildings by the sixteenth-
century Italian architects Palladio and
Scamozzi, specifically the Villa
Rotonda near Vicenza and the Rocca
Pisana at Lonigo. He had also traveled
in Italy and acquired a collection of
drawings by Palladio and his pupils.
Thus Lord Burlington, while by no
means the founder of the eighteenth-
century Palladians in England, for
Colen Campbell and Giacomo Leoni
had preceded him, was well equipped
to be the patron and leader of the
movement both as a knowledgeable
architect and an important political
figure.

Chiswick follows its prototypes in a
less doctrinaire way than Campbell's
Mereworth, built in 1723, and perhaps for that reason it is a more successful adaptation to the English
climate, where warmth and light were
more important than coolness and
shade. Similarly, Jefferson, although
also an admirer of Palladio, whom
he knew only through engravings, felt
free to adapt his models to the less
sophisticated world of Virginia, where

it was more difficult to find experienced workmen to carry out his designs, and he used materials, especially
wood, in keeping with the indigenous
architecture. The parallels between
Monticello and Chiswick must not be
pressed too far, because there are
other influences, particularly French,
also discernible in the creation of
Monticello. However, the resemblance
of the west or entrance front of
Monticello to that of Chiswick cannot
be accidental. Jefferson visited the
villa when he stayed in London, and
while the Monticello portico is much
simpler than Burlington's, without the
flight of steps and with four Tuscan
instead of six Corinthian columns,
the general effect, with the same low
dome on its octagonal base, pierced
by circular or semicircular windows,
is so striking that the influence of
Chiswick is undeniable. Jefferson was
to later project a similar scheme of a
domed central hall in the plan for
Barboursville (see no. 481). R.W.

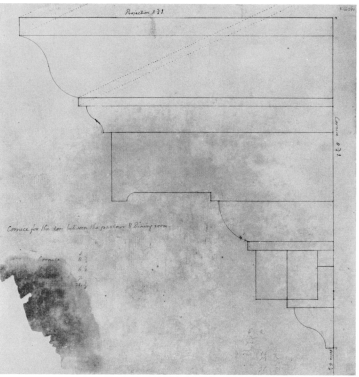

468 Drawing of a cornice for a door at Monticello

THOMAS JEFFERSON 1743–1826
Ink (and pencil in another hand)
on laid paper c. 1803
25.4 x 24.4 (10 x 9⅝)
*Lent by the Massachusetts Historical
Society, Boston*

Jefferson made this simplified and
slightly modified Corinthian cornice
"for the door between the parlour
and dining room" at Monticello.

In his *Notes of a Tour into the
Southern Parts of France and Northern
Italy* of 1787, Jefferson gives us a
good illustration of the close study
which he had given to the classical
orders:

The Sepulchral pyramid, a little way
out of the town, has an order for
its basement, the pedestal of which
from point to point of its cap, is
twenty-four feet one inch. At each
angle is a column, engaged one
fourth in the wall. The circumference of the three fourths disengaged is four feet four inches. Consequently, the diameter is twenty-
three inches. The base of the column
indicates it to be Ionic, but the
capitals are not formed. The Cornice,
too, is a bastard Ionic, without
modillions or dentils. Between the
columns on each side is an arch of
eight feet four inches opening, with
a pilaster on each side of it. On
the top of the basement is a zocle, in
the plane of the frieze below. On
that is the pyramid, its base in the

plane of the collanno of the pilaster
below. The pyramid is a little truncated on its top.

F.N.

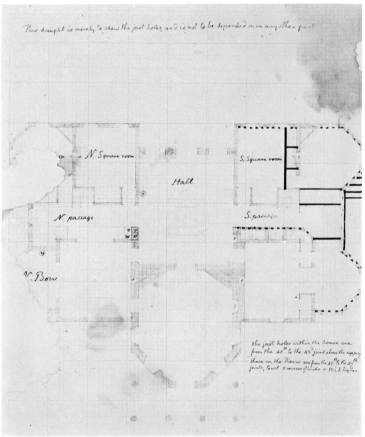

This draught is merely to shew the joist holes, and is not to be depended on in any other point.

N. Square room

S. Square room

Hall

N. passage

S. passage

N. Bow

the joist holes within the house are from the 40ᵗʰ to the 42ᵈ joint above the copping those on the Bow are from the 45ᵗʰ to the 47ᵗʰ joints, coart 2 courses of bricks or 15¼ J. higher

469 First floor plan for Monticello

THOMAS JEFFERSON 1743–1826
Pencil and ink on laid paper 1796?
22.8 x 29.2 (9 x 11½)

Lent by the Massachusetts Historical Society, Boston

Jefferson brought with him on his return from France many ideas for improvements to Monticello, based on the architectural ideas he had absorbed in France. "All new and good houses are of a single story," he wrote, "That is of 16. or 18 f. generally, and the whole of it given to rooms of entertainment; but in the parts where there are bedrooms they have two tiers of them of from 8. to 10 f. high each, with a small private staircase."

This plan differs only slightly from the final Monticello, as it stands today. It is the most complete plan that we have of Monticello in Jefferson's hand. There are fewer windows and their placement is different, and some of the smaller rooms were changed. But the most prominent difference is the plan of the parlor, which shows that at one time Jefferson considered making the room a full octagon. The dotted lines in the hall show the skylight, intended for this room but never built, as he decided to place the dome room over it. His notes refer to joist holes, which sug-gest that the drawing was made well after the remodeling had begun. F.N.

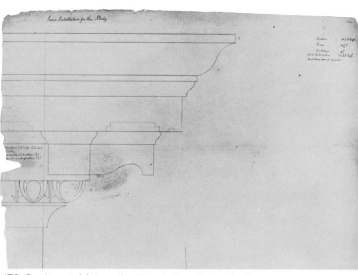

Ionic Entablature for the Study.

470 Ionic entablature for the study at Monticello

THOMAS JEFFERSON 1743–1826
Ink on laid paper 1775 or after
54.6 x 38.1 (21½ x 15)

Lent by the Massachusetts Historical Society, Boston

Jefferson showed only the cornice and part of the frieze in his drawing for an Ionic entablature, which he took directly from Palladio's *First Book*. The drawing includes the egg and dart but typically omits the water leaf molding. Jefferson probably preferred the unornamented molding, and it was also simpler to build. He also substituted a flat frieze for Palladio's cushion frieze, which had become old-fashioned by that time.

The entablature was intended for the large library with a mezzanine, the room above the parlor at the early Monticello. When Jefferson later altered the house, the upper space was lowered, the dome installed, and the entablature removed.

Specifications for this entablature are given on page 47 of Jefferson's notebook for building at Monticello. It indicates Jefferson's method of design:

Study
Ionic Palladio Book I, pl. 18–22
The frieze to be ornamented with human figures as in Palladio, Book IV, pl. 13, 14, and 15

Following this are noted the dimensions for the entire room, carried out to five decimals. F.N.

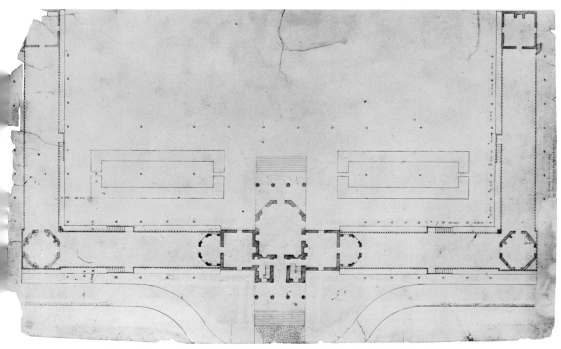

471 Final drawing of first floor with dependencies

THOMAS JEFFERSON 1743–1826
Ink on laid paper 1772–1784
51.4 x 34.2 (20¼ x 13½)

*Lent by the Massachusetts Historical
Society, Boston*

The dependencies for Monticello as
finally proposed in 1784 consist of two
long L-shaped blocks that form an
open U toward the west. They have a
plan similar to plate 41 in *Palladio,
Book II*, by which they may have been
inspired.

At the ends of the terraces are the
outchambers, while at the turns are
"corner temples." The corner temples
went through a number of designs
varying from square Chinese temples,
derived from William Chambers'
Chinese Designs, to Tuscan temples,
to Monopteros derived from Perrault's
Vitruvius, and finally to octagonal
structures with domes as they appear
on this drawing. The corner temples,
however, were never built.

This drawing was altered many
times from 1772, when it was begun,
until Jefferson's departure for Europe
in 1784, in order to keep it current
with Jefferson's changing ideas. For
some forty years, Jefferson worked on
his beloved home, and he wrote, "I
am as happy nowhere else, and in no
other society, and all my wishes end,
where I hope my days will end, at
Monticello." F.N.

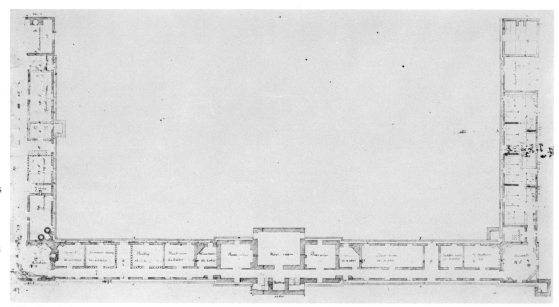

472 Final drawing of the basement and dependencies of Monticello

THOMAS JEFFERSON 1743–1826
Ink, before August 1772
52.7 x 34 (20¾ x 13⅜)

*Lent by the Massachusetts Historical
Society, Boston*

A significant aspect of Jefferson's
design for Monticello was the relationship of the main dwelling to the
many dependencies required for its
management. After numerous studies,
Jefferson resolved on a scheme unique
in American building; it combined
the dependencies in long L-shaped
wings connected to the flanks of the
main house. Jefferson may have taken
the idea from Palladio, whose own
designs for villas show similar solutions. Jefferson took Palladio's idea one
step further, however, by exploiting
the potential of his sloping site. By
suppressing the wings in the hillside
he was able to preserve an almost
uninterrupted view of the mountaintop
from the garden front of the main
house as well as provide level access to
both the working areas at the cellar
level and the terraces above. In one
sense, Jefferson turned the Palladian
villa plan inside out by designing
the access to the dependencies from
the outside of the L-shaped wings
rather than from a courtyard formed
in front of the house. The drawing
shows numerous changes, and it seems
that Jefferson worked on it at least
through the decade of the 1770s. The
wings, however, were not constructed
until after 1800 and then only on a
somewhat diminished scale without
the offices leading from the house to
the angles. F.N.

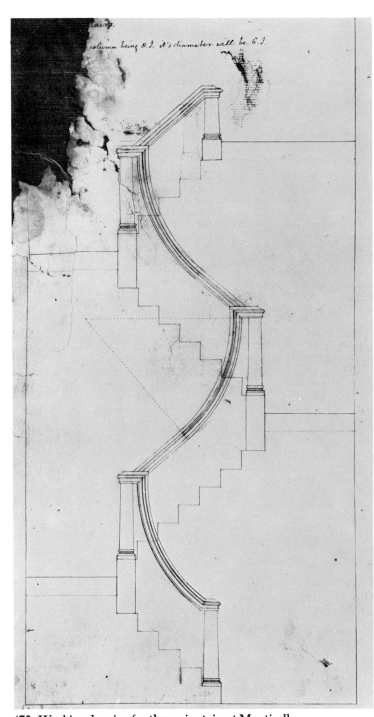

473 Working drawing for the main stairs at Monticello

THOMAS JEFFERSON 1743–1826
Ink on laid paper c. 1771–1776
18.4 x 27.6 (7¼ x 10⅞)

*Lent by the Massachusetts Historical
Society, Boston*

During the building of the first version
of Monticello from 1769 to 1783,
Jefferson seems to have personally
attended to every detail and supervised
much of its construction. His activities as a lawyer and delegate and later
his involvement in the cause of revolution, however, often took him away
from Monticello. So it is not surprising that it was 1775 before the
upper story of the house was begun.
It was about that time that Jefferson
wrote out the specification for the
construction of the stairs, and it was
probably then that this drawing was
prepared. F.N.

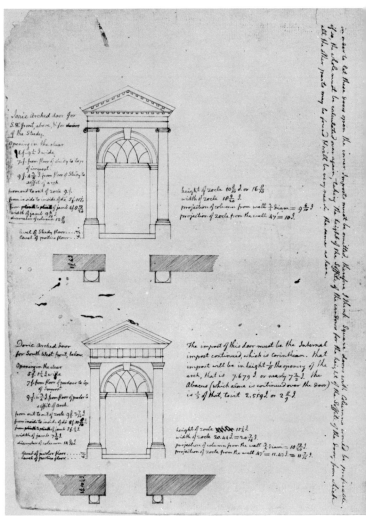

474 Study for the exterior doors for the west front of Monticello

THOMAS JEFFERSON 1743–1826
Ink on laid paper c. 1770
48.2 x 29.8 (19 x 11¾)

*Lent by the Massachusetts Historical
Society, Boston*

Jefferson's earliest and perhaps most
trusted source of architectural details
for Monticello seems to have been
Gibbs' two books. A page from Jefferson's notebook for building indicates that the exterior parlor arched
door was to be modeled after plate 39,
figure 2 from Gibbs' *Rules for Drawing the Several Parts of Architecture*.
A note on the drawing which dates
after the memorandum, establishes
that the design was to be changed
to a square door because of the difficulties of clearing the inner impost when
the door was opened. This change
was incorporated in the final drawing
of the elevation. F.N.

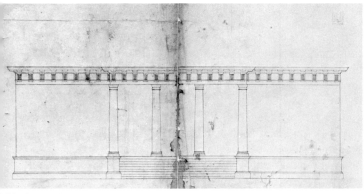

475 Study for the elevation of Monticello

THOMAS JEFFERSON 1743–1826
Ink on laid paper probably 1768–1770
67.3 x 47.6 (26½ x 18¾)

*Lent by the Massachusetts Historical
Society, Boston*

This elevation of the first story was
probably drawn to accompany the plan
for Monticello shown at number 476.
From the position of the drawing
on the paper it can be determined that
it was an incomplete study and that
an upper story was intended. The
important classical features are the
portico and the entablature, which is
carried around the body of the house.
The architectural order is the Doric
from James Gibbs' *Rules for Drawing
the Several Parts of Architecture*,
shown here at number 51, which was
probably in Jefferson's library by this
time. Jefferson solicited estimates in
England and Scotland in 1769 for
executing the molded elements of the
architectural order in stone but, after
discovering that the expense was excessive, determined to execute them in
wood and molded brick. F.N.

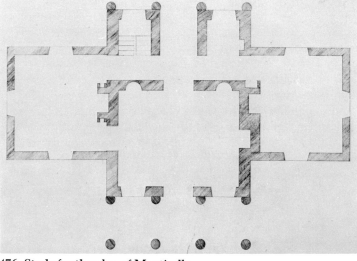

476 Study for the plan of Monticello

THOMAS JEFFERSON 1743–1826
Ink on laid paper 1768–1770
48.2 x 33.6 (19 x 13¼)

*Lent by the Massachusetts Historical
Society, Boston*

Combining elements from earlier
studies, this plan seems to correspond,
for the most part, with specifications
written out by Jefferson in his account book in 1769. It can be determined from the thickness of the walls
that the central block was to be two
full stories and each of the wings one
full story with attic above. Porticos
front both ends of the central block.
The entrance lodge is flanked by stair
alcoves, and it can be seen that even at
this early date Jefferson favored the
narrow enclosed stair. A transverse hall
connects the two wings, and the
parlor with its niches at one end opens
directly from the lodge. F.N.

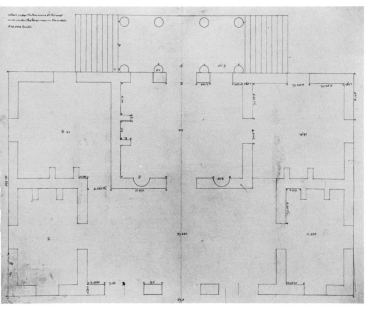

477 Study of the plan for Monticello

THOMAS JEFFERSON 1743–1826
Ink on laid paper 1768–1770
36.8 x 29.8 (14½ x 11¾)

*Lent by the Massachusetts Historical
Society, Boston*

Jefferson may have based this plan,
presumably for Monticello, indirectly
on plates from either a Leoni edition
of Palladio's *Four Books of Architecture* or from James Gibbs' *Book of
Architecture*. The drawing would
appear to be an intermediate study,
since the exact length of the house and
the salon, with niches opening onto
a portico with engaged columns, are
retained in a later plan, exhibited here
at number 476. F.N.

POPLAR FOREST

Poplar Forest, the country retreat to which Jefferson increasingly resorted in his later years, stood on 4,300 acres bequeathed to him by his wife. The property was located in Bedford County a few miles south of Lynchburg, in Jefferson's day about eighty miles from Monticello.

Jefferson's first recorded trip to Poplar Forest was in September 1773, and in 1781 he and his family sought refuge there from the British. On that visit, in fact, he began putting together material for *Notes on the State of Virginia*, completed the following year and published during his stay in France. Though Poplar Forest was a working plantation at that time, the house seems to have been architecturally undistinguished, if not primitive. Jefferson's interest in establishing a more comfortable seat there may date from his enforced stay due to the British, since in the next year he first sent fruit trees and shrubs to be planted and made a visit of inspection.

The house he eventually built was an octagonal design, novel in America, and originally planned for the Pantops farm of his daughter Maria and her husband John Eppes. Maria's death in 1804 caused that project to be abandoned, and by the summer of 1806 Jefferson, aged sixty-three, had transferred his scheme for an octagonal house to his land at Poplar Forest.

The building was habitable, though unfinished, by 1809, and interior work continued for years, with moldings and friezes still being installed in 1823, when Jefferson was eighty.

From 1809 on, Jefferson's habit was to visit the house three or four times a year, often accompanied by children and grandchildren, for visits of two or three weeks. Its function was not unlike that of Palladio's farm villas of the sixteenth century, built to be used in season by the landowner to supervise farming and harvesting details. In 1823, Jefferson's grandson Francis Eppes, son of Maria, and his bride settled there as the house's first permanent residents, and ownership passed to them at Jefferson's death. Poplar Forest left the Jefferson family in 1828, however, when Eppes sold it to William Cobbs, in whose family it remained for more than a century. s.h.b.

478 Model of Poplar Forest

Made by THEODORE CONRAD, Jersey City, New Jersey, from drawings prepared by the School of Architecture, University of Virginia, under the supervision of PROFESSOR FREDERICK DOVETON NICHOLS See nos. 479, 480.

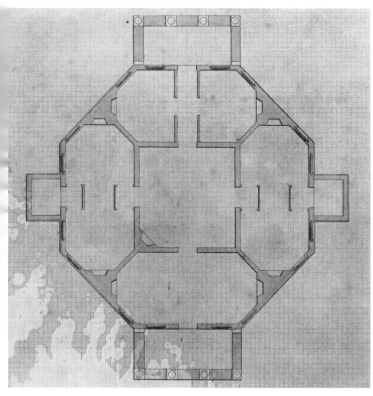

479 Poplar Forest, first floor plan

CORNELIA JEFFERSON
RANDOLPH (?) 1799–1871
Ink and wash c. 1820
29.2 x 22.9 (11½ x 9)

*Lent by the University of Virginia,
Alderman Library, Charlottesville*

Jefferson fully exploited his love of the octagon in his house at Poplar Forest. The outline of the house and three of the rooms were octagonal, as well as two small semioctagonal chambers. The large room in the center, lit by skylights, was the dining room with the drawing room beyond, opening onto a tetrastyle portico, matching the one on the entrance front overlooking the garden. Two suites of rooms with center bed alcoves flanked the dining room. The small rectangular projections on the left and right contained staircases to the raised basement. It was a simple but ingenious plan, and, unlike Monticello, the house was centralized and open, without lateral and private suites.

Jefferson used the octagonal form in a significant number of projects and studies, and perhaps it was inevitable that he would eventually use it as the dominant theme for a house. At one time he wrote, "We shall have the eye of a brick-kiln to poke you into, or an octagon to air you in." He may have been inspired by octagonal houseplans seen in William Kent's *Designs of Inigo Jones*, published in 1727. Except for the general plan, however, Jefferson's houses have no relationship to Kent's plates, and the interior of Poplar Forest is his own invention. F.N.

480 Poplar Forest, garden elevation

CORNELIA JEFFERSON
RANDOLPH (?) 1799–1871
Ink and watercolor c. 1820
29.2 x 22.9 (11½ x 9)

*Lent by the University of Virginia,
Alderman Library, Charlottesville*

Jefferson's granddaughter, Cornelia Jefferson Randolph, frequently visited Poplar Forest and probably did this rendering as a drawing exercise in about 1820, when the house was complete except for a few interior details. A description of the house, written by one of Jefferson's granddaughters in 1856, survives:

The house at Poplar Forest was very pretty and pleasant. It was of brick, one story in front, and, owing to the falling of the ground, two in the rear. It was an exact octagon, with a centre-hall twenty feet square, lighted from above. This was a beautiful room, and served as a dining-room. Round it were grouped a bright drawing-room, looking south, my grandfather's own chamber, three other bedrooms, and a pantry. A terrace extended from one side of the house; there was a portico in front connected by a vestibule with the center room, and in the rear a verandah, on which the drawing-room opened, with its windows to the floor....

F.N.

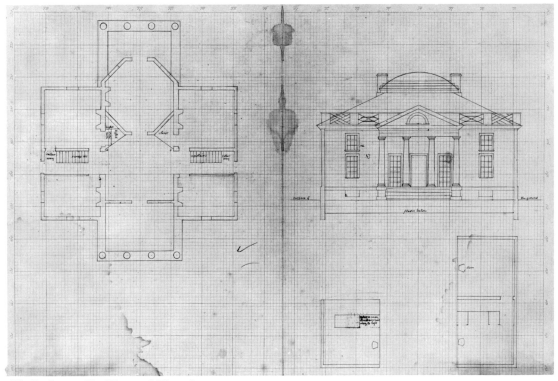

481 Barboursville, Plan and Elevation

THOMAS JEFFERSON 1743–1826
Ink on laid paper 1817
52.1 x 33.3 (20½ x 13⅛)
Specifications on verso

Lent by the Massachusetts Historical Society, Boston

Jefferson designed this house for his friend, Governor James Barbour, in 1817. In plan, it is a development from earlier rejected studies for the house at Poplar Forest, having two stories and a dome as at Monticello. Jefferson stated in his notes on the reverse of the drawing that the addition of the dome was entirely optional, and it was omitted in execution. Otherwise, the house seems to have conformed exactly with Jefferson's design, according to evidence in a painting completed before a fire left the house a ruin in 1888.

A letter from Barbour to Jefferson, dated March 29, 1817, indicates the method by which Jefferson's architectural ideas were disseminated. "The bearers of this, James Bradley and Edward Ancel, are the undertakers of my building—the former a carpenter—the latter a bricklayer. I have resolved on the plan you were good enough to present me and for which I return you my sincere thanks. You were kind enough to accompany the plan with a suggestion that it would be well for my workmen to see your building and receive such verbal explanations as might facilitate their labors. To that end I have directed

them to repair to Monticello. . . ." Jefferson was deeply involved with his work on the University of Virginia at this time. F.N.

NOTES ON THE RECONSTRUCTED
ROOMS OF BARBOURSVILLE
Two rooms from Barboursville, the entry and an adjoining octagonal room, have been reconstructed for the exhibition. Their design is based on Jefferson's drawings and specifications, on evidence from the surviving Barboursville ruin, and on precedent from other Jefferson designs. Since certain minor changes in Jefferson's plans were made during the original construction, the present reconstruction is a balance between what was specified and what was actually built.

Jefferson's plans for the fireplace, for example, specified a projecting "Rumford" fireplace, similar to that in the Monticello dining room; but Barbour built a more elegant, recessed fireplace with a projecting mantel, which is reproduced here. The recessed fireplace was also used extensively by Jefferson and was obviously copied from a Jefferson design by Barbour's workmen.

For moldings in the octagonal room, Jefferson specified "Ionic with Modillions," but gave no further details. Although the Ionic order usually has no frieze decoration, Jefferson had added a Corinthian frieze from the temple of Antoninus and Faustina to the Ionic moldings in the

entry of Monticello; accordingly this same order and frieze are here used in the reconstructed cornice, fireplace and window and door treatments for Barboursville. The window and door decoration, too, were not specified but are based here on precedent from Monticello.

Jefferson gave specific details and dimensions for the octagonal room's triple-hung windows and sash doors, and existing drawings by him have been adapted to the Barboursville dimensions for the reconstruction. Similarly, Jefferson's sketch for a parquet floor, shown here at number 537, has been adapted for use in the octagon room.

No specifications or evidence remain to give clues to the appearance of the entry room. The details indicated here are conjectural, using drawings made by Jefferson for similar architectural situations at Monticello and elsewhere. The order here is Doric, as used by Jefferson in his dining room. Some changes in the original structure of the room have been made for the reconstruction: one of the side doors in the entry has been eliminated for display purposes, and the room is a few feet shorter than the original. In addition the ceiling is lower than the original by two feet.
F.N.

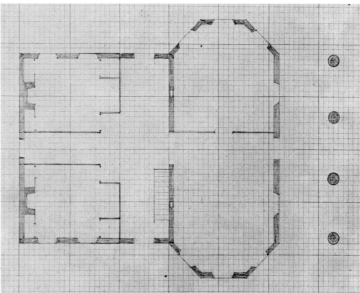

482 Elevation of Farmington, Albemarle County

THOMAS JEFFERSON 1743–1826
Ink on wove paper 1802 or earlier
18.4 x 26 (7¼ x 10¼)

*Lent by the Massachusetts Historical
Society, Boston*

Designed for Jefferson's friend, George
Divers, this building was well along
in construction by the summer of
1803. The design shows a less strict
adherence to a single story than appeared in the designs for Edgehill and
for rebuilding Shadwell, perhaps as a
concession to the conservatism of
Divers, or a wish to emulate Monticello. The large circular windows are
of Portland stone and were ordered
from London in 1792 for use in the
dome room at Monticello. The house
was not ready to receive them upon
arrival, and they were used at Farmington instead.

Jefferson viewed the house after a
long absence and found that the
column capitals were much too small
for the portico, but nothing was ever
done by Divers to correct the mistake.

F.N.

483 Plan of Farmington, Albemarle County

THOMAS JEFFERSON 1743–1826
Ink on laid paper 1802 or earlier
20.3 x 28 (8 x 11)

*Lent by the Massachusetts Historical
Society, Boston*

This plan shows the addition of an
octagonal wing to a preexisting, traditional two-room, sidehall plan of
typical townhouse design. The exploration of the possible combinations of
an octagon with a rectangle furnished
motifs for many of Jefferson's later
designs. The addition of alcove beds
show the influence of Jefferson's stay
in France.

As the plan shows, the octagonal
wing was originally planned to consist
of two rooms on the ground floor,
with the large salon being two stories
and an additional bedroom on the
second floor over the smaller room.
The plan was never completed, and the
wing now survives as one large room.

F.N.

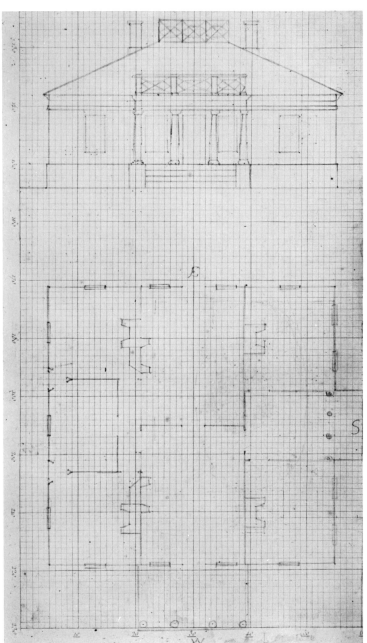

485 View of Bremo

EDWARD TROYE 1808–1874
Oil on canvas before 1836
48.2 x 63.5 (19 x 25)

*Lent by Mr. and Mrs. John Page Elliot,
Charlottesville*

The original low roof of Bremo, shown here, was made up of "rooflets," which Jefferson had designed as a series of small valleys to give the appearance of a flat roof. Even though Jefferson had warned against the use of parapet walls and gutters, General Cocke used them, and he later had to substitute a hipped roof, due to leakage. Cocke noted in his diary on September 19, 1836, "Commenced taking off Roof of the House to be replaced by a new one to get rid of the evils of flat roofing and spouts and gutters, or in other words to supersede the Jeffersonian by the common sense plan."

Edward Troye also painted the distinguished equestrian portrait of General Cocke which now hangs in the White House. F.N.

484 Edgehill

THOMAS JEFFERSON 1743–1826
Ink on laid paper before 1798
20.3 x 28 (8 x 11)

*Lent by the Massachusetts Historical
Society, Boston*

Edgehill, first proposed in 1790 and begun in 1798, was built for Jefferson's daughter Martha and her husband, Thomas Mann Randolph, who occupied it, though it was still unfinished, in 1800. Because the owners found the house too small, in 1828 it was moved to the rear of the property and a larger two-story brick house was constructed on the original site.

Edgehill shows Jefferson's favorite one-story design, undistorted by any conflicting requirements. An awkward room arrangement, however, caused him to return to the T-shaped plan he had developed at Monticello. F.N.

486 Plan of Bremo

Elevation of Bremo, Fluvanna County
CORNELIA JEFFERSON
RANDOLPH (?) 1799–1871
Ink and wash
Two drawings on the same sheet of
paper, 35.5 x 50.8 (14 x 20)
Lent by the University of Virginia,
Alderman Library, Charlottesville

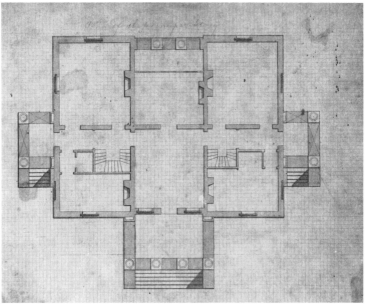

Bremo, built by General John Hartwell Cocke between 1817 and 1820,
was designed by John Neilson, a Jefferson disciple, and has many characteristic Jeffersonian features, including the T-shaped arrangement, which
was present in many of Jefferson's
house designs to effect air circulation.
The entrance hall has lateral corridors,
which contain stairs and which are
connected with outlying pavilions by
passageways partly below grade, similar
to the side passageways at Monticello. The four porticos, one on each
front, are a feature derived directly
from Palladio's Villa Rotonda. The
spaces and the detail are all by Jefferson, including the stair brackets, which
are taken directly from *The Young
Carpenter's Assistant*, a pattern book
by Owen Biddle, published in 1810,
which Jefferson owned. The tulip
motif on the console stair ends was also
used in the pavilions at the University of Virginia.

The plan afforded the advantages
of a large living or entrance hall, in this
case without a fireplace. Next to it
on the south is a winter "parlour" with
long windows to the floor, a projecting Rumford fireplace, and a shallow
portico, which permitted a maximum of sunlight in the winter. The
two large chambers in each corner
of the south side have carefully designed, built-in storage cupboards. The
library, an equally sunny room on

the ground floor, has tambour fronted
shelves to protect some of the books.
The dining room is also on the ground
floor, in the southeast corner. It has
a black and white marble floor and a
revolving door fitted with shelves on
which the kitchen help could place the
food, which was handed around by
the servants. Much of the interior was
painted and grained. In the west outbuilding, the school room remains
with its original benches.

Cocke, who before beginning his
house had designed and begun construction in fieldstone of a Palladian
barn, consulted several of his friends
on the plans for his house. One of
them, Colonel Isaac Coles, showed
Cocke's plan to Jefferson, with whom
Cocke was not yet acquainted. A
wonderful letter written by Coles to
General Cocke on February 23, 1816,

describes much of Jefferson's architectural philosophy:

With Mr. Jefferson I conversed at
length on the subject of architecture.
Palladio he said "was the Bible."
You should get it & stick close to it.
He had sent all his Books &c. &c. to
Washington, or he would have
drawn yr. House for you—it would
have been a pleasure to him—but
now he could not undertake to do it
before the fall, when he expected
other Books from Paris. He dis-
approved of parapet walls—no House
could be made perfectly tight with
them—there must be a gutter along
the Wall which in heavy falls of
rain &c. would sometimes overflow—
as was the case with the Presidents
House in Washington & every other
House similarly constructed that
he had ever seen—the roof should

cover the walls & the Balastrade
could be raised above it as at Monticello which tho not handsome was
safe, The flat roof he thought very
practicable—the sort he most approved of was the one I descrived to
you of sheet Iron with a rise of half
an inch in each foot—viz. of 12½
Inches to your House 50 ft wide.
Your cross gutters &c. &c. would
never do, & ought not to be thought
of. He lays it down as a rule never
to be departed from "That a gutter
over a hall can never be safe". Your
South Portico would be very handsome & should be supported on
arches as you proposed—the height
not to be less than 16 ft. The rule
was that the height of a room should
be equal to its width—20 ft therefore would not be too much but
16 ft would do—his was 18 ft which
gave chambers over all the smaller
rooms on the north of his House
which you might have in yours. The
Tuscan order was too plain—it would
do for your Barns &c. but was not
fit for a dwelling House—the Doric
would not cost much more & would
be vastly handsomer—his was doric.
You could get drawings of the columns, cornice &c. &c. from him.
Dinsmore who is now in Petersburg
he recommends to you as a good &
faithful workman or Oldham who is
(I think) in Richmond—either of
them would build you a House
without any false architecture, so
much the rage at present. The Italian
rule for windows is a third of the
whole space—viz.—7 feet of light to
every 21 feet of wall. He is a great
advocate for light and air—as you
predicted he was for giving you
Octagons. They were charming. They
gave you a semi-circle of air & light.
He thought the window you proposed would be very handsome for a
passage or Hall &c. but seemed not to
know that they were in use & fashionable for rooms— In a word the
old Gentleman entered as he always
does in to every thing with great
zeal into your building scheme and I
now regret more than ever that you
did not see him.

F.N.

THE UNIVERSITY OF VIRGINIA

The great achievement of Jefferson's architectural career was the University of Virginia. As early as 1804–1805 he had been considering buildings in the form "of an academical village rather than one large building." By 1810 his ideas had crystallized into a complex of buildings with "a small and separate lodge for each professorship, with only a hall below for his class, and two chambers above for himself; joining these lodges by barracks for a certain portion of the students, opening into a covered way to give a dry communication between all the schools. The whole of these arranged around an open square of grass or trees." The general scheme was probably inspired by Louis XIV's favorite château at Marly, which Jefferson had visited with Maria Cosway during his stay in Paris.

Jefferson had written to Dr. William Thornton, asking for his opinions on the design for the college, and Thornton suggested the use of columns instead of piers for the colonnades, and porticos over arcades. Jefferson also corresponded with Benjamin Latrobe, whose most important suggestion was that of using a focal building, preferably a rotunda. Jefferson wrote the word *Latrobe* on his drawings for Pavilions VIII and IX, indicating the architect's influence, which is supported stylistically by the designs.

Finding that his site would not allow the quadrangle he had originally planned, Jefferson made the lawn into a long rectangle, and to increase the apparent length, he enlarged the distance between each pavilion as they are located farther from the rotunda In the French manner he terminated his great lawn with small porticos *à point*, which frame the terminal pavilions. The pavilions themselves he wished to make "models of taste and good architecture, and of a variety of appearance, no two alike, so as to serve as specimens for the Architectural lecturer." Their orders were based on Errard and de Chambray's *Parallèle de L'Architecture* and on Palladio. For covering the dormitories Jefferson planned to use flat roofs, despite protests of some members of the Board of Visitors. He called them *rooflets* and built them of valleys of wood about eighteen inches deep covered with tin, like a series of gutters. In time the "rooflets" leaked, and had to be replaced with pitched roofs. The two parallel rows of ranges had three pavilions each to be used for student dining halls. The students' rooms between the dining halls, or hotels, as Jefferson called them, open on arcades whose proportions were taken almost directly from Palladio.

Recently, the Chinese trellis railings included in the original structure have been restored to the colonnades, and it has been discovered that the railings were designed to be increasingly higher toward the south, to increase the sense of perspective.

The cornerstone of the first pavilion, number VIII, West Lawn, was laid on October 6, 1817, but construction of the rotunda was not begun until 1823, for want of funds. The rotunda had cost $55,000 and was practically complete when Jefferson died in 1826 at the age of eighty-three. While the exterior of the rotunda was based upon that of the Pantheon in Rome, simplified and reduced to one-half scale, the interior was divided into two floors with a high basement. For the domed ceiling of the circular library he planned a planetarium and a sky blue dome with gilt stars and planets against it; there would be a seat for an operator, and the stars could be changed to conform to their varying positions. With the rotunda dominating the northern end, the lawn opened to a beautiful vista of the mountains, a similar view to that of the château at Marly.

As Jefferson said, the rotunda was the capstone of his university, and it is the masterpiece of his career. In this building he managed to express to perfection the visionary ideals of the French architects Ledoux and Boullée. Like them, he was concerned with architecture for large groups of people and for housing them in finite geometrical forms. Combining utility with this aesthetic philosophy, Jefferson created one of the great buildings of Western civilization. Due to the slope of the land, Jefferson was able to maintain the interior proportions of the Pantheon for the dome room, while providing six useful oval rooms for lectures, laboratories, and meetings. All this he combined in a perfect sphere. The dome room for the library occupies the upper section of the sphere, and it is most fitting that the Pantheon was used for his inspiration, for Jefferson believed in education as the cornerstone of freedom, and his gods were books. With its three great oval rooms on the main floor and its free-form hall, the rotunda had the finest suite of oval rooms in America. The idea for the design of ovals in a circle came from the Désert de Retz, which Jefferson had visited with Maria Cosway. He showed his enthusiasm for it in a letter written to her in 1786: "How beautiful was every object! . . . the Désert. How grand the idea excited by the remains of such a column. The spiral staircase, too, was beautiful." F.N.

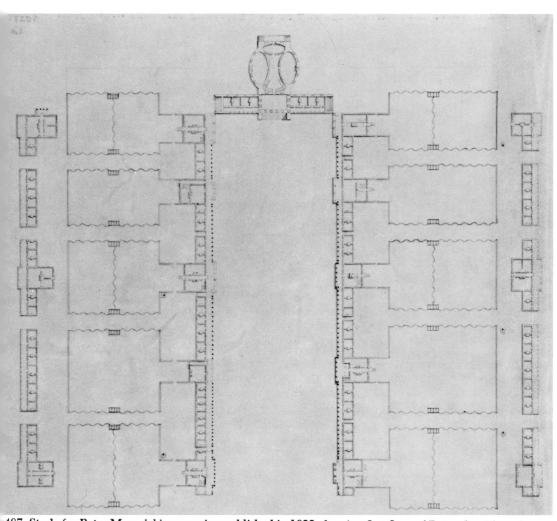

487 Study for Peter Maverick's engraving published in 1822 showing first floor of Rotunda with oval rooms and sixteen rooms in wings

JOHN NEILSON (?) d. 1827

Ink

43.2 x 49.5 (17 x 19½)

Lent by the Virginia State Library, Richmond

On November 30, 1821, the Board of Visitors resolved to commission an engraving of a "ground plat" of the university. William J. Coffee of New York, who had supplied architectural elements for Monticello and Poplar Forest as well as the university, delivered a drawing of the university to Peter Maverick, a New York engraver. Maverick's engraving, for which this study was made, was the first published plan of the University of Virginia. Neilson's study differs from the later published engravings in that the dormitories are unnumbered, a dormitory is missing from the south end of the West Range, and steps are shown on the east and west ends of the wings of the rotunda in Neilson's study. An explanation of the Maverick plan including the university rules and expenses was printed on a separate sheet, and the pair was sold primarily to prospective students.

Neilson's study clearly shows the ten pavilions and their flanking dormitories arranged in two parallel rows on terraces descending to the south. At the north end is the rotunda, with its wings extending to the east and west. The first floor plan of the rotunda with its original oval rooms is shown with the dome room shown as an inset, while only the first floors of the pavilions, where professors had their offices and classrooms, are engraved. Behind each pavilion is a walled garden, and alternating gardens are subdivided and shared with the "hotels" or dining halls on the ranges, the eastern and western rows of buildings. In the gardens are "necessary houses" or privies.

The gardens on the west side are shallower than those on the east side because the steep slope on the eastern side had to be terraced. The pavilions are spaced further and further apart to the south, and this is reflected in the width of the gardens. Jefferson left no plan for the planting of the elegant walled enclosures. The present period gardens were planted in the 1940s and 1950s by the Garden Club of Virginia.

This innovative design grew from Jefferson's dislike of the common plan for American colleges:

I would strongly recommend to their consideration, instead of one immense building, to have a small one for every professorship, arranged at proper distances around a square, to admit extension, connected by a piazza, so that they may go dry from one school to another. This village form is preferable to a single great building for many reasons, particularly on account of fire, health, economy, peace and quiet . . . more may be said hereafter on the opportunity these small buildings will afford, of exhibiting models in architecture of the purest forms of antiquity, furnishing to the student examples of the precepts he will be taught in that art.

. . . it should be in fact, an academical village, instead of a large and common den of noise, of filth and of fetid air. It would afford the quiet retirement so friendly to study, and lessen the dangers of fire, infection and tumult. Every professor would be the police officer of the students adjacent to his own class of preference, and might be at the head of their table, if, as I suppose, it can be reconciled with the necessary economy to dine them in smaller and separate parties, rather than in a large and common mess. These separate buildings, too, might be erected successively and occasionally, as the number of professors and students should be increased, as the funds become competent.

F.N.

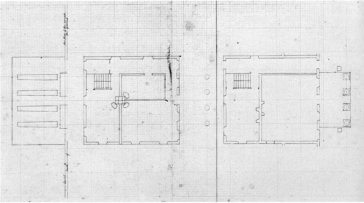

489 Early study for the plans and elevation of a pavilion for Central College, later Pavilion III, University of Virginia

THOMAS JEFFERSON 1743–1826
Ink on laid paper 1817
29.2 x 44.4 (11½ x 17½)

Lent by the Massachusetts Historical Society, Boston

This study shows the placement of four columns in front of the mass of the pavilion, before Jefferson added bases and capitals. As the pavilion was executed, the low pedestals shown on this drawing were omitted. This was the second pavilion to be constructed and the first with the colossal order, and Jefferson was obviously experimenting with several ideas. The plan of the first floor (bottom) shows the pavilion as it was constructed, with two front entrances, one for students and one for family, and an office in the rear for the professor. In front Jefferson suggested one possibility for terminating the covered ways on each side by ending them with piers rather than columns, a system he subsequently discarded. In the rear was planned another portico, but it was not executed. Upstairs, of course, are the professor's private quarters, the design of which Jefferson later changed. F.N.

488 Early plan of the University of Virginia

THOMAS JEFFERSON 1743–1826
Ink on laid paper May 9, 1817
21.6 x 26 (8½ x 10¼)

Lent by the University of Virginia, Alderman Library, Charlottesville

In the spring of 1817, when the beginning of construction for Central College was imminent, Jefferson wrote to William Thornton and Benjamin Latrobe for ideas for the pavilions. In the letters he included a sketch of a rectangular quadrangle with one of the long sides open, seven pavilions arranged more or less equidistantly, dormitories between the pavilions, and a covered way. The center was to be simply "grass & trees." The description Jefferson gave to Thornton and Latrobe of his plan for the college is proof that neither of these two architects were responsible for the general idea of pavilions, dormitories, and covered ways, although both (particularly Latrobe) influenced its final form. Noticeably missing here is the rotunda and porticos of pavilions extending into the space of the quadrangle. Jefferson later changed the configuration of the lawn to its final form, because of characteristics of the site, and added additional streets of "hotels" and dormitories not shown here.

"We are commencing here the establishment of a college," wrote Jefferson,

and instead of building a magnificent house which would exhaust all our funds, we propose to lay off a square of about 7. or 800 f. wide, the outside of which we shall arrange separate pavilions, one for each professor and his scholars. Each pavilion will have a schoolroom below, and 2 rooms for the professor above and between pavilion and pavilion a range of dormitories for the boys, one story high, giving to each room 10 f. wide & 12 f. deep. the pavilions about 36. wide in front and 24 f. in depth. this sketch will give you an idea of it. the whole of the pavilions and dormitories to be united by a colonnade in front of the height of the lower story of the pavilions, under which they may go dry from school to school. the colonnade will be of square brick pilasters (at first) with a Tuscan entablature. now what we wish is that these pavilions as will show themselves above the dormitories, shall be models of taste & good architecture, & of a variety of appearance, no two alike, so as to serve as specimens of the Architectural lectures. Will you set your imagination to work & sketch some designs for us, no matter how loosely with the pen, without the trouble of referring to scale or rule; for we want nothing but the outline of the architecture, as the internal must be arranged according to local convenience. a few sketches such as need not take you a moment will greatly oblige us. . . .

F.N.

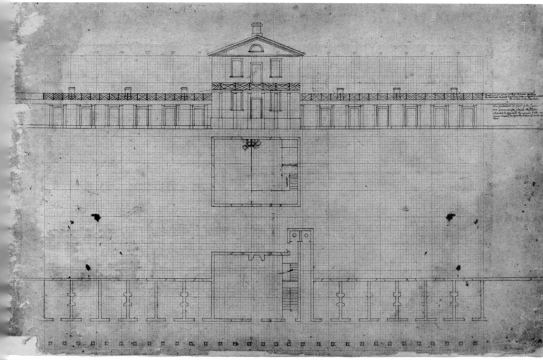

90 Study for the plan and elevations of a pavilion and flanking dormitories for Central College, later Pavilion VII, the University of Virginia

THOMAS JEFFERSON 1743–1826
Ink on laid paper 1817
53.3 x 34.2 (21 x 13½)

Lent by the University of Virginia,
Alderman Library, Charlottesville

Jefferson's early plans for the university buildings were simple and unpretentious. This drawing was made when Jefferson was planning Central College, which did not become the University of Virginia until 1819. Here Jefferson experimented with his idea for pavilions for classrooms and living quarters for professors, dormitories for students between the larger buildings, and a continuous covered passage for circulation. This early drawing of Pavilion VII (the first to be constructed) shows the square freestanding piers Jefferson called "pilasters" before he decided to use Tuscan columns. It also shows the use of the piers rather than an arcade in front of the pavilion and the awkward proportions of an idea not fully developed. Yet the drawing aptly demonstrates how Jefferson considered the functional aspects of the design before decorative aspects were seriously considered. We see that Jefferson at this early stage was particularly interested in varying the treatment of the covered way in front of the pavilion, in using the pediment-front temple-form building, and in installing railings in Chinese lattice on the open upper levels of the covered way. His notes on the drawing refer to errors—he wanted the panels of the railing to line up with the piers and the piers to line up with the edge of the pavilion.

The plan of the pavilion shows a single classroom with its own entrance, a stairway to the professor's suite above with a private entrance, a drawing room with an octagonal end, and two privies, one accessible to the students. The present pavilion is similar to this except that the location of the privy has been changed. For obvious reasons, Jefferson finally constructed them in the gardens away from the pavilions and dormitories.

F.N.

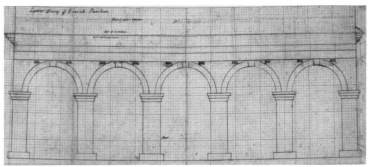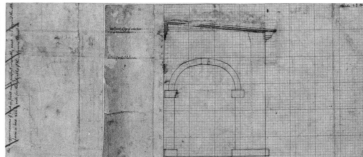

491 Study for the front and side elevation of the lower story of a pavilion for Central College, later the University of Virginia

THOMAS JEFFERSON 1743–1826
Ink on laid paper 1817
63.5 x 15.2 (25 x 6)

*Lent by the University of Virginia,
Alderman Library, Charlottesville*

This early study for a pavilion shows Jefferson working out the arrangement of floors and windows of a pavilion in relation to the projecting arcade. The arcade itself is probably not drawn in final form because the moldings are only roughed out in blocks. At one point Jefferson changed his mind about the design of the entablature because he pasted over a thin strip and reworked the design.

The side elevation shows a wider arch and a sloping roof. The design for the roof must have been giving him some trouble, too, because a new piece of ruled paper is pasted over the earlier work.

The study is probably for Pavilion VII, the only pavilion to have a lower arcade. Jefferson noted "Dorick Pavilion," the order eventually used.

F.N.

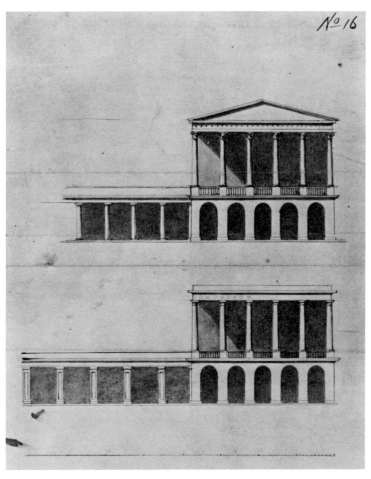

492 Studies for pavilions for the University of Virginia

WILLIAM THORNTON 1759–1828
Ink on wove paper 1817
19 x 24.1 (7½ x 9½)

*Lent by the University of Virginia,
Alderman Library, Charlottesville*

The idea for pavilions, dormitories, and covered ways was Jefferson's, which he fully explained to William Thornton in a letter of May 9, 1817. Thornton sent these drawings to Jefferson in response to a request for ideas for designs of façades.

Two designs submitted to Jefferson by Thornton that summer contain arches on the lower floor with porticos above. His proportions are more attenuated than those of Palladio, preferred by Jefferson. The top drawing shows a Corinthian portico with pediment and Doric columns on the colonnade. The lower design proposes a Doric portico without pediment, arches below, and paneled piers instead of columns for the colonnade. Stylistically these two pavilions are in the current neoclassical manner, but Jefferson's personal tastes were more academic. Nevertheless, these designs had an influence on the façade of Pavilion VII, which was begun during the summer of 1817. F.N.

493 Study for pavilions and dormitories for Central College, later the University of Virginia

WILLIAM THORNTON 1759–1828
k and watercolor on wove paper
obably 1817
x 23.5 (13 x 9¼)

*nt by the University of Virginia,
derman Library, Charlottesville*

esumably Thornton sent this draw-
g to Jefferson as a suggestion for
e plan of the college, but it did not
eet the terms of Jefferson's descrip-
on, as there was no continuous
vered way and the dormitories were
o stories high. The drawing may

have suggested three ideas to Jefferson
which were also proposed by Latrobe:
the colossal order running through
two stories instead of an arcade with a
single story porch above, unpedi-
mented porticos, and a center building
of greater size and importance.
Thornton's scheme was more in keeping with traditional neoclassical for-
mulae and unsuitable for inclusion in
Jefferson's plan, though Jefferson
may have been influenced by several
of its aspects. F.N.

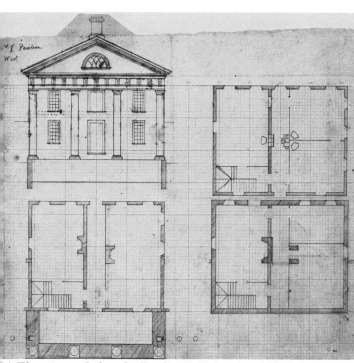

94 Elevation and plans for Pavilion I, University of Virginia

THOMAS JEFFERSON 1743–1826
k on laid paper
.9 x 25.4 (11¾ x 10)

*nt by the University of Virginia,
derman Library, Charlottesville*

vilion I demonstrated the Doric
der of the Baths of Diocletian, illus-
ted in Fréart de Chambray. Jef-

ferson's drawing, of course, is not fully
detailed. The staircase is placed in
front of a window because of the demand of the plan.
    Scorched rafters in the attic indicate
that the pavilion was damaged in the
fire of 1895 that destroyed the rotunda.
The aid of students and townspeople
saved the buildings on the lawn from
sustaining further injury. F.N.

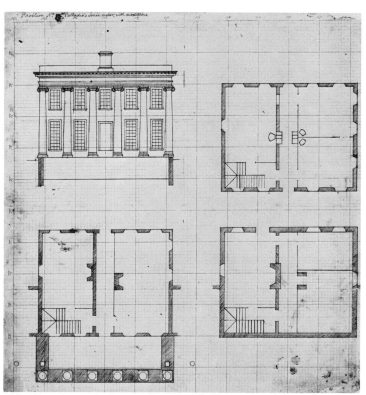

495 Elevation and plans for Pavilion V, University of Virginia

THOMAS JEFFERSON 1743–1826
Ink on laid paper before 1821
29.2 x 31.1 (11½ x 12¼)

*Lent by the University of Virginia,
Alderman Library, Charlottesville*

For Pavilion V, the third to be erected,
Jefferson chose a hectastyle portico
to extend across the entire front of
the pavilion. A similar portico was used

by Palladio on the Villa Malcon-
tenta near Venice. The capitals, carved
from Carrara marble, were adapted
from Palladio's Ionic order in Book I
of the *Four Books of Architecture*. No
pediment was intended, but Jefferson
indicated a low parapet to crown
the entablature. Inside Jefferson proposed a center-hall plan, with flanking
rooms and stair hall. F.N.

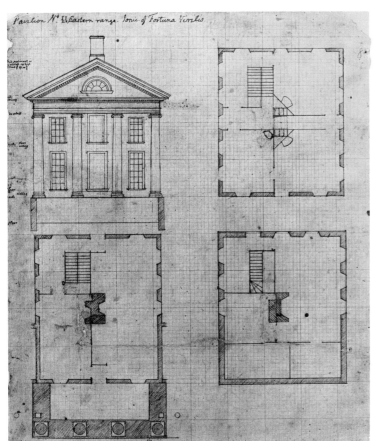

496 Elevation and plans for Pavilion II, University of Virginia

THOMAS JEFFERSON 1743–1826
Ink on laid paper 1819
25.4 x 30.5 (10 x 12)

*Lent by the University of Virginia,
Alderman Library, Charlottesville*

The Ionic order from the Temple of
Fortuna Virilis in the Roman Forum
is demonstrated on Pavilion II. Jefferson wanted each pavilion to serve as an
illustration for architectural lectures,
and for this purpose he borrowed
from several specific monuments.
However, it is only the designs of the
bases, capitals, and entablatures (exterior and interior) that come from
ancient buildings, generally not the
form of the structures themselves. This
pavilion, however, does bear a striking resemblance to its model.

This full temple-form building was
devised by Jefferson presumably
without suggestions from Thornton or
Latrobe. Jefferson favored fully pedimented fronts, with roofs carried
continuously from front to back, for
his own designs, which were more
literal than those of Thornton or
Latrobe. Both of them provided Jefferson with designs that were fashionably neoclassical, reflecting European
tastes with which Jefferson was equally
familiar. F.N.

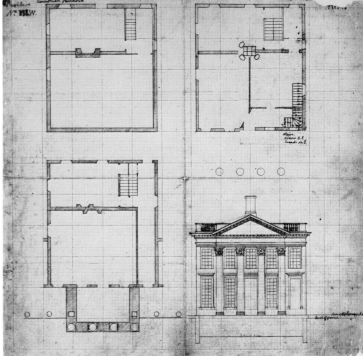

497 Elevation and plans for Pavilion III, University of Virginia

THOMAS JEFFERSON 1743–1826
Ink on laid paper 1818 or 1819
30.5 x 29.2 (12 x 11½)

*Lent by the University of Virginia,
Alderman Library, Charlottesville*

Pavilion III, the second to be constructed, demonstrated the Corinthian
order from Palladio. Italian stonecutters, brought to Virginia by Jefferson to make the capitals for the
columns, found the local stone unsuitable for delicate carving. Their extreme homesickness may have had a
great deal to do with their lack of
enthusiasm. Jefferson sent them back
to Italy and had the four capitals
carved there in marble from the
famous Carrara quarries near Florence.
The entablature, of course, was
executed in wood and the columns are
brick covered with plaster. They
project into the lawn beyond the
colonnade. The tetrastyle portico does
not extend across the pavilion's
façade, and the break in the roof is
hidden by the parapet. Unfortunately
the parapets on various pavilions were
not maintained. They have since
been removed from Pavilion III and
from the other pavilions but plans
have been made to reconstruct them.

The plan shows the inclusion of
an office or study for the professor
next to his classroom, and a separate
entrance. Pavilions VII and III were
the only ones to provide such a dual
entrance system. As usual, the flues for
the fireplaces and second floor Franklin stoves were designed for one
central chimney. This pavilion and
Pavilion IV are the only ones that have
not had extensions on the garden
side.

Typically, the verso of the drawing
contains brief specifications and estimates of the number of bricks necessary for the pavilion and its flanking
dormitories. F.N.

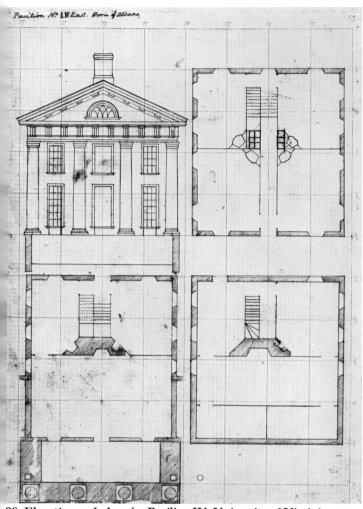

98 Elevation and plans for Pavilion IV, University of Virginia

THOMAS JEFFERSON 1743–1826
Ink on laid paper 1819
2.2 x 30.5 (8¾ x 12)

*Lent by the University of Virginia,
Alderman Library, Charlottesville*

For Pavilion IV, Jefferson turned to Roland Fréart de Chambray's *Parallèle*, which depicted the Doric order of the Temple of Albano, located in the hills south of Rome. Like Pavilions I, III, and V, this pavilion is one of Jefferson's pure temple-form designs. All four pavilions, with their more academic façades, were placed near the Rotunda, and the more unorthodox pavilions were placed toward the south end of the lawn.

The main floor of Pavilion IV has a classroom across the entire front. Above are four rooms, each with Franklin stoves. The plans for all the pavilions are similar, though there are occasional variations. This pavilion, for instance, is the only one with a room across the entire façade. Pavilions III and VII have side hall entries, Pavilions II and VI have entry into

a small center vestibule, and Pavilions I, V, VIII, IX, and X have the most common plan, with a through center hall. F.N.

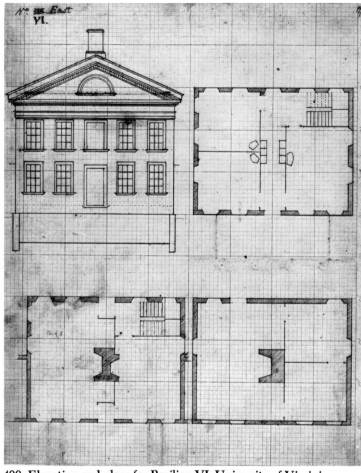

499 Elevation and plans for Pavilion VI, University of Virginia

THOMAS JEFFERSON 1743–1826
Ink on laid paper 1819
21.6 x 28 (8½ x 11)

*Lent by the University of Virginia,
Alderman Library, Charlottesville*

The Ionic order from the Theatre of Marcellus Jefferson found in Fréart de Chambray's *Parallèle*. He used it for the entablature of Pavilion VI, but the portico was omitted. "This pavilion," noted Jefferson on the reverse, "is to have no columns." Jefferson intended the flat façade to be part of the systematic variety of the design for the lawn.

Across the façade Jefferson imposed the Tuscan colonnade or covered way, but to express the pavilion he broke the colonnade and extended it slightly forward. This is not shown in the elevation but is included in the plan.

The interior plan features a small entrance vestibule to prevent cold air and mud from entering the classroom.
F.N.

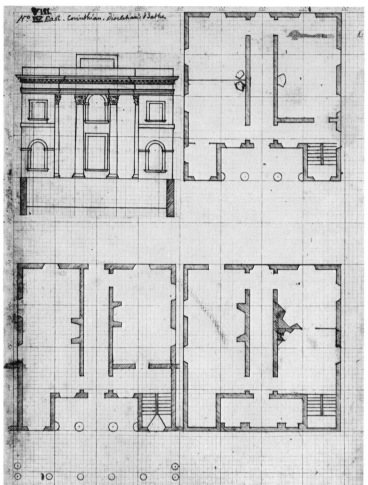

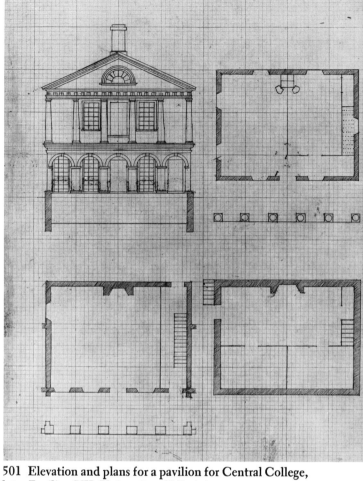

500 Elevation and plans for Pavilion VIII, University of Virginia

THOMAS JEFFERSON 1743–1826
Ink on laid paper 1819
21.6 x 28 (8½ x 11)

*Lent by the University of Virginia,
Alderman Library, Charlottesville*

For Pavilion VIII Jefferson used the colossal order from the Baths of Diocletian illustrated in Fréart de Chambray. The design for the façade may have been inspired by Latrobe—in fact, Jefferson called it "Latrobe's Lodge Front." It contains a recessed portico with two Corinthian columns *in antis* and Corinthian half columns. To each side are wings with arched windows. Later, in the recessed portico, Jefferson added additional windows, which are not shown in the elevation but appear in the plan. He undoubtedly regarded these windows as necessary to light the entrance, but he may have thought that they compromised the design. The pavilion is sited opposite Pavilion VII, and its arched windows seem to relate to that pavilion's arcade.

Like Pavilion VI, Jefferson drew no Tuscan colonnade across the façade of this pavilion. The covered way was built, of course, to conform with the general plan of the university, but the executed plan admittedly is architecturally unsatisfying. For the pavilions of the university Jefferson favored flat façades and projecting porticos, because this approach admirably lent itself to the inclusion of the colonnade. But the large columns of the recessed portico behind the small columns of the covered way presented special visual problems which are unresolved in the finished work.

Originally, the upper portion of the colonnade was connected to the second floor of the pavilion by a ramp. Light could enter the ground floor of the portico through two open wells, a feature not unlike that in Pavilion IX.

On the interior Jefferson placed the staircase in one of the flanking wings, but the other wing was for the most part "leftover" space. Jefferson did the drawings and specifications for the five pavilions on the East Lawn in three weeks, in June 1819. F.N.

501 Elevation and plans for a pavilion for Central College, later Pavilion VII, University of Virginia

THOMAS JEFFERSON 1743–1826
Ink on laid paper 1817
27.3 x 29.8 (10¾ x 11¾)

*Lent by the University of Virginia,
Alderman Library, Charlottesville*

Pavilion VII, the first pavilion to be constructed, may have been inspired by designs of William Thornton, but Jefferson made the proportions conform to those of Palladio. This design, however, related to an early study made by Jefferson for Monticello as closely as it did to Thornton's proposed façade. On the first level are Tuscan arches (the only arcade on the lawn) and above are Doric columns (also from Palladio). This use of the temple form was one of the earliest for domestic building in America.

Jefferson originally intended all the pavilions to have arches on the first floor, with columns above. Probably at Thornton's and Latrobe's suggestion, Jefferson adopted full porticos for most of the other pavilions.

The first floor plan shows a single classroom, where the professor lectured. He had his own entrance on the right with stairs to the upper apartment. Like the other pavilions, the upper rooms were equipped with Franklin stoves (more correctly called Pennsylvania stoves), because they produced heat more efficiently than fireplaces. F.N.

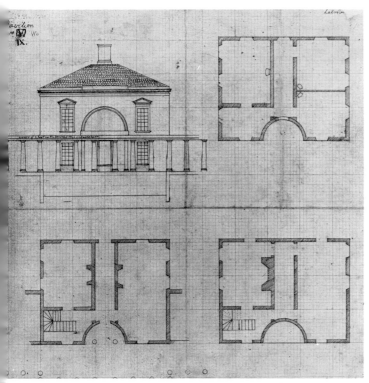

502 Elevation and plans for Pavilion IX, University of Virginia

THOMAS JEFFERSON 1743–1826
Ink on laid paper before 1821
28.5 x 28.5 (11⅛ x 11⅛)

Lent by the University of Virginia, Alderman Library, Charlottesville

Pavilion IX is one of the most unusual of the ten pavilions, because it does not derive from an ancient form but rather from a leading contemporary French architect, Claude-Nicolas Ledoux (1736–1806), whose work Jefferson knew at first hand. Ledoux's earlier work followed the very latest neoclassical styles, but his later work was severely geometrical and displayed an interest in pure, simple forms decorated with a minimum of classical ornament. Apparently Latrobe also had something to do with the design (see "Latrobe" written in the upper right). The second floor very much suggests Latrobe, while the entrance motif derives from the French architect.

Jefferson used the exedra, or niche with a semidome, for the entrance to the pavilion, with two Ionic columns *in antis* forming a screen in front of the exedra, which was open so that light could enter directly from above. When the morning sun shines it casts splendid abstract patterns on the surface of the exedra, and at night the soft exterior lamps make the interior of the niche glow with a rich, warm, and even light.

Above, no portico was planned, but the proportions were taken "as they might be" from "an order entire of pedestal, column and entablature. . . ." Jefferson specified the Doric of the Temple of Fortuna Virilis (which he slightly modified) for the columns of the exedra and for the thin entablature, which rings the interior of the niche.

There is no pediment across the façade, but Jefferson indicated a truncated parapet. The aedicular windows on the second floor were not executed. The present fenestration is simple, and of the standard type. F.N.

503 Pavillon de Mlle Guimard

SIR WILLIAM CHAMBERS
1726–1796
Ink 1774
21.5 x 36.2 (8½ x 14¼)

Lent by the Royal Institute of British Architects, London

When the noted British architect Sir William Chambers visited Paris in 1774 with his brother John, he made a series of invaluable drawings of the latest buildings in the neoclassic style then being built. Among these were buildings by his friends de Wailly, Soufflot, Antoine, and Peyre, and other leading French architects, such as Ledoux, who had completed the design for the pavilion at Louveciennes in 1771 (see nos. 296–298) and, just a year later, the new residence for Mlle Guimard, shown here. Whether Jefferson met Ledoux during his stay in Paris ten years after Chambers' visit is unknown, but his eye, like Chambers', was attracted by some of the same buildings by this French architect, including the pavilion of Mlle Guimard, on which he later modeled Pavilion IX at the University of Virginia. J.H.

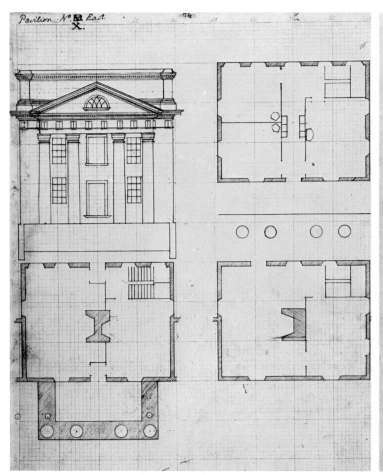

504 Elevation and plans for Pavilion X, University of Virginia

THOMAS JEFFERSON 1743–1826
Ink on laid paper 1819
22.9 x 29.2 (9 x 11½)

*Lent by the University of Virginia,
Alderman Library, Charlottesville*

"The columns to have no bases," Jefferson specified in his notes on the back of this drawing. Jefferson took the order from the Theatre of Marcellus in Rome, shown in Fréart de Chambray's illustrations. It was unusual because it was the only Roman Doric without bases. The design for the parapet (no longer extant) came partly from another ancient monument. "I have never seen an Attic pilaster, with the measures of it's parts minutely expressed except that of the Temple of Nerva Trajan. (Palladio, B. III, pl. 18) That temple is overloaded with ornaments, and it's Pilaster frittered away so minutely in it's mouldings as to lose all effect. I have simplified these mouldings to suit our plainer style, still however retaining nearly their general outlines and proportions," Jefferson wrote.

As in Pavilion III, Jefferson designed a modified temple form with a portico extending across only the center three bays of the façade. Its large size and its projecting tetrastyle portico anchor the south end of the lawn and relate it to the north end, establishing a coherence in the lawn. F.N.

505 Notes for the construction of the Rotunda

THOMAS JEFFERSON 1743–1826
Ink on wove paper c. 1823
19.7 x 27.3 (7¾ x 10¾)

*Lent by the University of Virginia,
Alderman Library, Charlottesville*

Jefferson made these notes for the library, or rotunda, on the number of bricks necessary for the construction (he estimated 1,171,889) and on the method for building the wood-frame dome. He planned to rest the ribs of the roof on curved plates attached to the wall with iron bolts. "The ribs (of the dome) are to be keyed together by cross boards at proper intervals for the ribs to head in as they shorten." On the back Jefferson made a sketch of the ribbing system of the dome. To strengthen the walls, he said that "the fireplaces & chimneys must be brought forward so that the flues may not make a hollow in the main walls. They will thus become buttresses."

For the design of the plate and "the crib of the skylight," Jefferson referred to Delorme, and the general design of the wooden dome was based on the advanced structural system of Molinos and LeGrand's Halle aux Bleds in Paris, which Jefferson had praised in his correspondence with Maria Cosway:

[We] must go and examine this wonderful piece of architecture; . . . it was the most superb thing on earth! . . . What you had seen there was worth all you had yet seen in Paris! . . . My visit to Legrand and Molinos had public utility for its object. A market is to be built in Richmond. What a commodious plan is that of Legrand and Molinos; especially if we put on it the noble dome of the Halle aux Bleds. F.N.

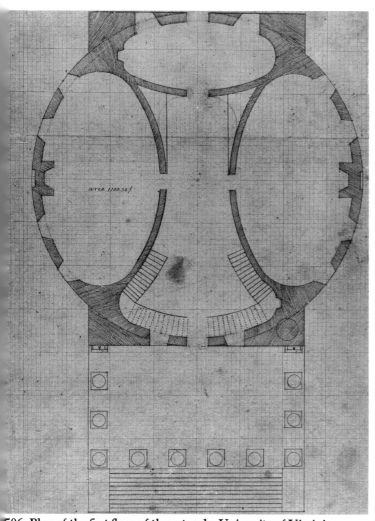

506 Plan of the first floor of the rotunda, University of Virginia

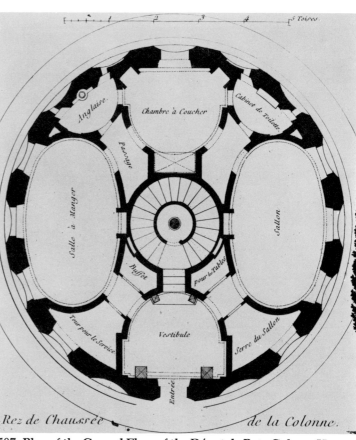

507 Plan of the Ground Floor of the Désert de Retz Column House

THOMAS JEFFERSON 1743–1826
Ink on laid paper probably 1821
31.1 x 22.2 (12¼ x 8¾)
*Lent by the University of Virginia,
Alderman Library, Charlottesville*

One of the masterpieces of the classical revival is Jefferson's rotunda. As the section shows, six classrooms on two floors and a dome room above for a library were inscribed in a sphere. The first floor of the rotunda contained three oval rooms and a splendid dumbbell-shaped center hall with a double staircase. Jefferson originally intended angled walls in the north end of the hall but later changed his mind to accomodate a curved end. This change is visible on the drawing, and there is a note to the builder as well.

Oval rooms were built in America in the eighteenth century and of course existed in Europe, but this suite of oval rooms was quite avant-garde in America. Like other interiors on the lawn, Jefferson used various entablatures illustrated in books. These oval rooms were decorated with the Ionic

of the Temple of Fortuna Virilis, the Doric of the Baths of Diocletian, and the Corinthian of the Pantheon, all ancient buildings in Rome. Straight grain pine floors were installed. Presumably the walls were white.

The oval rooms were used for a variety of purposes. On October 4, 1824, the Board of Visitors decided that the rooms were to be used for examinations, lectures, religious worship, drawing, music, "or any other of the innocent and ornamental accomplishments of life." Provision was made for classes too large for the pavilion classrooms to be held in the larger rooms of the rotunda.

Jefferson designed a portico for the south side of the rotunda and provided for a respond on the north side. He considered this the "back" of the rotunda. Undoubtedly a portico was planned for the north side, but there was never a surplus of funds for building and no portico was ever added to the original building. The present portico on the north side was added by Stanford White between 1895 and 1898. F.N.

JEAN-NICOLAS LE ROUGE
active late 18th century
Engraving (facsimile)

Jefferson knew the Désert de Monville, as the Désert de Retz was then called, and visited it with Maria Cosway. The picturesque assemblage of buildings ranging from a pyramid to a ruined gothic church must have been a great attraction to the visitor, and the column house was the most imposing and the most unusual of all the structures. In his famous "Head" and "Heart" letter to Maria Cosway, Jefferson particularly mentioned the column house: "How grand the idea excited by the remains of such a column!" He also saw the inside, for he added, "The spiral staircase too was beautiful." When he came to design the oval rooms of the rotunda in the University of Virginia, Jefferson must have remembered the floor plan of the Column House, as they are very similar. Both have oval rooms on the left and right of the entrance, Jefferson's design making them more

ovoid. The smaller rooms at the back are less closely linked, but the general idea is close enough to speculate that the semicircular bedroom of the Column House suggested the small oval room of the rotunda, where Jefferson had more space to extend the original circle to an oval. R.W.

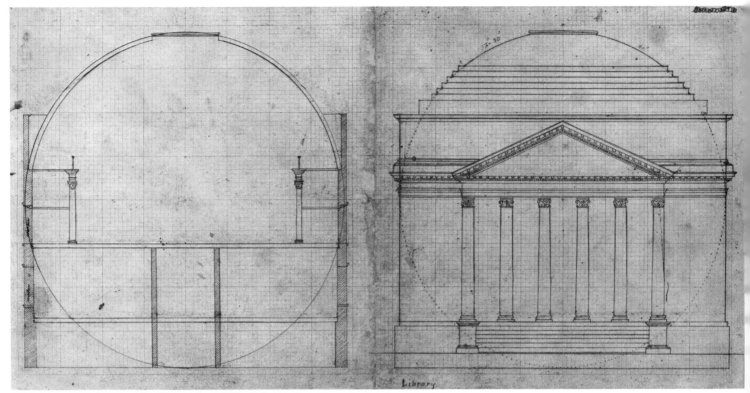

508 Section of the rotunda, University of Virginia

THOMAS JEFFERSON 1743–1826
Ink on laid paper probably 1821
43.8 x 22.2 (17¼ x 8¾)

*Lent by the University of Virginia,
Alderman Library, Charlottesville*

The section of the rotunda shows
three levels: the raised basement with
four low oval rooms, the principal
suite of rooms and center hall, and the
dome room above. The dome springs
from behind the columns and from a
setback in the wall, a system quite
unlike that of the Pantheon, Jefferson's
model. Jefferson was too great an
artist by this time to copy an interior
literally; what he planned was the
proportions of the Pantheon with
functional galleries. Behind the columns were two gallery levels; above, a
skylight instead of an open oculus.
Jefferson originally wanted the dome to
be painted blue and decorated with
gilt stars. But no bills for blue paint
could be found in the university
archives and the dome was painted
white, when the rotunda interior was
recently reconstructed.

Jefferson's genius for neoclassical
design is brilliantly shown in this section. Here he combined one of the
greatest interiors of Roman architecture with two functional floors of oval
rooms to produce a design at once
aesthetic and practical. F.N.

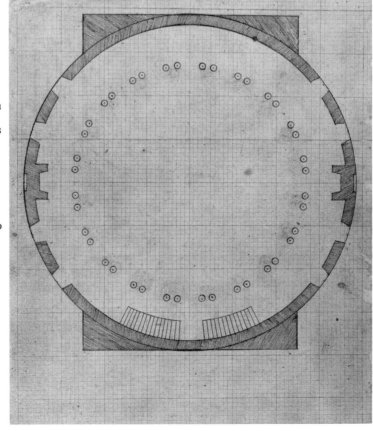

509 Plan for the dome room of the rotunda, University of Virginia

THOMAS JEFFERSON 1743–1826
Ink on laid paper probably 1821
21.6 x 31.1 (8½ x 12¼)

*Lent by the University of Virginia,
Alderman Library, Charlottesville*

The dome room, or "library room,"
of the rotunda was a single space about
as high as it was wide, exactly the
interior proportions of the Pantheon.
Arranged around the space were
twenty pairs of columns of the Composite order from Palladio, forming a
low aisle for bookcases. Photographs
taken before the fire of 1895 show
two gallery levels behind the columns
included in the drawing. The top
gallery had balusters and pedestals.

Behind the chimneys were false
windows to maintain the regularity of
the exterior. The chimneys also acted
as buttresses to support the dome.
In the drawing, Jefferson did not show
the windows as they were built,
opening onto the portico from the
dome room. He wanted a "folding sash
door" of glass with a railing for the
center opening, but no exterior gallery
was planned, because, as Jefferson
told Arthur Brockenbrough, the proctor, on August 10, 1823, it "would
injure the grandeur of the portico."
F.N.

510 Elevation of the rotunda and Pavilions IX and X, University of Virginia

Attributed to CORNELIA
JEFFERSON RANDOLPH 1799–1871
Ink and tinted washes on wove paper
c. 1820?
44.4 x 28 (17½ x 11)
*Lent by the University of Virginia,
Alderman Library, Charlottesville*

It was probably Cornelia Jefferson
Randolph, Thomas Jefferson's granddaughter, who made this drawing of
the lawn from the south end. It shows
the rotunda, with its flanking wings,
and the southernmost pavilions with
dormitories. They have their parapets
and Chinese trellis railings. Omitted
are the two terraces descending from
the rotunda and the serpentine walls
behind the pavilions. F.N.

**511 Design for a planetarium,
University of Virginia**

THOMAS JEFFERSON 1743–1826
Ink on wove paper 1819
12.7 x 20.3 (5 x 8)
*Lent by the University of Virginia,
Alderman Library, Charlottesville*

Jefferson was famous for his interest in
science. This drawing contains instructions for making the dome of the
proposed rotunda into a planetarium.
The dome room, itself, was planned
and used as a library.

Jefferson had a great admiration
and interest in the restoration of the
Pantheon in Rome, as evidenced by
this letter to William Short, penned in
1791: "Pray get me by some means
or other a compleat set of Piranesi's
drawings of the Pantheon, and especially the correct design for it's restoration as proposed by I forget whom,
which was not executed, and of which
I have heard you speak. I wish to
render them useful in the public
buildings now to be begun at Georgetown. . . ." This interest had a direct
effect on the design of the rotunda
at the university, and Jefferson wrote
later, "The library is to be on the
principle of the Pantheon, a sphere
within a cylinder of 70 feet diameter—
to wit, one-half only of the dimensions of the Pantheon, and of a single
order only." F.N.

512 Bird's eye view of the University of Virginia

THOMAS JEFFERSON 1743–1826,
shaded by CORNELIA JEFFERSON
RANDOLPH (?) 1799–1871
Ink and wash on heavy, cold-pressed
paper c. 1820?
31.8 x 14.6 (12½ x 5¾)

*Lent by the University of Virginia,
Alderman Library, Charlottesville*

Drawn by Jefferson and probably
shaded by his granddaughter Cornelia,
the bird's-eye view from the east side
shows the ten pavilions and dormitories of the lawn on the inner rows
and the hotels and dormitories of the
ranges on the outside rows, parallel to
the lawn. Conspicuously absent are
the serpentine walls between the lawn
and ranges and the rotunda on the
right, not yet built. Construction of
the rotunda was begun after all the
pavilions and ranges were complete or
underway. F.N.

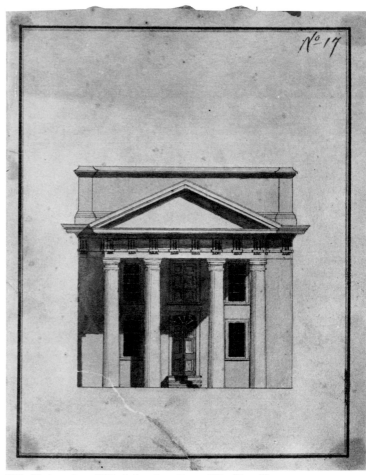

513 University of Virginia, elevation of Pavilion X

Attributed to CORNELIA
JEFFERSON RANDOLPH 1799–1871
Ink and wash, on thin paper c. 1820
17.1 x 20.3 (6¾ x 8)

*Lent by the University of Virginia,
Alderman Library, Charlottesville*

This drawing, probably by Jefferson's
granddaughter Cornelia Jefferson
Randolph, shows the end pavilion on
the East Lawn with its unusual tetrastyle Roman Doric portico with columns without bases and tall pilastered
parapet (see no. 504). F.N.

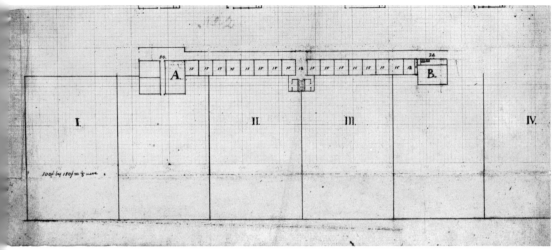

514 Plan of dormitories, West Range, with Hotels A and B

THOMAS JEFFERSON 1743–1826
Ink on laid paper 1817?
37.4 x 15.8 (14¾ x 6¼)

*Lent by the University of Virginia,
Alderman Library, Charlottesville*

Behind the lawn of the University of
Virginia are two parallel rows of dormitories and "hotels," small houses
which contained dining rooms and
apartments for the housekeepers who
operated the dining facilities. As in
the pavilions, kitchens were in the
basement.

Hotels were first mentioned in 1818,
when the group of Virginians commissioned by the Commonwealth
to choose a site for the university met
in August. Their report mentioned
dormitories and hotels for the students
"to be lodged and dieted." Apparently none had been built by the
spring of 1819, when Jefferson rejected
a suggestion for multi-story dormitories. He settled on a plan to put the
hotels and dormitories behind the
pavilions, facing outward to the fields
and woods, with the professors'
gardens directly behind their pavilions.
"It forms in fact a regular town, capable of being enlarged to any extent
which future circumstances may call
for," wrote Jefferson to James Breckin-
ridge, a member of the Board of
Visitors, on July 18, 1819.

This is an early drawing, made
before Jefferson had decided on this
arrangement. Here the hotels face the
rear of the pavilions. Only two hotels
are shown on this drawing, but Jefferson finally planned three on each
side. F.N.

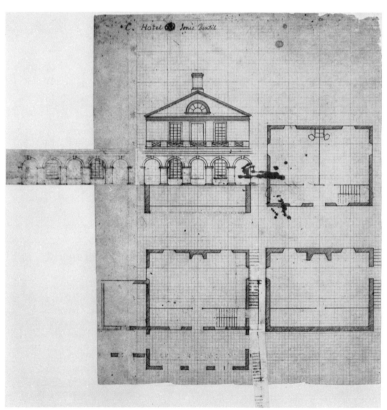

515 "C Hotel, Ionic Dentil" elevation and 3 plans

THOMAS JEFFERSON 1743–1826
Ink on laid paper before 1822
23.5 x 30.5 (9¼ x 12)

*Lent by the University of Virginia,
Alderman Library, Charlottesville*

Jefferson planned three hotels for each
of the two ranges. They served as
dining halls for students and contained
small apartments for housekeepers.
Kitchens were in the basement.

Like the pavilions on the lawn, the
hotels were connected to the dormitories by covered ways. Jefferson chose
the Tuscan arcade, rather than colonnade, for the exterior passages, but
for this hotel Jefferson specified "Ionic
Dentil" for the cornice. Only one
hotel was built with two stories. The
drawing shown here was not executed;
its temple form reflects the design
of the pavilions. When Hotel C was
built it had a full pediment but there
was only one story.

This design was apparently unfinished, as the elevation shows five
arches across the façade and the plan
shows only three. F.N.

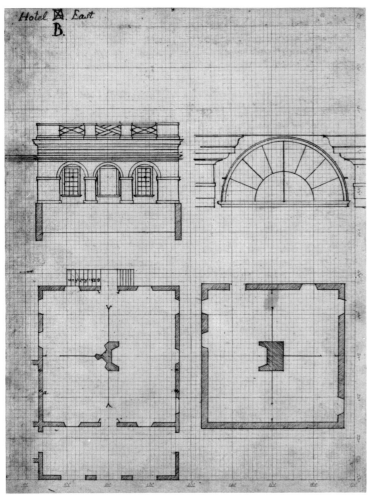

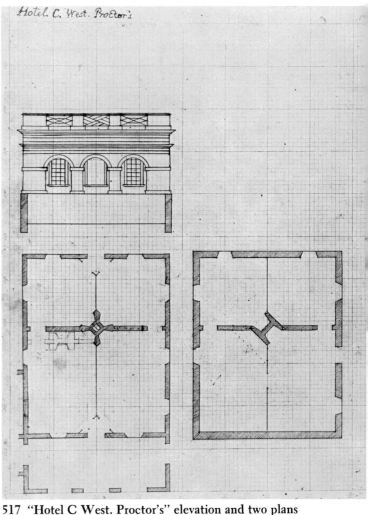

516 "Hotel B East" elevation and two plans, with detail of arched window set in cornice

THOMAS JEFFERSON 1743–1826
Ink on laid paper before 1822
22.2 x 29.2 (8¾ x 11½)
Specifications on verso

Lent by the University of Virginia, Alderman Library, Charlottesville

For Hotel B Jefferson devised a scheme similar to that of Hotel C west, with three widened arches, a flat roof, a high cornice, a single story, and a Chinese railing. Inside were planned three rooms, all of which had the semioctagonal effect created by corner fireplaces and unusual small triangular entrance ways. Below, of course, was the kitchen.

The semicircular fan light, for which a detail is shown, was intended to be placed in the front room on the left in the position marked *a*. Jefferson thought that room "poorly lighted and aired," surrounded as it was on three sides by other rooms and a dormitory. He placed the rounded light in the entablature, making sure that the height of the window equaled the height of the entablature. "The window should open on pivots placed horizontally (as the upper windows in the Monticello house) to be managed by a cord, or (being but 8-8 from the floor) may be opened and shut by hand, mounting into a chair," wrote Jefferson on the back. F.N.

517 "Hotel C West. Proctor's" elevation and two plans

THOMAS JEFFERSON 1743–1826
Ink on laid paper before 1822
22.2 x 29.2 (8¾ x 11½)
Specifications on verso

Lent by the University of Virginia, Alderman Library, Charlottesville

For this hotel Jefferson specified "3. arches and 4. piers of same height with those of dormitories, but different breadths." He also noted that "the body of the Hotel must rise above (the arcade) by its whole entablature. . . ." He planned a low roof with a "Chinese parapet 4. f. high."

The plan of the main floor of the interior indicates four rooms with corner fireplaces and corner entrances, which suggest a semioctagonal effect found in some of the other hotels and pavilions. Below were four more rooms, two with fireplaces.

The drawing of the façade is similar to hotels at present lettered B and E, though Jefferson noted the drawing "Hotel C West. Proctor's." Since other drawings exist for Hotel B, this was most likely intended for E. Actually, no hotel was constructed on these floor plans. F.N.

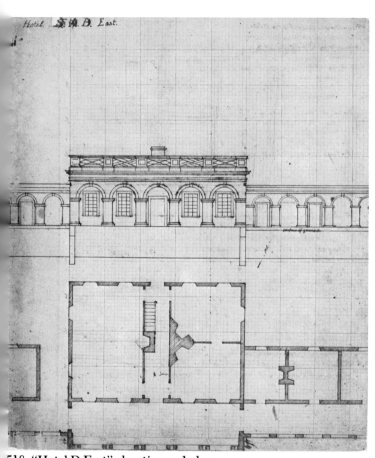

518 "Hotel D East" elevation and plan

THOMAS JEFFERSON 1743–1826
Ink on laid paper before 1822
26 x 30.5 (10¼ x 12)
Specifications on verso

*Lent by the University of Virginia,
Alderman Library, Charlottesville*

"Hotel with refectory and 2. family
rooms. with a flat roof and Chinese
railing. to be Tuscan also, but so much
higher than the adjacent dormitories
that it's entablature may be clear
above theirs," described Jefferson on
the back of the drawing. Unlike similar
hotels, this one has a five-bay arcade,
and a central hall with staircase running front to back. It was constructed
on this plan. The basement kitchen
is not shown. F.N.

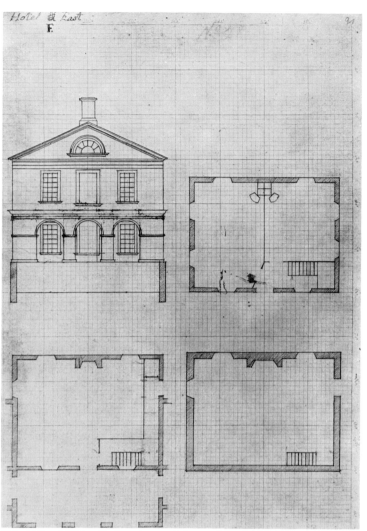

519 "Hotel F East" elevation and three plans

THOMAS JEFFERSON 1743–1826
Ink on laid paper before 1822
21 x 29.2 (8¼ x 11½)
Specifications on verso

*Lent by the University of Virginia,
Alderman Library, Charlottesville*

Hotel F is the only hotel of two
stories built at the university. Like the
other, unexecuted two-story design
shown here at number 515, it has a
full pediment roof.

The basement contains the kitchen,
which is a single room, and on the
ground level is an odd-shaped room
with a stair hall. This was later built
to form a rectangular space. Above
were smaller rooms with Franklin
stoves and a small hall.

As usual, Jefferson made notations
on the back of the design indicating
the increased breadth of the arches of
the arcade in front of the hotel, dimensions of the building, construction
of the staircases, and the window
panes "of glass 12. I. square." F.N.

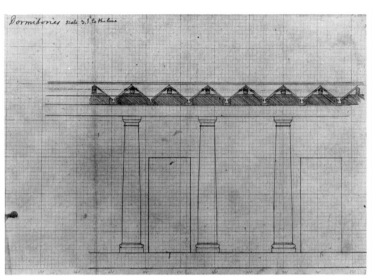

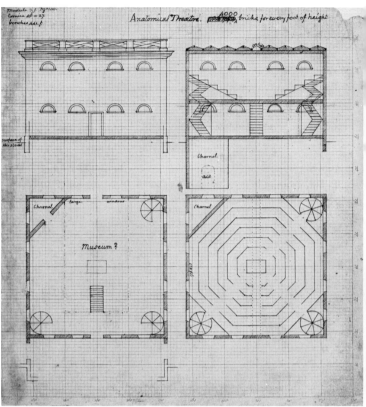

520 Elevation and section of dormitories, showing colonnades and "rooflets"

THOMAS JEFFERSON 1743–1826
Ink on laid paper
55.8 x 18.4 (22 x 7¼)

*Lent by the University of Virginia,
Alderman Library, Charlottesville*

The elevation of the colonnade and dormitories shows simple Tuscan columns supporting the flat roof. The entablature is cut away to show the series of short sawtooth ridges Jefferson called "rooflets" and the method of their construction. The rainwater was intended to be carried off in the rear. Unfortunately, the tin roofs leaked and were later replaced with more old-fashioned pitched roofs of slate. F.N.

521 Elevation, plans and section of an anatomical theater, University of Virginia

THOMAS JEFFERSON 1743–1826
Ink on laid paper 1825
28 x 30.5 (11 x 12)

*Lent by the University of Virginia,
Alderman Library, Charlottesville*

On March 9, 1825, Jefferson wrote to the proctor of the university, regarding the projected anatomical theater, that "the plan shall be delivered to you as soon as I shall have had a consultation on it with Dr. Dunglison," a physician and professor at the university. The building was not completed until after Jefferson's death. Earlier, on January 11, Jefferson told Joseph C. Cabell, a member of the Board of Visitors, that "an anatomical theatre . . . is indispensible to the school of anatomy. There cannot be a single dissection until a proper theatre is prepared giving an advantageous view of the operation to those within, and effectively excluding observation from without."

This theater, built after the completion of the rest of the university's buildings was assured, was the only building Jefferson designed outside of the system of the four rows of buildings and their covered ways. Constructed during 1826, it contained two stories and large rooms. The ground floor, labeled "Museum?", had four staircases (three circular) and semicircular windows, which admitted light but prevented passersby from observing the medical lectures and specimens. On the second level was the actual theater, with seats banked on the sides and a dissecting table in the center. The spaces labeled "charnel" on both levels and below grade were used, of course, for the storage of corpses needed for lectures and demonstrations.

The octagonal shape of the lecture room was one of Jefferson's favorite, but he did not use it so directly elsewhere at the university. His design for the theater bore a striking resemblance to his unexecuted plan for an octagonal chapel (see no. 24). The roof was flat with a Tuscan cornice and railing in Chinese lattice. The cross section shows "rooflets" and the placement of a skylight. Unfortunately, the theater was razed in 1938 to make way for a new library. Except for the rotunda, which was destroyed by fire in 1895, the anatomical theater is the only building of Jeffersonian design at the university to have been lost. F.N.

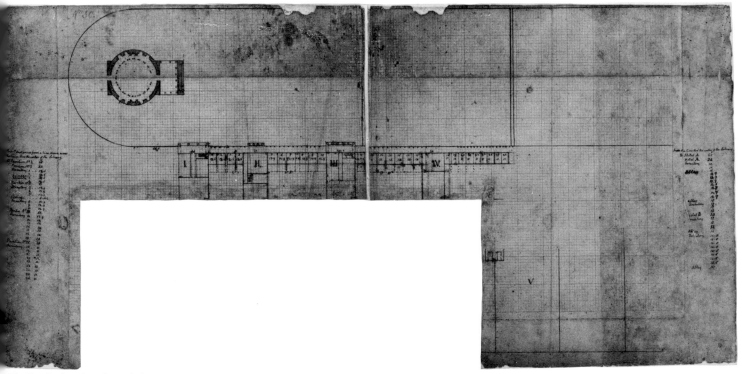

22 Study for the plan of the Lawn

THOMAS JEFFERSON 1743–1826
Ink on laid paper 1823 or before
9.2 x 32.4 (27¼ x 12¾)

Lent by the University of Virginia,
Alderman Library, Charlottesville

This drawing of part of the lawn shows three of the western pavilions, their dormitories, and covered ways, and the position of the rotunda. Though here Jefferson labeled the pavilions consecutively, later he assigned the odd numbers to the west and the even to the east. The passage between Dormitories 2 and 3 was not built.

Another drawing, of the West Range, shown here at number 514, was cut from this drawing. When it was part of the single sheet, Jefferson intended to have the ranges face inward on the pavilions. Later when he changed his mind, Jefferson must have clipped that portion from the drawing. The gardens were then placed behind the pavilions. The wings extending from the portico of the rotunda are not shown on this early plan. F.N.

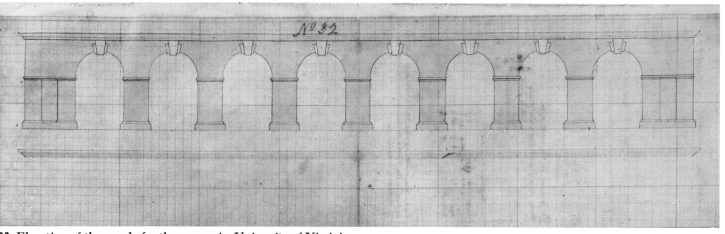

523 Elevation of the arcade for the gymnasia, University of Virginia

THOMAS JEFFERSON 1743–1826
Pencil and wash on wove paper 1824
11.1 x 40.6 (4⅜ x 16)

Lent by the University of Virginia,
Alderman Library, Charlottesville

From each side of the rotunda portico extended low wings called gymnasia. They were to be used for "Gymnastic exercises and games of the students . . ." resolved the Board of Visitors in 1824. This drawing shows the north side of the wings with the arcade similar to the arcades of the ranges. There are no full Tuscan moldings shown, only simple blocked bands to the imposts of the arches. The gymnasia, like the colonnades and arcades, had flat roofs with rooflets. After the 1895 fire, Stanford White made significant changes to the railings, substituting typical colonial revival designs, and enclosed the arched openings. Two similar wings were added to the north front of the rotunda. F.N.

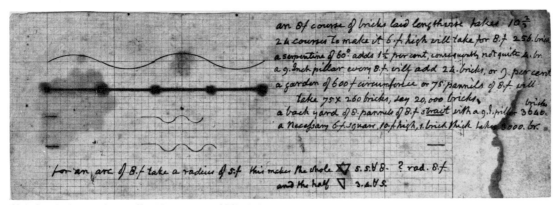

524 Study for garden walls, University of Virginia

THOMAS JEFFERSON 1743–1826
Ink on laid paper c. 1817–1822
7 x 20.3 (8 x 2¾)

*Lent by the University of Virginia,
Alderman Library, Charlottesville*

For the gardens at the university,
Jefferson designed serpentine walls one
brick thick. He thought they were
more economical because they required
fewer bricks than straight walls, and
the masons were paid the same amount
whether the bricks were laid in a
straight wall or in a curved one.

The curves were designed partly for
stability and were effective in preventing the collapse of the walls in high
winds. The walls were not otherwise
structurally successful, because the
narrow four-inch brick could not adequately protect the mortar from the
deleterious effects of freezing water.
Because of this, none of the original
walls survive. They have all been reconstructed since 1949, on the original
foundations, but still require constant
maintenance.

Undoubtedly Jefferson's intentions
were aesthetic as well as practical.
The curved walls reflected the established English and French taste for
curves and ovals in gardening. Curving
walls are known in parts of England,
particularly in Suffolk, where one
scholar has counted at least forty-five
of them, and though Jefferson did not
see them, he could easily have heard
or read of them. The English found
these were practical as well as beautiful, as they held the scanty heat of
the sun in a small area and helped to
force plants growing in the curves.

The extensive specifications accompanying this drawing read as follows:

an 8 f. course of bricks laid length-
wise takes 10⅔ 24 courses to make
it 6 f. high will take for 8 f. 256
brick
a serpentine of 60° adds 1½ percent,
consequently not quite 4 br.
a 9 Inch pillar every 8 f. will add
24 bricks or 9 percent
a garden of 600 f. circumference or
75 pannels of 8 f. will take

75 x 260 bricks, say 20,000 bricks
a back yard of 8 pannels of 8 f.
strait with a 9 I. pillar 3640 bricks
a Necessary 6 f. square, 10 f. high,
1 brick thick takes 3000 br.

_____

for an arc of 8 f. take a radius of 5 f.
this makes the whole ▽5.5 ⩚8- ?
rad. 8 f.
half ▽3.4 ⩚5.

F.N.

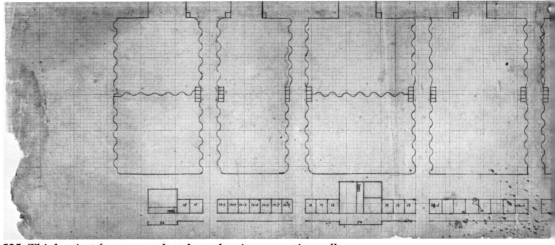

525 Third variant for range and gardens, showing serpentine walls

THOMAS JEFFERSON 1743–1826
Ink on laid paper
40 x 16.5 (15¾ x 6½)

*Lent by the University of Virginia,
Alderman Library, Charlottesville*

Jefferson's preference for the serpentine wall over other types of enclosure
extended even to his plans for a
botanical garden, which he proposed
in the last year of his life to Dr. John
P. Emmett, professor of natural history at the university. He wrote,

It is time to think of the introduction
of the school of Botany into our
institution. . . . For that branch, I
presume, can be taught advantageously only during the short season
while nature is in general bloom, say
during a certain portion of the
months of April and May. . . . Our
first operation must be the selection
of a piece of ground of proper soil
and site. . . . Enclose the ground with
a serpentine brick wall seven feet
high. This would take about 80,000

bricks and cost $800, and it must
depend on our finances whether they
will afford that immediately, or
allow us, for awhile, but enclosure
of posts and rails.

F.N.

526 Thomas Jefferson

GILBERT STUART 1755–1828
Oil on wood panel 1805
53.3 x 68.6 (21 x 27)

*Lent by Mr. and Mrs. Donald B.
Straus, New York*

It is likely that Jefferson, at age sixty
two, sat for this portrait in Stuart's
studio at F and Seventh Streets in
Washington not long before the
seventh of June, 1805. Stuart was
forty-nine and, as a friend told Dolley
Madison, "all the rage."

The life portrait remained unfinished in Stuart's studio for sixteen
years. The protracted commission,
though infuriating to Jefferson, was
deliberate on the part of the painter.
Stuart characteristically refused to
finish life portraits of his more distinguished subjects so he could use them
as sources for the numerous replicas
he produced for ready sale. After
persistent attempts by Jefferson to
obtain possession of this portrait, it was
finally Henry Dearborn who procured

it from the painter and shipped it to
Monticello in August 1821. It was
there that it hung for the rest of Jefferson's life, descending to his family
at Edgehill, where it hung for seventy-
five years and thus came to be known
as the "Edgehill Stuart," to distinguish it from Stuart's two other life
portraits of Jefferson.

Late in Jefferson's second term,
prints of this likeness began displacing
the prints of the 1800 Rembrandt
Peale image in public popularity. The

likeness was persistently reproduced
in America and in France during his
later life, and after Jefferson's death—
especially after the Stuart likeness
was adopted by the government as the
official image of Jefferson for use on
postage stamps and currency—it
triumphed over the Peale to become
unquestionably the preeminent icon of
Jefferson. A.B.

DECORATIVE ARTS

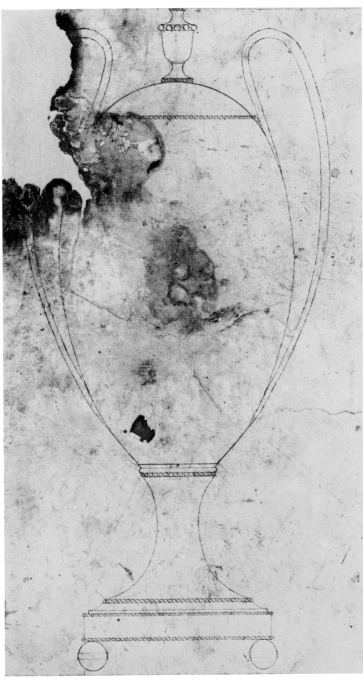

527 Design for an urn

THOMAS JEFFERSON 1743–1826
Ink on laid paper
31.4 x 41.5 (12⅜ x 16⅜)

Lent by the Massachusetts Historical Society, Boston

This drawing of an urn is very similar to a silver coffee urn now at Monticello, made in 1789 by Jacques-Louis-Auguste Leguay. The drawing differs from the silver urn only in the shape of the lid. It is possible that this drawing is the one referred to in Jefferson's invoice from the Paris silversmith Jean-Baptiste-Claude Odiot. In this invoice, dated June 3, 1789, Odiot charged Jefferson 423 livres for "une Fontainne, pareille au desin." In his account book entry for this purchase, Jefferson noted that he paid Odiot 423 livres for a "coffee pot as a present to Clerissault [*sic*]." Charles-Louis Clérisseau, the noted French architect,

had assisted Jefferson in the design of the Virginia state capitol building, and originally Jefferson had considered presenting Clérisseau with a silver copy of a Roman askos unearthed at the site of the Maison Carrée at Nîmes, the building after which the capitol had been modeled. Instead he gave Clérisseau the silver coffee urn, which Jefferson felt was "moins singulier, mais antique et beau." C.G.

528 Coffee urn

JACQUES-LOUIS-AUGUSTE LEGUAY
active late 18th century
Silver 1789
34 (13⅜) high; 11.1 (4⅜) diam.

Lent by the Thomas Jefferson Memorial Foundation, Charlottesville

This silver coffee urn was made in Paris in 1789 by the silversmith Jacques-Louis-Auguste Leguay, whose mark appears on the base and the lid. The discovery of Greek and Roman vases and urns during the mid-eighteenth century led to the development of highly conventionalized urns such as this one, and similar examples were made in both England and America during the last quarter of the eighteenth century.

This urn by Leguay may have been the inspiration for Jefferson's drawing of an urn, shown at number 527, which is identical except for the shape of the lid. It is possible that Jefferson's drawing is the design referred to in the silversmith Jean-Baptiste-Claude Odiot's invoice of June 3, 1789, in which he billed Jefferson 423 livres for "une Fontainne, pareille au desin." There is no doubt that this urn was intended as a present for the French architect Charles-Louis Clérisseau, for Jefferson noted that he "pd. Odiot for a coffee pot as a present to Clerisault [sic] for his assistance about the draughts & model of capitol and prison, 423⫣." Unfortunately the whereabouts of the urn given to Clérisseau is not known, but it would be interesting to know whether it matches the urn by Leguay with those modifications to the lid shown in Jefferson's drawing.

It would appear that Jefferson purchased as many as three coffee urns while in Paris, for in addition to the Leguay urn and the one bought from Odiot on June 3, 1789, there is what appears to be an earlier purchase of an urn from Odiot on February 6, 1789. In his accounts for that date, Jefferson noted:

pd for a silver coffee pot 309⫣
pd for mending my own coffee pot, 12⫣

After the entry for the coffeepot costing 309 livres, Jefferson lined out, "present for Clerisault [sic] for his troubles about the draughts and model for Capitol & prison 309 to be charged to Virginia." In his payment to Odiot on June 3 for the urn given to Clérisseau, Jefferson mentioned that he was paying Odiot an additional 100⫣ to correct an error in his February account, thus making the payments for the two urns more equal: 409 livres for the first urn, and 423 livres for the second. It is possible that the coffeepot that Odiot mended on February 6 was the one purchased earlier from Leguay. This leaves two urns accounted for, the Leguay urn now at Monticello and the Odiot urn presented to Clérisseau. The fate of the first urn by Odiot is not known, for it cannot be accounted for either as a gift or as part of Jefferson's personal possessions.
C.G.

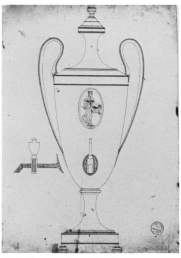

529 Design for a Coffee Urn

JEAN-BAPTISTE-CLAUDE ODIOT
1763–1850
Pen 1785–1790

Lent by M. J. Gaube du Gers, Paris

530 Pair of goblets

After JEAN-BAPTISTE-CLAUDE
ODIOT 1763–1850
Silver

Lent by Mme Georges Pompidou, Paris

The goblets are part of a set of six modern copies made for presentation to President Pompidou in 1969 from a surviving pair, now in a private collection. The original goblets were made by Odiot from a design by Jefferson (see no. 531). Odiot's invoice of June 3, 1789, indicates that there was, in addition, a model, presumably in some base metal, that Jefferson had had made. At the same time the silversmith charged Jefferson for the

second of the coffee urns he had made, also to a design of Jefferson's (see no. 527). The shape and profile of the goblets are fully in accord with his neoclassical ideas of simplicity, and their effectiveness lies in their shape rather than in details of decoration.
R.W.

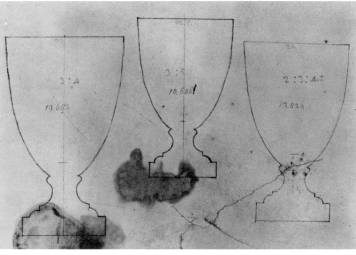

531 Profiles for goblets

THOMAS JEFFERSON 1743–1826
Pencil
20.3 x 31.1 (8 x 12¼)

Lent by the Massachusetts Historical Society, Boston

This drawing of three goblets of varying proportions was executed while Jefferson was in France. A pair of silver goblets virtually identical in design, bearing the Paris date letter for 1789, were part of Jefferson's estate at the time of his death, and descended to the widow of his grandson Meriwether Lewis Randolph. These goblets may be the pair mentioned in Jefferson's invoice of June 3, 1789, from the silversmith Jean-Baptiste-Claude Odiot. This invoice lists, in addition to the silver coffee urn that Jefferson presented to Clérisseau, "Deux Goblet, Pareille au Model," at a cost of 223 livres.

Unfortunately neither goblet bears a legible maker's mark. The largest goblet in the drawing has a diameter, at its mouth, of 27 lignes, while the silver goblets have a diameter of approximately 33 lignes each. This may indicate that Jefferson used this drawing to determine the proportions, and then made another drawing to the proper scale. Since Odiot notes that he made the goblets from a model, it is possible that Jefferson had a wooden or base metal model made from one of his drawings which Odiot used for a pattern. C.G.

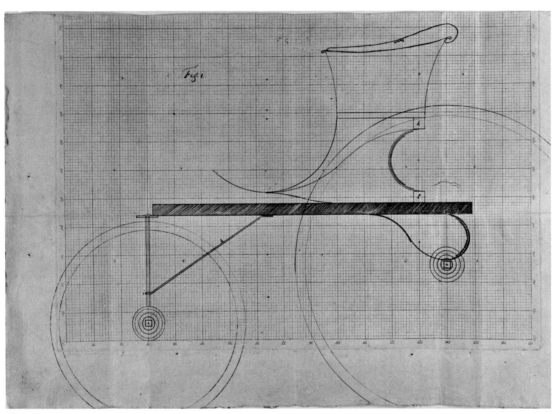

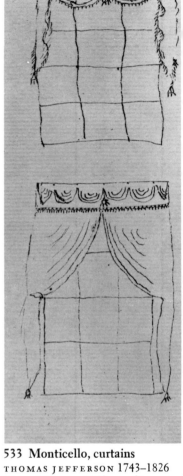

532 Carriage

THOMAS JEFFERSON 1743–1826
Ink 1788–1789?
53.2 x 34.3 (20¹⁵⁄₁₆ x 13½)

Lent by the University of Virginia, Alderman Library, Charlottesville

While in Paris Jefferson was interested in having a simple but elegant carriage made. As this drawing shows, it had great distinction, and the following letter to baron de Geismer dated November 20, 1789, throws some light on the transaction:

You have had great reason, my dear Sir, to wonder that you have been so long receiving an answer to your request relative to the drawing of a cabriolet and phaeton. Your object was to have such drawings as that a workman could work by them. A painter's eye draught would not have answered this purpose, and, indeed, to be sure of having them done with the accuracy necessary to guide a workman, I could depend on nobody but myself. But the work was to be done principally in an open court and there came on between two

and three months of such intense cold as rendered this impossible. Since the season has become milder I have devoted such little scraps of time to this object as I was master of, and I now enclose you the drawings. They are made with such scrupulous exactness in every part that your workman may safely rely on them. I must except from this the drawing of the carriage—*la train*—of the phaeton. I took less pains about this because I did not like it. They make light crans-necks which are preferable. This drawing was made for the sake of the body—*la caisse*—the circular ribs of that are round rods of iron about a half inch diameter. If you would have the body of the cabriolet higher it is made so by raising the lock between the shaft and axle, or by putting in its place an iron in this form, ⏛ . . . . F.N.

533 Monticello, curtains

THOMAS JEFFERSON 1743–1826
Ink on laid paper 1803 or earlier
6.6 x 20.6 (2⅝ x 8⅛)

Lent by the Massachusetts Historical Society, Boston

There are no records of curtains for the original house at Monticello. Just after the revolution, when Jefferson was in Philadelphia, he purchased some curtains. During his last illness in 1826, he told his grandson, Thomas Jefferson Randolph, that the curtains of his bed "had been purchased from the first cargo that arrived after the peace of 1782." In the account book for 1783, Jefferson wrote, just before he left Philadelphia:

April 8. paid for printed linens £6
 " 10. 9½ yd. linen £5⅝:
22½ do. £7-6

These linens, amazingly durable to have lasted for so long, probably were *toiles de Jouy*, which were newly fashionable prints made from engraved copper plates, which had been invented in the 1770s by Oberkampf.

They were usually sold in mono-
chrome, chiefly in red.

While Jefferson was in Paris, his
account books reveal many purchases
of textiles for curtains. They show
that from December 20, 1784, to
February 2, 1786, he ordered both
toiles de Jouy and damask. A specific
order was placed on March 2, 1785,
for seven pairs of lawn curtains, three
pairs of red damask window curtains,
three pairs of blue damask window
curtains, blue damask bed curtains, two
pairs of red calico window curtains,
and two sets of red calico bed curtains. These curtains were listed in the
contents of eighty-six packing cases
of Jefferson's furnishings, shipped to
Philadelphia in 1790, after his return
home. When he retired to Monticello in 1793, the silk curtains were
probably used in Jefferson's own room,
in the drawing room, the dining
room, and the pair of bow rooms. At
that time all of the windows were
of the same size. The only material in
sufficient quantity for the windows of
the drawing room was the blue damask.
There were six large curtains and
eight medium size ones, which would
have been sufficient for the ten large
curtains needed. The six red damask
curtains would just barely have been
sufficient for the four pairs of curtains
then needed for Jefferson's bedroom
and the dining room.

In 1801, when Jefferson had moved
into the president's house in Washington, he added to the furnishings. In
a drawing dated January 12, 1803,
he shows the manner of treating one
of the dimity curtains which had been
used for the large dining room and
for many of the bedrooms. Since the
red damask curtains from Paris were
almost twenty years old, they must
have begun to show some wear, and
as the dimensions on the drawing show
how Jefferson had reduced the size
to suit the dining room window at
Monticello (which was 5 ft. 8 in. wide),
we can assume that he was planning
to adopt the blue and white Wedgewood color combination which he used
in his later years at Monticello.

In the years 1804–1805 Jefferson
made a "list of red curtains" which
included twelve old red ones, which he
planned to use in the new mezzanine
windows at Monticello. As there were
only six crimson damask curtains,
these were probably the toiles de Jouy
which were made over into the seven
pairs of window curtains and three
pairs for alcove beds.

On March 2, 1808, Jefferson
ordered new curtains and referred to a
drawing enclosed with his order. He
asked for "drapery for the tops of
4 windows (no curtains being desired)
somewhat in the style here drawn,
of crimson damask silk, lined with

green and a yellow fringe. In the House
of Representatives are two small
prints with drapery in this style which
will give a just idea of what is desired."
For his own bedroom he also planned
a counterpane of the same crimson
silk as the draperies, again writing to
John Rea in Philadelphia to ask for
"a counterpane of such crimson
mantua silk as the draperies which
Mr. R. formerly furnished to Mr. J.
2½ yds. long and the same width with
a crimson fringe or other suitable
bordering at the side and foot. No
lining as it is to be lined with furs
which are here; and not to be hollowed
over the bolster in the French manner, but plain as is usual with us."
This fur-lined coverlet may have been
for the "couch on which Jefferson
reclined while studying" referred to
on Cornelia Jefferson Randolph's plan
of the house, and it may also have
been used for the bed alcove.

The drawing for draperies with a
striped calico valance was intended for
one of the "square rooms" also at
Monticello. It is now used in the south
square room, which was the room
of Jefferson's daughter Martha Jefferson Randolph.

Due to his generosity in signing a
note for a cousin who went bankrupt,
Jefferson's last years were spent in
extreme poverty. In the inventory
made after his death in 1826, now in
the collection of the Massachusetts
Historical Society, only six sets of curtains, the draperies to two windows,
and three curtains for the lower parts
of windows were left in the large
house of twenty rooms. F.N.

534 Clock

CHANTROT active late 18th century
Black marble, brass and ormolou;
the works are brass and have a
pin-pallet escapement
43.8 x 31.1 x 15.8 (17¼ x 12¼ x 6¼)
Marked at the top of the dial.
Chantrot A Paris

Lent anonymously

After his return to America in 1790,
Jefferson sent to William Short in
Paris a list of instructions for procuring
household furniture. Included in the
list were specifications for a clock
and a sketch showing the general design for the base and case, which
Jefferson described as follows:

This, Mr. Short may recollect, was
the form of the little clock which
was stolen from the chimney of my
study. The parts a.b. c.d. were parts
of a cone, being round and tapering to the top, where a gilt head was
put on. I would wish one to be
made like that, as to the pedestal
part, but with obelisks as is represented here a.b. c.d. instead of

conical columns as the former had.
No gilt head to be on the obelisk,
but to be in plain marble, cut off
obliquely as is always done in the
obclisk. The section of an obelisk,
you know, is a square; I mean its
iconography.

The clock to have a pendulum
vibrating half seconds exactly, To
have a second hand, but none for the
days of the week, month, or moon.
To strike the hours and half hours.
The dial plate to be open work, or as
the French workmen say, le cadran
a jour, of black marble. The superintendant of the Salle des ventes
(where I bought mine) undertook
to have a clock on the above plan
made for me, for either 12. or 15.
guineas, I forget which. He required
only 3. or 4. weeks. I shall be obliged
to Mr. Short to have one made
immediately for me, that it may be
done in time to come with my other
things.

While Jefferson specified that Short
apply to the superintendant of the
Salles des ventes to have the clock

535 Folding music stand
Walnut
29 x 30.5 (11½ x 12)

Lent by the Thomas Jefferson Memorial Foundation, Charlottesville

This stand has five adjustable rests to hold sheet music. When not in use, these rests may be folded down to form a small box. When open, the stand provides places for five musicians, one of whom stands and uses the top rest. The present base, upon which the stand revolves, is a replacement. Originally the stand probably sat on a tripod base, permitting it to be placed in the center of a quartet or quintet.

It is very likely that this music stand was made in the cabinet shop at Monticello by one of Jefferson's workmen, and is almost certainly of Jefferson's design. C.G.

made, there were difficulties in agreeing on a price, and, as the work did not progress as rapidly as promised, Short instead engaged Chantrot to make the clock, which was finished in 1791. The clock was first shipped to Jefferson in Philadelphia, and then forwarded to Monticello in 1793 with his other furnishings.

Jefferson's desire for a clock supported by obelisks is undoubtedly related to his long-standing interest in obelisks as architectural elements. He was familiar with obelisks prior to his stay in France through the published designs of James Gibbs and Inigo Jones, and as early as the 1770s he had contemplated incorporating obelisks in his designs for Monticello. That this form continued to hold his interest, even in later life, is evident in his choice of an obelisk for his gravestone in the Monticello cemetery.
C.G.

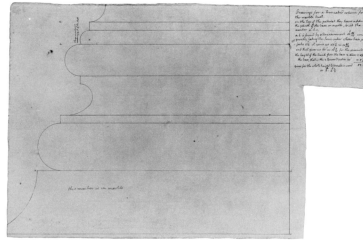

536 Drawing of a base for a pedestal for a bust at Monticello
THOMAS JEFFERSON 1743–1826
Ink on laid paper c. 1803
40 x 24.8 (15¾ x 9¾)

Lent by the Massachusetts Historical Society, Boston

In Europe Jefferson had seen the uses of decorative pedestals to support both antique and modern busts. He made use of these observations at Monticello, where he had an extensive collection of sculpture decorating the main public rooms and halls. No pedestal from this design survives, but a number have been fabricated for this exhibition from the original specifications. F.N.

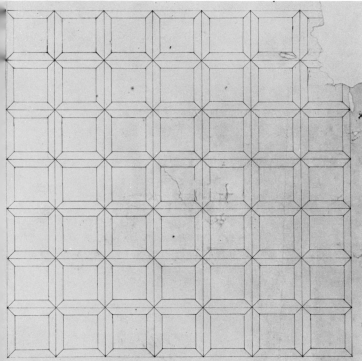

537 Study for parquet floor

THOMAS JEFFERSON 1743–1826
Ink on wove paper c. 1803
27.5 x 29.2 (10⅞ x 11½)

Lent by the Massachusetts Historical Society, Boston

In 1804 Jefferson installed in the parlor at Monticello one of the first parquet floors in America. The floor, according to the diarist Mrs. William Thornton, who visited Monticello in 1806, cost $200. The design, identical to the plan and small section reproduced for this exhibition, was executed with a center square of cherry and a border of beech.

Jefferson's other studies, undoubtedly inspired by similar floors seen in France, include a basket weave pattern and two of concentric squares and hexagons. An undated letter from Gouverneur Morris, believed to be from 1802, indicates that Jefferson provided a plan for a parquet floor that Morris intended to use if his carpenters had not gone too far with a floor of their own design.

W.L.B.

538 Sketch for a candlestick

THOMAS JEFFERSON 1743–1826
Included in a letter from Thomas Jefferson to John Trumbull, August 5, 1789
Facsimile

The security of the Hôtel de Langeac against breaking and entering seems to have worried Jefferson throughout his stay in Paris. In 1789 he mentioned that he was afraid to keep a large sum of money in the house for fear of robbers, and on July 8, 1789, he wrote that, "My hotel having been lately robbed for the third time, I take the liberty of uniting my wish with that of the inhabitants of this quarter, that it coincide with the arrangements of the police to extend to us the protection of a guard."

During those tumultuous days of July 1789, burglars appeared to have worried Jefferson more than the mobs. He wrote to John Trumbull on August 5, 1789, "Tranquillity here is pretty well restored. It has never been what the Londoners believed in their hopes. I never was more tranquil in my house than thro the whole of it. I went much too into the city, and saw there was no danger but for a very few characters. Property was sacred thro' the whole. About a week before those tumults began, I suffered by common robbers, who broke open my house and rifled two apartments."

Among the articles stolen at this time were all of Jefferson's candlesticks, one of which Jefferson sketched in the margin of his letter to Trumbull. As no identical replacements were available in Paris, he wished Trumbull to purchase four pairs in London. He included along with the sketch, the following description of the candlestick: "It was a fluted Corinthian column, with the capital of it's order, and the bottom of the candlestick was of the form in the margin. I recollect to have once seen the undermost form, which I thought very handsome. Mine were about 12. Inches high. I must trouble you therefore to find one of these patterns for me, and indeed I think you will find them in any great shop of plated ware. I think no form is so handsome as that of the column."

Trumbull was successful in obtaining the candlesticks, for he mentioned in a letter of October 3, 1789, that they had been sent to France. On October 10, he enclosed to Jefferson his accounts for articles purchased for Jefferson in London, including, "For Candlesticks £13.13.6." C.G.

539 Two side chairs

Cherry c. 1775–1800
99 x 50.8 x 43.2 (39 x 20 x 17)

Lent by the Thomas Jefferson Memorial Foundation, Charlottesville

Almost certainly of Virginia manufacture, these chairs may have been obtained by Jefferson in Williamsburg. Both the general design of the chairs as well as construction details such as the lack of corner blocks, the shoe for the splat and the rear seat rail made in one piece, and the horizontal shaping of the rear seat rail are consistent with other examples of Williamsburg chairs.

The chairs are numbered on the inside of the rear seat rail, the highest number being XX, indicating that they were probably part of a full set of dining room chairs, perhaps including two armchairs and eighteen side chairs. None of Jefferson's inventories list a specific set of chairs that large, raising the possibility that they were part of a set belonging to George Wythe of Williamsburg, at least seven of which Jefferson inherited. Five of these chairs are at Monticello. C.G.

such as this, perhaps modeled after a French étagère, may be unique in American furniture.

In keeping with every piece of furniture of known Jefferson design, this dumbwaiter displays simple lines and sparse ornamentation. The only decorative elements are the pulls, the small bead along the top of each gallery and the edge of the top, and the tapering legs. It is not known where Jefferson obtained this dumbwaiter. Those that he owned in Paris were not brought back to America, so it must be assumed that this one was made by one of the numerous cabinetmakers that Jefferson patronized in Philadelphia and Washington. At least one dumbwaiter, virtually identical to this one, was made in the cabinet shop at Monticello for use at Poplar Forest. The maker is unknown, but it could have been James Dinsmore, Jefferson's master builder, who is credited by one overseer with having made "a great deal of nice mahogany furniture." The dumbwaiter made at Monticello differs from the one exhibited only in that the moldings are larger, to correspond with the thicker gallery rails; in addition, it lacks the marble top and brass pulls. c.g.

540 Dumbwaiter

Mahogany with brass castors and pulls and marble top
89 x 46.3 (35 x 18¼)

Lent by Mr. R. M. Graham, Baltimore, and Estate of Miss Ellen C. Burke

This rectilinear table, or dumbwaiter, as Jefferson called it, is one of two known examples used at Monticello. Jefferson first used dumbwaiters while serving as minister to France, and he continued their use in the president's house, at Monticello, and at Poplar Forest. Margaret Bayard Smith, a frequent visitor to the president's house during Jefferson's administration, described the use of dumbwaiters:

When he had any persons dining with him, with whom he wished to enjoy a free and unrestricted flow of conversation, the number of persons at table never exceed four, and by each individual was placed a *dumb-waiter*, containing everything necessary for the progress of the dinner from beginning to end, so as to make the attendance of servants entirely unnecessary, believing as he did, that much of the domestic and even public discord was produced by the mutilated and misconstructed repetition of free conversation at dinner tables, by these mute but not inattentive listeners.

Circular dumbwaiters, common in England, were familiar to Jefferson, who had even made a drawing of one; however, a rectilinear dumbwaiter

PLEASURES OF NATURE

The greatest service which can be rendered any country is, to add a useful plant to its culture.
JEFFERSON, a list of services, c. 1800

Mr. Madison and myself . . . visited . . . the principal scenes of General Burgoyne's misfortunes. . . . We were more pleased, however, with the botanical objects which continually presented themselves.
JEFFERSON to Thomas Mann Randolph, June 5, 1791

My old friend Thouin of the National garden at Paris has sent me 700 species of seeds. I suppose they will contain all the fine flowers of France, and fill all the space we have for them. . . .
JEFFERSON to Martha Jefferson Randolph, October 18, 1808

I take the liberty of making it known to the botanist by the name of Jeffersonia, in honour of Thomas Jefferson, Esq., Secretary of State. . . . I have had no reference to his political character. . . . My business was with his knowledge of natural history. In the various departments of this science, but especially in botany and in zoology, the information of this gentleman is equalled by that of few persons in the United States.
BENJAMIN SMITH BARTON, Transactions of the American Philosophical Society, 1798

By his own testimony, Thomas Jefferson would have preferred to be a gardener than to have held any of the high posts that fell to his lot during his lifetime. "I have often thought," he wrote from his retreat at Poplar Forest to the artist, Charles Willson Peale, "that if heaven had given me choice of my position and calling, it would have been a rich spot of earth, well watered, and near a good market for the productions of the garden. No occupation is so delightful to me as the culture of the earth, and no culture comparable to that of the garden."

He believed that the earth belonged to the living, and its care, its cultivation, and the documentation of its infinite variety and mysterious laws made nature the most absorbing interest of the things that engaged his eye, his imagination and his talents.

The first entry in his *Garden Book*, started when he was twenty-two, opens with poetry, "Purple hyacinth begins to bloom," and continues to the end of his life, recording his love affair with growing things, the cycle of growth, perfection, failure and renewal.

With the exception of affairs of state, no subject occurs more frequently in his correspondence. His heritage was that of a planter and farmer. The extensive farmlands he inherited and acquired at an early age, and the detailed attention he had to devote to this large establishment, required an awesome range of practical knowledge, but the skill which he brought to its management was impressive even in a predominantly agricultural age.

But aside from the endless efforts to improve the production of his estates with constant experimentation, Jefferson was also concerned with its visual improvement and ornamentation. The importance of the landscape as a setting for architecture first attracted his imagination as he pored over the books of design and architectural theory in preparing the first plans of Monticello. In his legal notebook of 1771, he sketched some of these ambitious plans, which far exceeded in their scale the romantic detail and architectural ornamentation of temples, grottoes and follies—anything that had been conceived of up to that moment in Colonial America.

Jefferson's youthful fantasies had undoubtedly been fueled by English poets like William Shenstone and philosophers such as Lord Kames, who had been steadily advancing the concept of the picturesque, romantic landscape throughout the early part of the eighteenth century. A number of the books Jefferson recommended to his friend, Robert Skipwith, in 1771 as a basic gentlemen's library included these writers, as well as Thomas Whately's influential *Observations on Modern Gardening*.

When Jefferson and John Adams toured English gardens in 1786, with Whately in hand, Jefferson had already studied and experimented with many of the English ideas and theories on the mountaintop at Monticello. Botany, horticulture, gardening techniques and new landscape designs constantly attracted his eye and interest during his travels. "Garden. Particularly worth the attention of an American," he wrote in his travel instructions to the young tourists, Thomas Shippen and John Rutledge, for America was "the country of all others where the noblest gardens may be made without expense. We have only to cut out the superabundant plants." His approach to the subject was clearly that of an artist capable of handling a very large canvas.

When Jefferson arrived in Paris in 1784, he quickly learned that the new circle of friends that he had met not only shared his interest in painting, sculpture, music and architecture, but were enthusiastic gardeners and landscape students as well. He was constantly asked to acquire native American plants for the gardens of his friends, and his correspondence during the Paris years records his efforts to carry out these commissions. Typical is his letter to John Bartram, Jr., the Philadelphia botanist, enclosing a long list that included the *Kalmia latifolia, Geranium maculatum, Magnolia grandiflora* and the *Chionanthus virginica.*

Wine making and the cultivation of the grape were of particular interest to Jefferson, and he later carried out many experiments of viticulture on his Virginia estates, but without much success. The fig, olive and other European staples were constantly observed and noted as possible candidates for American cultivation. His interest in the famous Italian rice and its introduction into America as a replacement for the wet rice of the Carolinas and Georgia prompted his travels to northern Italy in 1787. Indeed, he had given so much time and attention to rice culture that he was not able to extend his travels further into the country of antiquity, but rather he limited himself as he later wrote to only a "peep into Elysium."

Jefferson's library on natural history and botany was extensive, and his own *Notes on the State of Virginia* was a major addition to the literature of natural philosophy of the eighteenth century. As a guidebook and encyclopedia, it not only discussed the political, legal, and educational institutions of the state but comprehended and described the natural resources of climate, plants, animals and minerals. His list of the birds of Virginia not only gives the popular name but the designations of Linnaeus and Catesby as well.

Jefferson adored birds and he was particularly pleased to receive "a living magpie" among the exotic plants, skeletons, Indian ornaments and minerals which Meriwether Lewis had shipped to the president from the upper Missouri as the expedition progressed westward. His earliest landscape plans for Monticello called for natural preserves as "an asylum for hares, squirrels, pheasants, partridges and other wild animals." During his travels in Europe the nightingale, like the fig tree, is singled out and considered as a possible immigrant to America, though he confides to his daughter that the song of the Virginia mockingbird surpasses anything he had heard in Europe. Margaret Bayard Smith, the early Washington diarist and friend of Jefferson, records an unforgettable portrait of the third president sitting alone in his study in the president's house on a summer evening among his favorite geranium plants and with his pet, uncaged mockingbird flying about in the room. "Whenever he was alone he opened the cage and let the bird fly around the room. . . . when he retired to his chambers it would hop up the stairs after him and while he took his siesta, would set on his couch and pour forth its melodious strains."

Jefferson's contributions to the beginning of landscape planning in America along the informal lines of the English developments must be viewed along with his heroic efforts to make his countrymen aware of good architectural design and proportion. So much of our early landscape architecture has been destroyed or altered that it is difficult to reconstruct the formal garden traditions of Elizabethan and Dutch design which existed at the time that Jefferson first turned his attention to the subject. Perhaps some idea may be gleaned by comparing the rigid, geometric garden designs of John James' *On Gardening*, which was translated from Le Blond's formal style guide, to the ground plan of the poet Shenstone's estate, Leasowes, a famous example of the new English landscape. The idea of an "ornamented farm" which the poet had described appealed strongly to Jefferson, and its influence can be seen in some of his later plans for the Monticello grounds.

From his mountain eyrie, Jefferson was caught up in the dramatic panorama of the Virginia valleys, endless vistas, and mountain ranges so that he had no difficulty in "leaping" the fence and seeing "that all nature was a garden," as Walpole had written earlier about William Kent.

"Love" and "passion" are frequently used by Jefferson to describe his emotions when confronting a piece of architecture or music, but gardening must also be reserved for his stronger feelings, for, as he wrote the comtesse de Tessé, it too "has always been my passion." And it was a passion that was to remain constant to the end. "But though I am an old man," he wrote a friend after leaving the presidency, "I am but a young gardener." W.H.A.

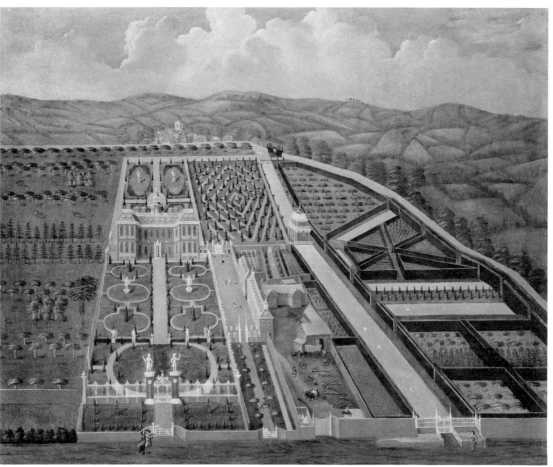

541 A Perspective View of Denham Place

Oil on canvas c. 1695
103.5 x 123.2 (39½ x 48½)

From the Collection of Mr. and Mrs. Paul Mellon

This late seventeenth-century view of Denham Place, Buckinghamshire, a good example of the formal English garden as established under Dutch and French influence. The splendid iron gates and railings are a fitting introduction to the imposing house which had just been built, and the symmetry of the sculpture, the clipped shrubs and hedges, and the patterns of the grass on the main axis are a further means of emphasizing its importance. No attempt at naturalism has been made, and there is still a sharp contrast between the garden and park and the countryside outside their walls. This barrier was to be broken down after the mid-eighteenth century when greater informality in garden design substituted irregularity for symmetry and a natural grouping of trees for the fantastic topiary to the right of the house. An English country house was still to some degree self-supporting, and the farmyard and vegetable and fruit gardens can be seen on either side of the canal.

The gardens of Virginia houses in the eighteenth century would not have been so elaborate as Denham Place, but in a modified form they must have appeared quite similar, with walks and parterres lined by clipped box hedges. The contrast between the "tamed" garden and the landscape outside must have seemed all the greater as the country had been settled so recently. R.W.

542 Formal Garden View

Watercolor, 18th century
26.7 x 43.5 (10½ x 17⅛)

Lent by the Dumbarton Oaks Garden Library, Washington

This view of a formal garden by an unknown artist may depict the central *allée* at Versailles. The symmetrically placed statues, formal parterre, and sweeping vista suggest the central garden court at Versailles designed under Le Nôtre's direction between 1662 and 1668 for Louis XIV. It was against the formal and geometric tradition of Le Nôtre that the French reacted, in the years immediately preceding the Revolution, in favor of the less formal and seemingly more natural English landscape school.

The influential *La théorie et la pratique du jardinage*, which described

COLONIAL INTERPRETATION

543 Plan of Mount Airy

Facsimile
Made by the American Institute of
Architects (reproduced from *Great
Georgian Houses of America*, 1937)

Mount Airy, the estate of Colonel
John Tayloe (1721–1779) in Richmond County, Virginia, was one of the
large houses, surrounded by land-
scaped grounds, that would have been
familiar to Jefferson during his youth
and college years at William and
Mary. Colonel Tayloe, whose grandfather had settled in Lancaster County
in 1650, was one of the wealthiest
men in Virginia and in 1747 had built
Mount Airy on a rising piece of
ground overlooking the Rappahannock
River. The design of the house and
gardens has been attributed to a certain
Colonel Thornton, about whom
little is known except that he was a
close friend. The house, a handsome
stone structure of baronial proportions,
was approached through a deer park,
and on the opposite side, formal
terraced gardens led down to the river
and to an orangerie, the remains of
which still exist.

Philip Vickers Fithian, who tutored
Robert Carter's children at Nomini
Hall and who was a frequent visitor to
Mount Airy, described the estate in
his journal in 1774:

Here is an elegant Seat!—The House
is about the size of Mr. Carters,
built with Stone, & finished curiously,
& ornamented with various paintings, & rich Pictures. . . . He has also
a large well formed beautiful Garden, as fine in every respect as I have
seen in Virginia. In it stand four
large beautiful Marble Statues—
From this House there is a good
prospect of the River Rappahannock.

Jefferson must have known Mount
Airy. Alice Corbin Tayloe of Mount
Airy was the stepmother of John
Page of Rosewell, Jefferson's youthful
companion at William and Mary
and his lifelong friend.

The plan for Mount Airy, reconstructed from surveys in 1916 by the
American Institute of Architects, is
comparable in its general arrangement
to that of Nomini Hall and other
large Virginia estates of the period.
The formal, geometric parterres, the
bowling green and orangerie are
characteristic features of the mid-
eighteenth-century plantation garden.
E.M.

544 Not in Exhibition

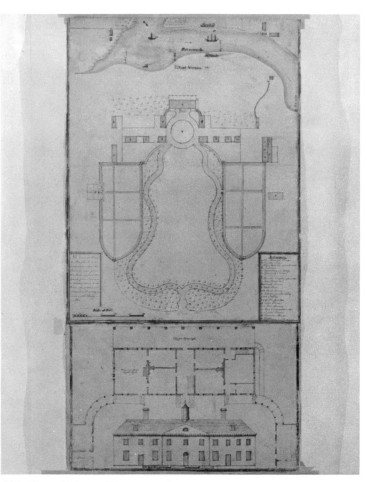

545 Plan of Mount Vernon garden

VON GLUMER after SAMUEL
VAUGHAN active late 18th century
Lithograph
*Lent by Mount Vernon Ladies'
Association of the Union, Virginia*

Washington, like Jefferson, was long
preoccupied with garden design. He
was well acquainted with the two
leading garden books of the period:
Phillip Miller's *Dictionary* and Batty
Langley's *New Principles of Gardening*. In the years 1785–1786 he cleared
the land for his "Wilderness," trans-
planted trees and began to lay out
the serpentine road enclosing the great
lawn on the west side of the mansion
house, Mount Vernon.

The plan of Mount Vernon, attributed to Samuel Vaughan and presented to General Washington in
November 1787, is based on notes by
Vaughan at Mount Vernon several
months earlier. Clearly shown are the
great serpentine road, the flower
and kitchen gardens and the adjoining
shrubberies.

The architect Benjamin Latrobe,
who visited Washington in 1796, gave
the following account of the gardens: "The ground on the west front
of the house is laid out in a level lawn
bounded on each side with a wide
but extremely formal serpentine walk
shaded by weeping willows. . . . On
one side of this is a plain kitchen
garden, on the other a neat flower
garden laid out in squares and boxed
with great precision. . . ." E.M.

e Nôtre's ideas, was first published
1709 and attributed to Joseph
ezallier d'Argentville and later to
lexandre Le Blond; it was published
an English translation in 1712.
utch and German translations in
any editions also appeared extending
e Nôtre's influence.

Earlier, the elaborate garden designs
André Mollet, characterized by
abesque scrolls and volutes similar
the parterre shown in the Dum-
arton Oaks watercolor, were intro-
uced in *Le Jardin de Plaisir*, pub-
shed in 1651.

The French garden style reflected
the lucid rules and engraved plans
f motifs, scrolls and even monograms
ontained in these and other books
uickly became the rage of Holland,
ermany, Sweden and to a lesser
xtent England.

The first English translation of *La
héorie et la pratique du jardinage*
y John James, called *The Theory and
ractice of Gardening*, went through
any editions and extended the
rench influence not only in England
ut to its North American colonies
s well. Something of these geometric
arden schemes can be seen in the
arliest Virginia gardens, and it is not
urprising that Jefferson's first book
n gardening was an edition of James
see no. 53). His own taste was more
ompatible, however, with the natural,
omantic plans based on the English
andscape theories. W.H.A.

546 View of William and Mary College

Engraving (facsimile) c. 1740

Jefferson knew well the gardens at Williamsburg, where he lived most of the time between 1759 and 1770, first as a student at the College of William and Mary and later as a lawyer. He disliked, however, the formal, geometric style of gardening he found there and as early as 1771 made clear his preference for the new English style of gardening, advanced by the contemporary garden theorists Horace Walpole and Thomas Whately.

This composite view of William and Mary is a modern restrike of a copper plate found at the Bodleian Library at Oxford University. It may be based on an original drawing of about 1740 by the Philadelphia botanist John Bartram, who also corresponded with Jefferson's grandfather, Isham Randolph, on plants. According to Isaac Stokes, the Bartram drawing may have been intended to illustrate William Byrd's *History of the Dividing Line,* a work circulated in manuscript form during Byrd's lifetime and published with this engraving in 1841. Bartram briefly visited William Byrd II in 1738 at his James River estate, Westover, and declared in a letter to Peter Collinson that with its "new gates, gravel walks, hedges and cedars finely twined . . . it was the finest seat in Virginia."

The plate is divided into three panels. In the upper panel is a view of the college, showing a formal topiary garden in the foreground. The second panel shows, from left to right, the southern façade of the colonial capitol, the western façade of the Wren building, and the southern façade of the governor's palace. In the bottom panel are unidentified botanical specimens and insects, flanked by two Indians. E.M.

546a Plan of a Garden—Rosewell?

Ink on laid paper mid-18th century
34.9 x 53.4 (13¾ x 21)

Lent by the Massachusetts Historical Society, Boston

This plan of a formal garden two hundred and forty feet wide, extending four hundred and fifty feet from the façade of a building, terminating with a ha-ha wall is an intriguing and

unidentified American landscape document. As a part of the collection of Jefferson drawings in the Coolidge Collection at the Massachusetts Historical Society, it was among the architectural drawings that were collected in Virginia by Thomas Jefferson Coolidge, but it is clearly not in Jefferson's hand, nor does it relate to any known garden designed by him.

It appears to be an eighteenth-century measured drawing of an existing garden and of a scale that would relate to only the most princely Virginian establishments, such as the governor's palace in Williamsburg, Mount Airy or Rosewell. From what is known of the palace grounds and of Mount Airy, they can be eliminated as likely candidates.

Because of Jefferson's early association with Rosewell and the Page family, Mr. John Bedenkapp, who has reconstructed the plans of Rosewell for the model (see no. 8), has suggested that the plan is of the garden of the famous Page manor house, begun in the 1720s. Jefferson's long visits there with John Page made him familiar with the Gloucester County, Virginia, estate on the York River and it is completely consistent with his interest in garden design to have secured a plan of such an imposing landscape scheme from a member of the Page family. By juxtaposing the floor plan of Rosewell onto the garden, following the few clues the drawing provides in the dimensions of the façade of a house and the location of the steps, Mr. Bedenkapp has further reinforced his supposition through an analysis of the close relationship of key architectural elements of the house to the garden layout itself. The long parallel hedges defining the central walk line up with the fenestration on either side of the entrance as indicated by the sketchy steps in the garden plan. The outer walks created by these hedges are on a line with the two cupolas on the roof of the house which are its chief vertical features.

No contemporary descriptions of Rosewell's garden have been discovered, but one can assume that its scale and development would have been in keeping with the grandeur of the manor house. If further research and detailed study of the physical remains of the grounds should confirm that the drawing is indeed of the gardens of Rosewell before the Revolution, it would be one of the earliest extant American landscape plans that has survived. W.H.A.

47 A View from the West Side of the Island in the Garden of the Hon. Charles Hamilton at Painshill near Cobham in Surry

WILLIAM WOOLLETT 1735–1785
Engraving, 1760, in Thomas
Whately, *Observations on Modern
Gardening* (London: West and
Hughes, 1801)

Signed lower right: W. Woollett del.
et sculp.

Lent by The Victoria and Albert
Museum

Painshill, the estate of Charles Hamilton near Cobham in Surrey, was one of the places visited by Jefferson in his tour of English gardens in 1786. The park and gardens had been laid out in the 1750s by Hamilton according to principles of picturesque landscape design. Hamilton, who had enthusiastically studied the paintings of Lorrain and Poussin, achieved at Painshill a total unity of design which Southcote at Woburn farm and Lyttleton at Hagley were less successful in attaining.

Thomas Whately, who was, with Horace Walpole, the leading garden critic of the period, gave high praise to Painshill: "Throughout the illustrious scene consistency is preserved in the midst of variety; all the parts unite easily. The groves the lawns and the declivities are elegant and rich; the fine expanse of the lake, enlivened by the gay plantations on the banks, and the reflections of the bridge upon the surface, animates the landscape; and the extent and the height of the

hanging wood an air of grandeur to the whole."

Jefferson agreed with Whately's judgment of Painshill and with his general principles of design. Jefferson, who counted landscape "the 7th fine art," recognized, too, the relationship of painting to landscape composition. Writing of Painshill in a memorandum of his tour, he noted, "323 as. garden and park all in one. Well described by Whately." He went on to say that he had particularly admired the Doric temple by the lake, though he did not like, as Walpole did not, what he considered to be Hamilton's overuse of evergreens.

At Monticello, Jefferson sought to carry out a plan along principles which would unite the upper and lower parts of the site by means of a series of "roundabouts" or walks encircling the mountain. Faced with a difficult topography, Jefferson's solution was ingenious, though in his mind imperfect. Writing to his friend William Hamilton of The Woodlands, near Philadelphia (no apparent relative of the Hamilton of Painshill), he described some of the difficulties he faced:

The grounds which I destine to improve in the style of the English gardens are in a form very difficult to be managed. . . . The hill is generally too steep for direct ascent, but we make level walks successively along its side, which in its upper part encircle the hill & intersect

these again by others of easy ascent in various parts. . . . You are sensible that this disposition of the ground takes from me the first beauty in gardening, the variety of hill & dale, & leaves me as an awkward substitute a few hanging hollows and ridges. . . .

E.M.

548 Plan for the Leasowes
Ink (facsimile), c. 1764

Jefferson had seen this plan for the Leasowes reproduced in William Shenstone's *Works*, which was one of the books he recommended for a basic library to young Robert Skipwith in 1771.

Designed by Shenstone, the Leasowes, near Birmingham, was one of the most celebrated farms in England, a place, as Dr. Johnson said, "visited by travelers and copied by designers." Thomas Whately called the Leasowes a perfect picture of Shenstone's mind: "simple, elegant and aimiable." It was, in Whately's phrase, "literally a grazing farm," and "in every part rural and natural."

Jefferson visited the Leasowes on the English garden tour he took with John Adams in April 1786 and seemed to find it too plain for his taste, noting, "The waters small. This is not even an ornamented farm. It is only a grazing farm with a path round it. Here and there a seat of board, rarely any thing better. Architecture has contributed nothing. The obelisk is of brick. . . ." He was pleased with "the 1st and 2nd cascades," however, and with the ninety-degree "prospect at 32," a high point in the walk where Jefferson could see the Welsh mountains from which his ancestors had come and which probably also reminded him of Monticello, with its mountainous vistas. E.M.

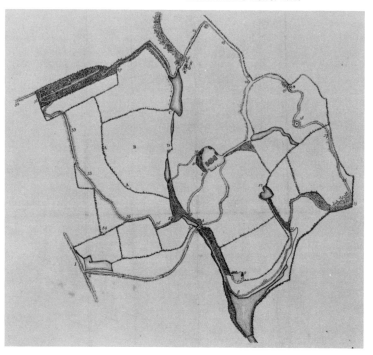

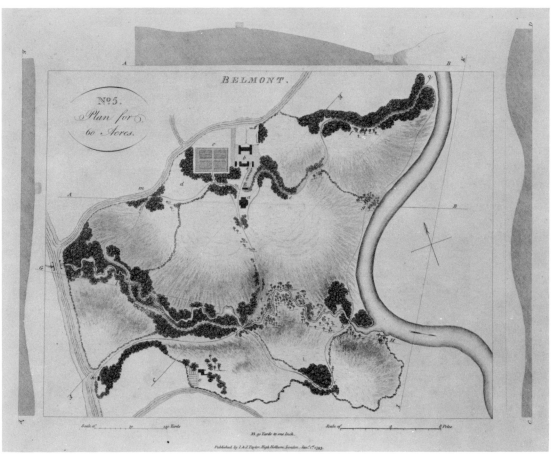

one of the first places that Jefferson visited on his garden tour of 1786. He was critical of the artificiality of the gardens and wrote in his "Notes of a Tour of English Gardens,"

Cheswick. Belongs to D. of Devonshire. Garden about 6. acres. The Octagonal dome has an ill effect, both within and without; the garde shews still too much of art; an obelisk of very ill effect. Another in the middle of a pond useless.

William Kent was born of humble parents in Yorkshire but attracted t attention of Lord Burlington for his remarkably varied designing skills, which are said to have encompassed everything from barges to wedding dresses. In 1724, Burlington persuade Kent to edit the *Designs of Inigo Jones*, and in 1730 Kent succeeded t "phlegmatic" Charles Bridgeman as designer of the gardens at Chiswick, ushering in a more naturalistic approach to garden design that was embraced by such influential critics as Whately and Horace Walpole, who said of Kent that he had "leaped the fence" and seen "that all nature was garden." In the gardens at Carleton House, Claremont and Stowe, Kent discarded geometric principles in fav of a freer approach, which, though classical in its references, emphasized serpentine walks, shadowy groves, and other features designed to give a more informal effect.

Kent's drawing of the exedra, a semicircular seat for relaxation and conversation, is characteristic of his rather fanciful approach to landscape. Ancient statues, memorial vases, and hermae are arranged against a background of architecturally cut hedges. Three leaping dogs in the foreground enliven the scene and seem to announce the arrival of strolling guests from another part of the garden. E.M.

549 Plan for Belmont

GEORGE ISHAM PARKYNS
1749–1820
Engraving 1793, in George Isham Parkyns, *Six Designs for Improving and Embellishing Grounds with Sections and Explanations* (London: printed for I. and J. Taylor, 1793)
From the Collection of Mr. and Mrs. Paul Mellon

Jefferson's enthusiasm for this *Plan of Belmont* by George Isham Parkyns, with its series of encircling walks that link together the various elements of a working farm, led him to try to obtain Parkyns' help in designing the grounds of Monticello. Parkyns, however, who had visited this country between 1794 and 1800 and had traveled as far south as Mount Vernon, had evidently returned to England by the time Jefferson sought his advice. In a letter to his friend William Hamilton in July 1806, Jefferson said, "I had once hoped to get Parkins to go and give me some outlines, but I was disappointed."

Parkyns had published "Six Designs," of which the plan for Belmont was one, in 1793 as an appendix to Sir John Soane's *Sketches in Architecture*. The "Six Designs" were hypo-

thetical plans for "ornamented farms" in Nottinghamshire, which he considered "one of the most romantic counties in Great Britain." Parkyns' object in each of the plans was to create a variety of visual experiences while respecting the natural topography of the site, a philosophy that must have appealed to Jefferson, faced with the recalcitrance of his particular topography at Monticello. E.M.

550 Exedra at Chiswick

WILLIAM KENT 1665–1748
Pen and ink with brown wash over pencil, c. 1730
29.2 x 40 (11½ x 15¾)
Lent by the Trustees of the Chatsworth Settlement, Devonshire Collection, Chatsworth

Chiswick, built in 1725 by Lord Burlington as a suburban retreat, was

551 Hagley, View from Thomson's Seat

Engraving (facsimile)

Jefferson had absorbed the important artistic and landscape theory of the period long before his tour of English gardens, and he was prepared to admire some places more than others. Hampton Court, for instance, he nearly dismissed because of its excessive formality, whereas Hagley, the estate of George Lyttleton, near Birmingham, was one of his favorites. Situated in a fertile valley not far from the Welsh border, Hagley seemed to combine, as Thomas Whately had said, "the excellencies of park and garden."

As early as 1770, Jefferson had read William Hogarth's *Analysis of Beauty*, which stressed the attractions of the serpentine line and the principle of intricacy and variety in art. Edmund Burke took the same view when he said that the "principal property of beautiful objects is that the line of their parts is continually varying its direction." A third influence on Jefferson's eye was Lord Kames' *Elements of Criticism*, in which the author extended the principle of variety in art to gardening. Gardens, according to Kames, were to be designed with "wildness and even surprise and wonder" in mind. Trees were to be distributed in groves to increase the illusion of depth. Straight walks were to be avoided. The winding walk, on the other hand, had the advantage of offering a fresh prospect at every step. Such ideas were marked with the stamp of "good taste" in 1780 by Horace Walpole in his essay, *Taste in Gardening*, which added to Whately's earlier *Observations on Modern Gardening* and which comprised the last word in romantic gardening criticism.

Hagley had been designed with the guidance of such principles of variety, wildness and wonder. Beyond the charm of the wooded park, the cascades which enlivened the terraced hillsides were "a dazzling prospect," said one contemporary writer, "full of a thousand objects, animated by gaiety, variety and rural magnificence."

Beyond the success of the physical design, the literary associations of Hagley must have pleased Jefferson. Alexander Pope's favorite walk was at Hagley, and the poet James Thomson said that "Hagley was the place in England he most desired to see." Lyttleton, who was himself an amateur poet, dedicated seats at Hagley to Thomson and Pope, lending both literary authority and charm to the natural scene. Jefferson noted, as Whately had, the blending of park and gardens and also noted the cascades and, near one cascade, "in a small, dark, deep hollow . . . a Venus pudique, turned half round as if inviting you with her into the recess."

E.M.

552 The House and Gardens at Woburn in Surrey, as laid out by Philip Southcote Esq.

WILLIAM WOOLLETT 1735–1785
Engraving (facsimile)

Woburn Farm, the estate of Philip Southcote, near the village of Chertsey in Surrey, is the first notable example in England of the ornamented farm. The idea, partly borrowed from the French *ferme ornée*, was particularly appealing to the English landed gentry, who sought to unite utility with art. "All my design at first was to have

a garden in the middle ground and a walk all round my farm for convenience as well as pleasure," said Southcote. "From the garden I could see what was doing in the grounds, and by the walk could have a pleasing access to either of them where I might be wanted." Southcote had probably been influenced, in the general scheme for Woburn, by Joseph Addison's *Spectator* essay of 1718, in which he had rhetorically inquired, "Why

may not a whole estate be thrown into a kind of Garden? If the natural Embroidery of the meadows were helpt and improved by some small Additions of Art, and the several rows of Hedges set off by Trees and flowers . . . a man might make a pretty landskip of his own Possessions."

Jefferson visited Woburn Farm in April 1786 and in his "Notes of a Tour of English Gardens" recorded briefly that the kitchen and pleasure

gardens were "intermixed . . . the pleasure garden being merely a highly ornamented walk through and round the divisions of the farm and the kitchen garden."

Jefferson adapted the ornamental farm idea to his own purposes at Monticello, and several sketches from the period 1806–1808 indicate his intention to unite the working elements of the farm by means of a series of walks, or roundabouts. In a note to Edmund Bacon, for many years his overseer, Jefferson wrote in February 1808, "In the open grounds on both of 3d. and 4th Roundabouts lay off lots for the minor articles of husbandry for experimental culture, disposing them into a ferme ornée and by interspersing occasionally the attributes of a garden." Added to experimental orchards were lots for clover and lucerne and, in one of Jefferson's most ingenious and attractive designs, a labyrinth of Scotch broom, designed for "winter enjoyment" in the form of a pinwheel.

Jefferson does not mention the abundance of American plants in the garden at Woburn, but they cannot have escaped his attention. Southcote' relative, Lord Petre, was one of the earliest sponsors of the botanists and hybridizers John Bartram and his son William, whose garden near Philadelphia attained international fame. In the planting plan for Woburn, preserved by Spence, were a number of American plants including holly, laurel, chestnut, and black poplar, all undoubtedly imported from the Bartram nursery. E.M.

553 Bird's Eye Perspective of Stowe House, Buckinghamshire

Attributed to CHARLES BRIDGEMAN
d. 1738
Ink, pencil and wash c. 1720
41.9 x 95.2 (16½ x 37½)
Lent by the Bodleian Library, Oxford

Jefferson visited Stowe, the estate of

the powerful Grenville family, in 1786. The gardens had been successively altered over a forty-year period, first by Charles Bridgeman in association with the architect, John Vanbrugh, then by William Kent, and finally by Capability Brown. It was

Bridgeman who provided the basic structure, still visible at the time of Jefferson's visit.

A *Bird's Eye Perspective of Stowe House*, attributed to Bridgeman, bears out Jefferson's observation of the "straight," which he called "very ill,"

approach to the house, and the essentially formal and geometric character of the gardens prior to their romantic revision in the 1730s and 1740s by Kent and Brown. E.M.

to by Jefferson in his *Notes on the State of Virginia* and in his *Garden Book*. Jefferson owned a copy of the 1768 edition of Miller's *Dictionary* as well as a French edition, published in 1785. Jefferson also owned Miller's *Gardeners Kalendar*, another useful and widely circulated book giving instructions on a variety of subjects of interest to Jefferson such as pruning fruit trees, forcing hyacinths and transplanting endive.

Through Peter Collinson and Dr. John Fothergill, Miller received at the garden in Chelsea a number of plants from the Bartram nursery at Philadelphia. Miller listed in 1735, and in subsequent editions of the *Dictionary*, dogwood, dwarf Virginia chestnut and Weymouth pine among the trees introduced from the American colonies. In response to the almost explosive demand for new plants and landscape information, Miller also gave, in the eight successive editions of his *Dictionary*, some practical advice on the subject of laying out gardens. Under the general heading "Wildernesses," Miller advised his readers to plant shades of American evergreens and to arrange walks in the "form of a serpent," an instruction which reflected growing interest in picturesque gardening as advanced by Walpole, Alexander Pope and others, who came to associate a freer approach in garden design with individual freedom.

Cole's perspective view of Chelsea Physick Garden, done in 1735, depicts a fanciful classical allegory of agriculture and gardening, above, and a schemtic plan of the gardens, below, showing the categories of garden mentioned in the subtitle: "The Kitchen, Fruit and Flower Garden and also the Physick Garden, Wilderness, Conservatory and Vineyard."

E.M.

554 Perspective View of Chelsea Physick Garden

B. COLE active early 18th century
Engraving, in Philip Miller, *The Gardeners Dictionary* (London: printed for the author, 1735)
Lent by the Dumbarton Oaks Garden Library, Washington

The Chelsea Physick Garden was the botanic center of Great Britain for the greater part of the eighteenth century. Now an enclosed site in a residential district of London, the garden once formed a part of the manor of Chelsea. Sir Hans Sloane, a wealthy London doctor and a Fellow of the Royal Society, purchased the property in 1712, deeding it to the Worshipful Society of Apothecaries of London, an organization with a strong interest in the importation of plants for their medicinal value, in 1722.

The garden was in its heyday under Philip Miller (1691–1771), a Scotch gardener who became director in 1722 and published in 1731 the first folio edition of the *Gardeners Dictionary*, one of the principal books referred

555 Gardens of Bagatelle

FRANÇOIS-JOSEPH BÉLANGER
1744–1818
Watercolor and ink c. 1784

Lent by the Bibliothèque nationale

Thomas Jefferson visited the gardens of the Bagatelle with Maria Cosway in the spring and summer of 1786, and later in his famous "Dialogue Between My Head and My Heart," he recalled their excursions to the Bagatelle, the Désert de Retz, and other gardens, remembering it as a time when "every moment was filled with something agreeable."

The property for the Bagatelle had been purchased in 1775 by the comte d'Artois, brother of Louis XVI and a man of vast energy, who had become associated with the follies and architectural extravagances of the last years of the Ancien Régime. On a bet of 100,000 francs, he offered to rebuild the château within two months. He won his bet and soon afterwards began work on the garden. It was François-Joseph Bélanger who designed the gardens in the so-called new English style. Bélanger's plan, which superseded the naive design of the Scottish gardener Thomas Blaikie (1750–1838), who had first shaped the gardens, was more sophisticated and better suited to the taste of the period. He had traveled extensively in England in the 1760s and seems to have combined in the plan for the Bagatelle everything he had seen at Kew, Stowe, Painshill and Hagley, as well as several fanciful elements of his own. Here for the amusement of Marie-Antoinette and members of her court were Chinese pavilions, Gothic hermitages, rockeries, and a philosopher's grotto. It was in the Bagatelle gardens that Bélanger arranged magical and musical performances for the queen. E.M.

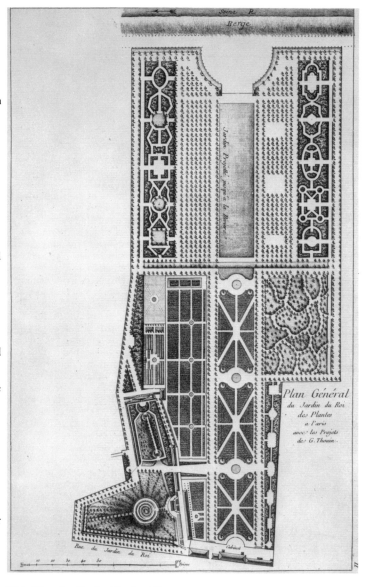

556 Plan for the Jardin des Plantes

GEORGE-LOUIS LE ROUGE
active 1776–1780
Engraving c. 1777

Jefferson often visited the Jardin des Plantes during the period of his residence in Paris, and after his return to the United States he corresponded for years with the head gardener André Thouin, who devoted a lifetime to the king's collection of living plants and seeds. Thouin, whom Jefferson referred to as "my antient friend," sent Jefferson an assortment of seeds, which Jefferson planted at Monticello and passed on to other American botanists including Bernard McMahon of Philadelphia and David Hosack, founder of the Elgin Botanic Garden in New York.

This plan of the Jardin des Plantes was drawn several years before Jefferson arrived in Paris by George Le Rouge, who had been instrumental in popularizing the Chinese influence in French landscape design. The organization of the garden, which was founded in 1626 as the Jardin du Roi, is reflected in the categories into which Thouin divided his seeds when he sent them to Jefferson, as described in this letter of May 4, 1811, to Bernard McMahon:

My old friend Thouin, Director of the National garden of France has just sent me a fresh parcel of seeds which he thus describes. 'They consist of about 200. species, foreign to N. America, selected from among 1. The large trees, the wood of which is useful in the arts. 2. small trees & shrubs, ornamental for shrubberies. 3. plants vivacious & picturesque. 4. flowers for parterres. 5. plants of use in medicine & all the branches of rural & domestic economy.'

E.M.

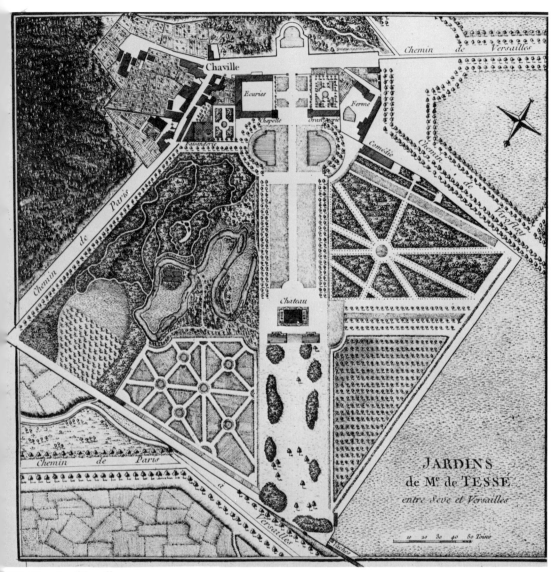

557 Plan for Chaville

GEORGE-LOUIS LE ROUGE
active 1776–1780
Engraving c. 1779
Lent by the Dumbarton Oaks Garden Library, Washington

The comtesse de Tessé, an aunt of the marquis de Lafayette, was one of the leading figures in liberal society in Paris before the Revolution and counted Jefferson one of the intimates of her salon at Chaville, which had been rebuilt in the late 1770s by her neighbor Etienne-Louis Boullée, the architect whose visionary schemes provoked criticism in his own day, and who is considered one of the founders of modern architecture (his *Project for a Museum* and his *Project of a Cenotaph for Newton* are exhibited at nos. 320–323 and 326–327).

Writing to their mutual friend Mme de Tott from Marseilles in April 1787, Jefferson recalled the "charming gardens of Chaville without" and the "charming society within." And in a letter to Mme de Tessé, Jefferson asked the witty and hospitable lady why she, who loved "the precious remains of antiquity, architecture, gardening, a warm sun, and a clear sky," had not thought of moving Chaville to Nîmes. "It would not be so impractical as you may think," continued Jefferson, "to move the Maison Carrée to Paris and bring Chaville to Nîmes."

The plan of the gardens at Chaville, done by the topographic artist George-Louis Le Rouge between 1776 and 1779, indicates some traces of the old style of landscape design, with the straight avenue of trees, the parterres and the axial arrangement of walks. The informal garden to the left of the château is, like Jefferson's garden at the Hôtel Langeac (here exhibited at nos. 559 and 560) consciously modeled after the English style. It was for this informal garden that Jefferson was "commissioned" by Mme de Tessé before he left for the United States to obtain from the botanists William Bartram and Richard Carey American plants such as cedar, laurel, and dogwood, plants which were also included in Boullée's garden nearby. The "botanical commission" of Mme de Tessé preoccupied Jefferson long after his return to America, and during his second term as president, in an affectionate letter to Mme de Tessé who had returned after years of exile in Switzerland to a rented house and garden in Paris, he wrote,

I own, my dear Madame, that I cannot but admire your courage in undertaking now to plant trees. It has always been my passion; insomuch that I rarely planted a flower in my life, but when I return to Monticello, which will be in 1809 at the latest (because then, at any rate, I am determined to draw the curtain between the political world and myself) I believe I shall become a florist.

E.M.

558 Vue du Parc d'Ermenonville

CONSTANTIN BOURGEOIS
1767–1841
Engraving in Alexander de Laborde,
*Description des Nouveaux Jardins de la
France* (Paris: Delance, 1808)

*Lent by Mrs. Thomas S. Kelly,
New York*

The marquis de Giradin (1735–
1808) published a book on landscape
design, *De la Composition des paysages sur le terrain*, in 1777 and at the
same period designed the gardens at
Ermenonville, his estate near Paris, in
the so-called English style. The
philosopher Rousseau, who was a close
friend of Giradin's, retired to
Ermenonville at the end of his life,
and it was there on the Island of
Poplars that Giradin dedicated a
memorial to Rousseau.

Jefferson must have visited the
celebrated gardens at Ermenonville
during the period of his residence in
Paris. They were like the gardens at the
Bagatelle, designed according to
English principles with emphasis on
seeming naturalness. The northern
part of the park was a skillfully engi-
neered piece of marshland—a stagnant
bog, transformed into an "enameled
meadow."

Alexander de Laborde gave the
following account of the park at
Ermenonville: "This enchanting meadow which is here represented was
once formerly a deep bog in which
canals were cut and constantly full of
stagnant water and surrounded with
beam hedges. The marsh has been
drained and there is now to be seen
only a beautiful enameled meadow
ornamented with groves and buildings
variegating and animating the landscape." E.M.

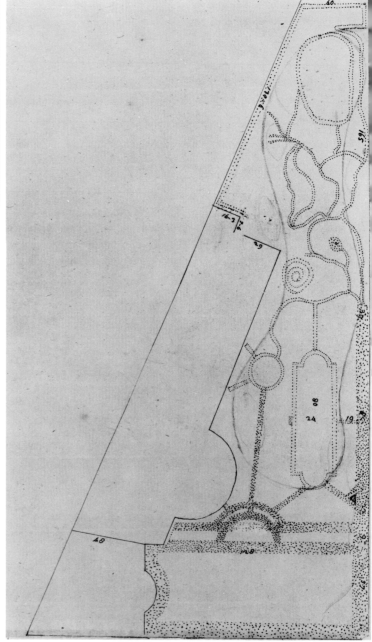

559 Hôtel de Langeac garden

THOMAS JEFFERSON 1743–1826
Ink and wash (facsimile),
1785–1789
*Original at The Huntington Library,
San Marino, California*
(See number 204)

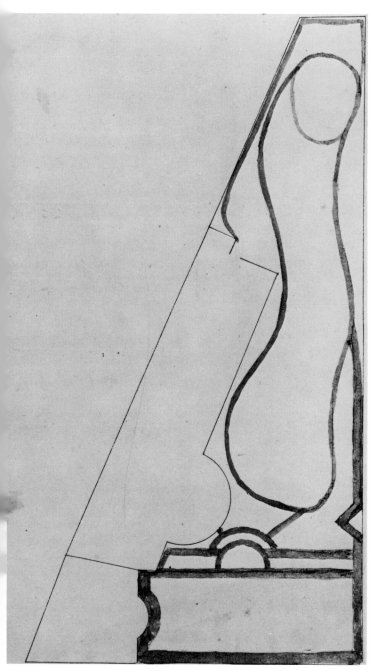

560 Hôtel de Langeac garden
THOMAS JEFFERSON 1743–1826
Ink and wash (facsimile),
1785–1789
*Original at The Huntington Library,
San Marino, California*
(See number 204)

561 Garden Scene
JEAN-DÉMOSTHÈNE DUGOURC
1749–1825
Gouache 1784
31.4 x 43.8 (12⅜ x 17¼)
Signed in pen and black ink on
pedestal: *J. D. Dugourc. Pinxit.*
MD.CC.LXXXIIII

*Lent by The Metropolitan Museum
of Art, Rogers Fund, 1966*

Dugourc's charming and airy garden
scene suggests the mood and spirit
of Jefferson's halcyon days in Paris,
particularly his excursions to gardens
with Maria Cosway in 1786. In
memory of them, Jefferson enclosed in
a letter to Mrs. Cosway, a copy of
his favorite operatic air, "Jours
Heureux" by the Italian composer
Sacchini: "I send you the song I
promised. Bring me in return its subject, Jours Heureux . . . Learn it I
pray you and sing it with feeling."

Jean-Démosthène Dugourc was born
at Versailles. He studied at Rome
and in 1779 published a work on
theatrical costume. Dugourc achieved
considerable reputation in Paris as a
theatrical designer and was closely
associated with the architect François
Bélanger, who designed the house
and gardens of the Bagatelle in 1777–
1778. Dugourc's appointment as
director of decorations and costumes
for the Paris opera in 1783 led to
commissions abroad for Catherine the
Great and the king of Sweden. The
artist turned his decorative talents to
industrial design during the Revolution
and later decorated the royal palace
in Madrid. E.M.

562 View of Washington
GEORGE ISHAM PARKYNS
1749–1820
Aquatint 1795
64.1 x 52.7 (25¼ x 20¾)
Lent by the Library of Congress

Parkyns' engraved view of the city of Washington from Georgetown is one of four known views of the Federal City executed by the British artist and landscape architect on his American tour of 1794–1796. This highly romanticized view, depicting Mason's Island, the seat of George Mason's son, General John Mason, and the port of Georgetown and Capitol Hill belongs to the series of *American Landscapes* announced by the artist in March 1795.

Parkyns began his landscape training as a military surveyor in the Nottingham district of England between the years 1785 and 1790. A talent for drawing and an understanding of topographic detail led to the publication in 1793 of *Six Designs for Improving and Embellishing Grounds,* a work much admired by Jefferson which undoubtedly influenced the retiring president when revising his designs for the grounds at Monticello in 1806 and 1807.

The view is taken not far from the site of Thomas Main's nursery, a spot frequently visited by Jefferson, who obtained there most of the trees and shrubs planted at Monticello in the spring of 1807. Jefferson helped Main to publish his pamphlet on thorn hedging and experimented with Main's methods of fencing with hawthorn trees at Monticello. E.M.

563 The Woodlands, Seat of William Hamilton
WILLIAM BIRCH 1755–1834
Engraving 1808, in William Birch, *Country Seats of the United States* (Springland near Bristol, Penn.: W. Birch, 1808)
Lent by the Library of Congress

William Birch's engraved view of the Woodlands, the estate of William Hamilton, is one of twenty views of Philadelphia estates published by the British artist in 1808. Birch described the Woodlands in his unpublished autobiography: "The Woodlands near the city has a beautiful water scene towards the Delaware. The ground is spacious and elegant. Mr. Wm. Hambleton was a man of taste and at that time first in Boterny."

William Hamilton (1745–1813), a wealthy and dedicated botanist and amateur landscape gardener, surrounded his house with extensive gardens and greenhouses, containing the most exotic collection of native and imported plants then known in the United States.

Jefferson became acquainted with Hamilton during his years in Philadelphia as secretary of state and shared Hamilton's enthusiasm for exotic botany and the new English style of naturalistic gardening. It was to Hamilton and the Philadelphia nurseryman Bernard McMahon that Jefferson entrusted the "botanic fruits" of the Lewis and Clark expedition, in 1807.

In revising his plans for the gardens of Monticello in 1806, Jefferson sought to model his grounds after the Woodlands.

In a letter to Hamilton, one of the key documents of American landscape history, Jefferson wrote that should Hamilton come to Monticello, "You would have an opportunity of indulging on a new field some of the taste which has made the Woodlands the only rival I have known in America to what may be seen in England. Thither we are to go no doubt, for the first models in this art."

Jefferson later referred to the Woodlands as "the chastest model of gardening" which he had seen "out of England." E.M.

564 Belmont, Seat of Judge Richard Peters
WILLIAM BIRCH 1755–1834
Engraving (facsimile) 1808, in William Birch's *Country Seats of the United States,* 1808

Belmont, the estate of Judge Richard Peters, was known to Jefferson when he lived in Philadelphia as secretary of state. Situated on the banks of the Schuylkill, Belmont was, like the Woodlands, one of the most celebrated estates of the region. Jefferson refers to "Judge Peters, an excellent farmer in this neighborhood," in a letter of 1793 to his son-in-law Thomas Mann Randolph.

Richard Peters (1744–1828) was not only a judge and a farmer, but was also the founder of the Philadelphia Society for the Promotion of Agriculture and experimented on his estate with new agricultural methods and with different breeds of sheep and cattle, an interest which was close to Jefferson's heart as well. Jefferson's friend the marquis de Chastellux described his visit to Belmont in 1780: "The tasty little box" of Mr. Peters, late secretary of the Board of War, is situated on the most enchanting spot that nature can embellish, and besides the variegated beauties of the rural banks of the Schuylkill commands the Delaware and the shipping mounting and descending it where it is joined by right angles by the former from hence is the most romantic ride up the river to the falls, in which the opposite bank is likewise seen beautifully interspersed with the country houses of the opulent citizens of the Capitol. E.M.

565 View of West Front of Monticello and Garden

JANE BRADICK (PETTICOLES)
active 19th century
Watercolor 1825
28 x 45.8 (11 x 18)

*Lent by Thomas Jefferson Coolidge Jr.,
Boston*

This watercolor of the west front and
garden at Monticello by Jane Bradick
(Petticoles) was commissioned by
Jefferson's granddaughter Ellen Wayles
Randolph and is thought to have
been completed in the year before Jefferson died. Three of Jefferson's other
grandchildren, George (age seven),
Mary (age twenty-two) and Cornelia
(twenty-six) are depicted in the
middleground.

In a letter to the Reverend H. W.
Pierson, Edmund Bacon described the
grounds at the time this view was
painted: "The grounds around the
house were most beautifully ornamented with flowers and shrubbery.
There were walks, and borders, and
flowers, that I have never seen or heard
of anywhere else. Some of them were
in bloom from early in the spring
until late in the winter. A good many
of them were foreign. Back of the
house was a beautiful lawn of two or
three acres, where his grandchildren
used to play a great deal." E.M.

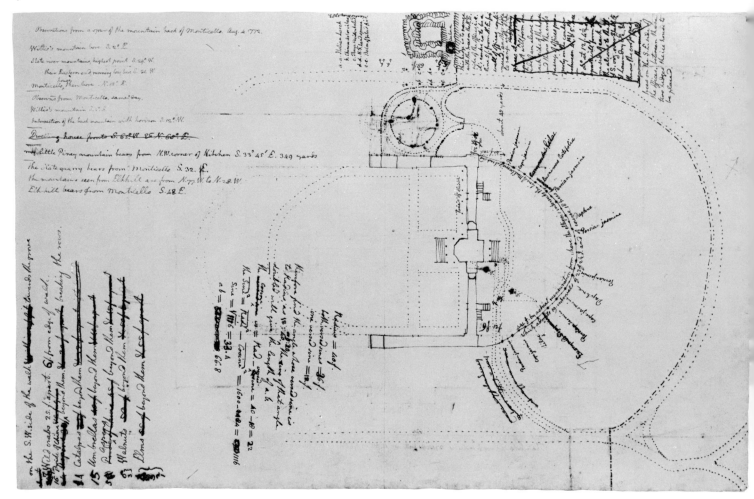

566 General plan of the summit of Monticello mountain

THOMAS JEFFERSON 1743–1826
Ink on laid paper, after Aug. 2, 1771,
and before Aug. 4, 1772
22.9 x 36.8 (9 x 14½)

*Lent by the Massachusetts Historical
Society, Boston*

This drawing was both a final plan,
circa 1772, of the house and L-shaped
dependencies, and a plan for landscaping the mountaintop. As late as
May 1783 notes were added to the
plan on the planting of trees, indicating that this drawing probably represented the extent of the designs for
the area around the main house
prior to Jefferson's departure for
Europe. F.N.

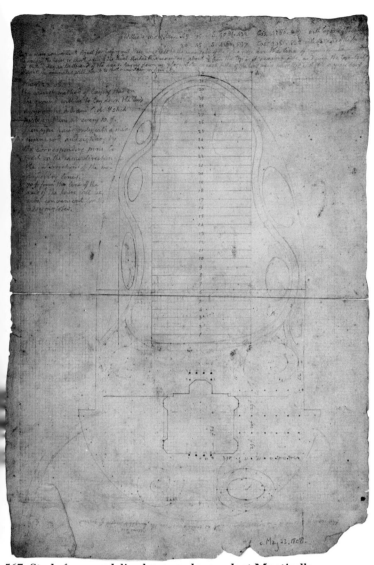

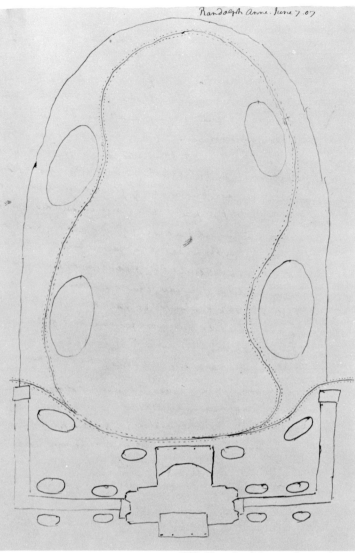

567 Study for remodeling house and grounds at Monticello

THOMAS JEFFERSON 1743–1826
Pencil on wove paper, 1785–1789?
27.3 x 40 (10¾ x 15¾)
Lent by the Massachusetts Historical Society, Boston

Jefferson learned to use engraved coordinate paper when he lived in Paris, and almost all of his drawings were made on it when he returned home. That is the basis for attributing this site plan for Monticello to the years Jefferson spent in Europe; in addition, the proportions of the mass of the house and the design of the portico for the east front were later significantly changed. Within the site, Jefferson sketched the serpentine walk and oval flower beds, which were partly executed in a similar design. The notes on the drawing, which were made later, refer to the method of laying out the plan by determining an axis

between the house and a nearby mountain and forming a coordinate perpendicular to it. He considered the climate an asset to his planning and in May, 1791, wrote to Martha Jefferson Randolph from Lake Champlain,

On the whole, I find nothing anywhere else, in point of climate, which Virginia need envy to any part of the world. Here they are locked up in ice and snow for six months. Spring and autumn, which make a paradise of our country, are rigorous winter with them; and a tropical summer breaks on them all at once. When we consider how much climate contributes to the happiness of our condition, by the fine sensations it excites, and the productions it is the parent of, we have reason to value highly the accident of birth in such a one as that of Virginia.

Evidence suggests that the hori-

zontal lines superimposed on the garden plan, numbered 1–31, were made in 1808, when the garden was being planted. F.N.

568 Not in Exhibition

569 Sketch of the garden and flower beds at Monticello

THOMAS JEFFERSON 1743–1826
Ink, June 7, 1807
19.7 x 24.5 (7¾ x 9⅝)
Verso: Letter from Jefferson to Anne Cary Randolph
Lent by the Massachusetts Historical Society, Boston

Throughout his life Jefferson was devoted to gardens and gardening, but other matters diverted his attention from the gardens at Monticello until relatively late in life. This sketch, on the reverse of a letter to his granddaughter Anne Cary Randolph in June, 1807, shows the serpentine walks, with flower borders indicated by dotted lines, and oval beds, which were planted with flowers and flowering shrubs.

I find that the limited number of our flower beds will too much restrain the variety of flowers in which we might wish to indulge, & therefore I have resumed an idea, which I had formerly entertained, but had laid by, of a winding walk surrounding the lawn before the house, with a narrow border of flowers on each side. this would give us abundant room for a great variety. I enclose you a sketch of my idea, where the dotted lines on each side . . . shew the border on each side of the walk. the hollows of the walk would give room for oval beds of flowering shrubs. . . .

Though Jefferson's exact plan has not survived, we know that he "indulged" in many varieties of flowers at one time or another. His granddaughter Ellen Randolph Coolidge, writing in later years to Jefferson's biographer Henry S. Randall, said, "I remember well when he first returned to Monticello, how immediately he began to prepare new beds for his flowers. He had these beds laid off on the lawn, under the windows, and many a time I have run after him when he went out to direct the work, accompanied by one of his gardeners . . . armed with spade and hoe, whilst he himself carried the measuring-line."

F.N.

JEFFERSON GARDEN BUILDINGS AND FURNITURE

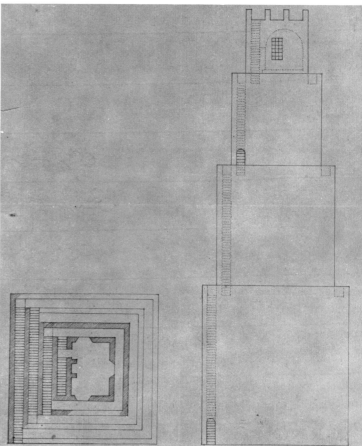

570 Decorative outchamber for Monticello
THOMAS JEFFERSON 1743–1826
Ink on laid paper, probably 1778
18.4 x 22.9 (7¼ x 9)
Lent by the Massachusetts Historical Society, Boston

This design, without indication of scale, is a castellated four-stage tower, with a small room on the top level, and may have been Jefferson's perception of a medieval tower. It is the most uncharacteristic work in Jefferson's oeuvre and may be original in America. The English fashion for Gothic buildings and *chinoiserie* (other than simple Chinese lattice) had not yet reached America, and Jefferson's design, though it was probably not intended to be built, seems to be one of the earliest evidences of interest in exotic, ornamental structures in this country.

The paper type and its association with other ornamental structures exhibited here at numbers 571 and 574, suggests the date for this drawing. F.N.

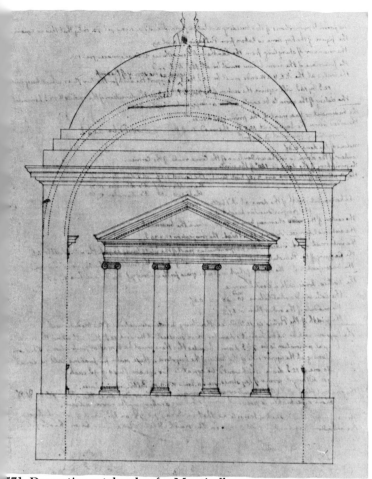

571 Decorative outchamber for Monticello

THOMAS JEFFERSON 1743–1826
Ink on laid paper, probably 1778
15.9 x 20.3 (6¼ x 8)
Notes and specifications on verso

*Lent by the Massachusetts Historical
Society, Boston*

English landscape gardens with any
pretensions to style had to include a
neoclassical monument. Though
Jefferson had not yet visited England
when he made this drawing, he was
certainly aware of the fashionable
jardin anglais and wished to incorporate the temple motif in the garden
at Monticello. On his tour of English
gardens eight years later, he particularly admired the temples in the gardens at Stowe and Hagley.

In his notes on the back of the
drawing, Jefferson noted that his source
for "form and proportions" were
taken from Kent's *Designs of Inigo
Jones*, published in 1727, in which
Jefferson copied a garden temple
designed and built by Lord Burlington,
which Jefferson later saw at Chiswick.
Lord Burlington's temple was round,
but perhaps for practical reasons,

Jefferson's design was square.

The cap of the dome was taken
from Bramante's *Tempietto*, which
was illustrated in Palladio's *Fourth
Book*. The cornice of the pedestal
was taken from Gibbs' *Rules for
Drawing the Several Parts of Architecture*, of which Jefferson owned the
second edition of 1738, and from the
Builder's Dictionary, published in
1734.

The "manner of shingling," interestingly enough, came from a crude
engraving of the so-called "Lantern
of Demosthenes" in Jacques Spon's
Voyage d'Italie, published in 1675–
1676. It was a round temple with a
roof *taille en écailles*, which the orator
and statesman was said to have
inhabited. F.N.

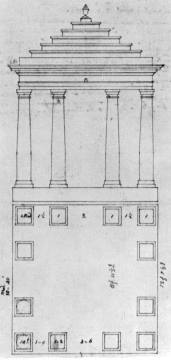

572 Design for a garden temple and dovecote

THOMAS JEFFERSON 1743–1826
Ink on laid paper, probably 1779
15.9 x 20.2 (6¼ x 8)

*Lent by the Massachusetts Historical
Society, Boston*

With few exceptions, Jefferson's ideas
for garden structures can be traced
to architectural books. In many cases
he copied the designs, only simplifying
them when a change of scale was
necessary or the construction was too
involved. However, an important early
example of a clearly imaginative
adaptation of a published design is his
drawing of a garden temple and dovecote dating from about 1779.

The only design resembling this
drawing illustrated in any of the architectural books owned by Jefferson
before 1785 is one for a small pavilion
in James Gibbs' *Book of Architecture*,
plate 77. Although Jefferson apparently consulted this work in preparing
several early studies for his house, it
was undoubtedly after he acquired a
copy in Williamsburg in December
1778 that the sketch was produced. At
that same time, Jefferson purchased
the *Designs of Inigo Jones*, from which
he made a tracing of William Kent's
garden temple at Chiswick. Inasmuch
as both the drawing based on Gibbs
and the tracing from *Inigo Jones* are
two of only four known examples
of drawings on paper with the same

watermark (and the other two are of
indeterminable date) one may reason-
ably conclude that they are contemporary with one another. Very
likely they date after the acquisition of
the two books and possibly from the
spring of 1779, when Jefferson resumed ideas for landscaping Monticello and before his election as governor in June consumed so much of his
time.

Gibbs' design is for a small enclosed
pavilion with entrances on each side.
A modified Venetian window motif is
adapted for the elevation of each
wall, with the tall central arch rising
into an attic space and solid walls
enclosing the flanking bays between
the pilasters. The roof is a stepped
pyramid and is surmounted by an urn.
The idea of a stepped roof comes
from antiquity, the most famous precedent being the Mausoleum of Halicarnassus. The idea appeared in ancient
tombs, in which the roof consisted
of stepped terraces, sometimes planted
with trees. This scheme is represented at Hadrian's Tomb in Rome,
now called the Castle of St. Angelo. In
classical architecture this type of roof
is associated mainly with monuments
for the dead. It was revived in the
eighteenth century by the visionary
architects, most notably by Boullée.

The combination of a stepped roof
and free-standing columns was original with Jefferson, though there are
other examples to be found in English
gardens. Jefferson's adaptation of
Gibbs' design is far more classical than
Gibbs' in feeling; the Venetian motif
and attic are abandoned and the
stepped pyramidal roof is supported
on twelve columns. The scale of the
building is also changed by the substi-
tution of the Tuscan for the Doric
order. Within the roof Jefferson
planned a dovecote with access holes
in the frieze, another good example
of his combining the aesthetic with the
practical.

On the reverse of the drawing,
Jefferson devised his own proportions
for the roof, carefully basing it on
the model of Palladio's Tuscan order.
In one instance, however, he broke
from Palladio's proportions and increased the projection of the abacus
(the top member of the capital) as a
way of preventing rats from entering
the roof space.

The reference to a north-south
orientation suggests that Jefferson had
considered a location for the temple,
but there is no evidence that it was
ever constructed. F.N.

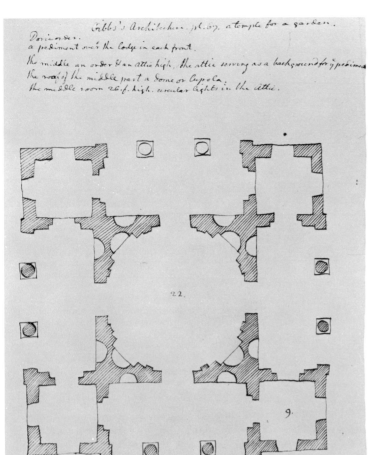

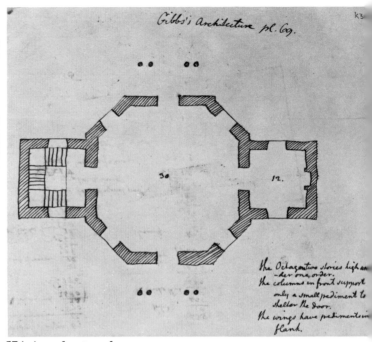

573 A temple for a garden

THOMAS JEFFERSON 1743–1826
Ink on laid paper c. 1778
19.3 x 25.1 (7⅝ x 9⅞)

Lent by the Massachusetts Historical Society, Boston

Jefferson acquired a copy of Gibbs' *Book of Architecture* in 1778. It was probably about that time that this tracing of plate 67 from that book was made. Gibbs identified the design as a "building of the Doric order in form of a temple, made for a person of quality, and propos'd to have been placed in the center of four walks; so that a portico might front each walk." Jefferson's notes on the reverse side indicate that this was to be built in a modified form. The proposed location at Monticello of this unexecuted design is unknown. F.N.

574 A garden temple

THOMAS JEFFERSON 1743–1826
Ink on laid paper c. 1778
16.8 x 16.5 (6⅝ x 6½)

Lent by the Massachusetts Historical Society, Boston

This drawing of a small domed pavilion is probably contemporary with another tracing from Gibbs' *Book of Architecture*, exhibited here at number 573. Jefferson's model here was plate 69, which Gibbs described as a garden pavilion with "an octagonal room of 30 feet, with a closet on one side, and on the other a stair-case which leads to the waiting rooms underneath." It is evident from Jefferson's dimensions of the central octagonal space that the pavilion was to be without the dome shown in Gibbs' design, because the space is not square. Like number 573, the drawing probably was done after Jefferson acquired his copy of Gibbs' *Book of Architecture* in December 1778. F.N.

575 Drawing for a gate in Chinese lattice at Monticello

THOMAS JEFFERSON 1743–1826
Ink on laid paper 1771?
12.1 x 18.4 (4¾ x 7¼)

Lent by the Massachusetts Historical Society, Boston

The pattern books of William and John Halfpenny, William Chambers, and Thomas Chippendale, which appeared in the latter half of the eighteenth century, popularized Chinese lattice, and it was widely used as a decorative motif in Virginia during this time. Jefferson made extensive use of lattice at Monticello and at the University of Virginia for railings and gates. This drawing shows a typical gate, for which Jefferson has indicated revisions. It is dated by the paper type. F.N.

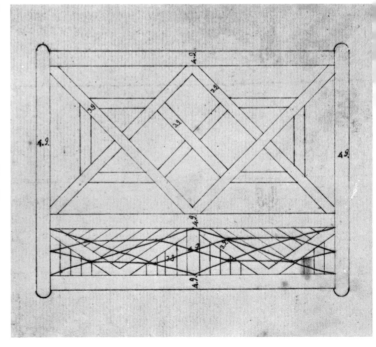

**76 Designs of Chinese Buildings,
Furniture, Dresses, Machines, and
Utensils** (London: published for
the author [etc.], 1757)

SIR WILLIAM CHAMBERS
1726–1796

*From the Collection of Mr. and
Mrs. Paul Mellon*

Fiske Kimball considered Thomas
Jefferson to have been ahead of his
time by his possession of a copy of
Sir William Chambers' *Designs of
Chinese Buildings*. The fact that Jefferson had books such as Chambers' is
one reason for calling his architectural library superior to most others in
the United States at that time.

Chambers visited China and published books on Oriental gardening
as well as on Chinese architecture. He
was the architect for a number of
mansions in England as well as public
buildings such as Somerset House
in the Strand and the Chinese pagoda
in Kew Gardens. Jefferson's calculations for Chinese pavilions at the
corners of his terraces at Monticello
are, according to Kimball, taken from
Chambers' *Designs of Chinese
Buildings*. J.M.E.

577 View of the Queen's Theater from the Rotunda at Stowe, Buckinghamshire

JACQUES RIGAUD 1681–1754
Ink and gray wash
(facsimile) c. 1733

*Original in The Metropolitan Museum
of Art*

The drawing of the queen's theater is
one of fifteen views of Stowe drawn
by Rigaud and then popularized in
engravings executed by Bernard Baron
(1696–1762) under the direction
of the landscape architect Charles
Bridgeman. These views were published by Bridgeman's widow Sarah in
1739 and form one of the most
comprehensive sets of eighteenth-
century drawings of any British landscape garden.

The rotunda, designed in 1721 by
the architect John Vanbrugh and
altered by Borra in 1752, may have
been in Jefferson's mind years after his
tour of Stowe, when he laid out the
grounds for the University of Virginia.
This exquisite little temple was placed
at a focal point of the old half-
geometrical gardens, with radiating
lines in three directions and an open
park across a ha ha wall (or concealed ditch) to the west. Jefferson's
own garden temple plans included a
structure of similar design (see
no. 574). E.M.

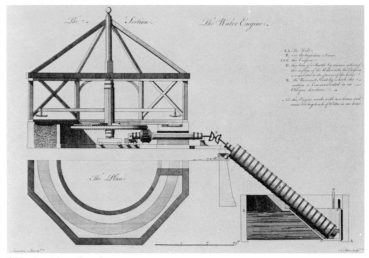

578 Archimedes Screw

SIR WILLIAM CHAMBERS
1726–1796

Engraving in Sir William Chambers,
*Plans, Elevations, Sections, and
Perspective Views of the Gardens and
Buildings at Kew*
(London: J. Haberkorn, 1763)

*Lent by the Dumbarton Oaks Garden
Library, Washington*

Jefferson visited the royal gardens at
Kew in 1786, and the feature that
interested him most was an "engine"
for raising water, the Archimedes
Screw. It had the capacity for raising
three hundred hogsheads of water
in an hour, and Jefferson made a rough
sketch of it in his notes, thinking

that a similar device might be used for
the springs at Monticello.

Sir William Chambers (1726–
1796), born in Stockholm, was educated in England and at age sixteen
joined the Swedish East India Company, with whom he made three
voyages to the Far East where he became acquainted with the architecture
and gardens of China. These were
the subject of two illustrated books,
which he subsequently published in
England: *Designs of Chinese Buildings* in 1757, and *A Dissertation
on Oriental Gardening* in 1772. In an
autobiographical note of his early
years, Chambers wrote that his strongest inclination was for architecture,
and that on his voyages to the East he

had "studied modern languages, mathematics and the liberal arts, but chiefly architecture." Within two years of his return, he studied at the Ecole des Beaux-Arts and spent five years in Rome, earning there a reputation for "greatness of thought and nobility of invention, drawing and ornamentation." When he returned to England, Chambers gained immediate favor with the Prince of Wales and his mother, the Dowager Princess Augusta, and in 1757 became chief architect of the royal gardens at Kew as well as architectural tutor to the prince and advisor to his mother.

Chambers devoted six years to the improvement of Kew, transforming it, as he modestly said, from a desert into an Eden. In the introduction to his book on Kew, published in 1763, Chambers described the site as low, with barren soil and no trees or water. Inspired by William Kent, he created an inward-looking park, defined by belts of trees and interspersed with groves and low-rising hills. A lake and several new architectural features enlivened the scene, including a Chinese pagoda and an orangery. Jefferson knew Chambers' books on Chinese architecture and gardens and copied at least one design, for a garden seat, from his book on Kew.

E.M.

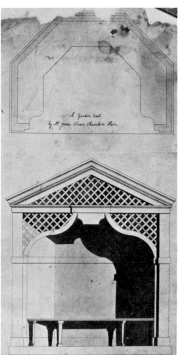

579 A garden seat by Mr. Jones. From Chamber's Kew

Attributed to CORNELIA JEFFERSON RANDOLPH 1799–1871
Ink on wove paper c. 1820
22.7 x 39.3 (9 x 15½)

Lent by the University of Virginia, Alderman Library, Charlottesville

This study in rendering was probably done by Cornelia Jefferson Randolph around 1820. The subject is incorrectly identified as "A garden seat by Mr. Jones," presumably the English architect Inigo Jones. It is actually a design by William Kent, as Chambers states in his 1763 book *Plans, Elevations, Sections and Perspective Views of the Gardens and Buildings at Kew in Surrey*, from which this drawing was copied. Kent executed the mansion and gardens at the new palace of Kew soon after 1730. This was a favorite design of Kent's, and he used it in other projects throughout his career. At Rousham, Oxfordshire, where Kent laid out the gardens between 1738 and 1741, there are still extant two garden seats identical to these designs. F.N.

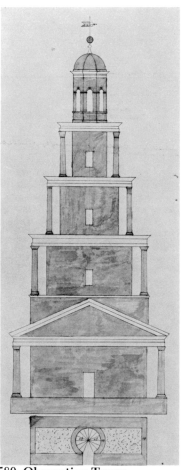

580 Observation Tower

THOMAS JEFFERSON 1743–1826
Ink on laid paper, probably 1771
22.9 x 36.8 (9 x 14½)

Lent by the Massachusetts Historical Society, Boston

This is one of Jefferson's most ambitious designs for a garden structure and probably was intended for the summit of the mountain which adjoins and rises above Monticello. Notes on the back indicate that the construction was to be of stone, the interstices of the wall filled with dry stone and the columns and entablature of plank "with the projections cut." The front windows were to be lower than those in the back, which together would have the effect of "directing the line of sight to Monticello." The upper story is based on plate 31, figure 2 from Gibbs' *Book of Architecture*. At the end of his notes Jefferson apparently changed his mind and wrote "a Column will be preferable to any thing else. it should be 200 f. high, & have a hollow of 5. f. in the center for stairs to run up. on the top of the capital a ballustrading." These designs, as well as proposals for other garden structures, were apparently never executed. F.N.

81 Linnaeus
WILLIAM RUSH 1756–1833
Painted wood, c. 1812
63 (24¾) high
Lent by the Corcoran Gallery of Art,
Washington

Jefferson as a botanist was a lifelong
disciple of Carl von Linné, known as
Linnaeus (1707–1778), the Swedish
naturalist who first defined a universal binomial system of classification
of plants and animals, thus "uniting
all nations under one language in
Natural History," as Jefferson wrote in
1814, in answer to a request for his
opinion of the different methods of
classification. For Jefferson, as for
scientists everywhere, it was of paramount importance to be able to communicate with others of like interests
and to share the growing knowledge of
the natural world. "To communicate
intelligibly with one another," as
Jefferson wrote in support of Linnaeus,
whether it was cataloguing orders,
genera and species or exchanging con-
stitutions and plans for a new political
system, was at the heart of the
eighteenth-century Enlightenment.

Through Miller's *The Gardener's
Dictionary* (seventh edition), Jefferson first studied the Linnaean system,
which he later adopted in his classification of native plants. He also
listed these plants according to their
popular names, in *Notes on the State
of Virginia.*

Jefferson's own interest in sculpture
may have indirectly affected the
career of William Rush (1756–1833),
generally considered to be the first
native American sculptor. In 1785,

Houdon, who had been invited by Jefferson to take the likeness of Washington (see no. 172), stopped in
Philadelphia on his way to Mount
Vernon, and Rush undoubtedly saw
the famous Frenchman's work. But
Rush's professional career was to be
that of a ship's carver, and he only occasionally found time to execute
portraits and allegorical figures that
reflected an unaffected native style and
simple integrity.

Rush was a friend of Charles Willson Peale, and together they worked to

form the Pennsylvania Academy of
Fine Arts, where the bust of Linnaeus
was exhibited in 1812, along with a
portrait of Philadelphia's own great
botanist and Jefferson's friend, William
Bartram. W.H.A.

582 Natural Bridge, Virginia
FREDERIC EDWIN CHURCH
1826–1900
Oil on canvas 1852
71.1 x 58.4 (28 x 23)
Signed lower center: *F. Church/1852*

*Lent by the University of Virginia
Art Museum, Charlottesville*

The date of Jefferson's first observation of the Natural Bridge is unknown,
but his Account Book for 1767 records his detailed description of this

wonder. The notations he made on this encounter were later utilized in his *Notes on the State of Virginia* (1785). Naming the Bridge "the most sublime of nature's works," he contrasted the heightened "painful and intolerable" emotions experienced by looking down from the top of the arch with the opposite extreme from below: "so beautiful . . . so elevated, so light, and springing as it were up to heaven! the rapture of the spectator is really indescribable!" Acquiring the Natural Bridge and adjoining land by patent from George III in 1774, Jefferson viewed his purchase "in some degree a public trust, and would on no consideration permit the bridge to be injured, defaced or masked from the public view. To another early admirer of the bridge, William Carmichael, who published the first printed description in hopes of inspiring C. W. Peale or any other artist to paint a landscape view, Jefferson wrote, "I sometimes think of building a little hermitage at the Natural bridge . . . and of passing there a [part] of the year at least." While never able to build his little hermitage, Jefferson retained ownership to the end of his life despite mounting financial difficulties.

Again and again Jefferson urged that this marvel of the American landscape be recorded on canvas. On three different occasions, he exhorted Maria Cosway to come to America and paint the Natural Bridge, a subject "worthy of immortality." Five years later he advised John Trumbull to "take to yourself and your country the honor of presenting to the world this singular landscape, which otherwise some bungling European will misrepresent." In fact, Jefferson was well aware that a view of the bridge already existed. In 1782 the marquis de Chastellux visited the bridge at Jefferson's urging. Unable to take exact measurements or to draw accurate sketches, he convinced the comte de Rochambeau to send the baron de Turpin of the Royal Corps of Engineers to prepare suitable sketches, two of which appeared in Chastellux's *Voyages en Nord Amérique* in 1786. Jefferson was dismayed with this introduction of the American wonder to European eyes as the platform was misrepresented, whereupon he made reference to a "bungling European." Later Jefferson owned an oil painting and an engraving of the Natural Bridge at Monticello, but their whereabouts and even the artists are unknown today.

Frederic E. Church painted one of the most dramatic and realistic views of the bridge in 1852. Sketching the bridge in the spring of 1851, Church was challenged by his traveling companion, Cyrus Field, who wagered that

Church would not match the colors of some rocks that Field had pocketed. When Church completed the painting the next winter, the colors corresponded perfectly and Field bought the painting. Church, a knowledgeable and consummate observer of nature, united both art and natural history in his landscape painting. He was profoundly influenced by the writings of Jefferson's friend and admirer, Baron von Humboldt. Owning editions of Humboldt's *Cosmos, Personal Narratives,* and *Aspects of Nature,* Church attempted to answer Humboldt's call for a new landscape art based on the natural forms of nature, particularly those of the tropics of the Western Hemisphere. G.V.

583 Harper's Ferry

REMBRANDT PEALE 1778–1860
Oil on canvas 1819
102.8 x 172.7 (40½ x 68)

Lent by the Walker Art Center, Minneapolis

The passage of the Patowmac through the Blue ridge is perhaps one of the most stupendous scenes in nature. You stand on a very high point of land. On your right comes up the Shenandoah, having ranged along the foot of the mountain an hundred miles to seek a vent. On your left approaches the Patowmac, in quest of a passage also. The moment of their junction they rush together against the mountain, rend it asunder, and pass off to the sea. . . . But the distant finishing which nature has given to the picture, is of a very different character. It is as placid and delightful, as that is wild and tremendous.

The artist, devoted to Jefferson and like him a romantic at heart, is illustrating this description from the *Notes on the State of Virginia,* which the book's great popularity had made famous. Dr. Samuel Latham Mitchill inquired of Jefferson in 1802 as to the exact spot from which he had viewed the scene, and was told that it no longer existed. Jefferson was of the opinion that some Federal soldiers, from political motivation, had dynamited it away. One reason for Rembrandt Peale's painting may have been to prove this report false. Certainly, Thomas Doughty's view of 1826, engraved much later by James W. Steel as *Harper's Ferry from Jefferson's*

Rock, would indicate that no serious vandalism had occurred.

This painting was first announced in the newspaper *Aurora,* January 9, 1812, as at "REMBRANDT'S NEW PICTURE GALLERY" in Philadelphia, featuring "His Great Equestrian Picture of NAPOLEON" and "his large view of HARPER'S FERRY at the junction of the Shenandoah with the Potomac." Jefferson must have seen and admired the painting, for Rembrandt makes special mention of it in applying to him, December 7, 1825, for a place on the fine arts faculty of the University of Virginia. It was then at the Peale Museum, Baltimore. C.S.

584 Jefferson's Rock, Harper's Ferry

BENJAMIN HENRY LATROBE
1764–1820
Watercolor and pencil 1810
20.3 x 32.2 (8 x 12¹¹⁄₁₆)

Lent by the Maryland Historical
Society, Baltimore, Papers of
Benjamin H. Latrobe

In Richmond during his first year in
America, Latrobe made the acquaintance of the French thinker C.F.C.
Volney and the physician-philosopher
Scandella. In these friendships,
Hamlin points out, Latrobe had a
source of intellectual stimulation unlike anything previously experienced
in his new country. Though Latrobe
had evidenced interest in geological
matters since his arrival in 1796,
Volney's commitment to geology is
likely to have provided Latrobe with
the impetus to greater work in the
field. It was to Volney in Philadelphia
that Latrobe sent his notations on
geological and related subjects. A large
body of technical correspondence
remains as evidence of these
relationships.

In 1798 Latrobe submitted his
"Memoir on the Sand Hills of New
Jersey" to the American Philosophical
Society in Philadelphia. The paper
was accepted, and in 1799 it was published in the society's transactions,
at which time Latrobe was elected to
the society's membership. It is thought
that Volney and Scandella, both
members, were responsible for alerting
the society to Latrobe's contributions to the field of geology.

In this watercolor, Latrobe clearly
describes the geological structure of
Jefferson's Rock. In a complementary
sketch made at the same time, he
depicted the "Plan of the Cave removing the upper Rock." In the lower
right of *Jefferson's Rock, Harper's
Ferry* is a view of the confluence of the
Potomac and Shenandoah rivers,
which Jefferson made famous in his
Notes on the State of Virginia. The
figure standing on the rock is thought
to be the artist. B.S.

585 Falls of the Schuylkill

CHARLES WILLSON PEALE
1741–1827
Ink and watercolor c. 1770
19.7 x 32.4 (7¾ x 12¾)
Inscribed across top: *the lower falls of
Schuylkill 5 miles from Philadelphia*

Lent by Charles Coleman Sellers,
Carlisle, Pennsylvania

John Adams, while visiting "Mr.
Peale's painter's room" on August 21,
1776, was shown among other things,
"sketches of gentlemen's seats in
Virginia, where he had been, Mr.
Corbin's, Mr. Page's, General Washington's. etc." This drawing of the
river along which Philadelphians'
summer homes were clustered may
well have been among those sketches.
In his portrait of John Dickinson,
whose *Letters of a Pennsylvania
Farmer* had given American resistance
to royal power a freshly logical,
legalistic cast, Peale adapts this view as
background, bringing the curve of
the stream into harmony with the
downward-flowing lines of the figure
and pensive mood of the whole.

It is not far downstream from this
spot to where the floating bridge once
crossed the river at Gray's Ferry and
Gray's Gardens, where too, on the
east bank looking across to Bartram's
gardens and mansion, was the small
cottage which Jefferson rented in
1793. Alexander Wilson taught his
school nearby, began work on his
American Ornithology here, and dwelt
upon the beauty of the spot in rhyme:

There market-maids in lovely row,
    With wallets white, were riding
    home,
And thund'ring gigs, with powdered
    beaux,
    Through Gray's green festive
    shade to roam.

Sweet flows the Schuylkill's winding
    tide
    By Bartram's emblossomed

bowers,
    Where nature sports in all her pride
    Of choicest plants and fruits and
    flowers.

Jefferson thought of adding a "salon
à la français" to the tiny cottage,
but he found life on the lawn under
the towering trees more pleasant than
anything within walls—"and under
them I breakfast, dine, write, read,
and receive my company. What would
I not give that the trees planted
nearest round the house at Monticello
were full-grown." C.S.

586 View of the Great Falls of the Potomac

BENJAMIN HENRY LATROBE
1764–1820
Watercolor and pencil 1809
20.3 x 32.2 (8 x 12¹¹⁄₁₆)

*Lent by the Maryland Historical
Society, Baltimore, Papers of
Benjamin H. Latrobe*

In his view of the Great Falls of the
Potomac from the south or Virginia
side, executed in September 1809,
Latrobe notes in the left rear the remains of a forge damaged by fire. The
river, he wrote, "was very low when
this view was taken. From the drift-
wood lying on the top of the large
Rock over which the tall trees are
growing it is evident that the Water
rised frequently over the top." Latrobe
makes clear his intention in recording views such as this when he further
notes, "At this visit I could stay little
more than an hour, and had time
only to take this hasty sketch, which
however is perfectly correct as far
as it goes." Latrobe continues in the
tradition of the earliest topographical
recorders of the American landscape.
His aim, furthered by his unaffected
style of painting, was an accurate
record of the land.

In a discussion of the use of rivers
and lakes for commerce in the eastern
states, Jefferson observed in his *Notes
on the State of Virginia* the potential advantages of the Potomac. "The
channel to the Chesapeak leads
directly into a warmer climate. The
southern parts of it very rarely freeze
at all, and whenever the northern

do, it is so near the sources of the
rivers, that the frequent floods to
which they are there liable, break up
the ice immediately, so that vessels
may pass through the whole winter,
subject to only accidental and short
delays. . . . But the channel to New-
York is already known to practice;
whereas the upper waters of the Ohio
and Patowmac, and the great falls of
the latter, are yet to be cleared of their
fixed obstructions." B.S.

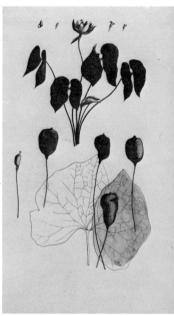

587 Jeffersonia diphylla

Attributed to BENJAMIN SMITH
BARTON 1766–1815
Engraving
55.5 x 40 (21⅞ x 15¾)

*Lent by the American Philosophical
Society, Philadelphia*

Benjamin Smith Barton, professor
of natural history and botany at the
University of Pennsylvania, played
a decisive role in the development of
botanical literature in the first decade
of the nineteenth century. He published in 1803 what is generally considered the first botanical textbook in
the United States and wrote numerous
articles on botanical and natural history subjects. Barton formed an
early association with Jefferson through
his membership in the American
Philosophical Society. It was Barton
who, in a paper read before the society,
on May 18, 1792, named the plant
Jeffersonia, previously known as
Podophyllum diphyllum:

Jeffersonia,

in honour of Thomas Jefferson, Esq.,
Sectretary of State to the United
States.

I beg leave to observe to you, in
this place, that in imposing upon
this genus the name of Mr. Jefferson,
I have had no reference to his
political character, or to his reputation for general science, and for
literature. My business was with his
knowledge of natural history. In
the various departments of this
science, but especially in botany and

zoology, the information of this gentleman is equalled by that of few persons in the United States. . . .

Jefferson planted *Jeffersonia* in one of the oval flower beds at Monticello in the spring of 1807. In a letter addressed to Jefferson on August 18, 1817, Francis Gilmer enclosed a few seeds of *Jeffersonia* with the following description: "I inclose for Mrs. Randolph a few seeds of the plant which has been dedicated to you, under the name of Jeffersonia. It is not very beautiful but is curious, and its name will I am sure recommend her to piety. It grows in deep, shady bottoms like the May apple (podophyllum peltatum). The seeds came from Harpers Ferry where all the regions of nature have conspired to do you honor. . . ." E.M.

588 Franklinia
WILLIAM BARTRAM 1739–1823
Ink and watercolor 1788
Signed lower right: *Will. M Bartram Delin. 1788*
Lent by the British Museum of Natural History, London

William Bartram, son of the Quaker botanist John Bartram, was sent by John Fothergill, a prosperous London doctor and enthusiastic collector of plants to east and west Florida, the Carolinas and Georgia in 1773. Fothergill, whose botanical collection at Upton, near London, was considered "second only to Kew" was a Quaker and had followed the work of the Bartrams through Peter Collinson. William Bartram was to send Fothergill, in exchange for fifty pounds a

year plus expenses, "curious plants and seeds, and to draw birds, reptiles, insects and plants on the spot."

The younger Bartram, who was described by one of his contemporaries as "one of the most ambitious lovers of nature" he had ever met, had accompanied his father to the St. John's River in 1765. He was eager to return to the aromatic groves and lush tropical forests of east and west Florida in 1773. The journey, which was to have lasted two years, lasted five and was the inspired subject of William Bartram's published account: *Travels through North and South Carolina, Georgia, East and West Florida*, published initially in Philadelphia in 1791.

"This world, as a glorious apartment of the boundless palace of the sovereign Creator, is furnished with an infinite variety of animated scenes, inexpressibly beautiful and pleasing, equally free to the inspection and enjoyment of all his creatures," wrote Bartram, in the introduction to his *Travels*.

Bartram's drawing of the rare *Franklinia* is one of several drawings executed for Robert Barclay and now preserved in the Fothergill album at the British Museum of Natural History. Bartram described his discovery of the plant, which he named after Benjamin Franklin, in a report to Fothergill: "This very curious tree was first taken notice of about ten or twelve years ago, at this place, when I attended my father on a botanical excursion; but it then being late autumn, we could form no opinion to what class or tribe it belonged."

The drawing bears Bartram's inscription: *Franklinia Alatamaha, a Beautiful Flowering Tree discovered growing near the Banks of the R. Alatamaha in Georgia.*

Jefferson began a long and intimate association with the Bartrams during the period of his residence in Philadelphia, when he lived opposite Bartram's garden, on the banks of the Schuylkill River. Jefferson subscribed to the first edition of Bartram's *Travels*, published in 1791, and through Benjamin Smith Barton sought to appoint Bartram chief botanist for the Lewis and Clark expedition in 1803. It was William who sent Jefferson in 1808 the seeds of the silk tree. Thanking Bartram, in a letter dated November 23, 1808, Jefferson wrote that he would plant the seeds and "cherish" them with care at Monticello. E.M.

Fragaria Chiloensis fructu maximo, foliis carnosis hirsutis Frez.

588a Fragaria chiloensis
WILLIAM BARTRAM 1739–1823
Etching
42.3 x 27.5 (16⅝ x 10¹³⁄₁₆)
Lent by the Historical Society of Pennsylvania, Philadelphia

William Bartram's undated etching of the *Fragaria chiloensis*, or Chili Strawberry, may belong to a series of illustrations executed by the Philadelphia botanist for English and American plant catalogues, or for a projected catalogue of the Bartram botanic garden at Kingsessing, Pennsylvania.

The Chili or Chile strawberry, a native of the Pacific coast, was introduced in Europe by M Frezier, a French botanist, in 1712. Jefferson's friend Bernard McMahon counted the Chili one of the five most delicious varieties in his *American Gardener's Calendar*. Jefferson, who was fastidious in all gardening matters, indicated his preference for the Chili in a letter to Thomas Mann Randolph, dated March 22, 1798. Writing from Philadelphia, Jefferson said that he had just shipped, together with a harpsicord for Maria, a box of plants including the "immensely valuable" Chili and Antwarp strawberries. And in a letter to Bernard McMahon, dated January 1810, Jefferson again referred to the Chili, indicating that he would select for his garden at Monticello "only one or two of the *best* species or variety of every garden vegetable." "Some plants of your gooseberry," Jefferson continued, "[and] of your Hudson and Chili strawberries . . . would be very acceptable." E.M.

589 Cypripedium acaule . . . Richmond—Lady Slipper from Blossom to Roots
BENJAMIN HENRY LATROBE
1764–1820
Watercolor, pen and ink, pencil 1798
26.0 x 17.8 (7 x 10¼)
Lent by the Maryland Historical Society, Baltimore, Papers of Benjamin H. Latrobe

Cypripedium acaule, or Lady Slipper, does not appear in the *Notes on the State of Virginia*, though Jefferson would probably have known of the plant. A member of the orchid family, it was once quite common in the wooded areas of the eastern United States, from Tennessee to New England. Its omission from Jefferson's notes can be understood from his introduction to the lists where he explains that "A complete catalogue of the Trees, Plants, fruits, &c. is probably not desired."

Several years later, with undiminished interest in matters of natural history, Jefferson encouraged the Lewis and Clark expedition in their aim of gathering specimens of flora, fauna, minerals and significant artifacts from the area west of the Mississippi. In April 1805, Meriwether Lewis sent Jefferson "67 specimens of earth salts, and minerals, and 60 specimens of plants" to increase his knowledge of native American natural history.

Latrobe's drawing was made near Richmond in 1798. By that date, two years after his arrival from England, Latrobe had established contacts with many of the significant men of late eighteenth-century Virginia, among them George Washington, Colonel Thomas Blackburn, Richard Randolph and Jefferson, and had already been appointed as architect of the new penitentiary at Richmond, for which his plan is exhibited at number 406. B.S.

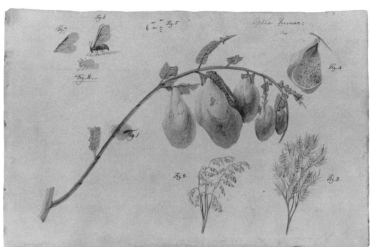

590 Representation of the Leaf of the Shumac Tree

BENJAMIN HENRY LATROBE
1764–1820
Watercolor and pencil 1809
20.3 x 32.2 (8 x 12¹¹⁄₁₆)

Lent by the Maryland Historical Society, Baltimore, Papers of Benjamin H. Latrobe

In 1796 Latrobe had noted in his journals the prevalence of the sumac in Amelia County, Virginia. The leaves, he said, were "used by the Indians, and many white people to mix with their tobacco in smoking. It bears a red berry which remains upon the tree all the winter, and has a pleasant acid taste" (May 11, 1796). In his sketchbook thirteen years later, Latrobe recorded his observations on an unusual natural phenomenon encountered in his travels, perhaps in search of building materials. "Under the Wall of the Canal of the Great Falls of Potowmac grow some of the largest Shumacs [sumacs] I have ever seen. One of those Shrubs, or Trees, had absolutely no leaves, and in their room the leaf stalks were hung with the nidi here represented." With characteristic thoroughness he records all aspects of the discovery: Figure 1 represents the actual size of a single sumac branch; figure 2 shows the relationship of the branch to other branches of the tree; figure 3 the appearance of figure 2 if it were not infested; figure 4 shows an open nide; figure 5 the actual size of the fly; figure 6 the appearance of the fly under a microscope; figure 7 a pair of its wings "marked and nerved"; and figure 8 the larval stage of the insect.

In his *Notes on the State of Virginia*, Jefferson devised a list of native flora whose attributes were "1. Medicinal, 2. Esculent, 3. Ornamental, or 4. Useful for fabrication." Sumac is included as an ornamental plant.

B.S.

591 Spiraea, Hanover County, Virginia

BENJAMIN HENRY LATROBE
1764–1820
Watercolor, pencil, pen and ink 1797
23.7 x 17.8 (9⁵⁄₁₆ x 7)

Lent by the Maryland Historical Society, Baltimore, Papers of Benjamin H. Latrobe

Spiraea trifoliata, also know in the eighteenth century as Indian physic, is a spring-blooming member of the rose family, whose flowers can be pink but are more often white. Jefferson includes it in his list of medicinal plants as "Spiria trifoliata" in his *Notes on the State of Virginia*; Latrobe notes that it had been described in the scientific literature as early as 1762 by Dr. Clayton in his *Flora Virginica*.

That the primary interest in the natural history of North America at that time was botanical was pointed out by the naturalist Benjamin Smith Barton in *A Discourse on Some of the Principal Desiderata in Natural History*, 1807. In 1792 Barton, a member of the American Philosophical Society —as Latrobe would be and Jefferson was—delivered a paper to the society on botany. In it he named a newly described plant family, *Jeffersonia*, after Jefferson, in acknowledgment of Jefferson's expertise in the field of botany (see no. 587). B.S.

592 Bloodwort, Hanover County, Virginia

BENJAMIN HENRY LATROBE
1764–1820
Watercolor, pencil, pen and ink 1797
23.7 x 17.8 (9⁵⁄₁₆ x 7)

Lent by the Maryland Historical Society, Baltimore, Papers of Benjamin H. Latrobe

One year prior to making the drawing of the bloodwort or *Sanguinaria canadensis*, and with his usual delight in matters of natural history, Latrobe discussed the folkloric medicinal qualities of the plant, reporting that a "horse was bit in the nose by a venemous snake. The animal immediately swelled all over his body, and was in terrible torment . . . took a large parcel of the Blood wort, root, leaves, and flowers, and having made it *Blood warm* in milk, he gave it to the Horse as a drench. In a few hours the horse was grazing as before." Latrobe's observations were corroborated for, by 1830, the root of the plant was acknowledged for the treatment of horses "to make them sweat, shet their coats," and for the treatment of humans as a "good prophylacted for intermittents, marshy fevers, and inward fevers."

Latrobe's drawing of the bloodwort was made at the Hanover County, Virginia, farm of the physician Dr. James McClurg (1746–1823), for whom Latrobe would later design a house to be built in Richmond. McClurg had been a fellow student with Jefferson at the College of William and Mary and was appointed by Jefferson to the Chair of Anatomy and Medicine at the college in 1779. In 1797, the year of Latrobe's commission for the Richmond Penitentiary (see entry nos. 406, 407), as well as in 1800 and 1803, McClurg was the mayor of Richmond. B.S.

593 Liriodendron tulipifera
P. BESSA 1772–1835
Engraving c. 1810, in François A.
Michaux, *Histoire des arbres forestiers
de L'Amérique septentrionale*
(Paris, 1813), vol. 3

*From the Collection of Mr. and
Mrs. Paul Mellon*

Jefferson's association with the leading
botanists of the day, with the
Bartrams and with the Michaux,
stemmed as much from a belief in the
idea of a community of scientists
as from a common interest in the
science of botany. Scientific exchange
was seen as a highly civilized form of
communication. In a letter to John
Hollins, dated February 19, 1809,
Jefferson expressed the view that
scientific societies transcended political
interests.

General Washington, in his time,
received from that Society (the
Board of Agriculture of London) the
seed of the perennial succory, which
Arthur Young had carried over
from France to England, and I have
since received from a member of it
the seeds of the famous turnip of
Sweden, now so well known here. I
mention these things, to show the
nature of the correspondence which
is carried on between societies instituted for the benevolent purpose
of communicating to all parts
of the world whatever useful is discovered in any one of them. These
societies are always in peace, however
their nations may be at war. Like
the republic of letters, they form a
great fraternity spreading over the
whole earth, and their correspondence is never interrupted by any
nation. . . .

André and François Michaux, John
and William Bartram, Frederick Pursh
and Benjamin Smith Barton enriched
the course of American and European
botany in the last quarter of the
eighteenth century and in the first
decade of the nineteenth. The Michaux were responsible for the introduction of countless American plants
abroad and founded one of the first
experimental tree plantations in this
country at Charleston, South Carolina. François Michaux warned against
the wanton destruction of American
forests and sought to introduce sound
forestry practices at a time when
virgin forests, particularly the southern pine barrens, were being stripped
for naval stores and ship construction
Michaux's book on American forest
trees, published in this country with
the help of the American Philosophical
Society, formed the basis for later
works on American trees by Thomas
Nuttall and Charles Sprague Sargent.

Bessa's drawing of the *Liriodendron*
or tulip tree showed one of the most
popular of American trees in Europe.
The tulip tree is one of the plants
Jefferson attempted to send through
the blockade to Nantes, and hence by
canal to Paris in October 1805. Writing to his friend Mme de Tessé,
Jefferson said that because of the war
he "despaired of being able to send
any seeds," but that he would send,
among other native Virginia species,
the tulip. The white oak he said,
in the same letter, was the Jupiter of
our forests and the tulip—the "Juno of
our groves." E.M.

594 Cornus florida
P. J. REDOUTÉ 1759–1840
Engraving c. 1810, in François A.
Michaux, *Histoire des arbres forestiers
de L'Amérique septentrionale*
(Paris, 1813), vol. 3, pl. 13
Signed lower left: P. REDOUTÉ.
Lower right: *Gabriel Sculp.*

*Lent by the Dumbarton Oaks Garden
Library, Washington*

François André Michaux, son of the
French botanist and explorer André
Michaux, accompanied his father to
this country at the age of fifteen,
coming first to New York and in 1787
to Charleston, South Carolina. The
younger Michaux returned to France
in 1790 to serve in the French Revolution and to complete his education
in medicine and botany. He returned
to Charleston in 1801, where, with the
help of Pierre Samuel du Pont de
Nemours, he launched a campaign to
save two tree plantations, which
his father had established for the
French government. He traveled in the
Alleghenies during the summer of
1802 and returned to France the
following year to publish a report on
the naturalization of American forest
trees. He published between 1810
and 1813 an important three-volume
work on North American forest trees,
one volume of which is exhibited
here, a work consulted by Jefferson
which laid the foundation for con-
servation and forestry in the United
States.

Jefferson had been associated with
the elder Michaux as early as 1792.
André Michaux had botanized as far
north as Hudson Bay and had sought
to interest the American Philosophical
Society in an expedition beyond the
Missouri. Some money was subscribed
for the purpose, and Jefferson was
asked by the society to draft a set of
instructions for the journey. The expedition failed for political reasons,
though Michaux was given letters
of introduction by Jefferson for his
tour of the Midwest in 1793.

Jefferson received from his friend
John Vaughn in 1806 a copy of
François Michaux's pamphlet on the
naturalization of forest trees and a copy
of his travels. Jefferson thanked
Michaux in a letter dated July 12,
1806, saying that both books were
"valuable additions" to his botanical
library.

P. J. Redouté's engraving of the
dogwood appeared in the third volume
of François Michaux's *Histoire des
arbres forestiers*, published in 1813.
Dogwood was one of the trees sent by
Jefferson to Mme de Tessé, together
with seeds of the hickory nut and
other native Virginia trees, in 1805.
In a note accompanying Redouté's
engraving, Michaux recommended the
dogwood as a remedy for fever, and
as one of the principal American trees
recommended to European foresters
for use in parks and gardens. E.M.

595 Hypericum ascyron
F. F. NODDER d. 1800
Engraving, in J. J. Rousseau, *Letters
on the Elements of Botany* (London:
printed for B. White and Son, 1794)

*Lent by the Dumbarton Oaks Garden
Library, Washington*

Rousseau, like Jefferson, found solace
and retreat from political life in the
study of botany. Rousseau, exiled in
1762 to Neuchâtel on the Swiss
frontier, for the controversial publication of *Emile* and the *Social Contract*,
found solitude and peace in the
valley of the Areuse. Encouraged
initially by Dr. Jean-Antoine

nd His Circle, 1953, no. 83; London, Thos. Agnew & Sons, Ltd., *Loan Exhibition of Pictures from the City Art Gallery, Birmingham,* 1957, no. 35; Munich, Residenz, Council of Europe Exhibition, *The Age of Rococo,* 1959, no. 239; Arts Council of Great Britain, *Johann Zoffany,* 1960–1961, no. 16; Prague, Národní Galerie, and Bratislava, *Two Centuries of British Painting,* 1969, no. 173; Sydney, Opera House, *All the World's a Stage,* 1973.

Literature: Lady Victoria Manners and G. C. Williamson, *John Zoffany, R.A.* (London: John Lane, The Bodley Head, and New York: John Lane Company, 1920), p. 313; A. C. Sewter, "Four English Illustrative Pictures," *BurlM,* 74, (Mar. 1939), 127, illus. p. 126; Malone, *Jefferson the Virginian,* p. 125; City of Birmingham Museum and Art Gallery: *Illustrations of One Hundred Oil Paintings,* 1952, illus. p. 50; Raymond Mander and Joe Mitchenson, *The Artist and the Theatre* (London: Heinemann, 1955), pp. 13–19, repr. pp. 12, 20; Arno Schönberger and Halldor Soehner, *The Rococo Age* (New York: McGraw-Hill Book Company, Inc., 1959), p. 69, pls. 155 and 170; Ellis Waterhouse, *Johann Zoffany,* exhib. cat. (London: Arts Council of Great Britain, 1960–1961), no. 16.

72 The March to Finchley 1746
WILLIAM HOGARTH 1697–1764
Provenance: Presented to the Foundling Hospital by the artist, who was a governor, in 1750.

Exhibitions: London, British Institution, 1814, no. 140; London, British Institution, 1843, no. 164; Manchester, *Art Treasures,* 1857, no. 26; London, *International Exhibition,* 1862, no. 6; London, Royal Academy of Arts, 1872, no. 45; London, Wembley, *Empire Exhibition,* 1925, no. V.1, illus. in *Souvenir,* pl. ii; London, 25 Park Lane, *English Conversation Pieces,* 1930, no. 137, illus. in *Souvenir,* 25; London, Royal Academy of Arts, *British Art c. 1000–1860,* 1934, no. 210, illus. in *Commemorative Catalogue,* pl. XXVII; London, St. Bartholomew's Hospital, 1936; The Arts Council of Great Britain, *British Life,* 1953, no. 72, in cat. pl. III; London, Tate Gallery, *Hogarth,* Dec. 2, 1971–Feb. 6, 1972, no. 149, illus. in cat.

Literature: J. Nichols, *Biographical Anecdotes of William Hogarth* (London: J. Nichols, 1781), pp. 112–113; John Nichols and George Stevens, *The Genuine Works of William Hogarth* (London: Longman, Hurst, Rees and Orme, 1808–1817), 1:155–170, 3:173; J. B. Nichols, *Anecdotes of William Hogarth* (Lon-

don: J. B. Nichols & Son, 1833), p. 360; John Ireland and John Nichols, *Hogarth's Works,* 2nd ser. (London, 1874), pp. 121–136, illus.; William Makepeace Thackeray, *The Works of William Hogarth* (Boston: James R. Osgood and Company, 1876), no. 71; Austin Dobson, *William Hogarth* (New York: Dodd, Mead and Company, 1891), pp. 129–131, 335; John La Farge, *The Works of William Hogarth* (Philadelphia: George Barrie & Son, 1900), 2:76–92, 6:51–59, illus.; François Benoit, *Biographie critique* (Paris: H. Laurens, 1904), p. 43; G. Baldwin Brown, *William Hogarth* (London and New York: The Walter Scott Publishing Co., Ltd., and C. Scribner's Sons, 1905), p. 162; Edward Garnett, *Hogarth* (London and New York: Duckworth & Co., and E. P. Dutton & Co., 1911), pp. 136, 143; I. Gibeme Sieveking, *The Memoirs of Sir Horace Mann* (London: Kegan Paul, Trench, Trubner & Co. Ltd., 1912), p. 250; Herbert B. Grimsditch, *William Hogarth* (London: The Studio, 1926), pl. X; André Blum, *Hogarth,* 2nd ed. (Paris: Librairie Félix Alcan, 1931), pp. 70–71; G. C. Williamson, *English Conversation Pieces* (London: B. T. Batsford Ltd., 1931), p. 9, pl. XIX; *George Vertue Notebooks,* The Walpole Society, 22, (1933–1934), 3:153; R. H. Nichols and F. A. Wray, *The History of the Foundling Hospital* (London: Oxford University Press, 1935), illus. opp. p. 255; R. B. Beckett, *Hogarth* (London: Routledge and Kegan Paul Ltd., 1949), p. 69, pl. 158; Frederick Antal, *Hogarth and His Place in European Art* (New York: Basic Books, 1962), pp. 2, 28, 119–120, 222–223; Gabriele Baldini, *L'opera completa di Hogarth* (Milan: Rizzoli, 1967), no. 161, pls. XXXV and XXXVI; Ronald Paulson, *Hogarth's Graphic Works,* rev. ed. (New Haven and London: Yale University Press, 1970), 1:16–17, 277–280; Ronald Paulson, *Hogarth: His Life, Art and Times* (New Haven and London: Yale University Press, 1971), 1:403, 2:10, 20, 85–96, 99, 102, 111, 116, 133, 140, 151, 175, 181–182, 196–197, 203, 298, 304, 359, 362, 400, 402, 417, 433, 460, 477, 498, 500, pls. 224a and b; Benedict Nicolson, *The Treasures of the Foundling Hospital* (Oxford: Clarendon Press, 1972), pp. 69–70, pl. 70.

73 Chiswick Villa from the North-West 1742
GEORGE LAMBERT 1710–1765
Provenance: Third Earl of Burlington and fourth Earl of Cork, whose daughter Charlotte married the fourth Duke of Devonshire.

Exhibitions: London, Royal Horticultural Society, *International Exhibi-

tion of Garden Design,* 1928; London, 35 Grosvenor Square, *Country Life Exhibition,* 1937; London, Kenwood, *George Lambert 1700–1765,* 1970, no. 14; Nottingham University Art Gallery, *Apollo of the Arts: Lord Burlington and His Circle,* Jan. 22–Feb. 17, 1973, no. 36 as *Chiswick Villa from the south-east* with incorrect measurements.

Literature: J. B. Nichols, *Anecdotes of William Hogarth* (London: J. B. Nichols & Son, 1833), p. 366; Maurice Harold Grant, *A Chronological History of the Old English Landscape Painters* (London: The Author, 1926), 1:38; Warwick Draper, *Chiswick* (London: P. Allan & Co., 1923), illus. opp. p. 110; Ellis Waterhouse, *Painting in Britain 1530–1790* (Baltimore: Penguin Books, 1953), p. 115; James Lees-Milne, *Earls of Creation* (London: Hamish Hamilton Ltd., 1962), pp. 148–156; Elizabeth Einberg, *George Lambert 1700–1765,* exhib. cat. (London: Kenwood, 1970), no. 14.

74 The Coursing Party c. 1755–1758
IN THE STYLE OF GEORGE STUBBS
1724–1806
Provenance: R. C. Wilson, Tranby Croft, near Hull; Walter Hutchinson, 1948; Christie, Manson & Woods sale, London, Dec. 14, 1951, lot 65; M. B. N. Wyatt; Sotheby & Co. sale, London, Dec. 7, 1960, lot 11, illus. in cat.

Exhibitions: London, Hutchinson House, *National Gallery of British Sports and Pastimes,* no. 119; Virginia Museum of Fine Arts, Richmond, *Painting in England 1700–1850: Collection of Mr. and Mrs. Paul Mellon,* 1963, no. 313, illus. in vol. of plates p. 182.

Literature: J. Blan van Urk, *The Story of American Foxhunting* (New York: The Derrydale Press, 1940), 1:30–43, 45–46, 55–56, 61; Ross Watson, "Stubbs in America," *The British Racehorse,* 22, no. 2 (Summer 1970), 173–174, illus.; Jefferson to Thomas Jefferson Randolph, Nov. 24, 1808 (Lipscomb, 12:197–198).

75 The Sharp Family on a Yacht on the Thames 1779–1781
JOHANN ZOFFANY 1734/5–1810
Provenance: By descent, through his daughter Mary, who married Thomas John Lloyd Baker of Hardwicke Court, Gloucestershire, from William Sharp who commissioned the painting for 800 guineas.

Exhibitions: London, Royal Academy of Arts, 1781, no. 85 as *A gentleman's family;* London, Royal Academy of Arts, *Old Masters Exhibition,* 1879, no. 27; London, Whitechapel Art Gallery, *Spring Exhibition,* 1906,

no. 148; London, Wembley, *Empire Exhibition,* 1925, no. V, 27, illus. in *Souvenir,* no. 15; Brussels, *Peinture Anglaise,* 1929, no. 200; London, 25, Park Lane, *English Conversation Pieces,* 1930, no. 56, illus. in *Souvenir,* no. 71; London Royal Academy of Arts, *British Art c. 1000–1860,* 1934, no. 295; London, The Arts Council of Great Britain, The New Burlington Galleries, *British Life,* May 29–July 11, 1953, no. 12, illus. in cat. pl. VII; London, Royal Academy of Arts, *European Masters of the Eighteenth Century,* 1954–1955, no. 120; The Arts Council of Great Britain, *Johann Zoffany,* 1960–1961, no. 13, illus. in cat. pl. VIII; Cologne, Wallraf-Richartz Museum; Zurich, Kunsthaus, *Englische Malerei der Grossen Zeit,* Oct. 8–Nov. 6, 1966, and Jan.–Feb. 1967, no. 74, illus. in cat.; London, Royal Academy of Arts, *Bicentenary Exhibition 1768–1968,* 1968, no. 62, illus. in vol. of illustrations pl. 37.

Literature: Lady Victoria Manners and G. C. Williamson, *John Zoffany* (London and New York: John Lane, the Bodley Head and John Lane Company, 1920), pp. 70–72, 175–176, illus. opp. p. 70; G. C. Williamson *English Conversation Pictures* (London: B. T. Batsford Ltd., 1931), pp. 18–19, pl. LII; C. H. Collins Baker and Montague R. James, *British Painting* (Boston: Hale, Cushman & Flint, 1933), p. 136; Sacheverell Sitwell, *Conversation Pieces* (London: B. T. Batsford Ltd., 1936), pp. 25, 30, 94–95, pl. 32; Ellis Waterhouse, *Painting in Britain 1530–1790* (Baltimore: Penguin Books, 1953), p. 231; Ellis Waterhouse, *Johann Zoffany* (London: Arts Council of Great Britain, 1960–1961), no. 13, pl. VIII; Mario Praz, *Conversation Pieces* (University Park, Pa., and London: The Pennsylvania State University Press and Methuen & Co. Ltd., 1971), p. 184, fig. 155; Cripe, pp. 6–8, 14, 17; Boyd, 2:196; *Grove's Dictionary of Music and Musicians,* ed. Eric Blom, 5 (New York: St. Martin's Press, Inc., 1955): 371, 373, 375.

76 The Dutton Family
JOHANN ZOFFANY 1734/5–1810
Provenance: James Naper, later Dutton; Lord Sherborne by descent; Christie, Manson & Woods sale, London, June 28, 1929, lot 72; Daniel H. Farr, New York; Viscount Bearstead, father of the present owner.

Exhibitions: London, Royal Academy of Arts, *Winter Exhibition,* 1907, no. 143; London, 25, Park Lane, *Conversation Pieces,* 1930, no. 134; London, *European Masters of the Eighteenth Century,* 1954–1955, no. 100.

Literature: John Burk, *The History of Virginia, From Its First Settlement to the Present Day*, 3 (Petersburg: Dickson & Pescud, 1805):401; Lady Victoria Manners and G. C. Williamson, *John Zoffany, R.A.* (London and New York: John Lane, the Bodley Head, and John Lane Company, 1920), pp. 154, 233, illus. opp. p. 233; G. C. Williamson, *English Conversation Pieces* (London: B. T. Batsford Ltd., 1931), pp. 14–15, pl. XL; Sacheverell Sitwell, *Conversation Pieces* (London: B. T. Batsford Ltd., 1936), pp. 24, 25, 34, 36, 37, 40, 43, 46, 47, 94, pl. 29; Mario Praz, *Conversation Pieces* (University Park, Pa. and London: The Pennsylvania State University Press and Methuen & Co., Ltd., 1971), p. 101, fig. 60; Norman F. Cantor, *Western Civilization: Its Genesis and Destiny*, 2 (Glenview, Ill. and London: Scott, Foresman and Company, 1967), illus. betw. pp. 114–115.

77 A Midsummer Afternoon with a Methodist Preacher 1777
PHILIP JAMES DE LOUTHERBOURG
1740–1812
Provenance: Colonel W. P. Tipping, Brasted Place, Kent; H. Avray Tipping, Harefield House, Middlesex; Sotheby & Co. sale, London, Dec. 10, 1930, lot 83; P. & D. Colnaghi and Co., Ltd., London; bought by the National Gallery of Canada, 1932.
Exhibitions: London, Royal Academy of Arts, 1777, no. 216; London, Whitechapel Art Gallery, *Georgian England*, 1906, no. 130; London, Burlington Fine Arts Club, 1927–1928, no. 80; London, Royal Academy of Arts, *British Art c. 1000–1800*, 1934, no. 594, illus. in cat.; Toronto Art Gallery, *Loan Exhibition*, 1935, no. 43; London, Ontario, University of Western Ontario, *English Masters*, 1952; Pittsburgh, Carnegie Institute, *Everyday Life, Genre Painting in Europe, 1500–1900*, 1954, no. 64; Toronto Art Gallery, *European Masters*, 1954, no. 39; Detroit Institute of Arts and Philadelphia Museum of Art, *Romantic Art in Britain*, Jan. 9–Feb. 18 and Mar. 14–Apr. 21, 1968, no. 60, illus. in cat.; London, Kenwood, *Philippe Jacques de Loutherbourg, R.A., 1740–1812*, June 2–Aug. 13, 1973, no. 25, illus. in cat.
Literature: W. T. Whitley, *Artists and Their Friends in England, 1700–1799* (London and Boston: The Medici Society, 1928), 2:351, pl. 7; "Pictures at the Burlington Fine Arts Club," *Country Life*, 63 (Feb. 4, 1928), 144–145, illus.; *Art News*, 30 (Jan. 3, 1931), 13; Hans Tietze, "Die offentlichen Gemäldesammlungen in Kanada," *Pantheon*, 17 (June 1936), 184; Sacheverell Sitwell, *Narrative*

Pictures (London: B. T. Batsford Ltd., 1936), pp. 53, 109, pl. 82; Geneviève Levallet-Haug, "Philippe Jacques Loutherbourg 1740–1812," *Archives Alsaciennes*, 16 (1948), illus. opp. p. 104; Ellis Waterhouse, *Painting in Britain 1530–1790* (Baltimore: Penguin Books, 1953), p. 234, pl. 192B; R. H. Hubbard, *European Paintings in Canadian Collections: Earlier Schools* (Toronto: Oxford University Press, 1956), pp. 128, 153, pl. LXI; R. H. Hubbard, *The National Gallery of Canada, Catalogue of Paintings and Sculpture* (Ottawa and Toronto: University of Toronto Press, 1957), 1:121, illus.; Frederick Antal, *Hogarth and His Place in European Art* (New York: Basic Books, Inc., 1962), p. 250, pl. 149b; Paul Bois and France Verpeax, *Histoire, les XVIIIe et XIXe siècles* (Paris: Librairie Armand Colin, 1966), illus. p. 21; Louis Bergeron, *Les révolutions européennes et le partage du monde* (Paris: Bordas, Laffont, 1968), 1: illus. p. 35; William Gaunt, *The Great Century of British Painting: Hogarth to Turner* (London: Phaidon Press, 1971), pls. 83, 84; John Hayes, *Rowlandson: Watercolours and Drawings* (London: Phaidon Press Limited, 1972), p. 31, fig. 21; Jean Sutherland Boggs, *The National Gallery of Canada* (Toronto: Oxford University Press, 1971), pl. 72; Rudiger Joppien, *Philippe Jacques de Loutherbourg, R.A. 1740–1812*, exhib. cat. (London: Kenwood, 1973), no. 25, illus.; Ralph Edwards, "Percy Maquoid and Others," *Apollo*, 99 (May 1974), 336, illus. p. 337.

78 Warley Camp: The Mock Attack 1779
PHILIP JAMES DE LOUTHERBOURG
1740–1812
Provenance: Presented to George III by General Pierson and the officers of Warley Camp.
Exhibitions: London, Royal Academy of Arts, 1779, no. 182; London, Iveagh Bequest, *Philippe Jacques de Loutherbourg, R.A., 1740–1812*, June 2–Aug. 13, 1973, no. 59, illus. in cat.
Literature: Oliver Millar, *The Later Georgian Pictures in the Collection of Her Majesty the Queen* (London: Phaidon Press, Ltd., 1969), 1:81, 2: pl. 83; Rüdiger Joppien, *Die Szenenbilder Philippe Jacques de Loutherbourgs. Eine Untersuchung zu ihrer Stellung zwischen Malerei und Theater* (Cologne, 1972), pp. 206–207.

79 Kneehole writing table, English, c. 1750
Provenance: Formerly in the collections of Sir James Horlick, Bart., and Walter P. Chrysler; given to the Metropolitan in 1971 by Irwin Untermyer.

81 Settee, English, c. 1750
Provenance: Collection of Lord Doverdale, Westwood Park, Worcestershire; given to the Metropolitan Museum by Irwin Untermyer, 1951.

82 Side chair, English, c. 1750
Provenance: Collection of Lord Doverdale, Westwood Park, Worcestershire; given to the Metropolitan Museum by Irwin Utermyer, 1951.
Literature: Hackenbroch, fig. 124, pl. 97.

83 Ribband-back chair, English, Chippendale c. 1755
Provenance: Formerly in the collections of Sir Edward J. Dean Paul, Twickenham, and Leopold Hirsch, London; given to the Metropolitan Museum in 1957 by Edwin C. Vogel.
Exhibition: London, Lansdowne House, *English Decorative Art*, 1928, no. 432; New York, Parke-Bernet Galleries, *Art Treasures Exhibition*, 1955, no. 231.
Literature: Anthony Coleridge, *Chippendale Furniture* (London: Faber and Faber, 1968), pls. 172, 175; Ralph Edwards and Percy Macquoid, *Dictionary of English Furniture* (London: Country Life Limited, 1954), 1:280, 282, fig. 170.

84 Tripod tea table, English, c. 1750
Provenance: Formerly in the collections of Gerard Phelips, Montacute House, Somerset; Frances Wolfe Carey, Haddonfield, New Jersey, and George Horace Lorimer, Philadelphia; given to the Metropolitan Museum by Irwin Untermyer, 1964.
Literature: Hackenbroch, fig. 255, pl. 216.

85 Pair of brackets, English, Chippendale, c. 1755
Provenance: Given to the Metropolitan Museum by Irwin Untermyer, 1964.
Literature: Hackenbroch, fig. 354, pl. 310.

86 Fire screen, English, c. 1760
Provenance: Bequeathed to the Metropolitan Museum by Bernard M. Baruch, 1965.

87 Dressing table, English, c. 1760
Provenance: Formerly in the collections of Percival Giffiths and H. James Yates.

88 Armchair, English, c. 1750
Provenance: Lord North, Clemham, Suffolk.
Literature: Ralph Edwards and Percy Macquoid, *Dictionary of English Furniture* (London: Country Life Limited, 1954), 1: fig. 197; Percy

Macquoid, *A History of English Furniture; The Age of Mahogany* (London: Lawrence and Bullen, 1904), figs. 188–190.

89 Chinoiserie mirror, English, Rococo
Literature: Helena Hayward, *Thomas Johnson and the English Rococo* (London: A. Tiranti, 1964), pl. 150.

90 Sideboard, English, c. 1775
Provenance: Formerly in the collection of Miss Bouverie, Delapre Abbey, Northamptonshire; given to the Metropolitan Museum in 1964 by Irwin Untermyer.
Literature: Hackenbroch, fig. 50, pl. 30.

91 Pair of sideboard pedestals and urns, English, c. 1775
Provenance: Same as no. 90.
Literature: Hackenbroch, figs. 51, 52, pl. 31.

92 Card table, English, c. 1780–1790
Provenance: Acquired by the Metropolitan Museum in 1921 through the Rogers Fund.

93 Knife box, English, c. 1770–1780
Provenance: Acquired by the Metropolitan Museum in 1911 through the Rogers Fund.

94 Card table, English, c. 1770–1780
Provenance: Acquired by the Metropolitan Museum in 1911 through the Rogers Fund.

95 Pair of pedestal candlestands, English, c. 1775
Provenance: Former collection at Padworth House, Berkshire; given to the Metropolitan Museum of Art by Irwin Untermyer, 1964.
Literature: Hackenbroch, fig. 210, pl. 174.

96 Pair of candlesticks 1767/68
JOHN CARTER active c. 1767–1789
Provenance: Dr. H. F. Parshall; Christie, Manson & Woods sale, London, June 19, 1963, lot 151.
Exhibitions: London, Victoria and Albert Museum, *The Age of Neoclassicism*, Sept. 9–Nov. 19, 1972, no. 1741.
Literature: *Leeds Art Calendar*, no. 53 (1964), pp. 2–3 illus.; Robert Rowe, *Adam Silver* (London: Faber and Faber Limited, 1965), p. 37, pl. 10; Judith Banister, *English Silver* (London: Ward, Lock, 1965), pl. 102.

97 Pair of candelabra 1774/75
JOHN CARTER active c. 1767–1789
Literature: Robert Rowe, *Adam Silver* (London: Faber and Faber, 1965), pp. 37–38.

98 Cup 1774/75
WILLIAM CRIPPS?
Provenance: Presented, 1875. Bond Gift.
Literature: Robert Rowe, *Adam Silver* (London: Faber and Faber, 1965), p. 78.

100 Cup 1776/77
MATTHEW BOULTON 1728–1809, and JOHN FOTHERGILL c. 1700–1782
Provenance: Purchased by the Museum of Fine Arts, Boston, through the Theodora Wilbour Fund in memory of Charlotte Beebe Wilbour.
Literature: Robert Rowe, *Adam Silver* (London: Faber and Faber, 1965), p. 65, pl. 42.

101 Pair of candlesticks 1774/75
MATTHEW BOULTON 1728–1809, and JOHN FOTHERGILL c. 1700–1782
Provenance: Purchased by the Museum of Fine Arts, Boston, through the Theodora Wilbour Fund, no. 2, in memory of Charlotte Beebe Wilbour.
Literature: Robert Rowe, *Adam Silver* (London: Faber and Faber Limited, 1965), pp. 28, 65, pl. 50.

102 Pair of sauce tureens 1776/77
MATTHEW BOULTON 1728–1809, and JOHN FOTHERGILL c. 1700–1782
Provenance: Mrs. Montagu.
Literature: Robert Rowe, *Adam Silver* (London: Faber and Faber, 1965), pp. 60–62, pls. 56A and 56B; Eric Delieb, *The Great Silver Manufactory* (London: Studio Vista, 1971), p. 87, illus., and illus. in col. opp. p. 41; Boyd, 11:26.

103 Tea urn 1777/78
THOMAS HEMING active 1745–1780
Provenance: James Hazen Hyde.
Exhibitions: New York, The Cooper Union Museum, *The Four Continents*, 1961, no. 90; The Cleveland Museum of Art, *Neo-classicism: Style and Motif*, Sept. 21–Nov. 1, 1964, no. 94, illus. in cat.

104 Exhuming the First American Mastodon 1806
CHARLES WILLSON PEALE 1741–1827
Provenance: Charles Willson Peale; Lloyd Rogers; George Reuling; Anderson Auction Galleries sale, New York, Apr. 26, 1905, lot 30; Bertha James White (Mrs. Harry White).
Exhibitions: New York, The Metropolitan Museum of Art, *Life in America*, Apr. 24–Oct. 29, 1939;

Pittsburgh, The Carnegie Institute, *Survey of American Painting*, Oct. 24–Dec. 15, 1940; Washington, D.C., The Corcoran Gallery of Art, *American Processional, 1492–1900*, July 8–Dec. 17, 1950; Cincinnati Art Museum, *Paintings by the Peale Family*, Oct. 1–31, 1954; Baltimore, Municipal Museum (The Peale Museum), *Rendezvous for Taste*, Feb. 24–Apr. 22, 1956; Baltimore, Municipal Museum, *The Peale Family and Peale's Baltimore Museum, 1814–1830*, Feb. 1965; New York, Whitney Museum of American Art, *Art of the United States, 1670–1966*, Sept. 28–Nov. 27, 1966; The Detroit Institute of Arts, *The Peale Family*, Jan. 8–Mar. 5, 1967; Utica, The Munson-Williams-Proctor Institute, *The Peale Family*, Mar. 28–May 7, 1967; Washington, D.C., National Portrait Gallery, *This New Man*, Sept. 28–Dec. 31, 1968; New York, The Metropolitan Museum of Art, *19th Century America; Paintings and Sculpture*, Apr. 16–Sept. 7, 1970.
Literature: Charles Coleman Sellers, *Charles Willson Peale, II: Later Life (1790–1827)* (Philadelphia: American Philosophical Society, 1947), pp. 127–148, 205; Oliver Larkin, *Art and Life in America* (New York: Rinehart, 1949), pp. 132–133; Charles Coleman Sellers, *Portraits and Miniatures by Charles Willson Peale* (Philadelphia: American Philosophical Society, 1952), no. 252, p. 75, figs. 285, 285A; Wilbur Harvey Hunter, *The Peale Museum, 1814–1964* (Baltimore: Municipal Museum, 1964), pp. 4–6; Charles Coleman Sellers, *Charles Willson Peale* (New York: Scribner, 1969), p. 344.

105 Portrait of Lavoisier and his Wife 1788
JACQUES-LOUIS DAVID 1748–1825
Provenance: David was paid the considerable sum of 7000 livres for the portrait on December 16, 1788; bequeathed by Mme Lavoisier to her great niece, the comtesse de Chazelles; collection of Etienne de Chazelles at the Château de la Canière, near Aigueperse; sold in 1924; acquired by John D. Rockefeller in 1925; entered the collection of the Rockefeller Institute for Medical Research, New York, in 1927.
Exhibitions: Paris, Exposition Universelle Internationale, *Centennale de l'Art Français 1789–1889*, 1889, no. 234; Paris, Petit Palais, *David et ses Elèves*, 1913, no. 20; New York, World's Fair, *Masterpieces of Art*, 1940; Paris, Orangerie, *David*, 1948, M.O. 23, illus.; Paris, Grand Palais, *De David à Delacroix, La peinture française de 1774 à 1830*, Nov. 16, 1974–Feb. 3, 1975, no. 33; Detroit,

The Detroit Institute of Arts, Mar. 5–May 4, 1975, *French Painting 1774–1830: The Age of Revolution*, no. 33.
Literature: "Correspondance de M. d'Angiviller avec Pierre," *Archives de l'Art français*, 1905–1906, 2 (Aug. 10, 1789), 264–265; Pierre Chaussard, *Le Pausanias français, ou Description du Salon de 1806*, 2nd ed. (Paris: F. Buisson, 1808), pp. 156–157; *Notice sur la vie et les ouvrages de M. J. L. David* (Paris, 1824), p. 43; A. Th [Thomé?], *Vie de David, premier peintre de Napoléon* (Paris, 1826), pp. 151 and 240 (as two portraits); P. A. Coupin, *Essai sur J. L. David peintre d'histoire, ancien membre de l'Institut, officier de la Légion d'Honneur* (Paris: Renouard, 1827), p. 54; Charles Blanc, *Histoire des peintres français au XIX* e *siècle*, 1, (Paris: Cauville frères, 1845): 209; Miette de Villars, *Mémoires de David, peintre et député à la Convention* (Paris, 1850), p. 100; E. J. Delécluze, *Louis David, son école et son temps. Souvenirs* (Paris: Didier, 1855), p. 137; J. du Seigneur, "Appendice à la notice de P. Chaussard sur L. David," *Revue universelle des Arts*, 18 (1863), 366; J. L. J. David, *Le peintre Louis David* (Paris: V. Havard, 1880), pp. 53 and 637, illus. p. 1882; E. Grimaux, *Lavoisier 1743–1794, d'après sa correspondance, ses manuscrits, ses papiers de famille et d'autres documents inédits* (Paris, 1888), 6: 364–365, frontispiece illus.; Victor de Swarte, "Les financiers amateurs d'art," *Réunion des Beaux-Arts des Départements en 1890*, 14th session, 1890, pp. 161–162; Charles Saunier, *Louis David* (Paris, 1904), p. 17, illus., and p. 124; Leon Rosenthal, *Louis David* (Paris, n.d. [1905]), p. 165; Prosper Dorbec, "David portraitists," *GBA*, April 1907, pp. 310–311, 324, illus.; G. Capon, *The portrait of Lavoisier and his wife by Jacques Louis David* (n.p., n.d. [1924]); Richard Cantinelli, *Jacques-Louis David, 1748–1825* (Paris-Brussels: G. Van Oest, 1930), no. 55, p. 104, pl. XIX; D. S. Mac Coll, "Jacques Louis David and the Ducreux Family," *Burl M*, 72 (1938), 264 and 268, illus.; Holma, p. 53, no. 61, p. 126, pl. XVII; Jacques Maret, *David* (Monaco: Les Documents d'Art, 1943), fig. 38; Hautecoeur, pp. 105, 107; Jack Lindsay, *Death of the Hero: French Painting from David to Delacroix* (London: Studio, 1960), p. 60; A. Gonzales-Palacios, *Chefs d'oeuvres de l'art. Grands peintres, David* (Milan, 1966; Paris, 1967), no. 17, cover illus.; Hugh Honour, *Neoclassicism* (Harmondsworth, 1968), pp. 72 and 198, fig. 28; R. L. Herbert, *David, Voltaire, "Brutus" and the French Revolution: an Essay in Art and Politics* (Lon-

don, 1972), pp. 58–59 and ns. 44–47, illus. 29; René Verbraeken, *Jacques-Louis David jugé par ses contemporains et par la postérité* (Paris: L. Laget, 1973), pp. 14, 28, 30, 32, 147, fig. 22; Daniel and Guy Wildenstein, *Documents complémentaires au catalogue de l'oeuvre de Louis David* (Paris: Fondation Wildenstein, 1973), nos. 205, 1810, 1938 (17); Jefferson to Lavoisier and others, Feb. 4, 1787; Lavoisier to Jefferson, Mar. 3, 1787; Jefferson to Madison, July 19, 1788.

106 The Astronomer
NICOLAS-BERNARD LÉPICIÉ 1735–1784
Provenance: E. Tondu sale, Apr. 1865; Baronne Nathaniel de Rothschild collection, 1876–1892; Baronne David Leonino; Baron Henri de Rothschild, bought by Gulbenkian, 1943.
Exhibition: Paris, Musée du Louvre, *Deuxième Exposition des Portraits du XVIII* e *Siècle*, 1885, no. 209; Leipzig, Leipziger Kuntsverein, *Cent Chefs-D'Oeuvre*, June 1892, no. 23; London, the National Gallery, *Pictures from the Gulbenkian Collection*, 1947–1950; Washington, National Gallery of Art, *European Paintings from the Gulbenkian Collection*, 1950–1960; Paris, Fundaçao Caloust-Gulbenkian, *Tableaux de la Collection Gulbenkian*, 1960, no. 17; Lisbon, Museu Nacio de Art Antiga, *Pintures da Coleccao da Fundaçao Gulbenkian*, 1961, no. 21; Porto, Museu Nacio de Soares dos Reis, *Artes Plasticas Francesas de Watteau a Renoir*, 1964, no. 8; Oeira, Palacio de Pombal, *Obras de Arte da Coleccao Calouste Gulbenkian*, 1965, no. 210; Lisboa, Museu Calouste Gulbenkian, 1969–1976, no. 620.
Literature: C. Lorice, *L'Art et les Artistes* (Paris, 1906), p. 231; Emile Dacier, *Gabriel de Saint-Aubin* (Paris: G. van Oest, 1929); Philippe Gaston-Dreyfus, *Catalogue Raisonné de Nicolas Bernard Lépicié* (Paris: A. Colin, 1923); Jefferson to Daniel Rittenhouse, July 19, 1778; Jefferson to Thomas Mann Randolph, Jr., Aug. 27, 1786.

107 Portrait of Balthazar Sage 1777
JEAN-FRANÇOIS GILLES, CALLED COLSON 1733–1803
Provenance: Offered by Société des Amis du Musée de Dijon, 1959.
Exhibitions: Mayence, *Kunst des 18. Jahrhunderts* au Dijon, 1966, no. 3; Dijon, Musée des Beaux-Arts, *Trois peintres bourguignons du XVIII* e *siècle, Colson, Vestier, Trinquesse*, 1969, no. 10 and pl. VI.
Literature: "La Chronique des Arts," *GBA*, Jan. 1960, p. 5, fig. 17; Pierre Quarré, "Tassel, Colson, Hoén," *Bulletin de la Société des Amis du*

Musée de Dijon, 1958–1960, p. 82, illus.; Pierre Quarré, "Musée des Beaux-Arts de Dijon, Nouvelles acquisitions," *La Revue du Louvre et des Musées de France*, 1964, nos. 4–5, p. 253, fig. 6; Gabriel Arlet, "Essai sur l'histoire des écoles des Mines," *Regards sur la France: Les écoles nationales supérieures des Mines*, no. 15 (Nov. 1961), 40, illus. p. 30; Thomas Jefferson, *Notes on the State of Virginia*, ed. William Peden (New York, 1954), pp. 26–29.
Related Works: An engraving brought to our attention by Mr. J. C. Garreta, after the portrait and printed by Beauvalet, *Inventaire du fonds français, graveurs du XVIIIe siècle*, 2 (Paris, 1932): no. 87; Jefferson to Dr. Joseph Willard, Mar. 24, 1789.

108 Robert Fulton c. 1803
JEAN-ANTOINE HOUDON 1741–1828
Literature: Louis Reau, "Houdon sous la révolution et l'empire," *GBA*, July–Aug. 1924, pp. 59–86; Paul L. Grigaut, "A Marble Bust of Robert Fulton by Houdon," *AQ*, 12, no. 3 (Summer 1949), 252–257; Paul L. Grigaut, "Houdon's Marble Bust of Robert Fulton," *Bulletin of the Detroit Institute of Arts*, 28, no. 4 (1949), 79–80; Edwin T. Martin, *Thomas Jefferson, Scientist* (London, New York: Abelard-Schuman, 1952), pp. 8–9, 78–81; James Woodress, *A Yankee's Odyssey: The Life of Joel Barlow* (Philadelphia: Lippincott, 1958), pp. 210–217, 227–229, 253; Jefferson to Fulton, Mar. 17, 1810 (Lipscomb, 12:380–381); Jefferson to George Fleming, Dec. 29, 1815 (Lipscomb, 14:366–369), on household uses of steam; Fulton to Ruth Baldwin Barlow, June 12, 1813 (Houghton Library, Harvard University).
Material in this and all subsequent entries contributed by Mr. Arnason is derived from: H. H. Arnason, *The Sculpture of Houdon*, London, Phaidon Press; New York, Oxford University Press, 1975.

109 Experiment with an Air Pump c. 1768
JOSEPH WRIGHT OF DERBY 1734–1797
Provenance: Dr. Benjamin Bates; Walter Tyrrell; presented by Edward Tyrrell to the National Gallery, 1863; transferred to the Tate Gallery, 1929.
Exhibitions: London, Society of Artists, 1768, no. 193, and again as a special exhibition for the king of Denmark in the same year, no. 131; Derby Museum and Art Gallery, on loan 1912–1947; Derby Museum and Art Gallery, *Wright of Derby*, 1934, no. 36, illus. in cat.; Derby Museum and Art Gallery and Leicester Museum and Art Gallery, *Joseph Wright of*

Derby Exhibition, 1947, no. 36; London, The Tate Gallery, and Liverpool, The Walker Art Gallery, *Joseph Wright of Derby 1734–1797*, Apr. 11–May 18, and May 31—June 21, 1958, no. 5.
Literature: Richard and Samuel Redgrave, *A Century of British Painters* (London: Smith, Elder and Co., 1866), 1:257, 263–264; William Bennrose, *The Life and Works of Joseph Wright, A. R. A.*, commonly called "Wright of Derby" (London and Derby: Bennrose & Sons, 1885), pp. 66–68; Francis Klingender, "The Industrial Revolution and the Birth of Romanticism," *Apropos*, 4 (1945), 20–24; Ruthven Todd, *Tracks in the Snow—Studies in English Science and Art* (London: The Grey Walls Press 1946); Francis Klingender, *Art and the Industrial Revolution* (London: N. Carrington, 1947), p. 47; Charles E. Buckley, "Joseph Wright of Derby," *Magazine of Art*, 44, no. 4 (Apr. 1952), 161–163, illus.; Ellis Waterhouse, *Painting in Britain 1530 to 1790* (Baltimore: Penguin Books, 1953), p. 208, pl. 174 B; Benedict Nicholson, *Joseph Wright of Derby* (London and New York: Routledge and Kegan Paul for the Paul Mellon Foundation for British Art and Pantheon Books, 1968), 1:17–18, 43–45, 50, 52, 104–105, 112–114, 117, 119–120, 235, and figs. 43, 49, 118, details, 2: pl. 58; J. H. Plumb, "The New World of Children in Eighteenth-Century England," *Past & Present*, no. 67 (May 1975), 80; *The Jefferson Cyclopedia*, ed. John P. Foley (1900; rpt. New York: Russell & Russell, 1967), 2:839; Jefferson to Charles Thomson, Apr. 22, 1786 and Dec. 17, 1786, Boyd, 9:400–401, 10:609–610; Jefferson to George Fleming, Dec. 29, 1815 (Lipscomb, 14:366–369).

110 The Cast Iron Bridge near Coalbrookdale 1782
WILLIAM ELLIS 1747–c. 1805, after Michael "Angelo" Rooker 1743–1801
Literature: Metius Chappell, *British Engineers* (London: W. Collins, 1942), illus. opp. p. 9; Alfred Owen Aldridge, *The Man of Reason, The Life of Thomas Paine* (Philadelphia and New York: J. B. Lippincott Company, 1959), pp. 108–117; Francis D. Klingender, *Art and the Industrial Revolution*, rev. ed. (Chatham: Evelyn, Adams and Mackay, 1968), p. 88; Marie Kimball, "Jefferson's Works of Art at Monticello," *Antiques*, 59, no. 4 (Apr. 1951), 311.

111 William Hunter Lecturing on Anatomy c. 1775
JOHANN ZOFFANY 1734/5–1810
Provenance: William Hunter; his

nephew, Matthew Baillie; presented to Royal College of Physicians by Mrs. Baillie, 1825.
Exhibitions: London, *International Exhibition*, 1862, no. 36; London, South Kensington Museum, *National Portraits Exhibition*, 1867, no. 506; London, Royal Academy of Arts, *Winter Exhibition*, 1871, London, Whitechapel Art Gallery, 1906, no. 23.
Literature: R. Kingston Fox, *William Hunter* (London: H. K. Lewis, 1901), pp. 9, 65; Lady Victoria Manners and G. C. Williamson, *John Zoffany, R.A.* (London and New York: John Lane, The Bodley Head and John Lane Company, 1920), p. 226, illus.; Gordon Wolstenholme and David Piper, *The Royal College of Physicians of London: Portraits* (London: J. & A. Churchill, 1964), p. 232, illus. p. 233; Jefferson to Dr. Caspar Wistar, June 1807 (Ford, 9:81).

112 An Inoculation
CONSTANT DESBORDES 1761–1827
Provenance: Commissioned by the minister of the interior (most writers repeat Duthilloeul who affirms without proof that the painting had been commissioned by the minister as early as 1812; however, it is then difficult to explain why the painting was not exhibited until 1822); deposited by the Musée du Louvre in the Musée de Douai, 1890.
Exhibition: Paris, Salon of 1822, no. 348; Paris, Salon of 1824, no. 491 ("Scène de Vaccine"); Douai, Bibliothèque municipale, *Marceline Desbordes-Valmore*, 1959, no. 71; Paris, Bibliothèque nationale, *Marceline Desbordes-Valmore*, 1959, no. 208, pl. II; London, Royal Academy and The Victoria and Albert Museum, *The Age of Neo-classicism*, Sept. 9–Nov. 19, 1972, no. 72.
Literature: H. Duthilloeul, *Galerie douaisienne, ou, Biographie des hommes rémarquables de la ville de Douai*, 1 (Douai: d'Aubers, 1844): 112; *Courrier de l'art*, 1890, p. 211; Lucien Descaves, *La vie douloureuse de Marceline Desbordes-Valmore* (Paris: Editions d'art et de littérature 1910), p. 30; Thieme-Becker, 9:108; Sowerby, 1:428–433; Jefferson to William Fleming, July 1, 1776; Jefferson to Benjamin Rush, Dec. 20, 1801, Ford, 10:303; Jefferson to Meriwether Lewis, June 20, 1803, Ford, 18:153; Jefferson to Edward Jenner, June 21, 1806, Ford, 19:152.

113 Coalbrookdale by Night 1801
PHILIP JAMES DE LOUTHERBOURG 1740–1812
Provenance: D. Reader; purchased from Pictura Ltd., London, 1952.
Exhibitions: London, Royal Academy

of Arts, 1801, no. 54 as *A View of Colebrook Dale by Night*; Manchester, City Art Gallery, *Art and the Industrial Revolution*, 1968, no. 32, illus. in cat. pl. V; Prague, Bratislava and Vienna, British Council Exhibition, *Two Centuries of British Painting from Hogarth to Turner*, 1969; Tokyo, The National Museum of Western Art and The Kyoto National Museum of Modern Art, British Council Exhibition, *English Landscape Painting of the 18th and 19th centuries*, Oct. 10–Nov. 23, 1970 and Dec. 1, 1970–Jan. 15, 1971, no. 18, illus. in cat.; London, The Tate Gallery, *Landscape in Britain c. 1750–1850*, Nov. 20, 1973–Feb. 3, 1974, no. 133, illus. p. 63 in cat.; London, Kenwood, *Philippe Jacques de Loutherbourg, R.A. 1740–1812*, June 2–Aug. 13, 1973, no. 52, illus. in cat.; Milan, British Council Exhibition, 1975.
Literature: *The Engineer*, 193 (Feb. 22, 1952), 268, illus.; *BurlM*, 110 (July 1968), illus. p. 419; Francis D. Klingender, *Art and the Industrial Revolution* (Chatham: Evelyn, Adams and Mackay, 1968), pp. 86–93; Leslie Paris, *Landscape in Britain c. 1750–1850*, exhib. cat. (London, The Tate Gallery, Nov. 20, 1973–Feb. 3, 1974), no. 133, illus. p. 63; Rudiger Joppien, *Philippe Jacques de Loutherbourg, R.A. 1740–1812*, exhib. cat. (London: Kenwood, 1973), no. 52, illus.

114 The Ascent of Lunardi's Balloon c. 1788–1790
JULIUS CAESAR IBBETSON 1759–1817
Provenance: Willson Brothers, London, purchased in 1915.
Exhibitions: London, Kenwood, *Julius Caesar Ibbetson*, 1957, no. 4.
Literature: Rota Mary Clay, *Julius Caesar Ibbetson (1759–1817)* (London: Country Life Ltd., 1948), pp. 11–12; Theodore Sizer, *The Works of Colonel John Trumbull* (New Haven and London: Yale University Press, 1967), p. 102; Boyd, 7:134–137, 602, 8:233.

115 The Interior of the Pantheon, Oxford Street c. 1778
MICHAEL "ANGELO" ROOKER 1743–1801
Provenance: Edward Basil Jupp (1812–1877) who formed an illustrated collection of exhibition catalogues of the Society of Artists of Great Britain and the Free Society of Artists in which the present drawing was included; Thomas William Waller; Elizabeth Stauffer Moore; by descent to her great-granddaughter Elizabeth Richard Simmons, New York; Christie, Manson & Woods sale, London, Nov. 12, 1968, lot 157, illus. in cat.; Appleby Bros., London.

Literature: Benjamin Wilson, *An Account of Experiments made at the Pantheon on the Nature and Use of Conductors* (London, 1778), illus. frontispiece, *Notes on the State of Virginia*, p. 64.

116 Comte de Buffon 1782
JEAN-ANTOINE HOUDON 1741–1828
Provenance: Appeared as no. 65, sale of Sussman Collection, May 1922; collection of Arnold Seligman of Rey and Co., New York, 1936; The Fine Arts Museums of San Francisco, Archer M. Huntington Fund Purchase.
Literature: Gaston Brière, "Notes sur quelques bustes de Houdon," *Mélanges offerts à M. Henry Lemonnier par la Société de l'histoire de l'art français, ses amis et ses élèves* (Paris, 1913), pp. 354–357; "Comte de Buffon: portrait bust," *Bulletin of the California Palace of the Legion of Honor, 1* (June 1943), 20–22; Dumas Malone, *Jefferson and the Rights of Man* (Boston: Little, Brown and Co., 1951), pp. 99–100.

117 Telescope
JOHN DOLLOND 1706–1761, and PETER DOLLOND 1730–1820
Provenance: Purchased by Jefferson, possibly in London in 1786; descended to Thomas Jefferson Randolph who presented it to the University of Virginia; currently on loan to the Thomas Jefferson Memorial Foundation from the University of Virginia.
Literature: Dollond Telescope, see Jefferson's account book for 1786, Mar. 21. Jefferson to Thomas Mann Randolph, Aug. 27, 1786.

118 Theodolite and Tripod
JESSE RAMSDEN 1735–1800
Provenance: It cannot be determined where or when Jefferson obtained this theodolite. It was purchased at the 1827 sale of Monticello furnishings by General J. H. Cocke from whom it descended to Mrs. Milton Elliott. The theodolite and tripod were purchased from Mrs. Elliott by the Thomas Jefferson Memorial Foundation in 1967.
Literature: re: Theodolites, see Jefferson to David Rittenhouse, July 19, 1778. PHi; Lipscomb, 19:183–184; Jefferson Memorandum dated Mar. 10, 1806, in the Massachusetts Historical Society.

119 Louis XVI, Accompanied by M. the Maréchal de Castries . . .
NICOLAS-ANDRÉ MONSIAU 1754–1837
Provenance: Executed by Monsiau 1816–1817 for the galerie de Diane at the Château des Tuileries.
Exhibition: Paris, Salon of 1817.
Literature: E. Soulié, *Notice du musée imperial de Versailles, 1* (Paris, 1859): no. 220, pp. 54–55; Bellier and Auvray, 2:112; Thième-Becker, 25: 74; Charles O. Ziexhiss, "Le décor pictural de la galérie de Diane aux Tuileries sous le premier empire," *Bulletin de la Société de l'histoire de l'art français,* 1966; G. and J. Lacambre, "La galerie de Diane aux Tuileries sous la Restauration," *La Revue du Louvre et des musées de France,* no. 1 (1975), 39, fig. 3, pp. 41, 50.

120 Sir Joseph Banks, Omai and Dr. Solander c. 1775
WILLIAM PARRY 1742?–1791
Provenance: Sir Robert Williams Vaughan, 2nd Bart., Dolgelley, Merioneth, and by descent to Brigadier C. H. Vaughan; Christie, Manson & Woods sale, London, Apr. 2, 1965, lot 35, illus. in cat.
Exhibitions: Cardiff, National Museum of Wales, *Portraits in Welsh Houses,* 1948, no. 53.
Literature: H. C. Cameron, *Sir Joseph Banks* (London: Batchworth Press, 1952), illus. opp. p. 236; John Steegman, *A Survey of Portraits in Welsh Houses* (Cardiff: National Museum of Wales, 1957), 1:232, pl. 40B; Stig Rydén, *The Banks Collection: an Episode in 18th Century Anglo-Swedish Relations* (Stockholm: Almqvist and Wiskell, 1963), fig. 6.

121 Matavai Bay, Tahiti 1776
WILLIAM HODGES 1744–1797
Provenance: H. T. de Vere Clifton; Spink and Son, Ltd., London, from whom purchased 1963.
Exhibitions: Possibly London, Royal Academy of Arts, 1776, no. 113, as *A View of Matavie Bay in the island of Otahiete;* London, Royal Academy of Arts, *Painting in England 1700–1850 from the Collection of Mr. and Mrs. Paul Mellon* 1964–1965, no. 37, illus. in *Souvenir,* p. 30; New Haven, Yale University Art Gallery, *Painting in England 1700–1850 from the Collection of Mr. and Mrs. Paul Mellon,* Apr. 15–June 20, 1965, no. 105.
Literature: Bernard Smith, *European Vision and the South Pacific, 1768–1850* (Oxford: Clarendon Press, 1960).

122 Rhinoceros c. 1772
GEORGE STUBBS 1724–1806
Provenance: Painted for John Hunter; bequeathed by Hunter with his collection to the British government who gave it to The Royal College of Surgeons of England.
Exhibitions: Liverpool, Walker Art Gallery, *George Stubbs,* 1951, no. 51; London, Whitechapel Art Gallery,

George Stubbs, 1957, no. 53.
Literature: Geoffrey Grigson, *The Harp of Aeolus* (London: Routledge, 1947), p. 19; *Annals of the Royal College of Surgeons,* 1949, p. 162; Adrian Bury, *Antiques Review,* 2, no. 7 (Mar./May 1954), fig. 10; Basil Taylor, *Animal Painting in England* (Harmondsworth: Penguin Books, 1955), pp. 36, 63, pl. 1; William Le Fanu, *A Catalogue of the Portraits in the Royal College of Surgeons of England* (Edinburgh and London: E. & S. Livingston, 1960), p. 88, illus. in opp. col.; Constance-Anne Parker, *Mr. Stubbs, the Horse Painter* (London: J. A. Allen, 1971), p. 86; Basil Taylor, *Stubbs* (London: Phaidon Press, 1971), pp. 30–31, 210, pl. 72; T. H. Clarke, "The Iconography of the Rhinoceros, Part II," *Connoisseur,* 185 (Feb. 1974), 121, illus. p. 115, with date of c. 1790; Ledyard to Jefferson, July 29, 1787; Jefferson to Harry Innes, Mar. 7, 1791 (Ford, 5:294) ("Natural history . . . is my passion").

123 Green Monkey 1774
GEORGE STUBBS 1724–1806
Exhibitions: Probably London, Royal Academy of Arts, 1775, no. 304, as *Portrait of a monkey;* Liverpool, Walker Art Gallery, on loan, June–Sept. 1972.
Literature: Jefferson Himself: The Personal Narrative of a Many-Sided American, ed. Bernard Mayo (Charlottesville: The University Press of Virginia, 1973), p. 19.

124 Meriwether Lewis 1803 or 1807
CHARLES-BALTHAZAR-JULIEN FEVRET DE SAINT-MÉMIN 1770–1852
Provenance: Sent to Locust Hill about time of departure on expedition, July 4 or 5, 1803; Lucy Meriwether Lewis Marks (mother of Meriwether Lewis) to Jane Lewis Anderson (his sister), to Dr. M. Lewis Anderson (her son), to Charles Harper Anderson, Dr. M. Lewis Anderson, and Meriwether Lewis Anderson, Jr., by whom it was presented to the Missouri Historical Society.
Exhibitions: Richmond, Virginia Historical Society, *Contemporary Personages Associated with the Colony and Commonwealth of Virginia between the Years 1585 and 1830,* 1929; Richmond, Valentine Museum, *Works of Charles Balthazar Julien Fevret de Saint-Mémin,* 1941; Washington, National Portrait Gallery, *This New Man,* 1968.
Literature: Alexander Weddell, ed., *A Memorial Volume of Virginia Historical Portraiture, 1585–1830* (Richmond: William Byrd Press, Inc., 1930), pp. 316–318; Fillmore Nor-

fleet, *Saint-Mémin in Virginia* (Richmond: The Dietz Press, 1942), p. 183; Donald Jackson, ed., *Letters of the Lewis and Clark Expedition with Related Documents 1783–1854* (Urbana: University of Illinois Press, 1962), pp. 2, 320, 589–591; Richard Dillon, *Meriwether Lewis, A Biography* (New York: Coward-McCann, Inc., 1965).

125 Portrait of Thomas Jefferson 1804
CHARLES-BALTHAZAR-JULIEN FEVRET DE SAINT-MÉMIN 1770–1852
Provenance: Collection of George Bancroft, to his son, John Chandler Bancroft; purchased by the Worcester Art Museum, Worcester, Mass., in 1954 from the estate of Wilder D. Bancroft.
Exhibition: National Gallery of Art and the Library of Congress, *The Thomas Jefferson Bicentennial,* 1943; The Detroit Institute of Arts, *The French in America 1520–1880,* July 14 to Sept. 16, 1951; Charlottesville, The University of Virginia Museum of Fine Arts, *The Life Portraits of Thomas Jefferson,* Apr. 12–16, 1962; National Portrait Gallery, Smithsonian Institution, Washington, D.C., *If Elected . . . Unsuccessful Candidates for the Presidency 1796–1968,* Apr. 14 to Nov. 19, 1972.
Literature: Clarence W. Bowen, ed., *The History of the Centennial Celebration of the Inauguration of George Washington* (New York: D. Appleton and Co., 1892), pp. 486–487; Charles Henry Hart, "The Life Portraits of Thomas Jefferson," *McClure's Magazine,* 11, no. 1 (May 1898), 47–55; Fillmore Norfleet, *Saint-Mémin in Virginia* (Richmond: The Dietz Press, 1942), pp. 30–31, 176–177; *The Thomas Jefferson Bicentennial Exhibition, 1743–1943,* exhib. cat. (Washington: The National Gallery of Art, 1943), no. 7; *The French in America, 1520–1880,* exhib. cat. (Detroit: Institute of Arts, (1951), pp. 167–168; Howard C. Rice, Jr., "Saint-Mémin's Portrait of Jefferson," *The Princeton University Library Chronicle,* 20, no. 4 (Summer 1959), 182–192; Louisa Dresser, "A Life Portrait of Thomas Jefferson," *Worcester Art Museum News Bulletin and Calendar,* 17, no. 3 (Dec. 1951), 9–10; *A Catalog of Portraits and Other Works of Art in the Possession of the American Philosophical Society* (Philadelphia: American Philosophical Society, 1961), pp. 53–54; Alfred L. Bush, *The Life Portraits of Thomas Jefferson,* exhib. cat. (Charlottesville: The University of Virginia Museum of Fine Arts, 1962), pp. 65–67.

126–129 Four Indian portraits
CHARLES-BALTHAZAR-JULIEN FEVRET
DE SAINT-MÉMIN 1770–1852
Portrait of an Osage Warrior c. 1807.
Portrait of Cachasunghia, an Osage Warrior c. 1807.
Portrait of a Chief of the Little Osages c. 1807.
Purchased from Elias Dexter by the New-York Historical Society, Mar. 1861.
Indian Chief of the Little Osages c. 1807.
Right Honorable Sir Augustus John Foster; descended in Foster family; Lady Foster sale, Sotheby & Co., London, Nov. 18, 1926; Mrs. Luke Vincent Lockwood sale, Parke-Bernet, New York, May 15, 1954.
Exhibition: Cachasunghia, an Osage Warrior, at Denver, Denver Art Museum, 1966; *Indian Chief of the Little Osages,* Detroit, Detroit Institute of Art, "Loan Exhibition of American and Early Federal Art," 1951.
Literature: Jefferson to William Dunbar, Jan. 12, 1801 (Ford, 7:483); Jefferson to John Adams, Feb. 1812 (Lipscomb, 13:130) (familiarity with Indians); Margaret Bayard Smith, *The First Forty Years of Washington Society,* ed. Gaillard Hunt (New York: Scribner's Publishing Co., 1906), p. 401; Luke Vincent Lockwood, "The Saint-Mémin Indian Portraits," *The New-York Historical Society Quarterly Bulletin,* 12, no. 1 (Apr. 1928), 3–26; Fillmore Norfleet, *Saint-Mémin in Virginia* (Richmond: The Dietz Press, 1942), p. 35 (Lewis paid Saint-Mémin); Dorothy Wollon, ed. (with note by Margaret Kinaid), "Sir Augustus John Foster and 'The Wild Natives of the Woods,' 1805–1807," *William and Mary Quarterly,* 3rd ser., no. 2 (Apr. 1952), 191–214; Thomas Jefferson, *Notes on the State of Virginia,* ed. William Peden (New York: W. W. Norton and Co., Inc., 1954), p. 101; Richard Beale Davis, *Jeffersonian America, Notes on the United States of America in the Years 1805–6–7 and 11–12 by Sir Augustus John Foster, Bart.* (San Marino, California: Huntington Library, 1954); Reuben Gold and R. G. Thwaites, eds., *Original Journals of the Lewis and Clark Expedition, 1804–1806* (1904–1905; rpt., New York: Antiquarian Press, Ltd., 1959); Jefferson to Meriwether Lewis, Oct. 26, 1806, in *Letters of the Lewis and Clark Expedition,* ed. Donald D. Jackson (Urbana: University of Illinois Press, 1962), p. 351 ("Indian Hall").

130 Indian peace medal
ROBERT SCOTT active c. 1800
Literature: Francis Paul Prucha, *Indian Peace Medals in American History* (Madison: The State Historical Society of Wisconsin, 1971), pp. 90–95; Bauman Lowe Belden, *Indian Peace Medals Issued in the United States* (New York: American Numismatic Society, 1927), pp. 22–24; Luke Vincent Lockwood, "The St. Mémin Indian Portraits," *The New-York Historical Society Quarterly Bulletin,* 12, no. 1 (Apr. 1928), 3–5, 8, 12, 14, 16; John C. Ewers, "Chiefs from the Missouri and Mississippi and Peale's Silhouettes of 1806," *Smithsonian Journal of History,* 1, (Spring, 1966), 1–9, 15; Jefferson to John Adams, Ford, 9:358.

131 Telescope c. 1800
CARY OF LONDON
Provenance: Owned by Meriwether Lewis and by family descent to Meriwether Lewis Anderson. Given by Mr. Anderson to the Missouri Historical Society.

131a Moon Globe
JOHN RUSSELL 1745–1806
Literature: W. F. Ryan, "John Russell, R.A., and Early Lunar Mapping," *Smithsonian Journal of History,* I, no. 1 (1966) pp. 26–48.

132 Alexander von Humboldt 1806
FRIEDRICH GEORG WEITSCH 1758–1828
Provenance: Alexander von Humboldt; Prussian Royal Collections; transferred 1861.
Exhibitions: Berlin, National-Galerie and Pergamon-Museum, *Schateze der Weitkultur von der Sowjetunion Gerettet,* 1958, no. H 76, illus. in cat.
Literature: Verzeichnis der Gemalde und Skulpturen in der Königlichen National-Galerie zu Berlin (Berlin: E. S. Mittler v. Sohn, 1911), p. 147; *Die Malerei des XIX, Jahrhunderts, 240 Bilder nach Gemalden den National-Galerie* (Berlin: Verlag Gabr. Mann, 1945), p. 3, pl. 8; Sowerby, 4: 290–292; Helmut de Terra, "Alexander von Humboldt's Correspondence with Jefferson, Madison and Gallatin," *Proceedings of the American Philosophical Society,* 103, no. 5 (Oct. 15, 1959), 783–795; Douglas Botting, *Humboldt and the Cosmos* (New York: Harper & Row, 1973), pp. 167–176, illus. p. 87; Jefferson to Humboldt, May 28, 1804, Ford, 19:140–141; Jefferson to Humboldt, Mar. 6, 1809, Ford, 12:263; Jefferson to Humboldt, Apr. 14, 1811, Ford, 13:35–36.

133 The Medici Venus; Aphrodite Rising from the Sea 1st century B.C.–1st century A.D.
Provenance: Reportedly found in or near Rome during the sixteenth century and acquired for the Villa Medici from the Carpanica-della Valle collection about 1584; transferred to Florence in 1677; after the French occupation of Italy, 1799, transported to Leghorn, Palermo, and then in 1802 to Paris, the Musée Napoléon; returned to the Uffizi Tribune, 1816.
Literature: François Perrier, *Segmenta nobilium signorum e statuarum* (Rome, 1638), pls. 81–83; J. Richardson, *An Account of Some of the Statues, Bas-Reliefs, Drawings and Pictures in Italy &c with Remarks* (London, 1722), pp. 45, 53, 55–56, 110, 127, 133, 134, 144, 149, 156, 163, 166, 167, 283, 285; Daniel Webb, *An Inquiry into the Beauties of Painting; and into the Merits of the Most Celebrated Painters, Ancient and Modern* (London: Dodsley, 1761), pp. 43, 52–53, 59, 159; Joseph Spence, *Polymetis: or an Enquiry Concerning the Agreement Between the Works of the Roman Poets and the Remains of the Ancient Artists* (London: R. Horsfield, 1765), pp. 65–69, 83, pl. 5; "The Sage of Monticello," *Niles' Weekly Register,* 11 [ed. H. Niles] (1816–1817), 318; A. Michaelis, "Der Schleifer und die mediceische Venus," *Archaologische Zeitung,* 38 (1880–1881), 11–17; John Morgan, *The Journal of Dr. John Morgan of Philadelphia from the City of Rome to the City of London Together with a Fragment of a Journal Written in Rome, 1764,* ed. J. M. Harding (Philadelphia: Lippincott, 1907), pp. 241–242, 247–249; Carl and Jessica Bridenbaugh, *Rebels and Gentleman* (New York: Reynal and Hitchcock, 1942), pp. 214–215, 217; F. P. Johnson, *Lysippos* (Durham, N.C.: Duke University Press, 1927), pp. 55–57, 187–188, pl. 36; Kimball, "Jefferson and the Arts," pp. 238–239, 241–242; A. Hyatt Mayor, "Jefferson's Enjoyment of the Arts," *BMMA,* 2 (1943), 145; Berman, p. 96; Georg Lippold, *Die griechische Plastik* (Munich: Beck, 1950), p. 312; B. M. Felleti-Maj., "Afrodite Pudica," *Archaelogica Classica,* 3 (1951), 33–65 (32 replicas); Fritz Muthmann, *Statuenstutzen und dekoratives Beiwerk an griechischen und romischen Bildwerken* (Heidelberg: C. Winter, 1951), pp. 28, 91–92; Gisela M. A. Richter, *Three Critical Periods in Greek Sculpture* (Oxford: Clarendon Press, 1951), p. 53, fig. 130; C. Alexander, "A Statue of Aphrodite," *BMMA,* 11 (1953), 241–243; O. Kurz, "Huis Nympha Loci," *JWarb,* 16 (1953), 171–173, 176; William B. O'Neal, *Jefferson's Fine Arts Library* (Charlottesville: University Press of Virginia, 1956), pp. 29–31, 45–47; Heinz Ladendorf, *Antikenstudium und Antikenkopie* (Berlin: Akademie-Verlag, 1953), pp. 69–70, 103, nn. 51, 178, figs. 99, 151; Sir Kenneth Clark, *The Nude* (New York: Pantheon Books, 1956), pp. 126–128, fig. 67; Kimball, *Thomas Jefferson, Architect,* pp. 120–122, 135–136, 164–166, figs. 11, 18, 24, 79, 150, 156; Randall, 1:45, 60, 63–64; Desmond Guinness and J. T. Sadler, *Mr. Jefferson, Architect* (New York: Viking Press, 1973), p. 48; *Horace Walpole's Correspondence,* ed. W. S. Lewis (New Haven: Yale University Press, 1937), 19:34, 20: 397, 539.

134 Charles Towneley in His Gallery 1782
JOHANN ZOFFANY 1734/5–1810
Provenance: Painted for Charles Towneley and by descent to third Lord O'Hagan; Christie, Manson & Woods sale, London, May 19, 1939, lot 92; bought for the Burnley Art Gallery.
Exhibitions: London, Royal Academy of Arts, 1790, no. 191 as "A nobleman's collection"; London, British Institution, 1814, no. 92; London, British Institution, 1849, no. 124; London, South Kensington Museum, National Portraits Exhibition, 1868, no. 913; London, Burlington Fine Arts Club, 1907, no. 25; Rome, International Fine Arts Exhibition (British Section), 1911, no. 113; London, Wembley, *British Empire Exhibition,* 1925; London, 25, Park Lane, *English Conversation Pictures,* 1930; London, Royal Academy of Arts, *The First Hundred Years of the Royal Academy, 1769–1868,* 1951–1952, no. 108; London, Royal Academy of Arts, *English Taste in the Eighteenth Century,* 1958–1959, no. 406; Rome, Palazzo delle Esposizioni, *Il Settecento a Roma,* 1959, no. 691; The Arts Council of Great Britain, *Johann Zoffany,* Nov. 1960–Apr. 1961, no. 23; London, Tate Gallery, Contemporary Arts Society: *50th Anniversary Exhibition,* Apr. 1–May 8, 1960; London, Royal Academy of Arts, *Primitives to Picasso,* 1961–1962, no. 173; Cleveland Museum of Art, *Neo-classicism: Style and Motif,* no. 83, illus. in cat.; Cologne, Wallraf-Richartz Museum and Zürich, Kunsthaus, *Englische Malerei der grossen Zeit,* Oct. 8–Nov. 6, 1966, and Jan.–Feb. 1967, also in Rome and Warsaw, no. 76, illus. in cat.; Bregenz, Vorarlberger Landesmuseum and Vienna, Österreichisches Museum für Angewandte Kunst, *Angelika Kauffmann und ihre Zeitgenossen,* July 23–Oct. 13, 1968 and Nov. 8, 1968–Feb. 1, 1969, no. 494, illus. in cat., pl. 124; Prague, Národní Galerie, and Bratislava, *Two Centuries of British Art,* 1969; London, Royal Academy of Arts, *The Age of Neo-classicism,* Sept. 9–Nov. 19, 1972, no. 285.

Literature: Amabel Strachey, "The Towneley Museum," *Country Life, 34* (Aug. 16, 1913), 233–234, illus.; John Thomas Smith, *Nollekins and His Times,* ed. Wilfred Whitten (London and New York: John Lane, The Bodley Head, and John Lane Company, 1920), 1:213–214, illus.; Lady Victoria Manners and G. C. Williamson, *John Zoffany, R.A.* (London and New York: John Lane, The Bodley Head, and John Lane Company, 1920), pp. 121–124, 223, illus. opp. p. 122; William T. Whitley, *Artists and Their Friends in England, 1700–1799* (London and Boston: The Medici Society, 1928), 2:397; G. C. Williamson, *English Conversation Pictures* (London: B. T. Batsford Ltd., 1931), pp. 15–16, pl. XLIII; C. H. Collins Baker and Montague R. James, *British Painting* (Boston: Hale, Cushman and Flint, 1933), p. 136; Sacheverell Sitwell, *Conversation Pieces* (London: B. T. Batsford, Ltd., 1936), pp. 33–34, 96, fig. 37; Ellis Waterhouse, *Painting in Britain, 1530–1790* (Baltimore: Penguin Books, 1953), p. 231; Ellis Waterhouse, *Johann Zoffany,* exhib. cat. (London, Arts Council of Great Britain, 1960–1961), pp. 8, 21–22; Mary Webster, "Zoffany's Painting of Charles Towneley's Library in Park Street, Westminster," *BurlM, 106* (July 1964), 316–323, fig. 8; Henry Hourley, *Neo-classicism: Style and Motif,* exhib. cat. (Cleveland: Museum of Art, 1964), no. 83, illus.; John Cornforth, "London's Lost Galleries," *Country Life, 143* (June 13, 1968), 1566, illus. on cover; Mario Praz, *Conversation Pieces* (University Park and London: The Pennsylvania State University Press, and Methuen & Co. Ltd., 1971), p. 37, fig. 6; Jefferson to Maria Cosway, Oct. 12, 1786.

135 The Towneley vase
1st century A.D.
Provenance: Found in 1773–1774 at Monte Cagnolo by Gavin Hamilton in the Villa of Antoninus Pius (?) at Lanuvium; thence to the Charles Towneley Collection, London; in 1805 part of the Towneley Bequest to the British Museum.
Literature: Charles Towneley, "A Catalogue of the Ancient Marbles in the Park Street Westm^t.," British Museum, Department of Greek and Roman Antiquities, case 65c; A. H. Smith, "Gavin Hamilton's Letters to Charles Towneley," *Journal of Hellenistic Studies, 11* (1901), 306–308, 313; P. F. Hugues d'Hancarville, *Recherches sur l'origine, l'esprit, et le progres des arts de la Grèce* (London: B. Appleyard, 1785), 1:199; *A Description of the Collection of Ancient Marbles in the British Museum* (London: n.p., 1812), 1:

pls. 7, 9; Sir Henry Ellis, *The British Museum, The Towneley Gallery* (London: Charles Knight and Co., 1836), 2:209–211 (room II, no. 7); William S. W. Vaux, *Handbook to the Antiquities in the British Museum* (London: n.p., 1851), p. 254; Sir Charles T. Newton, *Synopsis of the Contents of the British Museum: Graeco-Roman Guide* (London: n.p., 1876), 2: no. 55; Paul Wolters and C. Friedrichs, *Die gypssabgusse antiken Bildwerke* (Berlin, 1885), no. 2119; Friedrich Hauser, *Die neu-attischen reliefs* (Stuttgart: K. Wittwer, 1889), pp. 104–105, no. 41; A. H. Smith, *A Catalogue of Sculpture in the Department of Greek and Roman Antiquities, British Museum* (London: n.p., 1904), 3:393–395, nos. 2500, 2501; W. Fuchs, *Die vorbilder der neu-attischen Reliefs* (Berlin: W. de Gruyter, 1959), 20th supplement of *Jahrbuch des deutschen archaeologischen Instituts,* pp. 85, 153, no. 3, pl. 23, fig. d; Fiske Kimball, "Domestic Architecture in the History of the Colonies and of the Republic," *American Historical Review, 27* (Oct. 1921), 47–57; Margarete Bieber, *The Sculpture of the Hellenistic Age* (New York: Columbia University Press, 1961), figs. 791, 792, 793; Ian Jack, *Keats and the Mirror of Art* (Oxford: Clarendon Press, 1967), pp. 214–217, 281, 282, 283, pl. 29; Desmond Guinness and J. T. Sadler, *Mr. Jefferson, Architect* (New York: Viking Press, 1973), pp. 58, 60, 62; Christine M. Havelock, *Hellenistic Art* (Greenwich, Conn.: New York Graphic Society, 1970), p. 236, pl. 2; Seymour Howard, "An Antiquarian Handlist and the Beginnings of the Pio-Clementino," *Eighteenth-Century Studies, 7* (1973), 40–42, 55–56, 58.

136 The Antique School of Old Somerset House 1779
EDWARD FRANCIS BURNEY 1760–1848
Provenance: Part of an album of drawings which remained in family possession until c. 1960 when it was purchased from P. & D. Colnaghi & Co., Ltd., London, by the Royal Academy (Sidney Lee Fund).
Exhibitions: London, Royal Academy of Arts, *Treasures of the Royal Academy,* 1963, no. 87; London, Royal Academy of Arts, *Bicentenary Exhibition 1768–1968,* 1968, no. 651; London, Sotheby & Co. for *The Burlington Magazine, Art into Art,* 1971, no. 71. London, Royal Academy of Arts, *The Age of Neo-Classicism,* Sept. 9–Nov. 19, 1972, no. 521.
Literature: J. Byam Shaw, "One more link in the history of the Leonardo Cartoon," *BurlM, 104* (May 1962),

212–213, illus. p. 215; Kimball, "Jefferson and the Arts," p. 241.

137 Design for the Ruin Room at Santa Trinità dei Monti c. 1765
CHARLES-LOUIS CLÉRISSEAU 1721–1820
Provenance: Rev. J. W. Whittaker Gift 1821.
Exhibition: London, The Arts Council of Great Britain in The Royal Academy, *The Age of Neo-Classicism,* Sept. 9–Nov. 19, 1972, no. 1053.
Literature: Johann Joachim Winckelmann, *Lettres familières,* ed. H. Janson (Amsterdam: Chez Couturier fils, 1781), 2:215; J. G. Legrand, "Notice historique sur la vie et sur les Ouvrages de J. B. Piranesi," Paris Bibliothèque nationale, nouv. acq. fr. 146r [this document is published in a somewhat abbreviated form in G. Morazzoni, *Giovanni Battista Piranesi Architetto ed Incisore 1720–1778* (Milan and Rome: Alfieri and Lacroix [1921]), pp. 70ff.]; A.T., "Documents pour servir à l'histoire des collections impériale, IV: Clérisseau," *Starye Gody,* July–Sept. 1913, pp. 43–52; Johann Joachim Winckelmann, *Briefe,* ed. Hans Diepolder and Walter Rehn (Berlin: Walter de Gruyter and Co., 1952–1957), 3:344–349; Thomas J. McCormick and John Fleming, "A Ruin Room by Clerisseau," *Connoisseur, 149* (Apr. 1962), 239–243; Thomas J. McCormick, "An Unknown Collection of Drawings by Charles-Louis Clérisseau," *Journal of the Society of Architectural Historians, 20* (1963), 119–126, fig. 9; Paul Zucker, *Fascination of Decay* (Ridgewood: The Gregg Press, 1968), pp. 240–243; Thomas J. McCormick, "Charles-Louis Clérisseau and the Roman Revival," Ph.D. dissertation, Princeton University, 1970, pp. 121–128, 328–329; The Arts Council of Great Britain, *The Age of Neo-Classicism,* exhib. cat. (London, The Arts Council of Great Britain, 1972), p. 516 repr.; Jefferson to John Rutledge, Jr., and Thomas Shippen, June 19, 1788.

138 The Triumphal Arch and Tomb of the Julii at St. Rémy 1769
CHARLES-LOUIS CLÉRISSEAU 1721–1820
Literature: Victoria and Albert Museum: *Catalogue of Water Colour Paintings by British Architects and Foreigners Working in Great Britain,* rev. ed. (London: Victoria and Albert Museum, 1927), p. 93, no. E 5151-1910; Thomas J. McCormick, "Virginia's Gallic Godfather," *Arts in Virginia, 4,* no. 2 (Winter 1964), 9–10, repr.; Thomas J. McCormick, "Charles-Louis Clérisseau and the Roman Revival," Ph.D. dissertation, Princeton University, 1970, pp. 153–157, 347–350; Jefferson, "Notes of

a Tour into the Southern Parts of France," Boyd, 11:425–426; Jefferson to John Rutledge, Jr., and Thomas Shippen, June 19, 1788.

140 Autre Vüe intérieure des restes du College . . . 1778
GIOVANNI BATTISTA PIRANESI
1720–1778
Provenance: Nathan Chaikin; Sotheby & Co. (July 11, 1974; nos. 103, 104); David Tunick.
Literature: William Bainier O'Neal, *Jefferson's Fine Arts Library for the University of Virginia* (Charlottesville: University of Virginia Press, 1956); S. Lang, "The Early Publications of the Temples at Paestum," *JWarb, 13* (1950), 48–64; Arthur M. Hind, *Giovanni Battista Piranesi* (London: Holland, 1967), pp. 19–20, 87; the portrait reproduced in Stefano Bottari, *Mostra di Incisioni di G. B. Piranesi* (Bologna: Alfa, 1963); Henri Focillon, *Giovanni-Battista Piranesi: Essai de catalogue raisonné de son oeuvre* (Paris: Henri Laurens, 1918), nos. 585 and 591.

141 Galleria grande di Statue 1723
GIOVANNI BATTISTA PIRANESI
1720–1778
Provenance: Sir Reginald Blomfield, A.R.A.; Sir Austin Blomfield; Georges Heilbrun.
Literature: Ferdinando Galli Bibiena, *L'Architettura Civile* (Parma: Paolo Monti, 1711); Giuseppe Galli Bibiena, *Architetture, e Prospettive* (Augsburg: Andreas Pfeffel, 1740); Arthur Samuel, *Piranesi* (London: B. T. Batsford, 1910); Henri Focillon, *Giovanni-Battista Piranesi: Essai de catalogue raisonné de son oeuvre* (Paris: Henri Laurens, 1918), pp. 11–12; Arthur M. Hind, *Giovanni Battista Piranesi* (London: Holland Press, 1967), p. 75; Andrew Robison, "Giovanni Battista Piranesi: Prolegomena to the Princeton Collections," *The Princeton University Library Chronicle, 31,* no. 3 (Spring 1970), 168–170; Andrew Robison, "Giovanni Battista Piranesi," exhib. pamphlet (Princeton: Princeton University Library, 1971), p. 3; Herbert Mitchell, *Giovanni Battista Piranesi,* exhib. cat. (New York: Avery Architectural Library, 1972), pp. 69–73.

142 Varie vedute di Roma antica e moderna 1748
GIOVANNI BATTISTA PIRANESI
1720–1778, et alii
Provenance: Cte. Chandon de Briailles.
Literature: Kimball, *Thomas Jefferson, Architect,* facs. 232; *Catalogue of the Library of the United States* (Washington: J. Elliot for The Library of Congress, 1815), p. 130; Sowerby,

4:371; William Bainter O'Neal, *Jefferson's Fine Arts Library for the University of Virginia* (Charlottesville: University of Virginia Press, 1956), pp. 21, 31, 36; *Catalogue of the Library of Congress in the Capitol of the United States of America* (Washington, 1840), p. 566; Henri Focillon, *Giovanni-Battista Piranesi: Essai de catalogue raisonné de son oeuvre* (Paris: Henri Laurens, 1918), pp. 15–17; Arthur M. Hind, *Giovanni Battista Piranesi* (London: Holland Press, 1967), pp. 76–78; Andrew Robison, "Giovanni Battista Piranesi: Prolegomena to the Princeton Collections," *The Princeton University Library Chronicle*, 31, no. 3 (Spring 1970), 176, 178–179.

143 Elevation of the reconstructed temple at Palestrina 1791
GEORGE HADFIELD 1763–1826
Provenance: Collection of Sir James Wright, Bart., minister to the Venetian Republic, who may have known Hadfield in Italy; collection of John Buonarotti Papworth, whose initials *JBP* appear on the drawings; to his son, John Woody Papworth, who gave them to the Royal Institute of British Architects in 1848.
Exhibition: Royal Academy of Art, 1765; Royal Institute of British Architects, May 15, 1848.
Literature: D.A.B., 8:76–77; John W. Papworth, "Notes on Some Drawings in Illustration of Praneste (Palestrina) Ancient and Modern, Read at an Ordinary Meeting Monday, 15 May, 1848," Royal Institute of British Architects, typescripts; H. F. Cunningham, J. A. Younger, and J. W. Smith, *Measured Drawings of Georgian Architecture in the District of Columbia, 1750–1820* (Washington, 1914); Helen Bullock, *My Head and My Heart* (New York: G. Putnam's Sons, 1945), p. 134; Ronriccio Bianchi Bandinelli, *Rome: The Center of Power* (New York, 1970), pp. 147, 148, 354; *The Portrait of Sir John Soane, R.A.*, ed. Arthur T. Bolton (London: Butler and Tanner, Ltd., 1927).

144 The Remains of the Roof of one of the Arches of the Temple on the 7th Platform 1791
GEORGE HADFIELD 1763–1826
Provenance: See entry 143.
Exhibition: See entry 143.
Literature: See entry 143.

145 Further Remains of the Interior of the Temple now converted into a Store House 1791
GEORGE HADFIELD 1763–1826
Provenance: See entry 143.
Exhibition: See entry 143.
Literature: See entry 143.

146 The Interior of one of the Square Temples on the 3rd Platform now converted into a cellar 1791
GEORGE HADFIELD 1763–1826
Provenance: See entry 143.
Exhibition: See entry 143.
Literature: See entry 143.

147 The Triumphal Arch and the Amphitheater in the City of Orange
HUBERT ROBERT 1733–1808
Provenance: Commissioned for a salon at the Château de Fontainbleau; stored in the artist's studio and sold by Mme Hubert Robert in 1822.
Exhibition: Paris, Salon of 1787, no. 48; Paris, Musée de l'Orangerie, *Hubert Robert (1733–1808)*, 1933, no. 16.
Literature: Villot, no. 485; Gabillot, pp. 132, 133, 245, 252, 268; Engerand, p. 430; de Nolhac, p. 66; Leclère, p. 94; Brière, no. 797; Robert Mesuret, "Les vues des provinces occitanes dans les salons de l'Académie Royale de Paris," *Mémoires de l'Académie des Sciences, Inscriptions et Belles-Lettres*, 1969, p. 212; *Musée National du Louvre, Catalogue des peintures, I, Ecole française* (Paris, 1972), p. 331; Marianne Roland-Michel, "A Taste for Classical Antiquity in Town Planning Projects: Two Aspects of the Art of Hubert Robert," *BurlM*, 64 (Nov. 1972), no. 836, p. cxiv.

148 The Interior of the Temple of Diana at Nîmes
HUBERT ROBERT 1733–1808
Provenance: Commissioned in 1786 for a room in the Château de Fontainbleau; collection of Louis XVI; entered the Louvre in 1794.
Exhibition: Paris, Salon of 1787, no. 46; Paris, Musée de l'Orangerie, *Hubert Robert*, 1933, no. 14; Munich, Residenz, *Le siècle rococo*, 1958, no. 178; London: The Royal Academy and the Victoria and Albert Museum, *The Age of Neo-Classicism*, Sept. 9– Nov. 19, 1972, no. 222.
Literature: Gabillot, pp. 132, 133, 212; Engerand, p. 430; de Nolhac, pp. 66, 67, 106; T. Leclère, p. 94; Brière, no. 799; P. Paul-Sentenac, *Hubert Robert* (Paris: Reider, 1929), pp. 24, 30; Jean Cailleux, *Hubert Robert*, coll. I Maestri del Colore, no. 246 (1968), pl. 2; Robert Masuret, "Les vues des provinces occitanes dans les salons de l'Académie royale de Paris," *Mémoires de l'Académie des Sciences, Inscriptions et Belles-Lettres de Toulouse* (1969), p. 212; *Musée national du Louvre. Catalogue des peintures, I., Ecole française* (Paris, 1971), p. 331; Marianne Roland-Michel, "A Taste for Classical Antiquity in Town Planning Projects: Two Aspects of the Art of Hubert

Robert," *BurlM*, 64, no. 836 (Nov. 1972), iv, fig. 3.

149 The Pont du Gard
HUBERT ROBERT 1733–1808
Provenance: Commissioned in 1786 for a room in the Château de Fontainebleau; collection of Louis XVI; exhibited at the Château de Fontainebleau, then transferred to the Musée du Louvre.
Exhibition: Paris, Salon of 1787, no. 49; Paris, Musée de l'Orangerie, *Hubert Robert*, 1933, no. 15.
Literature: Renou, *Journal de Paris*, Sept. 1, 1787; Anonymous [Stanislas Koska Potocki], *Lettre d'un étranger sur le Sallon de 1787* (n.p., n.d.), p. 13; Gabillot, pp. 56, 132, 133, 212, 237, 268, 278; Engerand, p. 430; de Nolhac, pp. 66, 67; Leclère, p. 94; Brière, no. 800; Jeanne Magnin, *Le paysage français des enlumineurs à Corot* (Paris: Payot, 1928), p. 152; P. Paul-Sentenac, *Hubert Robert* (Paris: Rieder, 1929), pl. 24; R. Mesuret, "Les vues des provinces occitanes dans les salons de l'Académie royale de Paris," *Memoires de l'Académie des Sciences, Inscriptions et Belles Lettres de Toulouse* (1969), p. 212; *Musée national du Louvre. Catalogue des peintures, I, Ecole française* (Paris, 1972), p. 331; Marianne Roland-Michel, "A Taste for Classical Antiquity in Town Planning Projects: Two Aspects of the Art of Hubert Robert," *BurlM*, 64, no. 836 (Nov. 1972), iv, no. 28.

150 The Maison Carrée, the Arena and the Tour de Magne at Nîmes
HUBERT ROBERT 1733–1808
Provenance: Commissioned in 1786 for a room in the Château de Fontainebleau; remained in the artist's studio and was bequeathed to the Louvre by Mme Hubert Robert in 1822.
Exhibition: Paris, Salon of 1787, no. 47; Paris, Musée de l'Orangerie, *Hubert Robert 1733–1808*, 1933, no. 17.
Literature: Villot, no. 486; Gabillot, pp. 56, 132, 133, 245, 252; Engerand, p. 430; de Nolhac, p. 66; Leclère, p. 94; Brière, no. 798; P. Paul-Sentenac, *Hubert Robert* (Paris: Reider, 1929), p. 30, pl. 25; Albert P. de Mirimonde, *Catalogue du musée Baron Martin* (Gray, 1959), p. 138; Robert Mesuret, "Les vues des provinces occitanes dans les salons de l'Académie royale de Paris," *Mémoires des Académies des Sciences, Inscriptions et Belles-Lettres de Toulouse* (1969), p. 212; *Musée national du Louvre, catalogue des peintures, I, Ecole française* (Paris, 1972), p. 331; Marianne Roland-Michel, "A Taste for Classical Antiquity in Town Planning Projects:

Two Aspects of the Art of Hubert Robert," *BurlM*, 64, no. 836 (Nov. 1972), iv.

151 Roman askos
Provenance: Found in the ruins of the Maison Carrée, in Nîmes; collection of Jean-François Seguier; currently in the collection of the Musée des Antiques, Maison Carrée, Nîmes, France.
Literature: Julien P. Boyd, "Thomas Jefferson and the Roman askos of Nîmes," *Antiques*, 54 (July 1973), 116–124, figs. 6, 7, 8; James A. Bear, Jr., *Report of the Curator* (Charlottesville: The Thomas Jefferson Memorial Foundation, 1957), pp. 7, 8, pl. 3; Boyd, 15:xxix–xxxii.

152 Model of a bronze askos 1789
SOUCHE active late 18th century
Provenance: Copied from a bronze askos in the Cabinet of Antiquities at Nîmes, France, in 1789 by Souche for Thomas Jefferson; given by Jefferson to Thomas Sully in 1821; bought by Mrs. Raymond Porter at an auction in Bucks County, Pennsylvania, in 1972; presented to the Thomas Jefferson Memorial Foundation by Mrs. Porter, through Julian P. Boyd, in 1974.
Literature: See no. 153.

153 Askos 1801
SIMMONS and ALEXANDER, Philadelphia
Provenance: Purchased by Thomas Jefferson from Simmons and Alexander in Philadelphia in 1801; descended in the family to Mr. Thomas Jefferson Coolidge III, who in 1957 presented it to the Thomas Jefferson Memorial Foundation.
Literature: Julian P. Boyd, "Thomas Jefferson and the Roman askos of Nîmes," *The Magazine Antiques*, 104 (July 1973), 116–124, figs. 6, 7, 8; James A. Bear, Jr., *Report of the Curator* (Charlottesville: The Thomas Jefferson Memorial Foundation, 1957), pp. 7, 8, pl. 3; Boyd, 15: xxix–xxxii.

154 Dr. John Morgan 1764
ANGELICA KAUFFMANN 1741–1807
Provenance: David T. Watson, in 1907.
Literature: John Morgan, *The Journal of Dr. John Morgan of Philadelphia* (Philadelphia: J. B. Lippincott Company, 1907), pp. 26, 38, 241–243, 247–256, illus. frontispiece; Lady Victoria Manners and G. C. Williamson, *Angelica Kauffmann* (New York: Brentano's, 1924), p. 219; Kimball, "Jefferson and the Arts," pp. 238–239; Brinsley Ford, "James Byres, Principal Antiquarian for the English Visitors to Rome," *Apollo*, 99 (June 1974), 451, 453.

155 Portrait of Winckelmann
ANTON RAPHAEL MENGS 1728–1779
Provenance: The artist; Don José
Nicholás de Azara, 1779; Cardinal
Dionisio Bardaji y Azara, Rome, his
nephew, 1804; Jean-Baptiste-Pierre Le
Brun, c. 1807–1808; Le Brun sale,
Paris, Mar. 20–24, 1810, lot 186;
Princess Isabella Lubomirska, Vienna,
and by descent to the Princes Lubomir-
ski, Cracow; purchased from Prince
Sebastian Lubomirski, Zürich, 1948.
Exhibitions: Florence, Palazzo
Vecchio, *International Portrait Ex-
hibition*, 1911, no. 66; Hartford, Con-
necticut, Wadsworth Atheneum,
Homage to Mozart, Mar. 22–Apr. 29,
1956, no. 40, illus. in cat. fig. 18;
London, Royal Academy of Arts, *The
Age of Neo-Classicism*, Sept. 9–
Nov. 19, 1972, no. 192, illus. in cat.
pl. 17; The University of Connecticut
at Storrs, The William Benton
Museum of Arts, *The Academy of
Europe: Rome in the Eighteenth
Century*, Oct. 13–Nov. 19, 1973.
Literature: Jean-Baptiste-Pierre
Le Brun, *Recueil de gravures . . .
d'après un choix de tableaux, . . .
recueillis dans un voyage fait en
Espagne, au midi de la France et en
Italie, dans les années 1807 et 1808*
(Paris: Didot jeune, 1809), 2:95,
no. 2; Jean-Baptiste-Pierre Le Brun,
Notice (Paris, 1809), no. 217; Julius
Braun, "Das Winckelmann-Porträt
von Anton Raphael Mengs," *Zeit-
schrift für Bildende Kunst*, 16 n.f.
(1905), 173–175, illus. opp. p. 173;
H. Uhde-Bernays, "Zu den Bildnissen
Winckelmanns," *Moatschefte für
Kunstwissenschaft*, 6 (1913), 55–56;
Hermann Voss, *Die Malerei des
Barock in Rom* (Berlin: Propylaen-
Verlag, 1924), p. 659; Kurt Gersten-
berg, *Johann Joachim Winckelmann
und Anton Raphael Mengs* (Halle:
M. Niemeyer, 1929), p. 20; Josephine
L. Allen, "Johann Joachim Winckel-
mann Classicist," *BMMA*, 7, n.s.
(1949), 228–232, illus. p. 229; Arthur
Schulz, *Die Bildnesse Johann Joachim
Winckelmanns* (Berlin: Akademie-
Verlag, 1953), p. 54, pl. 2; Dieter
Honisch, *Anton Raphael Mengs und
die Bildform des Frühklassizismus*
(Recklinghausen: Bongers, 1965),
p. 70, no. 13; L. D. Ettlinger, "Winckelmann," introduction to *The Age
of Neo-Classicism*, exhib. cat. (London: Royal Academy of Arts, 1972),
pp. 30–34; Jefferson to Maria Cosway,
July 1, 1787 ("I am born to lose
everything I love"); Jefferson to
Gaudenzio Clerici, Aug. 15, 1787
("Milan was the spot").

**167 The Declaration of
Independence, 4 July 1776** 1787–1820
JOHN TRUMBULL 1756–1843
Provenance: By bequest of the artist

to Yale University Art Gallery.
Literature: Trumbull Papers, Yale
University Library, Manuscripts Division; Trumbull file, Yale University
Art Gallery; John Trumbull, *Catalogue
of Paintings by Colonel Trumbull*
(New York, 1831), pp. 15–17; entry
repeated in *Catalogue of Paintings
by Colonel Trumbull* (New Haven,
1832, 1835, 1852, 1860, 1864), and in
the artist's *Autobiography, Reminiscences and Letters of John Trumbull from 1756–1841* (New York
and London: Wiley and Putnam, and
New Haven: B. L. Hamlen, 1841),
pp. 96, 147, 148, 150–151, 164, 166,
345–346, 358–367, 399, 402, 416–
418; Benjamin Silliman, "Notebook,"
Yale University Library, Manuscripts
Division, pp. 72–73; Henry T. Tuckerman, *Book of the Artists* (New
York: G. P. Putnam and Sons, 1867),
pp. 85–86, 90; William Dunlap,
*A History of the Rise and Progress
of the Arts of Design in the United
States*, ed., with additions, Frank
Bayley and Charles Goodspeed (Boston: C. E. Goodspeed and Company,
1918), 2:38, 56–57, 74, 75n; John
Hill Morgan, *Paintings by John
Trumbull at Yale University* (New
Haven: Yale University Press, 1926),
pp. 35–43, 79–82, 84, illustrated
with *Key*; Berman, pp. 79–80, 85, 88,
98–99, 260, fig. 5; Boyd, 12:645,
13:391, 525; Theodore Sizer, *The
Works of Colonel John Trumbull*,
2nd rev. ed. (New Haven: Yale Uni-
versity Press, 1967), p. 96, fig. 158,
Key, fig. 159; Irma B. Jaffe, "Fordham
University's Trumbull Drawings:
Mistaken Identities in The Declara-
tion of Independence and Other
Discoveries," *AAJ*, 3, no. 1 (Spring
1971), 5–14, fig. 2, *Key*, fig. 3; Irma B.
Jaffe, "Trumbull's *The Declaration
of Independence:* Keys and Dates,"
AAJ, 3, no. 2 (Fall 1971), 41–49,
fig. 1, *Keys*, figs. 3, 4, 5; Irma B. Jaffe,
*John Trumbull: Patriot-Artist of the
American Revolution* (Boston: New
York Graphic Society, in press), illus-
trated, with *Key*; Irma B. Jaffe, *John
Trumbull's 'Declaration of Independence'* (New York: The Viking
Press, in press), illus. with *Key*; Maria
Cosway to Jefferson, Aug. 19, 1788.
Engravings: The only important engraving is that by Asher B. Durand,
1823. A late print published by Leggo
Brothers and Company after 1877
is inscribed *A. B. Durand Sculp* but
differs from the 1823 print. Others
include J. E. F. Prudhomme, 1842;
William Lilly Ormsby, c. 1863 (used
on reverse side of the one-hundred-
dollar national currency note, 1863,
1864, and on U.S. postage stamp
no. 120, twenty-four cents, green and
violet, 1869; Jean Pierre Marie Jazet,
aquatint.

**168 The Death of General Mercer
at the Battle of Princeton,
3 January 1777** 1787–1831
JOHN TRUMBULL 1756–1843
Provenance: By bequest of the artist.
Literature: C. A. Munn Collection,
Fordham University; Trumbull file,
Yale University Art Gallery; John
Trumbull, *Catalogue of Paintings by
Colonel Trumbull* (New York, 1831),
pp. 19–23; entry repeated in *Cata-
logue of Paintings by Colonel Trum-
bull* (New Haven, 1832, 1835, 1852,
1860, 1864); Benjamin Silliman,
"Notebook" (1857), Yale University
Library, Manuscripts Division, pp. 79–
83; John Trumbull, *Autobiography,
Reminiscences and Letters of John
Trumbull from 1756 to 1841* (New
York and London: Wiley, and
Putnam; New Haven: B. L. Hamlen,
1841), pp. 399, 421–424; Henry T.
Tuckerman, *Book of the Artists* (New
York: G. P. Putnam and Sons,
1867), p. 90; William Dunlap, *A
History of the Rise and Progress of the
Arts of Design in the United States*
(1834; Boston: C. E. Goodspeed
and Company, 1918), 2:75; John Hill
Morgan, *Paintings by John Trumbull
at Yale University* (New Haven:
Yale University Press, 1926), pp. 47–
51, illus. with *Key*; Sizer, pp. 315–316;
Theodore Sizer, *The Works of
Colonel John Trumbull* (1950; rev.
ed., New Haven: Yale University Press,
1967), pp. 98, 143–146, fig. 169,
Key, fig. 170; Howard C. Rice, Jr.,
"Lost Horizon," *The Princeton Uni-
versity Library Chronicle*, 29, no. 2
(Winter 1968), 118–128; Irma B.
Jaffe, "Fordham University's Trum-
bull Drawings: Mistaken Identities in
The Declaration of Independence
and Other Discoveries," *AAJ*, 3, no. 1
(Spring 1971), 19; Irma B. Jaffe,
*John Trumbull: Patriot-Artist of the
American Revolution* (Boston: New
York Graphic Society, in press),
illus. with *Key*.

**169 The Surrender of General
Burgoyne at Saratoga, 16 October 1777**
c. 1822–1831
JOHN TRUMBULL 1756–1843
Provenance: By bequest of the artist.
Literature: C. A. Munn Collection,
Fordham University; John Trumbull,
*Catalogue of Paintings by Colonel
Trumbull* (New York, 1931), pp. 23–
26; entry repeated in *Catalogue of
Paintings by Colonel Trumbull* (New
Haven: 1832, 1835, 1852, 1860,
1864), and in John Trumbull, *Auto-
biography, Reminiscences and Letters
of John Trumbull from 1756 to 1841*
(New York and London: Wiley and
Putnam, New Haven: B. L. Hamlen,
1841), pp. 424–427; Benjamin Silli-
man, "Notebook" (1857), Yale
University Library, Manuscripts Divi-

sion, pp. 83–87; Henry T. Tuckerman,
Book of the Artists (New York:
G. P. Putnam and Sons, 1867), pp. 83,
86–87; Stan V. Henkels, *The Very
Important Col. John Trumbull Collec-
tion* [Silliman Sale Catalogue] (Phil-
adelphia, 1896), pp. 3–4; William
Dunlap, *A History of the Rise and
Progress of the Arts of Design in the
United States* (1934; Boston: C. E.
Goodspeed and Company, 1918),
2:59, 75n; John Hill Morgan, *Paint-
ings of John Trumbull at Yale Uni-
versity* (New Haven: Yale University
Press, 1926), pp. 51–55, illus. with
Key; Sizer, pp. 257–260, 309–310,
Key, fig. 185; Irma B. Jaffe, "Fordham
University's Trumbull Drawings;
Mistaken Identities in 'The Declara-
tion of Independence' and Other
Discoveries," *AAJ*, 3, no. 1 (Spring
1971), 24; Irma B. Jaffe, *John Trum-
bull: Patriot-Artist of the American
Revolution* (New York Graphic
Society, in press), illus., with *Key*.

**170 Surrender of Lord Cornwallis at
Yorktown, 19 October 1781**
1787–c. 1828
JOHN TRUMBULL 1756–1843
Provenance: By bequest of the artist.
Literature: C. A. Munn Collection,
Fordham University; John Trumbull,
*Catalogue of Paintings by Colonel
Trumbull* (New York, 1831), pp. 27–
28; entry repeated in *Catalogue of
Paintings by Colonel Trumbull* (New
Haven, 1832, 1835, 1852, 1860,
1864); John Trumbull, *Autobiography,
Reminiscences and Letters of John
Trumbull from 1756 to 1841* (New
York and London: Wiley and Putnam;
New Haven: B. L. Hamlen, 1841),
pp. 148, 151, 164, 166, 399, 428–
429; Benjamin Silliman, "Notebook"
(1857), Yale University Library,
Manuscripts Division, pp. 87–90; William Dunlap, *A History of the Rise
and Progress of the Arts of Design in
the United States* (1834; Boston:
C. E. Goodspeed and Company,
1918), 2:56, 57, 75n; John Hill Morgan, *Paintings by John Trumbull
at Yale University* (New Haven: Yale
University Press, 1926), pp. 55–64,
illus., with *Key*; Berman, p. 80; Sizer,
p. 100, fig. 187, *Key*, fig. 188; Irma B.
Jaffe, "Fordham University's Trumbull Drawings: Mistaken Identities in
The Declaration of Independence
and Other Discoveries," *AAJ*, 3, no. 1
(Spring 1971), 25; Irma B. Jaffe,
*John Trumbull: Patriot-Artist of the
American Revolution* (Boston: New
York Graphic Society, in press),
illus., with *Key*; Irma B. Jaffe, *John
Trumbull's 'Declaration of Inde-
pendence'* (New York: The Viking
Press, in press), illus.

171 The Resignation of General Washington, 23 December 1783
c. 1824–1828
JOHN TRUMBULL 1756–1843
Provenance: By bequest of the artist.
Literature: Trumbull Papers, Yale University Library, Manuscripts Division; Trumbull file, Yale University Art Gallery; John Trumbull, Catalogue of Paintings by Colonel Trumbull (New York, 1831), pp. 28–31; entry repeated in Catalogue of Paintings by Colonel Trumbull (New Haven, 1832, 1835, 1860, 1864), and in John Trumbull, Autobiography, Reminiscences and Letters of John Trumbull from 1756 to 1841 (New York and London: Wiley and Putnam; New Haven: B. L. Hamlen, 1841), pp. 429–432; Benjamin Silliman, "Notebook" (1857), Yale University Library, Manuscripts Division, pp. 90–92; William Dunlap, A History of the Rise and Progress of the Arts of Design in the United States (1834; Boston: C. E. Goodspeed and Company, 1918), 2:59, 75n; John Hill Morgan, Paintings by John Trumbull at Yale University (New Haven: Yale University Press, 1926), pp. 64–66, illustrated with Key; Theodore Sizer, The Works of Colonel John Trumbull (1950; rev. ed., New Haven: Yale University Press, 1967), p. 102, fig. 203, Key, fig. 204; Irma B. Jaffe, John Trumbull: Patriot-Artist of the American Revolution (Boston: New York Graphic Society, in press), illus. with Key; Irma B. Jaffe, John Trumbull's 'Declaration of Independence' (New York: The Viking Press, in press) illus. with Key.

172 George Washington c. 1785
JEAN-ANTOINE HOUDON 1741–1828
Provenance: Collection of comte Henri de Bayle de Malmont, through family descent until acquired by present owner.
Literature: Sherwin McRae, Washington, his person as represented by the artists, The Houdon statue, its history and value (published by the order of the Senate of Virginia, 1873; photostat, Frick Art Reference Library, New York); Gaston Brière, "La statue de Washington par Houdon" in Musées de France (Paris, 1910), pp. 82–85; Florence Ingersoll-Smouse, "Houdon en Amérique," La Revue de l'art ancien et moderne, 35 (Jan.–June 1914), 279–298; André Michel, Statue de Washington par Houdon (Paris, 1918); Mabel Munson Swan, The Athenaeum Gallery, 1827–1873 (Boston: The Boston Athenaeum, 1940), pp. 160–168 and passim; Charles Seymour, "Houdon's Washington at Mount Vernon Reexamined," GBA, 6th series, 35 (Mar. 1948), 137–158; Marie Kimball, Jef-

ferson: The Scene of Europe (New York: Coward-McCann, Inc., 1950), pp. 56–67; Jefferson to George Washington, Dec. 10, 1784; Jefferson to Benjamin Harrison, Jan. 12, 1785; Jefferson to George Washington, Aug. 14, 1787.

173 Benjamin Franklin 1778
JEAN-ANTOINE HOUDON 1741–1828
Provenance: Collection of Pierre Samuel du Pont de Nemours; sold c. 1836 to John Church Cruger; to his daughter and her husband, Dr. and Mrs. Samuel Bard; to their son, John Bard, who gave it to the Metropolitan Museum in 1882.
Literature: Kimball, "Jefferson and the Arts," p. 243; Kimball, The Scene of Europe, pp. 81, 83; Réau, pp. 401–403.

174 Marquis de Lafayette c. 1785
JEAN-ANTOINE HOUDON 1741–1828
Provenance: Collection of Thomas Jefferson, Monticello; 1828, deposited in the Boston Athenaeum by Mr. and Mrs. Joseph Coolidge, Boston.
Literature: Mabel Munson Swan, The Athenaeum Gallery, 1827–1873 (Boston: The Boston Athenaeum, 1940), pp. 160–168; Kimball, The Scene of Europe, pp. 63–66; Boyd, 15:xxxvii; Jefferson to the governor of Virginia, Aug. 22, 1785; Jefferson to James Madison, Mar. 18, 1785 and Jan. 30, 1787.

175 John Paul Jones 1781
JEAN-ANTOINE HOUDON 1741–1828
Provenance: Collection of the duc d'Orléans; by descent through his family to the duc de Nemours; bought by a New York dealer in 1940; collection of Marshall Field, Chicago, who presented it to the U.S. Naval Academy.
Literature: Jefferson to Monroe, Nov. 11, 1784; Abigail Adams, Letters of Mrs. Adams, introductory memoir by Charles Francis Adams (Boston: Charles C. Little and James Brown, 1840), p. 208; Florence Ingersoll-Smouse, "Quelques documents et lettres relatifs au voyage (1785) et aux oeuvres de Jean-Antoine Houdon aux Etats-Unis" in Bulletin de la Société de l'histoire de l'art français (Paris, 1914), pp. 11–31; Georges Giacometti, La vie et l'oeuvre de Houdon (Paris: A. Camoin, 1929), 2:99–101; George Pudelko, "A Marble Bust of John Paul Jones by Jean-Antoine Houdon," ArtAm, 27 (Oct. 1939), 151–155; information provided in letters from Samuel Eliot Morison, 1959; Samuel Eliot Morison, John Paul Jones: A Sailor's Biography (Boston: Little Brown, and Co., 1959); Boyd 15: illus. xxxvii.

Medals
Literature: Zigrosser, pp. 289–304; Boyd, 16:xxxv–xli, 53–79.

176 De Fleury Medal 1780
PIERRE SIMON BENJAMIN DUVIVIER 1730–1819
Provenance: See no. 179.
Literature: Zigrosser, pp. 289–290; Boyd, 15:55–56.

177 Libertas Americana Medal 1783
AUGUSTIN DUPRÉ 1748–1833
Provenance: See no. 179.
Literature: Zigrosser, pp. 290–294.

178 Benjamin Franklin Medal 1786
AUGUSTIN DUPRÉ 1748–1833
Provenance: See no. 179.
Literature: Zigrosser, pp. 296–298.

179 General George Washington medal 1789
PIERRE SIMON BENJAMIN DUVIVIER 1730–1819
Provenance: George Washington; purchased by Daniel Webster when the offer to the United States was refused in 1827; collection of Peter Harvey, a close friend of Webster's, 1852; presented by Peter Harvey to the Massachusetts Historical Society, 1864.
Literature: Boyd, 16:xxxv–xxxvi, 65, 66, 77, 78, 288, 289

180 Lieutenant-Colonel John E. Howard medal 1789
PIERRE SIMON BENJAMIN DUVIVIER 1730–1819
Provenance: See no. 179.
Literature: Boyd, 16:xxxvii, 54, 56–57, 59–61, 65, 66, 67, 72, 74, 77, 289.

181 General Daniel Morgan medal 1789
AUGUSTIN DUPRÉ 1748–1833
Provenance: See no. 179.
Literature: Zigrosser, pp. 299–300; Boyd, 16:xxxvii–xl, 54, 56–57, 59–61, 63, 65, 67, 71, 73, 74, 76, 288.

182 General Nathaniel Greene medal 1787
AUGUSTIN DUPRÉ 1748–1833
Provenance: See no. 179.
Literature: Zigrosser, pp. 298–299; Jefferson to John Jay, Feb. 14, 1787; Boyd, 16:xxxvii, 54, 57, 59–64, 67, 69, 72, 73, 75, 76.

183 General Horatio Gates medal 1787
NICOLAS-MARIE GATTEAUX 1751–1832
Provenance: See no. 179.
Literature: Boyd, 16:xxvi, 54, 55, 56, 59–61, 63, 64, 67, 69, 70, 73, 75, 76.

184 General Anthony Wayne medal 1789
NICOLAS-MARIE GATTEAUX 1751–1832
Provenance: See no. 179.
Literature: Boyd, 16:xxxvii, 54, 55, 56, 59, 60, 64–66, 70–71, 73–76, 289.

185 Major John Stewart medal 1789
NICOLAS-MARIE GATTEAUX 1751–1832
Provenance: See no. 179.
Literature: Boyd, 16:xxxvii, 54, 59, 71–75.

186 Lieutenant-Colonel William Washington medal 1789
PIERRE SIMON BENJAMIN DUVIVIER 1730–1819
Provenance: See no. 179.
Literature: Boyd, 16:xxxvii, 54, 56–57, 59–61, 65, 66, 67, 71–72, 73, 74, 76, 77, 289.

187 John Paul Jones medal 1789
AUGUSTIN DUPRÉ 1748–1833
Literature: Zigrosser, pp. 299–301; Boyd, 16:xli, 54, 55, 57, 63, 65, 71, 73–76, 77; John Paul Jones to Jefferson, Aug. 29, 1788; Jefferson to John Paul Jones, Mar. 23, 1789.

188 Diplomatic medal 1791
AUGUSTIN DUPRÉ 1748–1833
Literature: Zigrosser, 301–303; Boyd, 16:xli–xlii; Jefferson to William Short, Apr. 30, 1790.

189 Plan of Paris with the New Wall of the Farmers-General
PIERRE-FRANÇOIS TARDIEU 1714–c. 1774
Literature: Boyd, 10:xxviii and ill. opp. p. 211; Jefferson to David Humphreys, Aug. 14, 1787; Marcel Raval and J.-Ch. Moreux, Claude-Nicolas Ledoux, 1756–1806 (Paris: Arts et Métiers Graphiques, 1945), pp. 65–67, pls. 258–329; Rice, Thomas Jefferson's Paris, chap. 1; Leon Vallée, Catalogue des Plans de Paris (Paris: Champion, 1905).

190 Proclamation of the Versailles Peace Treaty between France and England on November 25, 1783
ANTOINE VAN YSENDICH 1801–1875
Provenance: Commissioned from the artist for the Musée de Versailles.
Exhibitions: Newport, 175ème anniversaire du débarquement de Rochambeau, 1955; Paris, Archives nationales, Hôtel de Rohan, La Fayette, 1957, no. 165, p. 61; Versailles, Musée National du Château, Les grandes heures de la diplomatie française, 1963, no. 236, p. 87; Tokyo, Versailles, symbole royal, 1970, no. 35, p. 140 and repr.
Literature: Soulié, 2nd ed., p. 54; Thieme-Becker, 36:364; Jefferson to Lafayette, Aug. 4, 1781.

191 Cul-de-sac Taitbout 1786
[BIT]TMAN active 1780, and JEAN JUNIÉ [ac]tive 1780
[L]iterature: Boyd, 7:442–443; H. C. [R]ice, Jr., "The Paris Depository for [N]otarial Archives," *American Archiv[es]t,* 14, no. 2 (Apr. 1951), 99–104; [R]ice, *Jefferson's Paris,* chap. 4.

[1]92 Project for the Façade of the [C]hurch and Buildings of the Royal [A]bbey of Panthemont . . . c. 1755
[R]OBERT BENARD b. 1734, after [F]rançois Franque 1710– after 1792
[l]iterature: Diderot, D'Alembert, et al., [E]ncyclopédie, *Recueil de planches,* (Paris, 1762): 8–9, pls. 16–21; [T]hiéry, 2:568–569; François Rousseau, "Histoire de l'Abbaye de Pentemont," *[M]émoires de la Société de l'Histoire [d]e Paris,* 45 (1918), 171–227; [L]. A. Weigert, "Un Centenaire: le [t]emple de Pentemont, 1846–1946," *[B]ulletin de la Société de l'Histoire [d]u Protestantisme français,* Jan.– [M]ar. 1947, pp. 13–32; George B. [W]atts, "Thomas Jefferson, the 'Encyclopédie' and the 'Encyclopédie [m]ethodique,'" *French Review,* 38, [n]o. 3 (Jan. 1965), 318–325; E. M. [B]etts and James A. Bear, Jr., eds., *The [F]amily Letters of Thomas Jefferson* [Columbia, Missouri: University of [M]issouri Press, 1966); Rice, *Jeffer[s]on's Paris,* chap. 6.

[1]93 Public Sale in the Auction Room [o]f the Hôtel Bullion
[P]IERRE-ANTOINE DE MACHY 1723–1807
[P]rovenance: G. Muhlbacher Collec[t]ion Sale, May 15–18, 1899, no. 9, [b]ought-in by the seller; sale, May 13– [1]5, 1907, no. 20, F. Doisteau col[l]ection; F. Doisteau sale, Galerie [G]eorges Petit, June 9–11, 1909, no. 17, [b]ought by F. David-Weill; gift to [t]he Musée Carnavalet by M and [M]me D. David-Weill, 1948.
[E]xhibition: Paris, Hôtel de la chambre [s]yndicale de la curiosité et des Beaux-[a]rts, *Exposition de petits maîtres peu [c]onnus du XVIIIe siècle,* Mar. 20– [A]pr. 30, 1928, no. 37.
Literature: D. Deville, "Paris aux [v]entes de 1909," *Société d'iconog[r]aphie parisienne,* 1910, p. xix and [f]ig. 2, pl. II; B. de Montgolfier, "Quelques oeuvres de la donation de M. et Mme. D. David-Weill," *Bul[l]etin du Musée Carnavalet,* June 1955, p. 10 and pl. 11; Editorial, "En[c]hantment and Intellectualism," *Apollo,* 97 (Jan. 1973), fig. 3, p. 4; J. Wilhelm, "Les principales acquisi[t]ions du musée Carnavalet de 1941 à 1972," *Bulletin du Musée Carnavalet,* 26th year (1973), nos. 1, 2, fig. p. 51; Le Curieux, "Le carnet d'un curieux— l'exposition des petits maîtres du XVIIIe siècle," *La Renaissance de l'art français et des industries de luxe,*

3rd year, no. 7 (July 1920), 300; Thieme-Becker, 23:516.

194 Place Louis XV, Paris 1786
JOHN TRUMBULL 1756–1843
Provenance: Descent through Silliman family to present owners.
Literature: Thiéry, 1:96–104; Jefferson to Virginia delegates in Congress, Paris, July 12, 1785 (re Bouchardon statue of Louis XV); Jefferson to L'Enfant, Philadelphia, April 10, 1791 (re Garde-Meubles), in Saul K. Padover, ed., *Thomas Jefferson and the National Capital* (Washington: Government Printing Office, 1946), pp. 58–59; Sizer, pp. 96–97; Theodore Sizer, *The Works of Colonel John Trumbull* (New Haven: Yale University Press, 1950), p. 86 and rev. ed. (1967), p. 116; Rice, *Jefferson's Paris,* chap. 3.

195 The Ditches around the Place Louis XV
HUBERT ROBERT 1733–1808
Provenance: Sale X, June 12, 1929, no. 14, acquired by Marius Paulme; given by M Paulme to the Carnavalet in 1949.
Literature: B. de Montgolfier, "Hubert Robert, peintre de Paris au musée Carnavalet," *Bulletin du Musée Carnavalet,* nos. 1, 2 (1964), 13–15, fig. 10; Marguerite Beau, *La Collection des dessins d'Hubert Robert au musée de Valence* (Lyon: Audin, 1968), no. 84b.

196 Paris seen from Franklin's former House at Passy 1786
JOHN TRUMBULL 1756–1843
Provenance: Descent through Silliman family to present owners.
Literature: Boyd, 8:92n (re Abbés Chalut and Arnoux); Sizer, p. 118; Theodore Sizer, *The Works of Colonel John Trumbull* (New Haven: Yale University Press, 1967), p. 116 (where it is incorrectly assumed that the Pearson-owned drawing is the unlocated pencil sketch that was engraved for Trumbull's *Autobiography,* 1841 edition); Rice, *Jefferson's Paris,* chap. 8.

197 The Construction of the Hôtel de Salm c. 1784
Provenance: Acquired in 1904 by the Musée Carnavalet from M Becker.
Exhibition: Sceaux, Musée de l'Ile de France, *Maisons de Paris et de l'Ile de France,* 1953; Paris, Grand Palais, *Benjamin Franklin and Thomas Jefferson,* winter 1974.
Literature: *Le musée Carnavalet, Guide du Visiteur* (1925), p. 29; *Guide du musée Carnavalet* (1928), p. 21.

198 Procession in Front of the Church of Sainte-Geneviève 1788
FRANÇOIS-DENIS NÉE 1732–1818, after Meunier active 1780
Literature: Thiéry, 2:240–242; Sebastien Mercier, *Tableau de Paris,* 2 (Amsterdam, 1782–1788), chap. 153, "L'Eglise de Sainte-Geneviève"; J. Monval, *Soufflot, sa vie, son oeuvre, son esthétique* (Paris: Lemerre, 1918); Kimball, *Thomas Jefferson, Architect,* pp. 54–55, 157–158, no. 132; James A. Bear, Jr., *Report of the Curator,* 1972 (Charlottesville: Thomas Jefferson Memorial Foundation, 1972), pp. 14–15 and repr. of Charpentier engraving belonging to Jefferson; Paul Lesourd, *Le Panthéon,* in series Petites notes sur les Grands Edifices (Paris: Caisse National des Monuments Historiques et des Sites, 1965); Alan Braham, "Drawings for Soufflot's Sainte-Geneviève," *BurlM,* 113 (Oct. 1971), 582–591.

199 Le Guichet du Louvre c. 1785
FRANÇOIS-DENIS NÉE 1732–1818, after Meunier active 1780
Literature: Jefferson, "Catalogue of Paintings etc. at Monticello," c. 1809, MS, University of Virginia; James A. Bear, Jr., *Report of the Curator* (Monticello: Thomas Jefferson Memorial Foundation) for 1962, pp. 15–16, 1963, pp. 12–13, 1969, pp. 11–12, 1971, p. 21, 1972, pp. 14–15; Thiéry, 1:327–380; Yvan Christ, *Le Louvre et les Tuileries, Histoire d'un double Palais* (Paris: Editions "TEL," 1949).

200 Interior View of the New Circus in the Palais Royal . . . 1788
CHARLES-FRANÇOIS-GABRIEL LE VACHEZ ET FILS active 1760–1820
Literature: Jefferson to David Humphreys, Aug. 14, 1787; Jefferson to comte de Moustier, Aug. 9, 1788; Jefferson to John Jay, Aug. 10, 1788; Mayeur de Saint-Paul, *Tableau du Nouveau Palais Royal* (London and Paris: chez Maradan, 1788), pt. 2, pp. 107–112; Sebastien Mercier, *Tableau de Paris,* 10 (Hambourg: Virchaux et compagnie, 1781), chap. 820; A. de la Vaissiere and B. de Montgolfier, "Une Tasse de Sèvres commemorant l'Ambassade de Tippo-Saib," *Bulletin du Musée Carnavalet,* June 1961, pp. 9–11; Marcelle Brunet, "Incidences de l'Ambassade de Tipoo-Saib (1788) sur la Porcelaine de Sèvres," *Cahiers de la Céramique,* no. 24 (1961), 275–284.

201 Place Louis XV at the Launching of the Balloon of MM Charles and Robert, December 1, 1783
Attributed to PIERRE-ANTOINE DE MACHY 1723–1807
Provenance: Destailleur sale, Paris,

May 23, 1896, no. 592; acquired in 1912 from M Jules Feral.
Exhibition: Paris, Musée Carnavalet, *Trois siècles de dessin parisien* (1946), no. 79; Paris, Musée Carnavalet, *Dessins parisiens du XVIIIe siècle* (1971), no. 67; Montrouge, Salle des Fêtes, *L'air et les peintres,* May 6– June 1, 1975, no. 11.
Literature: M. Benisovich, "Etienne de Lorimer dessinateur de Montgolfières," *Le Courrier Graphique,* Jan.–Feb. 1948, pp. 59–67; Madison to Jefferson, Apr. 28, 1784; Jefferson to Philip Turpin, Apr. 28, 1784; Jefferson to Madison, Nov. 11, 1784; Jefferson to John Page, Nov. 11, 1784; Jefferson to David Rittenhouse, Nov. 11, 1784; Jefferson to Charles Thomson, Nov. 11, 1784; Jefferson to James Currie, Nov. 11, 1784.

202 Plan for remodeling the Hôtel de Langeac. Circular room of mezzanine 1785–1789
THOMAS JEFFERSON 1743–1826
Literature: Nichols, pp. 5, 39; Rice, *Hôtel de Langeac.*

203 Hôtel de Langeac. Study for changes 1785
THOMAS JEFFERSON 1743–1826
Literature: Kimball, *Thomas Jefferson, Architect,* p. 118; Nichols, pp. 5, 39, 47; Rice, *Hôtel de Langeac.*

204 Plan for the garden of the Hôtel de Langeac
THOMAS JEFFERSON 1743–1826
Literature: Nichols, p. 39; Rice, *Hôtel de Langeac.*

205 The Rising of the Sun with Aurora's Chariot
JEAN-SIMON BERTHÉLEMY 1743–1811
Provenance:
Literature: Rice, *Hôtel de Langeac.*

206 A Cloister of the Hermits at Mont Valérien A Monk's Cell, Mont Valérien
Literature: Randolph, p. 48 (quoting Martha Jefferson Randolph MS); Jefferson, Account Book; Jefferson to Mme de Corny, Paris, Oct. 18, 1787; Fremyn de Fontenille to Jefferson, Paris, Oct. 23, 1787, Jefferson (in French) to Fremyn de Fontenille, Paris, Oct. 24, 1787; R.-F. du Breil de Pontbriand, *Pélerinage du Calvaire sur le Mont Valérien, avec des figures en taille douce* (Paris: Chez Babuty, 1779); Sowerby, 2:128; Sébastien Mercier, *Tableau de Paris,* 7 (Amsterdam, 1782–1788): 70–72; Jacques Hérissay, *Le Mont-Valérien* (Paris: Librairie Académique Perrin, 1934); H. C. Rice, Jr., "Jefferson in Europe a Century and a Half Later: Notes of a Roving Researcher,"

Princeton University Library Chronicle, 13, no. 1 (Autumn 1950), 19–35; H. C. Rice, Jr., "Les Visites de Jefferson au Mont-Valérien," *Bulletin de la Société Historique de Suresnes*, 3, no. 13 (1953–1954), 46–49.

207 Château de Marly 1724
PIERRE-DENIS MARTIN LE JEUNE 1663–1742
Literature: Anthony Blunt, *Art and Architecture in France 1500–1700*, 2nd ed. (Baltimore: Penguin Books, 1970), p. 207; Jefferson to Maria Cosway, Oct. 12, 1786.

208 The Terrace of the Château at Marly
HUBERT ROBERT 1733–1808
Provenance: Baron Gustav de Rothschild, to his daughter and son-in-law Baron and Baroness Leonius, to Charles Michel, Paris.
Exhibition: Paris, Château de Bagatelle, *Peintres des Jardins des XVIII et XIX Siècles*, June–July 1928, no. 79; Nice, Musée Jules Cheret, *Exposition de l'Art des Jardins*, Mar.–Apr. 1929, no. 201 repr.; New York, Metropolitan Museum of Art, *Exhibition of 18th Century Painting and Sculpture*, Nov. 4, 1935 to Jan. 5, 1936, p. 10, no. 53 repr.; Pittsburgh, The Carnegie Institute, *French Painting, 1100–1900*, Oct. 18 to Dec. 2, 1951, no. 91 repr.; Hartford, The Wadsworth Atheneum, *Homage to Mozart*, Mar. 7 to May 15, 1956, no. 52; San Antonio, Marion Koogler McNay Art Institute, *The French Tradition*, Jan. 25 to Mar. 21, 1961; Poughkeepsie, Vassar College Art Gallery, *Hubert Robert, The Paintings and Drawings*, Oct. 9 to Nov. 11, 1962, no. 15; Chicago, Art Institute of Chicago, *Great French Paintings: An Exhibition in Memory of Chauncey McCormick*, Jan. 20 to Feb. 20, 1955, no. 36; Kansas City, William Rockhill Nelson Gallery of Art, *The Century of Mozart*, Jan. 15 to Mar. 4, 1956, no. 94, pp. 13, 31; Indianapolis, John Herron Museum, *Romantic Era: Birth and Flowering 1750–1850*, Feb. 21–Apr. 11, 1965, no. 5 repr.
Literature: "Revue de l'Exposition au Bagatelle," *Bulletin de l'Art*, no. 75 (1928), 305–307, repr. 309; Georges Isarlov, *La Peinture à l'Exposition de Londres 1932* (Paris: J. Corti, 1932), p. 26; "Nelson Gallery of Art Special Number," *Art Digest*, Dec. 1, 1933, p. 13, repr. p. 20; Georges Isarlov, "L'Exposition Hubert Robert," *Notes d'Art*, *La Concorde*, Jan. 5, 1934; Dorothy Adlow, "Terrace of the Chateau of Marly," *Christian Science Monitor*, Feb. 17, 1942, p. 12; Sizer, pp. 97, 118;

BMMA, 22, no. 1 (Summer 1963), repr. 26; *Connoisseur*, 158, no. 638 (Apr. 1965), 257; Ralph T. Coe, "The Baroque and Rococo in France and Italy," *Apollo*, 96, no. 130 (Dec. 1972), 69, pl. 15.

209 Perspective View of the Machine de Marly
PIERRE AVELINE, LE VIEUX 1656–1722
Literature: Jefferson, Account Book, Aug. 6, 1784; Jefferson to Maria Cosway, Paris, Oct. 12, 1786; Thiéry, 2:490.

210 Halle aux Bleds, exterior 1786
JEAN-BAPTISTE MARÉCHAL active 1780
Literature: Thiéry, 1:413–419; Gabriel Vauthier, "La Halle au Blé, 1758–1811," *Bulletin de la Société d'Histoire de Paris*, 55 (1926), 62–68; Rice, *Jefferson's Paris*, chap. 2.

211 Pavilion of Louveciennes 1774
SIR WILLIAM CHAMBERS 1726–1796
Literature: Jefferson to Maria Cosway, Oct. 12, 1786; John Harris, "Sir William Chambers and his Parisian Album," *Architectural History*, 6 (1963), 54–90.

212 The Pavilion of Bagatelle, three views
FRANÇOIS-DENIS NÉE 1732–1818, after L. Bélanger active late 18th century
Literature: Jefferson to John Trumbull, Paris, Aug. 24, 1788; Jefferson to Robert Skipwith, with List of Books for a Private Library, Monticello, Aug. 3, 1771; plans for the development of the grounds at Monticello, in Jefferson's Account Book for 1771, printed in Betts, pp. 25–27; the prince de Ligne, *Coup d'oeil sur Beloeil et sur une grande partie des Jardins de l'Europe*, Ernest de Ganay, ed. (Paris. Bossard, 1922), p. 225; Abbé Delille, *Les Jardins, ou l'Art d'embellir les paysages, Poëme*, 6th ed. (Reims: Chez Cazin, Librarie, 1785), pp. 14, 104–105; G. L. Le Rouge, comp., *Jardins Anglo-Chinois* (Paris, 1776 . . .), bk. 12, pl. 2; Thiéry, 1:25–30; Ernest de Ganay, *Châteaux et Manoirs de France: Ile-de-France*, 5 (Paris: Vincent, Fréal & Cie., 1939): 5–9, pls. 1–5.

213 Gardens of Bagatelle, showing Philosopher's Grotto
FRANÇOIS-JOSEPH BÉLANGER 1744–1818
Literature: See no. 212.

214 View of the Column House and Temple of Pan 1785
Attributed to LOUIS CARROGIS, CALLED CARMONTELLE 1717–1806
Exhibition: London, Royal Academy

and Victoria & Albert Museum, *The Age of Neo-classicism*, Sept. 9–Nov. 19, 1972, cat. no. 997.
Literature: Lyman H. Butterfield and H. C. Rice, Jr., "Jefferson's Earliest Note to Maria Cosway, with Some New Facts and Conjectures on His Broken Wrist," *William & Mary Quarterly*, 5, 3rd series, no. 1 (Jan. 1948), 26–33, illus.; Osvald Sirén, "Le Désert de Retz," *Architectural Review*, 56, no. 635 (Nov. 1949), 327–332; Osvald Sirén, *China and the Gardens of Europe in the Eighteenth Century* (New York: Ronald Press, 1950); Colette, "Le Désert de Retz," in *Paradis terrestre*, photos by Izis-Bidermanas (Lausanne: Guilde du Livre, 1953), pp. 59–81; Cyril Connolly and Jerome Zerbe, *Les Pavillons: French Pavilions of the Eighteenth Century* (New York: Macmillan, 1962), pp. 150–151; Michel Gallet, *Stately Mansions: Eighteenth Century Paris Architecture* (New York: Praeger, 1972), pp. 35, 141 (s.v. Barbier).

215 The Studio of Houdon
LOUIS-LÉOPOLD BOILLY 1761–1845
Provenance: Given to the museum in 1835 by Thomas Henry.
Exhibition: London, The Royal Academy and the Victoria and Albert Museum, *The Age of Neo-classicism*, Sept. 9–Nov. 19, 1972, no. 36.
Literature: H. Harisse, *Boilly, sa vie, son oeuvre, 1761–1845* (Paris, 1898), pp. 40, 111, no. 312; Paul Marmottan, *Le peintre Louis Boilly* (Paris: H. Gateau, 1913), p. 86; André Mabille de Poncheville, *Boilly* (Paris: Plon, 1931), pp. 107–108, 168; Réau, pp. 190–192, pl. CLVII; Boyd, 8:xxvii–xxviii, illus. opp. p. 215; Sizer, p. 99.

216 Marquis de Condorcet 1785
JEAN-ANTOINE HOUDON 1741–1828
Literature: William Short to Jefferson, Oct. 21, 1819 (Lipscomb, 15: 223); Florence Ingersoll-Smouse, "Houdon en Amérique," *La Revue de l'art ancien et moderne*, 35 (Jan.–June, 1914), 279–298; *Catalogue of Portraits and other Works of Art in the Possession of the American Philosophical Society* (Philadelphia, 1961), pp. 15–16, fig. 11.

217 Christoph Willibald von Glück c. 1775
JEAN-ANTOINE HOUDON 1741–1828
Provenance: Acquired from a private source in the U.S.A.
Exhibition: Notre Dame, Indiana, Art Gallery of the University of Notre Dame, *Eighteenth Century France: A Study of Its Art and Civilization*, Mar. 12–May 15, 1972, no. 47.

Literature: Benjamin Franklin, *Writings*, 7 (New York: Macmillan, 1907): 207; Berman, pp. 178–179.

218 Madame de Wailly 1789
AUGUSTIN PAJOU 1730–1809
Provenance: Mme Camille Lelong, Paris (sale catalogue, Galerie Georges Petit, Apr. 27–May 1, 1903, no. 298, listed as Mme de Fourcroy); princesse de Wagram, Paris; David David-Weill, Neuilly-sur-Seine; Seligmann, Paris; Mrs. William Salomon, New York (sale catalogue, American Art Association, New York, Jan. 4–7, 1928, no. 748); J. Horace Harding, New York (sale catalogue, Parke-Bernet Galleries, New York, Mar. 1, 1941, no. 748); Baronne Cassel van Doorn, Englewood, N.J. (sale catalogue, Galerie Charpentier, Paris, May 30, 1956, no. 75); purchase, Fletcher Fund, 1956.
Exhibition: Paris, Salon of 1789, no. 207; New York, The Metropolitan Museum of Art, *Fiftieth Anniversary Exhibition*, 1920, p. 12; New York, The Metropolitan Museum of Art, *French Painting and Sculpture of the XVIII Century* (1935–1936), p. 19, fig. 35.
Literature: Chaussard, "Liste des oeuvres de Pajou," *Pausanias Français* (1806), reprinted by J. du Seigneur in *Revue Universelle des Arts*, 16 quaire de l'Ile Saint-Louis," *Revue de l'art ancien et modern*, 13 (1903), 254; Henri Stein, *Augustin Pajou, sa vie et ses oeuvres* (Paris, 1912), pp. 26–29, 35, 415; *GBA*, 1 (1923), 192 (on Bethmann bust); Edmund Hildebrandt, *Malerei und Plastik des achtzehnten Jahrhunderts in Frankreich* (Wildpark-Potsdam, 1924), pp. 93–94; Preston Remington, "French Painting and Sculpture of the XVIII Century," *BMMA*, 30, no. 11 (1935), 214; Michel N. Benisovich, "Drawings by the Sculptor Augustin Pajou in the Art Museum," *Princeton University Art Museum Record*, 14 (1955), 9, no. 2; John Goldsmith Phillips, "Recent Accessions of European Sculpture," *BMMA*, 15, no. 6 (1957), 151.

219 The comte d'Angiviller c. 1779
JOSEPH-SIFFRED DUPLESSIS 1725–1802
Provenance: Charles, comte d'Angiviller, to Emily de Flahaut, to the Marchioness of Lansdowne, to Baroness Nairne and Keith, to Lady Emily Digby; A. E. H. Digby, sale, Sotheby's, June 20, 1951, no. 18 (sold as by Carle van Loo).
Exhibitions: London, Agnew's, *European Pictures from an English County* (Hampshire), 1957, no. 32; London, Royal Academy of Arts, *France in the Eighteenth Century*, 1968, no. 212 and fig. 314.

Literature: J. Belleudy, *J. S. Duplessis, peintre du roi (1725–1802)* (Avignon: Éditions de l'Académie de Vaucluse, 1913), pp. 87–90, 316; L. Bobe, *Mémoires de Charles-Claude Flahaut comte de la Billarderie d'Angiviller* (Copenhagen: Levin and Munksgaard, 1933), pp. 189–190; H. Stein, *Dictionnaire de biographie française, 2* (Paris, 1936), col. 1132; Kimball, "Jefferson and the Arts," p. 243.

220 Portrait of Architect Ledoux and His Family
MARGUÉRITE GÉRARD 1761–1837
Provenance: Purchased by Mary Frick Jacobs in 1909 from Eugene Fischhof at Felix Doistau sale, Galérie Georges Petits, Paris.

Exhibition: Indianapolis, Herron Museum of Art, *Jewelry and Finery,* Feb. 18–Mar. 26, 1967; Baltimore, Walters Art Gallery, *Old Mistresses,* Apr. 16–June 18, 1972.

Literature: Jefferson to David Humphreys, Aug. 18, 1787; Henry Barton Jacobs, *The Collection of Mary Frick Jacobs* (Baltimore: published by the author, 1938), pl. 24.

221 Jacques-François Desmaisons 1782
JACQUES-LOUIS DAVID 1748–1825
Exhibition: Paris, Salon of 1783, no. 163 ("Two portraits under the same number"); New York, The Century Association, *Exhibition,* Feb. 15–Apr. 10, 1947; Toronto, Art Gallery of Toronto, *Fifty Paintings by Old Masters,* Apr. 21–May 21, 1950, no. 8; Worcester, Mass., Worcester Art Museum, *Condition Excellent,* Mar. 22–Apr. 22, 1951, no. 11; Pittsburgh, Carnegie Institute, *French Painting, 1100–1900,* pl. 98; Buffalo, Albright Art Gallery, *Painters' Painters,* Apr. 16–June 1, 1954, no. 16, repr. p. 28; Minneapolis, Minneapolis Institute of Arts, *French Eighteenth Century Painters,* Oct. 5–Nov. 2, 1954, no. 6; New York, Wildenstein & Co., benefit for Minneapolis Institute of Arts, Nov. 16–Dec. 11, 1954, no. 6; Kansas City, Mo., Nelson-Atkins Gallery of Art, *The Century of Mozart,* Jan. 15–Mar. 4, 1956, no. 18, fig. 10; Hartford, Wadsworth Atheneum, *Homage to Mozart,* Mar. 22–Apr. 29, 1956, no. 10, pl. 6; Toronto, Art Gallery of Toronto, *Exhibition,* Sept. 23–Oct. 1; Buffalo, Albright Art Gallery, *Trends in Painting 1600–1800,* Oct. 2–Nov. 4, 1957, p. 60, repr. p. 61; Hamilton, Ontario, The Art Gallery of Hamilton, *Old Masters,* Nov. 1958, no. 10; Rochester, Memorial Art Gallery, *Paintings and Sculpture from the Albright Art Gallery,* Jan. 15–Mar. 5, 1961; New Haven, Yale University Art Gallery, *Paintings and Sculpture*

from the Albright Art Gallery, Apr. 26–Sept. 4, 1961, no. 13; Cleveland, Cleveland Museum of Art, *Style, Truth and the Portrait,* Oct. 1–Nov. 10, 1963, no. 58; Indianapolis, Herron Museum of Art, *The Romantic Era,* Feb. 21–Apr. 11, 1965; Milwaukee, Milwaukee Art Center, *The Inner Circle,* Sept. 15–Oct. 30, 1966, no. 26.

Literature: Coll. Deloynes, 13:970, no. 311 and 997, no. 312; Daniel and Guy Wildenstein, *Documents complémentaires au catalogue de l'oeuvre de Louis David* (Paris, 1973), nos. 108 (p. 14), 114 (p. 15), 1810 (p. 208), 1938 (11) (p. 226); Michel Gallet, "L'oeuvre de Pierre Desmaisons architecte du Roi de 1733 à 1791," *Bulletin de la société d'histoire de l'art français,* 1953, p. 99, n. 1; J. M. Fort, "Pierre Desmaisons," *Dictionnaire de biographie française, 55* (Paris, 1962): 1431.

222 Joseph-Marie Vien 1784
JOSEPH-SIFFRED DUPLESSIS 1725–1802
Provenance: Offered by Duplessis to the Royal Academy of Painting in 1785; the Academy's collections; in the Year II in the Petits Augustins; Musée National du Château de Versailles; in 1826 in the Ecole des Beaux-Arts; in 1887 in the Musée du Louvre.

Exhibitions: Paris, Salon of 1785, no. 43; Rennes, Musée des Beaux-Arts, *Peintures françaises du XVIIIᵉ siècle du Musée du Louvre,* 1964–1965, no. 14.

Literature: Procès-Verbaux de l'Académie Royale, 1771–1774, 8 (Paris: A. de Montaiglon, 1888): 67, 103, 154; *Coll. Deloynes,* nos. 327 (p. 147), 331 (p. 296), 335 (p. 408), 336 (p. 438), 337 (p. 480), 339 (pp. 549, 561), 340 (p. 586), 344 (p. 656), 345 (p. 690), 351 (p. 824); Henri-Auguste Jouin, *Musée de portraits d'artistes* (Paris: H. Laurens, 1888), p. 192; Philippe de Chennevières-Pointel, *Souvenir d'un directeur des Beaux-Arts,* 5th pt. (Paris: aux bureaux de l'artiste, 1889), p. 19; André Fontaine, *Les collections de l'Académie Royale de peinture et de sculpture* (Paris: H. Laurens, 1910), pp. 122, 177, nos. 375–369; Jules Belleudy, *J. S. Duplessis* (Avignon: Editions de l'académie de Vaucluse, 1913), pp. 1, 112, 116–119, 144, 147, 171 and no. 141 (p. 335), illus. opp. p. 184; F. Schmid, "Some Observations on Artists' Palettes," *AB,* no. 4 (Dec. 1958), 334; Anne-Marie Passez, *Adélaïde Labille-Guiard 1749–1803: Biographie et catalogue raisonné de son oeuvre* (Paris: Arts et métiers graphiques, 1973), p. 53; P. Rosenberg, N. Reynaud, I. Compin, *Musée du Louvre, Catalogue illustré*

des peintures, Ecole française XVIIᵉ et XVIIIᵉ siècles (Paris, 1974), 1, fig. 254, p. 121; Brière, no. 277; *Musée national du Louvre, Catalogue des peintures, I, Ecole française* (Paris, 1972), p. 151.

223 Thomas Jefferson 1786
MATHER BROWN 1761–1831
Provenance: By family descent from John Adams.

Exhibition: National Gallery of Art and the Library of Congress, "The Thomas Jefferson Bicentennial," 1943; Charlottesville, The University of Virginia Museum of Fine Arts, *The Life Portraits of Thomas Jefferson,* Apr. 12–16, 1962.

Literature: John Trumbull to Jefferson, Mar. 6, 1788; William Short to Jefferson, Mar. 6, 1788; Bowen, p. 486; Charles Henry Hart, "The Life Portraits of Thomas Jefferson," *McClure's Magazine,* 11, no. 1 (May 1898), 49; Kimball, "Life Portraits," pp. 499–501; William Kelby, *Notes on American Artists 1754–1820* (New York: The New-York Historical Society, 1922); Massachusetts Historical Society, *Proceedings, 47* (1913), 32–34; Bush, pp. 15–16, repr.

Engravings: Timothy House, in George Bancroft, *History of the United States,* 10 vols. (Boston: Little, Brown and Company, 1835–1875), vol. 8, frontispiece; A. B. Hall, in *Appleton's Cyclopaedia of American Biography* (1887), s.v. "Thomas Jefferson."

224 Martha Jefferson 1789
JOSEPH BOZE 1744–1826
Provenance: 1789–1966, at American Embassy in Paris; removed to the Department of State in 1966.

Literature: Jefferson to Francis Eppes, Aug. 30, 1785; Jefferson to Martha Jefferson, Mar. 6, 1786; Abigail Adams to Jefferson, July 23, 1786; Jefferson to Martha Jefferson, Mar. 28, 1787; Martha Jefferson to Jefferson, May 3, 1787; Jefferson to Martha Jefferson, May 21, 1787; Boyd, 14:xli–xlii, 355, illus. opp. p. 361; Nathaniel Cutting's travel diary, Oct. 1789; Boyd, 15:498.

225 Louis XVI
JOSEPH-SIFFRED DUPLESSIS 1725–1802
Provenance: Collection of Louis XVI.

Exhibition: Paris, Salon of 1775, no. 128.

Literature: Jefferson to John Jay, June 17, 1785; Jefferson to Abigail Adams, Aug. 9, 1786 (on the popularity of the king); Jefferson to John Jay, Oct. 8, 1787 (his revised opinion of Louis XVI); Jefferson's Autobiography, Ford, 1:121–122, 141; Soulié, 3rd ed., 3: no. 3966; Jules Belleudy, *J.-S. Duplessis: peintre du*

roi 1725–1802 (Chartres: Imprimerie Durand, 1913), pp. 59–60 and no. 91, pp. 326–327.

226 Marie-Antoinette
MARIE LOUISE ELISABETH VIGÉE-LEBRUN 1755–1842
Provenance: Bought from the artist by Louis XVIII to be hung at Saint-Cloud.

Exhibition: Vienna, *Souvenir de Marie-Antoinette et de ses enfants,* 1930; Versailles, *Marie-Antoinette,* 1955, no. 81.

Literature: P. de Nolhac and A. Pératé, *Le musée national de versailles* (1896), p. 240; P. de Nolhac, "Marie-Antoinette et Mme Vigée-Le Brun," *Revue de l'art,* Dec. 1898, pp. 523–524; P. de Nolhac, *Madame Vigée-Le Brun* (Paris, 1908), pp. 24–25; Thomas Jefferson, *Autobiography* (Ford, 1:140).

227 Charles-Alexandre de Calonne 1784
MARIE LOUISE ELISABETH VIGÉE-LEBRUN 1755–1842
Provenance: Collection of Calonne; collection of George IV, who acquired it as early as 1806; the portrait was listed in the account books of Carlton House in 1816 (no. 270) and in 1819 (no. 291).

Exhibitions: Paris, Salon of 1785, no. 87; London, The Royal Academy, *Exhibition of the King's Pictures,* 1946–1947, no. 406; London, The Royal Academy, *European Masters of the Eighteenth Century,* 1954–1955, no. 339; London, The Queen's Gallery, *George IV and the Arts of France,* 1966, no. 6 and fig. 5; London, The Royal Academy, *France in the Eighteenth Century,* 1968, no. 711 and fig. 26.

Literature: Jefferson to Mme de Corny, Oct. 18, 1787; Coll. Deloynes, no. 327 (p. 149), no. 330 (p. 260), no. 331 (p. 297), no. 341 (p. 614), no. 343 (p. 629), no. 344 (p. 662), no. 345 (p. 697), no. 346 (p. 728), no. 351 (pp. 829–830); Marie Louise Elisabeth Vigée-Lebrun, *Souvenirs de Mme. Vigée-Lebrun* (Paris: H. Fournier, 1835–1837), 1:105–106, 111–112, 153; Charles Pillet, *Mme Vigée-Lebrun* (Paris: Librairie de l'Art, 1890), pp. 26–27; Pierre de Nolhac, *Mme Vigée-Le Brun, peintre de la reine Marie-Antoinette* (Paris: Goupil et Cᵉ, Manzi, Joyant et Cᵉ, succ., 1912), pp. 57–62; W. H. Helm, *Vigée-Lebrun, Her Life, Works, and Friendships* (London: Hutchinson and Co., 1915), pp. 67–75, 190–191; Louis Hautecoeur, *Mme Vigée-Lebrun* (Paris: H. Laurens, 1914), pp. 68–69; C. H. Collins-Baker, *Catalogue of the Principal Pictures in the Royal Collection at Windsor*

Castle (London, 1937), p. 120, and repr. pl. 72.

228 Alessandro, Conte Cagliostro 1786
JEAN-ANTOINE HOUDON 1741–1828
Provenance: Sir John Murray Scott to Sir Richard Wallace, to George Petit; bought at auction Mar. 4, 1921, by Jacques Seligman; sold to Samuel H. Kress, who gave it to the National Gallery of Art, 1952.
Exhibition: Paris, *Exposition de l'art au XVIIIe siècle*, 1883; Paris, *Exposition de Marie-Antoinette et son temps*, 1894, no. 212; Paris, *Exposition des cents pastels*, 1908, no. 131; London, The Royal Academy, *Exhibition of French Art*, 1932.
Literature: Réau.

229 Madame de Tott Painting the Portrait of the Comtesse de Tessé
Literature: Gilbert Chinard, *Trois amitiés françaises de Jefferson d'après sa correspondance inédite avec Madame de Bréhan, Madame de Tessé, and Madame de Corny* (Paris: Société d'édition "Les Belles lettres," 1927); Bush, p. 28; Boyd, 10: xxvii, 157–160, illus. opp. p. 178, 14: 704; Mme de Tott to Jefferson, Dec. 1786; Jefferson to Mme de Tott, Feb. 28, 1787; Mme de Tott to Jefferson, Mar. 4, 1787; Jefferson to Mme de Tott, Apr. 5, 1787; Jefferson to Mme de Tessé, Mar. 20, 1787; Mme de Tott to Jefferson, May 19, 1787; Mme de Tessé to Jefferson, May 22, 1788; Mme de Tessé to Jefferson, Mar. 10, 1789; Jefferson to Mme de Tessé, Aug. 27, 1789; Jefferson to William Short, Mar. 14, 1790; William Short to Jefferson, June 12, 1790; Mme de Tott to Jefferson, July 20, 1786; Mme de Tott to Jefferson, Sept. 28, 1786.

230 Madame d'Houdetot
VALLIÈRES, active late 18th century
Provenance: By family descent.
Literature: Jefferson to Saint John de Crèvecoeur, Dec. 8, 1786; Mme d'Houdetot to Jefferson, Aug. 26, 1788; Jefferson to Mme d'Houdetot, Sept. 13, 1789; Mme d'Houdetot to Jefferson, Sept. 16, 1789; Mme d'Houdetot to Jefferson, Sept. 3, 1790; Mme d'Houdetot to Jefferson, Oct. 26, 1790.

231 Tea in the Salon des Quatre Glaces of the Hôtel du Temple . . . 1777
MICHEL-BARTHÉLÉMY OLLIVIER 1712–1784
Provenance: Commissioned in 1766 by the prince de Conti; Collection of the prince de Conti; Musée Napoléon; transferred by the Musée du Louvre to the Musée de Versailles on November 15, 1974.
Exhibitions: Salon of 1777, no. 135; Paris, Musée Carnavalet, *Les grands salons littéraires*, 1927, no. 57 repr.; Paris, Bibliothèque nationale, *La musique française du Moyen Age à la Révolution*, 1934, no. 555; Paris, Musée Galliéra, *Huit siècles de vie britannique*, May–Aug. 1948, no. 260; Paris, Bibliothèque nationale, *Mozart en France*, 1956, no. 35 repr.; Rome, Palazzo Venezia, *Il ritratto francese da Clouet a Degas*, 1962, no. 152; Paris, Musée Carnavalet, *Le Marais*, 1962, no. 136; Vienna, Oberes Belvedere, *Kunst und Geist Frankreichs im 18. Jahrhundert*, 1966, no. 431.
Literature: Les tableaux du Louvre (1777), p. 20; *Les lettres pittoresques à l'occasion des tableaux exposés au Salon de 1777*, p. 29; Soulié, 2nd ed., no. 3824; Vienne, "L'ancienne Académie de peinture et sculpture," *Revue universelle des arts*, 1861, p. 231; L. Both de Tauzia, *Notice supplémentaire des tableaux exposés dans les galeries du musée national du Louvre* (Paris, 1878), no. 821; P. de Chennevières, "Les dessins des maîtres anciens," *GBA* series 2, 20 (Sept. 1879), 194; Bellier and Auvray, 2:176; Léonce Bénédite, "M. B. Ollivier," *L'Art*, Oct. 1, 1888, pp. 136–139; Léonce Bénédite, "Michel-Barthélémy Ollivier," *GBA* series 3, 14 (Dec. 1895), 453–470, repr.; E. Biais, "Les grands amateurs angoumoisins, XVe–XVIIIe siècles," *Réunion des Sociétés des Beaux-Arts des départements*, Apr. 1898, p. 895; Emile Dacier, *Catalogues de ventes et livrets de Salons, illustrés par Gabriel de Saint-Aubin* (Paris, 1910), 4:50; Raymond Bouyer, "L'exposition de la vénerie française au pavillon de Marsan," *GBA*, series 5, 8 (July 1923), 21–26; Brière, no. 665; A. P. de Mirimonde, "Musiciens isolés et portraits de l'école française du XVIIIe siècle dans les collections nationales," *La Revue du Louvre et des musées de France*, no. 15 (1966), 197–200 and repr. p. 198; *Musée du Louvre. Catalogue des peintures, I, école française* (1972), p. 286; P. Rosenberg, N. Reynaud, I. Compin, *Musée du Louvre. Catalogue illustré des peintures. Ecole française, XVIIe et XVIIIe siècles* (Paris, 1974), no. 603 and repr.; Cripe, p. 87.

232 Saint John de Crèvecoeur
VALLIÈRES, active late 18th century
Provenance: By family descent.
Literature: Howard C. Rice, *Le Cultivateur américain; étude sur l'oeuvre de Saint John de Crèvecoeur* (Paris: H. Champion, 1933); DAB, 4:542–544; de Crèvecoeur to Jefferson, Jan. 23, 1784; de Crèvecoeur to Jefferson, Apr. 16, 1787; de Crèvecoeur to Jefferson, May 18, 1785; Jefferson to de Crèvecoeur, Aug. 22, 1785; Jefferson to William Short, Mar. 29, 1787; de Crèvecoeur to Jefferson, Oct. 20, 1788; de Crèvecoeur to Jefferson, May 20, 1789; Jefferson to de Crèvecoeur, Aug. 9, 1789.

233 Thomas Jefferson 1789
EDMÉ QUENEDEY 1756–1830
Provenance: This example of the aquatint was acquired in 1946 by the Yale University Art Gallery as part of the Mabel Brady Garvan Collection.
Exhibition: Yale University Art Gallery; Charlottesville, The University of Virginia Museum of Fine Arts, *The Life Portraits of Thomas Jefferson*, Apr. 12–16, 1962.
Literature: Kimball, "Life Portraits" (1944), 497; René Hennequin, *Les Portraits au Physionotrace* (Troyes: J.-L. Paton 1932), pp. 59–60; Howard C. Rice, Jr., "A 'New' Likeness of Thomas Jefferson," *William and Mary Quarterly*, 6, n.s. 3, no. 1 (Jan. 1949), 84–89; Bush, pp. 20–22.
Engravings: Neither the copper plates engraved by Chrétien, nor any of the twelve prints (almost certainly showing the profile against a circular background) which Jefferson purchased has ever been found. Only three examples of the aquatint, engraved by Quenedey most probably about 1801 (depicting the profile against an irregular oval background), have been located. Besides the Yale example, the Bibliothèque nationale possesses one with and one without an inscription.

234 Gouverneur Morris 1789
GILLES-LOUIS CHRÉTIEN 1754–1811, after EDMÉ QUENEDEY 1756–1830
Provenance: Gift from the American Antiquarian Society, 1939.
Literature: Gouverneur Morris, *A Diary of the French Revolution*, ed. Beatrix Cary Davenport (Boston: Houghton Mifflin, 1939); René Hennequin, *Les Portraits au Physionotrace* (Troyes: J.-L. Paton, 1932), pp. 85–86, no. 421; Rice, *Jefferson's Paris*, chap. 2; Gouverneur Morris, *The Diary and Letters*, ed. Anne Cary Morris (New York: C. Scribner's Sons, 1888), 1: frontispiece; Schreider, p. 471.

235 Meeting of the Assemblée des Notables Presided Over by Louis XVI and Held in the Hôtel des Menus Plaisirs at Versailles
JEAN-MICHEL MOREAU, CALLED MOREAU LE JEUNE 1741–1814
Provenance: Bruun Collection, Neergard; Paris, sale of the Bruun Collection, Neergard, Aug. 29, 1814, no. 257, purchased by the Musée du Louvre; deposited at Versailles, 1899.
Exhibition: Paris, Salon of 1787, no. 316.
Literature: Renouvier, p. 313; J. F. Maherault, *Catalogue raisonné et descriptif de l'oeuvre de Moreau le Jeune* (Paris: A. Labitte, 1880), no. 470; E. Bocher, *Les graveurs françaises du XVIIIe siècles, ou Catalogue raisonné des estampes, vignettes, eaux-fortes, pièces en couleur au bistre et au lavis de 1700 à 1800*, 6 fasc., *Jean-Michel Moreau le Jeune* (Paris: Librairie des Bibliophiles, 1882), p. 692; Edmond and Jules de Goncourt, *L'art du XVIIIe siècle* (Paris: A. Quantin, 1882), pp. 217, 235; Thomas Jefferson, *Autobiography*, Ford, 1:97.

236 Meeting of the Etats-Généraux in the Room of the Menus Plaisirs at Versailles
JEAN-MICHEL MOREAU, CALLED MOREAU LE JEUNE 1741–1814
Provenance: Acquired at the Hôtel Druot, Paris, June 22, 1953, no. 60.
Exhibition: Paris, Salon of 1789, no. 324.
Literature: Thomas Jefferson, *Autobiography*, Ford, 1:125–126.

237 The Oath of the Tennis Court 1791
JACQUES-LOUIS DAVID 1748–1825
Provenance: Commissioned from David by the Société des Amis de la Constitution, June 20, 1790. Sold by estate of Louis David, Apr. 17, 1826, no. 26; bought by Eugène David, the painter's son; collection of Jules David, the painter's grandson; left to the Musée du Louvre in 1892 by M. David-Chassagnol, and moved to the Musée de Versailles.
Exhibition: Paris, Salon of 1791, no 132; Paris, 26 Blvd. des Italiens, 1863, no. 26; Paris, Orangerie, *Louis David*, 1948, no. 97; London, The Royal Academy and the Victoria and Albert Museum, *The Age of Neoclassicism*, Sept. 9–Nov. 19, 1972, no. 553.
Literature: Renouvier, 1:76; David, pp. 88–91, 96–97, 108, 655–656; J. Guiffrey and P. Marcel, *Inventaire Général des Dessins du musée du Louvre et du musée de Versailles, Ecole Française*, VI (Paris, 1909), no. 3197; Holma, pp. 59–60, pl. 21; D. Lloyd Dowd, *Pageant Master of the Republic, Jacques Louis David and the French Revolution* (Lincoln: University of Nebraska, 1948), pp. 36–41, repr.; Virginia Lee, "Jacques-Louis David: The Versailles Sketchbook I," *BurlM*, Apr. 1969, p. 201, fig. 21; Andrew A. Kagan, "A Classical Source for David's Oath of the

Tennis Court," *BurlM*, no. 856 (July 1974), 395–396.

238 The Bastille During the First Days of Its Demolition
HUBERT ROBERT 1733–1808
Provenance: Lafayette Collection; Remusat Collection (on the back of the painting is written: *ce tableau representant la demolition de la Bastille, peint par Robert, peintre assez distingué du XVIIIe, a appartenu à M^r. Lafayette et apres à M^r. Remusat*); Charles Kaufmann Collection; given in 1929 by les amis du Musée Carnavalet.
Exhibition: Paris, Salon of 1789, no. 36?; Paris, Galerie Charpentier, *Hubert Robert et Louis Moreau*, 1922, no. 40; Paris, Musée Carnavalet, *Paris et la Révolution*, 1931, no. 66; Paris, Musée de l'Orangerie, *Hubert Robert, 1733–1808*, 1933, no. 153; Paris, Musée Carnavalet, *Le Révolution française*, 1939, no. 74; Paris, Archives Nationales, *La Fayette*, 1957, no. 216.
Literature: J. Cloquet, *Souvenirs de la vie privée de La Fayette* (Paris: 1836), p. 183; Gabillot, p. 136; de Nolhac, p. 78; Pierre de Nolhac, "Un artiste en prison sous le Terreur," *Journal des Debats*, Oct. 12, 1919; Louis Réau, "Hubert Robert peintre de Paris," *Bulletin de la Société d'histoire de l'art français* (1927), p. 217; G. Pascal, "Les Hubert Robert de Carnavalet," *Beaux-Arts*, 20 (Feb. 1930), 2, 3 repr.; B. de Montgolfier, "Hubert Robert, peintre de Paris au Musée Carnavalet," *Bulletin du musée Carnavalet*, nos. 1 and 2 (1964), p. 14, fig. 13, p. 20; Jefferson to Mme Denise Broutin, July 13, 1789; Jefferson to Thomas Paine, July 13, 1789; Jefferson to John Mason, July 16, 1789; Jefferson to Maria Cosway, July 25, 1789.

239 Belisarius 1784
JACQUES-LOUIS DAVID 1748–1825
Provenance: Executed in 1784 for d'Angiviller; seized during the Revolution (Year II) from the collection of the duchesse de Noailles (Archives Nationales F^17–372); entered the Musée du Luxembourg in 1818.
Exhibitions: Salon of 1785, no. 104; Paris, Orangerie, *David*, 1948, no. 104, M.O. 73.
Literature: Coll. Deloynes, 14: no. 325 (p. 81), no. 327 (p. 140), no. 329 (pp. 190–191), no. 330 (p. 256), no. 333 (p. 321), no. 334 (p. 333), no. 336 (p. 444), no. 339 (pp. 535–536), no. 340 (pp. 590–591), no. 343 (p. 630), no. 344 (p. 665), no. 345 (p. 699), no. 349 (pp. 777–778), no. 351 (pp. 831–832), no. 363 (p. 907); Landon, 29–30, pl. 13 and 2nd ed., 1 (1832): 39–40, pl. 20;

P. A. Coupin, *Essai sur J. L. David* (Paris: Renouard, 1827), p. 53; Villot, no. 152; David, p. 635; Jean Locquin, *La peinture d'histoire en France de 1747 à 1785* (Paris, 1912), p. 220; Marc Furcy-Raynaud, "Ces tableaux et objets d'art saisis chez les émigrés et condamnés et envoyés au Museum Central," *Archives de l'Art français*, 4 (1912), 308; Marie-Juliette Ballot, *Une élève de David, La comtesse Benoist* (Paris: Plon, 1914), pp. 68, 75; Brière, no. 192; Philippe-Auguste Hennequin, *Mémoires*, ed. Jenny Hennequin (Paris: Calmann-Levy, 1933), pp. 54–63; Fernand Beaucamp, *Le peintre lillois Jean-Baptiste Wicar (1762–1834): son oeuvre et son temps*, 1 (Lille: E. Raoust, 1939): 74–75; Holma, p. 40 and no. 43, p. 126; Sizer, p. 108; Hautecoeur, pp. 51–52, 55–61; Jean Seznec, "Diderot critique d'art," *L'Information d'histoire de l'art*, Jan.–Feb. 1957, no. 1, p. 13; Gerard Hubert, "Notes sur deux oeuvres retrouvées du sculpteur Chaudet," in *Etudes et documents sur l'art français du XIIe au XIXe siècle, Archives de l'art français*, 22 (1959), 289; Charles Sterling and Helene Adhémar, *Musée du Louvre, Peintures; Ecole française, XIXe siècle*, 2 (Paris: Editions des Musées nationaux, 1959): no. 538 and pl. 168; Rosenblum, pp. 30–33; Robert Rosenblum, "Jacques-Louis David at Toledo," *BurlM*, 107 (Sept. 1965), 473 and n. 4, p. 475; *107*; Musée du Louvre—*Catalogue des peintures, I, Ecole française* (Paris, 1972), p. 116; René Verbraeken, *J. L. David jugé par ses contemporains et la postérité* (Paris: L. Laget, 1973), p. 24 and n. 82; Daniel and Guy Wildenstein, *Documents complémentaires au catalogue de l'oeuvre de Louis David* (Paris: Fondation Wildenstein, 1973), pp. 1, 20; Antoine Schnapper, *De David à Delacroix*, exhib. cat. (Paris: Musée du Louvre, 1974), no. 30, p. 365; Arlette Serullaz, *Le Néo-classicisme français: dessins des musées de province*, exhib. cat. (Paris: Grand Palais, 1974), no. 15, p. 24; Philippe Bordes, "Girodet et Fabre camarades d'atelier," *La Revue du Louvre et des Musées de France*, 1974, no. 6, p. 393 and n. 3, p. 398; Antoine Schnapper, "Les Académies peintes et le 'Christ en noix' de David," *La Revue du Louvre et des Musées de France*, no. 6 (1974), 389–390; Philippe Bordes, "François-Xavier Fabre, peintre d'histoire I," *BurlM*, 117 (Feb. 1975), 92 and n. 8; Antoine Schnapper, *De David à Delacroix: La peinture française de 1774 à 1830*, exhib. cat. (Paris, Grand Palais, Nov. 16, 1974, Feb. 3, 1975), no. 30.

240 M. de Chabanon
JOSEPH-SIFFRED DUPLESSIS 1725–1802
Provenance: Gift of M. Auvray-Fédou to the Musée d'Orléans in 1825.
Exhibitions: Paris, Salon of 1785, no. 45; Paris, *Exposition des portraits nationaux*, 1878, no. 576.
Literature: Coll. Deloynes, no. 326 (p. 120), no. 331 (p. 296), no. 337 (p. 480), no. 345 (p. 691), no. 363 (p. 924); *Catalogue des tableaux statues et dessins exposés au musée d'Orléans* (Orléans: Musée d'Orléans, 1876), p. 48, no. 111; Jules Belleudy, *J. S. Duplessis peintre du roi 1725–1802* (Avignon: Editions de l'académie de Vaucluse), pp. 109, 112, 113, 114, 247 and no. 39, pp. 318–319.

241 Self-Portrait with Two Pupils 1785
ADÉLAÏDE LABILLE-GUIARD 1749–1803
Provenance: Descended in the Griois family; offered to the Louvre in 1876 by Mme August-François Griois, but refused by the Ministry in December 1878. Sold in 1905 by Mme Veuve Auguste Griois to Gimpel and Wildenstein. Sold by R. Gimpel to Edward Berwind in 1918; in the collection of Edward and Julia Berwind, Newport, until given to the Metropolitan Museum of Art, New York, by Miss Julia Berwind in 1953; entered the collection on her death in 1961.
Exhibitions: Paris, Salon of 1785, no. 101; Paris, Galerie Bonne-Nouvelle, *Exposition des ouvrages au profit de la Caisse de secours et pensions de l'association des artistes*, 1848, no. 53; Paris, Salle du Jeu de Paume, *Cent portraits de femmes des écoles anglaise et française du XVIIIe siècle*, 1909, no. 85; London, Royal Academy, *Exhibition of French Art (1200–1900)*, 1932, no. 284; Paris, Grand Palais, *David to Delacroix*, Nov. 16, 1974–Feb. 3, 1975, no. 112, also at the Detroit Institute of Arts, Mar. 5–May 4, 1975, and at the Metropolitan Museum of Art, New York, June 12–Sept. 7, 1975, p. 75, no. 112.
Literature: Coll. Deloynes, 14: no. 325 (p. 91), no. 326 (p. 121), no. 327 (p. 150), no. 329 (pp. 206–207), no. 334 (pp. 360–361), no. 339 (p. 549), no. 341 (p. 614), no. 343 (p. 623), no. 344 (pp. 662–663), no. 345 (p. 698), no. 348 (pp. 757–758), no. 350 (pp. 830–831); J. Lebreton, "Notice necrologique sur Madame Vincent née Labille," *Nouvelles des Arts*, 2 (1803), 5; Renouvier, p. 360; Spire Blondel, *L'art pendant la Révolution* (Paris: H. Laurens, 1887), p. 58; G. de Leris, "Les femmes à l'Académie de Peinture," *L'Art*, 45 (1888), 130; M. Bouchot, "Le portrait miniature en France," *GBA*, 1 (1894), 246; Roger,

baron Portalis, "Adélaïde Labille-Guiard," *GBA*, 2 (1901), 491; Roger, baron Portalis, *Adélaïde Labille-Guiard* (Paris, 1902), pp. 38–41; M. Bouchot, *La miniature française* (Paris, 1907), p. 62; Pierre de Nolhac, *Madame Vigée-Le Brun, peintre de la reine Marie-Antoinette* (Paris: Goupil et Cie, Manzi, Joyant et Cie, succ., 1912), p. 54; Armand Dayot and Claude Phillips, *Cent portraits de femmes d'écoles françaises et anglaises* (Paris: G. Petit, 1910), p. 70, repr.; Ch. Oulmont, *Les femmes peintres du XVIIIe siècle* (Paris: Rieder, 1928), p. 41 repr.; Guy Wildenstein, "L'exposition de l'art français à Londres, le XVIIIe siècle," *GBA*, 1 (1932), 54, 76, fig. 28; Arnauld Doria, *Gabrielle Capet, biographie et catalogue critique, l'oeuvre et l'artiste* (Paris: Les Beaux-Arts, 1934), pp. 5, 15, 88; Paul Ratouis de Limay and Emile Dacier, *Pastels français des XVIIe et XVIIIe siècles* (Paris: Musée du Louvre, 1925), p. 105; Michel Florisoone, *La peinture française, le XVIIIe siècle* (Paris: P. Tisne, 1948), p. 118, repr.; E. Gardner, "Four French Paintings from the Berwind Collection," *BMMA*, 1962, pp. 265–270, repr.; A. M. Passez, *Adélaïde Labille-Guiard, Biographie et catalogue raisonné de son oeuvre* (Paris, 1973), pp. 19, 26–27, 48–49, 156–159, repr. no. 49, p. 157; *De David à Delacroix*, exhib. cat. (Paris: Musée du Louvre, 1974), pp. 512–513.

242 The Painter Charles-Amédée van Loo 1785
ADÉLAÏDE LABILLE-GUIARD 1749–1803
Provenance: Presented to the Académie Royale as a second reception piece at the meeting of July 30, 1785. Collection of the Académie Royale; Musée des Monuments Français in the convent of the Petits Augustins; Musée Spécial de l'école française, Château de Versailles, 1798; sent to the Musée Royal in 1818; transferred from the Musée du Louvre to the Musée de Versailles on September 13, 1921.
Exhibition: Paris, Salon de l'Académie royale, 1785, no. 98.
Literature: Louis-Petit de Bachaumont, *Mémoires secrets pour servir à l'histoire de la Republique des lettres en France, depuis 1762 jusqu'à nos jours, ou Journal d'Observateur*, 30 (Paris: n.p., 1785): 184; Joachim Lebreton, "Notice necrologique sur Madame Vincent née Labille," *Nouvelles des Arts*, 2 (1803), 3; Emile Bellier de la Chavignerie, "Les artistes français du XVIIIe siècle oubliés ou dedaignés," *Révue universelle des Arts*, 21 (1865), 184; Octave Fidière, "Les femmes artistes à l'Académie royale de peinture et de sculpture," *Bulletin de la Société de l'Histoire de*

l'Art Français, 1885, p. 43; Henry Jouin, *Musée de portraits d'artistes* (Paris: H. Laurens, 1888), p. 188; Anatole de Montaiglon, *Procès-verbaux de l'Académie royale de peinture et de sculpture 1648–1793*, after the original records in the Ecole des Beaux-Arts (Paris: J. Baur, 1889), 9:248; Röger, baron Portalis, *Adélaïde Labille-Guiard* (Paris, 1902), pp. 19, 22, 34, 35; Haldane Macfall, *The French Pastellists of the Eighteenth Century* (London: Macmillan and Co., Ltd., 1909), p. 192; André Fontaine, *Les collections de l'Académie royale de peinture et de sculpture* (Paris: Société de propagation des livres d'art, 1910), pp. 80, 122, 177; Charles Oulmont, "Amédée van Loo, peintre du roi de Prusse," *GBA*, 2 (1912), 229; Louis Réau, *Histoire de la peinture française du XVIIIe siècle*, 2 (Paris-Bruxelles: G. van Oest, 1926): 36; Georg Biermann, "Doppelbildnis der Madame Labille-Guiard," *der Cicerone*, 19 (1927), 8; Pierre Lespinasse, *La miniature en France au XVIIIe siècle* (Paris-Bruxelles: G. van Oest, 1929), p. 127; Paul Ratouis de Limay, "Une portraitiste du XVIII siècle, Madame Labille-Guiard," *Le Dessin*, no. 3 (1947), 104; Anne-Marie Passez, *Adélaïde Labille-Guiard, Biographie et catalogue raisonné de son oeuvre* (Paris: Arts et métiers graphiques, 1973), pp. 22, 26, 53, 122–145, repr. no. 58, p. 148.

243 The Farmyard 1784
NICOLAS-BERNARD LÉPICIÉ 1735–1784
Provenance: Siezed during the revolution from the collection of de Mailly, duc de Châlons, 1794.

Exhibition: Paris, Salon of 1785, no. 6?; Toledo, Toledo Museum of Art, *Eighteenth Century France, Paintings from the Louvre*, 1964–1965, no. 12; Montreal, Musée des Beaux-Arts, *Peintures françaises du XVIIIe siècle en provenance du Louvre*, 1965, no. 12; Troyes, Musée des Beaux-Arts, *La scène de genre et le portrait dans la peinture française du XVIIIe siècle, Tableaux du Louvre*, 1973, no. 21.

Literature: "Procès-verbaux de la Commission des Monuments," *Nouvelles Archives de l'Art français*, 18, n.s. 3 (1902), 140; M. Furcy-Raynaud, "Les tableaux et objets d'art saisis chez les émigrés et condamnés et envoyés au Museum central," *Archives de l'Art français*, 1912, p. 272; Philippe-Gaston Dreyfus and Florence Ingersoll-Smouse, *Catalogue raisonné de l'oeuvre peint et dessiné de Nicolas-Bernard Lépicié (1735–1784)* (Paris, 1923), no. 211, p. 81; Brière, no. 549.

244 The Body of his Son Lausus being Brought to the Wounded Mezentius 1785
JEAN-JOSEPH TAILLASSON 1745–1809
Provenance: Vaudreuil auction, Nov. 26, 1786, no. 164; given to Musée des Beaux-Arts, Nancy, in 1939 by M Munier-Jolain.

Exhibition: Paris, Salon of 1785, no. 118; Nancy, Musée des Beaux-Arts, 1965; Paris, Grand Palais, *Le Néo-classicisme français—Dessins des musées de province*, Dec. 6, 1974–Feb. 10, 1975, no. 125, repr. p. 121.

Literature: Coll. Deloynes, no. 339, p. 547; Bellier and Auvray, 2:539; H. Bardon, "Les peintures à sujets antiques au XVIIIe siècle d'après les livrets de Salons," *GBA*, 61 (Apr. 1963), 230.

245 Autolion . . . Wounded by the Ghost of Ajax
JEAN-JOSEPH TAILLASSON 1745–1809
Provenance: Bonnet gift to the Musée Fabre, Montpellier.

Exhibition: Paris, Salon of 1785, no. 118.

Literature: Bellier and Auvray, 2:539; "Essai de repertoire," in *Le Néo-classicisme français—Dessins des musées de province*, exhib. cat. (Paris: Grand Palais, 1975), pp. 121, 157–158; H. Bardon, "Les peintures à sujets antiques au XVIIIe siècle d'après les livrets de Salons," *GBA*, 61 (Apr. 1963), 226, 240.

246 Seated Bacchante 1785
MARIE-LOUISE-ELISABETH VIGÉE-LEBRUN 1755–1842
Provenance: Collection of Lady Rolleston; The Hallsborough Gallery, Ltd., London; purchased by Fine Arts Museum of San Francisco, Mildred Anna Williams Collection.

Exhibition: Salon of 1785, no. 86.

Literature: Coll. Deloynes, 15: no. 326 (p. 118), no. 327 (pp. 149–150), no. 331 (p. 297), no. 333 (pp. 323–324), no. 334 (pp. 338–339, 361), no. 335 (p. 410), no. 337 (pp. 489–491), no. 339 (pp. 548–549), no. 340 (p. 588), no. 341 (p. 613), no. 343 (p. 629), no. 344 (p. 660), no. 345 (p. 697), no. 351 (p. 830), and 50: no. 1345 (pp. 291–292); "Works of Art Now on the Market," *Connoisseur*, 135, no. 543 (Mar. 1955), 50, no. 6, color illus. also included in advertisement for William Hallsborough Ltd.; *AQ*, 19, no. 3 (Autumn 1956), 305, 307; *Handbook of the Collections* (San Francisco: California Palace of the Legion of Honor, 1960), p. 63 repr.; William Davenport, *Art Treasures in the West* (Menlo Park: Sunset Books, 1966), p. 155.

247 The Countess de Ségur 1785
MARIE-LOUISE-ELISABETH VIGÉE-LEBRUN 1755–1842
Provenance: Bequeathed July 1923 to the Musée National du Château de Versailles by the comte Louis de Ségur.

Exhibition: Salon of 1785, no. 88; Paris, Orangerie, *L'art de Versailles et les nouvelles acquisitions du musée de Versailles*, 1932, no. 239; Versailles, Musée National du Château, *Deux siècles d'histoire de France*, 1937, no. 300; Hamburg, Kunsthalle, Munich Alte Pinakothek, *Meisterwerke des französischen Malerei von Poussin bis Ingres*, 1952–1953, no. 67; Tokyo, *L'art français au Japon*, 1954–1955, no. 27; Versailles, Musée National du Château, *Marie-Antoinette*, 1955, no. 364; Tokyo, *Versailles symbole royal*, 1970, no. 36.

Literature: Mme Vigée-Lebrun, *Mémoirs*, trans. Lionel Strachey (New York: Doubleday, Page & Company, 1903), pp. 176–177, 202, 220; W. H. Helm, *Vigée-Lebrun, Her Life, Works and Friendships* (London: Hutchinson and Co., 1915), p. 220.

251 Coriolanus among the Volscians. . . . 1788
JEAN-JACQUES-FRANÇOIS LE BARBIER, CALLED LE BARBIER L'AÎNÉ 1738–1826
Provenance: Sale, Collection Detienne, Paris, Apr. 29, 1807, no. 175; sale, Paris, Feb. 26, 1900, no. 76; given anonymously to the Musée de Pontoise in 1900.

Exhibition: Paris, Salon of 1787, no. 100; Pontoise, Musée Tavet, *Aquarelles et dessins du musée de Pontoise*, 1971–1972, no. 67, fig. 23; Paris, Grand Palais, *Le Néo-classicisme français—Dessins des musées de province*, Dec. 6, 1974–Feb. 10, 1975, no. 90, repr. p. 89.

Literature: Bellier and Auvray, 1:936.

252 View of the Cascades at Tivoli and the Temple of the Sibyl 1786
JEAN-FRANÇOIS HUE 1751–1823
Provenance: Collection of President Bernard; seized during the Revolution, with a pendant, *l'Ile d'amour*, from his home on the rue Saint-Marc in Paris; at the Hôtel de Nesles during Years I and II; at the Louvre; Ministry of the Interior, 1892.

Exhibition: Paris, Salon of 1787, no. 86.

Literature: Bellier and Auvray, 1:785; Jean Vergnet-Ruiz and Michel Laclotte, *Petits et grands musées de France, La peinture française des primitifs à nos jours* (Paris: Editions cercle d'art, 1962), p. 240; B. Lossky, *Inventaire des collections publiques françaises no. 7—Tours, musée des Beaux-Arts, peintures du XVIIIe*

siècle (Paris, 1962), no. 50 repr.; B. Lossky, "Identifications et acquisitions récentes de peintures françaises aux musées de Tours," *Bulletin de la Société de l'histoire de l'art français*, 1962, p. 46, n. 2.

253 Madame Adélaïde
ADÉLAÏDE LABILLE-GUIARD 1749–1803
Provenance: Collection of the marquis de Cazeaux; Wildenstein and Co., New York; acquired by the museum in 1964.

Exhibitions: The Los Angeles Museum, *Five Centuries of European Painting*, 1933, no. 36; New York, Wildenstein and Co., *Four Centuries of Portraits*, 1945, no. 45; New York, Wildenstein and Co., *The Woman in French Painting*, 1950, no. 31; New York, Wildenstein and Co., *Treasures of French Art*, 1964, no. 45; London, Royal Academy of Arts, *France in the Eighteenth Century*, 1968, no. 356.

Literature: James Harithas, *Paintings, Drawings and Sculptures in the Phoenix Art Museum Collection* (1965), p. 57, no. 64, illus. p. 69; F. M. Hinkhouse, "The Phoenix Art Museum," *Apollo*, 82 (Oct. 1965), pl. II; Jean Cailleux, "Portrait of Madame Adélaïde of France, daughter of Louis XV," *BurlM*, 111 (Mar. 1969), 112–114; Anne-Marie Passez, *Adélaïde Labille-Guiard 1749–1803 Biographie et catalogue raisonné de son oeuvre* (Paris, 1973), no. 82, p. 188, pl. LXVII, p. 189; Madame Campan, *Mémoires sur la vie privée de Marie Antoinette* (Paris, 1822), 1:290; Sizer, p. 111.

254 View of the Port-au-Blé . . .
LOUIS-NICOLAS DE LESPINASSE 1734–1803
Provenance: Collection of Pierre-Gabriel Berthault, 1787; gift of M. Forsyth Wickes, 1946.

Exhibition: Paris, Salon of 1787, no. 157; Paris, Musée Carnavalet, *Dessins parisiens du XVIIIe siècle*, 1971, no. 60, detail repr. p. 33.

Literature: Coll. Deloynes, 15: no. 372 (p. 137), no. 373 (p. 166), no. 375 (p. 250), no. 379 (p. 378); Bellier and Auvray, 1:1029; H. Bourin, "Le Chevalier de Lespinasse," *Société d'Iconographie parisienne* (1910), pp. 26, 27; M. Roux, *Bibliothèque nationale, Département des Estampes —Inventaire du fonds français: graveurs du XVIIIe siècle*, 2 (Paris, 1933): 359, 387; F. Boucher, "Deux aquarelles du chevalier de Lespinasse," *Bulletin du musée Carnavalet*, Oct. 1948, pp. 12–13 repr.; J. Wilhelm, "Les principales acquisitions du musée Carnavalet de 1941 à 1972," *Bulletin du musée Carnavalet*, 1973, nos. 1, 2, repr. detail p. 49.

55 View of the Port Saint-Paul . . .
1782
LOUIS-NICOLAS LESPINASSE 1734–1803
Provenance: Collection of P. G.
Berthault (1787); Martini Collection;
gift of M. Martini, 1917.

Exhibitions: Paris, Salon of 1787,
no. 159; Paris, Musée Carnavalet,
Trois siècles de dessin parisien, 1946,
no. 216; Berlin, Hambourg, *Le dessin
français*, 1958; Paris, Musée Carnavalet, *Dessins parisiens du XVIIIe
siècle*, 1971, no. 59 and repr. (detail)
on the cover.

Literature: Coll. Deloynes, 15: no. 372
(p. 137), no. 373 (p. 166), no. 375
(p. 250), no. 379 (p. 378); Bellier
and Auvray, 1:1029; H. Bourin, "Le
chevalier de Lespinasse," *Société
d'Iconographie parisienne*, 1910,
pp. 26–27; M. Roux, *Bibliothèque
nationale, Département des Estampes
—Inventaire du fonds français:
graveurs du XVIIIe siècle*, 2 (Paris,
1933): 359 and 387; F. Boucher,
"Deux aquarelles du chevalier de
Lespinasse," *Bulletin du musée Carnavalet*, Oct. 1948, pp. 12–13;
J. Wilhelm, "Le Marais, de la rue
Saint-Antoine à la Seine," *Médecine
de France*, no. 118 (1960), fig. pp.
26–27.

**256 View of the Demolition of the
Church of the Saints-Innocents . . .**
1787
PIERRE-ANTOINE DE MACHY 1723–1807
Provenance: Sale David-Weill, Paris,
Hôtel Drouot, June 9–10, 1971,
no. 165, bought by the musée
Carnavalet.

Exhibition: Paris, Salon of 1787,
no. 25.

Literature: Coll. Deloynes, 15: no. 375
(pp. 236–237), no. 376 (pp. 268–
269), no. 379 (p. 363), no. 386 (pp.
582–583), no. 387 (p. 600); Bellier
and Auvray, 1:402; "La Chronique des
Arts—Nouvelles acquisitions," *GBA*,
no. 1237 (Feb. 1972), fig. 48, p. 17;
B. de Montgolfier, "La demolition
de l'église des Saints Innocents, vue
par de Machy," *Bulletin du Musée
Carnavalet*, 1973, nos. 1, 2, repr.
p. 22.

**257 Electra at the Tomb of
Agamemnon** 1785
JEAN-JOSEPH TAILLASSON 1745–1809
Provenance: Bought on the Paris art
market, 1965.

Exhibition: Paris, Salon of 1787,
no. 123.

Literature: Journal de Paris, no. 269
(Sept. 26, 1787), 1165; Coll.
Deloynes, no. 373 (p. 20), no. 394
(p. 768), no. 397 (pp. 865–866);
Bellier and Auvray, 2:539; H. Bardon,
"Les peintures à sujets antiques au
XVIIIe siècle d'après les livrets de
Salons," *GBA*, Apr. 1963, p. 236.

**258 Cicero Discovering the Tomb of
Archimedes at Syracuse**
1787
PIERRE-HENRI DE VALENCIENNES
1750–1819
Provenance: Reception piece for the
Royal Academy, Feb. 28, 1787; Collections of the Royal Academy, musée
spécial de l'Ecole française at Versailles, no. 296; Musée du Louvre,
no. 8243; given to the Musée de l'Ain
at Bourg-en-Bresse in 1953; transferred to Musée des Augustins,
Toulouse, in 1961.

Exhibition: Paris, Salon of 1787,
no. 171; Toulouse, Musée Paul
Depuy, *Pierre-Henri de Valenciennes*,
1956–1957, no. 101.

Literature: Jean-Baptiste Deperthes,
*Histoire de l'art du paysage depuis
la Renaissance des Beaux-Arts jusqu'au
XVIIIe siècle* (Paris: Le Normant,
1822), pp. 524–525; Anonymous,
"Le Salon de 1787," *Magasin Pittoresque*, 20 (1852), 107; Duvivier,
"Sujets des Morceaux de réception
des Membres de l'ancienne Académie,"
Archives de l'art français, 2 (1852–
1853), 389; Henri Delaborde, *Etudes
sur les beaux-arts en France et en
Italie*, 2 (Paris: J. Renouard, 1864):
p. 162; Villot, no. 582; Paul Mantz,
"Les paysagistes du XVIIIe siècle,"
l'Artiste, 4 (1858), 156; Paul Lacroix,
"L'amateur polonais au salon de
1787," *Revue universelle des Arts*, 16
(1862), 372–373; Charles Blanc,
*Histoire des peintres de toutes les
écoles. Ecole français*, 3 (Paris:
Renouard, 1865): 37; Montaiglon, p.
329; G. Lanoe and T. Brice, *Histoire
de l'Ecole française de paysage (depuis
le Poussin jusqu'à Millet)* (Paris,
1901), p. 83; Louis Hourticq, *Les
tableaux du Louvre* (Paris: Hachette,
1921), p. 147; Marie-Louis Desazars
de Montgailhard, *Les artistes tou-
lousains et l'Art à Toulouse au XIXe
siècle*, 1 (Paris: Librairie Marqueste,
1924): 112; Henri Focillon, *La
peinture au XIXe siècle* (Paris:
Renouard, 1927), p. 304; P. Lespinasse, "Le peintre toulousain Valenciennes et les origines du paysage
romantique," *L'Archer*, Nov. 1931,
p. 318; Alcantes de Brahm, "L'Ecole
toulousaine de peinture du XVIe au
XIXe siècle," *Cahiers mensuels de
littérature et d'art*, 57 and 58 (Sept.–
Oct. 1935), 119–120; Bellier and
Auvray, 2:609; Thieme-Becker, 34:
62; André Fontaine, *Les collections de
l'Académie royale de Peinture et de
Sculpture* (Paris: H. Laurens, 1910),
p. 204, no. 576; J. Vergnet-Ruiz and
M. Laclotte, *Petits et grands musées
de France, La peinture française des
primitifs à nos jours* (Paris, 1962),
p. 254.

**259 The Ancient City of
Agrigento . . .**
PIERRE-HENRI DE VALENCIENNES
1750–1819
Provenance: Collection of the marquis
de Crillon, 1787–after 1861; 1942,
Collection of Jean Schmit, Paris; given
to the Louvre in 1950 by the office
des biens privés.

Exhibition: Paris, Salon of 1787,
no. 172; Toulouse, Musée Paul Depuy,
Pierre-Henri de Valenciennes, 1956–
1957, no. 105; London, Royal
Academy and the Victoria and Albert
Museum, *The Age of Neo-Classicism*,
Sept. 9–Nov. 19, 1972, no. 257;
Anvers, Internationaal Cultureel
Centrum, *Neoklassieke schilderkunst
in Frankzijk*, 1972, no. 35.

Literature: Horsin-Déon, "Les cabinets
d'amateurs à Paris," *L'Artiste*, 1861,
p. 246; Comte Potocki, "Critique
du Salon de 1787," *Revue universelle
des arts*, 1862, p. 372; Bellier and
Auvray, 2:609; Marie-Louis Desazars
de Montgailhard, *Les artistes tou-
lousains et l'art à Toulouse au XIXe
siècle* (Paris: Librairie-Marqueste,
1924), p. 112; Thieme-Becker, 34:62;
Germain Bazin, *Corot* (Paris:
P. Tisné, 1942), p. 29; C. Sterling and
H. Adhémar, *Musée du Louvre:
Peintures: Ecole française XIXe siècle*,
4 (Paris, 1961): no. 1941, pl. 752;
G. Bazin, "P. H. de Valenciennes,"
GBA, May 1962, pp. 358–359, fig. 7;
*Musée du Louvre—Catalogue des
peintures, I. Ecole française* (Paris,
1972), p. 378.

**260 Eugène-Joseph-Stanislas Foulon
d'Ecotier** 1785
ANTOINE VESTIER 1740–1824
Provenance: Formerly in a private
collection in Paris; collection of an
unidentified London art dealer, who
offered it for sale at Sotheby's,
March 24, 1965, lot 84, as a portrait
by Vestier of M. Foulon Ecotier,
governor of Guadeloupe.

Exhibition: Paris, Salon of 1787,
no. 148.

Literature: Lanlaire, *Au Salon
académique de peinture* (Paris, 1787),
pp. 28–31; Jules Guiffrey, "Table
des portraits exposés aux Salons du dix-
huitième siècle jusqu'en 1800,"
Nouvelles archives de l'art français, 5
(1889), 35; Denys Sutton, "Pleasure
for the Aesthete," *Apollo*, 90 (Sept.
1969), 238, no. 6 and repr. p. 238;
Everett Fahy and Sir Francis Watson,
The Wrightsman Collection, 5,
no. 33 (New York: Metropolitan
Museum of Art, 1973), pp. 322–329,
repr.

**261 The Marquise de Pezé and the
Marquise de Rouget . . .**
MARIE-LOUISE-ELISABETH
VIGÉE-LEBRUN 1755–1842

Provenance: Private collection, France;
gift of the Bay Foundation in
memory of Josephine Bay Paul and
Ambassador Charles Ulrick Bay, 1965.

Exhibition: Paris, Salon of 1787,
no. 98; Cleveland, Cleveland Museum
of Art, *Style, Truth and the Portrait*
(1963), no. 67.

Literature: Coll. Deloynes, 15: no. 375
(p. 245), no. 379 (p. 373); Marie
Louise Vigée-Lebrun, *Souvenirs de
Mme Vigée-Lebrun*, 2nd ed. (Paris:
H. Fournier, 1869), 1: 63, 2:363;
J. J. Foster, *French Art from Watteau
to Prud'hon* (London, 1907), pp. 157,
168; Pierre de Nolhac, *Mme Vigée-
Le Brun, peintre de la reine Marie-
Antoinette* (Paris: Goupil et Cie,
Manzi, Joyant et Cie, succ., 1912),
pp. 72, 151, 251; W. H. Helm, *Vigée-
Lebrun, Her Life, Works, and
Friendships* (London: Hutchinson and
Co., 1915), pp. 215, 219, repr. opp.
p. 82; A. Blum, *Madame Vigée-
Lebrun* (Paris, 1919), p. 98; R. G.
Saisselin, *Style, Truth and the Por-
trait*, exhib. cat. (Cleveland: Cleveland Museum of Art, 1963), no. 67,
repr.; I. Bischoff, "Vigée-Lebrun
and the Women of the French
Court," *Antiques*, 42, no. 5 (Nov.
1967), 711, fig. 10.

267 M. Sue
GUILLAUME VOIRIOT 1713–1799
Provenance: Collection of the
Académie de Peinture; Musée
Napoléon (no. 8485); deposited at the
Musée de Versailles.

Exhibition: Paris, Salon of 1789,
no. 336.

Literature: Soulié, 3rd ed., no. 4548,
pp. 395–396; Bellier and Auvray,
2:700; L. Dumont Wilden, *Le portrait
en France* (Paris, 1909), p. 268;
Thieme-Becker, 34:513.

**268 Drawing for the Pulpit of
Saint-Sulpice**
CHARLES DE WAILLY 1729–1798
Provenance: Collection of the duc
d'Aiguillon; collection of Leon
Decloux.

Exhibition: Paris, Salon of 1789,
no. 54.

Literature: Bellier and Auvray, 2:709;
G. Gaillard, "Un dessin de Charles de
Wailly pour la chaire de Saint-
Sulpice," *Bulletin de la Société de
l'histoire de l'art français*, 1957, p. 55;
J. Wilhelm, "Un projet de Charles
de Wailly pour l'aménagement du
Salon du Louvre," *Bulletin du musée
Carnavalet*, June 1963, no. 1, p. 10;
A. Braham, "Charles de Wailly and
Early Neo-classicism," *BurlM*, 114
(Oct. 1972), 670; M. Gallet, "Un
dessin de Charles de Wailly pour la
chaire de Saint-Sulpice," *Bulletin du
musée Carnavalet*, 1972; D. Rabreau

and M. Gallet, "La chaire de Saint-Sulpice, sa création par Charles de Wailly et l'example du Bernin en France à la fin de l'Ancien Régime," *Bulletin de la Société de l'Histoire de Paris et de l'Ile de France*, 98th year (1971), pp. 120–123, fig. 10.

269 The Deluge
JEAN-BAPTISTE REGNAULT 1754–1829
Provenance: Godefroi Sale, Paris, Apr. 2, 1794, no. 25; Sale, Paris, Dec. 17, 1821 ("*une collection de tableaux de choix . . . recueillie par feu Monsieur Paignon-Dijonval et continuée par Monsieur le vicomte de Morel Vindé*"), no. 89, purchased for 277 francs by M de Langeac (annotation on the copy of the sales catalogue in the bibliothèque Doucet); acquired by Louis XVIII from M de Langeac in 1822; Château de Saint-Cloud; Musée du Louvre; sent from the Louvre to Compiègne Aug. 22, 1874; returned to the Louvre in 1956.

Exhibitions: Paris, Salon of 1789, no. 91; Paris, Salon of 1791, no. 211; Paris, Grand Palais, *De David à Delacroix, la peinture française de 1774 à 1830*, Nov. 16, 1974–Feb. 3, 1975, no. 149, pl. 50; *French Painting 1774–1830: The Age of Revolution*, Detroit, The Detroit Institute of Arts, Mar. 5–May 4, 1975; New York, The Metropolitan Museum of Art, June 12–Sept. 7, 1975, no. 149, pl. 92.

Literature: Coll. Deloynes, 16: no. 410 (pp. 84–85), no. 415 (pp. 171–172); Landon, 3: repr. 21; Chaussard, pp. 249–250; Antoine Chrysotome Quatremère de Quincy, *Suite du recueil de notices historiques* (Paris: A. le Clere et c^ie, 1837), pp. 42–43, 49; Renouvier, p. 126; G. Levitine, "Some Unexplored Aspects of the Illustrations of Atala: the Surenchères visuelles of Girodet and Hersent," *Actes du Congrès de Wisconsin pour le 200ème anniversaire de la naissance de Châteaubriand* (Geneva, 1970), pp. 142–144; Charles Sells, "Esquisses de J. B. Regnault," *La Revue du Louvre et des Musées de France*, 1974, no. 6, pp. 408, 410; *Musée national du Louvre, catalogue de peintures, I. école française* (Paris: Louvre, 1972), p. 317; J. P. Luzin, notice in *De David à Delacroix*, exhib. cat. (Paris, 1974), no. 149, pp. 572–573; Pierre Rosenberg, notice in *De David à Delacroix*, exhib. cat. (Paris, 1974), no. 26, pp. 357–358.

270 The Lictors returning to Brutus the Bodies of his Sons 1789
JACQUES-LOUIS DAVID 1748–1825
Provenance: Anonymous sale, Paris, Dec. 12, 1925; Wildenstein and Co., New York, 1932; purchased by The Wadsworth Atheneum, 1934.

Exhibition: Salon of 1789, no. 88; Springfield, Mass., Springfield Museum of Fine Arts, *From David to Cézanne*, Feb. 9–Mar. 10, 1935, no. 10; Northampton, Mass., Smith College Museum of Art, June, 1935; Rochester, Memorial Art Gallery, *Rebels in Art*, Dec. 1936–Jan. 1937, repr. p. 9; Baltimore, The Baltimore Museum and Walters Art Gallery, *The Greek Tradition*, May 15–June 25, 1939, pp. 22, 34, repr. opp. p. 20; Springfield, Mass., Springfield Museum of Fine Arts, *David and Ingres*, Nov. 20–Dec. 17, 1939, no. 8, repr.; New York, Parke-Bernet Galleries, *French and English Art Treasures of the Eighteenth Century*, Dec. 20–30, 1942, no. 8; New York, Wildenstein and Company, *The French Revolution*, Dec. 1943, no. 50, repr. p. 115; Providence, The Rhode Island School of Design, *The French Revolution and the Napoleonic Period*, Oct. 1–28, 1945; Toledo, Ohio, The Toledo Museum of Art, *The Spirit of Modern France: An Essay on Painting in Society*, Nov.–Dec. 1946, no. 14; Middletown, Conn., Wesleyan University, *Exhibition of Eighteenth Century Art*, Feb. 20–29, 1948; Northampton, Mass., Smith College Museum of Art, *Pompeiana*, Nov. 18–Dec. 15, 1948, no. 109; Providence, Rhode Island School of Design, *Isms in Art since 1800*, Feb. 3–Mar. 9, 1949, no. 1; Pomona, California, Los Angeles County Fair Association, *Masters of Art from 1790–1950*, repr.; Buffalo, Albright Art Gallery, *Expressionism in American Painting*, May 10–June 29, 1952, no. 1, repr. p. 10; Kansas City, Mo., Nelson Gallery-Atkins Museum, *The Century of Mozart*, Jan. 15–Mar. 4, 1956, no. 20, repr. fig. 17; Hartford, the Wadsworth Atheneum, *Homage to Mozart*, Mar. 22–Apr. 29, 1956, no. 9, repr. fig. 4; New York, Knoedler and Co., *Masterpieces from the Wadsworth Atheneum, Hartford*, Jan. 21–Feb. 15, 1958, p. 96 repr. in *Handbook 1958*; Sarasota, The John and Mable Ringling Museum of Art, *A. Everett Austin, Jr.: A Director's Taste and Achievement*, Feb. 23–Mar. 30, 1958; Raleigh, N.C., The North Carolina Museum of Art, *W. R. Valentiner Memorial Exhibition*, Apr. 6–May 17, 1959, no. 105, repr. p. 167; Andover, Mass., Addison Gallery of American Art, Phillips Academy, *Significant Forms, The Changing Character of Western Art*, July 8–Sept. 25, 1961 (extended through October 1); Cleveland, The Cleveland Museum of Art, *Neo-Classicism, Style and Motif*, Sept. 21–Nov. 1, 1964, no. 115, repr.

Literature: *Bulletin*, 16 [Cleveland Museum of Art] (Nov. 1929), 166 repr.; *Bulletin of the Wadsworth Atheneum*, Oct.–Dec. 1934, pp. 36–38, repr. p. 37; J. L. Clarke, Jr., "David and Ingres," *Art News*, 38 (Nov. 25, 1939), repr. p. 9; R. Cortissoz, "David, Ingres and the Classical Hypotheses," *New York Herald-Tribune*, Jan. 14, 1940, repr.; H. Devrée, *Magazine of Art*, 33, Jan. 1940, pp. 41–42, repr. p. 41; Regina Shoolman and Charles Slatkin, *The Enjoyment of Art in America* (New York: J. B. Lippincott and Co., 1942), pl. 512; David Lloyd Dowd, *Pageant Master of the Republic, Jacques-Louis David* (Lincoln: The University of Nebraska Press, 1948); Michel Florisoone, *David, exposition en l'honneur du deuxième centenaire de sa naissance* (Paris: Orangerie des Tuileries, 1948), p. 56; Michel Florisoone, "Premières conclusions à l'exposition David," *Musées de France*, Nov. 1948, p. 261; John Canaday, "The World Dividing: The Eighteenth Century," *Metropolitan Seminars in Art*, portfolio G (New York: The Metropolitan Museum of Art, 1959), pl. G12; Germain Bazin, *The Loom of Art* (London: Thames and Hudson, 1962), p. 267; Rosenblum, pp. 30, 33; Robert L. Herbert, *David, Voltaire, "Brutus" and the French Revolution: an Essay in Art and Politics* (New York: Viking Press, 1973).

271 Jacob Coming to find the Daughters of Laban 1787
LOUIS GAUFFIER 1762–1801
Provenance: Painted in Rome in 1787 for Anne-Gabriel-Henri Bernard, marquis de Boulainvilliers; bought by the Ministry of the Interior; given in October 1874 to the Elysée; given to the Ministry of Public Health in 1932; entered the Louvre in 1970.

Exhibition: Rome, Mancini Palace, *Exhibit of the works of pensioners*, Aug. 29, 1787; Paris, Salon of 1789, no. 346.

Literature: David, pp. 39, 41–42, 45; Anatole de Montaiglon and Jules Guiffrey, *Correspondance des Directeurs de l'Académie de France à Rome*, 15 (Paris, 1906): no. 8715, p. 84 (Apr. 12, 1786), no. 8722, p. 90 (May 9, 1786), no. 8732, p. 96 (Aug. 23, 1786), no. 8754, p. 112 (Oct. 11, 1786), no. 8758, p. 115 (Oct. 30, 1786), no. 8763, p. 117 (Nov. 12, 1786), no. 8790, pp. 133–134 (May 16, 1787), no. 8794, p. 137 (June 8, 1787), no. 8833, p. 167 (Aug. 28, 1787), no. 8845, p. 174 (Sept. 19, 1787), no. 8847, p. 176 (Sept. 26, 1787); Bellier and Auvray, 1:679; Paul Marmottan, "Le peintre Louis Gauffier," *GBA*, May 1926, p. 282; René Crozet, "Louis Gauffier 1762–1801," *Bulletin de la Société de l'Histoire de l'art français*, 1947, pp. 102–108; A. Lecoy de la Marche, "L'Académie de France à Rome d'après la correspondance de ses directeurs (1666–1792) suite des lettres de Lagrenée," *GBA*, Nov. 1872, pp. 413–414.

272 Naval Battle off the Island of Grenada. . .
JEAN-FRANÇOIS HUE 1751–1823
Provenance: Commissioned from the artist for king Louis XVI; presented at Versailles Oct. 5, 1788.

Exhibition: Paris, Salon of 1789, no. 69.

Literature: Soulié, 1st ed., no. 1437; Soulié, 2nd ed., no. 1428, p. 441; Bellier and Auvray, 1:785.

273 The Death of Cleopatra 1791
NICOLAS-ANDRÉ MONSIAU 1754–1837
Provenance: Acquired by the museum in 1972.

Exhibition: Salon of 1789, no. 194; Paris, Grand Palais, *Le Néo-classicisme français—Dessins des musées de province*, Dec. 6, 1974–Feb. 10, 1975, no. 103, repr. p. 102.

Literature: Pierre Rosenberg and N. Butor, *La "Mort de Germanicus" de Poussin du musée de Minneapolis*, Les dossiers du departement des peintures no. 7 (Paris, 1973), p. 53.

274 Louis-Jean-François Lagrenée, called l'Aîné 1788
JEAN-LAURENT MOSNIER 1746–1808
Provenance: Reception piece for the Royal Academy, May 31, 1788; in the collection of the Academy; at the Musée Napoleon, no. 6810; École des Beaux-Arts; given to the Louvre, 1887; sent to Musée de Versailles, 1920.

Exhibition: Paris, Salon of 1789, no. 125; Paris, Musée des Arts Décoratifs, *Les artistes français en Italie de Poussin à Renoir*, 1934, no. 256; Paris, Musée Carnavalet, *La Révolution française*, 1939, no. 1090; Versailles, Musée National du Château de Versailles, *Marie-Antoinette*, 1955, no. 319.

Literature: Johann Georg Wille, *Mémoires et Journal* (Paris: V. J. Renouard, 1857), 2:178–179; Bellier and Auvray, 2:132; H. Jouin, *Musée de portraits d'artistes* (Paris: H. Laurens, 1888), p. 104; D. Roche, "Jean-Laurent Mosnier et ses portraits à l'huile," *Renaissance de l'art français et des industries de luxe*, no. 4 (Apr. 1921), 170–171, Gaston Brière and E. Communaux, "Musée du Louvre. Emplacements actuels des peintures de l'école française antérieurement cataloguées et retirées des galeries," *Bulletin de la Société de l'Histoire de l'art français*, 1924, p. 324; Thieme-Becker, 25:186; Georges Lafenestre, *Notice des portraits d'artistes exposés dans la salle Denon*

au musée du Louvre (Paris: Im-
primeries réunies, 1888), no. 47, p. 29;
Montaiglon, 9:361–362; Edmond
and Jules de Goncourt, L'art du dix-
huitième siècle (Paris: A. Quantin,
1882), p. 82; Louis Dumont-Wilden,
Le portrait en France (Brussels:
G. van Oest, 1909), p. 221; Phillipe de
Chennevières, Souvenirs d'un directeur des Beaux-Arts (Paris: Aux
bureaux de l'artiste, 1889), p. 19.

**275 Project for the Remodeling
of the Salon of the Louvre in 1789**
CHARLES DE WAILLY 1728–1798
Provenance: Bought in Paris, 1896,
at the sale of the collection of old
drawings by the architect Destailleur,
no. 705.
Exhibition: Vienna, L'art et la Pensée
en France au XVIIIe siècle, 1966;
Paris, Musée Carnavalet, Dessins
Parisiens du XVIIIe siècle, 1971,
no. 132.
Literature: C. Aulanier, Histoire du
Palais et du Musée du Louvre, Le
Salon Carré (Paris: Editions des
musées nationaux, 1950), pp. 37–38,
pl. 16; J. Wilhelm, "Un projet de
Charles de Wailly pour l'aménagement
du Salon du Louvre," Bulletin du
Musée Carnavalet, no. 1 (June 1963),
5–10, fig. pp. 8–9; J. Wilhelm and
B. de Montgolfier, Dessins Parisiens
du XVIIIe siècle, exhib. cat. in
Bulletin du Musée Carnavalet, 1971,
no. 1 and 2, no. 132, pp. 58–59;
Robert L. Herbert, Art in Context,
J. L. David's Brutus (London, 1972),
p. 55, fig. 28.

**281 The Discovery of the Laocoön
1773**
HUBERT ROBERT 1733–1808
Provenance: Baron Maurice de
Rothschild, Pregny, Switzerland.
Exhibitions: Kansas City, Nelson
Gallery and Atkins Museum, The
Century of Mozart, Jan. 15–Mar. 4,
1956, no. 93; Hartford, the Wads-
worth Atheneum, Homage to Mozart,
Mar. 22–Apr. 29, 1956, no. 51;
Vassar College Art Gallery, Hubert
Robert, Oct. 9–Nov. 11, 1962, no. 6;
Cleveland Museum of Art, Neo-
classicism, Style and Motif, Sept. 23–
Nov. 1, 1964, no. 36; London, Royal
Academy of Arts, France in the
Eighteenth Century, Winter 1968,
no. 587, repr. fig. 253; New York,
Wildenstein, and Co., Gods and
Heroes, Oct. 29, 1968–Jan. 4, 1969,
no. 36, repr. pl. 41.
Literature: Jefferson to L'Enfant,
Apr. 10, 1791; Gabillot, pp. 250–252,
263, 270; de Nolhac, p. 121; Paul L.
Grigaut, "Ruins and Rose Petals,"
Arts in Virginia, Winter 1964, pp.
26–29; Henry Hawley, Neo-classicism:
Style and Motif (Cleveland: Cleve-
land Museum of Art, distributed by

H. N. Abrams, New York, 1964),
p. 36; Robert Rosenblum, "Neo-
classicism Surveyed," BurlM, 107
no. 742 (Jan. 1965), 30–33; European
Art in the Virginia Museum of Fine
Arts, A Catalogue (Richmond:
Virginia Museum of Fine Arts, 1966),
no. 60, repr. p. 43; Sheldon Nodel-
man, "After the High Roman
Fashion," Art News, 67, no. 7 (Nov.
1968) pp. 34–36, 65–66, repr. p. 36.

282 Hôtel de Langeac, elevation
Provenance: Gift of Dennelle de
Saint-Leu, 1843, to the Bibliothèque
nationale.
Literature: Thiéry 1:54; Rice, Hôtel
de Langeac, p. 22.

283 Nouvelle Amérique project, plan
FRANÇOIS-JOSEPH BÉLANGER
1744–1818
Provenance: Fonds Bélanger.
Literature: Charles Marrionneau,
Victor Louis (Bordeaux: Imprimerie
G. Gounouilhou, 1881), 477–522;
Jean Stern, A l'ombre de Sophie
Arnauld, François-Joseph Bélanger, 1
(Paris: Plon, 1930): 93–103.

284 Hôtel d'Argenson
Literature: Jean Charles Krafft and
Nicolas Ransonnette, Plans, coupes et
élévations des plus belles maisons
et des hôtels construits à Paris et dans
les environs entre 1771 et 1802 (Paris:
C. Pougens, s.d., 1802), pl. 2; Michel
Gallet, Demeures parisiennes.
L'époque Louis XVI (Paris: Le
Temps, 1964), p. 190.

**285 Vue de la Maison de Mme
Brunoy**
J. A. LE CAMPION, active late
18th century, after Antoine Louis
François Sergent 1751–1847
Provenance: Collection Destailleur.
Literature: Jean-Marie Pérouse de
Montclos, Etienne-Louis Boullée
1728–1799, l'architecture classique à
l'architecture révolutionnaire (Paris:
Arts et métiers graphiques, 1969),
pp. 103–108; Robin Middleton,
"Revolutionary Urge," Architectural
Design (July 1970), pp. 358–361;
Jean-Marie Pérouse de Montclos,
Etienne-Louis Boullée 1728–1799.
Theoretician of Revolutionary Archi-
tecture (New York: Braziller, 1974),
pp. 16–20.

286 Hôtel de Brunoy
Literature: Krafft and Ransonnette,
Plans, coupes et élévations des plus
belles maisons et des hôtels construits
à Paris et dans les environs entre 1771
et 1802 (Paris: C. Pougens, 1802),
pl. I; "Voyage à Paris d'un gentil-
homme breton en 1782," Revue de
Bretagne, 23 (1900), 15; Jean-Marie

Pérouse de Montclos, Etienne-Louis
Boullée 1728–1799, l'architecture
classique à l'architecture révolutionnaire (Paris: Arts et métiers graphiques,
1969), pp. 103–108; Robin Middleton, "Revolutionary Urge," Architectural Design, July 1970, pp. 358–361;
Jean-Marie Pérouse de Montclos,
Etienne-Louis Boullée 1728–1799.
Theoretician of Revolutionary Architecture (New York: Braziller, 1974),
pp. 16–20.

**287 Reconstruction of the Salon,
Hôtel Grimod de la Reynière 1782**
JEAN-CHRISTIAN KAMSETZER
1753–1795
Literature: Albert Babeau, "L'hôtel
de la Reynière," Bulletin de la Société
historique du XVIIIème arrondissement, 1904, pp. 29–34; Fiske Kimball, "Les influences anglaises dans la
formation du style Louis XVI,"
GBA, 5, series 6 (Jan. 1931), pp. 29–
44; Louis Riau, "La décoration de
l'hôtel Grimod de la Reynière d'après
les dessins de l'architecte polonais
Kamsetzer," Bulletin de la Société de
l'Histoire de l'art français, 1937,
pp. 7–16; Edward Croft-Murray, "The
Hôtel Grimod de la Reynière: The
Salon Decorations," Apollo, 78 (Nov.
1963), 377–383.

288 Model of the Hôtel de Salm
Literature: Jefferson to Mme de Tessé,
Mar. 20, 1787; Frédéric Contet, Les
vieux hôtels de Paris, 4 (Paris:
F. Contet, 1920–1930): 20–26;
Andrée-Madeleine Duchet, "Châteaux
et châtelains de Rochefort-en-
Yvelines," Pays d'Yvelines, de
Hurepoix et de Beauce (1966),
pp. 3–17.

289 Hôtel de Mlle Guimard,
FRANÇOIS-JOSEPH BÉLANGER
1744–1818
Provenance: Destailleur Collection.
Literature: Paul Jarry, "Mlle Guimard
et son hôtel de la Chaussée d'Antin,"
Le Vieux Montmartre, Sept. 1926,
pp. 21–33; Wolfgang Herrmann, "The
Problem of Chronology in Claude-
Nicolas Ledoux's Engraved Work,"
AB, 42 (Sept. 1960), 191–210; John
Harris, "Sir William Chambers
and his Parisian Album," Architectural
History, 6 (1963), 54–90.

**290 Perspective View of the Hôtel
de Thélusson**
CLAUDE-NICOLAS LEDOUX 1736–1806
Literature: Geneviève Levallet-Haug,
Claude-Nicolas Ledoux, 1736–1806
(Paris and Strasbourg: Librarie Istra,
1934), pp. 53–59; Oscar Reutersvärd,
"De Sjunkande Cenotafierna,"
Konsthistorisk Tidskrift, 28 (1959)
110–124; Johannes Langner, "C. N.
Ledoux und die Fabrike," Zeitschrift

für Kunstgeschichte, 26 (1963), 1–36;
Visionary Architects, exhib. cat.
(Houston: University of St. Thomas,
1968), pp. 82–85.

**291 Cross Section of the Hôtel de
Thélusson**
CLAUDE-NICOLAS LEDOUX 1736–1806
Literature: See no. 290.

**292 Perspective view of the houses
of M. Saiseval**
CLAUDE-NICOLAS LEDOUX 1736–1806
Provenance: L'Architecture de C. N.
Le Doux, 2nd vol. (Paris: Lenoir,
1847).
Exhibition: Houston, University of
St. Thomas, Visionary Architects,
Oct. 19, 1967–Jan. 3, 1968, p. 89.
Literature: Marcel Raval, "Claude-
Nicolas Ledoux, 1736–1806; com-
mentaires, cartes et croquis de J. Ch.
Moreaux," Les Architectes français, 1
(Paris: Arts et métiers graphiques,
1945), p. 51.

**293 Proposed plan for execution.
Front elevation of the Château de
Bagatelle**
FRANÇOIS-JOSEPH BÉLANGER
1744–1818
Provenance: Don Stern, 1955.
Exhibition: London, Royal Academy
and the Victoria and Albert Museum,
The Age of Neo-classicism, Sept. 9–
Nov. 19, 1972, p. 492, no. 999.
Literature: Jefferson to Maria Cosway,
Oct. 12, 1786; Jean Stern, A l'ombre
de Sophie Arnauld, François-Joseph
Bélanger, 2 vols. (Paris: Plon, 1930),
pp. 56–72; Friedrich Gilly, "Descrip-
tion de Bagatelle," L'Oeil, no. 126
(June 1965), 17–23; Richard Paul
Wunder, "Bagatelle and Two Draw-
ings by Bélanger in the Cooper
Union," Connoisseur, 148, no. 596
(1961), 171–174.

**294 Proposed plan for execution.
Elevation from the Courtyard of the
Château de Bagatelle**
FRANÇOIS-JOSEPH BÉLANGER
1744–1818
Provenance: See no. 293.
Literature: See no. 293.

**295 Proposed plan for execution.
Cross section of the Château de
Bagatelle**
FRANÇOIS-JOSEPH BÉLANGER
1744–1818
Provenance: See no. 293.
Literature: See no. 293.

**296 Plan for the pavilion at
Louveciennes**
CLAUDE-NICOLAS LEDOUX 1736–1806
Literature: Geneviève Levallet-Haug,
Claude-Nicolas Ledoux, 1736–1806

(Paris and Strasbourg: Librarie Istra, 1934), pp. 17–26; Wolfgang Herrmann, "The Problem of Chronology in Claude-Nicolas Ledoux's Engraved Works," *AB*, *42* (Sept. 1960), 191–210.

297 Front elevation of the pavilion at Louveciennes
CLAUDE-NICOLAS LEDOUX 1736–1806
Literature: See no. 296.

298 Project for the château at Louveciennes: front elevation
CLAUDE-NICOLAS LEDOUX 1736–1806
Provenance: Acquired in 1957 on the art market.
Literature: See no. 296.

299 Plans and elevation of the column house, Désert de Retz
JEAN-CHARLES KRAFFT 1764–1833, after Boullay active late 18th and early 19th century
Provenance: Jean-Charles Krafft, *Recueil d'architecture civile* (Paris: Imprimerie de crapelet, chez Bance aîné, 1812).
Exhibition: Houston, University of St. Thomas, *Visionary Architecture,* Oct. 19, 1967–Jan. 3, 1968, p. 222, no. 137.
Literature: Jefferson to Maria Cosway, Oct. 12, 1786; Ernest de Canay, "Fabriques aux jardins du XVIIIe siècle," *GBA*, *45* (May–June 1955), 287–298; Olivier de Janvry, "Avant que disparaisse à jamais le Desert de Retz," *L'Oeil*, nos. 151–153 (July–Sept. 1967), 31–41; *The Age of Neo-classicism*, exhib. cat. (London: The Royal Academy and the Victoria and Albert Museum, 1972), no. 997.

300 Project for a hunting lodge for the prince de Bauffremont, perspective view
CLAUDE-NICOLAS LEDOUX 1736–1806
Literature: Wolfgang Herrmann, "The Problem of Chronology in Claude-Nicolas Ledoux's Engraved Work," *AB*, *42* (Sept. 1960), 191–210.

301 Barrière de l'étoile
Literature: Jacques-Guillaume Legrand and Charles-Paul Landon, *Déscription de Paris et de ses édifices* (Paris: Treuttel und Wurz, 1808); Cte. E. Fremy, "L'enceinte de Paris construite par les Fermiers generaux," *Bulletin de la Société historique de Paris et de l'Ile de France,* 1912, pp. 115–148; Geneviève Levallet-Haug, "L'architecte Ledoux et la cloture de Paris," *Société d'iconographie parisienne,* 1932, pp. 7–68; Geneviève Levallet-Haug, *Claude-Nicolas Ledoux* (Paris and Strasbourg: Librarie Istra, 1934), pp. 113, 158; Rice, *Hôtel de Langeac,* p. 9.

302 Tollgate at the Etoile in 1859
MARVILLE, active mid-19th century
Provenance: Marville estate.
Literature: See no. 301.

303 Loursine tollgate, elevation
CLAUDE-NICOLAS LEDOUX 1736–1866
Literature: See no. 301.

304 Tollgate at la Villette
Literature: See no. 301.

305 Elevation of the buildings on the Place Louis XV
JACQUES-ANGES GABRIEL 1698–1788
Provenance: Commissioned by the Direction de l'Architecture.
Literature: Solange Granet, *Images de Paris, La place de la Concorde, La revue géographique et industrielle de France,* no. 26 (Paris: n.p., 1963).

306 The Church of Sainte-Geneviève (now called the Panthéon) Paris
Literature: Michael Petzet, *Soufflots Sainte-Geneviève und der Francosische Kirchenbau des 18. Jahrhunderts* (Berlin, 1961), p. 185; Allan Braham, "Drawings for Soufflot's Sainte-Geneviève," *BurlM, 113* (Oct. 1971), 582–592.

307 Ecole de Chirurgie, plan of the ground floor
JACQUES GONDOIN 1737–1818, and CLAUDE-RENÉ-GABRIEL POULLEAU b. 1749
Provenance: Jacques Gondoin, *Description des écoles de chirurgie* (Paris: the author, 1780), pl. 6.
Exhibition: London, The Royal Academy and the Victoria and Albert Museum, *The Age of Neo-classicism,* Sept. 9–Nov. 19, 1972, pp. 545–546, pl. 170b.
Literature: Jean Adhémar, "L'Ecole de Medecine, sa place dans l'architecture du XVIIIeme siècle," *L'Architecture,* Mar. 1934, pp. 105–108; Louis Hautecoeur, *Histoire de l'architecture classique en France,* 4 (Paris: A. and J. Picard, 1943–1955): 242–247.

308 Ecole de Chirurgie, street elevation
JACQUES GONDOIN 1737–1818, and CLAUDE-RENÉ-GABRIEL POULLEAU b. 1749
Provenance: Jacques Gondoin, *Description des écoles de chirurgie* (Paris: the author, 1780), pl. 8.
Exhibition: See no. 307.
Literature: See no. 307.

309 Ecole de Chirurgie, interior view of the amphitheater
JACQUES GONDOIN 1737–1818, and CLAUDE-RENÉ-GABRIEL POULLEAU b. 1749

Provenance: Jacques Gondoin, *Description des écoles de chirurgie* (Paris: the author, 1780), pl. 29.
Exhibition: See no. 307.
Literature: See no. 307.

310 Halle aux Bleds, project section
JACQUES MOLINOS 1743–1831
Literature: Jefferson to Maria Cosway, Oct. 12, 1786; Dora Wiebenson, "The Two Domes of the Halle au blé in Paris," *AB, 55* (June 1973), 262–279.

311 Halle aux Bleds, plan
NICOLAS LE CAMUS DE MÉZIÈRES 1721–1789
Literature: See no. 310.

312 Théâtre de l'Odéon, section 1776
CHARLES DE WAILLY 1730–1798
Exhibition: London, The Royal Academy and the Victoria and Albert Museum, *The Age of Neo-classicism,* Sept. 9–Nov. 19, 1972, p. 646, no. 1378.
Literature: Monika Steinhauser and Daniel Rabreau, "Le théâtre de l'Odéon," *Revue de l'art,* no. 19 (1973), 8–49; Michel Gallet, "Projet de Charles de Wailly pour la Comédie française," *Bulletin du Musée Carnavalet,* no. 1 (June 1965), 3–13; Daniel Rabreau, "Charles de Wailly dessinateur," *Information d'histoire de l'art,* no. 5 (Nov.–Dec. 1972), 219–228.

313 Plan of the level of the first tier of boxes of the Bordeaux Theater
NICOLAS (CALLED VICTOR) LOUIS 1731–1800
Provenance: Victor Louis, *Salle de spectacle de Bordeaux* (1782), pl. V.
Literature: Charles Marionneau, *Victor Louis* (Bordeaux: Imprimerie G. Gounouilhou, 1881), pp. 103–476.

314 Front elevation of the Bordeaux Theater
NICOLAS (CALLED VICTOR) LOUIS 1731–1800
Provenance: Acquired in 1850 by the city of Bordeaux from M. Miquel.
Literature: See no. 313.

315 Cross section facing the stage, Bordeaux Theater
NICOLAS (CALLED VICTOR) LOUIS 1731–1800
Provenance: See no. 314.
Literature: See no. 313.

316 Cross section of the auditorium of the Bordeaux Theater
NICOLAS (CALLED VICTOR) LOUIS 1731–1800
Provenance: See no. 314.
Literature: See no. 313.

317 Eye reflecting the interior of the Besançon Theater
CLAUDE-NICOLAS LEDOUX 1736–1806
Literature: Geneviève Levallet-Haug, *Claude-Nicolas Ledoux* (Paris and Strasbourg: Librarie Istra, 1934), pp. 77, 97; Helene Leclerc, "Le théâtre de Besançon," *Revue de l'histoire du théâtre,* 2 (1958), 16–32.

318 Perspective view of the city of Chaux
CLAUDE-NICOLAS LEDOUX 1736–1806
Literature: Geneviève Levallet-Haug, *Claude-Nicolas Ledoux* (Paris and Strasbourg: Librarie Istra, 1934), pp. 63–76; Helen Rosenau, *The Ideal City in its Architectural Evolution* (London: Routledge and Kegan Paul, 1959), p. 168; Wolfgang Herrmann, "The Problem of Chronology in C. N. Ledoux's Engraved Work," *AB, 42* (Sept. 1960), 191–210.

319 Project for a large metropolitan church, interior view
ETIENNE-LOUIS BOULLÉE 1728–1799
Provenance: Given in 1838–1839 to the Royal Institute of British Architects by Sir John Drummond-Stewart, who probably acquired it in 1817 from the estate of Pierre-Nicolas Benard, the heir of Boullée.
Literature: Jean-Marie Pérouse de Montclos, *Etienne-Louis Boullée* (Paris: Arts et métiers graphiques, 1969), pp. 155–162.

320 Project for a museum, plan
ETIENNE-LOUIS BOULLÉE 1728–1799
Provenance: Collection left by Boullée to the Bibliothèque royale (today the Bibliothèque nationale).
Exhibition: Houston, University of St. Thomas, *Visionary Architects,* Oct. 19, 1967–Jan. 3, 1968, pp. 54–57.
Literature: Jean-Marie Pérouse de Montclos, *Etienne-Louis Boullée* (Paris: Arts et métiers graphiques, 1969), pp. 163, 164.

321 Project for a museum, section
ETIENNE-LOUIS BOULLÉE 1728–1799
Provenance: See no. 320.
Exhibition: See no. 320.
Literature: See no. 320.

322 Project for a museum, interior view
ETIENNE-LOUIS BOULLÉE 1728–1799
Provenance: See no. 320.
Exhibition: See no. 320.
Literature: See no. 320.

323 Project for a museum, interior view
ETIENNE-LOUIS BOULLÉE 1728–1799
Provenance: See no. 320.
Exhibition: See no. 320.

326 Elevation, Newton's cenotaph, exterior by night
ETIENNE-LOUIS BOULLÉE 1728–1799
Provenance: Collection left by Boullée to the Bibliothèque royale (today the Bibliothèque nationale).
Exhibition: Houston, University of St. Thomas, Visionary Architects, Oct. 19, 1967–Jan. 3, 1968, no. 7, p. 26, repr. p. 27.
Literature: H. Sedlmayr, "Die Kugel als Gebaude," Das Werk des Kunstlers, 1 (1939), 1–53; Etienne-Louis Boullée, Architecture, Essai sur l'art, with introduction and notes by Jean-Marie Pérouse de Montclos (Paris: Arts et métiers graphiques, 1969), pp. 132–143; Adolf-Max Vogt, Boullées Newton-Denkmal, Sakralbau und Kugelidee (Basel: Birkhäuser, 1969), p. 400; Werner Oechslin, "Pyramide et Sphere," GBA, 77 (1971), 207–238.

327 Section, Newton's cenotaph, interior by day
ETIENNE-LOUIS BOULLÉE 1728–1799
Provenance: See no. 326.
Exhibition: Houston, University of St. Thomas, Visionary Architects, Oct. 19, 1967–Jan. 3, 1968, no. 10, p. 29 repr.; London, The Royal Academy and the Victoria and Albert Museum, The Age of Neo-classicism, Sept. 9–Nov. 19, 1972, p. 502–504.
Literature: See no. 326.

328 Vision inspired by the cemetery at Chaux
EDMÉ BOVINET 1767–1832, after Claude-Nicolas Ledoux 1736–1806
Literature: Hans Sedlmayr, "Die Kugel als Gebaude," Das Werk des Kunstlers, 1939; Wolfgang Herrmann, "The Problem of Chronology in C. N. Ledoux's Engraved Work," AB, 42 (Sept. 1960), 191–210; Adolphe-Max Vogt, Boullées Newton-Denkmal, Sakralbau und Kugelidee (Basel: Birkhäuser, 1969).

329 Project for a sepulchral monument for the sovereigns of a great empire, elevation
PIERRE-LÉONARD FONTAINE 1762–1853
Provenance: Collection of the former Académie d'Architecture.
Exhibition: Houston, University of St. Thomas, Visionary Architects, Oct. 19, 1967–Jan. 3, 1968, no. 146, p. 232 repr.; London, The Royal Academy and the Victoria and Albert Museum, The Age of Neo-classicism, Sept. 9–Nov. 19, 1972, no. 1101, p. 535.
Literature: Marie-Louise Biver, Pierre-Léonard Fontaine, premier architecte de l'Empereur (Paris: Plon, Editions d'histoire et d'art, 1964), p. 16.

331 The Death of Socrates 1787
JACQUES-LOUIS DAVID 1748–1825
Provenance: Commissioned before April 1786 by Charles-Michel Trudaine de La Sablière (Charles Sterling, 1955, verified by the Archives Nationales, F17 1267, 190), and not, as was formerly believed, by his older brother Charles-Louis Trudaine de Montigny. The two brothers were guillotined in 1794; collection of Mme Trudaine de Montigny; left at her death in 1802 to her brother, Micault de Courbeton; collection of the marquis de Verac; to his son-in-law, the comte de Rouge, at whose sale (April 8, 1872, no. 1, 17,600 francs) it was purchased by Marius Bianchi, husband of Mathilde Jeannin, David's great-granddaughter; to their son-in-law, the marquis de Ludre; acquired in 1931 by the Metropolitan Museum.
Exhibition: Paris, Salon of 1787, no. 119; Paris, Salon of 1791, no. 299; Paris, Galerie Lebrun, Ouvrages de peinture exposés au profit des Grecs, 1826, no. 37; Paris, Galerie des Beaux-Arts, Exposition au profit de la Caisse de secours et pensions de la société des artistes peintres, sculpteurs, graveurs, architectes et dessinateurs, Jan. 11, 1846, no. 7; Paris, Palais de la Présidence du Corps Legislatif, Société de protection des Alsaciens et Lorrains demeurés français, Apr. 23, 1874, no. 761; Paris, Palais des Beaux-Arts, David et ses élèves, 1913, no. 23; Paris, Orangerie, David, 1948, no. 21; Boston, Museum of Fine Arts, Masterpieces of Painting in the Metropolitan Museum of Art, 1970, p. 72; London, The Royal Academy and the Victoria and Albert Museum, The Age of Neo-classicism, Sept. 9–Nov. 19, 1972, no. 63, repr. 2; Paris, Grand Palais, De David à Delacroix. La peinture française de 1774 à 1830, Nov. 16, 1974–Feb. 3, 1975, no. 32, pl. 36; Detroit, The Detroit Institute of Arts, French Painting 1774–1830: The Age of Revolution, no. 32.
Literature: Coll. Deloynes, 15: no. 373 (pp. 157–158), no. 374 (pp. 193–194), no. 375 (p. 244), no. 376 (p. 275), no. 378 (p. 319), no. 379 (p. 374), no. 381 (pp. 376, 412–413), no. 382 (p. 462), no. 384 (pp. 524–525), no. 385 (pp. 547–562), no. 386 (p. 585), no. 387 (p. 603), no. 390 (pp. 683, 687–688), no. 394 (pp. 765–766), no. 395 (pp. 836–838), no. 397 (pp. 863–865), no. 402 (pp. 957–959), and 50: no. 1360 (p. 389); T. C. Bruun-Neergaard, Sur la situation des Beaux-Arts en France ou Lettres d'un Danois à son ami (Paris, Year IX [1801]), p. 89; Landon, 3:1802; Chaussard, pp. 155–156; C. P. Landon, Musée royal du Luxembourg, recréé en 1822, et composé des principales productions des artistes vivants, extracted from Annales du musée et de l'école moderne des Beaux-Arts (Paris, 1823); Notice sur la vie et les ouvrages de M.J.L. David (Paris, 1824), pp. 32–34; A. Th[ome?], Vie de David, premier peintre de Napoléon (Paris, 1826), pp. 45–46, 187–188, 324; P. A. Coupin, Essai sur J. L. David peintre d'histoire, ancien membre de l'Institut, officier de la Légion d'Honneur (Paris: Renouard, 1827), pp. 19, 53; Charles Blanc, Histoire des peintres français au XIXe siècle, 1 (Paris: Cauville frères, 1845): 171–172, 209; Charles Baudelaire, "Le musée classique du bazar Bonne-Nouvelle," Corsaire-Satan (Jan. 21, 1846), reprinted in Ecrits sur l'Art (1971), 1: 131; Miette de Villars, Mémoires de David peintre et député à la Convention (Paris, 1850), pp. 100, 189, 232; Etienne-Jean Delécluze, Louis David, son école et son temps, Souvenirs (Paris: Didier, 1855), pp. 119, 348, 399; A. Cantaloube, "Les dessins de Louis David," GBA, Sept. 1860, p. 291; J. du Seigneur, "Appendice à la notice de P. Chaussard sur L. David," Revue Universelle des Arts, 18 (1863), 366; David, pp. 46–51, 63; Léon Rosenthal, Louis David (Paris: Librairie de l'art ancien et moderne, 1904), pp. 33, 37, 44; Louis Hautecoeur, Rome et la renaissance de l'Antiquité (Paris: Fontemoing et cie, 1912), p. 194, repr.; Charles Saunier, "David et son école au palais des Beaux-Arts de la ville de Paris," GBA, May 1913, pp. 273, 280; Léon Rosenthal, "L'exposition de David et ses élèves au Petit Palais," Revue de l'art ancien et moderne, 33 (May 1913), 339; Richard Cantinelli, Jacques-Louis David 1748–1825 (Paris and Brussels: G. van Oest, 1930), pp. 24, 104, repr.; B. Burroughs, "A picture by Jacques Louis David," BMMA, June 1931; A. Bonnardet, "Comment un oratorien vient en aide à un grand peintre," GBA, May–June 1938, pp. 311–315; Holma, pp. 50–51, 55, 126; Jacques Maret, David (Monaco: Les Documents d'Art, 1943), repr. p. 41; E. Wind, "A lost article on David by Reynolds," JWarb, 6 (1943), 223–224; Gaston Brière, "Sur David portraitiste," Bulletin de la Société de l'histoire de l'art français, 1945–1946, p. 179; Boyd, 12:xxxiv; W. Friedlaender, David to Delacroix (Cambridge, Mass.: Harvard University Press, 1952), p. 17, repr. p. 4; J. Adhémar, David, Naissance du genie d'un peintre (Paris: Raoul Solar, 1953), pp. 42–43; Hautecoeur, pp. 90–94; Charles Sterling, A Catalogue of French Paintings of the 15th to 18th Centuries at the Metropolitan Museum of Art (Cambridge, Mass., 1955), pp. 192–196; Jean Seznec, Essais sur Diderot et l'Antiquité (Oxford, 1957), p. 20, repr. 9; Jack Lindsay, Death of the Hero. French Painting from David to Delacroix (London: Studio, 1960), pp. 55–56, repr. p. 2; A. Salmon, "Le Socrate de David et le Phedon de Platon," Revue belge de Philologie et d'histoire, 40 (1962), no. 1, 90–111; A. Brookner, "J. L. David. A Sentimental Classicist," Akten des 21 Internationalen Kongresses fur Kunstgeschichte in Bonn (1964), p. 189, repr.; Robert Rosenblum, Transformations in Late Eighteenth Century Art (Princeton: Princeton University Press, 1967), pp. 73–76, 81, 103, 125, repr. p. 74; René Verbraeken, Jacques-Louis David jugé par ses contemporains et par la posterité (Paris: L. Laget, 1973), pp. 24, 28–30, 33, 46, 54–55, 80, 82, 85, 87–88, 94, 106, 108, 149–150, repr. p. 21; Daniel and Guy Wildenstein, Documents complémentaires au catalogue de l'oeuvre de Louis David (Paris, 1973), nos. 162, 180, 188, 189, 191, 192, 195, 303, 327, 352, 1165, 1167, 1543, 1810, 1929, 1938; A. Schnapper, notice, De David à Delacroix, exhib. cat. (Paris, 1974), no. 32, pp. 367–368.

332 The Oath of the Horatii 1784
JACQUES-LOUIS DAVID 1748–1825
Provenance: Bequest of Jean-Baptiste Wicar (1762–1834), pupil and friend of David, in 1834.
Exhibition: Paris, Orangerie, David, 1948, no. 93; London, Heim, From Poussin to Puvis de Chavannes, 1974, no. 13, pl. 45.
Literature: L. Gonse, "Le musée Wicar," GBA, 1 (1877), 88; David, p. 654; Henri Pluchart, Ville de Lille. Musée Wicar. Notice des dessins, cartons, pastels, miniatures et grisailles exposés (Lille, 1889), no. 823; L. Gonse, Les chefs d'oeuvre des musées de France, sculptures, dessins, et objets d'art (Paris: Librairie d'art ancien et moderne, 1904), pp. 223–225; Fernand Beaucamp, Le peintre lillois Jean-Baptiste Wicar (1762–1834), son oeuvre et son temps (Lille: E. Raoust, 1939), 1:60; Holma, pp. 5, 46; Hautecoeur, p. 71; F. H. Hazlehurst, "The Artistic Evolution of David's Oath," AB, 42, no. 1 (Mar. 1960), 62–63; A. Calvet, "Unpublished studies for 'The Oath of Horatii,' by Jacques-Louis David," MD, 6, no. 1 (1968), 40, pl. 28.

333 Marius Imprisoned at Minturnae 1786
JEAN-GERMAIN DROUAIS 1763–1788
Provenance: Collection of Mme Drouais, the artist's mother; offered to the museum in 1795; acquired by the Louvre from Mlle Marie-Jeanne Doré, the artist's aunt, in 1816 (no. 4143).

Exhibition: Paris, Grand Palais, De David à Delacroix, la peinture française de 1776 à 1830, Nov. 16, 1974– Feb. 3, 1975, no. 52, pl. 32; Detroit, The Detroit Institute of Arts, French Painting 1774–1830, The Age of Revolution, Mar. 5–May 4, 1975, no. 52.

Literature: Coll. Deloynes, 15: no. 374, p. 195; Correspondance des Directeurs de l'Académie de France à Rome, 15 (May 3, 1786) 89, (June 5, 1786) 92, (Aug. 23, 1786) 96, (Oct. 11, 1786) 112–113, (Aug. 24, 1787) 124; Procès-verbaux de l'Académie royale de peinture et de sculpture, 9 (Paris: J. Baur, 1889): 334; T. C. Bruun-Neergaard, Sur la situation des Beaux-Arts en France ou Lettres d'un danois à son ami (Paris: Dupont, Year IX [1801]), pp. 102–103; Landon, 5:147–148; J. D. Fiorillo, Geschichte der Zeichnenden kunste von ihrer Wiederauflebung bis auf die neuesten Zeiten, 5 (Gottingen, 1805): 466–467; J. B. A. Guard, "Eloge de Drouais," Mélange de Littérature, 3 (1806), 278; P. M. Gault de Saint-Germain, Les trois siècles de la peinture en France (Paris, 1808), p. 262; Chaussard, pp. 341–342; Filhol and J. Lavalée, Galerie du musée Napoléon, 11 (Paris, 1828): 1–3, pl. 37; C. P. Landon and E. F. Mill, "Notice sur Jean-Germain Drouais," Annales de la Société libre des Beaux-Arts, 1836, p. 58; Etienne-Jean Délécluze, David, son école et son temps, Souvenirs (Paris: Didier, 1855), pp. 249–251; A. de Montaiglon, "Lettres écrites par Pierre-Paul Prud'hon à MM Devosge et Fauconnier pendant son voyage d'Italie," Archives de l'Art français, 1857–1858, pp. 164, 168, 170; F. de Villars, "Les trois Drouais," Revue universelle des Arts, 1859, p. 313; Charles Coligny, "La vie et la mort de Drouais," L'artiste, Mar. 1, 1862, p. 100; J. du Seigneur, "Le dernier Drouais," Revue universelle des Arts, 17 (1862), 50; Renouvier, p. 222; C. Blanc, Histoire des peintres de toutes les écoles; école française, 3 (Paris: J. Renouard, 1865): 3, 5, 8; A. Jal, Dictionnaire critique de Biographie et d'histoire (Paris, 1867), p. 509; A. Lecoy de la Marche, "L'Académie de France à Rome d'après la correspondance de ses Directeurs (1666–1792); suite des lettres de Lagrénée," GBA, 2 (Nov. 1872), 413; A. Lecoy de la Marche, L'Académie de France à Rome; correspondance inédit de ses Directeurs (Paris, 1874), p. 343; Bellier and Auvray, 1: 449; C. Gabillot, "Les trois Drouais," GBA Mar. 1906, pp. 257–258; Thieme-Becker, 9:579; Brière, no. 270; H. Lapauze, Histoire de l'Académie de France à Rome, 1 (Paris: Plon-Nourrit et cie, 1924): 411; J. P.

Alaux, L'Académie de France à Rome, ses Directeurs, ses pensionnaires, 1 (Paris, 1933): 200; Hautecoeur, p. 95; D. and G. Wildenstein, Documents complémentaires au catalogue de l'oeuvre de Louis David (Paris, 1973), nos. 168, 1368; J. Villain, "Un tableau de J. G. Drouais récemment acquis par le musée du Mans," LRL, 1974, no. 6, p. 400.

334 Voltaire 1778
JEAN-ANTOINE HOUDON 1741–1828
Provenance: Collection Lamorinière family, who acquired it from the artist; Alfred Morrison of Fonthill, England, who sold it to Duveen's before 1900; Widener Collection; given to the National Gallery of Art.
Literature: Louis Réau, "Correspondance artistique de Grimm avec Catherine II," Archives de l'art français, 1931–1932, pp. 30–34; Michel Benisovich, "Houdon's Statue of Voltaire Seated," AB, no. 30 (Mar. 1948), 70–71; Theodore Besterman, "The terra-cotta Statue of Voltaire made by Houdon for Beaumarchais," Studies on Voltaire and the Eighteenth Century, 12 (1960), 21–27; Willibald Sauerlander, Jean-Antoine Houdon: Voltaire (Stuttgart, 1963); H. H. Arnason, Sculpture by Houdon, exhib. cat. (Worcester, Mass.: Worcester Art Museum, 1964), pp. 48–53; N. B. Petrusevic, "The Statue of Voltaire by Houdon," Leningrad, 1970 (in Russian).

335 Diana 1778
JEAN-ANTOINE HOUDON 1741–1828
Provenance: Comtesse de Fresnes; Comtesse Greffulhe; given to the National Gallery of Art in 1958 by Miss Syma Busiel.
Exhibition: Salon of 1777, no. 248.
Literature: Louis Courajod, "La Diane en bronze de Houdon du Musée du Louvre," Archives de l'art français, 1879–1880, pp. 269–271; Jacques Darl, Le buste de la Diane de Houdon (Paris, 1906); Paul Vitry, "La 'Diane' et l' 'Apollon' de Houdon," Les Arts, no. 61 (Jan. 1907), 9–16; L. Roger-Miles, Les Dianes de Houdon, et les caprices de la pudeur esthetique à la fin du XVIIIe siècle (Paris, 1913); H. H. Arnason, "Note on the Diana of Houdon," AQ, 2, no. 4 (Autumn 1939), 402e–402f; Perry B. Cott, "A Note on Houdon's Bust of Diana," Studies in the History of Art (Mel Suida), 1959, pp. 364–367; Louis Réau, "La Diane et l'Apollon de Houdon à la Fondation Calouste Gulbenkian de Lisbonne," Coloquio, June 1960; Réau, 1:43–47, 50, 223–224, 2: 12–13, pls. 4–8; The Frick Collection Catalogue, 4, (1970), 114–119, 127–139; H. H.

Arnason, The Sculptures of Houdon (London and New York, 1975), pp. 43–45, pls. 39–42.

336 Jacob Blessing the Sons of Joseph c. 1710–1720
ADRIAEN VAN DER WERFF 1659–1722
Provenance: Possibly sale, Amsterdam, June 5, 1765, lot 1; Frederick II of Prussia, Sanssouci, Potsdam, by 1770, probably bought from the Paris dealer Mettra in 1767; by descent in the House of Hohenzollern until 1925; private collection, London; Christie, Manson & Woods sale, London, May 24, 1963, lot 152, bought in; purchased through the Mrs. F. F. Prentiss Fund, 1963.
Exhibitions: Sanssouci Gallery, 1770– c. 1833; Berlin Museum, 1837–1906.
Literature: G. Hoet and P. Terivesten, Catalogus of naamlyst van schilderijen, 3 (The Hague, 1770): 451; M. Oesterreich, Beschreibung der Königlichen Bildergallerie und des Kabinetts im Sanssouci (Potsdam, 1770), p. 112; C. Decker, Arrangement du Cabinet à côté de la Grande Galerie Royale des Tableaux de Sans-Souci (Berlin, 1773); Friedrich Nicolai, Beschreibung der königlichen Residenstädte Berlin und Potsdam, 2nd ed. (Berlin, 1779), 2:924 and 3rd ed. (Berlin, 1786), 3:1211; Friedrich Rumpf, Beschreibung der äussern und innern Merkwürdigkeiten der Königlichen Schlösser in Berlin, Charlottenburg, Schönhausen, in und bey Potsdam (Berlin, 1794), p. 178; John Smith, A Catalogue Raisonné of the Works of the most Eminent Dutch, Flemish and French Painters (London: Smith and Son, 1833 and 1842), 4:212, no. 114, and 9:558, no. 30; C. Hofstede de Groot, Beschreibung und kritisches Verzeichnis der Werke der hervorragendsten holländischen Maler de XVII Jahrhunderts, 10 (Stuttgart and Paris: Paul Neff Verlag and F. Kleinberger, 1928): 241, no. 17; Sir Francis Watson, The Choiseul Box (London: Oxford University Press, 1963); Wolfgang Stechow, "Jacob Blessing the Sons of Joseph, by Adriaen van der Werff," Allen Memorial Art Museum Bulletin, 22, no. 2 (Winter 1965), 69–73, illus. p. 68; Richard D. Buck, "Adriaen van der Werff and Prussian Blue," Allen Memorial Art Museum Bulletin, 22, no. 2 (Winter 1965), 74–76; Catalogue of European and American Paintings and Sculpture in the Allen Memorial Art Museum (Oberlin, Ohio: Oberlin College, 1967), pp. 159–160, fig. 81; Lipscomb, 18:254; Boyd, 10:440; Kimball, The Scene of Europe, p. 227.

337 Hercules and Lichas after 1796
ANTONIO CANOVA 1757–1822
Provenance: Given to the museum in 1968 by the Medical Auxiliary of Wake County.
Exhibition: Raleigh, North Carolina Museum of Art, Reopening Exhibition, Mary Duke Biddle Gallery, 1969; Raleigh, North Carolina Museum of Art, Exhibition Number One from the Permanent Collection, 1970; Storrs, The William Benton Museum of Art, University of Connecticut, The Academy of Europe, Rome in the Eighteenth Century, 1973; Roanoke, Roanoke Fine Arts Center, The Male Image, Sept. 12– Oct. 27, 1974.
Literature: Jefferson to Nathaniel Macon, Jan. 22, 1816 (Lipscomb, 14:408–412); Antoine Chrysotome Quatremère de Quincy, Canova et ses ouvrages (Paris: A. Le Clerc et cie, 1834), pp. 81–86; Robert D. W. Connor, Canova's Statue of Washington (Raleigh: North Carolina Historical Commission, 1910); Elena Bassi, Canova (Rome: Instituto italiano d'arti grafiche, 1943), pl. 59; Hugh Honour, "Antonio Canova and the Anglo-Romans; part II, The First Years in Rome," Conoisseur, 64 (Jan. 1960), 230; Elena Bassi, La Gipsoteca di Possagno, scultere e dipinti di Antonio Canova (Venice: N. Pozza, 1957), p. 107; Elena Bassi, Museo Civico di Bassano, I Disegni di Antonio Canova (Venice: N. Pozza, 1959), pp. 82–83; Rudolf Zeitler, Klassizismus und Utopia (Stockholm, 1954), pp. 104–108, 117, pp. 104–108; Philipp Fehl, "Thomas Appleton of Livorno and Canova's Statue of George Washington," in Festschrift Ulrich Middledorf (Berlin, 1968), pp. 523–552; Philipp Fehl, "Canova's Hercules and Lichas, Notes Regarding a Small Bronze in the North Carolina Museum of Art," North Carolina Museum of Art Bulletin, 8, no. 1 (Sept. 1968), 3–25; Robert Rosenblum, Transformations in Late Eighteenth Century Art (Princeton: Princeton University Press, 1969), pp. 14–15.

338 Thomas Jefferson 1800
REMBRANDT PEALE 1778–1860
Provenance: Collection of Rembrandt Peale; to his brother Rubens with contents of Peale Museum in Baltimore in 1822; with the remnants of the museum it survived many moves, at least two fires and a number of disinterested proprietors, the last being Charles Getz, who sold the Jefferson to Charles J. M. Eaton, on whose death the family presented it to the Peabody Institute. It was acquired in 1962 by the Fine Arts Committee of the White House with funds provided for that purpose by

Mr. and Mrs. Paul Mellon.
Exhibition: Charlottesville, The University of Virginia Museum of Fine Arts, *The Life Portraits of Thomas Jefferson,* Apr. 12–16, 1962.
Literature: Bowen, pp. 478–479; Charles Henry Hart, "The Life Portraits of Thomas Jefferson," *McClure's Magazine,* 11, no. 1 (May 1898), 51; Kimball, "Life Portraits," p. 498; Peabody Institute Gallery of Art, *List of Works of Art on Exhibition Including the Collections of John W. McCoy and Charles J. M. Eaton* (Baltimore, 1949), p. 17; Wilbur H. Hunter, Jr., *Rendezvous for Taste, Peale's Baltimore Museum,* exhib. cat. (Baltimore: Baltimore Municipal Museum, 1956), p. 6; Alfred L. Bush, "Rembrandt Peale's Earliest Life Portrait of Thomas Jefferson," unpublished typescript; Bush, pp. 52–55; *The White House, An Historic Guide,* exhib. cat. (Washington, D.C.: The White House Historical Association, n.d.).

Copies: The painting was first reproduced by David Edwin in a stipple engraving dated 1800 and in the following year in the same medium by Cornelius Tiebout. These two engravings, the only likenesses taken directly from the life portrait, became the sources for at least fifty other versions of the portrait which were painted, engraved and lithographed in the nineteenth century.

Among the notable likenesses derived from this life portrait through these two prints is the handsome crayon drawing by Bouch, dated 1801 and drawn from Tiebout's 1801 engraving. This crayon was itself copied in the engraving by August Gaspard Louis Boucher, later the Baron Desnoyers, that created the image of Jefferson which is the type followed in France even today. The Desnoyers engraving was also copied in a line engraving by William Holl the Younger in England and, with further derivatives, became perhaps the most important of the British images of Jefferson.

339 Thomas Jefferson 1788
JOHN TRUMBULL 1756–1843
Provenance: By bequest of Maria Cosway to the Collegio de Maria SS Bambina in Lodi, Italy.
Literature: Bowen, p. 486; Charles Henry Hart, "The Life Portraits of Thomas Jefferson," *McClure's Magazine,* 11, no. 1 (May 1898), 47; Kimball, "Life Portraits," 501–505; Theodore Sizer, *The Works of Colonel John Trumbull* (New Haven: Yale University Press, 1950), pp. 35, 72–73, pl. 13; Sizer, pp. 152, 285–288; Elizabeth Cometti, "Maria Cosway's Rediscovered Miniature of

Jefferson," *William and Mary Quarterly,* 9, 3rd ser. (1952), 152–155; Boyd, 10:xxix–xxx, 12:358, 405, 603, 645, 14:364–365, 440; Bush, pp. 17–19.
Copies: The life portrait hangs in the Yale University Art Gallery. The replica painted for Angelica Schuyler Church is now in the Metropolitan Museum of Art; that painted for Maria Jefferson is at Monticello. Two further replicas were painted in duplications of the complete *Declaration of Independence:* the first, with figures the size of life, is in the rotunda of the capitol in Washington; the second is owned by the Wadsworth Atheneum. The earliest of the uncountable progeny of prints was engraved by Asher B. Durand in 1823.

340 Maria Cosway
RICHARD COSWAY 1742–1821
Provenance: Collection at Wellsford Manor, Salisbury, England; collection of Mrs. George R. Balch.
Literature: George C. Williamson, *Richard Cosway, R.A. and his Wife and Pupils* (London: George Bell & Sons, 1897), pp. 14–17, 52–53; Jefferson to Maria Cosway Oct. 12, 1786; Jefferson to Mrs. Bingham, Feb. 7, 1787.

341 Maria Cosway c. 1785
RICHARD COSWAY 1742–1821
Provenance: By bequest of Maria Cosway to the Convent of the Dame Inglesi, Lodi.
Literature: George C. Williamson, *Richard Cosway, R. A. and His Wife and Pupils* (London: George Bell & Sons, 1897), pp. 11, 24, 62, illus. opp. p. 62; Helen Duprey Bullock, *My Head and My Heart* (New York: G. P. Putnam's Sons, 1945), p. 182.

342 Mrs. Cosway and Her Daughter
JOHN RAPHAEL SMITH 1752–1812
Provenance: Manning Galleries, Ltd., London, from whom acquired, 1967.
Literature: George C. Williamson, *Richard Cosway, R.A.* (London: George Bell & Sons, 1897), pp. 17–18; Helen Duprey Bullock, *My Head and My Heart* (New York: G. P. Putnam's Sons, 1945), pp. 141, 144, 146, 148.

343 Self-Portrait c. 1785
RICHARD COSWAY 1742–1821
Provenance: By bequest of Maria Cosway to the Convent of the Dame Inglesi, Lodi.
Literature: George C. Williamson, *Richard Cosway, R.A. and His Wife and Pupils* (London: George Bell & Sons, 1897), p. 62, illus.

344 Self-Portrait 1777
JOHN TRUMBULL 1756–1843
Provenance: Percy Webb McClellan, grandnephew of the artist, Haverhill, Mass.; George Nixon Black, Boston, c. 1914.
Exhibition: Boston, Copley Society, *Portraits by American Painters Before the Revolution,* 1922, no. 64; New Haven, Yale University Art Gallery, *Connecticut Tercentenary,* 1935, no. 42; Cambridge (Mass.), Harvard University, *Tercentenary,* 1936, no. 33; New London, Conn., Lyman Allyn Museum, *Trumbull and His Contemporaries,* 1944, no. 2; New Haven, Yale University Art Gallery, *Makers of History in Washington, 1800–1950,* 1950, no. 131, repr. p. 157; Hartford, Conn., Wadsworth Atheneum, *Trumbull, Bicentennial of His Birth,* 1956, no. 7; Washington, D.C., International Exhibitions Foundation, *American Self Portraits,* 1974, no. 8, repr. color cover.
Literature: Trumbull Papers, Yale University Library, Manuscripts Division; John Trumbull, *Autobiography, Reminiscences and Letters of John Trumbull from 1756 to 1841* (New York and London: Wiley and Putnam, and New Haven: B. L. Hamlen, 1841), p. 60; Theodore Sizer, *The Works of Colonel John Trumbull* (1950; rev. ed. New Haven: Yale University Press, 1967), p. 72; Irma B. Jaffe, *John Trumbull: Patriot-Artist of the American Revolution* (Boston: New York Graphic Society, in press), illus.

345 William Short with the Temple of Paestum in the Background 1806
REMBRANDT PEALE 1778–1860
Provenance: By family descent from the sitter to William Short, great-nephew of the sitter; to Fanny Short Butler and Mary Churchill Short; gift in the name of William Short, Fanny Short Butler and Mary Churchill Short, 1938.

346 Joel Barlow 1803
JEAN-ANTOINE HOUDON 1741–1828
Provenance: Pennsylvania Academy of Fine Arts since 1812.
Literature: Louis Réau, "Houdon sous la révolution et l'empire," *GBA,* July–Aug. 1924, pp. 59–86.

347 John Adams 1788
MATHER BROWN 1761–1831
Provenance: Thomas Jefferson, 1788–1826; Jefferson heirs, 1826–1833, when sold at Chester Harding's auction house; probably the Parkman family of Boston, 1833–1908; bequeathed to the Boston Athenaeum by George Francis Parkman, 1908.
Exhibitions: Boston, the Athenaeum,

1828; Boston, Chester Harding's Gallery, 1833; Washington, Corcoran Gallery, *United States Constitutional Sesquicentennial,* 1937; New London, Lyman-Allyn Museum, *Trumbull and his Contemporaries,* 1944; New York, Century Club, *Exhibition of Brouère Life Masks,* 1947; Chicago, Art Institute, *From Colony to Nation,* 1949; Williamsburg, Colonial Williamsburg, *They Gave Us Freedom,* 1951; Quincy, Adams National Historic Site, 1955; Dallas, Museum of Fine Arts, *Portraits of the American Presidents,* 1956; Washington, National Portrait Gallery, *This New Man,* 1968.
Literature: Jefferson to John Page, May 4, 1786; Jefferson to W. S. Smith, Oct. 22, 1786; Jefferson to Benjamin Rush, Dec. 5, 1811; Jefferson to John Adams, Jan. 21, 1812; T. W. Coburn, "Mather Brown," *Art in America,* 11 (Apr. 1923), 252–259; *The Adams-Jefferson Letters, The Complete Correspondence between Thomas Jefferson and John Adams,* ed. Lester J. Cappon (Chapel Hill: The University of North Carolina Press, 1959); *Diary and Autobiography of John Adams,* ed. L. H. Butterfield (Cambridge: The Belknap Press, 1961).

348 Abigail Adams c. 1785
RALPH EARLE? 1751–1801
Provenance: Owned in 1928 by H. A. Hammond Smith; Parke-Bernet Galleries, Erskine Hewitt sale, October 20, 1938; Harry Shaw Newman Gallery, 1948; Miss Frances Eggleston, Oswego, New York; left to the New York State Historical Association, Cooperstown, New York.
Exhibition: New York, Museum of the City of New York, *Inaugural Exhibition,* 1932.
Literature: Charles Francis Adams, *Letters of Mrs. Adams, the Wife of John Adams* (Boston: Wilkins, Carter, and Company, 1848); T. W. Coburn, "Mather Brown," *Art in America,* 11 (Apr. 1923), 252–259; F. F. Sherman, "The Painting of Ralph Earl," *Art in America,* 27 (Oct. 1939), 168, 178; Kimball, *The Scene of Europe;* Howard C. Rice, Jr., *The Adams Family in Auteuil* (Boston: the Massachusetts Historical Society, 1956); Laurence B. Goodrich, *Ralph Earle, Recorder of an Era* (New York: State University of New York, 1967); Andrew Oliver, *Portraits of John and Abigail Adams* (Cambridge: The Belknap Press of Harvard University Press, 1967).

349 The Amphitheater at Nîmes
WILLIAM MARLOW 1740–1813
Provenance: Dr. T. C. Girtin, c. 1850; Mrs. Barnard; Mrs. Sutton; T. R. C.

Blofield; Tom Girtin; John Baskett, London, from whom acquired in 1970.

Exhibitions: Arts Council of Great Britain, *Three Centuries of British Watercolours,* 1951, no. 112; London, Guildhall Art Gallery, *William Marlow,* 1956, no. 72; Leeds, City Art Gallery, *Early English Water-colours,* 1958, no. 71; New York, Pierpont Morgan Library and London, Royal Academy of Arts, *English Drawings and Watercolors 1550–1850 in the Collection of Mr. and Mrs. Paul Mellon,* Apr. 13–July 28, 1972 and Feb. 24–Apr. 30, 1973, no. 29, illus.

Literature: Jefferson to Mme de Tessé, March 20, 1787; John Baskett and Dudley Snelgrove, *English Drawings and Watercolors 1550–1850 in the Collection of Mr. and Mrs. Paul Mellon,* exhib. cat. (New York and London: Pierpont Morgan Library and Royal Academy of Arts, 1973), no. 29, illus.

350 Nîmes from the Tour Magne
WILLIAM MARLOW 1740–1813
Provenance: Palser; T. Girtin; Tom Girtin; John Baskett, London, from whom acquired, 1970.

Exhibitions: Cambridge, Fitzwilliam Museum, *Drawings by the Early English Watercolourists,* 1920, no. 15; Sheffield, Graves Art Gallery, *Early Water-colours from the Collection of Thomas Girtin, Jnr. Esq.,* 1953, no. 74; London, Guildhall Art Gallery, *William Marlow,* 1956, no. 59; London, Royal Academy of Arts, *The Girtin Collection,* 1962, no. 5.

Literature: Elizabeth Cometti, "Mr. Jefferson Prepares an Itinerary," *The Journal of Southern History,* 12, no. 1 (Feb. 1946), 105; Boyd, 2:254, 239–241, 424.

351 Map of the Royal Canal in Languedoc 1787
DEZAUCHE active late 18th century
Provenance: Acquired in France by Jefferson; sent with letter of May 2, 1788 to Washington; Library of Congress with Washington's Papers.

Literature: Jefferson, "Notes of a Tour into the Southern Parts of France, &c.," Boyd, 11:xxxiii, 415–464; Jefferson to Martha Jefferson, May 21, 1787; Jefferson to William Short, May 21, 1787; Jefferson to Washington, May 2, 1788; Washington to Jefferson, Aug. 31, 1788; Edward Dumbauld, *Thomas Jefferson, American Tourist* (Norman, Oklahoma: University of Oklahoma Press, 1946), pp. 104–105.

352 Voyage pittoresque de la France...
JEAN-BENJAMIN DE LABORDE et al.
Literature: Jefferson to William Short, Mar. 27, 1787 (on Aix); Jefferson

to William Short, Apr. 7, 1787 (on wrist); Jefferson to Martha Jefferson, May 21, 1787; André Monglond, *La France révolutionnaire et impériale: Annales de bibliographie et Description des livres illustrés,* 5 (Grenoble: Editions B. Arthaud, 1938): 921–969; Pierre Quarré, comp., *J.-B. Lallemand, Paysagiste dijonnais du XVIIIe siècle,* exhib. cat. (Dijon: Musée de Dijon, 1954), pp. 8–9, nos. 104, 104 bis, 105, 106; Boyd, 11:xxxii–xxxiii.

353 The Interior of the Port of Marseilles, Seen from the Clock Tower in the Park 1754
JOSEPH VERNET 1714–1789
Provenance: Second of the Vues des Ports de France commissioned by Louis XV from J. Vernet in 1753. Collection of Louis XV; Musée du Louvre, no. 8294; deposited at the Musée de la Marine in July 1943.

Exhibition: Paris, Salon of 1755, no. 98.

Literature: Villot, no. 941; Florence Ingersoll-Smouse, *Joseph Vernet, peintre de marines* (Paris: E. Bignou, 1926), p. 22, no. 568, p. 79, fig. 122; General Thiervoz, "Les ports de France de Joseph Vernet," *Neptunia,* no. 58 (1960), 10; Jefferson to John Trumbull, Apr. 4, 1787.

354 View of the City and the Port of Bordeaux Taken from the Side of the Saltworks 1758
JOSEPH VERNET 1714–1789
Provenance: The ninth of fifteen paintings of French ports commissioned by Louis XV in 1753; collection of Louis XV; Musée du Louvre, no. 8301; placed in the Musée de la Marine in July, 1943.

Exhibition: Paris, Salon of 1759, no. 65.

Literature: Villot, no. 600; L. Lagrange, *Joseph Vernet et la peinture au XVIIIe siècle, avec le texte des livres de raison et un grand nombre de documents inédits* (Paris, 1864); Engerand, p. 505; Ernest Labadie, *Les deux vues du port de Bordeaux au XVIIIe siècle de Joseph Vernet, gravées par Cochin et Lebas. Notice historique et iconographique* (Bordeaux, 1907), pp. 21–25; Jean Loquin, *La peinture d'histoire en France de 1747 à 1785* (Paris, 1912), p. 20; Brière, no. 948; Florence Ingersoll-Smouse, *Joseph Vernet, peintre de marine* (Paris: E. Bignou, 1926), p. 24, no. 692, p. 88, fig. 159; Betts, p. 462; Boyd, 11:457; Pierre Gassier, "Luis Paret et Joseph Vernet," *Cahiers de Bordeaux,* 3ème année (1956), p. 28; Général Thiervoz, "Les Ports de France de Joseph Vernet," *Neptunia,* no. 58 (1960), 14–15; Pierre du Colombier, "Vernet vu de

près," *ConndArts,* no. 126 (July 1962), 62, detail repr. p. 65; Jacques Thuillier and Albert Chatelet, *La peinture française de le Nain et Fragonard* (Geneva: Skira, 1964), pp. 233–237; *Catalogue du musée de la Marine,* no. 296; M. A. Tippetts, *La marine des peintres vue par les littérateurs de Diderot aux Goncour* (Paris: A. G. Nizet, 1966), p. 17.

355 View of the Pagoda of Chanteloup taken from the grand Salon
Literature: Jefferson, "Notes of a Tour into the Southern Parts of France, & c.," in Boyd, 11:415–464; Thomas Jefferson, "Hints to Americans Travelling in Europe," in Boyd, 13:264–276; Arthur Young, *Travels during the years 1787, 1788 and 1789, undertaken more particularly with a view of ascertaining the cultivation, wealth, resources, and national prosperity of the kingdom of France,* 2nd ed. (London: W. Richardson, 1794); André Hallays, R. Edouard André, Roland Engerand, *Chanteloup* (Tours: A. Mame et fils, 1928), pp. 25–26; Douglas Cooper, "Richard Wilson's Views of Kew," *BurlM,* 90 (Dec. 1948), 346; W. G. Constable, *Richard Wilson* (Cambridge, Mass.: Harvard University Press, 1953), pp. 179–180, pl. 41b; Alfred Cobban, ed., *The Eighteenth Century* (New York: McGraw-Hill, 1969).

356 Somerset House, St. Paul's Cathedral and Blackfriar's Bridge
JEAN-LOUIS DESPREZ 1743–1804
Provenance: Sir William Chambers; Christie sale, London, June 6, 1811, lot 104, one of "Three Large Views of Somerset House by Despres"; Major and Mrs. W. H. Gibson-Fleming; P. & D. Colnaghi & Co. Ltd., London, from whom acquired, 1960.

Literature: John Harris, *Sir William Chambers* (London: A. Zwemmer Ltd., 1970), pp. 229, illus. p. 167.

357 Kew Gardens with the Pagoda and Bridge 1762
RICHARD WILSON 1713–1782
Provenance: Dr. John Wolcot; Richard Winstanley; Christie and Manson, sale, London, Mar. 6, 1858, lot 34; Louis Huth; Christie, Manson & Woods, sale, London, May 20, 1905, lot 136; Henry Yates Thompson; Sir Christopher Chancellor; Sotheby & Co. sale, London Feb. 20, 1952, lot 81; Edward Speelman, Ltd., London from whom acquired 1962.

Exhibition: London, Society of Artists, 1762, no. 131; Birmingham City Museum and Art Gallery, *Richard Wilson and His Circle,* Nov. 17, 1948–Jan. 9, 1949, no. 11; London, Tate Gallery, *Richard Wilson and His Circle,* 1949, no. 10; Richmond, Virginia Museum of Fine Arts, *Painting in England 1700–1850: Collection of Mr. and Mrs. Paul Mellon,* 1963, no. 20, illus. in vol. of plates p. 209;

London, Royal Academy of Arts, *Painting in England 1700–1850 from the Collection of Mr. and Mrs. Paul Mellon,* 1964–1965, no. 55; Yale University Art Gallery, *Painting in England 1700–1850 from the Collection of Mr. and Mrs. Paul Mellon,* Apr. 15–June 20, 1965, no. 224.

Literature: Thomas Wright, *Some Account of the Life of Richard Wilson, Esq., R.A.* (London: 1824), pp. 103–104; Betts, p. 114; Adrian Bury, *Richard Wilson, "the Grand Classic"* (Leigh-on-Sea: F. Lewis, 1947), pp. 25–26; Douglas Cooper, "Richard Wilson's Views of Kew," *BurlM,* 90 (Dec. 1948), 346; W. G. Constable, *Richard Wilson* (Cambridge, Mass.: Harvard University Press, 1953), pp. 179–180, pl. 41b; Alfred Cobban, ed., *The Eighteenth Century* (New York: McGraw-Hill, 1969).

358 Smeaton's Engine at Kew
FREDERIK MAGNUS PIPER 1746–1824
Literature: Boyd, 9:373.

359 Pope's Villa, Twickenham c. 1726
JOSEPH NICKOLLS active 1726–1748
Provenance: Spink & Son, Ltd., London, from whom acquired in 1960.

Exhibitions: Richmond, Virginia Museum of Fine Arts, *Painting in England 1700–1850: Collection of Mr. & Mrs. Paul Mellon,* 1963, no. 15, illus. in vol. of plates p. 144.

Literature: Betts, p. 111; *Country Life,* 83 (May 2, 1963), 989, illus.; John Walker, *Engraved Views of the Thames in English and Chinese Painting* (unpublished article), 1967.

360 The North Terrace of Windsor Castle, Looking West c. 1768
PAUL SANDBY 1730–1809
Provenance: Honorable Sir Richard Molyneux, presented in 1922 to H. R. H. The Princess Royal on the occasion of her marriage; Earl of Harewood, her son; Christie, Manson & Woods sale, London July 13, 1965, lot 173, illus. in cat.; P. & D. Colnaghi & Co., Ltd., from whom acquired, 1965.

Literature: Tancred Borenius, *Catalogue of the Paintings and Drawings at Harewood House* (Oxford: The University Press, 1936), p. 174, no. 429 (it has been confused with its pendant *The North Terrace of Windsor Castle, Looking East* dated 1768 [Borenius 430] also in the Mellon Collection); A. P. Oppé, *The Drawings of Paul and Thomas Sandby in the Collection of His Majesty the King at Windsor Castle* (Oxford and London: The Phaidon Press, Ltd., 1947), p. 20. Of the six views of the

North Terrace Looking West, at Windsor, the closest is Oppé no. 4.

361 View of Painshill 1779–1780
FREDERIK MAGNUS PIPER 1746–1824
Literature: Osvald Sirén, *China and Gardens of Europe of the Eighteenth Century* (New York: The Ronald Press Company, 1950), p. 43, pl. 30.

362 Plan of the Grotto at Painshill 1780
FREDERIK MAGNUS PIPER 1746–1824
Literature: Osvald Sirén, *China and Gardens of Europe of the Eighteenth Century* (New York: The Ronald Press Company, 1950), pp. 44–46; Alison Hodges, "Painshill, Cobham, Surrey: the Grotto," *Garden History*, 3, no. 2 (Spring 1975), 23–25, illus.; Boyd, 9:370.

363 Merton College, Oxford 1771
MICHAEL "ANGELO" ROOKER 1743–1801
Provenance: Fine Art Society, London, from whom acquired, 1960.
Exhibition: Royal Academy of Arts, London, 1771, no. 166; Richmond, Virginia Museum of Fine Arts, *Painting in England 1700–1850: Collection of Mr. and Mrs. Paul Mellon*, 1963, no. 46, illus. in vol. of plates, p. 159.
Literature: *The Oxford Almanack*, 1772, illus.; Helen Mary Petter, *The Oxford Almanacks* (Oxford: University Press, 1974), p. 74.

364 Turin with the Palazzo Reale c. 1745
BERNARDO BELLOTTO 1720–1780
Provenance: A. G. Turner, Hungerford Park, Berkshire.
Exhibitions: The Art Gallery of Toronto; Ottawa, The National Gallery of Canada; Montreal, The Museum of Fine Arts, *Canaletto*, Oct. 17–Nov. 15, 1964, Dec. 4, 1964–Jan. 10, 1965, Jan. 29–Feb. 28, 1965, no. 138, illus. in cat.
Literature: Kimball, "Jefferson and the Arts," 238, 239, 241; W. G. Constable, *Canaletto*, exhib. cat. (Toronto: The Art Gallery of Toronto, 1964), no. 138, illus.; *Bernardo Bellotto, genannt Canaletto*, exhib. cat. (Vienna: Oberes Belvedere, 1965), p. 96; Stefan Kozakiewicz, *Bellotto*, 2 (Greenwich, Conn.: New York Graphic Society Ltd., 1972): 477, no. z365, illus. p. 474; George Green Shackelford, "Thomas Jefferson and the Fine Arts of Northern Italy: 'A Peep into Elysium,'" in *America: the Middle Period; essays in Honor of Bernard Mayo*, ed. by John B. Boles (Charlottesville: The University Press of Virginia, 1973), pp. 14–35; Sowerby, 4:106; "Jefferson's Notes of a Tour into the Southern Parts of

France &c"; Boyd, 11:435; Jefferson to John Page, Jan. 20, 1763; Jefferson to William Short, Apr. 7, 1787; Jefferson to William Short, Apr. 12, 1787; Jefferson to Maria Cosway, July 1, 1787.

365 View of the Façade of the Country House Called Welgelegen... 1791
H. P. SCHOUTEN 1747–1822
Literature: Lipscomb, 17:250; J. A. G. van der Steur, *Oude Gebouwen in Haarlem* (Haarlem: Bohn, 1907), pp. 130–131; G. Lerouge, "Jardins Anglo-Chinois," *Cahier XX* (1788), pls. 16–17.

366 View of the Westerkerk, Amsterdam 1778
ISAAK OUWATER 1750–1793
Provenance: Hirschl and Adler Galleries, Inc., New York from whom acquired 1957.
Exhibitions: Vancouver Art Gallery, British Columbia, *Rembrandt to Van Gogh*, Sept. 17–Oct. 13, 1957, not in cat.; The Minneapolis Institute of Arts, *Dutch Masterpieces of the Eighteenth Century: Paintings & Drawings 1700–1800*, Oct. 7–Nov. 14, 1971, no. 60, illus. in cat. pl. 66 and in col. on cover.
Literature: *The National Gallery of Canada Annual Report, 1957/58*, p. 11; Willem A. Blom, *The National Gallery of Canada Bulletin*, 2, no. 1 (1964), 24–29, illus. in col.; Earl Roger Mandel, *Dutch Masterpieces of the Eighteenth Century: Paintings & Drawings 1700–1800*, exhib. cat. (Minneapolis: The Minneapolis Institute of Art, 1971), p. 76; Boyd, 13:xxv, illus. opp. p. 16.

367 Court Pond at The Hague, near the "Binnenhof" 1762
PAULUS CONSTANTIJN LA FARGUE 1729–1782
Provenance: C. F. L. de Wild, The Hague, 1902.
Exhibitions: Delft, Stedelijk Museum "Het Prinsenhof," *Van Intimiteit to Theater*, Dec. 1951–Jan. 1952, no. 18; Brussels, Palais des Beaux-Arts, I.C.O.M. Exhibition, *Kunst en Stad*, June–Aug. 1963, no. 662, illus. in cat. pl. 5; Delft, Stedelijk Museum "Het Prinsenhof," *De Hugenoten in Nederland*, Nov. 1963–Jan. 1964, no. 230; The Minneapolis Institute of Arts, the Toledo Museum of Art and the Philadelphia Museum of Art, *Dutch Masterpieces from the Eighteenth Century*, Oct. 7–Nov. 14, 1971, Dec. 3, 1971–Jan. 30, 1972, Feb. 17–Mar. 19, 1972, no. 21, illus. in cat. pl. 62.
Literature: H. E. van Gelder, *Kunstgeschiedenis der Nederlanden van de

Middeleeuwen tot onze tijd* (Utrecht: W. de Haan, 1955), p. 358; L. J. van der Haer, "De Werkwijze van Paulus Constantijn," *Die Haghe Jaarboek*, 1960, p. 111, illus. p. 114; Dienst voor Schone Kunsten der Gemeente's-Gravenhage, *Beknopte Gids voor de Afdeling Haagse Historie* (The Hague, 1967), p. 68; Jefferson's *Autobiography*, Ford, 1:101, 114–116.

368 Main Square at Dusseldorf 1791
THOMAS ROWLANDSON 1757–1827
Provenance: Sotheby's, no. 99 in sale March 19, 1958; collection of C. B. Boerner, Dusseldorf; acquired by museum, March 29, 1958.
Literature: Elizabeth Cometti, "Mr. Jefferson Prepares Itinerary," *The Journal of Southern History*, 12, no. 1 (Feb. 1946), 96; John Hayes, *Rowlandson, Watercolours and Drawings* (London: Phaidon Press Limited, 1972), pp. 18, 19, 51, fig. 5; Lipscomb, 17:254.

369 Canapé
Provenance: Purchased during the Revolutionary sales of 1793–1794 by Gouverneur Morris; by descent to the present owners.
Literature: Watson, p. 139, no. 162, pl. 162; Verlet, pp. 162–168, pls. 30a, 30b, 30c, 30d, and 30f; Schreider, figs. 14, 17.

370 Fauteuil à la Reine
Provenance: See no. 369.
Literature: See no. 369.

371 Bergère
Literature: See no. 369.

372 Bergère à la Reine
Provenance: Presented by Lafayette to Dolley Madison, and given by her to Mrs. William Thornton, who passed it on to Dr. Thomas Miller; Dr. Miller's great-granddaughter gave it to the White House in 1972.
Literature: For the similar chair given to Jefferson by Monroe, see Marie Kimball, "The Original Furnishings of the White House, part II," *The Magazine Antiques*, 16, no. 1 (July 1929), 34, fig. 2.

373 Fauteuil en Cabriolet
Provenance: Purchased by Washington from the comte de Moustier. A brass label attached to the top rail of the back is inscribed: "Presented by members of the Washington family to Admiral Shurbrick, afterwards presented by the Admiral to J. B. Cannon, Baltimore, Md."
Literature: For the similar chair given to Jefferson by Monroe, see Marie

Kimball, "More Jefferson Furniture Comes Home to Monticello," *The Magazine Antiques*, 38, no. 1 (July 1940), 20, fig. 3.

374 Fauteuil à la Reine
Provenance: Purchased by James Monroe in Paris between 1794 and 1796 and later sold to Thomas Jefferson; descended in the family to Mrs. J. M. Bloch, who, in 1940, donated the chair to the Thomas Jefferson Memorial Foundation.
Literature: Celia J. Otto, "French Furniture for American Patriots," *Antiques*, 79, no. 4 (Apr. 1961), 370–373, fig. 371; James A. Bear, Jr., "The Furniture and Furnishings of Monticello," *Antiques*, 52, no. 1 (July 1972), 118, pl. III; Watson, pp. 139–140, pl. 165.

375 Boiseries
CLAUDE-NICOLAS LEDOUX 1736–1806
Provenance: Bouvet de Vezelay to Edward Preble Deacon, 1848; to Boston Athenaeum, 1879; later to the Museum of Fine Arts, Boston.
Literature: Watson, "Boston," pp. 481, 482; Raval, p. 49, figs. 22–24; Emile Kauffman, *Three Revolutionary Architects* (Philadelphia: American Philosophical Society, 1952), pp. 480–481; Yvan Christ and Ionel Schein, *Ledoux, l'oeuvre et ses rêves* (Paris: Chêne, 1971), pls. 18, 19.

376 Framed Panel of embroidery
Provenance: See no. 369.
Literature: See no. 369.

377 Bureau à Cylindre
Provenance: Probably from the collection of Gouverneur Morris. Mr. Louis Schreider III has given some reason for thinking that Morris may have bought it in Paris between April and July 1792; then by descent to the present owners.
Literature: Schreider, p. 478, fig. 7.

378 Commode
JEAN FERDINAND SCHWERDFEGER active 1786–after 1799
Provenance: From the Swan collection. For history see no. 381 (text).
Literature: Richard H. Randall, Jr., *Bulletin of the Boston Museum*, 59, no. 316 (1961), 36–38, figs. 5, 6.

379 Console
ADAM WEISWEILER active 1778–after 1810
Provenance: Bequest of Miss Elizabeth Howard Bartol, from the Swan Collection (see no. 381, text, for history).
Literature: Sir Guy Francis Laking, *The Furniture of Windsor Castle*

(London: Bradbury, Agnew and Co., 1905), pl. 41.

380 Fauteuils en cabriolet
Provenance: Bequest of Miss Elizabeth Howard Bartol (screen), and gift of Mrs. Edward Law, Mrs. Helen Howard Hudson Whipple and Mrs. Alice Weyland Hudson White.
Literature: Howard C. Rice, Jr., "James Swan, Agent of the French Republic 1794–1796," *New England Quarterly*, Sept. 1937, pp. 464–486; Howard C. Rice, Jr., "Notes on the Swan Furniture," *Bulletin of the Boston Museum of Fine Arts*, June 1940, pp. 43–48; Verlet, pp. 179–180; Watson, "Boston," pp. 477–479.

381 Firescreen
Provenance: See no. 380.
Literature: See no. 380.

382 Pair of Firedogs (Feux)
Provenance: Bequest of Miss Elizabeth Howard Bartol, from the Swan Collection. For history see no. 381 (text).
Exhibition: Boston, Museum of Fine Arts, *Paul Revere, Boston 1738–1818*, Apr. 18–Oct. 12, 1975, exhib. cat. p. 161, repr., p. 236.
Literature: *George IV and the Arts of France* (London: The Queen's Gallery, 1966), exhib. cat. p. 72; Watson, "Boston," p. 479 repr.; Svend Eriksen, *Early Neo-Classicism in France* (London: Faber and Faber, Ltd., 1974), pl. 328.

383 Pair of vases
Provenance: Bequests of Miss Elizabeth Howard Bartol and the heirs of Helen L. Jacques, to the Museum of Fine Arts, Boston. From the Swan collection. For history see no. 381.
Literature: Pierre Verlet, "Some Historical Sèvres Porcelains Preserved in the United States," *AQ*, 17 (Autumn 1954), 238–241, repr. 240; Howard C. Rice, Jr., "A Pair of Sèvres Vases," *Bulletin of the Boston Museum of Fine Arts*, Summer 1957, pp. 31–37; Watson, "Boston," pp. 475, 479.

384 Mantle clock
Provenance: Bequest of Miss Elizabeth Howard Bartol to the Museum of Fine Arts, Boston. From the Swan Collection, see no. 381 for history.

385 Aristotle surprised by Alexander while pulling the Chariot of Aspasia c. 1792
Provenance: Acquired by Gouverneur Morris during the Revolution; by family descent to the present owner.
Literature: J. Badin, *La Manufacture de Tapisseries de Beauvais depuis les*

origines jusqu'à nos jours (Paris: Société de Propagation des Livres d'art, 1909), pp. 40, 67; Schreider, pp. 472, 476.

386 Alcibiades surprised by Socrates playing among the Women c. 1792
Provenance: See no. 385.
Literature: See no. 385.

387 Long case clock
Provenance: Presumably acquired by Gouverneur Morris during his residence in Paris, 1789–1794; by family descent to the present owner.
Literature: Schreider, p. 474, fig. 9; F. J. B. Watson, *Wallace Collection Catalogues: Furniture* (London: The Wallace Collection, 1956), cat. no. F 270, pp. 133–134, pl. 49.

388 Governor's House, first floor plan c. 1780
THOMAS JEFFERSON 1743–1826
Provenance: Collection of W. H. Loudermilk, Washington, D.C.; purchased by the University of Virginia, March 15, 1940.
Literature: Nichols, pp. 7, 39, 40, 47.

389 Governor's House, second floor plan c. 1780
THOMAS JEFFERSON 1743–1826
Provenance: See no. 388.
Literature: See no. 388.

390 Study for Governor's House 1780
THOMAS JEFFERSON 1743–1826
Literature: See no. 388.

391 Study for Governor's House c. 1780
THOMAS JEFFERSON 1743–1826
Literature: See no. 388.

392 Study for the plan of a Governor's House c. 1779
THOMAS JEFFERSON 1743–1826
Literature: See no. 388.

393 Model of the Virginia Capitol, Richmond 1786
BLOQUET, active late 18th century
Provenance: Property of the Commonwealth of Virginia since its construction.
Literature: Jefferson to James Buchanan and William Hay, Aug. 13, 1785; Jefferson to James Madison, Sept. 20, 1785; Kimball, *Jefferson, Architect*, pp. 142–148; Kimball, "Richmond," 303–310; Kimball, *The Scene of Europe*, pp. 69–77; Karl Lehmann, *Thomas Jefferson, American Humanist* (New York: Macmillan, 1947), pp. 55, 164–165, repr. p. 162; Nichols, p. 39; Thomas J. McCormick, "Virginia's Gallic Godfather," *Arts in Virginia*, 4, no. 2 (Winter 1964),

2–3, repr.; Thomas J. McCormick, "Charles-Louis Clérisseau and the Roman Revival" (Ph.D. dissertation, Princeton University, 1970), pp. 212–223, 383–388.

394 Plan of the first floor of the Virginia Capitol
THOMAS JEFFERSON 1743–1826
Literature: See no. 393.

395 Plan of the second floor of the Virginia Capitol
THOMAS JEFFERSON 1743–1826
Literature: See no. 393.

396 Plan of the first floor of the Virginia Capitol
THOMAS JEFFERSON 1743–1826
Literature: See no. 393.

397 Side elevation of the Virginia Capitol
THOMAS JEFFERSON 1743–1826
Literature: See no. 393.

398 Side elevation of the Virginia Capitol
THOMAS JEFFERSON 1743–1826
Literature: See no. 393.

399 Front elevation of the Virginia Capitol
THOMAS JEFFERSON 1743–1826
Literature: See no. 393.

400 Study for the plan of a rotunda house, probably a new governor's palace for Williamsburg 1772–1773
THOMAS JEFFERSON 1743–1826
Literature: Jefferson to James Oldham, Dec. 24, 1804, quoted in Sowerby, 4:360; Kimball, "Williamsburg," 115–120; Nichols, pp. 7, 44, 47.

401 Plan of a prison, description
FRANÇOIS-PHILIPPE CHARPENTIER 1734–1817, after Pierre-Gabriel Bugniet d. 1806
Literature: James Buchanan and William Hay to Jefferson, Mar. 20, 1785; Jefferson to James Buchanan and William Hay, Aug. 13, 1785; Jefferson to Buchanan and Hay, Jan. 26, 1786; Jefferson to Governor James Wood, Mar. 31, 1797 (Virginia Archives); Lipscomb, 1:69; Marius Audin and Eugène Vial, *Dictionnaire des Artistes et ouvriers d'art du Lyonnais* (Paris: Bibliothèque d'Art et d'Architecture, 1918), 1:136, s.v. *Bugniet*; Howard C. Rice, Jr., "A French Source of Jefferson's Plan for the Prison at Richmond," *Journal of the Society of Architectural Historians*, 12, no. 4 (Dec. 1953), 28–30; Kimball, *Jefferson, Architect*, pp. 43–45.

402 First floor plan of a prison
FRANÇOIS-PHILIPPE CHARPENTIER 1734–1817, after Pierre-Gabriel Bugniet d. 1806
Literature: See no. 401.

403 Plan of a prison, elevation
FRANÇOIS-PHILIPPE CHARPENTIER 1734–1817, after Pierre-Gabriel Bugniet d. 1806
Literature: See no. 401.

404 Plan of a prison, cross-section
FRANÇOIS-PHILIPPE CHARPENTIER 1734–1817, after Pierre-Gabriel Bugniet d. 1806
Literature: See no. 401.

405 A prison with a cell for solitary confinement
THOMAS JEFFERSON 1743–1826
Literature: Thomas Jefferson, Autobiography (Ford, 1:63–65); Howard C. Rice, Jr., "A French Source of Jefferson's Plan for the Prison at Richmond," *Journal of the Society of Architectural Historians*, 12 (Dec. 1953), 28–29; Nichols, pp. 6, 45, 48.

406 Ground Plan of the Richmond Penitentiary 1797
BENJAMIN HENRY LATROBE 1764–1820
Provenance: In the possession of the Commonwealth of Virginia since the building of the penitentiary.
Literature: Hamlin, pp. 120–126, 534, 560 and pl. 11; M. Demetz and Abel Blouet, *Rapports à Monsieur le Comte de Montolivet sur les penitenciers des Etats-Unis* (Paris: Imprimerie Royal, 1837), pp. 42–44; Howard C. Rice, Jr., "A French Source of Jefferson's Plan for the Prison at Richmond," *Journal of the Society of Architectural Historians*, 12, no. 4 (Dec. 1953), 28–30; Kimball, "Richmond," 115–120, 303–310; for various early views of the prison see Alexander Weddell, *Richmond, Virginia, in Old Prints, 1737–1887* (Richmond: Johnson, 1932).

407 Internal Elevations of the Infirmary and Women's Court, and Perspective of the Gate, Richmond Penitentiary 1797
BENJAMIN HENRY LATROBE 1764–1820
Provenance: In the possession of the Commonwealth of Virginia since the building of the penitentiary.
Exhibition: London, Royal Academy and the Victoria and Albert Museum, *The Age of Neo-classicism*, Sept. 7–Nov. 19, 1972, p. 571, no. 1193.
Literature: Hamlin, pp. 120–126, 534, 560; M. Demetz and Abel Blouet, *Rapports à Monsieur le Comte de Montalivet sur les penitenciers des Etats-Unis* (Paris: Imprimerie Royal, 1837), pp. 42ff.; Howard C. Rice, Jr.,

"A French Source of Jefferson's Plan for the Prison at Richmond," *Journal of the Society of Architectural Historians*, 12, no. 4 (Dec. 1953), 28–30; Kimball, "Richmond," 115–120, 303–310; Fiske Kimball, "Early Prisons," *Journal of the Society of Architectural Historians*, 12, no. 4 (Dec. 1953), 26–28. For various early views of the prison see Alexander Wilbourne Weddell, *Richmond, Virginia, in Old Prints, 1737–1887* (Richmond: Johnson, 1932).

408 View of the City of Richmond from the South side of the James River 1798
BENJAMIN HENRY LATROBE 1764–1820
Provenance: By family descent to Mrs. Ferdinand C. Latrobe, II, Baltimore. Maryland Historical Society, Baltimore.
Literature: Latrobe's Sketchbook, III-33a, Papers of Benjamin Henry Latrobe, Maryland Historical Society, Baltimore, Maryland; Malone, *Jefferson the Virginian*, p. 302.

409 View of Richmond from Bushrod Washington's Island 1796
BENJAMIN HENRY LATROBE 1764–1820
Provenance: By family descent to Mrs. Ferdinand C. Latrobe, II, Baltimore. Maryland Historical Society, Baltimore.
Literature: Boyd, 1:598–602, 2:271–272; Kimball, "Richmond," 303–310.

410 Preliminary study for the competition design. Elevation 1792
THOMAS JEFFERSON 1743–1826
Literature: Kimball, *Jefferson, Architect*, pl. 126.

411 Preliminary study for the competition design. Plans 1792
THOMAS JEFFERSON 1743–1826
Literature: Kimball, *Jefferson, Architect*, pl. 125; Padover, pp. 348–349.

412 Original competition drawing. Elevation 1792
THOMAS JEFFERSON 1743–1826
Literature: Desmond Guinness and Julius Sadler, Jr., *Mr. Jefferson, Architect* (New York: Viking Press, 1973), p. 38; Fiske Kimball, "The Genesis of the White House," *Century Magazine*, 95 (Feb. 1918), 523–526; Kimball, *Jefferson, Architect*, pl. 129; Padover, repr. opp. p. 348; *The White House. An Historic Guide*, 12th ed., rev. (Washington, D.C.: White House Historical Association, 1975), p. 108; Thomas Jefferson Papers, series three (pertaining to Washington, D.C.), Manuscripts Division, Library of Congress; Fiske Kimball and Wells Bennett, "The Competition for the Federal Buildings,

1792–1793," *Journal of the American Institute of Architects*, 1, no. 1 (Jan. 1919), 9–11 and 2, no. 3 (Mar. 1919), 98–102.

413 Original competition drawing. First floor plan 1792
THOMAS JEFFERSON 1743–1826
Literature: Kimball, *Jefferson, Architect*, pl. 127, and references cited at no. 412.

414 Original competition drawing. Second floor plan 1792
THOMAS JEFFERSON 1743–1826
Literature: Kimball, *Jefferson, Architect*, pl. 128, and references cited at no. 412.

415 Original competition drawing. Third floor plan 1792
THOMAS JEFFERSON 1743–1826
Literature: Kimball, *Jefferson, Architect*, pl. 128, and references cited at no. 412.

416 Study for a rotunda plan house. Plan c. 1801–1803
THOMAS JEFFERSON 1743–1826
Provenance: Collection of W. H. Loudermilk, Washington, D.C.; purchased by the University of Virginia March 15, 1940.
Literature: Nichols, p. 43.

417 A rotunda house. Drawing exercise. Elevation and plan 1803
ROBERT MILLS 1781–1855
Literature: Helen M. Pierce Gallagher, *Robert Mills, Architect of the Washington Monument, 1781–1855* (New York: Columbia University Press, 1935), pp. 85–87 repr. opp. p. 88; Desmond Guinness and Julius Sadler, Jr., *Mr. Jefferson, Architect* (New York: Viking Press, 1973), pp. 37–40; Kimball, *Jefferson, Architect*, pl. 181; Nichols, pl. 16 and p. 43.

418 A rotunda house. Drawing exercise. Second floor plan 1803
ROBERT MILLS 1781–1855
Provenance: Collection of Graham Clark, Charlottesville; acquired by the University of Virginia June 14, 1940.
Literature: See no. 417.

419 A rotunda house. Drawing exercise. Section 1803
ROBERT MILLS 1781–1855
Provenance: See no. 418.
Literature: Nichols, p. 43; Desmond Guinness and Julius Sadler, Jr., *Mr. Jefferson, Architect* (New York: Viking Press, 1973), pp. 37–40.

420 Original competition drawing. Elevation 1792
JAMES HOBAN c. 1762–1831
Literature: Glenn Brown, *History of

the United States Capitol*, 2 vols. (Washington, D.C.: Government Printing Office, 1900–1903), 1:6, 94–95; Wilhelm B. Bryan, *A History of the National Capital*, 2 vols. (New York: The Macmillan Co., 1914), 1:194–195; Commissioners Letter Book, 1 (1791–1793): 96, 99, in the National Archives; Martin I. J. Griffin, "James Hoban, the Architect and Builder of the White House and the Superintendent of the Building of the Capitol at Washington," *American Catholic Historical Researches*, N.S.3, no. 1 (Jan. 1907), 35–52; Francis W. Kervick, "James Hoban," in his *Architects in America of Catholic Tradition* (Rutland, Vt.: Charles E. Tuttle Co., 1962), pp. 65–68; Fiske Kimball, "The Genesis of the White House," *Century Magazine*, 95 (Feb. 1918), 524–526; *DAB*, 5:91–92; Kimball, *Jefferson, Architect* pp. 54, 176–179; *Letters Received by the Commissioners*, 1 (1791–1792): nos. 97–98, in the National Archives; Ethel Lewis, *The White House. An Informal History of Its Architecture, Interiors, and Gardens* (New York: Dodd, Mead & Co., 1937), pp. 23–28; Charles Moore, "Historical Notes on the White House," in *Restoration of the White House* (Washington, D.C.: Government Printing Office, 1903), pp. 43–44; Frederick D. Owen, "The First Government Architect: James Hoban, of Charleston, S.C.," *Architectural Record*, 11, no. 2 (Oct. 1901), 581–589; Alfred C. Prime, *The Arts and Crafts in Philadelphia, Maryland, and South Carolina*, 2 vols. (Philadelphia: The Walpole Society, 1929–1932), 1:295, 2:293; *Proceedings of the Commissioners*, 1 (1791–1795): 123–124, in the National Archives; Beatrice St. Julien Ravenel, "James Hoban," in her *Architects of Charleston*, 2d ed., rev. (Charleston, S.C.: Carolina Art Association, 1964), pp. 76–80; *The White House. An Historic Guide*, 12th ed., rev. (Washington, D.C.: White House Historical Association, 1975), pp. 106–110.

421 Original competition drawing. Principal floor plan and section 1792
JAMES HOBAN c. 1762–1831
Literature: See no. 420.

422 Original competition drawing. Front elevation and principal floor plan, scheme A 1792
JACOB SMALL, JR. 1772–1851
Literature: Robert L. Alexander, "William F. Small, 'Architect of the City,' " *Journal of the Society of Architectural Historians*, 20, no. 2 (May 1961), 63–77; Wilbur F. Coyle, *The Mayors of Baltimore* (Baltimore: Baltimore Municipal

Journal, 1919), pp. 33–35; "Recollections of George A. Frederick" (Unpublished MS, 1912, deposited at the Maryland Historical Society Library), pp. 15–16; "Jacob Small" material, Dielman and Hayward Files, Maryland Historical Society Library; Joseph F. A. Jackson, "Development of American Architecture. VII: South of the Mason and Dixon Line," *Building*, 4, no. 11 (Nov. 1924), 18–19; Fiske Kimball and Wells Bennett, "The Competition for the Federal Buildings, 1792–1793. III: The Competitors and Their Designs," *Journal of the American Institute of Architects*, 7 (May 1919), 202–203, 205, 206, 207; J. Thomas Scharf, *Chronicles of Baltimore* (Baltimore: Turnbull Brothers, 1874), pp. 354, 378, 421, 432.

423 Original competition drawing. Front elevation and principal floor plan, scheme B 1792
JACOB SMALL, JR. 1772–1851
Literature: See no. 422.

424 Original competition drawing. Front elevation and principal floor plan, scheme C 1792
JACOB SMALL, JR. 1772–1851
Literature: See no. 422.

425 Original competition drawing. Front elevation and principal floor plan, scheme D 1792
JACOB SMALL, JR. 1772–1851
Literature: See no. 422.

426 Original competition drawing. Front elevation and principal floor plan 1792
JAMES DIAMOND died c. 1797
Literature: Fiske Kimball and Wells Bennett, "The Competition for the Federal Buildings, 1792–1793. IV," *Journal of the American Institute of Architects*, 7, no. 8 (Aug. 1919), 359–361; Alfred C. Prime, Arts and Crafts in Philadelphia, Maryland, and South Carolina. Part I, 1721–1785 (Philadelphia: Walpole Society, 1929), p. 294; William S. Rusk, "Early Maryland Architects," *Americana*, 35, no. 2 (Apr. 1941), 268–269.

427 Original competition drawing. Section and rear elevation 1792
JAMES DIAMOND died c. 1797
Literature: See no. 426.

428 Original competition drawing. Ground and second floor plans 1792
JAMES DIAMOND died c. 1797
Literature: See no. 426.

429 Original competition drawing. Front elevation and principal floor plan 1792
ANDREW MAYFIELD CARSHORE

active late 18th century
Literature: "Andrew Mayfield Carshore," in *Biographical Review. A Volume Containing Biographical Sketches of the Leading Citizens of Columbia County* (Boston: Biographical Review Publishing Co., 1894), p. 50; Edward A. Collier, *A History of Old Kinderhook* (New York and London: G. P. Putnam's Sons, 1914), pp. 189, 283–284; Franklin Ellis, *History of Columbia County, New York* (Philadelphia: Everts and Ensign, 1878), pp. 195, 242; Elizabeth L. Gebhard, *The Parsonage Between Two Manors* (Hudson, N.Y.: Hudson Press, 1909), p. 45; Sherwood B. Speed, "The Hudson Academy," *Bulletin of the Columbia County Historical Society*, no. 54 (Oct. 1941), 5; F. H. Webb, *Claverack Old and New* (Private publication c. 1892), p. 37; M. Williams, *Columbia County at the End of the Century: A Historical Record of Its Foundation*, 2 vols. (Hudson, N.Y.: Record Printing & Publishing Co., 1900), 1:59, 150–151, 374, 465.

430 Original competition drawing. Perspective drawing and elevation of front door 1792
ANDREW MAYFIELD CARSHORE
active late 18th century
Literature: See no. 429.

431 Original competition drawing. Roof plan and elevations of canopy and hall doorway 1792
ANDREW MAYFIELD CARSHORE
active late 18th century
Literature: See no. 429.

432 East Front of the President's House 1807
BENJAMIN HENRY LATROBE 1764–1820
Provenance: Collection of Library of Congress since early 19th century.
Exhibition: Washington, The Library of Congress, *District of Columbia Sesquicentennial of the Establishment of the Permanent Seat of the Government*, Apr. 24, 1950–Apr. 24, 1951, no. 244.
Literature: Hamlin, pp. 300–301; Margaret Brown Klapthor, *Benjamin Latrobe and Dolley Madison Decorate the White House 1809–1811* (Washington: Smithsonian Institution, 1965); Kimball, *Jefferson, Architect*, pp. 66–67.

433 South Elevation of the President's House 1817
BENJAMIN HENRY LATROBE 1764–1820
Provenance: Collection of Library of Congress since early 19th century.
Exhibition: Washington, The Library of Congress, *District of Columbia Sesquicentennial of the Establishment of the Permanent Seat of Govern-*

ment, Apr. 24, 1950–Apr. 24, 1951, no. 245.
Literature: Hamlin, pp. 293–295, 300; Kimball, *Jefferson, Architect*, pp. 66–67.

434 Study for the capitol building, Washington 1792
THOMAS JEFFERSON 1743–1826
Literature: Jefferson to Major Pierre Charles L'Enfant, Apr. 10, 1791; Malone, *Rights of Man*, pp. 371–373; Nichols, pp. 5, 6, 43, 48.

435 Tracing by Jefferson of Hallet's modifications of Thornton's design of the capitol, Washington 1796–1803
THOMAS JEFFERSON 1743–1826
Literature: Jefferson to Daniel Carroll, Feb. 1, 1793 (Lipscomb, 9:18); Jefferson to George Washington, July 17, 1793 (Padover, pp. 184–185); Padover, pp. 171, 387; Nichols, pp. 5, 6, 43, 47; Kimball, *Jefferson, Architect*, p. 132.

436 Elevation of the North Wing of the Capitol 1795–1796
WILLIAM THORNTON 1759–1828
Provenance: Collection of Library of Congress since founded.
Literature: Brown; Fiske Kimball and Wells Bennett, "William Thornton and the Design of the U.S. Capitol," *AS*, 1 (1923).

437 West Elevation of the Capitol at Washington
STEPHEN HALLET active 1789–1796
Provenance: Collection of Library of Congress since its founding.
Literature: Brown; Fiske Kimball and Wells Bennett, "William Thornton and the Design of the United States Capitol," *AS*, 1 (1923), 76–92; Jefferson to Dr. Stewart, or to all the Gentlemen, Jan. 31, 1793 (Lipscomb, 9:17–18).

438 U.S. capitol in the course of construction 1806
BENJAMIN HENRY LATROBE 1764–1820
Provenance: By family descent to Mrs. Ferdinand C. Latrobe, II, Baltimore. Maryland Historical Society, Baltimore.
Literature: Hamlin, pp. 257, 259–286; Paul Foote Norton, "Latrobe, Jefferson and the National Capitol," Ph.D. diss., Princeton University, 1952, pp. 152–158; Brown, pp. 4–13.

439 View of the Capitol 1800
WILLIAM BIRCH 1755–1834
Literature: DAB, 2:284.

440 Interior view of the Halle aux Bleds
Literature: Luc-Vincent Thiéry,

Guide des amateurs et des étrangers voyageurs à Paris, 1 (Paris: Hardouin & Gattey, 1787): 413–419; Jefferson to Benjamin H. Latrobe, Sept. 8, 1805 (District of Columbia Letters and Papers on the Site and Buildings for the Federal City, Manuscript Division, Library of Congress); Gabriel Vauthier, "La Halle au Blé, 1758–1811," *Bulletin de la Société d'Histoire de Paris*, 55 (1926), 62–68; Paul Foote Norton, "Latrobe's Ceiling for the Hall of Representatives," *Journal of the Society of Architectural Historians*, 10, no. 2 (1951), 5–10; Paul Foote Norton, "Jefferson's Plans for Moth-Balling the Frigates," *U.S. Naval Institute Proceedings*, 82, no. 7 (July 1956), 736–741; Howard C. Rice, Jr., *Thomas Jefferson's Paris* (Princeton: Princeton University Press, 1976), chap. 2.

441 Preliminary section of the House of Representatives 1804
BENJAMIN HENRY LATROBE 1764–1820
Exhibition: Washington, The Library of Congress, *District of Columbia Sesquicentennial of the Establishment of the Permanent Seat of Government*, Apr. 24, 1950–Apr. 24, 1951, no. 162.
Literature: Jefferson to Benjamin Henry Latrobe, Sept. 8, 1805 (Thomas Jefferson Collection, District of Columbia Miscellany, Library of Congress no. 849); Benjamin Henry Latrobe to Jefferson, May 21, 1807 (Letterbooks, Maryland Historical Society); Brown, 1: pl. 42; Paul Foote Norton, "Latrobe's Ceiling for the Hall of Representatives," *Journal of the Society of Architectural Historians*, 10, no. 2 (May 1951), 5–10; Hamlin, p. 272, pl. 22; Kimball, *Jefferson, Architect*, pp. 64–65.

442 Cross section of the House of Representatives 1804
BENJAMIN HENRY LATROBE 1764–1820
Literature: See no. 441.

443 Ceiling of the House of Representatives 1805
BENJAMIN HENRY LATROBE 1764–1820
Exhibition: Washington, The Library of Congress, *District of Columbia Sesquicentennial of the Establishment of the Permanent Seat of the Government*, Apr. 24, 1950–Apr. 24, 1951, no. 164.
Literature: Benjamin Henry Latrobe to Jefferson, May 21, 1807 (Letterbooks, Maryland Historical Society); Brown, 1:41–42; Paul Foote Norton, "Latrobe's Ceiling for the Hall of Representatives," *Journal of the Society of Architectural Historians*, 10, no. 2 (May 1951), 5–10.

444 Principal story of the United States capitol 1806
BENJAMIN HENRY LATROBE 1764–1820
Exhibition: Washington, The Library of Congress, *District of Columbia Sesquicentennial of the Establishment of the Permanent Seat of the Government*, Apr. 24, 1950–Apr. 24, 1951, no. 179.
Literature: Padover, pp. 473–476; Hamlin, p. 453.

445 View of the capitol from my shop 1813
BENJAMIN HENRY LATROBE 1764–1820
Provenance: By family descent to Mrs. Ferdinand C. Latrobe, II, Baltimore. Maryland Historical Society, Baltimore.
Literature: Jefferson to Benjamin Henry Latrobe, July 12, 1812 (Lipscomb, 8:178); Charles E. Fairman, *Art and Artists of the Capitol of the United States of America* (Washington: United States Government Printing Office, 1927), pp. 39–41; Hamlin, pp. 291–292 (appropriations) and pp. 449–452 (resignation).

446 Letter concerning the tobacco plant and the capital derived from it. November 5, 1816
BENJAMIN HENRY LATROBE 1764–1820
Literature: Brown, 1:45, 52, pls. 53, 69; Charles E. Fairman, *Art and Artists of the Capitol of the United States of America* (Washington: United States Government Printing Office, 1927), p. 29; Padover, pp. 394–396, 462, 479, 481–483, 485, 490; Hamlin, pp. 270, 446, 454, 553; Nichols, p. 43.

447 Sketch for a classical figure
BENJAMIN HENRY LATROBE 1764–1820
Provenance: By family descent to Mrs. Ferdinand C. Latrobe, II, Baltimore.
Literature: Hamlin, pp. 267–270; Charles E. Fairman, *Art and Artists of the United States Capitol*, Senate Document 95 (Washington: Government Printing Office, 1927), pp. 1–18.

448 Egyptian Design of the Library of Congress
BENJAMIN HENRY LATROBE 1764–1820
Exhibition: Washington, The Library of Congress, *District of Columbia Sesquicentennial of the Establishment of the Permanent Seat of Government*, Apr. 24, 1950–Apr. 24, 1951, no. 180.
Literature: Jefferson to Samuel H. Smith, Sept. 21, 1814 (Lipscomb, 14: 190–194); Benjamin Henry Latrobe, *Message from the President of the United States Transmitting a Report of the Public Buildings of the United States, in the City of Washington,*

December 1, 1808 (City of Washington: A. and G. Way, Printers,
1808), p. 9; Brown, 1: pl. 47; I. Frary,
*Thomas Jefferson: Architect and
Builder* (Richmond: Garrett and
Massie, 1931), p. 4; Hamlin, pl. 25,
p. 288.

**449 Elevation and Plan for the
Capitol** 1832
ANDREW JACKSON DAVIS 1803–1892,
after George Hadfield, 1763–1826
Provenance: From the Machen
collection.
Literature: DAB, 8:76; Sizer, pp. 176–
177; *Documentary History of the
Construction and Development of the
U.S. Capitol Building and Grounds*
(Washington: United States Govern-
ment Printing Office, 1904), pp. 26–27.

**450 Elevation and Plan of the
City Hall, Washington** 1832
ANDREW JACKSON DAVIS 1803–1892,
after George Hadfield, 1763–1826
Provenance: From the Machen
collection.
Literature: DAB, 8:76–77; H. F.
Cunningham, J. A. Younger, and
J. W. Smith, *Measured Drawings of
Georgian Architecture in the District
of Columbia, 1750–1820* (New York:
Architectural Book Publishing Com-
pany, 1914); Journal of A. J. Davis
(ms.), vol. 2, leaf 9, verso: "1832 at
Washington, in the Capitol, made
highly finished copies from Geo.
Hadfield," Davis Collection, Metro-
politan Museum of Art; Sizer, p. 177.

**451 Elevation and Plan of the
City Hall (Corinthian Order)** 1832
ANDREW JACKSON DAVIS 1803–1892,
after George Hadfield, 1763–1826
Provenance: From the Machen
collection.
Literature: Helen Bullock, *My Head
and My Heart* (New York: G. P.
Putnam's Sons, 1945), p. 181, quotes
Jefferson's letter to Mrs. Cosway,
Oct. 24, 1822.

452 Christ Church, Charlottesville
Literature: Randall, 3:672.

**453 The Church of Saint-Philippe
du Roule, longitudinal section**
After JEAN-FRANÇOIS CHALGRIN
1739–1811
Exhibition: London, The Royal
Academy and the Victoria and Albert
Museum, *The Age of Neo-classicism,*
Sept. 9–Nov. 19, 1972, nos. 1038,
1039, p. 510.
Literature: Louis Hautecoeur, *His-
toire de l'architecture classique en
France,* 4 (Paris: A. Picard, 1952):
213–216, 219, 279, 341, 342, 348,
350, 353, 355–356, 473, 533.

**454 The Church of Saint-Philippe
du Roule, latitudinal section**
After JEAN-FRANÇOIS CHALGRIN
1739–1811
Exhibition: See no. 453.
Literature: See no. 453.

455 A Church with Tuscan Portico
c. 1820
CORNELIA JEFFERSON RANDOLPH(?)
1799–1871
Provenance: Former collection of the
Rotunda Restoration Committee,
University of Virginia.
Literature: Nichols, p. 44.

456 Thomas Jefferson c. 1799
BENJAMIN HENRY LATROBE(?)
1764–1820
Provenance: It is presumed that this
sketch passed at the time of the
architect's death in 1820, as part of
his papers, into the hands of his son,
John H. B. Latrobe. On the death
of John H. B. Latrobe in 1891 the
papers were given by his widow to
John E. Semmes. On the latter's death
in 1925 the papers were divided
among his children, the portion containing this portrait becoming the
property of Miss Frances C. Semmes.
In 1953 the portrait was presented
to The Maryland Historical Society.
Exhibition: The Maryland Historical
Society; Charlottesville, The University of Virginia Museum of Fine Arts,
*The Life Portraits of Thomas Jeffer-
son,* Apr. 12–16, 1962.
Literature: Kimball, "Life Portraits,"
523–524; *Maryland History Notes,* 11,
no. 3 (Nov. 1953); Hamlin, p. 93
and pl. 37; Bush, pp. 46–48.
Copies: This likeness was redrawn by
an unidentified copyist and reproduced
in John E. Semmes, *John H. B.
Latrobe and His Times (1803–1891)*
(Baltimore: The Norman, Remington
Co., 1917), opp. p. 4.

457 Benjamin Henry Latrobe c. 1804
CHARLES WILLSON PEALE 1741–1827
Provenance: Probably the picture
painted for the Peale Museum;
Thomas & Sons sale, Philadelphia,
Oct. 6, 1854, lot 146; Ferdinand C.
Latrobe; Mrs. Ferdinand C. Latrobe.
Literature: Charles Coleman Sellers,
*Portraits and Miniatures by Charles
Willson Peale* (Philadelphia: Ameri-
can Philosophical Society, 1952),
no. 461, p. 122, fig. 289; Hamlin,
p. 140.

458 James Hoban
Provenance: By family descent to the
present owner.
Exhibition: On loan to the Department of State, Washington.
Literature: Kimball, pp. 54, 176–
179; *DAB,* 9:91–92.

459 William Thornton c. 1799 or
1804
CHARLES-BALTHAZAR-JULIEN FÉVRET
DE SAINT-MÉMIN 1770–1852
Literature: Elias Dexter, *Saint-Mémin
Collection* (New York: E. Dexter,
1862); Fiske Kimball and Wells
Bennett, "William Thornton and the
United States Capitol," *AS,* 1 (1923),
76–92; Mary Martin, "The Physi-
onotrace in France and America,"
Connoisseur, 74 (1926), 144–152;
I. T. Frary, *They Built the Capitol*
(Richmond: Garrett and Massie,
1940); Malone, *The Rights of Man*
(Boston: Little, Brown, and Co.,
1951), pp. 384–387; Pierre Quarre,
*Charles-Balthazar-Julien Févret de
Saint-Mémin, archeologue, Con-
servateur du Musée de Dijon* (Dijon:
Musée de Dijon, 1965); Alfred
Nicolson, "Dr. Thornton, who prac-
ticed everything but medicine,"
Smithsonian Magazine, 2, no. 1 (Apr.
1971), 66–75.

**460 Elevation of the first executive
office for the Treasury Department,
Washington** 1796–1797
GEORGE HADFIELD 1763–1826
Literature: Kimball, *Jefferson, Archi-
tect,* pp. 61, 67, 179; *DAB,* 8:76;
Brown, pp. 21, 23, 95; Boyd, 15:351,
413, 414; W. B. Bryan, *A History
of the National Capitol,* 1 (New
York: The Macmillan Company,
1914–1916): 306; *History of Public
Buildings* (Washington, D.C.: United
States Government Printing Office,
1901), p. 83; Michael Richman,
"George Hadfield (1763–1826): His
Contribution to the Greek Revival
in America," *Journal of the Society of
Architectural Historians,* 32, no. 3
(Oct. 1974), 234, 235; Sizer, p. 177;
James Stuart and Nicholas Revett,
Antiquities of Athens, 2 (London:
J. Haberkorn, 1787): pls. 1, 3, 4, 7, 8,
9, pp. 16–22; Benjamin H. Latrobe,
Journal (New York: D. Appleton,
1905), p. 133.

**462 Final first-floor plan of the
first version of Monticello** after
April 1771
THOMAS JEFFERSON 1743–1826
Exhibition: Boston, Massachusetts
Historical Society, 1960.
Literature: Kimball, *Jefferson, Archi-
tect,* pp. 25, 124, fig. 24; Kimball,
The Road to Glory, pp. 157, 158;
Nichols, p. 35; Waterman, p. 390.

**463 Final elevation of the first version
of Monticello** after April 1771
THOMAS JEFFERSON 1743–1826
Literature: Kimball, *Jefferson, Archi-
tect,* pp. 25, 123, fig. 23; Kimball,
The Road to Glory, pp. 153, 154;
Nichols, p. 35; William H. Pierson,
American Buildings and Their Archi-

tects, the Colonial and Neoclassical
Styles (Garden City, New York:
Doubleday, 1970), p. 293, fig. 210;
Waterman, p. 393.

464 Early plan for Monticello
1768–1770
THOMAS JEFFERSON 1743–1826
Literature: Kimball, "Williamsburg,"
p. 116; Kimball, *Jefferson, Architect,*
pp. 22–24, 118, 119, fig. 6; Kimball,
The Road to Glory, pp. 150, 151,
321; Clay Lancaster, "Jefferson's
Architectural Indebtedness to Robert
Morris," *Journal of the Society of
Architectural Historians,* 10, no. 1
(1951), 4; Nichols, p. 34; Waterman,
pp. 388, 389.

465 Early plan for Monticello
1768–1770
THOMAS JEFFERSON 1743–1826
Literature: Kimball, "Williamsburg,"
p. 116; Kimball, *Jefferson, Architect,*
pp. 22–24, 118, 119, fig. 5; Kimball,
The Road to Glory, pp. 150, 320;
Clay Lancaster, "Jefferson's Architectural Indebtedness to Robert Morris,"
*Journal of the Society of Architec-
tural Historians,* 10, no. 1 (1951), 4;
Nichols, p. 34; Waterman, pp. 388,
389, 393.

**466 West elevation of the final
version of Monticello** 1803?
Attributed to ROBERT MILLS
1781–1855
Exhibition: Boston, Massachusetts
Historical Society, 1960.
Literature: Jefferson to William B.
Giles, Mar. 19, 1796 (Lipscomb,
9:326); Jefferson to Constantin
François de Volney, Jan. 8, 1797
(Lipscomb, 9:360); Hamilton W.
Pierson, *Jefferson at Monticello* (New
York: Scribner, 1862), p. 293,
fig. 211; Nichols, p. 37; Kimball,
Jefferson, Architect, pp. 165–166,
frontispiece.

**467 Chiswick Villa from the
southeast** c. 1730
WILLIAM KENT 1685–1748
Provenance: Third Earl of Burlington
and fourth Earl of Cork, whose
daughter Charlotte married fourth
Duke of Devonshire.
Exhibitions: Nottingham University
Art Gallery, *Apollo of the Arts:
Lord Burlington and His Circle,* 1973,
no. 73.
Literature: James Lees-Milne, *Earls of
Creation* (London: Hamish Hamilton,
1962), illus. opp. p. 128.

**468 Drawing of a cornice for a door
at Monticello** c. 1803
THOMAS JEFFERSON 1743–1826
Literature: Boyd, 11:423; Nichols,
p. 37; Kimball, *Jefferson, Architect,*
p. 167.

469 First floor plan for Monticello
1796?
THOMAS JEFFERSON 1743–1826
Literature: Hamilton W. Pierson, *Jefferson at Monticello* (New York: Charles Scribner, 1862), pp. 300–301; Nichols, pp. 6, 36; Kimball, *Jefferson at Monticello* (New York: Charles Scribner, 1862), pp. 300–301; Nichols, pp. 6, 36; Kimball, *Jefferson, Architect*, pp. 164–165, fig. 150.

470 Ionic entablature for the study at Monticello 1775 or after
THOMAS JEFFERSON 1743–1826
Literature: Kimball, *Jefferson, Architect*, p. 131, fig. 46; Nichols, p. 36; Frederick D. Nichols and James A. Bear, Jr., *Monticello* (Charlottesville: Thomas Jefferson Memorial Foundation, 1967).

471 Final drawing of the first floor with dependencies 1772–1784
THOMAS JEFFERSON 1743–1826
Literature: Kimball, *Jefferson, Architect*, p. 32; Nichols, pp. 4, 35, 47.

472 Final drawing of the basement and dependencies of Monticello before August 1772
THOMAS JEFFERSON 1743–1826
Exhibition: Boston, Massachusetts Historical Society, 1960.
Literature: Kimball, *Jefferson, Architect*, pp. 27, 125, 126, fig. 31; Kimball, *The Road to Glory*, p. 158; Nichols, p. 35.

473 Working drawing for the main stairs at Monticello c. 1771–1776
THOMAS JEFFERSON 1743–1826
Literature: Kimball, *Jefferson, Architect*, p. 124, fig. 26; Nichols, p. 35.

474 Study for the exterior doors for the west front of Monticello c. 1770
THOMAS JEFFERSON 1743–1826
Literature: Kimball, *Jefferson, Architect*, pp. 26, 123, fig. 20; Nichols, p. 35.

475 Study for the elevation of Monticello probably 1768–1770
THOMAS JEFFERSON 1743–1826
Literature: Kimball, "Williamsburg," p. 116; Kimball, *Jefferson, Architect*, pp. 26, 122, 123, fig. 19; Kimball, *The Road to Glory*, p. 153; Nichols, p. 35.

476 Study for the plan of Monticello 1768–1770
THOMAS JEFFERSON 1743–1826
Literature: Kimball, "Williamsburg," p. 116; Kimball, *Jefferson, Architect*, pp. 24, 25, 122, fig. 18; Kimball, *The Road to Glory*, pp. 152, 153; Clay Lancaster, "Jefferson's Archi-

tectural Indebtedness to Robert Morris," *Journal of the Society of Architectural Historians*, 10, no. 1 (1951), 4, fig. 3; Nichols, p. 35.

477 Study of the plan for Monticello 1768–1770
THOMAS JEFFERSON 1743–1826
Literature: Kimball, "Williamsburg," p. 116; Kimball, *Jefferson, Architect*, pp. 24, 120, fig. 11; Kimball, *The Road to Glory*, pp. 152, 322; Nichols, p. 34; Waterman, pp. 389, 390.

479 Poplar Forest, first floor plan c. 1820
CORNELIA JEFFERSON RANDOLPH(?) 1799–1871
Provenance: Collection of W. C. N. Randolph; acquired by the University of Virginia October 25, 1938.
Literature: Nichols, pp. 7, 8, 41, 42; Kimball, *Jefferson, Architect*, pl. 14; Frederick D. Nichols, "Poplar Forest," *The Ironworker*, 38, no. 2 (Spring 1974), 2–13.

480 Poplar Forest, garden elevation c. 1820
CORNELIA JEFFERSON RANDOLPH(?) 1799–1871
Provenance: Collection of W. C. N. Randolph; acquired by the University of Virginia October 25, 1938.
Literature: Nichols, pp. 7, 8, 42; Kimball, *Jefferson, Architect*, pl. 15; Frederick D. Nichols, "Poplar Forest," *The Ironworker*, 38, no. 2 (Spring 1974), 2–13.

481 Barboursville, Plan and Elevation 1817
THOMAS JEFFERSON 1743–1826
Literature: Nichols, p. 34.

482 Elevation of Farmington, Albemarle County 1802 or earlier
THOMAS JEFFERSON 1743–1826
Literature: Nichols, p. 34.

483 Plan of Farmington, Albemarle County 1802 or earlier
THOMAS JEFFERSON 1743–1826
Literature: Nichols, p. 34.

484 Edgehill before 1798
THOMAS JEFFERSON 1743–1826
Literature: Nichols, p. 34.

485 View of Bremo before 1836
EDWARD TROYE 1808–1874
Provenance: General John Hartwell Cocke; to Miss Betty Cocke; to Miss Elliot; to John Elliot.
Literature: Peter Hodson, *The Design and Building of Bremo: 1815–1820*, M.A. Thesis, University of Virginia, 1967.

486 Plan of Bremo
Elevation of Bremo, Fluvanna County
CORNELIA JEFFERSON RANDOLPH(?) 1799–1871
Provenance: Collection of Mrs. Thomas H. Wyllie; given to the University of Virginia September 20, 1963.
Literature: Nichols, p. 42; Marcus Binney, "Bremo, Virginia," *Country Life*, Jan. 3–10, 1974, pp. 18–21.

487 Study for Peter Maverick's engraving published in 1822 . . .
JOHN NEILSON(?) d. 1827
Literature: Jefferson to Governor Wilson C. Nicholas, Apr. 2, 1816 (Lipscomb, 14:453); Nichols, pp. 8, 42, 43.

488 Early plan of the University of Virginia May 9, 1817
THOMAS JEFFERSON 1743–1826
Provenance: Gift of W. C. N. Randolph, date unknown.
Literature: Nichols, p. 41.

489 Early study for the plans and elevation of a pavilion for Central College, later Pavilion III, University of Virginia 1817
THOMAS JEFFERSON 1743–1826
Literature: Nichols, p. 40; Kimball, *Jefferson, Architect*, p. 187, fig. 211.

490 Study for the plan and elevations of a pavilion and flanking dormitories for Central College, later Pavilion VII, the University of Virginia 1817
THOMAS JEFFERSON 1743–1826
Provenance: Gift of W. C. N. Randolph, 1938.
Exhibition: Boston, Massachusetts Historical Society, 1960.
Literature: Nichols, fig. 23, p. 40; O'Neal, *Pictorial History*, fig. 9, p. 12; Lambeth & Manning, pl. V.

491 Study for the front and side elevation of the lower story of a pavilion for Central College, later the University of Virginia 1817
THOMAS JEFFERSON 1743–1826
Provenance: See no. 490.
Literature: Nichols, p. 40.

492 Studies for pavilions for the University of Virginia 1817
WILLIAM THORNTON 1759–1828
Provenance: See no. 490.
Literature: Nichols, p. 41.

493 Study for pavilions and dormitories for Central College, later the University of Virginia probably 1817
WILLIAM THORNTON 1759–1828
Provenance: See no. 490.
Literature: Nichols, p. 40.

494 Elevation and plans for Pavilion I University of Virginia
THOMAS JEFFERSON 1743–1826
Provenance: See no. 490.
Literature: Nichols, p. 42; O'Neal, *Pictorial History*, p. 16, fig. 14; Adams, pp. 14–15; Barringer and Garnett, 1:270; Frary, pl. LV; Schuyler, p. 71.

495 Elevation and plans for Pavilion V, University of Virginia before 1821
THOMAS JEFFERSON 1743–1826
Provenance: See no. 490.
Literature: Nichols, p. 42; O'Neal, *Pictorial History*, p. 17, fig. 16; Adams, pp. 14–15; Barringer and Garnett, 1:272; Schuyler, p. 70.

496 Elevation and plans for Pavilion II, University of Virginia 1819
THOMAS JEFFERSON 1743–1826
Provenance: See no. 490.
Exhibition: Richmond, Virginia Museum of Fine Arts, 1969; Charlottesville, University of Virginia, 1969.
Literature: Nichols, p. 41; O'Neal, *Architectural Drawing*, p. 2, fig. 3; O'Neal, *Pictorial History*, p. 20, fig. 22; Adams, pp. 14–15; Barringer and Garnett, 1:270; Schuyler, p. 71.

497 Elevation and plans for Pavilion III, University of Virginia 1818 or 1819
THOMAS JEFFERSON 1743–1826
Provenance: See no. 490.
Literature: Nichols, pp. 40–41; O'Neal, *Pictorial History*, p. 17, fig. 15; Adams, pp. 14–15; Barringer and Garnett, 1:270; Schuyler, p. 71.

498 Elevation and plans for Pavilion IV, University of Virginia 1819
THOMAS JEFFERSON 1743–1826
Provenance: See no. 490.
Exhibition: Richmond, Virginia Museum of Fine Arts, 1969; Charlottesville, University of Virginia, 1969.
Literature: Nichols, p. 41; O'Neal, *Architectural Drawing*, p. 2, fig. 3; O'Neal, *Pictorial History*, p. 20, fig. 22; Adams, pp. 14–15; Barringer and Garnett, 1:270; Schuyler, p. 71.

499 Elevation and plans for Pavilion VI, University of Virginia 1819
THOMAS JEFFERSON 1743–1826
Provenance: See no. 490.
Exhibition: Richmond, Virginia Museum of Fine Arts, 1969; Charlottesville, University of Virginia, 1969.
Literature: Nichols, p. 41; O'Neal,

ictorial History, p. 22, fig. 24; O'Neal, *Architectural Drawing*, p. 6, fig. 7; *Adams*, pp. 14–15; Barringer and Garnett, 1:272; Schuyler, p. 70.

500 Elevation and plans for Pavilion VIII, University of Virginia 1819
THOMAS JEFFERSON 1743–1826
Provenance: See no. 490.
Exhibition: Richmond, Virginia Museum of Fine Arts, 1969; Charlottesville, University of Virginia, 1969.
Literature: Nichols, p. 41; O'Neal, *Architectural Drawing*, p. 8, fig. 9; O'Neal, *Pictorial History*, p. 23, fig. 25; Adams, pp. 14–15; Barringer and Garnett, 1:272; Schuyler, p. 70.

501 Elevation and plans for a pavilion for Central College, later Pavilion VII, University of Virginia 1817
THOMAS JEFFERSON 1743–1826
Provenance: See no. 490.
Literature: Nichols, p. 40; O'Neal, *Pictorial History*, p. 17, fig. 17; Adams, pp. 14–15; Barringer and Garnett, 1:272; Frary, pl. LVI.

502 Elevation and plans for Pavilion IX, University of Virginia before 1821
THOMAS JEFFERSON 1743–1826
Provenance: See no. 490.
Exhibition: Boston, Massachusetts Historical Society, 1960.
Literature: Nichols, p. 42; O'Neal, *Pictorial History*, p. 19, fig. 20; Adams, pp. 14–15; Barringer and Garnett, 1:274; Schuyler, p. 70.

503 Pavillon de Mlle Guimard 1774
SIR WILLIAM CHAMBERS 1726–1796
Literature: Paul Jarry, "Mlle Guimard et son hôtel de la Chaussée d'Antin," *Le Vieux Montmartre*, Sept. 1926, pp. 21–33; John Harris, "Sir William Chambers and his Parisian Album," *Architectural History*, 6 (1963), 54–90.

504 Elevation and plans for Pavilion X, University of Virginia 1819
THOMAS JEFFERSON 1743–1826
Provenance: See no. 490.
Exhibition: Richmond, Virginia Museum of Fine Arts, 1969; Charlottesville, University of Virginia, 1969.
Literature: Nichols, p. 41; O'Neal, *Architectural Drawing*, p. 10, fig. p. 11; O'Neal, *Pictorial History*, p. 23, fig. 26; Adams, pp. 14–15; Barringer and Garnett, 1:274; Schuyler, p. 70.

505 Notes for the construction of the Rotunda c. 1823
THOMAS JEFFERSON 1743–1826
Provenance: See no. 490.
Literature: Nichols, p. 41; Lambeth and Manning, pl. XVIII.

506 Plan of the first floor of the rotunda, University of Virginia probably 1821
THOMAS JEFFERSON 1743–1826
Provenance: See no. 490.
Exhibition: Richmond, Virginia Museum of Fine Arts, 1969; Charlottesville, University of Virginia, 1969.
Literature: Nichols, p. 41; O'Neal, *Architectural Drawing*, p. 14, fig. p. 15; O'Neal, *Pictorial History*, p. 30, fig. 38; Lambeth and Manning, pl. XVI.

507 Plan of the Ground Floor of the Désert de Retz
JEAN-NICOLAS LE ROUGE active late 18th century
Literature: Jefferson to Maria Cosway, Oct. 12, 1786.

508 Section of the rotunda, University of Virginia probably 1821
THOMAS JEFFERSON 1743–1826
Provenance: See no. 490.
Exhibition: Boston, Massachusetts Historical Society, 1960; Richmond, Virginia Museum of Fine Arts, 1969; Charlottesville, University of Virginia, 1969.
Literature: Nichols, fig. 27; O'Neal, *Architectural Drawing*, p. 20, fig. p. 21; O'Neal, *Pictorial History*, p. 32, fig. 41; Frary, pls. LIII, LIV; Lambeth and Manning, pl. XV.

509 Plan for the dome room of the rotunda, University of Virginia probably 1821
THOMAS JEFFERSON 1743–1826
Provenance: See no. 490.
Exhibition: Richmond, Virginia Museum of Fine Arts, 1969; Charlottesville, University of Virginia, 1969.
Literature: Nichols, p. 41; O'Neal, *Architectural Drawing*, p. 16, fig. p. 17; O'Neal, *Pictorial History*, p. 31, fig. 39.

510 Elevation of the rotunda and Pavilions IX and X, University of Virginia c. 1820?
Attributed to CORNELIA JEFFERSON RANDOLPH 1799–1871
Provenance: Gift of Hartwell Cabell, New York, 1946.
Literature: Nichols, p. 42; O'Neal, *Pictorial History*, p. 33, fig. 43.

511 Design for a planetarium, University of Virginia 1819
THOMAS JEFFERSON 1743–1826
Provenance: Gift of William Andrews Clark, Los Angeles, California, 1932.
Literature: Jefferson to William Short, Nov. 24, 1821 (Lipscomb, 18:315); Nichols, pp. 9, 41; Sowerby, 4:371.

512 Bird's eye view of the University of Virginia c. 1820?
THOMAS JEFFERSON 1743–1826, shaded by CORNELIA JEFFERSON RANDOLPH(?) 1799–1871
Provenance: See no. 490.
Literature: Nichols, p. 41; O'Neal, *Pictorial History*, p. 29, fig. 37; Adams, pp. 14–15; Barringer and Garnett, 1:298; Frary, pl. LII.

513 University of Virginia, elevation of Pavilion X c. 1820
Attributed to CORNELIA JEFFERSON RANDOLPH 1799–1871
Provenance: See no. 490.
Literature: Nichols, pp. 9, 42; Bernard Mayo, *Jefferson Himself* (Charlottesville: The University Press of Virginia, 1973), pp. 325, 327.

514 Plan of dormitories, West Range, with Hotels A and B 1817?
THOMAS JEFFERSON 1743–1826
Provenance: See no. 490.
Literature: Nichols, p. 40.

515 "C Hotel, Ionic Dentil" elevation and 3 plans before 1822
THOMAS JEFFERSON 1743–1826
Provenance: See no. 490.
Literature: Nichols, p. 42.

516 "Hotel B East" elevation and two plans, with detail of arched window set in cornice before 1822
THOMAS JEFFERSON 1743–1826
Provenance: See no. 490.
Literature: Nichols, p. 42.

517 "Hotel C West. Proctor's" elevation and two plans before 1822
THOMAS JEFFERSON 1743–1826
Provenance: See no. 490.
Literature: Nichols, p. 42.

518 "Hotel D East" elevation and plan before 1822
THOMAS JEFFERSON 1743–1826
Provenance: See no. 490.
Literature: Nichols, p. 42.

519 "Hotel F East" elevation and three plans before 1822
THOMAS JEFFERSON 1743–1826
Provenance: See no. 490.
Literature: Nichols, p. 42.

520 Elevation and section of dormitories, showing colonnades and "rooflets"
THOMAS JEFFERSON 1743–1826
Literature: Nichols, p. 42.

521 Elevation, plans and section of an anatomical theater, University of Virginia 1825
THOMAS JEFFERSON 1743–1826
Provenance: See no. 490.
Literature: Nichols, p. 42; O'Neal, *Pictorial History*, p. 35, fig. 45.

522 Study for the plan of the Lawn 1823 or before
THOMAS JEFFERSON 1743–1826
Provenance: See no. 490.
Literature: Nichols, p. 42; O'Neal, *Pictorial History*, p. 14, fig. 11; Lambeth and Manning, pl. VIII.

523 Elevation of the arcade for the gymnasia, University of Virginia 1824
THOMAS JEFFERSON 1743–1826
Provenance: See no. 490.
Literature: Nichols, p. 42; O'Neal, *The Rotunda*, I, pl. III, pp. 54–55.

524 Study for garden walls, University of Virginia c. 1817–1822
THOMAS JEFFERSON 1743–1826
Provenance: Gift of Samuel Herbert McVitty, Salem, Virginia, 1952.
Exhibition: Boston, Massachusetts Historical Society, 1960.
Literature: Nichols, fig. 28, p. 40.

525 Third variant for range and gardens, showing serpentine walls
THOMAS JEFFERSON 1743–1826
Literature: Jefferson to Dr. John P. Emmett, Apr. 26, 1826 (Lipscomb, 16:163–166).

526 Thomas Jefferson 1805
GILBERT STUART 1755–1828
Provenance: The painting descended from Jefferson to his heirs at Edgehill; in 1902 it was purchased by a collateral descendant of Jefferson, Burton Harrison, who took the painting to his residence in Scotland. John B. Winant purchased the panel from Harrison in 1927 who sold it to Percy S. Straus from whom it passed by inheritance to its present owner.
Literature: Bowen, pp. 483–485; Charles Henry Hart, "The Life Portraits of Thomas Jefferson," *McClure's Magazine*, 11, no. 1 (May 1898), 47–55; Kimball, "Life Portraits," pp. 512–523; Fiske Kimball, "Gilbert Stuart's Portraits of Jefferson," *GBA*, 26, n.s. 6 (July–Dec. 1944), 95–112; Bush, pp. 71–73.
Copies: Of the four recorded replicas of the painting, only two are now in public collections. The earliest,

painted for James Bowdoin between 1805 and 1807, survives in the Bowdoin College Museum of Fine Arts. The second, in the possession of James Madison in 1814, now hangs in the governor's palace at Colonial Williamsburg. A third replica, commissioned by George Gibbs, is now owned by Mrs. Gilbert L. Steward. The fourth, commissioned by John Doggett, was destroyed in the 1851 fire in the Library of Congress. It was the Doggett version of this image that was chosen to represent Jefferson officially on United States postage stamps, currency and certificates. At least eighty paintings and prints were derived from the Edgehill panel during the nineteenth century. Some thirty copies have been counted of the Bowdoin replica—many of them derived from Robert Field's 1807 engraving, which first set Stuart's portrait before the public. Less than a dozen copies of the Madison replica are known. Matthew Harris Jouett's copy of 1816, perhaps the first of the many painted from Stuart's 1805 *Jefferson*, was itself duplicated with some frequency.

527 Design for an urn
THOMAS JEFFERSON 1743–1826
Literature: Boyd, 15:xxvii–xxix, illus. p. 280; Julian P. Boyd, "Thomas Jefferson and the Roman Askos of Nîmes," *Antiques,* 54 (July 1973), 116–124; Jefferson's Account Book, July 3, 1789; Odiot's invoice to Jefferson, June 3, 1789, Vi; Jefferson to Charles-Louis Clérisseau, June 7, 1789.

528 Coffee urn 1789
JACQUES-LOUIS-AUGUSTE LEGUAY, active late 18th century
Provenance: Procured by Jefferson in Paris in 1787 and used at Monticello until his death; descended to Frank M. Randolph who sold the urn to Jefferson M. Levy in 1892; descended from Jefferson M. Levy to Mrs. Charles Mayhoff, from whom the urn was purchased in 1940 by the Thomas Jefferson Memorial Foundation.
Literature: Julian P. Boyd, "Thomas Jefferson and the Roman Askos of Nîmes," *Antiques,* 54 (July 1973), 116–124, fig. 4, 5; Boyd, 15: illus. p. 280; Jefferson's Account Books, Feb. 6, 1789, June 3, 1789; Jefferson to Charles-Louis Clérisseau, June 7, 1789; Odiot's invoice to Jefferson, June 3, 1789, Vi.

530 Pair of goblets
After JEAN-BAPTISTE-CLAUDE ODIOT 1763–1850
Provenance: Part of a set of six made at Colonial Williamsburg in 1969 and presented to President Pompidou

of France in 1970.
Literature: James A. Bear, "Thomas Jefferson's Silver," *Antiques,* 74 (Sept. 1958), 235; Boyd, 15:xxvii, xxviii, xxix, illus. opp. p. 281.

531 Profiles for goblets
THOMAS JEFFERSON 1743–1826
Literature: Boyd, 15:xxxiv, illus. p. 280; James A. Bear, Jr., *Catalogue of an Exhibition of Thomas Jefferson Silver* (Charlottesville: The Thomas Jefferson Memorial Foundation, 1958); Jean-Claude-Baptiste Odiot to Jefferson, invoice for silver, June 3, 1789.

532 Carriage 1788–1789?
THOMAS JEFFERSON 1743–1826
Provenance: Collection of Walter Schatzki, New York; purchased by the University of Virginia November 2, 1949.
Literature: Jefferson to Baron de Geismer, Nov. 20, 1789.

533 Monticello, curtains 1803 or earlier
THOMAS JEFFERSON 1743–1826
Literature: Nichols, p. 36; Fiske and Marie Kimball, "Jefferson's Curtains at Monticello," *The Magazine Antiques,* 52 (Oct. 1947), 266–268; Randall, 3:543.

534 Clock
CHANTROT active late 18th century
Provenance: Purchased by Thomas Jefferson in 1791; belonged to his daughter, Mrs. Thomas Mann Randolph; bequeathed by her to her son-in-law Nicholas Trist; to his grandson N. P. T. Burke, and by his widow to the present owners.
Literature: Boyd, 16:xxxiii, illus. 52, 321; Short to Jefferson, June 14, July 16, and Aug. 4, 1790, and Mar. 30, Apr. 26, May 2, and July 17, 1791; Jefferson to Short, Jan. 24, 1791; Chantrot to Jefferson July 24, 1791.

535 Folding music stand
Provenance: Probably made at Monticello, this music stand descended in the family to Mrs. Hollins N. Randolph, from whom it was purchased, in 1938, by the Thomas Jefferson Memorial Foundation.
Literature: Cripe, pp. 75, 76, pl. 3; Helen Cripe, "Thomas Jefferson's Delightful Recreation," *Antiques,* 102 (July 1972), 126, pl. I.

536 Drawing of a base for a pedestal for a bust at Monticello c. 1803
THOMAS JEFFERSON 1743–1826
Literature: Nichols, p. 37; Kimball, *Thomas Jefferson, Architect,* p. 168.

537 Study for parquet floor c. 1803
THOMAS JEFFERSON 1743–1826
Literature: Frederick D. Nichols and James A. Bear, Jr., *Monticello* (Monticello: Thomas Jefferson Memorial Foundation, 1967), pp. 34, 37; Nichols, p. 37.

538 Sketch for a candlestick 1789
THOMAS JEFFERSON 1743–1826
Literature: Jefferson to the Commissioners of the Treasury, Aug. 12, 1786; Jefferson to John Trumbull, Aug. 5, 1789; John Trumbull to Jefferson, Oct. 3, 1789; John Trumbull to Jefferson, Oct. 10, 1789; Marie Kimball, "Thomas Jefferson's French Furniture," *The Magazine Antiques,* 15, no. 2 (Feb. 1929), 128, fig. 10.

539 Two side chairs c. 1775–1800
Provenance: Sold at the Dispersal Sale of Monticello furnishings in 1827; donated by Mrs. Martha Farish in 1935 to the Thomas Jefferson Memorial Foundation.
Literature: James A. Bear, Jr., "The Furniture and Furnishings of Monticello," *Antiques,* 102 (July 1972), 118, pl. 2.

540 Dumbwaiter
Provenance: Purchased by Jefferson; descended in the family to Mrs. Ellen Coolidge Burke.
Literature: Margaret Bayard Smith, *The First Forty Years of Washington Society,* ed. Gaillard Hunt (New York: Frederick Ungar Publishing Co., 1965), pp. 387–388; Nichols, p. 45, no. 498; Charles F. Montgomery, *American Furniture of the Federal Period* (New York: The Viking Press, 1966), pp. 393–394, pl. 390; James A. Bear, ed., *Jefferson at Monticello* (Charlottesville: University Press of Virginia, 1967), p. 70; James A. Bear, *Report of the Curator* (Charlottesville: The Thomas Jefferson Memorial Foundation, 1971), pp. 10–12, pl. 2.

541 A Perspective View of Denham Place c. 1695
Provenance: Collection Lady Vansittart; sold Sotheby & Co., London, Dec. 18, 1968, lot 210, as by Danckerts, illus. in cat.
Literature: John Harris, "The Building of Denham Place," *The Records of Bucks,* 1957, pp. 193–197, illus. pl. XII.

543 Plan of Mount Airy
Reproduced from *Great Georgian Houses of America,* 1937
Literature: Frank Conger Baldwin, "Early Architecture of the Rappahannock Valley: Mt. Airy," *Journal of the American Institute of Architects,* Nov. 1916, pp. 448–457; Hunter

Dickinson Farish, ed. *Journal & Letters of Philip Vickers Fithian 1773–1774: A Plantation Tutor of the Old Dominion* (Williamsburg: Colonial Williamsburg, Inc., 1957), pp. 94–95; Paul Wilstach, *Tidewater Virginia* (Indianapolis: Bobbs Merrill, 1929), pp. 243–244.

544 Mount Vernon garden
Literature: Diaries of George Washington 1748–1799, ed. John C. Fitzpatrick (New York: Houghton and Mifflin, 1925), 2:334–354; Alice Lockwood, *Gardens of Colony and State* (New York: Charles Scribner's Sons, 1934), 2:54–65.

545 Plan of Mount Vernon garden 1787
Attributed to SAMUEL VAUGHAN active late 18th century
Literature: See no. 544.

546 View of William and Mary College c. 1740
Literature: Isaac Stokes, *American Historical Prints; Early Views of American Cities, Etc., from the Phelps Stokes and Other Collections* (New York: The New York Public Library, 1932), p. 15; Alice B. Lockwood, *Gardens of Colony and State* (New York: Charles Scribner's Sons, 1934), 2:49; Betts and Perkins, pp. 1–3; Pierre Marambaud, *William Byrd of Westover, 1674–1744* (Charlottesville: The University Press of Virginia, 1971), pp. 158, 159; Randall, 1:10.

547 A View from the West Side of the Island in the Garden of the Hon. Charles Hamilton at Painshill near Cobham in Surrey 1760
WILLIAM WOOLLETT 1735–1785
Literature: Thomas Whately, *Observations on Modern Gardening . . . A New Edition with Notes by Horace (Late) Earl of Orford; and Ornamented by Plates, chiefly designed by Mr. Wollet* (London: West and Hughes, 1801), p. 104; Isabel Wakelin Urban Chase, *Horace Walpole: Gardenist, An Edition of Walpole's The History of Modern Taste in Gardening with an Estimate of Walpole's Contribution to Landscape Architecture* (Princeton: Princeton University Press, 1943), pp. 230–232, 257; Betts, pp. 322–324 (Jefferson to William Hamilton), 303–304 (Jefferson on gardening as the "7th fine art"); Boyd, 9:370.

548 Plan for the Leasowes c. 1764
Literature: Thomas Whately, *Observations on Modern Gardening* (London: West and Hughes, 1801), pp. 90–97; William Shenstone, *Works,* ed. J. Dodsley (London: printed for R. and J. Dodsley, 1764),

2:333–369; Jefferson to Robert Skipwith, Aug. 3, 1771 (Lipscomb, 4:237); Boyd, 9:371–372; Betts, pp. 113, 323–324.

549 Plan for Belmont 1793
GEORGE ISHAM PARKYNS 1749–1820
Literature: G. I. Parkyns, "Six Designs for Improving and Embellishing Grounds. With Sections and Explanations," published as an appendix to Sir John Soane's *Sketches in Architecture* (London: Taylor and Holborn, 1793); Betts, pp. 323, 350, 356; Eleanor M. McPeck, "George Isham Parkyns, Artist and Landscape Architect, 1749–1820," *Quarterly Journal of the Library of Congress*, 30, no. 3 (July 1973), 171–182.

550 Exedra at Chiswick c. 1730
WILLIAM KENT 1665–1748
Literature: Boyd, 9:369; Isabel Wakelin Urban Chase, *Horace Walpole: Gardenist* (Princeton: Princeton University Press, 1943), pp. 25–35; R. Wittkower, "Lord Burlington and William Kent," *Archaeological Journal*, 102 (1947) [published by the Royal Archaeological Institute of Great Britain and Ireland]; James Lees-Milne, *Earls of Creation* (London: Hamish Hamilton, 1962), pp. 140–148; John Summerson, *Architecture in Britain, 1530–1830* (Harmondsworth: Penguin Books, Ltd., 1970), pp. 338–346.

551 Hagley, View from Thomson's Seat
Literature: Edmund Burke, *A Philosophical Inquiry into the Origin of Our Ideas of the Sublime and the Beautiful* (London: J. Dodsley, 1770), p. 299; Joseph Heely, *Letters on the Beauties of Hagley, Envil and the Leasowes* (London: printed for R. Baldwin, 1777), 1:162, 202; Boyd, 9:372; Isabel Wakelin Urban Chase, *Horace Walpole: Gardenist* (Princeton: Princeton University Press, 1943), pp. 15, 109, 111, 113, 130, 181, 205; Betts, pp. 303–304; William Hogarth, *Analysis of Beauty*, ed. Joseph Burke (Oxford: Clarendon Press, 1955), p. liv; *James Thomson (1700–1748), Letters and Documents*, ed. Alan Dugald McMillop Lawrence: University of Kansas Press, 1958), pp. 163, 165–167.

552 The House and Gardens at Woburn in Surrey, as laid out by Philip Southcote Esq.
WILLIAM WOOLLETT 1735–1785
Literature: Boyd, 9:370; Thomas Whately, *Observations on Modern Gardening* (London: West and Hughes, 1801), pp. 98–101; Betts, pp. 357, 360, 384; Nichols, p. 38; R. W. King, "The 'Ferme Ornée':

Philip Southcote and Woburn Farm," *Garden History*, 2, no. 3 (Summer 1974), 27–60.

553 Bird's Eye Perspective of Stowe House, Buckinghamshire c. 1720
Attributed to CHARLES BRIDGEMAN d. 1738
Literature: Peter Willis, "From Desert to Eden: Charles Bridgeman's Capital Stroke," *BurlM*, Mar. 1973, pp. 150–155; Lawrence Whistler, Michael Gibbon, and George Clarke, *Stowe, A Guide to the Gardens* (Buckinghamshire: E. N. Hillier & Sons, 1968), pp. 5–7; Peter Willis, "Jacques Rigaud's Drawings of Stowe in the Metropolitan Museum of Art," *Eighteenth Century Studies*, 6, no. 1 (Fall 1972), 85–98.

554 Perspective View of Chelsea Physick Garden
B. COLE active early 18th century
Literature: Jefferson to John Bartram Jr., Jan. 17, 1786; Jefferson to Richard Cary, Aug. 12, 1786; Philip Miller, *The Gardeners Dictionary* (London: printed for the author, 1735); Philip Miller, *The Gardeners Kalendar* (London: printed for the author, 1765); William Thomas Stearn, "Botanical Gardens and Botanical Literature," in *Catalogue of Botanical Books in the Collection of Rachel McMasters Hunt*, 2, pt. 1 (Pittsburgh: Hunt Botanical Library, 1961): lxxiii–lxxxvi.

555 Gardens of Bagatelle c. 1784
FRANÇOIS-JOSEPH BÉLANGER 1744–1818
Literature: Thomas Blaikie, *The Diary of a Scotch Gardener at the French Court at the End of the 18th Century*, ed. Francis Birrell (New York: E. P. Dutton, 1932); Oswald Siren, *China and Gardens of Europe of the 18th Century* (New York: Ronald Press Company, 1950), pp. 107–120; Thiéry, 2:274; Adrienne Koch and William Peden, *The Life and Selected Writings of Thomas Jefferson* (New York: Random House, 1944), pp. 395–406; Jefferson to Maria Cosway, Oct. 12, 1786; Jean Stern, *A L'ombre de Sophie Arnoud, François-Joseph Bélanger* (Paris: Librairie Plon, 1930), 1:66–77.

556 Plan for the Jardin des Plantes c. 1777
GEORGE-LOUIS LE ROUGE active 1776–1780
Literature: George Le Rouge, *Des Jardins Anglois-Chinois* (Paris: Le Rouge, 1776–1779), pl. 11; Jefferson to André Thouin, Apr. 29, 1808 (Betts, p. 370), and Dec. 14, 1813 (Betts, p. 520); Jefferson to Bernard McMahon, Dec. 28, 1808 (Betts,

pp. 383–384), May 4, 1811 (Betts, pp. 456–457), and Feb. 16, 1812 (Betts, pp. 479–480); Jefferson to Ellen Randolph, Oct. 18, 1808 (Betts, p. 378); Jefferson to David Hosack, July 13, 1816 (Betts, pp. 559–560); André Thouin to Jefferson, Feb. 5, 1823 (Betts, p. 609).

557 Plan for Chaville c. 1779
GEORGE-LOUIS LE ROUGE active 1776–1780
Literature: George-Louis Le Rouge, *Des Jardins Anglois-Chinois* (Paris: Le Rouge, 1776–1779), pl. 23; Emil Kaufmann, "Three Revolutionary Architects, Boullée, Ledoux, and Lequeu," *Journal of the American Philosophical Society*, 42 (1952), 455; Jefferson to Mme de Tessé, Mar. 20, 1787; Jefferson to Mme de Tessé (Betts, pp. 122, 131, 149, 284, 287, 299, 305, 339, 454, 519); Mme de Tessé to Jefferson (Betts, pp. 138–139).

558 Vue du Parc d'Ermenonville
CONSTANTIN BOURGEOIS 1767–1841
Literature: Alexandre de Laborde, *Description des Nouveaux Jardins de la France et Ses Anciens Châteaux* (Paris: Delance, 1808), p. 92, pl. 38.

559 Hôtel de Langeac garden 1785–1789
THOMAS JEFFERSON 1743–1826
(See number 204)

560 Hôtel de Langeac garden 1785–1789
THOMAS JEFFERSON 1743–1826
(See number 204)

561 Garden Scene 1783
JEAN-DÉMOSTHÈNE DUGOURC 1749–1825
Provenance: Peter Gregory, London; Ann Phillips, New York; Sale, New York, Parke-Bernet Galleries, Mar. 6–7, 1964, no. 285, repr.; purchased in London, 1966, by The Metropolitan Museum of Art.
Exhibition: London, Wildenstein Gallery, *French Paintings and Drawings*, 1946, no. 16; London, Matthiesen Gallery, Oct. 1950, no. 20; New York, The Metropolitan Museum, *French Drawings and Prints of the Eighteenth Century*, 1972, no. 17.
Literature: Denys Sutton, *French Drawings of the Eighteenth Century* (London: Pleiades Books, 1949), p. 49 and frontispiece; Helen Duprey Bullock, *My Head and My Heart* (New York: G. P. Putnam's Sons, 1945), p. 27.

562 View of Washington 1795
GEORGE ISHAM PARKYNS 1749–1820
Literature: G. I. Parkyns, "Six Designs

for Improving and Embellishing Grounds. With Sections and Explanations" published as an appendix to Sir John Soane's *Sketches in Architecture* (London: Taylor and Holborn, 1793); Thomas Main to Jefferson, Nov. 18, 1805 (Betts, p. 308); Thomas Main to Jefferson, Mar. 4, 1807 (Betts, p. 342); Joseph C. Cabell to Jefferson, July 4, 1816 (Betts, p. 558); Jefferson to Joseph C. Cabell, July 13, 1816 (Betts, p. 559); Thomas Main, *Directions for the Transplantation and Management of Young Thorn or Other Hedge Plants, Preparative to their Being Set in Hedges: With some Practical Observations on the Method of Plain Hedging* (Washington: A. & G. Way, 1807).

563 The Woodlands, Seat of William Hamilton 1808
WILLIAM BIRCH 1755–1834
Literature: Jefferson to William Hamilton, July 1806 (Betts, pp. 322–323); Jefferson to Bernard McMahon, Mar. 20, 1807 (Betts, pp. 343–344), and Mar. 22, 1807 (Betts, p. 344); Jefferson to William Hamilton, Mar. 22, 1807 (Betts, p. 344), and May 7, 1809 (Betts, p. 411); "The Life and Anecdotes of William Russell Birch, Enamel Painter, by Himself," Pennsylvania Historical Society; Sarah Stetson Davis, "William Hamilton and his Woodlands," *Pennsylvania Magazine of History and Biography*, 73 (Jan. 1949), 26–33; Paul Russell Outright, *Lewis and Clark: Pioneering Naturalists* (Chicago: University of Illinois Press, 1969), pp. 349–392.

564 Belmont, Seat of Judge Richard Peters 1808
WILLIAM BIRCH 1755–1834
Literature: Jefferson to Thomas Mann Randolph, Aug. 11, 1793 (Betts, pp. 202–203); Thomas Wescott, *The Historic Mansions of Philadelphia* (Philadelphia: Porter and Coates, 1877), pp. 381–395; marquis de Chastellux, *Travels in North America in the Years 1780, 1781 and 1782*, ed. Howard C. Rice, Jr. (Chapel Hill: University of North Carolina Press, 1963), 1:325.

565 View of the West Front of Monticello and Garden 1825
JANE BRADICK (PETTICOLES) active 19th century
Provenance: Through family descent to the present owner.
Literature: Betts and Perkins, p. 43; Betts, pp. 636–637.

566 General plan of the summit of Monticello mountain after Aug. 2, 1771, and before Aug. 4, 1772

THOMAS JEFFERSON 1743–1826
Literature: Kimball, "Williamsburg," 117; Kimball, *The Road to Glory*, p. 157; Nichols, p. 35; Kimball, *Jefferson, Architect*, pp. 128, 129, fig. 34.

567 Study for remodeling house and grounds at Monticello 1785–1789?
THOMAS JEFFERSON 1743–1826
Literature: Jefferson to Martha Jefferson Randolph, May 31, 1791, from Sarah N. Randolph, *The Domestic Life of Thomas Jefferson* (Charlottesville: Thomas Jefferson Memorial Foundation, 1947), pp. 166–167; Nichols, p. 36; Kimball, p. 160, fig. 138; Betts and Perkins, fig. 13.

569 Sketch of the garden and flower beds at Monticello June 7, 1807
THOMAS JEFFERSON 1743–1826
Literature: Betts, pp. 111–114, 349, pl. 24; Nichols, p. 37; Betts and Perkins, p. 35, fig. 14.

570 Decorative outchamber for Monticello probably 1778
THOMAS JEFFERSON 1743–1826
Literature: Nichols, p. 36; Kimball, *Jefferson, Architect*, p. 133, fig. 64.

571 Decorative outchamber for Monticello probably 1778
THOMAS JEFFERSON 1743–1826
Literature: Nichols, p. 36; Kimball, *Jefferson, Architect*, p. 133, fig. 62.

572 Design for a garden temple and dovecote
THOMAS JEFFERSON 1743–1826
Literature: Nichols, p. 36.

573 A temple for a garden c. 1778
THOMAS JEFFERSON 1743–1826
Literature: Kimball, *Jefferson, Architect*, pp. 27, 129, fig. 35; Nichols, p. 35.

574 A garden temple c. 1778
THOMAS JEFFERSON 1743–1826
Literature: Kimball, *Jefferson, Architect*, pp. 27, 129, fig. 36; Nichols, p. 35.

575 Drawing for a gate in Chinese lattice at Monticello 1771?
THOMAS JEFFERSON 1743–1826
Literature: Nichols, p. 35; Kimball, *Jefferson, Architect*, p. 130.

577 View of the Queen's Theater from the Rotunda at Stowe, Buckinghamshire c. 1733
JACQUES RIGAUD 1681–1754
Literature: John Harris, "Some English Architectural and Decorative Drawings in the Museum's Collection," *BMMA*, Feb. 1963, pp. 215–216; Peter Willis, "Jacques Rigaud's Drawings of Stowe in the Metropolitan

Museum of Art," *Eighteenth Century Studies*, 6, no. 1 (Fall 1972), 85–98; Peter Willis, "From Desert to Eden: Charles Bridgeman's Capital Stroke," *BurlM*, Mar. 1973, pp. 150–155.

578 Archimedes Screw
SIR WILLIAM CHAMBERS 1726–1796
Literature: John Harris, *Sir William Chambers* (London: A. Zwemmer Ltd.), pp. 3–18, 32–39; *Sir William Chambers, Plans, Elevations, Sections, and Perspective Views of the Gardens and Buildings of Kew*, facsimile ed. (London: Gregg Press, 1966), pls. 35, 36.

579 A garden seat by Mr. Jones. From Chamber's Kew c. 1820
Attributed to CORNELIA JEFFERSON RANDOLPH 1799–1871
Literature: Nichols, pp. 45, 48; Kimball, p. 1.

580 Observation Tower probably 1771
THOMAS JEFFERSON 1743–1826
Literature: Nichols, p. 35; Kimball, *Jefferson, Architect*, pp. 27, 129, 130, fig. 39.

581 Linnaeus c. 1812
WILLIAM RUSH 1756–1833
Provenance: Purchased from an estate in New Jersey by Mr. Kendrick Scofield, Doylestown, Pennsylvania; then to Leon F. S. Stark, Philadelphia; acquired by the Corcoran Gallery of Art from Mr. Stark in 1951.
Exhibition: Philadelphia, Society of Artists, Pennsylvania Academy of Fine Arts, 1812.
Literature: Henri Marceau, *William Rush, 1756–1833: The First Native American Sculptor* (Philadelphia: Pennsylvania Museum of Art, 1937), no. 18, pp. 34–35; *The Eighty-first Annual Report, The Corcoran Gallery of Art Bulletin*, 5, no. 3 (June 1952), ill. p. 4; William Dunlap, *History of the Rise and Progress of the Arts of Design in the United States*, ed. Alexander Wyckoff, rev. and enl. (New York: Benjamin Blom, Inc., 1965), pp. 374–375; Wayne Craven, *Sculpture in America* (Newark, Del.: University of Delaware Press, 1968), pp. 20–26; on Jefferson and Linnaeus, Betts, pp. 528–531; *Notes on the State of Virginia*, pp. 38–43, 66–69.

582 Natural Bridge, Virginia 1852
FREDERIC EDWIN CHURCH 1826–1900
Provenance: Cyrus West Field; Thomas Fortune Ryan; given to the University of Virginia, 1912.
Exhibitions: New York, National Academy of Design, *Annual Exhibition*, 1853; Washington, D.C.,

National Collection of Fine Arts, Smithsonian Institution, *American Landscapes: A Changing Frontier*, 1966.
Literature: Jefferson to Maria Cosway, Oct. 12, 1786; Jefferson to William Carmichael, Dec. 26, 1786; Jefferson to John Trumbull, Feb. 20, 1791; Jefferson to William Caruthers, May 15, 1815, quoted in Boyd, 19: xxxi; *Notes on the State of Virginia*, pp. 24–25; Albert T. Gardner, "Scientific Sources of the Full-Length Landscape: 1850," *BMMA*, 4 (Oct. 1945), 59–65; Richard Beale Davis, *Intellectual Life in Jefferson's Virginia, 1790–1830* (Chapel Hill: University of North Carolina Press, 1964), pp. 228, 333, 337; David Huntington, *The Landscapes of Frederic Edwin Church* (New York: George Braziller, 1966).

583 Harper's Ferry 1819
REMBRANDT PEALE 1778–1860
Provenance: Dr. Conrad Gold; Clarke's Art Room sale, New York, Feb. 8, 1912, lot 74.
Exhibitions: New York, National Academy of Design, 1826, no. 134; Baltimore, Municipal Museum (The Peale Museum), *The Peale Family and Peale's Baltimore Museum, 1814–1830*, Feb. 1965; The Detroit Institute of Arts, *The Peale Family*, Jan. 18–Mar. 5, 1967; Utica, The Munson-Williams-Proctor Institute, *The Peale Family*, Mar. 28–May 7, 1967.
Literature: Peale Papers, American Philosophical Society; Rembrandt Peale to Jefferson, Massachusetts Historical Society; *Notes on the State of Virginia*, p. 19; "Dr. Mitchill's Letters from Washington: 1801–1813," *Harper's New Monthly Magazine*, 58 (1878–1879), 744; The Walker Art Galleries, *Alphabetical List of Artists with Biographical Sketches*, illus. ed. (Minneapolis: Walker Art Galleries, 1927), no. 225, p. 120, attrib. to Charles Willson Peale.

584 Jefferson's Rock, Harper's Ferry 1810
BENJAMIN HENRY LATROBE 1764–1820
Provenance: By family descent to Mrs. Ferdinand C. Latrobe II, Baltimore; Maryland Historical Society, Baltimore.
Literature: *Notes on the State of Virginia*, p. 261.

585 Falls of the Schuylkill c. 1770
CHARLES WILLSON PEALE 1741–1827
Provenance: By descent from the artist.
Exhibitions: Hagerstown, The Washington County Museum of Fine Arts,

The Peale Heritage, 1763–1963, Sept. 15–Oct. 30, 1963; The Detroit Institute of Arts, *The Peale Family*, Jan. 8–Mar. 5, 1967; Utica, The Munson-Williams-Proctor Institute, *The Peale Family*, Mar. 28–May 7, 1967; Philadelphia, The Pennsylvania Academy of the Fine Arts, *Philadelphia Painting and Printmaking to 1776*, Mar. 26–Apr. 25, 1971 (with no. 20).
Literature: Charles Coleman Sellers, *Charles Willson Peale with Patron and Populace, a Supplement to 'Portraits and Miniatures by Charles Willson Peale'* (Philadelphia: American Philosophical Society, 1969), no. S16, p. 13, fig. 5.

586 View of the Great Falls of the Potomac 1809
BENJAMIN HENRY LATROBE 1764–1820
Provenance: By family descent to Mrs. Ferdinand C. Latrobe II, Baltimore; Maryland Historical Society, Baltimore.
Literature: *Notes on the State of Virginia*, p. 16.

587 Jeffersonia diphylla
Attributed to BENJAMIN SMITH BARTON 1766–1815
Literature: Joseph Ewan, *A Short History of the Botany of the United States* (New York: Hafner Publishing Co., 1969), pp. 37, 38, 40, 47, 48, 115; Betts and Perkins, pp. 12–13; Betts, pp. 172, 173, 353, 574.

588 Franklinia 1788
WILLIAM BARTRAM 1739–1823
Literature: Francis Harper, *The Travels of William Bartram, Naturalist's edition* (New Haven: Yale University Press, 1958), pp. 337, 416, 417; N. Bryllion Fagin, *William Bartram, Interpreter of the American Landscape* (Baltimore: Johns Hopkins Press, 1933), pp. 10, 12; Ernest Earnest, *John and William Bartram Botanists and Explorers 1699–1777* (Philadelphia: University of Pennsylvania Press, 1940), pp. 71, 81; Joseph Ewan, *William Bartram Botanical and Zoological Drawings, 1756–1788, reproduced from the Fothergill Album in the British Museum of Natural History* (Philadelphia: American Philosophical Society, 1968), pp. 6, 9, 16, 17, 37, 39, 62, 151, 154, 167; Jefferson to William Bartram, Nov. 23, 1808 (Betts, p. 380); William Bartram to Jefferson, Oct. 29, 1808 (Betts, p. 379).

588a Fragaria chiloensis
WILLIAM BARTRAM 1739–1823
Literature: Bernard McMahon, *The American Gardener's Calendar* (Phil-

adelphia: A. McMahon, 1828), pp. 484–486; L. Bailey, *Standard Cyclopedia of Horticulture*, 6 (New York: Macmillan, 1917): 3265; Jefferson to Thomas Mann Randolph, Mar. 1798 (Betts, p. 261); Jefferson to John Bartram Jr. June 11, 1801 (Betts, p. 275); Jefferson to Bernard McMahon, Feb. 8, 1809, Jan. 13, 1810 (Betts, pp. 430–431).

589 Cyprepedium acaule . . . Richmond—Lady Slipper from Blossom to Roots 1798
BENJAMIN HENRY LATROBE 1764–1820
Provenance: By family descent to Mrs. Ferdinand C. Latrobe II, Baltimore; Maryland Historical Society, Baltimore.
Literature: Jefferson to Mme de Tessé, Dec. 8, 1813 (Lipscomb, 14:28); Hamlin, pp. 60, 67, 89.

590 Representation of the Leaf of the Shumac Tree 1809
BENJAMIN HENRY LATROBE 1764–1820
Provenance: By family descent to Mrs. Ferdinand C. Latrobe II, Baltimore; Maryland Historical Society, Baltimore.
Literature: Papers of Benjamin Henry Latrobe, Maryland Historical Society; *Notes on the State of Virginia*, p. 38.

591 Spiraea, Hanover County, Virginia 1797
BENJAMIN HENRY LATROBE 1764–1820
Provenance: By family descent to Mrs. Ferdinand C. Latrobe II, Baltimore; Maryland Historical Society, Baltimore.

592 Bloodwort, Hanover County, Virginia 1797
BENJAMIN HENRY LATROBE 1764–1820
Provenance: By family descent to Mrs. Ferdinand C. Latrobe II, Baltimore; Maryland Historical Society, Baltimore.
Literature: C. S. Rafinesque, *A Medical Flora, A Manual of the Medical Botany of the United States of North America* (Philadelphia: Atkinson and Alexander, 1830), 2:80.

593 Liriodendron tulipfera c. 1810
P. BESSA 1772–1835
Literature: François André Michaux, *Histoire des arbres forestiers de L'Amérique septentrionale* (Paris: Hausmann et D'Hautel, 1813), 3:13; Gilbert Chinard, "Les Michaux et leurs Précurseurs," in *Les Botanistes Français en Amérique du Nord Avant 1850* (Paris: Centre Nationale de la Recherche Scientifique, 1957), pp. 263–284; Jefferson to John Hollins, Feb. 19, 1809 (Lipscomb, 12:252); Jefferson to Mme de Tessé Oct. 26, 1805 (Betts, pp. 305–306).

594 Cornus florida c. 1810
P. J. REDOUTÉ 1759–1840
Literature: François André Michaux, *Histoire des arbres forestiers de L'Amérique septentrionale* (Paris: Hausmann et D'Hautel, 1813), 3:13; Joseph Ewan, ed., *A Short History of Botany in the United States* (New York: Hafner Publishing Company, 1969), pp. 38–39; Gilbert Chinard, "Les Michaux et leurs Précurseurs" in *Les Botanistes Français en Amérique du Nord Avant 1850* (Paris: Centre Nationale de la Recherche Scientifique, 1957), pp. 263–284.

595 Hypericum ascyron
F. F. NODDER d. 1800
Literature: *Lettres sur la botanique par Jean-Jacques Rousseau*, ed. Bernard Gagnebin (Paris: Club des Libraires de France, 1962), pp. IX–XXXV; Jean-Jacques Rousseau, *Les Reveries du promeneur solitaire*, ed. Henri Roddier (Paris: Editions Garnier Frères, 1960), pp. 75–86.

596 Luna Moth on a Marble Slab 1796
BENJAMIN HENRY LATROBE 1764–1820
Provenance: By family descent to Mrs. Ferdinand C. Latrobe II, Baltimore; Maryland Historical Society, Baltimore.
Literature: Benjamin Henry Latrobe, *The Journals of Latrobe, Being the Notes and Sketches of an Architect, Naturalist and Traveller in the United States from 1796 to 1820* (New York: D. Appleton and Co., 1905), pp. 99–113.

597 The Ground Squirrel 1796
BENJAMIN HENRY LATROBE 1764–1820
Provenance: By family descent to Mrs. Ferdinand C. Latrobe II, Baltimore; Maryland Historical Society, Baltimore.
Literature: Hamlin, p. 539 and, on Latrobe's general interest in nature, pp. 60, 67, 89.

598 View of Elgin Garden c. 1812
HUGH REINAGLE 1790–1834
Provenance: Collection of I. N. Phelps Stokes; given to the New York Public Library, 1930.
Literature: Bernard McMahon to Jefferson, Dec. 24, 1809 (Betts, pp. 417–418); Jefferson to Bernard McMahon, Jan. 13, 1810 (Betts, pp. 430–431); Jefferson to Dr. David Hosack, July 13, 1816 (Betts, pp. 559–560), and Feb. 18, 1818 (Betts, p. 587); Frederick Pursh, *Flora Americae Septentrionalis Or, a Systematic Account of the Plants of North America* (London: White Cochrane and Co., 1814); Joseph Ewan, "Frederick Pursh 1774–1820

and his Botanical Associates," *Proceedings of the American Philosophical Society*, 96, no. 5 (Oct. 1952), 599–628; Isaac Stokes, *American Historical Prints; Early Views of American Cities, Etc. from the Phelps Stokes and other Collections* (New York: The New York Public Library, 1932), p. 54.

599 William Bartram 1808
CHARLES WILLSON PEALE 1741–1827
Provenance: Charles Willson Peale's Museum; Thomas & Sons sale, Philadelphia, October 6, 1854, lot 175; City of Philadelphia; transferred in 1951 to the Independence National Historical Park Collection, Philadelphia.
Exhibitions: Charles Willson Peale's Museum, Philadelphia; Philadelphia, The Pennsylvania Academy of the Fine Arts, *Exhibition of Portraits by Charles Willson Peale and James Peale and Rembrandt Peale*, Apr. 11–May 9, 1923.
Literature: Charles Coleman Sellers, *Charles Willson Peale, II: Later Life (1790–1827)* (Philadelphia: American Philosophical Society, 1947), p. 203; Charles Coleman Sellers, *Portraits and Miniatures by Charles Willson Peale* (Philadelphia: American Philosophical Society, 1952), no. 26, p. 28, fig. 283; Charles Coleman Sellers, *Charles Willson Peale* (New York: Scribner, 1969), pp. 326, 472 n. 29; John C. Milley, *Faces of Independence, Portrait Gallery Guidebook* (Philadelphia: Second Bank of the United States; Independence National Historical Park, 1974), n.p.

600 Rubens Peale with a Geranium 1801
REMBRANDT PEALE 1778–1860
Provenance: Mrs. Sabin W. Colton, Jr. (a descendant of the artist); Mrs. Robert P. Esty; Lawrence A. Fleischman.
Exhibitions: Philadelphia, The Pennsylvania Academy of the Fine Arts, 1807; Philadelphia, The Pennsylvania Academy of the Fine Arts, *Exhibition of Portraits by Charles Willson Peale and James Peale and Rembrandt Peale*, Apr. 11–May 9, 1923; University Park, The Pennsylvania State University, *Pennsylvania Painters*, Oct. 7–Nov. 6, 1955; New York, Kennedy Galleries, Inc., *The Fabulous Peale Family*, June 13–July 8, 1960; New York, The Metropolitan Museum of Art, *American Art from American Collections*, Mar. 6–Apr. 28, 1963; Baltimore, Municipal Museum (The Peale Museum), *The Peale Family and Peale's Baltimore Museum, 1814–1830*, Feb. 1965; The Detroit Institute of Arts, *The Peale Family*, Jan. 8–Mar. 5, 1967; Utica, The

Munson-Williams-Proctor Institute, *The Peale Family*, Mar. 28–May 7, 1967; New York, The Metropolitan Museum of Art, *19th Century American Paintings and Sculpture*, Apr. 16–Sept. 7, 1970.
Literature: Charles Coleman Sellers, *Charles Willson Peale, II: Later Life (1790–1827)* (Philadelphia: American Philosophical Society, 1947), fig. 12, opp. p. 147; Baltimore, The Peale Museum, *Rendezvous for Taste; Peale's Baltimore Museum 1814–1830*, exhib. cat. (Baltimore: Municipal Museum, 1956), no. 82, p. 28 (not exhibited); "The Fabulous Peale Family," *The Kennedy Quarterly*, 1, no. 3 (June 1960), 76–77; Stuart P. Feld, "Loan Collection, 1965," *BMMA*, 23, n.s. (Apr. 1965), 283; William H. Gerdts and Russell Burke, *American Still-Life Painting* (New York: Praeger Publishers, 1971), p. 36; Margaret Bayard Smith, *The First Forty Years of Washington Society* (New York: Ungar, 1965), p. 385.

601 François André Michaux
19th century
HENRY BRYAN HALL 1808–1884, after Rembrandt Peale 1778–1860
Literature: American Philosophical Society, Philadelphia, *A Catalogue of portraits and other works of art in the possession of the American Philosophical Society* (Philadelphia: American Philosophical Society, 1961), pp. 65–66.

602 Passenger Pigeon c. 1725
MARK CATESBY 1679–1749
Literature: Mark Catesby, *The Natural History of Carolina, Florida and the Bahama Islands: Containing the figures of birds, beasts, fishes, serpents, insects, and plants . . .* (London: printed for Benjamin White, 1771); George Frederick Frick and Raymond Phineas Stearns, *Mark Catesby, the Colonial Audubon* (Urbana: University of Illinois Press, 1961), p. 38.

603 Stewartia c. 1725
MARK CATESBY 1679–1749
Literature: Jefferson to John Banister Jr., Aug. 9, 1788; Mme de Tessé to Jefferson, Aug. 8, 1788; Mark Catesby, *Natural History of Carolina, Florida and the Bahama Islands: Containing the figures of birds, beasts, fishes, serpents, insects, and plants . . .* (London: printed for Benjamin White, 1771), 2: pl. 13, Appendix; George Frederick Frick and Raymond Phineas Stearns, *Mark Catesby, the Colonial Audubon* (Urbana: University of Illinois Press, 1961), p. 92; Alan Stevenson, ed., *Catalogue of the Books in the Collection of Rachel McMasters

Hunt, 2, pt. 2 (Pittsburgh: Hunt
Foundation, 1961): 142–147.

604 Mockingbird c. 1810
ALEXANDER WILSON 1766–1813
Literature: Jefferson to Abigail Adams,
June 21, 1785; Jefferson to Martha
Jefferson Randolph, June 10, 1793
(Betts, p. 189); Alexander Wilson,
American Ornithology (Philadelphia:
Bradford and Inskeep, 1810), 2:13–25;
Betts, pp. 42, 93, 283, 290; Margaret
Bayard Smith, *The First Forty Years
of Washington Society* (New York:
Ungar, 1965), p. 385; Cripe, p. 385.

605 Magpie c. 1805
ALEXANDER WILSON 1766–1813
Provenance: Gift of John E. Thayer to
the Museum of Comparative Zoology,
1910.

Literature: Alexander Wilson, *American Ornithology* (Philadelphia:
Bradford and Inskeep, 1811), 4:75–
78; Robert Cantwell, *Alexander
Wilson, Naturalist and Pioneer* (Philadelphia: J. B. Lippincott Co.,
1961); Donald Jackson, ed., *Letters
of the Lewis and Clark Expedition
with Related Documents* (Urbana:
University of Illinois Press, 1962),
pp. 255, 256, 260, 264, 267, 271, 291,
298.

SELECTED BIOGRAPHIES

The following biographical notes were compiled by Anna Voris and Ross Watson, museum curators at the National Gallery of Art.

ROBERT ADAM
Kirkcaldy, Fifeshire 1728–1792 London

Robert Adam was the son of William Adam, a successful Scottish architect. He entered Edinburgh University in 1743, and in 1754 went to Italy, where he met Piranesi and Clérisseau. In 1757 he visited Split with Clérisseau where he explored and measured the ruins of the palace of Diocletian and published his results in *Ruins of the Palace of the Emperor Diocletian at Spalatro* (1764), a magnificent volume engraved by Bartolozzi and others. Adam returned to London early in 1758 and established himself as senior partner in the family firm. Through the influence of Lord Bute, the king's first minister, he was appointed architect of the king's works in company with Sir William Chambers. He was also elected a member of the Society of Arts and, in 1761, became a fellow of the Royal Society. In place of the Palladian style Adam substituted in his architectural projects a new and elegant repertoire of architectural ornament based on a variety of classical sources ranging from antiquity to the cinquecento. Among architects, only Sir William Chambers remained resolute in his refusal to have anything to do with Adam's "affectations," and there can be no doubt that it was owing to Chambers' disapproval that Adam never became a Royal Academician. Adam ignored the Academy, however, sending none of his designs there for exhibition. In 1773 there appeared the first volume of the *Works in Architecture of Robert and James Adam*, followed in 1779 by the second volume; the third volume was published posthumously in 1822. Robert Adam was one of the two or three busiest architects in England; several of his important projects include the screen-wall at the Admiralty, Whitehall (1760), Buckingham House (1762), the Riding School, Edinburgh (1764), Lansdowne House, Berkeley Square (1762), Kenwood House (1767–1769), the Royal Society of Arts, London (1772–1774), and the University of Edinburgh (1789–1791).

JOHN BANISTER
Twigworth, Gloucestershire 1650–1692 Henrico County, Va.

Banister attended Magdalen College, Oxford (1667–1674), finishing with a Master of Arts degree. After graduation he worked at Magdalen College for several years as a clerk and chaplain and, while there, began collecting specimens and preparing a manuscript catalogue of the plants in the Oxford Physick Garden and vicinity. In 1678 Banister arrived in Virginia, apparently as a minister for the colonists, probably having visited Barbados and St. George, Grenada, en route. He remained in Virginia for fourteen years, continuing his investigation of natural history, and in 1680 he sent to John Ray a lengthy catalogue of Virginia plants, which was published in the *Historia Plantarum*. Banister was an entomologist as well as botanist, and he published papers on the insects, mollusks and plants of Virginia in the *Philosophical Transactions*. In 1692 Banister joined an exploration trip, organized by William Byrd I, to inspect some of Byrd's property on the lower Roanoke River, and was accidentally shot while he was examining plants along the Roanoke riverside by Jacob Colson, probably one of the woodsmen in the Byrd party. Banister's notes and papers were sent to Compton; his dried plants were acquired by Sir Hans Sloane, and are now in the British Museum.

BENJAMIN SMITH BARTON
Lancaster, Pa. 1766–1815 Philadelphia

Barton attended the York Academy until he was fifteen, when both his parents died and he moved to Philadelphia to live with an older brother. There he studied literature, the sciences, and medicine at the College of Philadelphia. In 1786 he went to England and studied medicine at Edinburgh and London, but he received his M.D. degree at Göttingen in 1789. He returned to Philadelphia to practice medicine and taught in the College of Philadelphia, which in 1791 was incorporated with the University of Pennsylvania. In 1790 he was appointed professor of natural history and botany, and on the death of Benjamin Rush in 1813, Barton succeeded him in the chair of theory and practice of medicine. Barton published articles on such diverse subjects as rattlesnakes, earthquakes of North America, the anthropology of the Indians, and the food of the hummingbird. His *Elements of Botany* (1803) was the first elementary botany written by an American.

WILLIAM BARTRAM
Philadelphia 1739–1823

William Bartram was born, was reared, and died in a stone house built by his father John Bartram in his botanic garden in Kingessing, on the Schuylkill River, now part of Philadelphia. The boy showed an early interest in drawing natural objects, and in 1765–1766 he accompanied his father in exploring the St. John's River in Florida. In 1768 he became a corresponding member of the American Society, which became the American Philosophical Society the next year. At the expense of Dr. John Fothergill, an English botanist, Bartram explored the southeastern part of the United States from 1773 to 1777. In return, Fothergill was to be sent seeds, specimens, and drawings; and journals and exquisite drawings, some colored, ultimately reached England. In 1782 Bartram was elected professor of botany at the University of Pennsylvania, but he declined the offer because of poor health. In 1791 Bartram published in Philadelphia his *Travels through North and South Carolina, Georgia, East and West Florida, the Cherokee Country, the Extensive Territories of the Muscogulges, or Creek Confederacy, and the Country of the Chactaws.*

FRANÇOIS-JOSEPH BÉLANGER
Paris 1744–1818

When, after studying with Le Roy and Contant d'Ivry at the Academy, Bélanger failed to gain the Prix de Rome in 1765, he went to England for two years. On his return he became, as Challe's assistant, *dessinateur des menus plaisirs*, building superintendent for Monsieur (later Louis XVIII) in 1770, and in 1777 *premier architecte* of the comte d'Artois, brother of Louis XVI. He built the stables at Versailles and in Paris (c. 1780) for the prince, made alterations to the Château de Maisons (1777–1784), and built the spectacular Bagatelle (1777). Bélanger was the favorite architect of the younger aristocracy and of the leading figures of the French theater, and he built for them luxurious pavilions and laid out their gardens in the English manner. After the Revolution and the death of his patrons, Bélanger devoted himself to public building and took part in many competitions, without much success. His only really important work was the dome of the Halle aux Bleds (1808–1811), which was erected after fire destroyed the wooden dome by Legrand and Molinos. Bélanger's dome, with cast-iron ribs tied by wrought-iron rings, was the first iron dome ever constructed.

BERNARDO BELLOTTO
Venice 1720–1780 Warsaw

Bellotto was a pupil of his uncle, Canaletto, with whom he is often confused, and his early paintings are close in style to his teacher. Bellotto settled in Dresden in 1747, where he remained until driven away by war in 1758. Thereafter he spent some time in Vienna with a short stay in Munich until he returned to Dresden in 1762. He remained there until 1767, when he finally settled in Warsaw.

WILLIAM RUSSELL BIRCH
Warwickshire 1755–1834 Philadelphia

Birch was trained in Bristol and London, and exhibited his first miniatures in London in 1775. He exhibited at the Royal Academy from 1781 to 1794. Birch copied portraits by Reynolds in miniature and executed enamel miniatures and engravings. In about 1794 he came to America with a recommendation from Benjamin West and settled in Philadelphia, where he published a series of twenty-eight engravings, *Views of Philadelphia* (1798–1800), and a smaller series of plates showing American country seats (1808).

ÉTIENNE-LOUIS BOULLÉE
Paris 1728–1799

Despite his promise as a painter, Boullée was forced by his father to study architecture and to attend the classes of Blondel. In 1746 he became a pupil of Boffrand, then with the firm of Lebon and Le Geay. At the age of eighteen, Boullée himself became a teacher at the Ecole des Ponts et Chaussées, and was able to impart his great enthusiasm to his students. In 1762 he was admitted with second-class membership to the Academy and in 1780 was accepted as a full member. He designed many residences for an elegant clientele in Paris, but most of the large projects he designed were never built. He was one of the academicians consulted for such major projects as the reorganization of the Louvre galleries (1785); the doming of the Paris Halle aux Bleds, proposed by Legrand and Molinos (1782); the reconstruction of the Cathedral of Rennes (1785); and the designs for the Church of the Madeleine by Couture (1786). He was one of nine academicians present at the final session of the Academy in 1793. During the Revolution, Boullée was denounced as a Royalist. In 1795 he became a member of the newly formed Institut de France and was nominated professor of architecture at the Ecoles Centrales. Boullée's unique qualities can best be seen in his drawings and in the manuscript of his *Architecture*, which he bequeathed to the nation.

CHARLES BRIDGEMAN
?–1738 London

Bridgeman's date and place of birth are unknown. He supervised the royal gardens and was the leading professional landscape gardener of his day. His most famous work is at Stowe, Buckinghamshire.

MATHER BROWN
Boston 1761–1831 London

At an early age Brown was taught drawing by Gilbert Stuart, and by 1777 he had become a proficient miniaturist. He went to Europe about 1780, first to Paris, then to London, where he became a pupil of Benjamin West. He exhibited at the Royal Academy during the years 1782–1808 and 1824–1831. From 1809 to 1824 he worked in Manchester and Liverpool and then returned to London, where he painted portraits of George III, George IV and Queen Charlotte, and was appointed painter to the Dukes of York and Clarence.

PIERRE-GABRIEL BUGNIET
Lyon ?–1806 Charly, Rhône

Bugniet worked mainly in his home province. He designed a monumental fountain for the Place des Cordeliers in Lyon (1764–1769) and, in 1765, published four engravings of his plan for a prison in Paris based on the idea of solitary confinement. Between 1777 and 1782, he worked on the Pont de l'Archevêché and in 1785, along with Thibière, started work on the Prison de Roanne, also in Lyon (1785–1837).

CHARLES BULFINCH
Boston 1763–1844

Bulfinch became interested in architecture on his graduation from Harvard in 1781, and from 1785 to 1787 he traveled in England and on the continent, visiting the monuments of Paris and following Jefferson's route through southern France and northern Italy, going on to Florence and Rome. On his return to Boston he was soon giving his friends advice on architecture. In 1788 the old Hollis Street church in Boston was built from his plans, and this was followed by designs for churches at Taunton and Pittsfield. The state house at Hartford was begun in 1792 from his plans, and his most ambitious project up to that time, the Massa-

chusetts state house on Beacon Hill, was completed in 1800. A designer of houses as well, he introduced the delicate detail of the Adam style and curved staircases into the domestic architecture of New England. In 1791 he was elected to the board of selectmen for the town of Boston. He was active on committees which, for the first time, lighted the streets of Boston, admitted children of both sexes to the public schools, and transformed Copley's pasture into a city park, the present Boston Common. In 1817, on the resignation of Latrobe as architect of the capitol in Washington, President Monroe offered the post to Bulfinch, who moved to Washington and remained in charge until the building was finished, completing the wings and constructing the central part according to the lines already established by the earlier architects, Hallet, Thornton and Latrobe. His principal contribution to this project was the detailed form of the western front.

GIOVANNI ANTONIO CANAL, CALLED CANALETTO
Venice 1697–1768

Canaletto was the leading view painter in Venice, producing works mainly for the tourist market, especially the English. Canaletto's subjects are almost entirely confined to Venice except for some views of England, which he visited on two occasions, between 1746 and about 1756.

ANTONIO CANOVA
Possagno 1757–1822 Venice

The most distinguished neoclassical sculptor, Canova settled in Rome in 1780 and spent his working life there. No artist of his day achieved such wide-ranging prestige. He received several important papal commissions and later helped in the recovery of Italian works of art taken by the French. Canova was patronized by Napoleon and members of his family, and also sculpted a statue of George Washington.

MARK CATESBY
London (?) c. 1679–1749

Catesby left England in 1712 to study the flora and fauna of America, and after staying with relatives in Virginia for seven years he brought back the largest natural history collection to come to England up to that time. On his second trip to America, from 1722–1725, he traveled through the Carolinas, Georgia, and Florida, spending some time in the Bahamas before returning to England in 1726. In London he published his important work, *Natural History of Carolina,*

Florida and Bahama Islands (1731–1743), for which he etched almost one hundred plates, coloring the first set himself. In his first volume, devoted to birds, he made observations about their migrations at a time when the subject was little understood. His second volume was devoted to fish, reptiles, and a few quadrupeds, including the bison. In 1733 Catesby was elected to the Royal Society.

JEAN-FRANÇOIS CHALGRIN
Paris 1739–1811

Chalgrin was a pupil of Servandoni, Boullée and Moreau. He received the Grand Prix de Rome in 1758 and studied in Rome from 1759 to 1763, and was specially interested in antiquities. When he returned to Paris he was attached to the staff of the architect Moreau. Later when he succeeded Moreau as architect of the city of Paris, Chalgrin collaborated on the design for the Hôtel de Saint-Florentin (1767), the Chapelle du Saint-Esprit (1768), and the gallery for the marriage of the Dauphin (1770). The Hôtel de Langeac, Jefferson's residence in Paris, was designed by Chalgrin in 1768. Chalgrin was elected a member of the Academy in 1770. His masterpiece in the field of church architecture was Saint-Philippe du Roule, built from 1772 to 1784. He also worked on the north tower of Saint-Sulpice (1777–1780) and the Collège de France (1780). Chalgrin became *premier architecte* to Monsieur (later Louis XVIII) and worked at Versailles on the Pavillon de Madame (1784). He worked on the reconstruction of the Odéon (begun in 1807). Napoleon began the Arc de Triomphe de l'Etoile from designs by Chalgrin but it was completed later. He became a member of the Institut in 1809.

MASON CHAMBERLIN THE ELDER
active 1763–1787

Little is known about Chamberlin; he was a pupil of Francis Hayman and exhibited in London as early as 1763. He was one of the original members of the Royal Academy and exhibited there from 1769 to 1786. Most of his patrons were merchants. He died in London.

SIR WILLIAM CHAMBERS
Gothenburg, Sweden 1723–1796 London

As a member of the Swedish East India Company Chambers visited China and so had first-hand knowledge of Chinese architecture. He then studied in Paris under Blondel and for five years in Italy. His appointment as

architectural tutor to the Prince of Wales, later George III, established him on the road to royal favors and success. He became the king's architect and eventually surveyor general in 1782 and thus the leading official architect. For much of his later career he worked on his masterpiece, Somerset House. He was also treasurer of the Royal Academy which he helped to found.

GILLES-LOUIS CHRÉTIEN
Versailles 1754–1811 Paris

Chrétien was a musician and engraver, and about 1786 invented the physiognotrace, whose mechanism is described in the biographical sketch of Edmé Quenedey, his collaborator in portraiture.

FREDERIC EDWIN CHURCH
Hartford 1826–1900 New York City

Church studied first in Hartford with Benjamin Hutchins Coe and Alexander Hamilton Emmons. Then in 1844 he went to Catskill, New York, and became a pupil and close friend of Thomas Cole. During the summer months Church went on many sketching trips to the Catskills, Hartford, the Berkshires, western New York, Vermont, the White Mountains, Maine, Virginia, Kentucky, the Upper Mississippi and Canada. He first exhibited at the National Academy in 1845 and was elected a full member in 1849, becoming the youngest Academician in this country. In 1853 and again in 1857 Church visited Ecuador and Colombia, where he found great inspiration for his landscapes. He later made visits to the coast of Labrador, the West Indies, Europe and the Near East in search of romantic subjects. After 1877 Church was crippled by rheumatism, and the last twenty years of his life were spent in enforced idleness.

CHARLES-LOUIS CLÉRISSEAU
Paris 1721–1820 Auteuil

Clérisseau began his architectural training at the French Academy under Blondel, and in 1746 he won a Prix de Rome but did not leave for Italy until 1749. He lived at the French Academy in Rome for six years, and becoming a pupil of Panini's, he developed a taste for composing fantasies of Roman ruins. He made friends in Rome with Piranesi, Winckelmann and Mengs, leaders of the neoclassic movement. In 1754 Clérisseau met Robert Adam and for the next eight years he was employed by the Adam brothers. Their debt to him was considerable. He infused their taste with his own passionate interest in the study of antiquity and its application to contemporary architecture and ornament. In 1757 Robert Adam commissioned Clérisseau to measure and to do drawings of Diocletian's palace at Split. By 1768 he was back in Paris and became a member of the Academy the following year. In 1771–1775 he was in England working for the Adam brothers again, and sometime after 1778 he was summoned to St. Petersburg, where he became architect for Catherine II of Russia and a member of the Academy in St. Petersburg. By 1782 he had returned to Paris. He became a member of the Academy of Rouen in 1810. His major works include a project for the Château Borély, Marseille (1767); decorations for the Hôtel Bouret, Paris (before 1777); and decorations for the Hôtel Grimod de La Reynière (1777).

JEAN-FRANÇOIS GILLES, CALLED COLSON
Dijon 1733–1803 Paris

Colson studied under his father and various artists in the towns where his family lived. As well as being a portrait painter, Colson was for many years chief architect to the duc de Bouillon at his Château de Navarre.

JOHN SINGLETON COPLEY
Boston (?) 1738–1815 London

Copley was the son of recent immigrants from Ireland. His father died shortly after his birth, and in 1748 his mother married the English-trained painter and engraver, Peter Pelham, who encouraged the boy in the arts. Influenced by engravings and copies of European masters and by John Smibert, Robert Feke, John Greenwood, and Joseph Blackburn, Copley began by working in Boston about 1753; but he also made trips to Philadelphia and New York City in 1771–1772. In 1774 he left for Europe, traveling in France and Italy before settling in London the following year, where he received advice from Benjamin West. Copley first exhibited at the Royal Academy in 1777 and was elected to full membership in 1779.

RICHARD COSWAY
Tiverton, Devonshire 1742–1821 London

A pupil of Thomas Hudson and William Shipley, Cosway first exhibited in London in 1760 and soon received many fashionable commissions. In 1771 he became a full member of the Royal Academy, and in 1781 he married the artist Maria Hadfield. His miniatures were very popular, and he became friendly with the Prince of Wales at Carlton House.

About 1786 he was appointed principal painter to the prince. In 1788–1789 Cosway executed pictures for the ceiling of the grand salon at Carlton House.

JACQUES-LOUIS DAVID
Paris 1748–1825 Brussels

On the recommendation of Boucher, a family friend, David in 1766 entered the studio of Vien, a pioneer of the neoclassic style. After three unsuccessful attempts he finally received the Grand Prix de Rome in 1774 and left for Italy the following year. David was unquestionably influenced by the wealth of antique sculpture he saw in Rome. He was in Paris again in 1780 and exhibited first in the Salon of 1781. He was nominated a member of the Academy in 1784, and in the same year he returned to Rome again for eighteen months. After his return to Paris he became the most fashionable painter of the day. An ardent revolutionary and dictator of the arts until the fall of Robespierre, David was arrested in 1794 and spent several months in prison. After his release he shifted his allegiance and became first painter to Napoleon in 1804. After the final defeat of Napoleon, David went into exile in 1816 to Brussels, where he remained active until his death.

FRANÇOIS-HUBERT DROUAIS
Paris 1727–1775

At first a pupil of his father, Hubert Drouais, François-Hubert also attended the studios of Carle van Loo, Natoire, and Boucher. In 1754 he was accepted at the Academy and exhibited regularly in the Salon from 1755 to 1775. In 1756 he was called to the court at Versailles to paint the two children of the dauphin. He was highly regarded at the court, particularly by Mme de Pompadour and later by Mme du Barry. In 1758 he was received as a full member of the Academy and in 1774 was appointed counselor of the Academy.

JOSEPH-SIFFRED DUPLESSIS
Carpentras, Provence 1725–1802 Versailles

First a pupil of his father Joseph-Guillaume Duplessis, Duplessis later studied for four years in Rome with Subleyras until the latter's death in 1749. After working in Carpentras for a few years, he went to Paris in 1752. In 1769 he was accepted at the Academy and was finally received as a full member in 1774. He was appointed counselor of the Academy in 1780. He painted many important people of his day, including the German composer Glück, Allegrain,

Vien, comte d'Angiviller and Louis XVI. He lost his fortune in the Revolution and in 1794 accepted the post of curator of the galleries at Versailles.

RALPH EARLE
Worcester County, Mass. 1751–1801 Bolton, Conn.

Earle had opened a studio in New Haven, Connecticut, by 1775, but was forced to flee to England early in 1778 because of his Loyalist sympathies. He studied with Benjamin West in London and painted portraits there and in the county of Norfolk and in Windsor. He also exhibited at the Royal Academy. After his return to America in 1785 he painted portraits in Vermont, New York and Connecticut. He was the brother of James Earle and the father of Ralph E. W. Earle, also painters.

PAULUS CONSTANTIJN LA FARGUE
The Hague 1729–1782

La Fargue came from a distinguished literary family. Two of his brothers and a sister were also artists, and they all concentrated on topography and landscape views.

BARON FRANÇOIS GÉRARD
Rome 1770–1837 Paris

Gérard's father was a servant in the employ of the French ambassador in Rome, and in 1782 Gérard came to Paris with his parents and soon became the pupil of the sculptor Pajou, with whom he worked for two years. He studied under Brenet and David (1786–1789). Under the influence of David he became a member of the Revolutionary Tribunal in 1792. He painted historical works in the style of David, but later he turned mainly to portraiture and successfully portrayed Napoleon, the Bourbons, and other members of the French ruling class. He was one of the original Knights of the Legion of Honor, became a member of the Institut de France in 1812, became first painter to Louis XVIII in 1817, and was made a baron in 1819.

GEORGE HADFIELD
Leghorn 1764–1826 Washington, D.C.

George Hadfield entered the Royal Academy Schools in 1781 and received a gold medal in 1784; in 1790 he was the first recipient of the traveling scholarship in architecture awarded by the Royal Academy, and was in Rome until 1794. In 1795 he exhibited some of his Italian drawings at the Royal Academy. Soon afterward, John

Trumbull recommended Hadfield to supervise the construction of the capitol in Washington, where work on the north wing proceeded under his direction until 1798, when he quarreled with the commissioners. In 1800 he patented the first machine for brick-making in the United States. He also designed other public buildings in Washington: the treasury and executive offices, which were burned by the British in 1814, the city hall, the arsenal, the county jail, and the Branch Bank of the United States. He also planned Commodore Porter's house, the Van Ness mausoleum in Oak Hill Cemetery, and "Arlington," the Custis mansion, which is now in the Arlington National Cemetery. It was Hadfield's sister Maria who married Richard Cosway.

WILLIAM HOGARTH
London 1697–1764

About 1720 Hogarth began his career under Ellis Gamble as an engraver on silver and copper. Later in the same year he was admitted to Cheron and Vanderbank's Academy in St. Martin's Lane, and achieved his first recognition in 1726 with his plates for Butler's *Hudibras*. Next he ventured into oil painting, after which followed his celebrated series of pictorial satires, including the *Harlot's Progress* (1730–1731), *A Rake's Progress* (1735), and *Marriage à la Mode* (1745). On the death of his father-in-law, Sir James Thornhill, in 1734, Hogarth took over his Academy, which flourished until 1768. He seems to have visited Paris in 1743 and again in 1748. In 1753 he published the *Analysis of Beauty*, and in 1757 he was appointed Sergeant Painter to King George II.

JOHN HESSELIUS
Philadelphia or Maryland (?) 1728–1778 near Annapolis

A pupil of his father, Gustavus Hesselius, who had come from Sweden, John Hesselius spent his youth in Philadelphia. After working in Maryland, Virginia, Delaware and Philadelphia, he settled in Annapolis. During the 1750s he was greatly influenced by John Wollaston, an English painter, who was active in Maryland and Virginia at this time. About 1762 Charles Willson Peale received his first lessons in painting from Hesselius in Annapolis. In 1763 Hesselius married a wealthy widow who lived near Annapolis and this insured him the patronage of the landholding aristocracy of the area.

JEAN-ANTOINE HOUDON
Versailles 1741–1828 Paris

Houdon's father was concierge of the Ecole des Elèves Protégés. In 1761 Houdon won first prize at the Academy school in Paris, and after three years at the Ecole des Elèves Protégés as a pupil of Michel-Ange Slodtz, he left for Rome in 1764. He returned to Paris in 1768, exhibiting for the first time at the Salon of 1769, and regularly thereafter until 1814. He was significantly influenced by Lemoyne and Pigalle. Two trips to Germany gave him some wealthy foreign patrons, and he executed portrait busts of the greatest personalities of the time. He was received at the Academy in 1777. In 1785 Houdon went to Mount Vernon to do studies for a marble statue of George Washington. A member of the Institut de France since its creation in 1795, and of the Legion of Honor in 1803, he was commissioned to model busts of both Napoleon and Josephine from life.

JEAN-FRANÇOIS HUE
St.-Arnould-en-Yvelines (Seine-et-Oise) 1751–1823 Paris

A pupil of Joseph Vernet, Hue devoted himself mostly to landscape and marine paintings, but did produce a few historical paintings. In 1781 he was accepted at the Academy and became a member in 1782. He exhibited in the Salon from 1781 to 1822. Hue was employed by the government to continue the series of paintings of ports of France begun by Joseph Vernet, who died in 1789.

ANGELICA KAUFFMANN
Coire, Switzerland 1741–1807 Rome

A pupil of her father, Joseph Johann Kauffmann, Angelica Kauffmann moved with her family to Milan in 1754 and to Rome in 1759. She spent several years in Florence and Venice before going to England in 1766. In 1768, when the Royal Academy was founded, she was one of the original thirty-six members, and she exhibited her portraits there from 1769 to 1797. She also carried out decorative wall and ceiling paintings in many English and a few Irish houses, some in collaboration with Antonio Zucchi, a Venetian painter, whom she married in 1781. In 1782 she retired to Rome with her husband.

WILLIAM KENT
Bridlington, Yorkshire 1684–1748 London

Kent began as a painter and studied in Rome, where he was befriended by Lord Burlington, who brought him back to England and became his life-long patron. From about 1730 Kent turned to architecture, although he is perhaps better known for his designs for furniture and interiors. Kent's greatest contribution was the creation of the informal English landscape garden.

SIR GODFREY KNELLER
Lübeck 1646–1723 London

In about 1660 Kneller was sent to the University of Leiden to study "mathematics particular to fortification." He became interested in painting, and about 1668 he studied in Amsterdam under Ferdinand Bol and received advice from Rembrandt. By 1672 he was in Rome, where he copied Raphael and made contact with Bernini and Maratta; he then went to Naples and Venice, where he studied Titian and apparently had some success as a portrait painter. In 1675 he returned to Germany. He arrived in London in 1676 and was soon introduced to the English court. In 1711 he was elected the first governor of the first Academy for Painting and Drawing in England. His mature style is based upon that of Lely.

ADÉLAÏDE LABILLE-GUIARD
Paris 1749–1803

Mme Labille-Guiard was a pupil of the miniature painter François-Elie Vincent, and later of his son François-André Vincent, whom she eventually married. In 1783 she became a member of the Académie Royale at the same time as her great rival, Mme Vigée-Lebrun.

GEORGE LAMBERT
Kent (?) 1700(?)–1765 London

George Lambert has been called "the father of English oil landscapes" and produced both imaginary views in the style of Gaspard Poussin as well as topographical paintings, which show an awareness of Kent's new ideas on landscape gardening. Lambert became chairman and later president of the Royal Society of Artists of Great Britain.

BENJAMIN LATROBE
Fulneck, near Leeds 1764–1820 New Orleans, La.

Latrobe, the son of the head of the Moravian congregation in England, grew up in England but was educated at the Moravian college in Saxony and at the University of Leipzig (1777–1783). After he returned to England, he studied engineering with John Smeaton from 1786 to 1788 and architecture with Greek revivalist Samuel Pepys Cockerel from 1788 to 1789. Latrobe designed several homes in England, but after the death of his first wife in 1793 he emigrated to Virginia in 1796. In 1797 he designed the Richmond penitentiary and completed the façade of the Virginia state capitol in 1798. He then moved to Philadelphia in 1799 to work on the Bank of Pennsylvania, the first example of Ionic Greek revival architecture in the United States. In 1803 President Jefferson appointed Latrobe surveyor of the public buildings in Washington, and he built the south wing of the capitol for the House of Representatives. In 1804 he designed the Baltimore Cathedral in the Gothic revival style. This was followed by the Pennsylvania Academy of Fine Arts in Philadelphia (1805), the Bank of Philadelphia (1807), and the Marine Hospital in Washington (1812). After the British burned Washington in 1814, Latrobe was put in charge of rebuilding the capitol, and he designed new Senate and House chambers. He retired from federal service in 1817 and went to New Orleans in 1818 to complete the waterworks started by his son Henry.

CLAUDE-NICOLAS LEDOUX
Dormans (Marne) 1736–1806 Paris

Ledoux went to Paris at an early age and enrolled at the Collège Beauvais. He began doing engravings at the age of fifteen and made a living by selling his battle scenes. But he soon decided to become an architect and entered the school of Blondel in 1757 and later worked under L.-F. Trouard. His first executed work was the interior decoration of the Café Militaire in Paris in 1762, which brought him acclaim. His commissions soon grew, and he found an increasing number of patrons from the court and among the great names of the royal administration. Mme du Barry's pavilion at Louveciennes was built by him in 1771; and in the same year he was appointed inspector of royal saltworks in the Franche-Comté, a position which he held for twenty-three years and which gave him the opportunity to build his largest work, the Saltworks of Arc-en-Senans near Besançon (1775–1779). Ledoux was accepted by the Academy in 1773, and in 1784 he was entrusted with the building of the tollhouses of Paris, but the commission was taken from him in 1789 because of the extravagance of his plans. When the Revolution broke out, he was the victim of political intrigues and spent a short time in prison, barely escaping the guillotine, though he was by no means unsympathetic to the new era. After his release from prison, he devoted the rest of his life to writing his book on architecture, which was published in 1804. He reflected the ideas of the era of Enlightenment, as well as the ideals of Rousseau. Ledoux believed that the architect had it in his power to alter society, that he should be the leader of the community and concern himself with every aspect of the community's life. Ledoux was prepared to investigate everything, down to the ventilation of stables. As a city planner, he foreshadowed the nineteenth century.

JACQUES-GUILLAUME LEGRAND
Paris 1743–1807 Saint-Denis

Legrand was a pupil of Perronet and Blondel and the son-in-law of Clérisseau. He became the architect for the Cathedral of Orléans (1773–1787) and was associated with Jacques Molinos for many years. They first collaborated on a wooden dome for the Halle aux Bleds, which they constructed on a girder system (1782–1783) and which eventually burned. In 1786 Legrand and Molinos built the market for the cloth merchants (Halle aux Draps), which was also later destroyed by fire. In 1788 Legrand, already famous, was commissioned to restore the Fontaine des Innocents, and he undertook the work with the help of Molinos. They collaborated again in the building of the Théâtre Feydeau (actually the Théâtre de l'Opéra-Comique, 1789–1791), which later burned. Legrand alone was responsible for the erection of the monument known as the Lantern of Diogenes, in the park of Saint-Cloud, which was destroyed during the war of 1870. Legrand also published two remarkable works: Essai sur l'histoire de l'architecture (1809) and Parallèle entre l'architecture ancienne et moderne (1799).

PIERRE-CHARLES L'ENFANT
Paris 1754–1825 Prince George's County, Md.

L'Enfant apparently received some instruction in engineering and architecture in Paris before his enthusiasm brought him to America at age twenty-three to fight in the war for independence. He received a commission as first lieutenant of engineers in December 1776 and sailed from France in February 1777, a month ahead of Lafayette, spending the winter at Valley Forge. In 1778 he was commissioned captain of engineers, attached to the inspector-general, Steuben.

L'Enfant was one of the early members of the Society of the Cincinnati, and when a design for a medal was requested, he proposed the use of an eagle instead. In 1783 he sailed for France to oversee the casting of these eagles.

The new government, temporarily located in New York, entrusted L'Enfant with converting the old Jacobean city hall at the head of Wall Street into Federal Hall. Here Congress met in 1789 and Washington was inaugurated on the balcony. L'Enfant surveyed the site for the new Federal city of Washington, and he also selected the site for the capitol and the president's house. He laid out the streets on a rectangular street plan, north-south and east-west, and then opened up others in various directions, as avenues to and from the principal places. He was greatly influenced by the plan of what was then the French capital, Versailles. The location of the capitol corresponds to that of the palace, the president's house to the Grand Trianon, the Mall to the parc.

On Hamilton's recommendation, L'Enfant was commissioned to lay out a plan for Paterson, New Jersey, a new town proposing to use the power of the falls of the Passaic for manufacturing. In Philadelphia, he designed rooms for the Philadelphia Assembly and built, for Robert Morris, a house which was left unfinished when Morris was forced into bankruptcy in 1798. In 1812 L'Enfant was offered an appointment as professor of civil and military engineering in the new Military Academy at West Point, but Monroe, then secretary of state, could not persuade him to accept. During the War of 1812 L'Enfant worked on the fortifications at Fort Washington on the Potomac. He lived on the estate of Thomas Digges, near Fort Washington, and later laid out the grounds and gardens for Green Hill, the estate of William Dudley Digges in Prince George's County, where he died.

MICHEL-NICOLAS-BERNARD LÉPICIÉ
Paris 1735–1784

Lépicié first studied engraving under his father, but because of bad eyesight he abandoned it for painting and became a pupil of Carle van Loo. In 1769 he was elected to the Académie Royale and the post of painter to the king.

LOUIS-NICOLAS DE LESPINASSE
Pouilly-sur-Loire 1734–1808 Paris

Lespinasse was a painter of architecture and watercolors. He was a knight of the Order of Saint-Louis. He became a member of the Academy in 1787 and exhibited in the Salon from 1787 to 1801, mostly views of Paris in oil, watercolor or gouache.

PHILIPPE-JACQUES (PHILIP JAMES) DE LOUTHERBOURG
Strasbourg 1740–1812 London

De Loutherbourg studied under Carle van Loo, Jean-Georges Wille and François-Joseph Casanova. He was elected to the Académie Royale at an unusually early age. In 1771 he came to London where he settled and for many years painted scenery at Garrick's theater, Drury Lane, an occupation that affected his style of landscape painting. He also painted battle scenes, marines and religious subjects. He became a member of the Royal Academy, London, in 1781.

PIERRE-ANTOINE DE MACHY
Paris 1723–1807

De Machy was a pupil of Servandoni and a painter of architectural perspectives and an engraver. In 1758 he was accepted at the Academy as a painter of architecture. In 1786 he became a professor of perspective at the Academy. On the grand staircase in the Palais Royal he painted three perspective views. He often worked with Clérisseau and Hubert Robert.

WILLIAM MARLOW
London 1740–1813

Marlow was a pupil of Samuel Scott and was influenced by Canaletto, who had spent some time in England. Marlow traveled in France and Italy, but his best-known paintings are of London and the Thames.

ANTON RAPHAEL MENGS
Bohemia 1728–1779 Rome

After training under his father Ismael Mengs in Dresden, Mengs went to Rome in 1741, where he studied the works of Michelangelo and Raphael and worked in the studio of Marco Benefial and Sebastiano Conca. He was greatly influenced by antique statuary in Rome. In 1746 he returned to Dresden and was made court painter to Elector Frederick Augustus II of Saxony. He was again in Rome 1747–1749 and 1752–1761, when he became acquainted with Winckelmann, to paint family portraits for Charles VII (son-in-law of the Elector). He was appointed court painter to Charles VII, who had by that time become Charles III of Spain, and Mengs lived in Madrid from 1761 to 1769. He was appointed chief court painter in 1766. During this time he began painting two ceiling frescoes in the royal palace, which were completed upon his return to Madrid in 1774, when he painted a third ceiling. In the meantime he had visited Rome, Naples and Florence, where he was elected Principal of the

Academy of St. Luke in 1770. He was elected a member of the Academy at Madrid in 1773.

JACQUES MOLINOS
Lyon 1743–1831 Paris

Molinos was a pupil of Blondel, and for many years he collaborated with Jacques-Guillaume Legrand. In 1782 they worked together on their first project, which was a wooden dome for the Halle aux Bleds, built on the girder system. This dome burned in 1803 and was replaced by one designed by Bélanger. Under the Consulate, Molinos was inspector general of the public buildings in Paris, and under the Empire he was official architect for the city of Paris. He produced a great number of drawings for various festivals celebrated during the Empire and the Restoration. In 1829 he became a member of the Institut de France.

NICOLAS-ANDRÉ MONSIAU
Paris 1754–1834

Monsiau was a pupil of Peyron and painted historical subjects and portraits. In 1787 he was accepted at the Academy and became a member in 1789. From 1787 to 1833 he exhibited in the Salon. Much of his time was devoted to book illustrations. Monsiau was enough in favor at the time of the Restoration to be granted some important commissions.

JEAN-MICHEL MOREAU LE JEUNE
Paris 1741–1814

Moreau was the younger brother of Louis-Gabriel Moreau. Jean-Michel produced paintings, drawings and engravings. He was a pupil of Louis-Joseph Le Lorrain, who went to St. Petersburg in 1758, taking his pupil with him. After Le Lorrain's death in 1760, Moreau returned to Paris and studied engraving in the studio of Lebas. In 1770 he was appointed dessinateur des menus plaisirs du roi, and later he became dessinateur du Cabinet du Roi. From 1781 to 1810 he exhibited a considerable number of drawings in the Salon. In 1785 he visited Italy. In 1793 he became a member of the Commission for Art, and in 1797 a professor at the Ecole Centrale in Paris. Toward the end of his life he fell out of favor, but on the restoration of Louis XVIII in 1814 he was appointed to his old office as dessinateur du Cabinet du Roi.

ISAAK OUWATER
Amsterdam 1750–1793

Ouwater continued the tradition of the seventeenth-century master, Jan van der Heyden, and painted views of many Dutch towns.

AUGUSTIN PAJOU
Paris 1730–1809

Pajou, the son of a craftsman sculptor and a pupil of Lemoyne, won first prize at the Academy school in 1748 and left for Rome (1751–1756) to study at the French Academy. On returning to Paris he became a fashionable portrait sculptor, making many busts and statues of important people. He exhibited for the first time in the Salon of 1759, was accepted at the Academy the same year, became a full member in 1760, an assistant professor in 1762, and rector in 1792. In 1770 he was commissioned to decorate the opera house at Versailles and in 1777 was made keeper of antique sculpture at the Louvre. He was also appointed designer to the Académie des Inscriptions, and for twenty years he was responsible for designing its medals. Pajou was the only sculptor on the committee appointed to organize the National Museum during the Directoire, and he was particularly concerned with the project of creating a museum at Versailles.

GEORGE ISHAM PARKYNS
Nottingham c. 1749/50–c. 1820 Cambridge

Parkyns exhibited engravings and landscapes in London (1772–1813) and published Monastic Remains and Ancient Castles in Great Britain. About 1794 he came to America and in 1795 announced the publication by subscription, in collaboration with James Harrison of New York City, of twenty-four aquatints of American cities. Only four were engraved—Annapolis, Mount Vernon, and two views of Washington.

CHARLES WILLSON PEALE
Queen Anne's County, Md. 1741–1827 Philadelphia

In 1762 Peale became a professional saddler in Annapolis and, shortly afterward, took his first lessons in painting from John Hesselius. In 1765 he visited Boston, where he saw paintings by Smibert and where he met Copley. From 1767 to 1769 he studied with Benjamin West in London. On his return his commissions took him to Annapolis, Philadelphia, Baltimore, Williamsburg, and in 1772 to Mount Vernon, where he painted his first life portrait of Washington. After three years in the Continental Army he settled in Philadelphia in 1778. In addition to his painting, Peale was a scientist, naturalist and inventor. In 1782 he opened a picture gallery, and in 1786 he established the Peale Museum in Independence Hall. In 1795 he helped to organize the Columbianum, or American Academy of Fine Arts in Philadelphia, and was also a founder of the Pennsylvania Academy of the Fine Arts. He taught most of his sons to paint, including Raphaelle, Rembrandt, Rubens, Franklin, and Titian Ramsay Peale.

REMBRANDT PEALE
Bucks County, Pa. 1778–1860 Philadelphia

A student of his father, Charles Willson Peale, Rembrandt painted his first portrait in 1791 and in 1795 did his first portrait of George Washington. He visited Charleston, S.C., in 1795–1796; in 1797 he and his older brother Raphaelle opened a museum in Baltimore. In 1802–1803 he studied in London under Benjamin West, and on returning to America he spent a few months in Charleston and Baltimore before settling down in Philadelphia. He was again in Europe in 1808 and 1809–1810, chiefly in Paris, where he became interested in historical painting. In 1814 he again opened a museum in Baltimore. In 1822 he moved to New York City and helped to found the National Academy of Design in 1826. He returned to Europe in 1829–1830, and again in 1831, before settling permanently in Philadelphia.

FREDRIK MAGNUS PIPER
Stockholm 1746–1824

Piper visited England twice, from 1772 to 1776 and from 1778 to 1780, with two years in Italy in between. He became vice-president of the Royal Academy and director of the School of Architecture.

GIOVANNI BATTISTA PIRANESI
Mestre 1720–1778 Rome

Piranesi was educated in Venice, mostly by his father, a stonemason, and his uncle, an engineer and architect. In Rome (1740–1744) he learned etching from Giuseppe Vasi and Felice Polanzani and published his first large volume, *Prima parte di architeture . . .* (1743). After returning briefly to Venice, he settled permanently in Rome in 1745 and had become one of its most famous inhabitants by the time of his death. In the late 1740s he began the series of *Vedute di Roma*, including 135 etchings in all, which he continued to work on until his death. These prints dramatized antique and baroque Rome, and they flooded Europe like travel posters. During his last summer he measured and drew the temples at Paestum for a publication which his son Francesco finished after his death. His major work as an architect was the rebuilding of S. Maria del Priorato on the Aventine hill (1764–1765).

MATTHEW PRATT
Philadelphia 1734–1805

From 1749 to 1755, Pratt was an apprentice to his uncle James Claypoole, a limner and general painter. In 1758 he began his career as a portrait painter in Philadelphia. In 1764 he accompanied Betsy Shewell, a relative, to London, where she married Benjamin West. Pratt remained in England for four years and was one of West's first pupils. After his return to America in 1768 Pratt spent most of his time in Philadelphia, though he also worked in New York City in 1772 and Virginia in 1773.

EDMÉ QUENEDEY
Riceys-le-Haut (Aube) 1756–1830 Paris

Quenedey was a pupil of Devosges and became a miniaturist and engraver, active in Brussels, Ghent, Hamburg (1796–1801) and Paris. He is known for his engraved physiognotrace portraits, which were made with an instrument first invented by Chrétien. According to Quenedey, in his prospectus, the instrument permitted one to trace the subject in four or five minutes through a real or imaginary glass with a view-finder, which did not leave the vertical plane, as a pencil registered the tracing at the other end of the instrument. These tracings were used as the basis of engraved portraits.

ALLAN RAMSAY
Edinburgh 1713–1784 Dover

Ramsay studied in London under Hans Hysing, a Swedish artist, and from 1736 to 1738 studied in Italy under Solimena and Francesco Imperiali. He set himself up in London as a portrait painter and his success was immediate; for many years he also had a studio in Edinburgh. On his second visit to Italy (1755–1757) Ramsay worked at the French Academy in Rome and studied work by Domenichino. In 1761 he was appointed Painter-in-Ordinary to King George III, and in 1769, when Reynolds was knighted, Ramsay declined a similar honor. He painted very little after 1766 except replicas of the royal portraits. He was president of the Society of Artists but never entered the Royal Academy.

PIERRE-JOSEPH REDOUTÉ
Saint-Hubert, Belgium 1759–1840 Paris

The art teacher of Marie-Antoinette, and later of Josephine, Redouté was also the friend of Audubon. Unlike Audubon, he did not attempt to create any suggestion of native habitat; rather, he placed his flowers on a white background, accentuating their fragility of form and exquisite colors. Except for a short trip to England he seems to have confined himself to France. His prints resemble watercolors, for Redouté engraved them and then hand-colored them. He mastered the Linnean botanical system, which had been published only a few years before, and with the botanist L'Héritier he explored the gardens of Paris, Malmaison, Navarre and Kew near London. Oblivious to the political upheavals of the Revolution and the Napoleonic era, which must have broken all around the gardens where he worked, he turned out hundreds of studies of roses, lilies and other plants. Redouté was awarded a gold medal by Louis XVIII and made a Legionnaire of Honor in the same group with Ingres and Sir Thomas Lawrence.

HUGH REINAGLE
Philadelphia c. 1788–1834 New Orleans

Reinagle was a son of the noted musician and composer Alexander Reinagle, who became musical director of the New Theater in Philadelphia soon after Hugh's birth. Reinagle presumably learned the art of scenery painting in the New Theater and by 1807 was employed as a scene painter at the New Theater in New York City, where he remained until about 1813. From 1815 to 1817 he was in Albany painting scenery and running a drawing academy, and in 1818 he opened an academy in Philadelphia. During the 1820s Reinagle was chief scene painter at the Park Theater, New York City, and in 1826 he was a founding member of the National Academy. Reinagle's large painting of *Belshazzar's Feast* was exhibited at Peale's Museum in New York City in 1830, and he took it to New Orleans for exhibition during the winter of 1833–1834.

SIR JOSHUA REYNOLDS
Plympton 1723–1792 London

In 1740 Reynolds was apprenticed to Thomas Hudson in London, where he remained for three years. He then worked in Devonshire, was back in London during 1744–1746, then returned to Devonshire. Early in 1750 he was in Rome, and when he returned to London in 1752, he soon built up a flourishing studio. As the first president of the Royal Academy in 1768, he became an arbiter of taste through his *Discourses* to the students; in the following year he was knighted. In 1781 he visited Flanders and Holland, and in 1784 he succeeded Ramsay as principal painter to King George III. After 1789 his

production of pictures gradually diminished with his failing sight.

HUBERT ROBERT
Paris 1733–1808

Robert received his first drawing lessons from the sculptor Michel-Ange Slodtz, and left for Rome in 1754 with the future duc de Choiseul, who had been appointed ambassador to Rome. Robert obtained lodgings at the French Academy in Rome, studying with Natoire. He became close friends with Panini and Piranesi, and later with Fragonard and the abbé de Saint-Non. In 1765 he returned to Paris and was accepted the following year by the Academy, as a "painter of ruins." Robert was appointed designer of the king's gardens in 1778, then keeper of the king's pictures in 1784, and he resided in the Louvre. He was arrested in 1793 but worked diligently while in prison. After the fall of Robespierre, he was released, and in 1795 he was given a position in the Louvre, along with Fragonard and Pajou, a post he held until 1802.

MICHAEL "ANGELO" ROOKER
London 1743–1801

Rooker was the son of an engraver. He studied at the Royal Academy and followed his father's profession, but was forced to turn to painting scenery because of bad eyesight. Many of his watercolors were done in walking tours he made in various parts of England. Rooker was an associate of the Royal Academy.

GEORGES LOUIS LE ROUGE
active late 18th century

Le Rouge worked in Paris. He was best known for his travel books and for engravings of gardens in *Jardins Anglochinois*.

THOMAS ROWLANDSON
London 1757–1827

Rowlandson studied at the Royal Academy schools. His prolific output included topographical views, satires, book illustrations and a few portraits in the form of drawings, watercolors and etchings.

WILLIAM RUSH
Philadelphia 1756–1833

At the age of fifteen, Rush entered the shop of Edward Cutbush, an Englishman who operated a busy wood-carving shop in Philadelphia. After serving with the Continental Army, Rush set up his own shop in Philadelphia. Although his income was derived mainly from ship carving, he also carved portrait busts, anatomal models and allegorical figures. Along with Charles Willson Peale he helped to organize the Columbianum and the Pennsylvania Academy of the Fine Arts, and he took part in their first exhibition in 1811. His serious work with the portrait bust took place between 1812 and 1824, and virtually all his busts from this period are in plaster or terra cotta, indicating that by then he had mastered the art of modeling.

CHARLES-BALTHAZAR-JULIEN FÉVRET DE SAINT-MÉMIN
Dijon 1770–1852

Saint-Mémin was educated for the army and joined the French anti-revolutionary forces in exile. In 1793 he went to North America and lived in various cities on the east coast of the United States mainly as a portraitist. Saint-Mémin returned to France in 1814 and became director of the Dijon Museum in 1817.

PAUL SANDBY
Nottingham 1725–1809 London

Sandby worked in the Military Drawing Office of the Tower of London and was later employed in the surveying of roads in Scotland. His brother Thomas, with whom he often lived, had an official position at Windsor, and as a result the castle and park are frequent subjects in Sandby's watercolors. The royal family were among his pupils, and he taught at the Royal Military College, Woolwich. Sandby was a founding member of the Royal Academy.

JOHN RAPHAEL SMITH
Derby 1752–1812 Doncaster

John Raphael Smith was employed as a linen draper and only practised painting and engraving in his spare time. He became an accomplished mezzotinter and had a flourishing business reproducing the works of English contemporary painters. Later he turned to portraiture in pastel, crayon and oils and exhibited frequently at the Royal Academy.

THOMAS SULLY
Horncastle, Lincolnshire 1783–1872 Philadelphia

Thomas Sully's parents, who were actors, came to Charleston, S.C., in 1792, and Thomas grew up there. His first painting lessons were from a schoolmate, Charles Fraser; then he studied with his brother-in-law Jean Belzons and in Norfolk and Richmond, Va., with his brother Lawrence, both of whom were miniaturists. In 1799 he also received some instruction from Henry Benbridge in Norfolk.

In 1801 he began work in Norfolk and Richmond, and in 1805 he married his brother's widow and the next year moved to New York City. He went to Hartford, Connecticut, in 1807, and on to Boston, where he received advice from Gilbert Stuart. In 1808 he settled permanently in Philadelphia. He visited England from 1809 to 1810 to study with Benjamin West but was profoundly influenced by the sleek portrait style of Sir Thomas Lawrence. When he returned to Philadelphia he quickly became the country's leading portrait painter. In 1838 he returned to London to paint a portrait of the young Queen Victoria.

GILBERT STUART
North Kingston, R.I., 1755–1828 Boston

In 1761, Stuart's family moved to Newport, where about 1769 he became a pupil of Cosmo Alexander, a Scottish artist, who took him to Edinburgh in 1772. Stuart returned to America in 1773 but left for London in 1775, where at first he had little success as a portrait painter. From 1777 to 1782 he worked in the studio of Benjamin West, and was also influenced by Gainsborough and Raeburn. In 1782 Stuart set up his own studio in London and enjoyed considerable success until 1787, when he moved to Dublin. In 1792 he returned to America, working in New York City (1793–1794), Philadelphia and Germantown, Pennsylvania (1794–1803), where he painted his first portrait of Washington in 1795. Stuart was also in Washington, D.C., 1803–1805, and in Bordentown, N.J., in 1805. In 1805 he moved to Boston, where he spent the remaining years of his life.

GEORGE STUBBS
Liverpool 1724–1806 London

George Stubbs was largely self-taught as a painter and through his own efforts came to have an unrivalled knowledge of human and equine anatomy. The results of these labors were finally published in *The Anatomy of the Horse* and *Comparative Anatomical Exposition of the Human Body with that of a Tiger and a Common Fowl* (unfinished), which he engraved himself. In addition to oil paintings Stubbs experimented with enamel painting on Wedgwood porcelain. He was the greatest animal painter in eighteenth-century England. Because of a disagreement with the Royal Academy, he was only an associate and not a full member.

JEAN-JOSEPH TAILLASSON
Blaye 1746–1808 Paris

Taillasson was a pupil of Vien and painted historical subjects. In 1769 he won the third Grand Prix of painting. In about 1773, he went to Rome, where he worked for four years. In 1782, he was accepted at the Academy and became a member in 1784. He exhibited in the Salon beginning in 1783. Taillasson also wrote several works on aesthetics.

JOHN TRUMBULL
Lebanon, Conn. 1756–1843 New York

After graduating from Harvard in 1773, Trumbull became an officer in the Continental Army, from 1775 to 1777, and an aide-de-camp to General Washington. In 1780 he went to London to study under Benjamin West but spent eight months in prison on the charge of treason for the Major André affair. After his release he returned to America, but by 1784 he was back in West's studio in London, where he worked until 1789. He also visited Paris and was greatly influenced by David and Vigée-Lebrun. From 1789 to 1794 he was in America making studies of those who participated in the Revolution. In 1794 he went to London a third time, as secretary of John Jay, and he remained there until 1804 as one of the commissioners under the Jay Treaty. From 1804 to 1808 Trumbull had a studio in New York City; he was in England again from 1808 to 1816 and back in New York from 1816 to 1837. In 1816 he started work on the commission for the Revolutionary War murals for the rotunda of the capitol in Washington. He was president of the American Academy of Fine Arts in New York from 1816 to 1835. In 1831 he sold to Yale College his collection of his own works, which became the nucleus of the Yale University Art Gallery.

PIERRE-HENRI VALENCIENNES
Toulouse 1750–1819 Paris

After first studying in his native city, Valenciennes went to Paris and entered the studio of Doyen. Then he went to Italy and studied the works of Claude Lorrain and Poussin. After returning to Paris he quickly acquired a reputation for his landscapes and founded a school for classical landscape, which attracted many pupils. In 1787 he was accepted at the Academy and became a member in 1789. From 1787 to 1814 he exhibited in the Salon. He wrote a book on the elements of perspective.

CLAUDE-JOSEPH VERNET
Avignon 1741–1789 Paris

Vernet was a pupil of his father and went to Rome to study under Bernardino Fergioni in 1732. He returned to France in 1753 and became a member of the Académie Royale.

MARIE-LOUISE-ELISABETH VIGÉE-LEBRUN
Paris 1755–1842

Vigée-Lebrun was first a pupil of her father, Louis Vigée, a pastel painter, and later received advice from Briard, Doyen, Greuze and Joseph Vernet. In 1774 she became a member of the Academy of St. Luke. In 1776 she married Pierre Lebrun, an artist and well-known picture dealer. She was summoned to Versailles in 1779 and soon became the official painter to Marie-Antoinette and was elected a member of the Academy in 1783. At the outbreak of the Revolution in 1789, she fled to Italy and later traveled to the courts at Vienna (1793–1794), Prague, Dresden, Berlin and St. Petersburg (1795–1800). She returned to France in 1801, but she was unable to adjust to the new society. Vigée-Lebrun then went to England for three years and to Switzerland, before returning to France in 1809. In 1835 she published her memoirs, which provide an insight into the social climate of her day.

CHARLES DE WAILLY
Paris 1729–1798

De Wailly, a pupil of Blondel, Legeay and Servandoni, was a painter, engraver and architect. In 1752 he won the Grand Prix for architecture and studied in Rome from 1754 to 1756. In 1767 he became a member of the Academy of architecture and in 1771 a member of the Academy of painting and sculpture. From 1771 to 1796 he exhibited in the Salon. He designed the decoration for the Palazzo Spinola at Genoa (1772), the Chapel of the Virgin in Saint-Sulpice (1774) and the Chancery of Orléans (1784). He collaborated with Peyre on the Theater of the Odéon in Paris (1786). He engraved genre subjects.

ADRIAEN VAN DER WERFF
Kralingen, near Rotterdam 1659–1722 Rotterdam

In Rotterdam, van der Werff was a pupil of Cornelis Picolet and Eglon van der Neer. There are dated works beginning from 1678, and in 1696 he began to work for the Elector Palatine, who appointed him court painter in 1697. Van der Werff visited Düsseldorf in 1697, 1698, 1703 and 1712 to deliver pictures and to execute a portrait of the elector, who made him a knight in 1703. He also painted for the king of Poland and the duke of Brunswick. His mature work was greatly influenced by contemporary French classical taste. Van der Werff was greatly admired in his own time, and he achieved greater fame and wealth than almost any other Dutch painter of the seventeenth and eighteenth centuries.

BENJAMIN WEST
Springfield (now Swarthmore), Pa. 1738–1820 London

West began to draw and paint at eight, and was a sign and portrait painter in Philadelphia by 1756. In 1759 patrons sponsored a trip to Italy. During three years of study in Florence, Rome, Bologna and Venice, he was profoundly moved by the art and monuments of Greek and Roman antiquity, by the High Renaissance masters and also by the new neoclassical teachings of Raphael Mengs. After visiting Paris, West settled in London in 1763 and was an immediate success. By 1773 he had been appointed historical painter to King George III. He was a charter member of the Royal Academy, and in 1792 he succeeded Reynolds as its second president, an office which he held, with only one year's interruption, until his death. He befriended many young American artists, including Matthew Pratt, Charles Willson Peale, Rembrandt Peale, Gilbert Stuart, Samuel F. B. Morse, Robert Fulton, Washington Allston, John Trumbull and John Singleton Copley.

ALEXANDER WILSON
Paisley, Scotland 1766–1813 Philadelphia

Wilson worked as a weaver and peddler in Scotland until 1794, when he emigrated to America. At first he taught school in New Jersey and Pennsylvania, but in 1802, after meeting the naturalist William Bartram, he began to collect material and make sketches for a work on American birds. The first volume of his classic *American Ornithology* appeared in 1808, with engravings by Alexander Lawson after Wilson's drawings, and the eighth volume was being printed at the time of Wilson's death. While working on his book Wilson had traveled widely throughout the United States, east of the Mississippi. In 1804 he made a sketch of Niagara Falls which was engraved for *Port Folio* in 1810.

JOHN WOLLASTON
active 1736–1767

Influenced by Sir Godfrey Kneller in London, Wollaston came to America in 1749 and remained there almost ten years, painting portraits in New York City (1749–1752), Annapolis (1753–1754), Virginia (c. 1755–1757) and Philadelphia (1758). He had a great influence on Benjamin West, Matthew Pratt, John Mare, John Hesselius and Jeremiah Theus. In 1758 he went to India for the East India Company. He returned to America briefly in 1767 but left later the same year for England.

JOSEPH WRIGHT OF DERBY
Derby 1734–1797

Wright of Derby was a pupil of Thomas Hudson in London (1751–1753) and worked briefly in Derby, but he returned to Hudson in 1756–1757. He then set up a flourishing studio in the Midlands, and first exhibited in London in 1765. From 1773 to 1775 he traveled in Italy, visiting Rome and Naples, and spent two years in Bath before settling in Derby in 1777. In 1781 Wright was elected an associate of the Royal Academy, and in 1784 he became a full member; but he preferred to remain independent of that body and at a later time ceased to be an associate. He held his first one-man show in London in 1785.

JOHANN ZOFFANY
Near Frankfurt 1734–1810 London

Soon after his birth, Zoffany's family moved to Ratisbon, where for three years he was a pupil of Martin Speer. In 1750 he went to Rome and for seven years studied with Maratta and with Raphael Mengs, after which he returned to Ratisbon, where he was painter to the Elector of Treves. In 1760 he went to England, where he worked as drapery painter to Benjamin Wilson. In 1762 he attracted the attention of David Garrick, who commissioned him to do a theatrical "conversation piece." From the success of this theater publicity Zoffany earned royal patronage, which enabled him to paint the domestic subjects for which he is best known. In 1769 the king nominated him to the Royal Academy and he exhibited there between 1770 and 1800. He visited Rome for a second time between 1772 and 1778, and from 1783 to 1789 he lived in India.

SELECTED BIBLIOGRAPHY

The following is a select bibliography of works related to Jefferson and his world. A key to those titles which have been abbreviated in the literature section is given here. Unless otherwise indicated, all Jefferson letters written before March 1791 are quoted from the Princeton edition of his papers edited by Julian Boyd.

Short Title

AAJ	*American Art Journal*
AB	*The Art Bulletin*
Adams	Adams, Herbert Baxter. *Thomas Jefferson and the University of Virginia.* Washington: U.S. Government Printing Office, 1888.
AQ	*The Art Quarterly*
ArtAm	*Art in America*
AS	*Art Studies*
Barringer and Garnett	Barringer, Paul, and Garnett, James. *The University of Virginia, Its History, Influences, Equipment and Characteristics, with Biographical Sketches and Portraits of Founders, Benefactors, Officers and Alumni.* 2 vols. New York: Lewis Publishing Co., 1904.
	Bear, James A., Jr. "The Furniture and Furnishings of Monticello." *Antiques* 102 (July 1972): 113–123.
	Bear, James A., Jr., ed. *Jefferson at Monticello.* Charlottesville: The University Press of Virginia, 1967.
	Bear, James A., Jr. "Thomas Jefferson's Silver." *Antiques* 74 (Sept. 1958): 233–236.
Bellier and Auvray	E. Bellier de la Chavignerie continued by L. Auvray. *Dictionnaire Général des artistes de l'école française depuis l'origine des arts du dessin jusqu'à nos jours.* Paris: Renouard, 1882–1885.
	Benisovich, Michel. "Thomas Jefferson, amateur d'art à Paris." *Archives de l'art français* (1959).
Berman	Berman, Eleanor D. *Thomas Jefferson Among the Arts.* New York: The Philosophical Library, 1947.
Betts	Betts, Edwin Morris, ed. *Thomas Jefferson's Garden Book.* Philadelphia: The American Philosophical Society, 1944.
	Betts, Edwin Morris, and Bear, James A., Jr., eds. *The Family Letters of Thomas Jefferson.* Columbia: University of Missouri Press, 1966.
Betts and Perkins	Betts, Edwin Morris, and Perkins, Hazlehurst Bolton, eds. *Thomas Jefferson's Flower Garden at Monticello.* Charlottesville: The University Press of Virginia, 1971.
	Binney, Marcus. "Bremo, Virginia." *Country Life* (Jan. 3–10, 1974), 18–21.
BMMA	*Bulletin of The Metropolitan Museum of Art*
Bowen	Bowen, Clarence W., ed. *The History of the Centennial Celebration of the Inauguration of George Washington.* New York: D. Appleton and Co., 1892.
Boyd	Boyd, Julian P., ed. *The Papers of Thomas Jefferson.* Princeton: Princeton University Press, 1950.
	Boyd, Julian P. "Thomas Jefferson and the Roman Askos of Nîmes." *Antiques* 54 (July 1973): 116–124.

Short Title

Brière	Brière, Gaston. *Musée national du Louvre, Catalogue des peintures exposées dans les galeries. I. Ecole française.* Paris: Musées nationaux, 1924.
Brown	Brown, Glenn. *History of the United States Capitol.* Washington, D.C.: U.S. Government Printing Office, 1900–1903.
	Bullock, Helen Duprey. *My Head and My Heart: A Little History of Thomas Jefferson and Maria Cosway.* New York: G. P. Putnam's Sons, 1945.
BurlM	*The Burlington Magazine*
Bush	Bush, Alfred L. *The Life Portraits of Thomas Jefferson.* Charlottesville: The University of Virginia Museum of Fine Arts, 1962.
	Butterfield, Lyman H., and Rice, Howard C., Jr. "Jefferson's Earliest Note to Maria Cosway, with Some New Facts and Conjectures on His Broken Wrist." *William and Mary Quarterly* 5 (Jan. 1948): 26–33.
Chastellux	Chastellux, Marquis de. *Travels in North America in the Years 1780, 1781, and 1782.* Edited by Howard C. Rice, Jr. 2 vols. Chapel Hill: University of North Carolina Press, 1963.
Chaussard	Chaussard, Pierre. *Le Pausanias français ou Déscription du Salon de 1806.* Paris: F. Buisson, 1806.
	Chinard, Gilbert. "Jefferson and the American Philosophical Society." *Proceedings of the American Philosophical Society* 87 (July 14, 1943): 263–276.
	Chinard, Gilbert. *Trois amitiés françaises de Jefferson d'après sa correspondance inédite avec Madame de Brehan, Madame de Tessé, et Madame de Corny.* Paris: Société d'édition "Les Belles Lettres," 1927.
Coll. Deloynes	Collection Deloynes. Paris: Bibliothèque nationale.
	Cometti, Elizabeth. "Mr. Jefferson Prepares an Itinerary." *The Journal of Southern History* 12 (Feb. 1946): 105.
Cripe	Cripe, Helen. *Thomas Jefferson and Music.* Charlottesville: The University Press of Virginia, 1974.
DAB	*Dictionary of American Biography.* Edited by Allen Johnson and Dumas Malone. 20 vols. New York: Charles Scribner's Sons, 1928–1937.
	Daiker, Virginia. "The Capitol of Jefferson and Latrobe." *Library of Congress Quarterly* (Spring 1975), 25–32.
David	David, Jacques-Louis Jules. *Le peintre Louis David 1748–1825, Souvenirs et documents.* Paris: V. Havard, 1880.
	Davis, Richard Beale. *Intellectual Life in Jefferson's Virginia, 1790–1830.* Knoxville: University of Tennessee Press, 1972.
de Nolhac	de Nolhac, Pierre. *Hubert Robert 1733–1808.* Paris: Goupil et cie, Manzi, Joyant et cie, successeurs, 1910.
	Dumbauld, Edward. *Thomas Jefferson: American Tourist.* Norman: University of Oklahoma Press, 1945.
Engerand	Engerand, Fernand. *Inventaire des tableaux commandés et achetés par la Direction des Bâtiments du Roi (1709–1792).* Paris: Leroux, 1901.

Foley, John P., ed. *The Jeffersonian Cyclopedia*. New York: Russell & Russell, 1967.

Ford   Ford, Paul Leicester, ed. *The Writings of Thomas Jefferson*. 10 vols. New York: G. P. Putnam's Sons, 1892–1899.

Frary   Frary, Ihna Thayer. *Thomas Jefferson, Architect and Builder*. Richmond: Garrett and Massie, 1931.

Gabillot   Gabillot, C. *Hubert Robert et son temps*. Paris: Librairie de l'art, 1895.

GBA   *Gazette des Beaux-Arts*

Guinness, Desmond, and Sadler, Julius T. *Mr. Jefferson, Architect*. New York: Viking Press, 1973.

Hackenbroch   Hackenbroch, Yvonne, ed. *English Furniture in the Collection of Irwin Untermyer*. Cambridge, Mass.: Harvard University Press, 1958.

Hart, Charles Henry. "The Life Portraits of Thomas Jefferson." *McClure's Magazine* 11 (May 1898): 47–55.

Haug   Levallet-Haug, Geneviève. *Claude-Nicolas Ledoux, 1736–1806*. Paris and Strasbourg: Librairie Istra, 1934.

Hautecoeur   Hautecoeur, Louis. *Louis David*. Paris: La Table Ronde, 1954.

Holma   Holma, Klaus. *David, son évolution et son style*. Paris: Imprimerie P. Lejay, 1940.

Notes on the State of Virginia   Jefferson, Thomas. *Notes on the State of Virginia*. Edited by William Peden. New York: W. W. Norton & Co., Inc., 1954.

JWarb   *Journal of the Warburg and Courtauld Institutes*

Kimball, "Jefferson and the Arts"   Kimball, Fiske. "Jefferson and the Arts." *Proceedings of the American Philosophical Society* 87 (July 1943): 238–245.

Kimball, Fiske and Marie. "Jefferson's Curtains at Monticello." *The Magazine Antiques* 52 (Oct. 1947): 266–268.

Kimball, "Williamsburg"   Kimball, Fiske. "Jefferson and the Public Buildings of Virginia: I. Williamsburg, 1770–1776." *The Huntington Library Quarterly* 12 (Feb. 1949): 115–120.

Kimball, "Richmond"   Kimball, Fiske. "Jefferson and the Public Buildings of Virginia: II. Richmond, 1779–1780." *The Huntington Library Quarterly* 12 (May 1949): 303–310.

Kimball, "Life Portraits"   Kimball, Fiske. "The Life Portraits of Jefferson and Their Replicas." *Proceedings of the American Philosophical Society* 88 (1944): 497–534.

Kimball, *Jefferson, Architect*   Kimball, Fiske. *Thomas Jefferson, Architect*. Introd. by Frederick D. Nichols. New York: Da Capo Press, 1968.

Kimball, *The Road to Glory*   Kimball, Marie. *Jefferson: the Road to Glory*. New York: Coward-McCann, Inc., 1943.

Kimball, *The Scene of Europe*   Kimball, Marie. *Jefferson: the Scene of Europe*. New York: Coward-McCann, Inc., 1950.

Kimball, Marie. *Jefferson: War and Peace*. New York: Coward-McCann, Inc., 1947.

Kimball, Marie. "More Jefferson Furniture Comes Home to Monticello." *The Magazine Antiques* 38 (July 1940): 20–22.

Kimball, Marie. "Thomas Jefferson's French Furniture." *The Magazine Antiques* 15 (Feb. 1929): 123–128.

Kimball, Marie. "William Short, Jefferson's Only 'Son.'" *North American Review* 223: 471–486.

Lambeth and Manning   Lambeth, William A., and Manning, Warren H. *Thomas Jefferson as an Architect and a Designer of Landscapes*. Boston and New York: Houghton-Mifflin Co., 1913.

Lancaster, Clay. "Jefferson's Architectural Indebtedness to Robert Morris." *Journal of the Society of Architectural Historians* 10 (1951): 4.

Landon   Landon, Charles Paul. *Annales du Musée et de l'Ecole Moderne des Beaux-Arts*. 8 vols. Paris: Imprimerie des Annales du Musée, 1808–1820.

Leclère   Leclère, Tristan. *Hubert Robert et les paysagistes français du XVIIIe siècle*. Paris: H. Laurens, 1913.

Lehmann, Karl. *Thomas Jefferson, American Humanist*. New York: Macmillan, 1947.

Lipscomb   Lipscomb, Andrew A., and Bergh, Albert E., eds. *The Writings of Thomas Jefferson*. 20 vols. Washington, D.C.: Thomas Jefferson Memorial Association, 1903.

LRL   *La Revue du Louvre*

Malone, Dumas, ed. *Correspondence between Thomas Jefferson and Pierre Samuel du Pont de Nemours*. Boston and New York: Houghton Mifflin Co., 1930.

Malone, Dumas, ed. *The Fry and Jefferson Map of Virginia and Maryland*. Princeton: Princeton University Press, 1950.

Malone, *Jefferson the Virginian*   Malone, Dumas. *Jefferson the Virginian*. Boston: Little, Brown and Co., 1948.

Malone, *Rights of Man*   Malone, Dumas. *Jefferson and the Rights of Man*. Boston: Little, Brown and Co., 1951.

Malone, Dumas. *Jefferson and the Ordeal of Liberty*. Boston: Little, Brown and Co., 1962.

Malone, Dumas. *Jefferson the President: First Term, 1801–1805*. Boston: Little, Brown and Co., 1970.

Malone, Dumas. *Jefferson the President: Second Term, 1805–1809*. Boston: Little, Brown and Co., 1974.

Martin, Edwin T. *Thomas Jefferson: Scientist*. New York: Henry Schuman, 1952.

MD   *Master Drawings*

Mayo, Bernard, ed. *Jefferson Himself: The Personal Narrative of a Many-Sided American*. Charlottesville: The University Press of Virginia, 1973.

Mayor, A. Hyatt. "Jefferson's Enjoyment of the Arts." *Bulletin of The Metropolitan Museum of Art* 2 (1943): 145.

Meade   Meade, Bishop. *Old Churches, Ministers and Families of Virginia*. Philadelphia: J. B. Lippincott Co., 1906.

Montaiglon   Montaiglon, A. de *Procès verbaux de l'Académie Royale de Peinture et de Sculpture*. Paris: J. Baur, 1889.

Nichols, Frederick D., and Bear, James A., Jr. *Monticello*. Charlottesville: The Thomas Jefferson Memorial Foundation, 1967.

	Nichols, Frederick D. "Poplar Forest." *The Iron-worker* 38 (Spring 1974): 2–13.
Nichols	Nichols, Frederick D. *Thomas Jefferson's Architectural Drawings.* 3rd ed. Boston: the Massachusetts Historical Society and Charlottesville: The Thomas Jefferson Memorial Foundation and The University Press of Virginia, 1961.
	Norton, Paul Foote. "Jefferson's Plans for Moth-Balling the Frigates." *U.S. Naval Institute Proceedings* 82 (July 1956): 736–741.
O'Neal, Arch. Drawing	O'Neal, William Bainter. *Architectural Drawing in Virginia.* Exhib. cat. Charlottesville: University of Virginia School of Architecture and the Virginia Museum of Fine Arts, 1969.
	O'Neal, William Bainter. *Jefferson's Buildings at the University of Virginia: The Rotunda.* Charlottesville: The University Press of Virginia, 1960.
O'Neal, Pictorial History	O'Neal, William Bainter. *Pictorial History of the University of Virginia.* Charlottesville: The University Press of Virginia, 1968.
Padover	Padover, Saul K., ed. *Thomas Jefferson and the National Capital.* Washington, D.C.: U.S. Government Printing Office, 1946.
	Padover, Saul K., ed. *The Complete Jefferson, Containing His Major Writings, Published and Unpublished, Except His Letters.* New York: Duell, Sloan and Pearce, Inc., 1943.
	Peterson, Merrill D. *Thomas Jefferson and the New Nation: A Biography.* New York: Oxford University Press, 1970.
	Pierson, Hamilton W. *Jefferson at Monticello.* New York: Charles Scribner's Sons, 1862.
Randall	Randall, Henry S. *The Life of Thomas Jefferson.* 3 vols. New York: Da Capo Press, 1972, republication of edition first published in New York in 1858.
Randolph	Randolph, Sarah N. *The Domestic Life of Thomas Jefferson.* 3rd ed. Charlottesville: The Thomas Jefferson Memorial Foundation, 1947.
Raval	Raval, Marcel. *Claude-Nicolas Ledoux.* Paris, 1945.
Réau	Réau, Louis. *Houdon, sa vie et son oeuvre.* Paris: F. de Nobele, 1964.
Renouvier	Renouvier, Jules. *Histoire de l'art pendant la Révolution.* Paris: J. Renouard, 1863.
	Rice, Howard C., Jr. *Le Cultivateur Américain.* Paris: Librairie Ancienne Honoré Champion, 1933.
	Rice, Howard C., Jr. "A French Source of Jefferson's Plan for the Prison at Richmond." *Journal of the Society of Architectural Historians* 12 (Dec. 1953): 28–30.
	Rice, Howard C., Jr. "Jefferson in Europe a Century and a Half Later: Notes of a Roving Researcher." *Princeton University Library Chronicle* 13 (Autumn 1950): 19–35.
Rice, Hôtel de Langeac	Rice, Howard C., Jr. *L'Hôtel de Langeac, Jefferson's Paris Residence, 1785–1789.* Monticello and Paris: The Thomas Jefferson Memorial Foundation, 1947.
Rice, Jefferson's Paris	Rice, Howard C., Jr. *Thomas Jefferson's Paris.* Princeton: Princeton University Press, 1976.
	Rice, Howard C., Jr. "Les Visites de Jefferson au Mont-Valérien." *Bulletin de la Société Historique de Suresnes* 3 (1953–1954): 46–49.
Rosenblum	Rosenblum, Robert. "Neoclassicism Surveyed." *The Burlington Magazine* 107 (Jan. 1965): 30–33.
Schreider	Schreider, Louis III. "Gouverneur Morris, Connoisseur of French Art." *Apollo* 93 (June 1971): 470–483.
Schuyler	Schuyler, Montgomery. *American Architecture, and Other Writings.* Cambridge, Mass.: Belknap Press, 1961.
	Shackelford, George Green. "Jefferson and the Fine Arts of Northern Italy: 'A Peep into Elysium.'" In *America: the Middle Period; Essays in Honor of Bernard Mayo,* edited by John B. Boles. Charlottesville: The University Press of Virginia, 1973, pp. 14–35.
Sizer	Sizer, Theodore, ed. *The Autobiography of John Trumbull.* New Haven: Yale University Press, 1953.
Soulié, 1st ed.	Soulié, Eudore. *Notice des peintures et sculptures composant le musée impérial de Versailles.* 1ère partie. Versailles, 1854.
Soulié, 2nd ed.	Soulié, Eudore. *Notice du musée impérial de Versailles.* 2ème partie. Paris, 1859.
Soulié, 3rd ed.	Soulié, Eudore. *Notice du musée impérial de Versailles.* 3ème partie. Paris: 1861.
Sowerby	Sowerby, E. Millicent. *Catalogue of the Library of Thomas Jefferson,* compiled with annotations. Washington: The Library of Congress, 1955.
Thieme-Becker	Thieme, U., and Becker, F. *Allgemeines Lexicon der Bildenden Kunstler.* Leipzig: Verlag von E. A. Seemann, 1907–1950.
Thiéry	Thiéry, Luc-Vincent. *Guide des Amateurs et des Etrangers voyageurs à Paris.* Paris: Hardouin & Gattey, 1787.
Verlet	Verlet, Pierre. *Royal French Furniture.* London: Barrie and Rockliffe, 1963.
Villot	Villot, Frederic. *Notice des tableaux exposées dans les galéries impérial du Louvre, 3ème partie, Ecole française.* Paris, 1855.
VMHB	*Virginia Magazine of History and Biography*
Waterman	Waterman, Thomas Tileston. *The Mansions of Virginia, 1706–1776.* Chapel Hill, The University of North Carolina Press, 1946.
Watson	Watson, F. J. B. *Louis XVI Furniture.* London: Tiranti, 1960.
Watson, "Boston"	Watson, F. J. B. "French Eighteenth Century Art in Boston." *Apollo* 90 (Dec. 1969): 474–483.
Weddell	Weddell, Alexander. *Virginia Historical Portraiture, 1585–1830.* Richmond: William Byrd Press, 1930.
YUAGB	*Yale University Art Gallery Bulletin*
Zigrosser	Zigrosser, Carl. "The Medallic Sketches of Augustin Dupré in American Collections." *Proceedings of the American Philosophical Society* 51 (Dec. 1957): 289–304.

INDEX

Entry numbers are in roman; page numbers in *italics*.

PHOTO CREDITS

Save for those listed below, all photographs in this catalogue were provided by the lenders to the exhibition. For their assistance and cooperation we are most grateful.
James T. Tkatch: 528, 535, 539, 153, 117, 118, 374; Photographie Giraudon, Paris: 201, 193, 195, 238, 254, 255, 256, 310, 303, 302, 312, 453, 454; Annon, Glasgow: 16; Judson Smith Studio, Fredericksburg, Va.: 27; Photographie Bulloz, Paris: 198, 199, 200; Johnson & Johnson of Jersey, Channel Islands: 60; Raymond Fortt Studios, England: 62; Robert Mates, New York: 108, 172; Alinari, New York: 133; George M. Cushing, Boston: 176–187, 347, 352; André Gontard, Paris: 229; Greenburg-May Productions, Inc.: 221; Gilbert Mangin, Nancy, France: 244; Koppes, Phoenix, Arizona: 253; Jacques Seligmann & Co., Inc., New York: 265; Robert Chanoine, Saint-Ouen-L'Aumone, France: 251; and Image, Washington: 581.

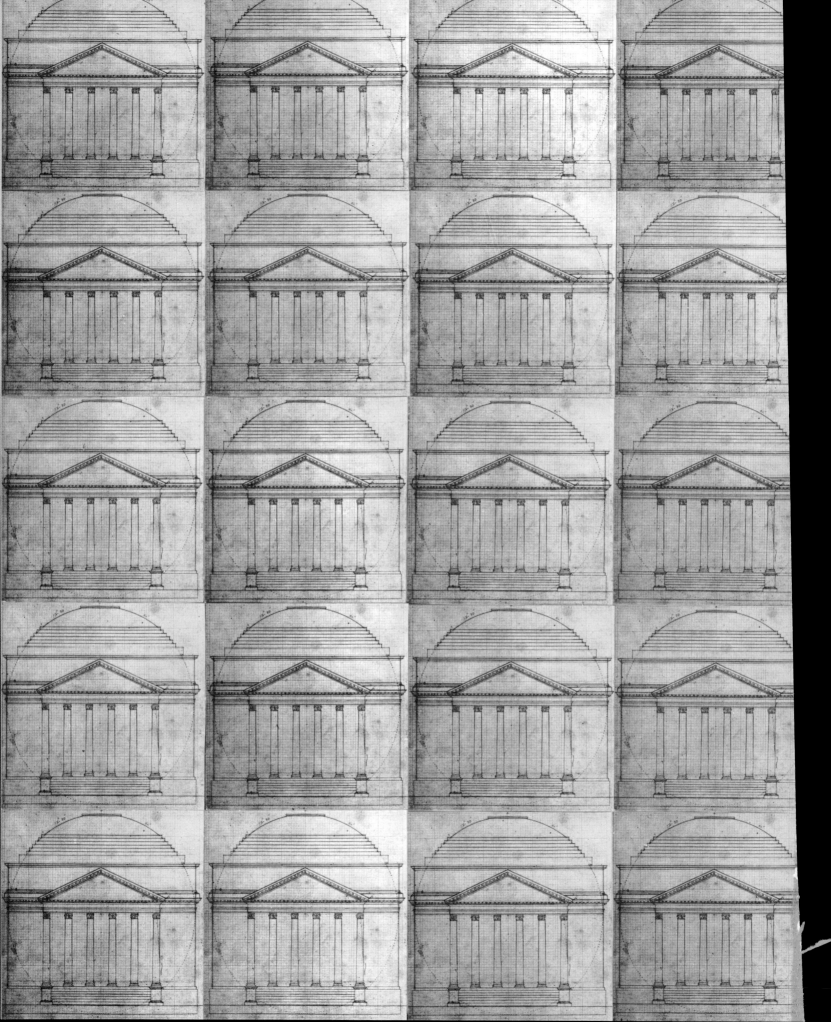